HENRY III

David Carpenter is professor of medieval history at King's College London. He is the author of numerous books including a new study of Magna Carta for the Penguin Classics series.

Further praise for *Henry III*:

'Carpenter is the foremost scholar of England's 13th century, and his spectacular erudition shines on every page . . . Above all, he has narrative gifts that root this history of our medieval country in reality rather than in romance, and makes the lives of our distant forebears feel as comprehensible as our own.' Simon Heffer, *Daily Telegraph*

'Outstanding. Through sustained scholarship Carpenter provides the reader with all sorts of insights into the decisions and daily experience of this ambitious and complex medieval king.' Michael Clanchy, author of *England and Its Rulers*

'This brilliant study by a leading historian of medieval England brings together a lifetime of research in a masterly way. Henry III is treated with humane understanding while his political failings and absence of a proper sense of priorities are emphasised with admirable clarity. Vivid and highly readable, this is a book of major significance.' Michael Prestwich, author of *Edward I*

'Rooted in his unrivalled understanding of the primary sources, Carpenter has created a sparkling and compelling narrative of this little-known English king.' Stephen Church, author of *Henry III*

'A monumental achievement. Never before has England's place in the wider history of medieval Europe been revealed on quite this epic scope, and with so sharp an eye for personalities. Revisiting fifty years of history, Carpenter reveals Henry III – a supposedly "non-descript king" – as one of the more fascinating failures ever to have sat on the English throne.' Nicholas Vincent, author of *A Brief History of Britain 1066–1485*

T0326737

The Yale English Monarchs Series

* Available in the U.S. from University of California Press

HENRY III

The Rise to Power and Personal Rule
1207–1258

David Carpenter

YALE UNIVERSITY PRESS
NEW HAVEN AND LONDON

For information about this and other Yale University Press publications, please contact:
U.S. Office: sales.press@yale.edu   yalebooks.com
Europe Office: sales@yaleup.co.uk   yalebooks.co.uk

Set in Baskerville by IDSUK (DataConnection) Ltd
Printed and bound by CPI Group (UK) Ltd, Croydon, CR0 4YY

Library of Congress Control Number: 2020934243

ISBN 978-0-300-23835-8 (hbk)
ISBN 978-0-300-25919-3 (pbk)

A catalogue record for this book is available from the British Library.

10 9 8 7 6 5 4 3 2 1

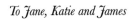

To Jane, Katie and James

CONTENTS

ILLUSTRATIONS

PLATES

MAPS

GENEALOGICAL TABLES

PREFACE

'Don't touch the Aga, it's hot.' These were the first words I remember spoken when I arrived at Westminster Abbey as a four-year-old boy in 1951, little taller than the Aga itself. My father had been appointed a canon of Westminster and we had travelled up together from Stanmore where he had been rector. I remember sitting in a car and seeing the flashing lights of London (it was already dark) through the window and then, when the car (driven by one of my father's old parishioners) broke down, sitting on the back seat of a bus and playing with a little blue plastic man. In 1985 I was with my father again when, having retired, he walked away from the Abbey, after thirty-four years as canon, archdeacon and latterly as dean.

It might be natural to think that, given my long association with Westminster Abbey, I was always destined to write a biography of its builder, King Henry III. But the truth is more complex. Growing up at the Abbey was in some ways a constricting experience with the constant fear of 'complaints' if I or my brother made too much noise in the cloisters or the Abbey garden. Compulsory attendance at the 10.30 Sunday service left me with a lifelong feeling of release at getting out of church. Later, as a teenager at Westminster school, and in the year before university working in the Abbey Library, I did begin to appreciate the beauty of the Abbey's architecture and sculpture but this hardly made me think very much about Henry III. Indeed, Henry was hardly celebrated at the Abbey. There was no effort to mark the 700th anniversaries of either the consecration of his new church on 13 October 1969 or of his death on 16 November 1972. As an undergraduate, reading history at Christ Church, Oxford, I spent an enjoyable summer term studying England in the central middle ages with my tutor, John Mason. And yet, curiously enough, we jumped from King John to King Edward I and left out Henry III altogether. We did the same the following year when studying Bishop Stubbs' *Select Charters Illustrative of English Constitutional History*. I never objected and indeed never asked why. For a third year special subject, I chose not the one on Henry III and Simon de Montfort, but 'British Policy and the making of the ententes 1898–1908'. For a while I thought of doing a doctorate on some related topic of diplomatic history.

In the event, my doctorate grew out of my work on Stubbs' *Select Charters*. My plan was to investigate how far magnates were able to corrupt the juries central to the new legal procedures introduced by King Henry II.

It was not a topic capable of much development, given the state of the evidence, but it did lead me, via some interesting cases, to Oxfordshire and an eventual thesis about the sheriffs of Oxfordshire in the first half of the thirteenth century. The thesis was hardly publishable as a book but, as my supervisor John Prestwich perceptively observed, it was good preparation for investigating many aspects of thirteenth-century history. It enabled me to explore the running of local government, the structure of local society and the course of high politics, for many of the sheriffs were leading ministers of the king. It led to articles on the changing nature of the sheriff's office, the social and economic position of the knightly class, and the fall of Henry III's great minister Hubert de Burgh. It was only with these and other articles out of the way that I began to think, with no one else aspiring to do so, that I might be qualified to write a full-scale biography of Henry III.

I began work on this biography in the 1980s and have written parts of it intermittently over the following years. When, however, the 2015 Magna Carta anniversary year was over, I wrote and rewrote the narrative of the whole reign from start to finish, so I hope the account is not disjointed. The resulting biography will appear in two volumes. This volume runs from Henry's birth in 1207 through to the great political revolution of 1258 that stripped him of power. It thus covers his early life, his minority and its aftermath, and then the whole of his personal rule from 1234 down to 1258.[1] Although I have yet to finish two thematic chapters, I hope there will be no significant interval between the volumes.[2]

In writing about the reign of Henry III, the first debt of all historians is to the wonderful sources on which accounts are based. These are firstly the records produced by the king's government and especially the rolls of the chancery recording the charters and letters issued by the king. Henry's letters in particular often take us very close to his personality and policies. Because, moreover, all the charters and letters end with the place and date of their issue, it is possible to see where Henry was on the great majority of days each year. Since the charters have witness lists, it is possible to see the leading figures with him at court.[3] Alongside the record sources, there are the accounts of the reign written by contemporary historians. Here one name stands out, that of the monk of St Albans, Matthew Paris. An

---

[1] Since I have covered the politics of the minority in great detail in my *Minority of Henry III*, published in 1990, I have sketched the course of events, especially in the early minority, when Henry was not involved, very lightly.

[2] In chapter 1 of volume 2, 'Henry III and his People', I will put the politics of the reign into its wider social and intellectual context.

[3] I remember going right up in the estimation of C.A.F. Meekings, doyen of the Public Record Office, when, as a young scholar, I pointed out that the fall of the king's steward Godfrey of Crowcombe in 1233 could be seen in his sudden disappearance from the witness lists. Subsequently Meekings allowed me to photocopy his detailed analysis of the witness lists and they have been a great help in writing this book.

historian of extraordinary energy, both prejudiced and perceptive, his account of the years 1235 to 1259 runs to over 1,400 pages in a nineteenth-century printed edition and has much to say, both good and bad, about the king.[4]

Mention of printed editions takes us to a second debt, namely that to the many editors who, since the nineteenth century, have put so much of the source material of the period into print. The Public Record Office itself was responsible for publishing, partly in full Latin, partly in English calendar, thirty volumes of chancery rolls. Its labours were completed by the Henry III Fine Rolls Project which has published online searchable English translations of the two million words of the fine rolls.[5]

Another debt, of course, is to all the historians who have written about the period. One naturally starts here with Sir Maurice Powicke's two-volume study of the reign, *Henry III and the Lord Edward*, published in 1947, the first to make full use of the then recently published chancery rolls. 'Powicke wrote until inspiration came' was a remark once made to me by John Prestwich, and certainly in *Henry III and the Lord Edward* there are sections where it is very difficult to see where he is going.[6] Yet, when inspiration did strike, Powicke could write passages of fine prose and great insight. Here he is, for example, on Henry: 'Though much too big a man to be content with little things, he was happiest while he was holding splendid feasts or moving about from one hunting lodge to another, or praying at shrines, or, most of all, when he was planning the decoration of his houses and supervising, with remarkable attention to detail, the construction of Westminster Abbey. There at any rate he had more than a vision of greatness, and could live with an intensity denied to the dilettante.'[7]

After Powicke, little appeared on the reign of Henry III for many years, apart from a thought-provoking article on whether Henry had a policy, published by Michael Clanchy in 1968.[8] There was, however, much to be done, for while Powicke mentioned the building of the Public Record Office in London's Chancery Lane, he never seems to have entered its portals to consult the mountain of legal and financial material preserved

---

[4] This is in his *Chronica Majora*. For Paris, see below, 170–2.

[5] https://finerollshenry3.org.uk/home.html. The charter roll witness lists have also appeared separately, see in the Bibliography under *RCWL*.

[6] When I first started to teach the period at Christ Church, I remember rescuing a student who was sitting in the Library trying to read the chapter on 'Reform at the Exchequer', a subject Powicke clearly did not understand himself.

[7] F.M. Powicke, *King Henry III and the Lord Edward* (Oxford, 1947), i, 156–7. Henry, however, rarely visited his hunting lodges. Powicke also covered the reign in his Oxford History: *The Thirteenth Century, 1216–1307* (Oxford, 1953). Powicke is buried in the Lake District's Eskdale, where he owned Christcliff cottage, a very humble abode with low ceilings and small rooms. When I visited it a few years ago, long after it had passed from Powicke's descendants, many of his books were still on the shelves, a curious experience.

[8] M.T. Clanchy, 'Did Henry III have a policy?', *History*, 53 (1968), 203–16.

there.[9] Its use by later scholars has transformed our understanding of many aspects of Henry's reign. An important stage in that transformation came in 1985 with the first of the Thirteenth Century England conferences. It was held in Newcastle upon Tyne and organized by Peter Coss and Simon Lloyd. I am proud to say that, by the luck of the draw, I gave the very first paper (on the gold treasure of Henry III). Since then the Conference has been held every two years and, after its move from Newcastle, has been organized by historians from the universities of Durham, Aberystwyth and Cambridge. Its printed proceedings contain a wealth of new thinking and information about the reign of Henry III. At the same time many important books on the period have been published as well as papers in periodicals and collections of essays. Much new work is also forthcoming and I am grateful to those who have sent me their discoveries and given me advanced sight of future books and papers. I thank them in the appropriate place. Every time I look at what has appeared in *Thirteenth Century England* and elsewhere I find myself wanting to add to what I have written. But that would make an already long book even longer. I apologize for all I have missed.

In preparing the book for publication, I owe a great debt to Michael Clanchy and Michael Prestwich who both read the text for Yale and made a series of valuable suggestions. Thanks to Michael Prestwich I am also much better informed about the nature of lampreys and the unpleasant images of them on line.[10] The book has been read too by Adrian Jobson and Richard Cassidy and I have profited greatly from their comments and information. Adrian has put the footnotes into proper form and compiled the Bibliography. Richard has compiled much of the index. I could not have produced the book without their help.

The book would not have appeared without the encouragement over many years of Heather McCallum at Yale and her final decision, difficult I know, to publish in two volumes, rather than to cut it all down to one. I am grateful for her confidence and support. At Yale I am also indebted to Marika Lysandrou, Clarissa Sutherland, Lucy Buchan, Percie Edgeler and Rachael Lonsdale for all their work on the book; to Chris Shaw for proofreading; to Martin Brown for creating the maps; and Heather Nathan and James Williams for marketing and publicity. I have been lucky to join forces again

[9] Powicke, *King Henry III and the Lord Edward*, i, 125. After the Second World War, Powicke, just beginning work on the Oxford History, observed to his new doctoral student, Hugh Lawrence (as Hugh himself told me), that he was 'looking for a man' to help with all the material in the Public Record Office (PRO). Hugh, who had fought against the Japanese, was not falling for that and so Powicke never got his 'man', as the absence of references to PRO material in the History shows. To be fair to Powicke, he had much new material to work on in the printed chancery rolls.

[10] For Heston Blumenthal cooking lampreys, see https://www.youtube.com/watch?v=ZteNjBgJgbU.

with Richard Mason, who has copy-edited *Henry III* with the same eagle-eyed expertise he showed in copy-editing my Penguin Classics book on Magna Carta.

I have, over the years, received much generous help from Matthew Payne, Tony Trowles and Christine Reynolds at Westminster Abbey, and from Jessica Nelson and Paul Dryburgh at The National Archives. The book has been written while a member of the History Department of King's College London. I could not have been in a more happy environment. Amongst the medievalists I have had a series of wonderful colleagues: Allen Brown (all too briefly), Jinty Nelson, Diana Webb, Anne Duggan, Serena Ferente, Stephen Baxter, Denis Stathakopoulos, Peter Heather, Alice Rio, Alice Taylor, Julia Crick, Alexandra Sapoznik, Rory Naismith and Simon Parsons. A special thanks to Alice Taylor for all the laughter and learning she has shared with me, although I realize this is absolutely not her kind of book. For many years at King's I have shared an office with Daniel Hadas and I have benefited greatly from our discussions of theology, liturgy and points of Latin translation.

My final debt is to all the students at undergraduate, MA and doctoral level who have studied the reign of Henry III with me over so many years.

The book is dedicated to my wife, Jane, and our children, Katie and James.

David Carpenter, King's College London, June 2019

A NOTE ON THE TEXT

MONEY AND ITS VALUE

In the reign of Henry III, save for a brief period in the 1250s when he launched a gold coinage, there was only one coin of the realm, namely the silver penny, or in Latin 'denarius'.[1] Although amounts of money were frequently expressed in terms of pounds (Latin 'libra'), shillings (Latin 'solidus'), as well as pence (hence l. s. d.), pounds and shillings were terms of account. There were no pound or shilling coins. There were 240 pennies in a pound, 12 pennies in a shilling and 20 shillings in a pound. Another term of account was 'mark', worth two-thirds of a pound, so 13s 4d or 160 pennies. Rather than convert all money into pounds, shillings and pence, I have for the most part followed the contemporary sources in using sometimes pounds and sometimes marks, so having 100 marks rather than the cumbersome £66 13s 4d. Unless stated, all money is expressed in terms of these English values.

In Henry's reign a day's wage for a male labourer was often 1½d and for a female 1d. When Henry III fed paupers, the cost was usually between 1d and 1½d per head per day. Bread came in halfpenny loaves. The day's wage for a professional knight was 24d or 2s. In 1244 landholders with incomes of £20 a year were obliged to take up knighthood. Many barons had incomes of several hundred pounds a year. The annual income of an earl could be several thousands. After it had recovered from collapse in the 1215–17 civil war, the ordinary annual income of the Crown was around £25,000 a year.[2]

FOOTNOTES AND BIBLIOGRAPHY

In the footnotes, works by contemporary authors appear for the most part under either the name of the author (so Paris) or, in the case of chronicles where the author is unknown, under the name of the place where the chronicle was written (so Dunstable). Record sources are cited by an

---

[1] It was, however, lawful to cut a penny into halves or quarters, so creating halfpenny and farthing coins.
[2] For standards of living, see C. Dyer, *Standards of Living in the Later Middle Ages: Social Change in England c.1200–1520* (Cambridge, 1989).

abbreviated form of the published title (so *CR*, with the relevant dates, for *Close Rolls*). Full references to all these sources may be found in the Bibliography. In references to unprinted sources BL stands for the British Library, TNA for The National Archives at Kew and WAM for Westminster Abbey Muniments. Other archival references are given in full. Secondary sources are cited by the surname of the author and a short form of the title of the work, italicized in the case of books, within inverted commas in the case of articles and chapters in volumes of essays. Full details may be found in the Bibliography under the name of the author. I have stuck to the division between primary and secondary sources although many printed primary sources have important introductions by their editors.

PERSONAL NAMES

In the case of toponymic surnames, the modern form of the place has been given preceded by 'of', so Stephen of Seagrave. The exceptions are where this would overturn established usage, so Hubert de Burgh, not Hubert of Burgh. If the place is in France, the modern form is given preceded by 'de', so Falkes de Bréauté, but again exceptions are made where this would overturn established usage, so William de Ferrers, not de Ferrières. Where places have not been identified, a common contemporary form is used preceded by 'de'. In general I have tried to follow the forms found in the translations of the fine rolls: https://finerollshenry3.org.uk/home.html.

1. England in the time of Henry III

2. Wales in the time of Henry III

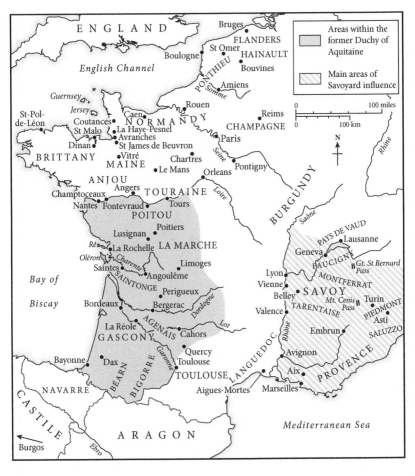

3. France and neighbouring regions in the time of Henry III

4. Gascony and neighbouring regions in the time of Henry III

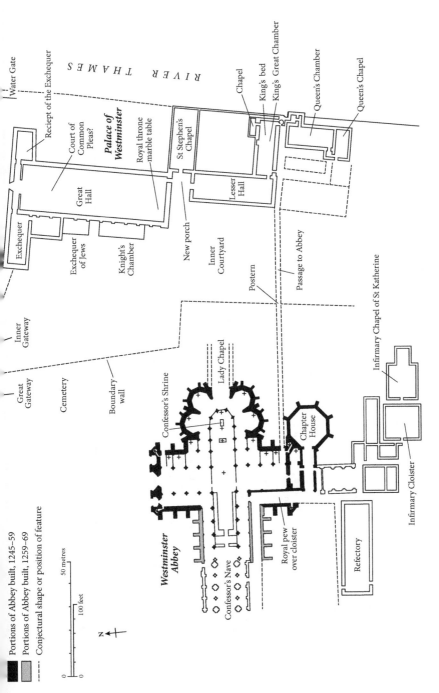

Portions of Abbey built, 1245–59

Portions of Abbey built, 1259–69

Conjectural shape or position of feature

50 metres

100 feet

N

Palace of Westminster

Water Gate

Reciept of the Exchequer

RIVER THAMES

Court of Common Pleas?

Royal throne marble table

Chapel

King's bed

King's Great Chamber

Queen's Chamber

Queen's Chapel

Great Hall

Exchequer

Exchequer of Jews

Knight's Chamber

St Stephen's Chapel

New porch

Inner Courtyard

Lesser Hall

Postern

Passage to Abbey

Inner Gateway

Great Gateway

Cemetery

Boundary wall

Westminster Abbey

Confessor's Shrine

Lady Chapel

Chapter House

Infirmary Chapel of St Katherine

Confessor's Nave

Royal pew over cloister

Infirmary Cloister

Refectory

5. The Abbey and Palace of Westminster in the time of Henry III

1. Henry III and his family

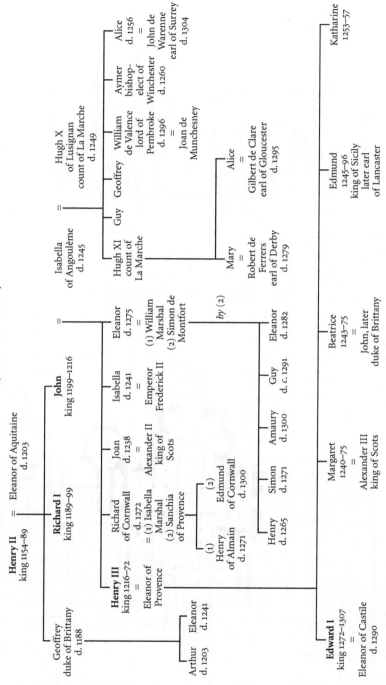

2. The House of Savoy

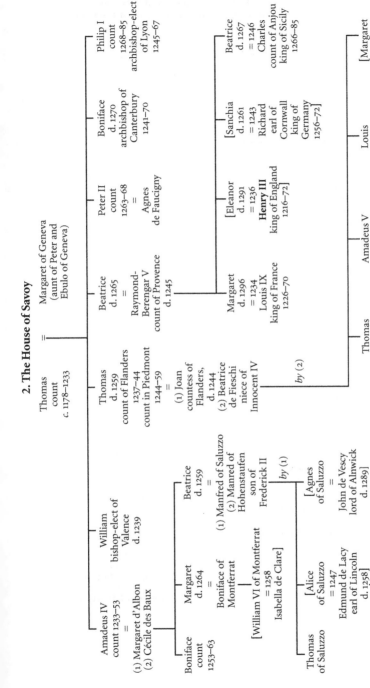

Thomas
count
c. 1178–1233
=
Margaret of Geneva
(aunt of Peter and
Ebulo of Geneva)

Amadeus IV
count 1233–53
=
(1) Margaret d'Albon
(2) Cécile des Baux

William
bishop-elect of
Valence
d. 1239

Thomas
d. 1259
count of Flanders
1237–44
count in Piedmont
1244–59
=
(1) Joan
countess of
Flanders,
d. 1244
(2) Beatrice
de Fieschi
niece of
Innocent IV

Beatrice
d. 1265
=
Raymond-
Berengar V
count of Provence
d. 1245

Peter II
count
1263–68
=
Agnes
de Faucigny

Boniface
d. 1270
archbishop of
Canterbury
1241–70

Philip I
count
1268–85
archbishop-elect
of Lyon
1245–67

Boniface
count
1253–63

Margaret
d. 1264
=
Boniface of
Montferrat

Beatrice
d. 1259
=
(1) Manfred of Saluzzo
(2) Manfred of
Hohenstaufen
son of
Frederick II

Margaret
d. 1296
=
Louis IX
king of France
1226–70

[Eleanor
d. 1291
= 1236
Henry III
king of England
1216–72]

[Sanchia
d. 1261
= 1243
Richard
earl of
Cornwall
king of
Germany
1256–72]

Beatrice
d. 1267
= 1246
Charles
count of Anjou
king of Sicily
1266–85

Thomas
of Saluzzo

[Alice
of Saluzzo
= 1247
Edmund de Lacy
earl of Lincoln
d. 1258]

[Agnes
of Saluzzo
=
John de Vescy
lord of Alnwick
d. 1289]

[William VI of Montferrat
= 1258
Isabella de Clare]

Henry de Lacy
earl of Lincoln
d. 1311

by (1)

by (2)

Thomas

Amadeus V
count
1285–1323

Louis

[Margaret
= 1257
Baldwin de Redvers
earl of Devon
d. 1262]

[English marriages in square brackets]

3. The descendants of William Marshal, earl of Pembroke and regent of England

*(shares of Marshal inheritances in **bold**)*

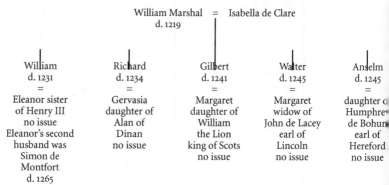

William Marshal = Isabella de Clare
d. 1219

William
d. 1231
=
Eleanor sister
of Henry III
no issue
Eleanor's second
husband was
Simon de
Montfort
d. 1265

Richard
d. 1234
=
Gervasia
daughter of
Alan of
Dinan
no issue

Gilbert
d. 1241
=
Margaret
daughter of
William
the Lion
king of Scots
no issue

Walter
d. 1245
=
Margaret
widow of
John de Lacey
earl of
Lincoln
no issue

Anselm
d. 1245
=
daughter of
Humphrey
de Bohun
earl of
Hereford
no issue

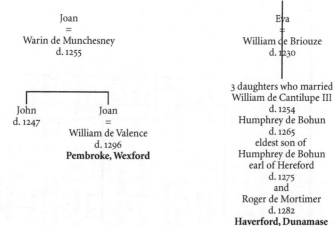

Joan
=
Warin de Munchesney
d. 1255

Eva
=
William de Briouze
d. 1230

John
d. 1247

Joan
=
William de Valence
d. 1296
Pembroke, Wexford

3 daughters who married
William de Cantilupe III
d. 1254
Humphrey de Bohun
d. 1265
eldest son of
Humphrey de Bohun
earl of Hereford
d. 1275
and
Roger de Mortimer
d. 1282
Haverford, Dunamase

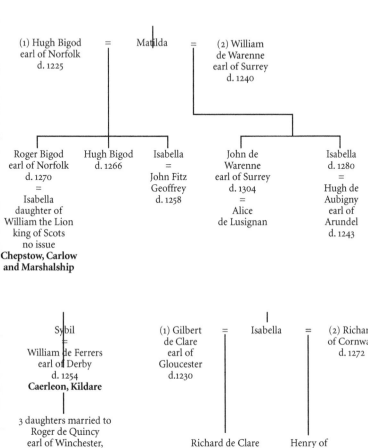

(1) Hugh Bigod
earl of Norfolk
d. 1225
= Matilda = (2) William
de Warenne
earl of Surrey
d. 1240

Roger Bigod
earl of Norfolk
d. 1270
=
Isabella
daughter of
William the Lion
king of Scots
no issue
**Chepstow, Carlow
and Marshalship**

Hugh Bigod
d. 1266

Isabella
=
John Fitz
Geoffrey
d. 1258

John de
Warenne
earl of Surrey
d. 1304
=
Alice
de Lusignan

Isabella
d. 1280
=
Hugh de
Aubigny
earl of
Arundel
d. 1243

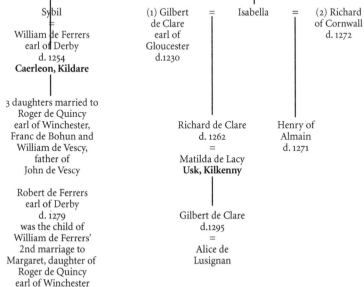

Sybil
=
William de Ferrers
earl of Derby
d. 1254
Caerleon, Kildare

3 daughters married to
Roger de Quincy
earl of Winchester,
Franc de Bohun and
William de Vescy,
father of
John de Vescy

Robert de Ferrers
earl of Derby
d. 1279
was the child of
William de Ferrers'
2nd marriage to
Margaret, daughter of
Roger de Quincy
earl of Winchester

(1) Gilbert
de Clare
earl of
Gloucester
d.1230
= Isabella = (2) Richard
of Cornwall
d. 1272

Richard de Clare
d. 1262
=
Matilda de Lacy
Usk, Kilkenny

Gilbert de Clare
d.1295
=
Alice de
Lusignan

Henry of
Almain
d. 1271

Chapter 1

FROM HENRY'S BIRTH TO THE END OF THE MINORITY
1207–1227

One day in late October 1216, William Marshal, earl of Pembroke, an old man of around seventy, but still vigorous in mind and body, rode south out of Malmesbury in the direction of Devizes. Across the plain riding towards him he saw a great company of armed men. At their centre, held by his master, Ralph de St Samson, was a boy, just past his ninth birthday, with blonde hair and a pleasant face. When the two groups met, the boy, breaking down in tears, commended himself to the Marshal's protection. The Marshal, crying now himself 'tenderly out of pity', promised faithful service as long as he lived.[1] The party then set out north for Gloucester, where on 28 October the boy was crowned and anointed king of England. The reign of King Henry III, the son of King John, had begun.

Henry was born on 1 October 1207 in the royal castle of Winchester. In later life he was occasionally called 'Henry of Winchester' and the castle became one of his favourite residences.[2] Henry was the first child of John's marriage to Isabella of Angoulême, politically an unfortunate union. John had good reasons for marrying Isabella for he thereby secured her strategic county of Angoulême to the south of Poitou. But he also grievously offended her previously intended husband, the great Poitevin baron Hugh de Lusignan, the count of La Marche. Hugh appealed for justice to John's overlord, the king of France, Philip Augustus. The result was the confiscation of John's continental fiefs and Philip's rapid conquest (in 1203–4) of Normandy and Anjou. These events ripped the heart from John's continental dominions and overshadowed the rest of his reign. John spent the next ten years largely in England, extorting the huge sums of money needed to recover his lost possessions. The failure of the eventual campaign in 1214, with his allies comprehensively defeated by King Philip at the

---

[1] This picture, as much else about the minority, comes from the life of William Marshal, commisioned by his family and written in the mid-1220s: Marshal, lines 262–7. For the blonde hair and pleasant face, see Paris, *HA*, ii, 196: 'venusta facies cum flava caesarie'.

[2] Guisborough, 221. For Henry being thus described in a plea roll of 1269, see TNA CP 21/1/7, m.25, a reference I owe to Paul Brand. That Henry thought of himself as 'Henry of Winchester' is suggested by the name being given to a Jew he had converted to Christianity, see below, 305.

I

battle of Bouvines, undermined John's power, and made possible rebellion in England.[3] As the price of peace, in June 1215, John conceded Magna Carta. His reneging on the Great Charter after little more than a month produced the civil war in which, as will be seen, Henry came to the throne.

For some years John's marriage lacked even the compensation of children. Since Isabella later proved extremely fertile, she was perhaps even younger than twelve (the one estimate of her age) at the time of her marriage in 1200.[4] As her pregnancy with Henry developed so did John's concern for her welfare. He described her in a letter as 'amica nostra', a term of endearment usually applied to his mistresses. He gave her 'a good saddle, plain and gilded with good reins and other appurtenances'. He begged her 'brother' to come to England 'to see the queen, our wife, your sister, who much desires to see you'.[5] John was at Winchester on 1 October for the birth, having hovered for the last few days of September within reach of the town. He stayed for three days and then hurried off to London.[6] That set the pattern for the future. John's hectic itinerary, rarely spending more than a few days at any one place, meant he was to see little of his son on any continuous basis. The queen was different. The evidence, while fragmentary, suggests she and her son were often together at Winchester and elsewhere.[7] The rather demure effigy at Fontevraud, which Henry many years later set up over her tomb, gives little impression of the strength of Isabella's body and the power of her personality. That strength was displayed in her childbearing. Henry's birth was followed by that of another son in 1209 (named Richard after John's heroic brother 'the Lionheart') and three daughters: Joan, born in 1210, Isabella in 1214, and Eleanor, the youngest (later the wife of Simon de Montfort), with whom the queen was pregnant at the time of John's death, in 1216. Isabella's second marriage (to Hugh de Lusignan, son of her originally intended husband) produced another six children. Her career shows she had a fiery sense of her queenly status. As she got older, she surely resented the way John, quite apart from dallying with mistresses, confined her to castles and denied her any political role. Stories of their tempestuous arguments abounded.

Isabella's proximity to Henry did not mean they had a close relationship. Indeed, judging from her return to France after John's death, she felt no deep bond with her children. In any case, women of high birth did not attend personally to the wants of their offspring. For a noblewoman to give suck herself, as twelfth-century romances make plain, was highly unusual.[8]

---

[3] For Bouvines, see Duby, *Le Dimanche de Bouvines*, and Barthélemy, *La Bataille de Bouvines*.

[4] Coggeshall, 103. For Isabella, see Vincent, 'Isabella of Angoulême'.

[5] *RLC*, i, 81; *RLP*, 71b. Isabella was the only surviving child of Aymer, count of Angoulême, and Amicie de Courtenay. The brother mentioned here, in fact her half-brother, was Peter de Joigny, product of Amicie's first marriage to the count of Joigny.

[6] Winchester, 80; Crowland, 199; Dunstable, 29; Gervase, ii, 106; Margam, 58; Osney, 54; Tewkesbury, 209; Waverley, 259; Wendover, iii, 520; Worcester, 395.

[7] Vincent, *Peter des Roches*, 71 n.128.

[8] Gillingham, *Richard I*, 32.

The nurses employed seem usually to have been commoners and this had important linguistic consequences. The vernacular language Henry grew up speaking, the language of the court and nobility, was French. It was in French that the two accounts of John's reign designed for the secular aristocracy were written. English, by contrast, was the vernacular language of the free-tenants and peasants who made up the great bulk of the population. Henry came into frequent contact with common people. Thanks to the language he learnt from his nurses he could speak with them directly. The best proof of this bilingualism comes in a remark Matthew Paris made about Henry's brother, Richard. He was considered suitable as king of Germany because of the similarity between the German and English tongue – 'linguam Anglicanam'. Clearly Richard could speak English and there was little difference between his upbringing and Henry's.[9]

We get a glimpse of Henry's attendants in 1210/11 when robes were bought for two women of his chamber, probably when he was staying at Winchester.[10] The one person specifically called Henry's nurse was usually named simply 'Helen', a good indication of her lowly origins. Since she occasionally appears as 'Helen of Winchester', and was young (living till the late 1240s), she may well have been Henry's wet nurse from the time of his birth.[11] Henry certainly remained attached to her. By the 1220s she was established with her husband, William Dun, at the royal manor of Havering in Essex, where she often received favours on the king's visits. Henry also remembered her at other times, giving her firewood in 1233, 1234, 1235, 1237, 1238, 1241, 1246 and 1247. As late as 1239 he increased by 2d a day the 6d a day pension she had received since 1213/14.[12]

Well might Henry, in his first years, be coddled by nurses, for the political significance of his birth was enormous. It was recorded in nearly all the contemporary chronicles. As late as 1221 the earl of Essex dated an event 'to the year in which the king was born'.[13] Henry's birth strengthened John's immediate political position and, so he might hope, secured the future of his dynasty, what he later called 'our perpetual hereditary succession'.[14] It was to stress dynastic continuity that John had named Henry after his mighty father Henry II. No wonder as much as £42 was spent in alms at Winchester during an early illness.[15] Henry's inheritance

[9] Paris, v, 603. For discussion, see Short, 'On bilingualism in Anglo-Norman England'; Lodge, 'Language attitudes and linguistic norms'. For a sketch of English society in the early thirteenth century as reflected in Magna Carta, see Carpenter, *Magna Carta*, chs. 4 and 5.

[10] *PR 1211*, 178.

[11] *PR 1211*, 171, 249; *CR 1227–31*, 516. Although as Michael Prestwich points out to me, Helen is a very rare name and an odd one for someone of low status.

[12] *CR 1227–31*, 516; *CR 1231–4*, 25, 214, 481; *CR 1234–7*, 133, 475; *CR 1237–42*, 79, 159, 297; *CR 1242–7*, 420, 514; *CLR 1226–40*, 140; *PR 1214*, 35, 54; *Pipe Roll 1242*, 129, 216. A penny was a day's wage for a female labourer.

[13] *CRR*, x, 139.

[14] *Guala*, no. 140b.

[15] *RLC*, i, 519.

should have included far more than just England. In all his charters and
letters John styled himself 'king of England, lord of Ireland, duke of
Normandy and Aquitaine and count of Anjou'. These titles, moreover,
gave no impression of how John had, for a while, subjected both the king
of Scotland and the native Welsh rulers to his overlordship. In 1212 the
Crowland chronicler credited him with a dominance over the British Isles
achieved by none of his predecessors. On the continent, as duke of
Normandy, count of Anjou and duke of Aquitaine, John's dominions
embraced the whole of the western side of France. Before the loss of
Normandy and Anjou, he was the mightiest ruler in Europe. How far his
son could recover that position was a major question for the reign.

As John's political difficulties mounted, so did Henry's significance.
Allegiance to the son became linked to allegiance to the father as a way of
testing and securing loyalty. In March 1209, Pope Innocent III placed
England under an interdict, John having refused to accept the papal
nominee, Stephen Langton, as the new archbishop of Canterbury. That
September, in great ceremonies around the country, climaxing in one at
Marlborough, all the free men of the kingdom were summoned to do
homage to the king and to Henry 'as the king's heir'.[16] John was also using
his son's marriage in diplomacy. By the Treaty of Norham, forced on
William the Lion, king of Scots, in August 1209, the latter's eldest daughter,
Margaret, was to marry Henry by the time he was ten years old.[17]
Whether John ever intended to go through with this low-status marriage
may be doubted. He had anyway eight years to think about it. Meanwhile,
the agreement helped get Margaret and her sister into his custody and
prevented them marrying anyone else. Three months later, in November
1209, with John still defiant, Pope Innocent proclaimed his excommunication. Although he never actually deposed the king, it was commonly
believed that he had done so. In 1212, thus encouraged, a group of barons
plotted against John's life. In his immediate panic, John thought at once of
his heir: only those bringing special letters of authorization were to be
allowed to see him. Further oaths of loyalty to Henry followed, one taken
by William Marshal himself.[18]

It was around this time in 1211 or 1212 that John made a major decision
about Henry's future by entrusting him to the guardianship of Peter des
Roches, bishop of Winchester. Bishop Peter was still impacting on Henry's
life and envenoming English politics more then twenty years later.[19] He
was in every way a remarkable man. Born at a guess around 1170, he came

---

[16] See Maddicott, 'Oath of Marlborough'.

[17] Carpenter, *Magna Carta*, 473–5. Margaret's sister Isabella was also handed over with
the promise of finding her a suitable marriage.

[18] *RLC*, i, 121b; *RLP*, 92, 95b.

[19] For a comprehensive treatment of Peter's career, see Nicholas Vincent's biography
Peter des Roches.

from the Touraine and was a member of the family that also produced William des Roches, a servant of Henry II who rose to be seneschal of Anjou. In the 1190s Peter entered the service of King Richard and then passed into that of King John. For both kings he acted as a clerk of the royal chamber and was thus intimately involved in their day-to-day expenditure of money. In 1205 John made this chamber clerk bishop of Winchester. Peter proved far more than a worldly prelate. He founded religious houses, conducted the first Dominican friars to England, and issued statutes bringing the life of his diocese into line with the reforming decrees of the 1215 Fourth Lateran Council. He was very much in touch with the religious currents of his age. Yet Peter, unique amongst his English episcopal colleagues, was also happy taking part in warfare. In 1217 he played a decisive part at the battle of Lincoln. He also, despite his episcopal duties, remained at the centre of royal government, sitting at the exchequer and in 1214 becoming 'justiciar', the king's chief minister. Arrogant and abrasive, he was very ready to push the king's policies to their limit. One (unfair) lampoon ran as follows:

> The warrior of Winchester
> Presides at the exchequer
> Indefatigable at accounting
> Indolent at the scripture
> Revolving the king's roll.[20]

There was also something else about Bishop Peter. He made no secret of his affection for his homeland in the Touraine. His loyalty was to the dynasty not to the land of England. He was quite capable of expressing contempt for English custom and contrasting his loyalty to the king with the disloyalty of native barons. Closely associated with other foreigners who felt much like himself, he increasingly stood out, in a period of increasing national feeling, as 'an alien in English politics'.[21]

In 1211 or 1212, when he became the king's guardian, much of this was in the future. What counted for John was Peter's absolute loyalty. He was at the time the only English bishop still at the king's side, the others having gone into exile during the Interdict, itself a stunning demonstration of papal authority.[22] Henry would be safe in Bishop Peter's hands. He is now found staying at episcopal residences as well as at Winchester castle, of which Peter became keeper.

The start of Bishop Peter's guardianship probably saw Henry move from the nursery to the schoolroom. (Around this time Helen of Winchester

---

[20] *Political Songs*, 10. For a different translation (although the sense is the same), see Clanchy, *England and its Rulers*, 129.

[21] This is the subtitle of Vincent's *Peter des Roches*.

[22] The bishop of Norwich, John de Grey, continued to serve John as justiciar of Ireland.

seems to have been pensioned off.)[23] It is possible that Henry's tutor was the poet Henry of Avranches, someone very much in Bishop Peter's circle. At any rate Avranches dedicated to Henry a metrical treatise on grammar, designed, so he said, to spare boys the difficulty of studying the multitude of contemporary books on the subject. However, at 2,200 lines, Henry may have found this hard going. Perhaps the work was more designed to impress the court than educate the pupil.[24] Ralph de St Samson, who held Henry at that first meeting with William Marshal, is never described as more than a 'serviens', which probably means in his case 'sergeant at arms'. In all likelihood, he was more Henry's bodyguard than anything else. That Henry was taught to speak and read Latin seems almost certain, even if there is no absolute proof. Latin was the language of the daily mass and the bible. It was also the language of all the documents produced by the royal chancery, exchequer and law courts. The clerk Walter Map stated that Henry's grandfather, Henry II, spoke Latin as well as French, and was for practical purposes 'literatus', which certainly meant he could read.[25] That Henry could do the same is suggested by poems and saints lives he later commissioned both in Latin and French (some from Henry of Avranches) and by the numerous occasions he demanded evidence in writing, for example about the state of his treasure. A joke he played on one of his clerks on the ship coming back from Gascony in 1243 depended very much on them both being able to read what Henry had ordered to be written on a roll.[26] Looking back from the 1220s, the biography of William Marshal acknowledged that, on his accession, the new king had been well brought up by Bishop Peter, and there is no reason to question that judgement.[27]

In 1215, as the rebellion against him gathered pace, John became increasingly concerned about the security of his wife and son. In May he brought them from Winchester castle to join him at Marlborough. Later in the year, after the breakdown of the Magna Carta peace, he sent them both to Corfe, the great stronghold where he had starved prisoners to death and lavished money on new fortifications and apartments. Later Henry was moved again, forty miles inland to the castle at Devizes. In July 1216, John had Gilbert son of Walter de Lacy removed from the castle 'since we do not wish so many boys to be there as there are now'.[28] Was John worried about security with so many boys running around? Was Gilbert seen as a bad influence? At least the order shows Henry had companions of his own age.[29]

---

[23] *PR 1211*, 171, 249.

[24] Henry of Avranches, 56–8. For Avranche's later career, see below, 403.

[25] Walter Map, 476–7.

[26] See below, 271–2.

[27] Marshal, lines 15267, 15604–10.

[28] *RLP*, 136, 191b (the 'Henry our son', one of the recipients of this order, was John's illegitimate son); Anonymous, 152.

[29] Earlier a son or brother of John de Lacy was with Henry: Vincent, *Peter des Roches*, 71 n.128. Gilbert de Lacy predeceased his father, dying in 1230.

HENRY'S ACCESSION

No king of England came to the throne in a more desperate situation than Henry III.[30] His grand titles had a very hollow ring. After John's rejection of Magna Carta, the rebel barons had deposed him and offered the throne to Louis, eldest son of the king of France. In May 1216, Louis arrived in England with a large army. He was cheered into London and accepted by the majority of the barons. Many previously loyal to John, such as the earls of Salisbury and Surrey and the chief forester, Hugh de Neville, deserted. They evidently felt he was finished. John had other ideas. In July 1216 he left Corfe and set off on a ravaging expedition that took him to the Welsh marches and then to East Anglia. But by early October he was grievously ill with dysentery. He died in Newark castle during the night of 18–19 October while a great storm battered the town and made the citizens fear for the safety of their houses. With John dead, leaving only a nine-year-old son, might not everyone go over to Louis and bring the war to an end?

The likelihood of that was increased by the causes of the rebellion. They went beyond John's personal failings – his cruelty, his murders, his sexual harassment of the wives and daughters of his barons.[31] Magna Carta was an attack on the dynasty as a whole. The king's financial exactions, his denial of justice, his seizures of property without legal process had got far worse under John, yet had been present in varying degrees under his brother Richard and his father Henry II. Why not then just get rid of the dynasty altogether?

Nothing like that happened. Here the oaths of allegiance John had demanded had some effect. William Marshal stressed again and again the loyalty he owed to Henry. If all else failed, he would bear him on his back to Ireland, the only place where the rebellion had no footing. There were also hard material reasons for remaining with the young king. John's captains and castellans, ruthless and often low born, could expect nothing from Louis. Some of the loyalist barons had disputes over lands and rights with the barons on Louis's side. If they could win the war, they might settle things in their own favour and also (a point made to the Marshal by his entourage) have much with which to reward their followers.

Henry's position, moreover, while desperate was not hopeless. Corfe and Devizes, his homes in 1215–16, were but two of many castles still in royal hands snaking across the land. There were also tensions in Louis's camp. He had been called in by the barons as the one person with the power to give them victory in their life and death struggle with John. But now there were quarrels over place and patronage between Louis's English

---

[30] I have covered the period between 1216 and 1225 in great detail in my *Minority of Henry III*, where full references to what follows may be found.

[31] For biographies of King John, see Warren, *King John*; Turner, *King John*, Church, *King John*, and Morris, *King John*.

and French supporters, as well as growing hostility in England more generally to these French invaders. And then there was the attitude of the pope. In 1213, John had finally accepted Stephen Langton as archbishop of Canterbury, bringing his excommunication and (in 1214) the Interdict to an end. In 1213 he had done homage to Pope Innocent for the kingdom of England, making it a papal fief. Then in 1215 he had taken the cross and promised to go on crusade. Once the pope's greatest enemy, now he was his greatest friend, a moving example, so Innocent thought, of 'the boundless and infinite goodness of God which makes just men of transgressors and turns sinners into saints'.[32] Accordingly, Innocent had quashed Magna Carta at John's behest and then excommunicated Louis and his supporters. This deprived Louis of senior ecclesiastical support and meant he could not be crowned. The pope's stand was reinforced by his legate in England, the formidable Cardinal Guala Bicchieri. The very look of him was impressive, astride his white palfrey, dressed in his red robes. He turned the war against Louis into a crusade and displayed a furious zeal in the royal cause, so much so that Innocent's successor, Pope Honorius, had to counsel him against excessive severity.[33]

The loyalists had one other advantage, namely Henry himself. The hated king had given way to his innocent son. Henry shrugged and the weight of John's crimes fell from his shoulders. 'Our father's quarrel has nothing to do with us,' he said in an early proclamation. A poet thus hoped 'the candle of the child' would 'call back the stars scared by the father's thunder'. The pope hoped the same. Perhaps a 'pious and merciful God' would convert John's death into good, the 'cause of the hatred' being now removed.[34]

In this situation of hope and fear Henry's supporters pressed on at once with his coronation at Gloucester 'for no one knows what the future holds'. Henry was first knighted by William Marshal – dressed in his small royal robes he made 'a fine little knight'. He was then carried on the shoulders of his great men to his coronation in the abbey church of St Peter at Gloucester, now Gloucester Cathedral, with the legate Guala presiding over the ceremony. The Romanesque columns witnessing the scene still hide behind the fourteenth-century tracery which laces Gloucester's choir.[35] Afterwards, Henry was carried back to his chamber in Gloucester castle where he was dressed in lighter robes before the coronation banquet. During the feast a messenger blundered in and announced that the Marshal's castle at Goodrich, less then fifteen miles away, was under siege. Nothing could

---

[32] *SLI*, 203.

[33] Innocent had died in July 1216 and was followed at once by Honorius.

[34] *F*, 145; *Political Songs*, 22; *Honorii III Opera*, ii, 105–6.

[35] The actual crowning and anointing was probably done by Peter des Roches assisted by other bishops, see Norgate, *Minority of Henry the Third*, 5 n.1. There is a stained-glass window in Gloucester Cathedral (dating to 1859) depicting the crowning. I am grateful to Michael Ray for sending me an image of it.

disguise the fact that the coronation was a makeshift affair. Westminster Abbey, its proper location, was under the control of Louis; the archbishop of Canterbury, Stephen Langton, who should have officiated, was abroad; silk for the king's robes had to be taken from the prior of Gloucester; and, with no time to make a proper crown, a gold circlet was used instead, perhaps taken from Henry's mother.[36]

After the coronation, the king's supporters considered the structure of the new government. There were no precedents to guide them for this was the first minority of an English king since that of Ethelred in 975. It was also, even if the war could be won, going to last a long time for the general view was that Henry would come of age at twenty-one, so not until October 1228. At least, no one disputed that, with the kingdom now a papal fief, the first place belonged to Guala as the pope's representative. But Guala, though soon granted full power in all things by Pope Honorius, did not aspire to control government on any day-to-day basis. What then was to be done? Here John had pointed the way. On his deathbed he had asked his men to entrust the guardianship of his son to William Marshal.[37] The choice was natural. The Marshal combined great prestige with great power. A landless younger son from a middle-ranking magnate family, he had, in tournaments across France, carved out a reputation as 'the greatest knight in the world'. In the service of John's father and brothers, he had also shown himself a clever politician. His reward came at the start of the reign of King Richard with his marriage to Isabella, daughter and sole heir of Richard fitzGilbert, or Strongbow as he was sometimes called. Her inheritance included Leinster in Ireland (conquered by fitzGilbert), Longueville in Normandy and Chepstow in Wales. At a stroke the Marshal thus became one of the greatest barons in the Anglo-Norman world. From John he received in addition the earldom of Pembroke and to John, despite several quarrels, he remained loyal.

The Marshal was, however, far too wise to stand on John's nomination. Instead, during the debates at Gloucester after the coronation, he insisted on waiting for the arrival of the only possible alternative, Ranulf, earl of Chester, and only with Ranulf's consent and the promise from Guala of remission of his sins did he shoulder the burden. The title he adopted was that of 'ruler of the king and the kingdom', which indicated his dual authority over both the king's person and the realm. The Marshal though could not take the young king with him round the country so he asked Peter des Roches to continue as Henry's immediate guardian.

In some respects Henry's accession to the throne made little difference to his life. He continued to spend time safely out of the way at episcopal residences and royal castles. In July 1217 he was back at Corfe. But he also

[36] Marshal, iii, 266–71.

[37] For the Marshal's career, see Crouch, *William Marshal*; Asbridge, *Greatest Knight*; Painter, *William Marshal*. The wonderful verse life commissioned by his family in the 1220s is published by the Anglo-Norman Text Society: see Marshal.

appeared on the public stage at assemblies of the king's supporters where his presence and his words gave authority to his governors' decisions. Those decisions shaped the whole future of England's polity.

The most fundamental decision was taken at once. After the coronation the new king and his governors moved to Bristol and there, on 12 November, in the king's name they issued a new version of Magna Carta. Since the young king had no seal, the new Charter was sealed by Guala, as papal legate, and William Marshal, as regent. For the Marshal and his baronial colleagues the decision was unproblematic. They had stuck to John from a mixture of idealism and self-interest, not from any hostility to the Charter. Indeed, they had as much to gain from it as had the barons on the other side. Guala himself was standing papal policy on its head, but doubtless calculated that Pope Honorius would see the wisdom of the decision. The immediate aim, of course, was to sap the will of the baronial rebels by accepting what they had been fighting for in the first place. The move had the more traction because Louis himself had made no commitment to the Charter. He said nothing about it in his proclamation on arriving in England. His English supporters had just to hope it would be unnecessary under benevolent Capetian rule.

If the issuing of Magna Carta weakened the resolve of Louis's supporters, it led to no flood of desertions. The war had still to be won. The climax came on 20 May 1217 at Lincoln, where the Marshal and Bishop Peter crushed Louis's Anglo-French army. Here the new version of Magna Carta did its work, for the English barons in Louis's army surrendered after hardly fighting very hard. Henry and Guala, anxiously awaiting the outcome at Nottingham, gave thanks to God, weeping tears of joy when the Marshal arrived with the news.[38] Louis himself was absent from the battle, being occupied with the siege of Dover. His last hope vanished on 24 August when the great fleet bringing reinforcements was shattered by Hubert de Burgh, Dover's castellan, in a sea fight off Sandwich.

The war was brought to an end by the Treaty of Kingston/Lambeth in September 1217. A week later Louis, resigning all claim to the English throne, left the country. On 29 October, Henry entered London, since 1215 the chief base of the rebels. Louis had secured good terms for his supporters. They were to recover without payment the lands they held at the start of the war. They were also to enjoy the protections of Magna Carta. In November 1217, Henry issued another version of the Charter, this time accompanied by an entirely new Charter governing the running of the royal forest. It was now that the name 'Magna Carta' was introduced to distinguish the 'Great Charter' from its physically smaller forest brother. Both Charters were sealed once again by Guala and the Marshal. Both together became fundamental to English political life.

---

[38] Wendover, iii, 24.

After the peace, a stream of former rebels came before Henry to renew their allegiances in acts of homage. At the Christmas court of 1217, held at Northampton, Henry also received the homage of King Alexander II of Scotland. Alexander, however, performed homage not for the kingdom of Scotland, as envisaged by the 1209 Treaty of Norham, but simply for the estates he held from Henry in England. Scotland had retained its independence and escaped John's noose. In its turn, the English government, while retaining hold of Alexander's sisters, made no move to marry the eldest, Margaret, to Henry, as the 1209 Treaty required. Henry could do better than that. Equally, nothing was said about Alexander's claims to England's three northern counties – Cumberland, Westmorland and Northumberland – which he had tried to assert during the war. This was a turning point. Neither Henry nor Alexander did much thereafter to revive their respective claims, the one to the overlordship of Scotland, the other to the northern counties. The foundations were being laid for a long period of Anglo-Scottish peace.

The minority government also reached a settlement with the ruler of Gwynedd, Llywelyn ap Iorwerth. This proud yet pragmatic man was to dominate Wales until his death in 1240. As John's authority collapsed, he had seized back the Four Cantrefs between the Conwy and the Dee ceded under a treaty in 1211, thus making himself master of the whole of Gwynedd. During the civil war Llywelyn had made major territorial gains further south at the expense of both the king and marcher barons. He had also established a practical hegemony over all the native rulers. Always more concerned with the reality of power than with titles and trappings, he called himself simply 'prince of North Wales' or, later, 'prince of Aberffraw and lord of Snowdon'. In reality Llywelyn was prince of Wales.[39] Now, in March 1218, he came to Worcester and did homage to Henry. He accepted that the other native rulers owed homage to the king, but in practice discouraged them from performing it. Meanwhile, he was allowed to retain all his territorial gains, including the Four Cantrefs, Cardigan and Carmarthen (until the king came of age), and, during the minority of their Welsh ruler, southern Powys and Montgomery.

Behind these capitulations to Alexander and Llywelyn lay the appalling weakness of the minority government. During the war, as John lost control of large parts of the country, his income had collapsed. His son's annual revenue, averaged over the first two years of peace, stood at £8,000, six or seven times below the level reached between 1207 and 1212, even leaving aside John's plunder of the church.[40] Major obstacles to the restoration of royal income and authority were the king's own local agents. The great freewheeling sheriffs and castellans who had done so much to win the

---

[39] For Llywelyn's titles, see Pryce, 'Negotiating Anglo-Welsh relations', 18–21.
[40] Carpenter, *Minority*, 113–14, 413. For John's revenues, see Barratt, 'Revenue of King John'; Carpenter, *Magna Carta*, 207.

war – Falkes de Bréauté, Philip Mark, Philip of Oldcoates, Peter de Maulay, Brian de Lisle and others – had become the villains of the peace. They now expected to continue in the same independent way, disdaining any control from the centre and spending the revenues they collected themselves, rather than paying them into the exchequer. Even worse, such men claimed they were irremovable, having, they said, taken a special oath to King John not to surrender their custodies until his heir came of age. They were also reluctant to restore lands and castles to former rebels, thus challenging the whole basis of the peace. Already at the Christmas court of 1216 there was a sign of the trouble to come. There, after numerous failed attempts, Henry himself had to order 'with his own mouth' an agent of Brian de Lisle to surrender Peverel castle.[41] The king's own commands, even when given in person, were not always enough. In July 1218 the Marshal took Henry with him to Newark. There a siege lasting nearly a week (the first of four Henry witnessed during the minority) was needed to oust John's Flemish captain, Robert de Gaugy, from the castle and restore it to the bishop of Lincoln. The final formal surrender was made to the king in person at Wallingford on 27 July.

The great council held in the king's presence at Westminster in November 1218 took an important step designed to enhance his authority. Hitherto all royal letters had been sealed with the Marshal's seal, this with the explanation that the king did not have one. Now the king's own seal was introduced. It followed the pattern of the seals of his predecessors and showed him not as boy but as man. On the front he was depicted sitting crowned and holding sword and orb. On the reverse he was in armour, sitting astride a stately war horse, brandishing a sword, and with his shield displaying the leopards of England. Whether Henry would live up to the image and revive kingship's majesty and might remained to be seen. The council entrusted the seal to the chancery clerk Ralph de Neville, who was to remain its keeper until 1238.

The introduction of the seal did not mark any change in the process of government. Royal letters were still attested by the Marshal and other ministers. There was now, however, a formal limitation placed on what they could do in the king's name. The first letter sealed with the new seal proclaimed that no charter or letter patent was to be issued making grants in perpetuity until the king came of age. In practice, the minority government, with one or two exceptions, was already abiding by this rule, one in accordance with both English custom and Roman law covering the property of underage children.[42] But it was still important to have the principle solemnly affirmed. Indeed, in an impressive display of unity, an oath supporting the 1218 proclamations was taken by the legate, the two archbishops, twelve bishops and eight abbots, together with the regent, the justiciar, and twenty-three earls

[41] *Patent Roll 1216–25*, 15.
[42] Carpenter, *Minority*, 18.

and barons, many of them former rebels.[43] The common will to protect the interests of the young king had been emphatically displayed.

LANGTON'S ARRIVAL, THE QUEEN'S DEPARTURE, THE MARSHAL'S DEATH

The introduction of the king's seal and the restrictions on its use were the first major decisions in which the archbishop of Canterbury, Stephen Langton, was involved after his return to England in May 1218. He was to play a major role in English politics down to his death in 1228. Born around 1165, Langton came from Langton by Wragby just east of Lincoln, where his father 'was a country gentleman of modest standing'.[44] At some time in the 1180s the young Stephen had gone to Paris to study at its famous university and there he had risen to be a professor of theology. His lectures and commentaries on the bible had built him a towering reputation. In 1206, Pope Innocent decided to make this academic superstar archbishop of Canterbury. King John was horrified and refused to accept him. University professors did not swing into his orbit very often and he did not know this one. That Langton was English (as Pope Innocent stressed) counted for nothing against the fact that he had resided for twenty years in Paris, the capital of John's greatest enemy. Langton would have been unsurprised by John's reaction. In his biblical commentaries he dwelt on God's warning to the Israelites about the tyranny and oppression which would follow from them choosing a king. It was absolutely necessary, Langton thought, for kings to be kept in check. They should study to obey the law given them by the priests. If they acted against individuals without lawful process, then resistance was justified. These views made Langton a passionate supporter of Magna Carta. In 1215 he had crafted the Charter's first chapter protecting the liberties of the church, and then, more than anyone else, he had struggled to preserve the peace the Charter was supposed to bring. In the circumstance of the minority, however, Langton also believed in the necessity of rebuilding royal power. Kings derived their authority from the church broadly defined as the clergy and people. Their duty was to protect the church with their 'arms', maintaining peace and giving justice. There was no way Henry could do that, Langton realized, in his current weakened state. To secure the revival of royal power within the limits of Magna Carta became, therefore, Langton's guiding political objective in the minority.[45]

Langton's arrival in England was balanced by two departures. One at the end of 1218 was that of Guala. His courageous and clever decision to accept Magna Carta at the start of the reign had done much to establish Henry on

---

[43] *Patent Roll 1216–25*, 177; *RLC*, ii, 75b.

[44] Powicke, *Stephen Langton*, 8.

[45] For Langton's ideas and career, see Powicke, *Stephen Langton*; D'Avray, 'Magna Carta'; Baldwin, 'Master Stephen Langton'; Vincent, 'Stephen Langton'.

his throne. Guala was replaced as legate by another wise Italian, Pandulf, since 1215 bishop-elect of Norwich and already well versed in English affairs. The other departure was that of Henry's mother, and John's queen, Isabella of Angoulême. Pregnant at the time of John's death, nothing is heard of her in the first months of Henry's reign. Although later involved in the negotiations for Louis's departure, she had by that time (September 1217) already decided to return to Angoulême. Indeed ships had been prepared for her departure as early as July. The only explanation given by the king in a letter to the barons of Poitou was that his mother longed to see again 'her native soil'. Had she also been snubbed by the minority government? The part she did play in the negotiations with Louis shows she wanted to be involved. Ten years later, in France, the queen mother, Blanche of Castile, would be the regent for the twelve-year-old Louis IX. Perhaps Isabella aspired to a similar role. In his letter Henry accepted his mother's decision although he found it, he said, 'sad and distasteful'. That at least shows the bond which was supposed to exist between a mother and her children. It may also have expressed Henry's real feelings.[46]

In the early months of 1219, William Marshal's health began to fail. His services to Henry had been immense. Had he faltered in October 1216, just as had Churchill faltered in May 1940, the whole history of England and Europe might have been different. As it was, the Marshal had won the war, established Magna Carta, and begun the restoration of royal authority. With his usual wisdom he now refused to choose a successor as guardian of the king and kingdom. In tense meetings in April 1219 around his bedside at Caversham beside the Thames (his favourite manor), he declared that the choice must be made by the barons.[47] This alarmed Bishop Peter, who pointed out that the king already had a guardian in himself; the only issue therefore was the guardianship of the kingdom. The Marshal would have none of it. He had, he said, been given dual authority at the start of the reign and the bishop was only the king's guardian by his delegation. Raising himself on his elbow, he now took the king by the hand and entrusted him to Pandulf, as representative of God and the pope. Then turning to Henry he prayed that God might make him 'a worthy man'. If on the other hand, he 'took after any wicked ancestor ('alcun felon ancestre')', 'then I pray to God, the son of Mary does not give you a long life'. 'Amen', said the king. The injunction not to follow in his father's footsteps could not have been clearer or spoken at a more awesome moment. Next day, the Marshal's eldest son entrusted Henry to Pandulf before the assembled barons. This time Bishop Peter, still trying to assert his claims, sprang forward and seized Henry's head, only to be repulsed by the young Marshal and a furious legate.[48]

[46] *Patent Roll 1216–25*, 113; *RLC*, i, 315; Vincent, 'Isabella of Angoulême', 198–9, 206.
[47] For what follows, see Marshal, iii, lines 18,038–114.
[48] Marshal, iii, 406–9.

HUBERT DE BURGH AND THE NEW GOVERNMENT

By entrusting the young king to Pandulf, the Marshal, as he knew, had merely postponed the baronial decision as to who should be in day-to-day charge of the king and the government of the country. The answer to these questions was formulated in a series of great councils held immediately after the Marshal's resignation. Pandulf was confirmed as the overall head of the government, holding much the same position as that of Guala. With Pope Honorius at his back, he was to play an important role in stiffening and energizing ministers. Bishop Peter, meanwhile, got his way and retained his place as the king's immediate guardian while also becoming second man in the government. That in practice meant demotion since he had held first place, attesting most of the king's letters, during the Marshal's illness. Peter's eclipse was beginning. The real victor of the new arrangements was the justiciar, Hubert de Burgh. During the Marshal's regency he had been virtually excluded from central government: he attests hardly a single royal letter. Instead Hubert concentrated on hearing judicial pleas in the counties and rebuilding Dover castle after the siege of 1216–17. Now, he was given control of the seal, with Ralph de Neville, as keeper, staying with him and taking his orders. Hence Hubert now becomes the normal witness of royal letters. He was at last in immediate charge of the king's government.

The justiciar, under John and his predecessors, had been the governor of England during the king's frequent absences on the continent and, when the king was present in England, his chief minister. At Westminster he was the head both of the exchequer and the central judicial court known as the bench or court of common pleas. King John had made Hubert justiciar at Runnymede in 1215, succeeding Bishop Peter. The position certainly gave Hubert a strong claim to the first place in the minority government. In 1216, besieged in Dover castle, and overshadowed anyway by the Marshal, he had not pressed his claims. In 1219 he was lucky that his most obvious rival, Ranulf, earl of Chester, was absent on crusade. Hubert had only to see off Bishop Peter, and that was not difficult. He was far more acceptable to the lay and ecclesiastical barons, something John himself had recognized in making him justiciar in Peter's place at Runnymede after the concession of Magna Carta.

Unlike Peter, Hubert was native born.[49] His Burgh was Burgh-next-Aylsham not far from Norwich. He came from a knightly family and still had his fortune to make. While gaining much from John, he held little in hereditary right. He had, therefore, none of the dangerous independence Bishop Peter derived from his overflowing episcopal revenues.[50] Because of their

---

[49] For a biography, see Ellis, *Hubert de Burgh*.
[50] For the steady rise of episcopal income in the minority, see Vincent, *Peter des Roches*, 147–9.

different situations and personalities the two men were sharply contrasting in their political approach. Peter was active, arrogant, acerbic and aggressive, very ready to brave opposition and bull ahead. Hubert could be minatory and decisive, but he was also, when he needed to be, cautious and conciliatory, very ready to wait, placate, and if necessary retreat. Sensibly he governed as 'justiciar of England' rather than demanding the Marshal's grander title.[51]

Vital to Hubert's appointment was the fame of his previous career, a fame, in his articulate and persuasive way, he was always ready to promote. (In later life he talked at length to Matthew Paris.) According to his own version of events, in 1204–5, after the fall of Normandy and Anjou, he had defended Chinon for a year and, when its fall became inevitable, had sallied out to do battle, being badly wounded before his capture. In 1216, on Louis's arrival, he had 'ventured his body' and taken command of Dover castle when no one else would do so. On John's death, he had gone to the postern gate of the castle, flanked by archers' arrows at the ready, and spurned Louis's overtures, proclaiming his fidelity to the young king. The following year, when cowards refused to sail out with him to confront Louis's fleet, he had confessed his sins to his chaplain Luke, received discipline till the blood ran, taken communion and enjoined his men, if he was captured, not to surrender Dover, even to save him from torture and death, 'since it is the key to England'.[52] True enough. Had Dover fallen at any time, Louis almost certainly would have won the war.

To Hubert's martial exploits and fidelity, just as much as those of William Marshal, Henry, therefore, owed his throne. Hubert had celebrated and commemorated his victory over the French fleet by founding a hospital at Dover dedicated to the Virgin Mary, 'the Maison Dieu' as it was called. A great patron of the Dominican friars, he was just as much in touch with the religious currents of the age as Bishop Peter. With a deep belief in the hand of God guiding human affairs, his piety was an important part of the bond he was to forge with the king.[53]

Hubert was well equipped in other ways to run the government. He was educated and could read Latin, a vital talent given the large number of letters of petition and complaint soon pouring in to him. He had appropriate experience, having been John's chamberlain early in the reign (working alongside Bishop Peter), and a sheriff of many counties, before long service on the continent, culminating as seneschal of Poitou. That proved another advantage because, out of the country, he was not, like Peter, tainted by the excesses of John's government. Indeed Hubert took pains to distance himself from John's crimes, spreading the story that, as

[51] *RL*, i, 116; *DD*, no. 223.

[52] Coggeshall, 154–5; Paris, iii, 3–4, 28–9; Paris, vi, 55; Paris, *HA*, ii, 218.

[53] For the hand of God in Hubert's affairs, see below, 90, 145, 156. His piety is discussed in Cazel, 'Religious motivation in the biography of Hubert de Burgh'.

castellan of Falaise, he had refused to blind John's nephew and rival, Arthur, an episode immortalized in Shakespeare's play.[54] Now, as Hubert made very clear, he was determined to do his job as justiciar – to dispense justice, maintain peace and recover the rights of the crown – but he recognized, far more than Bishop Peter, that such recovery must take place within the framework set by a public acceptance of Magna Carta.

These then were the characteristics which brought Hubert to the fore. They were to keep him in power for the next thirteen years.

HENRY'S SECOND CORONATION IN 1220

Down to 1221 England was ruled by something of a triumvirate. Hubert witnessed most royal letters and thus directed the government. At Westminster he presided over the exchequer and the bench. Bishop Peter, meanwhile, was guardian of the king. He also sat at the exchequer and sometimes stood in for Hubert as the witness of royal letters. Behind them was Pandulf, counselling, reassuring, sympathizing, bullying, complaining, occasionally commanding. His support was vital, for the task of restoring royal authority was very much incomplete. Many sheriffs and castellans were still unwilling to account for their revenues and to surrender what they held either to the king or former rebels. In September 1219 the constable of Tickhill, as Pandulf indignantly told Hubert, 'calls the king by way of derision not a king but a boy'.[55] This was the background to an important decision taken in 1220, namely to seek the pope's sanction for a second coronation. It would enhance the king's authority and remedy the defects of the first coronation at Gloucester. It could take place in Westminster Abbey, be presided over by Archbishop Langton and be graced by the proper robes and crown. Langton's pleasure at the decision was all the greater thanks to the personal affection he had developed for the young 'innocent' king. What a contrast to King John![56]

On 16 May 1220, Henry laid the foundation stone of the New Lady Chapel of Westminster Abbey. Next day, he was anointed, and crowned with the crown of Edward the Confessor (as it was called), by Archbishop Langton. The date was specially chosen for it was the feast of Pentecost, the feast celebrating the day when the light of the Holy Spirit descended upon the Apostles.[57] At least £760 was spent on the ceremony and the celebrations, the annual income of a rich baron. Something of the display can be glimpsed from the list of regalia handed in to the treasury afterwards, some of it having

---

[54] Coggeshall, 139–40.

[55] TNA SC 1/1/39; Carpenter, *Minority*, 160–1. For manhood and youth in politics in the reign of Richard II, see Fletcher, *Richard II*.

[56] Crowland, 244.

[57] It was likewise on Whitsunday that Henry proclaimed his recovery of power in 1261, as I discuss in volume 2.

been brought up (with Henry's brother Richard) from Corfe: the spurs, the gilded rod, the tunic, the dalmatic and mantle of red samite bordered with precious stones, the two brooches to pin the vestments together, one set with a sapphire, one with a pearl, the sandals and shoes of red samite fringed with gold, and the golden crown decorated with diverse stones, presumably the crown of St Edward, which had to be altered to fit Henry's head. The ceremonies were linked to government policy. The day after the coronation everyone took an oath, on pain of disinheritance, to surrender the king's castles at his command and account faithfully for his revenues.[58]

After the coronation, Henry went with Hubert to York for a meeting with King Alexander. It was agreed that the Scottish king would marry Joan, Henry's eldest sister. As for Alexander's two sisters, still in English custody, they were to be found husbands within a year from October 1220. The quid pro quo for this high-status marriage for Alexander was probably his accepting a low-status one (although it would not have been put like that) for his eldest sister, Margaret. Negotiations now started for her to marry not Henry, as agreed in the treaty of 1209, but Hubert de Burgh. Both Alexander's marriage and Hubert's were solemnized in the following year. By allying himself to the head of the English government, Alexander hoped there would be no attempt to make Scotland once more a subject kingdom. The minority government, for its part, hoped Alexander would not revive his claims to the northern counties. The marriage alliances between the courts set a pattern for the future and were another element in the coming period of Anglo-Scottish peace.[59]

After the meeting at York, the government moved at once to vindicate the king's authority. The sheriff of Northumberland, Philip of Oldcoates, had been ignoring a stream of orders (one issued by Henry 'viva voce') to return Mitford castle to its lord, the former rebel Roger Bertram. At York he at last capitulated. Then, on the way south, Henry and Hubert made a sudden diversion to Rockingham where a brief siege prized the castle from William de Fors, the earl of Aumale.

From Rockingham, Henry and Hubert hurried on to Canterbury for what was to be the greatest ecclesiastical ceremony of the reign and Archbishop Langton's crowning achievement. This was the translation of Thomas Becket's body to its new shrine in Canterbury Cathedral.[60] Langton, had carefully calculated the date for the ceremony, thus investing it with all the more significance. The translation took place on 7 July, which was the fiftieth anniversary of the martyrdom (29 December 1170)

---

[58] Dunstable, 57; Carpenter, *Reign of Henry III*, 460–1.

[59] For a full account of Anglo-Scottish relations in the 1220s and 1230s, see Oram, *Alexander II*, 108–48.

[60] Anonymous, 208–9 (a long account which shows the impact on the secular nobility); Crowland, 245–6; Dunstable, 58; Duggan, 'Cult of St Thomas Becket', 37–41, and Eales, 'The political setting of the Becket translation'.

according to the instructions for calculating a jubilee given in the book *Leviticus*. It was also a Tuesday, Tuesday having been the day of Becket's birth, consecration as archbishop and martyrdom. The ceremony was attended by the archbishop of Reims, an archbishop from Hungary and up to twenty-five bishops including those of Amiens and Tournai. Queen Berengaria, Richard I's widow, was there as also were many foreign nobles. The English barons courteously gave over Canterbury itself for their accommodation. The saint's body, found entire with the wounds, so it was said, still fresh, was raised from the crypt where it had lain since the martyrdom and carried to its magnificent golden shrine in the Trinity Chapel. Afterwards, Langton, in the gigantic hall he had completed for the occasion, threw a stupendous feast for all who had come, rich and poor alike. The date of 7 July was added to the ecclesiastical calendar as a day to be celebrated for ever.

Langton, in sermons he preached after the event, portrayed Becket as a lantern lit by God to enlighten the world. His career showed how bishops must renounce secular affairs and devote themselves to their spiritual responsibilities. It showed too all the courage and sacrifice needed to protect the church from a tyrannical king. Langton himself, in his resistance to King John, had shown that spirit. Indeed, in deliberate imitation of Becket, he had spent his years of exile at the monastery of Pontigny in Burgundy. He was also doing all he could to promote the cult of another bishop whose career taught much the same lessons. This was Hugh of Avalon, bishop of Lincoln between 1186 and 1200. In February 1220 he was canonized by the pope, after Langton had investigated his miracles.[61] For the young Henry, Becket's translation in 1220 was more problematic.[62] It naturally reminded everyone of his dynasty's greatest crime. Yet Henry's attendance showed his reverence for the saint. It continued the process of reconciliation begun by his grandfather Henry II himself in his penance at Canterbury after the murder. It also suggested that Henry's own rule would be consensual and quite different from his father's.[63]

Having put Henry right with Becket, the government was the better placed to continue its forward policies. In September, Henry and Hubert went to Exeter and removed Henry fitzCount from the sheriffdom of Cornwall. In February of the following year, 1221, they were at Bytham in Lincolnshire, where a siege removed the garrison of the earl of Aumale and returned the castle to its lord, the former rebel William de Coleville. Thus the government reassured former rebels and showed its determination to uphold the terms of the 1217 peace.

[61] Wendover, iii, 58–9.

[62] For Henry and Becket, see below, 316–17.

[63] For the Becket cult standing for 'a reconciliation with rightful royal power', see Eales, 'The political setting of the Becket translation', 138; and see also Binski, *Becket's Crown*, 130–1.

HENRY'S EARLY ENTOURAGE

Down to 1221, Bishop Peter retained control of the person of the king. He determined the personnel of Henry's household and attested the writs securing funds to meet its expenses. Although present at sieges and councils, Henry still spent much of his time living at episcopal and royal residences, apart from the justiciar, as before he had been apart from the regent William Marshal.[64] The royal castle at Wallingford, in particular, was fitted out for his use with a new wardrobe, pantry (for baking bread), buttery (for providing ale and wine), tables for the hall and a chimney for the king's 'high chamber'.[65] Henry's initial establishment is seen in the robes, differentiated according to rank, distributed to his household at Christmas 1217. There were seven knights and five 'servientes', the second group including the king's chaplain, his cook and Ralph de St Samson. The twenty-eight others included a huntsman, baker, tailor, two trumpeters, the ushers of the chamber and wardrobe, two messengers, two boys and the men who looked after the fire in the hall, the water in the king's chamber and the horses which either bore on their backs or drew in carts the contents of the wardrobe, chapel, kitchen, buttery and almonry. There was one female, a washerwoman.[66]

The list did not include the two clerks of the king's chapel, Walter de Lench and William of Winchester. They sang the daily mass and also, on the great ecclesiastical festivals, the 'Christus Vincit', the celebratory hymns calling down God's blessing on the king, his people and the whole Christian community. In 1221 the two were provided with new albs, amices, maniples, stoles and copes of samite, together with a new tunicle and a dalmatic, although the cost ($£6$ 10s) was nothing like what Henry spent on such vestments later in his reign.[67]

In overall charge of this household establishment were the king's stewards, all connected with Bishop Peter. These were men of knightly status, two of them, Eustace de Grenville and John Russel, appearing as knights in the 1217 list. The most senior was John's old steward William de Cantilupe. He came from a Norman family, but was now established as lord of Aston Cantlow (as it became called) in Warwickshire and Eaton Bray in Bedfordshire.[68] When separated from the government, it was Cantilupe's seal that Henry used to authenticate his letters. Two other people were important in Henry's early establishment. One was the 'vigorous knight', Philip de Aubigny, of the same family as the de Aubigny lords of Belvoir. Described by the chronicler Roger of Wendover as the king's 'most faithful master and teacher', in 1221 his work was commended

---

[64] Vincent, *Peter des Roches*, 153–5.
[65] *RLC*, i, 393, 443, 488, 491.
[66] *RLC*, i, 345b.
[67] *RLC*, i, 471–71b, 486b.
[68] For the Cantilupes, see Julian-Jones, 'Corbets and Cantilupes'.

by Pope Honorius. Probably his role was to educate the king in knightly exercises.[69] The other important person was Bishop Peter's nephew (some said his son), the clerk Peter de Rivallis. Peter acted as Henry's treasurer, receiving into the wardrobe the money for the king's day-to-day expenses.[70]

From the first, therefore, Henry was surrounded by a substantial establishment. He certainly needed one for, even when separated from the government, he welcomed and entertained a constant stream of visitors. Within a few months in 1219–20, he received the earl of Warenne, the countess of Eu, Falkes de Bréauté, Nicola de Hay, the abbot-elect of Fountains, Henry fitzCount and a messenger from the lepers of Lancaster.[71] Some of those who approached him in person or by letter were hoping he would bring pressure to bear on his ministers. 'Speak with your council on behalf of Roger of Acaster', urged Peter de Maulay in one letter. Others hoped he would act himself. 'The issues have been explained to you. Give me justice in your own person against Llewelyn and show you consider him a liar', wrote William Marshal, earl of Pembroke, the old regent's son.[72] Others again wanted simply to win Henry's favour with gifts and flatteries. Everyone was aware of how vital in the future such favour would be. 'Act now so that you will deserve the king's grace when he arrives at mature age', Hubert de Burgh warned in one letter.[73] Henry's reactions, presumably counselled by William de Cantilupe, who sealed the resulting letters, were usually cautious. Although the bishop-elect of Ely arrived at Wallingford with a letter from Pandulf telling Henry to take his oath of allegiance, Henry decided not to do so without the consent of Hubert and Bishop Peter. On another occasion he simply asked Hubert to 'do what you ought to do'.[74] Fittingly, for a king who later achieved such a reputation for piety, Henry's first known order (in April 1220) was on behalf of the lepers of Lancaster. Learning that the sheriff was preventing the lepers receiving their due alms from the crown, Henry instructed Hubert to issue letters putting matters right. Hubert duly did so.[75]

There are other signs of Henry's gradual emergence. In the financial year 1218/19 the total revenue assigned to meet the expenses of his household was £680, equivalent to the annual income of a major baron. In 1220/1 it was £2,350, the annual income of a richer earl. The household was also expanding in size. At Christmas 1217 robes were given to thirty-nine

---

[69] Archivio Apostolico Vaticano Honorius III Regesta X, fo.117; Wendover, iii, 67; Vincent, *Peter des Roches*, 155. For Wendover, a monk of St Albans, see below, 171.

[70] *RLC*, i, 391b.

[71] *RL*, i, 42, 73, 104–5; TNA SC 1/1/106; *CRR*, viii, 323.

[72] TNA SC 1/4/74; SC 1/1/11; *RL*, i, 179–80, 271–3. I paraphrase both letters. Maulay and William Marshal also wrote to Hubert.

[73] *RLC*, i, 435–35b.

[74] *RL*, i, 74–5; TNA SC 1/1/106; *Patent Roll 1216–25*, 224.

[75] *RL*, i, 104–5; *RLC*, i, 414b.

members. At Christmas 1220 the number was ninety-eight. The household knights had increased from seven to twenty-five.[76]

THE REMOVAL OF BISHOP PETER

The king's increasing prominence raised the question of Bishop Peter's governorship. If he remained as guardian, might he not use Henry's growing authority to destroy his enemies and recover control of central government? This prospect filled Langton and his fellow bishops with alarm. It was Peter who had suspended Langton from office for refusing to excommunicate John's opponents in 1215. Before that, he alone of the bishops had remained by John's side during the Interdict. Peter was equally anathema to many barons. If he gained power would he not school the king in John's obnoxious rule? Pandulf evidently shared these misgivings. Already in 1220 the pope had authorized him to make a change. The king was to be entrusted to men 'not distrusted either by himself or his kingdom . . . who will teach him to fear God and love his vassals'.[77] The reflection on Bishop Peter was obvious.

The approach of the king's fourteenth birthday on 1 October 1221 made the issue all the more acute. It increased the necessity for a change and could also justify it.[78] The general consensus in England was that the king would come of age when he was twenty-one in October 1228. Twenty-one was after all the age when his barons came of age, as a new clause in the 1216 Magna Carta stated. There was, however, nothing set in stone about this. The pope could authorize the king's assumption of power at any time. There was also a feeling that some change might take place on the king's fourteenth birthday. The government occasionally made concessions lasting until then, as though at that point Henry might decide things for himself.[79] Fourteen was when Frederick II had come of age in the kingdom of Sicily, also a papal fief. In educational theory it marked the dividing line between 'pueritia' and 'adolescentia'. In Roman law it was the point where the 'tutor's' authority over his 'pupil' ceased. The Crowland chronicle indeed has Peter's governorship ending because the king 'had exceeded the age of a pupil'.[80]

Hubert and his allies had, then, powerful arguments to use against Peter, but they were far from conclusive. While the age of fourteen could mark a division in the educational process it did not signal its end. Later in the century Giles of Rome assigned the years from seven to fourteen or

---

[76] Carpenter, *Minority*, 242.

[77] Archivio Apostolico Vaticano Honorius III Regesta X, fo.186 (*CPReg*, 71).

[78] Carpenter, *Minority*, 123–4, 240–1, 257–8; Orme, *From Childhood to Chivalry*, 6.

[79] *RLC*, i, 400b.

[80] Crowland, 260. That the so-called 'Barnwell' chronicle was produced at Crowland abbey is shown in Ispir, 'A critical edition of the Crowland chronicle'.

thereabouts for study and 'moderate exercise' and the period thereafter for learning how to ride and fight. In April 1221, Pope Honorius thought Henry's training far from complete because he tried to prevent Philip de Aubigny leaving on crusade before the king had been 'perfectly educated'.[81] Although in Roman law the authority of the 'tutor' ended at fourteen, he was then replaced by a 'curator', a role Bishop Peter could perfectly well aspire to play. Since there was no prospect of Peter going quietly, Hubert staged a coup.

In April 1221, Bishop Peter left England on a short pilgrimage to Santiago de Compostela, a measure of this many-sided man. Evidently he anticipated no immediate threat to his position. But his enemies saw their chance. On 30 May, Peter de Maulay, castellan of Corfe and Bishop Peter's closest associate in England, dined with the king at Winchester, as part of the Whitsun festivities. At Corfe he had in his keeping both the king's younger brother, Richard, and also a great state prisoner, the king's cousin Eleanor of Brittany. She was the daughter of John's elder brother, Geoffrey of Brittany, and thus the sister of Arthur, the rival for the throne whom John had murdered. Indeed Maulay was rumoured to have been the actual murderer, just as Hubert claimed to have been Arthur's protector. There were some who now regarded Eleanor herself as 'the true heir of England'. After the meal, Maulay was summoned into the king's chamber 'as if secret matters were to be discussed'. Instead, Hubert and his accomplices hurled insults at him, tore his clothes and had him thrown into chains. All this was pressure to confess his part in a treason plotted by none other than Bishop Peter himself. For had not the bishop gone abroad to arrange for the handing over of Eleanor to the king of France? The charge was trumped up. When Bishop Peter returned to England in July (accompanied by the first Dominican friars – what better way to show his purity) he cleared both himself and Maulay. But Maulay never recovered the castellanship of Corfe, and Bishop Peter appears no longer as the guardian of the king.[82]

Bishop Peter had been Henry's guardian for nearly ten years and was thus 'in a position to exercise more personal influence than anyone else over the growing king'.[83] Yet when it came to it in 1221 and in the years thereafter this counted for nothing at all. There is no sign Henry tried to stick up for his old tutor. What had gone wrong in the relationship between the boy and the bishop can only be guessed. Was Bishop Peter at turns remote and overbearing? Perhaps the occasion at the Marshal's deathbed, when Peter seized the king by the head, did not stand alone. If he had tried to vindicate John's methods of government and vilify the rebellious barons, that too seems to have had little effect. There was certainly an impulsive streak in the king, and a desire to act without restraint. Years

[81] Archivio Apostolico Vaticano Honorius III Regesta X, fo.117.
[82] Crowland, 260; Carpenter, *Minority*, 249–52.
[83] Clanchy, *England and its Rulers*, 130.

later Bishop Peter would exploit such characteristics to the full. But there was another side of Henry's personality, an uncertainty, a readiness to draw back, a desire for tranquillity, which fitted very well with Hubert's mode of rule. Hubert was to prove far more adept at managing the king than his deadly rival.

There was another area where the instructions of Bishop Peter and Philip de Aubigny were a failure, if indeed the latter's task was to educate Henry as a knight. By 1221, Henry had already been present at three sieges – those of Newark, Rockingham and Bytham. Yet Henry, although he wanted the rewards of victorious war, had little interest in its business. He gained a reputation neither as a gallant knight nor as a calculating general. He was instead a 'rex pacificus'. One aspect of that was Henry's lack of enthusiasm for tournaments. Taking the form of mock battles fought over large tracts of ground, these created local disorder and could be breeding grounds for plots and political agitation. Stamford and Brackley, well-known tournament grounds, had been the places where the rebel barons mustered in 1215.[84] Consequently, throughout the minority and indeed thereafter, the government, with the full support of the church, issued both blanket bans on tournaments and a whole series of individual prohibitions. There is no sign that Henry regretted this policy. Perhaps there were health and safety reasons for him not participating directly, but if he did not even attend tournaments, how was he to learn about warfare? There was a related area of physical endeavour where Henry failed to impress, unlike many of his predecessors and successors. This was hunting. Falconry, altogether less taxing, was different, as will be seen. One of the king's gerfalcons in training around 1221 was called 'Blackman', perhaps an indication that Henry spoke English with his falconers.[85]

If Bishop Peter's guardianship had limited impact on the king, the consequences of his dismissal were still fateful.[86] Peter could never forgive or forget what had happened. A deep fissure was opening up in English politics. On one side there was Hubert, in charge of central government, supported increasingly both by Langton and by an alliance, formed in 1220–1, with two earls, William Longespée of Salisbury and William Marshal of Pembroke, son of the old regent. Pandulf had helped here by agreeing (in 1221) that William Marshal might marry Henry's youngest sister, Eleanor, although in the event opposition prevented the match being celebrated until 1224. On the other side, Peter was close to Ranulf, earl of Chester. Chester had increasingly regretted his decision to stand aside in 1216 and allow the Marshal to become regent. In 1218 he had left England

---

[84] For the political bearing of tournaments see Barker, *Tournament in England*, ch. 3.

[85] *RLC*, 400b, 401b, 407b, 412, 441b, 470. Since gerfalcons were white, Michael Prestwich wonders whether the name was a joke. For Henry and falconry, see below, 409–12.

[86] I do, however, suggest Peter's possible influence on Henry's religious life, see below, 282, 284, 286.

on crusade. He returned in 1220 to find Hubert in the place he might have held. Despite periods of uneasy co-operation the two men never got on. Chester was later described by Hubert as 'one of his greatest enemies'.[87] While Chester was a great Anglo-Norman baron, the bulk of the bishop's associates were out-and-out foreigners like himself. Peter de Maulay, William de Fors, earl of Aumale, Engelard de Cigogné, castellan of Windsor, and Philip Mark, castellan of Nottingham, all came from Poitou or the Touraine. Falkes de Bréauté, rumoured to be the son of a serf, was from Normandy. He now wielded immense power as a sheriff of six counties and their castles across the midlands. In the early 1220s the divisions between natives and foreigners were deeply felt by the actors themselves and added an extra venom to their conflicts. 'All the native born men of England are traitors', Falkes cried out in 1221 or 1222, an outburst that the earls of Pembroke and Salisbury hastened in letters to pass on to Hubert.[88]

1223: THE FIRST STEP IN THE KING'S ASSUMPTION OF POWER

The hostility of Bishop Peter and his party made Hubert de Burgh all the keener to carry through the programme being urged on him by Pope Honorius and Pandulf, namely to take back into the king's hands all the royal castles, manors and sheriffdoms. Since Bishop Peter and his opponents had by far the largest share of local offices (Peter himself was sheriff of Hampshire and castellan of Winchester), this would undermine their power. Hubert had, however, to proceed without Pandulf's support. In July 1221 the latter left England and was not replaced. This was Archbishop Langton's doing. Buoyed up by Becket's translation, he had gone to Rome (thus missing the attack on Maulay) and secured Pandulf's removal on the grounds that the legate's authority interfered with his own position as head of the English church.

Bereft of Pandulf, Hubert relied increasingly on Langton's support. It was thus 'by the counsel of the archbishop of Canterbury and the bishops of England', as well as the earls and barons, that in June 1222 the order went out to resume the royal manors into the king's hands.[89] The following month Henry and Hubert went together on a tour to Gloucester. It marked a major change in Henry's life. Thereafter, he and Hubert are rarely found apart. Henry thus said goodbye to Wallingford, never to live there again. Later it was to become a principal residence of his brother Richard. There was no formal change in Henry's position but he no longer needed to send letters to Hubert authenticated by the seal of William de Cantilupe. The king could influence decisions direct, decisions

---

[87] Paris, iii, 229.

[88] *RL*, i, 220–2.

[89] Carpenter, *Minority*, 281; Waugh, 'The origins of the office of escheator', 232.

going out in his name in letters attested by Hubert and sealed by the great seal. When occasionally Henry and Hubert were separated from the great seal, then it was the seal of the justiciar which authenticated royal letters. Hubert had thus captured the king. He could exploit Henry's authority and shield him from rival influences. Although Peter de Rivallis remained as keeper of the wardrobe, Cantilupe now disappears as steward. Hubert began the process of placing his own men into the royal household, beginning with the knight Godfrey of Crowcombe.

This change in Henry's position is reflected in other ways. In the year from Michaelmas 1222, £3,785 were assigned to meet the costs of the royal household as against £2,350 two years before. There was also a sharp increase in the number of gifts of game, wine and timber made by royal letters, gifts to magnates, ministers, leper houses, hospitals and monasteries. There were eighty-eight of these in the regnal year 1222/3, as opposed to around thirty-five in each of the two years before. It was at this time that Henry began to take a personal interest in the welfare of two young women in receipt of his alms at the nunnery of Kington in Wiltshire. He built them a house to live in, warmed them with presents of firewood, and sustained them with gifts of money, expressing astonishment and the offence to his 'honour' when his orders were not promptly carried out.[90]

Henry's role is also seen in a matter of greater moment, as described by Roger of Wendover. In January 1223, at a great council, Hubert proposed an inquiry into the 'customs and liberties' which King John had enjoyed before the war. Its results were to be immediately implemented. In response, Archbishop Langton and other magnates demanded that the king first confirm Magna Carta only for one of John's old ministers, William Brewer, to argue that Magna Carta had no validity having been extracted by force. Langton at once rebuked him: 'William, if you loved the king, you would not disturb the peace of the kingdom.' Henry himself, seeing Langton moved to anger, now intervened. 'We have sworn to all these liberties and what we have sworn we will observe.' So Henry had in effect issued a verbal confirmation of Magna Carta. This is his first known political pronouncement. Although the inquiry went ahead, the implementation of its results was soon suspended, a retreat very typical of Hubert's style of government. 'It was not our intention,' the king declared, 'to raise or have observed evil customs in our kingdom.'[91]

In the early part of 1223, Bishop Peter made a move designed to unclasp Hubert's grip on central government. Concealing his partisan intent, he persuaded Pope Honorius to issue a dramatic set of letters. These, while not declaring Henry of age, opined that the maturity of his understanding and the 'vigour of his mind' made up for his lack of years.

---

[90] *RLC*, i, 479, 480b, 494b, 513b, 538b, 546, 573b, 581b, 598, 625; *RLC*, ii, 33.

[91] *RLC*, i, 569; Carpenter, *Minority*, 295–8, where Wendover's account is dated in accordance with the record evidence.

Consequently he should be given 'free disposition of his kingdom'. The keeper of the seal, Ralph de Neville, was henceforth to take orders solely from the king and seal nothing save at his will. The attack on Hubert, who had hitherto given the orders, was palpable. The papal letters also said that the royal castles were to be surrendered into the king's hands. If that threatened Peter's own allies, he knew that, having got rid of Hubert, he could soon shuffle them back into office. These letters arrived in England in the early summer. For a while they lay like an unexploded bomb which no one dared to touch. Peter needed to arrange the detonation at a moment favourable to himself. He never managed it. Instead the letters were eventually detonated by his enemies (as will be seen).

At first there was much else to claim attention. In July 1223 came the death of the king of France, Philip Augustus. The government summoned an army for an invasion, only for the rapid accession of Louis VIII (the erstwhile claimant to the English throne) to kill off the idea. There was, however, a real war in Wales. In April 1223, William Marshal gained revenge for Llywelyn's attack on Pembroke in 1220 and ejected the prince's men from Cardigan and Carmarthen. Hubert backed the campaign to the hilt. He allowed the Marshal to retain Cardigan and Carmarthen, instead of resuming them into the hands of the king. He also mustered a royal army and removed Llywelyn from another of his gains during the 1215–17 war, namely Montgomery. There, in early October, expert in siege warfare as he was, Hubert found a magnificent site for a new castle, one which, in Wendover's words, 'seemed untakeable to everyone'.[92] Henry had been fully involved in the campaign, the first of his many in Wales. He gained his first suit of armour. He also saw warfare's attractive trappings: the surcoats, banners and pennons made in red silk and adorned with his coat of arms – the leopards in yellow silk embellished with gold leaf.[93]

Encouraged by this triumph, in early November, at Westminster, Hubert made a cautious start in implementing the part of the papal letters calling for the surrender of the king's castles. The reaction was instantaneous, as though he had touched a sore. His enemies, led by Ranulf, earl of Chester (ally of the worsted Llywelyn), the earl of Aumale and Falkes de Bréauté, decided to go to the king and expose the justiciar's 'malice'. Hubert, getting wind of their intention, informed Henry there was a plot to seize him. The two then fled to Gloucester, a castle controlled by the Marshal and not far from the latter's great base at Chepstow. At the end of the month, having gathered substantial forces, Hubert and Henry returned to London and installed themselves in the Tower.

It was at this point that Archbishop Langton intervened. In the hope of brokering a settlement, he summoned the rival parties to meet in London on 4 December in the presence of the king. The meeting was a disaster.

---

[92] Carpenter, *Minority*, 311–3. For the castle, see below, 74–5.
[93] *RLC*, i, 550b.

Bishop Peter professed his loyalty to the king but angrily demanded Hubert's removal. Hubert branded Peter a traitor and the author of all the ills from which the kingdom suffered. Peter then rose up and swept out of the assembly with his allies, declaring that, if it cost him all he had, he would pull the justiciar from power.[94]

With the kingdom standing on the brink of civil war, Langton made up his mind. In 1222 he had pronounced a sentence of excommunication against all who disturbed the peace of the kingdom and unjustly detained the rights of the king.[95] Now he decided that Peter and his party were doing both. He would join with Hubert in implementing the papally commanded programme. Down to 10 December, Hubert had witnessed the great majority of royal letters. On 10 December he was replaced as the witness by Henry himself. Thereafter, nearly all royal letters were witnessed by the king. The Latin formula was 'teste me ipso'. In form, at least, Henry thus took ultimate responsibility for the writing and sealing of his letters. Now sixteen, he was in charge of central government. In practice, Hubert remained the controlling force, but there were two restrictions on his power, both almost certainly introduced by Langton as conditions of their alliance. The first was that two bishops were placed alongside Hubert to monitor his activities. One was Richard le Poore of Salisbury. He was a former pupil of Langton and a considerable scholar in his own right. Since 1220 he had been building the new cathedral at Salisbury. He also issued an influential set of reforming statutes for his diocese (one chapter stressed the role of parish priests as peacemakers).[96] The other bishop was Jocelyn of Wells, bishop of Bath, a hard-headed former chancery clerk of King John, but an exile during the Interdict. His brother, Hugh of Wells, bishop of Lincoln, had done much to support Magna Carta both in 1215 and 1217. The second restriction was that the ban on the king making grants of a permanent nature until he came of age remained in force. Thus Henry still issued no charters. The pope himself in his letters of April 1223 had imposed no such restriction, but it was sensible to postpone the scramble for patronage which the lifting of the ban was bound to introduce.

The king's authority thus enhanced, Hubert and Langton moved to resume the king's castles and sheriffdoms. Hubert, with the help of the bishops and many former rebels, assembled a large military force at Northampton for the Christmas court. With Langton threatening excommunication, the dissidents gave way and surrendered their custodies. Hubert did so too but his surrenders were nominal, and he quickly placed his own men into the positions vacated by his opponents. He also strengthened his control of the king's household, putting his faithful chaplain,

---

[94] Dunstable, 84, probably from the report of an eyewitness.
[95] C&S, i, 106–7, cap. 2.
[96] C&S, i, 64, cap. 12.

Luke, in charge of the wardrobe in place of Peter de Rivallis.[97] Bishop Peter was now absolutely out. He might still entertain the court at his manors, but at this point he disappears from the exchequer and from any role in central government.

Those removed from their sheriffdoms and castles at the end of 1223 were deeply embittered but decided to await better times. Only one person did not wait. This was Falkes de Bréauté. On 17 June 1224 his brother William de Bréauté seized a royal judge and imprisoned him in Bedford castle. The government, nearby at Northampton, moved at once to Bedford and placed the castle under siege. Falkes hurried to his friends and begged for their support. He received sympathy from the earl of Chester and others, but nothing more. His affront to royal authority was too blatant to condone. Bishop Peter and his associates loyally if sullenly brought their forces to the siege. With wrongheaded courage, William de Bréauté refused to surrender the castle without his brother's leave. He was, thanks to Falkes' work, in command of a mighty fortress which had to be taken piece by piece. The siege lasted a full eight weeks from 20 June to 14 August. Then with smoke filling the keep, their last refuge, and a crack appearing in the masonry, William and his men came out and flung themselves at the king's feet, begging for mercy. William himself knew Henry well since he had been a knight of the royal household. But there was no mercy. According to Roger of Wendover, Henry had sworn that if those besieged were taken by force they would all be hanged. Falkes, in his own account, admitted that Henry was provoked to anger, although for that he blamed the incitement of Langton and the bishops. Certainly Hubert and the bishops were determined to make an example. William and the rest of the garrison, upwards of eighty knights and men at arms, were hanged. Falkes himself, having tearfully viewed the bodies, went into exile, where he died in 1226. This is the first known example of Henry's anger, which flared on occasions throughout his reign. Yet the episode was untypical and set no precedent. There was hardly a single political execution in the rest of Henry's reign.[98]

THE LOSS OF POITOU, 1224; THE DEFINITIVE MAGNA CARTA OF 1225

During the siege of Bedford disaster overtook what remained of the dynasty's continental possessions in Poitou and Gascony. In the early part of 1224 the government had been confident that Louis VIII would renew the truce agreed by his father back in 1220. But on 5 May he suddenly

---

[97] Tout, *Chapters*, i, 192, 195–6. Under Luke were Walter of Brackley (from 1222) and Walter of Kirkham (from 1224).
[98] There were, however (discussed in volume 2), deliberate killings at the battle of Evesham.

refused to do so. Prevented from invading Toulouse by the pope's reconciliation with its count, he would invade Poitou and Gascony instead. To
ease the way, he reached an agreement with the greatest of the Poitevin
barons, Hugh de Lusignan. What made Hugh's defection all the worse
was that in 1220 he had married none other than Henry's mother, Isabella
of Angoulême. He had thus achieved the marriage coveted by his father
before John's intervention back in 1200. Isabella was a far stronger personality than her easygoing husband (a pleasant change from John), and must
have condoned the abandonment of her son. The reward indeed was
great. If Gascony was conquered, Hugh was promised Bordeaux, far and
away its greatest town.[99] In the event, Louis, despite divisions in his army,
secured Poitou with comparative ease, the key port of La Rochelle surrendering in August 1224.[100] Hugh de Lusignan and Louis's seneschal in
Poitou then moved on into Gascony and received the submission of all the
towns save Bordeaux and Bayonne. In their original agreement, Hugh had
been promised by Louis the wages of 200 knights and 600 foot-soldiers for
seven years to complete the conquest. Clearly Henry would have to make
an immense effort if he was to save Gascony.

To make that effort one thing was needed above all, money. It could
only come from the kind of tax John had levied on England in 1207. Paid
as a thirteenth of the value of everyone's moveable property – chiefly corn
and farm animals – it had raised around £60,000, more than double the
crown's ordinary annual income. The 1215 Magna Carta, however, had
laid down that such taxes could only be levied with the common consent
of the kingdom. Even though the chapter was omitted from the Charters
of 1216 and 1217, it remained well known and in practice in force. No tax
could be levied without such consent.

Accordingly, a great council was summoned to meet at Westminster in
February 1225. In return for the tax – this time a fifteenth of everyone's
movable property – the assembly demanded a quid pro quo. The king
must formally accept both Magna Carta and the Charter of the Forest.
On 11 February 1225, Henry thus issued what became the final and definitive versions of the Charters. They enjoyed a status possessed by none of
their predecessors, for the challenge of invalidity due to coercion, made by

---

[99] Bordeaux was to be compensation for the dower Isabella would lose in England. (It
was indeed immediately confiscated.) Until Bordeaux was acquired, Hugh was to have a
pension of 2,000 Parisian pounds a year. Hugh was also confirmed in his possession of
Saintes and promised the isle of Oléron when acquired (see Carpenter, *Minority*, 178–9,
193, 345, 349). The text of Hugh's demands and of Louis's concessions are printed in
Amplissima Collectio, i, cols. 1162–4, 1184–5. I thank Amicie Pelissie du Rausas for bringing
them to my attention.

[100] To intercede for Louis's success during the siege, a penitential procession through
Paris was staged by three queens, Louis's wife Blanche of Castile, Blanche's niece the
queen of Jerusalem, and Philip Augustus's widow, Ingebourg of Denmark: Grant, *Blanche
of Castile*, 72–3.

William Brewer in 1223, was definitively answered. The Charters now proclaimed they had been granted by Henry of his spontaneous and free will – something John had not said in 1215 or Henry in 1216 or 1217. The Charters were also authenticated by the king's own seal as opposed, in 1216 and 1217, to the seals of the legate and the regent. Henry was now seventeen and, while still banned from issuing charters (so Magna Carta was here an exception), could certainly speak for himself. But the main reason why the Charters were manifestly freely given went beyond the status of the king. It was a reason announced in the Charters themselves so that there could be no doubt about it. A new chapter near the end thus stated that in return for the liberties Henry had granted, everyone in the kingdom had given him a fifteenth of their movable property.

This proved the Charters were consensual, part of a freely made bargain between king and kingdom. The consensus was displayed by the extensive witness list at the end. The Charters of 1215, 1216 and 1217 had hardly been given witness lists at all. Now nearly all the good and great of the realm were there whatever side they had taken in the civil war. The list was headed by Langton, eleven bishops and twenty abbots. Hubert de Burgh, as justiciar, came next followed by nine earls and twenty-three other magnates. Eight of the rebel barons who had been appointed to enforce the 1215 Magna Carta were there, rubbing shoulders with such loyalists as the earl of Chester and William Brewer. Sensing the importance and novelty of this, the copy of the Charters made soon afterwards at Cerne abbey in Dorset set out the witness list in beautifully elaborate fashion, and then wrote out the place and date of issue in capital letters.[101]

Archbishop Langton and Hubert de Burgh were the essential begetters of the 1225 Charters. Hubert's acceptance of them was pragmatic, Langton's was ideological. But the two men came to the same conclusion about their necessity. Given the new consensual nature of the Charters, Langton was able to do something more in their support, something again never done before. He and his fellow bishops issued sentences of excommunication against all who contravened them. The church thus stood full square behind the Charters. In 1225 both king and kingdom had taken ownership of them.

THE EMERGENCE OF THE KING

In February 1225 there were still well over three years to go before October 1228 when Henry would come of age. Yet there were growing pressures for him to enter full power before that date and thus start issuing his own charters. There was no legal barrier to that happening. The papal letters of April 1223 had already given the king full power. It was his councillors'

---

[101] Carpenter, *Magna Carta*, 422.

decision to restrict their implementation. They could always change their minds.

One factor encouraging them to do so was the increasing role being played by the king himself. Henry must have known that his brother-in-law, Alexander II of Scotland, had assumed full power on William the Lion's death in 1214, although not yet seventeen. While many of the royal letters Henry attested in 1225 and 1226 have a note saying he acted in the presence of the justiciar, or the justiciar and the bishops of Bath and Salisbury, many others did not. Petitioners were very clear that Henry himself was the source of patronage and (as with many kings) best approached through a friend at court. In 1224, William Brewer urged Ralph de Neville to use all his influence with the king so that his clerk might be presented to a certain living. In August 1225, William Marshal asked the bishop of Bath to persuade the king to grant him a wardship, or at least postpone its bestowal 'until we can come into his presence and your own'. At the end of the year John de Lacy begged Hubert de Burgh 'to help me with the king' over the postponement of a lawsuit.[102]

One episode at this time highlights the king's will and temper, and also his ignorance. In May 1226, Richard de Marsh, bishop of Durham, Henry's absentee chancellor, died. This cleared the way for his deputy, Ralph de Neville, keeper of the seal and since 1222 bishop of Chichester, to take over as chancellor. It also created a vacancy at Durham. When a delegation from the cathedral monks came to court, Henry urged them to elect as the new bishop his keeper of the wardrobe, Luke, the former chaplain of Hubert de Burgh. When the monks demurred, Henry, according to the testimony of one present, 'ordered the justiciar to demolish [Durham] castle if they did not obey his will'. This was not a well-judged threat as Hubert made all too clear. 'The demolition of the castle,' he interjected, 'will please the monks a great deal, not harm them,' the point being that the castle belonged not to the monks but to the sometimes oppressive bishop. How often in the future did Henry's ministers have to pull him away from tempestuous and ill-judged orders and initiatives.[103]

In 1225, Henry and Hubert spent around 200 days at Westminster. In 1226 it was around 150. Hubert, one suspects, wished to remain at the centre of government given the financial, diplomatic and military exigencies of the crisis overseas. But time was also spent at traditional royal residences, notably Winchester and Marlborough, while in 1226 there was a journey to Nottingham and then a tour of the Welsh marches. What becomes very clear in these years is what might be called Henry's itinerary of alms and prayers, one which continued throughout his reign. Wherever he stopped, wherever he stayed, he gave alms and other favours to the neighbouring hospitals, leper houses, recluses and monasteries. In return, what Henry

---

[102] TNA SC 1/6/48; TNA SC 1/2/9; TNA SC 1/11/48.
[103] Evers, 'Disputes about episcopal elections', 107; Powicke, *King Henry III*, i, 266–70.

sought to harvest were the prayers of those receiving his alms. It was as though he lived under a pergola of spiritual light. In 1225 the beneficiaries included the recluse at Sutton at Hone near Dartford (a pension of a penny a day), the prioress of Ankerwyke near Windsor (firewood), the nuns of Clerkenwell in London (pardoned a tax because of their poverty), the parson of Brill in Buckinghamshire (timber to repair his church), the nuns of nearby Studley (a gift of 20s), and the lepress received at the king's petition into the hospital at Harbledown near Rochester (20s to buy clothes). In December when he visited the Cistercian monastery of Waverley in Surrey the king was met by a solemn procession of the monks. Entering the chapter house, he sought and received all the spiritual benefits which came from membership of the order.[104] Next year, in the Welsh marches, Henry gave firewood to the two hospitals at Bridgenorth (one a leper house) and timber to the prior of Llanthony Gloucester to build a new refectory. At Gloucester, hearing that the Premonstratensian canons were about to hold a general chapter, Henry begged twice over to be remembered in their 'assiduous prayers'.[105] Prominent in this pattern of piety were also gifts to widows and 'poor little women', 'pauperculae' (they were often one and the same). In 1227, Henry found land for two poor sisters who had come to see him at Ripon. He also made a series of concessions to a certain Gunhilda from the royal manor of Ludgershall. Convicted of homicide, her husband had been hanged and her daughter, Matilda (arrested on the king's orders), burnt. Henry allowed Gunhilda to stay in her husband's house and made provision for Matilda's soul. In the same year Henry pardoned 'for God' the widows of Somerset the tallage being levied in the county.[106]

A new dimension was added to Henry's pious itinerary in 1226 by the first of his pilgrimages to the East Anglian holy sites, a pilgrimage which was to recur throughout his life. That April he visited Walsingham, Bury St Edmunds and Bromholm, a priory famous for housing supposed relics of the Holy Cross. In all probability this was Hubert's doing. His ancestral home at Burgh was under ten miles from Bromholm and he entertained Henry there on the day after the pilgrimage to the priory.[107] These years in the mid-1220s were important for Henry's spiritual life in another way. The Dominican friars had arrived in England in 1221. The Franciscans came in 1224. Bishop Peter and Hubert de Burgh were at one in their enthusiasm for the new orders. Henry did not lag behind. In April 1227, following a petition from the mayor and men of York, he gave a chapel and a place in the city for the foundation of a Dominican friary, this for the benefit of his soul and the souls of his ancestors and successors. Later in the year arriving at Northampton, he gave timber to the Franciscans to

[104] Waverley, 301.
[105] Patent Roll 1225–32, 60.
[106] CR 1227–31, 8; RLC, ii, 189, 190, 201b; CFR 1226–7, no. 265.
[107] Henry had been at Bury in 1225 but he did not go to Walsingham or Bromholm.

build a chapel there.[108] The pattern was set. As the number of friaries multiplied through the country, often with Henry's help, so they slotted in to his itinerary of alms and prayers.[109]

The king's emergence was also reflected in the central role now being played by the wardrobe in the kingdom's finances. In the financial year 1224/5 its expenditure, most of the money coming from the exchequer, amounted to nearly £10,000, well over half the ordinary revenue of the crown at the time.[110] Fragmentary accounts for 1225/6, recording the daily cost of the household's food and drink, also reveal for the first time the full extent of the king's domestic establishment. Separate entries were made for the pantry, buttery, kitchen, scullery, saucery, hall, chamber and stables. There was also a record of the expenditure on wax for candles, on firewood for the hall and chamber, and on the wages of grooms and livery of horses. The usual daily cost was between £6 and £7, although the real cost was greater since the sum excludes wine (bought separately) and the food coming from the king's own manors. The cost more than doubled later in the reign, but even at £6 or £7 it was approaching half the annual income considered (in 1255) necessary for a knight. On feast days the cost was much greater. On Christmas Day 1225, celebrated at Winchester (and *not* at the bishop's expense), it approached £51. Over £20 of this was spent by the kitchen (always the largest cost centre). The consumption of wax amounted to 136 pounds.[111]

THE PRESSURE FOR PATRONAGE

As the king grew in 'vigour of mind', so his ministers could argue the more plausibly for the lifting of the last restrictions on his authority. They had very personal reasons for doing so. The gifts of deer, wine and wood they received from Henry were important marks of his favour, but they were no substitute for more substantial and permanent rewards. Only when Henry could issue charters and make grants in perpetuity could they hope for that. The members of the regime thus wished to increase the king's power so as to profit from it themselves, to increase his authority to diminish his resources. But did not the faithful men who had won the war and secured the peace deserve their reward? And they had waited so long. In October 1226 it was ten years since Henry's accession. These feelings

---

[108] *RLC*, ii, 180, 196.

[109] For further discussion of Henry and the friars see below, 281–5.

[110] Wild, *WA*, liv, lxii; Carpenter, *Minority*, 413–14. In 1224/5 the wardrobe's receipts and expenditure were swollen by over £3,000 of expenditure on Gascony being channelled through it.

[111] *DA*, 95; Carpenter, 'Household rolls', 34–8. The accounts run together for Christmas Eve and Christmas Day probably because the cost of food and drink on Christmas Eve was small. For further discussion of Henry's food and drink, see below, 380–3, and for his almsgiving in 1225/6, see below, 287.

were not confined to laymen. The bishops of Salisbury and Bath were preparing long lists of local government privileges they hoped to extract from the king. No one, however, felt the need to empower the king more strongly than Hubert de Burgh himself.

Despite his long service to John and Henry, despite indeed saving the dynasty, Hubert had received little in the way of permanent reward. Through his first wife, Beatrice de Warenne, he held the barony of Wormegay in Norfolk, but only for life, his wife having had an heir by a previous marriage. By his second marriage in 1216, to Isabella, the aged countess of Gloucester, he gained nothing thanks to her almost immediate death. Hubert held the Three Castles, as they were called, in Upper Gwent – Grosmont, Skenfrith and Whitecastle – but this was by a dubious grant from Reginald de Briouze. Hubert desperately needed that to be confirmed by a royal charter. His greatest gains from King John were the honours of Haughley in Suffolk and Rayleigh in Essex. But John had merely given these to Hubert during the king's pleasure. Henry was later to accuse Hubert of lifting the ban on alienations precisely to obtain these honours by royal charter.[112]

This situation was aggravated rather then alleviated by Hubert's third marriage in 1221 to Margaret, eldest daughter of King William the Lion of Scotland, and sister to King Alexander II. This was an extraordinarily high-status match for someone from a knightly family. After all, under the Treaty of Norham in 1209, Margaret was supposed to marry Henry III himself. In 1225, Isabella, Margaret's younger sister, married the earl of Norfolk. The marriage rocketed Hubert up the social scale. It alone made him earl-worthy. The earldom of Kent he later obtained was entailed on his issue by Margaret and was not to pass to John de Burgh, the son of his first marriage. The marriage to Margaret, however, did not transform Hubert's material position in the same way as marriage had transformed the position of the old regent, William Marshal, for Margaret came without a landed endowment. Alexander doubtless thought assenting to the marriage at all was favour enough. Margaret herself was a proud and forceful woman, very conscious of her royal status. She certainly expected a landed estate worthy of her and, if they arrived, her children.[113]

Hubert was also under pressure to reward his supporters. 'You are to know that my sole hope is in God and you . . . in no way can I remain in the king's service unless you provide for me,' wrote Ralph de Trubleville in 1220. John Marshal, nephew of the old regent, in complaining that he had received nothing to maintain himself in Ireland, told Hubert bluntly, 'make up your mind whether my service in these parts is useful to the king or not'.[114]

[112] Paris, vi, 69.
[113] For Margaret, see Annesley, 'The countess and the constable'.
[114] TNA SC 1/1/202; TNA SC 1/1/141.

Hubert could give money from the king's revenues, but what men wanted above all was land held in hereditary right. And here there was another problem. John had indeed sometimes rewarded people with land but rarely on a permanent basis. Much of what he gave came from the lands seized in England from Normans who in 1204 had entered the allegiance of the king of France. Rarely granted in hereditary right, these 'lands of the Normans' as they were called could be resumed by the crown at any time.[115] What made them all the more vulnerable was the practice of threatening great men through seizing this type of property from their followers. Henry of Audley's tenure of Edgmond, John Marshal's of Hingham and Peter de Maulay's of Upavon depended very much on the fortunes their patrons, respectively the earl of Chester, William Marshal and the bishop of Winchester. Hubert could not always protect his own clients. In 1225, William de Gamages reminded him of how the earl of Chester 'on your account has dispossessed me unjustly and without judgement of my land at Cottesmore'. Gamages added that 'both because of your financial straits and your great expenditures, I demand nothing from you at present against your will, but wait until God improves your circumstances, which, with God's will, will be soon'.[116] That improvement could only really come when the king gained full power. Indeed the king himself had hinted as much. In 1225 the bishop of Durham was told he could not be granted various privileges because of the ban on permanent alienations. But, Henry added, 'we will be most ready to agree to your wishes . . . at an opportune time so that you will be grateful and content'.[117] In effect Hubert and Henry were having to rule with one of the most vital hands of monarchy, the hand of patronage, tied behind their backs. The sooner that ended the better.

Hubert's political insecurity added a final push in the same direction. The dissidents of 1223 remained his bitter enemies, however much Hubert sometimes tried to co-operate with the earl of Chester. In addition, his close alliances with the earls of Salisbury and Pembroke had ended. In 1225 both earls were doing stirling work for the regime, William Longespée the commander of the king's army in Gascony, William Marshal the justiciar in Ireland. Then came problems, in both cases thanks to Hubert's desire to advance the interests of his family. The rift with Longespée began with a rumour of his death. Hubert, according to the account in Roger of Wendover, at once proposed that Raymond de Burgh, his nephew, should marry Ela, Longespée's widow, in her own right countess of Salisbury. Raymond, according to the story, even went to see Ela, dressed in fine robes, to press his suit. She rejected him with contempt: 'the nobility of her lineage' prevented any such union. Doubtless many thought the same

---

[115] For the lands of the Normans, see Moore, 'The loss of Normandy and the invention of *Terre Normannorum*', and Power, 'The treaty of Paris'.

[116] TNA SC 1/1/100.

[117] *RLC*, ii, 75b.

consideration should have prevented Hubert's marriage to Margaret of Scotland. When Longespée returned to England early in 1226, he complained bitterly about what had happened. Hubert's response was typical of the arts that kept him in power for so long. 'He confessed his fault, and recovered the favour of the earl with precious horses and other rich gifts.'[118] The gifts, however, were wasted. Longespée died in March 1226, to be commemorated in a magnificent effigy in Salisbury Cathedral.

William Marshal had gone to Ireland as justiciar in 1224, encouraged by the final celebration of his marriage to Eleanor, the king's sister (later the wife of Simon de Montfort). The Marshal's task was to prevent the insurgent Hugh de Lacy taking over Ulster. In that he was successful.[119] But then there was trouble. It arose from Hubert de Burgh's determination to install his nephew Richard de Burgh in Connacht. Richard was the son of William de Burgh, Hubert's elder brother. William had gone with John to Ireland in 1185 and been established in Munster. He had also been given a grant of Connacht, effectively as an incentive to conquer it from its native Irish rulers. Richard de Burgh had inherited this claim to Connacht, and in 1226 Hubert at last judged the time right to make it good. The problem was that, as justiciar of Ireland, William Marshal would not agree.

Faced with this obstruction, at a great council held at Winchester in June 1226, Hubert persuaded Henry to remove the Marshal from the justiciarship and replace him with Geoffrey de Marsh, the justiciar between 1215 and 1221. At first the Marshal, who attended the meeting, said he would now go on a pilgrimage to Santiago de Compostela, but then, his resentment boiling over, he set off back to Ireland, evidently to cause trouble. He was pursued by a pained and reproachful royal letter.[120] The king denied suspecting him of disloyalty, after all the Marshal had married his sister. But if he was indeed going back to Ireland he must first surrender Cardigan and Carmarthen. (The Marshal had held these since wresting them from Llywelyn in 1223.) Hubert and Henry were playing a dangerous game, but they knew their man. The Marshal remembered his father's loyalty to King John despite many ups and downs. He had a genuine affection for the king, his brother-in-law. He now capitulated and surrendered Cardigan and Carmarthen to the king, who entrusted them to the earl of Chester's man Henry of Audley. The Marshal then returned to Ireland but to help not hinder Geoffrey de Marsh. There were compensations, as usual with Hubert. The Marshal was allowed to retain the castle of Caerleon for another four years, when his much disputed rights would be decided (in accordance with Magna Carta) 'by the judgment of his peers'. John Marshal was also returned to Hingham in Norfolk.[121]

---

[118] Wendover, iii, 101–4.
[119] Hugh was restored to Ulster in 1226–7, but only for life.
[120] *Patent Roll 1225–32*, 81.
[121] *Patent Roll 1225–32*, 58–9, 82–3; *RLC*, ii, 133.

These events were a victory for Hubert. He had begun the installation of his nephew in Connacht, recovered Cardigan and Carmarthen for the crown, and disciplined one of the most powerful barons without driving him into rebellion. Yet it would have been easier had the king's authority been greater and his own power more secure.

THE REASSERTION OF THE KING'S RIGHTS

The desire of ministers to reap their just rewards was not the only reason for empowering the king. Such power would also facilitate the maintenance and recovery of his rights both in England and overseas. King Henry had issued his new version of Magna Carta and the Charter of the Forest in 1225 'benignly and happily', as the Crowland chronicler put it. But he and his ministers soon suspected that in the localities, in the name of the Charters, far more was being taken than was justified. In July 1225 a sharp letter was sent to the men of Yorkshire and Cumberland about the way, under cover of the Charter, they were impeding the king's officials in the performance of their tasks.[122] Next year the knights of Lincolnshire obstructed the sheriff in his holding of local courts, arguing that he was acting in breach of Magna Carta.[123] The two knights leading the opposition, Theobald Hautein and Hugh of Humby, were brought before the king, only for the case against them to be dropped, a typical Hubertian retreat.[124] In their disputes with the sheriffs, the counties had the support of the great lords. At the petition of the magnates, gathered at Winchester in June 1226, the men of eight counties, including Lincolnshire, were to send knights to the king to explain the arguments over the Charter. Although the meeting was postponed, the issue resurfaced in 1227.[125]

These disputes paled before that over the implementation of the Charter of the Forest.[126] In the first chapter of the Charter the king promised that he would remove from the royal forest all the areas afforested by Henry II, once, that is, their extent had been established by local juries. But did this mean everything Henry put in without qualification or everything he put in having made good the extensive losses to the royal forest under his predecessor, King Stephen? The counties said the first, the government the second. On the difference could turn whether large areas of a county were in or out of the royal forest. Because no agreement could be reached, the minority government refused to implement the verdicts of

---

[122] *RLC*, ii, 79b.

[123] They were appealing here to cap. 35 of the 1225 Charter, which regulated the holding of the county, hundred and wapentake courts, a chapter introduced in 1217.

[124] *CRR*, xii, nos. 2142, 2312; Holt, *Magna Carta*, 391–3; Maddicott, 'Magna Carta', 33–4.

[125] *RLC*, ii, 153, 154b, 212b–13.

[126] For the dispute in Nottinghamshire, see Crook, 'The struggle over the forest boundaries'.

the juries made after the first issue of the Forest Charter in 1217. In 1225, however, anxious to do everything to facilitate the payment of the tax, it gave way. The verdicts of the new juries (staffed by local knights) were accepted and extensive deforestation took place. Roger of Wendover wrote lyrically of how in the liberated areas men now sold off timber and turned hitherto uncultivated tracts into arable land.[127]

Hubert and Henry were, however, but holding their fire. 'It is necessary at the moment to put up with it until at some opportune time we can put it right,' the king observed while ordering his officials to accept the exorbitant demands for deforestation in Dorset. Next year, in October 1226, the king stopped the deforestations in Yorkshire, Shropshire and Hampshire. He also said he would come to Huntingdonshire to investigate the demands of the knights, although, in fact, events abroad prevented him doing so. It was obvious that Henry would be far better placed to assert his rights once he had assumed full power. He would then, as Hubert de Burgh put it, 'be more greatly feared in his kingdom and of greater authority'.[128]

CONTINTENTAL AMBITIONS, THE ASSUMPTION OF FULL POWER

The tax levied to save Gascony proved a prodigious success, raising around £40,000. In a very responsible fashion, the money was kept apart from the king's ordinary revenues so that it could be devoted, as it largely was, to the Gascon cause. With funding flowing, the campaign in Gascony was an equal success. The leader of the expedition sent out in 1225 was William Longespée, earl of Salisbury, but the titular head was the king's younger brother, Richard, now sixteen. He was knighted, granted Cornwall during the king's pleasure, and given the title count of Poitou. By December 1225 the recovery of Gascony was complete. This was a decisive moment in English and Gascon history. Gascony was to remain under the king of England for another 225 years. Henry was lucky that Louis VIII proved far more interested in Toulouse than he was in Gascony. And without Louis, Hugh de Lusignan lacked the power to finish the conquest on his own. He evidently never received the promised 200 knights and 600 footmen.[129] There was also one fundamental factor binding England and Gascony together: the wine trade. Much of Gascony was a land of vineyards, as it is today, and the English market was open as never before, now that there was less competition from Anjou and Poitou with their loss to the king of France. In August 1225 the Cinque Ports assembled a great

---

[127] Wendover, iii, 94–5. Since Wendover was at this time prior of the St Albans daughter house at Belvoir, very close to the Nottinghamshire, Leicestershire and Rutland forests, this is very much an eyewitness account. See Crook, 'Roger of Wendover, prior of Belvoir'.

[128] Paris, vi, 69. Hubert was here referring to the events of 1223.

[129] See above, 30.

fleet to bring the Gascon harvest to England.[130] The Gascons themselves, with their own language and history, had no desire to exchange the remote and benign lordship of the king of England for what might be the intrusive rule of the king of France. Indeed, their view was that Gascony had never been a fief of the king of France and thus was not involved in the forfeiture of John's continental possessions.

With the saving of Gascony, might not the recovery of Poitou follow? Richard's title after all was 'count of Poitou'. And after that perhaps there might be the reconquest of Anjou and Normandy. This certainly was Henry's dream. The disaster of 1224 had left a deep mark. Years later he blamed Hubert for prosecuting the siege of Bedford instead of defending Poitou. In the life of the regent, William Marshal, written at precisely this time, the hope was expressed that the young king would revive all the chivalric virtues and recover the land he had lost. The permanency of 1204 and 1224 is far more apparent in retrospect than it was at the time. Henry, however, now found himself stuck in England while his younger brother laid siege to towns and defeated Hugh de Lusignan. Without realizing how ill fitted he was to a military campaign, Henry burned with the desire to lead one. Hubert de Burgh was far more aware of the difficulties and the disadvantages. This contrasting approach was to be an increasing source of friction between the king and his justiciar.

If the continental empire was to be recovered, allies were vital. In the years after 1224, there seemed good prospects of securing them. Perhaps Hugh de Lusignan and Henry's mother might be tempted back on side. Perhaps there could be an alliance with Henry's kinsman and neighbour to the east of Gascony, Raymond VII, count of Toulouse. Raymond, like Henry after all, had been the great victim of Capetian expansion. The Albigensian crusade against the Cathar heretics infesting his dominions had left the French monarchy installed in Carcassone and Béziers and the other conquests of the crusade's leader, Simon de Montfort (father of the English Simon). Louis, before his accession, had himself led two expeditions against Toulouse. In 1224 the pope, hoping for a rapprochement with Raymond, had stopped a third, but he could easily change his mind. Then Louis might conquer both Toulouse itself and Raymond's lordships in Provence, stretching north from Avignon up the Rhone valley.

Another potential ally for Henry was Peter de Dreux, since 1213 duke of Brittany in right of his wife. Peter was a member of the French royal house and had done homage for Brittany to Philip Augustus. But the duke of Brittany, before 1204, had been the vassal not of the king of France but of the duke of Normandy and thus of the king of England. The duke had also traditionally held the honour of Richmond in Yorkshire. Proud, ambitious and very keen to play an independent role, Peter might well be

---

[130] Carpenter, *Minority*, 378.

open to English offers. In that case the strategic importance of Brittany, with its frontiers adjoining Normandy, Anjou and Poitou, would be immense. In due course, an alliance with Peter would indeed become the cornerstone of Henry's continental policy.

There were also possibilities of alliances with the princes of Germany and its boy king, Henry VII, the king of the Romans. Henry was the son of the emperor of the Romans, Frederick II, the ruler, clever, cultivated and cruel, who was to dominate European politics down to his death in 1250. Born in 1194, Frederick's father was the Hohenstaufen Emperor Henry VI, his mother Constance, heiress to the Norman kingdom of Sicily. Henry VI died in 1197, leaving Frederick to grow up in Sicily and finally take control of the kingdom in 1208. He had gone on to defeat King John's nephew, Otto of Brunswick, and establish himself as king of the Romans, thus gaining authority over the princes of Germany. Then, in 1220, he had been crowned emperor by the pope, thus gaining authority over the north Italian towns. As a sop to the pope, worried about any junction between the empire and Sicily, he had established his nine-year-old son, Henry, as king of the Romans and thus his titular deputy in Germany.[131]

This backstory was important for Henry III and his councillors. On the face of it, given John's wholehearted support for Otto of Brunswick, Frederick would hardly welcome English overtures. Indeed, under the treaty of Catania in 1223 with Louis VIII he had promised to make no alliance with Henry III.[132] Still, Frederick might be tempted by English money, all the more so since Otto had died in 1218. A way round the treaty might be a marriage involving Frederick's son or a child of one of the German princes. Fortunately, Henry VII's regent in Germany, Engelbert, archbishop of Cologne, was a self-proclaimed Anglophile, 'he did not know why', although one reason was probably the trading links between Cologne and England.[133]

In negotiating an alliance, Henry and Hubert had one trump card. They could offer Henry's own hand in marriage. How lucky that Hubert had saved Henry from Margaret of Scotland by marrying her himself! In January 1225 the bishop of Carlisle, Walter Mauclerc, an experienced diplomat, left England for Cologne. His letters home spoke of the great storm in the channel, long daily rides with borrowed horses, the hardness of the roads, the unpleasant air and the fear of ambush. It was no better when he got there. 'God knows, I would rather be sent to Acre . . . than to this people so mad and lacking in reason,' wrote his colleague, the chancellor of

---

[131] It was the princes of Germany who had the right to elect the king of the Romans, the expectation being that whoever was elected would then be crowned emperor by the pope. However, the pope claimed the right to consent to the election and was very concerned to prevent any union between the empire and Sicily.

[132] Weiler, *Henry III of England and the Staufen Empire*, 25.

[133] *DD*, no. 160. A fascinating report of his attitudes.

St Paul's, Henry of Cornhill. The archbishop of Cologne, however, was optimistic. A marriage might be arranged between Henry and the daughter of Frederick, duke of Austria. Another possibility was a German marriage for one of Henry's sisters, perhaps indeed to Henry VII. The archbishop was confident that by such alliances the king would 'recover all his lost land', thus defining the aim of English diplomacy over the next quarter century. The only problem, as the archbishop said, was that 'the emperor thirsts for nothing save money and its accumulation'. When he gave examples of the current state of the marriage market, Mauclerc was so shocked he had to write home asking for fresh authority. He also reported that Frederick was anyway thinking of a French marriage for his son.[134]

Henry and Hubert were themselves wondering what could be done on the French front by diplomacy. Pope Honorius, in response to their complaints about the French invasion of Poitou, had sent to France as legate the wily Cardinal Romano Bonaventura. The legate professed his goodwill towards Henry but would do nothing to offend Louis, who might soon be needed for another crusade against the count of Toulouse. Such a crusade would, however, be helped by a peace with England, and so the legate went on to explore the possibility of Henry marrying a daughter of Louis VIII, with one of Henry's sisters marrying Louis's eldest son, the future Louis IX. Mauclerc was thus told to soft pedal on the German negotiations by demanding more for Henry's marriage and offering less for his sister's. If that broke the matter entirely, he was to feign indignation and leave immediately. Although, as he said, they endangered both his body and soul, Mauclerc agreed to follow these instructions and that was the end of Henry's projected Austrian marriage.[135]

The efforts of the legate did not stop the English government trying to arrange an alliance with the count of Toulouse. Indeed, the prospect might make Louis more amenable to a settlement. Letters from Henry, stressing their mutual sufferings at the hands of the king of France, were sent to the count in August 1225 and were followed in January 1226 by a subvention of 2,500 marks.[136] Unfortunately, in the very same month the legate excommunicated the count. In May, Louis mustered a great army and headed south, beginning the siege of Avignon early in June.

Henry had been disappointed by the collapse of his projected Austrian marriage, and later blamed Hubert for obstructing the negotiations.[137] Now, with Louis away attacking Count Raymond, he thought his moment for invasion had come. As Roger of Wendover put it, he 'thirsted with an ardent desire to cross overseas in hostile fashion'. He would join up with

---

[134] *DD*, nos. 160, 163–4, 172, 187; Powicke, *King Henry III*, i, 159. There is full discussion of the diplomacy of these years in Weiler, *Henry III of England and the Staufen Empire*, ch. 1.

[135] *RLC*, ii, 72b; *DD*, no. 172.

[136] *F*, 179; *DA*, 53, 58, 91.

[137] *RLC*, ii, 72b; *DD*, no. 172; Wendover, iii, 221.

his brother Richard, and then together they would go to help the count of Toulouse. Henry, therefore, summoned his magnates to muster in arms at Winchester, while assembling ships at Portsmouth and transporting his tents to Portchester. When, however, the magnates gathered at Winchester in mid-June 1226, letters from the legate were read out forbidding, on pain of excommunication, any action against Louis and any help to the count. Henry reluctantly backed down. While reinforcements were sent to Richard, the king dispersed the rest of his fleet 'as we have counsel that we should not proceed further at present'. He was, however, 'greatly exhilarated' when Master William de Pierrepont, a man skilled in astrology, prophesized that Louis's expedition would end in disaster.[138] Hubert was less disappointed by the postponement, indeed perhaps he engineered it. The Winchester council had also seen the dismissal of William Marshal as justiciar of Ireland and the beginnings of the installation of Richard de Burgh in Connacht. This was no time to invade France.

At first the prophecy of the astrologer seemed quite unfulfilled. In September 1226, Avignon fell to the French king. But then suddenly a sequence of extraordinary events seemed to prove the prophecy exactly right. The starting point here was the disaffection of Peter, duke of Brittany, and Hugh de Lusignan. The former was infuriated by the way his ingenious scheme to secure control of Flanders was stymied by Louis. The latter was disillusioned by Louis's failure to help him in Gascony. The two men entered an alliance which also included Theobald, count of Champagne. Duke Peter now sought to exploit his English connections. He was welcomed with open arms. On 19 October 1226, Henry announced that he would marry Peter's daughter, Yolande, as soon as he could get a dispensation from the pope. If Yolande survived her brother, Henry would obtain Brittany, saving Peter's life interest. Meanwhile he would receive Peter's homage for Brittany and recognize him as earl of Richmond. He would also cross over with an army as soon as the duke advised it. Henry's dreams of reconquest were becoming a reality.[139]

Better was to come. On 8 November 1226, Louis VIII died quite suddenly on his way home to France. He left a twelve-year-old son as his heir. Henry thought of an immediate invasion and summoned ships to Portsmouth to be ready to sail on the first wind. When news came of Louis IX's coronation at Reims on 28 November, the fleet was disbanded but Henry remained optimistic. The coronation had been boycotted by Duke Peter, Hugh de Lusignan and the count of Champagne. In December envoys from Hugh and other Poitevin magnates were in England and they took back elaborate offers designed to tempt their masters back into Henry's allegiance. Royal letters in this month breathed the king's

---

[138] Wendover, iii, 111; Tours, 314; *Patent Roll 1216–25*, 33, 35–61; *RLC*, ii, 113b, 119b, 151.

[139] *Patent Roll 1216–25*, 153–4. Although recognized as earl of Richmond, he was only to get all the lands of the honour if he lost his lands in France.

enthusiasm. He begged for money and offered everlasting thanks for help 'in this our urgent necessity . . . having been presented with the opportunity of recovering our rights and conquering our inheritance through the death of the king of France'.[140]

There was, however, one snag. The promises made to the Poitevin nobles were attested by Hubert, the earls of Chester and Gloucester, Archbishop Langton and eight bishops. But the nobles had to be reassured that the promises were valid despite the king being underage. Nor could the promises be embodied in charters. Instead they were put into awkward hybrid documents. Here then was the final spur to lifting the last restrictions on the king's authority. It would now be Louis not Henry who would be derided as a boy rather than a king.

Thus it was that on Sunday 9 January 1227, at a great council held in Oxford, Henry announced that by the counsel of his lay and ecclesiastical magnates (led by Archbishop Langton), he would henceforth issue charters and confirmations under his seal. Although technically Henry remained underage until he was twenty-one in October 1228, he had now, aged nineteen and three months, entered into the fullness of royal power.

THE IMPACT OF THE MINORITY

The events of Henry's minority were decisive for England's political future. The government, led by William Marshal, had won the war and established Henry on the throne. England was not to have a Capetian king with all its incalculable consequences for the political shape of Europe. Thereafter, the Marshal, followed by Hubert de Burgh, had gradually rebuilt royal power from its state of near collapse. England was not to dissolve into semi-independent shires ruled by earls, sheriffs and castellans acting more or less as they liked and absorbing much of the king's revenues. By 1225, the ordinary annual revenue of the crown, at over £16,000, was still below the £24,000 averaged by John even at the start of his reign. In real terms, taking account of inflation, the contrast was much worse. Still, at over £16,000 the revenue was double the level of the years 1218 to 1220.[141] And the ordinary revenue of 1225 was boosted by the £40,000 produced by the great tax to save Gascony. The government, meanwhile, had kept the peace both by ensuring former rebels were returned to their lands and by promising that royal power would be exercised within new limits: the limits set by Magna Carta and the Charter of the Forest. If the Charters were obeyed, Henry's kingship would be very different from his

---

[140] *Patent Roll 1225–32*, 101, 104–5; *RLC*, ii, 205b. In the quotation I have combined two passages.

[141] Carpenter, *Minority*, 413; Barratt, 'Revenue of King John', 848–51, and (for the recovery of exchequer authority) Barratt, 'Another fine mess'. For inflation, see below, 111, n. 26.

father's. The minority would be a watershed between lawless and lawful rule. Important changes were also taking place in the spiritual life of the country. The friars arrived in England, and Archbishop Langton, at Oxford in 1222, promulgated legislation introducing the decrees of the Fourth Lateran Council. Surviving in some sixty manuscripts, the legislation 'came . . . to form the basis of the local law of the English Church in the later Middle Ages'.[142]

In terms of the impact of these first years on Henry himself, central was the coronation. It was that which set him apart and above everyone else in his kingdom. I myself attended the coronation of Queen Elizabeth in 1953 and have a series of episodic memories of the day:[143] the breakfast at number 2 Little Cloister beforehand; the top hat someone placed on the ledge of the triforium by our seats high up in the north transept; the little sandwiches my grandmother made for me to eat; the standing up and gripping the railings in front of me, so I could see; and above all – I told myself 'remember this' – the crown descending from the hands of the archbishop onto the queen's head. Afterwards, I remember too attending a buffet in Church House, though that can hardly have compared with Henry III's coronation banquet! In 1953 I was six. Henry was nine at the time of his first coronation in 1216 and thirteen for the far more splendid affair in 1220. How vivid and numinous must have been his memories: the shouted acclamation at the start to the question whether the people would accept him as king; the coronation oath; the stripping down to a shirt open to the shoulders; the anointing with Holy Oil on head, breast and arms; the vesting in tunic, dalmatic and mantle; the girding with the sword; the fixing of spurs to his feet; the crowning with (in 1220) Saint Edward's crown; and the placing of the sceptre in one hand and the rod in the other. In the oath, the coronation testified to the obligations of Henry's kingship, in the anointing to its God-given nature, in its crowning to its glory, and in its insignia – the sword, sceptre and rod – to its power and authority.[144]

Henry never forgot his coronation. Years later, in a private conversation with Robert Grosseteste, the greatest scholar bishop of the age, he recalled how the legate Guala 'consecrated and crowned us and raised us up to the throne of the kingdom'.[145] In later years, he sometimes stated he would observe undertakings as 'a crowned and anointed king'.[146] He even hankered after a third coronation to coincide with the translation in 1269

[142] C&S, i, 100–25, with the quotation at 100.

[143] My father, as a canon of Westminster, carried the orb at the coronation.

[144] For the coronation, see English Coronation Records. Particularly relevant (between 30 and 53) are a twelfth-century ordo and (from Roger of Howden) a description of the coronation of Richard I. Translations of some of the prayers in the twelfth-century ordo are found in the coronation ordo of Charles I (between 255 and 65). For the coronation under Henry's predecessors, see Aurell, L'Empire des Plantagenêt, 123–33.

[145] Robert Grosseteste, 356.

[146] F, 288–9; Paris, v, 377.

of Edward the Confessor to his new shrine in Westminster Abbey, thus linking together what for him were the two greatest spiritual celebrations of the reign.[147]

The spiritual climax of the coronation was the anointing. Derived from the prophet Samuel's anointing of King David, it meant the king was established over his people by God and ruled through his grace. 'King by the grace of God' featured in the titles at the start of all royal letters and charters. In 1246, aware that many kings (including those in Scotland) were not anointed, Henry asked Grosseteste what the ceremony added to royal dignity.[148] Grosseteste, in reply, explained in detail how it poured into the king all the gifts of the Holy Spirit – those of fear (of doing anything unlawful), piety, knowledge, fortitude, counsel, understanding and wisdom. In outline this was probably what Henry believed already. The prayer before the anointing called on God to 'water' the king 'plentifully with the blessings of his grace and the dew of heaven'.[149] Other prayers asked him to be given the wisdom of Solomon, the fortitude of Joshua and the faith of Abraham as well as the humility of David and the clemency of Moses. In Henry's case, the gifts of the Holy Spirit did indeed work their magic when it came to piety. They were less efficacious in giving Henry wisdom and understanding.

Anointing at the coronation did not mean the king had any priestly functions. Grosseteste was very firm on the point and Henry accepted what was said. In 1253, during a great sentence of excommunication against violators of Magna Carta, he refused to hold a candle, declaring he was not a priest.[150] Equally, there was nothing in the God-given nature of his rule that placed Henry above the law or justified absolutist theories of kingship. Rather the stress throughout the ceremony was on how he should rule justly for the benefit of his people. As the prayer before the anointing put it, he would govern in peace and plenty, protecting his country, comforting the church, loving his subjects, vanquishing his enemies, and dazzling everyone with the splendour of his court and power of his rule. 'After the glorious and happy days of this life' he would 'attain everlasting joy and happiness'.[151] Before the anointing the king's obligations were encapsulated in the coronation oath. Here Henry swore to give peace and honour to God and the church, to give justice to his people, and to eradicate bad laws and customs and introduce and keep good ones.

---

[147] This is discussed in volume 2.

[148] *Letters of Grosseteste*, 366–9; Southern, *Robert Grosseteste*, 268–9.

[149] *English Coronation Records*, 32–3, 258.

[150] Paris, v, 377. Recalling, under the year 1253, the sentence of excommunication launched in 1237, Paris has Henry holding a candle (Paris, v, 360–1). It is possible that Henry changed his mind about his priestly status after hearing Grosseteste's views, but more likely that Paris's later account of the 1237 excommunication is embellished. Henry holding a candle does not feature in the account under 1237 itself: Paris, iii, 382–3.

[151] *English Coronation Records*, 32–3, 258.

He also swore to maintain the rights of the crown.[152] The politics of the minority itself, with the struggle to recover control over the royal manors, castles and counties, had likewise educated Henry, or so it might be hoped, in the need to preserve his rights. There was no contradiction between that need and the obligation to rule justly for the common good. Unless the king was strong and secure in his rights (as Langton realized) he would lack the power to maintain peace and protect the rights of everyone else. Henry in later life referred on several occasions to his coronation oath.[153] How far he would live up to its standards and obligations would go a long way towards determining the success or failure of the reign.

As king there was no way Henry could escape his father's shadow. From start to finish of his reign he was called in official documents 'Henry son of King John'. He was even so described in the epitaph on his tomb. From Peter des Roches, Henry must have heard many justifications of John's rule and denigrations of those who had rebelled against him. Were not all native-born Englishmen traitors as Falkes de Bréauté claimed? Did not the king need loyal men from elsewhere in his dominions to keep them in order? Perhaps Henry also heard from Bishop Peter a view of Magna Carta similar to that expressed by William Brewer: it had been extracted by force and had no validity. When he finally achieved power between 1232 and 1234, Peter both ridiculed the Charter's principles and encouraged Henry to rule very much in the aggressive and arbitrary spirit of King John.

From the start, however, Henry also heard very different views about his father's rule: from William Marshal, who prayed Henry would not live long if he followed the path of a 'criminal ancestor'; from Pandulf, who sought permission to place Henry under a tutor who would teach him to 'love his vassals'; from Archbishop Langton, who in 1223 reprimanded Brewer and secured Henry's verbal confirmation of the Charter; and from Hubert de Burgh, who distanced himself from John's crimes and ruled in a cautious and conciliatory fashion very different from that later practised by Peter des Roches. Henry remained very aware of the disasters of his father's reign. He later described how the country before his time had been devastated by general war and oppressed by an Interdict. He had come to the throne with the kingdom not merely alienated but actively against him.[154]

Outside the brief period of Bishop Peter's supremacy between 1232 and 1234, it was the dangers of John's mode of rule that most impacted on Henry, hence, in part at least, his frequently indulgent treatment of leading

---

[152] The precise words of Henry's oath are unknown. I follow here Richard's coronation oath as found in *English Coronation Records*, 49, 51–2, reprinted from Howden, *GR*, ii, 81–2. There is no mention of an oath to protect the rights of king and kingdom, but it was certainly taken by Henry and may go back to 1154: see *RL*, i, 551; *F*, 229; Richardson, 'The coronation', 153–61.

[153] *RL*, 551; *F*, 229; *DBM*, 256–7.

[154] *F*, 408–9; *Robert Grosseteste*, 356.

magnates. There was in any case no way Henry could avoid Magna Carta and the Charter of the Forest. His first political statement had been a verbal confirmation of the Charters: 'we have sworn to all these liberties, and what we have sworn we will observe'.[155] The first charters to which he put his seal were the final and definitive versions of Magna Carta and the Forest Charter in 1225. He had granted these specifically of his own free will in return for a tax. As the lengthy witness lists showed, the Charters were now consensual documents agreed by the good and great of the land. As such, Langton and the bishops had supported them with sentences of excommunication against all contravenors. Magna Carta asserted fundamental principles about just and lawful rule. No free man was to be arrested, imprisoned, deprived of property, outlawed, exiled or in any way destroyed or proceeded against 'save by the lawful judgement of his peers or by the law of the land'. To no one was the king to deny, delay or sell right and justice. In other provisions, fines (or amercements as they were called) were to match the offence and to be assessed by local men; earls and barons were to succeed to their inheritances on the payment of a £100 relief (as against the hundreds or thousands of pounds John had sometimes charged); widows were not to be forced to remarry and were to enter their dowers, inheritances and marriage portions without payment; and rules were laid down for the behaviour of the sheriffs in running the county and hundred courts. The Forest Charter, meanwhile, promised large reductions in the forests' boundaries. The struggle of county knights to exploit these clauses showed how valued Magna Carta and the Forest Charter were by local society. Taken as a whole, the Charters, if obeyed, would reduce royal revenue and royal power and bring to an end the arbitrary and extortionate kingship practised by John and his predecessors.

Henry's commitment to the Charters at the end of the minority was sincere, however much he resented their illegitimate exploitation. But it was hardly the kind of settled, principled and informed commitment that would mean the Charters were fully secure. Henry was later to be driven in a very different direction by Peter des Roches. He was also to face persistent complaints that, whatever lip service was paid to the Charters, they were not being obeyed, especially by his officials. Here a problem arose from a key change made to the 1215 Magna Carta. Omitted from the subsequent versions was the 'security clause' under which twenty-five barons were empowered to force the king to keep the Charter if he or his agents sought to break it. The clause was omitted from the Henrician charters since it seemed a recipe for civil war. In setting up a parallel authority, it also seemed to violate the rights of kingship. But no more acceptable processes were put in its place. As a result, the Charters were left without constitutional means of enforcement. The sentences of excommunication launched by the bishops gave

---

[155] Wendover, iii, 76.

them status but were hardly a way of enforcing their detail. How far Henry's rule was congruent with the Charters, how far the Charters were a remedy at all for the problems set by his rule, were to be key questions during his reign.

There was another constitutional legacy of the minority with which Henry had to deal. This was the place of great councils, or parliaments as they were soon to be called, in public life. That kings should rule with the counsel and consent of their leading men was an old principle, sometimes observed, sometimes breached. The circumstances of the minority meant it was put into practice as never before. Great councils had thus chosen the king's ministers and decided a whole range of other issues.[156] Although the chapter in the 1215 Magna Carta saying that taxes needed to be levied with common consent was omitted from Henry's Charters, in practice it remained in force.[157] It was thus a great council in 1225 that conceded the tax for the relief of Gascony. Henry was to live with this legacy. He knew he must get the consent of parliament to any levy of taxation. He also had to face parliament's demand to choose his ministers. In the end, in 1258, a revolt in parliament would bring his personal rule to an end.

The restrictions in the Charters, even if obeyed to the letter, still left much of kingly power intact. Henry was very far from being a monarch in chains, one of high prestige but little authority. In one area, indeed, the Charter had called for more kingship, not less. The procedures of the common law for settling disputes over property were popular and were to be made more available. Henry's reign was to witness a huge expansion in the number of people, from wide sections of society, litigating in the king's courts.[158] More contentiously, the Charter left Henry still able to choose his local agents – his sheriffs and castellans. He could likewise decide the financial terms on which the sheriffs held office.[159] In the area of ecclesiastical affairs, Henry's claim to influence episcopal elections, as he had tried to do at Durham, was helped by the way Magna Carta's confirmation of John's charter guaranteeing that bishops might be freely elected (by the canons or monks of their cathedrals) was omitted after 1215, this for fear it might lead to the election of rebel prelates.[160] As for control over central government, Magna Carta was completely silent. Henry was still free to have whom he liked at court and appoint whom he liked as his leading ministers. He was equally free when it came to disbursement of patronage. He could give away land, wardships,

---

[156] Carpenter, *Minority*, 407–9.

[157] For the omission, see Carpenter, *Magna Carta*, 426–7. The baronial leaders may have feared the chapter would restrict their ability to tax their own men. They may also have felt it was unnecessary, thinking that taxes on the kingdom could never in practice be levied without their consent.

[158] See Moore, 'Fine rolls as evidence for the expansion of royal justice'.

[159] This was thanks to the omission of chapter 25 of the 1215 Charter saying that the counties were to be held at their ancient farms without any increments.

[160] John's concession was, however, characteristically hedged around. See Harvey, *Episcopal Appointments*, 19–28.

marriages and money almost as he pleased. And there was nothing in the Charter about the direction of policy. Henry might be unwise to make war and peace without the consent of a great council, but the Charter did not say so.

Another framework of Henry's rule was provided by the growing strength of English national feeling. Here the loss of Normandy in 1204 was important.[161] It meant there was no longer an elite, a hundred or so strong, of great barons who held land in both the kingdom and the duchy and probably felt Anglo-Norman rather than exclusively English. Henceforth the nobility of England would live and be born in England. They could share the Englishness of the county knights, the bedrock of local society, and the Englishness of the free tenants and peasants, free and unfree, beneath them. These feelings of Englishness were strengthened under John and during the minority by the belief the country was under threat from foreigners. The aliens, Peter des Roches and the rest, inserted by John into the government, had been followed by a war portrayed as rescuing England from the French.[162] And then there had been the politics of the minority where, or so it could be thought, a gang of foreigners led by Bishop Peter and Falkes de Bréauté disturbed the peace of the kingdom and had to be repressed by Hubert de Burgh and Archbishop Langton. The way Langton celebrated Becket as the great English martyr saint, following on from St Alphege and St Edmund, was another strand in the growing sense of national identity.[163] How far a great baron such as William Longespée, earl of Salisbury, identified with England is shown by his reaction to Falkes de Bréauté's outburst.[164] Falkes had declared, so Longespée told Hubert de Burgh, that 'all *we* native born men were traitors and wanted war'. Clearly Longespée included himself (and Hubert) in the 'we'.[165] Born and living largely in England, Henry was well placed to exploit this sense of national identity. Unfortunately it grew in strength during his reign in reaction to rather than in support of his policies.

The minority had given Henry a grounding in England's administrative and social structure. From the summer of 1222, he spent a great deal of time at Westminster, the base of the bench of judges hearing civil pleas according to the forms of the common law.[166] He must equally have been

---

[161] For a sketch related to what follows, see Carpenter, *Struggle for Mastery*, 4–11, 269. The major study is Thomas, *English and Normans*.

[162] Carpenter, *Minority*, 29. The war is described as being 'between the English and the French' in a charter of 1217 in which the former rebel Geoffrey de Say (captured at the battle of Lincoln) makes an agreement with the regent's nephew John Marshal: BL Add. MS 27982, fo. 21v (a discovery of Nicholas Vincent).

[163] Eales, 'The political setting of the Becket translation', 137–9.

[164] For Longespée, see Strickland, 'William Longespée'.

[165] *RL*, i, 220–1.

[166] Henry was 111 days at Westminster in 1223, 149 in 1224, 199 in 1225 and 149 in 1226: Craib, Brindle and Priestley, *Itinerary of King Henry III*, 10–11. For the contrast with John and the pre-eminence of Westminster in the minority, see below, 351. For the common law legal procedures, see Hudson, *Formation of the English Common Law*.

aware of the visitations (or eyres) of his judges in the localities, such visitations having commenced in both 1218 and 1226.[167] This apparatus enabled Henry to perform kingship's most important public function, that of maintaining peace and dispensing justice. Under the procedures of the common law, his free subjects could bring all manner of civil disputes over rights and property before the king's judges where they would be decided by the verdicts of juries composed of local men. When litigating at the eyre, the writs ordering the sheriffs to summon the juries to come before the justices only cost 6d, and were bought in great numbers.[168] The justices in eyre also heard the criminal pleas arising from breaches of the king's peace, the pleas reserved for the crown being treason, homicide, robbery, arson, serious theft and rape. Here juries from each hundred appeared before the judges and answered a whole series of questions about events in the county since the last eyre, including those relating to crime and to usurpation of royal rights. Those they accused of criminal offences then went to trial by jury. It was in this area of crown pleas that the eyres made most of their money for the king. A whole series of amercements were imposed on local juries and communities for such things as giving false evidence and failing to arrest criminals. In addition, the chattels of those hanged or, as much more often, outlawed (for few criminals were caught) went to the king.[169]

Alongside the judicial eyres, there were eyres trying offences against the law of the royal forest. The struggle over the bounds of the forest in the minority had made Henry well aware of this valuable and vexatious resource.[170] Royal forest was found in over twenty counties and, extending far beyond the king's own demesne woods, embraced land held by

[167] Crook, *Records of the General Eyre*, 71–85. A general eyre (a term invented by historians) means the visitation of the judges was part of a circuit designed to cover the whole kingdom with panels of judges assigned to particular groups of shires.

[168] See Clanchy, *Berkshire Eyre*.

[169] A general eyre took a long time to complete and an individual county would only see the judges once every several years. Indeed a seven-year interval came to be accepted as normal. Given the financial burden of the crown pleas, there would have been strong opposition to any lesser interval. (When Magna Carta in 1215 called for the king's judges to visit the counties four times a year it was only to hear civil pleas.) The interval between the eyres was why in increasing numbers litigants paid extra to have their cases heard by ad hoc judges in the localities. They also paid to move their cases to the court *coram rege* or, more often, to the bench at Westminster (see below, 528). The amounts involved were not large and this was not regarded as the selling of justice. Between eyres, the king would also commission justices of gaol delivery to try those imprisoned in local gaols. The classic analysis of how the crown pleas worked is found in Meekings' introduction to *Crown Pleas of the Wiltshire Eyre*, and see Summerson, 'The structure of law enforcement in thirteenth-century England'. For new work in the area, see Duggan, 'Communal justice in thirteenth-century England' and 'The hue and cry in thirteenth-century England'.

[170] For the royal forest see G.J. Turner's introduction to *SPF*; Bazeley, 'The extent of the English royal forest'; Young, *The Royal Forests of Medieval England*; and Winters, 'The forest eyre', with a comprehensive catalogue of the eyres and their financial proceeds.

ecclesiastical institutions, earls, barons, knights and free tenants. Forest law forbad the hunting of deer and boar. It also forbad the cutting down of trees ('waste'), the creation of new arable land ('assart'), and the erection of buildings and enclosures ('purpresture'). Such offences were liable to heavy financial penalties on the periodic eyres of the justices of the forest. Those unlucky enough to have lands within the bounds of the forest were thus prevented from exploiting them to the full. No wonder the counties were intent on securing the removal of areas from the forest, as promised (they thought) by the Forest Charter.

The money due from the judicial and forest eyres was exacted for the king by the greatest of all institutions of English medieval government. Based at Westminster, this was the exchequer. Henry was there with his council in July 1225, and made many more appearances during his personal rule.[171] The exchequer's task was to exact and audit the revenue due to the crown. The revenue was collected for the most part by the king's chief agent in each county, the sheriff. He both answered for a fixed annual payment or 'farm' and collected the money owed the king by individuals.[172] The sheriffs paid this revenue into the exchequer half at Easter and half at Michaelmas.[173] They then returned, one after the other, for the exchequer's annual audit of the money owed the crown, the results being recorded on great documents called 'pipe rolls'.[174] It is by laboriously adding up the payments in the pipe rolls that historians have attempted to calculate the crown's annual revenue.[175]

Henry would have been well aware of the multiplicity of ways individuals could owe him money; the reliefs (the payments to inherit) owed by his tenants-in-chief;[176] the scutages owed by tenants-in-chief in place of performing military service; the offers of money to purchase wardships, marriages and a multitude of other favours; the payments for writs to prosecute lawsuits; and the amercements imposed for offences tried before the king's forest judges and justices in eyre. Henry had the right to impose a tax or 'tallage' on royal towns and manors, and also on the Jews since they were regarded as the property of the crown. When a bishopric or abbey was vacant he took the revenues till a new appointment was made. Henry would also have known, from the experience of 1225, that he could

---

[171] *CFR 1224–5*, no. 226.

[172] For the farm, see below, 190. Towns often answered for their farms directly to the exchequer rather than through the sheriff.

[173] Revenue could also come in at other times.

[174] Barons could pay their own money in and appear in person, or more often through their stewards, at the audit. The exchequer also kept receipt rolls, issue rolls, memoranda rolls and plea rolls.

[175] The pipe rolls, of which there is a continuous annual sequence from 1155, are being published by the Pipe Roll Society, publication having currently reached the 1220s. As the series continues to 1833, there is a long way to go!

[176] Tenants-in-chief are defined in what follows.

double or triple his ordinary annual revenue if he could get consent to a tax levied on movable property. The burden of the king's financial demands ran from top to bottom of society. At the top, there were few men of any consequence who did not owe him money, sometimes large sums of money. At the bottom, peasants and peasant communities bore a large share of the amercements arising from the crown pleas heard by the justices in eyre.[177]

The exchequer kept the money it received in its treasury and disbursed as ordered by the king, sending (as in 1224/5) a large proportion to the king himself where it was paid into his wardrobe, hence the importance of the keeper of the wardrobe, or treasurer as he was sometimes called.[178] Henry could use this wardrobe cash to do whatever he liked, although much of it always went in funding his household's daily food and drink. Also permanently with the king, alongside the clerks of the wardrobe, were the clerks of the chancery who wrote and sealed the letters on which his rule depended. From the end of 1223, as we have seen, Henry was witnessing all the letters himself and thus taking formal responsibility for the output. Some of that was prosaic; some highly political; some highly personal. Recorded on the rolls of the chancery (new ones were opened for each regnal year), Henry's letters are the reason why the history of his reign can be written in such richness and detail.[179]

By the end of the minority, Henry knew England well, its monasteries and cathedrals, its royal and baronial castles, its dioceses and their bishops, its counties and their sheriffs, its towns and their ruling elites.[180] He had made a triumphal entry into London at the end of the war and his long residence at Westminster meant he was very familiar with the city. During the crisis of 1223 he had sought the protection of the Tower. Henry had seen the sea at Dover and the hills of the Welsh marches at Montgomery. He had been to York to meet King Alexander, to Worcester to meet Llywelyn, and to Exeter to dispossess Henry fitzCount. He had attended Becket's translation at Canterbury and been on pilgrimages to Bury St Edmunds, Walsingham and Bromholm. He had spent time at Windsor, Winchester, Marlborough and Woodstock, all to be major residences.

Henry's almsgiving and concern for the poor had brought him into contact with the English-speaking majority of the population. The struggles over the bounds of the forest and Magna Carta's chapters on local courts had shown the power of county knights, in John's reign a body four to five

---

[177] See above, n. 51.

[178] Individual debts could also, on the king's orders, be paid directly into the wardrobe rather than into the exchequer, something which happened with increasing frequency later in the reign.

[179] For a full discussion of Henry's court and household, see below, ch. 7.

[180] For books putting the politics of the period into their wider social context, see Harding, *England in the Thirteenth Century*, and Prestwich, *Plantagenet England 1225–1360*.

thousand strong.[181] Many of these men held just a single manor, or its equivalent, and enjoyed incomes of perhaps £15 or £20 a year. But others had
collections of manors and were just as wealthy as many barons. Through his
maintenance of the peace and the exaction of money, Henry had a direct
relationship with all his subjects. All swore an oath of fealty to him. But
Henry was also very aware of his special relationship with a select band of
subjects, namely his tenants-in-chief, the earls, barons, and several hundred
others of knightly and less than knightly status, who held their land directly
from him.[182] Perhaps already he could name 250 English baronies, as he did
later in a conversation with Matthew Paris.[183] He could certainly have named
the dozen or so English earldoms. Nine earls attested the 1225 Magna Carta.
A rich earl in Henry's reign might have an annual income of several thousand pounds, a middle-ranking baron one of several hundreds.[184] The
tenants-in-chief were bound to Henry by the act of homage in which they
swore to give faithful service for the land they held. After the stream of former
rebels doing homage at the end of the war, Henry was constantly receiving
the homage of new tenants-in-chief as they entered their inheritances.
Magna Carta had restricted the amount of the relief he could demand in
such circumstances, but had left intact his rights of wardship, and thus to the
revenues of the estate while the heir was underage. He also retained the right
to marry off the wards themselves, the heirs and heiresses in his custody.[185]
Closely associated with wardships were 'escheats', land that had come into
the king's hands, often through forfeiture.[186] How Henry exploited these valuable sources of revenue and patronage became major issues in the reign.

Given the number of armies summoned during the minority, Henry
was very familiar with the most basic obligation of the tenant-in-chief,
namely to muster with a number of knights when he summoned an army.
By Henry's reign few were expected to come with more than a handful of
knights but that could still mean an army of around 500.[187] It was also the
tenants-in-chiefs who were summoned to Henry's great councils and

[181] Faulkner, 'Transformation of knighthood'; Carpenter, *Magna Carta*, 129–31. The
numbers of those taking up knighthood declined in Henry's reign, as will be discussed in
chapter 1 of volume 2.

[182] For the number of minor tenants-in-chief, see Maddicott, ' "An infinite multitude of
nobles" ', 20.

[183] Paris, v, 250.

[184] For baronial incomes, see Painter, *Studies in the History of the English Feudal Barony*,
ch. VII; Maddicott, *Simon de Montfort*, 55.

[185] The Charter did, however, say that heirs were to be married without disparagement,
meaning married to those of lesser social status. It also laid down rules to prevent land in
wardship being overexploited. For the exploitation of wardships and marriages, see
Waugh, *The Lordship of England*.

[186] For the particular importance of the lands seized from Normans who had taken the
French allegiance after 1204, see below, 95–6.

[187] For the levels of military service demanded in Henry's reign, see Prestwich, *Armies and
Warfare in the Middle Ages*, 68–71.

parliaments.[188] Probably the procedure followed that outlined in the 1215 Magna Carta, where the earls and 'greater barons' were to receive individual letters of summons, while the rest were to be summoned generally through the sheriffs. Given the composition of 'the rest', this meant there were many knights present at Henry's parliaments. When Henry named 250 baronies he was already going beyond those held by the 50 to 90 men who might be reckoned 'greater barons'.[189] Much would depend on how far he could reach out to this wider constituency.

If in terms of knowledge and experience Henry was well equipped to rule, whether he was in terms of personality is another matter. He certainly had one great strength, already becoming apparent in the minority, namely his religiosity. Did this owe something to a fear of being like his father? There were aspects of John's religious life that Henry might admire.[190] He supported the Cistercian monastery John established at Beaulieu in Hampshire, and attended the final consecration of its church in 1246. But Henry certainly regarded the Interdict as a disaster, hence his boast that in his time the country had never suffered from one.[191] He could not be unaware of his father's crimes for he was holding captive Eleanor of Brittany, sister of the murdered Arthur. In later life he made a major gift to Amesbury abbey for the souls of both Eleanor and Arthur.[192] Even if he was shielded from wilder stories of John's irreligion (his refusal to take the eucharist, his desire to convert the country to Islam), Henry must surely have wondered and worried where his father was in the afterlife: not in a good place according to the 'horrible and fantastic visions told by many people about him'.[193] One of John's former clerks gave up praying for his master, having been told in a vision to read the fifty-second psalm with its warning that God would destroy for ever those who loved evil more than good. In another vision, recorded under the year 1226, a monk of St Albans witnessed John 'in inferno' tortured by burning robes of intolerable weight.[194] Henry was determined to avoid any such fate himself.

Another facet of Henry's character was less helpful to his rule. From an early date he was charged with 'simplicity' and one wonders whether that characteristic was aggravated by the conditions of the minority.[195] Coming to the throne at the age of nine, surrounded by ministers who took the

---

[188] For the composition of parliament, see below, 457–8.

[189] For these numbers, see Maddicott, ' "An infinite multitude of nobles" ', 21.

[190] For a measured assessment of John's religious practices, getting beyond the surrounding myths, see Webster, *King John and Religion*.

[191] *F*, 408–9.

[192] *CChR 1257–1300*, 100. For the treatment of Eleanor by John and Henry, see Seabourne, 'Eleanor of Brittany'.

[193] Coggeshall, 184.

[194] Guisborough, 156; Wendover/Paris, iii, 112–13; Carpenter, *Reign of Henry III*, 457; Webster, *King John and Religion*, 185.

[195] For discussion of the meanings of 'simplicity', see below, 166, 168–9.

decisions themselves while at the same time seeking his favour, cannot have been the best education for all the difficult choices integral to kingship. Henry's immediate predecessors, Henry II, Richard and John, and his successor, his son Edward I, kings who, whatever their strengths and weaknesses, could never be called 'simplex', had all enjoyed a long experience of politics before ascending the throne.

About some other features of Henry's personality one can likewise only speculate. Was his fidelity to his wife and his devotion to his children the result of losing so early both his father and mother? More certainly, the events of the minority, as Henry himself said, left him with a lifelong devotion to the papacy. He was, he told Robert Grosseteste, tied to the Roman church more closely than any other prince thanks to the way, through the agency of the legate Guala, it had rescued his kingship and re-established peace at the start of the reign. He hoped his eyes would be plucked out and his head cut off (a good example of his emphatic way of speaking) if he ever deserted his spiritual father.[196] Henry knew, of course, that John had made England a papal fief. He also had a more general understanding of papal authority. The pope, he said, was established by God over everyone, and enjoyed the plenitude of power. Kings and princes were placed under the pope with part of the care, and with a special duty to protect churches and help the oppressed. It was natural, therefore, for kings to have recourse to the pope in their difficulties. Henry was indeed to do so again and again.[197]

By the time he assumed full power at the age of nineteen, Henry must have been more or less fully grown, no longer the rather anxious boy shown in Matthew Paris's drawing of the 1220 coronation. Perhaps he was already sporting the short beard shown in some of Paris's drawings, although in others he appears clean-shaven. Unfortunately, neither those drawings nor other images of Henry, including the splendid effigy on his tomb, are attempts at portraiture, so they provide no clue as to his actual features. Did he in manhood still have the blonde hair and pleasant face Matthew Paris gives him at the start of the reign?[198] That Henry lived to be sixty-five, despite several serious illnesses (one at Marlborough in 1226), shows he had a sound constitution. In the only surviving physical description, by the friar Nicholas Trevet, he is depicted as of middle height, compact of body and strong in build. A physical defect was that the lid of one eyelid drooped so that it hid part of the black pupil. Trevet was writing of Henry late in life so perhaps the compactness owed something to thickening with age.[199] That Henry had a drooping eyelid is confirmed

---

[196] *Letters of Grosseteste*, 356.

[197] *RG*, i, no. 1206, a letter of 1242.

[198] See above, n. 1.

[199] Trevet, 280, with a translation by Gransden, *Historical Writing*, 506 and 501–5, for a discussion of his work. Trevet was writing in the 1320s but he had been born around 1258 and was the son of one of Henry III's judges.

by one of Paris's drawings.[200] Probably he suffered from congenital ptosis, a benign condition but one sometimes causing psychological problems in children. Whether it troubled Henry we cannot know. It seems to have had little effect on his self-confident son, who had the same condition.[201] That Henry was of average height is confirmed by his coffin in Westminster Abbey. In November 1871 the then dean of Westminster, A.P. Stanley, was going to open it but then changed his mind after an intervention, according to one story, by Queen Victoria. (She was unamused by the plans to tamper with the body of her predecessor.)[202] Stanley, however, did measure the coffin and found its length to be six foot one and a half inches.[203] Since coffin length is obviously greater than body length, Henry was perhaps much the same height as his father, whose body measured five foot six and half inches when his tomb was opened in 1797.[204]

Henry, therefore, lacked his son's impressive stature (Edward was over six foot), but he was of reasonable height and was strong and manly. He was later to father five children. There was nothing physically to prevent him earning a reputation as a 'miles strenuus, a vigorous knight'. His tutors in the minority must have pushed him in that direction. They had certainly given him a burning desire to recover his lands in France: Normandy and Anjou lost under his father, Poitou, even more grievous, lost under himself. Here Henry was very much a king with ambition. The trouble was he lacked the martial ardour and expertise to attend it. Henry was strong but physically lazy. He hawked rather than hunted. His anger was easily lit but easily extinguished. There was no 'devil in his play'.[205] Yet he still coveted the rewards of successful war. That contradiction between ambition and aptitude became very clear in the years immediately following his assumption of power.

[200] That in the gallery of kings at the start of the *Historia Anglorum*: http://www.bl.uk/manuscripts/Viewer.aspx?ref=royal_ms_14_c_vii_f008v. In the drawing it is Henry's left eye.

[201] For congenital ptosis see https://www.ncbi.nlm.nih.gov/pmc/articles/PMC5338973. The problem is caused by the mutation of the FOXL2 gene. This also causes problems with the ovaries, but that will not have affected Henry. I owe the information about congenital ptosis to Michael Prestwich.

[202] I owe the story to Lawrence Tanner (born in 1890), long-serving librarian and keeper of the muniments at the Abbey. For Stanley's own explanation, see Carpenter, *Reign of Henry III*, 427.

[203] Stanley, 'On an examination of the tombs of Richard II and Henry III', 317–22. Stanley did open the tomb of Richard II and some of the royal coffins in Henry VII's chapel. According to Lawrence Tanner he had one advantage in such explorations: no sense of smell.

[204] Green, *Account of the Discovery of the Body of King John*, 4. A less authoritative account gives the height as five foot five inches: Poole, *From Domesday Book to Magna Carta*, 486, n. 2.

[205] A remark made by the Leeds United manager, Don Revie, about the winger Eddie Grey.

Chapter 2

HENRY AND HUBERT DE BURGH
1227–1231

In January 1227, with the lifting of the last restrictions on his power, the whole nature of Henry's kingship changed. The pleasures and pitfalls of giving patronage were now before him. Able to issue charters and make permanent grants of lands and rights, he could at last reward those who had served him so well. But he needed to be careful. If he was over-generous he would diminish the resources and damage the rights of the crown. If he was overly partisan, he would create political discontent. Henry's assumption of power opened other vistas. With his authority enhanced, he might lead the campaign to recover his continental empire. Within England, he could reverse the damaging inroads made since 1225 into the royal forests. There was also money to be made from those seeking confirmation of old charters and fresh concessions in new ones.

All this took place within a framework set by the justiciar, Hubert de Burgh. Indeed his star seemed to shine more brightly than ever. 'He was joined to the king in such great familiarity,' wrote Roger of Wendover, having narrated the events of January 1227, 'that he considered all the other counselors of the kingdom beside himself as nothing.'[1] Such was his dominance that unpopular policies were often blamed on the minister not the monarch. Henry, however, was never mere putty in Hubert's hands. Warm-hearted and effusive, he very much had a will of his own. After 1227, as before, Hubert had often to curb the king's more ill-judged ideas and reactions. As the chronicler Thomas Wykes put it, he 'restrained the arbitrary motions (motus voluntarios) of the king, lest the king should harm himself'. Wykes accordingly commended Hubert as a man of 'the greatest discretion, prudence and probity'.[2] Yet with the king's emancipation in 1227, Hubert had another ambition, one, beyond a certain point, less commendable. It was to direct the flow of Henry's patronage towards himself.

Hubert's enemies later accused him of bewitching the king with magic charms and sorceries.[3] That was hardly necessary. Almost continually in Hubert's company since the summer of 1222, when he was fourteen, Henry was awed by the career and qualities of his chief minister: the fame

---

[1] Wendover, iii, 122.
[2] Wykes, 62.
[3] Paris, iii, 223.

of his military exploits, the sincerity of his piety, the depth of his knowledge and the force of his intelligence. Henry was far less clever. That emerges all too clearly from the charges he brought against Hubert in 1239. Although then an old man, Hubert swatted them away with ease, in the process demonstrating Henry's ignorance both of recent history and the workings of government. It was a contest between ignorant bluster and informed argument.[4] Hubert was also 'family', for both he and Henry were brothers-in-law of King Alexander of Scotland, Hubert through his marriage to Alexander's eldest sister Margaret, Henry through his eldest sister Joan's marriage to Alexander. It was a relationship Hubert was adept at exploiting by arranging meetings between the courts.

Had Henry been different, he might have found living in Hubert's shadow intolerable and sought to escape. Save in brief moments of frustration, there is no sign he tried to do so. Although the king was hot-tempered, he was also easily calmed down, counselled and, in effect, controlled. He is often seen in these years asking for advice and making appropriate pronouncements surrounded by his ministers. He trusted Hubert's judgement more than he did his own. With so much more experience, it was Hubert who knew how things worked.

There was also something else which made a match between the two men. Hubert's sedentary, Westminster-centred form of government, as practised before 1227, suited Henry very well. Between 1227 and 1229 the king spent time at Windsor, Woodstock, Marlborough, Guildford and Winchester, all traditional royal residences. But Westminster and London still absorbed 39 per cent of his time, down (but not decisively so) from the 46 per cent of his time spent there between 1220 and 1226. Even in 1229, when there was a tour of the Welsh marches, a pilgrimage to East Anglia, a muster at Portsmouth and a Christmas at York, Henry spent over 100 days in the capital. His stays in any one place frequently lasted for longer than a week. There was absolutely no return to the high-pressure itinerary of his father. King John rarely remained stationary for more than a few days and spent, over the reign as whole, only 7 per cent of his time in Westminster and London.[5]

If Henry had wished to escape Hubert's embrace, it would not have been easy. Hubert was always with him. He witnessed nearly every royal charter issued between 1227 and 1231, apart from those in his own favour. When Henry was separated from the chancellor Ralph de Neville and the great seal, he used the justiciar's seal to authenticate his letters.[6] If Henry had a privy seal, he was not encouraged to use it.

---

[4] Paris, vi, 63–74.

[5] Kanter, 'Itineraries of John and Henry III', 13–17, 20–1. The Westminster/London figure for John rises to 10% in years he was not, for some of the time, on the continent. For further discussion of Henry's itinerary, see below, 350–7.

[6] For example, *RLC*, ii, 173b, 174b; *CR 1227–31*, 158–9; *CFR 1227–8*, no. 281.

Hubert had also stitched up Henry's entourage. Nobles of the king's own age seem to have spent little time at court. That was true of Roger Bigod, heir to the earldom of Norfolk, and two years Henry's junior, although he was married to King Alexander's younger sister, Isabella. It was equally true of Henry's brother, Richard, despite Henry's respect and affection for him. Instead Henry was surrounded by middle-aged men who had mostly built their careers under John and now owed everything to Hubert. It was Hubert who had put in place the stewards of the royal household, the knights Ralph fitzNicholas, Godfrey of Crowcombe, Richard de Argentan and Osbert Giffard. He had also made his chaplain, Luke, keeper of the wardrobe and appointed as Luke's assistants two conscientious clerks, Walter of Kirkham (later bishop of Durham) and Walter of Brackley. When Luke left to become archbishop of Dublin, he was replaced by Hubert's clerk, Ranulf le Breton.[7] Hubert was intimate with the other great minister usually with the king, the chancellor 'his dearest friend in Christ', Ralph de Neville, bishop of Chichester.[8] The two had worked closely together since 1219 when Neville, as keeper of the great seal, had been put under Hubert's orders. Now nearly all the royal charters Henry issued, besides being witnessed by Hubert, were 'given by the hand of Ralph bishop of Chichester, our chancellor', meaning Ralph had authorized their writing out and sealing.

Outside the court, Hubert kept a close eye on the exchequer. Indeed to do so was one reason why he spent so much time at Westminster. The exchequer's memoranda rolls thus recorded his orders about the payment of debts and noted matters to be discussed with him.[9] They give no equivalent sign of the king's involvement. Under the justiciar, the head of the exchequer, was its treasurer, who from 1228 was Walter Mauclerc, bishop of Carlisle. Mauclerc freely acknowledged that it was 'through' Hubert that he had been placed in office.[10] Also sitting at the exchequer, and often at court attesting royal charters, were the two bishops whom Stephen Langton had introduced to the government in 1223, Jocelyn of Wells, the bishop of Bath, and Richard le Poore, bishop of Salisbury, although Richard became less prominent after his translation to the bishopric of Durham in the summer of 1228.[11] When Henry and Hubert were separated from the great seal, Jocelyn usually took over as the witness of the king's letters. Another exchequer official was Hubert's nephew Thomas de Blundeville. In 1226, Hubert engineered his election to the bishopric of Norwich. The bishops of Chichester, Carlisle, Bath, Salisbury and Norwich

---

[7] Tout, *Chapters*, i, 196–8.

[8] *DD*, no. 223.

[9] For example in 1227/8: TNA E 159/9, mm. 2, 5d, 7d–8, 9–9d, 13, 14d, 18d.

[10] TNA SC 1/1/152.

[11] For the two bishops at the exchequer in 1227/8, see TNA E 368/11, mm. 1–2, 3d–4d, 5d–6, 12.

were thus all props of the regime. In 1230, Hubert's chaplain observed that the church and its prelates were 'in all things your guardians and supporters'.[12]

Hubert and his allies were not just dominant at the centre. They also stretched their tentacles into the localities through holding sheriffdoms and royal castles. Hubert himself retained Dover castle and the Tower of London. Yorkshire was under his steward Robert of Cockfield and Kent under Ranulf le Breton's brother William. The steward Godfrey of Crowcombe held Oxfordshire, his colleague fitzNicholas held Herefordshire and Nottinghamshire–Derbyshire (a joint sheriffdom), while the treasurer Bishop Mauclerc had Cumberland. Such men held their sheriffdoms on terms very favourable to themselves, retaining a good slice of the revenues rather than paying them into the exchequer. That was both a form of patronage and a way of increasing their local power.

Hubert, therefore, had pocketed the king, or so he could hope. It was unlikely Henry would hear criticism of the justiciar from within the regime or receive any encouragement to escape. What of criticisms from without? That prospect too seemed reduced by a long-awaited event. In the summer of 1227, Bishop Peter at last set sail on his crusade. To hasten his departure a settlement was reached over his debts, but he still left in an angry mood. Doubtless through Hubert's intervention, the royal charter for which Peter offered £500 gave him significantly less than he wanted.[13] But for Hubert what did it matter? Bishop Peter was gone. Indeed he was out of England for the next four years. Hubert had little to fear from the rest of the party that had been worsted in 1223–4. The great earls and barons were another matter. How would they react to the honours Hubert now hoped to extract from the king? If help was needed in any future quarrel, one other person, moreover, would be missing. Archbishop Langton's health was giving way. His consent to the king's assumption of power in January 1227 was his last appearance on the national stage.

1227: A CAMPAIGN IN FRANCE?

By far the most exciting prospect on Henry's horizon in early 1227 was that of leading an expedition to France. It was to help forge the necessary alliances, in the aftermath of the death of Louis VIII in November 1226, that the last restrictions on his authority had been lifted. 'Since through the grace of God, an opportunity has been given of recovering our inheritance . . . it behoves us to cross the sea soon, God willing,' Henry announced in January.[14]

---

[12] *DD*, no. 222.
[13] See Carpenter, 'The bishop of Winchester's fine in 1227'.
[14] *RLC*, ii, 208b.

To build up the war chest for the expedition, a tallage was levied on London and the other towns and manors of the royal demesne. Meanwhile, masters of ships were warned that the king would need their services at the latest by Easter (11 April). A little silver ship was sent as an offering to Bromholm.[15] The vital alliances, however, both with the duke of Brittany and with Henry's stepfather and mother, Hugh de Lusignan and Isabella of Angoulême, were proving hard to negotiate. The fact was Henry now faced a formidable opponent. The regent for the young Louis IX was his mother, Blanche of Castile, widow of Louis VIII and a granddaughter of Henry II. Combining a remarkable political ability with a steely determination to uphold the interests of her young son, she now leapt into the bidding.[16] In December 1226 her messengers, offering Hugh de Lusignan 'many things', arrived on the same day as Henry's. Hugh naturally passed the news on to Henry and warned him to reply as soon as possible 'to our petitions'.[17] Blanche, moreover, was not waiting passively for any English invasion. She advanced with an army to Loudun and then (in March 1227) to Vendôme. One by one she bought off her opponents. Henry had promised Hugh and Isabella the return of Isabella's dower lands in England. Blanche countered by offering 'an infinite sum of money' as compensation for their loss. Henry had also promised Hugh and Isabella both Saintes and the isle of Oléron in hereditary right. But these were not his to give, being in the hands of the king of France. Blanche's offer had thus far more reality. She suggested that Saintes and Oléron be the marriage portion of Louis IX's younger brother, Alphonse, on his marriage to one of Hugh and Isabella's daughters. Their eldest son, meanwhile, was to marry one of Louis's sisters.[18] Had Henry given Bordeaux to Hugh, the situation would have been different, but that was impossible to contemplate. Blanche's was thus much the better offer and Hugh and Isabella accepted it.

Blanche was equally successful with Peter of Brittany, despite the agreement that his daughter, Yolande, was to marry Henry. Duke Peter certainly hankered after the rewards of an English alliance. He styled himself earl of Richmond even in his agreement with Blanche.[19] But Henry had failed to give him all the lands of the earldom, this because Richmondshire itself was held by Ranulf, earl of Chester, as compensation for his losses in Normandy.[20] So Peter decided to throw Henry over and accept Blanche's offers. Yolande would marry not the king of England but John, count of Anjou and Maine, another of Louis's younger brothers. Until John was twenty-one, Peter was to hold Angers, Saumur and Loudun. He was to

[15] *RLC*, ii, 172b; *Patent Roll 1225–32*, 110.
[16] For Blanche's role in these years, see Grant, *Blanche of Castile*, 83–91.
[17] *DD*, no. 199.
[18] Tours, 319–20; *Layettes*, ii, no. 1924.
[19] *Layettes*, ii, no. 1922.
[20] *Patent Roll 1225–32*, 124, 153–4.

hold them for twenty-one years even if John died and the marriage did not proceed. He was, therefore, to be the master of Anjou. There was no way Henry could match that.[21]

'And thus,' wrote the Dunstable annalist, 'the hope of the king of England for a confederation with the count of Brittany and the Poitevins was frustrated although the archbishop of York and the bishop of Carlisle and other solemn envoys had laboured for it amidst much danger and at great expense.'[22] When he heard the news, Henry, angry and bruised, seized the lands of Duke Peter. While the possibility of some future rapprochement was kept open, Earl Ranulf now was only to lose his Richmond lands if he first recovered his lands in Normandy.[23] For the moment, the Breton alliance seemed dead.

Despite these reverses, Henry was still set on his expedition overseas. Early in June 1227 he ordered ships to assemble at Portsmouth and an army to muster on 1 August at Winchester. Henry explained that the magnates of Poitou and Gascony were urging him to come, 'if ever we intend to look after our affairs across the sea'.

Not for the first or last time, it all ended in an anti-climax. On 11 July, Henry ordered his tents to be sent to Winchester by 1 August. On 13 July he dispatched his siege engines to Portsmouth. And then on 17 July the expedition was called off. The fact was that while preparations proceeded for the crossing, Henry's envoys (Bishop Mauclerc and Philip de Aubigny) had been negotiating with Queen Blanche. They had now come back with both the offer of a truce lasting until July 1228 and suggestions about a possible comprehensive peace. When the truce was renewed again the following year, Henry declared he found this 'painful', given he was still deprived of his 'patrimony'.[24] He probably felt the same way about accepting the truce in 1227, given the pleas from Poitou and Gascony and the preparations for the crossing. But he allowed himself to be overruled by the cautionary counsels of his justiciar. He hardly appeared a very martial or masterful king.

THE ENRICHMENT OF HUBERT, THE DOMESTIC CRISIS OF 1227

Regrets over the abandonment of the campaign were soon lost in a domestic crisis. The foundations here were laid both by Henry's assertion

[21] *Layettes*, ii, no. 1922. Peter was also given a life interest in the earl of Chester's castles of Bellême and St James de Beuvron in Normandy. They were then to become Yolande's marriage portion: *Layettes*, ii, no. 1926.

[22] Dunstable, 103.

[23] *RLC*, ii, 181; *CFR 1226–7*, nos. 206–7; *Patent Rolls 1225–32*, 124. For Ranulf's dealings with Duke Peter, see Eales, 'Henry III and the end of the Norman earldom of Chester', 105–6.

[24] *RLC*, ii, 192, 212; *CLR 1226–40*, 39, 41; *Patent Roll 1225–32*, 134–5, 213.

of his rights and his distribution of patronage now he had come to power. In 1225, Henry and Hubert had resented the way the Charter of the Forest was being exploited by local society. The knightly jurors determining the forests' bounds had put out of the forest not merely what Henry II had put in de novo but also what he had merely restored to the forest after the losses of King Stephen's reign. Now was the time to do something about it. Henry assumed full power on 9 January 1227. On the very next day the knights who had perambulated the forests in Shropshire, Rutland, Nottinghamshire and Leicestershire were summoned to come before the king on 3 February to explain themselves. The perambulators in Hampshire, Berkshire, Oxfordshire and Huntingdonshire soon followed.[25] All admitted their errors with the result that substantial areas were subject again to forest law. According to Roger of Wendover, 'all judged' the justiciar the author of this policy. It amounted, he thought, to quashing the Forest Charter.[26] Hubert would have denied that. He was not quashing the Charter. He was insisting it be interpreted correctly. Once, moreover, the knights had confessed their faults, the king exempted them from further punishment. One can imagine the swingeing fines they would have suffered under King John.

A second forward policy in 1227 derived directly from the king's new power to grant charters. On 21 January, Henry announced that all those who claimed to have lands and liberties by the gift of his predecessors or by his own order were to show their 'warrant' to them 'as they wish to retain these things'. There was nothing illegitimate about Henry's procedure here. After a long minority, it was reasonable to check that lands and liberties were held justly and had not been usurped. Henry also proclaimed that anyone wanting a new charter, or a confirmation of an old one, should come before him. In the event, down to October 1227 no fewer than thirty-three religious houses offered money to obtain charters.[27] Some of these granted new privileges, some confirmed old ones, some did both. A good number of towns secured similar concessions with the payment for the charter being sometimes included in the amount owed for a tallage. The total offered in the fine roll of 1226/7 for charters was around £3,000 out of a total for fines of £7,820. This was by far the largest sum achieved so far under Henry. In 1225/6 the recorded amount had been less than £2,000.[28]

Wendover's view was that Henry 'considered ancient charters to be of no moment'. As a result, religious institutions and others were forced to renew their charters, paying exorbitant sums fixed arbitrarily by the

---

[25] *RLC*, ii, 206–9b; *Patent Roll 1225–32*, 109–10.

[26] Wendover, iii, 122.

[27] See Ambler, 'The fine roll of 11 Henry III', and Carpenter, 'Fines made with Henry III for the confirmation of charters'.

[28] *CFR 1224–34*, vii–viii (figures calculated by Paul Dryburgh and Beth Hartland).

justiciar.[29] This was unfair. It was customary for kings at the start of their reigns to issue charters confirming lands and rights granted by their predecessors. Henry went much less far than John, who had instructed his judges not to uphold earlier royal charters unless he had confirmed them.[30] Under Henry royal charters continued to be valid whether or not they were confirmed. Indeed, very few laymen bothered to seek such confirmations. On the whole the amounts charged were not excessive. The £7,820 offered in the fine roll for 1226/7 paled before the £40,000 offered to John in the first year of his reign.[31] This was a very different monarchy. The government was also treading carefully in other areas. Between March and May 1227 the tallages imposed on around fifty towns and royal manors were reduced in size, with the order that the remaining debt be fairly assessed without burdening the poor.[32] Wendover thought a 5,000-mark tallage imposed on London was punishment for the city's conduct in the civil war, but it obtained as well the confirmation of London's charters, including the one John had issued in 1215 allowing the citizens to elect their own mayor.[33] Hubert was hardly straining every nerve to build up a treasure chest for a campaign in France. In truth he had a different priority: to create an atmosphere of calm in which the king could concentrate on rewarding his faithful servants.

Reward them he did. Between February and March 1227, Henry made Hubert de Burgh earl of Kent and granted him in hereditary right the honours of Haughley and Rayleigh, together with five valuable manors, two of them from the royal demesne.[34] In July, in another charter, Henry went a long way towards exempting Hubert's estates from the local jurisdiction of the sheriff. He also gave him the wardship of the lands of the earl of Arundel during the minority of the heir. Equally looked after were Hubert's nephews. Richard de Burgh now obtained a royal charter establishing him and his heirs in Connacht, while Raymond de Burgh, having failed in his suit for the countess of Salisbury, married the widowed countess of Essex.[35] Alongside the rewards to the justiciar, Henry made Ralph de Neville chancellor for life, and gave the stewards Ralph fitzNicholas and Godfrey of Crowcombe manors in hereditary right. Bishop Mauclerc

---

[29] Wendover, iii, 122.

[30] Holt, 'Magna Carta 1215–1217', 12.

[31] *CFR 1224–34*, vii–viii. The amount offered in the fine roll of 1227/8 was £2,768.

[32] *RLC*, ii, 178b–86b; *CFR 1226–7*, no. 265.

[33] Wendover, iii, 121; Mitchell, *Studies in Taxation*, 172–3; *CChR 1226–57*, 23–4. The pipe roll, however, puts London's tallage at 4,120 marks. The burgesses of Northampton gave 200 marks for their tallage and a charter, not the £1,200 Wendover alleged: *CFR 1226–7*, no. 160.

[34] *CChR 1226–57*, 11–13, 25. The royal demesne manors were Soham in Cambridgeshire and Aylsham in Norfolk. The other manors were escheats: Ospringe and Eastbridge (Kent) and Arley (Staffordshire).

[35] *CChR 1226–57*, 42, 49, 54; *RLC*, ii, 186b.

received a life grant of the royal demesne manor of Melbourne in Derbyshire on very advantageous terms. His colleagues at the exchequer, the bishops of Bath and Salisbury, obtained charters removing their episcopal lands from the jurisdiction of the sheriff, and giving them the amercements imposed by the king's judges on their men. The bishop of Bath had now the same local jurisdiction as that enjoyed by the king 'before the grant of these liberties'. Both bishops paid for their concessions, Bath 500 marks and Salisbury 300 marks. No one else did.[36]

Years later Henry complained bitterly over this bonanza of patronage. Hubert had 'usurped' royal demesne manors and secured charters giving him Haughley and Rayleigh and other lands and liberties of which King John 'had died seized'. Ecclesiastics and others had likewise obtained 'lands and liberties . . . to the great diminution of the dignity of the lord king and his crown'.[37]

In some ways Henry had only himself to blame. He certainly needed to reward his ministers for their long and laborious service. The problem was to know when to stop or at least when to become sticky. Henry did not know. The rewards of 1227 were but the start of a tide of favour sweeping riches and rights to Hubert and his circle. Henry's warm-hearted and uncalculating personality was surely a factor here. For all his criticisms of Hubert, he was to treat later ministers and favourites in much the same open-handed way. Henry delighted in giving, and he could be careless of the consequent damage to the rights and revenues of the crown. Compared to his father, he was a soft touch. After more than ten years' service as a household knight, Godfrey of Crowcombe had received nothing permanent from King John. Between 1227 and 1232 he received five manors in hereditary right from Henry. These included the very royal demesne manor (at Pitney and Wearne in Somerset) that Godfrey had been forced to surrender in the general resumption of the demesne in 1222.[38]

Yet one has great sympathy for Henry. To judge what to give and where to stop cannot have been easy. In many cases he might think he was merely putting the final and fitting hereditary finish to gifts made by his father. John, after all, had given Haughley and Rayleigh to Hubert in 1215 and the royal demesne manor of Soham in Cambridgeshire as far back as 1202. Equally the local government liberties granted to the bishops of Bath and Salisbury and Hubert de Burgh were no more than what others had long enjoyed by custom or by grant of the king. Hubert and his followers, moreover, were expert in leading the king gradually towards their objectives, getting him to swallow alienations in small helpings rather than in

---

[36] *CChR 1226–57*, 1, 6–7, 9, 24, 39, 52, 54. Ambler, 'The fine roll of 11 Henry III'; Carpenter, 'The bishop of Winchester's fine in 1227'. The bishop of Bath also secured a confirmation of his patronage of Glastonbury abbey, a long-standing ambition of bishops of Bath.

[37] Paris, vi, 69; *CR 1231–4*, 567.

[38] Carpenter, 'The career of Godfrey of Crowcombe', 33–4, 37–41.

great gulps all at once. In the minority Hubert had held the royal manor of Aylsham in Norfolk (close by his home at Burgh) first as sheriff of the county, and then, a significant change, as a private individual. In 1227 he gained the manor by royal charter in hereditary right, but still had to answer at the exchequer for its traditional rent. Next year another charter replaced the rent with nominal military service. The manor had effectively ceased to be part of the royal demesne but it had been a gradual process.[39]

There were few if any cautionary voices close to the king. Hubert and his allies, led by the bishops of Bath and Salisbury and the stewards of the royal household, effectively formed a ring in which they helped each other and witnessed each other's charters. Only two earls in 1227, those of Gloucester and Aumale, appear in the witness lists of the numerous charters issued in Hubert's favour. This was no accident. Getting Henry alone was an important part of the process. One supplicant for a favour, writing to Ralph de Neville, observed that 'the time and place for prosecuting this affair is now most favourable since the king, as it is said, has set out for Gloucester with a small company, and with not many magnates with him'.[40] Henry had taken an oath at his coronation to protect the rights of the crown. He had witnessed the resumption of royal demesne manors in 1222, and doubtless knew of the view that they were inalienable. But he was protected by no hard and fast rules. John himself, for favoured individuals, had occasionally granted away royal demesne manors in hereditary right, if usually in return for the payment of a rent. Hubert (like some courtiers) was able to find a way round even that limitation. In return for the lifting of the rent of Aylsham he returned other properties to the crown.[41]

Henry, of course, had never witnessed his father's cagy, canny and calculated approach to patronage and it is doubtful whether he remembered any paternal advice on the subject. Louis IX, by contrast, perhaps thanks to his mother Blanche, could recall the advice of his grandfather Philip Augustus: 'that you should reward the members of your household in accordance with the quality of the service they give – one more, another less. He also said that no man can be a good governor of lands unless he knows how to withhold just as firmly as to give.'[42] This was not a lesson taught by Hubert de Burgh. It was not a lesson Henry ever learnt.

Hubert, with his usual prudence, did his best to defuse opposition to his sudden enrichment. Concessions from the king won the acquiescence of the earls of Aumale and Gloucester.[43] Hubert even persuaded William

---

[39] *PR 1224*, 172; *CChR 1226–57*, 25, 82, 98; *CR 1227–31*, 133.

[40] TNA SC 1/6/139.

[41] *CChR 1226–57*, 82.

[42] Joinville, cap. 662.

[43] *RLC*, ii, 172; *CFR 1226–7*, nos. 1–3. Gilbert de Clare, earl of Gloucester, in return for a fine of 2,000 marks, was allowed to marry his eldest daughter to the heir of the earldom of Devon.

Marshal to witness the charter giving Connacht to his nephew Richard de
Burgh. But in general the earls and barons neither consented to nor profited from this first outpouring of royal patronage. Not a single earl
received a royal charter between January and July 1227. 'The princes of
the kingdom were indignant,' recorded the annalist of Dunstable, having
summarized Hubert's gains.[44] Despite the concessions over the tallage,
there was also wider discontent, especially because of the policies over the
forest. The justiciar had 'incurred the hatred of the whole kingdom',
wrote Matthew Paris later.[45]

To this groundswell of discontent a spark was provided by the grievances
of Richard, the king's brother, now eighteen. With the collapse of the
schemes for continental alliances, Richard had returned to England in May
1227. He was warmly welcomed by the king and on Whitsunday made earl
of Cornwall.[46] Richard had, however, enjoyed the revenues of Cornwall
since 1224 so the title added little to his resources. He must have looked
enviously at the favours his brother was raining down on Hubert and his
allies. He certainly determined to make the best he could of Cornwall's
resources. Hence when he discovered that the knight Waleran the German
was holding eight of the best manors belonging to the county, he promptly
disseised him and took the manors into his own hands, pending an investigation.[47] In early July, Waleran, an old and trusted servant of King John,
complained to Henry, and Henry promptly ordered the restoration of his
manors. This brought Richard himself to court. Speaking 'without any
advocate', he asserted his rights to the manors and demanded judgement
by the magnates of the kingdom. Henry was infuriated by this defiance.
According to Roger of Wendover's account, 'in a voice tumultuous and
unseemly he ordered his brother to return the manors to Waleran at once,
or he should leave the kingdom not to return'. Richard tartly replied that
he would do neither and withdrew. Then, hearing a rumour that the justiciar intended to arrest him that night, he escaped on a solitary horse to
Reading, his knights following next morning.[48]

Henry had some grounds for his anger. Waleran had indeed been
granted the manors by the king before Richard received the county.[49]
Although his tenure was probably during the king's pleasure, he should
not have been disseised without judgement. Richard was now demanding
judgement for himself, having denied it to Waleran. In the charged atmosphere of 1227, however, Richard easily won support. He joined up with

[44] Dunstable, 103. The comment was written after 1232 as it mentions the marriage of
Hubert's daughter Meggotta.
[45] Paris, HA, ii, 293–4.
[46] Paris, iii, 123; Waverley, 303.
[47] For the manors, see Denholm-Young, Richard of Cornwall, 11 n. 3.
[48] Wendover, iii, 122–4.
[49] RLC, i, 555, 601.

the earl of Chester and with his brother-in-law William Marshal. A muster in arms at Stamford (echoes of 1215) included the earls of Gloucester, Surrey, Hereford, Derby and Warwick. Blaming the justiciar for what had happened, they demanded justice for Richard. They also, widening their support, took up the complaints in the localities about the forest boundaries and the sheriffs breaking chapters of Magna Carta.

As the tension mounted, Henry and Hubert made efforts to shore up their position. On 22 July, Henry granted the royal manor of Edgmond to Henry of Audley in hereditary right, clearly an effort to appease Audley's lord, the earl of Chester. On 28 July, Henry gave way to Archbishop Langton's long-standing plea and allowed his brother Simon Langton, exiled for supporting Louis VIII in the war, to return to England. The crisis, however, deepened. The archbishop himself was evidently too infirm to intervene as he had in 1223. On 3 August 1227, Henry summoned an army to rendezvous at Northampton: the messengers with the letters were to travel 'with great haste day and night'.[50]

In the event, both sides decided to parley rather than to fight. Already on 4 August, before the government left London, safe conducts were issued for Richard, William Marshal and the earl of Chester to come and speak with the king. Henry reached Northampton on 9 August and in the next days Richard and his supporting earls were all at court. Something was done for local society. On 13 August each county was instructed to elect four knights to come before the king in October to air their complaints about the sheriffs breaking Magna Carta. The perambulators of the forests in nineteen counties were summoned to appear on the same date to justify their verdicts.[51] Concessions also defused the discontent amongst the magnates. Henry in charters granted escheats in hereditary right to William de Ferrers, earl of Derby, and to Gilbert and Thomas Basset, two knights in the entourage of William Marshal. A gift of a deer to William Marshal's wife, Henry's sister, soon followed. Henry also allowed the clerk Robert Passelewe to return to England, a favour to the earl of Chester and the other dissidents of 1223, whose agent at Rome Passelewe had been. Richard himself now received the dower forfeited by his mother in England, including Berkhamsted castle. Yet there were still tensions. In November, against Henry's wishes, Richard went to Scotland to seek the hand of the third sister of King Alexander. He was followed as far as Durham by Henry and Hubert, and their opposition helped prevent the marriage. Richard returned via Carlisle to avoid meeting his brother, but by the end of the year the two were reconciled.[52]

[50] *CChR 1226–57*, 55; *Patent Roll 1225–32*, 136; *RLC*, ii, 212b.

[51] *Patent Roll 1225–32*, 137; *RLC*, ii, 212b–13.

[52] Bower, 5, 140–1; Oram, *Alexander II*, 114–15. For the sister (Margaret), see below, 106. Richard's high demands were another reason why the marriage was looked on unfavourably in Scotland.

Richard never became a standard bearer around whom opposition to Hubert might rally. It was another ten years before he openly resisted his brother. After that he never did so again. Richard and Henry were in fact very different personalities. Richard was cooler, cleverer, more calculating and less pious. Unlike Henry, he husbanded his resources and grew rich. Yet fundamentally the brothers got on. Matthew Paris, describing years later the settlement of 1227, observed that Henry 'deservedly loved his brother and desired above all to enrich and pacify him'.[53] Had Richard been a more refractory personality, the history of Henry's reign would have been very different.

'And thus everyone returned home in peace,' wrote Roger of Wendover. The 'mouths' of those indignant with Hubert 'were stopped up with gifts', observed the Dunstable annalist. In September the earls of Pembroke, Gloucester and Aumale and John de Lacy dutifully set off on a diplomatic mission to the German princes.[54] The outcome of the proposed meeting with the county knights about Magna Carta is unknown, but the following year the government steered a middle course when it came to the forests. In April 1228 the knights who had perambulated the boundaries in seven counties came before the king at Westminster and admitted their errors.[55] The deforestations they had implemented in 1225 were thus modified or reversed. These events rankled for a long time. The men of Surrey were complaining about them in 1258. Yet in practice what emerged in the next few years was a compromise typical of Hubert's style of government. Some counties, such as Huntingdonshire, found themselves back to square one, whereas others secured a substantial measure of deforestation. The forest boundaries never returned to their extent before 1215. Despite the complaints they were not modified in the period of revolution and reform between 1258 and 1265.[56]

There is just one sign that the crisis of 1227 shook Henry's confidence in his justiciar. When, that November, the king's judges in Essex challenged the liberties Hubert was claiming as lord of Rayleigh, Henry sided with the judges, only then for Hubert to persuade him to change his mind.[57] In general Hubert seemed as dominant as ever. The summer crisis was hardly over before Henry, on 25 August, granted him in hereditary right the royal demesne manor of Archenfield in Herefordshire with its

[53] Paris, *HA*, ii, 296–7.

[54] *Patent Roll 1225–32*, 159–60.

[55] *CR 1227–31*, 90, 101–4. The counties were Staffordshire, Shropshire, Worcestershire, Northamptonshire, Surrey, Hampshire and Wiltshire.

[56] Carpenter, *Minority*, 391–3. For the final removal of Leicestershire from the forest in 1235, see Crook, 'Roger of Wendover, prior of Belvoir', 173–4. Forest eyres were staged in sixteen counties between 1229 and 1232, with the amercements imposed totalling £2,049. This doubtless added to Hubert's unpopularity. In general, however, the amounts raised by the forest eyres were modest before the late 1240s. See Winters, 'The forest eyre 1154–1368', 25–6, 163–71, and below, 545–6.

[57] *CR 1227–31*, 6; *Patent Roll 1225–32*, 302.

attendant hundred.[58] For the Christmas of 1227, Henry and Hubert were at York and it was there they were reconciled to Richard of Cornwall. Early the following year, Hubert extended his power to the north by securing the Vieuxpont wardship. This meant that until the heir came of age in 1231 or 1232, Hubert was master of Westmorland.[59] In the same month (February 1228) he also wove his tentacles more tightly around Ireland by making Richard de Burgh its justiciar. This was followed later in the year by the election of his former chaplain, Luke, now keeper of the wardrobe, as archbishop of Dublin. The vestments and ornaments he received for his consecration from a delighted king cost all of £73.[60]

These Hubertian advances, striking though they were, paled before those achieved in April 1228. First, on 25 April, at Westminster, Henry recognized John de Briouze's title to the Three Castles in Upper Gwent – Grosmont, Skenfrith and Whitecastle. This cleared the way for John to grant them to Hubert in hereditary right.[61] Then, two days later, Henry issued a charter granting Hubert the justiciarship of England for life.[62] The charter also gave him a life tenure of the castles of Dover, Rochester, Canterbury and Montgomery, with an annual payment of 1,200 marks for their upkeep. Hubert's power now seemed utterly entrenched. There was no precedent for a grant of this kind. No previous justiciar had been given his office for life. Henry might think he was strengthening the position of his faithful minister against attacks like that of the year before, yet to have made such a concession spoke ill of his judgement and concern for the rights of the crown.

There was something else remarkable about the grant. Whereas previous concessions to Hubert had largely been attested by bishops and household officials, this one claimed to command general consent. The king had made his concession, so the charter said, 'by the counsel of our magnates at our petition'. Henry, therefore, had made the proposal but the magnates had accepted it. This was more than mere words. The charter was attested by the bishops of London, Bath and Carlisle, and then by the earls of Chester, Pembroke, Gloucester and Surrey. How on earth had this been achieved? As ever, it was by Hubert the master manipulator.

In the first place he had squared William Marshal, earl of Pembroke. On 27 April, the same day as the grant of the justiciarship for life, Henry gave the Marshal and his heirs what was evidently a grand house (formerly that of a Jew) in London. Four days earlier Henry had taken the manor of Upavon in Wiltshire from Bishop Peter's man, Peter de Maulay, and given

---

[58] *CChR 1226–57*, 57–8, 83; *RCWL*, i, 45.

[59] *CR 1227–31*, 17; Holt, *Northerners*, 221 and n. 3; *CFR 1231–2*, no. 287.

[60] *CLR 1226–40*, 170, 179. This was in 1230.

[61] *CChR 1226–57*, 74, 83; *CRR*, xiii, no. 592.

[62] *CChR 1226–57*, 74; *RCWL*, i, 56. There is a photograph of the charter as enrolled on the charter rolls in Ellis, *Hubert de Burgh*.

it to the Marshal familiar Gilbert Basset. Hubert had threatened Maulay (so he later complained) with imprisonment in a dungeon 'where he would not see his hands and feet' if he did not vacate the manor. Next year Gilbert received the manor from the king in hereditary right, thus realizing a major Basset/Marshal ambition. Basset, moreover, was made one of the king's household knights, and became increasingly prominent at court where, of course, he could represent the Marshal's interests.

Hubert also tried to give Ranulf, earl of Chester, comforting connections with the regime. His familiars, Henry of Audley and the brothers Hugh and Geoffrey Despenser, were established at court. Audley was also sheriff of Shropshire and Staffordshire, the counties the earl had been forced to resign in 1223. Equally significant was the place of Stephen of Seagrave. In 1228 he became (on terms favourable to himself) sheriff of Northamptonshire and Bedfordshire–Buckinghamshire. In 1229 he added Warwickshire–Leicestershire, and became the senior judge at the judicial bench. Hubert must have thought Seagrave completely trustworthy, wrongly as it turned out. He provided a useful link to the earl of Chester, having once been his steward.[63] Henry and Hubert also gave numerous favours to John de Lacy, lord of Pontefract, and the earl of Chester's nephew. In 1225, John thanked Hubert 'many times over for all the good things and honours which you have always conferred on me and still will if it pleases you'.[64] It may well be that this period saw Henry's agreement to the scheme by which John would inherit Chester's second earldom of Lincoln.[65]

THE DEATH OF ARCHBISHOP LANGTON

In July 1228, Henry and Hubert made a brief visit to Canterbury. One reason was to meet the envoys of the king of France and renew the truce for another year. Another was to attend on 7 July the feast of Becket's translation. Archbishop Langton, however, was absent. He was a hundred miles away on his deathbed at Slindon in Sussex, one of his favourite manors (not surprisingly as the village has a beautiful situation on the lower slopes of the South Downs). He died there on 9 July. On 13 July his body was brought back to Canterbury and next day was buried in the cathedral before the altar of St Michael. By then Henry and Hubert had returned to Westminster. They had at the last been on good terms with the archbishop. Henry had protected him from the demands of the king's justices touring Kent and had brushed aside an offer of money for a confirmation of

---

[63] For a biography of Seagrave see Turner, *Men Raised from the Dust*, ch. 7. There is a full study of the family with a calendar of the Seagrave cartulary in Letters, 'The Seagrave family c.1160–1295'.

[64] TNA SC 1/1/108.

[65] For the whole question of the fate of Ranulf's inheritance, see Eales, 'Henry III and the end of the Norman earldom of Chester'.

Canterbury's liberties.[66] There were no miracles around Langton's tomb. At Canterbury, Becket dominated all, just as Langton wished. There was also something commendably unexciting about Langton personally. During the Interdict he had suffered exile not martyrdom. In 1215, despite stories to the contrary, he had been a peacemaker not a partisan. His academic writings showed the same practical common sense he brought to the affairs of church and state. Exemplary though it was, there were no extremes in his piety and religious life. It was, as the Waverley annalist put it, 'in theological knowledge' that he was 'second to none in his time'.[67]

How far Henry's political outlook and religious practices were influenced by Langton's counsel we cannot know.[68] What is certain is that Langton had helped shape the whole nature of Henry's kingship. He had supported the recovery of royal power, yet insisted it should be limited by the acceptance of Magna Carta. In 1225 he had helped make the definitive Magna Carta a consensual and inclusive document supported by the church's sentences of excommunication. Without Langton the Charter would never have gained its central place in English life.

A few days after Langton's burial, a delegation of Canterbury monks appeared before Henry at Westminster asking for the licence to elect a successor. Henry received them with due honour and said he would give his answer on the morrow. Next day, cheerful, friendly and surrounded by his bishops and barons, Henry replied 'wisely and prudently'. 'Since,' he declared, 'it is not fitting for a catholic prince knowingly to breach the holy canons, of my free and pure will, I consent most readily. I love your church most warmly and will love it unless you do anything to make it otherwise. I ask you to study to agree on such a person who will benefit God and the English church, together with myself and my kingdom.'

Henry thus acted very differently from two years before when he had threatened to pull down Durham castle if the monks refused to elect his candidate as their new bishop. He seemed to show proper respect for his father's charter of November 1214 promising the church free elections, a charter which indeed the monks read out before proceeding with their choice. At the same time, however, Henry was hoping his words, mixing friendship and threat, would lead to the election of one of the obvious curial candidates, most notably the chancellor Ralph de Neville. In the event, Henry was disappointed. With proper procedures and proper emotion, with tears, chants and attention to the rule book, the monks elected one of their number, Master Walter of Eynsham. Henry refused to accept him and appealed to the pope. Here again he was acting having taken counsel, indeed after long deliberation according to Roger of Wendover. Eynsham would be useless to king and kingdom. He had been

---

[66] For the dispute, see Cazel, 'Last years of Stephen Langton', 674–7.
[67] Waverley, 304.
[68] For Langton and Henry's piety see below, 277, 284, 300.

disloyal to King John. His father had been hanged for theft. He himself had fathered children by a nun. So at any rate ran the stories. The bishops also appealed to the pope, feeling they should have been involved in the election. It was not until 1229 that a successor to Langton was appointed.[69]

THE CERI CAMPAIGN, 1228

Since the campaigns of 1223, relations with Llywelyn ap Iorwerth had been on a relatively even footing. His ambition was to pass on his principality and power intact to Dafydd, his son by King John's illegitimate daughter Joan. He would thus exclude his illegitimate son Gruffudd from any share of the inheritance. Henry was happy to fall in with this plan. Llywelyn after all was his brother-in-law, Dafydd his nephew. Henry, therefore, sanctioned the oaths taken by 'the great men' of Wales to Dafydd as Llywelyn's heir. He also welcomed (in April 1226) Joan's legitimization by the pope.[70] When Henry met Llywelyn and Joan at Worcester in August 1226 he added the royal manor of Condover in Shropshire to Rothley in Leicestershire, which she had held since 1224.[71] The only source of tension lay in Llywelyn's failure to return to the marcher barons lands he had taken from them or their ancestors during and after the 1215–17 civil war. He was thus in breach of both the 1218 Treaty of Worcester and the settlement at Montgomery in October 1223. The Mortimers were still excluded from Maelienydd and the Briouzes from Elfael. Other claimants included Thomas Corbet and Fulk fitzWarin. In August 1226, Llywelyn promised to make amends that coming October. He did not.[72]

It was not until 1228 that Henry and Hubert decided they must react. They deprived Joan of Condover and Rothley, and in July, having taken counsel from the same group of magnates who witnessed the speech to the Canterbury monks, set off for the Welsh marches, staying on the way at the Marshal's manor of Hamstead Marshal. Any hope of arranging a peaceful settlement of the disputes was soon blown away. At the end of August, while they were at Shrewsbury, disturbing news came in from Montgomery. A party clearing the surrounding woods had been attacked by the Welsh and the castle was now under siege.

This touched a raw nerve in Hubert. The new castle at Montgomery, started in October 1223, was one of his proudest achievements. Disdaining and deserting the old Norman castle down in the plain, he had built it on a new site high above the Severn valley on a final outcrop of the Ceri hills. Right in the centre of the middle march, the castle commanded a famous ford over the Severn and one of the main roads from north to south Wales.

---

[69] Gervase, 115–24; Wendover, iii, 157.

[70] CPReg, 109; Walker, 'Hubert de Burgh and Wales', 478.

[71] RLC, ii, 18, 138.

[72] RLC, ii, 154b–5; Patent Roll 1225–32, 205; Walker, 'Hubert de Burgh and Wales', 475–6.

By 1228 the great drum towers of the gatehouse and the walls of the inner bailey behind it, some 10 feet thick, must have been complete. In April 1228, Montgomery was one of the royal castles Hubert had obtained from the king for life. His intention, almost certainly, was to secure it eventually in hereditary right.

Not surprisingly, therefore, on hearing the news of the attack, Hubert (very different from his caution when it came to France) persuaded Henry to act at once. Although they had no substantial forces with them, the two left Shrewsbury and by 3 September had reached Montgomery. They raised the siege, such as it was, and immediately determined on a much greater action. Henry summoned his barons and household knights to come to Montgomery with horses and arms. Eventually a considerable army assembled comprising 425 knights brought by his tenants-in-chief and 120 household knights. The avowed purpose of the campaign was to force Llywelyn to return the lands he had taken from the marcher barons.[73] The form of the campaign, however, suggested a different or at least a parallel objective. Hubert and Henry did not march south into Maelienydd and Elfael to restore Ralph de Mortimer and William de Briouze. They did not march north towards Llywelyn's heartland in Gwynedd. Instead, around 23 September the army advanced into Ceri, the Welsh commote just to the south of Montgomery. There Hubert, with Henry's consent, ordered the building of a castle on a site that seemed 'untakeable'. The site is indeed spectacular. High on a hill, it looks down on the road through the vale of Ceri, and commands wide views westwards over the commote of Cedewain and parts of Arwystli. A castle there could protect Montgomery, control the vale of Ceri, and project royal (or rather Hubertian) power into central Wales.[74]

The Welsh reaction to this threat was robust. According to one native chronicle, 'all the Welsh, gathered together in unity with their prince, made fierce attacks on their enemies and caused a great confusion amongst them'. In the skirmishing, the baron, William de Briouze, who had just succeeded to the family estates, 'a man eminent in arms though young', was captured. According to Roger of Wendover, food supplies ran short and some of the king's army secretly allied with Llywelyn.[75] Llywelyn certainly tried to exploit divisions in the royal camp. His declaration that he would send envoys to the king only when Henry had councillors with him was obviously aimed at Hubert. It provoked the indignant reply, 'we

---

[73] Walker, 'Hubert de Burgh and Wales', 480; *CR 1227–31*, 115; *Patent Roll 1225–32*, 202.

[74] For the location and significance of the site (grid reference SO20668971), I am grateful to David Stephenson. For the definitive account see Spurgeon, 'Hubert's Folly'. The site is best approached from the hamlet of Sarn where excellent meals and teas may be had at 'The Sarn'.

[75] Brut, 101; Wendover, iii, 159; Walker, 'Hubert de Burgh and Wales', 481.

were never so destitute of counsel but that it was sufficient to deal with much greater and more difficult matters than posed by you!'[76]

In this unpleasant situation Henry and Hubert decided to open negotiations. Around 13 October they reached a settlement and called off the campaign. Llywelyn agreed to pay an indemnity of £2,000 and the Welsh princes renewed their homages to the king. Henry, however, abandoned the attempt to control Ceri, and pulled down the new castle. (Today only earthworks remain.) It was to be no Montgomery. He also accepted that Ceri should be held by the Welsh lord of Ceri, 'the just heir'.[77] Little was done for the marcher barons still excluded from their lordships. William de Briouze's release was secured but only by waiving the £2,000 indemnity.[78]

The campaign of 1228 has been called 'perhaps the poorest show put up by a royal army in Wales in the whole of the thirteenth century'.[79] Contemporary choniclers joined in a chorus of disapproval. William de Briouze was captured, several knights were killed and the king 'achieved little', remarked the Tewkesbury annalist. The king was forced to conclude 'a shameful agreement' and 'returned home ignominiously', said Roger of Wendover. 'The king returned home with little honour,' opined the Dunstable annalist, 'but the shame was imputed to the justiciar.' According to Roger of Wendover, Hubert had come up with a name for the new castle, 'Hubert's folly', doubtless confident that it would prove the reverse. As it was, 'many laughed and declared that the justiciar was not only a prophet but more than a prophet'. In other words he was a fool.[80] Hubert, however, still achieved one of his objectives. On 28 November 1228, Henry granted him the town and castle of Montgomery in hereditary right for the service of one knight. What a reward for failure. Hubert's episcopal allies attested the charter, but not a single earl.[81]

On 1 October 1228, in the midst of the Ceri campaign, Henry had turned twenty-one. He was in the full vigour of youth. Camping with his army in the vale of Ceri, with the new castle going up, with skirmishes taking place all round, with William de Briouze captured while out foraging, were not Henry's military instincts stirred? He was certainly under pressure to show some martial mettle. Earlier in the year in London, in the presence of the earl of Chester and other earls and barons, he had agreed that a tournament could take place at Stamford on 8 September. Later, he postponed the tournament until October, and switched the venue to Northampton, while informing his household knights that they should meet him there. So he was going to attend. His reasons for the

[76] CR 1227–31, 116.
[77] Wendover, iii, 159; Dunstable, 110, 117; Brut, 101.
[78] Patent Roll 1225–32, 205, 241; CR 1227–31, 155.
[79] Walker, 'Hubert de Burgh and Wales', 480.
[80] Wendover, iii, 159.
[81] CChR 1226–57, 81; RCWL, i, 64.

postponement did not, however, suggest any great enthusiasm for tournaments. He had, he said, remembered the sentence passed by the late Archbishop Langton against all who tourneyed without ecclesiastical licence and felt he needed to get it lifted by the pope.[82] One can imagine the reaction of ardent barons and knights to that! In the event, the tournament was replaced by the real thing in Wales. But there is no indication that Henry performed any martial exploits during the campaign. Perhaps it was all too uncomfortable. After a while he abandoned his tents in the vale of Ceri and moved into accommodation in Ceri itself.[83] There is no evidence that Henry ever did attend a tournament.

THE ALLIANCE WITH PETER, DUKE OF BRITTANY

Henry's failure in Wales did nothing to diminish his enthusiasm for a campaign in France. This, however, was impossible without powerful allies, and none seemed available after the defection of Duke Peter of Brittany and Hugh de Lusignan in 1227. In July 1228, therefore, while lamenting the continued exclusion from his patrimony, Henry renewed his truce with the king of France for another year.[84]

What Henry could still do was to consolidate his position in Gascony. Here he had done well, doubtless on Hubert's advice, by appointing in 1227 an able seneschal, the household knight Henry de Trubleville. Gascon revenues being so limited, Henry and Hubert supported him with cash sent out from England, although, with the tax of 1225 now spent, the amounts involved were limited. At one point, pawning his horses to continue the work, Trubleville did all he could to strengthen the king's castles in the major towns: 'through your castles when they are completed all your land in these parts may be brought to order,' he declared.[85] He also advised concessions to consolidate the loyalty of the towns themselves and, in February 1229, the toll on the wines coming from Bordeaux and Bayonne into Sandwich was reduced.[86] Another tack was to spend money securing the allegiance of the nobles of Gascony and those further north in the Saintonge and Poitou.[87] Here Henry had won over to his side the great Poitevin baron, Savary de Mauléon. Savary had deserted in 1224 only to return to Henry's allegiance at the end of 1226. In 1227 he visited

---

[82] *CR 1227–31*, 113.
[83] *CLR 1226–40*, 96, for the transport of the king's tents to Montgomery.
[84] *Patent Roll 1225–32*, 193–4, 213–15; *Layettes*, ii, no. 1967.
[85] *RL*, i, 317–18.
[86] *CR 1227–31*, 153.
[87] Annual payments were made to Raymond, vicomte of Fronsac, Ranulf, lord of Talmont, and William Larchevêque, lord of Parthenay, in the centre of Poitou: *CR 1227–31*, 125; *CLR 1226–40*, 93, 109, 119, 124, 134, 152, 156, 158; *Patent Roll 1225–32*, 503. Others in receipt of fees were Robert de Rancon and Peter Raymond: *CLR 1226–40*, 52, 65; *CChR 1226–57*, 61, 63. Both hoped to recover land in Poitou.

England to assure Henry of his loyalty, complain of his losses, and receive his due rewards, including custody of the lands of the earldom of Devon. In the three years between 1227 and 1230 he enjoyed an annual pension of £200 and gifts totalling at least £2,633.[88]

All of this might consolidate royal power in Gascony and lay the foundations for the recovery of the Saintonge and Poitou. But it was not nearly enough, in Hubert's view, to launch an immediate campaign. The Christmas court of 1228 was held at Oxford. It was attended by Gérard de Malemort, the new archbishop of Bordeaux. In 1227 his predecessor had berated Henry for failing to support the nobles of Gascony and warned of their desertion. Now, Gérard begged the king to come in person. The magnates of Gascony and Poitou would join Henry with horses and arms and he would recover his lost inheritance. The court was also attended, according to Roger of Wendover (the only source for all this), by 'solemn messengers' from Normandy, who likewise urged Henry to take action. 'The king,' however, 'who was still perplexed by great simplicity', sought counsel from the justiciar and was advised 'to defer the matter until a happier hour'.[89]

This is the first association of Henry with the 'simplicity' of which he was again and again accused. Matthew Paris, when he rewrote the passage, linked the simplicity to the king's tender years, and perhaps Wendover too was thinking of that. But Henry was now twenty-one.[90] He was enthusiastic about an expedition to France. What he lacked was confidence in his own judgement. In a way he appreciated his simplicity. Not for the first or last time he bowed to Hubert's advice. That advice was understandable. The king had no war chest. The overtures from Normandy cannot have amounted to much. There were no Norman nobles actually in Henry's pay. There also remained the prospect of a peace brokered by the legate in France. In December 1228 the abbot of Cleeve set off to see him with a range of proposals. They showed just how limited English ambitions now were. There was an acceptance that Normandy was lost save perhaps for the two dioceses of Avranches and Coutances in the Cherbourg peninsula. There was also an acceptance that Maine and Anjou north of the Loire might be ceded as part of a marriage agreement involving Henry's sister, Isabella. The only real objective, so the proposals implied, was the recovery of Poitou. Even that was unrealistic short of Queen Blanche's defeat in war.[91]

And then suddenly everything changed. Duke Peter of Brittany had reappeared on the scene. After the treaty of Vendôme in 1227, Peter had

---

[88] *Patent Rolls 1225–32*, 129, 133–4; *CLR 1226–40*, 37, 40, 43, 50, 52, 65, 68, 70, 87, 91, 108, 121, 124, 127, 131, 134, 141, 151, 154, 157, 163–5, 168; for his losses, *RLC*, ii, 214b–15.

[89] Wendover, iii, 164–5.

[90] Wendover, iii, 164–5; Paris, *HA*, ii, 306. For signs of the archbishop in England, see *CLR 1226–40*, 114, 117; *Patent Roll 1225–32*, 284–5.

[91] *CLR 1226–40*, 114; *CR 1227–31*, 230–1; *DD*, no. 215.

hoped to become the virtual head of Louis IX's minority government. Instead, Queen Blanche excluded him from her counsels and took advice simply from the papal legate and from Theobald, count of Champagne. With both she was rumoured to be enjoying carnal relations. An attempted settlement at a meeting arranged for just after Christmas 1228 collapsed when (so Peter later complained) Louis IX and his governors failed to turn up.[92] In these circumstances Peter looked once again to England. He proposed a revival of the marriage alliance of 1226 and suggested Henry should cross the channel as soon as possible with his army. The only problem was that Peter's daughter, Yolande, was now in the custody of Queen Blanche, and so not available as Henry's bride. Still, at least the pope had forbidden her marriage to Louis IX's younger brother and doubtless she would become available after any victory.

Henry was delighted at the prospects now opening up. On 6 February 1229 he stalled the negotiations with the legate.[93] On the same day he told his tenants-in-chief and household knights of news which 'will make you very happy and joyful'. They were to be ready with horses and arms so that 'when God gives an opportune time, which by the grace of God will be soon, you will be able to cross in honourable fashion with our body'.[94] Henry was not acting without counsel. The earls of Chester, Pembroke, Derby and Gloucester, and John de Lacy, were all at court around this time. When the truce with the king of France expired on 22 July it was not renewed. The very next day Henry held a great council at Northampton. It was agreed to muster an army and fleet at Portsmouth on 13 October. 'At the request of certain of our friends from parts overseas and by the counsel of the earls and barons of England, we firmly intend to cross, God willing,' wrote Henry.[95] The earls and barons were indeed prepared to support the expedition with money. With their consent a scutage was to be paid at the high rate of £2 a fee by the tenants-in-chief not joining the expedition.[96]

Meanwhile, Henry tried to gather more overseas supporters, if not with any great success. One obvious target was John's ally Ferrand, count of Flanders, who had languished for years in a French prison after his capture at the battle of Bouvines. In 1225, on a false rumour of his release, Henry had written hoping that their ancient alliance might be renewed and they might assist each other against the king of France. In 1227 the count had indeed come to England. He was given 1,000 marks and promised for his

---

[92] The precise chronology of Peter's revolt is very unclear and has been the subject of much debate; see Berger, *Blanche de Castile*, 125 n. 2; Painter, *Scourge of the Clergy*, 131–7; Grant, *Blanche of Castile*, 88–90.

[93] *DD*, no. 216. For the negotiations, see *Patent Roll 1225–32*, 243–4.

[94] *CR 1227–31*, 232.

[95] *CR 1227–31*, 248; *Patent Roll 1225–32*, 259.

[96] Mitchell, *Studies in Taxation*, 181–9.

homage and service the 500 marks annual fee traditionally received by counts of Flanders from the king of England. In March 1229, 500 marks were indeed sent out to him.[97] But Ferrand, while happy to take Henry's money, had learnt the lesson of Bouvines and would not move against the king of France. Henry had no better luck with Raymond, count of Toulouse. In March 1229 messengers set out with news too secret to put in writing 'concerning the alleviation of our grievances and your tribulation'.[98] But the count was a beaten man. In April 1229 he concluded the Treaty of Paris which conceded the seneschalships of Carcassonne and Beaucaire to the king of France. At the same time Raymond's daughter and heir was to marry one of Louis IX's brothers, thus opening the prospect of Toulouse falling to the French royal house.

There was equally little chance of help from the empire. Back in 1227, after the collapse of the Brittany marriage, Henry had wondered whether he might marry a daughter of the king of Bohemia. 'We are still single,' he enthused. In September 1227 he sent envoys to Antwerp with the aim of negotiating a 'confederation' with 'the king of Germany and the empire'. But nothing came of these initiatives. That same month Frederick II reached an agreement with Louis IX, one replicating the restrictions on an English alliance found in the Treaty of Catania. In September he was excommunicated by the pope for failing to set out on his crusade. Henry begged both sides to resolve the quarrel but until that happened he hesitated over closer relations with Frederick.[99] At least that did raise the possibility of an alliance with Henry's kinsman, Otto of Brunswick, the son of King John's old ally, and Frederick's rival, the Emperor Otto. 'We cannot hide from you,' Henry wrote in March 1229, 'with what injustice the power and violence of our enemies and your enemies has kept us both disinherited and excluded from our rights. However, we trust in God, who does not desert those placing their hope in him, that our rights and yours, which he permitted to be taken away, soon through his grace we will recover.'[100] Henry could not have revealed more clearly how he felt about his own disinheritance. The rest was parchment talk. Otto had just been released from prison, and faced a hard struggle to establish himself as duke of Brunswick. There was no prospect of him helping Henry or of Henry helping him.[101]

The papal imperial quarrel went beyond Frederick's excommunication. It also involved armed conflict in Italy. Frederick's departure on his crusade in the summer of 1228, still excommunicated, brought no resolution. All

[97] F, 177; Patent Roll 1225–32, 143; CLR 1226–40, 54, 58, 123. For the 'false Baldwin', see Weiler, Henry III of England and the Staufen Empire, 22.

[98] CR 1227–31, 233; CLR 1226–40, 123.

[99] RLC, ii, 210; Patent Roll 1225–32, 161–2; Weiler, Henry III of England and the Staufen Empire, 26, 36–8, 43.

[100] CR 1227–31, 233.

[101] For discussion, see Weiler, Henry III of England and the Staufen Empire, 40–3.

this impacted on England in ways that would become familiar during Henry's reign. The taxes demanded by the papacy to finance its wars against Frederick and his successors (the first for causes other than the crusade) became deeply unpopular. They also damaged Henry since he was blamed for failing to protect the church from such impositions. This pattern emerged for the first time in 1229. Apart from the general taxes, the papal envoy, Master Stephen, also demanded a special payment from Henry himself. One thousand marks now, he said, would be worth two or three times as much later. Faced with this request, Henry (apparently uncounselled by the justiciar or anyone else) observed that he could give no certain answer until the return of his envoys from the legate in France. This sensible reply was then immediately undermined by what followed: 'however, nonetheless, he said he would freely agree to the petition of the lord pope'.[102] Since there is no sign any payment was made, it looks as though here again Henry was persuaded to backtrack by his ministers.

THE ABORTED EXPEDITION OF 1229

After the great council held at Northampton in April 1229 had agreed to launch the expedition in October, Henry and Hubert pressed on with the necessary preparations, spiritual as well as material. Henry went immediately on pilgrimage to Walsingham, Bury St Edmunds, and probably also to Bromholm, doubtless to pray for the success of his arms. The kingdom, meanwhile, seemed stabilized by the appointment of a new archbishop of Canterbury. Pope Gregory had indeed quashed the election of the Canterbury monk Walter of Eynsham, and had provided in his place the chancellor of Lincoln Cathedral, Master Richard Grant, here acting on the suggestion of the king and the English bishops. In March 1229, Henry gave his assent to the appointment.[103] Grant was no courtier. He was famous for his learning and conspicuous for his physical stature, hence his nickname 'le Grant, the Great'. It is a measure of how carefully Henry and Hubert were treading over Canterbury that they accepted this scholar and churchman. Grant, hearing the news of his appointment, promised the king 'all reverence with due devotion' and begged Chancellor Neville for help in undertaking his onerous task. Both Henry and Hubert gave him generous gifts and in September attended the ceremony at Canterbury when Grant received the pallium from the pope.[104]

From Canterbury, Henry returned to Westminster, and there, in early October made arrangements for the government of the kingdom in his

[102] *DD*, no. 216. The episode is narrated in a letter from the treasurer, Walter Mauclerc, to the chancellor, Ralph de Neville.

[103] Harvey, *Episcopal Appointments*, 107, 131, 149.

[104] Wendover/Paris, iii, 169–72, 205; Paris, *FH*, ii, 196–7; TNA SC 1/6/157; *CLR 1226–40*, 122; *CChR 1226–57*, 100.

absence. It was to be run by Chancellor Neville and Stephen of Seagrave, now, through the death of Martin of Pattishall, the senior justice at the bench.[105] On 10 October the exchequer was ordered to release 20,000 marks to be taken across the sea. Another 2,000 marks was to be given to Hubert de Burgh himself. At this time before departure, Henry's regard for his justiciar burnt very bright. Hubert had, or so it seemed, brought about the expedition on which Henry's heart was set. He was also constantly easing Henry's task in smaller matters. When Henry, in September, entered the chapter house at Canterbury and witnessed the prior of Canterbury give the sub prior of Rochester the kiss of peace, it was Hubert who had worked out the settlement.[106] In the same month Hubert was granted in hereditary right the castle, manor and honour of Knaresborough, thus establishing himself, so he might hope, permanently in the north. Here he was profiting from one of King John's most notorious exactions because Knaresborough was in the king's hands only through the failure of the Stutevilles to pay a 10,000-mark relief slapped on them in 1205. At this time in 1229, Knaresborough was held for the king by the archbishop of York, Walter de Grey, in return for an annual rent of £200. He declared himself quite ready to surrender the custody provided it was 'committed to the honour and advantage of the lord king'. Whether he thought the eventual grant to Hubert in hereditary right and at a rent of £100 not £200 was to the king's advantage may be doubted.[107]

Even more remarkable was the grant to Hubert early in October of Cardigan and Carmarthen in hereditary right.[108] Hubert may well have argued that this would help keep the peace in Wales during Henry's absence. Concern for the peace was the reason why Henry, at the same time, took the homage of Dafydd as Llywelyn's heir and granted him an annual fee of £40 until converted into land.[109] Yet the grant of Cardigan and Carmarthen surely amounted to a major diminution in the possessions and power of the crown. Carmarthen, if with intermissions under Welsh rule, had been the great base of royal power in south Wales since the time of Henry I. Cardigan, 'the lock and stay of all Wales' (as a Welsh chronicle put it), had been acquired in perpetuity by King John from its Welsh ruler early in his reign. Although Llywelyn had seized Cardigan and Carmarthen in 1215, he had been ousted by William Marshal in 1223. Thereafter the Marshal and his successors had controlled Cardigan and

---

[105] Patent Roll 1225–32, 275.

[106] Dunstable, 118–20; CRR, xiii, no. 2787; Paris, FH, ii, 196–7.

[107] CChR 1226–57, 99–100; TNA SC 1/6/113; CFR 1225–6, no. 74; Patent Roll 1225–32, 254. Grey's response (in a letter) also shows how Hubert was moving secretly and gradually towards his ultimate objective.

[108] CChR 1226–57, 100.

[109] Patent Roll 1225–32, 275.

Carmarthen as royal custodians. Now, Hubert had made Cardigan and Carmarthen a marcher barony, answering merely for the service of five knights. Already holding Montgomery and the Three Castles in heredi-tary right, Hubert was to be far more dominant in Wales than the king.

On 12 October, Henry at last left Westminster for Portsmouth, thus missing the feast of the translation of Edward the Confessor on the thir-teenth, something he would never have done ten years later, having adopted the Confessor as his patron saint. He reached Portsmouth on 15 October. There he was greeted by Duke Peter, who now did homage for Brittany.[110] By 18 October the earls of Cornwall, Chester, Pembroke, Derby, Hereford, Surrey, Aumale and Huntingdon were all at court. According to the muster roll an army of 548 knights eventually assembled, no mean force.[111] The great men may have looked askance at the favours being heaped on Hubert. Not a single earl witnessed the charters for Knaresborough, Cardigan and Carmarthen. Yet Hubert, working through the king, remained adept at disarming his critics with gifts and concessions. On 18 October Henry made grants to both the Marshal and the earl of Chester, ones in both cases involving the permanent alienation of royal demesne.[112]

The campaign was all ready to be launched. On 19 October letters of protection were issued for those taking part. And then suddenly, appall-ingly, a couple of days later, it was all called off. The reason, according to Roger of Wendover, was a lack of shipping. When the king learnt this, Wendover continued:

He was absolutely furious and blamed the whole crime on Hubert de Burgh, the justiciar. And in everyone's hearing, called him a traitor, alleging that he had brought about the lack [of shipping] for 5000 marks which he had received from the king of France. And drawing his sword, as if filled with madness, he wished to kill the justiciar. But the earl of Chester and others who were there, placing themselves in the way, saved him from death. And he withdrew from the king's presence until the king's anger subsided and calmed down.[113]

We have no means of checking the accuracy of this story, but it does not seem improbable. After the cancellation of expeditions in 1223, 1226 and 1227, and after the colossal build-up for this one, Henry's disappointment and frustration must have been intense. It was natural to blame Hubert whom he had trusted so much and rewarded so well. It was natural too to question Hubert's enthusiasm for the enterprise and suspect his motives, given the way he had cautioned against previous expeditions. Henry's

---

[110] *Patent Roll 1225–32*, 255.
[111] *RCWL*, i, 78–9; Sanders, *Feudal Military Service*, 115–29.
[112] *CChR 1226–57*, 101–2; *Patent Roll 1225–32*, 224, 277; *PR 1230*, 329–30.
[113] Wendover, iii, 190–1.

anger seems also to have flared up against the two senior stewards of the royal household, Ralph fitzNicholas and Godfrey of Crowcombe, both of whom he now removed (if temporarily) from their sheriffdoms. None of this, however, was revealed in the letters of 22 October which announced the cancellation of the expedition. Henry had acted, so he said, on the advice of his earls and barons and the duke of Brittany. The reason was the lateness of the season – as though no one had thought of that before. The crossing was now postponed until the following Easter.[114]

So the duke of Brittany returned home, taking with him a good proportion of the money assembled for the expedition. Roger of Wendover says that Henry and Hubert were reconciled, but tensions persisted. On 8 November, Hubert's protégé Ranulf le Breton, now keeper of the wardrobe, was convicted of a disseisin in a case heard before the king.[115] The justiciar could no longer protect his own. Two days earlier Henry had despatched an impatient letter to Hubert himself. The justiciar was to instruct the Londoners to pay their debts 'in full' by 13 December. If they failed to do so, 'by the faith in which he is held to the king and under the due oath taken to him' he was to seize the city into the king's hands and suspend all its liberties until further orders. It sounds as though Henry was utterly exasperated by Hubert's failure to deal with the Londoners. Hubert, however, was nothing if not resilient. He calmed Henry down, for the Londoners neither paid their debts in full nor had their liberties seized.[116] On 12 November, a sign both of strength and anxiety, Hubert obtained a charter acquitting him of all accounts as justiciar up to the present time. Hubert also played yet again the Scottish card. Once more Christmas was at York with King Alexander. It was doubtless there that Alexander promised 2,000 marks for the forthcoming expedition.[117]

On the way to York, Henry appears in a very different guise from the angry monarch seen at Portsmouth. When he reached the royal manor of King's Cliffe in Northamptonshire, the men of the manor and the surrounding area came before him and tearfully complained about the oppression of the forest officials. Henry, 'having merciful compassion on their poverty', and acting 'for God', ordered the oppression to cease. At the same time he arranged for 300 robes of russet and 300 pairs of shoes to be given as alms to the poor. On 15 December, now at Nottingham (the centre of a county where the forest was a major issue), he clarified his attitude to the Charter of the Forest. At the instance of many complainants, he had, so he said, now remembered the Charter's stipulation that no one living outside the forest could be summoned routinely before the forest judges. The judges were thus ordered to uphold the provision. 'We have

---

[114] Wendover, iii, 190–1; Tewkesbury, 73; *CR 1227–31*, 255–6.

[115] *CRR*, xiii, nos. 2757–9.

[116] *CR 1227–31*, 383; *PR 1230*, 105–8.

[117] *CChR 1226–57*, 107; Wendover, iii, 193; *Patent Roll 1225–32*, 332.

sworn to maintain the liberties in our Charter of the Forest and we wish them to be preserved unharmed.'[118] Thus Henry sought to sedate discontent before his departure and win God's favour for the coming expedition.

THE CAMPAIGN OF 1230

In the early months of 1230, Henry and Hubert did all they could to rally the earls and barons to the expedition. They welcomed them to court, gave them favours and took their counsel. On 7 February a decision was made at the exchequer by the king in the presence of Hubert and the earls of Chester, Cornwall, Gloucester, Surrey, Aumale, Hereford and Huntingdon.[119] A particular effort was made to conciliate Richard of Cornwall, who became twenty-one in January, and was, of course, the heir to the throne. He was given 1,000 marks and the honours of Eye and Wallingford, Wallingford castle becoming one of his main residences. Although he had yet to receive anything in hereditary right, Richard had been prepared to witness the charter acquitting Hubert of accounts as justiciar.[120]

It was at this moment that Simon de Montfort first enters English history. Simon was a younger son of the most famous French nobleman of the age: the Simon de Montfort who had led the Albigensian crusade and been killed in 1218 at the siege of Toulouse. Although in the allegiance of the king of France (his Montfort was Montfort l'Amaury near Paris), Simon the crusader had a claim through his mother, Amice, to the earldom of Leicester in England. (She was a sister of the childless earl Robert of Leicester who had died in 1204.)[121] This claim King John had briefly recognized. Now, early in 1230, with clever timing, young Simon arrived in England and sought to recover his father's position, his elder brother Amaury having resigned the family claims in his favour. Henry wanted allies and was impressed by Simon. Some two years his junior, persuasive and plausible, here was someone who might give long years of faithful and fruitful service. In February it was agreed that Montfort could have the lands and rights enjoyed by his father once these had been resigned by the current tenant, the earl of Chester. (Henry had earlier agreed that Chester would not be dispossessed until he had recovered his lands in Normandy.) In April, after Montfort had promised 'to stand in the king's service in England and elsewhere', he was granted 400 marks a year

---

[118] *CR 1227–31*, 274–5, 385; *CLR 1226–40*, 159; TNA E 368/11, mm. 4d, 5; *PR 1230*, 97, 245. For the forest eyre at this time in Nottinghamshire, see Winters, 'The forest eyre 1154–1368', 165.

[119] TNA E 368/11, m. 5d.

[120] *Patent Roll 1225–32*, 313; *CR 1227–31*, 287; *CLR 1226–40*, 172; *RCWL*, i, 84.

[121] The claim was only to half the lands of the honour of Leicester, the other half passing to Amice's younger sister Margaret, married to Saer de Quincy, earl of Winchester.

until he received the Leicester lands.[122] It was the beginning of a fateful relationship.

Montfort did not come on the 1230 expedition but the muster at Portsmouth was joined by the earls of Cornwall, Pembroke, Chester, Derby, Gloucester, Aumale, Hereford and Huntingdon, as well as John de Lacy (soon to be earl of Lincoln) and the heirs to the earldoms of Norfolk and Winchester. As far as is known, the question of whether tenants-in-chief owed service overseas was not raised.[123] All told, letters of protection were issued to 370 barons and knights. With their retinues the total force must have been much larger. This time there was no problem over transport. Lists were drawn up of the ships and their masters (each was to carry at least sixteen horses), and Henry found himself with a surplus. The army was eventually carried over in some 230 ships with 160 being let go.[124] Evidently Henry would have liked a bigger army. With money from the scutage, a clerical aid, tallages levied on the Jews and the royal demesne, and 4,300 marks from Ireland, Henry took with him a treasure chest worth at least £20,400.[125] Given that it had taken a tax of £40,000 to save Gascony in 1225–6, the expedition was hardly adequately funded.[126]

Henry himself arrived at Portsmouth on 17 April. Two days later he received the new regalia which he had ordered for the expedition: a royal robe of white silk, with sandals and gloves, and a crown, sceptre and rod of silver gilt. Henry then asked for his ring with the small ruby to be sent as well, adding that it was kept in the same box as his gold crown. He clearly recognized the importance of sitting in state and displaying the majesty of kingship. Henry also recognized the importance of gift-giving and took with him eight coffers filled with jewels.[127]

The fleet set sail on 1 May: *Welfare, Goodyear, Goodchild, Falcon, Godale of Portsmouth, Countess, Stockstrong* were the names of some of the ships. 'On the day on which he boarded his ship, led by a spirit of humility, the king kissed all the poor, infirm and lepers and caused many good things to be given to them', recorded a mendicant chronicle.[128] This was the first time Henry

---

[122] *Patent Roll 1225–32*, 124, 325; *CR 1227–31*, 316; Maddicott, *Simon de Montfort*, 8–9.

[123] The early schedule of baronial demands in 1215, 'the Unknown Charter' (Holt, *Magna Carta*, 427, cap. 7), accepted that service was due in Normandy and Brittany, and Brittany was the immediate destination in 1230. For all Henry's overseas campaigns (in 1230, 1242–3 and 1253–4), there are no detailed records of payments out of the wardrobe. There is, therefore, no means of knowing how far the armies were supported with money in the form of wages or loans (the latter much used by John). If Henry did give loans, he never sought their repayment. For the development of loans, see Church, 'The 1210 campaign in Ireland'.

[124] *CR 1227–31*, 387; *Patent Roll 1225–32*, 344–6, 370–5.

[125] *CLR 1226–40*, 161; *CR 1227–31*, 302; *Patent Roll 1225–32*, 329–30, 335, 337–8, 341. Mitchell, *Studies in Taxation*, 180–95, analyses the taxation for the campaign.

[126] For other comparisons, see below, 568, 598.

[127] *CR 1227–31*, 323, 329, 335; *Patent Roll 1225–32*, 335.

[128] BL Cotton Nero A IX, fos. 69r–69v.

had been to sea. It must have been an exciting, perhaps alarming experience. Of course, had the old continental empire been still in place, he would by now have crossed to Normandy many times. As it was, he sailed past the Norman ports of Dieppe, Le Havre and Caen, where his ancestors had so often disembarked, rounded the Cherbourg peninsula and then, allowing part of the fleet to continue, put into Guernsey for the night of 2 May, the Channel Islands being the one part of the duchy of Normandy still in his hands. His reason was that his sister Isabella (brought along presumably with a view to some marriage) was seasick. Henry finally reached his destination, the Breton port of St Malo, around the third hour on 3 May. Already the alliance with Duke Peter was showing its worth. Without it, Henry's destination would have been Bordeaux.

Hearing of the king's landing, Duke Peter, in 'the march of Anjou', hurried to St Malo and arrived on 6 May. The next day there was a council of war. Its decisions shaped the whole future of the campaign. St Malo is in the north-eastern corner of Brittany hard by the Norman frontier. Peter already had a foothold over the frontier through holding the great castle of St James de Beuvron. Stretching northwards were the Norman dioceses of Avranches and Coutances, the very parts of the duchy the English government had hoped to retain in the peace proposals of 1228. In this area there were Norman nobles who might be tempted onto Henry's side. Henry at this moment had the initiative. At the time of his arrival, as a letter home reported, Louis IX was still 'in France preparing to come with an army to meet us'.[129] Clearly Louis would have to respond to whatever Henry did. His army, moreover, was riven by faction with conflicts swirling around the count of Champagne and the count of Flanders. It had taken a truce to bring it together at all.

In these circumstances, did Henry hope for an advance with all his forces into Normandy? If Louis came to meet him, as surely he would, might not some great battle in the Cherbourg peninsula reverse the verdict of Bouvines? If Henry argued for that, he soon gave way to other counsels. The decision taken was to split the army. Henry, Hubert, William Marshal and the great bulk of the English forces were to head south. The aim was to recover Poitou, not Normandy. Meanwhile, Duke Peter and Ranulf of Chester were to remain in the north-east of Brittany. There they could defend the duchy from French attack and try to regain the lands in Anjou of which Peter had already been deprived.[130] They also had more particular objectives. Duke Peter and Earl Ranulf had reached an agreement and done a swap. Peter gave Ranulf St James de Beuvron, which was an ancestral castle of the earls of Chester. In return, Ranulf gave Richmond castle and Richmondshire to Peter. So at last Peter had

[129] *DD*, nos. 218–20.
[130] Painter, *Scourge of the Clergy*, 131–2.

full possession of the honour of Richmond.[131] Probably Chester's first move (as early as 17 May he was commanding his own section of the king's army) was to assert his control over St James and the surrounding area.[132] Duke Peter and Earl Ranulf also had a mutual enemy in Andrew de Vitré. Andrew was lord of Vitré, near the Breton border with Maine, and had long been a thorn in Peter's side. He also held some of the earl of Chester's lands in Normandy.[133] Not surprisingly he now threw in his lot with the king of France. In revenge Peter and Ranulf destroyed his castle at Marcillé-Robert and engaged in concerted action against Vitré itself.[134]

Henry and his army, meanwhile, headed south. The plan was for him to go first to Dinan to see his mother, who was expected there on 11 May. He would then go on to Nantes to meet his stepfather Hugh de Lusignan.[135] If he could win them over, he would have struck a major blow towards the recovery of Poitou. Henry was indeed at Dinan on 11 May and at Nantes on the 17th. But there is no sign that he met Hugh and Isabella there. He did, however, have the opportunity of meeting someone else, for Louis had now arrived with 'a large army'. On 8 June he was astride the Loire at Champtoceaux only twenty miles from Nantes.[136] Henry thus had the chance to fight the great battle for the recovery of his empire.

But Henry never stirred. He remained stationary in Nantes from 17 May until the end of June. His strategy was absolutely the reverse of seeking battle. It was explained with crystal clarity by Hubert de Burgh in a letter home to Chancellor Neville. The king had stayed at Nantes, he reported:

> . . . because of the arrival of the king of France and his army, who stayed in those parts both to obstruct our way and prevent us proceeding further, and to tempt us by diverse means so that through an attack of our own, or in some other way, he might find a chance of attacking us.[137]

The 'proceeding further' here meant proceeding further into Poitou, and at least something was being done on the diplomatic front to further that strategy. 'The king has stayed at Nantes for three weeks,' the king's steward Ralph fitzNicholas reported on 8 June, 'waiting for and drawing to him the magnates of Poitou.' FitzNicholas then gave a long list of those who were expected to come into the king's service. Unfortunately the

---

[131] Wendover, iii, 198; *CR 1227–31*, 410–11. See Eales, 'Henry III and the end of the Norman earldom of Cheshire', 105–6.

[132] *CR 1227–31*, 410.

[133] Powicke, *Loss of Normandy*, 335–6, assuming that Andrew retained the lands granted by Philip Augustus to his father.

[134] *DD*, nos. 221, 223; Wendover, iii, 195; *Layettes*, ii, nos. 2057–8.

[135] *DD*, no. 219.

[136] *DD*, no. 220; Painter, *Scourge of the Clergy*, 68.

[137] *DD*, no. 223.

biggest prize had already slipped away. 'You should know,' fitzNicholas confessed, 'that [Hugh de Lusignan] has wholly departed from the fealty of the king and rides with the king of France since [the latter] has given him great gifts and a new convention has been made between them.' This was all too true, the agreement, reached on 30 May, being essentially a renewal of the 1227 treaty of Vendôme.[138]

A letter home on 20 June from the royal clerk Geoffrey of Wolford shows there was disquiet at this stationary strategy: 'one thing you should know displeases the world here as is openly said both by our circle and by others, namely the king's long delay at Nantes. As a result some of our French adherents . . . have lost hope in us, men who are anxious for our welfare and progress, because we are spending the time idly doing nothing.' Similar reports reached Roger of Wendover: the king's army, he opined, remained idle at Nantes, drinking, womanizing and consuming treasure.[139]

Wendover blamed Hubert de Burgh for this situation: he would not permit the earls and barons to move arms against the enemy. There are some signs that Henry was frustrated by this inaction. In July, in a letter to Chancellor Neville, he denied that 'sharp words, verba aspera' had passed between him and his justiciar. 'We have never held him so dear as we do now, as he who, above all our faithful men, attends to our affairs most diligently and devotedly'.[140] The implication was surely that sharp words had indeed passed between them. Henry, moreover, sought to find a way out of the impasse, though it was hardly a military one. At the end of June, Hubert's chaplain, Richard de St John, wrote an anxious letter to Neville. The king, 'I do not know by whose devious and sinister suggestion' and 'against the wise counsel of the justiciar and everyone else', had insisted (the 'royal will bursting out in such fervour') on dispatching envoys to Rome asking for Cardinal Giovanni de Colonna to be sent to England as a legate. St John was horrified at the possible consequences for the English church but 'neither through myself nor through the justiciar was I able to change the king's intention while he waxed hot in the matter'. The heat, however, did not last and St John was able to report that, in the end, Henry had backed down, persuaded by Hubert's 'various clever arguments' to do so. Unfortunately it was too late to recall the envoys and the pope expressed astonishment at Henry's change of mind.[141]

At this very time, however, the clouds were clearing. Henry and his army had not been mindlessly stationary in Nantes. They had been playing a waiting game. They knew that the fragile truce holding the French army together was due to expire on 1 July. As early as 20 June there

---

[138] *DD*, no. 220; *Layettes*, ii, no. 2052. Louis also reached an agreement with another great Poitevin baron, Raymond, vicomte of Thouars: *Layettes*, ii, nos. 2055, 2060–1.

[139] *DD*, no. 221; Wendover, iii, 199.

[140] *DD*, no. 224.

[141] *DD*, no. 222. For Giovanni, see *DD*, nos. 19, 168; *Reg. Gregoire IX*, no. 3298.

were rumours Louis was planning to return to France. By the end of the month he was gone and his army had disintegrated with one faction launching an attack on the count of Champagne.[142] At last the way was open for Henry, but where should he go? In June, Duke Peter and Earl Ranulf had been in negotiations with the Norman noble Fulk de Paynel. He was the lord of a substantial barony in the diocese of Coutances centred on La Haye-Pesnel. Towards the end of June he and his brother William, and 'a great part of the knights of his family' (as a letter home put it), entered Henry's allegiance. According to Wendover, they begged Henry to invade Normandy 'with the certain hope of subjugating the land'. Henry, Wendover says, was up for this only for the justiciar to quash the idea. It was far too dangerous. So Poitou remained the priority with Normandy a poor second. As Henry explained, the submission of the Paynels meant that 'having finished our business in Poitou, we will be able to approach the march of Normandy, and it is believed undoubtedly that many more will come to us'. It hardly sounded as though he was thinking of advancing very far into the duchy.[143]

THE MARCH THROUH POITOU TO GASCONY

On 1 July, therefore, Henry left Nantes and set out for Poitou. His excitement must have been great. As well as Hubert, he had with him William Marshal, the earls of Derby and Hereford, and John de Lacy. There was a real sense that something 'big' was about to happen. Hubert wrote home to Chancellor Neville asking for his prayers and hoping that God, without whom nothing could be achieved, would grant 'prosperity and happiness to our expedition'.[144] Henry had many of the barons of Poitou in his pay and promises from others. Yet it soon became clear that he was engaged in a promenade through the county not a war of conquest. As Ralph fitzNicholas observed, the king 'will be able to ride well and safely through the parts of Poitou to the parts of Gascony and, if it is necessary, he will easily be able to return to the parts of Brittany'.[145] Was that all it was about? Indeed, it was.

There were two reasons for these limited ambitions. The first was the result of Louis IX securing Hugh de Lusignan. His castles ran through Poitou and formed a barrier to any outright conquest.[146] Hugh also held Saintes, the capital of the Saintonge. The clerk Geoffrey of Wolford, writing on 20 June, thought there was a 'certain hope' of Hugh coming

---

[142] *DD*, no. 221; Wendover, iii, 196.

[143] *Patent Roll 1225–32*, 382; *DD*, no. 224; Wendover, iii, 197–8; Powicke, *Loss of Normandy*, 324; Stevenson, 'England and Normandy 1204–1259', 335–454.

[144] *DD*, no. 223.

[145] *DD*, no. 220.

[146] For Lusignan castles in Poitou see below, 248–9, 256.

over, but he never did.[147] The second reason was so obvious and irremedi-
able that it was not mentioned in any of the letters home. Poitou was
dominated by its towns. The king of France had held Poitiers itself since
1204. The conquest of 1224 had brought him Niort, St Jean d'Angely, and
finally the great port of La Rochelle, the key, as everyone acknowledged,
to Poitou. In 1230 all the towns were held firmly for Louis IX. Henry did
not go near them, let alone put them under siege. Although, moreover,
many of the Poitevin barons had entered Henry's allegiance, their loyalty
was fragile. It rested on pensions and promises. These men were very
aware that they might be in difficulties once the king was gone. Essentially,
therefore, in his progress through Poitou, Henry avoided the towns and
moved from the castle of one questionable supporter to that of another.
He was like a man crossing a fast-flowing stream by jumping from one wet
and slippery stepping stone to another, in the process avoiding a series of
large rocks.

Having left Nantes, Henry thus moved to Luçon where the lord Aimery
de Thouars had just accepted a fee of 100 marks a year. He then moved
to Marans where he promised its lord, William de Mauzé, a fee of £50 a
year if he lost his land in the king's service. Here Henry was twelve miles
from La Rochelle. But that was close enough. He gave the town a wide
birth and headed on south to Tonnay at the mouth of the Charente,
where the lord, Hugh de Tonnay, had been in receipt of gifts since 1227.
Henry now faced another barrier to any recovery of the Saintonge, for he
had yet to reach an agreement with Geoffrey de Rancon, whose great
castle of Taillebourg, fifteen miles away, controlled the passage up the
Charente.[148] From Tonnay, therefore, Henry, avoiding both Taillebourg
and Saintes, moved on south to Pons, having secured the allegiance of its
lord, Reginald de Pons, with a promise of 200 marks a year until (optimistically) land could be given him 'in the areas of our conquest'. Still
Reginald, leader of the opposition to Hugh de Lusignan in the Saintonge,
was worth buying. Henry stayed in the castle at Pons with its great keep
from 15 to 19 July and there reached an agreement with Iter de Barbezieux,
promising him a lump sum of 1,240 marks and 200 marks a year. Henry
de Trubleville, as seneschal of Gascony, was to put a large garrison into
Barbezieux castle for the duration of the war or 'until the march may be
further enlarged', a striking indication of the shaky military situation.[149]

Having done what he could on the line of Charente, Henry moved south
towards Gascony. At Mirambeau, just to the east of the Gironde estuary,
having summoned help from the Gascon towns, and borrowed mangonels

[147] *DD*, no. 221.
[148] *CLR 1226–40*, 37; *Patent Roll 1225–32*, 384. For offers to Geoffrey, see *CR 1227–31*,
423–4; *Patent Roll 1225–32*, 392.
[149] *Patent Roll 1225–32*, 387; *Layettes*, ii, no. 3049. See Chenard, *L'Administration d'Alphonse
de Poitiers*, 200.

and a trebuchet, he took the castle after a ten-day siege (21–31 July), his only military activity in the campaign.[150] He then headed south again, reaching Bordeaux on 5 August. Henry was at last in the great capital of Gascony. The Gascons had long cried out for his presence. Would he now make Bordeaux his base and tour the duchy, reasserting his authority? The answer was no. Henry stayed in Bordeaux for just five days (5–9 August). He then set off back to Brittany, at the same time arranging a short truce with King Louis and Hugh de Lusignan. 'The reason we will tell you when we next see you,' Henry told his supporters, somewhat shamefacedly. The reason was to allow him a safe exit from the Saintonge and Poitou.[151]

Henry had not merely decided to return to Brittany. He had also decided, doubtless with Hubert's counsel and consent, to return home altogether. Henry announced the decision on 6 September by which time he was back at Luçon. Ten days later, now at Nantes, Henry explained himself. He was acting on the counsel of his earls and barons and Duke Peter. The reason was an illness. Although he had now recovered, he could not 'spend this coming winter safely in parts overseas'. Henry wanted his home comforts. At the end of the month, Henry gave another reason, one more designed to encourage his Poitevin supporters. He was departing 'especially so that we can make provision against a future time both in men and money, so that we may be able to return . . . to resist our enemies more strongly'.[152]

There was something in both these explanations. Illness had indeed ravaged Henry's army. The earl of Gloucester, Nigel de Mowbray, Maurice de Gant, Geoffrey de Say, Thomas Basset and William de Coleville of Bytham all died during the expedition. Richard of Cornwall and several others fell ill. Henry had also run out of money. 'If we had an abundance of money instead of suffering from its lack', we could succeed in everything, he told the regents in a letter of 18 July. Two days later Ralph fitzNicholas was more forthright. The king was 'astonished' that since his departure he had received no money at all: 'if he had an abundance of money, he would recover the greatest part of his land'. As it was, not until early September did fresh supplies arrive from England, and then only to the tune of £6,000.[153]

At least Henry did not depart leaving his allies entirely in the lurch. Out of the money arriving from England, he ordered around £3,000 to be paid out to his 'Poitevin barons'. Failing any success in negotiating a truce, he promised Duke Peter 6,000 marks and a force of 400 knights and 100 horse

---

[150] *CR 1227–31*, 422; *Patent Roll 1225–32*, 388; Wendover, iii, 198. The castle was on the hill above the town. The site, with views over the estuary, is now occupied by a Renaissance chateau converted into a luxury hotel.

[151] *CR 1227–31*, 446; *Patent Roll 1225–32*, 394.

[152] *Patent Roll 1225–32*, 395–7; *CR 1227–31*, 450–1.

[153] *DD*, nos. 224–5; *Patent Roll 1225–32*, 397–8.

sergeants, although only 100 knights were immediately available.[154] Henry also persuaded William Marshal to stay as 'captain' of the king's forces, 'making war in our place'. In return, the Marshal was to hold in hereditary right the royal demense manor of Awre in Gloucestershire. The earl of Chester, with St James de Beuvron to protect, also remained, and was promised 1,000 marks.[155]

After being detained by adverse winds, Henry finally set sail from St Pol de Léon on 26 October, reaching Portsmouth on the following day. In his absence, William Marshal and Earl Ranulf led raids into Anjou and Normandy, destroying both the castles of Châteauneuf-sur-Sarthe, north of Angers, and that of Pontorson, close to St James de Beuvron just over the Norman border. 'So,' as Matthew Paris commented, 'more seemed to be done with the king absent than present'.[156]

THE FAILURE OF THE 1230 CAMPAIGN

Henry had one solid achievement to show from the 1230 campaign. He had managed to wrest the isle of Oléron from Hugh de Lusignan and place it under his seneschal of Gascony, Hugh de Trubleville.[157] Given its strategic situation, the isle would facilitate a blockade of La Rochelle in any future campaign.[158] For the rest, however, the 1230 expedition was rightly judged an abject failure. Henry had crossed to Poitou with a large army, commented the Margam annalist, 'where he lost many of his men, expended a great deal of money, and recovered little or nothing of his lands'.[159] Henry himself later wrote feelingly of how he had suffered 'grievous harm to our body and irreparable loss of our magnates and men'.[160] But the loss had been due not to fighting but to illness, or, in the case of Hubert's nephew Raymond de Burgh, accident. He was drowned trying to ford the Loire on horseback. In melancholy fashion the bodies came back for burial in England: Raymond and Geoffrey de Say to Hubert's foundation the Maison Dieu in Dover; Maurice de Gant to Bristol, where his body was divided between the priory of St Augustine's and the Dominican friars; and Gilbert de Clare, earl of Gloucester, to Tewkesbury, where he was patron of the monastery.[161]

Henry left Brittany uttering brave words about a return with fresh forces. There was every reason for that given a French descent on the duchy was generally expected. In March 1231, Henry tried to muster forces

[154] CR 1227–31, 430–2; Patent Roll 1225–32, 399–400, 403.
[155] Patent Roll 1225–32, 400–1, 404; CChR 1226–57, 174.
[156] Wendover, iii, 200; Paris, HA, ii, 329.
[157] Patent Roll 1225–32, 387–8, 490.
[158] See below, 248.
[159] Margam, 38.
[160] CR 1234–7, 169.
[161] Tewkesbury, 76; Winchester, 85; Dunstable, 125; Wendover, iii, 199.

to go out and help Duke Peter, later expressing surprise and astonishment at the poor turnout. But he made no move to go himself. When the French invasion came in June 1231, it was Duke Peter and Ranulf of Chester who led the resistance, resistance which resulted in a three-year truce being concluded on 4 July.[162] So at least for the next three years Peter continued to hold Brittany from the king, and the Poitevin barons remained in Henry's pay and allegiance. The failure of the 1230 expedition, nonetheless, marked a sea change in Henry's approach to his lost continental empire. Down to 1230 he had actively planned its recovery and summoned army after army to go with him overseas to bring it about. After 1230 such planning virtually ceased. It was to be more than ten years before Henry summoned an army to go with him again. This was not because he had given up hope of recovering his empire. He continued to make substantial payments to nobles in Poitou and the Saintonge. When the opportunity came in 1242, he was as enthusiastic as ever. Rather it was because there seemed no prospect of gaining the necessary allies. The year 1230 had clearly shown that Duke Peter alone was not enough. Henry had also learnt just how thoroughly unpleasant a continental campaign could be.

The course of the campaign had been governed by two critical decisions. One was to sit tight in Nantes instead of bringing Louis IX's army to battle. Without knowing the respective size of the two forces, how justified this was we cannot know. It may well be that Louis's army, riven though it was by faction, was very much bigger, as certainly were his financial resources. The English did not want another Bouvines. The other decision was to prioritize the recovery of Poitou over that of Normandy. This was understandable too, given the paucity of Henry's Norman support and the number of his potential allies in Poitou. Normandy's revenues, towns and castles made it far and away the most valuable part of the old Angevin empire, but by the same token it was by far the most difficult to recover. Already, in the proposals for a settlement in 1228, the English government had accepted that for the most part it was lost, though it was true that the events of 1204 had far from severed all the connections between England and the duchy.[163] In 1227 a burgess of Caen wrote to Henry explaining how Normandy might be recovered. In 1230 itself Henry gave licence to ships from Caen, Barfleur and Dieppe to carry on trading throughout his power. Indeed, ships from Barfleur and Dieppe helped to ferry over Henry's army.[164] But the fact was that the king of France held Normandy in a vice. Many of the royal officials established after 1204 came from the French royal demesne. That might make them unpopular as outsiders but it also meant they were fiercely loyal. For the

---

[162] *CR 1227–31*, 579–80; *Layettes*, ii, 2144.

[163] The subject is studied in Stevenson, 'England and Normandy', and in Power, 'The treaty of Paris'. More publications from Power are forthcoming.

[164] *Patent Roll 1225–32*, 323, 369–70, 413.

few nobles who did go over to Henry, retribution was swift. Thomas
de Gorges, Enguerrand de Sancto Philiberto and others lost their lands
and had to flee Normandy, taking refuge in England or the Channel
Islands.[165]

For the burgess of Caen, writing to Henry, the route to the recovery of
Normandy was easy. Henry should promise the Normans the restoration
of their lands in England and the English the restoration of their lands in
Normandy.[166] It was far from as simple as that. The kind of neat swap
made by the earl of Chester and the duke of Brittany was rarely possible.
The fact was that any reunion of kingdom and duchy would open a
Pandora's box of conflicting claims to land: far better, many must have
thought, to keep it firmly shut. Normans who had lost lands in England
knew those lands were hardly being kept warm in the king's hands all
ready to be given back. Many had been given away by John and Henry III
to ministers and magnates to reward their service and consolidate
loyalty.[167] True, in nearly all cases, tenure was only to last until Normandy
was recovered. The implication was that the Normans would then recover
their English estates. But how easy would that be to effect? The experience
of Fulk de Paynel himself was hardly encouraging. His lands in England
were held by his kinsman Hugh de Paynel and two household knights,
Nicholas de Lettres and William de Gaugy, both of whom went on the
1230 expedition. Henry felt unable to dispossess these men of their lands
and had to fob Fulk off with promises. And this was how he treated his
greatest Norman supporter! Not surprisingly in 1231 Fulk returned to the
allegiance of the king of France. The episode revealed another problem.
Henry had promised Lettres that if he did lose his Paynel estate, he would
be given compensation. Such promises were common and meant that the
dispossession of those holding lands of the Normans would be a costly
exercise for the king.[168] The French king, meanwhile, was adept at using
the lands seized from the English in Normandy to keep on side those who
counted most. Andrew de Vitré, on the face of it, should have been tempt-
able into the English camp for he had lost lands in Cornwall after 1204.
Philip Augustus, however, seeing the danger, had compensated him with

[165] Stevenson, 'England and Normandy', 231–2; *Patent Roll 1225–32*, 405; Strayer,
Administration of Normandy, 6.
[166] For discussion and more detail, see Power, 'The treaty of Paris', and for the lands of
the Normans, see Moore, 'The loss of Normandy and the invention of *Terre Normanorum*',
behind which is Power's AHRC-funded 'Lands of the Normans' project.
[167] A survey in 1237 covered about 120 properties from the lands of the Normans in
fifteen counties with an estimated value of about £3,000 a year. Most had been given away
to reward royal servants: Power, 'The treaty of Paris', 150.
[168] *Patent Roll 1225–32*, 357–8, 362, 399–400, 403; *CChR 1226–57*, 84, 132; *CPR 1258–66*,
165–6; Stevenson, 'England and Normandy', 452. For Bingham, the property granted to
Nicholas de Lettres, see Crook, 'The "lands of the Normans" in thirteenth-century
Nottinghamshire', 102–3.

lands of the earl of Chester in Normandy. In 1231, Louis IX added the honour of the Mowbrays.[169]

On the English side, many of those taking part in the expedition had little to gain from a reunion of England and Normandy. This created a virus affecting the very top of the expedition. William Marshal himself must have been perfectly content with the status quo. His father, the old regent, almost uniquely amongst the great Anglo-Norman barons, had managed to retain his Norman lands, and they were now held by William's younger brother Richard. The earl of Chester had certainly lost extensive lands across Normandy, but having obtained St James de Beuvron, through his deal with Duke Peter, he concentrated on defending that. Another baron on the expedition with nothing to gain was William Bardolph. In a very unusual and surprising way, he had recovered his father's estates at Beronville and Putot. This was surely thanks to the influence of Bardolph's stepfather, none other than Hubert de Burgh. Hubert indeed took a close interest in these Norman estates since one of his knights was a William de Putot.[170] When in 1229 Henry accused Hubert of being in the pay of the king of France, perhaps he was not so wrong.

Enthusiasm for the recovery of Norman estates was also dulled by the commensurate prospect of losing the lands of the Normans in England with which some leading nobles had been compensated for their Norman losses. Geoffrey de Say and the earls of Gloucester and Hereford were all in that position, as was William de Warenne, earl of Surrey. Perhaps the fear of losing Stamford and Grantham in Lincolnshire explains his absence from the expedition. There was also a large body of barons and knights on the campaign, headed by Hubert de Burgh himself, and including the stewards Ralph fitzNicholas and Godfrey of Crowcombe, who had no land to recover in Normandy, yet much to lose from the lands of the Normans in England.[171] If then the magnates and ministers on the expedition had limited enthusiasm for the recovery of Normandy, that was even more true of Anjou and Poitou, counties in which they had no stake at all and could hardly hope to gain one. Geoffrey of Wolford might have said that the king's delay in Nantes displeased all the world, but he added that 'the greater part of our magnates' seemed to care little about it.

[169] Andrew's sister still held land in both England and Normandy: *RLC*, i, 207, 407, 541b; Stevenson, 'England and Normandy', 484–5; Stapleton, *Magni Rotuli*, ii, xlvi; Powicke, *Loss of Normandy*, 336, 346, 356. For families profiting from land confiscated in Normandy, see Power, 'The treaty of Paris', 147–8.

[170] Stevenson, 'England and Normandy', 395, citing Stapleton, *Magni Rotuli*, ii, ccxvii; *BF*, i, 270. For Putot attesting a charter of Hubert, see Canterbury Cathedral Archives and Library, Dean and Chapter Register B, fo.404, a reference I owe to David Crouch.

[171] The list includes the earls of Cornwall and Derby, Roger de Quincy (heir to the earldom of Winchester), Peter de Brus, Philip de Aubigny, Richard de Argentan, Gilbert Basset, Drogo de Barentin, William de Cantilupe, Engelard de Cigogné, John fitzPhilip, Luke de Drumare, John de Plessis, William Talbot and Ralph de Trubleville.

The one person who had everything to gain from a victorious battle, from a Crécy, Poitiers or Agincourt, was Henry himself. Instead, in those June days in 1230, as the tide flowed up and down the Loire, with the armies only twenty miles apart, the life flowed out of the Angevin empire. Whatever the material calculations, the earls and barons of England had come with Henry on the expedition. They had not quibbled over this being service overseas. The king's household knights had come too. These men were brought up to bear arms. They were frustrated by Henry's repeated ban on tournaments in England. Their heroes were men like the old William Marshal who had won fame through deeds of derring-do. It was up to Henry to exploit these feelings and galvanize his army into action. Even if there was no full-scale battle, he could surely lead into French territory the ravaging expeditions so central to the exercise of war. Yet Henry did none of these things. Neither the letters home nor the writings of the chroniclers suggest any kind of personal military effort.

Writing shortly before the launch of the expedition in 1230, a poet in the circle of Savary de Mauléon wrote optimistically about its potential results. The great Poitevin nobles would join the king, Poitiers itself would be his:

> Now that the king is young and vigorous he should come and make war on the king of France, engage in assaults and combats, equip his troops well, give great blows and strike with his hands. For a young king who breaks his lance well, who is brave, gallant, courageous, wise and generous, charming and intrepid, of him it is said that a land is well placed in his hands.

Alas, the poet already suspected Henry was not like that:

> Good sauce, clear wine, white bread, chambers and tapestries, and the like, to drink, to consult with quibblers, to ride like a dean on docile mounts, the king loves better all that than to put on a coat of mail. Hauberks and haberjons, helms, cuirasses, pourpoints, and hoquetons, would be far better for him now while he has neither thinning hair nor a grey beard. Ah king of England do not be either cowardly or indolent, it is not thus that you will take La Rochelle. It is necessary to have archers, and Brabançon mercenaries, knights and master engineers, who will give you a better counsel than lawyers.[172]

The poet's fears could not have been more justified.

---

[172] Jeanroy, 'Un sirventès politique de 1230', 277–8.

HENRY AND HUBERT BACK IN ENGLAND, 1230–1

Henry landed at Portsmouth on 27 October and four days later was received into Winchester Cathedral by the convent, Archbishop Richard and his suffragans. One thing Henry did not do on his return was to blame Hubert de Burgh. Instead, his anger turned on one of Hubert's knights, who had managed to offend Margaret, countess of Kent and Hubert's wife. The whole episode suggests the pressure Hubert was under from the pride and pretensions of his royally born spouse. Before departure for Brittany, Henry had allowed the countess to stay as long as she liked in any royal castle she wished to enter. The castellans were to give her due honour, assistance in such affairs of the king as she explained, and as much wine as she wished.[173] Nonetheless, Bertram de Criel, left behind as Hubert's deputy, refused to allow Margaret entry into Dover castle. Responding doubtless to her indignant complaints, Henry on his return reacted with fury. He ordered Criel to leave the kingdom and took possession of his lands. Even after the king calmed down, Criel was still forbidden to enter his sight. Henry did at least justify the seizures on the grounds that Criel held his lands at royal pleasure. In other words he could be lawfully dispossessed. In fact, at least some of the property was held by Henry's gift in hereditary right, so the king, knowingly or not, was committing an unlawful disseisin in breach of Magna Carta. Characteristically Hubert soon sought to restore Criel to his lands, admitting he had been disseised 'by will of the king'. But the following year Criel still threw in his lot with Hubert's enemies.[174]

While Criel was punished, Hubert was rewarded. The deaths on the expedition had created a series of lucrative wardships and it was Hubert who got them.[175] Most important of all was the wardship of the lands of Gilbert de Clare, together with the right to marry off the heir, Gilbert's son Richard, born in 1222. So Hubert now controlled Glamorgan and the earldoms of Gloucester and Hertford. Hubert did at least offer money for these concessions, some of it given cash down, some of it set against his loans to the king on the Breton expedition – loans which reflected the plenitude of Hubert's resources and the paucity of the king's. But Hubert was still getting all this very much on the cheap. The 7,000 marks he offered for the Clare wardship could be recouped from its revenues in two or three years. It would be thirteen years before Richard de Clare came of age. Hubert justified receiving the wardship on the grounds of an agreement made with the late earl and already accepted by the king, an agreement under which Richard de Clare was to marry Hubert's only child by Countess Margaret. (She was named Margaret after her mother

[173] *Patent Rolls 1225–32*, 341.

[174] *CFR 1230–1*, nos. 16, 40; *CR 1227–31*, 475–6; *CChR 1226–57*, 117; *CR 1231–4*, 29. For the whole episode, see Annesley, 'The countess and the constable'.

[175] *CFR 1230–1*, nos. 18–22; *CR 1227–31*, 441. See also Carpenter, 'Hubert de Burgh, Matilda de Mowbray'.

but was universally known as Meggotta.) Eventually, then, assuming Hubert had no more children, Richard would combine Glamorgan with Montgomery, the Three Castles, and Cardigan and Carmarthen. Was Henry wise to accept the prospect of this vast baronial fiefdom in Wales? Surely not.

If Henry was happy with these new concessions to Hubert, others were not. The charter granting him the Clare wardship was attested simply by Hubert's episcopal allies and household officials.[176] In February 1231, William Marshal arrived back in England from Brittany. Given that Gilbert de Clare had been married to his sister, and that Richard de Clare was thus his nephew, given that Glamorgan marched with his lordships in south-east Wales, he might have expected the Clare wardship for himself. Equally disaffected was the Marshal's brother-in-law and the king's brother Richard of Cornwall, still without an unambiguous hereditary title to his lands.[177] The two men reached an agreement and decided to pay Henry back.

On 30 March, at Fawley, a manor of William Marshal high up in the Chilterns a few miles from Marlow, Richard married Isabella, Gilbert de Clare's widow and William's sister, a woman of great beauty or so it was said. Henry was not merely absent (he was sixty miles away at Marlborough). He had not even been consulted. He was naturally enraged at both the snub and the violation of his rights. Even Magna Carta had accepted that widows of tenants-in-chief needed the king's consent for any remarriage. But any thoughts of punishment were soon forgotten. On 6 April, so a week after the wedding, William Marshal died. He had honoured his father's memory by commissioning the verse life which is such a key source for the politics and culture of the age. He had given much to the king. At the battle of Lincoln in 1217 he had led the decisive charge. In 1223 his alliance with Hubert de Burgh had underpinned the king's recovery of his castles and sheriffdoms. In 1224, as justiciar in Ireland, he put down the revolt of Hugh de Lacy. His marriage with Eleanor, Henry's youngest sister in the same year, made him family. If relations were sometimes uneasy thereafter that was largely the result of de Burgh ambitions in Ireland. The Marshal had come on the 1230 expedition and had acted as captain of the king's forces after Henry's departure. Now his death, as a royal letter put it, was 'vehemently lamented' by the king. On 15 April, Henry attended the funeral at the Temple Church in London, where the Marshal was laid to rest beside his father. Later in the year Henry decided he would be buried at the Temple Church himself. The death of the Marshal led not to revenge but reconciliation. Richard was immediately forgiven and on 11 April given the Briouze wardship previously in the Marshal's hands.[178]

---

[176] *CChR 1226–57*, 126; *RCWL*, i, 98.

[177] *CChR 1226–57*, 129.

[178] Tewkesbury, 178; Wykes, 72; Paris, iii, 201; *CChR 1226–57*, 135; *Patent Roll 1225–32*, 428, 435. The nature of the Briouze wardship is explained in what follows.

THE PAINSCASTLE CAMPAIGN, 1231

'England lamented the death of that knight; Wales rejoiced, fearing his wars and menace when alive,' declared the Waverley abbey annals on the Marshal's death.[179] With the menace removed, Llywelyn saw his chance. The result was Hubert and Henry's third and last campaign in Wales.

The Marshal's death came on top of a series of events that destabilized Wales and created Llywelyn's opportunity. Here Llywelyn had played his own part by bringing about the destruction of the great Briouze fiefdom centred on the castles and lordships of Radnor, Builth, Hay, Huntington, Brecon and Abergavenny. As the price for his release from captivity after his capture in 1228, William de Briouze had agreed that his daughter Isabella should marry Dafydd, Llywelyn's heir, with Builth as her marriage portion, that vital centre at the southern end of the middle march where the deep valleys of the Wye and Irfon meet. More was to follow. During his time as Llywelyn's captive Briouze had started a 'liaison dangereuse' (very dangerous as it turned out) with Joan, Llywelyn's wife. Invited to the Easter festivities in 1230, the feckless couple had renewed their intrigue and been surprised in Llywelyn's chamber. On 2 May, William de Briouze, as a letter informed the regents in England, was 'hanged on a certain tree in full daylight before more than 800 men', many drawn from those the Briouzes had injured.[180] Llywelyn was doing far more than simply punishing the insult to his person. He was also ending the oppression of the Briouzes once and for all, for William had no male heir and his inheritance would be divided between his four daughters. Out in Brittany there was little Henry could do. He entrusted the wardship of the Briouze estates, with the marriage of the daughters, free of charge, to William Marshal.[181] The Marshal had certainly the power to resist any further advances from Llywelyn, but the situation was very different once the wardship passed, on his demise, to Richard of Cornwall, a man with no previous stake in Wales.

If this was not bad enough, even before the Marshal's passing the death of Gilbert de Clare had created instability in Glamorgan where his heavy hand had antagonized the native rulers. Doubtless Hubert, in making his case for the wardship, argued that only he could control the situation, established as he was in Cardigan and Carmarthen, as well as the Three Castles and Montgomery. But how far that was true remained to be seen. And then there was a final element in the mix, a dispute over the Marshal succession.

William Marshal's heir was his next eldest brother, Richard Marshal. Henry and Hubert knew Richard well. He held lands in England at Long

---

[179] Waverley, 309. This comment is made in two lines of verse.

[180] *RL*, i, 366–7.

[181] *Patent Roll 1225–32*, 377. The marriage between Isabella and Dafydd had not taken place by 1230 but subsequently went ahead.

Crendon and elsewhere. By marriage he was lord of Dinan in Brittany, where Henry had stayed during the 1230 campaign. But Richard also held the Marshal lordships of Longueville and Orbec in Normandy from the king of France and had been active in French affairs. In 1230 he had seemed to play a double game, making Henry and Hubert suspect his loyalty. William Marshal, foreseeing difficulty, had secured a promise that, if he died overseas in Henry's service, Richard's succession would not be blocked 'because of his stay in the land and power of the king of France'. Henry and Hubert now accepted that Richard was the rightful heir and denied 'sinister rumours' that they were trying to disinherit him. But, not unreasonably, they wished to know whether he would 'leave the allegiance of the king of France, the king's greatest enemy'. Meanwhile, they sought to take the Marshal lands in England, Wales and Ireland into the king's hands. They also ordered Richard's arrest if he landed in England, the fear being he was going to enter his lands before any agreement with the king. He certainly did that in Ireland.[182] The dispute rumbled on through the summer and it was not until 8 August that Henry at last took Richard's homage and gave him possession of his lands.[183]

It was into this vacuum of power within the marcher baronies of south Wales that Llywelyn now strode with characteristic force and decision. On 25 April 1231, Henry announced his intention of spending Whitsun at Gloucester, probably to pressurize the Marshal bailiffs into surrendering their Welsh custodies. Two days later, in urgent tones, he informed various marcher barons that he was sending his brother, Richard, to give them protection and was following himself as quickly as possible. He had probably heard of Llywelyn's attack on the Briouze lordships of Radnor and Huntington.[184] On the way at Oxford, Henry refounded the hospital of St John the Baptist by giving it the garden of the Jews outside the eastgate as its new site, a conspicuous act of piety commended by Matthew Paris, and doubtless designed to win God's favour for the forthcoming campaign.[185] Henry reached Gloucester on 8 May and then moved on to Hereford, freeing as he did so Richard of Bletchingdon from attending local courts in person: it was 'cruel and inhuman' to make him do so when he was blind.

These acts of piety seemed to be rewarded. Negotiations began with Llywelyn and the Marshal castles of Chepstow and Caerleon (though not those further west) were surrendered into the king's hands. At the end of May, with a sigh of relief, Henry placed his tents in Hereford castle and set off back to Westminster, leaving Hubert de Burgh behind to deal with the situation. The fall guy was Richard of Cornwall. In a resounding vote

---

[182] *CR 1227–31*, 582; *Patent Roll 1225–32*, 435–6; Smith, 'Irish politics', 18. For Richard's position, see Power, 'The French interests of the Marshal earls', 213–22.

[183] See below, 104.

[184] *CR 1231–4*, 497, 503, 585–6; Wendover, iii, 201–2.

[185] *CJB*, iii, vi, xiv–xvi; *CR 1227–31*, 500; Paris, iii, 262–3.

of no-confidence he was removed from the Briouze custodies and replaced by Hubert himself. The tenants expelled by Llywelyn, Henry explained, could now return to their lands 'since beyond our royal protection' the justiciar 'will vigorously maintain you under his protection', a remarkable acknowledgement of the duality of power.[186] Henry further punished his brother, doubtless after angry words had passed between them, by depriving him of the castle and honour of Wallingford.[187]

If Llywelyn needed further encouragement, this disarray in the royal camp was it. In June he struck. With the native rulers of south Wales recognizing his authority and swelling his armies, he burnt Radnor and Hay in the Wye valley and then Brecon and Caerleon in the valley of the Usk. He took the Clare castle at Neath and the Marshal castle at Kidwelly. His forces then went on to burn the town of Cardigan and, triumph of triumph, force Hubert de Burgh's garrison in the castle to surrender. The whole campaign was a stunning demonstration of Llywelyn's power.

Henry's reaction was stuttering to say the least, partly because he was separated from the justiciar. He summoned the bishops to convene in London and then, to make it easier for Hubert to attend, switched the venue to Oxford. There, on 13 July, Llywelyn was excommunicated, not with any great effect on his activities. The Oxford assembly meant Henry could not immediately join the military forces summoned to Gloucester and Hereford. Instead, he sent (on 6 July) an apologetic letter explaining his absence, 'although we greatly desire to hasten to your area and will hasten when we are able'. Meanwhile, one of the king's sergeants was sent to inform the troops by word of mouth about the king's 'situation and health'. On the same day Henry made arrangements for the burial of his body in the Temple Church. A sensible precaution perhaps, but one hardly suggesting any great confidence in the coming campaign.[188]

In the event, English chroniclers acknowledged that a 'large' army was assembled, and indeed the cavalry forces seem to have numbered at least 600.[189] The army did not, however, wreak vengeance on Llywelyn. It did not seek to retake Builth and Cardigan. It did not seek to invade Gwynedd. Instead, it sat down and built another castle. The tactics, doubtless reflecting Hubert's judgement and Henry's mood, were thus the same as in 1223 and 1228. The chosen site was at Painscastle in the uplands of Elfael. It was usually called 'Castle Matilda' after the famous defence of the old castle in the 1190s by Matilda de Briouze. At Painscastle, therefore, Henry and his army remained from the end of July until 20 September

[186] *Patent Roll 1225–32*, 434.

[187] *Patent Roll 1225–32*, 434; *CR 1227–31*, 510; *CFR 1230–1*, no. 202.

[188] *CR 1227–31*, 590, 592, 594–5; *CChR 1226–57*, 135; Wendover, iii, 202. Henry's relationship with the Temple Church is discussed below, 331–2.

[189] Wendover, iii, 202; Tewkesbury, 79; Walker, 'Hubert de Burgh in Wales', 488; TNA C 72/2 (a scutage roll for the campaign).

while ditchers, carpenters and masons laboured over their work. The site was well chosen. Painscastle is only five miles from Hay and sits astride the ancient road running down from Radnor, past Huntington and on to Builth. A great castle there might well obstruct the kind of attack that Llywelyn had just mounted. And great castle it was with a stone tower on top of a motte, two lines of concentric earthworks bearing stone walls, and the whole defended by deeply dug dry moats. Roger of Wendover acknowledged that the castle, built 'elegantly' at great cost with stone and cement, and well garrisoned, restrained the incursions of the Welsh. Instead of 'Hubert's folly' the castle was known as 'Maugre Llywelyn' ('In spite of Llywelyn').[190]

The trouble was Llywelyn had been impeded but not repressed. On his way back to London at the end of September, Henry acknowledged that the Welsh prince was still 'persecuting us and devastating our land'. Henry was already thinking of another campaign in the following summer, this one indeed to attack Gwynedd itself. The idea, however, was soon abandoned. At the end of November, Henry agreed to a one-year truce. The verdict of the Dunstable annalist on the events of 1231 was withering: 'while the king of England repaired Castle Matilda, Llywelyn in the march of Wales destroyed ten castles'.[191] Painscastle itself, for all the expenditure, never became a royal castle and in 1233 was given to the marcher lord Ralph de Tony with whose descendants it remained.[192]

POLITICS AT PAINSCASTLE

In the fields around the rising castle in these summer days the tents of Henry and Hubert were surrounded by those of the great barons. The earls of Surrey, Derby, Aumale and Hereford were all there as was John de Lacy. They were to be joined by the men who next year were to ruin Hubert and plunge England into a civil war. They were joined too by the man who more than thirty years later was to capture Henry in battle and rule England in his name.

Having concluded the truce with the king of France back in June, Ranulf, earl of Chester, had returned to England. By 10 August he was at Painscastle. He brought with him Simon de Montfort. Back in 1230, Henry had agreed that Montfort could have Ranulf's half of the honour of Leicester, provided Ranulf agreed to the cession. Accordingly, Montfort had sought Ranulf out at St James de Beuvron and pleaded his case. Ranulf was in his sixties and his heirs, all well provided for, were his sisters. He was bowled over by Montfort's youthful spirits and martial ardour, by his eloquence and intelligence, and by his conviction that the Leicester

[190] Wendover, iii, 203; Worcester, 422; St Werburgh, 56.
[191] *CR 1227–31*, 600; *Patent Roll 1225–32*, 453; Dunstable, 127.
[192] *CR 1231–4*, 268–9; Paris, iii, 254.

lands were indeed his right. He agreed to make the cession at once, instead of merely arranging for Montfort to inherit after his death. Thus it was at Painscastle, on 13 August, that Henry took Montfort's homage 'for the lands held by his father Simon de Montfort once earl of Leicester of the honour of Leicester which belong to Simon by hereditary right'.[193] Montfort was not yet recognized as earl but his dramatic and disruptive career in England had begun.

That was for the future. More important in the short term was something else occurring at Painscastle. On 8 August, Henry at last took the homage of Richard Marshal as the heir of his brother. What was agreed about the Norman estates is not known, but Richard Marshal seems to have held on to them.[194] He was to play a central part in the politics of the next two years, ultimately waging war against the king. At Painscastle, Henry, rarely angry for long, also reached a settlement with Richard of Cornwall. Already on 5 July he had presented his brother with two magnificent goshawks as a peace offering. Now, on 10 August, Richard's landed position was at last made permanent. He was granted in hereditary right the county of Cornwall and the honour of Wallingford. He was also promised exchanges if ever deprived of the honour of Eye, the lands of Robert de Dreux (which included Beckley in Oxfordshire) and the dower lands of his mother Isabella. Outside Cornwall, Wallingford, Beckley and Berkhamsted (from his mother's dower) were to become Richard's principal residences. In contrast to so many charters making important gifts to Hubert, the charters for Richard were attested by five earls and John de Lacy.[195]

The equable atmosphere achieved by these settlements, if such it was, did not last for long and Earl Ranulf departed in anger for Chester. Hubert, however, had been dealing with these kinds of alarms and excursions for years. With Stephen of Seagrave (a conciliatory choice) sent after him, Ranulf was back at Painscastle before the king's departure.[196] The real threat to Hubert came from another quarter. Indeed, he may well have encouraged the settlements with Richard Marshal and Richard of Cornwall to gain allies in the coming struggle. Peter des Roches, bishop of Winchester, had at last returned from his crusade. On 1 August, the day Henry and Hubert were arriving at Painscastle, he was received into his cathedral in a solemn procession. His offering was a precious relic, the foot of Saint Philip.[197] Peter then set off to meet the king at Painscastle. He was there by

---

[193] Bémont, *Simon de Montfort*, 333; *CR 1227–31*, 543–4; Maddicott, *Simon de Montfort*, 9. On the same day Ranulf received a generous gift of timber from the king.

[194] *CR 1227–31*, 541; Power, 'The French interests of the Marshal earls', 221–2.

[195] *CR 1227–31*, 523; *CChR 1226–57*, 139; *RCWL*, i, 106. He was also restored to the Briouze wardships.

[196] St Werburgh, 56–9; Dunstable, 127; *RCWL*, i, 107. For suggestions as to the reasons for the quarrel, see Eales, 'Henry III and the end of the Norman earldom of Chester', 107–8; Vincent, 'Simon de Montfort's first quarrel', 171.

[197] Winchester, 86; Wendover, iii, 204.

10 August when he headed the witnesses to the charters in favour of Richard of Cornwall. Also amongst the witnesses, evidently having come with Peter, was Peter de Maulay, the very man whom Hubert had accused of treason in 1221 and later threatened with imprisonment in a dungeon so dark he would neither see his hands nor feet.[198] Hubert must have dreaded the bishop's return. He was right to do so. Bishop Peter was determined to fulfil his oath sworn in 1223, namely, to eject the justiciar from power. Hubert would soon be fighting for his position, indeed for his life.

[198] See above, 23, 72.

Chapter 3

THE REGIME OF PETER DES ROCHES
1232–1234

As Henry journeyed back from Painscastle to Windsor and Westminster, he was about to enter the most traumatic political period of his life, barring the later years of reform, rebellion and civil war. Henry would be pulled one way and another by the struggle for power between Hubert de Burgh and Peter des Roches. With de Burgh gone, he would be driven by Bishop Peter into a series of lawless acts and an unsuccessful war against Richard Marshal. In the end he would be reined in by a great council and forced to admit his faults. The principles of Magna Carta would be vindicated and the difficulty of returning to anything like the rule of King John exposed.

After the discomfort and disappointment of the Painscastle campaign, there was at once something to lift Henry's spirits, the prospect of marriage.[1] He was now twenty-four. His brother Richard had married Isabella, William Marshal's sister, earlier in the year. His eldest sister was married to King Alexander and so queen of Scotland. Yet Henry had seen proposal after proposal for his own marriage come to nothing. His piety may well have discouraged a resort to mistresses. At least there is no evidence he fathered any bastards, unlike King John. The purely 'mechanical' reasons for marriage, as Dr Johnson termed them, were strong. Henry's idea now was that he should marry Margaret, the third and youngest sister of King Alexander of Scotland.[2] In mid-October, at Westminster, he ordered a new set of silver dishes and sauce boats to be made and sent to him at York by 9 November. Apparently he was planning to entertain King Alexander with a feast there and celebrate his forthcoming marriage.[3]

---

[1] For a comprehensive and compelling account of the events between 1232 and 1234, covering some 200 pages, see chs. 8–13 of Nicholas Vincent's *Peter des Roches*. There are points of detail and emphasis where our accounts differ, but I leave those interested to discover them for themselves.

[2] Wendover, iii, 206, is the main source here. She was called Margaret despite that also being the name of her eldest sister married to Hubert de Burgh.

[3] *CR 1227–31*, 569–70; Oram, *Alexander II*, 115–16. *ASR*, 40–1, shows there had been an agreement about the marriage.

Henry's scheme was soon in disarray. Indeed, its timing was singularly inept. At the very moment he was issuing his orders about York, a great council was opening at Westminster. The assembled magnates protested against the Scottish marriage; it was 'unfitting' that the king should marry the youngest sister of King Alexander when Hubert de Burgh was married to the eldest. Peter, duke of Brittany, seconded the protests. He had come to England for his money and returned home with 5,000 marks.[4] He pointed out that Henry was still betrothed to his daughter Yolande. True, Yolande remained in French custody but that might change. Faced with this barrage of opposition Henry abandoned his Scottish plans and reaffirmed his agreement to marry Yolande, with the duke promising to make her available by Michaelmas 1232.[5]

Henry, therefore, cancelled his visit to York to seek a bride. Instead, he went to Marlborough to see a sister. This was Isabella, she who had been seasick during the voyage to Brittany. The result of their meeting was an elaborate order for new clothes. Henry was to have robes of scarlet and black burnet lined with red deer skin, plus a new bed; Isabella robes in blue of Ypres and green of Ghent lined with minever. In a remarkable and revealing slip, the chancery clerk headed this order 'robes for the king and Isabella his wife'.[6]

The collapse of the Scottish marriage was a setback for Hubert de Burgh. He had doubtless promoted the scheme for the very reason the magnates opposed it. If the marriage undermined the expensive Breton alliance, perhaps so much the better. Hubert, however, with his usual agility, quickly switched attention from his rejected policies to his respected piety. During the great council Henry thus became the patron of the religious house founded at Creake in Norfolk by Hubert's cousin, a foundation very close to Hubert's heart. At the same time he confirmed all Hubert's gifts to the Maison Dieu at Dover, the hospital Hubert had established after his great victory in the battle off Sandwich. The relevant charters were witnessed by seven bishops (including Peter des Roches), the duke of Brittany, the earls of Cornwall and Chester and Simon de Montfort. Then in December, Henry, Hubert and a few courtiers travelled to Dover itself for the dedication service of the hospital.[7] Henry's love for his justiciar seemed secure. But the assault on Hubert was about to begin. The political situation resembled a stream where on the surface the waters move slowly, are even stagnant, but beneath they are running fast and will soon sweep all away.

---

[4] This is according to Wendover, iii, 206. The 'liberate' rolls are missing between October 1230 and October 1232.

[5] *CR 1231–4*, 151.

[6] *CR 1227–31*, 507; *CR 1231–4*, 4.

[7] *Monasticon*, vi, 688; *CChR 1226–57*, 141–2; *RCWL*, i, 108; *Patent Roll 1225–32*, 455; Vincent, 'Simon de Montfort's first quarrel', 170–1.

HUBERT DE BURGH'S WEAKNESS, BISHOP PETER'S ATTACK

Bishop Peter had seen the king at Painscastle in August and been present at the great council held at Westminster in October. He had not, however, been in regular attendance at court. The Christmas festivities of 1231 changed all that. They were staged by Bishop Peter at Winchester and his nearby manor of Marden. The opulence contrasted with the king's own straitened circumstances. 'With wonderful generosity', recorded the Dunstable annalist (whose prior was probably present), 'he dispensed so much food, clothes, and gifts of gold, silver and horses, that the solemnity would have done justice to a coronation.' The following January, Peter was almost constantly at court, receiving free of charge from the king (what a contrast to 1227) a munificent grant of local government privileges for his church.[8] Henry was enthralled. The discredited and disgruntled tutor of the minority was now replaced by a statesman of international renown. In his late fifties (much the same age as Hubert), the bishop was still vigorous in mind and body. Indeed he still hunted with enthusiasm.[9] And what tales he had to tell of his exploits on crusade! The Dunstable annalist narrated them as Peter himself probably recounted them to Henry. He had mediated between pope and emperor and won the favour of both; in the Holy Land he had rebuilt the city of Ascalon and the castle of Joppa; he had refounded the house dedicated to Thomas Becket in Acre. On his way back to England, he had arranged the truce between Henry and the king of France.[10] Once home, with Henry's help, he immediately set about founding a religious house at Titchfield in Hampshire.[11]

Buoyed up by his remarkable achievements, Peter now looked to a future in which he would at last remove Hubert de Burgh from power. His chances of doing that were far greater than in 1223. In the words of Sir Maurice Powicke, Hubert had become 'isolated in his greatness'.[12] Although light-years away from the oppressions of King John, his government had become unpopular in the localities. The great tax of 1225 had been followed by a succession of scutages, by the fines for the renewal of charters, by burdensome judicial and forest eyres, by two tallages imposed on the Jews (which meant pressure on their Christian debtors), and by all the controversy over the bounds of the royal forest. 'The yoke of servitude and especially that of the forest was much worse than ever before,' commented the Waverley annalist, not entirely fairly.[13] In 1223, Hubert had been supported by his alliance with the earls of Salisbury and Pembroke, but Salisbury was now dead and in place of William Marshal

---

[8] *CChR 1226–57*, 145–6.

[9] *Patent Roll 1225–32*, 478.

[10] Dunstable, 126–7. For Peter's crusade, see Vincent, *Peter des Roches*, ch. 7.

[11] *CFR 1231–2*, no. 338; Vincent, *EEA Winchester*, 58–60.

[12] Powicke, *The Thirteenth Century*, 47.

[13] Waverley, 311.

there was his younger brother Richard Marshal, whose succession to the family's great inheritance Hubert had obstructed. Hubert's relations with the old earl of Chester and the young Richard of Cornwall remained edgy as well. He had also offended another young noble, namely Simon de Montfort, by refusing to return to him lands given to Creake abbey from the honour of Leicester.[14] Having outlined Hubert's material gains, the Dunstable annalist observed how 'indignant' these made 'the princes of the kingdom'. He 'lacked nothing of royal power save only the dignity of the royal diadem', added the Waverley annalist.[15] Hubert, of course, was a master at defusing opposition with well-targeted concessions, usually at the king's expense. In the event, it was not the magnates who would bring him down. Yet they would accept his fall readily enough. In the great struggle that was to come not one magnate stood by him.

Another contrast with earlier years was that Hubert had nothing like his old alliance with Archbishop Langton. Aware that the prelates were his greatest supporters, he always treated the church with respect. In 1230–1, when Langton's successor, Archbishop Richard Grant, objected to the scutage levied on the church for the Poitevin expedition, Hubert persuaded Henry to back down and accept a freely given aid in its place.[16] Around the Easter of 1231 the archbishop had, nonetheless, set off for Rome to complain about the justiciar. The immediate bone of contention was Tonbridge castle. During the minority of Richard de Clare did it belong to the archbishop or to Hubert as Clare's custodian? But the archbishop also complained about bishops acting as royal ministers and demanded an investigation into Hubert's marriage on the grounds that Margaret of Scotland was related to his second wife, the countess of Gloucester. He thus sought to weaken Hubert's government, where bishops were prominent, and damage Hubert personally, since only his marriage to Margaret had made him earl-worthy. In the event, Archbishop Richard died in August 1231 before he could return to England. For a moment the clouds seemed to clear. In September the Canterbury monks elected none other than Hubert's old friend and ally Chancellor Neville, asking the pope to translate him from Chichester. Pope Gregory would have none of it. After two great scholar bishops in Langton and Grant, Neville's lack of learning made him quite unsuitable. The monks were told to hold another election. In the event it was not until 1234 that a new archbishop was in place (Edmund of Abingdon). Hubert's fortunes might have been very different had there been a sympathetic archbishop of Canterbury during the coming crisis.

Bishop Peter doubtless marked the decay in the outworks of Hubert's power. He also sought to undermine its very centre, namely the control

---

[14] Vincent, 'Simon de Montfort's first quarrel', 170–2.

[15] Dunstable, 103; Waverley, 311.

[16] *CFR 1231–2*, nos. 66–7, 137; Wendover, iii, 200; Tewkesbury, 77; *CR 1227–31*, 475; *Patent Roll 1225–32*, 429; Mitchell, *Studies in Taxation*, 192.

over the king. Henry in 1231 must have seemed a very different individual from the one Peter had last seen in 1227. His interests were expanding, his emotions less restrained, his desires more pronounced. On 4 December 1231, on his way to Dover, Henry issued detailed orders for images of St Stephen and St John the Baptist to be painted on panels behind their respective altars in the palace of Westminster. The paintings were to be ready by his return to London.[17] This is the first surviving writ in which Henry reveals his interest in religious imagery and his impatience to see his commissions completed. It stands at the head of a long line of such orders. Three days later, Henry wanted made, again by his return to London, a 'good cope of good red samite, great and well decorated with good orphreys (strips of elaborate embroidery)'; an early example of the magnificent vestments in which Henry sought so often to clothe those celebrating divine service. Around this time the king's desire to light up his services with a multiplicity of candles also becomes apparent. At Worcester for Christmas in 1232, judging existing arrangements inadequate, he ordered beams with spikes a foot apart for candles to be placed across the bishop's chapel and around its altar.[18]

Another new departure was Henry's foundation of religious institutions. In 1231 he had assumed the patronage of the hospital of St John the Baptist in Oxford. In October he became the patron of Creake. In January 1232 he made a foundation all his own, one for which he was widely commended. With enthusiastic (if unfulfilled) promises of an annual endowment worth 700 marks, he established in New Street (now Chancery Lane) off the Strand in London the 'Domus Conversorum', a house for Jews converted to Christianity. His involvement in the conversion of the Jews was to become one of the hallmarks of his piety.[19]

The paintings of Stephen and John ordered for the chapels at Westminster were part of Henry's growing concern for the expansion and embellishment of his homes. At Clarendon in 1231/2 he ordered the painting of the great chamber and the glassing of its windows, while in the hall he replaced the old-fashioned Romanesque windows with Gothic ones with gabled heads. At Woodstock there was a new porch and a staircase leading up to the king's great chamber as well as two new images for the chapel.[20] The king's impatience to see his projects completed and his will obeyed had its counterpoint in other areas. In 1231 his letters expressed irritation at having to repeat orders and declared that 'it was improper for those things done in the king's presence and by his authority' to be

---

[17] *CR 1231–4*, 9–10.

[18] *CR 1231–4*, 10; *CLR 1226–40*, 191.

[19] See below, 298–307.

[20] *CR 1231–4*, 4, 14, 16, 34, 46; TNA E 372/76, mm. 18, 34d; Colvin, *History of the King's Works*, ii, 912, 1011.

invalidated.[21] In December 1231 comes the first evidence that Henry possessed a privy seal. Whereas in the past, when separated from the chancellor, he had used the seal of Hubert de Burgh or Godfrey of Crowcombe, now he could act independently of those ministers.[22]

The numerous candles burning during the dedication of the Domus Conversorum in January 1232 illuminated a very different political scene from that at the dedication of the Maison Dieu in Dover the month before. Hubert was now sharing the stage with Bishop Peter. Indeed, the presiding bishop was the latter's own suffragan, John, bishop of Ardfert.[23] Bishop Peter exploited his proximity to the king for all it was worth. In conversations described by Roger of Wendover, he declared it was 'a great scandal to the crown' that the ravages of the Welsh went every year unpunished.[24] Equally shameful was the king's inability to sustain Duke Peter in Brittany. When Henry lamented that he had barely the money for his own food, clothes and alms, he was told to blame himself. Whereas his predecessors, 'rich and powerful kings', had husbanded their resources, Henry had given his lands and offices away to others so that 'not in gold and silver, but only in name are you a king'.

What made this critique so devastating was that it was all too true. Hubert had certainly increased the king's revenues from the low levels of the early minority, a considerable achievement. Indeed, in the financial year 1229/30 they reached some £24,700.[25] Henry's revenue was thus much the same as King John's at the start of his reign, the problem being that thanks to the inflation in the early 1200s, it was worth at most half as much.[26] The kind of income John generated between 1207 and 1212, even leaving aside his spoliation of the church, at well over £55,000 a year, Henry could only dream about.[27] By 1214, John had amassed a treasure of £130,000, four or five times more than the treasure Henry took to Brittany

---

[21] *CR 1231–4*, 502, 508.

[22] *CR 1227–31*, 461–2; *CChW*, 17; Tout, *Chapters*, i, 210–11, 318.

[23] TNA E 372/76, m. 16d; Vincent, *Peter des Roches*, 289.

[24] Wendover, iii, 219–20.

[25] I owe this figure to Nick Barratt. For a breakdown of the 1230 revenue, see his 'English royal revenue in the early thirteenth century', 75–7.

[26] Early in John's reign prices had tripled and then fallen back to something like double their old level. Prices in Henry's reign into the 1250s were fairly stable, especially the staple of wheat, allowing, of course, for yearly fluctuations according to the state of the harvest: see Bolton, *Money in the Medieval English Economy*, 176–83. For the inflation in John's reign, see Latimer, 'The English inflation of 1180–1220'.

[27] Calculated from Barratt, 'Revenue of King John', 839. See also Carpenter, *Magna Carta*, 207. The £55,000 figure (an average for the years 1207–12) was partly due to the tax of 1207, which brought in over £60,000 as against £40,000 for the tax of 1225: Mitchell, *Studies in Taxation*, 91; Cazel, 'Fifteenth of 1225', 70–1. The figures for Henry's revenues in Ramsay, *History of the Revenues of the Kings of England*, i, 262–365, have to be treated with caution, even where not merely estimates. Thanks to misdating the pipe rolls, the politics of each year are also related to the revenue of the year before.

in 1230.[28] Henry was a far less powerful king than his father. This lack of money left Henry scrabbling around to meet his continental commitments, as Bishop Peter pointed out. In April 1231, burdened with payments to knights after the 1230 campaign, he was unable to pay a pension of 40 marks a year requested by the pope: 'we can scarcely satisfy those to whom we are at present obliged,' he wrote apologetically. In 1232 he had to find £8,000 for the duke of Brittany and around £2,400 for Poitevin nobles.[29] Equally telling was Bishop Peter's diagnosis of the causes of the crisis. For Henry had indeed loaded Hubert de Burgh and his supporters with wardships, lands and liberties instead of keeping them in his own hands. He had also allowed the sheriffs of the regime to retain a large slice of their revenues rather than pay them into the exchequer. As late as Christmas 1231, Godfrey of Crowcombe was made sheriff of Oxfordshire for life on such easy terms.

Bishop Peter was equally clear about the remedy. He should himself return to the exchequer and reform the finances of the kingdom, ensuring that the sheriffs accounted properly for their revenues and that wardships and escheats were henceforth kept in the king's own hands. The implication of the critique was, of course, that Hubert and his acolytes should be removed from office and deprived of the 'demesnes and other things' they had 'illicitly usurped', as Henry put it later.[30] One might think that Peter was here pushing at an open door. Had not Henry outgrown Hubert's sluggish regime, with its failure to find him a wife, its fiascos in Brittany and Wales, its constricting poverty, its profiteering at the king's expense, and its frustrating emphasis on 'don't' rather than 'do'? Bishop Peter spread out before Henry an altogether more sunlit world, one in which he would at last be a 'rich and powerful' king like his predecessors.

Yet the most remarkable feature of the next six months is Henry's refusal to part with his justiciar. Hubert, from the moment Bishop Peter reappeared at court, knew he was in deadly danger. He fought back with stubborn courage, deploying all the arts of persuasion that had kept him in power for so long. Doubtless he reminded Henry of his lengthy and loyal service and warned of Peter's disastrous record. Had not the bishop brought the kingdom to the brink of civil war in 1223? Had not his harshness as justiciar helped provoke the rebellion of 1215? Around Hubert at court, seconding his arguments, and shielding Henry from rival influences, were Hubert's men – the stewards of the royal household, the household knights, the clerks of wardrobe and chamber. Many of them would suffer from Hubert's fall. So would Bishop Mauclerc at the exchequer. These men had every reason for keeping Hubert in office.

[28] Jolliffe, 'Chamber and the castle treasures', 135.

[29] *CR 1227–31*, 583; *Patent Roll 1225–32*, 465–6, 501; *CLR 1226–40*, 210. The requested pension was for a citizen of Rome.

[30] *CR 1231–4*, 567.

THE STRUGGLE FOR POWER IN 1232

Battered by the conflicting voices of Bishop Peter and Hubert de Burgh, Henry could not make up his mind. While he gradually entrusted a large part of the financial administration of the country to Bishop Peter and his nephew Peter de Rivallis, he retained Hubert by his side, and bestowed on him fresh favours. If there was more here than a weak man being pulled one way and then another, Henry's aim was to accommodate both sides and create a regime in which Peter and Hubert would somehow share power. With both of them at daggers drawn (whatever the surface formalities) that was never going to be easy.

The first sign that Henry was succumbing to the bishop's arguments came towards the end of January 1232. On 27 January, Peter was with Henry at Havering in Essex. Later in the same day he was sitting at the exchequer at Westminster. Peter's return to the arena he had dominated for so long must have caused a sensation. It represented the first breach in Hubert's walls and doubtless sent shivers down his spine and that of Bishop Mauclerc. Peter arrived at the exchequer in the middle of the accounts for Shropshire and Staffordshire and thus could inform the king how the sheriff was unable to collect debts thanks to the war with Llywelyn.[31] In the next months Peter combined time at court with work at the exchequer. He may have been behind the appointment on 8 February of two knights in each county to keep the king's escheats and wardships, answering for their issues at the exchequer. The implication was that these were no longer to be sold at a small price or given away free to Hubert and his supporters.[32]

Having made the initial break in, events moved rapidly in Peter's favour as the king's financial predicament worsened. In February the duke of Brittany arrived in England to get his hands on more money. Henry expressed joy at his coming and stopped him purchasing provisions, thus making him accept royal hospitality![33] This was the kind of opulent, masterful king that Henry now hoped to be. The reality was very different. The Hospitallers and Templars agreed to act as sureties for the £4,000 owed the duke only when Henry placed the crown jewels in their keeping and vowed to spend nothing save on household expenses until the debt

---

[31] On 27 January, Peter attests both a royal charter at Havering and an exchequer writ at Westminster. Havering is twenty miles from Westminster so such a journey is not impossible even in January. But it may be that one or other of the dates is out: *RCWL*, i, 112 (where Westminster as opposed to Havering is a mistake in the transcription, see *CChR 1226–57*, 148); *MR 1231–3*, nos. 783–4, 1452.

[32] *CR 1231–4*, 129–31; *CFR 1232–2*, no. 57 (which probably also dates to 8 February); Waugh, 'The origins of the office of escheator', 245. If Bishop Peter was behind this initiative, he soon replaced it with the far more radical scheme of placing all wards and escheats under his nephew Peter de Rivallis.

[33] *CR 1231–4*, 128.

was paid. At the same time Henry had to borrow £3,186 from Italian merchants.[34] To these financial difficulties Hubert had no answer. Trying to rival Bishop Peter, he entered the exchequer and ordered the sheriffs to be arrested if they did not account properly for the Brittany scutage, but no great sums were likely to come from that.[35] The only real solution was to get a tax to clear the king's debts. At a great council which met at Westminster in March 1232, Hubert appealed for just that. The earl of Chester led the opposition, pointing out that he and other barons had wasted their money on the 1230 expedition and come home paupers. They would therefore grant no tax.[36]

Despite this humiliating rebuff, Hubert was still able to promote his men. Around this time his chaplain, Richard de St John, became chaplain of the king and then keeper of the wardrobe.[37] Hubert also had a golden opportunity to rub into Henry the disasters of King John's rule, disasters with which Bishop Peter was so closely associated. In May 1232 the court left Westminster for the Welsh marches. Its ultimate destination was a meeting with Llywelyn, but beforehand there was to be a very special event at Worcester. The monks of Worcester, faced with a challenge from Beaulieu abbey for possession of King John's body, had taken steps to consolidate their ownership. They had prepared a new tomb for the king, and commissioned the Purbeck marble effigy that is still there above it. The date chosen for John's translation was 19 May, the eve of Ascension Day, and so the eve of the day of John's coronation. Henry and Hubert were both present at the ceremony, but Bishop Peter, making his own way to the Welsh marches, was absent.[38] For almost the last time the court had an exclusively Hubertian appearance.[39] Henry was surely prompted to reflect on the events bringing his father to this tomb at Worcester instead of lying at Fontevraud with his father (Henry II), brother (Richard the Lionheart) and mother (Eleanor of Aquitaine). In this same month he pardoned the abbot of St Albans an amercement imposed by John 'by will rather than by reason'.[40] Henry was certainly concerned about his father's soul. Before leaving Worcester he granted to the monks the church of

---

[34] *Patent Roll 1225–32*, 465–6, 490–1.

[35] *MR 1231–3*, no. 1370. The amount paid in, as recorded in the pipe rolls of 1231/2 and 1232/3, was £1,593: Mitchell, *Studies in Taxation*, 191.

[36] Wendover, iii, 211–12.

[37] *CR 1231–4*, 67; *Monasticon*, ii, 81.

[38] Des Roches attested neither of the charters given at Worcester on 21 May. Nor does he attest at Reading on 12, 13 May as the court made its way to Worcester: *RCWL*, i, 116.

[39] On 20 May, the day after John's translation, in a great mass in the cathedral celebrated by Bishop Neville, the new abbot-elect of Tewkesbury was presented to the bishop of Worcester by Richard de St John. Henry begged the bishop to spare the 'poor monks' expense as they were burdened with many debts. Hubert, for his part, as patron of Tewkesbury via the Clare wardship, counselled the new abbot 'to put aside the pomp of the world and diligently look after his house and his monks': *Monasticon*, ii, 81.

[40] *CFR 1231–2*, no. 94. See Clasby, 'Abbot of St Albans'.

Bromsgrove in return for commemorating each year the anniversary of John's death.[41]

The meeting with Llywelyn at Shrewsbury led to nothing and another was fixed for 4 August. In the interval Henry, on 7 June, decided to make a pilgrimage to Bromholm. Since this would take him into Hubert's home-land and indeed to Burgh itself, the decision showed the continuing influence of the justiciar. Yet Bishop Peter, back at court by 22 May, found much he could exploit. On 7 June itself Henry confessed he had no money with him, and was in the greatest need.[42] Previously Peter had attacked the exchequer. Now his target could be the household. If Henry was out of money, he should surely blame the incompetence and dishonesty of the household officials and particularly those of the wardrobe who were responsible for receiving, storing and spending all the money for the king's daily expenses. Peter also had at hand the man who could replace them, none other than his nephew Peter de Rivallis, so unjustly removed from the keepership of the wardrobe at the end of 1223.[43] Faced with his obvious poverty, Henry was convinced. On 11 June, when the court was at Oddington, at the head of Oxfordshire's Evenlode valley, he once more made de Rivallis keeper of the wardrobe. It was to be no temporary appointment. De Rivallis was to remain keeper for life. At the same time, he was given life custody of the chamber with the right to appoint and dismiss all subordinate wardrobe and chamber officials. Four days later life custody of the small or privy seal followed. While there is little evidence of it being used during his supremacy, it gave de Rivallis the power to bypass Chancellor Neville should he prove difficult.[44]

Having done all this, Henry, now at Woodstock, granted a pauper a pension 'inspired by God', and made gifts to his new Oxford hospital, to the Oxford friars and to the nearby religious houses of Coldnorton, Brackley, Bruern, Nutley and Biddlesden.[45] At Bishop Peter's devising he had shattered Hubert's hold over the household. To place its key offices in the hands of one man was unprecedented. To do so for life showed there was to be no turning back. Hubert's men, Richard de St John and Ranulf

---

[41] CChR 1226–57, 154–5. He also gave the bishop a hundred oaks for the new cathedral being raised around John's body: CR 1231–4, 64.

[42] CR 1231–4, 70. On 10 June money was supplied to Peter for the work on the great hall at Winchester castle, Peter having recovered custody of the castle, together with the sheriffdom of Hampshire, back in March: Patent Roll 1225–32, 466–7, 480.

[43] In the secondary literature de Rivallis (the most usual form in the primary sources) is often rendered mistakenly as 'des Rivaux'. The place itself is unidentified. It might have been in Poitou but Roches d'Orival near Rouen in Normandy is another possibility. See Vincent, Peter des Roches, 27.

[44] All these concessions were made by charter: CChR 1226–57, 156–7. So there should be no misunderstandings about his authority, de Rivallis was also given life custody of the treasury of the household although this was really coterminous with custody of the wardrobe.

[45] CR 1231–4, 73–5.

le Breton, were out. Richard managed to remain at court but Ranulf was disgraced, and later had to offer £1,000 for the king's favour. His brother, William, was sacked as sheriff of Kent and later penalized 1,000 marks. His successor was Bertram de Criel, the castellan of Dover disgraced the year before for his treatment of Hubert's wife.[46]

Henry, however, still wished to combine all factions together at court. He soothed Neville's anxieties over the grant of the privy seal to de Rivallis by confirming his life tenure of the chancery and the great seal. He reassured Hubert by making him justiciar of Ireland for life, Richard de Burgh thus becoming his deputy. While Hubert attested the charters in favour of de Rivallis, Bishop Peter attested those in Hubert's favour.[47] When, therefore, Henry left Woodstock on 16 June, Bishop Peter's victory was far from complete, yet he did not accompany the king on his pilgrimage to East Anglia. On 25 June, by which time Henry was at Ely, Peter was sitting at the exchequer at Westminster.[48] He was doubtless preparing the schemes of administrative reform which were soon to unfold. He also believed that his nephew Peter de Rivallis could look after himself. He was proved right, but only just.

Peter de Rivallis was far more than a mere stooge of his uncle. Clever, industrious and ruthless, confident in success and tenacious in adversity, he coveted both public power and private wealth. Having known Henry since his youth, he was perfectly able to make his own case to the king. Thus it was that at Norwich on 28 June, Henry agreed to more of the two Peters' programme. In a series of completely unprecedented grants, the king gave de Rivallis life custody of wards and escheats, coasts and ports, and the mint and exchange. De Rivallis was also to have for life the custody of the Jews and responsibility for all the king's purchases and prises. When Chancellor Neville refused to take responsibility for these concessions, Henry forged ahead anyway. The charters in question (witnessed by Hubert de Burgh no doubt reluctantly) were 'given' by Henry's own hand, as against the almost universal custom for charters to be 'given' by the chancellor. Henry, however, still wanted everyone to get on. On 27–28 June he tried to appease Neville by granting local government privileges to the see of Chichester. He also exempted Hubert from all accounts as justiciar of England and Ireland.[49]

---

[46] *CFR 1231–2*, nos. 153, 255–9; Dunstable, 130; Wendover, iii, 220. After his disgrace (in September 1231), Hubert had brought Ranulf back to court, see Carpenter, *Reign of Henry III*, 51. Ranulf's depredations in the manors he had received from the king were a factor in his downfall. After Hubert's dismissal Criel followed him as castellan of Dover.

[47] *CChR 1226–57*, 156–7; *RCWL*, i, 117–18.

[48] *MR 1231–3*, no. 1133.

[49] *CChR 1226–57*, 163–4. For Neville in this period, see Carpenter, *Reign of Henry III*, 60–9.

THE OATHS OF BURGH

The attempt to reassure old ministers reached a climax a few days later. On 1 July, Henry arrived at Bromholm where he offered gold and silks before the relics of the Holy Cross. Next day he stayed at Burgh, Hubert's ancestral home. There he could pray in the exquisite chancel Hubert had added to the parish church and view the scenes of the justiciar's early life. Surrounded by Hubert's servants and supporters, he took an extraordinary oath. Kings very rarely swore oaths in person; a minister usually did so on their behalf. But now, on 2 July, Henry swore personally on the Holy Gospels that 'without any fraud and guile' he would observe the charters he had granted to various ministers. If he broke his word, he placed God in pledge he would subject himself to excommunication by the pope. The beneficiaries of Henry's undertaking were Hubert and his wife Margaret of Scotland, the stewards Godfrey of Crowcombe and Ralph fitzNicholas, Peter de Rivallis, Chancellor Neville (probably without his consent) and Treasurer Mauclerc. To ensure the absent Mauclerc reaped the full benefit from these arrangements, also on 2 July Henry issued a charter granting him the treasurership of the exchequer for life. De Rivallis had already been eyeing up the exchequer. Indeed, he had established a clerk there to keep a roll of the money coming in.[50] No wonder Mauclerc's position needed support.

The king's oath on 2 July did not conclude the proceedings for the day. Later, in what was clearly a very private episode, Henry again contemplated or was made to contemplate the possibility that he might renege on his undertakings. As a further safeguard, he ordered Hubert to take an oath of his own. And so the justiciar swore to impede 'with all his power' any move by the king to overthrow the charters mentioned in the earlier undertaking. Apart from Peter de Rivallis, the only witnesses to Hubert's oath were his household officials William of Blockley and Philip of Eye. The charter embodying the undertaking, like that recording the oath of the king, was again 'given' by Henry himself rather than by the chancellor.[51] It is difficult to think in any age of a parallel to Hubert's oath, an oath in which a king voluntarily empowers a minister to take action against him.

Henry later claimed that in swearing his oath he had acted out of fear, which seems incredible. The reverse was the case. His devotions at Bromholm and his entertainment in Hubert's house had rekindled his love for his justiciar. His swearing in person on the Gospels, his giving the charters with his own hand, his placing of God as his pledge, his acceptance of papal excommunication, his order to the justiciar to force him to keep his word, all these were emotional and impulsive responses to Hubert's

---

[50] *CChR 1226–57*, 157.
[51] Mauclerc's charter was also given by the king.

pleas for reassurance. Quite probably the two men concocted the details of the oaths together. Hubert thus accepted the massive advances made by Peter de Rivallis, but preserved for himself and his supporters the huge array of lands and offices granted them by royal charters, including, in Hubert's case, the justiciarships of England and Ireland. Hubert's wife Margaret was included amongst the beneficiaries because so many concessions of land had been made to them jointly. De Rivallis, without the support of his mighty kinsman, doubtless had to swim with the tide, although he ducked out of attesting the charter granting the treasury for life to Mauclerc. He also extracted an immediate quid pro quo. On 2 July at Burgh he was granted by charter, in hereditary right, the honour of Pevensey in Sussex, an escheat in the hands of the crown. This was an early indication of the hypocrisy and self-interest soon tainting Bishop Peter and his nephew's programme of reform.

At Burgh, Henry still hoped to bring all parties together. The project was laudable, the process lamentable. The oaths of Burgh were one of the lowest points of his kingship. Next year they were quashed by the pope as clean contrary to Henry's coronation oath to uphold the rights and dignities of the king and kingdom. He had acted 'circumvented by the counsel of certain people and led astray by his juvenile nature'.[52] Henry was now twenty-four! It was bad for him to make any group of ministers irremovable; it was worse to admit that he might be foresworn; it was shameful to submit himself to such humiliating sanctions. In the emotion of the moment, Henry had totally forgotten how to behave as a king. He had agreed to be treated like a child whose promises are unreliable and whose good behaviour only the threat of punishment can guarantee.

Hubert must have hoped the oaths of Burgh would end the revolution in government. He was soon disappointed. Bishop Peter was back at court by 10 July and must have protested at once over what had happened. He was able to exploit anxieties within Hubert's own regime. Bishop Neville, as chancellor, had not merely refused to take responsibility for the oaths and the surrounding concessions. He seems for a few days to have left court altogether. On his return, he had his name expunged from the list of beneficiaries of the king's oath. In effect, he was disowning his old friend.[53] The two Peters now pushed the king into further administrative reforms. Between 7 and 11 July, as Henry journeyed back to Westminster, he made life grants to Peter de Rivallis of the royal forests, and then amazingly of nearly all the sheriffdoms. Although most of the existing sheriffs continued as de Rivallis's deputies, there was absolutely no precedent for this concentration of local office in the hands of one man, let alone it being for life. Hubert de Burgh must have been appalled. Yet he still could

[52] RL, i, 551; and (from 1235) F, 229 (CPReg, 148): 'juvenili facilitate seductus'.

[53] See Carpenter, Reign of Henry III, 63–9. My view of Neville's attitude is to some extent conjectural.

sway the king. On 7 July, in the last charter 'given' personally by Henry, he received a life grant of the Tower of London and the castles of Windsor and Odiham.[54] It needed an entirely new and utterly devastating accusation to bring him down.

Since December 1231 there had been attacks in several parts of England on foreign clerks provided by the papacy to English livings.[55] Henry confessed his shame to the count of Savoy, whose son had been amongst the victims. He had also to listen to sarcastic letters from the pope: 'Here is the king of England; here the devoted pupil; here the faithful vassal; here filial reverence; here fitting reward for benefits received.'[56] The pope had also commissioned his own inquiries into the outrages. They were to be carried out by none other than Bishop Peter. Wittingly or unwittingly the pope had placed a lethal dart in the hands of Hubert's greatest enemy. Bishop Peter proceeded to fling it with all his might. As the court travelled towards the Welsh march for the meeting with Llywelyn, he accused Hubert of instigating the disorders in revenge for the pope's inquiry into the validity of his marriage. Nothing was more likely to appall the pious and papally minded king. Hubert, of course, fiercely denied the charges, but he was now surrounded by his enemies. By 28 July at Woodstock the vultures had gathered round, for the earls of Cornwall, Chester and Pembroke, and Chester's former steward Stephen of Seagrave, had all arrived at court. Still Hubert doggedly hung on. On 28 July he attested a humiliating charter placing Ireland's financial administration under Peter de Rivallis. Was it now that Hubert directed 'verba probrosa et turpia' at the king in the presence of Ralph fitzNicholas and Godfrey of Crowcombe?[57] At any rate, on the next day, 29 July, Henry at last told Hubert to go. On 30 July, as the king, Bishop Peter, the earls and the long wagon trains of the court moved down the Evenlode valley to spend the night at Oddington before continuing on to Worcester and Shrewsbury, Hubert was not with them. Henry had at last escaped from his justiciar. He was to find his new masters much less congenial.

HUBERT'S FATE

The conference with Llywelyn at Shrewsbury was as inconclusive as those in the past, and another (in fact postponed) was fixed for October.[58] Meanwhile the dominating question was what to do with Hubert de Burgh. Resentful and suspicious, Henry wanted revenge. 'Hubert had

---

[54] *Patent Roll 1225–32*, 488–9; *CChR 1226–57*, 163–4.

[55] The provision of Italians to English livings had gathered pace during Guala's legation: *Guala*, lxvii–xxiv (Vincent's introduction). For the riots see Vincent, *Peter des Roches*, 303–7.

[56] *CR 1231–4*, 135; *F*, 203–4.

[57] Paris, vi, 74. This was one of the charges Henry brought against Hubert in 1239.

[58] *CR 1231–4*, 93.

been almost the heart of the king', commented the Margam annalist, 'but the king's love suddenly turned to the most atrocious hate.'[59]

Hubert had ridden away from Woodstock still possessed of all his lands, castles and offices. It was not to last. On 8 August, Henry ordered him, still styled justiciar of England and Ireland, to surrender the royal castles in his custody: Dover, Canterbury, Rochester, Windsor, Odiham, Hertford, Colchester and the Tower of London – quite a list. Just over a fortnight later, Henry went further and ordered Hubert, now just 'earl of Kent', to leave England altogether.[60] The king then changed his mind and decided to put Hubert on trial, inviting accusations from the people and levelling numerous charges of his own. Some of the latter, as Wendover recounts them, were fantastic. Had Hubert really stolen a magic gem from the treasury and given it to Llywelyn, thus making him invincible in battle? Other charges, bearing on the usurpation of the king's rights and properties, had more substance.[61]

Hubert meanwhile took shelter at Merton priory in Surrey. When in mid-September he failed to appear for his trial, Henry ordered the Londoners to fetch him dead or alive. Egged on by Bishop Peter from his palace at Southwark, they accordingly set out, only for Ralph de Neville and the earls of Chester and Pembroke to persuade Henry to recall them, thus avoiding a scandalous breach of sanctuary. Henry now adjourned proceedings until the following January, here influenced by the pleadings of Archbishop Luke of Dublin, who had hurried to England in his old master's cause.[62] Henry insisted, however, that Hubert surrender all he had received from the crown. And so back into the king's hands came Hubert's great haul: Haughley and Rayleigh, Knaresborough, Montgomery, the Three Castles, Cardigan and Carmarthen, the Arundel, Avranches, Mowbray and Clare wardships, and all the manors obtained from the royal demesne.

Persecuted in this way, Hubert decided to leave Merton and join his wife in the liberty of Bury St Edmunds. By 25 September he had reached the house at Brentwood in Essex of his nephew Thomas, bishop of Norwich. There, however, he learnt that Henry was sending a posse through the night to arrest him. Rising from his bed he fled half-naked to an adjoining chapel. The posse was actually led by Hubert's old protégé, the steward Godfrey of Crowcombe, but Godfrey's 'fear of the king', as Henry later admitted, now overrode all considerations of past obligation and present propriety. He dragged Hubert from the chapel and brought him back to the Tower of London, though not before a gallant smith, as Hubert loved to recall, had refused to put fetters on this 'saviour of

[59] Margam, 39–40.
[60] *Patent Roll 1225–32*, 496–8.
[61] Wendover, iii, 220–3.
[62] Wendover/Paris, iii, 222, 224–6.

England'. Henry, who had waited up for news, went to bed happy. Next day he reaped the consequences. The bishop of London protested about the breach of sanctuary and conducted Hubert back to the chapel.[63]

It says everything about Hubert's strength of mind and body that for the next month he stuck it out in the chapel, disdaining the alternatives offered him by the king through Archbishop Luke, namely exile or perpetual imprisonment provided he openly confess that he was a traitor. Henry, meanwhile, issued a stream of vindictive orders, all eloquent of his frustration and fury. The sheriff of Essex was to surround the chapel: if he had guarded it well before, he was now to do so even better; if Hubert came out he was to be taken immediately to the Tower on pain of a £4,000 penalty; Hubert's privy seal was to be broken before his eyes; his psalter was to be taken from him; he was not to hear 'any word' from 'any man'; his food was to be reduced to one half-penny loaf and one measure of ale a day; he was to receive no food at all. And then finally, when none of this seemed to work, Henry began proceedings for Hubert's outlawry.[64]

At the end of October, Hubert finally surrendered and was taken to the Tower. When brought to trial on 10 November he refused to plead and threw himself on the mercy of the king. He thus escaped a judgement which, so Henry indicated, threatened him with death and disinheritance, doubtless what Bishop Peter wanted. Instead, Hubert formally surrendered everything he held from the crown with all the attendant charters. He also surrendered his treasure at the New Temple, so Henry could now gaze on an array of rings, cups, basins, belts, brooches and candelabras.[65] Hubert remained, however, earl of Kent (perhaps in deference to his royal wife) and was allowed to keep his ancestral manors and the manors acquired from everyone bar the king.[66] Since these amounted to over thirty properties, he was far from poor. But it was nothing, of course, to what he had been. Nor could Hubert enjoy what remained of his wealth. He was sent to Devizes castle, there to be guarded by knights of the earls of Cornwall, Surrey, Pembroke and Lincoln until he went on crusade as a Templar or was released by decision of the king and magnates. Henry promised to do Hubert no further 'grace or cruelty', and instructed the four earls to resist him if he broke his word, another undignified concession which Bishop Peter did not witness. Henry, so he said, had agreed to this settlement 'at the instance of the magnates of England' and 'moved by piety'. Henry's mood indeed had changed. He spoke of Hubert's past services and refused to execute him. 'Note the mercy of the king,' observed

---

[63] Wendover/Paris, iii, 226–9; *F*, 207–8.

[64] *CR 1231–4*, 118, 153–5, 161.

[65] *CPR 1232–47*, 5; Wendover, iii, 232–3.

[66] These included his life interest in the honour of Wormegay, the inheritance of his first wife.

Matthew Paris later. Wendover has Henry saying, 'I prefer to be thought a king foolish and remiss than cruel and tyrannical.'[67]

There was much which could be fairly said against Hubert de Burgh. The rewards he extracted from a gullible and grateful king went far beyond what were justified and damaged the rights and possessions of the crown. If there were reasons for Hubert controlling Montgomery, Cardigan and Carmarthen as bulwarks against Llywelyn, there was no need for him to hold them in hereditary right. In his private dealings, Hubert could be as ruthless as anyone. He made the widow Matilda de Mowbray pay to obtain her dower and remain single, in clear breach of Magna Carta.[68] Yet Hubert's services to the king in the winning of the war and the recovery of royal power had been immense. There was at least some truth in Henry's statement that, 'above all our faithful men', Hubert had 'attended to our affairs most diligently and devotedly'.[69] At Dover, the three solid beaked towers blocking the gateway brought down by the siege of 1216, the sally port beneath and the new gateway to the south still stand as visual testimonies to the justiciar's achievement. Hubert had seen the necessity of a public acceptance of Magna Carta and, with Archbishop Langton, was the chief architect of the final consensual Charters of 1225. He thus helped to forge a new framework for relations between king and kingdom. If Poitou was lost on his watch, at least Gascony was retained. However governed by self-interest, his scepticism about the chances of recovering Normandy was probably justified. Above all, Hubert's style of government, with all its compromises and concessions, kept the peace in England (apart from the siege of Bedford) for thirteen years. His successors, by contrast, were at war within months.

BISHOP PETER'S EARLY REGIME

After the fall of Hubert de Burgh, contemporary chroniclers all agree that Bishop Peter, magnificent and triumphant, became the king's chief minister. Henry himself later said the bishop had been his 'father and spiritual counsellor', enjoying 'the fullest grace of our intimate friendship'.[70] Peter remained active at the exchequer and was frequently at court. Between August 1232 and October 1233 he witnessed royal charters in every month bar one. His pre-eminence can be seen in the numerous letters, often embodying important decisions, that Henry authorized with him or in his presence. Linked inseparably to Bishop Peter was his nephew Peter de Rivallis. A fixture at court as keeper of the wardrobe, he was

---

[67] *F*, 207–8; *RL*, i, 408–9; *CR 1231–4*, 166–7, 188; Wendover/Paris, iii, 230–4, with the quotation at 233. The return of property excluded the Three Castles.

[68] See Carpenter, 'Hubert de Burgh, Matilda de Mowbray'.

[69] See above, 89.

[70] *TR*, no. 15.

responsible for receiving and spending a large share of the king's revenues. He also attended to a wide range of other business, authorizing more royal letters than anyone else. If that was not enough, de Rivallis, through his deputies, controlled much of local government as sheriff of numerous counties, keeper of the king's wards and escheats, and chief justice of the royal forest.

Initially the new regime had something of a balanced, almost consensual look. Ralph de Neville remained as chancellor and Bishop Mauclerc as treasurer of the exchequer. The senior stewards of the royal household were still Ralph fitzNicholas and Godfrey of Crowcombe. All these men had been close to Hubert. This was less so of Hubert's replacement as justiciar, namely Stephen of Seagrave, the senior justice at the bench and regent alongside Bishop Neville in 1230. Hubert had accepted his promotion as a way of conciliating the earl of Chester. Now his appointment, according to the Waverley annalist, was agreed by a great council, probably that which met in September 1232.[71] Seagrave had nothing like Hubert's position but, second only to de Rivallis, he handled a great deal of business, as the authorization notes to royal letters show.[72] There was one other person who gave the government its balanced appearance, none other than Richard Marshal, earl of Pembroke, since his homage to the king at Painscastle back in August 1231, fully possessed of the family estates in England, Wales and Ireland. Between Hubert's fall at the end of July 1232 and February 1233 he was almost permanently at court.

Henry's confidence in the new regime was enhanced by a stupendous early success. The great council which met in September 1232 agreed to the very tax refused to Hubert de Burgh back in March. The council agreed it, moreover, without any concessions in return, the only time this happened in the whole of Henry's reign. Evidently the new regime was popular. Admittedly the tax was at a much lower rate than in 1225, a fortieth of the value of everyone's movable property rather than a thirteenth. Lords were also allowed to raise the tax themselves within their own baronies and liberties before passing it to the king. Nonetheless the tax was collected efficiently and soon raised £16,475.[73] Henry could think he was rich.

Henry and his ministers also dealt confidently and consensually with another early test, namely that arising from the death of the earl of Chester. For much of October 1232, Henry hovered within reach of Wallingford where Earl Ranulf laboured in extremis. Henry's aim was to ease the earl's passing, not to profit from it. He made gifts for Ranulf's soul, and expressed the fervent hope that even now God would restore his

---

[71] Waverley, 311.

[72] It is a testimony to the political uncertainty of the period that large numbers of notes appear in the chancery rolls showing on whose authority royal letters were issued.

[73] CR 1231–4, 155–6; RBE, iii, 1064; DA, 63–73; Lay Subsidy Rolls, 106–19; Stacey, Politics, Policy and Finance, 42 n. 38; Mitchell, Studies in Taxation, 199–208.

health. On 26 October, at or near the end, he visited the deathbed. Earl
Ranulf's passing left a void. Since the 1190s he had strode the military and
political stage, like the old Marshal frequently quarrelling with his kings
yet never rebelling against them. The survival of the dynasty in the
1215–17 civil war owed much to his testy loyalty. The earl's equally testy
accommodation with Hubert de Burgh had helped keep the justiciar in
power. When Hubert, in the chapel at Brentwood, heard of Ranulf's
death, he took his psalter and standing before the altar read it through for
the earl's soul.[74]

Henry's task now was to divide the earl's far-flung properties amongst
his sisters, their husbands and descendants. He did so without difficulty or
dispute. At a great council at Northampton in November he formally
invested John the Scot, earl of Huntingdon, with the earldom of Chester
and John de Lacy with the earldom of Lincoln, while assigning William de
Ferrers, earl of Derby, the castle of Chartley and the lands between the
Ribble and the Mersey. King John might well have charged large sums for
his favour in this matter, playing one party off against another. Henry
charged nothing at all. His government seemed very different from his
father's. That, however, was due more to Hubert de Burgh than Bishop
Peter, if, as seems likely, it was under Hubert that the divisions of 1232 had
been agreed.[75]

Henry and his ministers were also at one about how to spend the
money coming in from the tax. It would be used not to punish Llywelyn
but to prop up the king's Breton and Poitevin allies. After the Northampton
council Henry journeyed to Shrewsbury and early in December concluded
a three-year truce with Llywelyn.[76] It was thus to run beyond the danger
point marked by the expiry of the truce with Louis IX in the summer of
1234. Evidently Henry had no stomach for another campaign in Wales.
His earlier plans for invading Gwynedd and recovering Cardigan were
forgotten. Richard Marshal agreed with this policy. As lord of Dinan in
Brittany, he wished to support Duke Peter. As lord of Pembroke and
Gwent, he thought he could deal with Llywelyn himself. After all his
brother William all alone had wrested Cardigan and Carmarthen from
the Welsh in 1223. A truce also suited Peter de Rivallis. In Wales he
had stepped into the shoes of Hubert de Burgh. He was now keeper of
the Three Castles, Glamorgan (via the Clare wardship), Cardigan and
Carmarthen. The truce meant his custody of Cardigan remained nominal,
but gave security to the rest of his Welsh empire. Bishop Peter himself was
little interested in Wales. He did not travel to the Shrewsbury meeting and

---

[74] *CR 1231–4*, 122; *CChR 1226–57*, 169; Paris, iii, 230. Paris may well have got this information from Hubert.

[75] *Patent Roll 1225–32*, 508; *CPR 1232–47*, 3; *CR 1231–4*, 169–70; Chester, 59. See also Eales, 'Henry III and the end of the Norman earldom of Chester', 103–6.

[76] Tewkesbury, 88.

thus was absent from court throughout December. With his homeland in the Touraine, it was the Breton alliance and the prospects of recovering Poitou which engaged his feelings. Henry felt the same way. In early January 1233, with Bishop Peter and Richard Marshal, he authorized payments for Poitou and Gascony totalling some £735.[77]

THE OVERTHROW OF ROYAL CHARTERS

If Henry hoped for a period of tranquility in which he could husband his resources and prepare for another campaign overseas, he was to be grievously disappointed. The trouble lay in the ambitions of the two Peters. They were far from finished with the fall of Hubert de Burgh. At court they were prepared to live with Chancellor Neville and Ralph fitz-Nicholas, but they wanted rid of Godfrey of Crowcombe. At the exchequer they wanted rid of Bishop Mauclerc. The two Peters also wanted more generally to transfer land and office from supporters of the old regime to their own supporters. They had come to power at the head of a faction, a faction created by the politics of the early minority and the crisis of 1223 when Hubert had ousted Bishop Peter and his party from local and central office. Those who had suffered during Hubert's supremacy now expected to recoup their losses, which often meant ejecting those currently in place. Bishop Peter was surrounded by hungry mouths which he could feed only by snatching other people's food. Those under threat, moreover, often held their lands and offices for life or in hereditary right under the terms of royal charters and letters patent. If these were overthrown, the king might be accused of acting 'by will' 'per voluntatem', in violation of law, custom and Magna Carta. And there was another danger: if Bishop Peter rid himself of rivals and concentrated favour on his own men, his regime could appear one increasingly dominated by foreigners.

There were already warning signs. Richard of Cornwall had virtually quit court after Hubert's fall. He was incensed that the Clare wardship, including Glamorgan, had gone to de Rivallis and not to himself. After all the late earl's widow was his wife.[78] Richard Marshal himself was at court not as some altruistic councillor but to protect his own interests from attack. Had Henry been stronger and more perceptive he would have seen these dangers and insisted on maintaining the status quo. Had Bishop Peter been wiser, he would have moved slowly and slyly towards his objectives. But that was not his style. He persuaded Henry to go for it all at once. When this sparked violent opposition, he urged Henry to advance not retreat, to make war not peace. Age and experience had not mellowed

---

[77] This was on top of £1,130 paid out in Poitevin fees in November 1232 and £4,000 owed the previous Michaelmas to the duke of Brittany: *CLR 1226–40*, 186–8, 194–5; *Patent Roll 1225–32*, 501.

[78] Hailes, 52.

the bishop. They had made him all the more militant. Elevated and exalted by his exploits on crusade and by his destruction of Hubert de Burgh, this armour-plated prelate would teach his old pupil now at last to act like a king.

Thus it was that, in an extraordinary period between October 1232 and February 1233, Henry, counselled and pressurized by the two Peters, moved against seven individuals, in the process overthrowing the concessions made in twelve royal charters and two letters patent. In many of these cases Henry admitted later that he had acted unjustly and 'by will'.[79] The first victim was Godfrey of Crowcombe. In October he was removed from the sheriffdom of Oxfordshire despite his letter patent granting him the office for life. He remained at court but not for long. Crowcombe's replacement was John of Hulcote, an old servant of Falkes de Bréauté, a telling sign of the make-up of the new regime. The king personally authorized Crowcombe's dismissal but the two Peters were probably behind it. Later Crowcombe described de Rivallis as his 'enemy'.[80]

De Rivallis was also behind another attack. In December he ordered the arrest of the king's sergeant, Henry de Heliun. Heliun's lands (a combination of royal demesne and lands of the Normans) were seized 'by will of the king' despite being held in hereditary right by royal charters. Another victim was Hubert's old esquire, John Lestrange. He later said it was through de Rivallis and 'by will of the king' that he was deprived of land at Roade in Somerset, again despite his royal charter.[81] A similar case involved someone altogether more illustrious. This was Richard de Argentan, a former steward of the royal household and a famous crusader, wounded at the siege of Bedford in 1224. Between 1227 and 1231, Argentan had secured three royal charters each making his hereditary tenure of lands of the Normans at Lilley and Willian in Hertfordshire more secure. He coveted the manors since they adjoined his ancestral seat at Wymondley. The only trouble was that King John had previously given them to Payn de Chaworth as compensation for the lands he had lost in Normandy. At the end of November 1232, Payn suddenly appeared at court and commenced a legal action for the recovery of Lilley and Willian. When Argentan failed to turn up, the judgement was that the properties should be taken into the king's hands for his 'default'. In mid-December they were returned to Pain de Chaworth. When Argentan arrived in early January, he could do nothing to reverse the decision. He then disappeared from court until Bishop Peter's fall. He later complained he had been disseised 'by will of the king'.[82]

---

[79] Full references to these cases are given in Carpenter, *Reign of Henry III*, 38. I have not included the Clatford case, for which see below, 130.

[80] *Patent Roll 1225–32*, 455, 507; *CRR*, xv, no. 1289.

[81] *CRR*, xv, no. 1427.

[82] *CRR*, xv, no. 1426; Carpenter, *Reign of Henry III*, 24.

Bishop Walter Mauclerc was next. In early January 1233, while at Woodstock with Bishop Peter, Henry dismissed him from the treasurership of the exchequer and replaced him with Peter de Rivallis. De Rivallis then appointed as his deputy to run the exchequer none other than Robert Passelewe, the former clerk of Falkes de Bréauté and agent of the 1223–4 dissidents at Rome. Having taken this momentous step, Henry sank back with relief and ordered a whole series of improvements to his great chamber at Woodstock, including painting the wainscoting green. Mauclerc, however, holding his position for life by a royal charter, refused at first to accept his dismissal. When the news reached Woodstock, it was Bishop Peter who struck. He left the king behind and, taking the great seal with him, dashed to London. On 17 January he entered the exchequer and two days later issued the great seal letter which confirmed Mauclerc's dismissal, de Rivallis's appointment and Passelewe's position as deputy in his place. The old tiger could still leap and gouge with venom.[83]

In the next few days, while Henry commissioned paintings of God's Majesty, the Four Evangelists, and St Edmund and St Edward for his chapel at Woodstock, he also knocked over Mauclerc's other charters one by one, like so many bowling pins. Mauclerc thus lost the royal demesne manor of Melbourne in Derbyshire, Carlisle castle, the sheriffdom of Cumberland and the manor of Horncastle in Lincolnshire, for which he had secured a cornucopia of liberties. Walter's men also suffered. Both his clerk, John le Francis, and his knight, William of Huntercombe, were deprived of property despite the support of charters and letters patent. Huntercombe later complained of disseisin 'by will of the king'. In his case the person who replaced him at Chalgrove in Oxfordshire was John de Plessis, a household knight of Norman origin beginning a long career in the king's service. Faced with this onslaught, Walter Mauclerc made terms. In February all complaints against him were dropped and Horncastle was restored. In return, he promised the king £1,000 and surrendered 'of his own will' his royal charters, including that embodying Henry's promises in the oath of Burgh.[84] What a long time ago that seemed! The settlement itself was far from permanent. Later in the year Mauclerc was deprived of Horncastle again and also of Gisland in Cumberland. In the Gisland case, Henry later issued an abject apology for acting in contravention of his own charter.[85]

THE BREAK WITH RICHARD MARSHAL

Did the two Peters have their hands full in January and February 1233 with their attack on Bishop Mauclerc? One might have thought so, but not a

[83] *CPR 1232–47*, 7–8; *CLR 1226–40*, 194; *MR 1231–3*, no. 3011.
[84] *CFR 1232–3*, nos. 136–7.
[85] *CR 1231–4*, 231, 242, 249, 401, 416; *CChR 1226–57*, 69, 76, 189; *CPR 1232–47*, 60.

bit of it. During this very period they engineered another disseisin, one which drove Richard Marshal from court, plunged England into a civil war, and set in train the events leading the following year to their own downfall. The disseisin in question involved the removal of Gilbert Basset from the manor of Upavon and his replacement by Peter de Maulay.

Between the hilly downs around Marlborough and the uplands of the Salisbury Plain lies the vale of Pewsey, overlooked in the north-west by the castle of Devizes and watered in the east by the river Avon. At the very point where the Avon enters the vale from the south, having run through a narrow pass from Amesbury, sits Upavon. Its benign aspect today, nestling in the mouth of a little defile, belies its ancient significance. Anyone wishing to travel from Devizes to Salisbury, Clarendon, Winchester and beyond had to travel through Upavon. It was also a large valuable manor worth at least £40 a year.[86]

It was this manor, an escheat from the lands of the Normans, that King John in 1204 had given to Peter de Maulay. Maulay hailed from the north of Poitou near the border with the Touraine. He became John's castellan of Corfe and also, through marriage, lord of a Yorkshire barony centred on Doncaster, an extraordinary elevation for a foreigner who had begun his career as a mere 'usher' in the king's household. With a common homeland, Maulay was Bishop Peter's closest associate in England. In 1221, as we have seen, they were jointly accused by Hubert de Burgh of treason.[87]

From the word go the possession of Upavon by Maulay was an affront to the Bassets and their patrons, the Marshal earls of Pembroke. That was King John's intention. He had loved to create discord between his own men. Upavon was deep in Basset and Marshal territory. Wootton Basset, Winterbourne Basset, Compton Basset, Berwick Basset were all within an eighteen-mile radius. The Basset's Marden was only three miles away. Hubert de Burgh, therefore, knew what he was doing when in 1228, with a view to restoring his alliance with William Marshal, he took Upavon from Maulay and gave it to Gilbert Basset. Next year Basset obtained a royal charter granting him the manor in hereditary right. By this time he was also a household knight of the king and constable of Devizes, a position he lost on Hubert's fall, an early warning of what was to come.[88]

A harsh and grasping man, tainted by rumours that he had murdered Arthur, Maulay caused trouble wherever he went. His tenure of Upavon

---

[86] *BF*, i, 381.

[87] See above, 23.

[88] Gilbert Basset was the son and heir of John's leading household knight, Alan Basset. A younger son, and thus with his own fortune to make, Alan's rewards from the king included the manors of High Wycombe and Woking. Gilbert was followed successively as head of this branch of the Bassets by his brothers, Fulk Basset, bishop of London, and Philip Basset, who became justiciar in 1261. For the family, see Stewart-Parker, 'The Bassets of High Wycombe'.

itself was marked by complaints of extortion.[89] Furious over his dispossession, having held the manor for twenty years, he now saw his chance of getting it back. He accompanied Bishop Peter out to Painscastle and from November 1232 was frequently at court. The reason why Richard Marshal stuck there so solidly was to ward off the attack on Gilbert Basset. Early in January he was joined there by Basset himself. The battle lines were drawn. When battle commenced a month later, Henry, acting on Maulay's complaint, summoned Basset to show 'by what warrant' he held the manor. Basset's answer was simple: he held it by the charter of Henry himself. Maulay was ready with his own reply. He had only surrendered the manor when threatened by Hubert with imprisonment in a place where he would neither see his hands nor his feet. Having been granted the manor by King John, he had been disseised 'unjustly and without judgement'. In the end, as was the customary procedure when royal charters were involved, the case was referred to the king himself. Only he could interpret his own acts. His duty, however, was to judge justly and on the whole justice seemed to favour Basset. Maulay after all had produced no charter or letter showing that John's gift was other than during the king's pleasure. He had not, therefore, been disseised unjustly. Henry, however, acted differently. On 4 February he ordered Upavon to be taken into his hands. Two days later, by a writ authorized by Bishop Peter and Stephen of Seagrave, he returned Upavon to Peter de Maulay. When Basset was finally restored a year and a half later, Henry admitted he had been disseised 'by will'.[90]

Fundamentally, Henry had made his decision because Bishop Peter had more influence over him than Richard Marshal. Both in these weeks must have been fighting for his ear. The bishop doubtless told Henry to be a king and the fuss would die down. Gilbert Basset would accept his dispossession just like Bishop Mauclerc. In saying that, however, Peter was grievously mistaken and the king grievously misled. Mauclerc and his fellows had lost their great protector in Hubert de Burgh. Gilbert Basset's protector was very much in place in the form of Richard Marshal. Indeed, with the earl of Chester's demise Richard was the mightiest baron in the realm. Now, as Matthew Paris observed, he embraced Basset's cause as his own.[91] On 9 February, after Henry's judgement, Richard left court, never to return. According to the annals of Dunstable, Henry was so angered by his protests that he told him to go.[92] Richard's conduct was not surprising. His prayers had been ignored and his man slighted. Failure to act would utterly destroy his reputation for good lordship. That would have been true at any time. But it was especially so for Richard, who until 1231 was

---

[89] *CRR*, xiii, no. 1168.
[90] *CRR*, xv, no. 131; *BNB*, ii, no. 857; *CFR 1232–3*, no. 107; *CR 1231–4*, 187, 437.
[91] Paris, *FH*, ii, 208.
[92] Dunstable, 136.

essentially a Franco-Breton lord. In these early days of his new career he had to prove himself both to the Marshal affinity and to the wider realm.[93]

Richard Marshal was absolutely up to the job. In Matthew Paris's picture, he was mighty in arms, abundant in courage, elegant in body and eloquent in speech.[94] He was also highly intelligent, and understood how to turn his cause into one with general relevance and appeal. 'He fought for the cause of justice and the laws of the English people against the oppressions of the Poitevins,' wrote Roger of Wendover.[95] There was here an element of hypocrisy. Richard had sat at court and accepted the disseisins suffered by Mauclerc and his colleagues. Indeed, he had engineered a dissesin of his own, persuading Henry to give him the manor of Clatford in Hampshire although Waleran the German held it in hereditary right by royal charter. Henry himself later confessed he had disseised Waleran 'by will'.[96] What Richard had inflicted on others he condemned only when suffered by himself. Yet Richard's inconsistency was never exposed. Many accepted Roger of Wendover's view of the situation. That was partly because the disseisin of Gilbert Basset seemed so blatant. Matthew Paris wrote of him being 'despoiled violently, unjustly and without judgement'. The annals of Dunstable had him disseised with 'the order of justice omitted'.[97]

JUSTIFICATIONS FOR HENRY'S CONDUCT

These months in 1232–3, with their plethora of dismissals and disseisins in contravention of royal charters, had no parallel in the rest of Henry's reign. They came on top of the overthrow of all the charters granted to Hubert de Burgh. Hubert himself had ruled in a very different manner. When he had moved against the dissidents in 1224, he had only seized property held at the king's pleasure. The same had been the case in his move against Peter de Maulay over Upavon. The disseisin of Bertram de Criel in 1231, itself reversed, is conspicuous precisely for being so untypical.[98] What happened now was disseisin 'by will' on an altogether different scale. 'Will' of course could be both good and bad. What made it bad, in contemporary thought, was when it was exercised in contravention of law and justice. For the king to break his own charters seemed a prime case of just that. Henry II himself had acknowledged that royal charters should be inviolate. Indeed, if, so he said, one of his predecessors had issued a charter granting away his manor of Clarendon 'which I dearly love', 'there would be no way justly for me to deny that it should be given up

---

[93] For this theme, see Vincent, *Peter des Roches*, 395–8.
[94] Paris, *HA*, ii, 334.
[95] Wendover, iii, 278.
[96] *CR 1242–7*, 304; Vincent, *Peter des Roches*, 320, 328–31.
[97] Dunstable, 136; Paris, *FH*, ii, 208.
[98] Carpenter, *Minority*, 346–7.

completely'. Likewise the *Dialogus de Scaccario*, the great book written during Henry's reign about the work of the exchequer, acknowledged that the king's gifts ought not to be revoked or reclaimed.[99]

What then was Henry to do? Surely he should not be held to foolish gifts he had made to beneficiaries now exposed as self-seeking and dishonest. One possible solution was to argue that such concessions were invalid as contrary to the king's coronation oath to preserve the rights of the crown. It was on those grounds that the pope quashed the oaths of Burgh. Henry, however, does not seem to have deployed this defence when it came to the charters he was now overturning. Another solution was to threaten the delinquent ministers with trial or having to account and then allow them instead to resign their charters. This had worked with Hubert and with Mauclerc. Where there were conflicting claims to property, the proper approach was through a lawsuit, and such cases had been commenced over Lilley and Willian, and over Upavon. True, the eventual judgements, especially that given in person by Henry over Upavon, were questionable, but how far was the king aware of that at the time?[100] Henry now had as his chief counsellor in matters legal his new justiciar, Stephen of Seagrave, a man acknowledged to be highly skilled in English law. Surely, Henry could think, Stephen's involvement guaranteed the lawfulness of what he was doing.

From this perspective, Henry could believe his conduct raised no great issues of principle and required no provocative political theory in justification. This, however, was far from the whole story. For Bishop Peter at this time was unfolding before Henry a far more exciting canvas, one which rose above legal palliatives, and justified acts of will straight out in terms of the elevated and all-encompassing nature of royal authority. It was in these terms that Henry gave the only explanation of what had happened in this period. In 1235 he explained how Bishop Peter had made him 'deviate from the observation of justice, and that we were able to do injury to our faithful subjects at our will, he attributed to the plenitiude of royal power'.[101]

'Plenitude of power' had long been ascribed to the papacy.[102] It distinguished the overall authority of the pope from the lesser responsibilities of bishops, prelates, kings and princes. It meant that in the life of the church, in particular, the pope was the supreme judge and legislator. He was not bound by laws because he made them. The privileges he conferred, he was

---

[99] Battle, 216–17; *Dialogus*, 74–5.

[100] For the overturn of the Upavon judgement, see below, 157. However, the judgement over Lilley and Willian, without going into the ultimate right in the matter, was later upheld: *CRR*, xv, no. 1426; Carpenter, *Reign of Henry III*, 24.

[101] *TR*, no. 15. Henry here was writing to Frederick II against the bishop. Henry was not criticizing the idea of the 'plenitude of royal power' but its misuse. The implication was that it was legitimate when possessed by Frederick but not by Henry. See below, 174.

[102] For Henry's own reference to it, see above, 56.

perfectly entitled 'if necessity impels' to cancel.[103] Bishop Peter, however, was thinking less of the pope than of his old friend, the emperor Frederick II. In a famous edict of April 1232, Frederick had explained how as emperor he possessed 'the plenitude of power' and wished to enhance the position of the princes in Germany since they were called with him to 'part of the care'. Accordingly, without any of the 'common consent' found in English legislation, he simply abolished the city communes throughout Germany, 'revoking and judging wholly worthless and empty' 'all privileges and letters open and close' which he and his predecessors had previously granted.[104] Issued in April 1232, it seems highly likely that Bishop Peter knew of this ordinance (or at least of the principles behind it) by the time the disseisins in England started. It fitted exactly the English situation. Henry too, it could now be argued, possessed plenitude of power within his own realm. On his authority, by his will, he could revoke the charters, and letters he had issued, not of course to do 'injury' to his subjects but to punish evil ministers and right the wrongs that good men had suffered. Whatever he said later, Henry was delighted at the idea that his authority paralleled that of the emperor. How grateful he was to Bishop Peter for revealing these truths. He would follow where the bishop led.

Perhaps he was grateful too in another area. In the 1220s, Henry's household choirs had chanted the 'Christus Vincit' hymn before him simply on the three great festivals of the church – Christmas, Easter and Whitsun. By 1233 they were doing so on seven other festivals as well: the purification, assumption and nativity of the Virgin Mary, the translation of Edward the Confessor and the feasts of Ascension, Trinity and Midsummer. Thus ten times a year Henry heard the chant:

Christ conquers, Christ reigns, Christ rules. Hear O Christ.
To the king of the English, crowned by God, salvation and victory.

Since the liberate rolls, from which the evidence for these performances come, are missing for the years 1230 to 1232, we cannot be sure that Bishop Peter encouraged this remarkable multiplication, testifying to the God-given and protected nature of kingship, but it seems possible.[105]

REFORM OF THE REALM?

Despite these justifications for his conduct, Henry should have seen the warning signs flashing. For the leaders of the new regime were proving just as acquisitive as the old. Peter de Rivallis was clearly intent on building up a base of private power in Sussex. Probably he intended at some point to

[103] See the full discussion in Burns, *Cambridge History of Medieval Political Thought*, 282–8.
[104] MGH, *Constitutiones*, 192–4, no. 156.
[105] Kantorowicz, *Laudes Regiae*, 175.

swap his clerical status for a knightly one. Back at Burgh in 1232 he had secured the honour of Pevensey in hereditary right. In February 1233, Pevensey castle itself was added. He also held the sheriffdom of Sussex on terms highly favourable to himself – so no reform there.[106] Custody of the Briouze wardship gave him control of Bramber and also of Gower.[107] In the Welsh marches he added to his possessions – another hereditary grant – the Three Castles once belonging to Hubert de Burgh.[108] Striking too were the gains of Stephen of Seagrave. Seagrave had criticized Hubert de Burgh for usurping royal demesnes, only then, as Henry later complained, to usurp them himself. But why hadn't Henry seen this coming at the time? As it was, no sooner had Henry recovered the royal demesne manor of Melbourne from Bishop Mauclerc than he granted it in hereditary right to Seagrave. Likewise, with Newcastle-under-Lyme back in his hands following the death of the earl of Chester, he gave it in hereditary right to Gilbert, Seagrave's son.[109] If Henry trusted Seagrave to advise him on the law, he was trusting a 'flexible man', as Roger of Wendover called him, flexible in his allegiances and his principles.[110]

What then of the much-vaunted reform of the realm that Bishop Peter had promised? Here there was one significant piece of legislation promulgated in April 1233 and directed against the Jews. Henceforth, proper records were to be made of their loans, interest was not to be charged at more than 2d a week in the pound, church vessels were not to be received as security, and no Jew was to remain in the realm unless he could serve the king and give pledges for his fidelity. Those who could not were to leave the kingdom by Michaelmas. Although there was little in the legislation that was new, this was 'the first attempt by secular authorities to embody the Lateran decrees [of 1215] into a coherent body of law'. The legislation was a clever move by Bishop Peter, for it won the favour of churchmen at a time when Peter was trying to get his own man elected to Canterbury. (It was at Canterbury that the legislation was promulgated.) And it was a bid for wider popularity at a time when the regime was coming under attack.[111]

In the financial sphere, the regime did, in one way, build on the tax granted in 1232. In March 1233, Bishop Peter was personally involved in

---

[106] Carpenter, *Reign of Henry III*, 164.

[107] In the minority of Henry III the Briouze inheritance had been split between Reginald de Briouze, father of the William hanged in 1230 by Llywelyn, and his nephew John de Briouze, whose portion was Bramber and Gower. John died in 1232, hence the wardship.

[108] *CChR 1226–57*, 185; *CPR 1232–47*, 58.

[109] *CR 1231–4*, 567; *CChR 1226–57*, 172, 175.

[110] Wendover, iii, 240.

[111] Richardson, 'Glanvill continued', 393; Richardson, *English Jewry under the Angevin Kings*, 293–4; Vincent, *Peter des Roches*, 363–4; Vincent, 'Jews, Poitevins and the bishop of Winchester', 126, 129–32. For further discussion of Henry and the Jews, see below 298–307.

imposing a 10,000-mark tallage on the Jews. It was payable in instalments, with the first £500 due at Michaelmas 1233.[112] Much less was achieved in respect of the sheriffdoms. It is possible that that there was some tightening up at the exchequer in the hearing of shrieval accounts, though the evidence is far from conclusive. If the concentration of sheriffdoms in the hands of de Rivallis was designed to increase the revenue from county farms (the fixed annual payments owed by the sheriffs), it led to nothing. The new sheriffs appointed by him in October 1232 answered for much the same sums as their predecessors. They were not required to detail the revenue they could raise from their farms, the first stage in any informed alteration of the terms on which they held office. The monopolization of office in Peter's hands seems to have been more an exercise in the grabbing of power than financial reform. A major barrier to reform, just as under Hubert, remained the number of sheriffdoms held by members of the regime on terms favourable to themselves. The number increased in the course of 1233 as the regime braced to meet opposition.[113] These circumstances, and perhaps also the money coming in from the 1232 tax on movables, meant the regime quickly lost interest in reform.[114]

That Henry failed to realize he was being let down was largely due to what contemporaries, as we have seen, called the king's 'simplicity'. For Roger of Wendover it was as 'rex simplex' that Henry fell in with Bishop Peter's mendacious counsels. The continuation of the Margam chronicle, in the same context, described Henry as 'boy king'. (He was now twenty-five!) Matthew Paris, likewise, believed that Richard Marshal 'constantly blamed the simplicity of the foolish king'.[115] Henry, in this period, often seems remote from events, as though just letting his ministers get on with it. In the liberate rolls for the regnal year 1232/3 de Rivallis authorized alone forty-seven letters and Seagrave thirty-four. Henry alone authorized only sixteen of which ten were concerned with acts of piety and devotion. When Henry authorized himself a concession to the bakers of Canterbury, it had to be altered next day to clarify what it was about![116]

---

[112] *CPR 1232–47*, 12–13; Vincent, *Peter des Roches*, 363; Vincent, 'Jews, Poitevins and the bishop of Winchester', 125.

[113] Carpenter, *Reign of Henry III*, 161–2. For a full discussion, see Vincent, *Peter des Roches*, ch. 10. In the regnal year 18, Henry III, so between 28 October 1233 and 27 October 1234, by a ruling of the king and his council, the exchequer no longer automatically allowed claims of religious houses to have the amercements imposed by the king's judges on their men. There now had to be a specific sanction from the king: *Reading Abbey Cartularies*, i, 91–2; Carpenter, *Reign of Henry III*, 85–6, and see below, 461. This was an important measure in defence of the rights of the crown but there seems no evidence as to whether it was promulgated during or after the regime of des Roches.

[114] Peter des Rivallis's custody of wards and escheats brought little in the way of reform. For a full appraisal, see Waugh, 'The origins of the office of escheator', 246–51.

[115] Wendover, iii, 241; 'Margam Continuation', 138; Paris, *FH*, ii, 208.

[116] *CR 1231–4*, 205–6.

THE DRIFT TO WAR

On 23 March 1233 great rolls of thunder rumbled over St Albans. They seemed to symbolize the angry turmoil into which the kingdom was descending. Henry felt torn. On the one hand, he longed for peace, and summoned great council after great council in the hope of reaching a settlement. But, on the other hand, provoked by the actions of Gilbert Basset and Richard Marshal, his anger flared. He would stand firm over Upavon and punish their defiance. In that resolution he was stiffened and stirred by Bishop Peter. As the king said later, 'at his counsel and urgent persuasion we moved arms [against our faithful subjects] nor for them was justice heard or the voice of supplication admitted'.[117]

On leaving court in February 1233, Richard Marshal had gone to Wales, where he helped another malcontent, his brother-in-law Richard of Cornwall, defend the former Briouze lands from the attacks of Llywelyn.[118] He then paid a brief visit to Ireland. If Henry hoped this was the end of the matter, he was mistaken. Returning to London after spending Easter (4 April) at Canterbury, he was met at Stratford by Gilbert Basset and envoys (including friars) from Richard Marshal. Henry was enraged by what was put to him. He expelled the Marshal's deputy, William of Rowden, from court, rehabilitated the Marshal's enemy, Morgan of Caerleon, and decided to celebrate Whitsun (22 May) at Gloucester, from where he could threaten the Marshal's lordship of Gwent. Yet Henry still remained true to his continental priorities. On 25 April, Duke Peter of Brittany, yet again in England, received a generous financial settlement. Substantial sums around this time were also assigned to the counts of Flanders and Boulogne.[119]

At Gloucester during the Whitsun festivities, Henry knighted two young earls, Roger Bigod of Norfolk and Hugh de Vere of Oxford, as well as William Longespée, later a claimant to the earldom of Salisbury. If this was a show of unity, it was illusory. At court there was turmoil. Survivors of the old regime feared for their futures. The two Peters were about to claim another victim. On 25 May they persuaded Henry to remove Godfrey of Crowcombe from court and from the custody of Woodstock and Oxford castle, although he held the last two for life by a charter granted only that January.[120] There was also tension in the country. In June, as Henry patrolled the Marches, he issued ordinances for the arrest of malefactors and forbad a tournament at Northampton, summoning the participants to come and speak with him at Worcester instead. The tournament was clearly intended as a political gathering and Henry soon

---

[117] *TR*, no. 15.

[118] For an exploration of the political culture and norms of conduct surrounding the Marshal's rebellion, see Weiler, *Kingship, Rebellion*, especially ch. 11.

[119] *CLR 1226–40*, 210, 239.

[120] *CChR 1226–57*, 174.

heard that Gilbert Basset had attended and spoken 'certain words in contempt of the king'.[121]

Henry had had enough. He ordered Basset to be arrested and brought to court to answer charges of disturbing the peace of the kingdom. At the same time his lands were to be seized. Walter of Clifford, a young marcher baron and 'choice knight', in the words of Matthew Paris, was given the same treatment. Measures were also taken, although less drastic, against Richard Marshal. The regime evidently feared the contagion was spreading to other marcher barons. On 13 June, in a throwback to the methods of King John, eight of them gave hostages to Henry (now at Worcester) for their faithful service 'until there is a firm peace in the kingdom of England'.[122] Peace was indeed Henry's ambition. Leaving the marches, he summoned a council to meet at Oxford and then retired to Woodstock where he ordered an image of Christ Crucified to be painted in the chapel and discussed the building and refurbishment works at Winchester castle with Elyas of Dereham: they agreed the king's chamber in the castle was too dark and needed new windows while the wainscoting should be painted green. If only Henry had given the same careful attention to the political mess he was creating.[123]

When the Oxford assembly opened on 24 June, Henry was in for a shock. The friar Robert Bacon declared in a sermon that there would never be peace until the two Peters were removed. As if to make the point, the assembly was boycotted by many barons, indignant, so Wendover says, at the way the king was surrounded by aliens. The opposition was probably co-ordinated by Richard Marshal, who held his own meeting at Worcester after the king's departure.[124] Henry was incensed by the boycott but eventually calmed down and asked how he could proceed against the absentees 'in judicial fashion'. In the end he summoned another assembly to meet at Westminster (on 11 July) where he promised to correct whatever needed correction in the kingdom. The Westminster council, however, was boycotted just like that at Oxford. According to Wendover, the magnates sent envoys demanding the dismissal of Bishop Peter and 'the Poitevins' on pain of their expulsion 'by the common counsel of the kingdom'. The magnates even threatened to discuss creating a new king. The echoes of King John's deposition in 1215 and the offer of the throne to the future Louis VIII could not have been clearer. Henry, thoroughly alarmed and still hoping for a settlement, summoned another council to meet at Westminster, this time in early August.[125]

The August council seemed at first to hold out more hope than its predecessors. Apart from Bishop Peter, it was attended by the bishops of Bath

---

[121] CR 1231–4, 309–10; CPR 1232–47, 17; BNB, ii, no. 857.
[122] CR 1231–4, 312–13; CFR 1232–3, no. 230.
[123] CLR 1226–40, 219–21.
[124] CFR 1233–4, no. 266; Dunstable, 136.
[125] Wendover, iii, 244–6.

and Salisbury, and by the earls of Cornwall, Surrey, Chester and Aumale, and probably also by the earls of Lincoln and Derby. Most important of all, Richard Marshal himself decided to attend. There must have seemed a real prospect of rapprochement. When, however, the Marshal neared London he received a warning – true or false we cannot tell – of a plot to seize him. The Marshal, therefore, held an armed muster of his immediate supporters at High Wycombe, the chief seat of Gilbert Basset. Both Roger Bigod, earl of Norfolk, and Walter of Clifford were there. Richard Marshal then hurried back to the safety of his Welsh lordships.

The Marshal's retreat owed something to other information. His lordships in Wales and Ireland were being placed under threat. While Henry had been fussing over councils, Bishop Peter had been urging him 'to move arms' against the rebels.[126] Up to a point Henry had agreed. By 18 July he had decided to take an army to Ireland. The muster was to be at Gloucester on 30 August. The ostensible aim was to subject the whole of Connacht to royal authority, ousting both the fallen justiciar, Richard de Burgh, and his rival, the Irish ruler Felim O'Connor. But, of course, an army at Gloucester might equally advance against the Marshal's Welsh lordships. In Ireland, it could move against the Marshal's Leinster. Bishop Peter must surely have reminded Henry of King John's triumphal Irish campaign of 1210 when he had disciplined the old Marshal and ousted the Lacys.

After the Marshal's muster at High Wycombe in early August, Henry, doubtless counselled by Bishop Peter, became yet more aggressive. He switched the port of departure for the Irish army from Ilfracombe to Milford Haven, so, starting from Gloucester, it was going to march through south Wales from the Marshal's Gwent to the Marshal's Pembroke. On 15 August, Henry went further. Now at Tewkesbury, he seized the lands of those present at High Wycombe and gave them to supporters of the regime. At the same time he ordered the destruction of Gilbert Basset's houses at Wooton Basset. Ten miners were employed there for a week doing the job. The Marshal, for his part, protecting the northern approaches to Upper Gwent, occupied the baronial castles of Hay-on-Wye and Ewyas Harold. In addition, 'which angers us especially', so Henry said, he destroyed the house of Philip le Bret, one of the king's household knights. None of this seemed to amount to much but it gave Bishop Peter and the king their excuse. On 23 August, Henry ordered the lands of Richard Marshal and Roger Bigod to be seized. At the same time, through the bishop of St David's, he issued Richard with a formal act of defiance. That severed all relations between them and created a state of war. In 1215 it was the barons who had taken the initiative and defied the king. Now, a measure of Bishop Peter's aggression and confidence, it was the other way

---

[126] Wendover, iii, 246.

round. Henry, if he had the power, could do with the Marshal's lands and person as he pleased. The Irish expedition was cancelled. The war against Richard Marshal was about to begin.[127]

DOWN WITH THE ALIENS

The hostility to Bishop Peter and his associates seen in the great councils of 1233 was not merely because of what they had done. It was because of who they were. They were foreigners, 'Poitevins', who had seized power and alienated the king from his native-born subjects and natural advisers. In exploiting these feelings, Richard Marshal could be accused again of double standards. After all, spending most of his time before 1234 on his estates in Normandy and Brittany, was he not in part a foreigner himself? This did not make his stand any the less emotive. The continuation of the Margam chronicle accepted completely the St Albans view of events. The war with Richard Marshal had started 'on account of the aliens' whom the two Peters 'brought to England to oppress the clergy and people as was done in the time of King John'. Accordingly, the barons of Ireland had sent the king a letter demanding he dismiss aliens 'and adhere to the counsels of the native men of the kingdom'. Likewise, the Dunstable annalist believed that the turmoil in 1233 was caused 'by the counsel of the Poitevins' and only ended with the dismissal of the two Peters 'and all other Poitevins' together with 'the fraudulent favourers of the Poitevins'.[128] So strong was the hostility to foreigners that the pope himself became concerned. In 1234, in an eloquent letter, he urged native-born men to form 'one people' with 'extranii' and not resent the patronage they received.[129]

Hostility to foreigners in high places had a long history behind it, as we have seen.[130] The Coggeshall chronicler thought that when Bishop Peter became justiciar in 1213, 'the great men of the kingdom murmured at an alien being placed over them'.[131] Such feelings had been exacerbated both by the civil war and by the politics of the minority. Now it seemed to Roger of Wendover that, counselled by Bishop Peter, the king was removing all native-born ministers and replacing them with foreigners from Poitou.[132] In fact Bishop Peter himself came from the Touraine but

---

[127] *CFR 1232–3*, nos. 311–14; *CR 1231–4*, 322.

[128] Wendover, 241; Dunstable, 135–7; 'Margam Continuation', 134, 138. See also Tewkesbury, 90, 93; Waverley, 315. The continuation of the Margam chronicle was not itself composed at Margam. It may have originated from the Cistercian house of Grace Dieu in Monmouthshire: 'Margam Continuation', 129.

[129] *RL*, i, 556. For discussion of the hostility to aliens, see Weiler, *Kingship, Rebellion*, 81–2, 84, 90–1, 97–8.

[130] See above, 50.

[131] Coggeshall, 168.

[132] Wendover, iii, 240.

given the porous borders between the Touraine and Poitou, 'Poitevin' seemed accurate enough. Peter de Maulay really was a Poitevin. (His Maulay is today a tiny village in the Vienne department of Nouvelle-Aquitaine.) Wherever Peter de Rivallis was born, he persisted in using his early title of 'capicerius' of Poitou (how acquired is unclear) even when showered with offices in England.[133] So labelling the regime 'Poitevin' could stick and it had a powerful emotional charge given the Poitevin nobility's reputation for treachery.

The foreign element in the regime, moreover, was far from confined to the two Peters and Peter de Maulay. Appointed as constable of Devizes was the Norman Walter de Goderville, a former knight of Falkes de Bréauté. (Bréauté and Goderville are only two miles apart.) Taking over Godfrey of Crowcombe's Oxfordshire offices in April 1233 was Engelard de Cigogné, an old associate of Bishop Peter, like him from the Touraine, one of the foreigners dismissed from office under the 1215 Magna Carta. As constable of Tonbridge castle, and as de Rivallis's deputy in Sussex, was Engelard's former knight and fellow Touraigneau, Aimery de Chanceux. The magnate closest to the regime was Bishop Peter's old friend the Poitevin William de Fors, earl of Aumale.[134] He was handsomely rewarded in July 1233 by a grant of the royal demesne manor of Dartford in hereditary right. Meanwhile two younger foreigners were beginning long careers at court: the household knight John de Plessis, a Norman by birth, and another member of the Chanceaux family, Matthias Bezill. In June 1233 the two Peters, the earl of Aumale, Peter de Maulay, John de Plessis and Matthias Bezill all attested royal charters, but not a single English earl or baron did so. As for the English members of the regime, several were former servants of that most disruptive of all foreigners Falkes de Bréauté: Robert Passelewe was in day-to-day charge of the exchequer; John of Hulcote was sheriff of Oxfordshire; and Ralph de Bray, Falkes' right-hand man, was sheriff of Warwickshire and Leicestershire. If only Falkes himself had been alive to see the day, he would doubtless have returned to England and recovered his lands from an apologetic king.

However much they were committed to careers in England, the foreign members of the regime were conspicuous by their foreignness. As late as the 1260s, Matthias Bezill was rejected as sheriff of Gloucestershire because he was a Frenchmen. Bishop Peter himself maintained many foreign clerks in his household and asked the poet Henry of Avranches to write in honour of St Martin of Tours, 'the saint of his native country'. Peter's basic loyalty was not to a people but to the dynasty, a dynasty which, when he began his career, was as much at home in Normandy, Anjou, the Touraine and

[133] Vincent, *Peter des Roches*, 17, 27. Vincent points out that the usual translation as 'treasurer' is not altogether accurate.
[134] William had probably grown up in Poitou. Fors is in the department of Deux-Sèvres; see English, *Lords of Holderness*, 37.

Poitou as in England. It was perfectly acceptable for the king, so Peter declared (according to Wendover), to bring in as many 'extranii' as he liked to 'compel his proud and rebellious men to perform their due service'. This came close to Falkes' declaration that all native-born men in England were traitors. Bishop Peter was indeed bringing in 'extranii'. In August, Baldwin de Guines, leading a band of Flemish mercenaries, arrived in England to help win the war against Richard Marshal.[135]

THE FIRST MARSHAL WAR, AUGUST–SEPTEMBER 1233

Henry's plan of campaign, doubtless devised by Bishop Peter, was clear and courageous. He would defeat the Marshal where he was strongest, defeat him, that is, in Gwent, the great bastion of Marshal power bounded to the east by the Wye and to the west by the Usk and guarded by the castles of Chepstow, Goodrich, Usk and Caerleon. After that, if the Marshal did not submit, Henry would march westwards, occupy Pembroke and carry the victorious campaign into Ireland. This strategy reflected the strengths of Henry's position, for all the growing unpopularity of the bishop's regime. The Marshal had many manors in England but no castles there to compare with his mighty strongholds in Wales. In England he had failed to stir up any general uprising. Around forty men had their lands seized for being in arms with him at High Wycombe, but they included only three major barons, the Marshal's nephew Roger Bigod, earl of Norfolk, Walter of Clifford and Thomas Grelle, a kinsman of Gilbert Basset. Beyond that, by far the largest group was provided by the Marshal's own followers, many from families with long records of service to the family – men such as Robert Musard, Henry of Earley, William of Rowden, Roger of Hyde, Hamon and William Crassus (le Gros), Ralph Bloet, Henry de Brayboef and William de Christchurch, as well as Gilbert Basset and his brothers Warin and Philip.[136]

The fact was that Bishop Peter had been busy. According to Wendover he had won over the earl of Lincoln and the Marshal's brother-in-law Richard of Cornwall by giving each of them £1,000. 'Alas the cupidity' of Richard, groaned Matthew Paris.[137] Other favours went to the earls of Hereford and Surrey, the latter also a Marshal brother-in-law. It was with some confidence, therefore, that Henry left Hereford on 30 August and marched westward down the Wye valley. Both Hay and Walter of

---

[135] Wendover, iii, 241, 248.

[136] *CFR 1232–3*, no. 297. The information here can be added to the discussion in Walker, 'The supporters of Richard Marshal'.

[137] Wendover, iii, 248; Paris, *HA*, ii, 357 n. 3. Paris later replaced this comment with a more diplomatic 'because he did not want to desert his brother'. In August 1233, Richard was granted custody of the lands of the earldom of Devon: *CR 1231–4*, 252; *CFR 1232–3*, no. 316.

Clifford's castle at Clifford, two miles away, were taken without a struggle. Encouraged by these successes, Henry progressed through the gentle slopes and fertile plains of the Golden Valley past Dore abbey, where he doubtless made suitable oblations, and Ewyas Harold, where he occupied the castle. He then followed the course of the river Monnow towards Abergavenny, with the looming mass of the Black Mountains to his right, terrain so very different from that of the home counties he knew so well. From Abergavenny, Henry marched twelve miles southward to Usk. The climax of the war was at hand. Usk the Marshal must defend, otherwise his lordship of Gwent would be overrun. Henry began the siege of the castle on 4 September – only to abandon it two days later and agree a truce. By 10 September he was back at Hereford and planning a new chapel 'fair and becoming' for his chamber in the castle; by 30 September he was at Oxford and entertaining the friars there to dinner; by 8 October he was back at Westminster in time to hear the monks 'at his command' sing the 'Christus Vincit' on the feast day of Edward the Confessor.[138] Commanding the monks was so much easier than commanding the Marshal. What had happened?

Roger of Wendover's explanation is that provisions had failed in the king's army. In all probability morale had failed as well. The whole course of the war suggests that the great barons dutifully turned up, pocketed their rewards and were then keen to go home. They would not fight for the Marshal but they were reluctant to fight against him, especially on the side of Bishop Peter. Henry's morale had failed as well. The reality of the campaign was very different to its rhetoric in the mouth of Bishop Peter in Hereford castle. The taking of Usk itself would be a long and dangerous business. The castle sits on a hill above the town, the land beneath falling away so rapidly as to make any frontal assault impossible. To the rear there were lines of deeply dug moats, while the regent had added a new gateway, curtain wall and flanking towers. When ecclesiastics intervened to propose a truce, Henry was only too pleased to accept it.

The terms of the truce, obscure now and probably ill-defined then, were, however, a recipe for future conflict, perhaps as Bishop Peter hoped. A great council was to meet at Westminster early in October where Henry, once again, was to correct whatever needed correction in the kingdom. Meanwhile the Marshal, Roger Bigod and, a little later, Walter of Clifford were restored to their lands. However, six other 'knights of the earl Marshal' – Gilbert, Warin and Philip Basset, William Crassus, Robert Musard and Henry of Earley – were only to gain like favour after they had come to the king and made their peace. Of these Warin Basset had certainly defied the king.[139] Probably the others had too. They were his 'capital' enemies whose lands and persons he was entitled to destroy. As

[138] *CLR 1226–40*, 230, 234.
[139] *CR 1231–4*, 252. He had 'returned his homage to the king'.

security for the observation of the truce, the Marshal formally surrendered Usk castle. He was, however, to recover it after fifteen days by which time the knights were to have made their peace.

In the event the knights did not make their peace. Probably there were arguments over safe conducts and the nature of any trial at court. Between 22 and 24 September, with the fifteen days up, Henry, counselled by de Rivallis and Stephen of Seagrave, abruptly halted the process of returning their lands. He also retained hold of Usk. Revenge was swift and it was taken by a man who now moves centre stage, the most famous 'miles strenuus' of the age, Richard Siward.[140] From obscure origins, Richard had fought alongside Hubert de Burgh in the sea battle off Sandwich, and been prominent in the service of the Marshals. In 1229 he had married Gilbert Basset's cousin, thus becoming lord of Headington in Oxfordshire. He had been at the High Wycombe muster and sometime before 1 September had defied the king. Now in the early morning of 27 September he descended from the Berkshire downs and attacked Bishop Peter's baggage train as it made its way from Winchester to Woodstock.[141] Robert Musard and Warin and Philip Basset were in his company and afterwards they went to the Marshal's manor of Hamstead where they ate the earl's bread and took one of his horses.

This exploit performed with wonderful confidence and daring (there was even a return to recover a hawk) marked a new stage in the war. It was the first in a series of raids by Siward on the properties of the king's hated ministers. A master of disguise and movement, his assaults were impossible to foresee and combat. The Marshal's party could not wage war in England. But, carefully avoiding attacks on the king himself, it had found a perfect way to humiliate and discredit his ministers.

Henry's reaction to Siward's outrage showed how much he was hoping for peace. He was angry but hoped the Marshal would disown his followers and help bring them to justice. The council at Westminster still went ahead, opening on 9 October. One reason for this response was Henry's anxiety over Brittany and Poitou, the end of the truce now being only ten months away. Between 15 and 20 October he personally authorized payments worth some £1,270 to his continental allies.[142] But the council itself was acrimonious, in large part due to Bishop Peter's offensive remarks. These brought to a head a complaint growing stronger and stronger during the course of 1233, namely that the king was denying his opponents 'judgment by their peers'.

Magna Carta, enshrining a centuries' old principle, had laid down that no free man was to be arrested, imprisoned, exiled, outlawed or deprived

---

[140] For Siward, see Crouch, 'The last adventure of Richard Siward'.

[141] For a graphic account drawn from the testimony of local jurors, see *CRR*, xv, no. 214; *CR 1231–4*, 326.

[142] *CR 1231–4*, 325; *CLR 1226–40*, 235–8.

of property, nor was the king to 'destroy' him or go against him, save by the lawful judgement of his peers or by the law of the land. But what had happened in 1233? Henry, as he later admitted, had committed numerous disseisins by will rather than by law. He had also refused, save in the most limited way, the safe conducts both the Marshal and Gilbert Basset sought through letters and messengers so they could come to court and receive the judgement of their peers.[143] Henry's own account of the breakdown of the August negotiations shows he wanted the Marshal's men to suffer simply the 'judgment of his court'.[144]

At the October council this whole issue came centre stage. A group of bishops begged the king to make peace with the magnates whom he had attacked 'without judgment of their peers'. The reply was given not by Henry but by Bishop Peter. In a speech as contemptuous as it was controversial he maintained that judgement by peers had no meaning. There were no peers in England as there were in France. He evidently meant, with deliberate obtuseness, that England had no equivalent to the small privileged group formed by the great French dukes and counts. It was thus lawful, Peter continued, for the king of England to judge and condemn anyone in the kingdom through judges whom he had himself appointed.[145] Peter's statement was full of menace. It meant that in any trial for treason those accused would be at the king's mercy. The bishops were horrified and threatened Bishop Peter with excommunication. At the same time they pointedly refused to excommunicate the Marshal and the other dissidents.[146]

Richard Marshal was not present to hear Bishop Peter's outburst. He had set off for the council and reached Woodstock, only then to turn back. He complained that Henry himself had broken the truce, leaving him in the same state as before it, a man defied by the king. So he returned to Wales and reoccupied Usk. On 18 October, having heard the news, Henry confiscated once again the Marshal's possessions and gave them to Richard of Cornwall. He summoned his barons and tenants-in-chief to join him at Hereford early in November. The second Marshal war was about to begin.

THE SECOND MARSHAL WAR, NOVEMBER 1233

That Henry was up for a winter war shows how much he remained under Bishop Peter's astringent and bracing influence. At least there were reasons for hoping that this campaign might prove more glorious than the last. At Hereford in November, Henry was joined by the earls of Cornwall,

---

[143] *BNB*, ii, 666. Henry would only give what amounted to safe conducts if they came 'alone'.

[144] *CFR 1232–3*, no. 311.

[145] *Bracton*, ii, 337; Carpenter, *Reign of Henry III*, 39–40.

[146] Wendover, iii, 251–2; *RL*, i, 554–6.

Chester, Derby, Hereford and Surrey. All were rewarded for their loyalty. Richard Marshal's affinity was also proving friable. Both Henry of Earley and Robert Musard, facing the destruction of their English possessions, made their peace, stipulating only that they should not have to fight against the Marshal. Even better, the regime had managed to prize away the Marshal's greatest allies, Roger Bigod, earl of Norfolk, Thomas Grelle and Walter of Clifford, the latter hoping for the pardon of the 1,000 marks he owed the Jew Hamo of Hereford.[147] His defection meant the loss of the Marshal's outer shield in the valley of the upper Wye.

In fact, however, by the time Henry arrived at Hereford in early November, he found a political and military situation transformed by Richard Marshal. The Marshal might have lost his English followers and allies, but his knightly tenants in Gwent (most without English interests) remained steadfastly loyal.[148] Far from waiting passively for Henry's invasion, Richard had gone on the offensive. In a diplomatic masterstroke, reversing all previous Marshal policy, he had made an alliance with Llywelyn. From being a spectator who exchanged compliments with the king in the first war, Llywelyn became a violent enemy in the second. He entered the valley of the upper Usk, ravaged the lordship of Brecon in the custody of Richard of Cornwall, and then began a siege of Brecon castle. The Marshal himself marched north from Usk and seized Abergavenny. Then he went south and invaded Glamorgan, the great Clare lordship in the custody of the 'notorious and noxious rascal' Peter de Rivallis.[149] On 15 October, with the king still at Westminster, the Marshal took Cardiff, Warin Basset being killed in the assault. Having secured the allegiance of the Welsh chiefs of the lordship and most of its knightly tenants, he was soon master of all Glamorgan – a stunning achievement.[150]

At the end of October the Marshal struck another blow, one less of military than of psychological significance. He sent Richard Siward and Gilbert Basset to rescue Hubert de Burgh from Devizes.

At Devizes, Hubert had been guarded in rotation by the knights of the four earls appointed as his custodians back in November 1232. At least Henry allowed him a visit from Archbishop Luke to speak about his confession and the health of his soul.[151] But then, in September 1233, the knight of Richard of Cornwall, on the king's orders and with Richard's consent, handed Hubert over to the castellan of the castle, Ralph of Wilton. Henry was to be informed 'at any time of the day' that the handover had taken place. Hubert now felt entirely in Bishop Peter's power and feared for his life, the more especially as Ralph of Wilton was

[147] CR 1231–4, 314, 434. For Hamo's career, see Hillaby, 'Hamo of Hereford',
[148] Walker, 'The supporters of Richard Marshal', 55–6.
[149] 'Margam Continuation', 138.
[150] Walker, 'The supporters of Richard Marshal', 57–60.
[151] CR 1231–4, 314.

a personal enemy.[152] What happened next, Hubert was later to describe in a conversation with Matthew Paris. He won over the two servants who brought his food, and on the night of 29 September they released him from his cell and got him out of the keep, the stronger carrying Hubert, who was still fettered, on his shoulders. Disaster nearly followed when Hubert fell into the dry moat, ending up in a bush, but the fetters made little noise, no bones were broken, and the party struggled out and reached the adjoining church of St John the Baptist, very visible against the night sky with its tall Norman tower. The escape, however, was soon discovered and, with the scene lit by lanterns and flaming faggots, Hubert was found in the chancel of the church, clutching the crucifix on the altar. Beaten and punched, he was dragged back to the castle and thrown into an even deeper dungeon. When Henry heard the news he ordered Hubert to be restored to his previous 'vault' and given sufficient food but to be loaded with three pairs of iron fetters. This could not last. The bishops at the Westminster council protested at the gross breach of sanctuary and Hubert was restored to St John's just as he had before been restored to the chapel at Brentwood. There he was guarded day and night by the whole posse of the county, while Bishop Peter with grim satisfaction set up a packed court to try him when he was finally forced out.[153]

In deciding to rescue Hubert, Richard Marshal was reviving the old alliance between his brother and the justiciar, an alliance which, after all, had brought Gilbert Basset the prize of Upavon. He was also linking his own cause to that of a man for whom there was now much sympathy. Here was the English hero who had saved the kingdom from foreign invasion in 1217 and governed in peace for more than a decade before being destroyed by a clique of lawless foreigners.

The rescue bid took place in the early morning of Saturday 29 October. It was market day and Devizes (which Basset knew intimately as a former constable) was shrouded in mist. Siward and Basset broke through to Hubert in the church, placed him on a horse and galloped away shouting the old battle cry 'God aids the Marshal'. By evening they had reached the Severn at Aust. A tense night in the woods followed. Hubert, as he later recalled, prayed earnestly to the Virgin and heard again and again a voice saying 'Fear not she will deliver you.' Sure enough, early next morning, galleys appeared to ferry the party across to Chepstow where Hubert was greeted by the Marshal himself 'with joy and honour'.[154]

Henry heard this astonishing news just after his arrival at Hereford. He ordered the outlawry of Siward and Basset (an illegal process it was later

[152] *CR 1231–4*, 276; Paris, vi, 73; Dunstable, 138.
[153] *CR 1231–4*, 325–7; *F*, 211 (*CPR 1232–47*, 27). For Hubert's version of his escape as told to Matthew Paris, see Paris, *HA*, ii, 359–60. The chancel of the church retains its twelfth-century vault and wall arcading.
[154] 'Margam Continuation', 136–8.

decided) and the destruction of all their property along with that of the Marshal. Nothing daunted by the loss of Glamorgan, he also pressed on with preparations for the campaign, even summoning galleys from Bordeaux to help with the blockade of Chepstow.[155]

At first things went well. The Marshal's castle at Goodrich was taken and Llywelyn was forced to abandon the siege of Brecon. Henry himself left Hereford on 10 November and next day was at Grosmont. From there he probably intended to continue on to Abergavenny and then march on Usk. It was not to be.

'The castle of Grossemount . . . standeth strongly on a rocke of hil drye ditched, and a village of the same name by it,' wrote John Leland around 1538. Hubert de Burgh during his tenure had rebuilt the parish church, giving it a fine chancel similar to that at Burgh itself. He had also transformed the castle so that it had a new hall and a curtain wall with formidable round towers. But if Henry, in the castle, was thus completely secure, the bulk of his forces sleeping in tents outside were vulnerable. In the early night of 11 November (with sunset around four o'clock) they were ambushed by the Marshal. He himself kept out of it, unwilling to attack the king, and his men only killed one knight, but they plundered the royal army of its money, armour and horses. The engagement was decisive for the whole course of the war. According to Wendover, many magnates who had lost everything returned home. Henry was left 'nearly alone'. By 18 November he was back at Hereford. He remained there for the next four weeks and then moved with the two Peters to Gloucester for a low-key and lonely Christmas. He never took the field again.[156]

The regime, nonetheless, nursed illusions that Richard Marshal might still submit. There were certainly those who urged him to do so. Robert Grosseteste, soon to be bishop of Lincoln, in a pained letter, urged him to turn the other cheek, endure evil rather than be its cause, and seek no revenge for injustice. But at least this acknowledged that he had suffered injustice.[157] Just before Christmas the Marshal also received an envoy from the court. This was none other than the chief minister of the Franciscan friars in England, Brother Agnellus of Pisa. His labours in travelling to Wales in the cold of midwinter were to hasten his death. Agnellus explained that if the Marshal threw himself on the mercy of the king, Henry would grant him life and limb and an estate in Herefordshire on which to live. In the debate which followed the Marshal skilfully widened the issue beyond his personal wrongs. He had, he said, been despoiled 'without judgment' when always ready to submit to the 'judgment of his peers'. If he submitted now to the king's 'erroneous will unsupported by reason', it would set an 'evil example' and do injury to the king's 'honour'

---

[155] CR 1231–4, 542–4.
[156] Wendover, iii, 253–4; Tewkesbury, 91; CR 1231–4, 338–9.
[157] Robert Grosseteste, 73–5.

and to the right and justice which he was supposed to give to his people. In all this, the Marshal was careful to exempt Henry himself from blame. It was the ministers who were his target. They had violated their agreement with Hubert de Burgh. They had broken their oaths to keep Magna Carta and were thus in a state of excommunication. Stephen of Seagrave had sworn to maintain the laws yet had corrupted them. Bishop Peter aspired to cover the land with aliens and indeed planned to bring England under the sway of the emperor.[158]

There was, of course, no chance of the Marshal accepting the court's offer. Indeed, given the course of the war it was little short of absurd. While Henry lay quiescent at Hereford, the Marshal was engaged in heroic activity. In a skirmish on 25 November he was wounded in the face yet hit out left and right with his sword and, with his horse killed beneath him, leapt onto another, pulling its rider from the saddle. A month later he ravaged the area around Monmouth while Richard Siward took off on another of his marauding raids, burning Richard of Cornwall's houses at Beckley, Stephen of Seagrave's at Seagrave and Bishop Peter's outside Winchester. In January, Llywelyn joined forces with the Marshal and together they laid waste the march between Hereford and Shrewsbury, leaving Shrewsbury itself in flames.

'While all these things were done,' observed Roger of Wendover, 'the king with the bishop of Winchester remained peacefully at Gloucester since he did not have the military force to dare to attack his enemies.' Henry finally set off home on 12 January, 'shamed and confounded, leaving the region to be depopulated by his enemies'.[159] At least Bishop Peter was able to show that he was more than a defeated general. At this very time he was completing the foundation of an Augustinian priory at Selborne. Henry himself was thinking of one of his own foundations. At Winchester on 26 January he set out the constitution for the hospital of St John he had refounded outside the East Gate of Oxford. It too was to follow the Augustinian rule. Henry, however, could not escape politics for long. For the beginning of February, he had summoned another great council to meet at Westminster.[160]

ARCHBISHOP EDMUND'S INTERVENTION

When Henry arrived back at Westminster on 1 February 1234 he was entering one of the most dangerous periods of his reign. He would be forced to dismiss the ministers to whom he had given so much trust. He

[158] Wendover, iii, 257–62; Thomas of Eccleston, 76; Powicke, *King Henry III*, i, 132, has an evocative description of this mission. For discussion of the debate, see Weiler, *Kingship, Rebellion*, 79–80, 91, 93, 114.

[159] Wendover, iii, 264–5.

[160] *Selborne Charters*, 8–10; *CJB*, iii, xvii n. 1; *CPR 1232–47*, 38.

would even be accused of complicity in murder. Yet through an engaging mixture of humility and piety he managed to emerge with his reputation in some ways enhanced.

Central to this remarkable performance was Henry's relationship with his new archbishop of Canterbury, Edmund of Abingdon. Since the death of Richard Grant back in August 1231, the monks of Canterbury had elected three successive archbishops, the king's chancellor, Ralph de Neville, their own prior, John of Sittingbourne, and Bishop Peter's friend the Oxford theologian John Blund. All had been rejected by the pope, who had then stepped in himself and nominated his own candidate for election, Edmund of Abingdon. Edmund was a distinguished scholar, a former pupil of Stephen Langton and a professor of theology at Oxford. Unlike Blund, he had no connections with the current regime.

When the great council opened at Westminster at the beginning of February, Henry duly confirmed Edmund's election and gave him the temporalities of his see. The king's intellect might be below Edmund's scholarship but his heart was open to his moral and spiritual teaching. Edmund was certainly a contrast to Bishop Peter. Where Peter had spent years at the exchequer, Edmund refused to hear even his own accounts. Where Peter loved hunting and display, Edmund counted riding and eating as so much time lost from study. He slept on the floor, rose in the middle of the night to pray, wore modest grey clothes and beneath them not a mere hair shirt but a knotted vest which he laced up with agonizing tightness.[161] Yet Edmund was no ivory tower ascetic. His most famous work, the *Speculum Ecclesiae*, was a practical manual of moral and pastoral theology, which ascends from elementary religious instruction to the heights of mystical devotion.[162] One of Edmund's themes as a preacher was how courts were full of flatterers and corrupt councillors, like those who had lured Achab, king of Israel, to his death in battle with false promises of victory. Listening to that, Henry might well think he had come close to succumbing to just such a fate himself.[163] Edmund brought to his new office the same intensity and endurance he devoted to his austerities and studies. Like Langton, he believed his duty was to maintain peace and counsel the king on all important affairs. Like Langton in 1223, he concluded that it was Bishop Peter and his party who were bringing discord to the realm.

At the Westminster council of February 1234, therefore, Edmund and his suffragans begged Henry to make peace and dismiss the two Peters. Henry agreed to negotiations, under episcopal auspices, for a truce with the Marshal and Llywelyn, but 'humbly' asked for a delay before making

[161] Lawrence, *St Edmund of Abingdon*, 187–94 (from the canonization proceedings).
[162] For discussion of the *Speculum Ecclesie*, see Binski, *Becket's Crown*, 193–7.
[163] Lawrence, *St Edmund of Abingdon*, 131.

a decision about his ministers.[164] He then set off on a pilgrimage to
Bromholm, just as he had before the fall of Hubert de Burgh in 1232.
When there he received on loan from Norwich cathedral a casket
containing the relics of a dozen saints and a piece of Aaron's rod. Henry
also visited Bury where, 'moved by piety', as Wendover put it, he was
reconciled to Hubert's wife, the countess of Kent.[165] Bishop Peter,
however, like Hubert before him, was not going down without a fight. He
accompanied Henry on his pilgrimage (as Edmund did not), and on 28
February received both a concession relating to Selborne priory and a gift
of timber.[166] Peter de Rivallis was equally tenacious. If he was threatened
by the return to court early in March of his enemy Godfrey of Crowcombe,
he still controlled much day-to-day business and spun the wheel of
patronage. On 3 March, while Henry (at Fotheringhay) distributed gifts to
the surrounding friars, lepers, hospitals and religious houses, he was able
to give away the lands of one of the Marshal's knights.[167]

Unfortunately for the two Peters, as Henry returned south, their regime
endured a fresh humiliation. When Stephen of Seagrave saw flames rising
from his manor house at Alconbury, a few miles from Huntingdon, he
went off to investigate, only to turn tail and gallop back in panic when he
realized the perpetrator was the fearsome Richard Siward![168] Against this,
however, there was at last a real military success. Henry de Trubleville,
sacked on Hubert's fall as seneschal in Gascony, had made terms with the
new regime and been given key commands in Wales. At some time in
February, with great daring, he sailed from Bristol and broke up Llywelyn's
three-month siege of Carmarthen. This, however, was little more than a
consolation goal near the end of the match. On 6 March the bishops of
Coventry and Rochester agreed a truce with the Marshal and Llywelyn. It
was to last until 25 July, by which time, through the auspices of the archbishop, peace was to be made.[169] Meanwhile all parties were to keep what
they held. So the Marshal remained as conqueror of Glamorgan. He was
now under threat in Ireland, but he had won the war in Wales. Bishop
Peter's grandiose plans to invade Gwent and Pembroke and break him, as
King John had broken William de Briouze, were in ruins.

The climax of the struggle for power was now at hand. On 2 April, a
day specially chosen as the Sunday of 'Rejoice Jerusalem', Henry was at
Canterbury for the consecration of Edmund of Abingdon as archbishop.[170] A week later a great council opened at Westminster. On 10 April

[164] Wendover, iii, 268–71; *RL*, i, 433–5; *CR 1231–4*, 551.
[165] Wendover, iii, 271; Tewkesbury, 92; *CR 1231–4*, 378, 380; *CPR 1232–47*, 39.
[166] *CR 1231–4*, 383.
[167] *CR 1231–4*, 383–4.
[168] Wendover, iii, 271.
[169] *AWR*, no. 269.
[170] For this Sunday, see below, 516.

Henry granted Bishop Peter's foundation at Selborne an array of liberties in a charter witnessed by the good and great of the land. But it was a form of farewell. 'The pious king,' as Wendover put it, 'in every way thirsted after peace' and now 'humbly submitted' to the counsel of Edmund and the other bishops. The Dunstable annalist spoke in similar terms. 'The most pious king' 'committed his body, soul, crown and kingdom to the archbishop with much devotion, which done the archbishop removed from the king's council and household Peter bishop of Winchester and Peter de Rivallis, the treasurer, and all other Poitevins'.[171]

Since Bishop Peter held no formal office, the precise moment he was barred from court is unknown, but the last writ he authorized, one dispatching crossbows to Henry de Trubleville at Carmarthen, was on 17 March, a fitting conclusion to the political career of this most military of bishops. Peter de Rivallis's end came on 15 April. On that day Henry personally authorized the writ removing him as treasurer of the exchequer and custodian of all wards and escheats. Around the same time de Rivallis lost his charge of the king's wardrobe. In the next few weeks he was deprived of all his other offices.[172] Henry had thus removed the two Peters and soon wanted them punished, but for the moment he retained Stephen of Seagrave as justiciar and Robert Passelewe as day-to-day head of the exchequer. This must reflect a distinction made by Archbishop Edmund between the leaders of the regime and their satellites, as it was also a distinction between the aliens and Englishmen. Seagrave, therefore, that 'flexible man', now had a hand in the rehabilitation of Bishop Mauclerc, although no one had profited more from Mauclerc's fall than himself.[173]

At the end of April, Henry set off from Westminster for a meeting of a great council at Gloucester where Archbishop Edmund hoped to finalize a general peace. When Henry reached Reading, where a Jew was baptized in his presence and then sent to the Domus Conversorum in London, he learnt that Richard Siward had shadowed him through Windsor Forest. Three days later Siward attacked the king's baggage train as it made its way to Woodstock and seized the possessions of Stephen of Seagrave. Around the same time he also ravaged a manor of Robert Passelewe.[174] If this was not bad enough, when Henry finally reached Woodstock, he received news which transformed the political situation and placed him in great danger.

THE DEATH OF RICHARD MARSHAL

Confident of his victory in Wales, Richard Marshal had left for Ireland. He had every reason to go there for the justiciar, Maurice fitzGerald, had

---

[171] Wendover, iii, 272–3; Dunstable, 135–7; Tewkesbury, 192; Margam, 139.

[172] *CR 1231–4*, 391; *CFR 1233–4*, nos. 196–8.

[173] *CR 1231–4*, 249, 401–2, 416–17.

[174] *CR 1231–4*, 415, 557–8; Wendover/Paris, iii, 289.

attacked his lordship of Leinster in alliance with Hugh and Walter de Lacy. They had been joined by Richard de Burgh, who calculated his best hope of keeping Connacht was to throw in his lot with the king. On arrival, the Marshal quickly gained hold of Limerick and then set about restoring his position in Leinster. But then, on 1 April, in fighting on the plain outside Kildare, he was wounded and captured by his enemies.[175] He was taken back to Kildare castle where he was soon eating, drinking, walking round his chamber and playing dice. Then his wounds festered, a doctor made matters worse, and on 16 April he died.[176]

Henry heard the news at Woodstock soon after 6 May. The shock was made all the greater by rumours that he and his ministers had plotted the Marshal's death. In fact, there was no murder plot for the Marshal was captured not killed. But it was easy to believe the contrary, the more especially as Henry had almost certainly issued letters confiscating the Marshal's lands in Ireland and giving them to his opponents. In this situation, potentially fatal to his reputation, if not his kingship, Henry's reaction was just right. 'To the admiration of all who were there,' wrote Wendover, he burst into tears, called the priests of his chapel and had a solemn mass sung for the Marshal's soul. Next day, after more masses, he distributed bountiful alms to the poor. 'Blessed, therefore, is such a king who loved his enemies and prayed with tears for his persecutors.' This praiseworthy reaction became widely known. 'The king, rendered penitent and moved by mercy, was shaken by vehement sorrow,' wrote the Waverley annalist. 'The king groaned for a long time as did David for the deaths of Saul and Jonathan,' wrote the annalist of Dunstable.[177]

Henry's behaviour was equally fitting when a shocked Archbishop Edmund arrived at Woodstock. The account of their meeting by Matthew Paris (in his life of Edmund) may be elaborated but probably catches its flavour. Henry rose reverently and kissed the archbishop. He then listened calmly as Edmund pleaded that the Marshal's younger brother Gilbert be allowed to succeed to the Marshal inheritance. When Edmund had finished the 'kind hearted king' was 'moved by piety' and exclaimed with a smile 'oh how beautifully you pray . . . pray in the same way for me and I do not doubt that when God is favourable, it will be because he has heard you . . . It will be done as you wish.' Accordingly on 12 May, at Woodstock, Henry gave a safe conduct to Gilbert Marshal and his brothers to come from Ireland to England to seek his grace and make their peace.[178]

'England weep for the Marshal,' cried a poet.[179] But at least the Marshal had died with his cause won. It was on the very day of his death

---

[175] For discussion, see Smith, 'Irish politics', 15–17.
[176] Wendover/Paris, iii, 278–9, 283–4; Wendover, *Flores*, iii, 86–7.
[177] Wendover, iii, 289–90; Waverley, 314–15; Dunstable, 137.
[178] Lawrence, *St Edmund of Abingdon*, 240–1; *CPR 1232–47*, 45.
[179] Waverley, 315.

that Henry authorized the writ dismissing Peter de Rivallis. In the ensuing weeks Gilbert Basset was restored to Upavon, and Gilbert Marshal succeeded to the whole of his brother's inheritance including the lordship in Ireland. The Marshal's defeat there was thus overturned by his victory in Wales and England. Richard Marshal was the last of the great Anglo-Norman barons. He came late to English politics and only opposed the arbitrary actions of the king when they affected his own interests. But, thereafter, he had converted his own cause into one with general appeal. He had seemed to stand for the fundamental laws and customs of the kingdom against a clique of foreigners seeking to subvert them. He was a precursor of Simon de Montfort.

THE GLOUCESTER COUNCIL OF MAY 1234

The great council which opened at Gloucester on or soon after 16 May 1234 was one of the most important in Henry's reign. It dismissed Stephen of Seagrave and Robert Passelewe, and rehabilitated the rebels, in the process affirming the principle of kingship guided by great councils and subject to the law. The council was attended by the archbishops of Canterbury and Dublin, the bishops of Bath, Durham, Carlisle, Coventry and Rochester, and by the earls of Cornwall, Derby, Hereford, Surrey and Warwick.

Seagrave's fall was sudden. As late as 21 May he was still justiciar and able to secure a substantial favour for his son. Then suddenly, in the midst of the assembly, he was accused by Archbishop Edmund of complicity in the Marshal's death. By 24 May he had resigned the justiciarship, given the king £500 (it was all paid into the wardrobe) and agreed to surrender the lands he had gained from the crown. Soon he was sheltering in Leicester abbey, with his head tonsured, claiming the status of a clerk.[180] Passelewe's removal from the exchequer took place around the same time. He was still there on 26 May; gone by 1 June.[181] Soon he was hiding in a cellar in the New Temple. The sweeping away of the old regime was not complete. Although Godfrey of Crowcombe recovered his Oxfordshire offices from Engelard de Cigogné, Engelard was allowed to live out his days as castellan of Windsor, the castle he had defended so gallantly during the 1215–17 civil war. The two young foreigners John de Plessis and Matthias Bezill, who had come to court during Bishop Peter's regime, both managed to remain there.

A series of safe and respectable appointments were made to replace the outgoing ministers. The new treasurer of the exchequer was the exchequer clerk Hugh of Pattishall, a son of the distinguished judge Simon of Pattishall. In Matthew Paris's view, Hugh carried out his duties blamelessly

---

[180] *CPR 1232–47*, 47; *CR 1231–4*, 427, 567; Wild, *WA*, 1.
[181] TNA E 159/13, mm. 7–7d; *CPR 1232–47*, 53.

until his election to the bishopric of Coventry in 1240. The new keeper of the wardrobe, replacing de Rivallis just as he had in 1224, was the clerk Walter of Kirkham, a man completely out of favour during Bishop Peter's regime. On his elevation to the bishopric of Durham in 1249, he was described by the Lanercost chronicler as 'pure and mild, small in body but pious and most noble minded who loved psalms not hunting'.[182]

The council also made an appointment to what was in effect a new position. As one of its first acts it summoned to Gloucester the chief justice of the judicial bench at Westminster, William of Raleigh. He must have ridden hard westwards for he left Westminster after 21 May and was at Gloucester by the 27th.[183] The immediate purpose was to involve Raleigh in the judicial decisions central to the rehabilitation of the former rebels. But Raleigh, probably as intended, became the professional judge presiding over a court that followed the king, the court *coram rege*, which now, for the first time, has a continuous life.[184] The appointment was highly political, for Raleigh, a protégé of the Pattishall dynasty of judges, believed passionately that the king was subject to the law and should rule in concert with great councils. His horror at Bishop Peter's doings was probably well known.

At the same time as it filled a new position, the great council left empty an old one. Stephen of Seagrave was not replaced as justiciar. Henry was in full agreement with the decision. Both Seagrave and de Burgh, after all, had enriched themselves at his expense. There was also, as Henry later observed, no need for a justiciar now that the king spent most of his time in England.[185] The exchequer could be run by its treasurer. Chancellor Neville, the stewards, the keepers of the wardrobe and others at court could carry the burden of day-to-day business. It was only in changed circumstances that parliaments of the 1240s and 1250s called repeatedly for the revival of the justiciarship, the very office suspended by common consent in 1234.

THE PUNISHMENT OF THE FALLEN MINISTERS

Henry did not merely wish to dismiss his old ministers. He also wished to punish them. His sense of betrayal was very great. He accused Seagrave both of hypocrisy and deception, hypocrisy in upbraiding Hubert de Burgh for 'usurping' the king's demesnes only then to do the same himself, deception in lying about the extent of the land he was seeking from the king.[186] The problem was that Seagrave, de Rivallis and others had all

[182] Lanercost, 69; Tout, *Chapters*, i, 244.
[183] *CRR*, xv, pp. xxvi–vii (by Meekings).
[184] See Meekings and Crook, *King's Bench and Common Bench*, 30–2, 49–50.
[185] *DBM*, 252–3.
[186] *CR 1231–4*, 567; *CRR*, xv, nos. 1136–8, 1883.

obtained concessions from the king in hereditary right under the terms of royal charters, just as before had Hubert de Burgh and his associates. Up to a point the method of proceeding was the same. Seagrave was forced to offer money for the king's goodwill and surrender his charters, just as had Bishop Mauclerc in 1233. Yet there was also a difference. Henry, under the new regime, to a far greater extent than under the old one, was made to cloak his actions in at least a semblance of justice and legal process.

Seagrave, therefore, was summoned *coram rege* to answer the charges against him, with Henry explaining that he wished to 'give full justice to everyone in the kingdom'. The demand that he should surrender Newcastle-under-Lyme (granted in hereditary right to his son) was justified on the grounds that its castle was needed by the king to defend the march between Wales and the lands of the earl of Chester.[187] De Rivallis was a far steelier character than Seagrave and also had the protection of a rather more genuine clerical status. He accepted that he had lost his offices but sought to bargain for the retention of the honour and castle of Pevensey, the Three Castles and the wardship of John de Briouze, which had brought him Bramber and Gower. Over these possessions Henry indeed acknowledged that de Rivallis had some rights. He insisted he was seeking 'nothing unjustly' and demanded the surrender of the castles only because of a decision 'by common counsel' that all castles on the sea coast and in the march of Wales should be taken into his hands because of the threat from France following the expiry of the truce.

Another method of attack, perfectly lawful, was to summon de Rivallis to account for all his erstwhile offices. When, through envoys, de Rivallis asked for letters of safe conduct, Henry lost his temper. According to the official record, he 'replied harshly, saying that he would make him no letters and that he wished him no good, but that he would seek to do him and his uncle evil and harm, and it would please him if anyone did them evil and harm'. Wendover even has Henry threatening to pull out de Rivallis's eyes. Henry was, however, soon calmed down by the bishops and magnates in attendance. 'His anger having abated', the official record continues, 'he replied courteously' and explained that a safe conduct was inappropriate for someone being summoned to account in time of peace. When de Rivallis still failed to appear, a group of bishops, earls, barons and ministers, forty-four strong, sat in judgement on him and decided he was in the king's mercy for default. Almost uniquely all their names were recorded on the roll of the court *coram rege*. This was on 30 June and on the same day orders were issued to take the honour and castle of Pevensey, the Briouze custody and the Three Castles into the king's hands.[188]

Eventually, on 14 July, de Rivallis did appear before the king and his judges at Westminster. According again to Wendover he flung himself to

---

[187] *CR 1231–4*, 475, 567; *CRR*, xv, no. 1059.
[188] *CRR*, xv, nos. 1031–2, 1064; *CPR 1232–47*, 58–9; *CR 1231–4*, 462–3.

the ground and begged for mercy: a painful and noisy gesture if, as Wendover asserts, he was wearing a coat of mail under his clerical garb! In fact, the official record shows de Rivallis still bargaining with the king. When his answers were deemed unsatisfactory, he was sentenced to imprisonment, although a few days later 'for love of the archbishop [Edmund] and for the honour of holy church', as Henry put it, he was released from the Tower and allowed to join his uncle at Winchester. His case rumbled on without reaching any conclusion. On one embarrassing occasion at Woodstock, still arguing with the king, he offered formally to surrender all the offices he had held by royal charter and 'adding that he wished to begin near Scotland' ran through from north to south a vast list of royal castles, sheriffdoms and other custodies. Henry's foolishness in granting him so much could not have been made more plain.[189] Peter de Rivallis was nothing if not hardy and resilient. His career was to have a remarkable final phase.[190]

Hardest to bring to book was the great author of Henry's miseries and misfortunes sitting in disdainful defiance at Winchester, Bishop Peter himself. He resisted pressure to loan the king £4,000, brought even Richard Siward to heel by a sentence of excommunication, and proved that he had not been sheltering Peter de Rivallis. A judgement pronounced before the king by Archbishop Edmund and 'the magnates of England', declared that he had done what he could to produce his nephew.[191] Since Peter had held no office (other than the sheriffdom of Hampshire), there was no point summoning him to account. His chief gains from the king had been the liberties conferred on the church of Winchester and Selborne abbey and Henry was not going to cancel those. Bishop Peter's contempt for Henry must have known no bounds. When asked in 1236 to go on a diplomatic mission he refused. Given all the criticism he had faced, for him now to be a royal envoy would merely highlight, he said, the instability of the king.[192]

REHABILITATION OF THE REBELS AND THE RULE OF LAW

The Gloucester council did not merely complete the dismissal of the old ministers. It also rehabilitated the former rebels. In the process, the council was determined to highlight the injustice of the king's actions and set new standards for the future. Henry was thus made to confess his faults and acknowledge that he had been both unwise and unjust. He had listened to 'evil counsel', denied his opponents judgement by their peers, deprived them of property by acts of 'will', and outlawed them without proper legal

---

[189] *CRR*, xv, nos. 1064, 1289; Wendover, iii, 294–5.
[190] See below, 672.
[191] *CPR 1232–47*, 47; Winchester, 86–7; *CRR*, xv, no. 1127.
[192] Paris, iii, 393.

process. Henry accepted all this with a mixture of penitence and emotion that took the edge off his humiliation and made him seem again 'a most pious king'.[193] Yet he also, in a way not unimpressive, sought to protect his own interests and make the best terms he could. Alone and brought low, he was not down and out.

Gilbert Marshal, Richard Siward, Gilbert and Philip Basset and Hubert de Burgh were brought to Gloucester by Archbishop Edmund, fresh letters of conduct being issued for them on 25 May. Hubert de Burgh led them into the king's presence 'bare foot and unbelted, heads uncovered and arms bare unto the elbows':

> They fell at the king's feet and mercy him cried vast
> The king could not forbear but he now wept at last
> And began in very pity in a swoon now to fall down
> But the earl of Hereford held him and Sir Godfrey of Crowcombe

So wrote (in English) a later poet basing his account on well-informed local annals.[194]

The ritual of submission was designed to obscure the realities of the situation and make it easier for Henry to comply with what must now happen. In Matthew Paris's account, probably derived from Hubert himself, Henry seemed indeed happy. He received Hubert 'with a cheerful face', embraced him and gave him the kiss of peace. 'Having recovered his mind and led by a similar spirit of piety', he likewise received Siward and Basset 'into his full and unfeigned grace'. Hubert, as he told Paris, saw his restoration as reward for having obeyed divinely conveyed instructions to spare a church from destruction during the 1215–17 civil war.[195]

These emotional scenes, however, did not reflect the totality of Henry's mood. He could not forget that these men had been in rebellion against him. When it came to the details, he proved sticky over the extent of their restoration. One issue here concerned the outlawries. On 26 May, Henry merely pardoned them whereas de Burgh, Basset and Siward wished them nullified altogether.[196] Here they had the full support of the Gloucester council, determined, as it was, to show Henry's conduct had been unlawful. On 27 May, therefore, 'since the king wished to give justice to everyone in his court', Henry brought together Archbishop Edmund, the bishops, earls and barons. Their judgement was pronounced by William of Raleigh. It was in every way remarkable. A great council laid down the law to the king, in the process restricting his use of the weapon of outlawry. The outlawries were thus pronounced null and void having been promulgated 'unjustly

---

[193] Dunstable, 137.
[194] *Robert of Gloucester*, ii, lines 10825–33; Hailes, 53.
[195] Paris, iii, 290–2.
[196] *RL*, i, 439–41; *CPR 1232–47*, 48–9.

and against the law of the land'. No one, the judgement said, could be outlawed if in a state of war with the king, as had been the case with Siward and Basset. No one could be outlawed on the simple order of the king, as had happened, to Hubert de Burgh. Instead an inquest must be held by the king's judges to establish guilt. Mere escape from prison, moreover, was not sufficient to incur the penalty.[197] The court, on 27 May, also made Henry acknowledge how he had erred in refusing to allow judgement by peers. As the official record stated, he 'came and recognized and remembered' how he had denied Richard Marshal and Gilbert Basset a proper safe conduct so that they could come and have such a judgement.

Henry also tried to argue over the extent of Basset's and Seagrave's restoration. On 26 May he merely offered to restore the lands they and their wives had inherited. Those they had acquired, often now given away by the king to others, they would have to recover by bringing legal actions. On 30 May all this changed. Siward, the Bassets and twenty-two more Marshal followers were restored to all the lands they had lost during the Marshal war.[198] This concession did not cover Upavon since Basset had lost that to Maulay before the war. Upavon, however, had already been dealt with by the great court held on 27 May. The history of the dispute was rehearsed up to the point where the king's justices and the magnates had refused to sit in judgement on the charters of the king.[199] 'Whereupon', as the record continued, 'the king by his will disseised Gilbert and gave the manor to Peter de Maulay.' The writ now putting all this right stated that Henry had restored Basset 'by judgment of the court', having 'disseised him by will'.[200]

Henry's toughest stand was reserved for Hubert de Burgh. He still resented the way Hubert had gorged himself at the crown's expense. In the terms offered on 26 May, therefore, Hubert was to resign the justiciarship and all the castles and lands given him by Henry from the royal demesne. In return, he could recover his inherited lands and would receive 'grace up to a certain point', in respect of land he had acquired from others. These terms were in some ways worse than those conceded in November 1232 when Hubert was to keep all his acquisitions.[201]

Henry had not finished. As Hubert later recorded, 'in the evening after peace was made at Gloucester', 'the king sent for him and led him to the altar saying that he wished him to swear on the altar that he would never speak about Richard de Clare, adding that he would never have his grace unless he swore that oath'. In this eerie episode, with its echoes of the oath of Burgh, Henry was thus demanding that Hubert resign all claims to the

---

[197] Paris, vi, 73; *CR 1231–4*, 566–7; *BNB*, ii, no. 857, interpreted in the light of *Bracton*, ii, 355, 357, 359; Pollock and Maitland, *History of English Law*, ii, 581.

[198] *RL*, i, 439–41; *CPR 1232–47*, 48–9; *CR 1231–4*, 435–7, 442.

[199] This was the correct procedure for only the king could judge his own acts.

[200] *BNB*, ii, 665; *CR 1231–4*, 437.

[201] *RL*, i, 440; *CPR 1232–47*, 48.

Clare wardship and with it the right to Richard de Clare's marriage. (Richard was, of course, intended for Hubert's daughter Meggotta.) Hubert gave this oath and also resigned the justiciarship and Dover castle. Further than that, however, he would not go. He refused to abandon his claims to Henry's gifts and to the lands Henry had given away.[202] In the event, having recovered the Clare wardship, Henry became more conciliatory. On 3 June he restored Hubert to all his non-royal acquisitions and in addition returned some manors granted him by King John. Hubert was also allowed to bring legal actions in the court *coram rege* for the recovery of property Henry had bestowed on others.[203]

The actions which followed all turned explicitly or implicitly on alleged disseisin 'by will of the king'. In one case, heard before Archbishop Edmund, and assorted bishops, earls and barons, Henry recognized that he had disseised Hubert of Apsley in Bedfordshire unjustly and had no right to give it to Robert Passelewe.[204] In another, when Hubert complained that he had been disseised of two manors 'by will of the king', Henry again 'came' to court and confessed his error. He had thought Hubert had been outlawed 'licitly' and thus that he could take the manors. Now he realized that was not the case.[205] The king equally acknowledged his faults in cases involving other individuals. Thus Henry appeared in person to acknowledge that he had disseised Eustace de Stuteville of the manor of Cottingham in Yorkshire 'by his will without summons and without judgment'.[206] A few days later (in July 1234) he described in abject terms how he had disseised Bishop Mauclerc of Gisland in Cumberland, led astray by the false suggestions of Robert de Vaux.[207] In January 1235, when the bishop of Bath complained that Henry, 'saving his grace', had 'unjustly and by will' taken trees from the episcopal woods, Henry accepted that he had done the bishop 'an injury', having forgotten all about the rights in the bishop's charters. 'And so', the record of the case concluded, 'it is considered in the king's presence that the woods should remain to the bishop and his successors . . . and the lord king pronounced this judgment with his own mouth.'[208]

GILBERT MARSHAL, WALES AND IRELAND

By far the most important of the nobles brought by Archbishop Edmund to Gloucester was Gilbert Marshal.[209] On 30 May, Henry took his homage

---

[202] *CR 1234–7*, 509; Paris, vi, 72–4; *CRR*, xvi, nos. 145, 1895.

[203] *CR 1231–4*, 443.

[204] *CRR*, xv, no. 1058.

[205] *CRR*, xv, no. 1475; *BNB*, ii, nos. 1136, 1141; *CChR 1226–57*, 24, 82, 182; *CR 1231–4*, 379.

[206] *CRR*, xv, no. 1026.

[207] *CPR 1232–47*, 60; *CChR 1226–57*, 189.

[208] *CRR*, xv, no. 1305. Henry's readiness to uphold his charters, did not, however, extend to those granted to peasants: see Carpenter, 'Peasants of Rothley', and below, 543.

[209] For Gilbert, see below, 169.

for the Marshal inheritance in England, Wales and Ireland.[210] He also acknowledged the Marshal victory in Wales by asking for no more than a nominal surrender of Glamorgan. On 3 June, Gilbert was ordered to hand the lordship over to none other than Richard Siward![211] Henry also accepted the advances of Llywelyn. The truce made by Edmund at Middle in Shropshire on 21 June returned the situation to the status quo before the war. That meant Llywelyn retained hold of Cardigan, having conquered it in 1231. He also retained Mold, southern Powys, Maelienydd and Builth. The truce was only meant to last for two years but in fact was renewed at intervals until Llywelyn's death in 1240. It was a triumph for Llywelyn and left him as the dominant power in Wales.

To some appearances, Henry accepted the succession of Gilbert Marshal with a good grace. Having knighted him and invested him with the earldom of Pembroke, he gave thirty deer towards the ensuing feast. Gilbert soon established himself at court and extracted, as will be seen, major concessions from the king.[212] Henry's feelings, however, were mixed. On 25 May, when he received Gilbert into his grace, he did so 'because of the death of Earl Richard his brother', which was rather different from condoning Richard's rebellion. Indeed, Henry, around the same time, was thanking the Irish magnates for resisting Richard so successfully 'as events have shown'. Later, according to Matthew Paris, he taxed Gilbert with Richard's rebellion and said the family should have been disinherited.[213] It was in Ireland that Henry was able to give vent to some of these feelings, although to a lesser extent than he might once have hoped.

At the time of the Marshal's capture and before the fall of Bishop Peter was known, a letter was sent to Henry by a royal agent in Ireland setting out the golden vistas now opening up. The letter shows very clearly how committed such men were to the expansion of royal power, and how strongly they felt this was the moment to bring it about. Henry was urged to hasten to Ireland himself where he would gain far more than even his father. The castles and lands of the Marshal, worth all of £20,000, were in the hands of the justiciar and Henry should come and receive them. He should defer answering the demands of the Irish barons (of whom the justiciar was one) while he inquired into their fidelity and valued the lands they sought. If he did return Connacht to Richard de Burgh, he should retain a city and castle in each cantref (administrative division) so as to control local courts and justice. He should beware the liberties sought by de Burgh, Walter de Lacy and others, 'since all wish to have nearly royal power and liberty'.[214]

[210] CR 1231–4, 435–6.
[211] CPR 1232–47, 53.
[212] Wendover, iii, 292; Tewkesbury, 93; CR 1231–4, 440.
[213] RL, i, 438–9; CPR 1232–47, 48, 65–6; CR 1231–4, 561; Paris, iii, 523–4; iv, 157–8.
[214] DAI, 2–3.

By the time this letter arrived in England, it was already out of date. Henry did not go to Ireland. Indeed, he never went there. The Marshal victory in England and Wales necessitated Gilbert's succession in Ireland also. But although the events of 1234 demonstrated the dependence of Irish politics on those of England and Wales, they also showed their independence. The defeat of the Marshal in Ireland did make a difference. Whereas Henry had to exempt Richard's followers in England from punishment, in Ireland he was able to demand fines from them for the pardon of their offences, recovery of their lands and if captured, release from prison.[215] Although the details are obscure, it was also in connection with Ireland that Henry, 'through great fear and violence', as the pope later put it, extracted 'a certain oath and obligation' from Gilbert Marshal. Here, however, a mark of the new regime, he was soon restrained. As the pope went on to explain, 'led by wiser counsel and becoming benevolent', Henry had remitted the oath 'mercifully recognizing the injury done to Gilbert'.[216]

Henry then made some money out of the Marshal defeat but that was all. He was also left with a simmering feud between Gilbert Marshal and his Irish enemies, enemies who had spearheaded the king's cause to victory (unlike their counterparts in England) and were now being fed with fair words, rather then a carve-up of the Marshal estates. These issues had to be faced again at a great council held later in 1234.[217]

KING HENRY III'S LESSON IN KINGSHIP[218]

In the tumultuous years between 1232 and 1234, Bishop Peter had driven Henry into a very different form of kingship from that practised under Hubert de Burgh. He had boasted about the plenitude of royal power and scoffed at the idea of judgement by peers. He had argued that the king could overturn the rights enshrined in royal charters, and appoint judges as he liked to pronounce judgement in cases being brought against disobedient subjects. This might have been acceptable had Henry been acting out of necessity in a national emergency. It was very different when he was simply rewarding members of the regime and punishing its enemies, all the more so when that regime was headed, so it seemed, by a gang of foreigners. England was being subjected to the tyranny of 'the Poitevins'.

The extent to which Bishop Peter's regime was at odds with prevailing legal and political culture is shown by one of the greatest books ever written about the laws and customs of England: Henry of Bracton's *De Legibus et Consuetudinibus Anglie*. In fact, Bracton himself, a *coram rege* judge

---

[215] *CDI*, nos. 2181, 2190, 2194, 2201, 2212, 2222, 2224, 2236, 2238–40, 2253–4.
[216] *Reg. Gregoire IX*, no. 2599.
[217] See below, 225.
[218] This heading is taken from the title of ch. 4 of Powicke's *King Henry III*.

in the 1240s and 1250s, was only the editor and custodian of the book. Its essential author, writing in the period between 1210 and 1234, was William of Raleigh himself.[219] What impresses about *Bracton* (as the work is conventionally called) is its 'constitutionality'. It continually insists that the king is subject to the law, must not rule 'by will', and should act in concert with his magnates. The king has no peer and is the Vicar of God, yet only so long as he rules justly. 'For the king must not be under man but under God and the law, because law makes the king . . . for there is no king where will rules rather than law.'[220] *Bracton* omits altogether the Roman law tag that the prince is 'freed from the laws, legibus solutus', and instead refers to the contrary Roman opinion that he was 'bound by the laws, legibus alligatus'.[221] In sharp contrast to the emperor's absolute authority to decide law as seen in the *Liber Augustalis*, *Bracton*'s king can make and change law only with the consent of great councils.[222] Thus *Bracton* is at pains to render harmless the Roman law maxim 'the will of the prince has the force of law': the will of the prince is 'not anything rashly put forward on his own will, but what has been rightly decided with the counsel of his magnates'.[223]

For William of Raleigh and those who thought like him, the regime of Bishop Peter was a shock and an affront. Just how great is seen from the passages Raleigh and his circle added to the text of *Bracton* in direct response to Peter's actions and pronouncements. One of these, drawing on Raleigh's judgement reversing the outlawries, explained that the king 'of his own will by his letters cannot cause someone to be proclaimed an outlaw'.[224] Another, refuting Bishop Peter's claim to the contrary, explained how the king must allow judgement by peers 'lest the king, in person, or through justices without peers, be both plaintiff and judge'.[225] Most striking of all is the passage in *Bracton* on resistance. This was inspired directly by the Upavon case and the question of what to do if the king disseised someone unjustly and broke his own charters. At first *Bracton* states the conventional view that there was little one could do other than charge the king with committing an 'injury' and 'petition him to correct his deed'. If that failed, then he must be left to 'the judgment of the living God'. But *Bracton* also canvassed a much less passive alternative, namely that 'the whole body (universitas) of the kingdom and the baronage may

---

[219] This was first shown by S.E. Thorne in his introduction to volume 3 of *Bracton*. The argument is clarified and taken further in Brand, 'Date and authorship of *Bracton*'. This is a response to the different view in Barton, 'Mystery of *Bracton*'.

[220] *Bracton*, ii, 33, 305–6.

[221] *Bracton*, ii, 305–6, and see ii, 110, 166, 169; iii, 43; iv, 79, 158–9.

[222] *Bracton*, ii, 19, 21; iv, 285, 289; and see also ii, 337; iii, 43, 73.

[223] *Bracton*, ii, 305. The sentiment is influenced by a passage in Justinian's *Institutes*. See also *LP*, 165, 296 and cxlviii.

[224] *Bracton*, ii, 358.

[225] *Bracton*, ii, 337; Ehrlich, *Proceedings against the Crown*, 49 n. 1.

and ought [to correct his deed] in the king's own court'. In another
passage *Bracton* was even more emphatic:

> The king has a superior, namely God. Also the law by which he is made
> king. Also his court, namely the earls and barons, because if he is without
> bridle, that is without law, they ought to put the bridle on him.[226]

The events of 1233–4 had emphatically vindicated the *Bractonian* view of
kingship. It had been challenged by Bishop Peter and the challenge had
failed. In a succession of great councils the 'universitas' of the kingdom
had resisted the Poitevin regime and in the end overthrown it. The final
Gloucester council in May 1234 had indeed put a bridle on the king. That
Henry must govern in concert with great councils, or 'parliaments' as they
were soon to be called, was clearly demonstrated. Equally insisted on in
1234 was that Henry must govern by law and not by will. There should be
no return to the governing style of King John and Bishop Peter. Behind
such an insistence stood Magna Carta. In justifying his actions, Richard
Marshal had accused Peter and his supporters of breaking Magna Carta
and being therefore in a state of excommunication. He was thinking of
the sentence passed by Archbishop Langton and the bishops in 1225
against all who contravened the Charters.[227] In the conflict of 1233–4,
Magna Carta had withstood its first great test.

THE END OF THE BRETON ALLIANCE

The year 1234 marked an end to Henry's continental policies just as it did
to his policies in England. Since 1229 the alliance with the duke of Brittany
had been central to Henry's continental ambitions. Amidst all the domestic
alarms and excursions, money had still been found to keep the alliance
alive and prepare for the moment when the truce with France expired in
June 1234. At the Westminster council in March 1234 there was yet another
financial settlement with Peter, duke of Brittany, with Henry promising to
have sixty knights at St James de Beuvron by 24 June, the day the truce was
to expire.[228] Henry's intentions were revealed in the instructions he gave

[226] *Bracton*, ii, 110; iii, xlvi n. 9 (Thorne's dating of the passage), 43; Carpenter, *Reign of Henry III*, 40–2.

[227] There is, however, one curious episode relating to the new regime's respect for Magna Carta. Under Bishop Peter, Eustace de Stuteville had offered the king £1,000 for justice in a case involving the manor of Cottingham in Yorkshire. This seems a clear breach of Magna Carta's cap. 40 laying down that justice was not to be sold. And yet in the event the offer was finally accepted not by Bishop Peter's government but, in June 1234, by that of Archbishop Edmund and William of Raleigh: Carpenter, *Reign of Henry III*, 37; *CFR 1233–4*, no. 231.

[228] *CR 1231–4*, 556. The earl of Chester had left St James to Henry and Henry had entrusted it to the duke.

personally, without any counsel he later confessed, to the envoys going to
the king of France. They were to enter negotiations only for a renewal of
the truce, and not therefore for a peace. Evidently, Henry still hoped one
day to win back his lost territories in a successful war. Here too he was
reined in and, on the insistence of Archbishop Edmund and the bishops
(mindful the pope was urging peace), he reversed his instructions.[229] In the
event, on the expiry of the truce, and with no agreement as to its continuation, let alone any progress towards a peace, Henry dispatched to Brittany
a substantial body of household knights and Welsh foot-soldiers. But only
a major expedition, like that in 1230, could have altered the situation. Peter
was powerless to resist the French invasion and soon made a truce lasting
until November. When a final visit to England produced only promises, he
submitted to the king of France without so much as notifying Henry.[230]
The Breton alliance, the cornerstone of Henry's continental plans since
1229, the alliance into which he had poured so much money and emotion,
was dead. With no peace available on anything like acceptable terms,
Henry was left to scramble around and arrange his own truce with the king
of France. In continental affairs too, after 1234 he would have to make a
new start.

HENRY'S PERFORMANCE

Henry's performance as king between 1232 and 1234 had been dismal. He
had wavered weakly over the dismissal of Hubert de Burgh. He had taken
a shameful oath quite inconsistent with regal dignity. He had failed to see
that the new regime was just as self-serving as the old. He had been driven
into a disastrous civil war. And, in the end, in humiliating fashion, he had
been forced by a great council to admit his errors and injustices. The only
compensation was that his reaction to the death of Richard Marshal and
his submission to Archbishop Edmund had enhanced his reputation as a
pious and Christian king. Had he learnt his lesson? It seemed so. In 1235
(in a letter to the emperor Frederick II) he would look back on the events
between 1232 and 1234 with genuine horror. His actions, he said, had
endangered his soul, offended divine majesty and violated his honour and
his obligations as a king. He had believed that the 'plenitude of royal
power' justified injurious acts of 'will'. He had refused to give justice to his
nobles and had waged war against them. The hearts of his faithful subjects
had been turned against him and he had lost both their devotion and
their service.[231] The sentiments were fine, but would they match up to the

---

[229] *CR 1231–4*, 559–60, 562. The bishop of Winchester was involved in the negotiations
with France, his last public role.

[230] Painter, *Scourge of the Clergy*, 83–8.

[231] *TR*, no. 15. For the circumstances of this letter to the Emperor Frederick, see
below, 174.

reality of Henry's rule? As Henry emerged from the chaos of the des Roches regime, a central question was whether he could indeed win the hearts of his subjects through just and consensual rule in co-operation with parliaments and in accordance with Magna Carta. Would he also be able to forge new alliances abroad more effective than that with the duke of Brittany?

Chapter 4

YEARS OF SUCCESS
1234–1241

The year 1234 marks a decisive break in Henry's reign. With the eclipse
of Hubert de Burgh and Peter des Roches, the days of great ministers
inherited from King John were over. Henceforth Henry would rule for
himself. For a few years he found this difficult. He hankered after some
de Burgh/des Roches substitute in the form of the legate Otto or his
wife's uncle William, bishop-elect of Valence. But with the adoption of
Edward the Confessor as his patron saint, and the birth of a son in 1239,
Henry's confidence grew. He soon felt quite able to govern without
some chief minister at his side. Henry's personal rule, as historians call it,
ended with the revolution of 1258, a revolution which deprived him
of power, and introduced wide-ranging reforms of law and local government. Yet the disastrous conclusion should not overshadow Henry's rule as
a whole. In some ways it was a success. Above all, as he himself later
boasted, it brought a long period of domestic peace. Indeed, Henry's peace
lasted beyond the revolution down to the final outbreak of civil war in 1263.

The personal rule itself falls into three distinct phases, divided by
Henry's continental expeditions of 1242–3 and 1253–4. The first phase
between 1234 and 1241 was for Henry the happiest. He adopted Edward
the Confessor as his patron saint and thereafter drew strength from the
Confessor's support. He married his second sister, Isabella, to the Emperor
Frederick II. He at last found a bride for himself in Eleanor of Provence,
and soon had a son and heir named Edward, after the Confessor. As an
additional fruit of the marriage, he established in England his wife's uncles
from the house of Savoy. He thus gained (or so he hoped) loyal and clever
councillors and an entirely new profile in international affairs. Henry
made a statesmanlike settlement with the king of Scots, exploited the
resources of Ireland without ever having to go there, gained the county of
Chester for the crown and, after the death of Llywelyn, reasserted royal
authority in Wales. He appears both as a legislator, concerned with the
welfare of his realm, and as a reformer, reordering the finances of the
crown. His accommodation with the political community was shown in
the concession of a tax by parliament in return for his confirmation of
Magna Carta. If there were quarrels with Richard of Cornwall, Gilbert
Marshal and Simon de Montfort (married in 1238 to Henry's sister
Eleanor), Henry rode them out. Indeed, in the end he put the Marshals

firmly in their place. The relative calm of this period was helped by a long truce with France. But Henry had not given up hope of recovering some or all of his continental dominions. He held on to Gascony, paid pensions to Poitevin nobles, and liked to think there would be help, when the time came, from Frederick II. This first phase of Henry's personal rule was the most successful period of the reign.

HENRY IN 1234

In October 1234, Henry III was twenty-eight years old. Much of his character and outlook were formed. 'Vir simplex erat et timens Deum', 'he was a simplex and God-fearing man,' wrote the Osney abbey annalist in his account of the year.[1] His words echoed the bible's description of Job – 'vir ille simplex, ac rectus, ac timens deum', 'a man simplex and upright and God-fearing'.[2] Here 'simplex' was a compliment, being used, as it often was of good and pious men, to mean honest, straightforward and innocent of any deceit or guile. A bishop of Ely could thus be described by Matthew Paris as a man 'simplex, just and free from all evil'. A bishop of Salisbury for another chronicler, Thomas Wykes, was 'a man of wonderful simplicity and innocence'.[3] But it was easy for the idea that someone was 'innocent' to slip over into the view that he lacked worldly wisdom and was guilty of a 'foolish simplicity'. For Roger of Wendover it was thus as a 'rex simplex' that Henry gave his trust to Peter des Roches.[4] Likewise Matthew Paris has Henry appointing Hugh of Pattishall as treasurer, 'understanding how his simplicity had been so often exploited by many people'.[5] These views were far from being confined to monastic chroniclers. Later Simon de Montfort was to say that Henry should be shut away like the Carolingian king, Charles the Simple.[6]

By 1234 key elements in Henry's religious life were well established, very much justifying the description of 'simplex' in its positive sense. His concern for the conversion of the Jews was shown in his foundation of the Domus Conversorum, the House of Converts, in London in 1232. His closeness to the friars was seen in numerous gifts, including in 1234 itself

[1] Osney, 77. The comment, however, was probably written later than 1234 and inserted into the account of that year.

[2] Job 1:1.

[3] Paris, *FH*, ii, 172; Wykes, 242. For Adam Marsh speaking of 'the truthful simplicity of the faithful' and (quoting the book of Job) 'the simplicity of the just man', see *Letters of Adam Marsh*, i, 144–5; ii, 342–3.

[4] Wendover, iii, 165 and see above, 78. For a comment in 1229, see Wendover, iii, 241. Edward the Confessor himself, in Matthew Paris's life, was himself accused (quite wrongly) of a 'foolish simplicity': Paris, *La Estoire*, lines 1265–6, and below, 326.

[5] Paris, *FH*, ii, 208, 214.

[6] See below, 262; and for an anecdote illustrating Henry's simplicity, see 405.

the oaks with which to build the Franciscan church at Reading.[7] His devotion to the Virgin Mary appeared in the way, by 1233, the 'Christus Vincit' was being chanted before him on the feasts of her Purification, Ascension and Birth.[8] His offerings to numerous churches of silver cups in which to hold the host showed his devotion to the Mass.[9] His care for the poor and sick was revealed in his refoundation of the hospital of John the Baptist outside Oxford. This was the framework in which, between 1233 and 1238, Henry adopted Edward the Confessor as his patron saint. Without in any way curtailing Henry's other forms of devotion, the Confessor was thereafter central to his life.[10]

The immediate purpose of Henry's devotions was naturally to win the support of God for success in this life and a safe passage to the next. Henry also had a genuine compassion for the poor and suffering, hence his concern for the 'cruel and inhuman treatment' of Richard of Bletchingdon, who was forced to attend courts despite his blindness; hence his pity for the 'poor little woman' from the royal manor of Ludgershall whose husband had been hanged and daughter burnt for homicide.[11] As a French Augustinian chronicler remarked in his entry for 1232, reflecting on Henry's alms to the poor and foundation of the Domus Conversorum, here was a king distinguished for his 'humanity'.[12] The fact and the forms of Henry's piety had made by 1234 an equal impression in England. A mendicant chronicler noticed how he kissed and gave alms to the poor and leprous before sailing for Brittany in 1230.[13] In 1234 both Roger of Wendover and the Dunstable annalist praised his masses and almsgiving on hearing of Richard Marshal's death. Here was a 'rex beatus', a 'rex piissimus'. That Henry's piety made this mark is not surprising for it was very public. By 1234 he was already illuminating his services with numerous candles and adorning his priests in splendid vestments. In 1233 a new set were to be made 'with all speed' so that they reached Reading early in the morning on Ascension Eve.[14] The king's piety was equally conspicuous when on the move. He visited the religious houses, friaries and hospitals along his route, giving timber for their building works and precious cloths for their altars and vestments. Between 1234 and 1236, 127 cloths of gold and 180 of 'arest' were distributed 'in offerings in divers churches throughout England'.[15]

[7] Thomas of Eccleston, 80; *CR 1231–4*, 415, 461. Note the king personally authorized the second of these writs.

[8] Kantorowicz, *Laudes Regiae*, 175. More generally, see Vincent, 'King Henry III and the Blessed Virgin Mary'.

[9] Wild, *WA*, 10.

[10] For a full discussion of Henry's religious life and his devotion to the Confessor, see below ch. 6.

[11] *RLC*, ii, 189, 201b; *CR 1227–31*, 71, 506.

[12] *Receuil*, xxi, 607h.

[13] See above, 86.

[14] *CLR 1226–40*, 165, 191, 213; *CR 1231–4*, 10.

[15] Wild, *WA*, 13. A cloth of arest was another type of cloth of gold with a ribbed weave.

Henry entered his personal rule with the lessons taught by the fall of Peter des Roches ringing in his ears. They were reinforced by his devotion to the Confessor, for the Confessor was famed for his just, peaceable and consensual rule. In some ways Henry's character was well suited to this framework. He was often ready to take advice, conciliate and draw back. If his conduct created crises, it also defused them. Here Hubert de Burgh remained his pattern, not Peter des Roches. Henry was also physically lazy. He liked the comfortable life. His itinerary centred on his palaces and palace castles in the south: Westminster above all and then Windsor, Winchester, Clarendon, Marlborough and Woodstock (the furthest north).[16] At his major residences he was already making his chambers and chapels more beautiful and comfortable with paintings, stained glass, tiled floors, wainscoting and privies.[17] His sedentary kingship was totally different from that of his father, who rarely spent more than a few days in one place. Not surprisingly, given his physical inertia, Henry was the reverse of a martial king. He disliked the business of war and knew little of how to wage it, as the 1230 campaign had all too clearly shown. A more aggressive king might have made far greater efforts to recover the lost lands in France, with all the resulting burdens on the kingdom.

Henry had another asset. He had a pleasant sense of humour and, affable and accessible, this helped create a happy light-hearted atmosphere at court. The humour is seen for the first time in a joke Henry played on his household clerks in 1237. When the king, in a letter patent, granted an individual 'full power' to do something, it was usually for a portentous purpose, so 'full power' to conclude a truce or a treaty. But now Henry used such a letter to give his clerk William de Peretot 'full power to cut the hair of the clerks of our household who have grown their hair long and cherish their fancy curls. If you don't do it properly, then we shall have to apply the scissors to your own locks.'[18]

One can imagine the ensuing fun as Peretot chased the clerks trying to cut their hair, ultimately perhaps having his own hair cut by the king himself.[19]

While there were many positive features of Henry's character and outlook, his 'simplicity', in its more negative sense, suggested there would be troubles ahead. Henry was articulate as his frequent speeches were to show. His grasp of detail appears in his artistic patronage and in his demands for exact information about his revenues. But down to 1234 he

---

[16] I discuss Henry's itinerary in more detail in ch. 7.

[17] For an evocative sketch of Henry along these lines, see Powicke, *King Henry III*, i, 303–4. Colvin, *History of the King's Works*, i, 93–5, catches well the enthusiasm and attention to detail with which Henry drove on his works.

[18] *CPR 1232–47*, 202. I owe the (abbreviated) translation here to the suggestions of Lesley Boatwright. See also Carpenter, 'The sense of humour of King Henry III'.

[19] For a discussion of Henry's sense of humour, see below, 405–7.

had shown none of the penetrating intelligence which enabled King John to think round all the angles of problems and devise clever solutions. Henry had also lacked the insight into character and the suspicion of motives so necessary in the treacherous world of the court. Other characteristics had aggravated the consequences of the king's naivety. Henry could be angry as both Hubert de Burgh and Peter des Roches had discovered. When his blood was up he could be sarcastic and sharp tongued, very ready to call people traitors and make the most violent threats.[20] Yet the storms quickly subsided. For much of the time Henry was warm-hearted and affectionate. He delighted in giving lavish, open-handed rewards to those he loved and trusted. But the combination of generosity and simplicity meant that, so far in his rule, he had failed to match reward and worth, as a good king should. He had been easily exploited by ministers far cleverer than himself, even to the extent of violating the very rights of the crown he was sworn to protect. The question for Henry, therefore, as he entered his personal rule, was whether age and experience would temper the negative side of his simplicity. And if it did not, how far would the positive side redress the balance.

Archbishop Edmund had played the central part in the fall of Peter des Roches, but his influence thereafter gradually waned. Outside great councils, he had no desire to spend time at court. Gilbert Marshal, earl of Pembroke, was quite different. He was small in stature and had been educated for the church. Down to 1234 he is sometimes styled 'Gilbert clericus'. This made him all the keener to prove himself both as a knight and as a lord who could defend and expand Marshal interests in Ireland, Wales and indeed in Scotland.[21] Winning over the king's stewards with judicious favours, he was very prominent at court in 1234–5.[22] Apart from Gilbert, a visitor at the end of 1234 might well have thought that the regime of Peter des Roches had never happened. Bishop Neville was still chancellor. The clerk Walter of Kirkham had returned to the keepership of the wardrobe. Godfrey of Crowcombe was back in place alongside Ralph fitzNicholas as a senior household steward. Together they authorized large numbers of letters between 1234 and 1236 and were at the centre of day-to-day affairs. While Walter Mauclerc, bishop of Carlisle, did not return as treasurer of the exchequer, he too was frequently at court. There too, in 1234–5, in some kind of ghostly afterlife, was Hubert de Burgh himself, still determined to recover more of his property, if resigned to his loss of the justiciarship.

The office of justiciar had been suspended by the Gloucester council and was not revived. Henry had no desire for another overbearing

---

[20] For Adam Marsh later being described as a traitor and an enemy, see *Letters of Adam Marsh*, ii, 446–9.

[21] See below, 225, 228, 231.

[22] *CChR 1226–57*, 188–9.

minister of that kind. The court *coram rege*, on the other hand, now had a continuous life. It kept its own rolls, and was presided over by a professional judge who sat with one of the household stewards and in important cases with a much larger group of magnates and ministers. The court's first task had been to reverse the injustices committed by the king himself between 1232 and 1234, and doubtless the Gloucester council hoped that it would prevent such transgressions in the future. The court, however, was also very much an instrument of the king where he could dispense justice and protect his rights. Thus it heard 'quo warranto' cases in which individuals and institutions were summoned to show 'by what warrant' they held rights and properties claimed by the crown. The court also exercised supervision over the other justices and heard complaints about official oppression and abuse. It had the potential to play a constructive part in Henry's kingship.[23]

The judge who presided over the court was William of Raleigh. He widened the scope of its business and helped shape the legislation of the mid-1230s.[24] He also played a leading part in the financial reforms, and took on an increasing range of general business. Until he left court in 1239 to become bishop of Norwich, he was central to Henry's success. Central too was Henry's co-operation with his great councils. They played an important part in furthering the two marriages which occupied so much of Henry's time in 1235-6.

MATTHEW PARIS

It is at the start of Henry's personal rule that a remarkable source becomes available to the historian. This is the account of the years from 1234 to 1259, written by the monk of St Albans Matthew Paris. Paris was born about 1200 and took the habit at St Albans in 1217. He died in 1259, working to the last.[25] His fame was such that the monk who continued historical writing at St Albans drew a large picture of Paris on his deathbed and added he was unworthy even to undo the latchet of his shoe. Paris's greatest work, his *Chronica Majora*, into the year 1234 is a copy, with many additions and alterations, of the *Flores Historiarum*, written by his predecessor

---

[23] For a full discussion, see Meekings and Crook, *King's Bench and Common Bench*.

[24] If he tried, he was, however, unable to stop Henry (in August 1234) treating the peasants of Rothley in Leicestershire unjustly when he refused to uphold their royal charter: see Carpenter, 'The peasants of Rothley' and below, 543.

[25] It is not known why he called himself Matthew 'Parisius' or 'Matthew of Paris', but given his interest in the French capital perhaps he had studied there. Amongst a vast literature on Paris, Richard Vaughan's *Matthew Paris* remains fundamental. For more recent studies, see Weiler, 'Matthew Paris on the writing of history', Carpenter, 'Chronology and truth: Matthew Paris and the *Chronica Majora*', and a new doctoral thesis, Greasley, 'Networks and information gathering in the *Chronica Majora* of Matthew Paris'.

at St Albans, Roger of Wendover.[26] Thereafter Paris continued on his own.[27] Although the *Chronica Majora*, as we have it, is a fair copy started in the 1240s, Paris from 1234 was making detailed notes of information as it came in and probably writing it up in a draft text.[28] He owed much to Wendover both in terms of method and opinion, but was far more energetic. Whereas the *Flores Historiarum*, in the twenty-two years between 1212 and 1233, in a nineteenth-century printed edition averages eighteen pages a year, the *Chronica Majora*, in the twenty-two years between 1236 and 1258, averages seventy-eight. This, moreover, takes no account of all the documents Paris copied into a large separate volume known as his *Liber Additamentorum*. As V.H. Galbraith commented, 'medieval history on this scale is unique'.[29]

Paris was a man of many parts and wide interests. He was an artist and illustrated his works with deft, sometimes dramatic drawings of both religious and secular subjects, including the elephant given to Henry III by Louis IX of France. He wrote saints' lives and drew maps of Britain, the Holy Land and the world.[30] His *Chronica Majora* reaches far beyond England and contains much about the Emperor Frederick II and the crusades.[31] Based at St Albans on a main road in and out of London, Paris was able to glean information from many informants, including Hubert de Burgh, Richard of Cornwall and Henry III himself. Between 1244 and 1257 he describes eight visits of Henry to the abbey.[32] By 1247 the king knew him well and knew he was a historian. Paris's attitude to the king was conflicted. He admired his piety yet cried out against his policies, notably his oppression of the church, and his partiality for foreigners. Modern historians have often shown how these opinions, so strongly held, affected the accuracy of Paris's narrative. In emphasizing the truth as he saw it, he was perfectly capable of putting words into people's mouths and even altering documents. Yet this should not detract from the great labour behind the accumulation of so much historical information, information that Paris arranged carefully in chronological order so the reader could see how God was working his purpose out. What Paris says needs always to be treated with care, but can never be ignored. Where it can be checked out,

[26] Wendover was prior of the St Albans daughter house at Belvoir from before the end of John's reign until 1226: Crook, 'Roger of Wendover, prior of Belvoir', 167–9. He then was presumably based at St Albans. He died in 1236.

[27] For Paris taking over from Wendover in the course of 1234, see Kay, 'Wendover's last annal'.

[28] The 1235–40 portion of the *Chronica Majora* thus shows knowledge of events in the 1240s.

[29] Galbraith, *Roger of Wendover and Matthew Paris*, 24, 42.

[30] Lewis, *Art of Matthew Paris*; Connolly, *Maps of Matthew Paris*.

[31] Paris produced three abbreviated versions of the *Chronica Majora*: his *Flores Historiarum*, *Historia Anglorum*, and *Abbreviatio Chronicorum*.

[32] Vaughan, *Matthew Paris*, 12–17.

it can prove remarkably accurate. It is Paris's chronicle and the king's letters on the chancery rolls together that enable the history of these years to be told in such unparalleled detail.

THE MARRIAGE OF A SISTER

In 1235, King Henry's mind was dominated by thoughts of his own marriage and that of his sister Isabella, subjects far more congenial than the awful politics of Bishop Peter's era. Diplomatic activity became so intense that the chancery opened a special roll to record all the correspondence.[33]

Back in the 1220s, Henry's councillors had declared that the king 'had no greater treasure than his own marriage and that of his sisters'. It should be used 'to secure great alliances in foreign parts'.[34] The need for such alliances was all the more imperative in 1235 with the submission of Peter, duke of Brittany, to Louis IX. To be sure, there was no immediate prospect of Henry renewing the struggle with France. In July 1235, with some grumbling, he agreed a five-year-truce with Louis.[35] But the truce would end and then allies would be vital. For all the disappointments of the years 1229 to 1234, Henry still hoped to recover some or all of his continental empire. In January 1235, with the full backing of a great council, he stoutly refused to surrender the isle of Oléron, the one conquest from the 1230 campaign, to his stepfather Hugh de Lusignan. He would be 'shamed and diminished in the eyes of all' if he did so.[36]

It was Pope Gregory IX who first suggested, probably in the early summer of 1234, a magnificent marriage for Isabella, a marriage to none other than Emperor Frederick II himself.[37] Frederick had returned from his crusade in 1229 in triumph. By the wiles of diplomacy rather than the rigours of war, he had actually recovered Jerusalem. In 1231 he was formally reconciled to the pope. For Gregory, Frederick's marriage to the sister of a faithful vassal would cement this rapprochement. It would also further the cause of European peace and prepare the way for another crusade: a crusade under papal auspices to consolidate Frederick's achievements. Gregory had pushed Henry and Louis IX into their long truce for the same reason. For Frederick, the marriage meant one thing above all else: money. How right the archbishop of Cologne had been to say he thirsted for it above everything![38] In the negotiations the emperor insisted

[33] *TR*, nos. 1–102.

[34] *DD*, no. 140.

[35] *TR*, no. 27; *DD*, no. 239.

[36] *CR 1234–7*, 160–1.

[37] For studies of Isabella's marriage, to which I owe much, see Weiler, *Henry III of England and the Staufen Empire*, ch. 2, and Wilkinson, 'The imperial marriage'.

[38] See above, 42.

that Isabella's dowry must not be less than 30,000 marks (£20,000). This was money he could use first of all to secure his position in Germany where his son Henry was raising the standard of revolt.[39]

Isabella was Henry's favourite sister. The two were frequently together. Henry showered her with gifts, and issued orders for her clothes at the same time as his own. We have seen how a chancery clerk once described her as Henry's wife.[40] How would this twenty-one-year-old English princess, used to the company of the celibate and psalm-singing holy woman Margaret Bisset, get on with a husband rumoured to delight in dancing girls and harems? Henry insisted that Frederick treat Isabella 'with imperial honour and marital affection' and give her a substantial dower.[41] But he also delighted in the match, as he made plain in a letter to his eldest sister Joan, queen of Scotland. After all, had not the pope told him to 'consider the utility and honour to you and your kingdom from a relationship with the pre-eminent prince amongst the kings of the earth'.[42] Frederick was, as Henry himself styled him, 'the most serene prince, by the grace of God emperor of the Romans, always Augustus'. He thus could claim both authority in Germany and northern Italy, and a vague overlordship over all the rulers of the Christian West. He was also king of Sicily, with its abundant wealth, and king too, since his crusade, of Jerusalem. Henry was not alone in welcoming the match, for a great council agreed to it after a formal debate. Henry and his realm seemed at one. As he told the pope, only dearth, following harvest failure in 1234, marred the kingdom's prosperity. All the magnates of the land agreed with his wishes and were joined with him in mutual love. He and his kingdom could breathe again after the conflicts of the past.[43]

Thus it was that in February 1235 the emperor's envoy, Master Peter de Vinea, arrived in England, viewed the prospective bride, and swore that Frederick would marry her. While waiting for the ambassadors who would take her to Germany, Henry set out on a pilgrimage to Bromholm, from where he sent Isabella, then staying in the Tower of London, a gift of 100 figs.[44] Matthew Paris marvelled at Isabella's amazing trousseau which included a crown on which were carved the four martyr saints of England to whose protection Henry had committed her. It was difficult to say, Paris joked, which attracted the emperor more, her person or her possessions. A surviving inventory shows that Isabella took with her three robes of gold silk, ten of other cloths and colours, six coverlets of hind and scarlet, three cloaks of scarlet and cendal, a tunic and super-tunic in burnet, a rain cloak and two

[39] F, 200 (TR, no. 9).

[40] CR 1231–4, 4–5, 43–4.

[41] TR, nos. 1, 19.

[42] CR 1234–7, 167; F, 220.

[43] TR, no. 5; Paris, iii, 305. For the great council standing shoulder to shoulder with Henry over another matter, see CR 1234–7, 160–1.

[44] CR 1234–7, 58, 73, 81.

dressing gowns of cendal lined with fur for rising in the night. She had two beds made from cloth of gold and several more from 'arest', all with mattresses made of cendal. Her chapel was equipped with a cope, chasuble, dalmatics in cloths of gold, two albs, two amices, four towels for the altar and one cloth of gold to hang behind it. New robes, graduated according to status, were provided for five knights, three squires, five chambermaids, a chaplain, a clerk, a physician, a washerwoman, three grooms, two messengers and fourteen kitchen and other menial staff.[45] How wise Frederick was to specify that the cost of the trousseau should not be deducted from the 30,000-mark dowry.[46] At least he did send back some gifts in return, including a great warhorse and three leopards, the latter a reference to the arms of England.[47] It is a measure of the consensual climate in which the marriage was agreed that Henry spread the emperor's bounty around with the earls of Lincoln, Derby, Pembroke and Cornwall, sharing in an assortment of precious cloths, Turkish bows and Saracen saddles and maces.[48]

Amidst the joy and display there was one anxiety. Peter des Roches had raised his head. In March 1235 he left England for the papal court, there to assist Pope Gregory in his conflict with the citizens of Rome. He did not return to England until September 1236. Henry welcomed Peter's absence while fearing the consequences. If Peter met the emperor in Italy what might he say about his pusillanimous monarch? Henry would hardly seem a king worthy of leopards and warhorses. In April, therefore, he wrote to Frederick the letter already mentioned setting out Bishop Peter's sins. The claim that Peter had ascribed to Henry 'the plenitude of royal power' was designed as a red rag to the emperor. In the secular sphere it was the emperor alone, Frederick would think, who had the plenitude of power. Other kings and rulers were merely his helpers.[49]

Having taken this precaution, Henry handed Isabella over to the archbishop of Cologne and the duke of Brabant at Westminster on 3 May 1235. The whole party then set off for the coast, entertained no doubt by the seven minstrels of the archbishop and the duke whom Henry had decked out in new green robes.[50] 'It was not without weeping that brother and sister parted,' Paris reported. Having passed through Cologne, where Isabella delighted the crowds in the streets and women on the balconies by removing her cap and hood, she was eventually married at Worms on 20 July. According to Matthew Paris, Frederick consummated the union at the hour ordained by astrologers, and then placed Isabella in safe custody

---

[45] For the whole trousseau, see Wild, 'Empress's new clothes'.

[46] *TR*, no. 1.

[47] *CR 1234–7*, 309, 417; Paris, iii, 324.

[48] Vincent, 'An inventory of gifts', 132, 139–42.

[49] *TR*, no. 15; Vincent, *Peter des Roches*, 471–3, though without my interpretation of the 'plenitude of power'.

[50] Wild, 'The empress's new clothes', 29, no. 103.

saying she was pregnant with a boy. He sent home her English attendants, and had her guarded by Moorish eunuchs and wizened old women.[51] Whether such tales reached Henry cannot be known, but he certainly noticed the sad trail of the attendants returning home. Before her death in 1241, Henry and Isabella never met again.

There was also the problem of raising the 30,000-mark dowry. In July 1235 a great council, showing again its support for the marriage, agreed that the tenants-in-chief should give an aid, levied at the rate of 2 marks for every knight's fee they held from the crown. But this would only raise a few thousand pounds. So Henry himself set out on a remarkable tour, taking him first west to Bath and then as far north as Nottingham. At all the major places along the route, the abbots and priors who did not hold in chief (and so had not contributed to the aid) were summoned 'to speak to the king on the affairs he will expound to them', meaning speak about giving him financial help. At least in return, many received gifts of chalices, cloth and timber. Despite these efforts, the problem of finding the money for the emperor hung over the king until the summer of 1237 when the last payment was made.[52]

What public benefit then did Henry gain for his private anxieties and public expense? The answer is not much. The imperial marriage was like a series of spiders' webs. On a damp, misty morning they appear in exquisite fineness. In the light of ordinary day they vanish. It was left to Henry, in a letter to the pope, to ask the acid question, thereby revealing his own doubts and anxieties. Would Gregory induce Frederick 'to assist us most powerfully, when opportunity offers, in the recovery of our rights?' He meant, of course, recover the rights lost to the king of France.[53] Perhaps Frederick made vague promises that he would do so, but at the same time both he and the pope were assuring Louis IX that he had nothing to fear from the alliance.[54] Of course, circumstances might change, but they never did. Frederick, having already seen off his son Henry, spent England's money on fighting his wars against the Italian cities. In 1239 he fell into his great quarrel with the pope. When for Henry 'opportunity' did offer in 1242, Frederick did nothing at all. The marriage was certainly prestigious but even that was double-edged. According to Paris, some thought Frederick was diminished by marrying a mere sister of the king of England. No one would have thought like that before 1204, and Frederick obliquely made the point. When a son was born to Isabella in 1238, he named him 'Henry', not after the boy's uncle, Henry III, but after his great-grandfather, Henry II, 'excited by meditating on his glorious memory'.[55]

[51] Paris, iii, 318–27.
[52] Mitchell, *Studies in Taxation*, 208–14; *CLR 1226–40*, 275; *TR*, nos. 54–5.
[53] *F*, 225–6 (*TR*, no. 8).
[54] Paris, iii, 325; Weiler, *Henry III of England and the Staufen Empire*, 63–4.
[55] *F*, 233.

THE KING'S MARRIAGE

Parallel with the negotiations for the imperial marriage ran those for Henry's own. He was desperate to bring them to a conclusion for all the obvious public and private reasons. At least the end of the Breton entanglement had helped clear the field by removing Yolande, daughter of Duke Peter, from the lists of prospective brides. One possibility was a marriage with Jeanne, eldest daughter of Simon Dammartin and Marie, in her own right countess of Ponthieu. Since the two had no son, Henry could hope eventually to obtain Ponthieu, the small but strategically placed county at the mouth of the Somme; an ideal perch for forays into Normandy. Despite some delays, negotiations proceeded so far that Henry, sometime before 8 April 1235, formally consented through intermediaries to the marriage.[56] Then difficulties arose. Henry learnt that he was related to Jeanne within the fourth degree, and would need papal dispensation before he could proceed. It soon became clear that thanks to Capetian opposition such a dispensation would not be forthcoming. So, in July 1235, on the advice of his council 'to which we are bound to give faith', Henry effectively called off the Ponthieu marriage. His envoys in Rome were not to 'breathe a word about it to a living soul'.[57] To make sure he was free to look elsewhere, the following year he secured a formal letter from the pope nullifying the marriage.[58]

Look elsewhere Henry had indeed been doing. In June 1235 he was already negotiating with Raymond-Berengar, count of Provence, about a marriage to his second daughter, Eleanor. The count's eldest daughter, Margaret, was unavailable as she was already married to King Louis IX of France. Henry's envoys returned from Provence early in October 1235 with a favourable response, and a great council, summoned to Windsor, agreed to the marriage. An imposing delegation was dispatched to receive Eleanor, equipped with six sets of letters empowering them to accept her with dowries ranging from 3,000 up to 20,000 marks. But Henry was still worried. On 19 October he sent a letter after the envoys saying that if disagreement over the dowry threatened to wreck the marriage, then they were to 'bring [Eleanor] back to us in England safely and securely without the payment of any money'.[59] Henry was determined to get his wife.

That determination was important in driving on the marriage for its material advantages were at best debatable. True, it might be seen to counter the king of France's advances in the south of France, advances with obviously threatening implications for English Gascony. But Louis's own marriage to the count's eldest daughter gave him influence over

---

[56] *F*, 216 (*TR*, no. 61), 231, 270.

[57] *F*, 218 (*TR*, no. 75); *TR*, nos. 81–2.

[58] *F*, 231. For a further nullification later, see the remarkable account in D'Avray, 'Authentication of marital status', and the documents printed in D'Avray, *Dissolving Royal Marriages*, 81–98.

[59] *TR*, no. 26.

Provence. He was also installed in the seneschalships of Carcassonne and Beaucaire, having, in the 1229 Treaty of Paris, wrested them from Count Raymond of Toulouse. By the same treaty his younger brother Alphonse was to marry Raymond's only child, with the promise of eventual succession to Toulouse itself.

The extent to which Henry's own marriage impeded these developments was questionable, however. Raymond-Berengar had no sons but said nothing about Eleanor, or Margaret for that matter, being his successor. Instead, in 1238, he willed Provence to his youngest daughter Beatrice, who was eventually snapped up by Louis IX's brother Charles of Anjou. With his eldest daughter married to Louis, the prospect of Raymond-Berengar joining Henry in some anti-Capetian coalition was non-existent. Given the conflicts between him and the count of Toulouse, the marriage would not help relations with the latter either. There were also no financial compensations. While Isabella was taking large sums of money out of England, Eleanor brought nothing in. She had been promised with 10,000 marks but it never materialized. Louis IX, promised the same amount, had done rather better, securing 2,000 marks and the castle of Tarascon in Provence as security for the rest.[60] Eleanor's trousseau too was exiguous, the only discoverable items being eighteen cups of gold and silver, of which one was melted down to make her crown at the coronation. It was Henry who supplied Eleanor with saddles, shoes, wimples, robes and all the vestments and books for her chapel, thus meeting the costs of two trousseaus in one year.[61]

In all this, however, there were blessings. Since the marriage was innocuous, the Capetian court did not oppose it, and thus, unlike the marriage to Jeanne of Ponthieu, it could actually go ahead. It also matched well with the five-year truce which was just being concluded. In the longer term, the family relationship between Louis and Henry, Margaret and Eleanor, between kings who were brothers-in-law and queens who were sisters, would draw the courts together in friendship and bring peace to their countries.

There was one other aspect of the marriage, both a blessing and a curse, which was to influence fundamentally both Henry's domestic and continental policies. This was the family of Eleanor's mother, Beatrice, daughter of the count of Savoy. From the mountains and lakes of Savoy, so much greater and grander than any in Britain, the family ranged westwards into the Rhone valley and eastwards across the alpine passes into northern Italy. They mingled and meddled in the affairs of the papacy and the empire, France and England. One of Eleanor's uncles, William, was bishop-elect of Valence on the Rhone south of Lyon; another, Thomas, held lordships in Piedmont. Through marriage, he was also to

[60] *Layettes*, ii, nos. 2719, 2280; Howell, *Eleanor of Provence*, 14.
[61] Wild, *WA*, 9–10.

become count of Flanders. Eleanor arrived in England as very much a
part of this family circle, and Henry was soon entranced by it. He was to
establish three of Eleanor's uncles in England, as well as many of their
satellites. He was also tempted by the Savoyards to play a part on the
Italian stage, ultimately with disastrous results.

Having dispatched the envoys to Provence, Henry waited. In November
1235 he went to Bury for the feast of St Edmund, offering a brooch and
nine rings with emeralds at the shrine.[62] For Christmas, as so often, he was
at Winchester, 'expecting with ardent desire' Eleanor's arrival. At last the
good news came. On 14 January, Henry galloped the twenty-eight miles
from Rochester to Canterbury in a few hours, embraced the envoys,
viewed his bride and married her on the same day, with Archbishop
Edmund presiding. Probably the marriage was consummated the same
night or a few days later.[63] Eleanor was twelve years old. Writing later,
Matthew Paris, who was to see her often, described her at this time as a
'puella speciosa', 'decoris expectabilis' and 'speciei venustissimae', words
which suggest a beauty informed by poise, grace and good manners.[64]
Evidently Eleanor had been well brought up at the Provencal court. There
she would have been surrounded both by the piety of the friars and the
poetry of the troubadours, of which her mother indeed was a patron.
Perhaps she looked on Britain first and foremost as the home of King
Arthur, and it was to Glastonbury, where Arthur was buried, that Henry
was to take her on a special visit later in 1236. Henry had good reasons to
be delighted with his bride.

Preparations now accelerated for Eleanor's coronation at Westminster,
the last great ceremony to be held in the old church built by Edward the
Confessor. However, there were problems. A dearth of wine forced prices
up to unheard-of levels, downfalls of rain threatened to flood Westminster
palace, fear of disorder consigned the Jews to the Tower, and disputes
broke out amongst the magnates about their roles at the ceremony. Simon
de Montfort, in defeating a challenge from the earl of Norfolk to his rights
as steward, showed himself remarkably informed about an agreement
between their predecessors, and very sure of correct procedures 'according
to the law of the land', an ominous foretaste of the grasp and tenacity with
which he would later pursue his rights.[65]

The great day, for which London was cleaned and decorated with
banners and bunting, was Sunday 20 January. Preceded by ministers and
magnates carrying the regalia, Henry and Eleanor, Henry wearing his

---

[62] Wild, *WA*, 9.

[63] Paris, iii, 334–6. For the likely consummation, see Howell, *Eleanor of Provence*, 15–16.

[64] Paris, iii, 335; Paris, *HA*, ii, 386; Howell, *Eleanor of Provence*, 5.

[65] *RBE*, ii, 757. The stewardship of England came with the Leicester inheritance.
Montfort made little of it until the 1260s: Maddicott, *Simon de Montfort*, 20, 200–1, 239–41,
332–3.

crown and coronation robes, processed along a specially laid carpet from Westminster palace to the Abbey. Above them were identical purple canopies, with golden bells at each corner, supported by gilded lances born by the barons of the Cinque Ports.

The ceremony in the Abbey, presided over by Archbishop Edmund, was deeply significant. The ring placed on Eleanor's finger symbolized fidelity, the sceptre and virge placed in her hands authority, and the crown placed on her head glory. Above all, Eleanor's anointing with Holy Oil meant that she was queen, as she said herself in her letters, 'by the grace of God'.[66] Now for the first time in the reign, the choirs chanting the 'Christus Vincit' could sing:

> Christ conquers, Christ reigns, Christ rules
> To the queen of the English, health and life

The acclamations in the Abbey, and the feasting afterwards, gave public acceptance to the new queen. She had been crowned (as King John had said of Henry's mother) 'by the common assent and will of the whole kingdom'.[67]

There was nothing in the ceremony which put the queen on a par with the king. It was the king, at his coronation, who swore to protect the church, maintain peace and dispense justice. The queen took no equivalent oath setting out her duties. Yet the ceremony, separated from the actual wedding, showed that the queen was not just the king's wife. She held a formal office and one of unique status. The prayers at the coronation, steeped in references to biblical women and the Virgin Mary, also indicated a queenly role. She should bear a son and she should act as an intercessor. An heir was vital for the future of the kingdom. Intercession might help its tranquillity by moving the king to mercy. On the very day of the coronation, it was arranged for Eleanor to intercede for a prisoner and secure his release.[68] Both roles might be avenues through which the queen could wield power.

If the coronation ritual promised much for Eleanor's queenship, the actual practice of her most recent predecessors did the reverse. There were no positive role models, for no queen regnant had played an active part in English affairs since Eleanor of Aquitaine in the 1160s. Having fomented the rebellion of 1173–4, Eleanor had then spent the remainder of Henry II's reign in semi-captivity. Her successor, Richard's queen, Berengaria of Navarre, had never come to England at all apart from attending Becket's translation in 1220. John's queen, Isabella of Angoulême, Henry's mother, had done nothing visible apart from bear children,

[66] Howell, *Eleanor of Provence*, 17–19.
[67] Kantorowicz, *Laudes Regiae*, 217; *RCh.*,28; Howell, *Eleanor of Provence*, 16.
[68] *CR 1234–7*, 229.

despite the splendour of her coronation and her feisty personality. Equally serious was the fact that, from the start of Henry II's reign in 1154, the practice of giving queens large landed endowments for their support had ceased. Instead they became dependent on money from the king, and were consequently less secure and independent. On her arrival in England, Eleanor was assigned a substantial dower, but she would receive it only on Henry's death. How she would be supported during his life was not mentioned.

Eleanor's fate within this ambiguous framework would depend absolutely on the relationship with her husband. The prospect must have been daunting. As a twelve-year-old girl she had to accept sexual intercourse with a man of twenty-eight. As a speaker of Occitan French, she had to understand his Anglo-Norman dialect. And beyond that she had to live in a country where the whole population, including her husband, also spoke another language, English, which she could not understand at all. Only gradually did it emerge that beneath the external 'decor' there was an intelligent, ambitious and courageous woman, a far stronger personality, in some ways, than her husband. Eleanor would play a larger part in English politics than any queen since the Norman Conquest. Here she had one advantage, not shared by her sister Queen Margaret in France. She had no dominant mother-in-law, no equivalent of Blanche of Castile, to cope with.[69]

In fact Eleanor must soon have been reassured about her husband. Despite the visit to Glastonbury, nothing could make Henry a king in the Arthurian mould, but equally he was not, like Frederick II, going to shut her away in some castle. Nor was he going to imitate the supposedly sexless marriage of his patron saint Edward the Confessor. Henry, warm-hearted and indulgent, doted on his new queen and delighted in her company. Nothing was too much trouble. Given Eleanor's age, moreover, she was very much his to mould.

In these early years Eleanor spent the great bulk of her time at court, yet she was never a rootless figure within it. From the start she had her own household. This was presided over by her steward Robert de Muscegros and the keeper of her wardrobe, the clerk John of Gatesden. Both had been selected by Henry as known and congenial figures: Muscegros, once a member of his sister Isabella's household, had been part of the delegation bringing Eleanor to England; Gatesden had met her when involved in the very first negotiations for the marriage. Henry also linked together his new-found wife and his lost sister by introducing into Eleanor's household Isabella's old companion Margaret Bisset. In addition, Eleanor had five ladies-in-waiting, four 'valetti' and (by Christmas 1237) nineteen clerks and other servants.[70] A good proportion of the entourage probably came

[69] Joinville, caps. 606–8; Grant, *Blanche of Castile*, 129.
[70] *CLR 1226–40*, 288; TNA E 372/81, mm. 27–8.

from Provence or Savoy. The chief of her ladies, Willelma, was to 'follow the queen' until her retirement in 1258, worn out by age and sickness. Willelma's daughter was also in Eleanor's service. There was no question of Henry sending his wife's people home.[71] Eleanor must also have got to know the wards growing up at court. One was the future earl of Gloucester, Richard de Clare, only two years Eleanor's senior, with whom she was later to forge an alliance.[72]

But it was Henry who was central to Eleanor's life. Soon after the coronation, he took her through the pouring rain on a tour of their future homes. In February they were at Winchester, Clarendon, Marlborough and Woodstock. In March and April, after a pilgrimage to Bury St Edmunds, they had their first real look at Westminster and Windsor. Henry's enthusiasm for building and decoration was now poured into providing worthy accommodation for his wife. In the next few years chambers and chapels for her, sometimes entirely new, sometimes refashioned from existing structures, arose at all the major palaces. Those at Westminster were especially impressive. Often linked to herb gardens for Eleanor's relaxation, the chambers were wainscotted, lit by 'beautiful' windows, and decorated with paintings and stained glass, much of it highly symbolic. At Winchester, in April 1236, Henry ordered that a window depicting the tree of Jesse be placed in the gable of Eleanor's chamber.[73]

Henry celebrated the unity with his queen in all kinds of visual ways. They both dressed in cloth of gold at Pentecost and participated jointly in the great gift-giving ceremonies on 1 January: in 1237 Henry gave 178 rings and Eleanor 65.[74] Henry gave Eleanor a great silver platter gilded with his arms. He commissioned for their chapels identical gold boxes to contain the host surmounted with gilded, jewelled and removable crowns. At Westminster, in the chapel of St Stephen, the seats of the king and queen had the same green surrounds and the same painted images of the crucifixion.[75] The two light windows in Eleanor's chamber (an entirely new structure) were modelled on the new ones in Henry's chamber, while on either side of the central lancet above the altar in her chapel were the sculpted heads of king and queen, evidently Henry and Eleanor themselves.[76] The apartments of the king and queen were also linked physically. At Westminster, nearly opposite the king's bed at the east end of his chamber, a door led into a little vestibule which opened into the chamber of the queen. Elsewhere, where the chambers were less adjacent, Henry

[71] Howell, *Eleanor of Provence*, 104–5.
[72] See below, 654, 692.
[73] *CLR 1267–72*, no. 2417.
[74] Wild, *WA*, 20, 28.
[75] *CLR 1226–40*, 268, 321–2; *CR 1234–7*, 239.
[76] Colvin, *History of the King's Works*, i, 501. For further discussion of the palace of Westminster, see below, 365–71.

linked them with covered passages: at Winchester one ran from the queen's chamber to her chapel and thence to the king's chamber. At Woodstock, the passage linking the queen's chamber and chapel was so that Eleanor could go back and forth 'with dry feet'.[77] In 1238 it was because he was sleeping in the queen's chamber at Woodstock that Henry escaped an assassination attempt.

Henry and Eleanor discovered similar tastes in food, an important bond. They agreed that they found all fish apart from lampreys 'insipid'.[78] They were also linked spiritually by sharing the same confessor in Nicholas of Farnham, a man widely admired for the purity of his life and the depth of his medical and theological learning. (He had taught at both Paris and Bologna.) He also became Eleanor's doctor.[79] Henry, of course, immediately introduced Eleanor to the general pattern of his piety. In 1236 he was sending recruits both to the Domus Conversorum in London and the Hospital of John the Baptist at Oxford. During the course of the year he made gifts, usually of game or timber, to eighteen friaries, nineteen religious houses, seven hospitals and five recluses. With religious practices of this kind Eleanor would have been familiar. But Henry also introduced her to something entirely new: the cult of Edward the Confessor. The cult and the marriage were closely linked, for Henry believed the Confessor's intercession had secured his bride. Indeed that belief was an important factor in consolidating the cult. On the day of her coronation, Eleanor was given a magnificent embroidered cope costing all of £23 to offer at the shrine.[80] A little later Henry commissioned from Matthew Paris a life of the Confessor designed to tell Eleanor all about him.[81]

THE PROVISIONS OF KING HENRY III, 1234–7

The celebrations of the queen's coronation at Westminster on 20 January were happy but truncated. Fear that the Thames, swollen by rain, would flood the palace, drove the court later the same day to Merton priory, eight miles away in Surrey. It was there, on 23 January, that the king, Archbishop Edmund, the bishops 'and the greater part of the earls and barons of England' agreed a series of provisions 'for the common utility of all the kingdom'.[82] The 'statute of Merton', as it became known, did not stand alone. Between 1234 and 1237 the king issued around a dozen provisions dealing with the law and government of the realm. On some occasions a

---

[77] CLR 1226–40, 372; Colvin, History of the King's Works, ii, 1013.
[78] CR 1234–7, 420.
[79] Paris, iv, 86–7.
[80] Wild, WA, 9.
[81] For a discussion of the life and the origins of the cult, see below, 319–29.
[82] CR 1234–7, 337–9, 353–5; Burton, 249–51; Paris, iii, 341–3. For the texts, see Powicke, King Henry III, ii, 769–71.

provision simply focused on an individual issue, on others a series of questions were addressed. The most important provisions were agreed in great councils by large numbers of lay and ecclesiastical magnates. They were very much the product of the co-operation between the king and the political community ushered in by Bishop Peter's fall. This was a period of legislative activity unique in Henry's reign.

The government kept no separate roll of its provisions, but clerks and chroniclers made collections of their own, thus showing they appreciated the importance of what was happening.[83] Protecting widows and orphans, restricting the activities of the Jews, regulating the composition and frequency of local courts, devising new legal rules and actions related to succession and disseisin, remedying the abuses of royal officials and restricting the king's rights of compulsory purchase, the legislation covered a whole range of issues and impacted on many sections of society. The statement at Merton that the legislation was conceived 'for the common utility of all the kingdom' reflected the consensus making it possible, while concealing the sometimes conflicting forces behind it.

For Henry the legislation was closely linked to his religion. According to Matthew Paris, he promulgated the statute of Merton 'for the salvation of his soul and the improvement of his kingdom, influenced by a spirit of justice and piety'. Henry himself, on another occasion, wrote of abolishing evil customs 'for the health of our soul and the souls of our ancestors and heirs'. This was as close as he ever came to acting in the spirit of his coronation oath to abolish bad laws and introduce good ones. He may well have been influenced by the example of Edward the Confessor, a legislator, so it was thought, deeply concerned with the welfare of his people. He was also inspired by his marriage, doing good in the hope, so Paris affirmed, that 'God would consummate a joyous beginning with a happy end by conferring the gift of children'.[84] The legislation reflected Henry's pious concern to protect widows, help the poor and bring the position of the Jews into line with the decrees of the Fourth Lateran Council. A provision in 1233, promulgated during the regime of Peter des Roches, had laid down that Jews were not to remain in the kingdom unless they could be of service to the king, a baleful step towards their eventual expulsion from England in 1290. Further measures in 1234 were prompted by the scandal in which a Norwich townsman accused a group of Jews of kidnapping and circumcising his son 'in contempt of Christ crucified and Christianity', a

[83] For one collection, including the provisions of Merton, made by a chancery clerk around 1236, see Richardson, 'Glanville Continued', 389–90. For another collection *ERW*, xcviii–civ, and see ciii n. 7. The Burton abbey annalist and Matthew Paris had texts of the Provisions of Merton, Burton also having the legislation promulgated at Kempton in January 1237: Paris, iii, 341–3; Burton, 249–53. See also Dunstable, 139–40.

[84] Paris, iii, 341; *F*, 227; Paris, *FH*, ii, 217.

case in which Henry took a close personal interest.[85] Henry was very ready to reform the abuses of his own officials but he was equally prepared to stand up for the rights of the crown. 'In no way will we permit them to perish for lack of sufficient defence,' he wrote in 1236. Next year, defending the rights and dignity of his crown, he entered the chapter house of Canterbury Cathedral and personally prohibited the prior and convent from prosecuting a secular case in an ecclesiastical court.[86]

In both the conception and the detail of the legislation, Henry owed a great deal to William of Raleigh. It is impossible to read the cases which Raleigh judged in the court *coram rege*, the letters he wrote for the king, the correspondence he received from Robert Grosseteste and the great law book *Bracton* on the laws and customs of England, which he created, without feeling that this was a man of passion, high intelligence and principle. Ambitious, self-confident, articulate, witty and no respecter of persons, he had a profound commitment to the corpus of usages and procedures which made up the laws of England, so different, as *Bracton* noted, from the written laws of other countries. He believed profoundly that the king was subject to the law, and must govern in concert with great councils.[87] He rebuked the bishop of Lincoln, Robert Grosseteste, for seeking to change the laws of England from arguments drawn from the Old Testament. He also declared in his court the king's determination not to 'alter the custom of England used and approved over many past times'.[88] This did not mean the laws were immutable. On the contrary, during these exciting years, Raleigh saw them very much as living things which could be changed with the assent of great councils. Hence in April 1236 his court entered a verdict, turning on a point of law, with the rider 'until it is decided otherwise by the common counsel of the kingdom'.[89] Raleigh drafted writs which initiated the legal actions required by the legislation, defended it when under attack and acted as the spokesman of the regime in parliament.

King and minister did not work in a vacuum. At the great councils they were faced by pressures from different sections of society. Raleigh himself drafted the legislation favouring lords rather than knights and free tenants when it came to exploiting the pasture in a manor. On the other hand, at the Merton council, Henry rejected a demand from the magnates that they be allowed to imprison malefactors taken in their parks.[90] In 1234, in some of the first legislation, steps were taken to meet a major grievance of local society, that of the burden of attendance both at royal courts and the

[85] *CRR*, xv, no. 1320.

[86] *CRR*, xvi, no. 136D; *CR 1234–7*, 356, 360, 390.

[87] See above, 160–2.

[88] *Letters of Grosseteste*, 123; *CRR*, xv, no. 1888; *Bracton*, iv, 360.

[89] *BNB*, iii, no. 1171; see *Bracton*, iv, 31.

[90] *Bracton*, ii, 447–8; *Bracton*, iii, p. xiv; Maitland, *Collected Papers*, ii, 147.

courts of magnates. In February 1234 it was 'provided by the common counsel of the kingdom' that henceforth freemen could attend through attorneys.[91] In August, in line, he said, with Magna Carta, Henry appeared to state that hundred courts (many in private hands) should only meet twice a year. Both in February and August, in insisting that this legislation should apply to the courts of magnates as well as those of the king, Henry drew attention to Magna Carta's stipulation that 'archbishops, bishops, earls, barons and other magnates' should obey the Charter in their dealings with their own tenants. This was a chapter given more force by a change in the 1225 Charter, one quite probably inspired by Archbishop Langton. It may well have been Archbishop Edmund who inspired the appeal to the chapter now.[92]

In the event the stipulation about the hundred courts caused chaos. It was not the general sessions of the hundred courts which the Charter had said should meet only twice a year, but simply the particularly well-attended sessions, known as the tourn. In October 1234, to clarify the issue, the Charter was read aloud before Archbishop Edmund and the assembled bishops, earls and barons 'of the whole kingdom'. As a result, the counties were told, the tourn was now to meet twice a year, and the hundred courts, whether royal or private, once every three weeks, anything less being incompatible with the maintenance of the peace.[93] Nonetheless, Henry explained, this was still a concession because hitherto fortnightly intervals had been customary. 'It gives us much pleasure to provide for the common utility of all our realm and the protection of the poor.'[94] This did not end the controversy. In one of the cases *coram rege* in 1237 the Lincolnshire baron John de Bayeux was accused of having the Charter read in public and stirring up the men of the county to attend the hundreds only twice a year.[95] The whole episode showed the power of local society and how carefully the government needed to tread in its dealings with it. It was not a lesson, unfortunately, that Henry learnt very well.

ROBERT GROSSETESTE AND THE DISPUTE OVER BASTARDY

The counsel and consent given by Archbishop Edmund to the legislation of these years was often made explicit in the documents which announced it. In one particular area he and his fellow bishops eased co-operation between

---

[91] For this great council, see above, 148.

[92] *CR 1231–4*, 551, 592–3; Carpenter, *Magna Carta*, 425–6. For Archbishop Edmund and Magna Carta, see Creamer, 'St Edmund of Canterbury and Henry III', 136–8. The change was the moving of the clause guaranteeing existing liberties so that it no longer qualified the obligation of lords to pass the king's concessions down to their own men.

[93] In a private hundred, the bailiff of the lord would preside over the court and take its proceeds. For private courts, see below, 529 n. 86.

[94] *CR 1231–4*, 588–9, 592–3.

[95] *CRR*, xv, nos. 31, 46, 112; Maddicott, 'Magna Carta', 34–6.

church and state. At the great council of October 1234 they agreed that in cases concerning bastardy they should, at the request of the king's judges, establish the facts as to whether birth had taken place before or after wedlock. They thus assisted the working of English law despite the fact that it was clean contrary to the canon law of the church. Under the first, a subsequent marriage left a child a bastard; under the second, the child would have been born legitimate. So matters might have remained, with the church co-operating with the secular authorities, had it not been for the new bishop of Lincoln, Robert Grosseteste, who now for the first time took the national stage.[96]

A Suffolk man of humble birth, any certain details of Grosseteste's studies, whether in Paris or in English provincial schools, are lost.[97] What is known is that around 1225 he established himself in Oxford and began a period of intensive lecturing and writing in theology, achieving such a dominance that he was elected chancellor of the university by the other masters. By the time he became bishop of Lincoln in 1235 he was already sixty-five but he teemed with intellectual energy, and still had before him twenty years of life. He brought to his post a passionate commitment to the cure of souls, and a steely confidence in his own judgement and integrity, the product no doubt of his vast intellectual superiority. He would not compromise on what he thought was right.

On reaching the bench, Grosseteste was immediately asked to carry out the inquiries into marriages to which his colleagues had agreed in 1234. He completely refused and instead began an extraordinary one-man campaign to bring the law of England into line with that of the church. With a combination of fervour and learning, so powerful one has a physical sense of Grosseteste springing from the page, he wrote a letter to William of Raleigh showing that English law was contrary to natural and divine law, the scriptures, nature and reason. Raleigh should do all he could to change it, 'as you do not wish to destroy the lord king by handing him over to the fires of Hell'.[98] In Raleigh, however, Grosseteste had met his match. Just as Grosseteste drew strength from a lifetime's study of science and theology, so Raleigh was strengthened by a lifetime working in the English law. His reply was witty and ironical. He began with a punning complaint about the length of Grosseteste's 'brevis' (a word meaning both 'brief' and 'letter'), accused him of trying to change the laws of England with arguments drawn from the Old Testament, and declared that since he evidently knew all the laws he should come and help support Raleigh's burden at the king's court.[99]

[96] For Grosseteste, see Southern, *Robert Grosseteste*; Callus, *Robert Grosseteste*; and Mantello and Goering's edition of the *Letters of Grosseteste*.

[97] For the debate, and the possibility that Grosseteste had a wife and children in Paris, see Schulman, 'Husband, father, bishop? Grosseteste in Paris'.

[98] *Letters of Grosseteste*, 108–22, with the quotation at 122.

[99] *Letters of Grosseteste*, 123–5.

The attack, however, which provoked Raleigh to ridicule, reduced Grossesteste's fellow bishops to a worried compliance. Thus, at the Merton council in January 1236, they executed an about-turn, and demanded that the law of England be brought into line with canon law. The response was deafening. 'All the earls and barons answered with one voice, that they did not wish to change the law of England which up to that time had been used and approved.'[100] The result was that the church ceased to hold inquiries to help the secular courts, which instead conducted inquiries of their own, the solution Raleigh perhaps wanted from the start.

WILLIAM, BISHOP-ELECT OF VALENCE, AND THE CRISIS OF 1236

Henry's legislative activity boded well for the co-operative form of kingship envisaged on the fall of Peter des Roches. Henry's growing attachment to Edward the Confessor, famed for his consensual rule, seemed to point in the same direction. King, magnates and community would now sail together in a great convoy. Yet, within months of the Statute of Merton in January 1236, Henry had taken on a foreign pilot. He had appointed as his chief councillor a total stranger to England: his wife's uncle William, bishop-elect of Valence. If this resulted in political tension, it also ushered in financial reform.

William had accompanied Eleanor to England, and remained at court thereafter. At Windsor, that April, when a small council of twelve ministers was formed, he was its head. William's sudden emergence was extraordinary. Indeed the appointment of a foreigner to be the king's chief minister on his first arrival in England seems without parallel in any age. It tells us a great deal about Henry's continuing lack of confidence and his need for a shoulder to lean on. Having relied for so long on a chief minister, first Hubert de Burgh and then Peter des Roches, he found it hard to be without one, however much Hubert and Peter had let him down.

Henry was not, however, acting without reason. William *was* immensely impressive. Even the hostile Matthew Paris acknowledged that he was 'famous, elegant and well bred'. Born in the early 1200s, and thus a few years older than the king, through business sense, diplomacy and warfare he had turned the diocese of Valence into an independent principality. In the process, like Peter des Roches, whom in some ways he resembled, William had gained a reputations as a 'a man of blood'.[101] His largely secular outlook was reflected in the way he neglected to become a priest, remaining simply bishop-elect. In the 1230s he had masterminded a family settlement between his brothers, and played the leading part in negotiating the marriages of both his nieces. William impressed Henry not merely

---

[100] *Bracton*, iv, 295–6.
[101] Paris, iii, 493–4; Cox, *Eagles of Savoy*, 71.

with his personality but also with his policies. Showing great financial acumen, he had already rescued the diocese of Valence from insolvency. He would now rescue the king of England.[102]

The details of the reforms (discussed in the next section) William probably owed to others, to William of Raleigh and to the treasurer of the exchequer, Hugh of Pattishall. What he supplied, having captured the trust of the king, was the power to force reforms through in the teeth of opposition and indifference. The stewards Ralph fitzNicholas and Godfrey of Crowcombe entrenched in local office, had vested interest in the status quo. The great men most at court were there for themselves. They were not interested in driving through administrative and financial reforms. Gilbert Marshal's aim was to restore his position in Ireland and achieve dominance in South Wales. Having obtained Henry's agreement (in July 1235) to his marriage to the sister of King Alexander of Scotland, he left court to digest his gains, never taking up residence there again. Hubert de Burgh too ceased to follow the court during the course of 1235, having succeeded, as far as he could, in recovering his lost lands and castles. With Richard of Cornwall largely busy on his own estates, the most prominent magnate at court in 1235–6 was John de Lacy.[103] Here was a remarkable throwback to the past, for Lacy had been one of the twenty-five barons chosen in 1215 to uphold Magna Carta. His aim now was probably to protect the interests of his mother-in-law in any litigation *coram rege* over the inheritance of the earl of Chester, the inheritance through which in 1232 he had become earl of Lincoln.[104]

Against this background, the bishop-elect of Valence appeared not so much as a breath of fresh air as a thunderclap. Ralph fitzNicholas, having survived the des Roches regime, was removed from court and from all his local offices, probably because he resisted the financial reforms. Also targeted was another 1232–4 survivor, none other than the king's chancellor, Ralph de Neville, bishop of Chichester. According to Matthew Paris, the king demanded he surrender the seal, only to be met by a refusal. Neville claimed that, having received the seal 'by the common counsel of the kingdom' (back in 1218), he could not resign it without similar 'common consent'.[105] Putting the authority of the great council on a par with that of the king, this was a statement of constitutional significance. It foreshadowed demands made throughout the 1240s and 1250s that great councils or parliaments should choose the king's chief ministers.

---

[102] Cox, *Eagles of Savoy*, 72–3.

[103] Richard was certainly not out of favour. In 1235 he was granted both Knaresborough in hereditary right and the wardship of the lands late of John de Briouze: *CChR 1226–57*, 89, 191.

[104] The mother of Lacy's wife was Hawisia, sister of Ranulf, earl of Chester.

[105] Paris, iii, 363–4.

The unease at these events became clear when a great council opened on 28 April 1236.[106] At its start Henry went not to the palace at Westminster, which was open and insecure, but to the Tower of London, a sure sign of crisis. The magnates refused to join him in the Tower and insisted that the parliament should be held at Westminster as customary. In Matthew Paris's account, they complained of William's influence and wondered ironically why he didn't seek to rule the kingdom of France where his other niece was likewise queen. Paris himself pointed out the contrast between Henry's conduct and that of Louis IX and Frederick II, both of whom had sent home the relations of their wives. Admittedly, Paris was writing in the 1240s, but his view of events, in itself hardly surprising, is reflected in the Tewkesbury annals where Henry, under the influence of William, dismisses Ralph fitzNicholas 'and several others of England'.[107]

In the event the crisis was defused. Henry left the Tower and came to treat with his magnates at Westminster. Neville kept his job, and the regime's local reforms, when explained, proved popular. Meanwhile, William continued at the summit of affairs. When he left England for a couple of months in February 1237, Paris declared that the king had committed to him 'the reins of all his council'.[108] The truth of the observation is amply confirmed in 1236–7 by the number of royal charters William witnessed, writs he authorized and rewards he received. The latter included the great lordship of Richmond in Yorkshire forfeited by the duke of Brittany. William thus gained an income of baronial proportions. In 1237, Henry pressed the Durham monks to make him their new bishop 'for love of the king and the security of the kingdom'.[109]

FINANCIAL REFORM

When the bishop-elect of Valence arrived in England, Henry III's immediate financial problem was obvious. He still owed a large part of the 30,000 marks due to the emperor with the final payment of 10,000 marks expected at Easter 1237.[110] His underlying problem remained the low level of his annual revenues, which in the early 1230s probably averaged around £24,000 a year.[111]

Henry knew that the best way of suddenly boosting his revenues was through a tax levied on the value of everyone's movable property like that of 1225 or 1232. But, given the tension created by the elevation of the bishop-elect of Valence, such a tax was out of the question in 1236. So it

---

[106] Paris, iii, 362–3.
[107] Tewkesbury, 102.
[108] Paris, iii, 387.
[109] Durham, 6.
[110] *TR*, no. 1.
[111] See above, 111.

was all the more imperative to get the best possible return from the ordinary revenues of the crown. To implement the necessary reforms, the bishop-elect of Valence saw there must be firm and formal control at the centre, hence the council set up at Windsor in April 1236. It was composed of twelve men, all sworn to give the king faithful advice, and William was the head.[112] During Henry's minority and thereafter, decisions had sometimes been taken by the king 'and his council'. Ministers and members of the king's household had also long taken a special oath to the king. Whether, however, the council before 1236 had a defined membership as opposed to being a more random and fluid body is questionable. The council of 1236 may well have marked a new start. Thereafter, although its membership and the nature of its meetings are obscure, the council seems to have had a continuous life. According to the annals of Dunstable, in 1236 Henry himself swore to obey his council's advice. The bishop-elect must have quickly sized Henry up and may well have suggested such an oath. If Henry's liberalities could be controlled (save, of course, to the bishop-elect himself) that would go a long way to restoring his finances.

Having set up the council, the bishop-elect turned his attention to the king's staple revenues, and in particular those from county farms and the royal manors.[113] Every sheriff owed a farm, a fixed annual payment, for his county. Their total worth at this time was about £2,000 a year, so around 8 per cent of annual income.[114] In order to raise them, the sheriffs could draw on the proceeds of the county and hundred courts, various fixed dues (such as sheriff's aid) and the revenues from such royal manors as were still in their hands. The king and the exchequer had long known that these revenues came to more than the ancient farms and had devised two ways of tapping the surplus. Either the sheriffs were made to account for a fixed increment above the farm or, called 'custodians', they had to account for all the revenue they received, the extra revenue above the farm (which might vary from year to year) being described as 'profit'. Both policies had been banned by chapter 25 of the 1215 Magna Carta, but the chapter had been omitted from its later versions. In 1224 the sheriffs were once again asked to account for revenue above the farm although in the following years the amounts involved had been modest either because the increments were small or because where the sheriffs were custodians they were given generous allowances for their expenses.

What was desperately needed in 1236 was a new policy exploiting much more effectively the farm revenues. There was, however, one great block

---

[112] Dunstable, 145–6, with Denholm-Young, *Collected Papers*, 141–6.

[113] There is comprehensive coverage of the financial reforms in Stacey, *Politics, Policy and Finance*, ch. 2. See also Carpenter, *Reign of Henry III*, 166–71, and Cassidy, 'Shuffling the sheriffs, 1234 and 1236'.

[114] Stacey, *Politics, Policy and Finance*, 57.

to reform. This was the significant number of sheriffdoms held by courtiers, on terms highly favourable to themselves. At the heart of this group was the king's steward Ralph fitzNicholas, who held the joint sher- iffdoms of Nottinghamshire–Derbyshire and Warwickshire–Leicestershire, while his brother Henry controlled Hampshire. Godfrey of Crowcombe, meanwhile, controlled Oxfordshire. Such men could be very cavalier when it came to accounting at the exchequer. In 1235, Richard de Grey had failed to appear for his Northumberland account and frankly admitted that, although a custodian, he had kept no record of his revenues. Thomas of Hengrave in Norfolk–Suffolk likewise acknowledged his 'negligence and incompetence'.[115] The disadvantages of such sheriffs (outside times of political crisis) must have been very clear to Hugh of Pattishall at the exchequer, and at court to William of Raleigh. Neither, however, had the power to oust the current curial clique and make a fresh start. Having captivated the king and captured the council, the bishop-elect of Valence possessed the power in abundance.

Thus it was that the formation of the new council at Windsor was quickly followed by a general dismissal of the curial sheriffs, including Ralph fitzNicholas. By the end of May seventeen counties were under new masters. Peter des Roches, of course, had also dismissed sheriffs and prom- ised financial reform, but it was now that a crucial difference between his situation and that of William emerged. For, whereas Bishop Peter had many followers, eager to return to office on terms favourable to themselves, the bishop-elect of Valence suffered no such incumbrance. In appointing the new sheriffs the government thus had *carte blanche*. Those it turned to were county knights. Attracted by local power and the prestige of the office, knights were prepared to hold sheriffdoms for far less financial profit than that traditionally expected by courtiers. Thus in 1236 the new sheriffs were all appointed as custodians, expected to hand in detailed lists of their revenues. They were also granted allowances significantly smaller than those enjoyed by their predecessors. A special list was drawn up recording the contrast. In the following months the reforms were extended to more counties so that in the financial year 1236/7 all but five were under custo- dians. In that year the reforms promised some £600 worth of extra revenue for the crown.

The reforms had one other advantage. They were politically sellable. Matthew Paris, in recounting the April 1236 parliament, alters his tone immediately when coming to the sheriffdoms. The changes there were 'laudable'.[116] The new sheriffs, Paris noted, took an oath not to receive gifts by which justice might be corrupted. As upstanding local knights, they were also just the kind of sheriffs the counties wanted. The

---

[115] TNA E 159/15, mm. 16, 17, 18, 23d.
[116] Paris, iii, 363.

desire for self-government was not surprising for the local elites naturally expected more sympathetic treatment from their own.[117]

The reform programme also embraced the manors of the royal demesne. Before 1236 their running was haphazard. Some manors were leased to their men, some were held by sheriffs and contributed to the county farm, others were held by separate keepers. A good deal more money could be made from them. Thus it was that in May 1236, in an unprecedented move, the royal manors south of the Trent were concentrated in the hands of the clerk Walter de Burgh, who eventually controlled around forty of them. The manors in Yorkshire, Lancashire and Cumberland, meanwhile, were placed under another experienced administrator, Robert of Crepping. Both acted as custodians, accounting for all the issues of the manors, and both were charged with increasing their value through restocking, expanding the inland and recovering land lost through alienation. In the first flush of office, Burgh in particular proved over-zealous, disseising tenants who held manors or parts of the manors in hereditary right by royal charter, actions which caused a storm and were quickly disclaimed and reversed. There was also a long struggle with forest officials over who should have custody of the woods attached to the manors. But the new arrangements were a success and remained in force until 1240. In his first accounts at Michaelmas 1238, Burgh ended by owing less than £40 on receipts of over £5,300. By the spring of 1240 he had raised annual demesne revenue between £600 and £700 above the pre-1236 levels, an increase of about 60 per cent. Crepping, in turn, upgraded the value of his manors by about a third, adding some £125–£150 a year to royal revenues.[118] Although there were fluctuations from year to year, the reforms of the shrievalities and the demesne together were worth some £1,500 annually to the king.

With regard to the royal demesne, the bishop-elect of Valence seems to have done something else for Henry's benefit. This was to reinforce the view that it was inalienable. Quite probably that was also a lesson taught at the Gloucester council in 1234. Before 1234, Henry, like his father, had been prepared to grant demesne manors away in hereditary right, if usually (although far from always) in return for a farm. Hubert de Burgh had been a particular beneficiary.[119] After 1234, Henry was still prepared to lease demesne manors to favourites, but grants in hereditary right more or less ceased. Henry thus preserved his rights and revenues, but at the expense of having less to give by way of patronage. It was a salutary change, given the dwindling stock of demesne manors, but its

---

[117] Holt, *Magna Carta*, 61–7; Carpenter, *Minority*, 81, 211–12. Paris described the new sheriffs as richer in land and more noble than their predecessors and thus less likely to be corrupted.

[118] Stacey, *Politics, Policy and Finance*, 82–3, 87–9.

[119] See above, 65–7.

necessity also reflected how much less powerful a king Henry was than his predecessors.[120]

In and after 1236 the reforms of the demesne and the county farms did not stand alone. The exchequer scraped in old debts, especially from taxation, and insisted that sheriffs and baronial stewards appeared promptly and in person with their money at the beginning of the Easter and Michaelmas sessions. The new broom was revealed by the complaint of John of Colemere, the purchaser of the king's wines, when told to account: 'he did not understand that he would have to account, nor was it said to him that he must do so.'[121] Most striking of all was the supervision the exchequer now exercised over the wardrobe. In 1236 it had been nearly ten years since a keeper of the wardrobe accounted at the exchequer. Now, between May 1236 and February 1240, Walter of Kirkham and his successor, Geoffrey the Templar, accounted on no fewer than five separate occasions. The accounts, moreover, were not merely for cash receipts and expenditure but also for all the cloths, jewels and precious objects going in and out of their keeping.[122] It may well be that the demand for Ralph de Neville to surrender the seal followed his refusal to account for all the issues of the chancery rather than keeping them all for himself.[123]

In Neville's case Henry backed down. In others, despite some wavering, he showed more mettle. When Henry de Hauville, keeper of the king's falcons at the royal manor of Brigstock, heard of the impending changes he hurried to court and extracted a letter ordering Walter de Burgh to leave him alone. Two months later this was reversed in another letter which laid out the whole basis of the new policy: 'since we have been given to understand,' Henry told him, 'that it would cede more to our advantage if we held the manor of Brigstock in our own hand than if you held it at the farm you have been accustomed to render, we order you to hand the manor over to our beloved clerk, Walter de Burgh'.[124]

MAGNA CARTA, 1237

The crisis of 1236 did not end the consensus between Henry and his subjects. It was reaffirmed at the great assembly meeting at Westminster in January 1237. This is the first referred to in an official document as a

[120] See Ridgeway, 'Foreign favourites', 598–9.
[121] TNA E 159/15, m. 16d; TNA C 60/36, m. 5; Stacey, *Politics, Policy and Finance*, 107–8.
[122] Wild, *WA*, lxiii–xciii.
[123] The treasurer of the exchequer himself was also to account: *CPR 1232–47*, 380. For other reforms, including the hearing of accounts for building works in more detail, see Stacey, *Politics, Policy and Finance*, 109.
[124] *CR 1234–7*, 275; *CFR 1235–6*, no. 444; TNA E 372/82, m. 6. For how Burgh increased the value of Brigstock, see Stacey, *Politics, Policy and Finance*, 85–6, 88, 90, 91 n. 158.

'parliament'.[125] It is also the first to be described in detail by Matthew Paris. It was this parliament that set the final seal on Magna Carta and the Charter of the Forest, and granted the king the last great tax he was to receive for thirty years.

When the assembly met, if we follow Paris's account, it was addressed by William of Raleigh, who explained the king's financial needs and requested a tax to meet them. This was badly received and the king himself intervened. Calmly and convincingly, he promised to confirm Magna Carta, thus 'conciliating in a wonderful fashion the hearts of all his hearers'. As a result he was conceded a tax of a thirtieth of the value of everyone's movable property.[126]

In explaining the king's need, Raleigh almost certainly concentrated on the costs of the imperial marriage. In fact Henry was able to pay off the last 10,000 marks owed to Emperor Frederick in June 1237 before the tax came in, but as a result he was left, as he said, with 'immense debts'.[127] The parliament's consent to the tax, having already agreed to the scutage of 1235, thus shows its continuing support for the imperial alliance. Indeed, the tax, as everyone knew, would be far more lucrative than the scutage. In the event, as against a few thousand pounds, it produce some £22,500, so roughly doubling the ordinary annual revenue of the crown.[128]

The parliament also showed that Magna Carta and the Forest Charter remained central to the political discourse. After the new versions Henry had issued in 1225, they had neither been forgotten nor discarded. Quite the reverse. The principles of Magna Carta had been threatened by the regime of Peter des Roches, and vindicated by its collapse. It was to ram home the point that both in February and August 1234, as we have seen, legislation turning on Magna Carta was promulgated about the running of local courts. In August Henry had ordered the Charters as a whole to be 'inviolably observed' throughout the kingdom, pointing out that there were copies in each county.[129] But there was still anxiety. Henry, after all, had issued the Charters in 1225 when still underage. Did this undermine their validity? Another problem was that the financial reforms begun in 1236 had seemed once again (probably through incompetence rather than intention) to threaten the arbitrary disseisin of those holding property from the crown. Indeed on 12 January 1237, fewer than ten days before the parliament opened, an order went out for the seizure of lands and woods alienated from royal manors.[130]

---

[125] CRR, xv, no. 2047. See also CR 1234-7, 399; Richardson, 'The earliest known official use of the term "parliament"'.

[126] Paris, iii, 380-4; Maddicott, Origins of the English Parliament, 173, 457.

[127] F, 232 (CPR 1232-47, 188); CLR 1226-40, 275; TR, nos. 54-5; CR 1234-7, 571-2.

[128] Mitchell, Studies in Taxation, 208-19.

[129] CR 1231-4, 592-3.

[130] CPR 1232-47, 173; Stacey, Politics, Policy and Finance, 110-11.

At the parliament, these worries about the Charters were soon put to rest. On 28 January, Henry granted a new charter confirming to everyone in the kingdom the liberties in 'our Magna Carta and in our Charter of the Forest' 'notwithstanding' their original concession 'while we were under age'. The witnesses included four of the councillors (including Hubert de Burgh) named by King John in the original Charter of 1215 and three of the twenty-five barons of its security clause. As Sir James Holt remarked, 'Magna Carta was secured within a generation, but only just.'[131]

Accompanying the new charter was a solemn and long-remembered ceremony. It took place in Westminster Abbey's infirmary chapel of St Katherine, now ruined but still redolent of all the important meetings that took place there in the medieval period.[132] Henry now 'with a serene face' promised to obey the Charters and caused Archbishop Edmund to excommunicate all who violated them, Henry, in Paris's account, crying out 'frequently and enthusiastically, Amen, Amen' as the candles were hurled into the ground and the smoke rose around him.[133] Henry and his barons then sought absolution from Edmund in case they had fallen under the previous sentence of excommunication pronounced by Stephen Langton in 1225. They received it but with a warning they would relapse into their previous excommunicated state if they transgressed again.[134]

To the confirmation of the Charters, Henry added another concession. He agreed that the parliament could appoint three members of his council. He thus responded to unease about the remodelling of the council under the bishop-elect of Valence. The concession set an important precedent, and prepared the way for more radical demands in the future. For the moment, however, it was innocuous. Although the new councillors were supposed to oversee the spending of the tax, there is no evidence that they actually did so. The three chosen were harmless enough: the old earl of Surrey, and the gout-ridden William de Ferrers, soon to be earl of Derby, both on good terms with the king. More significant was the third councillor, John fitzGeoffrey, a former sheriff of Yorkshire and son (by his second marriage) of King John's justiciar, Geoffrey fitzPeter. FitzGeoffrey now replaced Godfrey of Crowcombe as one of the stewards of the royal household, going on to enjoy a long career at the highest levels of the king's service.

Early in February the parliament moved from Westminster to Kempton, where it promulgated a further set of legislative reforms. These included a

---

[131] SR, 28 (CChR 1226–57, 225–6); Holt, Magna Carta, 394.

[132] Situated to the south of the chapter house, the chapel (as now) could be entered from the palace without going into the Abbey, hence it was often used for meetings. As a small boy I cultivated a little garden between the chapel's ruined pillars. For what follows, see Paris, iii, 382–3; iv, 186; v, 360–1; Letters of Grosseteste, 253–4; C&S, i, 205–7.

[133] This is from Paris's account (Paris, v, 360–1) under the year 1253.

[134] For the theory behind such sentences of excommunication, see Hill, 'Damnatio eternae mortis'.

new legal action, that of 'cosinage', devised by William of Raleigh, extending the range of those who could sue for their inheritance under the assize of *mort d'ancestor*. Here Raleigh had first to defeat a challenge from the magnates, who argued that the new action infringed the chapter in Magna Carta protecting the jurisdiction of their courts.[135] Also at Kempton, new rules were issued governing the process of compulsory purchase by royal agents, while, at the same time, the provocative order about resuming lands and woods alienated from royal manors was withdrawn. Henry agreed he would respect existing charters and proceed 'according to the law of the land'. Later in the year, in restoring land seized under the January order, he repeated the point: 'if we have right, we will claim it according to the law of the land'.[136]

During the course of the Westminster parliament of January 1237, if we can follow Matthew Paris, Gilbert Basset (now very much back in favour) had suggested that Henry should send one of his men effectively to spy on baronial deliberations. This sparked an anguished question from Richard de Percy, one of the 1215 Magna Carta's twenty-five barons who attested the new Charter of 1237: 'are we aliens and not also the friends of the king'? Henry's conduct during the parliament seemed to offer reassurance, as did a gift of fish to Richard soon afterwards. Henry had, in Paris's words, 'given himself to the counsel of his faithful and native born men'.[137] In coming to parliament at all and asking for consent to a tax, he was obeying the 1215 Magna Carta, although the chapter on taxation had been left out of the subsequent versions. In other ways, in these years, Henry's rule seemed congruent with the Charter. In asking consent for the scutage of 1235, he was actually going beyond it since a tax for marrying the king's daughter was one of those it permitted. A provision issued in December 1235, laying down that interest on debts owed to Jews should not accrue during minorities, restored a concession of the 1215 Magna Carta omitted in later versions.[138] A decision (in June 1236) made by the court *coram rege* that villagers could only be amerced by other villagers (and so not by the court *coram rege* itself) was in line with the Magna Carta's chapter on amercements. Another provision made before the king, in laying down that no one imprisoned for homicide or other felony should be deprived of his lands before conviction, was likewise very much in the Charter's spirit.[139]

Unfortunately the co-operation of the years 1234 to 1237 was more an end than a beginning. The tax on movables of January 1237 was the last

---

[135] *BNB*, iii, no. 1215; *Bracton*, iii, 318–19. *Mort d'ancestor* was a legal action by which free tenants could obtain their inheritances on the death of ancestors of whom they were the heirs.

[136] *CPR 1232–47*, 173; *CR 1234–7*, 482, 521–2; see *CRR*, xv, p. lvii n. 1.

[137] Paris, iii, 382; *CR 1234–7*, 447.

[138] *CR 1234–7*, 214; *ERW*, p. ci (no. 20).

[139] *BNB*, iii, no. 1170; *CR 1231–4*, 587–8.

granted during Henry's personal rule, despite him begging again and again for another. A major reason was the gradual disintegration of the consensus achieved with the fall of Peter des Roches. According to Paris, there were vociferous complaints at the parliament of 1237 about Henry trusting once more to foreigners. Paris may exaggerate. He did not write up his account until the 1240s when the problem seemed more acute. But still the elevation of the bishop-elect of Valence was at least a portent of what was to come. Another factor in Henry's difficulties was his failure to reform the realm. Although legislative provisions continued during his personal rule, their frequency and importance never approached those promulgated between 1234 and 1237. Perhaps something was due here to the departure of William of Raleigh from court on his election to the bishopric of Norwich in 1239. But the blame lay with the king himself, both in terms of outlook and other preoccupations, as will be seen.[140]

THE LEGATE OTTO

Soon, Henry had another foreigner as his prop and stay. Back in May 1236 he had written to the pope asking for the dispatch of a legate to England. His tone was emotional. The Apostolic see, as a pious mother, should give 'solace and help to her sons, desolate and oppressed'.[141] The request was as controversial as it was surprising. A legate would impact profoundly on the church in England, and affect the authority of Archbishop Edmund, yet there is no sign that Henry consulted with him and other bishops.[142] Only Bishop Mauclerc of Carlisle seems to have been at court around the time the request was made. Why should Henry want to make it now, just as he was embracing the bishop-elect of Valence as his chief minister?

The explanation lies both in the buffeting Henry had faced at the April 1236 council and the fear that William would not always be there to support him in such troubles. For William saw himself less as a permanent chief executive than as a trouble-shooting chairman of the board. He would sort matters out and then add England to his portfolio of director-ships. At this time he had much else on his agenda, including the scheme to make his brother Thomas, through marriage, count of Flanders. Henry's envoys sent to ask for a legate thus obtained a papal letter urging William to remain in England.[143] Henry must have hoped a legate would maintain the pressure on William to do so, while also providing comfort and counsel if, periodically, he was absent. The two together would succour and solace the worried king. There was also a more pointed reason behind the request. Henry was beginning to regret, doubtless

[140] See below, 527–33, 566–7, 711–15.
[141] TR, nos. 32–3; Reg. Gregoire IX, no. 3298 (CPReg, 157).
[142] Paris, iii, 395–6.
[143] Reg. Gregoire IX, nos. 3298–9 (CPReg, 157).

under the influence of the bishop-elect of Valence, the munificent grants he had made in 1234/5 to Gilbert Marshal and Hubert de Burgh. With papal authority, could he perhaps revoke them? Henry's initial letter of 25 May thus referred to the needs of 'the royal dignity', and the legate, when eventually appointed, was empowered by the pope to revoke alienations made contrary to the king's coronation oath.[144]

Henry, therefore, as in 1230, appealed for outside help to sort out his problems, rather than sorting them out himself. On this occasion, however, Pope Gregory was sceptical. He reminded Henry of his change of mind in 1230, and delayed for a while acceding to this new request. It was not, therefore, until July 1237 that Henry set off for Dover to meet the legate. In the event he got no further than Plumpstead in Kent, where he offered his welcome, with a bow, as Matthew Paris contemptuously described it, as low as the legate's knees.[145]

The legate appointed was Otto, cardinal deacon of St Nicola in Carcere. With his main base the bishop of Durham's London house on the Strand (in royal hands as the see was vacant following the death of Richard le Poore), he was to remain in England until January 1241, playing a major part in the business of both church and state. Otto was a good choice. Wise and circumspect, he had visited England as a papal nuncio in 1226 and thereafter had kept in close touch with its affairs. He had previously acted as a legate in northern Germany and Denmark, convening councils and issuing reforming statutes.[146]

Otto's situation in England, however, was not easy, especially as time wore on. The burden of his support through money payments from the church ('procurations'), the many benefices he obtained for his clerks and relations, and his unenviable role in 1240 as a papal tax collector (which coloured Matthew Paris's later account of his legation) were all potent grounds for criticism. There was also a particular flash in April 1238 when Otto was staying at Osney abbey just outside Oxford. An affray between his servants and clerks of the university led to the death of his chief cook (a kinsman) and forced him to shelter in the abbey's tower, before escaping to the king at Abingdon. Otto punished the clerks – they processed on foot through London without cloaks and mantles to his Strand house – but he then 'mercifully and kindly' relaxed the interdict he had imposed on the university.[147] This was of a piece with his general conduct. He won the trust of Archbishop Edmund, and disarmed criticism, as even Matthew Paris acknowledged, by refusing many of the gifts that were offered him. Twelve silver dishes and salt cellars (weighing nearly twenty pounds) made for him

[144] CPReg, 159; Paris, iii, 368; Paris, FH, ii, 223.
[145] CR 1234–7, 541; Paris, iii, 396.
[146] Williamson, 'Some aspects of the legation of cardinal Otto', 161.
[147] Paris, iii, 485.

by the king were thus given instead to the bishop-elect of Valence, a telling indication of how the two men were linked in Henry's mind.[148]

For all its burdens, Otto's legation benefited the English church. He confirmed privileges and agreements, ordained vicarages and, through his court 'at once a delegacy of the curia, a court of appeal and a court of first instance', dealt with a great deal of business which would otherwise have made the long journey to Rome.[149] Otto's greatest achievement was the canons issued by the great ecclesiastical council he convened at St Paul's in London in November 1237. Running to thirty-one separate chapters and surviving in over sixty manuscripts, they were based on the canons of the Fourth Lateran Council of 1215 but were adapted to local conditions. They became an absolutely standard source for church law, and profoundly influenced bishops in their work of reform.[150]

Otto also played an important role in affairs of state. According to Paris the king 'appeared to worship his very footsteps', and declared he could do nothing important without the consent of pope and legate.[151] As an impression of both the king's attitude and the constitutional position, this was not so far from the truth. Bereft of the bishop-elect of Valence, who left England in May 1238, Henry begged the pope to extend the legate's stay. At the farewell Christmas feast in 1240 he placed him in the royal seat.[152] And why not? 'The kingdom of England is known to belong to the Roman church,' the pope wrote in 1238, referring to the way King John had made England a papal fief.[153] In the original letters announcing the legation, the pope empowered Otto to revoke alienations and told the king to obey his orders. There was no expectation that Otto would act as a chief minister, but many important decisions in this period were made in his presence and by implication with his counsel and consent.[154] Indeed, Henry promised to spend none of the money coming from the tax granted in January 1237 without Otto's sanction. Formally at least, Otto thus had control of the crown's most important financial resource.[155]

Before Otto's arrival, Henry had already denied he would use papal authority to revoke previous alienations, but this was not the end of the matter. In February 1238 the pope ordered Henry once again to recall alienations of crown possessions made 'with improvident liberality . . . led by less than wise counsel' and 'to the enormous harm of the kingdom'. He was to do so notwithstanding previous oaths to the contrary. The pope had some

---

[148] *CR 1234–7*, 508; Paris, iii, 403, 412.

[149] Williamson, 'Some aspects of the legation of cardinal Otto', 154.

[150] Williamson, 'Some aspects of the legation of cardinal Otto', 159–61; *C&S*, i, 237–59.

[151] Paris, iii, 412.

[152] *CPR 1232–47*, 235; Paris, iii, 473, 530; Paris, iv, 83–4.

[153] *F*, 234 (*CPReg*, 167).

[154] For example, those connected with the futures of the earldoms of Salisbury and Leicester: *BNB*, iii, no. 1235; *CChR 1226–57*, 242–3.

[155] *CPR 1232–47*, 205, 211.

expectation of opposition and wrote of the losers coming to some 'amicable composition'.[156] In the event nothing came of the initiative. Probably Otto placed the kingdom's peace and tranquillity before anything else.[157]

THE CRISIS OVER THE MONTFORT MARRIAGE, 1238

In January 1237, when he confirmed Magna Carta, Henry had seemed at one with the great and good of the kingdom. A year later, in marrying his sister to Simon de Montfort, he totally ignored them. The result was a political crisis.

The origins of the marriage lay in a relationship formed at Henry's court. Montfort had been little there in 1235. In 1237 he was almost a fixture. Indeed, during the year he attested more royal charters than anyone save the king's stewards. Eleanor was often there too. The cost of the candles to light her chamber feature in her brother's wardrobe accounts.[158] For Eleanor, Montfort must have seemed a dream come true. He was silver tongued, hence his success in persuading Henry and the earl of Chester to give him the Leicester inheritance. He was sharply intelligent, hence he knew all about his rights as steward at the coronation. He was properly pious, hence his immediate expulsion of the Jews from Leicester. And he was the son of a heroic father, killed in the service of the cross, and often spoke of following in his footsteps.[159] In 1237, Montfort was about twenty-nine, Eleanor twenty-two, so they were both in the bloom of youth. How different from Eleanor's first marriage in 1224 when she was a child bride and her husband, William Marshal, earl of Pembroke, old enough to be her father. Widowed in 1231, Eleanor had taken a vow of chastity but without donning the religious habit.[160] By 1237 the impression from the stream of gifts she received from her brother – game for her food, timber for her buildings, a black palfrey to ride, Odiham castle in which to live – is that of a wealthy young woman with a large entourage, moving restlessly round her properties, and thoroughly bored with her single life. She certainly knew how to get her way. Henry had initially denied her custody of the park at Odiham. He soon changed his mind.[161]

What more natural than that the young couple should fall in love, but in Montfort's case love was inseparable from calculation. Earlier schemes to marry the countess of Boulogne or the countess of Flanders (he always

[156] *F*, 234 (*CPReg*, 167).

[157] On his arrival Otto had tried to reconcile Hubert de Burgh and Peter des Roches.

[158] Wild, *WA*, 20.

[159] *TR*, no. 46, where I suspect the reference to his father comes from Montfort himself. The influence of his father's career is a major theme in Sophie Ambler's new biography of Montfort: *The Song of Simon de Montfort*. For Eleanor, see Wilkinson, *Eleanor de Montfort*.

[160] Paris, iii, 487.

[161] *CPR 1232–47*, 161; *CR 1234–7*, 387.

aimed high) had come to nothing. (Perhaps such schemes explain his absences from court in 1235 and 1236.) Now marriage to Eleanor would place him at the heart of the English royal family, making him the king's 'beloved brother'. It would also bring him substantial wealth. True, Henry failed to provide Eleanor with a marriage portion (later a great bone of contention), but she kept Odiham and enjoyed a substantial dower as the widow of William Marshal. That meant, for the duration of her life, Montfort gained lands worth nearly £500 in England, as well as a £400 annual cash payment from the Marshal earls in place of her dower in Wales and Ireland. The marriage would roughly triple his income. It also brought, thanks to Henry's generosity, custody of the royal castle at Kenilworth, a mighty fortress with many tenants of the honour of Leicester living in the surrounding area.[162]

The same attendance at court which had brought Montfort and Eleanor together meant they could persuade Henry to agree to their match. It was not that difficult. Henry was delighted to satisfy and settle his sister. He must also have thought he was securing a brother-in-law who would support him through thick and thin. If Henry here was grievously mistaken, he saw very clearly the only way to bring the marriage about. It had to be suddenly and in secret. Henry's other sisters, Joan and Isabella, had married the king of Scotland and Emperor Frederick II respectively. Against that who was Montfort? A man of illustrious birth, certainly, but a younger son, possessed of only half the honour of Leicester and with an income of about £500 a year as against the thousands enjoyed by the greatest English earls.[163] While Henry in the occasional private letter styled Montfort 'earl of Leicester', there had been no formal investiture and no public recognition of the title.[164] Eleanor, after her marriage, continued to be styled 'countess of Pembroke'.

Henry, therefore, had to choose his moment, and he chose it well. Archbishop Edmund, before whom Eleanor's vow of chastity had been taken, left England for Rome just before Christmas 1237. Richard of Cornwall had been absent from court since the end of September. Thus at Westminster, on 7 January 1238, Montfort and Eleanor were married, 'in the little chapel of the king in the angle of his chamber', by a royal chaplain. The chapel itself left something to be desired because next month Henry had its floor covered with painted tiles.[165]

---

[162] Maddicott, *Simon de Montfort*, 44–51. There seems no evidence as to when and on what terms the Montforts were first given Kenilworth, but their first child was born there in November 1238.

[163] On the death of the last Beaumont earl of Leicester in 1204, his heirs were his sisters, Amice, the mother of Montfort's father, and Margaret, married to Saer de Quincy, earl of Winchester. As the eldest, Amice could carry with her the claim to the title, but the lands of the honour were divided between the sisters.

[164] *TR*, no. 46. See also *CChR 1226–57*, 230.

[165] Paris, iii, 470–1; Colvin, *History of the King's Works*, i, 497–8.

When he heard the news of his sister's clandestine marriage, Richard of Cornwall was outraged. Backed by a substantial group of magnates, including Gilbert Marshal, he held armed gatherings at Southwark and Kingston, won support in London and moved to secure the backing of the Cinque Ports. The efforts of the Legate Otto and the bishop-elect of Valence to broker a settlement seemed to underline how Henry was influenced by foreigners, of whom indeed Montfort could be seen as one. As the situation became more threatening, Henry fled to the Tower where he remained from 23 February through to 2 March. According to Matthew Paris, a document was drawn up and sealed by the legate, binding the king to act henceforth with baronial advice, only then for Richard to back down and reach private settlements with Montfort and Montfort's main baronial ally, John de Lacy, earl of Lincoln. (In January, Lacy had been squared by the bethrothal of his daughter to the king's ward Richard de Clare, the future earl of Gloucester.)[166] Certainly the crisis quickly evaporated without Henry making constitutional concessions.

Montfort himself soon left for Rome where he secured papal confirmation of his marriage. Between February 1238 and the summer of 1239 he received loans from the king's wardrobe totalling £1,565, an extraordinary mark of Henry's favour. The next largest sum was the £184 received by the bishop-elect of Valence.[167] In November 1238, Henry dashed to Kenilworth to stand as godfather at the baptism of Simon and Eleanor's first child, named Henry after himself. For Christmas 1238 he sent Eleanor a robe, tunic, quilt, mattress and coverlet, costing (with transport from London to Kenilworth) over £30.[168] Henry had established Montfort in England. It was a considerable achievement and one he would come to regret.

In an important respect the crisis set no precedent. In the ensuing years, Richard of Cornwall was sometimes exasperated by his brother, but he never again raised the standard of revolt. Instead of being a centre of opposition, as he might easily have been, he became a pillar of the regime.[169] Henry came to value his counsel and depend on his loans. He was also lucky in Richard's personality: a cool, level-headed man who generally preferred compromise to confrontation and diplomacy to warfare. Richard also wished to be rich, and, looking beyond England, to play a part on the international stage. Both these characteristics played a part in settling the crisis of 1238.

In 1236, Richard and a group of nobles (including again Gilbert Marshal) had taken the cross.[170] They were responding to papal preaching of the crusade prompted by the expiry of the 1229 truce under which the

---

[166] *CPR 1232–47*, 208.

[167] *CLR 1226–40*, 410; Wild, *WA*, 38.

[168] Stacey, *Politics, Policy and Finance*, 124 n. 168; *CLR 1226–40*, 356.

[169] Denholm-Young, *Richard of Cornwall*, 37, gets this point well.

[170] For an account of Richard's crusade, see Tyerman, *England and the Crusades*, 101–8.

Emperor Frederick II had recovered Jerusalem. Doubtless Richard was also inspired by the example of his uncle and namesake, Richard the Lionheart. In 1238, for all the anger at his sister's marriage, his real focus was gathering the money for his projected expedition. Henry was unenthusiastic, fearing (testimony to their underlying good relations) his brother's absence from the country, but he now gave £4,000 to Richard himself and another £1,000 to his 'chief of staff', the prior of the English Hospitallers, both sums coming from the proceeds (and amounting to some 22 per cent) of the 1237 tax. This was Richard's price for forgiving his brother.[171]

The crisis of 1238 had consequences for London. As he peered over a largely unturreted curtain wall, and over a moat which was dry, Henry realized that the Tower's defences were quite out of date. He began, therefore, the construction of a new curtain wall with eight towers, one of them containing a great new gateway towards the city. When the gateway collapsed, the Londoners rejoiced thinking correctly the new fortifications were designed as much to control as protect them. Indeed, one story was that the collapse was due to the miraculous intervention of that most famous of all Londoners, Thomas Becket. While rebuilding the Tower's defences, Henry also attended to his personal quarters. On 2 March 1238, the day he left the Tower, he ordered the chimney in the queen's chamber to be completed and a screen to be made between his chapel and chamber in what became known as the Wakefield Tower.[172] Later in the year the walls of the queen's chamber were to be whitewashed and painted with points and flowers. Henry spent over £5,000 on the Tower down to 1241. Although the gateway (soon rebuilt), was superseded by the work of Henry's son Edward I, Henry's walls and towers survive to this day. It is easy to forget that this most pacific of kings was one of the major builders of the Tower of London.[173] The strength he thus gained was a factor in the many confrontations he had with London over the following years. These began in 1239 itself when Henry, in breach of the city's liberties according to the protests, tried to influence the mayoral elections in favour of his own candidate, the alderman Simon fitzMary.[174]

1238: THE DISMISSAL OF RALPH DE NEVILLE

On 9 June 1238, Peter des Roches, bishop of Winchester, died. Having plunged the kingdom into civil war, and exacerbated native hostility to foreigners, his influence over Henry had been almost entirely negative. Yet it is a measure of the man, and the breadth of his interests, that the long

---

[171] Stacey, *Politics, Policy and Finance*, 126, and 125–8 for a general analysis of how the money was spent.

[172] For the Wakefield tower, see below, 363.

[173] *CLR 1226–40*, 315–16, 352; Colvin, *History of the King's Works*, ii, 713; Paris, iv, 80, 93–4.

[174] FitzThedmar, 7–8; Williams, *Medieval London*, 204–6.

obituary penned by Matthew Paris was almost entirely favourable. It
ignored his political career in England and concentrated on his crusade,
his religious foundations and his patronage of the friars.[175]

Henry was determined that the bishop-elect of Valence should be des
Roches' successor. The great man had departed in the previous month to
help the emperor in his war against the north Italian towns. If he became
bishop of Winchester, he would be tied more firmly to England.
Throughout August 1238, Henry stayed either at Winchester or at neighbouring episcopal manors in order to put pressure on the cathedral monks
who would make the election. On one occasion he even harangued them
in their own chapter house. To no avail. The bishop-elect of Valence, like
Peter des Roches, was a foreigner and a man of war. But at least Peter had
been based in England. What threatened now was a bishop who might
ruthlessly exploit the see to further his continental ambitions. So the
monks tried desperately to find another candidate acceptable to the king.
The first was William of Raleigh. 'He has killed more men with his tongue
than the elect of Valence has with his sword,' was the joke Matthew Paris
put into Henry's mouth.[176] The second was Henry's long-serving chancellor, Ralph de Neville, bishop of Chichester. When Neville, duly postu-
lated by the monks, would not stand down, Henry appealed to Rome and
demanded he surrender the seal. In 1236, Neville had refused to obey such
an order, claiming that, having been appointed by a great council, only a
great council could dismiss him. Now he complied. Perhaps he felt that his
position was weaker being engaged in a purely personal quarrel. Perhaps
he hoped that his emancipation from secular affairs would help his cause
with the pope.

The episode was doubly significant. In the event, the dispute over who
should be the new bishop (eventually it was William of Raleigh) lasted
down to 1244, damaging Henry's reputation, yet improving his finances:
between £2,300 and £3,000 a year flowed into his coffers from the revenues of the vacant see.[177] Neville's departure also impacted on the structure of central government and Henry's relations with the wider realm.
Neville retained the title and revenues of the chancellor until his death in
1244. Henry evidently hesitated to overturn the charter of 1227 granting
him the chancery for life. But from then onwards day-to-day charge of the
seal was in the hands of officials who, whatever their merits, lacked
Neville's status and independence. Henry liked such men for that very
reason. For those in the localities, outside the magic circle of the court, it
was a different story. They might wonder who was in control of the seal
and thus to whom they should address their petitions and complaints.
Henry's government was becoming increasingly remote and, some thought,

[175] Paris, iii, 489–90.
[176] Paris, iii, 494.
[177] Howell, *Regalian Right*, 229.

increasingly corrupt. The parliaments of the 1240s began to demand the restoration of an elected chancellor on the Bishop Neville model.

THE BIRTH OF EDWARD, 1239

In early September 1238, Henry was at Woodstock, busy sending off his proctor to Rome to appeal against Neville's election. One night a man (Henry described him later as a 'ribald') crawled through a window into the king's chamber armed with a knife, evidently intent on murder. Fortunately Henry was absent, in fact sleeping with the queen, and the alarm was raised by her lady Margaret Bisset, who was still up reciting psalms by candlelight. Having been arrested, the would-be assassin was eventually torn limb from limb by horses at Coventry, probably while the king was there on 16–17 September. Not surprisingly after this, Henry ordered the windows of his chambers to be barred.[178]

There was soon to be disruption at court of a different kind. King and queen spent Christmas Day 1238 at Winchester making offerings of gold at no fewer than three masses, one, 'the greater mass', presumably being in the cathedral. The king also washed the feet of 300 paupers, and then (at a cost of over £25) clothed and shod them.[179] When, however, Gilbert Marshal, earl of Pembroke, arrived for the Christmas feast he was roughly turned away by the king's marshals and ushers brandishing their staffs of office.[180] Gilbert had received handsome gifts of game and timber from the king the previous July, so had clearly been forgiven his protests over the Montfort marriage. Now, however, he had failed to make the payments due to Eleanor de Montfort for her dower in Wales and Ireland, leaving the king as the surety to pick up the bill. Montfort's own reception at the Christmas court was very different. On Christmas Day itself he was conceded as 'earl of Leicester', the third penny of the county.[181] In February 1239 he was finally invested with the title, Montfort's elder brother, Amaury, coming to England two months later to make a formal resignation of his claims.[182]

The breach in relations with Gilbert Marshal was not quickly healed. He was absent from court throughout 1239, thus missing one of the greatest celebrations of Henry's reign. Henry's nights in the queen's chamber had produced the desired result, for by the late autumn of 1238 Eleanor was pregnant. Henry was assiduous in seeking divine aid for the forthcoming birth. Between December 1238 and January 1239 he ordered the feeding of 200 paupers a day. In February 1239 he went on a pilgrimage

---

[178] Paris, iii, 497–8.
[179] TNA C 47/3/44.
[180] Paris, iii, 522–3; see Kjaer, 'Matthew Paris and the royal Christmas', 145.
[181] TNA E 159/17, m. 6.
[182] Maddicott, *Simon de Montfort*, 23.

to Canterbury where he made offerings at 'the crown of St Thomas', 'the two altars by the great altar', the fragment of the sword which had killed Becket, the altar of the Virgin Mary in the crypt, and finally 'at the tomb of the blessed Thomas' himself.[183] At Westminster, close to the birth, he paid over £10 for a great cloth to hang on St Edward's altar. During the course of 1239 he gave gifts to one or both orders of friars at Canterbury, Newcastle on Tyne, Lichfield, Winchester, Oxford, Reading, Derby, Durham, Salisbury and Carlisle, as well as paying for all the food on the first day of the Dominicans' general chapter at Stamford. Eleanor finally gave birth at Westminster during the night of 17–18 June, and it was a boy. Henry named him Edward after his patron saint.[184]

Henry's household choir chanted 'Christus vincit, Christus vincit', the Londoners celebrated with music and bonfires, and the earl of Surrey conferred £10 a year on the messenger who brought him the news. Gifts poured in, although Henry, according to Paris's tale, sent back those he thought inadequate, demanding better. 'God has given us this child but the king has sold him,' ran the joke.[185] In ceremonies attended by large numbers of noblemen and women, including Simon and Eleanor de Montfort, the royal baby was baptized by the legate Otto and confirmed by Archbishop Edmund. Henry thanked Sybil Giffard by granting her £10 a year 'for her diligence towards the queen at the time of her confinement'. He thanked 'the glorious Confessor and King Edward' in a whole series of gifts and offerings 'for us and our queen', one on 20 June just three days after the birth.[186] And he protected his son both materially and spiritually. Edward's chamber at Windsor (where he chiefly lived with his mother) was wainscotted and its windows barred. 'A tunic of good samite of the length of Edward our son' was placed on the crucifix at St Mary Southwark, while at Windsor a chaplain was appointed to celebrate the mass of the Virgin 'in perpetuity' for Edward's 'good estate and health'.[187]

Joy was utterly justified. Queen Eleanor, by producing a son, had secured the future of the dynasty and solidified her husband's political position. Richard of Cornwall (present at the court for the celebrations) was no longer heir to the throne, and thus all the less likely to be a centre of opposition. Henry had also been positive and innovative in naming his son Edward, for this broke with all previous practice since 1066. He thus honoured his patron saint, and also seemed to reposition the monarchy in the new post-imperial world, stressing its English rather than continental roots.

---

[183] CLR 1226–40, 356; TNA C 47/3/44, m. 1. The 'crown of St Thomas' was the top of Becket's head preserved in the corona chapel.
[184] Paris, FH, ii, 231. The birth seems to be dated to 18 June (the morrow of St Botolph) in CLR 1226–40, 406.
[185] Paris, iii, 540.
[186] CLR 1226–40, 418; CChR 1226–57, 244; CR 1234–7, 155.
[187] CR 1234–7, 149; CLR 1226–40, 435.

The celebrations, however, were soon clouded. On 31 July there was another great gathering of lords and ladies at Westminster, this time for the queen's purification. The royal choir again chanted the 'Christus Vincit' and 500 candles were burnt.[188] One couple, however, were absent: the Montforts. They had arrived in London the night before, to be met by Henry's order for Simon's arrest and dispatch to the Tower, something only prevented by the intervention of the earl of Cornwall. The king's anger had been building for some days – by 29 July the Montforts had been deprived of Odiham.[189] The anger had been ignited by Montfort, without consultation or permission, putting Henry down as the pledge for a large debt he owed the queen's uncle Thomas of Savoy, now, through marriage, count of Flanders.[190] The whole business had been revealed by Thomas himself who had come to England to press for payment. Through Montfort's default, that meant payment by the king. Henry, in his rage, went on to accuse Montfort of seducing his sister before their marriage, Paris's story here being confirmed by Montfort's own reference to Henry's 'grievous and shameful words which are hard to record'.[191] The accusation of seduction was unsupported by the date of their first child's birth and there is every sign that Henry was initially happy with the marriage. But Montfort could gain no forgiveness. He and Eleanor sailed down the Thames in a small vessel and then on to France.

Montfort's fall has much in common with that of Gilbert Marshal. There is the same climactic exclusion from a great ceremony, and the same royal anger over being left to pick up a bill. But, however extreme and disruptive Henry's reaction, he was right to show he could not be taken for granted.

THE TRIUMPH OF THE QUEEN

There was one conspicuous absentee from the celebrations surrounding Edward's birth in July 1239, namely the queen's uncle and the king's chief councillor, William, bishop-elect of Valence. During the summer his return to England was eagerly awaited with business being postponed until his arrival.[192] Instead, towards the end of December news arrived of his death at Viterbo. The queen wept. The king tore his clothes and threw them in the fire. Numerous chaplains were appointed to celebrate masses daily for the bishop-elect's soul.[193]

---

[188] The date of 9 August given in Paris, iii, 566–7, is clearly wrong: *CLR 1226–40*, 406.

[189] *CLR 1226–40*, 404.

[190] See Maddicott, *Simon de Montfort*, 23–5.

[191] Bémont, *Simon de Montfort*, 334; Maddicott, *Simon de Montfort*, 26.

[192] *CFR 1238–9*, no. 190; TNA E 159/17, m. 9d.

[193] Paris, iii, 623; *CLR 1226–40*, 436. This episode took place in the chapel of St Stephen in Westminster Palace.

Did the demise of this great man end or at least curtail Savoyard influence? Not a bit of it. Indeed, in the next two years Henry bound himself to the queen's kin as never before. Alongside a host of lesser Savoyards, there were three stars, yet more uncles of the queen: Thomas of Savoy, count of Flanders and champion of the family claims in Piedmont, who was given a money pension;[194] Peter of Savoy, who became lord of Richmond in Yorkshire; and Boniface of Savoy, who was elected archbishop of Canterbury. Henry hoped to secure wise and loyal councillors who would support the dynasty in England and open up all kinds of exciting prospects on the continent. He was certainly associating with some very clever men, men far cleverer and with far wider horizons than himself.

Henry had reasons for establishing the Savoyards but he did not narrowly calculate the pros and cons. He stands forth in these years as an impulsive, emotional, warm blooded king, acting sometimes out of anger, sometimes out of compassion, often, as in his enthusiastic orders for building works, giving his orders by word of mouth.[195] When Gerard Bat, elected mayor of London against Henry's wishes, complained in 1240 about being made to give up a traditional £40 payment – 'Alas, my lord, I could have married my daughter with the money' – Henry flew into a temper and swore by St Edward 'You will not be mayor this year, and for a little I would say never.'[196] Conversely, when in the same year the abbot of Waverley 'with sighs and tears' complained to Henry about a breach of the house's liberties, 'without delay' Henry gave him what he wanted.[197]

The arrival of Edward had given Henry confidence in himself and the whole future of his dynasty. In 1240 he ordered everyone in the kingdom, from villeins upwards, to swear oaths of fealty to Edward as his heir.[198] The desire to govern by himself, without the irksome objections of some chief minister, explains why down to 1258 Henry steadfastly refused to revive the office of chief justiciar and why there was no successor to the bishop-elect of Valence, let alone Hubert de Burgh and Peter des Roches. Yet there remained another side. While Henry was perfectly capable of sticking to his guns, he could still at times feel perplexed and uncertain. He was often ready to take advice, compromise and draw back. He soon promised that his treatment of Gerard Bat 'by will' should not harm London's liberties. In the Waverley abbey case he withdrew his concession and, on the advice of his council, insisted the abbot show proper warrant

---

[194] Cox, *Eagles of Savoy*, 52–7. In late 1237, Thomas had married Margaret, countess in her own right of both Flanders and Hainault. She had been widowed in 1233 with the death of Ferrand of Portugal.

[195] *CR 1237–42*, 224–5, 353; *CLR 1240–5*, 16.

[196] FitzThedmar, 8; Paris, iv, 94–5. This was part of a wider dispute over the king's attempt to influence mayoral elections: Williams, *Medieval London*, 204–6.

[197] Waverley, 325–7; *CRR*, xvi, p. xxxvi.

[198] *CR 1237–42*, 236; Paris, iv, 9; Tewkesbury, 114; Waverley, 321; Osney, 431.

for his liberties.[199] When organizing the oaths of fealty to Edward, he abandoned his impossible demand for lists to be supplied of all those who had sworn.[200] Although none of the new Savoyards achieved (or indeed aspired to) the position accorded the bishop-elect of Valence, Henry could find their confident counsels immensely reassuring.

Henry would never have turned to the Savoyards to the extent he did had it not been for the triumph of the queen in giving birth to a son and heir. Here she had done better than her sister Queen Margaret of France, who was yet to have a child and did not produce a son until 1244. Soon, moreover, Eleanor gave birth again. This time, in October 1240, it was a girl. She was called Margaret, so Matthew Paris tells us, after the queen's sister (now herself pregnant) and because the queen had cried out to St Margaret in the pains of childbirth.[201] Again Henry was overjoyed. His choir chanted the 'Christus Vincit' before him on the day of the birth, and thousands of paupers were fed 'so that Omnipotent God deigns to prosper our state and that of our queen and people'.[202] More children followed: Beatrice in 1242, and the much prayed for second son, Edmund, in 1245.

The royal children were based at Windsor castle and Eleanor divided much of her time between there and Westminster. Henry's desire to see his son Edward and daughter Margaret, support Eleanor in her pregnancies, and father more children was one reason why, during these years, he spent so much time at Westminster and Windsor: in 1239, 156 days and 35 days respectively; in 1240, 206 days and 72 days; in 1241, 133 days and 53 days.[203] In 1240 he spent fifty consecutive days at Westminster before and after Margaret's birth. Of course, another reason for that was to be close to the Confessor.

Henry continued his efforts to create a fitting environment for his queen.[204] At Westminster, in January 1240, the chimney in her chamber was to be raised and painted with an image of winter, as a contrast

---

[199] CR 1237–42, 254; Waverley, 326–7. For another example of Henry making a concession (to the executors of the archbishop of Canterbury) and then immediately changing his mind, see CR 1237–42, 273.

[200] CR 1237–42, 236.

[201] CLR 1226–40, 496, which fixes the date. Paris, iv, 48, gives 29 September but he later altered it to 2 October in FH, ii, 239, a good example of his attention to correct detail.

[202] CR 1234–7, 227, 233, 248.

[203] Craib, Brindle and Priestley, Itinerary of King Henry III, 16.

[204] During 1240 and 1241 work was going on for her at Havering, Hereford, Kempton, Kenilworth, Ludgershall, the Tower of London, Marlborough, Oxford, Winchester, Windsor and Westminster. At Kenilworth (back in the king's hands from the Montforts) the king ordered two seats to be made in the chapel, one for himself and one for Eleanor. There was also to be a painted seat for Eleanor in the chapel in the tower. During the royal couple's brief visit to the castle in September 1241, Henry ordered the windows in the queen's chamber to be widened and its walls to be wainscotted, lined and whitened: CLR 1240–5, 32–3, 71.

presumably to the cheery fire.[205] At the Tower, in the church of St Peter within the bailey the decorative scheme was a veritable celebration of the royal family. Before the altars of St Katherine, the queen's patron saint, and St Nicholas, the patron saint of children, 'great and beautiful stalls' for the king and queen were set up. Then, a few months later, Henry added images of the Virgin Mary and St Christopher holding the infant Jesus together with paintings of the histories of St Nicholas and St Katherine. In addition, standing to right and left of the great cross in the chapel, there were to be two cherubims 'with cheerful and joyous countenance'. The ensemble was surely meant to remind the royal couple of their two children and the happiness they had brought.[206]

It was above all at Windsor, the main base for the children, that these years saw the most striking architectural developments. In January 1240 the king issued orders for new chambers for himself and the queen. They were to be under the same roof and both 28 feet wide, the king's 60 feet in length and the queen's 40. There was also to be a garden and a new chapel 70 feet long and again 28 feet wide.[207] This set in train the 'great work of the reign, the building of an entirely new set of royal apartments' at Windsor.[208]

Concerned though he was with the material environment of his family, its spiritual welfare was even more important. When in 1241 the Franciscans gathered over Pentecost for their general chapter, Henry fed them on successive days for himself, for the queen and for his children. Later in the year he commanded four great candles, weighing 100 pounds each, to burn around the feretory of St Edward until his return to Westminster, for 'the health of the king, the queen and their children'. Henry's decision in 1241 to make a new shrine for the Confessor 'of purest gold with precious gems' was in part surely a thank-offering for Edward's arrival.[209]

The king's new family seems also to have inspired a huge escalation in the scale of his almsgiving for it was now he began the practice of mass feeding paupers in the halls of his castles and palaces.[210] For Christmas Eve 1239, Henry arranged simply for fifteen paupers to be fed and clothed at Windsor for Edward's spiritual and material health. But then, on Holy Innocents Day, 28 December, he ordered the great hall of the castle to be filled with paupers while poor children were to be fed in the smaller hall. Henry had already appointed a chaplain at Windsor to celebrate perpetually the mass of the Virgin for Edward's 'health' and the next great feeding

---

[205] *CLR 1226–40*, 444; Colvin, *History of the King's Works*, i, 501.

[206] *CLR 1226–40*, 452–3; *CLR 1240–5*, 14–15. I owe the interpretation to a communication from Margaret Howell.

[207] *CLR 1226–40*, 439.

[208] *CR 1242–7*, 141; Colvin, *History of the King's Works*, ii, 868–9; Brindle, *Windsor Castle*, 58–73; and see below, 362–3.

[209] Paris, iv, 156–7; Colvin, *History of the King's Works*, i, 147; *CR 1242–7*, 294, 374.

[210] For the whole subject, see Dixon-Smith, 'Image and reality'.

was related to the Virgin. In 1240, on the feast of her Purification (2 February), with its obvious reminders of Eleanor's own purification after Edward's birth the year before, the hall at Windsor was to be filled to capacity and a candle offered for Edward in the chapel.[211] At Westminster the first of the mass feedings was directly linked to Eleanor's second pregnancy. Both the great hall and the lesser hall, Henry instructed, were to be filled with paupers for the queen, 'who is near to giving birth'.[212] It may be around this time that Henry also began the practice of feeding 500 paupers at court every day.[213]

Eleanor was very far from being a passive recipient of these material and spiritual comforts, confined in the luxury of her new chambers and chapels. Aged sixteen in 1240, the increasing sums of money received by her wardrobe for the support of her household are a sign of her growing role. They averaged £28 a month in 1236/7, £41 a month between 1237 and 1240 and £60 a month between 1240 and 1242.[214] Above all, Henry came to think that it was Eleanor more than anyone else whom he could trust with Edward's future. Thus in February 1241, in the event of his death, Henry ordered the castles of Nottingham, Montgomery, Shrewsbury, Bridgnorth and Chester to be surrendered to her for Edward's use. This was a way of ensuring her power in any minority. She was not to be brushed aside as Henry's mother had been.[215] Eleanor's umbilical link to Edward also enhanced the position of the Savoyards. How natural to support the queen with her own kinsmen, Henry's 'uncles' as he described them.

THOMAS AND PETER OF SAVOY

The first of the new Savoyards with whom Henry made a permanent connection was the queen's uncle Thomas of Savoy. Since 1237 he had been count of Flanders in right of his wife.[216] Ambitious, plausible and polished, Thomas had come to England in the summer of 1239 soon after his niece had given birth, which was good timing. Henry ordered London to be decked out for his arrival, and listened with disgust to his complaints about the money he was owed by Simon de Montfort. Later in the year he loaned Thomas 1,000 marks and supported his case against Montfort at the court of Rome.[217] During the visit he also received Thomas's homage in return for an annual pension of 500 marks. By the time of his death

[211] *CLR 1240–5*, 433, 435, 446.
[212] *CR 1237–42*, 217.
[213] Stacey, *Politics, Policy and Finance*, 239–40. For a fuller discussion of Henry's almsgiving, see below, 285–97.
[214] Tout, *Chapters*, i, 253–5; v, 267–8.
[215] *CPR 1232–47*, 244.
[216] Cox, *Eagles of Savoy*, 52, 56, 95–107.
[217] *CLR 1226–40*, 433; *CR 1237–42*, 234–5.

early in 1259, Thomas had received no less than 8,375 marks from the exchequer and perhaps more from other sources.[218]

Henry's desire as he put it 'to labour for the profit and advantage of our beloved uncle and fidelis' was not simply because he was family, important though that was.[219] The relationship would have counted for less had Henry not taken to him personally. There were also good strategic reasons for forging a connection. As Matthew Paris recognized, the pension Henry now revived was one often enjoyed by counts of Flanders. Although the count owed his primary allegiance to the king of France (as Paris also stressed), England and Flanders were linked commercially, with the Flemish cloth industry depending on English wool. Counts of Flanders had been valuable allies in the past and might be again.

There was another reason why Henry could do with new friends in 1239. The great ally he had secured through the marriage of his sister Isabella was now in disgrace. That March, Pope Gregory had excommunicated Emperor Frederick II.[220] At least this did nothing to affect the alliance with the Savoyards. They had changed sides. Indeed, Thomas himself had quarrelled with the emperor. After becoming count of Flanders he had tried to secure the election of his brother, the bishop-elect of Valence, to the vacant bishopric of Liege, this in defiance of Frederick, who had his own candidate. In May 1239, Pope Gregory, in a hit against the emperor, had confirmed William as the new bishop while allowing him to continue also at Valence.[221]

Count Thomas returned to England in spring 1240, secured the payment of his pension, and then visited Edward at Windsor. His close relationship with the queen is seen in the way they interceded jointly for the pardon of a criminal.[222] It was doubtless the two of them together who now secured another extraordinary Savoyard advance, one which profoundly influenced the political environment for the next quarter century.[223] This was the establishment of Peter of Savoy, uncle of the queen and Thomas's younger brother, as lord of the honour of Richmond. The honour, once held by the duke of Brittany, and briefly by the bishop-elect of Valence, brought Peter Richmond castle in Yorkshire, numerous demesne manors and the lordship of many knightly tenants. Its income was estimated (in 1261) at some £1,200 a year.[224] Henceforth, Peter, in terms of resources, ranked with England's greatest barons. Whereas,

---

[218] CR 1264–8, 366. It is hard to disentangle Paris's accounts of Thomas's visits in 1239 and 1240, during both of which he has him doing homage: Paris, iii, 616–17; Paris, iv, 19–20.

[219] CR 1234–7, 234.

[220] This is more fully discussed in the next chapter.

[221] Cox, Eagles of Savoy, 74–5, 97.

[222] Paris, iv, 19–20; CR 1237–42, 185–6, 195.

[223] For Peter, see Andenmatten, Bagliani and Pibiri, Pierre II de Savoie.

[224] CChR 1226–57, 252; CPR 1258–66, 160; CIPM, ii, 210–22.

moreover, the bishop-elect of Valence had held the honour during the king's pleasure, Peter was granted it at once in hereditary right.

The grant, made by a royal charter on 20 April 1240, was doubly remarkable in that Peter was not in England and there is no evidence that Henry had ever met him! The grant commanded no wide consent. The witnesses included the archbishop of York and the bishop of Carlisle, but not a single English earl, and only one man of baronial status, John fitz-Geoffrey.[225] Peter's activity, moreover, had hitherto lain in the Alps, not an area, like Flanders, brimming with English interests. What then had Eleanor and Thomas said to persuade Henry to endow Peter with one of the greatest baronies in the kingdom? It is not difficult to see.

Born perhaps in 1203, and thus a few years older than Henry, originally destined for a clerical career (and thus a man of some education), Peter was lord of family castles in the mountains of Bugey, and was married to a daughter of the baron of Faucigny (east of Geneva). In the 1230s, surviving wounds and capture, he had led the fight to make the house of Savoy rather than that of Geneva dominant in the pays de Vaud. 'If the inhabitants of western Switzerland today speak French instead of German, it is partly because French was the language of its thirteenth-century conqueror, Peter of Savoy, and his family.'[226] Henry was evidently entranced by news of this man, who had also arranged the funeral of the beloved bishop-elect of Valence. The connection would enhance Henry's international standing, and add to the circle of those he could really trust.

There was one significant factor which made it easier for Henry now to advance the Savoyards. This was the absence, through death, minority, crusade and political eclipse of so many great men who might have opposed it.[227] The old earl of Surrey, William de Warenne, a veteran of King John's reign, died in May 1240. He left the king a hawk, and Henry had a cross erected in his memory outside Merton priory.[228] Two months later, John de Lacy, earl of Lincoln, died after a long illness, another veteran of John's reign, and Henry's leading councillor for a time in the late 1230s. Both Warenne and Lacy left underage heirs. Richard de Clare too was still under age. He finally entered his inheritance in 1243.

Meanwhile the crusade claimed both Simon de Montfort and Richard of Cornwall. Montfort had returned to England in April 1240. In the first of several reconciliations over the years, Henry now welcomed him 'with great honour', and the queen (at the king's expense) gave him a present of silver cups.[229] With Henry's help a settlement was arranged with Thomas of Savoy, although one which left Montfort, so he complained, having to

---

[225] *RCWL*, i, 177.

[226] Cox, *Eagles of Savoy*, 9, 15, 16, 40–3, 82–7.

[227] For an analysis of these changes, see Stacey, *Politics, Policy and Finance*, 139–40.

[228] *CR 1237–42*, 225, 233, 517; *CLR 1226–40*, 474.

[229] Paris, iv, 7; *CR 1237–42*, 191.

sell his woods to finance his crusade.[230] Richard of Cornwall's crusade had been long in preparation, and with a 1,000-mark gift from his brother out of the current tallage of the Jews, he finally set sail from Dover in July, Henry and the papal legate Otto being there to see him off.[231]

The Christmas celebrations in 1240 were on a grand scale. Fifty new surplices with 'R' embroidered in red silk on the collars were made. Orders were issued for the gathering of 1,500 lambs, 5 bulls, 7,000 hens, 80 porkers, 500 rabbits, 150 salmon pies, 200 kids, 40 roes, 312 pheasants, 1,230 partridges, 90 peacocks, 900 hares, 60 herons, all possible swans and cranes, and 68 boars of which 12 were to have their heads cut off, the brains taken out and then the heads well cooked and soused. For Eleanor, the king devised a wonderful present: a cup of gold enamelled within, weighing 2 marks or more and worth 20 marks, with a 'foot' on which to stand. It was to be worked on day and night 'so that the queen can drink from it at the foresaid feast . . . and so that both king and queen can then be content'.[232]

This was the Christmas at which the king said goodbye to the legate Otto, placing him in his own seat. A few days later Peter of Savoy arrived. On 5 January 1241, the feast day of Edward the Confessor, he was knighted by the king in Westminster Abbey. Peter, 'our beloved uncle' as Henry called him, measured up to all expectations. Prepared to give far more time to England than Count Thomas, he was placed at once on the king's council and spent much of 1241 at Henry's court. In attesting royal charters he came next after the earls.[233] He displayed his business acumen by obtaining a new charter outlining in more detail his rights over the honour of Richmond.[234] He displayed his concern for Edward's health by advising that all the dung should be removed from Windsor castle (the more quickly if it was rainy) and no horses should be stabled within the walls until August or September.[235] From dung to diplomacy, the range of Savoyard activity was indeed remarkable. In June 1241, Peter left England (returning in November), with power to offer annual fees 'for homage and service' to the count of Chalon, to William de Vienne and any others he thought fit.[236] There was an early warning here that Savoyard interests might not always coincide with Henry's. After all how was Henry helped by alliances with nobles in the valleys of the Rhone and Saone beyond the western frontiers of Savoy? Nothing, however, shook Henry's confidence

---

[230] Paris, iv, 7; *CR 1237–42*, 191; *CLR 1240–5*, 100; *CLR 1226–40*, 472; Bémont, *Simon de Montfort*, 334; Maddicott, *Simon de Montfort*, 29.

[231] *CR 1237–42*, 197.

[232] *CLR 1240–5*, 11–12, 15; *CR 1237–42*, 258.

[233] *RCWL*, i, 179–81, 184; *LMB*, 78.

[234] Peter's attention to this kind of detail is a theme in Huw Ridgeway's forthcoming article 'An English cartulary roll of Peter of Savoy'.

[235] *CR 1237–42*, 308.

[236] *F*, 242 (*CPR 1232–47*, 253); Cox, *Eagles of Savoy*, 112.

in his uncle. Later in 1241, having given him the honour of Pevensey and custody of the Surrey and Sussex lands of John de Warenne (heir to the earldom of Surrey), Henry made Peter castellan of Dover in place of the earl of Hereford. This 'key to England', as Hubert de Burgh called it, was now in foreign hands.[237]

BONIFACE OF SAVOY BECOMES ARCHBISHOP OF CATERBURY

Soon after Peter's arrival in England, Henry achieved another prodigious Savoyard advance. This was to secure the election of Boniface of Savoy, Peter's younger brother and thus another uncle of the queen, as archbishop of Canterbury. The vacancy had been created by the death of Edmund of Abingdon. Edmund's later years had been depressing. Although he maintained reasonable relations with the legate, he became embroiled in a bitter dispute with the Canterbury monks. This was over his misguided revival of the old archiepiscopal scheme to set up a college of secular canons in the Canterbury diocese so that archbishops could reward their clerks by appointing them to the canonries. Henry sided with the monks and, with the full backing of his council, fiercely prohibited work on the new college (at Maidstone). He considered Edmund's defiance as gravely prejudicial to his crown and royal dignity.[238] Eventually, in October 1240, Edmund left England both to lay his grievances before the pope and to attend the recently summoned great council of the church. He died on the way at Soisy in Burgundy on 16 November 1240, his body being taken back for burial to the great monastery at Pontigny where he had been a few days earlier.

It was on Christmas day 1240 that Henry gave the monks of Canterbury licence to elect Edmund's successor, at the same time making it very clear who it should be. Boniface would give security to both king and kingdom and protect the infant Edward from danger in the event of Henry's death.[239] Since Henry had never met Boniface, he must have relied here on character references from the bishop-elect of Valence, Thomas of Savoy and, after his opportune arrival, from Peter of Savoy himself. Doubtless what they said was seconded by the queen.

Boniface was probably around the same age as the king, and since 1232 had been bishop-elect of Belley in the Savoy. Matthew Paris in his initial account of the election spoke of him as a man 'unknown' to the monks and 'insufficient, as it was said', in every respect for such a great position. Yet later he erased this verdict and wrote of Boniface's noble birth and

---

[237] *CPR 1232–47*, 259–60, 265–6.

[238] *CR 1237–42*, 234.

[239] *AWR*, no. 294. This was said in a letter to the pope written on Henry's behalf by Dafydd, son of Llywelyn.

handsome appearance.[240] Boniface was certainly an able and impressive man. As archbishop, at turns honey-tongued and mail-fisted, he freed Canterbury from debt (he was a fine man of business) and vigorously defended his rights as archbishop. Despite absences in Savoy, he presided over councils which promulgated reforms and drew up lists of complaints about the abuses of royal government.[241]

Henry's problem now was how to get Boniface elected. After all no royal candidate had become archbishop since Hubert Walter in 1193. Henry was not helped by the disputes raging over the elections to Winchester, Durham and Hereford. Robert Grossseteste fired off passionate letters warning that Henry's behaviour imperiled his soul.[242] At a great council in January 1240 a whole series of complaints were made about how Henry's courts and officials, in violation of Magna Carta, were encroaching on the jurisdiction and immunities of the church.[243] The king's reputation was also damaged by one unfortunate consequence of the papal imperial quarrel. This was the taxation the pope imposed to support his war against Emperor Frederick. There were two forms, both set in motion in October 1239. First, all foreign clergy beneficed in England were required to pay to the pope a fifth of their annual revenues. Second, there was to be a subsidy from the English church as a whole. Henry was in an impossible situation. With the papal legate Otto in the kingdom, he had no alternative but to support the Roman church in what he called its 'great persecution'. His only protests, by letter and word of mouth, were on behalf of his own clerks whom he wanted to be exempted from the taxes.[244] As a result he was accused of doing far too little to protect the church in general from papal oppression.[245]

Yet none of this seemed to matter when it came to Canterbury. On 1 February 1241 the monks unanimously elected Boniface as their new archbishop. Well primed they wrote to the pope about the fame of his noble birth and virtuous way of life. Doubtless Henry's support in their quarrel with Archbishop Edmund, the hope of his continuing favour, and the desire to escape the tribulations at Winchester were the factors in their choice. In the event the death of Pope Gregory later in 1241 meant it was not until September 1243 that Boniface's election was confirmed by his successor, Innocent IV. It was not until 1244 that Boniface arrived in England. But at least that meant the revenues of Canterbury continued to flow into royal coffers. For Henry the election was a triumph. Boniface was the only royal candidate to become archbishop of Canterbury in the

---

[240] Paris, iv, 103–5. For a study of Boniface, see Williams, 'Aspects of the career of Boniface of Savoy'.

[241] For an example of Boniface's honeyed words, see *DD*, no. 256.

[242] *Letters of Grosseteste*, 208–11, 283–5.

[243] *C&S*, i, 280–5; Creamer, 'St Edmund of Canterbury and Henry III', 137–8.

[244] *CPR 1232–47*, 253; *CR 1237–42*, 174–6, 345, 347–8, 353, 361. For the whole subject, see Lunt, *Financial Relations*, 197–205.

[245] Paris, iv, 35–43, 137, 160–1.

whole course of the thirteenth century. He was, however, to prove much less a king's man than Henry had hoped.

Henry's success over the Canterbury election did not stand alone. In 1239 the treasurer of the exchequer, Hugh of Pattishall, was elected to Coventry. He bade a moving farewell to his exchequer colleagues: 'God has called me to the cure of souls.'[246] Then in January 1241 the Durham dispute was settled by the election of Master Nicholas of Farnham, the confessor of the king and queen. Henry and Eleanor went to Gloucester for his consecration in June.[247] There was also another Savoyard advance to the ranks of the episcopate. In August 1240 the Hereford chapter elected as their new bishop Peter de Aigueblanche, a protégé of the bishop-elect of Valence and keeper of the king's wardrobe.[248] Although the following year he resigned as keeper, he remained prominent in the king's service and acted frequently as a diplomat. For his consecration, Henry gave him a mitre costing £82. Encrusted with jewels it must have been a sight. Pattishall's had only cost £20.[249]

Aigueblanche was only the most high profile of the Savoyard satellites to whom Henry gave his favour. Between 1236 and 1272 he granted land to some thirty-nine Savoyards. At least a dozen of the estates were worth 50 marks per annum; and a dozen more were worth over 100 marks. In addition, 40 men, both laymen and clerics, received money pensions worth 100 marks or more per annum.[250] All told, 170 Savoyards or those with Savoyard connections came to England. While most of these never stayed for any length of time, others achieved permanent places in the service of the king and queen. Important here was Bernard of Savoy, perhaps an illegitimate son of Count Thomas. In December 1241 he became castellan of Windsor, thus giving the Savoyards control of the castle housing the heir to the throne.[251] Another important Savoyard was Imbert Pugeys; his ironic surname meant 'worthless thing'. Imbert, who came with the queen from Savoy (he was occasionally called Imbert of Savoy), became a valet of the king's chamber and ultimately a steward of the royal household. Amongst other rewards he married the widow of the baron Ralph fitzBernard and received escheated land worth £30 a year in the Oxfordshire manor of Bampton. Settling in England, the family later gave its name to Stoke Poges in Buckinghamshire.[252]

Alongside these Savoyards, there were other foreigners increasingly prominent in the king's service. Two had first come to the fore during the

---

[246] Paris, iii, 542–3; Paris, iv, 1–2.

[247] Paris, iv, 86–7, 134–5; DA, 9. The king's itinerary shows that Paris's date is the correct one.

[248] Aigueblanche is just north of Moûtiers in the Tarentaise: Cox, *Eagles of Savoy*, 107.

[249] *CLR 1240–5*, 29; *CLR 1226–40*, 461.

[250] Ridgeway, 'King Henry III and the "aliens"', 81–2, 84.

[251] *CPR 1232–47*, 268; Howell, *Eleanor of Provence*, 32.

[252] For Imbert's career, see Ray, 'Three alien royal stewards', and ch. 7 of his 'Alien courtiers of thirteenth-century England'.

regime of Peter des Roches, namely John de Plessis (of whom more later) and Matthias Bezill. In 1240 the latter became marshal of the queen's household.[253] All told, in February 1240, Henry gave the legate a list of nineteen clerks 'from parts across the seas' in his service. One of these, Master Simon the Norman, or Simon de Ételan, was keeper of the seal.[254] Like the Savoyards, these were able men, prepared indeed to tell the king what they thought. The story eventually reached Matthew Paris that Simon the Norman had been dismissed (in April 1240) for refusing to seal a charter giving Thomas of Savoy the proceeds of an export duty on wool. Presumably he thought, if the story is true, that such a grant (which never materialized) would infringe the rights of the crown.[255]

HENRY'S COUNCILLORS FROM 1239 TO 1241

The way the king's court and council developed between between 1239 and 1241 meant that Henry, in one view, 'cut his lines of communication with his baronage'.[256] This was certainly the perspective of Matthew Paris, who lambasts the king again and again for wasting the substance of England on foreigners and spurning the counsel of his native-born subjects. Paris was not alone. The Tewkesbury annals have Gilbert Marshal in 1240 refusing to submit his quarrel with the king to the judgement of 'aliens and adversaries'.[257]

The king's preferences were clear to a wide variety of his subjects: clear to the cathedral monks and chapters pressurized to elect Savoyards; to the Surrey and Sussex jurors who revealed how Peter of Savoy's agents had wasted the woods of John de Warenne while in his custody; to Roger Bigod whose officials were soon clashing with those of Peter of Savoy; to the Buckinghamshire jurors who reported that the king had married the widow of Ralph fitzBernard to 'Imbert of Savoy who came with the queen into England';[258] and to all who had dealings with the court where the wardrobe was under Peter de Aigueblanche, the seal under Simon the Norman and where, in 1240 and the first half of 1241, native earls were rarely present.[259]

---

[253] For Bezill and Plessis, see Ray, 'Three alien royal stewards', and chs. 5–6 of his 'Alien courtiers of thirteenth-century England'.

[254] *CR 1237–42*, 176; Powicke, *King Henry III*, i, 296 n. 2; ii, 772–3.

[255] Paris, iii, 629 (where misdated to 1239); Paris, iv, 63–4; Paris, v, 91; Powicke, *King Henry III*, ii, 780–3. The official reasons given for his disgrace were his 'debts and trespasses': *CChR 1226–57*, 255, 258.

[256] Stacey, *Politics, Policy and Finance*, 143.

[257] Tewkesbury, 115. It was probably looking back from this period that Paris wrote up Richard of Cornwall's 1238 speech voicing these sentiments: Paris, iii, 475–6.

[258] *CIM*, no. 16; *BF*, ii, 1373, 1379; Morris, *Bigod Earls of Norfolk*, 18–21.

[259] Spencer, 'Dealing with inadequate kingship', 79. Roger Bigod attests no royal charters in 1240. On the other hand, he was commissioned with Richard of Cornwall to renew the truce with France.

Henry would have been upset by the hostility to the Savoyards. Brilliant and internationally famous men, their establishment was, in his view, for the common good. Hence the way Henry thought the kingdom would be made more secure and, in the event of his death, his son Edward be protected from danger if Boniface was elected archbishop.[260] Henry might also think Paris's picture of an alien court was exaggerated. When it came to major decisions it could expand to include many of the great and good of the land. In the event, the Marshal was not judged by 'adversaries and aliens'.[261] Nor were the divisions between the English and the foreigners as sharp as Matthew Paris imagined. When in 1241 a tournament was proposed at Northampton between Peter of Savoy and Roger Bigod, the king, as Paris admitted, encouraged Gilbert Basset and some other English magnates to take Peter's side. Paris was reduced to saying that 'the English ... detested the ignoble pliability of the English'.[262]

Some of Henry's foreigners, moreover, were able to pursue their careers with surprisingly little hostility. No one exemplified this more than John de Plessis, the Teflon man of the reign of Henry III. He was one of a small group of Norman household knights in Henry's service in the 1220s. A colleague was Drogo de Barentin, and perhaps John came from Plessis just to the north of Barentin in upper Normandy.[263] John's first break came during the regime of Peter des Roches when he established himself at court amongst the circle of those attesting royal charters. He survived the bishop's fall and remained a favourite of the king.[264] The extent became clear between 1242 and 1247. Henry first bullied Margaret, in her own right countess of Warwick, into marrying John.[265] Then, when it was clear there would be no children, John was allowed to reach an agreement with the Mauduit heirs to the earldom by which he secured its lands for the rest of his life. From 1247 onwards John was styled earl of Warwick. In the 1250s he was granted in hereditary right his wife's honour of Hook Norton after it had been adjudged an escheat of the lands of the Normans. One might have thought this meteoric rise of an obscure Norman knight would have created intense resentment. Magna Carta had laid down that heiresses were neither to be forced into re-marriage nor disparaged through marriage to social inferiors, and John's marriage was surely an example of both. Yet, far from being expelled from England in

[260] *AWR*, no. 294.

[261] See below, 241.

[262] Paris, iv, 88. In the event the king forbad the tournament: *CPR 1232–47*, 249.

[263] Ray, 'Alien courtiers of thirteenth-century England', 93.

[264] According to an analysis of Andrew Spencer (see his ' "Vineyard without a wall" '), between 1236 and 1257 Plessis attested 297 royal charters, more than any earl and more than any of the king's foreign relatives, although their score does come from a shorter period.

[265] For further discussion of the marriage, see below, 264–6.

1258, John was co-opted by the barons to help choose the revolutionary council and given a place upon it! Clearly he had personal qualities which just somehow made him trusted and acceptable.[266]

Even on a day-to-day basis, Henry's court in the early 1240s was hardly swamped by foreigners. Matthew Paris's view that Henry felt 'there is scarcely today any English man who deserves trust' was simply untrue.[267] In April 1240, Simon the Norman was replaced as keeper of the seal by the abbot of Evesham, Richard le Gras, a former monk of Westminster, who had done much to introduce Henry to the cult of the Confessor. He was commended by Paris for his prudence and fidelity.[268] All four of the stewards of the royal household in 1240–1 were English. Two, John fitz-Geoffrey and William de Cantilupe II, were of baronial status.[269] Bertram de Criel, veteran from the days of Hubert de Burgh, came from the topmost ranks of the knightly class. Paulinus Peyvre, another man whom Paris described as 'prudent and circumspect', was one of several 'literate knights' at Henry's court.[270] The eight councillors named by Barnwell priory as giving a judgement in 1241 were headed by Aigueblanche and Peter of Savoy, but the rest were English, including le Gras, Cantilupe and Criel.[271]

Another name on the Barnwell list was that of John Mansel. His long career at the highest level of the king's service was now beginning. The illegitimate son of a Sussex priest, Mansel first appears in the king's service in 1234, having probably owed his entrée to the bishop of Chichester, Ralph de Neville.[272] He was then a young man. As Henry said later, 'he was trained under my wing. I have tested his ability, his character and merits since boyhood. He has always been serviceable and loyal in my affairs and those of my kingdom.'[273] Mansel's big break came in 1238

---

[266] Ray, 'Alien courtiers of thirteenth-century England', ch. 5, for a full study of John's career; Mason, 'Resources of the earldom of Warwick', 67–75; Carpenter, *Reign of Henry III*, 33–4; Coss, *The Lady in Medieval England*, 121–3; Hanchett, 'Women in thirteenth-century Oxfordshire', 81–97.

[267] See Meekings and Crook, *King's Bench and Common Bench*, 51–4.

[268] Paris, iii, 629; Paris, iv, 191.

[269] William de Cantilupe II was the son of John's steward and Henry's early governor William de Cantilupe I. He became a steward of the household in 1239 and was one of the governors of the kingdom during Henry's absence in 1242–3. His son, another William, married a Briouze heiress and became lord of Abergavenny. Walter de Cantilupe, bishop of Worcester, was a son of William de Cantilupe I. Although only really established in England under John, the family came to be regarded as sprung from 'the noble stock of the barons of England'. Their manor at Eaton Bray in Bedfordshire was held as a barony: Carpenter, *Reign of Henry III*, 293; Julian-Jones, 'Corbets and Cantilupes', 51–9; Sanders, *English Baronies*, 39–40.

[270] *CRR*, xvi, pp. xxv–vi, l–li; Paris, v, 242–3, 294.

[271] *LMB*, 79.

[272] For John's early career, see Liu, 'John Mansel', 22–9.

[273] *F*, 414; Powicke, *King Henry III*, i, 294.

when he went out to Italy as the paymaster of the king's forces sent to help the emperor. He distinguished himself in the fighting and throughout his career was very much a 'clericus militaris'. On his return, Henry persuaded the convent of Durham to appoint him to the rich living of Howden, refusing to take no for an answer. Later Mansel was said to joke of another living, 'This will provide for my dogs.'[274] Mansel, however, put his wealth to good use, founding the Augustinian house at Bilsington in Kent. He was completely loyal to the king, but was also prepared to proffer unpalatable advice, having the happy knack of being able to do so without giving offence. For many people he acted as a friend at court, appearing indeed as an executor of the saintly Richard of Wich, bishop of Chichester.[275] In 1258 he was the other king's man, alongside John de Plessis, appointed to the ruling council. Mansel was very ready to smooth over troubles and come to the rescue of fellow ministers at odds with the king, something that was easier to do given his closeness to the queen. Perhaps there was here one disadvantage. An insider, with a network of personal connections, Mansel was never likely to encourage Henry in any thoroughgoing reform of the royal administration. Still, over many years, this wise, courageous and humane man did his best to steer Henry round corners and help him out of difficulties. He gave far better value than the Savoyards.

An early sign of Mansel's wisdom came in August 1241 in a dispute where Matthew Paris praises both his conduct and the king's. As soon as Mansel saw that his appointment to a prebend at Thame in Oxfordshire had provoked the ire of the bishop, Robert Grosseteste, he resigned the position: 'let not such discord and scandal arise because of me'. Grosseteste, appeased, preached a sermon at the king's request in which he commended the king's humility and compared his justice to the rays of the sun. Henry, acting as a peacemaker, then went on to settle the dispute between the bishop and the abbot of Westminster.[276]

Another person on the Barnwell list of Henry's councillors was none other than Stephen of Seagrave. His disgrace in 1234 had not ended the career of this 'vir flexibilis'. As will be seen, he played a significant part in securing Chester for the crown. He then became the senior judge in the court *coram rege*, following William of Raleigh's departure to be bishop of Norwich. He remained there, both senior judge and leading councillor, until his death in October 1241. During this time he was involved in significant changes to the financial reforms of 1236.

[274] Durham, 159–61, 226; Paris, iv, 154.

[275] *Saint Richard of Chichester*, 68–9.

[276] *CPR 1232–47*, 257; Paris, iv, 152–4. For Mansel accepting the loss of a manor so it could be granted to Simon de Montfort, see *CPR 1247–58*, 209, 210, 267. For him accepting that a manor he had acquired should be held directly from Roger Bigod, earl of Norfolk, see TNA CP 40/59, m. 81d (a reference I owe to Paul Brand). Mansel knew his place!

THE FINANCIAL CHANGES OF 1240–1

One change was thoroughly retrograde and due entirely to Henry's indulgent attitude towards the Savoyards. Since 1236, keepers of the wardrobe had accounted regularly at the exchequer for their income and expenditure. By contrast, Peter de Aigueblanche, in office from February 1240 to October 1241, never accounted at all. Indeed Henry formally exempted him from any need to do so.[277] His successor, the Poitevin clerk Peter Chaceporc, did not account until 1245.

In 1240 there were major changes to the running of the sheriffdoms. The sheriffs ceased to be custodians with allowances and instead answered for fixed increments above the traditional county farms. Here Seagrave had a direct hand since it was he who determined the size of the new increments.[278] Around the same time, this by a formal decision of the council, the royal demesne was taken from Walter de Burgh and Robert of Crepping and instead entrusted to men from the individual manors who answered not for all the issues but for farms topped up with increments.[279]

These changes, and the reappointment of some curial sheriffs in 1239, have been seen as a retreat from the reforms of 1236. Some of the curial sheriffs (most notably Emery de Sacy in Hampshire) did prove very difficult for the exchequer to control.[280] Yet in other respects the changes of 1240 were a logical conclusion to the reforms of 1236. Having obtained proper information about shire revenues from the custodian sheriffs, it was possible to fix the increments at a realistic level and thus return to a system which was far simpler to run. On the demesne side, the new policy of leasing manors to their men was introduced with care. Henry ordered a detailed inquiry into the value of the manors, and, as so often, showed himself sympathetic to the grievances of their men. The inquiry was to hear their complaints and reserve judgement for Henry himself.[281] The changes certainly made a difference financially since in 1241/2 the increments demanded from the sheriffs were £400 to £500 more than the profits, less allowances, of the previous custodial system. They were also some £750 more than the sums due above the county farms in 1230.[282] The system introduced in 1240 remained in place down to 1258. King and exchequer clearly thought it a success, although it became increasingly unpopular in the counties. This was because the increments were steadily

---

[277] *CPR 1232–47*, 240.

[278] *RBE*, ii, 771–2: a copy of TNA E 371/8A, m. 4, sched. 2; TNA E 368/13, m. 3.

[279] *CFR 1234–42*, nos. 244–5; Stacey, *Politics, Policy and Finance*, 89–90.

[280] Stacey, *Policy, Politics and Finance*, 132–6. I am unclear about the reasons for the curial appointments in 1239, some in the middle of the financial year. They suggest a degree of political anxiety.

[281] *CR 1237–42*, 220; Stacey, *Politics, Policy and Finance*, 80–1.

[282] Carpenter, *Reign of Henry III*, 171–2.

increased in size, making the sheriffs all the more grasping.[283] There was also no return to the general appointment of county knights, which had made the reforms of 1236 popular. The curial sheriffs disappeared from the counties since the rising increments, depriving them of power and profit, made the office unattractive. But while some of the new sheriffs were county knights (and sometimes oppressive for all that) others were strangers in their counties and men of scant substance. The reformers of 1258 made radical changes and sought in effect to put the clock back to 1236.[284]

The most striking of the new policies around this time was that relating to the Jews. This period saw the start of the heavy taxation which broke the financial back of the Jewish community and thus prepared the way for their eventual expulsion from England in 1290.[285] In July 1240 a special inquiry was launched into the wealth of the Jews, combined, 'an extraordinary innovation', with a census of all Jews, male and female, over the age of twelve.[286] Then, in February 1241 the representatives of the Jewish communities were brought before the king at Worcester where they were forced to agree a 20,000-mark tallage, payable within the year.[287] From the king's point of view the tallage was a great success. Most of it was paid in cash, not just in assigned debts, and nearly all of it had come in by April 1242.

Another aim in 1240 was to build up a reserve of treasure 'as if hidden' in the Tower of London.[288] The background here was partly the sense that the tax of 1237 had been frittered away.[289] During the course of 1240/1 what remained of it in the Tower was joined by the money from the Jewish tallage, from a tallage levied on the king's demesnes, and by the revenues from wardships, ecclesiastical vacancies, the exchange and Ireland.

Henry himself was directly involved in all these financial policies. If he could be irresponsible spending money, he was acutely aware of the need to accumulate it. In November 1240 he ordered the feeding of paupers at Westminster and the burning of candles around the shrine of the Confessor for the soul of himself, his queen and children. He then went on, in the same writ, to demand precise information from the exchequer about its receipts and expenditure and 'by how many sacks' the money in its possession had increased. Henry's attitude to his 'hidden' treasure shows him at his most hands-on and his most wavering. In January 1241 nothing was to

[283] See below, 659.

[284] Carpenter, *Reign of Henry III*, 174–9.

[285] Stacey, *Politics, Policy and Finance*, 143–59, for what follows; and see his '1240–1260: a watershed in Anglo-Jewish relations?', and for a summary of the new financial pressures, Huscroft, *Expulsion*, 86–91.

[286] *CR 1237–42*, 238–9; Stacey, *Politics, Policy and Finance*, 147.

[287] *CR 1237–42*, 346–7.

[288] *CR 1237–42*, 252.

[289] For the expenditure of the tax, see Stacey, *Politics, Policy and Finance*, 125–8.

be touched without the sanction of 'the great men of our council'. A week later, the king took more personal control: nothing was to be removed save by a 'special mandate from the mouth of the king'. And yet the king, as so often, mistrusted himself. Later in the year he ordered that nothing be taken from the treasure 'for any order that the king may make'![290]

Thanks to the new policies with regard to the county and manorial farms, thanks to the Jewish tallage, the tallage on the royal demesne, a lucrative judicial eyre and the number of wardships and ecclesiastical vacancies in the king's hands, Henry's revenues in the early 1240s were buoyant, even without any taxation on movables. Although the figures are subject to all kinds of qualifications, there are indications that between 1240 and 1242 Henry was spending considerably less than his income, hence his ability to accumulate a treasure in the Tower.[291] The expendable income for 1241/2, at some £51,000, may well have been the highest in the reign, outside that is the years of general taxation. The average annual income between 1240 and 1245 at some £36,500 was some £10,000 more than in the last years of Hubert de Burgh.[292]

Henry took steps to see his money was spent sensibly. In November 1240, by a provision of king and council, all the king's prises, so all the goods compulsorily purchased from merchants, were to be paid for at quarterly intervals at four specified fairs.[293] Henry undertook a great deal of work on royal castles following an investigation into their defects and the cost of putting them right.[294] He pushed on with the new walls of the Tower of London, 'much desiring their completion'. In 1241 he finished the great round towers which still dominate the west front at Windsor.[295] Perhaps there was something in Matthew Paris's story that Henry was, in rebuilding castles, trying to imitate his brother 'whom fame declares to be more prudent than me'.[296] Still, in the financial policies of these years Henry had surely been prudent enough.

ABSENCE FROM IRELAND

If Henry's domestic policies had a fair measure of success, that was equally true of his policies in Britain and Ireland. The end of the Marshal

---

[290] *CR 1237–42*, 252, 268, 376.

[291] *RIR*, xxxi–ii; Stacey, *Politics, Policy and Finance*, 227, table 6.6. In this table expenditure authorized by writs of 'computate' should not be set against the exchequer's cash receipts as this was money spent locally, not money coming from the exchequer.

[292] Stacey, *Politics, Policy and Finance*, 208, table 6.2. The revenue in 1241/2 was boosted by a scutage taken for the Poitevin campaign.

[293] *CPR 1232–47*, 238–9. This scheme did not last long, however.

[294] *CR 1237–42*, 345–6.

[295] *CR 1237–42*, 275; *CLR 1240–5*, 33; *CIM*, no. 77; Colvin, *History of the King's Works*, ii, 866 and n. 9; Brindle, *Windsor Castle*, 49–55.

[296] Paris, iii, 532.

war in 1234 had left Ireland in a state of chaos.[297] Gilbert Marshal, restored to the lordship of Leinster, was threatening the justiciar, Maurice ftzGerald, with revenge for Richard Marshal's death. Many of the Marshal followers were embittered by heavy fines imposed for their part in the rebellion. On the other side, Maurice and his allies, Hugh and Walter de Lacy, Walter de Ridlesford and Richard de Burgh, had been denied their promised share of the Marshal lands and indeed had now to return what they had seized.[298]

In September 1234, Henry convened a great council at Marlborough and attempted to sedate these conflicts. Those present included Archbishop Edmund, Gilbert Marshal and Maurice fitzGerald, although Maurice insisted on guarantees for his personal safety before attending. The council produced some kind of settlement, although its terms are largely unknown.[299] Henry forgave 1,000 marks of the fines imposed on Marshal followers, and probably at this time remitted a vexatious oath extracted from Gilbert.[300] On the other hand he reaffirmed the policy of imposing fines and congratulated the Marshal enemies on their success.[301] While the fines made with the king seem to have precluded, at least in theory, the Irish magnates demanding ransoms of their own, the king did allow them to retain the lands of rebels held from their fees.[302] Amongst the Anglo-Irish nobility the great gainer was Richard de Burgh. In October 1234, in return for a fine of £2,000, he was restored to Connacht. The following year, Richard began its conquest in earnest and secured easier terms on which to pay his fine.[303]

The tensions in Ireland soon spilled over into one of the most sensational murders of the thirteenth century.[304] In the early hours of 14 May 1235 those sleeping in tents outside the gates of Westminster palace heard the noise of men on the causeway by the river, the neighing of horses in the cemetery by the Abbey, and then the sound of blows from swords. A king's messenger had a closer view. Five or six armed men barged into the hall in which he was sleeping, told him to keep quiet and he would not be hurt and then ran up the stairs. At the top, they broke down the door of the solar and there, under the light of a huge flaming torch, found their

[297] For this period, see Crouch, 'Gilbert Marshal and his mortal enemies', and Smith, 'Irish politics'.

[298] See for example, CPR 1232–47, 70.

[299] Osney, 81; Crouch, 'Gilbert Marshal and his mortal enemies', 401; CPR 1232–47, 72; TR, no. 97 (CDI, nos. 2168, 2284); Reg. Gregoire IX, no. 3198 (CPReg, 154, 165–6).

[300] See above, 160.

[301] CR 1231–4, 524; CR 1234–7, 54; CPR 1232–47, 71, 87–8 (CDI, nos. 2174, 2177, 2201, 2224, 2236); Reg. Gregoire IX, no. 2599 (CPReg, 147).

[302] CDI, nos. 2253–4; CPR 1232–47, 69.

[303] CChR, 42; F, 213 (CPR 1232–47, 73); CR 1231–4, 534–5; CR 1234–7, 134. For de Burgh's fine, see Hartland, 'Administering Irish fines', 81.

[304] For what follows, see CRR, xv, no. 1438; Powicke, King Henry III, ii, 740–59.

quarry, Henry Clement, a clerk of Maurice fitzGerald. Clement knew what was coming. He rushed to the window, but drew back when he saw the men outside. His enemies extinguished the torch and killed him. They then fled with drawn swords to their horses in the cemetery and escaped.

The king was shocked by the scandalous crime outside the very gates of the palace, but who was to blame? One rumour pointed to the men of Gilbert Marshal but Gilbert quickly cleared his name and his good relations with the king continued for a while longer. Another rumour, more believed, was that William de Marsh and his men were the murderers. Clement had been threatened with death by William when they were at court together at Windsor; he had then suffered an attempted assault on Rochester bridge when he was following the king to Sandwich to see Henry's sister Isabella off to Germany; and finally 'a small messenger of William with minute buttons' had inquired daily as to where Clement was staying. No wonder Clement, on the day before his death, had said he feared for his life and wished he was back in Ireland.

The motives for the murder were fairly clear. William de Marsh and his father Geoffrey had rebelled with Richard Marshal and had forfeited their Irish lands and castles in consequence. Some of these were still in the hands of Maurice fitzGerald, and fitzGerald, through his clerk Clement, was now obstructing the Marshes' efforts at court to obtain their recovery.[305] After the murder, Geoffrey de Marsh was able to prove his innocence but William fled to Lundy island in the Bristol Channel, where his nephew, a respectable Somersetshire knight, was the lord. From there, William preyed on passing shipping, and plotted (or so it was rumoured) the attempted assassination of the king at Woodstock in 1238. The suspicion that Gilbert Marshal, controlling much of the Bristol Channel coastline, connived in Marsh's activities was perhaps a factor in his deteriorating relations with the king.[306] Eventually, in 1242, after Gilbert's death, Marsh was captured and met a pious end on the gallows with all the ghastly ceremonies of drawing, evisceration and quartering.[307]

Over the next few years, not surprisingly, rumours persisted that civil strife was about to break out in Ireland.[308] Henry, on more than one occasion, said he would go there. In October 1237 he got as far as asking the justiciar whether he should come with or without provisions and with a large or small body of men.[309] But Henry never went and, not for the last time, he did well out of doing nothing. When urged to intervene on the death of Richard Marshal, he had been promised rich pickings. There were none to be had after Gilbert's restoration. As it was, Maurice

---

[305] *CPR 1232–47*, 69; but see Orpen, *Ireland under the Normans*, iii, 62n.
[306] Crouch, 'Gilbert Marshal and his mortal enemies', 402.
[307] Paris, iv, 193–7.
[308] *TR*, no. 97 (*CDI*, no. 2284); *CPReg*, 154, 165–6.
[309] *CR 1234–7*, 312, 511, 571–3.

fitzGerald, who remained as justiciar until 1245, managed to keep the peace. Here Ireland benefited from Gilbert Marshal's wise restraint. Whatever his feelings and the pressures from his men, he did not pursue Maurice fitzGerald with mortal enmity. In 1240 they were formally reconciled with Maurice agreeing to found a monastery for Richard Marshal's soul.[310] Peace meant a flow of money from Ireland into the English treasury, rising from £1,000 a year in the 1240s to double that in the 1250s.[311] An Irish contingent led by Richard de Burgh joined Henry's continental campaign in 1242. Henry also found sources of patronage falling into his lap without the need for exertion.[312] The deaths of Walter de Lacy, Walter de Ridlesford and Gerard de Prendergast, leaving only female heirs, the reversion of Ulster to the crown on the death of Hugh de Lacy in 1242, and the partition of Leinster following the death of the last Marshal earl in 1245 presented Henry with wonderful opportunities to reward his servants and kinsmen. In 1244 Peter of Savoy's kinsman Peter of Geneva married one of the granddaughters of Walter de Lacy, with her share of the lordship of Meath. Three years later, Peter's younger brother Ebulo married a Ridlesford heiress.[313] In return, the brothers ultimately resigned to Peter of Savoy all their claims to the county of Geneva. As has been remarked, 'how neatly was Henry III's patronage made to play Peter's game'.[314]

The 1230s were critical years in the history of Ireland. Had events fallen out differently, had Henry been a more aggressive king, he might have come to Ireland, kept Leinster and Connacht, or parts of Connacht, for the crown, and curtailed the freedom of the Lacies in Meath and Ulster, all along the lines of that letter of advice he received just after Richard Marshal's death in 1234.[315] The political structure of Ireland would have been transformed and royal power there hugely increased. But nothing like that happened. Another chance came in the next decade when Hugh de Lacy's death brought the king control of Ulster. But again, in circumstances we will see, royal possession was not sustained.[316] Ireland was becoming a 'peripheral lordship', of interest to the king mainly as a source of revenue and patronage. Equally, although they maintained close ties with the court, and solicited Henry's help in their quarrels, the great Anglo-Irish barons had no desire for any direct intervention by the king.[317]

---

[310] Dunstable, 151.

[311] Stacey, *Politics, Policy and Finance*, 208; Lydon, 'Edward II and the revenues of Ireland', 55.

[312] See Frame, 'King Henry III and Ireland', 193–202.

[313] *CPR 1232–47*, 261; *CPR 1247–58*, 15.

[314] Howell, *Eleanor of Provence*, 50–1 (the quotation is hers); Cox, *Eagles of Savoy*, 295; Von Wurstemberger, *Peter des Zweite*, nos. 507–8.

[315] See above, 159.

[316] This is discussed in volume 2.

[317] For these themes, see Smith, 'Irish politics', 14, 19–20; Frame, 'King Henry III and Ireland'.

PEACE WITH SCOTLAND, 1238

The eclipse of Hubert de Burgh, married to King Alexander's sister Margaret, had necessarily weakened the family ties between the English and Scottish courts. Indeed, Henry and his council specifically contrasted their policies with those under Hubert, 'friend and family' of the king of Scots.[318] For a moment in 1235 it seemed that Hubert's place linking the courts might be taken by Gilbert Marshal. That July, Henry happily agreed to his marriage with Margaret, youngest sister of King Alexander, the Margaret whom Henry himself had hoped to marry back in 1231. Gilbert received her with 10,000 marks and a 'noble dowry' in Scotland.[319] But, having obtained Henry's consent to the marriage (and much else besides), he left court never to return on any regular basis. Another weakening of the ties came with the death in June 1237 of Alexander's nephew John the Scot, earl of Chester and Huntingdon. The earldom of Huntingdon long held by or from the king of Scotland had been an important link between the kingdoms, but now the lordship was split between John's heirs and the earldom came to an end.[320]

Henry's own changing attitude is seen in his reassertion of the king of England's claim to overlordship over Scotland. Hubert de Burgh (in 1221) had obstructed Alexander's plans to be crowned by a papal legate, but had not raised the claims to overlordship in any proactive way.[321] Now this changed. Early in 1235 the pope advised Alexander to respect the liege homage he owed King Henry, evidently meaning the liege homage owed for the kingdom. He was acting at Henry's behest, having been informed of the treaties of 1174 and 1209.[322]

Alexander, for his part, had his own ambitions and grievances. He was raising once again the Scottish claims to Northumberland, Cumberland and Westmorland, claims he had tried to make good during the 1215–17 civil war. Despite his youngest sister Margaret's marriage to the Marshal, he also complained of Henry's failure to marry her himself under the agreement of 1231. And he pointed out that the king of England himself had broken the treaty of 1209, thinking here of the way his eldest sister, also Margaret, had never married Henry. A meeting between the courts at Newcastle in September 1236 achieved nothing, and Henry began to fear a Scottish invasion of the north. He garrisoned and strengthened his

---

[318] *CRR*, xvi, no. 18. This was in relation to Alexander's claims to overlordship over the earldom of Huntingdon. For what follows in this section, see Oram, *Alexander II*, 139–48.

[319] *CPR 1232–47*, 126; Dunstable, 143. For the marriage, see Nelson, 'The daughters of William the Lion', 127-8; Oram, *Alexander II*, 117.

[320] *CRR*, xvi, no. 18; *CR 1234–7*, 454–5.

[321] *CPReg*, 83. Scottish kings were inaugurated in a ceremony at Scone but not crowned or annointed.

[322] *ASR*, no. 6. The pope was confused over the details of the treaties, however.

northern castles, and worried that Alexander was recruiting Flemish knights, who were passing through England disguised as merchants.[323]

One of the legate Otto's duties, enjoined on him by the pope, was thus to make peace between England and Scotland.[324] The kings met in Otto's presence, at York, in September 1237, with Henry making generous gifts to the Franciscan and Dominican friars established in the city. A settlement was soon reached. Alexander remitted his complaints about the treaties, and abandoned his claims to the northern counties. In return, Henry promised Alexander land worth £200 a year in Northumberland and Cumberland. The treaty, in finally ending Scottish claims to the north, was an achievement for Henry. Even the grant of land had advantages since it meant Alexander owed allegiance for something more substantial than a small estate in Tynedale and the overlordship of a divided honour of Huntingdon. Henry had at last brought security to the northern counties, areas coveted, invaded and sometimes controlled by kings of Scotland since the eleventh century.

Alexander himself, in coming to terms with Henry, was being realistic. He had failed to secure the north during the 1215–17 civil war and, while circumstances might change, he probably calculated he would never have a better chance. After the failure he had reorientated his kingship, seeking to expand north and west rather than south into England. Since 1234 he had been busy asserting royal authority in Galloway. It made sense to settle with King Henry for what he could get. The lordship he was promised was only the equivalent of a small barony, but it fitted well with his existing manor in Tynedale and its extensive liberties made it virtually a state within a state.

Alexander also gained something else, something which, although not in the treaty, was really Henry's most significant concession. In 1235 the pope had backed Henry's claims to overlordship over Scotland. Now, a settlement produced under papal auspices said nothing at all about them, and treated Alexander as a sovereign ruler. Indeed, under the terms of the treaty Henry now returned all the documents relating to the noxious treaty of 1209. In effect, Henry passed over his claims to overlordship in order to end the king of Scotland's threat to the northern counties. It was a statesmanlike exchange. Henry had truly shown himself to be a peacemaker. The importance of the treaty was reflected in the size of its audience. Archbishop Edmund was absent, but it was witnessed by the archbishop of York, the bishop-elect of Valence, three English bishops and one Scottish bishop, six English earls (including Richard of Cornwall), Simon de Montfort, seven Scottish earls, two clerks of the legate and over twenty other English magnates and ministers.

Of the queens and countesses who were also present, we hear nothing. The influence at the Scottish court of Henry's sister Queen Joan must

---

[323] *CR 1234–7*, 313, 443, 529.

[324] *CPReg*, 160–2. Otto was empowered to act as legate in Scotland as in Ireland.

have been reduced by her failure to produce an heir. But doubtless she still played a part in smoothing relations between her husband and her brother. At the time of the meeting back in September 1236, Henry had strengthened her hand with a life grant of the valuable Yorkshire manor of Driffield.[325] Alexander's marriage, of course, made him 'family', Henry's 'beloved brother', as he was called in letters, and this too was a factor in the desire for peace. The fraternal relationship was celebrated in mutual gifts. Henry gave Alexander a gold garland studied with precious stones, and received from Joan a pair of basins.[326]

After the York meeting, Joan remained in England and celebrated the Christmas of 1237 with her brother at Winchester, Henry supplying the robes both for her and her eight clerks and servants. After the festivities, the two queens, Joan, twenty-seven, and Eleanor, fourteen, set off on a pilgrimage to Canterbury, perhaps both to pray for fertility. Then Joan prepared to return home, only to fall ill. She died in the arms of her brothers on 4 March 1238. Henry was grief-stricken. He immediately commissioned a marble tomb to cover Joan's body, and attended her burial at the nunnery of Tarrant in Dorset.[327]

After the 1237 settlement Henry wrote joyfully of a firm peace, and scaled down the costs of his northern castles. 'There is no need to fear as before,' he declared. In August 1238 he told Alexander through an envoy that despite Joan's death he wished them to be unified more strongly than ever.[328] It was not quite like that. The assignment of the £200 of land, despite the early involvement of the legate, was not effected until 1242. Meanwhile, Alexander's second marriage in 1239 to Marie, daughter of the great French noble Enguerrand de Coucy, inevitably weakened connections with England. The relationship was subject to further tensions in the 1240s. Yet the peace of 1237 lasted for nearly sixty years. The Treaty of York was one of Henry's greatest achievements.

WALES UNDER LLYWELYN AND THE MARCHER BARONS

In the aftermath of the Marshal war, Henry had virtually abandoned Wales to Llywelyn and the marcher barons. The castle of Montgomery remained as a lone royal outpost in the middle march. Seven years later, at the end of 1241, the situation looked very different. Henry had broken the power of Dafydd, Llywelyn's son and successor, and secured for

---

[325] *CChR 1226–57*, 222–3; *CR 1234–7*, 314.

[326] Wild, *WA*, 27–8.

[327] Howell, 'Royal women in England and France', 169; *CLR 1226–40*, 316–17; Wild, *WA*, 33, 41. That Joan died in the arms of Henry and Richard comes from Melrose, 510; Broun and Harrison, *Chronicle of Melrose*, 145 and n. 42. Tewkesbury, 106, says Joan died on 4 March at Havering, whereas chancery attestations place Henry at Westminster on both the third and fourth. This does not quite rule out a visit to Havering, however.

[328] *CR 1237–42*, 143, 498.

himself the eastern segment of Gwynedd in the process. He had also acquired the county of Chester for the crown, and recovered the Three Castles from Hubert de Burgh, and Cardigan and Carmarthen from the Marshal earls of Pembroke. He had transformed the situation in Wales very much to his advantage.

In the months after his rehabilitation in 1234, Hubert de Burgh spent a great deal of time at court with the aim of recovering more of his former possessions. His greatest success was in the Welsh marches. 'On the intercession of the earls, barons and magnates of England', Henry restored him to the Three Castles, the castles, that is, of Grosmont, Skenfrith and Whitecastle in Upper Gwent. Hubert also recovered the castle he had built at Hadleigh in Essex on a splendid site above the Thames estuary.[329]

Even more prominent at court in 1234–5, as has been seen, was Gilbert Marshal. Seizing the moment when there was no one much around, in December 1234 he extracted from the king possession of Cardigan and Carmarthen. The two lordships had been held both by his father and his eldest brother but only as bailiffs of the crown. Now, Gilbert was granted them in hereditary right. He followed this up by securing custody of Glamorgan during the Clare minority, thus gaining formal control of what he held already thanks to Richard Marshal's conquest in 1233. Here Gilbert did offer 500 marks for the favour.[330] Since the minority still had around ten years to run, this seems an amazing bargain. 'He possessed all the sea coast as far as St David's', commented the Tewkesbury annalist.[331] Nor was this all. Gilbert, with Henry's consent, also purchased from Richard of Cornwall the wardship of the Briouze lands in Wales, so he was now master of Brecon, Radnor, Huntington, Abergavenny and Gower.[332]

Gilbert topped all this off with his marriage to Margaret, the youngest sister of King Alexander of Scotland. In effect, he was rearranging the bases of Marshal power. On the death of Richard Marshal in 1234 the family estates in Normandy had been confiscated by Louis IX. The chances of ever recovering them, Gilbert must have known, were slim. Since 1066 great barons holding lands in England and Normandy had dominated much of the political scene. Richard Marshal was the last of the line. Gilbert now was setting up the Marshals as barons of the British Isles. Leinster in Ireland would march with expanded territories in Wales and altogether new connections with Scotland.

Not for the first time, one wonders what Henry was doing. If he was pressed by the 'magnates of England' to restore Hubert de Burgh, not a single earl, apart from Hubert himself, witnessed the charter granting

---

[329] Margam Continuation, 140; *CPR 1232–47*, 100, 101.

[330] *CChR 1226–57*, 189; *RCWL*, i, 139; *CPR 1232–47*, 96; *CFR 1234–5*, no. 152.

[331] Tewkesbury, 96.

[332] *CChR 1226–57*, 192. This was the wardship of both branches of the Briouze family. Gilbert was also given the marriages of the heiresses.

Gilbert both Cardigan and Carmarthen.[333] Perhaps Henry thought that he was giving Gilbert the power and incentive to resist any further advances by Llywelyn. Indeed, since Cardigan was still held by the Welsh prince, Gilbert was essentially being invited to conquer it. But that was still no reason for permanently alienating these royal bases in the south of Wales. Another motive apparently lay in Henry's feeling that Gilbert needed compensation for the loss of his Norman estates. Thus if they were ever recovered, Gilbert was to return Cardigan and Carmarthen to the king. Henry also granted Gilbert the honour of Pevensey in Sussex (valued at £300 a year) on the same terms.[334] King John had occasionally given compensation for Norman losses, but there was no obligation to do so. Henry, subjected to Gilbert's assiduous pressure, had gone far beyond what was necessary or appropriate. He was soon to regret what he had done.

If Henry saw the Marshal as a bastion against Llywelyn, that reflected, of course, his reluctance to take on Llywelyn himself. The reluctance was good for Wales because it led to a series of truces and six years of peace between 1234 and Llywelyn's death in 1240. The truces left the edifices of Llywelyn's power very much intact. He ruled an undivided Gwynedd from the Dee to the Dyfi, thus excluding a kinsman from Meirionnydd. He also wielded great territorial power outside Gwynedd, indeed through the length and breadth of Wales. Thus he still controlled Mold, southern Powys, Kinnerley (just over the border into Shropshire), Maelienydd, Builth, St Clears and Cardigan (for the Marshal did nothing to dislodge him), this at the expense of both Welsh ruler and marcher baron alike. To be sure, he failed in his last years to achieve the permanent peace with England that he craved. By the same token he failed to consecrate his power by constructing a formal principality of Wales with all the native rulers doing homage to him, and only he doing homage to the kings of England.[335] On this point Henry was firm. When in 1238 it seemed that Llywelyn's son Dafydd was about to take the homage of a group of Welsh 'magnates', Henry forcefully reminded Llywelyn that such homages belonged to the king.[336]

In the event, on this occasion, Llywelyn backed down. When 'all the princes of Wales' met at Strata Florida in October 1238, they swore fealty to Dafydd not homage.[337] Llywelyn was always more concerned with the realities rather than with the rhetoric of power. He never took the provocative title prince of Wales, contenting himself with the style prince of

---

[333] *RCWL*, i, 139.

[334] *CChR 1226–57*, 192. See also Power, 'The French interests of the Marshal earls', 222–3.

[335] See Smith, *Llywelyn ap Gruffudd*, 26–7, for analysis of Llywelyn's difficulties in his last years.

[336] *CR 1237–42*, 123–5; *AWR*, no. 240.

[337] *Cronica de Wallia*, 38; *Brut*, 234–5; *Brut/Peniarth*, 104; Smith, *Llywelyn ap Gruffudd*, 30–1.

North Wales and later Prince of Aberffraw and lord of Snowdon. But the truces, in a series of ways, recognized the reality of his authority over the other Welsh rulers.[338]

THE ACQUISTION OF CHESHIRE FOR THE CROWN

The first step in transforming this situation came with the acquisition of the county of Chester for the crown, another of Henry's greatest achievements.[339] The opportunity came with the death of John the Scot, earl of Chester and Huntingdon, on 6 June 1237. John left four co-heiresses. The first and second, in order of seniority, were the two daughters of his eldest sister, one married to William de Fors, son and heir of the earl of Aumale, the other to John de Balliol; the third co-heiress was John's second sister, married to Robert de Brus, the lord of Annandale; and the fourth was his youngest sister, married to Henry de Hastings. The king's ability to acquire the county turned on the legal opinion that Cheshire should be divided between the four co-heiresses and their husbands. It should not, in other words, pass intact to William de Fors as married to the most senior of the heiresses. If, then, partition was the rule, the king could hope to buy out the shares of the four co-heiresses and acquire the county for himself. It was true that when Ranulf, earl of Chester, had died in 1232, the county had passed intact to John the Scot, the son of Ranulf's eldest sister. But, so the king's lawyers argued, this was just because it was his fair share of the earl's extensive inheritance. Now, with a smaller pot to ladle out, the county would have to be divided, leaving William de Fors, married to the senior co-heiress, with a claim simply to the empty title of earl and perhaps to Chester itself.

It was not until 1239 that the court *coram rege* gave judgement for the king on these legal points and dismissed the counter-claims of William de Fors. Confident of success, Henry had already been putting his plan into action. So, after John the Scot's death, Cheshire remained under royal control and only his other lands were parcelled out between the heirs. By December 1237, Henry had struck a deal with John de Balliol, giving him various royal manors in return for his share of the county. Other deals followed and the whole process was completed by October 1241. Cheshire now belonged to the king.

Henry's determination to keep Cheshire was as impressive as his determination to acquire it. Here this sometimes irresponsible king was thoroughly responsible. His resolve was strengthened by the influence of the queen and the birth of their son Edward, for it was with Eleanor and

---

[338] *F*, 229–30; *CR 1234–7*, 350, 364–5, 369–70, 374, 381; and see *CR 1231–4*, 594–5. For Llywelyn's titles, see Pryce, 'Negotiating Anglo-Welsh relations', 18–21.

[339] For what follows, see Stewart-Brown, 'The end of the Norman earldom of Chester', 36–54; Eales, 'Henry III and the end of the Norman earldom of Chester', 108–13.

Edward that Cheshire became associated. In the 1240s, Henry assigned
the county to Eleanor as her dower, an indication, as he said, that it was
always to remain a possession of 'the crown'. In the 1250s, Cheshire was
part of the appanage granted to Edward on his marriage.[340]

In acquiring Cheshire, Henry had acted within the law. The critical
judgement in his favour was pronounced before both archbishops, five
bishops, the earls of Derby and Hereford, and an assortment of magnates
and ministers.[341] This was no rigged court. The compensation seems to
have been fair and there were advantages to the heirs in having manors in
England. Who put the whole scheme into Henry's mind? The answer, one
suspects, is his legal advisers, for it was they who held the key: William of
Raleigh, head of the court *coram rege*, and Stephen of Seagrave, whom the
king immediately appointed as justiciar of Chester.[342] This was the start
of his way back into the king's service.

The revenues of Cheshire were now the king's. In the first full year of
accounts (1237/8) no less that £704 was paid into the treasury.[343] The
compensations, however, must eventually have wiped out the financial
gains. The chief value in having Cheshire was rather political and strategic. Alone of the English earls, the earl of Chester had effectively
controlled the government of his county. It was almost a state within a
state. Ranulf of Chester had been a dignified if sometimes disgruntled
loyalist, but in other hands Cheshire might well support a rebellion against
the crown. That danger was now ended. Even more profound were the
consequences for the king's relations with Llywelyn and his successors as
rulers of Gwynedd. Gwynedd's eastern borders now adjoined a county
under not the earl of Chester but the king of England. Llywelyn had maintained good relations with Earl Ranulf. Indeed John the Scot, heir to the
earldom, had married one of Llywelyn's daughters. The result was that
any invasion of Gwynedd by the king was effectively impossible. It had not
been attempted in the campaigns of 1223, 1228 and 1231. Now everything
had changed. The king of England was ideally placed to threaten, discipline and demote the ruler of North Wales.

If one suspects Stephen of Seagrave's hand in the acquisition of
Cheshire, one detects it even more in the recovery from Hubert de Burgh
of the Three Castles in Upper Gwent, Grosmont, Whitecastle and
Skenfrith. In 1239, on William of Raleigh's retirement, Seagrave had taken
over as chief of the court *coram rege*.[344] Settling scores against his old
enemy, it was surely he who stirred up Henry III once more against Hubert

---

[340] *CPR 1232–47*, 501; Stewart-Brown, 'The end of the Norman earldom of Chester', 52.
In general, see Studd, 'Lord Edward's lordship of Chester'.

[341] *BNB*, iii, no. 1273, and see *CRR*, xvi, no. 136C.

[342] *CPR 1232–47*, 185, 188.

[343] *CheshirePR*, 36.

[344] *CRR*, xvi, p.xxi.

de Burgh. Thus it was that in the summer of 1239 Henry brought a whole series of charges against his former minister. Most of these related to Hubert's time as justiciar but one was of more recent origin, namely that Hubert had failed to hand over the marriage of Richard de Clare as he had promised the king at Gloucester in 1234. Instead (as Henry had discovered to his rage in 1236), Richard had been married to Hubert's daughter Meggotta. Hubert was old but his brain was sharp. He answered most of the charges with ease, making the king at times look both ignorant and credulous: one accusation was that to succour Poitou in 1224, Hubert had sent out stones rather than money! As for the marriage, Hubert pointed out that it had been carried through by his wife without his knowledge while he was awaiting trial in 1232. Anyway, Meggotta's death meant the king had suffered no loss. (Indeed, Richard was now married to the daughter of the earl of Lincoln).[345]

Hubert, however, declined trial and bought the king's pardon for all past offences by surrendering the Three Castles and Hadleigh.[346] Probably to force such a surrender had been the object of the attack in the first place, the king (as Matthew Paris said) appreciating that Hubert was too old and decrepit to resist.[347] The Three Castles, like Cheshire, Henry retained, later including them in Edward's appanage. He had planted royal power very firmly in a strategic part of Upper Gwent. Henry never seems to have clarified the terms on which he returned Hadleigh and the Three Castles to Hubert in 1234–5, so at least he was not guilty here of overturning royal charters. But this last attack on his old servant is a disreputable and unpleasant episode.

LLYWELYN'S DEATH AND DAFYDD'S SUCCESSION

Llywelyn died on 11 April 1240. A warrior and a diplomat,[348] a visionary and a realist, this extraordinary man had been the dominant force in Wales since the collapse of King John's power in 1215–16. He was rightly described by both Welsh and English chroniclers as Llywelyn the Great. In the next few years, Henry, building on his acquisition of Cheshire, was to replace Llywelyn's dominance with his own. Yet Henry had no burning desire to undermine the power of Dafydd, Llywelyn's son and successor. The recovery of his continental possessions had a far higher priority.

[345] Paris, vi, 63–74; *CR 1234–7*, 509; Nelson, 'The daughters of William the Lion', 129–31. The formal record of the charges and Hubert's replies, through Master Laurence of St Albans (Paris, vi, 63–74), can be compared with Matthew Paris's fanciful elaboration: Paris, iii, 618–20.

[346] Later the custody of Hadleigh was given to Ebulo of Geneva: *CPR 1247–58*, 454.

[347] *CChR 1226–57*, 248; Paris, iii, 618–20.

[348] For a beautifully written assessment, see Davies, *Conquest, Co-Existence and Change*, 250–1.

Henry had long accepted that Dafydd should indeed be Llywelyn's successor, just as Llywelyn had wished. The king was equally clear that the inheritance did not include the homages of the native Welsh rulers. They belonged to him. These principles guided the settlement with Dafydd made at Gloucester in May 1240. It laid down that 'all the homages of the barons of Wales' were the king's, and many indeed now did him homage. Henry, however, made no effort to break up Gwynedd. Dafydd himself did homage 'for his right of North Wales', which meant the whole of Gwynedd from the Dee to the Dyfi.[349] Henry, therefore, had not sought to return to the treaty of 1211, when King John had gained for himself the Four Cantrefs between the Dee and the Conwy. Equally he made no effort to exploit the fissures within the house of Gwynedd by taking up the cause of Llywelyn's illegitimate elder son, Gruffudd, who, supported by one interpretation of Welsh inheritance law, was vociferously and violently demanding his 'share' of the inheritance of his father.[350] Henry was also sympathetic, at least in part, to the question of Dafydd's status. True, in letters, he addressed him simply as 'Dafydd, son of Llywelyn once prince of North Wales' instead of 'Prince of North Wales', the title Dafydd used himself.[351] Yet in the ceremony at Gloucester, according to the Tewkesbury annalist, Dafydd 'wore the small diadem, which is called a garland, the insignia of the principality of North Wales'. Likewise on his seal (to which Henry never objected) he appeared enthroned and holding a sceptre, quite different from the seal of any English earl or baron.[352]

The problem with the settlement lay not in the ambitions of the king but in the grievances of the Marcher barons and the Welsh rulers. Under the Treaty of Worcester in 1218, Llywelyn had agreed to return all the lands he had seized during the civil war. He had never done so. That left Roger of Mold still excluded from Mold and Ralph de Mortimer from Maelienydd. Equally, Llywelyn had never returned southern Powys to Grufudd ap Gwenwynwyn although his tenure, under the Treaty of Worcester, was to be only during Gruffudd's minority.

Henry did nothing immediately to deprive Dafydd of Llywelyn's gains. Instead he hoped everything might be sorted out by legal processes and arbitrations presided over by the legate Otto.[353] For Henry, the Gloucester settlement was to bring a 'peace' in which both the English and the Welsh forgave the 'homicides, burnings and other evils' they had each committed

---

[349] *AWR*, no. 291.

[350] Paris, iv, 8, 47–8; Williams, 'The succession to Gwynedd', 401–8. Under Welsh custom (against which Llywelyn protested) legitimate and illegitimate children could enjoy the same rights of inheritance.

[351] For example, *AWR*, nos. 289, 292, 296, 298.

[352] Tewkesbury, 115; *AWR*, no. 304.

[353] *CR 1237–42*, 243, 359–60; *AWR*, no. 291; *CFR 1240–1*, no. 380.

and 'were fully reconciled one to another'. In all this, Henry was very conscious that Dafydd was family, the son of his half-sister Joan (the illegitimate daughter of King John who had died in 1237). In his letters he often addressed him as his 'beloved nephew'.[354]

The problem was that the process of arbitration seemed endless. The arbitrators had to be changed on Otto's departure at the end of 1240 and anyway Dafydd had no interest in expediting procedures from which he could only suffer. His capture of his half-brother, Gruffudd, in September 1240 made him the more confident and the more obstructive.[355] When a judgement was passed returning Maelienydd to Ralph de Mortimer he impeded its implementation.[356] He also introduced grievances of his own, notably over the inheritance of his wife as one of the heirs of William de Briouze. As the process dragged on, with Dafydd failing to turn up at meetings or adequately to empower representatives, Henry was in turns exasperated and emollient. As late as February 1241, he refused to believe that Dafydd was acting 'maliciously'. Finally a day was given for judgement on 16 June at Montfort Bridge just outside Shrewsbury, only for Dafydd neither to come nor send anyone in his place.[357]

Still Henry did not react. He left the Welsh marches and retreated to the comforts of Clarendon. Perhaps because of the situation arising from the sudden death of Gilbert Marshal (of which more later), it was not until 14 July that Dafydd was sent a letter both plaintive and threatening: he had, amongst other things, 'contemptuously' ignored the Shrewsbury meeting, tempted Welsh rulers from the king's homage and service, and helped drive Ralph de Mortimer from Maelienydd. Henry was angry but hesitant. His experience of Welsh campaigns was hardly happy. Dafydd, therefore, was simply told to put matters right. Only if he failed to do so would Henry take punitive action, 'which we do not wish'.[358]

Henry was, however, now beginning to raise an army. Early in July 1241 the barons and knights of Cheshire were put on standby for military service, a first indication of the crucial difference made by Henry's acquisition of the county.[359] For the first time in his reign he would be able to campaign in the north and take direct action against Gwynedd. Henry did not neglect the spiritual side, and hoped in particular for aid from the Virgin Mary. On 4 August he ordered the sheriff of Norfolk to feed all the paupers he could find and place 3,000 candles in the chapel of St Mary at Walsingham on the feast of the Virgin's assumption (15 August). Another 3,000 candles were to burn on the feast of her nativity (8 September), half

[354] *AWR*, no. 291; *CR 1237–42*, 280.
[355] Paris, iv, 47–8.
[356] *CR 1237–42*, 202, 359.
[357] *CR 1237–42*, 350, 359–60.
[358] *CR 1237–42*, 359–60.
[359] *CPR 1232–47*, 254.

in the church of St Mary le Strand and half in the chapel at the Marshal manor of Caversham, now in Henry's hands.[360]

Henry was equally active on the diplomatic side. Having previously ignored the pleas of Gruffudd's wife, Senana, at Shrewsbury on 12 August he reached an agreement with her.[361] In return for her promise of 600 marks, Henry undertook to free Gruffudd from Dafydd's prison and give judgement of the king's court 'according to Welsh law' as to the portion due to him from the inheritance of his father. This then was a major change of policy. Hitherto Henry had always accepted Dafydd's succession to an undivided Gwynedd. Now he envisaged Gwynedd's partition. It would thus be far more subject to his control. The strength of Henry's position and the depth of hostility to Dafydd is revealed in the list of those who backed Senana's fine. It combined Ralph de Mortimer, Walter of Clifford and Roger of Mold with the Welsh rulers (or would-be rulers) of northern and southern Powys, Gruffudd ap Madog and Gruffudd ap Gwenwynwyn. The bringing together of this grouping has been described as 'a diplomatic feat for which it would be difficult to find as fiendish a parallel in the whole history of Anglo-Welsh relations'.[362] The feat was certainly impressive, but to say it was 'fiendish' overstates perhaps the nationalistic divisions at this time between Welsh ruler and Marcher baron. Mortimer and Clifford after all had married daughters of Llywelyn and thus were brothers-in-law of both Gruffudd and Dafydd.

From Shrewsbury, Henry progressed to Chester, and then moved eastwards into Gwynedd until he reached Rhuddlan. There he remained in camp, living in his great tent, until the end of August. Henry had issued no general summons for the campaign but his army was large enough, especially given the summer heat which had dried up the marshes and rivers and thus made an invasion of Gwynedd easy. For once Wales was not 'wet'!

Faced with being overrun, Dafydd came to terms. Negotiations were begun even before Henry left Chester, and on 29 and 30 August Dafydd issued letters recording his submission, a submission ratified the next day in Henry's tent at Rhuddlan. Henry then set off for home, reaching Westminster on 20 September. Next month Dafydd himself came to the capital and renewed his homage to Henry on terms considerably more exigent than those agreed back in August. Henry's triumph seemed complete.[363]

The first beneficiaries of Dafydd's defeat were those so long disinherited by him and his father. Ralph de Mortimer recovered Maelienydd, Gruffudd ap Gwenwynwyn, southern Powys, and the Welsh rulers, ousted

---

[360] *CLR 1240–5*, 65–7. For Caversham as a Marian cult centre see Vincent, 'Henry III and the Blessed Virgin Mary', 135.

[361] *AWR*, no. 284. For what follows, see Carpenter, 'Dafydd ap Llywelyn's submission'.

[362] Smith, *Llywelyn ap Gruffudd*, 34.

[363] *AWR*, nos. 300–5, sets out the various letters on which the following discussion is based. See also Paris, iv, 150–1; *Cronica de Wallia*, 39.

by Llywelyn, Meirionydd. After a few years in the hands of the king, Roger of Mold recovered Mold.

Henry also looked after the interests of the crown. The treaty underlined that the homages 'of all the Welsh nobles' belonged to the king. Although not mentioned in the agreement, Henry took possession of Builth, the marriage portion of Dafydd's wife as a daughter of William de Briouze. It thereafter remained an important royal base.[364] In addition, having left the possibility open in August, when Dafydd got to London, Henry made him surrender in perpetuity Gwynedd's easternmost cantref, that of Englefield or (in Welsh) Tegeingl. This was now ruled by the justiciar of Chester, and soon held down by a mighty new castle with polygonal towers placed on the great rock of Dyserth high above the valley of the Clwyd.[365] Under the October agreement, Henry also took permanent possession of the castle of Deganwy. Dafydd had destroyed the castle before his withdrawal, but in 1244 Henry started to rebuild it.[366] The three cantrefs remaining to Dafydd east of the Conwy thus came to be pinioned by Henry's castles at Deganwy and Dyserth.

For Dafydd, there was one compensation, although it came at a price. The provision in the treaty relating to the partition of Gwynedd was never implemented. Instead Gruffudd simply swapped Dafydd's prison at Criccieth for Henry's at the Tower of London. Henry had changed his mind in part because, for all his misdemeanours, Dafydd remained kin, a point Matthew Paris stressed in explaining the settlement. When Dafydd begged not to be disinherited, Henry conceded this 'benigne'. With Gruffudd, there was no such family connection.[367] There was also a more material reason for Henry's choice. Dafydd, in a last desperate bid to stave off the partition, had made an offer Henry could not refuse. At Westminster he announced that, if he died without heirs by his wife, then Henry and his heirs would succeed to all the land of 'the principality of North Wales'.[368] In other words, the whole of Gwynedd would fall to the king of England. There was a good prospect of this happening for Dafydd had no children and had been married to Isabella de Briouze since 1230. By contrast, no equivalent resignation could be made by Gruffudd since his marriage to Senana had produced a brood of sons. By avoiding partition, therefore, Henry could hope the whole of Gwynedd might fall easily into his hands. For his part, Dafydd doubtless calculated that anything was better than an immediate division with his brother. What the future might hold, who could tell.

[364] *CLR 1240–5*, 74, 112–13, 275.

[365] *CPR 1232–47*, 258; *CR 1237–42*, 327; *Cronica de Wallia*, 39; Colvin, *History of the King's Works*, ii, 644–5.

[366] *AC*, 85 n. 3; Colvin, *History of the King's Works*, ii, 624–5.

[367] Paris, iv, 150–1.

[368] *AWR*, no. 305.

Henry's campaign of 1241 was a magnificent victory, and was regarded as such on all sides. 'The king subjugated the Welsh to himself,' a Welsh chronicle grimly noted. Matthew Paris wrote of how 'the king, having subjected Wales to himself, without the shedding of blood and the uncertain chances of battle, had triumphed over his enemies, thanks be to God'.[369]

THE HUMBLING OF THE MARSHALS

In 1240–1, Henry had not merely Dafydd to worry about. An equal anxiety concerned the activities in South Wales of Gilbert Marshal. There for a while Gilbert, not the king, threatened to be the great gainer from Llywelyn's death. In the event, Henry managed to cut the Marshals down to size just as much as Dafydd, in the process recovering Cardigan and Carmarthen for the crown.

As soon as he heard of Llywelyn's death, Gilbert had sent his brother Walter Marshal with an army to seize hold of Cardigan. After this coup, Gilbert proceeded to encroach on other lands held by Llywelyn and his satellites. In the summer of 1240, Henry, reacting to these unlicensed advances, brought a series of charges against Gilbert. There is no record of their content but the most serious probably was Gilbert's demand that Maredudd ap Rhys (of Cantref Bychan) do homage to him rather than the king. Having denied Llywelyn and Dafydd the homages of the Welsh rulers, Henry was not about to give them away to Gilbert Marshal.

In the event, in June 1240, just before he departed on his crusade, Henry's brother Richard of Cornwall was able to broker a settlement. Henry took Maredudd ap Rhys's homage and pardoned Gilbert all his offences. In return, Gilbert surrendered to the king the castle and honour of Pevensey, granted him in hereditary right back in 1234, a foolish concession Henry had long regretted. The original grant had allowed for the restoration of Pevensey to the king, if the Marshals were ever restored to their Norman lands. Now Henry permitted Gilbert to hold his Norman lands if they could be recovered, but this was merely for form's sake. Both sides knew it was unlikely ever to happen. The charges against Gilbert must have been serious and sustainable to have forced him into this capitulation, but he was also making a calculation. He extracted from Henry a promise that he could keep all his other lands and castles in England and Wales. Gilbert, as he said the following year, thus felt he had secured his conquest of Cardigan.[370]

Henry, rarely angry for long, resumed something of his old relationship with Gilbert. He allowed him to keep the timber felled in the Pevensey lands, gave him a present of deer and (in November) welcomed him and

[369] *AC*, 83; Paris, iv, 151.

[370] *CR 1237–42*, 198; *CRR*, xvii, no. 1493; *CChR 1226–57*, 191, 252–3; Dunstable, 151; Paris, iv, 3–4, 56.

his brother Walter to court.[371] He also, at the time of the June 1240 settlement, arranged the reconciliation already mentioned between Gilbert and the justiciar of Ireland, Maurice fitzGerald. Here Matthew Paris was full of praise for the king's activities.[372] Good relations, however, were not to last. Gilbert seems to have thought he now had a free hand in South Wales. He was quickly reconciled to Maredudd ap Rhys and installed him in Emlyn and Ystlwyf, having expelled the Welsh ruler Cynan ap Hywel. Next, over Christmas 1240, while the king was saying goodbye to the papal legate Otto and hello to Peter of Savoy, Gilbert seized Maelgwn ap Maelgwn (a cousin of Maredudd ap Rhys) and forced him to do homage for the lands he held between the Aeron and the Dyfi, this on the grounds that they belonged to the honour of Cardigan. So the issue of homage arose all over again. Early in January 1241, fearing the pattern might be catching, Henry sent a sharp order to the Welsh rulers threatened by the Marshal, including Maelgwn ap Maelgwn, and the bishop of St David's. They were not to do homage for their baronies to anyone but the king. He then summoned Gilbert to court to answer for his conduct. When Gilbert failed to turn up, saying he was going to Ireland, Henry sent him an irate letter ordering him to appear 'as you love those things which you hold from us'. This had the desired effect. At the end of February 1241, Gilbert dutifully appeared at Woodstock to answer the complaints of the king and Maelgwn ap Maelgwn.[373]

After lengthy pleadings, the verdict of the court went in favour of the king.[374] He recovered the homage of Maelgwn and Gilbert was placed in mercy. This was a striking demonstration of royal authority, yet also of authority exercised within the law. The official record carefully named those giving judgement and they formed no kangaroo court. If they included Peter of Savoy and the bishop of Hereford, also present were the archbishop of York, the bishop of Carlisle, the earls of Hereford and Devon, and several marcher barons including John of Monmouth, Fulk fitzWarin and Walter of Clifford. Nor did the verdict go all the king's way. His exaggerated claim for 10,000 marks worth of damages was dismissed with the English words 'nameles fremeles' (nameless, frameless), meaning apparently that the king had quite failed to give details justifying such an amount. The amercement imposed on Gilbert by the court was only £100, about as small as it could be. During the case Gilbert was far from cold-shouldered even by the king for he appears as a witness to royal charters.[375]

[371] *CR 1237–42*, 209, 213; *RCWL*, i, 179.

[372] Paris, iv, 56–7; Dunstable, 151. According to Paris, Henry reminded Gilbert of the parable of the unmerciful servant: Matthew 18:23–35.

[373] *CPR 1232–47*, 242–3; *CR 1237–42*, 348–9; *CRR*, xvi, no. 1493.

[374] *CRR*, xvi, no. 1493.

[375] *CFR 1240–1*, nos. 227, 437 (but see TNA E 368/13, m. 8d); *RWCL*, i, 180. The amercement was pardoned for Walter Marshal in 1243.

After these setbacks, qualified though they were, Gilbert turned his attention to tournaments. He had always been addicted to them, partly because, as Matthew Paris observed, small in stature and intended for the church, he wished to prove his prowess. In April he had hoped to join Roger Bigod at Northampton, tourneying against Peter of Savoy, only for the event to be forbidden by the king. In June another tournament was planned at Hertford, and this time it took place, with fatal consequences. Gilbert, his reins breaking, was thrown from his great Italian horse and dragged for a long distance with his foot caught in the stirrup, an incident graphically drawn by Matthew Paris. Gilbert was taken up alive and born to Ware, but died during the night. His body was buried at the Temple Church in London beside his father and eldest brother.[376]

Henry heard the dramatic news at Marlborough on 29 June 1241, after his return from the Welsh marches. At once he ordered the Marshal castles in South Wales – Chepstow, Usk, Caerleon, Carmarthen, Cardigan, Kilgerran and Pembroke – to be taken into his hands.[377] This was a perfectly proper procedure pending Gilbert's heir coming to do Henry homage. Since Gilbert's marriage to Margaret of Scotland had proved childless, that heir was his younger brother Walter Marshal. For reasons that are unclear, however, Walter prevented the king's agents from taking possession of the Marshal castles, or at least gave the impression that he was doing so.[378] For a moment in July, Henry thought he might have to secure the castles by force, indeed would have to do so before moving against Dafydd in the north. Thus from Marlborough he travelled to Gloucester, and from there sent his wines on to Monmouth. Under this pressure, Walter submitted, but Henry did not take his homage.[379] That could wait until after the campaign against Dafydd. Henry had Walter on the back foot and intended to drive a hard bargain.

In the end it was not until October 1241 at Westminster that Henry took Walter's homage, this after both Nicholas of Farnham, bishop of Durham, and the queen (a significant sign of her influence) had interceded for him. The price, however, was high for, in return, Walter surrendered Cardigan and Carmarthen to the king, this despite their concession in hereditary right to Gilbert Marshal back in 1234. The only quid pro quo was permission for Walter to do homage to the king of France for the Marshal lands in Normandy, but that was no more likely to happen under Walter than it had been under Gilbert.[380] Henry, therefore, had at last recovered what he

---

[376] Paris, iv, 135–6; Waverley, 328.

[377] *CFR 1240–1*, nos. 506–7, 510–11; *CPR 1232–47*, 254. Although still underage Richard de Clare had recovered Glamorgan from Gilbert Marshal in 1240 in return for a fine of 500 marks: Tewkesbury, 117.

[378] *CR 1237–42*, 365.

[379] *CLR 1237–42*, 63, 65; *CR 1237–42*, 321.

[380] Paris, iv, 157–8; *CR 1237–42*, 365; *CPR 1232–47*, 265–6; *F*, 239 (*CPR 1232–47*, 261).

had misguidedly given away. He did not make the same mistake again. Cardigan and Carmarthen, like Chester, remained with the crown and formed part of the appanage granted later to his son Edward. They were to be the bastions of royal power in South Wales.

It was also in October 1241 at Westminster that Henry completed the acquisition of Cheshire. In return for a grant of royal manors and other concessions, William de Fors and his wife, Christina, surrendered their claims to a share of the county. Since, as the quitclaim stated, these were the claims of the senior heiress, they effectively involved the surrender of Chester itself. Just to make sure, the following year Henry secured the specific resignation of both the castle and the now empty comital title.[381]

Given that around this time Henry gave Peter of Savoy the honour of Pevensey, recovered earlier in the year from Gilbert Marshal, and also made Peter castellan of Dover in place of Humphrey de Bohun, earl of Hereford, surely now he was facing a wave of baronial discontent. But that was not the case. Indeed, not the least of his achievements, Henry's deals and dealings with Walter Marshal and William de Fors took place openly during a well-attended parliament and commanded some kind of general consent. Fors's charter of resignation was attested by the bishops of Ely and Lincoln (as well as Hereford), and also by the earls of Hereford, Norfolk and Oxford. The settlement at the same time with another Chester heiress, Isabella de Brus, was witnessed in addition by the earls of Winchester and Arundel.[382]

A major factor in bringing all this about was Henry's triumph in Wales. It both increased his prestige and united him with the magnates who had joined the campaign. Roger Bigod, long absent, now reappeared at court, and received significant marks of favour. So did Humphrey de Bohun, earl of Hereford. Bohun, enjoying reasonable terms for the repayment of his debts, surrendered Dover without a fuss. He was at court at the time and later attended the 1241 Christmas festivities.[383] Henry equally avoided any breach with Walter Marshal. Having done homage, Walter remained at court and received generous gifts of deer and timber.[384] Personality perhaps was a factor here. Matthew Paris stresses Walter's 'humility and friendliness'. There may also have been a feeling that, in Cardigan and Carmarthen, Henry was only recovering what should never have been alienated from the crown. Paris, often critical of Henry's perceived injustices, was not critical

[381] Stewart-Brown, 'The end of the Norman earldom of Chester', 45, 54; *CChR 1226–57*, 262–3. Fors had succeeded his father on the payment of £100 relief (of which 100 marks were soon pardoned) in September 1241. In October his debts were attermed at £40 a year: *CFR 1240–1*, nos. 655, 748.

[382] Stewart-Brown, 'The end of the Norman earldom of Chester', 54; *RCWL*, i, 182; Morris, *Bigod Earls of Norfolk*, 20; Maddicott, *Origins of the English Parliament*, 459.

[383] *RCWL*, i, 182, 184–5; *CLR 1240–5*, 59; *CR 1237–42*, 326, 329; *CFR 1238–9*, no. 67; *CFR 1240–1*, no. 142, *CFR 1241–2*, nos. 129, 249; Morris, *Bigod Earls of Norfolk*, 20.

[384] *RCWL*, i, 184–5; *CR 1237–42*, 373, 378; *CPR 1232–47*, 265–6.

here. He has Henry restoring Walter to his inheritance 'retaining only two castles in Wales, Carmarthen and Cardigan which the king had once committed to William Marshal and then Hubert de Burgh'. There was no suggestion that the Marshals held in hereditary right and had been disseised unjustly. The retention of the castles, Paris added, was also necessary because of the need to strengthen the king's position in the newly acquired parts of Wales.[385]

Between 1234 and 1237, Henry had heeded the lesson in consensual kingship taught by the fall of Peter des Roches. With the support of great councils, he had married his sister to the Emperor Frederick and found a wife for himself in Eleanor of Provence. He had legislated for the good of the realm and issued a resounding confirmation of Magna Carta. He had reformed his finances and secured a tax from parliament. True, Henry had also at times acted impulsively without any kind of general consent. The patronage given to Gilbert Marshal, the invitation to the legate Otto and the bishop-elect of Valence's sudden appointment as head of the council were cases in point. Such actions were equally apparent in the years after 1237, notably in the Montfort marriage and the establishment of Peter and Boniface of Savoy in England before Henry had ever met them. The king had not outgrown his 'foolish simplicity'. The consensus of the period from 1234 to 1237, with its attendant legislation and taxation, was to prove a false dawn.

Henry, however, would have looked at things differently. In his view the kingdom was strengthened by the arrival of the Savoyards. Between 1238 and 1241 he could point to many other achievements. He had fathered a son and heir, secured Chester for the crown, made peace with the king of Scotland, defeated Dafydd in Wales and recovered Cardigan and Carmarthen from the Marshals. By the end of 1241 the Welsh campaign had put relations with his magnates on a more even keel. The relative quietude of the years owed much to Henry's lack of martial spirit and love of a comfortable life, not qualities universally celebrated in a king. A more aggressive monarch might well have intervened in Ireland (the peace there was another of Henry's achievements), refused concessions to King Alexander, made war much earlier in Wales and sought proactively to renew hostilities with the king of France. Now, however, at the end of 1241, in a quite unexpected way, the chance to renew those hostilities had come and Henry was determined to seize it.

[385] Paris, iv, 158.

Chapter 5

DEFEAT: POITOU AND GASCONY
1242–1243

On 14 December 1241, King Henry III summoned his magnates to London at the end of January 'to discuss arduous affairs specially touching our state and that of our kingdom'.[1] His aim was to explain a project to which he was already passionately committed, namely an expedition to Poitou to recover the province lost to the king of France back in 1224. Far more than in 1230, this project was to be Henry's own. There was no longer Hubert de Burgh beside him to guide policy and counsel caution. Nor was there any other mentor of the stature of Peter des Roches, William, bishop-elect of Valence, or the legate Otto. Success or failure would be Henry's alone.

Henry's opportunity had come from an extraordinary *bouleversement* in Poitou. In 1230 the rock on which his campaign had foundered had been the alliance between the king of France and the greatest magnate in Poitou, Hugh, lord of Lusignan and count of La Marche, the second husband of Henry's long-lost mother, Isabella, who ruled in her own right in Angoulême. Since 1230, Henry had tried to maintain contacts with Hugh and Isabella. He had even paid in advance the money owed them under the truce of 1240. He seems to have got little in return. His mother sent him a ring; Hugh a jester. Henry's offer (in 1237) to marry Richard de Clare to one of their daughters went unanswered.[2] Now suddenly everything was different. Hugh and Isabella themselves were up in arms against the French and wanted Henry's help. They were prepared to return to his allegiance to get it.

The course of events creating Henry's opportunity had begun in June 1241. In that month, at a great court held at Saumur, King Louis IX had knighted his younger brother Alphonse and invested him with the county of Poitou.[3] The French court had then moved south to Poitiers where, in July, Alphonse had taken the homages of the Poitevin nobles. None of this was very palatable to Hugh de Lusignan. His overlord would no longer be a remote king, but a very present count. Already at Saumur, embroidered on the clothes of Alphonse's numerous servants, Hugh saw all around him

---

[1] *CR 1237–42*, 428.
[2] *CPR 1232–47*, 199–200; *CR 1237–42*, 145–6, 190; *CLR 1226–40*, 277, 496; Wild, *WA*, 40.
[3] Paris, iv, 137–8; Joinville, cap. 93.

the coat of arms of his new master.[4] There was also material loss for Louis IX now demanded the return of St-Jean-d'Angély which Hugh had held under the agreement of 1224.[5] Hugh, however, regarded by contemporaries as an easygoing character, would have done nothing without his wife. It was at her 'instigation', as his sons later recorded, that he made war on the king of France.[6] Isabella remained every inch a queen (she still appeared as such on her seal) and expected all the consideration due to her status. What 'killed' her now, she lamented, was less the material loss than her 'grief, shame and anger' about the way she had been treated. Accompanying Hugh on his trips from Lusignan to Poitiers, she had been kept waiting for an audience, and then made to stand in the royal chamber, like some 'fatuous servant', while Louis IX, his queen and his two sisters lolled before her on the royal bed. When Hugh went on to entertain the French at Lusignan it was all too much. She ransacked the castle and took its contents back to Angoulême. When Hugh followed her, she refused to see him for three days and declared he would henceforth be a stranger to her bed until he took action. At last Hugh stirred. He held meetings with 'all the barons and castellans' of Poitou first at Parthenay and then, with Isabella, at Angoulême. Feelings ran high. The French, so it was said, had always hated the Poitevins and now, through tyrannous officials, intended to treat them even more vilely than they did the Normans and Albigensians. Oaths were sworn to rise up and resist such a fate, and envoys were sent from Hugh and Isabella seeking Henry's intervention. They arrived in England around the start of December.[7]

THE DIPLOMATIC SITUATION

Now that the great moment had come, what could Henry hope from his alliance with the emperor? He had done much to keep it warm. In 1238, as Frederick plunged into his conflict with the north Italian towns, Henry had spent 8,000 to 9,000 marks sending out a military force to help him. So, with the money for his sister Isabella's marriage, nearly 40,000 marks had been invested in the imperial alliance.[8] But, in truth, the likelihood of any return on the investment had never been great. Frederick, with his hands full in Germany and Italy, had little interest in quarrelling with the king of France. Henry also faced a new constraint in forging any imperial alliance. In 1239 the brief period of papal imperial rapprochement had

[4] Joinville, cap. 93.

[5] *Layettes*, ii, nos. 2065, 2928.

[6] Bibliothèque Nationale de France Clairambault 1188, fos. 18d–19; Joinville, cap. 99.

[7] This account comes from a remarkable contemporary letter (much cited hereafter) written by a citizen of La Rochelle to Louis IX's mother, Queen Blanche: 'Lettre à la Reine Blanche', 525–6; Vincent, 'Isabella of Angoulême', 211.

[8] Stacey, *Politics, Policy and Finance*, 126.

ended with Frederick's excommunication by Pope Gregory IX. There was no way Henry could ignore the excommunication. The legate Otto pronounced it with great publicity in the chapter house of St Albans. An awestruck Matthew Paris copied out the long propaganda letters the conflict produced. Henry himself must have been shocked by some of Frederick's conduct, notably his capture of cardinals (including Otto) on their way to the papal council in 1241. He had no alternative but to agree with the taxes demanded by the pope. So, hardly had Henry finished paying out money to support the emperor's wars than he found himself paying out money to support the wars against the emperor![9] Frederick's understandable annoyance dissipated some of the goodwill generated by Richard of Cornwall's crusade, which had taken place very much under imperial auspices. The situation had changed again with the death of Pope Gregory in August 1241, for there seemed a good chance Frederick would be reconciled to his successor. But, in the event, Innocent IV was not elected until June 1243 and he then continued the policies of his predecessor with even more vigour and venom. While Henry still felt able to seek an alliance with the emperor, he was under great constraints in doing so.[10]

Little could also be expected from the other continental alliances Henry had forged since 1234. There was obviously no chance of help from his father-in-law, the count of Provence, with his eldest daughter married to the king of France. There was equally no prospect of opening up a second front in Flanders as King John had done in 1214. The count, Thomas of Savoy, might be the uncle of Henry's queen, a frequent visitor to England and recipient of a 500-mark annual pension, but he only held the county in right of his wife and no less than a hundred Flemish towns and nobles had pledged in writing to rise up if he deserted his liege lord, the king of France.[11] Conflicted as they were, Henry could expect little help from the Savoyards in general, despite Peter of Savoy now being head of his council. This was not their war. Indeed, one suspects Peter was one of those cautioning against the enterprise. He certainly did not go on the expedition. There was one more difficulty. So little had Henry anticipated his sudden opportunity that in July 1240, probably under pressure from the pope (fearing the diversion of English resources from the struggle with the emperor), he had renewed the truce with the king of France for a full five years.[12]

---

[9] I owe this *aperçu* to Nicholas Vincent's unpublished paper 'Henry III, Frederick II and the council of Lyons'.

[10] Paris, iv, 161; *CLR 1240–5*, 80–1. For much of the above, see Weiler, *Henry III of England and the Staufen Empire*, ch. 4, at 102–3 for Richard and Frederick.

[11] *CLR 1226–40*, 394, 409, 420, 433, 472, 496; *CLR 1240–5*, 78; *CR 1264–8*, 366; *Layettes*, ii, nos. 2583–2605, 2611–91.

[12] The five years' duration is clear from *CR 1237–42*, 190; *CLR 1226–40*, 496. The truce had been renewed by the earls of Cornwall and Norfolk.

THE ALLIANCE WITH THE LUSIGNANS

Henry, however, knew it was now or never. Indeed he had been long preparing for this hour, however surprised by the way it had struck. Poitou itself was dominated not by the count but by a small group of regional nobles, made even smaller by the eclipse of Savary de Mauléon's family after his death in 1233.[13] Throughout the 1230s, Henry had continued to pay pensions to these men and their fellows to the south in the Saintonge, the vital area between Poitou and Gascony. Indeed over a third of the revenue from the 1237 tax on movables went on such payments. Between October 1240 and October 1241 itself over £1,900 was distributed to around thirty individuals.[14] Of the great lords, Henry never gained the allegiance of Aimery de Thouars, but he had in his pay William Larchevêque, lord of Parthenay, whose holdings, in a block around that great walled town, controlled central Poitou. Further south another pensioner was Reginald de Pons, lord of the key castle in the centre of the Saintonge. Reginald claimed that if Henry could recover Poitou he would gain an income of 20,000 marks a year and have 1,000 knights at his call![15] And then, along the south-east border of Gascony, Henry was making payments to the count of Bigorre. He too was involved in the uprising. From Gascony itself there were promises of 500 paid knights, 500 mounted sergeants and 1,000 foot-soldiers. Meanwhile, Bordeaux and Bayonne, 'lords of the sea', had plans to blockade La Rochelle.[16] Here Henry had one prized asset, namely the isle of Oléron, situated between La Rochelle and the mouth of the Charente at Rochefort. Its capture had been Henry's one success in 1230. He had held on to it tenaciously ever since. Fertile and well fortified, it provided a base both for a blockade of La Rochelle and attacks on the mainland.[17] If Henry no longer had help from the Breton ports, as he had in 1230, the many linkages between Bayonne, Bordeaux, Oléron, the Channel Islands, Bristol, Dublin and Waterford meant much of the Angevin seaborne empire remained in place.[18]

Henry's greatest assets of all, of course, were the Lusignans. Quite apart from La Marche and Angoulême, Hugh and his kinsmen had no

---

[13] For the political geography of Poitou, see Hajdu, 'Castles, castellans', and Chenard, *L'Administration d'Alphonse de Poitiers*, 192–204.

[14] *CLR 1240–5*, 2–5, 8, 42, 44, 46–7, 49–50, 53–4, 59, 62, 73, 76–7, 79, 81.

[15] *DD*, no. 245, interpreting the duchy of Aquitaine here as essentially Poitou.

[16] 'Lettre à la Reine Blanche', 527–9; *CLR 1240–5*, 2–3, 47, 73, 108, 269, 300, 321.

[17] The strategic importance of the strait between Oléron and the coast was recognized by Napoleon, who began the building there of Fort Boyard, now of TV fame as the site of an adventure game show. On boat trips from La Rochelle (as the music of the show plays) it attracts far more attention than does the isle of Oléron.

[18] I owe this picture and other aspects of what follows to Amicie Pelissie du Rausas's forthcoming doctoral thesis: 'Les relations franco-anglaises sous Louis IX et Henri III'. See also her 'The reconfiguration of Plantagenet Power in Gascony, 1242–1243'.

fewer than twenty-four castellanies in Poitou. Alphonse, as the new count, had five.[19] That was not all. Hugh came with a great ally, one whose support Henry had often solicited in vain. On 15 October 1241, Hugh had reached an agreement with Raymond, count of Toulouse, an agreement to be confirmed, it was hoped, by the count's marriage to one of Hugh and Isabella's daughters. This was a natural alliance, for just as Hugh wished to keep Louis IX's brother Alphonse out of Poitou, so the count wished to keep him out of Toulouse, to which he was due to succeed (under the 1229 Treaty of Paris) through his marriage to the count's daughter. Count Raymond also brought with him into the alliance none other than King James of Aragon, whose father had been killed in 1213 resisting the French invasion of Toulouse.[20] Already famous for wresting Majorca and Valencia from the Moors, might he now take revenge on the French?

Henry, therefore, could think he was joining a great coalition which would throw back the Capetians and utterly transform the situation in the south of France. He did not hesitate. On 8 December at Reading he took an oath to abide by 'certain writings and covenants' agreed with the envoys of his 'mother and father'.[21] In return for the homage they were now to give him, Henry quitclaimed to their children all his rights in the county of Angoulême. So Henry was to inherit nothing from his mother. In addition, Henry quitclaimed to Hugh, Isabella and their children his rights in Saintes and whatever belonged to them in the isle of Oléron. These renunciations were also to be made by his brother Richard of Cornwall and Henry's sisters the Empress Isabella and Eleanor de Montfort.[22] The agreement included provision for Hugh, Hugh and Isabella's eldest son. He was to do liege homage to Henry 'his brother' for a pension of 400 marks a year until converted into wards, escheats or other land. If through the coming war he lost the marriage portion of his wife, he was to be given rents in England worth 1,000 marks a year, these in places to be decided by his mother! Since the young Hugh was married to none other than Henry's erstwhile intended, Yolande, daughter of Peter, duke of Brittany, now a staunch loyalist, such a loss was almost inevitable.[23]

In some ways the conflict to come must have been painful for Henry, given he and Louis IX had married sisters. Back in October 1240, Henry's new daughter was named Margaret after Queen Margaret of France.

[19] Hajdu, 'Castles, castellans', 34–6. For the expansion of Lusignan power before 1242 see also Chenard, *L'Administration d'Alphonse de Poitiers*, 196–7, 200–1.

[20] *Layettes*, ii, no. 2941; Puylaurens, 102–3; Paris, iv, 179; Weiler, *Henry III of England and the Staufen Empire*, 88; James of Aragon, 3–4, 22–5.

[21] The oath was sworn on Henry's behalf by his steward Bertram de Criel.

[22] Eleanor is still called the countess of Pembroke in the agreement.

[23] I am grateful to Amicie Pelissie du Rausas for bringing to my attention the text of Henry's concessions in *Cartulaire des Comtes de la Marche*, 19–24. See also *CPR 1232–47*, 268; *CLR 1240–5*, 95; *RIR*, 86.

When the latter gave birth around the same time, Henry joyfully gave £10 to the messenger who brought the news.[24] But Henry was utterly committed. He had, wrote Matthew Paris, 'conceived such a fixed intention of crossing [to Poitou] that he could not be recalled from it by any arguments of his familiars and well wishers'. It was 'his heart's irrevocable purpose'. He drove it forward with praiseworthy courage and determination.[25]

HENRY'S PREPARATIONS

Henry was, however, taking a considerable risk. Perhaps believing that the affair brooked no delay, he had charged ahead without any proper consultation with the good and great of the realm. No bishops were present at court and probably no earls either when he signed up in December. His concessions were never recorded on the chancery rolls and were not drawn up in proper chancery form. The Welsh campaign of 1241 had brought Henry closer to his magnates but selling them the Poitevin enterprise at the forthcoming January parliament would not be easy. Henry began the process at his Christmas court. Held at his 'great palace' of Westminster, it lasted fifteen days and was attended by Peter of Savoy, the archbishop of York (soon to be appointed regent) and the earls of Hereford and Pembroke, the latter receiving a gift of deer.[26] On 8 January, Henry felt confident enough to order a fleet to assemble at Portsmouth by 13 April.[27]

Before the parliament met, Henry faced a more immediate problem. In mid-January his brother Richard of Cornwall arrived back in England from his crusade. How would Richard react to the position now accorded to Peter of Savoy, to an agreement with the Lusignans requiring him to make a series of renunciations, and to a campaign in Poitou likely to breach the truce with the king of France he himself had negotiated. Richard, moreover, was returning as a figure of international renown.[28] At least that was how he presented himself in conversations with Matthew Paris and doubtless also with the king. In the Holy Land, acting as the emperor's delegate, he had ratified a truce which restored the frontiers of the kingdom of Jerusalem and freed many French nobles from captivity. On his way home, as he progressed through the imperial cities of Italy, he had been welcomed by processions, one at Cremona including an elephant bearing the town band on its back. At the imperial court, where he had

---

[24] Paris, iv, 48; *CLR 1226–40*, 501. For the suggestion that the tension in 1241 between Louis IX and Margaret was due to her pro-English sympathies, see Grant, *Blanche of Castile*, 123.

[25] Paris, iv, 181.

[26] Paris, iv, 177; *RCWL*, i, 184. See Morris, *Bigod Earls of Norfolk*, 19–20.

[27] *CR 1237–42*, 429. For Hugh's messenger, see *CLR 1240–5*, 101.

[28] For Peter as head of the council, see Paris, iv, 187.

private talks with his sister the empress, he was invigorated by hot baths and entertained by Saracen dancing girls balancing on rolling spheres (especially alluring for Richard who, unlike his brother, was a noted womanizer).[29]

Henry, both calculating and spontaneous, did all he could to welcome and honour his brother. Loaded with gifts, he went with Eleanor and a great entourage of nobles down to Canterbury to meet him and rushed joyfully into his arms. In London, specially decked out for the occasion, Richard was met by processions (alas without elephants) at St Paul's and Westminster Abbey and then entertained to a great feast. At both St Paul's and the Abbey, Henry offered expensive cloths in thanksgiving for his brother's return.[30] In explaining his Poitevin plans, Henry had one trump card, for the great gainer from a successful expedition was potentially Richard himself. Since his expedition to Gascony in 1225, he had born the title (a nominal one to be sure) of count of Poitou, so, if the usurper Alphonse could be expelled, Richard could at last hope to make a reality of the position.

Richard was also, in a remarkable coup, drawn into the circle of the Savoyards. Peter of Savoy, with a tact commended by Matthew Paris, cleared the way by offering to surrender Dover castle, fearful that his position there would give offence.[31] Backed by the king and queen, he also suggested that Richard, a widower since 1240, should marry none other than the queen's younger sister, Sanchia, daughter of the count of Provence.[32] With Sanchia's eldest sister married to the king of France, this was a match of the highest status, but not one (to go from Henry's experiences with Eleanor) likely to bring much material gain to a very materially geared man. Henry, therefore, agreed to fill the gap. He gave Richard £400 and four valuable manors with the promise of more in the future. In return Richard agreed both to marry Sanchia and go with his brother to Poitou, if with safeguards against the breach of the truce. The Savoyard bishop of Hereford, Peter de Aigueblanche, immediately set off to negotiate the marriage agreement.[33]

---

[29] Paris, iv, 141–3, 146–8, 166–7; Denholm-Young, *Richard of Cornwall*, 42–3.

[30] Paris, iv, 180; Waverley, 329; *CLR 1240–5*, 121.

[31] Paris, iv, 177–8.

[32] The suggestion was made possible by the failure of a scheme for her to marry the count of Toulouse: Puylaurens, 100–2. For Sanchia, see Adrian Jobson's forthcoming article 'A queen in the shadows'. Richard's first wife, Isabella, daughter of the regent William Marshal, and widow of the earl of Gloucester, had wanted to lie with her first husband at Tewkesbury but instead was buried, at Richard's insistence, at Beaulieu (founded of course by King John). However, her heart, relic collection and contents of her chapel went to Tewkesbury: Tewkesbury, 114. She had prepared for death (in childbirth) by confessing her sins and having her long hair cut off: Paris, iv, 2.

[33] *CR 1237–42*, 400, 433; *CChR 1226–57*, 276; *CLR 1240–5*, 111; *F*, 242; *CPR 1232–47*, 274–6; *RCWL*, i, 185; Paris, iv, 190; Howell, *Eleanor of Provence*, 53–4.

Henry had less success at the parliament when it opened at the end of January. What he needed above all was a grant of taxation like that saving Gascony in 1225. Hugh de Lusignan had stressed that, while obviously Henry needed to come with a military force, what was needed above all was money, money with which Henry (or rather Hugh) could hire forces locally. This request reflected a basic attitude to English rule. Hugh and his allies were not going to replace an intrusive count in Alphonse with an intrusive king of England. As a citizen of La Rochelle put it, 'The land is theirs [the Gascons] and they do whatever they wish since for the king of the English, even at Bordeaux and Bayonne, they do not care an egg; and he gives to them and the barons quite sufficient.' The Poitevins and Gascons wanted to keep it that way.[34]

At the parliament, accordingly, Henry made his case for a tax both through spokesmen and in person only to be 'contradicted to his face'. He then tried soft talk in a series of individual meetings, but did no better. Henry was angry but undeterred. Nothing, he swore, would prevent him trying the fortunes of war with the king of France. Within a few days of the close of the parliament he summoned all his tenants-in-chief to appear with horses and arms at Winchester after Easter, ready to cross with him to Poitou.[35] In fact, the refusal of help at the parliament was not absolute. Although there were general complaints about financial exactions, breaches of Magna Carta and the wasted tax of 1237, the official record concentrated simply on the issue of the truce and indeed promised Henry help if Louis broke it.[36] Henry already had Richard of Cornwall on side (he was a spokesman at the parliament), and was working hard on other magnates. Between January and his departure in May eight earls appeared at court. None apart from Richard had anything to gain in Poitou, but Henry encouraged them with a series of concessions (a loan of 200 marks went to Roger Bigod).[37] Perhaps Henry was not the best man to speak of the excitement of warfare and the honour to be won, but everyone of any spirit would have felt that. In the event, the earls of Cornwall, Hereford, Norfolk, Pembroke, Devon, Winchester and Aumale all joined the expedition, a pretty full turnout of earls, allowing for those who were old and sick. The question of whether the obligations of tenants-in-chief extended to military service in Poitou seems not to have been raised.[38] Although,

[34] 'Lettre à la Reine Blanche', 527.

[35] CR 1237–42, 431. This letter, a general summons through the sheriffs, was presumably accompanied by individual letters to the major tenants-in-chief.

[36] In Matthew Paris's long account (Paris, iv, 181–8) the extent of the official record is not entirely clear, but I think it is confined to p. 185. For different views, see Stacey, Politics, Policy and Finance, 185 n. 113; Maddicott, Origins of the English Parliament, 181 n. 96.

[37] For example, CPR 1232–47, 278, 281, 283; CLR 1240–5, 118; RIR, 91; TNA E 368/14, m. 20d.

[38] 'The Unknown Charter' of 1215 had acknowledged service was due in Normandy and Brittany, but by implication excluded service further south: Holt, Magna Carta, 426–7, cap. 7.

moreover, there was no tax on movables, at some point before departure (perhaps at the final muster), 'by the common counsel of the kingdom', a scutage at the high rate of 3 marks a fee was imposed on those who did not take part in the expedition. Various changes in the form of the levy also promised to make it more lucrative than scutages in the past.[39]

Henry, meanwhile, was doing all he could to raise money in other ways.[40] He ordered the sheriffs 'as you love your own lands and chattels' to bring personally to the Easter exchequer all the money they could raise;[41] he appealed to the religious houses of the kingdom to earn his gratitude by gifts of money and horses, the king being in 'much want' of both. Many obliged, although Tewksbury abbey regarded its contribution of 20 marks as 'extortion'.[42]

Henry also busied himself gathering all the other necessaries for the campaign. Orders went out to secure 50,000 crossbow bolts, 15,000 horse-shoes, 100,000 nails, 18 great containers of hide to hold the king's wine, and 12 long carts each with 2 horses to draw the 100 barrels containing the king's treasure. The king's pavilions were moved from Hereford to Winchester, and a great new one, costing 200 marks, was bought for the king himself. All ships which could take sixteen horses and more were pressed into service, with twenty being reserved for the king and his household.[43]

In his last weeks, Henry made final arrangements for the security of his kingdom during his absence. He munitioned his new castle at Dyserth and promised to do justice in the continuing dispute over the possession of Mold. He began negotiations for a possible marriage between his infant daughter Margaret and the son of King Alexander, while also hastening the assignment of the land in Northumberland due under the treaty of 1237.[44] There was also the question of the governance of the kingdom in the king's absence. This, with general consent, Henry entrusted to wise old Walter de Grey, archbishop of York, counselled by Walter Mauclerc, bishop of Carlisle, and the steward William de Cantilupe II. They were to use the exchequer seal to authenticate their orders, Henry taking the great

---

[39] For the taxation of 1242, see Mitchell, *Studies of Taxation*, 224–39; Stacey, *Politics, Policy and Finance*, 187–8; *CR 1237–42*, 486; Madox, *History and Antiquities of the Exchequer*, i, 609 n.(c), 681 n.(p). The scutage was to be levied on all the tenants holding from a lord by knight service, not just on the number of knights the lord owed the king. It was also to be collected by the sheriff, not (as in 1235) by the lord. A clear distinction was made between the scutage and the fines to avoid personal service: *CFR 1241–2*, nos. 410, 412, 423; *PR 1242*, 18 and passim. The fines raised some £1,500: Stacey, *Politics, Policy and Finance*, 188. The scutage was linked to an inquiry into fees which produced the surveys in *BF*, ii, 637–1130.

[40] See Stacey, *Politics, Policy and Finance*, 187–90.

[41] *CR 1237–42*, 397. The proceeds of the Easter term were £7,200, an excellent result so the order had an effect: *RIR*, 66.

[42] *CPR 1232–47*, 271–2, 277; Tewkesbury, 121–2; *BF*, ii, 1130–41.

[43] *CPR 1232–47*, 278; *CLR 1240–5*, 109, 118–19, 127, 132, 134.

[44] *CLR 1240–5*, 102, 119–20; *CPR 1232–47*, 272–3, 291, 294; Paris, iv, 192–3.

seal with him.[45] Lord Edward, the heir to the throne, naturally stayed
behind at Windsor. Surely Eleanor would do so too. After all she was over
seven months pregnant. But no. Eleanor was evidently determined to go
and Henry wanted her with him. They eventually sailed in the same ship,
one fitted out with Eleanor's own oven and wainscoted chamber. How
integral she and her Savoyard kin were to the realm and its future was
clear from Henry's order that, in the event of his death, Dover and other
strategic castles were only to be surrendered to Eleanor or to one of her
Savoyard uncles not in the allegiance of the king of France (so to Peter or
Boniface but not Thomas of Savoy). Before his departure, Henry gave the
queen £50 worth of jewels and also, a first step in her financial independence, a valuable wardship.[46]

For all his material preparations, nothing was more important, in
Henry's mind, than winning God's favour for the campaign. In March,
having completed his deal with Richard of Cornwall, he left Westminster
on a pilgrimage to Bury St Edmunds, Bromholm and Walsingham, at
each place arranging for hundreds of candles to burn on his arrival.[47] He
also issued a heartfelt plea to archdeacons throughout the country:

> Since, led by God, we will shortly cross overseas, and we have a certain
> faith that by means of the prayers of the faithful, the All Highest will
> wish our journey and our acts to prosper, we ask you, most attentively,
> through all your archdeaconry, to have prayers offered up to the All
> Highest for us and our queen, that by his mercy we may be able happily
> to accomplish our project and return home with prosperity; and also
> cause prayers to be offered for our children that the Lord will preserve
> them safe.[48]

In all this, Henry did not, of course, forget the Confessor. A proper
endowment was made for the candles burning around his shrine; money,
during the king's absence, was provided for the goldsmiths and marblers
working on the new shrine; and orders were given for twelve gold coins to
be laid on the high altar of the Abbey, 'for the safety of the souls' of the
king, the queen and their children on each of the Confessor's feast days.[49]

Henry got back from his Norfolk tour in time to spend Easter at
Westminster, and then, on Easter Monday (22 April), giving three great
cloths to the Abbey, he journeyed first to Winchester and thence to

---

[45] *F*, 244 (*CPR 1232–47*, 280). Grey was able to act because no archbishop of Canterbury
was in place. Otherwise conflicts over precedence would have kept Grey in his northern
province.

[46] *CR 1237–42*, 405; *CLR 1240–5*, 115, 127, 133; *CPR 1232–47*, 280, 283, 294; Howell,
Eleanor of Provence, 32–3, 64–5, 274.

[47] *CLR 1240–5*, 113–14.

[48] *CR 1237–42*, 436.

[49] *CChR 1226–57*, 268; CLR 1240–5, 119, 134.

Portsmouth, arriving on 4 May.[50] In terms of money, Henry was able to send out £2,000 in advance to Poitou. After some hesitation, he assigned this to Hugh de Lusignan, although only until he asked for it back![51] As for the money he took with him, Henry cleaned out the exchequer and his treasure in the Tower of London. A posse of twenty sergeants guarded the largest consignment on its journey from London to Winchester.[52] In the end, Henry probably took with him around £30,000, along with hundreds of pounds worth of rings and broaches for distribution as favours. This compared with the roughly £20,000 taken in 1230 and the £15,000 in 1253. Henry, however, had hoped for more and indeed had ordered barrels to be made for £60,000.[53] The treasure he took was certainly far less than King John had assembled for his campaign in 1214.

At the core of the army were Henry's household knights, sergeants and crossbow men.[54] Then there were the earls and barons with their retinues. Henry, following Hugh's advice, had prioritized money over men and been very ready to accept fines from tenants-in-chief for exemption from the campaign. He had, however, hoped for a larger army, as he had hoped for more money. The force eventually sailed in around 90 ships as against the 200 Henry had thought might be necessary – that being the size of the fleet in 1230. Letters of protection were only issued to around 200 people, as against 370 in 1230, so the army was probably smaller than in the earlier year.[55] The paucity of Henry's force was to have dire consequences in the confrontation to come.

THE 1242 CAMPAIGN: ITS DISASTROUS START

Henry finally embarked at Portsmouth on Friday 9 May. The sea, as he said later, was 'placid and tranquil', and he landed safely on 13 May at Royan on the northern mouth of the Gironde. After a day or so he advanced to Pons, his base for the next month, where he was greeted by Reginald and other nobles of the Saintonge.[56] Henry's meeting with his

---

[50] *CLR 1240–5*, 121.

[51] For this saga, see *CPR 1232–47*, 273–4, 277; *CR 1237–42*, 402; *RG*, i, no. 670.

[52] *CLR 1240–5*, 121–2, 124; *RIR*, 89–91.

[53] *CR 1237–42*, 390, 407; *CLR 1240–5*, 403, 407. Stacey, *Politics, Policy and Finance*, 189–90, calculates that the king took with him around £35,000, but since the treasure in the Tower was transferred to the exchequer (*CPR 1232–47*, 281) it may be included in the sums the exchequer sent.

[54] *CLR 1226–40*, 379, 394–5. It is difficult to be sure about the number of household knights at this time: Walker, 'The Anglo-Welsh wars', 93; Stacey, *Politics, Policy and Finance*, 186.

[55] *CR 1237–42*, 401; *CLR 1240–5*, 140; *CPR 1232–47*, 294–7. Many of the 200 would have had their own retinues.

[56] *CR 1237–42*, 497–8; Paris, iv, 192. A detailed account of the campaign is found in Bémont, 'La campagne de Poitou'. It is studied in depth in the forthcoming doctoral thesis of Amicie du Pelissie du Rausas.

mother, Queen Isabella, whom he had last seen as an eleven-year-old boy nearly a quarter of a century before, is nowhere described, but it must have been as emotional personally as it was fraught politically: politically because the deteriorating military situation in Poitou was all too apparent. The problem was that Hugh and Isabella had moved too soon. At the time of their negotiations with Henry early in December 1241, they had been strengthening their castles and plotting a land and sea blockade of La Rochelle, but they had not actually declared war. All this changed at Alphonse's Christmas court. There Hugh publicly renounced his homage and departed with Isabella, having ceremonially burnt down the house in which he was staying.[57] This was a terrible mistake that shaped the rest of the campaign, for it meant King Louis could now act before Henry himself was ready.

Louis mustered his army at Chinon in late April, and at once received control of the castles of the loyalist Aimery de Thouars.[58] In the next couple of months he swept through Poitou taking a dozen castles from Hugh, his kinsman and his allies. The climax came at Frontenay, where siege operations started on 8 June. Its fall after fifteen days was a devastating blow, for Frontenay was the most formidable of Hugh's castles and the key to any landward blockade of La Rochelle. Having taken the castles, Louis either garrisoned them or, as at Frontenay, destroyed them. A true 'roi de guerre', he ravaged the lands of his opponents and punished in 'atrocious' fashion a spy taken in his camp. The destruction wrought by the war featured both in a poem by John of Garland and the complaints later made to Louis's inquiries.[59] Yet Louis also showed chivalric punctilio and refused to punish those who were merely following their lords. Faced with this advance, both fearsome and conciliatory, many Poitevin nobles deserted to the French army, including Ralph de Beaumont, who simply swapped the pension he was receiving from Henry for one from Louis.[60]

While Louis was free to act, Henry, on his arrival, was still restrained by the truce. What had it to do with Henry, Louis asked, if he punished rebels? With Louis observing all the proper procedures, conduct much admired by the English army, it behoved Henry to do the same.[61] Even before leaving England, he had issued a formal document allowing the earls of Cornwall and Norfolk, the negotiators of the truce, to return home if he broke it without due cause. Now, scraping together an assortment of

[57] Paris, iv, 178–9. Paris has Hugh refusing to do homage, rather than renouncing it, but *Layettes*, ii, no. 2928, shows this is wrong.

[58] *Layettes*, ii, no. 2972.

[59] I owe these details and the general perspective to Amicie Pelissie du Rausas's chapter on 1242. I am grateful to Martin Hall for letting me see his translation of the 1242 sections of John of Garland's poem, '*De Triumphis*'.

[60] Nangis, 335–6; Paris, iv, 202, 206–8; *Layettes*, ii, no. 2975; *CLR 1240–5*, 45, 95–6; *RG*, i, no. 268.

[61] Paris, iv, 202–4, 206–7; *Layettes*, ii, no. 2976.

grievances, he sent envoys twice (on 24 and 30 May to Louis) to complain about breaches of the truce, on the first occasion dictating personally the terms of the commission. It was not until 8 June, the day the siege of Frontenay began, that he was able formally to announce that the truce was at an end.[62]

In conjuring up support for the rising of 1242, one poet imagined that the English 'leopard' had all the courage of the sons of Henry II.[63] But now the traps were open no Henrician leopard came bounding out. Instead of crossing the Charente and doing battle with Louis in Poitou, Henry simply moved (on 7 June) to Saintes itself, the ancient capital of the Saintonge, where he stayed for the next fortnight. Here Henry could admire the Roman triumphal arch, wander over the ruins of the gigantic amphitheatre, and offer up his prayers in the cathedral of St-Pierre, the Cluniac monastery of St-Eutrope and the Abbaye aux Dames, whose many-sided bell tower could be seen far and wide from the surrounding countryside. The terrible truth was that Henry's army was deemed too small to take on Louis's much larger force. Those in arms against the French king, as the citizen of La Rochelle opined in a favourite phrase, were 'not worth an egg'.[64]

This was partly the fault of Hugh and Isabella, whose unpopularity was stressed by the same commentator.[65] It was also because of the limited response to the summons Henry had issued on 25 May to the towns and nobles of Gascony, the Saintonge and further afield to join him with horses and arms on 12 June.[66] As early as 8 June, realizing his mistake in coming with so small an army, Henry ordered the home government to send out to him 200 knights and 100 sergeants from England, 100 knights and 200 mounted sergeants from Ireland, and 500 good Welsh foot-soldiers. Those who had previously offered money to be excused their service, Henry added, should be pardoned their fines if they would now join him, a revelation of his miscalculation he sought to obscure by pretending that the ending of the truce had taken him by surprise![67]

At least Henry seems to have made some progress in the war at sea and the blockade of La Rochelle. In June he ordered the men of the Cinque Ports to pillage and burn the French coast (though sparing churches) and

---

[62] *RG*, i, nos. 262, 266–9; *CR 1237–42*, 497–9, 524–6. Gaining a bit of time for his preparations, Louis was not informed until 16 June: *RG*, i, no. 278.

[63] Aurell, *L'Empire des Plantagenêt*, 100, citing Jeanroy, 'Un sirventès historique de 1242', 122 v. 21.

[64] 'Lettre à la reine Blanche', 527–9

[65] See Chenard, *L'Administration d'Alphonse de Poitiers*, 202.

[66] *CR 1237–42*, 524–7; *RG*, i, nos. 411, 497. Bordeaux did send service though Henry had to acknowledge it was not owed outside the diocese of Bordeaux: *RG*, i, no. 281. La Réole did not: *RG*, i, nos. 306, 308.

[67] *CR 1237–42*, 496–8.

they were presumably the English sailors who forced the inhabitants around La Rochelle to pay protection money. The same inhabitants saw their lands ravaged by landing parties from galleys sent from Bayonne, if, that is, Henry's orders were obeyed.[68] The king's position was strengthened by gaining control of Ré, the small island north of Oléron sitting just above the channel leading into La Rochelle. In June he conceded the men there the right to chose their mayor and have a commune.[69] All this, however, would have been more threatening had Hugh de Lusignan still controlled the hinterland. It was rather less so now it was in French hands. Louis bolstered the garrison in La Rochelle and stationed a substantial force in the surrounding area to combat attacks from the sea.

Henry, moreover, was already running out of money. His expenditure at this time, handled by the wardrobe, was vast. In a normal year wardrobe expenditure stood at around £10,000. In the year October 1241 to October 1242 it reached an astronomical £31,410. Of this £22,485 went in payments to knights, sergeants and sailors and gifts to Queen Isabella, Hugh de Lusignan, the count of Toulouse and 'knights and others in parts across the sea'. Some 2,300 marks were received by Richard of Cornwall.[70] The great bulk of this expenditure almost certainly took place in the early days of the campaign. The letter of 8 June to the regents in England declared that 'the king has fallen into such great necessity that he needs money beyond measure'.

Henry was also disappointed in the great alliances Hugh had seemed to promise. There was no immediate help from the count of Toulouse, both because of a serious illness and because he was busy seeking absolution from numerous sentences of excommunication.[71] Nothing materialized from the king of Aragon either.[72] Faced with these disappointments, Henry's thoughts turned once again to Emperor Frederick. Here he was bound to wonder how the relationship would be affected by the death of his sister, the Empress Isabella, in December 1241. When Henry eventually heard the news (in April 1242), he ordered over 100,000 paupers to be fed for Isabella's soul, the largest ever of his mass feedings. But at least Frederick, in announcing the news, had assured Henry that their alliance would survive, one pledge of that being the two children produced by the marriage. So in June, while he was at Saintes, Henry despatched envoys to the emperor empowered to conclude a treaty 'for peace and war against all men'. Henry, also, rather sadly, reminded Frederick of the empress's last words, evidently

---

[68] *CR 1237–42*, 495–6, 501. The detail about protection money comes from Pelissie du Rausas's forthcoming doctoal thesis.

[69] *F*, 247; *CPR 1232–47*, 309, 316.

[70] Wild, *WA*, lxxviii, lxxxvii, xciv, 47.

[71] *Layettes*, ii, no. 2962; Puylaurans, 103–4.

[72] Powicke, *King Henry III*, i, 193, has a good analysis of 'the tugs and strains' which in the end kept James quiet.

words in his favour. Frederick, however, cannot have been pleased with the qualification to Henry's offer – the treaty was to be saving Henry's agreements with the Roman church. Nothing came of the initiative.[73]

None of this diminished Henry's commitment to the campaign. The letter to the regents on 8 June declared that he would 'either recover his honour in parts across the sea or, let it not happen, incur perpetual ignominy and irreparable loss'. Precisely for that reason the one thing Henry was not prepared to do was reduce his almsgiving. Of the 500 paupers he wished to feed every day, the regents were instructed to look after 350.[74] They spent over £1,000 in doing so, despite all the financial pressures they were under.[75] The other 150 paupers were presumably fed at Henry's court, as was Henry's later custom, 100 for himself and 50 for the queen.[76] Poitevins and Gascons could see at first hand that this was a king doing everything possible to win God over to his side.

Despite the urgency of the orders on 8 June, there was nothing the regents could do to influence the immediate campaign. Henry did, however, gain one further source of strength. In early July he welcomed back to court Simon de Montfort. Montfort had been in Burgundy, on his way home from his crusade, when he received Henry's summons. He did not come unrewarded. He was pardoned 600 marks of debt and received a gift of another 500 marks to be paid at the Michaelmas exchequer. The regents were ordered to implement the concessions if the exchequer made any difficulties, a good example of Montfort's attention to detail and determination to get his due. Despite giving the king a golden cup, Montfort remained unhappy about his treatment, but at least he now added his military expertise and martial ardour to the campaign, a vibrant and disruptive presence.[77]

THE BATTLES OF TAILLEBOURG AND SAINTES

Around 23 June, Henry at last left Saintes and marched north-west through the Saintonge, to the town of Tonnay astride the Charente. From

[73] CLR 1240–5, 124, 281; Paris, iv, 175–6; RG, i, no. 854; CR 1237–42, 530–2; F, 252 (CPR 1232–47, 399); Weiler, Henry III of England and the Staufen Empire, 105–6. Thomas, count of Flanders, was involved in this approach to the emperor. This wily politician thus showed willing while being pretty sure nothing would ever materialize to damage his relations with the king of France.

[74] CR 1237–42, 497.

[75] CLR 1240–5, 151, 160, 166, 169, 172, 174, 180, 184, 187. The money included some other almsgiving, including the feeding of 1,000 paupers on the anniversary of King John's death and 4,000 on the 5 January feast of the Confessor.

[76] When the queen was not with Henry, she would feed the 50 on her own.

[77] RG, i, no. 191 (CLR 1240–5, 153); CFR 1241–2, no. 560; Pipe Roll 1242, 180; Wild, WA, 57; Bémont, Simon de Montfort, 334; Maddicott, Simon de Montfort, 31–2.

here he could, as he said later in explanation of the move, send his men into Poitou to attack the king of France. In fact, nothing like that happened, at least on any scale. The concern soon became to use the bridge at Tonnay not to advance into Poitou but to secure it against a French advance into the Saintonge.[78] Indeed, the only significant English presence in Poitou during the whole campaign seems to have been at Parthenay, where Henry sent a force (one including the young Surrey knight Roland of Oxted) both to strengthen the garrison and attack the king's enemies.[79] Henry's strategy had thus become purely defensive, and one weak point in the defence was Taillebourg. The town stood on a loop in the Charente between Tonnay and Saintes, and had a bridge Louis might use to cross the river. The trouble was that the lord of Taillebourg, Geoffrey de Rancon, had never entered Henry's allegiance and had a personal feud with Hugh de Lusignan. Indeed, he had sworn to wear his hair long like a woman until he gained revenge, a vow he proclaimed on his seal, which depicted his long-haired head.[80]

Aware of this danger, towards the end of June Henry left Tonnay for Taillebourg where he and his army pitched their tents in the meadows (they are much the same today) beside the Charente and looked across the river to Geoffrey's great castle which dominated the town. As Henry later reflected, at this point he should either have crossed the river and taken the castle or destroyed the bridge and denied Louis access to the Saintonge. Instead, fatally, he was persuaded, chiefly by Reginald de Pons, that Geoffrey with proper reparation would come over to his side. Having heard that, at the start of July Henry returned to Saintes and remained there.[81] Hardly very inspiring.

Of course, Geoffrey de Rancon did not come over. Instead, when Louis approached Taillebourg, probably on Saturday, 19 July, Geoffrey welcomed him into the town. Next day, the plan was for Louis to cross the river and advance into the Saintonge.[82] For Henry, less than ten miles away in Saintes, the situation was critical, and for a moment he was its equal. On

[78] CR 1237–42, 529, 531; RG, i, nos. 314, 333, 589 (CPR 1232–47, 310, 312, 337).

[79] RG, i, no. 316 (CPR 1232–47, 310–11); CLR 1240–5, 156. For Roland, see Meekings and Crook, Surrey Eyre, i, 225–6.

[80] Joinville, cap. 104; Bibliothèque Nationale de France MS Latin 5480/1, fo. 231. For Geoffrey de Rancon, see Beauvoit, 'La famille de Rancon'. The seal is illustrated on p. 36. It is not clear whether the protagonist in 1242 was Geoffrey IV or his son Geoffrey V.

[81] CR 1237–42, 531; RG, i, no. 299.

[82] The main sources for events at Taillebourg and Saintes are Henry III's letter of explanation to the emperor (CR 1237–42, 511); Paris, iv, 209–13; Nangis, 336 (his life of St Louis); Joinville (in his life of St Louis), cap. 100–1. There are also details and reflections in John of Garland's poem 'De Triumphis', especially book 3, lines 329–698. These sources are sometimes both hard to interpret and contradictory. The fullest modern accounts are found in Bémont, 'La campagne de Poitou', 302–7, and in Pelissie du Rausas's forthcoming thesis. Matthew Paris cannot, I think, be wrong in saying the truce was on a Sunday and the rest of my chronology follows from that.

Hugh de Lusignan's urging, he came up from Saintes during the night, and on the Sunday morning his army was back in its old station in the meadows beside the Charente, this time looking across the river to the tents and pennants of the French army and the oriflamme, the great red banner of Louis himself. Henry's aim was to block the bridge and thus keep Louis at bay, but the French brought up specially constructed wooden bridges and also started to get across the river in small boats. Henry braced himself for the battle which might recover all his lost empire. He was never closer to that golden objective than now. According to Jean de Joinville's much later reminiscences, a battle 'fierce and strong' indeed took place, with Louis putting himself in danger, the scene depicted in a dramatic painting by Delacroix. In fact, as contemporary sources make plain, it was far tamer than that. One thing had become crystal clear as the two armies glared at each other across the Charente. Henry's force was by far the smaller, too small in fact either to prevent the French crossing the river, as they were beginning to do, or to have much hope in a battle thereafter. To save the situation, therefore, Richard of Cornwall went across the bridge, carrying only a staff, and managed to secure a truce until the morrow. Under cover of night, Henry and his army then retreated back to Saintes. On Monday morning Louis crossed the river and pitched his tents in the very place the English had been the day before. He had thus got across the Charente unopposed.[83]

Next day, Tuesday 22 July (the feast day of Mary Magdalene), Louis advanced early on Saintes itself, hoping, Henry later said, to catch him and his army in their beds or at table.[84] This time though there was 'a great and very formidable conflict' in the vineyards and narrow ways outside Saintes, with men on both sides being killed or captured. Here Hugh de Lusignan, first into the fray, at last distinguished himself, as (according to Matthew Paris) 'gaining eternal praise' did Simon de Montfort, William Longespée, Roger Bigod, John de Burgh and the steward Ralph fitzNicholas.[85] No mention is made of Henry himself or to be fair of Louis. In the end both sides claimed victory, the French thinking they had driven Henry's forces back into Saintes and the English that Louis's men had withdrawn to their tents defeated.[86]

For all 'the eternal praise' thus won, Henry's situation in Saintes on the night of 22–23 July was parlous. Only a small proportion of the French

---

[83] A monument on the field at Taillebourg, put up in 1892, celebrates the victory of Louis, 'a most ardent defender' of the 'libertatem patriae'.

[84] John of Garland seems to have thought Louis was here violating the truce.

[85] Paris, iv, 213. John of Garland has a similar list and may have shared Paris's source. For a prisoner captured by Warin de Munchensey (also in Paris's list), see *CR 1242–7*, 31. FitzNicholas had been restored to favour just before the campaign.

[86] A plaque placed in 1893 on the west front of the cathedral of Saint Pierre is dedicated to Louis, 'vainqueur des Anglais sous les murs de Saintes'.

army had been engaged in the day's skirmishes, and Henry plainly lacked the forces to go out and fight a set-piece battle. If, on the other hand, he stayed in the town he faced ultimate capture, however long the siege. The French prisoners taken back to Saintes heard of a violent quarrel between Henry and Hugh de Lusignan (as did Matthew Paris), Henry furiously demanding where was all the support Hugh had promised and Hugh blaming everything on Henry's mother, Isabella.[87] Simon de Montfort himself thought that Henry's conduct had been pathetic. It was probably at this moment, certainly it was at Saintes, that 'in great anguish of spirit' (as he later said) he declared that 'it would be well if [Henry] was taken and kept apart as was done with Charles l'Assoté', referring here to the imprisonment of the Carolingian king Charles the Simple after the battle of Soissons in 923.[88] This is the first example we have of the sharpness of tongue Montfort displayed throughout his career. The characteristic worried even his friends, and his spiritual counsellor, Adam Marsh, addressed a little homily to him on the subject. While it behoved the earl, Marsh said, 'to speak openly, freely and boldly the thoughts in his heart', he should nonetheless govern his tongue lest his lack of restraint caused offence.[89] His remark certainly caused Henry grave offence and was recalled bitterly by him many years later.

With his position in Saintes untenable, there followed some of the most unpleasant and humiliating days in Henry's life, days in which he sought a safe haven in one place after another while all around him the allies whom he had trusted so much and rewarded so well submitted to King Louis. Henry left Saintes during the course of 23 July and, with Hugh de Lusignan doing nothing to defend it, the city fell at once to King Louis. Henry then stayed a few days at Pons, only, as Louis approached, to hurry the twenty miles to Barbezieux where he was by the evening of the twenty-sixth. Here, however, disastrous news came in. Reginald de Pons, having kissed Henry farewell (the kiss of a Judas, Henry later complained), had promptly deserted to Louis. Even worse, there were rumours that Hugh and Isabella themselves were about to submit and were offering to capture Henry and hand him over. So, without eating a prepared meal, and after what had already been a long day, Henry fled from Barbezieux and, as he put it, 'travelled all night and all day' to reach Blaye forty miles away on the evening of 27 July; a terrible journey both for Henry (who lost relics and ornaments from his chapel) and the hungry and exhausted army

---

[87] Joinville, cap. 102; Paris, iv, 210–11.

[88] Bémont, *Simon de Montfort*, 341; Maddicott, *Simon de Montfort*, 32. For good measure, Montfort added that 'the houses barred with iron' at Windsor would be good to keep Henry in, presumably referring to the way many windows had been barred after the assassination attempt in 1238.

[89] *Letters of Adam Marsh*, ii, 349. I owe the significance of Marsh's passage here (in a letter to Montfort) to Ambler, *The Song of Simon de Montfort*, 98.

which straggled behind him. The earl of Hereford, for one, lost his weapons and baggage in a broken cart.[90]

Henry had now put distance between himself and Louis, and could, if necessary, retreat across the Gironde estuary into Gascony. It was soon necessary to do so. At the start of August, outside Pons, Louis received the formal submission of Hugh and Isabella. They kept Lusignan, Angoulême and La Marche, but they had to surrender Saintes and everything else Louis had captured. When Geoffrey de Rancon saw Hugh and Isabella, all their pride gone, kneeling with their children before Louis, and crying for mercy, he called for a stool and had his hair cut in their presence.[91] Louis had not finished. He now advanced towards Blaye and it was at Marcillac, only twelve miles away, that in August he received the formal submission of Reginald de Pons.[92] Henry made no attempt to resist. Instead he crossed the Gironde and set up camp in the fields on the southern bank.

The battle for Poitou and the Saintonge was over. Was the battle for Gascony about to begin? The English certainly thought so but at last mercifully there was relief. Louis and his army had succumbed to illness. They had done enough. Secure in his conquests, Louis set off for home and by the end of August was already at Tours where he received the submission of William Larchevêque of Parthenay, Henry's last remaining Poitevin ally.[93] Henry himself, no doubt with a sigh of relief, retreated to Bordeaux. There he was greeted by his queen. Whatever she felt about his failure, and it must have been as humiliating for her as it was for him, she 'honoured him' and presented him with a daughter, born on 25 June and named Beatrice after her mother.[94]

Henry was very aware that he had been defeated and, what perhaps was even worse, humiliated. It was not just the Poitevins' desertion that counted, it was the way they had done it, as thieves in the night behind Henry's back, without explanation or excuse. Only one, Ponce de Mirambeau, behaved correctly, going to Henry, explaining his predicament and being given permission to seek terms. Henry complained bitterly to the emperor of 'the treachery done us by our traitors of Poitou', and begged him not to believe 'frivolous' stories 'damaging to our fame', a request which shows how concerned Henry was about his reputation.[95]

Not surprisingly many in the English camp had now had enough. Seven of the earls who had joined Henry's expedition were at court in

---

[90] *CR 1237–42*, 511; Paris, iv, 217–20; *RG*, i, no. 507. By contrast, my wife and I had one of our best meals in France at La Boule d'Or at Barbezieux.

[91] Joinville, cap. 104.

[92] *Layettes*, ii, nos. 2980, 2984–5, 2987.

[93] *Layettes*, ii, nos. 2989–90.

[94] Howell, *Eleanor of Provence*, 35–6.

[95] *CR 1237–42*, 530–2; *RG*, i, no. 1197.

August and September, but all but one left for England shortly thereafter, if with the king's permission and sometimes thanked with pardons of debts and presents of deer.[96] The most damaging and damning departure was that of Henry's brother Richard. Since he had most to gain from a French defeat, this was the best indication that all was over. Matthew Paris picked up stories, which grew over the years, of a quarrel between the brothers, even that Richard fled home fearing arrest. Henry, while at Saintes, had certainly promised Gascony itself to his brother, only then, influenced by the queen (so Paris thought), to change his mind.[97] Probably she already thought of Gascony as part of her son Edward's appanage. Paris also thought that Richard had protested about the treatment of the northern baron William de Ros, whose lands had been seized (not without some justification) for failing to join the Portsmouth muster.[98] Whatever the tensions, Henry was quick to smooth over any quarrel. He praised Richard's service, sanctioned his return and promised him £2,000 to go with his marriage to Sanchia of Provence, as well (a much more personal touch) as placing at his disposal all the royal houses, forests, castles, falcons and goshawks back in England.[99]

Henry's own thoughts also turned to home. In September, for his new chapel at Windsor castle, he commissioned both a 'a most beautiful royal seat' and paintings from the Old and New Testaments. The latter were to be like those at Wolvesey, the palace of the bishop of Winchester. The queen's chapel (doubtless after consultation with Eleanor) was to have pictures of the wise and foolish virgins.[100] Henry was also reminded of home by the stream of people coming out with their complaints and petitions, just as in the old Angevin empire. They included 'two poor little women' from Chalgrove in Oxfordshire. Henry, 'moved by pious compassion' at their 'lamentable' sufferings, ordered the home government to give them full justice, notwithstanding the alleged oppressors being the household knights John de Plessis and Drogo de Barentin.[101]

HENRY, MAGNA CARTA AND WIDOWS

In another episode a few months later, prompted by intelligence from England, Henry behaved very differently both towards a woman and towards John de Plessis. It is an example of him struggling with the constraints imposed by Magna Carta's chapters on the treatment of

[96] *RG*, i, no. 584, for Walter Marshal.
[97] *F*, 254 (*CPR 1232–47*, 437).
[98] Paris, iv, 228–31 (not entirely accurate); *CR 1237–42*, 427, 453; *CR 1242–7*, 91; *CFR 1243–4*, no. 24.
[99] *CPR 1232–47*, 318, 320, 327, 331.
[100] *CR 1237–42*, 514.
[101] *RG*, i, no. 543 (*CPR 1232–47*, 333); *CR 1242–7*, 82.

widows of tenants-in-chief. As a general rule Henry did not, in contravention of the Charter, either charge widows for entry into the inheritances, marriage portions and dowers or force them into second marriages. Likewise he did not demand money for permission to stay single.[102] On one occasion he stated specifically that there should be no coercion in marriage 'since marriages should be free'.[103] What Henry did demand, although far less onerously than under King John, was money from widows for permission to marry whom they wished.[104] Such payments, Henry could argue, were allowed by the Charter since it laid down that widows needed the king's consent to remarry and did not forbid him charging for it. Henry also accepted that, since widows could choose to remain single, he had no absolute right to grant away their marriages. All he could grant, in the last resort, was any fine they might make to marry whom they wished. If they elected to stay single there would be no fine.

The frustration of these restrictions were shown towards the end of 1242 when Henry learnt that Margaret, in her own right countess of Warwick, was a widow.[105] As she had no children, she would bring Warwick castle and the lands of the earldom to any future husband.[106] On Christmas Day 1242, at Bordeaux, Henry granted her marriage to John de Plessis. Aware, however, of the Charter's restrictions, Henry added, that, if she refused the marriage, John was simply to have any fine she might make to marry freely.[107]

As it turned out, Margaret was indeed reluctant to marry John. She was after all surely being disparaged by the match. Henry, therefore, tried to exploit his right under the Charter to take security from widows that they did not marry without the king's consent. He also saw the need to justify his conduct to the probably sceptical governors at home. The result was a letter sent from Bordeaux in March 1243, one in a way so unkingly that

---

[102] See Waugh, *The Lordship of England*, 159–61; Carpenter, *Magna Carta*, 450–2; Annesley, 'The impact of Magna Carta on widows'. Since the Charter said widows were not to forced into remarriage, it clearly implied they should not have to offer money (as they frequently did under John) for permission to stay single.

[103] *RG*, i, suppl., no. 4552.

[104] In Henry's reign there were 44 such fines with an average value of 87 marks. In John's reign (where the fines often included permission to stay single), there were 149 fines with an average value of 278 marks: Waugh, *The Lordship of England*, 159, 161.

[105] She inherited after the death of her brother Thomas in June 1242. It is sometimes said that she subsequently married John Marshal, but the evidence cited shows no more than that she was married to him: *RG*, i, no. 396 (*CPR 1232–47*, 318). This is clarified in Ray, 'The lady doth protest'.

[106] The lands were, however, depleted by the dowers of previous countesses: Mason, 'Resources of the earldom of Warwick', 67–75.

[107] *RG*, i, no. 720 (*CPR 1232–47*, 352). For discussion of the marriage, see Mason, 'Resources of the earldom of Warwick', 67–75; Coss, *The Lady in Medieval England*, 121–3; Hanchett, 'Women in thirteenth-century Oxfordshire', 81–97; and Ray, 'The lady doth protest'.

Henry can only have dictated it himself.[108] He thus lamented rather
pathetically, but probably truly, that many noble ladies were spurning the
security they needed to give, and were going ahead and marrying whom
they pleased, this to the shame and damage of the crown.[109] The regents
were now to take possession of Warwick castle and other lands as a guarantee that Margaret did not do the same. With a rather loose sense of
geography, Henry added it was vital she married someone he trusted since
Warwick castle was near the Welsh march! By the end of the year
Margaret had indeed married John. Henry had certainly broken the spirit
of Magna Carta, but his efforts to stay within its letter show the Charter's
power.[110] It was a power before which, for the most part, he gave way.
Earlier in 1243, he had no success in pushing Isabella, widowed countess
of Arundel, into marrying Peter of Geneva.[111] The widows of tenants-in-
chief were far better off under Henry than they were under his father.

HENRY CONTINUES THE STRUGGLE

As his handling of the Warwick marriage at Bordeaux in December 1242
shows, Henry had not in fact gone home. Indeed, he was to remain in
Gascony until September 1243. This was the complete opposite of his
conduct in similar circumstances in 1230, when, under the tutelage of
Hubert de Burgh, Henry had gone home and left the earls of Chester and
Pembroke to continue the fighting. This time the earls went and Henry
stayed. He was moved by the sense of honour seen in his letters to the
emperor, by a genuine belief that the war could still be won, and then,
when clearly it could not, by the desire to set Gascony in order.

If, however, Henry showed here a stubborn determination, it was, as so
often, of sedentary kind. Of the roughly fourteen months in Gascony
between August 1242 and September 1243, he spent all but four of them in
Bordeaux itself, making indeed only three excursions from the city. During
these fourteen months the military forces of Gascony were summoned on no
fewer than seven occasions to carry on the war or deal with internal unrest,
but this did not mean the king was there to lead them. Those mustering in
September were told that they would meet either the king 'or one of our men
whom we will send'. Understandably, if unfairly, Matthew Paris thought the
king with his queen was just idling in Bordeaux wasting money.[112]

---

[108] *CR 1242–7*, 61.

[109] In the fine rolls between 1234 and 1258 there are seventeen fines from men for having
married widows without the king's permission. There seems to have been no organized
system for taking security.

[110] Carpenter, *Magna Carta*, 450–1.

[111] *CPR 1232–47*, 377. For Isabella, see below, 553–4.

[112] *RG*, i, no. 594.

During this period, with the earls back home, Henry was very much guided by ministers such as John Mansel and John fitzGeoffrey, who were both briefly seneschals of Gascony, and William Longespée, who acted as the captain of Henry's military forces. Longespée was encouraged by a promise that his claims to Salisbury castle and the county of Wiltshire would receive immediate judgement on the king's return.[113] John de Burgh, son of Hubert, also remained with Henry. When Hubert died in May 1243, 'full of days after many variations of fortune', Henry allowed John to succeed to his father's estates without paying a relief. Mansel himself 'strenuous in arms and unafraid in spirit', as Paris put it, had his leg broken during a siege by stones throne by the defenders. Henry rewarded Mansel's doctor (sent by Peter of Savoy) with a valuable benefice and later was able to laugh about the affair: in humorous verses by the court poet, Henry of Avranches, he threatens the doctor with death if Mansel's leg does not heal.[114]

Henry's stay depended very much on local support. In return for pay he was able to raise military forces of several hundred knights and sergeants from the local nobility. He was also supported by loans especially from Bordeaux. During his period overseas the wardrobe received nearly £5,000 from the mayor, commune, individual citizens and the archbishop.[115] Henry's credit rating remained high. Most of the loans were repayable at the English exchequer, where the Gascons knew there was a regular flow of money. The exchequer was also sending large sums of money out to Gascony: 5,100 marks in October 1242, another 10,000 marks in December, 12,000 marks in March or April 1243 and 6,000 marks in October, a total of 33,100 marks or £22,066. In addition the king received £1,000 from the issues of the bishopric of Winchester and 2,000 marks from Ireland. The wardrobe accounts show that, between October 1242 and September 1243, Henry spent nearly £24,000 in Gascony. Of this, £17,550 went on 'diverse gifts to the countess of Bigorre, the count of Bigorre and others in parts across the sea'. Only £288 came from local revenues (mostly from a hearth tax).[116]

---

[113] *RG*, i, nos. 528, 531; Paris, iv, 243–4; *CFR 1242–3*, no. 527. The claim to the 'comitatus' of Wiltshire seems also to have been a claim to the earldom of Salisbury. William Longespée was the son of Ela, in her own right countess of Salisbury, and her husband William Longespée, who died in 1226. On his mother becoming a nun at Lacock abbey in 1238 (she was subsequently abbess and died in 1261), he sought to prove his right to the earldom, as well as Salisbury castle and the county of Wiltshire. He was ultimately unsuccessful, apparently because it was considered that Ela did not hold in hereditary right. In a conversation with the pope in 1247, narrated by Matthew Paris, Longespée acknowledged that he had been denied the earldom 'judicaliter' and not 'in anger or by an act of will'. Paris, iv, 630 and *BNB*, iii, 248–9. For a discussion, see Ellis, *Earldoms in Fee*, 202–3.

[114] Paris, iv, 236–7; *CPR 1232–47*, 384; Henry of Avranches, 137–9, 157; Liu, 'John Mansel', 33–5, where there is a translation of the poem by Lesley Boatwright.

[115] Wild, *WA*, ciii, 45.

[116] Wild, *WA*, ciiii–iv, 48; *CPR 1232–47*, 355, 372, 384, 394; *CLR 1240–5*, 179.

Henry, therefore, with Louis IX out of the way, was quite able to remain in Gascony and try to reverse the verdict of the previous summer. He seized the lands of Lusignans and other deserters in the isle of Oléron, began to construct a castle on the isle of Ré, and, with help from Bayonne, sought to reinforce the blockade of La Rochelle.[117] Indeed, Henry persuaded himself that the men of the town, hearing a secret message from the mayor of Bayonne, might come over to his side.[118] In the sphere of diplomacy, Henry's immediate hopes centred on his alliance with Raymond, count of Toulouse. The count's fortunes during the summer had fluctuated. On the one hand, he had gained possession of Narbonne, and many had joined his cause including the citizens of Albi. Yet he had also been excommunicated once again for conniving, so it was said, in the murder of papal inquisitors investigating the Cathar heresy in Avignonet.[119] The count now came to see Henry at Bordeaux and, at the end of August, they swore a lifelong pact to help each other against the king of France.[120] Supported by this alliance, Raymond went off to make good his claim to the Agenais, while Henry summoned Gascon nobles to join William Longespée in the Perigord.[121]

Henry had other reasons for optimism. In September, Richard de Burgh arrived with forces from Ireland.[122] Next month there were further reinforcements led by Philip Basset and John de Grey, household knights, who stayed for the rest of the campaign. Henry had big plans. He asked the regents to send him 50,000 marks, 400 knights, 800 sergeants and 5,000 Welsh and Irish foot-soldiers. They were also to continue the king's alms in England and maintain the work on the feretory of St Edward: 'there is no one,' Henry told them, 'who can impede the king's alms and works without incurring his indignation'.[123]

All of these requests were urged on in a series of passionate letters filled with a mixture of aspiration, frustration and recrimination. The regents were told that nothing prevented the king recovering his inheritance save lack of money.[124] They were accused of growing cold in their affection for the king now he was absent. After mounting criticism of his personal performance, Bishop Mauclerc was eventually dismissed. 'It is time,' Henry told him waspishly, 'that you attend to the salvation of your soul.' Characteristically, the dismissal was soon reversed. Roger the king's almoner was also recalled despite the 'sharp words' Henry had addressed to him.[125]

[117] CR 1237–42, 505; CPR 1232–47, 340–1, 352.
[118] RG, i, no. 508 (CPR 1232–47, 329).
[119] Puylaurens, 102–6.
[120] F, 248–9; CPR 1232–47, 319, 338.
[121] RG, i, nos. 11, 24.
[122] Richard died in Gascony in January 1243.
[123] CR 1237–42, 514–15, 518, 522.
[124] CR 1237–42, 532–3.
[125] CR 1237–42, 514–15, 518–19, 532–3; CR 1242–7, 58.

It was all in vain. Count Raymond was soon confronted by the forces Louis sent against him led by his former ally Hugh de Lusignan. By 20 October negotiations for a settlement had begun with the count blaming the evil counsel that had led him into war. Eventually, by the peace of Lorris, in January 1243 the count accepted all the terms of the 1229 peace of Paris, which meant that Louis's brother, Alphonse, would be his successor.[126] Raymond's decision was not surprising. At Bordeaux he must have sized Henry up and seen he was not a man to lead a successful military campaign. Henry had also, in their treaty, hedged around his promises of support. He would do nothing to fall foul of the pope and so would not help the count if Louis IX invaded Toulouse under the papal banner. Raymond had also come at a bad time for, until the arrival of 5,100 marks in October, Henry was out of funds. He had to apologize to William Longespée for failing to send all the troops demanded.[127] The 5,100 marks itself was soon exhausted. In order to raise 500 marks for the countess of Bigorre, Henry was reduced to handing over to her the vestments and ornaments of his chapel stored at Bordeaux. When John Mansel told him these would only raise 200 marks, he threw in 'the most precious image of the Virgin Mary' as well, although begging the countess to pawn the items in a reputable place so he could recover them.[128]

Under the blow of Raymond's defection, Henry remained resolute. In November (when he probably knew what was afoot), he left Bordeaux and went to La Réole, where the castle was strengthened. He still hoped something might come from a blockade of La Rochelle, although the castle on the isle of Ré was taking longer than expected.[129] In January 1243 he told the emperor he intended to stay in Gascony to attack his enemies and 'restore his state'. He stopped his father-in-law, the count of Provence, from using his good offices to broker a truce.[130] Henry was encouraged by the presence at his Christmas court of the countess of Béarn. Her son, Gaston, did homage to Henry on Christmas Day. (The same day Henry gave the Warwick marriage to John de Plessis.)[131] Yet a truce was inevitable. The regents did their best, but there was no way they could send Henry 50,000 marks or the military forces he demanded. Henry could deal with local troubles in Gascony but totally lacked the resources to carry the war back into the Saintonge and Poitou. He was also under pressure from home because the ships of the Cinque Ports and elsewhere had lost as much as they had gained from the war at sea. In addition Thomas

---

[126] *Layettes*, ii, nos. 2995–6, 3012–13, 3017.

[127] *RG*, i, no. 464.

[128] *CR 1237–42*, 519, 523–4; *CR 1242–7*, I.

[129] *CPR 1232–47*, 343.

[130] *RG*, i, nos. 676, 1197, 1200–1 (*CPR 1232–47*, 348, 399).

[131] *RG*, i, no. 721 (*CPR 1232–47*, 352).

of Savoy, the count of Flanders, the king's 'beloved uncle', warned that from February 1243 he would have to declare war on English merchants.[132]

Thus it was that a truce was agreed to run from 21 March 1243 to Michaelmas 1248. It left Louis in possession of the lands and allegiances he had gained during the war, which meant he had control of Poitou and the Saintonge. Henry also had to give up, despite all his efforts, his stake in the isle of Ré. Whereas Henry asked for three adherents to be included in the treaty, Louis asked for over thirty, all of them men who had been on Henry's side during the war: the count of Toulouse, Hugh de Lusignan, Geoffrey de Lusignan, William Larchevêque, Reginald de Pons and so on down the list of Henry's old adherents and pensioners; a humiliating indication of the scale of his defeat.[133]

Having agreed the truce, Henry decided to return to England after Easter (12 April). He ordered fifteen candles of his height to burn around the shrine of Edward the Confessor at Westminster until his arrival. The sword of St Paul, the keys of St Peter and the crowns of Saints Edward and Edmund on their statues at Westminster were to be gilded. In addition, two great lions were to be painted in the gable of the king's chamber, as if to make up in art for the failures on the battlefield.[134] But in the event Henry did not come home. Instead he remained in Gascony until September, another five months. Henry's aim was altogether laudable. He realized he needed to stay longer for 'the better conservation of the peace and stability of our land of Gascony', a land riven by factional disputes in the towns (one broke out in Bordeaux in April) and subject to external threats.[135]

At the end of April, Henry, therefore, embarked on the kind of governmental tour he so rarely undertook in England, one which took him to Bazas, St-Sever, Dax and Bayonne, before returning to Bordeaux where he remained for the final four months of his stay. Henry now displayed his piety to his subjects. He made gifts to the local friars, gave vestments to the churches and at Bayonne ordered a chapel to be constructed in honour of St Edward.[136] His aim, acting 'for the public health', was to find compromises between the factions in the towns, while at the same time, in modest fashion, maintaining his own rights. These were the kind of palliating policies at which he was good.[137] In Bordeaux, where there were two dominant factions, Henry laid down that they should be equally represented each year amongst the ruling jurats.[138] Perhaps as a result of this

---

[132] *RG*, i, no. 753; Paris, iv, 238–9; *F*, 250 (*CPR 1266–72*, 725).

[133] *RG*, i, no. 1212 (*CPR 1232–47*, 401–3).

[134] *CR 1242–7*, 19–21.

[135] *RG*, i, no. 980 (*CPR 1232–47*, 376); *CR 1242–7*, 21. For Henry in this period, see Pelissie du Rausas, 'The reconfiguration of Plantagenet Power in Gascony, 1242–1243'.

[136] *CR 1242–7*, 25; *RG*, i, nos. 1769, 1781, 1783–5.

[137] For settlements, see *RG*, i, nos. 980, 1022, 1210, 1214–15, 1230 (*CPR 1232–47*, 376, 381, 401, 403–4, 406).

[138] *RL*, ii, 89–90 (*CPR 1247–58*, 158).

compromise, in April 1243 the mayoralty passed from the Solers family to the Coloms, where it remained for the next three years. Gailard Colom, the head of the family, had been the greatest lender to Henry (to the tune of £990) and thus the city was in the hands of someone very ready to support the English connection: not surprisingly he was deeply engaged in the wine trade.[139]

Henry took steps for the future government of Gascony. In June he made one of his best household knights, Nicholas de Molis, seneschal and put the office on a firm footing with a fee of 1,000 marks a year.[140] He also appointed his clerk Henry of Wingham to receive the local revenues at the abbey of Holy Cross at Bordeaux. With the seneschal he was to audit the accounts of the individual bailiffs.[141] Henry eventually summoned a general gathering of Gascons to Bordeaux for the last week of July to say goodbye, but alarms detained him further, although they did not shift him from Bordeaux.[142] In one portent of trouble to come, the vicomte of Gramont (on Gascony's southernmost frontier) left Henry's allegiance for that of the king of Navarre. Henry advised Molis and Longespée not to provoke the king, unless they were sure of a good outcome, but otherwise he left the matter to their discretion: 'you know far more about the area than I do'.[143]

During these last months Henry felt a great deal of gratitude to his queen, who had stood by him through all the tedium and traumas. On 17 August he gave Eleanor the county of Chester as her dower in place of various scattered manors, a tremendous increase in her potential power after Henry's death. The witnesses to the relevant charters were the Savoyard bishop of Hereford and Eleanor's uncle, Philip of Savoy, who had just brought Sanchia out to Gascony, prior to her journey to England for her marriage to Richard of Cornwall. Henry gave strict orders to the exchequer to pay Philip 1,000 marks for his expenses.[144]

Henry finally set sail in mid-September. The atmosphere on board ship was light-hearted and Henry had some fun at the expense of his clerk Peter the Poitevin. He made up a whole series of debts that Peter had incurred for various fanciful misdemeanours and ordered these to be enrolled on the fine roll. They included five dozen capons owed for an unspecified trespass on board ship, £100 that Peter had promised the king also on the ship, and money owed for selling wine at ridiculously high prices. The idea, obviously, was for Peter to look at the roll and think

[139] Marsh, *English Rule in Gascony*, 92–3; Wild, *WA*, 45.

[140] *RG*, i, nos. 648, 651–2, 819, 936, 1000, 1009 (*CPR 1232–47*, 345, 361, 372, 379–80).

[141] *RG*, i, nos. 1034–5, 1166, 1228, 1232; Studd, 'Reconfiguring the Angevin empire', 36. Molis's fee was smaller than the £1,000 received by Henry Hoese (*CLR 1226–40*, 361), but it was sugared by a gift of 500 marks.

[142] *CR 1242–7*, 35, 57.

[143] *CR 1242–7*, 70.

[144] *RG*, i, no. 1143 (*CPR 1232–47*, 394), 1180; Howell, *Eleanor of Provence*, 36–7.

'Great heavens, what is going on?!' Henry, however, was careful not to let the joke go too far and cause confusion when the copy of the fine rolls reached the exchequer. When Peter was not looking, he ordered the entry to be crossed out![145]

Henry landed at Portsmouth to an elaborate welcome organized by the regents, his treasure being replenished by all the gifts of gold, jewels and silver. At Winchester and London he was met by processions of citizens in their best clothes. For his arrival at Westminster, Henry had ordered as many candles to burn as on the feast of Edward the Confessor. In the event, he was able, with perfect timing to arrive on 13 October, the day itself. Matthew Paris thought the number of candles burnt 'incredible'.

As sometimes with Henry, the ritual had a mixed response. Matthew Paris spoke of the 'pomp of inane glory'.[146] Henry, of course, had failed. That failure was decisive for the future of southern France for it meant the county of Toulouse would indeed fall to the Capetians after the count's death in 1248. It was equally decisive for the future of Henry's continental possessions. He never made another attempt to recover them. The failure of the 1242 campaign thus laid the foundations for the surrender of his claims to Poitou, Anjou and Normandy in the 1259 Treaty of Paris. Henry had shown courage and determination in seizing the golden opportunity presented by the rebellion of the Lusignans. He was right to do so. The trouble was he had neither the character nor resources to drive forward a successful campaign. He was no English leopard. Yet Henry's piety still won respect. Matthew Paris quoted Louis IX as telling Henry's critics to be silent: 'his alms and masses will save him from all shame and dangers'.[147]

[145] See Carpenter, 'The sense of humour of Henry III'.

[146] *CR 1242–7*, 41–2, 129–30; *CLR 1240–5*, 205–6; Paris, iv, 254–5; Dunstable, 162; Wild, *WA*, 46.

[147] Paris, iv, 231–2, 255.

Chapter 6

THE PIETY OF HENRY III

King Henry III was widely regarded by his contemporaries as a 'rex Christianissimus', 'a most Christian king'. Everything we know about his religious practices confirms that opinion. In some areas, notably the distribution of alms and the hearing of masses, he was doing what all his predecessors had done, but on a new scale and with a new intensity. In other areas, notably in his efforts to convert the Jews to Christianity and his adoption of Edward the Confessor as his patron saint, he was doing something very new. His devotion to the Confessor, in particular, became central to his life and led to the greatest monument of his kingship, the rebuilding of Westminster Abbey.

One reason for Henry's piety was almost certainly his father's reputation for impiety. He was bound to wonder about King John's sufferings in the afterlife and wish to avoid anything like them himself.[1] Henry also lived in a new spiritual environment, one created by the decrees of the Fourth Lateran Council, the work of pastorally minded bishops, the preaching and example of the friars, and the ideas developed in the twelfth century about purgatory, confession, penance and the eucharist.[2]

THE FUNDAMENTALS OF THE FAITH

In the diocescan statutes, issued early in Henry's minority by Richard le Poore, bishop of Salisbury, the clergy were urged to instruct their parishioners in 'the articles of the faith without which there is no salvation'. In those articles, we may be sure, Henry had a good grounding. His guardian, Peter des Roches, in his own statutes for Winchester told his priests to teach the Lord's Prayer, the Apostles' Creed and the faith of the Trinity, passion and incarnation. Henry in later life called himself a 'friend of the Holy Trinity' and had its image set up in the chamber of the Franciscan friars at Clarendon. Representations of Christ's passion on the cross were ubiquitous in his chapels. The Annunciation of the Virgin Birth was painted at the entrance to the queen's chapel at Havering, and featured in

---

[1] See above, 55.
[2] For a study of art and religion between 1170 and 1300 which connects at many points with the discussion in this chapter, see Binski, *Becket's Crown*.

the great statues of the angel Gabriel and Mary still surviving above the inner door of Westminster Abbey's chapter house.[3]

Henry heard the Lord's Prayer every day at mass and almost certainly made it the centrepiece of his private devotions.[4] According to the statutes of the bishop of Coventry issued between 1224 and 1237, every Christian man and woman was to say it seven times a day:[5]

Pater noster qui est in celis sanctificetur nomen tuum. Adveniat regnum tuum. Fiat voluntas tua sicut in celo et in terra.

(Our father who art in Heaven, hallowed be thy name. Thy kingdom come. Thy will be done in earth as it is in heaven.)

Panem nostrum cotidianum da nobis hodie.

(Give us this day our daily bread.)

Et dimitte nobis debita nostra sicut et nos dimittimus debitoribus nostris.

(And forgive us our trespasses as we forgive those who trespass against us.)

Et ne nos inducas in temptacionem. Sed libera nos a malo. Amen.

(And lead us not into temptation. But deliver us from evil. Amen.)

'Give us this day our daily bread . . . deliver us from evil', bread and evil, here, of course, being both material and spiritual. For a king so often in perplexity and sometimes in danger, how consoling and strengthening these words were. How earnestly Henry must have prayed with them.

If Henry followed the practice enjoined in the Coventry statutes, he would have said the Creed twice every day. So with all the faithful Henry affirmed his belief in God making Heaven and Earth; in Christ, the son of God, 'for us men and our salvation' coming down from Heaven and, incarnate by the Holy Ghost and the Virgin Mary, been made man. Crucified 'for us' and buried, he had risen again and ascended into Heaven to sit with the father. In the end he would come again to judge both the quick and the dead. His kingdom would have no end. 'I look for the resurrection of the dead and the life of the world to come', the Creed concluded. How earnestly Henry must have prayed those words too.

The Lord's Prayer and the Creed showed God's saving power but gave no precise instructions about behaviour on earth. Here, of course, there were other teachings. Robert Grosseteste, in his statutes for the Lincoln

---

[3] *CLR 1245–51*, 297, 372; Borenius, 'Cycle of images', 47–50. For Henry as friend of the Holy Trinity, see below, 347.

[4] For Louis IX at prayer, see Le Goff, *Saint Louis*, 766–74.

[5] *C&S*, i, 213, cap. 20. The bishop was Alexander of Stavensby.

diocese, told his priests to expound the Ten Commandments to their parishioners with their warnings against idolatry, Sabbath breaking, murder, adultery, theft, slander and covetousness and their injunctions to honour parents and not take the name of the Lord in vain. The priests were also to warn against the seven deadly sins.[6] In the Coventry diocese they were given a special tract going into detail about the nature of pride, envy, anger, sloth ('called in English "idleness" in the service of God'), avarice, luxury and gluttony.[7] Henry himself doubtless heard and marked sermons along such lines. In the window splays of his great chamber at Westminster were painted figures of the Virtues triumphing over the Vices, including 'debonereté' trampling down 'anger' and 'largesse' trampling down covetousness.[8]

For all his famed 'simplicity', Henry was far from a passive recipient of what he was told. He lamented that the friar William of Abingdon no longer engaged him in spiritual conversation and just said 'give, give, give'.[9] He commissioned Lives of the Confessor from Matthew Paris and the poet Henry of Avranches. He asked Robert Grosseteste what the ceremony of anointing added to the royal dignity. He bothered the legate Ottobuono with the question of whether 'remission of sins' was the same as 'remission of all sins'. Ottobuono was dismissive and told Henry he should stick to secular affairs, but Grosseteste sent back a long letter explaining all the gifts of the Holy Spirit that unction brought. How far Henry was familiar with Grosseteste's works of pastoral instruction we do not know. He would have profited from the view that virtues were a 'mean between two vices' so that 'largesse' was the opposite not just of 'cupidity' but also of 'prodigality'![10]

At the heart of Henry's religion was his belief in the guiding hand of God.[11] In 1255 he observed that 'the governance of kingdoms cannot prosper, nor be happily administered, without him in whose disposition are all kingdoms and through whom all things are governed'. In the same year, Henry decided to pursue a project against all advice, 'directing our eyes to the king of heaven and commander of the stars, who since he is able to rule the sea and the winds . . . will be able to convert turmoil into tranquility and darkness into light'.[12] For some these might have been conventional statements. Henry nevertheless believed them profoundly.

[6] C&S, i, 268, cap. 1.

[7] C&S, i, 214–20.

[8] Binski, Painted Chamber, 41.

[9] Thomas of Eccleston, 46. According to Eccleston, he called William a 'serpent'.

[10] Letters of Grosseteste, no. 124; Graham, 'Letters of Cardinal Ottoboni', 102–3; Grosseteste, Templum Dei, 51–2; Binski, Becket's Crown, 186.

[11] For Hubert de Burgh expressing the same sentiments, see above, 90, 145, 156.

[12] CR 1254–6, 215–16, 407, and below, 637. The project was to make his second son king of Sicily.

HELL, PURGATORY AND HEAVEN

Like all devout Christians, Henry grew up facing the prospect of judgement after death. Peter des Roches, during his period as Henry's guardian, explained its consequences. To those who had practised works of piety and mercy, God promised 'the glory of a celestial kingdom'. To those who had neglected them, he would mete out 'the punishment of eternal fire'.[13] Henry himself ordered the last 'dread judgement' to be painted both in Nottingham castle and in St Stephen's chapel, the principal chapel in his palace at Westminster. Almost certainly the same subject was sculpted above the main entrance to Westminster Abbey.[14] The message of such depictions was all too clear. Beneath Christ, seated in judgement, were, on his right, the blessed ascending into heaven, on his left the damned being dragged down by gloating devils into the jaws of hell. When he met John, soon to be king, beneath the Last Judgement portal at Fontevraud in 1199, Bishop Hugh of Lincoln gave a homily on the subject. Pointing to the kings in full regalia descending to hell, he told John to 'fix your mind always on their howls and perpetual torment, and let your heart dwell on their unceasing punishment . . . you will thus learn the great risks those incur who for a short space of time are set over others as rulers, and, by not ruling themselves, are eternally tortured by demons'.[15]

Henry received similar warnings. Grosseteste told William of Raleigh that government policy (over the law of bastardy) risked the king being handed over to the fires of hell.[16] Grosseteste also waxed lyrical about the 'ineffable joys' of heaven. As he explained in a letter to Richard Marshal, the blessed would bask in a light with no shadows, possess a knowledge of all truth, rest from all activity and, looking upon God, sing his praises for evermore.[17] Henry was naturally determined to get there. In 1255 he asked for prayers that God might 'so mercifully direct our acts to the praise of his name and the exaltation of the catholic faith, that having completed the curriculum of this present life, we may attain the reward of eternal felicity'.[18]

As Henry pondered portrayals of the Last Judgement, he was faced with many questions.[19] The most obvious was when it would be. Grosseteste's view was that the date was 'altogether uncertain but it is certain to be in a short time'.[20] There was indeed a proliferation of literature in the

[13] Vincent, *EEA Winchester*, 50 (in an indulgence for St Thomas' Hospital, Southwark).

[14] *CLR 1251–60*, 11; *CR 1247–51*, 311. For suggestions about the Last Judgement portal, see Roberts, 'Relic of the Holy Blood', 132–42.

[15] Adam of Eynsham, 140. The account is, however, coloured by John's later conduct, being written in the midst of the Interdict.

[16] For this issue, see above, 185–7.

[17] *Letters of Grosseteste*, 70–3, 122, 210, 237.

[18] *CR 1254–6*, 215–16.

[19] I am grateful to David D'Avray for many discussions of the subject.

[20] *Letters of Grosseteste*, 360. For a discussion, see Southern, *Robert Grosseteste*, 282–5.

thirteenth century prophesying that the last days were nigh. In England in 1248 a rumour spread that the Day of Judgement was to be 17 September and Henry, according to the Waverley annalist, spent the night without sleep in fear, prayer and devotion.[21] Another much favoured date was 1250. Matthew Paris, however, while recording prophecies and portents, remained far from convinced the Last Judgement was imminent and perhaps Henry, outside scares like that of 1248, took the same view.[22] The date for the end of the world given in a riddle on the High Altar pavement he installed in Westminster Abbey was 19,683![23]

If then there was still some time to go, Henry, like all Christians, faced another question. What happened to the soul after death while awaiting the Last Judgement?

Fortunately, by Henry's time new light had been shed on the whole question by the Paris school of theologians led by Peter the Chanter, a school of which Stephen Langton was a leading member.[24] Here there was an initial judgement immediately after death.[25] Those who had died with mortal sins, unrepented, unconfessed and heavy of their heads, went straight to hell. The pure and the righteous went at once to heaven. The great bulk of mankind, however, in different degrees neither wholly bad, nor wholly good, went to purgatory. There those who had failed to confess their sins, perhaps through ignorance as to their faults, would be both purged and punished. Those who had confessed and were already purged through the church's absolution would simply be punished, punished if they had failed to complete the penance laid down by the church or if the penance enjoined was considered insufficient, which, in the case of mortal sins, was highly likely to be the case.

Much light on the progress of those in purgatory was shed by visions of the afterlife. In 1226, King John appeared to a monk of St Albans. He was being tortured in heavy burning robes, but expressed the hope that, through the 'ineffable grace and mercy of God', he would be saved, so evidently he was in purgatory rather than in hell. Six years later the bishop of Rochester saw both King Richard and Stephen Langton exit from purgatory on the same day, Richard after thirty-three years and Langton after only four. Both entered 'the sight of the divine Majesty', so this was heaven very much as envisaged by Grosseteste.[26] One Franciscan friar, Warin of Orwell, made quicker progress and 'passed through purgatory without delay and went to the Lord Jesus Christ'. Another friar was less

---

[21] Waverley, 343–4. Henry was not that shaken for the next day he was busy ordering building works at Oxford: CLR 1245–51, 200.

[22] For Paris, see Weiler, 'History, prophecy and the apocalypse'.

[23] Foster, Patterns of Thought, 98.

[24] Le Goff, La Naissance du Purgatoire, 224–7; Watkins, History and the Supernatural, 180–2.

[25] See Paul in I Corinthians 3:10–15; Le Goff, La Naissance du Purgatoire, 297.

[26] Wendover/Paris, iii, 112–13, 212, and see also 143–5.

lucky. He went confidently into purgatory only to find himself grievously suffering in his feet, this because he had frequently gone to visit a certain woman. She was devout so no problem there, but he should have been devoting himself to his lectures instead. Here was an example of a sin unconsciously committed and thus unconfessed, so needing both purgation and punishment after death. At least the form of punishment showed the friar had gone on foot. One wonders what would have happened had he, contrary to the rules of his order, gone on horseback![27] Some visions gave very detailed pictures of the afterlife. One recorded by Roger of Wendover, in the year before Henry's birth, runs to over eighteen printed pages in a modern edition, and was later copied verbatim by Matthew Paris into his own chronicle. Since Henry got to know Paris well, he may well have heard about it.[28] Here, in an out-of-body experience, a peasant from Stisted in Essex, Turchill by name, witnessed the excruciating tortures suffered by the damned in hell, the painful passage of souls through purgatory and then the joys of heaven where the souls now purged and punished were welcomed by their patron saints and presented to the sight of God. Turchill's tour, however, ended abruptly. It was realized that the friends pouring water over his apparently lifeless body back in Stisted were in danger of suffocating the poor chap, so he was hurried home. The relation of his experiences in after times moved many to tears and repentance.

In another vision, related by Wendover and Paris under the year 1228, the baron Roger de Tony, suffering in purgatory, said he hoped to be saved at least in part by the good works of his brother.[29] Here he touched on a central feature of purgatorial thinking, namely the belief the living could help the dead, most notably by offering up alms and masses and doing other good works for the benefit of their souls. In Turchill's vision, one reason why souls spent so long in purgatory was because they lacked the assistance of such special masses. The unfortunate friar tortured in his feet begged for masses from his friends on earth. King John too, in Matthew Paris's version of Wendover's story, hoped to be saved 'by the large distribution of alms by my son Henry and by the honour he gives, devoted to God, to divine service'.[30]

Henry certainly believed in the value of alms and masses for the dead.[31] On the demise of his mother, he fed all the clerks and friars of Oxford and Cambridge, and made a grant to Westminster Abbey so that, in perpetuity,

---

[27] Thomas of Eccleston, 52, 97–8.

[28] Wendover, *Flores*, ii, 16–35; Paris, ii, 497–511; with a translation in Giles, *Flowers of History*, ii, 221–35.

[29] Wendover/Paris, 143–5.

[30] Wendover/Paris, 112–13.

[31] For what follows, see Dixon-Smith, 'Feeding the poor', ch. 4 (Who was remembered?), and see her 'Image and reality', 89–91. For John's concern for the souls of his mother, father and other relations, see Webster, *King John and Religion*, 88–95.

a chaplain could celebrate mass daily for her soul.[32] On the death of his favourite sister, the empress Isabella, the numbers to be fed rose to 102,000.[33] Other beneficiaries included Henry's sister Joan, queen of Scotland, his wife's uncle William, bishop-elect of Valence, his cousin and captive Eleanor of Brittany, his father-in-law, Raymond Berengar, count of Provence, his youngest daughter Katherine and his sister-in-law Sanchia, wife of Richard of Cornwall. Henry clearly thought purgatory might last a long time. In 1244, 10,000 poor were fed for the soul of Edith, queen of Edward the Confessor, who had died in 1075. If Henry had heard of Richard's purported passage out of purgatory, he took no chances, and continued to feed paupers for the benefit of his soul.[34]

As for King John, did Henry altogether measure up to his father's hopes? There were some curious lapses. Henry failed to keep up to date with the annual payment John conceded to Reading abbey. (John was here honouring its most famous relic, a hand of St James.)[35] He also back-tracked on a promise to give Croxton abbey (where John's entrails were buried) an endowment within the royal manor of Finedon, finding what seems a less satisfactory substitute.[36] On the other hand, in 1232 he granted the monks of Worcester the church of Bromsgrove so they had funds to celebrate John's anniversary and then, 'desiring to help our father's soul', took steps to see they made as much money from the gift as possible. In 1242 he had 1,000 poor fed on John's anniversary and later gave Worcester a valuable cope 'for his commemoration'. (Mass was to be celebrated in it on Christmas day.) Henry also supported the work on John's foundation at Beaulieu and was present, with the rest of the royal family, at its consecration in 1246.[37]

PENANCE AND PREACHING

Roger de Tony, in the pains of purgatory, was not entirely dependent on the suffrages of his friends and relations to get him out. He also gained hope from the good deeds he had done on earth, notably one in honour of the Virgin Mary. Clearly central to salvation was the individual's behaviour as a Christian. Here, keeping men and women on the right path, an essential role was played by the sacraments of the church. 'I believe in one

---

[32] *CLR 1245–51*, 71; *CChR 1226–57*, 304.

[33] *CLR 1240–5*, 124.

[34] *CLR 1240–5*, 210.

[35] *Reading Cartulary*, i, nos. 42, 46, 58, 74; Webster, *King John and Religion*, 53–5.

[36] For this saga, see *RLC*, i, 295b, 296b; *RLC*, ii, 175b; *Patent Roll 1225–32*, 55, 264–5; *CFR 1226–7*, no. 141; *CChR 1226–57*, 131. In 1230, Finedon was given to Stephen of Seagrave: *CChR 1226–57*, 116.

[37] *CChR 1226–57*, 154; *CR 1234–7*, 341; *CLR 1240–5*, 151; *CR 1242–7*, 270; *CR 1253–4*, 143. See Engel, *Worcester Cathedral*, 160–2; Webster, *King John and Religion*, 178–9, 184–90. The initial gift to Worcester was made while attending John's reburial in the cathedral.

catholic and apostolic church. I acknowledge one baptism for the remission of sins', ran the creed. As Bishop Poore's statutes explained, baptism,
the first of the sacraments, the door to all the others, washed away original
sin (that incurred by the fall in the Garden of Eden), and was to be
followed immediately by confirmation, thus strengthening the faith of
those baptized and arming them against the works of the devil.[38] Baptism
and confirmation, however, would never be enough, for, as Bishop
Cantilupe of Worcester explained, 'every age of man from youth onwards
is inclined to evil ... and human frailty falls into sin'. Fortunately,
Cantilupe continued, 'divine mercy' had provided a 'remedy', 'namely the
sacrament of penance'. Through this the new nature achieved by baptism
but lost again through subsequent sin could be restored.[39] Thinking about
the sacrament, like the thinking about purgatory, had been transformed by
the work of the Paris schools in the latter part of the twelfth century. As
a tract attached to the Coventry statutes explained, reflecting closely the
views of Peter the Chanter, the sacrament was broken down into three
distinct elements: 'contrition of heart, confession by mouth, and satisfaction by works'.[40] Priests, therefore, had first to discover whether those
coming to confession were truly penitent and then decide an appropriate
penance. As a famous provision of the Fourth Lateran Council put it, they
needed, like a practised doctor pouring wine and oil into the wounds of
the injured, to enquire diligently into the circumstances both of the sinner
and the sin. They were then to choose intelligently what type of advice
to give and what type of remedy to apply, with 'various means availing to
heal the sick'.[41]

The canons of the Council laid down that everyone was to confess at
least once a year and at least once a year receive the sacrament of the
eucharist. The two sacraments were inextricably linked, for without
penance (in the threefold sense described above) one could not be purged
of sin and thus could not proceed to the vivifying unity with Christ promised in the eucharist. All this placed an awesome responsibility on the
priest. A series of manuals were prepared to help his work. The one
attached to the Coventry statutes explained (in conventional fashion)
the enquiries to be made as to the circumstances of the sin: 'who, what,
where, with whose help, why, in what way, when', providing detailed
examples under each heading. It then refused (turning its back on old
practices) to define any certain penances. The priest, echoing the decree
of the Fourth Lateran Council, was not to be like a foolish doctor
prescribing one remedy for all the sick. The tract did, however, explain

---

[38] *C&S*, i, 65–71.
[39] *C&S*, i, 303, cap. 21. I owe the translation to Daniel Hadas, as also discussion of the
passage.
[40] *C&S*, i, 220.
[41] *EHD*, 654–5, cap. 21.

that 'satisfaction consisted in three things especially: fast, prayer and alms'. Fast was suitable for carnal sins; prayer for spiritual ones; alms covered everything. Best were all three together.[42]

The sacraments of penance and the eucharist were intimately linked to preaching and teaching, for, unless the individuals knew the rules of right behaviour, how could they know they had transgressed, how could they receive the 'infusion of grace' leading to contrition and confession and thence to communion? The Franciscan friar Hamo of Faversham thus preached to the people on Easter Sunday 'lest any should communicate in mortal sin'. As a result, many put off their communion until they had confessed to Hamo, and indeed he sat in church for three days hearing confessions.[43]

When it came to preaching, a revolution in practice was taking place, as the activity of Hamo indicated. The canons of the Fourth Lateran Council instructed bishops to appoint men to travel their dioceses and carry out 'the office of sacred preaching'.[44] The men to whom the bishops turned were the friars. St Dominic, a priest from Castile, had conceived his movement as an order of preachers to battle against the Albigensian heretics. In 1217 he extended the mission worldwide and his followers were soon organized into territorial provinces with an elaborate system of elected officials. Dominic was inspired by the vision of 'the apostolic life', the life led by Christ and his apostles. This was equally the case with St Francis, the son of a cloth merchant from Assisi. A revelatory passage for him had been Matthew 10:7–9, where Christ sent out the apostles, declaring, 'As you go preach, saying the kingdom of heaven is at hand . . . provide neither gold, nor silver, nor brass in your purses . . . neither two coats, neither shoes, nor yet staves for the workman is worthy of his meat'.[45] The Franciscans were not, however, to wander as individuals. Like the Dominicans, they were to live in a disciplined way as members of a family, usually in town houses. It was in towns they could reach the largest audiences, although both orders also carried their ministry to the countryside.

The Dominicans arrived in England in 1221, the Franciscans in 1224. No one could doubt their commitment given their abject poverty. Nor was their message in any way simplistic, an important feature given a sometimes sophisticated audience. The preaching was often based on model sermons circulated from Paris. It was followed up by the hearing of confessions and

---

[42] *C&S*, i, 224–6, and in much more detail, Grosseteste, *Templum Dei*, 39–67.

[43] Thomas of Eccleston, 28. Hamo later became minister-general of the Franciscans. For a concession made by Henry at Hamo's petition, while Hamo was proctor of the Oxford Franciscans, see *Patent Roll 1225–32*, 469.

[44] *EHD*, 650–1, cap. 10. The decree 'marks, even if it did not cause, the beginning of a new age in the history of preaching': D'Avray, *Preaching of the Friars*, 15–16.

[45] *EHD*, 678.

the setting of penances, as seen in the case of Hamo of Faversham. The Dominicans were all priests (so they could hear confessions) and learned, designedly so. 'The purpose of study is preaching and of preaching the salvation of souls,' remarked Humbert of Romans, master-general of the order. The Franciscans too, for the same reason, became increasingly a learned order, and one dominated by the priestly element. Indeed, the Franciscan theological school in Oxford, established initially under Grosseteste, became one of the most famous in the university.

Townsmen, knights, academics and monks rushed to join the orders. The famous scholar Adam Marsh became a Franciscan 'for love of most high poverty'. Within twenty years of their arrival in England, the Dominicans had established nineteen town houses and the Franciscans thirty-nine. By the mid-1250s there were forty-nine Franciscan houses with 1242 occupants. The London house had around eighty members.[46]

This then was the framework of Henry's religious life, one set by pastoral bishops and preaching friars. He knew intimately many of the bishops – Langton, le Poore, des Roches, Grosseteste, Cantilupe – who were striving in their diocesan statutes to improve the work of their clergy as preachers, confessors and celebrants of the mass. From the first Henry was a patron of the friars, encouraged almost certainly by both Peter des Roches and Hubert de Burgh. In 1221 des Roches returned to England in the company of the first Dominicans. In his statutes, 'on account of the religion of the friars preachers and for the profit of souls', he allowed the faithful to go to them for confession.[47] One of the earliest Franciscan recruits came from Hubert's household. Hubert himself was a great benefactor of the Dominicans and was buried in their London Holborn church.[48]

Henry was not blind to criticisms of the friars, as his complaint about William of Abingdon shows, but he made numerous gifts to both the Dominicans and the Franciscans, gifts of money, food, clothes and building timber. Thomas of Eccleston, whose account of the coming of the Franciscans was finished by 1259, mentions as particular beneficiaries the houses at London, Cambridge, Shrewsbury and Reading. All told between 1226 and 1260 some fifty houses, twenty Dominican and thirty Franciscan, in thirty-seven different places, benefited from Henry's patronage, some of them many times over. Henry made seventeen gifts to the Franciscans at Winchester alone, including the ground on which to found their house.[49]

[46] Thomas of Eccleston, 10–11.

[47] C&S, i, 133, cap. 45. It was necessary, however, to have permission from one's own priest.

[48] Thomas of Eccleston, 14–15; Paris, iv, 243–4. Paris's statement that Hubert left his London palace to the Dominicans appears to be incorrect: Survey of London, 3.

[49] Thomas of Eccleston, 21–3, 80, 81n. I get the figures from the indexes of the CLR under 'Religious Institutions'.

Often his gifts took place after his arrival in a town, so clearly he always contacted the local friars. In 1259, when Henry established the Franciscans in Dunstable (against opposition from the priory), he spoke of his 'special devotion' to them as 'viros evangelicos, ministers of the most high king'.[50] He would have said the same of the Dominicans.[51]

Equally striking was the presence of friars at court. Henry had buildings made for both orders at Clarendon. (They were to be 24 feet long by 12 feet wide, with fireplaces and outer chambers.)[52] In 1256 he provided the Dominican John of Darlington and some of his colleagues with clothes, palfreys and saddles. They were described as being in the king's service so evidently they were following the court, presumably with a dispensation allowing them to ride. Probably it was now that John of Darlington began to act as Henry's confessor.[53]

An important feature of Louis IX's piety was his enthusiasm for sermons. During calm weather he even made the sailors of his ship hear them.[54] According to one story, Louis once advised Henry to hear sermons as well as masses, only for Henry to say he preferred to see his God (in the elevation of the Host) than to hear about him.[55] But Henry certainly did hear sermons. In one preached at his request, Grosseteste, in congratulatory mood, compared the righteousness of Henry's justice to the rays of the sun.[56] Henry had evidently no need to tell him to hurry up and finish, as King John had once done with Bishop Hugh of Lincoln. The friars at court were certainly well equipped to give relevant and resonant sermons. Some of the models circulated from Paris, in their use of allegory, were impregnated with the practices and values of aristocratic society. So Christ might be pictured as the just son of a good prince while obedience to the statutes of a ruler was considered 'natural and normal'.[57] In the case of the Franciscan Ralph of Rochester, it was his 'grace' in preaching that won Henry's favour. Adam Marsh was less acceptable. One of his sermons angered Henry and he was banished for a while from court.[58] Perhaps he had discoursed on the characteristics of good and bad rulers (such as Hugh of Lincoln before John in 1199) and gone on to criticize Henry's treatment of the church. Apart from listening to their sermons, Henry also engaged in spiritual discussions, as initially with William of Abingdon. Here John of Darlington was particularly well

---

[50] *CPR 1258–66*, 20; Dunstable, 213, which also mentions the agency of the queen.

[51] For Louis IX's equal affection for the two orders, see Geoffroi de Beaulieu, cap. 12.

[52] *CLR 1267–72*, no. 1212.

[53] Trevet, 296, 300, 310; *CLR 1251–60*, 282, 285; see Lawrence, 'John of Darlington'. For mendicants as Louis IX's confessors, see Le Goff, *Saint Louis*, 748.

[54] Geoffroi de Beaulieu, cap. 23; Le Goff, *Saint Louis*, 748–9, 776.

[55] Carpenter, 'Meetings of kings', 25–6. The episode is discussed in volume 2.

[56] Paris, iv, 154; see above, 221.

[57] D'Avray, *Preaching of the Friars*, 216–25.

[58] Thomas of Eccleston, 30–1; *Letters of Adam Marsh*, 348–9.

equipped, having been part of the team helping the Paris theologian
Hugh de St Cher produce a concordance of the bible. A later Dominican,
Nicholas Trevet, actually thought John was its sole author. As soon as John
joined the court in 1256, he was given £10 by the king to buy a 'scriptura',
presumably a bible.[59]

If there are no texts of the sermons preached before Henry, nothing
equally is known about how often he confessed and how severe were the
penances imposed by his confessors. In November 1240, Henry referred to
the oath by which he had been confessed that day at the altar of St
Stephen in Westminster palace, and perhaps this confession was part of a
regular weekly cycle. Louis IX was said to have confessed every Friday and
sometimes more frequently when he feared he had fallen into sin, the
night being an especially dangerous time for assaults of the devil.[60] Of
Henry's bodily austerities in general there is little evidence. Several references in Matthew Paris show he fasted and dressed humbly on the day
before the feasts of Edward the Confessor on 13 October and 5 January.[61]
He probably did the same before the other great ecclesiastical festivals,
hence in his household accounts at Easter, Pentecost and Christmas a
single sum is given for expenditure on food and drink both for the vigil and
the feast day, presumably because the expenditure on the vigil was very
small. It was not, however, through bodily austerities that Henry won his
reputation as a most Christian king. Conceivably, Peter des Roches had
some influence here. In an indulgence issued during his time as Henry's
governor, he conspicuously played down austerity's value. He first quoted
I Timothy 4:8, 'bodily exercise profiteth little', and then gave his own
examples – 'fasts, vigils and other macerations of the flesh'![62] (It was true
piety that counted.) Langton himself took the view that fasting without
alms was of no value although he did add, unlike des Roches, that fasting
and alms together were a double goodness.[63]

Henry revered the friars but was he altogether in tune with their lifestyle? Those rooms at Clarendon with their fireplaces and outer chambers
were surely at odds with the houses made of twigs, mud and refuse recom-
mended by St Francis. The chapel Henry built for the Franciscans at
Reading, with its wainscoting and painted altarpiece decorated with gold
stars, was disapproved of so much by the minister general of the order,
Albert of Pisa, that he hoped God would destroy it. (He could not do it

[59] *CLR 1251–60*, 297.

[60] FitzThedmar, 8; Geoffroi de Beaulieu, caps. 16, 16bis; Le Goff, *Saint Louis*, 763–4.
Henry's oath was taken on the third day after his arrival in London, which would seem to
indicate it was on a Wednesday or Thursday rather than a Friday.

[61] For example, Paris, v, 47–8.

[62] Vincent, *EEA Winchester*, 50. See also Webster, *King John and Religion*, for relevance to
John.

[63] Rubin, *Charity and Community*, 64.

himself for fear of offending the king.)[64] Henry thus appears very different from Louis IX, whose lifestyle was impregnated by the example of the friars. Louis dressed modestly where Henry loved to appear in cloth of gold. Louis ate frugally where Henry loved feasts. And there is no evidence that Henry wished to wear a hair shirt or suffered penitential flagellations. Perhaps the picture would be different had John of Darlington written an account of Henry's religious life to parallel that by Louis's confessor, Geoffroi de Beaulieu. But there are enough descriptions of Henry's devotional practices to say, at the very least, that such austerities played no conspicuous part in his religious life.[65]

HENRY'S ALMSGIVING

If little is known of Henry's austerities, a great deal is known about his almsgiving. Indeed, it was one of the most striking features of his piety. In speeches put into their mouths by Matthew Paris, King John hoped his son's alms would help him out of purgatory, Llywelyn declared he feared Henry's alms more than any military force, and Louis IX said they would save Henry from all shames and dangers.[66] Alms could play a central penitential role. The tract on confession and penance attached to the Coventry statutes thus cited a key passage in the Book of Daniel where the prophet urged King Nebuchadnezzar to 'redeem your sins with alms and your iniquities by mercies to the poor'.[67] A well-known proverb declared that as 'water extinguishes the burning fire, alms extinguishes sin'.[68] There was here a wider background. The giving of alms to the poor had always been a fundamental Christian practice. As Bishop Poore declared in his Salisbury statutes, 'it is not sufficient to avoid evil unless we do good' and one cardinal way of doing good was by 'the distribution of alms'.[69] Numerous passages in the Bible showed how almsgiving might bring reward both in this life and the next. 'Blessed be the man that provideth for the sick and needy: the Lord shall deliver him in the time of trouble' (Psalms 41:1). 'Charge them who are rich in this world, that they be ready to give . . . laying up for themselves a good foundation against the time to come, that they may attain eternal life' (Timothy 6:17–19). Most fundamental of all were the passages in the book of Matthew 15:31–46. Here, in a description of the Last Judgement, it was those who had fed and clothed Christ who would be saved, while those who had failed to do so would be

---

[64] Colvin, *History of the King's Works*, i, 157; Thomas of Eccleston, 46, 80, and 47 for the way a prayer to St Francis brought about the collapse of the spacious Paris house of the Franciscans.

[65] Geoffroi de Beaulieu, caps. 16 bis, 17; Le Goff, *Saint Louis*, 139, 757–60. For a shirt perhaps with Louis's spots of blood, see Le Pogam and Vivet-Peclet, *Saint Louis*, 202–4.

[66] Paris, iii, 290; Paris, iv, 231–2.

[67] *C&S*, i, 225; Daniel 4:27 (24 in the Vulgate Bible).

[68] Rubin, *Charity and Community*, 64.

[69] *C&S*, i, 64, cap. 14.

damned. But how could one feed and clothe Christ? The answer was by feeding and clothing the poor for, as Christ explained, he was present in the poor: 'Verily, I say unto you, inasmuch as you have done it unto the least of these my brethren, you have done it unto me.'[70]

All Christians, therefore, were wise to give alms according to their means, and none, of course, had more means than kings and princes. Indeed, the *Dialogue of the Exchequer*, written in the reign of Henry II, saw the bestowal of alms as integral to kingship. In war the king would lavish money on fortifying castles and paying soldiers; in peace (alluding to the passage in Matthew) he would use it to feed and clothe Christ 'in the poor'.[71] Henry's predecessors were well aware of their obligations in this area. Henry II was praised by William of Newburgh for distributing alms with an open hand and for having a care for widows, orphans and the poor. King Richard likewise was commended by Roger of Howden for feeding large numbers of paupers every day both at court and in cities and vills, this after having recalled the injunction in Psalm 41.[72] King John, as is known from record evidence, gave extensive alms both to atone for his own sins and help the souls of the departed.

Henry, therefore, stepped into a tradition of royal almsgiving. His eleemosynary obligations were equally expounded by his mentors in the minority. Peter des Roches was very familiar with the passage in Matthew for he began his indulgence in favour of the Southwark hospital with a long disquisition upon it.[73] Stephen Langton, as mentioned, took the view that fasting without alms had no value, whereas alms without fasting did. The school of Peter the Chanter from which he came even believed the ruler should enforce the duty of the rich to relieve the poor.[74] The kind of mendicant sermons Henry probably heard condemned the sin of avarice, argued that almsgiving and other good works alone justified riches, and again picked up on Christ dwelling in the poor.[75]

Henry's response to these injunctions is seen in the images he commissioned for his palaces and castles. The story of Dives and Lazarus was strategically placed in the halls at Ludgershall, Guildford and Northampton, and showed all too clearly the fate awaiting rich men who failed to give alms to poor beggars. The episode depicted again and again from the life of the Confessor (it had pride of place in Westminster Abbey) was that of the king giving alms in the form of the ring from his finger to a poor pilgrim. (The pilgrim turned out later to be St John the Evangelist.) The verse, 'he who does not give what he loves, does not receive what he desires', was painted

---

[70] For Christ's presence in the poor, see Rubin, *Charity and Community*, 59, 93–4.

[71] *Dialogus*, 4–5.

[72] Newburgh, i, 282; Howden, iii, 290.

[73] Vincent, *EEA Winchester*, 50.

[74] Rubin, *Charity and Community*, 58, 62, 64.

[75] D'Avray, *Preaching of the Friars*, 214–15.

(in French, so all the more readable) in the gable of the great chamber at Westminster. It was also featured in the hall at Woodstock.[76]

How far Henry's almsgiving was penitential there is no means of knowing. One may doubt whether, like his father, he had to feed paupers to atone for feasting on fast days and hunting on feast days, although given the nature of the records it is impossible to be quite sure.[77] Henry gave alms for the souls of dead family and friends, as we have seen. He gave them too for benefits in this life, so for the health of his children and the safety of the queen during pregnancy. In 1240, in one of his fullest statements of motive, Henry fed paupers 'so that Almighty God shall deign to prosper our state and that of our queen and people'. In 1242, in an order issued while on campaign in Poitou, he declared that 'no one can impede our alms giving without incurring our indignation'.[78]

Henry's most direct and personal involvement in the bestowal of alms took the form of his feeding paupers at court. Between the 1220s and the 1240s he both greatly increased the numbers fed and substantially improved their fare. A fragmentary household roll surviving from 1225/6 suggests that early in the reign daily alms simply took the form of doles of bread and ale to perhaps a hundred paupers, together with a money payment of a penny to a further twenty-four.[79] The next evidence comes from the 1240s and shows a dramatic change. Henry now seems to be feeding no fewer than 500 paupers every day![80] Just when this transformation took

---

[76] *CR 1234–7*, 271; *CLR 1240–5*, 3–4. See Dixon-Smith, 'Image and reality', 81–5.

[77] Webster, *King John and Religion*, 115–17. For the contrasting evidence under the two kings, see below, n. 121.

[78] *CR 1237–42*, 217, 227, 515; *CR 1242–7*, 150, 281, 390.

[79] *DA*, 94. Normally the roll here makes no record of expenditure on alms. However, it is revealed on 21 December 1225, when the king was entertained 'in all things' by the bishop of Winchester 'save alms'. On those alms, the pantry spent 50d (so enough for 100 halfpenny loaves) and the buttery 20d (probably enough to give ale to the same number of paupers). Whether this was a typical or exceptional daily sum we do not know. The date of 21 December was the feast day of Thomas the Apostle but no special alms were given on the same feast in the next surviving roll, that for 1259/60. The only other item recorded for the day is the consumption of thirteen and a half pounds of wax. Perhaps some of this was to provide candles for the almonry. In the same roll, in the course of 1226 itself, daily payments of money in 'external alms' begin to appear, the usual sum being around 2s or 24d: *DA*, 100–2.

[80] Writing home from Saintes in June 1242, Henry declared that, of the 500 paupers he was accustomed to feed each day, he wanted, until his return, 350 to be fed in England by John the almoner: *CR 1237–42*, 496–7. Writs issued by the regents providing John with money show that Henry's order was indeed carried out: *CLR 1240–5*, 160, 169, 172, 174, 180, 184, 187, 192. The most likely interpretation of the order is that, prior to his departure, Henry's custom had been to feed 500 paupers each day at court. Once overseas, he decided to reduce the number to 150, leaving the remaining 350 to be fed by his almoner in England. When Henry got home in 1243, the payments to the almoner ceased, so it looks as though the full 500 were once more being catered for at court. This interpretation is confirmed by a measure Henry took at the end of 1244. His almoner (now Robert the Templar) was sent ahead to Westminster, with instructions to carry out half the king's alms until the king's arrival. The number he was to feed was 250: *CR 1242–7*, 281.

place is not known. Perhaps it was after Henry's marriage in 1236, perhaps after the birth of Edward in 1239.[81] From this high point in the 1240s there seems later to have been a decline. In 1250, Matthew Paris records Henry, as part of a general cost-cutting exercise, reducing his customary distribution of alms.[82] His motive was pious, he wished to save money for his crusade. Later in 1255 the pope himself urged Henry to curtail his 'pious expenses'. His commitment to the Sicilian project should supersede all other 'works of piety'.[83] Since the cost of feeding 500 paupers a day was around £1,000 year (in 1242/3 the sum per pauper averaged out at 1.27d a day), Henry was spending enough to hire twenty-seven knights a day or, over ten years, to build a very substantial castle. One can see, therefore, why preparing for a crusade in the Holy Land or Sicily he might indeed feel justified in reducing the cost of his almsgiving.

That Henry had indeed ceased to feed 500 paupers daily is shown by the first household roll to survive since 1225/6, one covering the regnal year from October 1259 to October 1260. (This is the only complete roll for the whole reign.)[84] Although a period when Henry was, to a greater or lesser extent controlled by a baronial council, that is unlikely to have impacted on his pious practices. The roll shows that Henry (outside special occasions) was now giving daily alms to 150 paupers when the queen was present at court and 100 when she was absent. (Eleanor's own accounts show that when alone she usually fed fifty paupers every day.)

Although the numbers now benefiting from alms was not perhaps very different from the 1220s, the 1259/60 roll indicates a very major change in what was received. Whereas in 1225/6 the paupers only had doles of bread and ale from the pantry and buttery, now they had a square meal for the daily costs of the kitchen are recorded as well.[85] The total cost each day varied but 14s 6d and 19s 11d were common figures when 150 were fed, which works out at food and drink worth 1.16d and 1.59d per head. When the 'square meal' policy was introduced is unknown, but it was probably of long standing by 1259/60. Another striking fact revealed by the roll is that the almsmen are described not as 'paupers' but as 'fratres'. This might seem to indicate that they were friars, but since Henry can scarcely have brought together 150 friars every day (and on special occasions many

[81] Between 6 December 1238 and 6 January 1239 (the feasts of St Nicholas and Epiphany), Henry ordered 200 paupers a day to be fed, perhaps in connection with Eleanor's pregnancy: *CLR 1226–40*, 356.

[82] Paris, v, 114, 137, 199.

[83] *F*, 302–3.

[84] For this roll, see Carpenter, 'Household rolls', 24, 39–40. It is calendared in Dixon-Smith, 'Feeding the poor', Appendix 4, and used extensively in Carpenter, 'Meetings of kings'.

[85] There was also a commensurate change in the record keeping. Whereas the doles of 1225/6 have to be deduced from a single exceptional entry, in 1259/60 the daily costs of the kitchen, pantry and buttery are formally recorded. In the 1259/60 roll the money payment in 'external alms' appearing in 1225/6 disappears.

more) friars probably just headed the list. Significantly, while the queen's household accounts likewise speak of feeding 'fratres', the corresponding record on the pipe rolls just speaks of 'paupers'. Perhaps Henry also called his paupers 'fratres' to emphasize his brotherhood with the poor and thence, since Christ was present in the poor, his brotherhood with Christ.

Fragmentary rolls from 1262, 1266 and 1271 show that Henry continued his practice of feeding 100 or 150 paupers every day until the end of the reign. He did so when he was in France in 1262 and when he was at the siege of Kenilworth in 1266. However much, therefore, Henry had reduced the scale of his almsgiving, he clearly saw its daily repetition on what remained a generous scale as absolutely integral to his spiritual health. There is no evidence of Henry personally serving food to small groups of paupers in his chamber, as did Louis IX, but given, as will be seen, he washed the feet of the poor, it seems highly likely that he did so. The poor were certainly fed in his chamber at Westminster, although the one order to that effect was for a feeding in his absence.[86] Given the numbers involved, probably the great bulk of the paupers were fed in the king's halls and the almonry buildings attached to most of Henry's major residences. The household accounts often record, as a joint item, the consumption of wax, presumably for candles, in the king's chapel and the almonry. The practice of giving subsidiary figures for this consumption is another development between the rolls of 1225/6 and 1259/60.[87]

There is no indication of who the 'fratres' actually were. Presumably, they cannot have travelled with the king, so a new clientele must have been gathered together at each new residence. If the body of almsmen remained stable for the duration of a stay, then some lucky paupers could enjoy a sustenance for weeks and sometimes months. In thirteenth-century England there were certainly large numbers of paupers about.[88] Not surprisingly, the king's almoners were important men, usually chaplains of the king. When John of Lewknor died in 1245, Henry paid for the tomb in which he was to be buried.[89] A later almoner and chaplain, John of Colchester, was rewarded with six livings and some of the spoils after the battle of Evesham (1265).[90]

---

[86] CR 1242–7, 150. Although there is no evidence of the practice, Henry presumably followed the usual custom of giving alms from the leftovers of his table. Perhaps this was the purpose of the great silver dish in which to place the king's alms (together with a bag to keep it in), which cost £14 in 1224; RLC, i, 584b.

[87] See Dixon-Smith, 'Image and reality', 86; Carpenter, 'Household rolls', 40 and n. 66. In the roll of 1259/60 a joint figure for the consumption of wax in the chapel and almonry is given for about 100 days in the year. For the other days the chapel features alone.

[88] There is little evidence that Henry increased his almsgiving in time of need, but had we the household roll covering, say, the famine in 1258, it might show he had done so.

[89] CLR 1240–5, 286.

[90] I take these details from Dixon-Smith, 'Feeding the poor', Appendix 3, where there is a list of Henry's almoners with biographical details.

It was common for Henry to announce his arrival in a town with a distribution of alms over and above the normal daily quota. On reaching Canterbury in November 1259 he fed 220 'fratres'. On his return to London in April 1260 (during a time of political crisis) the number fed rose to 344, with 322 on the following day. Two arrivals at Westminster in June were marked by the feeding of 294 'fratres', on the second occasion with 322 on the following day. Arriving at Winchester in August, where he was greeted by the monks in a solemn procession, Henry fed 282 'fratres'. The usual quota of paupers was also exceeded on the major feast days of the church. In 1259/60, presumably not untypical, the numbers fed were as follows: All Saints Day, 390; Christmas Day, 450 (vigil and feast); Maundy Thursday, 321; Pentecost (vigil and feast), 464; Nativity of John the Baptist, 200; vigil of the Virgin's Assumption, 300.[91]

These exceptional figures were, however, dwarfed by those reached on the two feasts of Edward the Confessor. On 5 January 1260, although in Paris, Henry fed 1,500 'fratres'. On 13 October 1260, now at Westminster, he fed 5,016! On this occasion the kitchen kept its costs down by drawing from stock but the pantry's expenditure totalled £10 9s, enough for 5,016 halfpenny loaves. Henry, however, did not wish his paupers to get drunk: the buttery's costs were 14s 7d, larger than when lubricating the usual 150 paupers but nowhere near to any commensurate degree.[92]

There was one other aspect of Henry's almsgiving in which the pantry above all was involved. Quite apart from feeding specified numbers of fratres, it seems on special days to have made mass distributions of bread to the poor. This is clear from a sharp rise in its costs and (though less conclusively) by the way an 'etc' sometimes appears after the number of the 'fratres'. At Westminster, on Good Friday 1266, for example, while only 150 'fratres' were fed, the pantry's expenditure was given as £18, enough to produce 8,640 halfpenny loaves.[93]

The mass feeding on 13 October 1260 connects to the most striking and original feature of Henry's almsgiving, namely his practice of feeding thousands of paupers in the halls of his palaces and castles, often filling those halls full in order to do so.[94] The practice seems to have begun at the end of 1239 and was probably inspired by the birth of Edward.[95] Henry, in his expansive way, thus thanked God for the safe delivery of his son and strove to secure God's favour in the future for himself, his queen (soon

[91] The queen was at court on all these days.

[92] The costs on 13 October also cover the vigil of the feast. A common cost of the buttery when catering for 150 paupers was 2s 10d.

[93] TNA E 101/667/50, m. 2. For another example, see Carpenter, 'Meetings of kings', 12. By 1266 the pantry may have been making regular doles of bread, although, judging from the costs, usually of several hundred loaves rather than many thousands. The 'etc' appears after every entry whereas in 1259/60 it only appears on around thirty occasions.

[94] Dixon-Smith covers the whole subject in her 'Image and reality'.

[95] See above, 210–11.

again pregnant) and his growing family. Henry also filled halls to help the souls of the departed. At the end of 1243, 4,000 paupers (a good indication of its supposed capacity) were to be fed in the great hall at Westminster for the soul of the empress Isabella, Henry's sister.[96]

The halls Henry ordered to be filled included those at Dover, Dublin, Oxford and Cambridge (where the beneficiaries were the poor clerks of the university).[97] The most common venues, however, were Windsor (where Eleanor and the children were based) and Westminster, where both the great hall, the lesser hall and the king and queen's chamber were sometimes utilized. When the king was present, the feedings were catered for by the household departments, as on 13 October 1260. But Henry also commanded feedings in his absence, though sometimes these were linked to his imminent arrival. In July 1240, for example, the sheriff of Kent, prior to the king 'coming to those parts', was to fill the new hall at Dover castle with paupers and find them food for a day.[98] In another order, 6,000 poor were to be fed at Westminster on the feast of the Circumcision, 1 January 1244, this for the state of the king, the queen and their children.[99] Thus when Henry arrived from Windsor for the feast of the Confessor a few days later, he found the whole palace purified by the good works of his alms and the prayers of his almsmen.

It is easy to think with these mass feedings at Westminster that the London citizenry simply piled in for free meals. Certainly, with such numbers involved, it must have been difficult to decide who was a pauper and who not. Still Henry clearly expected differentiations to be made. For the feedings on 1 January 1240 the old and weak were to be in the great and lesser halls at Westminster, the middle-aged and less weak in the king's chamber, and the children in the queen's chamber. A feeding at Windsor in 1244 had a different target. Here, before a good fire (it was January), the hall was to be filled with poor and needy boys. How closely related this was to the welfare of the king's own children is shown by the accompanying order for them to be weighed and the weight (in food obviously) be given to the poor.[100]

In issuing his Windsor order, Henry added the rider, as he did on some other occasions, 'if so many paupers can be found'. Indeed, when Henry ordered 10,000 poor to be fed in London, for the soul of his father-in-law, the count of Provence, he acknowledged it might be necessary to feed them in instalments until the number was reached.[101] But that large numbers could be found is proved by the accounts for 13 October 1260 where 5,016 can hardly be a notional figure and must come from an actual

---

[96] *CLR 1240–5*, 204.

[97] *CLR 1226–40*, 377; *CR 1237–42*, 227; *CLR 1245–51*, 71.

[98] *CLR 1226–40*, 477.

[99] *CR 1242–7*, 150.

[100] *CR 1242–7*, 150.

[101] *CLR 1245–51*, 324, a reference I owe to Sally Dixon-Smith.

count of those involved. When, however, Henry reached for even higher numbers he saw the need to spread the distributions geographically. In the case of the 102,000 paupers to be fed in 1242 for the soul of the empress Isabella, 25,000 apiece were to be catered for at Oxford and Ospringe, 1,000 apiece at the nunneries of Broomhill and Ankerwyke, and the remaining 50,000 at London, Windsor and other unspecified places. Since the order says each person was 'to have a 1d for food' it looks as though here money was given rather than victuals, the £425 assigned exactly meeting the cost.[102] The same happened when Henry spent £62 10s feeding 15,000 poor (at exactly a penny a head) on the feast of the conversion of St Paul. Here the numbers could not be accommodated in any hall and the paupers received their alms in the churchyard of St Paul's.[103]

When Henry ordered 25,000 to be fed both at Oxford and Ospringe for the soul of the empress, he probably intended his hospitals to play a part. These were the hospital of St John the Baptist outside Oxford's east gate and the hospital of St Mary astride Watling Street at Ospringe in Kent. Of both he was the founder or refounder and both were close to his heart. He saw Ospringe on his many journeys to and from Canterbury and Dover, and Oxford, of course, whenever he was in the town. In one of his initial grants to the east gate hospital, he promised it funds to feed 100 paupers on the day of his arrival in Oxford.[104] Both hospitals were to say mass for the soul of William, the bishop-elect of Valence, both were exempted in the same way from taxation, both were conceded identical liberties, and both were placed under the same senior royal officials – the almoners Geoffrey and John, and then in the 1250s the keepers of the seal. To the care of both, in what were very personal acts of charity, Henry sent individual recruits, both men and women, some of them blind.[105]

Henry's connection with the Ospringe hospital had begun in the early 1230s when he provided his almoner with funds for its repair.[106] Three years before, he had refounded the Oxford hospital by granting it as a new site the garden of the Jews outside the east gate of the town. In the following years he made numerous gifts, particularly of timber for the new buildings. These came to include a chapel, infirmary, refectory, dormitories, chapter house and (on Henry's orders in 1240) a chamber for women labouring in childbirth.[107] Unfortunately the buildings, apart from

---

[102] *CLR 1240–5*, 124.

[103] *CLR 1240–5*, 306. There are other cases where one suspects money was given rather than food.

[104] *CJB*, i, 77.

[105] *CLR 1226–40*, 347, 436; *CR 1234–7*, 48, 148; *CR 1242–7*, 39, 44, 68; *CChR 1226–57*, 253, 294; *CJB*, iii, pp. xxvi, xxxiii.

[106] *CR 1231–4*, 492.

[107] *CLR 1226–40*, 455; Colvin, *History of the King's Works*, i, 158–9. The introduction to *CJB*, iii, by Henry Salter, has a detailed history of the house while Appendix III, by R.T. Gunther, covers its architecture.

portions of wall, have disappeared under Magdalen College. Ospringe has
been luckier and some medieval buildings survive.[108] Henry paid close
attention to the constitution of the Oxford hospital. Under rules issued in
1234 (in the heat of the crisis over Peter des Roches) there were to be three
priests, six lay brethren and six sisters. They were to look after the poor
and infirm, and follow the rule of St Augustine. Showing unaccustomed
caution, Henry added that the numbers of priests, brethren and sisters
were not to increase until they had fitting means of support.[109]

The hospital of St John the Baptist was not a leper hospital since
Oxford had a separate house for lepers, St Bartholomew's near Cowley,
like many such houses safely outside the town. There was also a leper
hospital at Ospringe, how far co-terminous with the main hospital is
unclear. Henry inherited a long tradition of kingly concern for lepers. The
St Bartholomew house had been founded by Henry I and was supported
by King John.[110] Not surprisingly, concern for lepers thus formed an
important part of Henry's piety. His first known intervention in government (in 1220) had been in favour of the lepers of Lancaster. In 1225 a
lepress was received into the leper hospital at Harbledown in Kent at his
petition. In 1227 he gave grain and bacon to the lepers of St John at
Berkhamsted. Such concessions continued throughout the reign.[111] The
leper hospitals at Oxford and Ospringe were linked together in his mind.
In 1244, John the almoner was given fifteen cows for their joint benefit.
Later Henry gave vestments and bells for the Ospringe lepers' chapel.[112]

There was nothing arms' length about Henry's support for lepers.
According to a mendicant chronicle, before setting sail for Brittany in
1230, he kissed the feet of lepers, the poor and infirm.[113] On one occasion,
Louis IX asked Joinville whether he washed the feet of lepers. When
Joinville said 'no', to do so would be unseemly, Louis continued 'very
unwillingly then would you do what the king of England does, who washes
the feet of lepers and kisses them'.[114] King Louis's compliment introduces
the most personal and intimate form of Henry's almsgiving, namely his
practice of washing the feet of paupers and providing them with clothes
and shoes. Henry described such ceremonies as his 'mandatum', so in
English his 'maundy', and they had a very ancient origin.[115] Since the
early church, popes and bishops had washed the feet of priests and
paupers on the Thursday before Good Friday (hence 'Maundy Thursday').

---

[108] Rigold, 'The medieval hospital', 3–14.

[109] *CJB*, iii, pp. xvi–vii.

[110] Webster, *King John and Religion*, 100–2.

[111] *RLC*, ii, 46b, 172.

[112] *CR 1242–7*, 214; *CLR 1251–60*, 133.

[113] BL Cotton Nero A IX, fos. 69r–69v.

[114] Joinville, cap. 688.

[115] There is a summary of the origins of the ceremony in Kellett, 'King John in
Knaresborough', 85–6.

This, of course, was in imitation of Christ's washing the feet of his twelve disciples before the last supper (John 13:1–17). The name for the ceremony derived from Christ's subsequent commandment, 'mandatum', that the apostles 'love one another as I have loved you' (John 13:34). The number of selected beneficiaries at such ceremonies was either twelve, after the twelve apostles, or thirteen following a legend involving Pope Gregory the Great – when he was ministering to twelve old priests on Maundy Thursday a thirteenth person appeared in the shape of an angel.[116]

King John himself, following perhaps the custom of his predecessors, clothed thirteen paupers on Maundy Thursday.[117] Henry was to go much further. From the early 1230s he clothed, shoed and washed the feet not of 13 but of 300, doing so not just on Maundy Thursday but at Christmas as well. By the 1240s he seems to have been doing the same at Whitsun.[118] In the 1250s, as with the rest of Henry's almsgiving, and doubtless for the same reasons, there was a decline in the scale of the king's maundy, first at Christmas and Whitsun and then at Easter also. A usual number of beneficiaries becomes 171: 150 for the king and queen and 21 for their children.[119] This still left the king a lot of washing to do. The wardrobe kept a great silver bowl, weighing over ten pounds, specifically 'for the use of the king to wash his feet and the feet of the poor at his maundies'.[120] It sounds as though Henry washed his own feet alongside those of the poor, a beautiful indication of their shared brotherhood. Some of the poor, in the later evidence, are described as converts, so Jewish converts to Christianity, of whom more later. Others presumably were lepers, hence King Louis's encomium.

How far Henry's almsgiving was exceptional compared with that of his predecessors is difficult to say. As mentioned, both Henry II and King Richard were commended for feeding the poor, but there is no indication of

---

[116] Kellett, 'King John in Knaresborough', citing Thurston, *Maundy Thursday*, 12.

[117] Kellett, 'King John in Knaresborough', 79–84; Webster, *King John and Religion*, 117–18.

[118] Most of the evidence comes from the king's orders embodied in chancery writs, but these only supplemented expenditure funded by the wardrobe for which, in terms of detail, there is limited evidence. For the clothing of 300 paupers at Christmas 1231 and 1232 and on Maundy Thursday 1233, see *CR 1231–4*, 1; *CLR 1226–40*, 191, 206. The evidence for the washing of feet (at Christmas 1238) comes from the oblation roll of 1238/9: TNA C 47/3/44. For Whitsun, see *CR 1242–7*, 311. Some 300 paupers were clothed and shod at Whitsun 1237, but this was not at court: *CR 1234–7*, 435 (this is one of the few orders where the king refers to need). In the wardrobe accounts from 1234 there is a regular item recording the cost of providing 'shoes and clothes for the poor and in the maundy of the poor': Wild, *WA*, 4. I owe some of the references here to Dixon-Smith, 'Feeding the poor', Appendix 5, where much of the evidence for Henry III's maundy distributions is calendared. In November 1229, while in the north, Henry arranged for the shoeing and clothing of 300 paupers by the treasurer in London: *CLR 1226–40*, 159; TNA E 368/11, mm. 4d–5; *PR 1230*, 97, 245. Perhaps this was the start of catering for the number of 300.

[119] For example, *CLR 1251–60*, 298, 344–5, 363; *CR 1256–9*, 13, 45.

[120] Wild, *WA*, 120, 127, 141, 154.

the scale of their activities. In 1204, King John, for fifteen weeks in various places across the country, fed a total of 2,200 paupers every day, with typical attention to detail giving precise instructions as to what they should receive.[121] If, as seems likely, these were feedings for the soul of his mother, Eleanor of Aquitaine, when totted up the total fed was more than double the 102,000 Henry fed for the soul of his sister the empress Isabella. On the other hand, for long periods in 1209/10, John's chamber was simply spending 3s a day in alms, at a penny a head enough to feed 36 paupers, a far cry from the 500 paupers fed daily by Henry in the 1240s.[122] Equally Henry seems to have increased the numbers receiving the annual maundy from John's 13 to 300. Perhaps Henry was also the first king on a regular basis to cram his halls full of paupers and feed 5,000 or more at a time. That there was something unusual and indeed inconvenient about the daily feedings at court is suggested by the conduct of his son, pious though he too was. After Edward's accession, the household rolls omit entirely the costs of the kitchen, pantry and buttery in feeding paupers. Instead, the daily alms were given in money, with the standard payment being 1½d per head per day. Initially, averaging about thirty beneficiaries a day, the numbers receiving alms from Edward were nothing like those fed by his father.[123]

If Henry owed nothing to King John in the numbers he fed daily, it is possible that he was influenced by the practices of Queen Margaret of Scotland, who died in 1093 and was canonized in 1250. According to the biography written by her chaplain, Turgot, she personally attended to the feeding of 300 paupers a day in the royal palace, thus 'serving Christ in the poor'. She also had twenty-four paupers permanently with her and saw them fed before dining herself. Given Henry's close connections with the Scottish court, he may well have known of Margaret's practices. Of the two sisters of King Alexander II named Margaret, he had wished to marry the younger himself, while the elder was married to Hubert de Burgh.[124] That Margaret was an Anglo-Saxon princess and kinswoman of the Confessor would have increased the appeal. Perhaps her example inspired

[121] *RLJ*, 95–6; *PR* 1204, 80, 94, 106, 121, 146, 176–7, 187, 248 and xxxvi; Webster, *King John and Religion*, 93–4; Harvey, 'Piety of King John', 22–3. John's almsgiving is fully discussed in Webster, *King John and Religion*, ch. 5. There is a disjunction between the records available for John and Henry. The rolls recording the money spent every day by John's chamber, with their frequent references to almsgiving, do not survive for Henry. Alternatively, no household rolls showing the expenditure of the food and drink departments on alms survive for John. There need, however, have been no consistency in where almsgiving was recorded.

[122] *RLJ*, 110; *DI*, 250; Webster, *King John and Religion*, 119. John, however, would regularly feed a hundred or more paupers when he broke one of the fast days of the church.

[123] Carpenter, 'Household rolls', 46, quoting Prestwich, 'Piety of Edward I', 120, 122. Edward's numbers greatly increased later in the reign, however.

[124] Henry's first daughter, born in 1240, and the eventual wife of King Alexander III, was herself called Margaret, but, according to Matthew Paris, this was after the queen's sister Queen Margaret of France and because the queen called out to Saint Margaret in the pains of childbirth: Paris, iv, 48.

Henry to go (for a while at least) even further and feed every day 500 paupers.[125]

What of Henry and his rival, friend and brother-in-law Louis IX? Here we are on uneven ground.[126] Whereas evidence for Henry's almsgiving comes from record evidence, for Louis it depends on the recollections of those writing after his death, and in the light of his sanctity, especially his confessor, Geoffroi de Beaulieu, and Guillaume de Saint-Pathus, the confessor of Louis's widow.[127] What they say is highly detailed and may be true. But it doubtless describes Louis's practices at their height and gives no indication of how they changed over time. If only we had for Louis the hard-record evidence available for Henry, if only we had for Henry the intimate details given by Beaulieu and Saint-Pathus.

In respect of daily feedings at court, neither Beaulieu nor Saint-Pathus claim for Louis anything like Henry's quota of 500 paupers. When, however, Henry's total comes down to 100/150, the two kings are comparable. Louis's practice was to feed 120 or 122 paupers each day 'in his house'.[128] He also gave two loaves of bread and money to a further 60 paupers, thus taking his total up to over Henry's, although Henry himself by 1266 seems to have been making daily distributions of bread. As for Henry feeding thousands in his halls, here too nothing similar is claimed for Louis. The numbers fed on feast days are only said to have risen to 200 or 300. On the other hand, Louis, on occasion, did make general distributions of bread and money to unnumbered multitudes – Saint-Pathus writes vaguely of ten or twenty thousand recipients a day when Louis visited his kingdom on return from his crusade. As for Maundy Thursday, here Louis's practice was to wash the feet of thirteen paupers. Henry was doing the same for 300. In the field of almsgiving, Henry's practices seem, therefore, quite on a par with those of Saint Louis. Indeed, both kings were criticized, Henry by Matthew Paris, Louis by his ministers, for what seemed excessive expenditure.[129]

---

[125] Turgot, 78–9. Margaret was the granddaughter of Edmund Ironside, the Confessor's half-brother.

[126] For what follows, see Carpenter, 'Meetings of kings', 17–19, where full references are given.

[127] Geoffroi de Beaulieu, cap. 19; Saint-Pathus, 57–70. I am indebted to Sally Dixon-Smith for sending me her translation and analysis of Saint-Pathus's long chapter on Louis's works of charity.

[128] Nothing is said as to whether this included a quota for the queen.

[129] Paris, v, 6 (where Henry's alms are seen as excessive given they depended, so Paris alleges, on seizing the necessary food from merchants); Geoffroi de Beaulieu, cap. 19; Saint-Pathus, 63; Joinville, cap. 726; Le Goff, *Saint Louis*, 818–19. I am not convinced by Frank Barlow's suggestion that after his visit to Paris in 1254, Henry began to imitate Louis IX's practice of touching for the 'king's evil' or scrofula, a tubercular infection leading to the swelling of glands in the neck. Henry may well have touched, for record evidence, not extant in his reign, shows the practice was well established early in the reign of his son (Edward gave a penny each to the many hundreds who came before him every year). But

More important than any precise numbers and comparisons is the impression made by Henry's almsgiving. That it was great is shown by the comments already quoted from Matthew Paris. Likewise in an obituary of Henry penned at Tewkesbury abbey in 1263, on a false rumour of his death, the generosity of his alms to the poor was singled out as one of his virtues.[130] The same was true at Osney abbey, where Henry was described by its chronicler as 'most devoted in the distribution of alms' and 'a father of the poor'. That the sheer scale of Henry's almsgiving was appreciated is shown by the ensuing story. One All Soul's day Henry told his men to go out into the highways and byways and gather together 10,000 paupers. When informed by a despairing servant that in the whole area it was not possible to find so many, Henry replied with a nice compliment to the abbot of Osney: 'I am astonished. The abbot of Osney at his nod gathers together 15,000 paupers and you cannot even get 10,000!'[131]

THE HARVESTING OF PRAYERS

In giving alms to the poor, Henry was performing good works and hoping for God's resulting favour. He also hoped to benefit from the prayers of the beneficiaries. As Thomas Aquinas later explained, there would be reward 'in the shape of the prayers our neighbor offers for us in return for the material assistance we have given him'.[132] Louis IX, therefore, having personally fed a leper with choice food, asked 'the sick man to pray to the Lord for him'.[133] Henry himself lived his life surrounded by prayers. Throughout the kingdom they were offered up in the daily mass for 'your servant our King Henry'. At court Henry's choirs sang the 'Christus Vincit' before him sixteen times in the year 1239/40: 'To the king of the English, crowned by God, salvation and victory. The redeemer of the world aid him.'[134] Henry was also assiduous in soliciting special prayers, most notably when religious orders met in their general chapters. In 1249,

---

Henry was perfectly capable of reviving or continuing the practice for which there is evidence under Henry II. He may well have been inspired by a miracle of Edward the Confessor, who cured a woman suffering from scrofula by anointing her face with the tips of his fingers and making the sign of the cross (Paris, *La Estoire*, lines 2606–83). Louis (according to Geoffroi de Beaulieu) introduced the sign of the cross into French practice, dare one suggest having heard of it from Henry in Paris in 1254? Touching for scrofula, however, does not seem to have played any large part in Louis's religious practices or reputation. Without any record evidence or contemporary comment, it is difficult to know how significant it was for Henry himself. For all this, see Barlow, 'The king's evil'; Vincent, *Holy Blood*, 193–4 and n. 19; Geoffroi de Beaulieu, cap. 35; Aurell, *L'Empire des Plantagenêt*, 126–7; and for Edward I, Prestwich, 'Piety of Edward I', 124–6.

[130] Carpenter, *Reign of Henry III*, 260.

[131] Osney, 77.

[132] Cited by Dixon-Smith, 'Image and reality', 85.

[133] Saint-Pathus, 66.

[134] Kantorowicz, *Laudes Regiae*, 175–6, 217.

when the Benedictine abbots met at Bermondsey, he asked them to agree that in future their houses should say every day during the mass of the Virgin the collect 'God in whose hands are the hearts of kings . . . and the protector of all hoping in him, give to our king and our queen, their children, and the Christian people the ability knowingly to cultivate the triumph of your virtue that through you they may always find favour.'[135]

Likewise, when, the following year, the Dominicans held their general chapter at Holborn, Henry came into their chapter house and begged for their prayers. He also provided them with food and ate with them.[136] Henry could hardly do the same with the Cistercian general chapter since it met at Cîteaux, but, in 1255, in an eloquent appeal, he still asked for prayers that God direct his acts aright. In the same year he intervened to ensure that Cîteaux received its annual pension from the manor of Stamford.[137] A particular occasion for prayer was when Henry was leaving the country. In 1242 he asked for prayers to be offered up through each archdeaconry for the success of his Poitevin expedition, his victorious homecoming and the health of his children.[138] In the early 1250s he wanted the whole kingdom to pray for the success of his crusade. In 1259, about to leave England to conclude the Treaty of Paris, he went to St Albans and secured daily masses and prayers from the convent until his return.[139]

The inmates of the hospital and leper houses he visited on his journeys, the poor fed on his arrival in a town, the 'fratres' fed every day at court, the thousands fed on special occasions, as well as the mendicant orders, the monasteries and the kingdom as a whole, all thus contributed to the dew of prayers rising up on Henry's behalf and the spiritual mist in which he hoped to move.

HENRY AND THE CONVERSION OF THE JEWS

In distributing alms to the poor, Henry was being completely conventional. He was doing, if on a grander scale, what all his predecessors had done and what all Christians should do. In another area of 'good works' Henry was far more original. In January 1232, 'in a suburb of London in

---

[135] Paris, v, 81; *Missale Westmonasteriensis*, ii, cols. 714, 1144; iii, col. 1310. The collect was part of the special mass for a king. Paris complained, however, that Henry made no provision for this extra liturgical burden.

[136] Paris, v, 127. The Dominicans were also fed by the queen.

[137] *CR 1254–6*, 163, 215–16; *CLR 1251–60*, 51, 271. Henry supported John's Cistercian foundation at Beaulieu but was not devoted to the order in the same way as Louis IX, who founded the Cistercian house of Royaumont and sometimes said he wished he could live there. See also Grant, *Blanche of Castile*, 206, 210, 233–4.

[138] See *CR 1237–42*, 436.

[139] St Albans Continuator, 433–4.

a neighborhood called Newstreet' (now Chancery Lane), he founded a house for Jews who converted to Christianity, his Domus Conversorum.[140] No other house for converted Jews was founded by a contemporary ruler.[141] Henry was also committing himself to the work of conversion at an early stage in its history. The polemic against the Jews, developed by the friars, with its accompanying drive for conversion, was not fully worked out until later in the century.[142] In France, Louis IX's own efforts, on any general scale, seem to have begun with his return from crusade in 1254.[143] In the mission of conversion, Henry was the leader, Louis the follower.

There were around 4,000 Jews in England around the time Henry founded the Domus Conversorum. Most were concentrated in major towns, with perhaps 500 to 700 in London.[144] Henry was very well aware of the church's attitude towards them. Around the very time the Domus was founded, Grosseteste himself wrote a long letter on the subject to the countess of Winchester.[145] Because of their sin in crucifying Christ, Grosseteste explained, the Jews had lost their homeland and been scattered through all lands and peoples. Grossteteste, however, was very clear that the Jews should be protected and not put to death. This was because, as Paul had explained in his epistle to the Romans, at the end of the world the Jews too would be saved. They were thus part of God's plan. They were also (here quoting from St Augustine's gloss on psalm 58, 12), 'witnesses to the Christian faith', this through being bearers of the books of the Old Testament with their prophecy and promise of Christ. Hence, as the psalm enjoined, 'slay them not less my people forget'. The occasion for Grosseteste's letter was the countess's reception of the Jews expelled by Simon de Montfort from Leicester, Montfort here acting to spare his men, as Grosseteste said, any further 'pitiless exploitation through usury'. Grosseteste did not instruct the countess to follow suit and remove the Jews from her lands in the suburbs of Leicester. But he did insist that princes should forbid the Jews from oppressing Christians with usury. Instead of

---

[140] *F*, 201 (*CChR 1226–57*, 143). There is a detailed history of the house in Adler, *Jews of Medieval England*, ch. 6. Stacey, 'Conversion of Jews', is the key work for the conversion in England.

[141] The uniqueness is recognized in Adler, *Jews of Medieval England*, 281, and Fogle '*Domus Conversorum*', 4. There is nothing in the later story that Robert fitzHarding founded a school for Jews in Bristol; see Hillaby, 'A *Domus Conversorum* in Bristol?' I am grateful to Joe Hillaby and Robert Paterson for help on this point.

[142] The polemic is fully examined in Cohen, *Friars and the Jews*.

[143] Jordan, *Louis IX and the Challenge of the Crusade*, 155–7; Jordan, *French Monarchy and the Jews*, 147–50; Le Goff, *Saint Louis*, 808–9.

[144] For these figures, see Stacey, 'Conversion of Jews', 269, 279. For the English Jewry, see Hillaby and Hillaby, *The Palgrave History of Medieval Anglo-Jewish History*, and, under Henry III, Huscroft, *Expulsion*, ch. 4.

[145] *Letters of Grosseteste*, 65–9. For a discussion of the letter, see Southern, *Robert Grosseteste*, 244–7. In his summary Southern 'softened rather than exaggerated the violence of Grosseteste's words'!

enjoying luxury and leisure from such illicit fruits, Jews should live in poverty through the hard labour of their hands. Princes, who profited from their usury, were committing the same sin as the Jews themselves and would share their punishment. God would ignore their prayers and their garments would be 'fuel for the fire' (Isaiah 9:5).

Alongside the hostility to usury, seen so well in Grosseteste's letter, Henry's attitudes were also affected by a whole series of measures against the Jews taken in the minority both by the regency government and by the church.[146] These measures introduced to England the decrees of the third and fourth Lateran councils and were designed above all to prevent Christians being undermined in their faith by contact with Jews. In March 1218 the minority government thus ordered all Jews to wear a distinguishing tablet on their clothes so that they could not be mistaken for Christians. The decrees of Archbishop Langton's council held at Oxford in 1222 took this further by specifying the tablet should be in a cloth of a different colour to the clothes and measure two inches by four inches. The council also banned Christian women from acting as Jewish servants, forbad Jews from entering churches, and laid down that no new synagogues were to be created.[147]

This growing hostility to the Jews placed Henry in a very difficult position. The Jews were the personal property of the crown and a major source of revenue, taxable at will. A year after Henry founded the house of the converts, he demanded the Jews pay a tallage of 10,000 marks. The trouble, of course, was that all Jewish wealth derived from usury. Indeed, the government itself enforced payment of Jewish debts and sometimes took them into its own hands, so that many Christians ended up owing the money to the king.[148] Magna Carta in 1215 had laid down that if Jewish debts came into the king's hands, he should demand only the capital not the interest. But the chapter was left out from the subsequent Henrician versions of Magna Carta, an omission much resented as concocted copies of the Charter with the chapter back in show.[149] The dilemma was encapsulated in a remarkable drawing made in 1233. It depicted the great Jewish financier Isaac of Norwich with three heads, burning in hell, and beneath him two of his associates, a man and a woman, being taunted by devils. Yet the drawing appeared on the record of payments made by Jews to the tallage of 1233. The government itself thus acknowledged the evil practices from which it was profiting.[150]

---

[146] Huscroft, *Expulsion*, 83–5.

[147] *RLC*, i, 378b; *C&S*, i, 120–1, caps. 46–7. Similar injunctions appeared in much episcopal legislation; see Watt, 'English episcopate, the state and the Jews'.

[148] This happened when Jews could not pay a tallage or when the king preferred to have in his hand the debts owed to a deceased Jew rather than allowing his relatives or connections to compound for them.

[149] Carpenter, *Magna Carta*, 213.

[150] For online images and discussion, see http://www.nationalarchives.gov.uk/education/resources/medieval-mystery/source-1b/

What made the pressure on Henry all the greater was the example of the French monarchy. In a series of legislative measures and pronouncements between 1223 and 1235 it insisted that Jews live either by the labour of their hands or by commerce without usury. When debts owed the Jews were taken over by the king (as in 1227/8), the Christian debtors were to pay only the principal, not the interest as well, just as Magna Carta wanted of King John. Louis IX, from 1234, in purifying acts of conscience, actually sought to restore the interest he had received.[151]

There was, however, no way Henry could follow the French example. The money to be made from the Jews was far too valuable. It was not until 1275, with Jewish wealth much diminished, that Edward I finally banned usury. That Henry was troubled by his failure is shown by what he did do. In April 1233, soon after the launching of the tallage, and as a spiritual salve for its questionable material gains, he declared that interest on Jewish loans should not be compounded and should escalate at no more than two pence in the pound per week. In some ecclesiastical thinking this might have been enough. The legislation of the Fourth Lateran Council merely said that interest should not be 'oppressive and excessive'.[152] But by this time the French monarchy was going much further. Henry's measure still left interest accumulating at 43 per cent a year and made him vulnerable to the dangers Grossesteste threatened. His added injunction that Jews who could not serve the king should leave the country showed how he still intended to profit from them.

Henry's foundation of the Domus has to be seen against this background. The foundation attempted to put Henry's relations with the Jews right with God, but left in place the main edifice of Jewish finance. For even Henry, naïve though he was, cannot have thought that all Jews would be converting to Christianity. There was also the prospect of profit from the chattels of converted Jews for these escheated to the crown. While most of the converts seem to have been poor, there were exceptions, the most prominent (in 1259) being Elyas L'Evesque, archpresbyter of the Jews, whose property was bought by a rival in return for a fine of 400 marks.[153]

From where though did Henry get the idea of a major effort to convert the Jews, given this was still early in its history? Grosseteste, while he was involved in the conversion of individual Jews, said nothing about conversion as the solution in his letter to the countess of Winchester.[154] The legislation

---

[151] Jordan, *French Monarchy and the Jews*, 95, 129–34.

[152] Richardson, *English Jewry under the Angevin Kings*, 293–4; Vincent, 'Jews, Poitevins and the bishop of Winchester', 126, 130.

[153] Hillaby and Hillaby, *The Palgrave Dictionary of Medieval Anglo-Jewish History*, 245–6. The debts owed Elyas were also taken over and amounted to more than £150 in Norfolk alone, information I owe to Richard Cassidy. The archpresbyter, appointed by the king, sat at the exchequer of the Jews.

[154] See Stacey, 'Conversion of Jews', 268.

issued by the bishops said nothing about it either.[155] None of Henry's predecessors as kings of England seem to have shown interest in the subject. In
the thought of the twelfth century, while the conversion of individual Jews
was applauded, 'there was a striking lack of interest in a missionary
program'.[156] The most probable answer is that Henry was influenced by the
mendicant orders for it was they who spearheaded the new assault on the
Jews. A particular role was probably played by the Oxford Dominicans, and
one Dominican in particular, Robert Bacon.[157] Bacon was established in
Oxford by the late 1220s where Henry came to know him well.[158] He
listened to a sermon Bacon preached in Oxford in 1233 and co-operated
with him in the conversion of the Jews. In 1236, on Henry's orders, a young
Jewish convert was entrusted to Bacon's care. In 1242 two more converts in
his charge were supported by the king. In 1245 the sheriff of Oxford was to
be informed by Bacon of a convert who had apostatized.[159] Henry's project
may also have been encouraged by Peter des Roches and Hubert de Burgh,
given their close connections with the Dominicans. Both witnessed the foundation charter of the Domus. Des Roches had indeed given alms to
converted Jews and it was his suffragan John, bishop of Ardfert who consecrated the Domus.[160] Hubert's own interest is shown in the foundation
charter where an unusual clause said the converts could send their petitions
to the king through the justiciar and chancellor. Both des Roches and de
Burgh were men of piety, yet both as long-standing servants of the crown
knew the value of its Jewish asset. For them too perhaps the Domus was part
of a compromise between God and mammon.

The arguments Henry heard about the importance of conversion
doubtless included the threat posed by Jews to the Christian faith. The
Oxford council of 1222 had handed over to the secular arm for execution
a deacon who had apostatized for the love of a Jewish woman.[161] There
was also a physical threat to Christians. Henry would have known all about
'St William of Norwich', the Christian boy in 1144 allegedly captured and
crucified by the Jews of Norwich in macabre parody of the crucifixion of
Christ.[162] Since then there had been numerous similar accusations, both in

[155] See Watt, 'English episcopate, the state and the Jews', 142–3.

[156] The whole subject is explored in Berger, 'Mission to the Jews'. The quotation is from
584. The few twelfth-century polemics against the Jews which do show signs of things to
come were, he argues, produced not from missionary objectives but to aid Christians in
debate with the Jews.

[157] Cohen, *Friars and the Jews*, 43, begins his account of the friars' 'aggressive missionary
spirit' with Oxford and Bacon.

[158] For Bacon, see Smalley, 'Robert Bacon and the early Dominican school at Oxford',
and Dunbabin, 'Robert Bacon'.

[159] *CR 1234–7*, 383; *CR 1242–7*, 298; *CLR 1240–5*, 99; *CFR 1242–3*, no. 773.

[160] Vincent, 'Jews, Poitevins and the bishop of Winchester', 122, 125.

[161] *C&S*, i, 100–6.

[162] For the events at Norwich see Monmouth, *William of Norwich* (with an introduction
by Miri Rubin).

England and abroad. A devotional shrine to an alleged victim was established at Bury St Edmunds in 1181. Between 1144 and 1290 'at least a dozen accusations that Jews had murdered a Christian child were recorded by English chroniclers, hagiographers, or royal justices'.[163]

How far Henry was aware of the arguments being developed in the mendicant attack on the Jews is less clear. These centred on the way the Jews had replaced the truths of the Old Testament with the desecrations of the later Talmud. The Talmud both blasphemed Christ and (so it was alleged) allowed Jews to commit all manner of crimes against Christians. Judaism thus attacked the basis of both Christian religion and society. The threat was acute and needed urgent remedy. Given the Jews could not be killed, they must be converted. In Paris, in the 1240s, these ideas led to the burning of the Talmud on the orders of Louis IX, here acting, after various inquiries and debates, on the instructions of the pope.[164] Nothing like that happened in England. Although the order of Gregory IX setting in motion the burning of the books was to be transmitted to Henry III, one wonders whether it ever was. The whole episode went unmentioned by Matthew Paris.

Once Henry was committed to the conversion of the Jews, a house in which the converts could stay was a logical step. Since the property of converts passed to the crown, they would in effect be left destitute, if given no other means of support, clearly a great disincentive to converting in the first place. In 1100, Archbishop Anselm was concerned lest poverty should cause one particular convert to regret his decision.[165] A house, therefore, where converts could live comfortably and securely would help solve the problem. It could also be a beacon drawing Jews into the faith as well as safe harbour once they had arrived there. For Henry conceived the house from the first as a school both for those converted and 'to be converted'.[166] Hence Henry wanted one Jew, evidently teetering on the brink of conversion, to experience the 'conversation' of the house in the hope he would be baptized.[167]

Henry endowed the Domus with 700 marks (£467) a year receivable from the exchequer until it was provided for in lands and rents. The money was to sustain the converts and also fund the construction of the church (dedicated to the Holy Trinity) and other buildings. The comparatively large amount showed Henry's enthusiasm for the project but was never realized. In 1233 the exchequer, in six separate payments, was ordered to give the house a total of £202. In 1246 the total was £87, and

---

[163] Stacey, '"Adam of Bristol" and tales of ritual crucifixion', 1; Hillaby, 'Ritual-child-murder accusation', 86.

[164] Cohen, *Friars and the Jews*, 60–8; Jordan, *French Monarchy and the Jews*, 137–41.

[165] Adler, *Jews of Medieval England*, 280 n. 6.

[166] *CChR 1226–57*, 199.

[167] *CR 1231–4*, 440.

thereafter the payments more or less cease.[168] By this time, however, the house, thanks to Henry's gifts, had obtained the church of St Dunstan by the Temple and a collection of houses and rents in London and elsewhere. In 1242, just before Henry sailed on his French campaign, it was given 200 marks to buy land.[169] Its buildings have long since disappeared beneath later structures culminating in the Victorian Public Record Office, now King's College London's Maughan Library. Only the chancel arch of the chapel survives fixed into a wall behind a bicycle shed. However, a statue of Henry III, holding the Domus, stands above the entry arch to the Victorian building.[170]

Henry's foundation of the Domus was widely commended, most notably by Matthew Paris. He made a drawing of the house and recorded how Henry:

> at his own cost, built a handsome church and sufficient for a conventual congregation with certain adjacent buildings ... to which house all Jewish converts who had abandoned the blindness of Judaism could come to be under a rule of honest living and enjoy a home and safe refuge and sufficient sustenance of life without servile labour or the profits of usury. As a result, in a short time, large numbers of converts gathered therein and, being baptized, were instructed in the laws of the Christians and lived in a praiseworthy manner under the direction of a competent warden especially appointed for the purpose.[171]

Henry himself had a direct hand in recruiting for the house, often sending converts on to it, both male and female. In 1234 one renamed Philip had been converted and baptized in his presence. Next year, when in Bristol, two local converts, brother and sister, were likewise sent to the Domus. In both these cases the writs commanding their admission were personally authorized by the king.[172] Henry took a close interest in the affairs of the house. He promised to do something if its resources were insufficient, drew up lists of inmates in receipt of robes, gave the chapel vestments of samite, contributed a silver cup to hold the host, and intervened in favour of converts who had been expelled or segregated.[173]

---

[168] *CLR 1226–40*, 196, 200, 202, 208, 216, 224, 226; *CLR 1245–51*, 47, 59, 83, 96, 100–1; Adler, *Jews of Medieval England*, 286; Stacey, 'Conversion of Jews', 267 and n. 22. In the 1240s payments to the Domus averaged 180 marks a year.

[169] *CChR 1226–57*, 199, 283, 292, 307, 309, 311, 322, 327, 336, 351; *CPR 1232–47*, 178; *CR 1242–7*, 22, 174, 198, 481, 496; *CLR 1240–5*, 128; Adler, *Jews of Medieval England*, 282–3.

[170] Colvin, *History of the King's Works*, i, 158.

[171] Paris, iii, 262; Giles, *Matthew Paris*, 580. Paris inserted this account in the 1240s into the chronicle of Roger of Wendover.

[172] *CR 1231–4*, 415; *CR 1234–7*, 134; Adler, *Jews of Medieval England*, 283–4.

[173] *CR 1237–42*, 97, 267; *CR 1242–7*, 141, 165; *CLR 1240–5*, 248, 268, 286. Henry's custom was to clothe the converts: *CLR 1245–51*, 101.

Within the Domus the inmates led a communal life, as in a monastery. They ate together and attended daily services celebrated by two chaplains. How far men and women were set apart is not known. Under his son Edward I there were between eighty and a hundred converts in the house and perhaps the numbers were much the same under Henry.[174] By the late 1240s the house was evidently full and, as a short-term measure, Henry began to send individual converts to monasteries around the country.[175] These arrangements not surprisingly broke down while he was abroad in 1253–4 and he returned to find a large backlog of converts unprovided for. His response was to dispatch 160 of them to some 140 monasteries with requests that, over a two-year period, they either be maintained or given a daily dole of one and a half pence instead.[176] Evidently the converts were unwelcome guests and around thirty, turned away, had to be sent back with letters expressing anger and astonishment at their treatment. The majority of the converts were single men and women (over seventy were women), but there were some family groups, husbands and wives, mothers and daughters, although they were not always kept together.

Assuming that at this time there were nearly 100 converts in the Domus itself, then Henry had managed to help with the conversion of some 250 Jews, 6 per cent of the total population, if that was around 4,000. From his point of view this was no small achievement. The numbers may indeed have been larger for there were evidently many converts living neither in the Domus nor in religious houses. Between 1255 and 1258 the 150 or 171 paupers who benefited from Henry's maundy provisions were regularly described as 'poor converts'.[177] Not all converts were poor, however, and some had successful careers in the king's service, none more so than Henry of Winchester. According to the later testimony of Edward I, he was converted (and subsequently knighted) by King Henry himself and thus was given the king's name. This seems to have been in 1252 when Henry of Winchester received £10 a year for life while £5 a year went to his wife.[178]

The list of converts sent to the monasteries in 1255 shows that Henry did not labour alone. Converts were thus named after John Mansel, John de Plessis and the king's Dominican confessor, John of Darlington. Later

---

[174] Stacey, 'Conversion of Jews', 267 n. 22, 273; Adler, *Jews of Medieval England*, 288; *CPR 1266–72*, 55.

[175] *CR 1247–51*, 100; Adler, *Jews of Medieval England*, 289 n. 3.

[176] *CFR 1254–5*, nos. 54, 124–5, 203, 981; Carpenter, 'Crucifixion and conversion', 140–2; Stacey, 'Conversion of Jews', 269; Greatrex, 'Monastic charity for Jewish converts'; Adler, *Jews of Medieval England*, 343–6, with a list of the names.

[177] *CR 1254–6*, 249; *CR 1256–9*, 13, 45, 51, 172–3, 203–4, 216, references I owe to Appendix 5 in Dixon-Smith, 'Feeding the poor'. And see Adler, *Jews of Medieval England*, 291.

[178] For Henry of Winchester, see Stacey, 'Conversion of Jews', 276–8. He worked at the exchequer of the Jews. For other careers, see Adler, *Jews of Medieval England*, 291–7.

Darlington was probably involved in converting one of the Jews accused of crucifying a Christian boy in Lincoln.[179] Henry certainly hoped that conversion would be voluntary and a matter of conviction, hence the way the Domus was also a school. When the Jews of Northampton took away the children of one convert, Henry ordered them to be placed before their father so they could decide whether they wished to follow him or 'remain in their error'.[180] Henry made special provision so converts could study the Catholic faith and allowed a Jew to help Master William of Arundel with his book about conversion, quite possibly a manual about how to do it.[181]

In fact, of course, many Jews must have converted because of the persecution suffered under Henry, persecution financial, religious and physical. The king's financial demands in the middle years of the century were steadily impoverishing the Jewish community.[182] The belief that Jews captured Christian boys for ritualistic purposes was gaining ground. One Norwich case, where the boy, so it was said, had been circumcised and named Jurnepin, came before Henry himself in 1235. Matthew Paris believed the Jews ultimately aimed to crucify the boy. In the end several Jews were executed.[183] Another accusation of ritualistic murder (this one gaining less traction) was made in London in 1244.[184] How necessary, Henry would have thought, was his legislation in 1253 with its attempt to limit as far as possible any contact between Christians and Jews.[185] How important to reduce the danger through multiple conversions. The legislation itself said no Jew should impede in any way a fellow Jew 'wishing to convert to the faith of Christ'.[186] Two years later the pressure on the Jews increased, and Henry's efforts at conversion seemed justified, by terrible events in Lincoln. After an accusation that Jews had indeed captured and crucified a Christian boy, Henry sanctioned the execution of nineteen Jews and imprisoned many more.[187]

Henry never lost interest in the conversion of the Jews. In April 1265, in the darkest days of his reign, while controlled by Simon de Montfort,

---

[179] Adler, *Jews of Medieval England*, 343–5; *F*, 335 (*CPR 1247–58*, 457). Another convert on the list was called Robert Grosseteste (he was sent to St Swithun's Winchester while his wife and son went to Horton Priory in Kent). Earlier a convert named after Grosseteste had been sent to the Domus itself: *CR 1242–7*, 493.

[180] *CR 1234–7*, 358.

[181] *CR 1242–7*, 12, 161; *CR 1237–42*, 238. William was archdeacon of Huntingdon; see *Letters of Adam Marsh*, 216–17.

[182] See Stacey, '1240–60: a watershed in Anglo-Jewish relations?'; Huscroft, *Expulsion*, 86–91.

[183] *CRR*, xv, no. 1320; *CR 1234–7*, 17, 39; Wendover, iii, 305; Paris, iii, 543; Paris, iv, 30–1.

[184] Paris, iv, 377–8; Carpenter, 'Crucifixion and conversion', 138.

[185] In 1234, Henry had personally authorized a writ forbidding Christian women from acting as nurses for Jewish children in Norwich and elsewhere: *CR 1234–7*, 13–14.

[186] *C&S*, i, 472–4. For the context, see below, 563.

[187] For the events in Lincoln, see below, 625–9.

he explained how a long time ago, 'inspired by charity', he had decided to provide a competent support for converts. Unfortunately, due to the arduous affairs of the kingdom, he had been unable to fulfil his wish. So now he asked the abbey of St Osyth in Essex to look after the convert Richard of Westminster.[188] Once Henry was free from Montfort and the civil war was over, he extended the buildings of the Domus and increased its chaplains froime two to three.[189]

THE MASS

Central to Henry's reputation as a most Christian king was his veneration of the mass, hence the way Mathew Paris linked together Henry's alms and his masses as key features of his piety. The Osney abbey annalist, in his obituary of the king, declared that more than all his predecessors he loved the 'beauty of the house of God and divine service'.[190] Nicholas Trevet, writing in the early fourteenth century, but well informed, said that Henry was accustomed to hear three sung masses a day and attended others celebrated privately.[191] All this was very different from the reputation of his father, King John. 'Look how fat that stag has got without ever attending mass', was one supposed remark. Another story, while it implied John attended mass, alleged that since his youth he had never taken communion.[192]

In his reverence for the mass Henry was very much the product of his age. Although debates about the precise nature of the transformation continued, the belief in Christ's real presence in the communion bread and wine was official and absolute.[193] In Richard le Poore's statutes for his Salisbury diocese the laity were instructed to have no misgivings 'concerning the true body and blood of Christ. For, without doubt, under the species of bread they receive what hung for us on the cross, in the chalice they receive what poured from Christ's side.'[194] Henry himself would certainly have had no doubts. One proof of Edward the Confessor's sanctity was the way, at the elevation of the host, he had seen the bread transformed into the Christ child himself.[195] The young son of Henry's courtier

---

[188] CR 1264–8, 109–10.

[189] CPR 1266–72, 25, 42, 55, 70, 79, 522, 530. The extension took place while the house was under the wardenship of the king's clerk Adam of Chesterton.

[190] Osney, 253–4.

[191] Trevet, 279–80. Trevet was born around 1258. His father was one of Henry III's judges.

[192] Adam of Eynsham, 143–4. For the rather different reality of John and the mass, see Webster, King John and Religion, ch. 1.

[193] For the whole subject, see Rubin, Corpus Christi, chs. 1–2. For discussion of 'what to do and think at mass', see Binski, Becket's Crown, 197–201.

[194] C&S, i, 77–8.

[195] Paris, La Estoire, lines 2514–73; Missale Westmonasteriensis, iii, col. 1347.

Geoffrey Despenser experienced a similar vision. Asked by his mother why he seemed scared of the priest who had celebrated mass, he replied he had seen him eat a baby and was frightened he might be eaten himself![196] If Henry, as is not unlikely, wished to delve more deeply into the mystery of the mass, his confessor John of Darlington was well equipped to provide answers, for John's master, Hugh of St Cher, had argued that the communion saw a complete transformation of Christ's body with nothing at all remaining afterwards of the bread – transubstantiation in other words, not consubstantiation.[197]

Everything in the mass revolved around the crucifixion, Christ's death on the cross to redeem the sins of the world, his death so everyone might live. No wonder Henry had the scene portrayed again and again. When the priest beseeched God to transform the bread and wine into the very body and blood of his son, he was asking him to recreate in a mystical way Christ's actions at the last supper, 'who on the day before he suffered took bread into his holy and adorable hands . . . blessed it, brake it and gave it to his disciples saying, take you all of this, for this is my body'. The priest then continued with the words Christ spoke in giving his disciples the chalice, words which showed how his death would give a new start to all mankind: 'for this is the cup of my blood of the new and everlasting testament . . . which shall be shed for you and for many for the remission of sins, as oft as you shall do this, you shall do it in remembrance of me'.

The prayers which followed made very clear the infusion of grace received by taking communion: 'O lord, grant me so worthily to receive this most holy body and blood of thy son, our lord Jesus Christ, that I may thereby receive forgiveness of all my sins and be filled with thy holy spirit, and have thy peace, and be freed from eternal damnation, and at the day of judgement attain fellowship with your saints in perpetual rest.'[198]

No spoken words were more familiar to Henry than those of the mass. He believed absolutely in the ceremony's revivifying power. The impact of

---

[196] Thomas of Eccleston, 97. The son, John Despenser, later became a Montfortian rebel.

[197] Rubin, *Corpus Christi*, 37, 174–6. Henry, however, does not seem to have celebrated the feast of Corpus Christi which Hugh promoted.

[198] I have here combined the versions of the prayer in the Salisbury and Westminster Missals: *Sarum Missal*, 317–18; *Missale Westmonasteriensis*, ii, cols. 517–18. The Salisbury statutes, in a section on 'the effect of the eucharist', quoted Christ in the same vein: 'who eats my flesh and drinks my blood will have eternal life': *C&S*, i, 78 (John 6:52, 55). Christ goes on: 'He that eateth my flesh and drinketh my blood dwelleth in me and I in him'. The Anglican prayer of humble access includes this line in a beautiful passage which gets to heart of what communion is all about: 'Grant us, therefore, gracious Lord, so to eat the flesh of your dear son Jesus Christ, and to drink his blood, that our sinful bodies may be made clean by his body, and our souls washed through his most precious blood, and that we may evermore dwell in him and he in us.' The Salisbury statutes also stressed the role of priests as 'mediators between God and man', for it was only priests, of course, who were able to call upon God to transform the bread and wine. One miracle of the mass was that he always responded.

the service was enhanced by its accompanying rituals, 'the unambiguous definitions of Christ's real bodily presence in the eucharist [having] turned communion into an enormous event'.[199] Diocesan statutes were concerned to ensure that the host was carefully and reverentially kept, hence Henry's numerous gifts of silver chalices in which 'to place the body of Christ'. The Salisbury liturgy, coming into use throughout England, gave detailed instructions to the celebrants about their movements and gestures: 'here let the priest raise himself and kiss the altar . . . here let the priest make three crosses over the chalice and the bread . . . here let the priest rise and join his hands and afterwards wipe his fingers'. At the supreme moment of transubstantiation where the priest intoned 'this is my body', he was to adore the host with bowed head and then 'elevate it above his forehead that it may be seen by the people'.[200]

The performance of Henry's masses was lit by numerous candles. From the earliest days of the established church, the provision of light had been central to Christian ritual, not surprisingly for light was a holy thing, associated continually in the scriptures with the understanding and salvation flowing from God himself. In numerous letters Henry gave precise and profuse instructions for the lighting up of his churches and chapels.[201] Between the 1220s and 1250s the number of candles burnt in his chapel and almonry increased so much that a special item was added to the household accounts recording the weight of wax consumed. On ordinary days it was generally around 10 pounds but on major feast days the candles could weigh over 200 pounds. On Easter Day 1266, at Westminster, 278 pounds of wax were consumed, so enough for 556 of the usual half-pound candles.[202] That the scale of Henry's activity was exceptional is shown by Matthew Paris's comment. In his critique of the king he linked together Henry's 'immoderate lights' and his excessive almsgiving.[203]

Henry's candles lit up the magnificent vestments of his priests. In acquiring them he spared no effort or expense. Bought for his chapel at Christmas 1240 were three copes, five chasubles, a tunicle, a dalmatic and an alb. They were made from red samite or cloth worked with gold. The alb had pearls and was decorated with orphreys (strips of elaborate embroidery), one showing Christ in majesty with two angels, the other, likewise with two angels, the Virgin Mary. The total cost was over £70. At the same time Henry had the censers and chalices of the chapel repaired. The following year no less than £43 were spent on an amice with precious

---

[199] Rubin, *Corpus Christi*, 65. Rubin discusses the rituals of the mass between pp. 35 and 82.
[200] *Sarum Missal*, 309–11. See Morgan, 'The Introduction of the Sarum calendar', and Binski, *Becket's Crown*, 198.
[201] For light, see Fouracre, 'Eternal light and earthly needs'.
[202] TNA E 101/667/50, m. 3.
[203] Paris, v, 6.

stones for the chapel and £21 on a gospel book.[204] Henry knew his copes intimately and could give detailed instructions for their enhancement. He was always on the lookout for better. English work was much prized, including Matthew Paris believed by the pope, but when Henry heard of a silk cope arriving in London 'which excels in beauty and decoration all English copes', he went all out to get it.[205]

And then there was the music. Henry's services were sung by the clerks of his chapel, led by Walter de Lench and later by Peter of Beddington. Their numbers are unknown but, like most choirs, the core group could be expanded. At Easter 1239, Henry gave a penny to each of the clerks singing the psalms on his order. The amount involved indicates there were 150 of them.[206] When, of course, Henry heard mass in Westminster Abbey, he could enjoy the full throated efforts of the monks there.[207]

Amidst all the chants, chasubles and chalices, how often then did Henry attend mass? The only documentary evidence comes from two rolls, one covering the period from 28 October 1238 to 30 April 1239, the other from 1 January to 1 July 1265.[208] The year 1265 was, of course, a highly unusual one since Henry was a virtual captive of Simon de Montfort. The rolls record the king's daily offerings in his chapel during and after mass. In the first roll the sums involved are generally just a few pennies, but on some feast days the post-mass offering rises to 5s. In the second roll for the post-mass offering 5s is standard.[209] Did Henry hear more than one daily mass? The answer is yes, sometimes. In the six months of 1238/9 there were eleven days when he heard two masses. Seven were major feast days, the others seem to have just been days when Henry wanted to hear two masses.[210] Only on Christmas Day itself at Winchester did Henry hear three masses, the last in 'the great church', evidently the cathedral. Another 'great church', in this case Westminster Abbey, was likewise the place for the second mass on the feast day of the Confessor in 1239. In 1265, by contrast, only on Easter Day were there two masses, the second again in the Abbey.[211]

The rolls of 1238/9 and 1265, therefore, give no support to Trevet's claim that Henry heard three masses a day and others in private. Generally

---

[204] *CLR 1240–5*, 22, 29; *CR 1237–42*, 255. The orphreys on the alb were to be like those on an amice at the New Temple.

[205] *CR 1237–42*, 309–10; *CR 1242–7*, 43, 274; Paris, iv, 547. For some idea of the magnificence of English medieval vestments, see *English Medieval Embroidery*, ed. Browne, Davies, Michael and Zösch.

[206] TNA C 47/3/44, m. 1.

[207] For example, *CLR 1226–40*, 496.

[208] TNA C 47/3/44 and TNA E 101/349/30.

[209] For comparison between the rolls, see Wild, 'Captive king', 51–5.

[210] The feast days were those of the vigil of All Saints, the deposition of the Confessor on 5 January, Epiphany, the purification of the Virgin, St Peter ad Cathedra, Palm Sunday and Easter Day.

[211] On 5 January 1265, the feast day of the Confessor, Henry did go into the Abbey to make an offering at the high altar.

he heard one mass, but sometimes two and at Christmas three. He thus did less well than Louis IX, if, that is, we can believe his biographers' claim that he generally heard two masses every day and sometimes three or four.[212] Had more Henrician rolls survived, of course, the picture might be different, as it might be had we record evidence for Louis. If Trevet did exaggerate, that is all the greater testimony to Henry's reputation.

There were also counterbalances to the virtual absence in the 1265 roll of two masses. One was the now standard 5s oblation after mass as opposed to the few pence usual in 1239. The other, more striking, is the appearance of large numbers of 'solemn masses'.[213] No 'solemn masses' are specifically mentioned in 1238/9. In 1265, Henry heard sixty-nine of them. Most of these were masses for a particular saint or the Virgin Mary. Henry was thus spending longer over mass for solemn masses had more singing and ritual than ordinary ones.

While there is some evidence of Henry's attendance at mass there is none on how often he took communion. When Henry told Louis he preferred to see his God rather than merely hear about him, he referred not to the communion but to the elevation of the host at the moment of transubstantiation. According to the later testimony of a St Albans chronicler, Henry's custom, at the elevation of the host, was to hold the priest's hand and kiss it.[214] In the thirteenth century the elevation had become a great event, accompanied by the ringing of bells and precise instructions as to the gestures to be used. It became for laymen almost a substitute for communion itself.[215] Whereas they could gaze daily at Christ's body, they only took communion (or so the church suggested) once, twice or thrice a year.[216] Communion was, of course, an awesome event, only to be undertaken, after instruction (like Hamo of Faversham's), confession and penance. Richard le Poore's Salisbury statutes quoted St Paul threatening damnation to all who took it unworthily.[217] But, with all his alms, offerings and good works, perhaps Henry had no such qualms. One wonders whether the occasions in the roll of 1239 when his offerings after mass were 5s rather than a few pence were also the occasions when he took communion. In that case, by 1265, just like the priest, he was taking communion every day. Here he was doing much better than Louis who, again according to his biographers, only took communion six times a year.[218]

Henry's chapel was itinerant. The clerks with their chalices, vestments and relics (of which more later) travelled with the king and performed

---

[212] Geoffroi de Beaulieu, cap. 21; Saint-Pathus, 65, 67; Le Goff, *Saint Louis*, 768.

[213] Wild, 'Captive king', 53–4.

[214] Rishanger, 73.

[215] For the elevation, see Rubin, *Corpus Christi*, 55–63, 69–70.

[216] The Fourth Lateran Council had only said that laymen should take communion once a year at Easter. Diocesan statutes often added Christmas and Pentecost.

[217] C&S, i, 78.

[218] Le Goff, *Saint Louis*, 764.

their rites in the chapels wherever Henry was staying. But when Henry
was absent, the chapels did not fall silent. As he put it in 1259, he wished
'service to be celebrated daily in the chapels of his castles throughout
England'.[219] Henry took great pains providing his chapels with books,
vestments, chalices, candles and chaplains (at the standard salary of £2 10s
a year).[220] In the first eighteen years of his majority he built at least
eighteen new chapels, ten for himself and eight for the queen.[221] All told,
in the 1250s, Henry was sustaining over fifty chapels, a considerable
increase on King John.[222] At major residences, where there was often
more than one chapel to serve, Henry increased the numbers of the chaplains. In the 1230s there was one each for the chapels of St Stephen and
St John at Westminster. By the 1250s the number had risen to seven. At
Windsor, where Henry built a magnificent new chapel, the numbers rose
from two to eight; at Dover from two to five.[223] The activities of Henry's
chaplains were not confined to the mass. They also performed the services
of the daily office, the canonical hours, that is, of Matins, Lauds, Prime,
Terce, Sext, None and Vespers. At Westminster, therefore, Henry and his
court were surrounded throughout the day by the sound of divine service
ringing out from the chapels of St Stephen and St John, the king's oratory
by his bed, and the queen's chapel by her chamber. One suspects the
scenario was much the same as at the court of Louis IX as described by
Guillaume de Saint-Pathus. 'The blessed king used to hear each day mass
and vespers sung, and all the canonical hours too. And he used to have
chaplains who day and night sang the mass, the matins and other offices
and he used to go to church to hear mass and the other canonical hours
even if he had lots of work.'[224]

How exceptional compared to his predecessors was Henry's devotion to
the mass? In terms of reputation there was certainly a big contrast with
his father and indeed his grandfather. According to Ralph Niger, Henry II
passed the time during mass in whispered conversation and doodling.[225]
While stories that King John never communicated are certainly false, the
picture of his misbehaviour, during the services conducted by Bishop
Hugh of Lincoln in 1199, seems quite believable. Indeed, they gain some

[219] *CLR 1251–60*, 474.

[220] For this in respect of Scarborough, see *CLR 1251–60*, 190, 474, 513.

[221] Colvin, *History of the King's Works*, i, 124.

[222] I get Henry's figure by combining the evidence in the pipe roll for 1258/9, kindly
given me by Richard Cassidy, with the list in *CLR 1251–60*, 659–60. The map of chapels
sustained by King John in Webster, *King John and Religion*, 25, has thirteen places on it. *PR
1214*, 239, lists around twenty royal chapels. In the pipe roll of 1258/9 around thirty are
mentioned.

[223] *CLR 1226–40*, 263; *CLR 1240–5*, 12, 141; *CLR 1245–51*, 112, 385; *CLR 1251–60*, 43, 75.
The Windsor figure seems later to have been reduced.

[224] Saint-Pathus, 26; Geoffroi de Beaulieu, cap. 21.

[225] Warren, *Henry II*, 211.

support from all the penances John performed for failing to observe the fast days of the church.[226] Richard's reputation, by contrast, was much closer to Henry's. Delighting in divine service, so Ralph of Coggeshall tells us, he adorned his chapel with precious vestments, conducted the singing of his choirs, and kept silence throughout the mass, devoting himself to prayers, even if faced with urgent business.[227] More impressive still was Saint Margaret of Scotland.[228] According to her biographer, Turgot, she had five or six masses performed for her privately before attending the public mass. She also told those worried about receiving communion (remembering St Paul's warning) that they had nothing to fear, provided, like her, they had confessed their sins and, 'scourged with penitence', had been cleansed by fasting, alms and tears. They could then eat Christ's flesh and drink his blood 'not for judgment but for remission of sins and for salutary preparation in eternal bliss'.[229] Perhaps this gets close to the spirit in which Henry himself took communion.

THE VIRGIN MARY, SAINTS, PILGRIMAGES AND RELICS

The Virgin Mary was woven into the fabric of the mass.[230] She was hailed as the mother of Christ. She was called upon again and again to act as an intercessor. Special masses could be said for her daily. Her feast days, each with variants of the Mass, ran through the Christian year: the Purification on 2 February, the Annunciation on 25 March, the Assumption on 15 August, the Nativity on 8 September and the Conception on 8 December. 'With exulting souls we ought to praise, to bless and proclaim her who didst both conceive thy only begotten son and, in glory of perpetual virginity, did pour on this world the eternal light of Jesus Christ our lord,' chanted the choirs. 'Grant we beseech thee that . . . by the glorious intercession of blessed Mary, ever virgin, we may be delivered from present sorrow and have the fruition of joy everlasting,' implored the priest.[231]

Given her centrality to Christian life, Henry hardly needed any special instruction about the Virgin's saving power. On that too his early mentors were naturally at one. Archbishop Langton composed hymns in the Virgin's honour. Peter des Roches dedicated to her many of his religious foundations. Hubert de Burgh founded in her honour the hospital celebrating his great sea victory in 1217 and introduced Henry to the Marian cult centre at Walsingham in 1226. In 1233, as he learnt in a vision, he was

---

[226] Adam of Eynsham, 142–3; see Webster, *King John and Religion*, 116.

[227] Coggeshall, 97; Gillingham, *Richard I*, 258.

[228] See above, 295.

[229] Turgot, 71–2, 78–9. Margaret also quoted John 6:53, 'Except you eat the flesh of the Son of Man and drink his blood, you have no life in you.'

[230] For a full treatment of Henry's devotion to the Virgin, see Vincent, 'King Henry III and the Blessed Virgin Mary'.

[231] *Sarum Missal*, 284–6, 307–8, 521–9.

saved by the Virgin from being captured by his enemies.[232] Westminster Abbey too was a cult centre with several relics of the Virgin given by the Confessor including her girdle and a fragment of the window in which she stood when learning from the angel Gabriel of the virgin birth.

The evidence for Henry's own devotion to the Virgin is overwhelming. He laid the foundation stone of Westminster Abbey's Lady Chapel before his second coronation in 1220, and later brought the building into line with his new Abbey. He adorned the chapel with two paintings costing all of £80 and replaced its two doubtless rather dim lamps with a perpetually burning candle.[233] He must have had a major say in the Marian themes of the Abbey's chapter house where he intended to address his parliaments. A roof boss in the Abbey itself depicted the Annunciation. There was also a beautiful painting of Mary on the retable Henry commissioned for the Abbey's high altar. She appeared alone, at the crucifixion and holding the Christ child in paintings and statues throughout Henry's residences.[234] And she featured in Henry's processions. Amongst the banners Henry commissioned for these in 1237 were ones depicting the Virgin, the coronation of the Virgin and the crucifixion with Mary and John on either side of the cross.[235] In 1253, in his only known will, Henry left his soul to the Virgin's care.[236]

On the Virgin's feast days Henry increased the numbers of masses heard, paupers fed and candles burnt. He made offerings in gold rather than silver and entered Westminster Abbey to venerate the Virgin's girdle.[237] On the feasts of the Virgin's Purification, Assumption and Nativity his choirs chanted the 'Christus Vincit'.[238] Henry also liked to hear the Virgin's mass outside her feast days, doing so on six occasions in the six months covered by the oblation roll of 1238/9, and on eleven occasions in the six months of the roll of 1265. In the second roll, while the

[232] Vincent, 'King Henry III and the Blessed Virgin Mary', 143–4.

[233] Flete, 69–70; CLR 1251–60, 424; Westminster Customary, 92. The sacrist, after Henry's death, replaced the candle with a lamp (presumably much easier to maintain), so, as the monks complained, in place of two lamps the chapel had ended up with one!

[234] Borenius, 'Cycle of images', 47–50. See CR 1242–7, 32, for a particularly elaborate order for a 'great' and 'beautiful' image of the Virgin and Child, with removable wooden crowns so they could be replaced by silver ones on feast days, this within a tabernacle 18 feet broad (so the image really was 'great'). Surviving fragments of the paintings (probably dating from the 1240s) show that the chapel at Chester castle had a cycle of the apocryphal miracles of the Virgin. This has been described as 'a milestone in the development of such iconography'. See Cather, Park and Pender, 'Henry III's wall paintings at Chester castle', 171–8, with the quotation at 178.

[235] CLR 1226–40, 260; CR 1247–51, 292.

[236] F, 496.

[237] Vincent, 'King Henry III and the Blessed Virgin Mary', 136–8; Carpenter, 'Household rolls', 41; TNA C 47/3/44; TNA E 101/349/27; TNA C 43/3/6; TNA E 10/667/50; TNA E 101/349/30.

[238] Kantorowicz, Laudes Regiae, 175.

Virgin was outshone by the Confessor, the next highest total for a special mass (Becket's) was three. How Henry must have hoped the Virgin would indeed deliver him from 'present sorrow'.[239] Both at Dover castle and the Tower, special chaplains were appointed to perform the Mary mass, and presumably it was celebrated daily throughout Henry's chapels.[240]

The rituals at court and the images in its chapels thus meant the Virgin was constantly at Henry's side. To worship her he also travelled. A dozen times in his reign he went on a pilgrimage to Walsingham, where Mary herself (so it was believed) had commanded the building of a house modelled on the one in Nazareth where the Angel Gabriel had announced the virgin birth. Let us hope the fragment of window frame at Westminster Abbey helped with the design. Twice Henry was at Walsingham for the feast of the Annunciation itself. When absent he would order the chapel there to be lit up with thousands of candles on the Virgin's feast days.[241]

Henry was particularly concerned to secure the Virgin's protection for his children. After Edward's birth, 'a tunic of good samite' measuring his length was placed on the crucifix at St Mary Southwark, while at Windsor a chaplain was appointed to celebrate the mass of the Virgin for his health and welfare.[242] A Mary mass was also to be celebrated daily for Henry's daughter Margaret, this while five candles burnt in veneration of the five joys of the Virgin. Many of the images of the Virgin that Henry ordered were for the queen, doubtless after mutual discussion. At Havering her chapel had a small statue of the Virgin and Child and a painting of the Annunciation. At Clarendon, this time in stained glass, another small figure of Mary with child was commissioned for Eleanor's chamber, while beneath it, at Mary's feet, was to be a queen (clearly Eleanor herself) with hands joined holding an 'Ave Maria'.[243] When Eleanor was enduring a difficult pregnancy in Gascony in 1242, the Virgin's girdle was sent out to her from Westminster Abbey with happy results.[244] During her mass, the Virgin was saluted as the queen of heaven and many of Henry's images must have shown her crowned. Eleanor was only queen of England, but she drew strength from the visual parallel between earthly and heavenly kingship.[245]

---

[239] Wild, 'Captive king', 53–4; Vincent, 'King Henry III and the Blessed Virgin Mary', 136–7. Vincent notes the way the masses in 1265, in contrast to 1238/9, were often heard on Saturdays. Henry thus seems to have become aware that Saturday had been instituted as Mary's day.

[240] *CLR 1226–40*, 499; *CLR 1240–5*, 129. Saint-Pathus has Louis hearing the Virgin's mass every Tuesday and Saturday, so more frequently than Henry.

[241] Vincent, 'King Henry III and the Blessed Virgin Mary', 133–4. A visit in 1234 can be added to Vincent's list.

[242] *CR 1234–7*, 149; *CLR 1226–40*, 435.

[243] *CLR 1240–5*, 372; *CLR 1245–51*, 324; Howell, *Eleanor of Provence*, 73, 255–6.

[244] *Westminster Customary*, 73; Howell, *Eleanor of Provence*, 35.

[245] *Sarum Missal*, 526–7; Howell, *Eleanor of Provence*, 256–7.

In the mass, the Virgin Mary was not a solitary intercessor. The priest also invoked the prayers of the apostles, martyrs and all the saints. Henry had portrayals of the four evangelists put up in his chambers, churches and chapels, both in painting and in glass. All twelve apostles probably featured in the sculpted statues on Westminster Abbey's great north door. Peter (with his keys), Paul and John all appeared in the Abbey's high altar retable. John had a special link with Edward the Confessor as will be seen. Peter was the supposed founder of Westminster Abbey and its dedicatee. The conversion of St Paul and another (unspecified) subject from his life were painted, at Henry's order, in Woodstock's chapel at Everswell. The rhythm of Henry's liturgical life was choreographed around saint's days, framing like so many stars the great feasts of the church at Christmas, Easter and Whitsun. Between the end of October 1238 and December 1239, Henry's oblation roll shows he offered pieces of gold (rather than the usual silver pennies) on the feasts of Simon and Jude, Martin, Edmund, Katherine, Andrew, Nicholas, Stephen, John the Evangelist and Thomas Becket. By 1265 he was hearing the solemn masses of numerous saints: in January and February those of Marcellus, Julian, Agnes, Bathild, Valentine, Matthias and Milburga.

Henry naturally honoured native saints. Between 1226 and 1258 he visited St Edmund at Bury on thirteen occasions and Becket at Canterbury on no fewer than twenty-two.[246] He was very concerned that his candles should add to their light. In 1246 four candles, each weighing 100 pounds, were to burn around their shrines on their respective feast days. When at Canterbury in 1239, Henry made offerings at Becket's 'crown' (the top of his head in the corona chapel), at the two altars by the great altar, at the fragment of the death-dealing sword, at the Virgin's altar in the crypt, and finally at the shrine of Becket itself.[247] One wonders, however, if there was an ambivalence in Henry's attitude to Becket. Although he attended Becket's translation on 7 July 1220, he only once (in 1228) returned to Canterbury on 7 July, although it became the major Becket feast day. Did Henry fear that Becket's influence might sometimes be less than benevolent? Thomas's miraculous intervention, after all, had supposedly destroyed the new gate Henry was building at the Tower of London. Later, parallels were drawn between Becket and Simon de Montfort.[248] It is striking how often Henry turned to the Confessor as though to offset or combat Becket's power. He thus filled Becket's chapel in Winchester castle with images of the Confessor.[249] Out in

---

[246] Bury: 1226, 1229, 1232, 1234, 1235 (twice), 1238, 1244, 1245, 1248, 1251, 1252, 1256; Canterbury, 1227 (twice), 1228, 1229, 1231, 1232, 1234, 1235 (twice), 1236, 1237, 1239, 1242, 1243, 1244, 1246, 1247, 1249, 1252, 1253, 1254, 1256. For new work in this area, see Shacklock, 'Henry III and the use of native saints'.

[247] *CLR 1245–51*, 93; and also *CLR 1240–5*, 374. For Canterbury in 1239, see above, 205–6.

[248] Ambler, *The Song of Simon de Montfort*, 277–8, 330.

[249] *CLR 1251–60*, 95, 308.

Bordeaux in 1243, only three days after the 7 July feast day of Becket, he gave orders for the establishment in Canterbury Cathedral of an altar dedicated to the Confessor along with paintings depicting him and his miracles. Perhaps it was with the same motive that he gave Becket relics (his hair shirt and vestments stained with his blood) to Westminster Abbey.[250]

When Henry travelled he was always on pilgrimage.[251] Before any considerable journey he would load up with the silks, jewels and chalices for his donations to the various religious institutions along his route.[252] Henry also made offerings of money, though here usually of a few pence. On his way to and from Canterbury in 1239 he made offerings at the crosses at Bermondsey, Sutton at Hone and Faversham, at the tomb of St William in Rochester Cathedral, at the high altar in Chatham church and at the image there of the Virgin Mary. The story of Henry, when going into the centre of Paris, entering every church along the route and staying until mass was over seems very believable.[253]

How often Henry journeyed specifically to visit a shrine, as opposed to simply venerating it as he passed through, is not always clear. Sometimes his presence at Canterbury was simply a by-product of a journey to and from Dover. Still, on several occasions, Henry does seem to have gone to Canterbury on pilgrimage for he went more or less straight there and back from Westminster.[254] A similar pattern can be seen at St Albans, where Matthew Paris gives such vivid pictures of Henry's devotions.[255] Sometimes Henry was just on his way in and out of London, but equally he might go straight there and back from Westminster, or take a circular route via St Albans back to Westminster from Windsor. He did the latter in 1259 when soliciting the prayers of Alban and the monks before setting off for France to conclude the Treaty of Paris.[256]

Henry's most spectacular pilgrimage was to the shrine of his erstwhile archbishop of Canterbury, Edmund of Abingdon, at Pontigny in Burgundy.[257] His most conspicuous pilgrimages in England were to East Anglia. There Bury and Walsingham formed a trio of holy sites with the priory of Bromholm on the Norfolk coast, where relics of the true cross were

---

[250] *RG*, i, no. 1848; Flete, 71.

[251] For this theme more generally, see Vincent, 'Pilgrimages of Angevin kings'.

[252] For example, *CR 1254–6*, 334. And for the resulting offerings see Wild, *WA*, 13, cited above, 167.

[253] Carpenter, 'Meetings of kings', 25–6.

[254] This was so in 1227 (twice), 1229, 1234, 1237, 1239, 1242, 1249 and 1253.

[255] See below, 454, 520, 551, 615, 642, 644.

[256] St Albans Continuator, 431–2, and (for the shrine) Clasby, *St Alban and his Shrine*. Henry often combined St Albans with a visit to Waltham abbey where he could venerate its Holy Cross. In March 1253, Henry went on a pilgrimage simply to Waltham, going there and back from Westminster.

[257] This visit is discussed in volume 2.

supposedly preserved. Henry's tours usually took in all three.[258] On these occasions Henry was on pilgrimage pure and simple for he had no residences in East Anglia and no political reasons to go there.[259] His dozen or so pilgrimages were sometimes directly linked to the desire for spiritual support in time of trial. He went in 1229 and 1242 before his expeditions to France, in 1232 and 1234 during the conflicts over Hubert de Burgh and Peter des Roches, in 1244 before confronting King Alexander, and in 1256 when worried about the Sicilian project and the health of his daughter Katherine.[260]

Henry, therefore, went on pilgrimage to the saints. He also had portions of the saints always with him, this thanks to his stupendous collection of relics. The idea that body parts, clothing and objects associated with the saints could possess something of their healing power is found in the New Testament. The Acts of the Apostles (19:11–12) affirmed that, when clothes and handkerchiefs of St Paul were brought to the sick, 'the diseases departed from them'.[261] Previous kings all had their relic collections, although since King John's was lost in the Wash, perhaps Henry had to make a new start.[262] He certainly set about collecting with a will. When he was at Bromholm in 1234, in those tense days before the fall of Peter des Roches, he received as gifts from Norwich Cathedral priory pieces from the bodies of Saints Gilbert, Euphemia, Stephen, Wulfstan, Leger, Theodore, Hermolaus, Nicholas, Bartholomew, Philip, Petronella and Zachariah, together with a portion of Aaron's rod.[263] A remarkable roll from 1234/5 recording gifts to the king shows that they often included relics. So in just a few months Henry accumulated a finger bone of St Augustine (from his brother Richard of Cornwall), a leg bone of St Osyth, relics of Saints George, Theodore and Pantaleon, a spine from the crown of thorns and portions of the golden gate at Jerusalem, the Holy Sepulchre, the altar on which Christ had been presented in the Temple and the burning bush from which God had spoken to Moses. Most of these were deposited in a 'coffer of relics' and probably travelled with the king. One hopes they were not among the relics lost during the flight from Barbezieux in 1242.[264]

---

[258] An exception was in 1235, when he made a special journey to Bury, across England from Woodstock, to be there on 20 November, Edmund's feast day. The ruins of Bromholm priory stand amidst farm buildings and cabbage fields in the outskirts of Bacton on the Norfolk coast and there is nothing to tell passers-by that this was once a place of pilgrimage. Walsingham by contrast is again a major pilgrimage centre.

[259] The only exception came in the last year of his life when shocking events forced Henry to go to Norwich, stopping at Bury on the way. Even this visit, however, turned into a pilgrimage, because, having finished his business in Norwich, he continued on to Bromholm and Walsingham.

[260] For the king ordering candles to burn on his arrival, see *CLR 1240–5*, 114, 244–6.

[261] See Bartlett, *Why Can the Dead?*, 244–5, with 276–82 about relic collections.

[262] For John's collection, see Webster, *King John and Religion*, 55–7.

[263] *CPR 1232–47*, 39.

[264] Vincent, 'Pilgrimages of Angevin kings', 35–6; Vincent, 'An inventory of gifts', 129–30.

Henry regarded the relics of Westminster Abbey as more or less his own, hence the way he had the Virgin's girdle sent out to the queen in Gascony. Here, however, he gave as well as took. He provided a new casket to contain one of the Abbey's major relics, the hand of the Apostle Thomas. The ring to be fitted on the casket's finger had a beautiful sapphire and an inscription including the lines 'blessed are those who do not see'.[265] As well as the Becket relics, Henry also gave the Abbey the arm of St Silvester, a tooth of St Athanasius and, more remarkable (and described in detail by Matthew Paris), a stone with an impression of Christ's foot as he ascended into heaven.[266] And then there was one more relic, greater than all the others, one more precious even than the relics of the passion that Louis IX had brought to Paris, namely a phial containing drops of the very blood Christ had shed on the cross. It was Henry's gift to the Abbey, to the Confessor and to the whole English people, a trinity at the center of the cult of the Confessor himself.[267]

EDWARD THE CONFESSOR

From the 1230s, Edward the Confessor was the central figure in Henry's religious life. His devotion to other saints paled in comparison. The household roll for 1259/60 shows Henry feeding 1,500 'fratres' on 5 January 1260, the anniversary of the Confessor's death, and 5,016 on 13 October 1260, the anniversary of his translation to Westminster Abbey. The next largest total was 464 'fratres' fed on the feast of Pentecost. Not a single saint's day, other than the Confessor's, registered at all. In the oblation roll of 1265 Henry heard twenty-one masses of the Confessor, eleven of the Virgin Mary and three of Becket. No other saint got more than one. Henry's gifts of silks, jewels and candles to the Confessor far outstripped those to any other saint. The new church he built at Westminster in the Confessor's honour far outshone all other churches in the country. All this, moreover, was quite new. None of his predecessors had adopted the Confessor as their patron saint. Nor was there any equivalent to Henry's overwhelming devotion to a saint in the religious life of King Louis.[268]

Edward the Confessor was the last Anglo-Saxon king of the ancient Wessex line. He died on 5 January 1066, and was buried in the Abbey he had built at Westminster – death, burial and Abbey all being depicted in the Bayeux Tapestry. Thanks to the efforts of the monks of Westminster,

---

[265] *CR 1237–42*, 270, 276. The inscription was written by Henry of Avranches. Henry wanted the queen to make the transfer from the old casket to the new. In the south transept of the Abbey, there is a large late thirteenth-century painting of Thomas putting his hand into Christ's side: Binski, *Westminster Abbey*, 171–3.

[266] Flete, 69, 72; Paris, v, 81–2.

[267] For the relic of the Holy Blood, see below, 474–8.

[268] Louis's relationship with St Denis offers little comparison: Carpenter, 'Meetings of kings', 16.

Edward was canonized in 1161, his translation to his shrine in the Abbey following in a great ceremony on 13 October 1163.[269] King Henry II had supported Westminster's campaign for Edward's canonization, and attended the 1163 translation, but there is little sign that either he or his successor, Richard I, felt any particular attachment to the saint. King John was more interested but still charged the abbot and convent a hefty 200 marks when confirming the Confessor's gift of Islip, his birthplace, to the Abbey.[270] He was never at Westminster for the 5 January feast, and only appeared twice at the more important feast on 13 October, on three occasions leaving London shortly beforehand.[271] Henry, therefore, hardly grew up in an aura of ancestral devotion to the Confessor. His own interest seems minimal in the first phase of the reign, despite his second coronation in the Abbey in 1220 with the Confessor's crown. In the household roll of 1225/6 the feast of 5 January was not marked in any way at all.[272] In 1227 it was Archbishop Langton, not Henry, who petitioned the pope for Edward's feast day to be celebrated by the English church.

The first sign of Henry's quickening interest comes in 1233. That January he ordered the images of St Edmund 'on the one side' and St Edward 'on the other' to be painted in his round chapel at Woodstock. If Edward and Edmund (the king of East Anglia martyred by the Vikings in 869) were here on a par, Edward was soon forging ahead. On the feast of his translation on 13 October 1233, Henry ordered the monks of Westminster to sing the 'Christus Vincit' before him. It was not until 1239 that Edmund was similarly privileged.[273] Sometime between October 1233 and October 1234, Henry ordered the Confessor's statue to be erected and his history painted in his chapel at Clarendon. He made no mention of Edmund. Whereas in 1236 Henry planned his offerings for the Confessor's feast of 13 October at Westminster weeks in advance, he only remembered Edmund's feast of 20 November on the day itself, with the result that his offerings, although to be made 'as quickly as possible', must have arrived at Bury St Edmunds ignominiously late.[274] Edmund was never, of course, forgotten. The 3,000 candles burning at Bury on his anniversary in 1244 invoked his aid during the queen's pregnancy. The resulting second son was named Edmund in his honour.[275] But it was Henry's first son who was called Edward. Of the two Anglo-Saxon royal saints, Edmund had to settle for a prestigious but very definite second place.

[269] For what follows, see Carpenter, 'King Henry III and Saint Edward the Confessor', where full references and more detailed discussion can be found.

[270] WAM, 15160, 15162; *RF*, 222. For a more positive view of John's attachment, see Webster, *King John and Religion*, 42–3, 59, 108–9, 197.

[271] The three occasions were in 1200, 1207 and 1209. He was there in 1204 and 1213.

[272] *DA*, 96.

[273] *CLR 1226–40*, 234, 441.

[274] *CR 1234–7*, 309; *CLR 1226–40*, 243.

[275] See below, 420.

The rise in the cult of the Confessor in the mid-1230s is also shown in Henry's relations with Westminster Abbey. In 1228, Henry did not mention the Confessor when granting the abbot and convent market rights. He also charged them the (fairly routine) sum of 15 marks for the privilege.[276] In November 1233, by contrast, another concession was made free of charge and 'out of reverence for King Edward our predecessor'. Then, in July 1235, when Henry, again gratis, gave a whole series of privileges to the Abbey, he described the Confessor not as his 'predecessor' but as 'the glorious king Edward, our special patron'.[277] The same ascent is clear from Henry's itinerary. In 1232 he left Westminster at the end of September and went on a tour to Woodstock, getting back to Westminster in early November. Manifestly he felt no overriding desire to be present at the 13 October feast. In 1235, by contrast, he left Windsor in good time to attend.[278] He made even greater efforts in 1236 and 1238, hurrying back from York in the first year and the Welsh marches in the second. Thereafter, save when abroad or on campaign, Henry never missed a 13 October feast. There was an equally striking change in Henry's behaviour in regard to the second feast on 5 January. Before 1238, Henry was never once at Westminster for it. Thereafter, save when abroad or campaigning, he missed only two such feasts in the remaining thirty-four years of his reign, frequently travelling up from the Christmas celebrations at Winchester to be there.[279]

It was then between 1233 and 1238 that the cult of the Confessor suddenly and securely entered the fibre of Henry's being. Why? The wider background here was provided by Henry's itinerary, for Henry, with no need to divide his time between England and the continent, was able to spend longer at his palace of Westminster than any king since the Conquest. There was no similar palace at Bury St Edmunds. Henry was at Westminster for eighty-five days in 1233, seventy-seven in 1234, and ninety-four in 1235. He lived, therefore, day after day close to the Confessor's body. He was very exposed to the group of men who pre-eminently extolled the Confessor's merits. These, of course, were the monks of Westminster. The monks at this time had two overriding reasons for needing Henry's support. The first was to gain help with constructing the new Lady Chapel, which had been making slow progress since its start in 1220. The second, related directly to the situation in the 1230s, was to defend the Abbey's jurisdictional privileges. Sometime in the regnal year 28 October 1233–27 October 1234 a ruling of the king's council threatened

---

[276] WAM, 154; CFR 1227–8, no. 75.

[277] WAM, 15163, 1493. The role of the patron is discussed below.

[278] It is possible Henry came up from Windsor for the feast in 1231 but there is a gap in the itinerary so one cannot be sure. In 1229 he left Westminster just before the feast.

[279] The two misses were in 1252, when Henry was in York for his daughter's wedding, and in 1272, the last year of his life, when he was ill at Winchester.

the ability of ecclesiastical institutions, such as Westminster Abbey, to receive the amercements imposed by royal justices on their own men, unless, that is, their title to them was expressly mentioned in a royal charter. A new visitation of the king's justices to hear pleas through the country in August 1234 gave topicality to the issue. By making the Confessor Henry's 'special patron', the monks could hope for help exactly on these issues. The standard life of the Confessor, written by Ailred of Rievaulx for the canonization in 1163, thus stressed how the Confessor had both built the Abbey and amplified and defended its privileges. Clearly the message was that Henry should do the same. And he did. In April 1234 he suddenly gave forty oaks for the works on the new Lady Chapel. In the great charter of 1235 he made absolutely explicit the Abbey's title to the amercements levied on its men. How crucial the charter was is shown by the number of times it was cited in the Abbey's defence over the ensuing years.

In introducing Henry to the Confessor, two Westminster monks stand out. The first was Richard of Barking, abbot between 1222 and 1246, and the donor of elaborate tapestries placed around the choir telling the story of the Confessor's life.[280] In 1234, a month after Henry's gift of oaks to the Lady Chapel, Barking set out on a mission for the king. Later he became a baron of the exchequer. The other monk, perhaps even more influential, was Richard le Gras, prior from 1231 of the Abbey's daughter house at Hurley. At the very time the cult was developing, Richard was beginning a meteoric rise in the king's service, one ultimately taking him to the keepership of the seal.[281] In June 1235 he went overseas to begin negotiations for Henry's marriage to Eleanor of Provence. Only a few days later, Henry, describing the Confessor as his special patron, issued the Abbey's great charter of liberties, surely no coincidence. After Richard's return, a great council met at Windsor and approved the marriage. Then Henry left Windsor in time to reach Westminster for the Confessor's feast on 13 October, the first time he made a clear effort to get there. Surely he was giving thanks for the bride the Confessor had secured. This was probably a key moment in establishing the cult. Next year, repeating his reference to the Confessor as his special patron, Henry conferred on Richard le Gras's priory of Hurley precisely the same privileges he had conferred on the Abbey itself.

As Richard le Gras and Richard of Barking talked about Edward, Henry began to see that this was a saint of mighty power who could support him through his troubles in this life and lead him to the next. As Ailred wrote, 'Saint Edward could not conceal from the world how influential he was in heaven . . . he restored sight to the blind, walking to the lame and health to the sick.'[282] Equally remarkable were the miraculous

---

[280] See Binski, 'Abbot Barking's tapestries'.
[281] By this time he was abbot of Evesham.
[282] Ailred, 96.

events associated with the Confessor in his lifetime. They were mentioned in the mass celebrated on the Confessor's feast days and were described at length in Ailred's book.[283] The Confessor had been able to sit back at table and watch as God choked to death the lying Earl Godwin. He had dissolved in laughter during mass when learning through a vision how God was, at that very moment, preventing an invasion by drowning the king of Denmark. (Henry had the altar at Westminster where the vision occurred lit up by candles.)[284] In the same vein, the psalm sung at the mass of the Confessor celebrated a king's victory over his enemies ('the Lord shall swallow them up in his wrath') and affirmed that God 'hast given him his heart's desire, and hast not denied him the request of his lips'.[285]

There could be no doubt the Confessor was at God's right hand, able to intercede on a disciple's behalf. The most striking proof of that was an episode Henry had depicted again and again in painting, tiles, glass and sculpture. This was of Edward giving his ring to a poor pilgrim about to set off to the Holy Land.[286] The overriding importance of the episode was shown by the sequel. For out in the Holy Land, the pilgrim, revealing himself as St John the Evangelist, had sent the ring back to the Confessor with a message: he was soon to die but would be conducted by John himself up to heaven.[287] An evocative illumination within Matthew Paris's version of Ailred's text depicts Edward's arrival in heaven with Peter standing by with his keys and John, with a delicately helping hand, ushering Edward into the presence of Christ.[288] What more proof did one need of the Confessor's whereabouts after that! Perhaps Henry knew of visions like Turchil's where, having passed through purgatory, the saints received their special disciples and prepared them for the sight of God. How Henry must have hoped the Confessor would do the same for him.

What Henry wanted from the Confessor, therefore, was precisely what the Confessor could provide: 'the patronage, protection, defence, advocacy' that a patron gave his disciple.[289] 'Entrust yourself to [the Confessor's] sedulous protection,' Ailred had told Henry II.[290] It was Henry III who took the advice. One of the stained-glass windows in Winchester castle

---

[283] For the mass, see *Missale Westmonasteriensis*, ii, col. 739.

[284] *CR 1242–7*, 427; *CChR 1226–57*, 304.

[285] *Missale Westmonasteriensis*, ii, cols. 738, 975. 'Domine in virtute', psalm 21 (20 in the Vulgate). The psalm was also sung at the coronation.

[286] Henry believed the meeting took place at the royal manor of Clavering in Essex. He commissioned a painting of it for the chapel of St John there: *CR 1245–51*, 342; *CLR 1251–60*, 268.

[287] In the Confessor's mass the episode is called the bringing back of the ring: *Missale Westmonasteriensis*, ii, col. 739.

[288] https://cudl.lib.cam.ac.uk/view/MS-EE-00003-00059, image 63. Binski, *Westminster Abbey*, 74, comments, 'the exchanged ring stands as a token of their union as peers, and of Paradise itself, since it betokens Edward's apotheosis'.

[289] For the role of patron, see Bartlett, *England under the Norman and Angevin Kings*, 464.

[290] Ailred, 16.

depicted the Confessor presenting a king to God's majesty, doubtless the Confessor presenting Henry himself.[291] It was, as Henry explained, 'helped by the protection of our patron and predecessor the blessed Edward that, through the mercy of Jesus Christ, we are able to rule'.[292]

This message from Westminster about the Confessor's saving power came to Henry at a crucial time. Indeed, that was a key reason why he fell under its spell. The year 1233, in which Henry's devotion first becomes apparent, was also the year of Peter des Roches. Having ousted Hubert de Burgh from power, Peter now dominated king and government. Perhaps he encouraged attachment to the Confessor as a way of dignifying Henry's kingship and disguising the new regime's very foreign hue. But his influence was brief. In 1233, Peter plunged England into a civil war. The following year he was sacked. If the cult of the Confessor was encouraged by des Roches to strengthen his regime, it took hold in order to salvage the king from its wreckage. Baffled and bruised, with his confidence shattered, and his kingship laid low, without any longer a great minister to lean on, Henry now sought solace and salvation from a spiritual minister who would always be there, and would never let him down. It is no accident that when Henry commanded the 'Christus Vincit' to be chanted before him by the monks of Westminster on 13 October 1233, he was in the middle of the parliament where des Roches's regime first came under sustained attack.[293]

The Confessor fitted the needs of the moment in another way. Henry, it could seem, was adopting the Confessor as his patron saint, not because he wanted to overthrow the political settlement after des Roches's fall but because he accepted it. The Confessor, in Ailred's picture, appears as a gentle, merciful king, concerned to bring peace and prosperity to his people. He acts a legislator, just like Henry between 1234 and 1237. He governs in concert with his magnates, taking their advice over his marriage, just as Henry was to do over his marriage. The Confessor thus epitomized the just and consensual rule required of Henry in the post-des Roches era. According to Ailred, under the Confessor there was 'peace for the people, honour for the nobles, liberty for the church.'[294] In his version of Ailred's life, almost certainly commissioned by Henry himself, Matthew Paris expanded on such passages. Once the Confessor ascended the throne:

Then is the land in good estate,
Count and baron and the prelate,

[291] *CLR 1251–60*, 308. Significantly this was a window in Becket's chapel.

[292] TNA SC 1/2/121. This is in a letter to the bishop of Waterford in November 1244, urging him, in accordance with the papal mandate, to celebrate the feast days of the Confessor in his diocese. Letters to the other bishops probably took the same form.

[293] *CLR 1226–40*, 234; see Carpenter, 'King Henry III and Saint Edward the Confessor', 870, n. 26.

[294] Ailred, 28. For the supposed legislation of the Confessor, see O'Brien, 'God's Peace and King's Peace'.

There is none whom the king does not please,
All are rich and all at ease.[295]

In another respect the cult of the Confessor fitted perfectly with Henry's situation in the mid-1230s. It enabled him to stress the Englishness of his kingship in a way highly acceptable to a political community so recently disgusted by the invasion of 'the Poitevins'. The point was made in a graphic illumination at the start of Matthew Paris's life of the Confessor with its depiction of Edward's forbears. It showed, enthroned and crowned, King Alfred 'first king of England', King Edgar and the Confessor's father, King Aethelred. Standing above them, touching their crowns, were two angels raining down 'peace and prosperity on the English'.[296] The appeal to Henry was all the greater because he was developing a more general interest in the sainted kings of the Anglo-Saxon past. In 1235 he entrusted his sister Isabella, about to set out on her daunting marriage to Emperor Frederick, to the protection of the four martyr and confessor saints of England.[297] Later, in 1257, in a conversation with Matthew Paris, he named all eleven of the sainted English kings.[298] The Confessor, however, remained unique. He not only joined Henry to the Anglo-Saxon past, but also smoothed over the great divide of 1066. According to well-known stories, he had both designated Duke William as his successor and, in a vision, foreseen the reunion of the Anglo-Saxon and Norman lines through the marriage of Henry I to the great-granddaughter of Edmund Ironside.

There was one other force behind the cult, for Henry must surely have appreciated the extraordinary parallels between himself and the Confessor in terms of their situation and experience. They had both come to the throne after their peoples had endured periods of war and oppression. They had both been abandoned by their mothers.[299] They had both been betrayed by treacherous servants. Indeed Ailred's description of how Godwin had become chief minister by removing all the king's friends, and had then done many things against right and law, might seem exactly to anticipate the conduct of Peter des Roches. Edward was also just as sedentary as Henry. In both Ailred's *Life* and in Paris's, 'he seldom does anything at all'.[300]

Henry could also believe he shared the Confessor's personal qualities. At the start of his work, Matthew Paris distinguished between kings who were

[295] Paris, *La Estoire*, lines 872–5. For the Paris life see below, n. 312.

[296] https://cudl.lib.cam.ac.uk/view/MS-EE-00003-00059, image 12.

[297] Wendover, iii, 319 n. 4. The four were Edmund, the Confessor, Edward the Martyr and Oswald.

[298] Paris, v, 617. They were Aethelbert, Edward the Martyr, Kenelm, Oswald, Oswin, Neithan, Wistan, Fromund, Edwulf, Edmund and Edward.

[299] For this point, see Vincent, 'Isabella of Angoulême', 215–16.

[300] Binski, 'Reflections on "La estoire de Seint Aedward le rei"', 344. Binski, *Westminster Abbey*, ch. 2, has a full exploration of the cult.

'mighty and very bold', like Arthur, and those, like the Confessor, who were 'wise and peaceable'.[301] In terms of wisdom, the Confessor was frequently compared to Solomon, just as Henry hoped to be.[302] He was also commended, for his 'debonereté', that calm and courteous conduct, the opposite of anger, to which Henry very much aspired, if not always success-fully. Most remarkable of all was the way the Confessor, just like Henry, was both praised for his 'simplicity' (his 'simplicité debonaire') and criticized, unfairly of course, for displaying a 'foolish simplicity' ('fole simplicité').[303] How reassuring for Henry to hear that his patron saint had also been traduced in that way. How reassuring too to learn that the path to successful kingship was not simply through being 'mighty and very bold.'

There was just one area where Henry had no intention of imitating the conduct of the Confessor. He had, reassuringly for Eleanor and the kingdom, no desire for a sexless marriage. Indeed, the Confessor's success in bringing Henry his bride was an important factor in establishing the cult. Thereafter, its consolidation owed much to the way Henry sought to call down Edward's blessings on his queen and children.

On the day of her coronation in January 1236, Eleanor thus offered at the Confessor's shrine in Westminster Abbey a great embroidered cope costing over £23. In June, when the royal couple were together at Clarendon, Henry ordered the image of a queen to be set up on the saint's feretory beside the image of a king already placed there. In September he was already making arrangements for their joint offerings at the forth-coming feast of the Confessor on 13 October.[304] It was probably around this time that Henry commissioned Matthew Paris to write his life of the saint, a life dedicated to Eleanor and quite specifically designed to make her love him. Paris's work was based on Ailred's but was made more acces-sible and engaging by being written in rhyming French verse, over 4,500 lines of it.[305] Near the start of the work, three lines encapsulated all the saint might do for Eleanor and of course for Henry:

---

[301] Paris, *La Estoire*, lines 1–22.

[302] Paris, *La Estoire*, lines 890–5, 1373–8. For the Solomonic references in Henry's palaces, see below, 366, 369.

[303] Paris, *La Estoire*, lines 911, 1053, 1265–6. For 'debonereté', see Vale, *The Angevin Legacy*, 23–5. Hyams, 'What did Henry III of England think in bed?', 116–20, discusses the Confessor as a royal role model.

[304] Wild, *WA*, 9; *CR 1234–7*, 278, 309; Howell, *Eleanor of Provence*, 24.

[305] Paris's original text and illustrations are lost. The text of the copy made probably in the 1250s is printed and translated in Paris, *La Estoire*, 1–311. *La Estoire de Seint Aedward*, edited by K.Y. Wallace, provides a modern edition of the French text. *The History of Saint Edward the King by Matthew Paris* is a new translation by Thelma Fenster and Jocelyn Wogan-Browne with a full introduction. The work is discussed in Binski, 'Reflections on "La estoire de Seint Aedward le rei"'. The illustrations are reproduced in M.R. James's *La Estoire de Seint Aedward*. Digitised images are available at https://cudl.lib.cam.ac.uk/view/MS-EE-00003-00059. In fact, they come up if one just puts into a search engine Cambridge University Library La Estoire.

By his virtues and his prayers
He governs you and comforts you,
He will cause to be opened for you the gate of Heaven.[306]

In this life the Confessor certainly did bring comfort. Having secured Henry's marriage to Eleanor in the first place, he then, triumph upon triumph, gave them a son and heir. In thanks, Henry named their son Edward, a totally innovative decision. Since 1066 no king or heir to the throne had been named after an Anglo-Saxon monarch. In effect, Henry was adopting the Confessor as the dynasty's patron saint and placing its future under his government and care.

In sustaining the Confessor's support, Henry knew one thing was vital, for it was the crux of all relationships between disciples and their saints. The saint had to believe the disciple was indeed a devoted follower and worthy of his help.[307] An obvious proof of devotion was through gifts. A steady stream of gold, jewels and precious cloths thus flowed from Henry's hand to the Confessor's shrine.[308] Henry also seems to have inaugurated an annual ceremony whereby he gave his ring to the Confessor and then had his chaplain buy it back.[309] There was an equal flow of vestments – amices, stoles, chasubles, dalmatics and above all copes, copes in white, gold, green and violet samite, decorated with orphreys and studied with jewels and pearls. They often had to be ready for offerings on Henry's arrival.[310] Perhaps most striking of all was the chasuble on which Mabel of St Edmunds laboured for years. It was to be offered to the Confessor for both king and queen. Henry took great pains to see Mabel was paid fairly, 'so that he committed no sin and she suffered no damage'.[311] Henry also gave the Confessor light. He endowed Westminster Abbey with £10 a year so that four candles could burn evermore around the shrine 'in addition to the old light there'.[312] The numbers were increased when he was absent on campaign. Through all the time the king was in Gascony in 1242–3, fifteen candles of his height burnt around the shrine at a cost of £51.[313]

The cult of the Confessor was far from confined to Westminster. His image was ubiquitous throughout the king's chapels and chambers. The new church Henry built in Bordeaux was dedicated to him as was the new

---

[306] *Lives of Edward the Confessor*, lines 80–2.

[307] See Bartlett, *Why Can the Dead?*, 106–12.

[308] So, for example, *CR 1242–7*, 156–7; Wild, *WA*, 37, 58–60, 62, 66, 68–9, 71–2, 74, 83, 89, 92, 97, 125, 128, 151. The gold was mostly in the form of money of Murcia and bezants.

[309] Wild, *WA*, lxx.

[310] For example, *CLR 1226–40*, 487, 501; *CLR 1240–5*, 8, 55; *CLR 1245–51*, 123; *CR 1242–7*, 206, 222, 270.

[311] *CR 1237–42*, 155, 282, 321–2, 372; *CLR 1226–40*, 427, 454, 462, 487, 496; *CLR 1240–5*, 8, 18, 38, 84, 86, 101.

[312] Book 11 (Westminster Abbey Domesday), fos. 399v–340r; *CChR 1226–57*, 250.

[313] *CLR 1240–5*, 306; *CR 1237–42*, 374; *CR 1242–7*, 199.

chapel in Windsor castle. His altar was set up in Canterbury Cathedral. His mass was celebrated daily at Ospringe hospital.[314] Henry also assumed the patronage and laid the foundation stone of the Cistercian house established at Netley in Hampshire by Peter des Roches's executors, a house called 'the place of Saint Edward' in Edward's honour.[315] But Westminster, of course, was the centre and here the high points every year were the feasts celebrated in Edward's honour on the anniversaries of his death on 5 January and of his translation on 13 October. Something of their nature can be gleaned from Henry's instructions for the feasts, never more detailed than when he feared he would be absent. One has some sympathy for the Westminster authorities, who were reprimanded in 1237 for failing to carry out the elaborate orders with due diligence![316]

On the vigil of the feasts Henry fasted on bread and water. He also arranged for the lighting of the shrine to begin. In 1237, for the 13 October feast, one hundred great candles were to burn around it from the ninth hour on the vigil to the ninth hour on the feast day and then another hundred from then on until next morning. At the same time 300 smaller candles were to burn around the shrine during vespers, the hours and the mass. On the feast day itself the whole church was 'illuminated' by the lighting of both the great candelabra in the nave and (in 1241) 500 candles, each of half a pound in weight. In 1246 the number of candles seems to have been much greater, for Henry ordered 10,000 pounds of wax to be ready for the October feast. Before the January feast in 1248, a massive candle weighing a record 1,000 pounds was to be placed in Westminster Abbey, or 'the monastery of the blessed Edward' as Henry described it.[317] On the feast days the Abbey was also decorated with great cloths of gold hung behind the cross on the high altar, one decorated with the arms of the king, his brother Richard and the count of Provence.[318]

Henry began the feast day with mass in his chapel where his offering was a piece of gold rather than the usual few silver pence. Then to the ringing of bells, he processed into Westminster Abbey for the great mass.[319] Invitations to an array of bishops and barons ensured a large

---

[314] CPR 1247–58, 37; CChR 1226–57, 391.

[315] Meekings, Studies in 13th-Century Justice, ch. 17; Colvin, History of the King's Works, i, 158 n. 2. For the name (not necessarily that given by des Roches), see Carpenter, 'King Henry III and Saint Edward the Confessor', 877 n. 71.

[316] CR 1234–7, 91–2. For a selection of other orders (not all directly related to the feasts), see CR 1234–7, 309; CR 1237–42, 333; CR 1242–7, 36, 41, 138, 153, 186, 331, 476–7; CLR 1245–51, 119; CR 1247–51, 493–4; CR 1254–6, 222; and CChR 1226–57, 268. What follows also draws on Matthew Paris, the oblation rolls of 1238/9 and 1265, and the household roll of 1259/60.

[317] CLR 1245–51, 81; CR 1247–51, 18–19.

[318] CR 1242–7, 153.

[319] Henry had a new bell tower built at the Abbey and told Edward of Westminster not to depart until he had hung a great new bell ready to be rung on the eve of the 5 January feast in 1253: Colvin, History of the King's Works, i, 143; CR 1251–3, 280 (BA, 192–4).

attendance at the October feast as, in later years, did the simultaneous opening of parliament. All the processions of the city of London came too with their candles and banners. They must have made a sight as they proceeded along the Strand and then turned at Charing to head down to Westminster. For the monks, the two feasts of the Confessor were naturally on a par with the greatest Christian festivals, so eight copes were worn by those officiating, doubtless ones given by Henry himself.[320] 'Let the church rejoice recollecting the wonderful works of King Edward', sang the choir, arrayed in surplices Henry had provided (all with 'R' woven in red silk into the collars), and accompanied by the tunes of the organs.[321] Henry's offerings included a piece of gold and thirty-six gold coins, the latter to be attached to the cross on the high altar for himself, his queen and their children.

After the mass came the great feast for which Henry had been accumulating food and drink for weeks. The cost on 13 October 1260 was over £200 with a colossal £133 spent by the kitchen, figures excluding much of the wine (bought separately) and the stocks of game from the king's forests.[322] In all this Henry did not forget the poor. His custom on the Confessor's feast days was to fill both great and small halls at Westminster full with paupers. On 13 October 1260 the number fed, as we have seen, was 5,016.[323] How this was achieved logistically is unknown. Perhaps some paupers joined in the feast of the great and good while others had to wait for second sitting. Henry at any rate was mindful of Christ's injunction: 'when thou makest a feast, call the poor . . . thou shall be recompensed at the resurrection of the just' (Luke 14:13–14).

The great mass in the Abbey did not end the liturgical celebrations. Like other saints, the Confessor had his own 'office' so that all the services through his feast days – Matins, Lauds, Prime, Terce, Sext, None and Vespers – were special to him. These were the 'hours' Henry ordered to be lit up in the Abbey with 300 candles. They were doubtless also performed and illuminated in his chapels within the palace. On 13 October 1260 over 200 pounds of wax were burnt in the chapel and the almonry, enough for 400 half-pound candles.[324] So on these great days the praises of the Confessor echoed continuously through the palace of Westminster just as they did through the Abbey.

---

[320] *Missale Westmonasteriensis*, iii, 1407.

[321] *Missale Westmonasteriensis*, ii, cols. 739, 976; *CLR 1240–5*, 15. In 1243, while in Gascony, Henry had ordered a great cloth, made of six samites 'if necessary', to be hung opposite the organs, so let us hope it did not dull their sound: *CR 1242–7*, 36.

[322] The cost includes that of the vigil.

[323] Carpenter, 'Household rolls', 41.

[324] For the office or hours of the Confessor, see *Missale Westmonasteriensis*, iii, cols. 1341–9. For the offices and masses of saints more generally, see Bartlett, *Why Can the Dead?*, 113–20.

WESTMINSTER ABBEY

Far and away Henry's greatest offering to the Confessor was the new shrine and new Abbey at Westminster. Henry began work on the first in 1241 and on the second four years later in 1245. On 13 October 1269 Henry's church was consecrated and the Confessor's body translated to the new shrine behind the high altar. This was the supreme moment of Henry's life.

In building his new church, Henry had necessarily demolished part of the old one built by the Confessor and depicted on the Bayeux Tapestry. Evidently the possibility the Confessor might be upset by the destruction of his work did not occur to Henry. This after all was an age where churches were constantly being rebuilt. The Confessor's Abbey was both outdated and (as the pope put it in 1245) 'old and decayed'.[325] He would surely be delighted by the construction of a magnificent new one in its place. Nothing would show more clearly the devotion of his disciple.

Henry's first object at Westminster, then, was to win the Confessor's favour for himself and his family. Part of him indeed wished to keep his devotion private. When, fearing he would be absent, he gave detailed instructions for the candles to be burnt at the October feast of 1238, he sought to conceal the fact he was the donor. If anyone asked they were to be told it was the prior of Hurley![326] But Henry also hoped the glowing core of his own devotion would radiate the benefits of the Confessor through all the realm. The Confessor would become England's national saint. Henry thus secured from the Cistercian general chapter in 1235 and the pope in 1236 orders commanding the observance of the Confessor's feast days, and had the papal mandate read at a legatine council in London.[327] For the feasts at Westminster, he assembled casts of thousands. 'Rejoice all the people of the English for [the Confessor] is an assiduous intercessor for the health of all the people,' ran one of the readings on the day.[328] Matthew Paris himself saw the construction of the new shrine as benefiting 'the state of the kingdom' as well as the material and spiritual health of the king, queen and their children.[329]

Henry, therefore, was offering the Confessor to his kingdom but he certainly wanted something in return. His desire to keep his patronage secret was but a momentary whim. His people were to show gratitude for all he was doing, all the more so since he manifestly ruled guided by the Confessor's protective hand. In broadcasting to everyone both the gift and

---

[325] WAM Book 11 (Westminster Abbey Domesday), fos. 405v–6; Colvin, *History of the King's Works*, i, 131–2.

[326] *CR 1237–42*, 91–2. Here, of course, Henry was following the example of Christ in concealing his miracles and indeed of the Confessor himself.

[327] Carpenter, 'King Henry III and Saint Edward the Confessor', 871.

[328] *Missale Westmonasteriensis*, iii, col. 1343.

[329] Paris, iv, 156–7.

the protection, the Abbey had one tremendous asset. Location, location, location. The Abbey was totally different from the Cistercian monastery that Richard of Cornwall was founding at Hailes, deep in the countryside. Instead it was at the very centre of the realm, adjoining London, and right beside the royal palace where the exchequer, the court of common pleas and parliament all met. It is no accident that the Abbey was conceived in the 1240s, the first decade of parliament's real power. Indeed, its conception was in a way a response to a parliamentary crisis, just as Henry's initial devotion to the Confessor was a response to the crisis of 1233–4.[330]

The Abbey therefore was a highly political building, reaching out to the realm, encouraging it to do Henry's bidding. There was also one other context. In the early 1240s, when the shrine and Abbey were being conceived, Henry was acutely conscious of what was happening in France. It is again no accident that he began work on the shrine in 1241, the same year Louis IX brought the crown of thorns and other relics of the holy cross to Paris. When work on the Abbey itself started in 1245, the dazzling chapel Louis built to house the relics was well under way. It was finally consecrated in 1248, the year after Henry brought to the Abbey his own relic of the cross, the phial of Christ's very blood.[331] In the Abbey Henry could think he was outdoing Louis and constructing a building of far more focused power than any in France.[332] There kings were crowned at Reims, buried at Saint Denis around the kingdom's national saint, and now had a new chapel, the Sainte Chapelle with its holy relics, at the heart of their Parisian palace. Westminster since 1066 had been England's coronation church. Henry now intended it to be his dynasty's mausoleum as well as the home of the kingdom's national saint. And Henry also regarded the Abbey as his chapel, one far grander than the Sainte Chapelle, and from 1247 housing a relic just as holy.[333] The Abbey was to be Reims, Saint Denis and the Sainte Chapelle rolled into one.

Henry's decision to be buried in the Abbey involved a change of mind and one which shows the Confessor's power. Back in 1231, Henry had wished to lie in London's Temple church.[334] He was influenced by the example of his brother-in-law William Marshal, whose funeral in the Temple Church Henry had attended earlier in the year. More immediately, he was making provision for his body before what might be a dangerous campaign in Wales.[335] Henry had no immediate intention of taking the cross, but leaving his body to the order most closely associated with the

[330] For a discussion of the political circumstances, see below, 428, 463–4.

[331] For a full discussion, see below, 474–8.

[332] A point developed from Colvin, *History of the King's Works*, i, 133.

[333] For the Abbey as the king's chapel, see *CR 1251–3*, 226; Binski, *Westminster Abbey*, 46.

[334] For a positive and wide-ranging view of Henry's relations with the Templars and the Temple church, see Stewart, 'A lesson in patronage'.

[335] See above, 102.

defence of the Holy Land, leaving it moreover to its church in the capital of the kingdom, was a way of vesting himself in a crusading aura. Henry remained attached to the Templars and often made gifts of wine and game when they celebrated their general chapters.[336] In the 1230s, Geoffrey the templar was the king's almoner and then keeper of the wardrobe.[337] With Henry's burial in view, the Templars started to rebuild the choir of the Temple Church as a fitting home for his body, creating the beautiful aisled church, with its elegant purbeck marble columns, surviving, if much restored, to this day.[338] But as Henry's devotion to the Confessor grew, the Templars worried about him changing his mind. In July 1235, the same month as the great charter to the Abbey where the Confessor was termed Henry's patron saint, they secured a confirmation that the Temple church would indeed be his place of burial. Later they obtained a charter from the queen saying she too would be buried there. A clause in Henry's charter stating that, should he found another religious house it was not to claim his body, suggests the Templars' anxieties.[339] In the end, with the creation of the new shrine and the new Abbey, Henry's desire to lie by his patron saint became overwhelming. In October 1246, with the new Abbey under way, he issued a charter affirming his desire, out of 'reverence for the glorious King Edward', to be buried in 'the monastery of Westminster'. At the same time, Queen Eleanor issued a similar charter.[340] Before the end of the reign both one of Henry's daughters and a grandson had been buried in the Abbey. It was already becoming the dynasty's mausoleum.

The Abbey was then to be coronation church, royal chapel, royal mausoleum and shrine for the kingdom's national saint. To fulfil these multiple and momentous functions, Henry's aim was clear. It was to build, as the pope put it, a church of 'wonderful beauty'.[341] Matthew Paris called the Sainte Chapelle 'incomparable'.[342] Henry absolutely intended the Abbey to be the same.

The Confessor's shrine itself was in two parts, the reliquary covering the wooden coffin, and the base designed to hold the reliquary aloft. As described by Matthew Paris in admiring alliteration, the reliquary was

---

[336] *CR 1242–7*, 182–3, 192, 307, 422, 424.

[337] For the end of Geoffrey's career, see Powicke, *Henry III*, ii, 782.

[338] For the architecture, see Stewart, 'A lesson in patronage', 352–72 with 343–6 for Henry's possible involvement with the building. For a comprehensive account of the church's history see the contributions in Griffiths-Jones and Park, *The Temple Church in London*.

[339] *CChR 1226–57*, 208, 210–11; Stewart, 'A lesson in patronage', 341–2, 345.

[340] WAM, 6318; WAM Book 11 (Westminster Abbey Domesday), fo. 62v. Henry's charter was issued on 23 October and was witnessed only by household officials, headed by the steward William de Cantilupe. The seal, contained in its silken bag, survives.

[341] WAM Book 11 (Westminster Abbey Domesday), fo. 407 (*CPReg.*, 262). Innocent IV is here (in 1250) issuing an indulgence for those who helped with the fabric.

[342] Paris, iv, 92; Paris, *FH*, ii, 447.

made from the most precious gems and from gold 'puro, primo et purissimo'. Its creators, he continued, were London goldsmiths, and the value of
their workmanship exceeded even that of the materials. Henry himself told
Paris with an oath that before its completion he would have spent more
than 100,000 marks.[343] Completion was indeed almost impossible because
there were always more gifts of gold, jewels and statuary coming in from
the king. In 1266, when Henry was forced to pawn the treasure destined for
the shrine, it consisted of hundreds of brooches, rings and cameos, a 'most
beautiful' sapphire worth 100 marks, a great head with a golden crown, a
golden majesty adorned with jewels (worth £200) and the bejewelled and
golden images of the Virgin and Child, St Peter with his keys trampling on
Nero, and numerous kings and angels. One of the kings (valued at £103)
held a shrine and was doubtless Henry himself.[344] The work on the reliquary was carried on in a special chapel constructed in the Abbey's
precincts and decorated with the Confessor's history.[345] It was there doubtless that Matthew Paris and other visitors viewed the extraordinary structure. Alas nothing now survives to show how 'incomparable' it was. There
were certainly major rivals in the shrines in England of Alban, Edmund
and, above all, Becket. Of the kingly images destined for the Confessor's
shrine, Edmund was the only one identified. Becket was not present.

Of the eventual base, more survives. Here Henry started out with a
conventional (in English terms) Purbeck marble structure, only to scrap it
and commission a replacement from the Italian Cosmati family. This
Cosmati base was dismantled at the Reformation but reconstructed during
the brief restoration of the Abbey under Queen Mary. Enough remains
of its glittering columns and porphyry stones to show its magnificence and
uniqueness.[346]

If the shrine base was radically new, so, on a far grander scale and in a
whole variety of ways, was the Abbey itself. Its east end, its windows, its
internal height and its main entrance were totally unlike anything seen
before in England. The reason is that these features were all derived from
the cathedrals of northern France, and in particular from Amiens and
Reims, Reims especially – Reims like the Abbey being a coronation
church. To be at Reims in the morning and at Westminster in the evening,
as I have sometimes been, is an uncanny experience, as though somehow
the great French cathedral has been transmuted into the Abbey. How
these similarities came about we know, for the name of the great master

---

[343] Paris, *FH*, ii, 454–5; Paris, iv, 156–7.

[344] *CPR 1266–72*, 135–40; WAM 9465; Colvin, *History of the King's Works*, i, 148. It may be
that some of these gifts had been offered to the temporary shrine in which the Confessor
rested before his translation. Henry sometimes ordered gifts fixed to the latter to be removable so they could adorn the new shrine.

[345] *CR 1251–3*, 290; Colvin, *History of the King's Works*, i, 148 and n. 3.

[346] The Cosmati base will be discussed further in volume 2 as I believe it was constructed
in the 1260s.

mason of the Abbey was Henry de Reyns.[347] Since 'Reyns' is a contemporary form of Reims, there seems little doubt that Henry derived his
surname from the French cathedral. That, however, he was an imported
Frenchman is unlikely. The uncertainty in the handling of some French
features, and the very English flavour of others, suggests the contrary.
More likely Henry was an English mason who had spent time in France
in the 1230s and had become thoroughly conversant with its great
churches. Above all, he knew Reims and hence came to be called, probably he called himself, Henry of Reims. He passed the surname onto his
son who described himself on his seal as 'Hugh de Reyns mason'.[348]

In 1243, Henry de Reyns is described as 'master of the masons of the
king' in a writ issued at Windsor. Probably he had been working on the
king's new chapel in the castle since its inception in 1240. In March 1245
he was sent to give advice about the castle the king was building at York.[349]
By this time he must have been well into plans for rebuilding Westminster
Abbey. In this perhaps he was helped by drawings he had brought back
from France, drawings of details, ground plans and elevations derived
both from existing buildings and from ideas of what might be built in the
future. Doubtless he was also teeming with ideas of his own.

King Henry was no passive recipient of Master Henry's advice. He had
as acute an eye for the details of buildings as he had for those of copes.
Out in Gascony in 1243 he ordered the roof of the new chapel at Windsor
to be made in wood like the roof of the new work at Lichfield, 'so that it
appears a work of stone'. The hall in Dublin castle was to have windows
like those in the hall at Canterbury. The lectern for the chapter house at
Westminster was to be like that at St Albans, although 'if possible even
more handsome and beautiful'.[350] Henry also had other advisers, notably
the clerk Edward of Westminster, who carried out many of the king's
commissions for the purchase of cloths and jewels. It was Edward who
suggested to the king that the leopards on either side of the throne at
Westminster would be more 'sumptuous' in bronze than in marble.[351]
Doubtless too there was input from the Westminster monks. In all the long,
earnest and impassioned debates over what to do, as plans were pored
over and alternatives discussed, the final decision was the king's. He as
much as Master Henry was the architect of the Abbey. The great church
breathes his generous and expansive spirit.

Henry de Reyns was master mason of the Abbey from its start until what
was probably his death in 1253. His successors were John of Gloucester

---

[347] He is so described in a charter of his son: WAM 17538.
[348] WAM 17538.
[349] *CR 1242–7*, 141, 293.
[350] *CR 1242–7*, 23, 39; *CR 1247–51*, 203; see also *CR 1237–42*, 333.
[351] *CR 1242–7*, 293. For a wonderful sketch of Edward, see Colvin, *History of the King's Works*, i, 103.

down to 1260 and then Robert of Beverley, who remained in place until the end of the reign. All historians agree that the main features of the design were settled (and a large part of the church built) in Master Henry's time. The sculptured head of a craftsman in a central place in the north transept triforium, bearded, lips slightly apart as though about to break into speech, is surely Master Henry looking proudly over his creation.

The first task, starting in July 1245, was to dismantle the Confessor's church and clear the site.[352] These masons had to be demolition experts as well as designers. Given the immensity of the task both of destruction and construction, it was decided to go forward in stages. So the initial demolition ran from the east end of the old church through to one bay beyond the transepts.[353] This necessarily involved moving the Confessor's shrine to a temporary site, probably in the remaining nave of the Confessor's church, where Henry's own seat was resited. The tomb of Edith, the Confessor's wife, was moved too, the orphrey found above her body being used by the king to decorate a cope.[354] The new church itself was begun early in 1246. The external walls were probably set up first to the level of the aisle windows. Work then progressed at great speed on the east end, the radiating chapels, the north front, the south transept, the east cloister and the chapter house. The north transept, with its rather different decorative motifs, especially in the triforium, came a little later, probably delayed by work on the north front. As early as November 1252 the king was getting timber for the roof of the church and for the stalls of the monks. The following year, the north front was being leaded and the chapter house windows filled with canvas, prior presumably to the arrival of glass. In 1254, Henry twice declared he wished the consecration to take place on 13 October 1255.[355] Nothing came of that, but by 1259 the new structure was evidently near completion for the decision was made to dismantle more of the Confessor's church and add four bays west of the central crossing, thus extending the area for the monks' choir.[356] The work, in a period of political turmoil, however, progressed slowly, and it

---

[352] The demolition would also have involved whatever lay between the east end of the Confessor's church and the new Lady Chapel, for which see next note.

[353] Given the position of the Lady Chapel started in 1220 and the likely east end of the Confessor's church, as revealed by the few remains beneath the current floor, it seems the latter was extended eastwards in the twelfth century, presumably to provide a fitting environment for the Confessor's shrine. For the Confessor's church, see Clapham and Tanner, 'Recent discoveries', and Fernie, 'Edward the Confessor's Westminster Abbey'.

[354] *CR 1242–7*, 344.

[355] *BA*, 192–4, 236–7, 282; *RG*, i, no. 2469 (*CPR 1247–58*, 281, 381). This then would have been the consecration of the church as far west as the transepts where the new structure adjoined the remaining church of the Confessor. Presumably Henry thought the new shrine would be ready for the translation of the Confessor's body at the same time.

[356] The circumstances of this decision and the changes in the design of this new work are discussed in volume 2.

was not until 13 October 1269 that the church was consecrated and the Confessor was translated to his new shrine. Henry's Abbey was incomplete, for it joined on to the remaining nave of the Confessor, but it was still an amazing achievement.

To construct the Abbey a gigantic work force was assembled. In the summer of 1253 it regularly numbered 300 to 400 personnel. In the first week of July, when activity was at its height, payments were made to 56 white stone cutters, 49 marblers, 28 layers, 23 carpenters, 15 polishers, 17 smiths, 14 glaziers, 4 plumbers and 220 labourers. They were nearly all men, although Agnes the limeburner supplied a great deal of lime.[357] The stone for the building came from Kent, from the isle of Purbeck in Dorset and from Caen in Normandy, where the quarries produced a much used stone easily shipped to England. A glimpse of the activity is seen in a letter to 'the venerable and wise man, master Robert of Beverley' from an agent at Purbeck: the king's works, he writes, have been expedited as much as possible and two shiploads of stone are being sent at a cost of £13 3s.[358] One wishes more of the Abbey had been built in Caen stone for, in its slightly pinkish hue, it remains as sharp as ever, whereas the whiter Kentish stone has proved friable like a bad tooth. Fortunately some of the best sculpture is indeed in Caen stone.

Behind everything was King Henry himself, inquiring, cajoling, commanding, driving on the work with all his might and money. All those with Kentish stone to sell were to be made to bring it to Westminster; 600 to 800 men were to be working on the Abbey when the king next arrived there; because the king wished operations to be greatly accelerated (this in October 1252), Master Henry was to raise all the marble he could during the winter provided it could be done without damage; twice urgent orders were issued to recall workmen who had left for lack of pay.[359]

Money of course was more important than anything else and here a pivotal role was played by a special exchequer, set up to receive and spend the funds, one presided over by Henry de Reyns, Edward of Westminster and a monk of the Abbey.[360] It was Henry's money too for there is no evidence that anyone else paid for the building. It was also the money of the kingdom, for Henry funded the Abbey out of his general revenues.[361] In April 1249 he ordered the exchequer to find £3,789 to cover the costs since Easter 1247. Thereafter, between 1250 and 1255 he found over, sometimes well over, £2,000 a year, this at a time he was saving hard for his

---

[357] BA, 7, 260–1; Colvin, History of the King's Works, i, 140.

[358] WAM 16000(g).

[359] BA, 190–5.

[360] See Colvin, History of the King's Works, i, 103–4 and 95–9, for how Henry's works in general were funded and organized. For further comment, see Stewart, 'A lesson in patronage', 379–82.

[361] For what follows, see Colvin, History of the King's Works, i, 155–7.

crusade and having to meet all kinds of emergencies in Gascony, including in 1253–4 his expedition to the province. Nothing shows better the supreme importance he attached to the Abbey. Henry wanted detailed information of how much he had spent, and doubtless boasted about it, as he did about his expenditure on the shrine. In 1259 he asked whether the £28,127 figure sent him by Master John of Gloucester included the costs of purchasing lead and repairing buildings.[362] All told, between 1245 and the end of the reign, Henry probably spent well over £40,000 on the shrine and Abbey combined, very considerably more than a normal year's annual revenue in the 1240s and 1250s. This was enough to build four of the great grim castles with which Edward I cemented his conquest of Wales. Henry's money was much better spent.

In architectural terms the first and most critical decision to be made at the Abbey was the form of its east end, the most holy part of the church housing, as it would, the high altar and behind it the shrine of the Confessor.[363] Henry knew well the solutions being propounded in contemporary English buildings. He saw the new east end going up at Worcester cathedral on his frequent visits to the city. Salisbury, begun in 1220, he knew better still for he spent time nearly every year at Clarendon palace on the hill above. Ely he sometimes took in on his pilgrimages to East Anglia.[364] All had square east ends. At Winchester, Henry himself gave detailed instructions about converting the round end of the chapel of St Judoc into a square one.[365] Yet he now turned his back on such examples. Looking at Salisbury one can see why, for the main vessel of the church ends in an uninspiring blank wall triforium with awkwardly framed lancets in the clerestory above.[366] By contrast, Henry's east end at the Abbey was circular and around it, combining with the existing Lady Chapel, were placed four radiating chapels. The whole design was derived from Reims down to the slight movement inwards of the last bay before the apse so that the turn seems to be made in a harmonious three bays rather than (as

---

[362] *BA*, 198–9.

[363] Works on the Abbey include Scott, *Gleanings*; Lethaby, *Westminster Abbey & the Kings' Craftsmen*; Lethaby, *Westminster Abbey Re-Examined*; Colvin, *History of the King's Works*, i, 130–57; Webb, *Architecture in Britain*, 109–16; Branner, 'Westminster Abbey'; Coldstream, *The Decorated Style*, 23–7 with 118–25 on Henry's artistic patronage; Binski, *Westminster Abbey* (with a comprehensive bibliography); Wilson, 'Calling the tune'; Jordan, *A Tale of Two Monasteries*; Church, *Henry III*, 34–9.

[364] For Henry ordering 1,500 candles to burn there ready for his arrival in 1244, see *CLR 1240–5*, 244. For the architecture of Ely's east end, see Maddison, 'Gothic cathedral', 119–24.

[365] Colvin, *History of the King's Works*, ii, 862 n. 5.

[366] The east end at Ely was more inspiring with triple lancets rising from the ground-floor wall arcade through the triforium level, but this arrangement was ruled out at Westminster, as it was at Salisbury, by the presence of the Lady Chapel.

at Amiens) a hurried five.[367] There is also the same wall walk above the wall arcade in the chapels and the delightful placing of a chapel window so that it contributes to the view looking eastwards down the aisles.[368]

The form of the windows throughout the church also came from Reims. In contemporary English churches the windows were usually composed of grouped lancets, two together in the aisles of Salisbury, three with the central one higher than the other two in its clerestory. At Westminster, on the other hand, two lancets were surmounted by a circular rose just as at Reims.[369] This type of window was achieved by adopting a French constructional technique, in which individual pieces of masonry were assembled so as to form the heads of the lancets and the rose above. Such 'bar tracery' (as it is called) could easily extend to far more elaborate designs and thus opened the way to the decorated windows of the later middle ages.[370]

Even more striking, for those familiar just with English churches, was Westminster Abbey's internal height. To the crown of the vault it was 104 feet, 20 feet more than at Salisbury, and nearly 40 more than at Worcester.[371] This was achieved by adopting a French constructional system in which the vaults were sprung not from the level of the triforium but from much higher up against the walls of the clerestory, with the resulting pressures being contained by rows of external flying buttresses. Nothing like this had ever been seen before in England. This system involved one sacrifice. Master Henry must have explained to the king that, as in the French cathedrals, there was no chance of the crossing between the transepts bearing the weight of a central spire. So it was still the great spire of St Paul's (drawn by Matthew Paris) that dominated London. No doubt, though, Henry intended to place spires on the towers planned for the west end of the new Abbey.

At Reims, Amiens and Notre Dame in Paris it was the west ends, with their twin towers, which formed the main entrance to the cathedrals. This, however, was no good for Henry for two reasons. First, beginning the church in the east, he might never get to the west end. Second, he wanted a grand entrance as close as possible to his royal palace and that lay to the Abbey's east. Henry's solution was thus to place the main entrance at the

---

[367] Scott, *Gleanings*, 24, comments on 'the beautiful gentleness' of the transition from the main arcades into the apse.

[368] There is a wall walk above the wall arcade at Worcester but in a form very different from that at the Abbey.

[369] At Reims the rose generally has six foils, at the Abbey five or six.

[370] The only place where this technique is found in England before Westminster Abbey is on the west front of Binham priory in Norfolk. Christopher Wilson suggests this may have been designed by Master Henry: Wilson, 'Chapter house', 48–9.

[371] For Worcester, see Engel, *Worcester Cathedral* (with 26–7 on its dimensions). For Salisbury, see Tatton-Brown and Crook, *Salisbury Cathedral*; Binski, *Becket's Crown*, ch.3 (also a study of Lincoln); Draper, 'Salisbury Cathedral'; and Jansen, 'Salisbury Cathedral'.

end of the north transept. But what form should it take? Here again, Henry had plenty of up-to-date English examples. At Wells, where he was in 1235, at the west end there was a low doorway beneath tiers of taber-nacles full of figure sculpture. Something comparable was going up at Salisbury. English churches also had imposing porches, projecting from the west end at Ely and from the north side of the nave at both Wells and Salisbury. Yet again, Henry turned his back on these models. Instead the north transept entrance at Westminster Abbey was modelled on the west front at Amiens and thus had three great gabled portals, the largest in the centre with sculpture almost certainly depicting the Last Judgment.[372] High up above the portals the Abbey had something even more spectac-ular, as the south transept did also. This was a great rose window. Unlike anything seen before in England, it was very similar to the south transept window at Notre Dame in Paris. Since this was probably put up in the 1240s, the Abbey's rose shows how up to date Master Henry was.

The two Henrys, king and mason, were the reverse of slavish in their following of French examples. They modified, developed and rejected as they thought fit. Thus the radiating chapels at Westminster were more spacious than those at Reims. In order to create the room a couple of square chapels to the west of the radiating ones were abandoned, but chapels in the transept aisles (longer than those at Reims as will be seen) provided compen-sation. As for the form of the windows, these were more harmonious than at Reims where the roses sometimes seem too large for the supporting lancets. On the nature of the windows, there was probably debate for Master Henry must have known that they were in some ways outmoded. At Amiens, the windows in the aisles repeated those at Reims, but in the clere-story the form was doubled so that the window was made up of two pairs of lancets each with their own rose, and with a larger rose above. That Master Henry had this type of window in his repertoire is shown by its use in the Abbey's chapter house. That he was perfectly capable of designing even more elaborate tracery is shown by the gable end of the north transept. Why then did the king choose to stick with the Reims windows? The answer is surely because they graced the French coronation church and thus seemed right for the coronation church of his own kingdom.

The triple portals of the north transept doorway at the Abbey came from Amiens, but above them the design became increasingly original. At Amiens, as at Notre Dame and Reims, the great portals were flanked by towers. The Abbey did not follow that example. Towers were reserved for the west end when that could be built. But neither did the Abbey go for a screen of lancets and sculpture hiding the main vessel of the church as at Wells, Lincoln (where Henry was in 1236) and at Salisbury. Instead, at Westminster, the

---

[372] Since Amiens was begun from the west, Master Henry could have seen the completed structure before his departure for England, if such it was, in the 1230s. Reims was built from the east and the west front was still being constructed in the 1240s.

main body of the church with its rose window stands up high, proud and clear supported on either side by the great arms of the flying buttresses reaching out, like sentinels standing guard, from the high pinnacled ends of the transepts. And then surmounting all was the gable, flanked on either side by pinnacles, and decorated with elaborate tracery – three pairs of lancets, the middle set higher than the other two, each supporting their own roundels, and above three large roses surmounted by a trefoil. This was a stunning entrance façade, partly derived from France, partly original, brilliantly calculated to impress both Henry's patron saint and his people.

Once inside the Abbey through the north door, another departure from any French design became apparent, one linked very much to the Abbey as a national church. This was the length of the transepts. At Reims, they projected just one bay beyond the main vessel of the church; at Amiens, two bays. But at Westminster, here following Lincoln and Salisbury, they projected three bays.[373] This was despite the new transepts extending much further than those of the Confessor and on the south side entailing the destruction of conventual buildings.[374] Why so much space? The answer is surely that Henry wanted it for the crowds who would attend great services in the Abbey, including of course coronations. It was in the central space between the transepts, lit (as was probably intended) by a lantern tower, and with the high altar, and the Confessor's shrine beyond, that the coronation would take place.

There was one final design decision at the Abbey, enhancing its function as a people's church, influencing its physical appearance and setting it apart from great churches going up both in France and in England. This was the decision to go for a galleried triforium with external walls and windows. These had been common in the twelfth century and were sometimes retained (as at Ely and Notre Dame) when old churches were remodelled. But in general they were now very much out of fashion. In the new east end at Worcester behind the triforium arches there was a blank wall. At Salisbury the space was left open but was covered by a sloping roof with no external windows so it was of no use to anyone. Both at Reims and Amiens behind the triforium arcade there was likewise a blank wall. In France itself this was evidently deemed unsatisfactory for in the later parts of Amiens the wall was replaced by glass windows. The same happened at both Saint Denis and Beauvais. That Master Henry knew of such possibilities is suggested by the treatment of the triforium in the end wall of the south transept. But if he suggested something similar to Amiens and Saint Denis for the whole church, the idea was firmly rejected. Henry wanted his galleried triforium. Indeed, he wanted it not merely over the aisles and

---

[373] The projection at Westminster, Reims and Amiens is as seen from the western side of the transepts.

[374] See the plan in Clapham and Tanner, 'Recent discoveries', 236. The transepts were effectively of four bays, if we include the bays above the aisles of the central vessel.

ambulatory but over the radiating chapels as well, thus creating an unprecedented amount of extra space. The Confessor's church may well have had a gallery but since Henry had no compunction about sweeping the church away this cannot have been a decisive influence. Rather he wanted a galleried triforium for two reasons: one prestigious, one practical. The gallery made the church grander and it also provided yet more space for the congregations attending great services. Henry fed thousands of paupers on the feast days of the Confessor. Before having their food, they surely went up into the triforium to hear the great mass and offer up thanks to the king and his patron saint.

When it came to the external windows of the triforium gallery, the two Henrys turned their back on the only current English example. This was at Ely where the external triforium windows of each bay in the new east end were formed by pairs of lancets. At Westminster, by contrast, the new bar tracery technique was used to create magnificent circular windows, each with eight foils. Nothing like them had been seen before in England. The inspiration came again from France, where identical windows were placed at the western ends of the aisles at Amiens and where circular windows were appearing in the remodelled triforium gallery at Notre Dame.[375]

The galleried triforium had a major impact on the Abbey's external appearance, giving it a whole new storey above the aisles and radiating chapels. This can be criticized. Standing close up the gallery obscures the base of the clerestory windows and gives the Abbey a rather high-shouldered look.[376] The original effect, however, before the total loss of the gallery's external finery – its pinnacles, gargoyles, trumpeting angels, colour and statuary – would have been much lighter and more exciting.[377] The triforium gallery, as well as performing an important function, certainly enhanced the majesty of the Abbey.

The use of French methods and motifs at the Abbey was profound, yet it was also, in places, uncertain, a major reason for thinking that Master Henry was not a fully fledged French architect. The way the clerestory windows were set in large areas of plain stonework contrasted clumsily with French practice, where they generally filled neatly all the space available.[378] This was part and parcel of the greater thickness of the masonry at this level. Indeed the triforium arcade was doubled so as to support the weight. Master Henry seems to have been worried whether the flying buttresses really would hold the Abbey up!

[375] At Notre Dame the windows were formed by a rose with six foils, with little trefoils in each corner.

[376] I used to think I had come up with the description 'high-shouldered' for myself, but rereading his superb appreciation of the Abbey, I now find it in Scott, *Gleanings*, 26.

[377] At Reims the appearance on the outside of the radiating chapels was itself thought unsatisfactory because their roofs were concealed behind a lancet arcade.

[378] There are some exceptions in, for example, some of the aisle windows at Reims.

There was also the question of the Abbey's height. At 104 feet it was certainly higher than any other church in England but it was still easily outstripped by the 122 feet at Reims and the 139 feet at Amiens. Here Master Henry had some excuse in the restrictions imposed by the existing site. The new church had to fit in with the Lady Chapel to the east, the cloisters to the south and the remaining choir and nave of the Confessor to the west. The width of the Confessor's church dictated that of the new work since their walls had more or less to abut. As a result, the width of the Abbey's main vessel was something over 30 feet whereas at Reims and Amiens it was over 40 feet. If Master Henry was thus to keep the same height to width ratio as at Reims, he was constrained as to how high he could go. Keep it he did, so the ratio at the Abbey was 3 to 1, the same as at Reims, hence the impression of the same slender height.[379] Meanwhile the division between the ingredients of each bay was the same as at Amiens, with the height to the top of the main arcade taking up three portions, the triforium one and the clerestory two.

In defending their church against a French critique, king and mason could have pointed to the length of the transepts and the galleried triforium. They could also have pointed to something else, something absolutely fundamental to the appearance of their church. This was the extraordinary richness of its internal decoration, so unlike the rather austere and clinical interiors of the French cathedrals. If Henry here was seeking to outdo the splendours of the Sainte Chapelle, to achieve his effect he drew on the long tradition of English church interiors decorated, as they were, with a profusion of marble, mouldings and sculpture.[380] In varying degrees Henry would have seen all these features in up-to-date

---

[379] Wilson gives the Abbey's ratio as 3:1 as against Reims's 2.9:1. He gives Amiens as 3.2:1: Wilson, 'Calling the tune', 75.

[380] A major theme in part 1 of Binski's *Becket's Crown* is the way the clerical critique of architectural 'sumptuosa' failed in the face of the desire, seen at Canterbury, Lincoln, Ely and (in more tempered fashion) at Salisbury, for architectural magnificence. I am less sure than some historians that the Sainte Chapelle influenced the detail of the Abbey's design. The form of the Abbey's external triforium windows comes from Amiens rather than the Sainte Chapelle. The shape of the Abbey's wall arcade is different from Sainte Chapelle's and in its spandrels there are figures of angels, diaper and foliage, whereas the Sainte Chapelle has only angels. More influential than Sainte Chapelle may have been Notre Dame with its north transept rose and remodelled triforium windows. Christopher Wilson has also noted the very close relationship between the form of a window in one of Notre Dame's nave chapels and those of the Abbey's chapter house (Wilson, 'Chapter house', 46–7). It has been suggested that Master Henry made a personal visit to Paris between 1241 and 1245 to familiarize himself with the latest developments. This seems unlikely in 1242–3, when England and France were at war. Early in 1244, however, Henry did think of appealing to the University of Paris (although, as he said, the capital of his greatest enemy) in the course of the Winchester election dispute. But cross-fertilization between the Abbey and Notre Dame (where the features mentioned above are hard to date exactly) does not necessarily require Master Henry's personal presence.

form at Worcester, Lincoln, Ely and Salisbury. The same spirit runs through the Abbey, hence the much quoted remark that it is 'a great French thought expressed in excellent English'.

One feature of this Englishness was the use of Purbeck marble for all the columns and shafts at the Abbey right up to those of the clerestory windows. This stone from the isle of Purbeck in Dorset is a freshwater limestone (shot through with tiny snails), which when polished (hence the polishers mentioned in the accounts) comes up like marble. Nothing like it was known in France, where the columns and shafts of the churches were in the same stone as the rest of the building. In their use the Abbey outdid one of its English exemplars. The piers of its main arcade were made up of a central drum and four detached shafts, as at Salisbury, but, whereas at Salisbury only the shafts were polished, at the Abbey the drum was too, adding greatly to the internal colour.[381]

Within the shimmering grey-green framework provided by the Purbeck marble, sculptured decoration was everywhere. The spacious spandrels of the perfectly designed ground floor wall arcade were filled with carvings, some-times of angels, sometimes foliage, sometimes diaper.[382] The wall arcades at Reims and Amiens had no carvings at all.[383] The arches of the main arcade had complex mouldings in the English fashion while the main arches of the triforium were moulded, or carved with stiff leaf foliage, dog tooths and diaper. The triforium arches at Reims and Amiens by contrast were left completely unadorned.[384] Whereas, moreover, the vaults at both those cathe-drals were capped with plain circular bosses, at the Abbey, again after the English fashion, they were highly carved, with biblical scenes in the aisles and stiff leaf foliage in the high vault. Over the form of the high vault itself was there debate between the mason and his patron? At Reims, Amiens and Salisbury, the ribs divided the vault into a simple four portions. Yet in the nave of Lincoln, Henry had seen a far more adventurous patterning with a multiplicity of ribs dividing the ceiling of each bay into fourteen segments. That Master Henry was perfectly up to that is shown by the twenty-four segments of the vault at the entrance to the chapter house. Did the king then want a multiplicity of ribs for the high vault in the Abbey? In the second phase of the work after 1259, in the vaults west of the crossing, this is certainly what he got. But perhaps Master Henry counselled caution, worried again about the structure. In the event the vault put up was an inspired compromise. It was quadripartite save that, as at Worcester and Lincoln, it had a longitu-dinal ridge rib. And, here very original, it also had bands of dark stone set

---

[381] The base of some of the piers was derived from Reims.

[382] Scott, *Gleanings*, 29, rightly comments on the 'exquisite design' of the wall arcade.

[383] There was no wall arcade at all in the nave of Reims.

[384] Perhaps surprisingly the foliage string course running under the triforium at Amiens was not picked up at Westminster.

horizontally across the lighter stone of the main vault, thus providing a most attractive pattern and more than substituting for the absence of extra ribs.

There was one other sculptural contribution to the decoration of the Abbey, indeed the one that often most impacts on any visitor. This was the use of diaper. Diaper consists of bands of small formalized roses made up of carved squares each with six or more petals emerging from a round central bud. Master Henry had seen diaper used on the west front of Amiens. The king had seen a fretwork pattern not dissimilar on Lincoln's west front and central tower. But these scarcely provided precedents for the use of diaper at the Abbey. For there, in a way utterly unique, diaper ran riot, filling the spandrels of every arch both in the main arcade and the triforium, and thus giving the Abbey its extraordinary overall patterned effect. One would love to know how such extensive diapering came about. It was certainly a major decision since it must have added greatly to the expense and duration of the work. Perhaps the king said to Master Henry, 'How can we make the inside even more sumptuous?', and Master Henry, in a moment of inspiration, came up with the idea of the diaper. If the diaper was gilded, then the effect would have been even more sumptuous.[385] The goldsmiths were creating the amazing reliquary for the Confessor's body. The church itself became a golden reliquary to place over the shrine.

In imagining the impact of the Abbey, we have thus to bear in mind its colour. The censing angels and the bosses at the end of the south transept still retain their splendid paintwork, and the statuary on the outside of the Abbey, now totally lost, was doubtless highly painted too. Also lost is all the glass, save for fragments of grisaille, three armorial shields, and a few lozenges with biblical scenes, including the Holy Spirit coming down to Christ's apostles at Whitsun.[386] The king must surely have wanted the Abbey's windows to be filled with stained glass, just as he had seen it in the chapels of Canterbury cathedral, and, as later (in 1254) he was to see it in France, notably at the Sainte Chapelle. The Abbey, therefore, was probably darker than it is now, more like the eastern parts of Reims where the glass in the clerestory survives. In that case, it was all the more mystical and magical when the interior was lit up with Henry's candles, their light glinting on the gilded diaper and mixing with a medley of colours from the sunlight filtering through the glass.

Master Henry, in concert with the king, did not merely design the Abbey. He also brought together the team of brilliant craftsmen responsible for its

---

[385] The gilding of the diaper in St Benedict's chapel is of course modern (I can remember it being done) but based on some earlier warrant. On the other hand, the diaper in the recess of the muniment room, although the paint in the area is well preserved, is not gilded. A head from the wall arcade retains gilding in its hair. It is now displayed in the Queen's Gallery at the Abbey. The head of the Virgin in the chapter house retains some of its original paint: see the remarkable photograph by Richard Foster in Foster and Tudor-Craig, 'Sculptural decoration', 176.

[386] These are all now on display in the Queen's Gallery at the Abbey.

decoration. The quality of the work is seen above all in the surviving sculpture – the tightly designed roof bosses, the vivacious portraits of craftsmen, the smiling faces of women and the censing angels of the south transept, swinging their censers with easy grace, their beautiful faces full of a calm assurance and humanity. These are supreme works of art. In expressing a range of character and emotion, the sculpture at the Abbey, so different from the facial impassivity of an earlier age, took its cue from Reims, doubtless thanks to Master Henry. But that the king himself was fully in tune with this new spirit, one marching so well with his personality, is shown by his written orders, hence the cherubims with 'joyous and cheerful countenance', he wanted in the church of St Peter at the Tower; hence the way a painting of winter on a chimney breast in Westminster palace was to recall the season by its 'sad looks and miserable portrayals of the body'.[387]

The decoration and design of the Abbey developed the themes mentioned earlier. The first of course was to honour the Confessor around whose shrine the church was built. Thus the first thing seen by all who entered through the north door were the great statues of the Confessor and the pilgrim high up in the triforium of the south transept, the pilgrim in the most moving of all the portrayals stretching out a beseeching arm to hold the ring. Either side were the censing angels and the whole scene was framed by the breathtaking beauty of the south transept façade, the greatest of all Master Henry's creations, with the rose window, the triforium windows and the windows of the cusped lancets beneath transforming the whole wall into a cascade of fretted glass.[388] Even before reaching the shrine, there was then no doubt what the Abbey was all about.

The second theme was that of the community of the realm. Henry did not want to keep the Confessor to himself. His patron saint was to become England's national saint. Indeed, who more suitable given the just, lawful and co-operative nature of his rule. The Abbey itself was a place for the people at coronations and at the great ecclesiastical feasts through the year, hence the length of the transepts and the galleried triforium. The sculpture in the gallery was very much for the entertainment of the people, some fearsome gargoyles, a smiling graceful woman in a wimple, a squatting, scowling craftsman, another craftsman this time full of cheer and humour (surely a caricature of a colleague) and a large devil's head with a red painted tongue, placed as a warning or a joke, at the very centre of the east end from where one could look down the whole length of the Abbey.

Beneath, in the main body of the Abbey, the community was celebrated in another way. Its leaders were of course the baronage and in the wall arcade of the choir, alongside Henry's leopards as king of England and the martlets of the Confessor, were shields bearing the coats of arms of the great English earls. These were put up after 1259 during the period of

---

[387] *CLR 1240–5*, 14–15; *CLR 1226–40*, 444. See Binski, *Becket's Crown*, 234–47.
[388] Compare the north transept glass at Chartres: Grant, *Blanche of Castile*, plate 1.

baronial rule, but were probably planned earlier, reflecting Henry's desire to be at one with his barons.

If, however, Henry believed in consensus, it was a consensus around agreeing with his wishes. The design and decoration of the Abbey thus shouted out that this was a royal church, a church belonging to Henry and his dynasty. Henry regarded the Abbey as his chapel. He had within it his own seat, moved into the Confessor's nave during the rebuilding and moved doubtless back into the new church after its consecration in 1269. He also had what was in effect his own private pew. Here Master Henry, in another flash of genius, had seen how he could exploit the way the existing eastern cloister prevented the Abbey having a western aisle to the south transept. What he did was to floor and vault the space above the cloister, giving it windows over the cloister garth on one side and leaving it open to the Abbey on the other. The sculpture proclaimed this was a place for the king. Entering the Abbey from the palace through what is now the Poet's Corner door, Henry could turn immediately leftwards into a staircase taking him up to the walkway across the south transept end and thus into the pew.[389] Entering, Henry saw immediately above him large sculptured heads of a king and queen, both highly painted with splendid crowns, both faintly smiling, calm and serene, very much in the spirit of the censing angels in the main body of the transept, very much in the spirit of 'deboneret̄e'. And above the heads were some of the finest bosses in the Abbey, the central one – how entertaining for Henry and Eleanor – showing a centaur spearing a dragon. From the pew, the king could listen to services of the monks, and impress chosen bishops and barons with the magnificent view, through a forest of arches, towards the High Altar and the shrine of the Confessor.

If the pew was for the privileged few, Henry also made his ownership of the Abbey very public. His coat of arms surely appeared again and again in the stained glass, just as did that of the king of France in the Sainte Chapelle. Quite probably the arms of Provence, in tribute to Eleanor, appeared many times too.[390] An inscription proclaimed Henry's role in installing the magnificent pavement before the High Altar.[391] Another inscription did the same for the Confessor's shrine, beside which Henry intended to be buried.[392] And then there was sculpture on the

---

[389] It is a walk I did many times myself in the 1960s and 1970s when leaving what is now the Muniment Room after working there late in the evening. In the arcading of the walkway there are sculptured heads of a king and a queen at the start, and another queen's head at the end.

[390] The only surviving armorial glass are three shields depicting the arms of England, Provence and Richard of Cornwall. One suspects they are the remnants of a much larger number. The same arms were displayed on the great cloth behind the high altar; above, 328. In the Sainte Chapelle, there were no arms of Provence, only those of Castile; here too Queen Margaret is being overshadowed by her mother-in-law.

[391] This is discussed further in volume 2.

[392] The inscription may have been added to the shrine after Henry's death, as discussed in volume 2.

inside of the north door. Here a Purbeck marble head of a young prince, evidently Edward, heir to the throne, gazed out over the Abbey, proclaiming to all who came and went that this was indeed a dynastic church. Above the head there was a carving of Samson tearing apart the Lion. 'And the spirit of the Lord came mightily upon him, and he rent [the lion] as he would a kid,' ran the verse in Judges 14:6, a prophetic text indeed given Edward's later violent and victorious career. Higher up on the transept end, in the splays of the lancet windows, were the figures of two kings, on the one side the Confessor, on the other Henry III, and above them, in the soffits of the lancets, joining the kings together, was a celebratory choir of angels, twenty-four in all, each playing their own instrument.[393]

The dynastic theme reached another climax in the chapter house.[394] Nearing completion in 1253, this was a wondrous creation by Master Henry, 'incomparable' as Matthew Paris called it, here indeed echoing what he had said about the Sainte Chapelle. It was the place where the monks held their daily meetings. It was also the place where Henry intended to address the realm. Indeed, he had a special lectern installed from which to do so.[395] Everything about the chapter house was designed to impress. In the cloister bay opposite the entrance was the complex vault already mentioned. Above the entrance was a statue of the Virgin and Child, flanked by angels, and surrounded by mazy scrolls of foliage, the whole entity painted and gilded.[396] Then down the vaulted passage, up the steps and into the chapter house itself and an extraordinary surprise awaited. For here at last were the four great lancet Amiens-style windows dissolving all the walls into glass and filling the chapter house with light. And then, high above, supported on a slender Purbeck marble column, was a vault, sprung unprecedentedly high so as not to obscure the windows and dividing, with a multiplicity of ribs, the ceiling into twenty-four separate segments.[397] The circular chapter house was traditional in England, but the treatment here at Westminster was utterly unique.

An inscription in the floor proclaimed Henry's responsibility for the building and described him as the 'friend of the Holy Trinity'. Why this rather than the friend of the Confessor (who did appear with St John in one of the tiles on the floor)? Does the answer lie in a passage from the Book of Revelation (4:1–11) that was read on Trinity Sunday? This conjures up a remarkable vision of the throne of God. 'In circuit' around

[393] See Cave and Tanner, 'Thirteenth-century choir of angels'. That the kings were the Confessor and Henry is, however, an assumption.

[394] There is a comprehensive treatment of the chapter house in Rodwell and Mortimer, *Westminster Abbey Chapter House*, with ch. 3 (Wilson, 'Chapter house') on its innovative architecture.

[395] For some of what follows, see Carpenter, 'King Henry III and the chapter house'.

[396] See Foster and Tudor-Craig, 'Sculptural decoration', 160–2.

[397] The springing of the vault here contrasts with the Sainte Chapelle where, from some angles, it obscures the top of the windows: Wilson, 'Chapter house', 42–6.

it are twenty-four seats with twenty-four elders who fall down and worship him 'sitting on the throne'. How Henry must have wished his parliaments were like that! Certainly the chapter house was designed to give all possible weight to his words. As he spoke he looked towards the magnificent lifesize statues of the Angel Gabriel and the Virgin Mary, Gabriel announcing the Virgin Birth and thus making the most important speech in history. Henry was also flanked on either side by bands of glinting tiles, running right across the floor, all bearing his coat of arms, thirty-one shields in each band, the three leopards, teeth bared, virile and menacing.[398] Who could resist the king's eloquence in such a setting? Who, in such a setting, would dare to question the royal word?

'As the rose is the flower of flowers, so this house is the house of houses,' ran the inscription on the floor of the chapter house. The same could be said of the Abbey itself. Henry and his master mason had indeed created a church of 'wonderful beauty', one of the greatest in Christendom.

* * *

Henry's religion was very much on display. When he arrived in a town he visited the hospitals and friaries, fed hundred of paupers, made gifts of silks and chalices to the churches and lit them up with candles. Equally, all coming to the capital saw the awesome Abbey he was building in honour of the Confessor. Henry was determined his acts of piety be known and remembered, hence the inscriptions and his coats of arms at the Abbey, hence the way at St Albans he asked how many silks he had given to the monks and whether they had all been signed as he ordered. The answer was thirty-one, more than any other king, and yes they had all been inscribed 'indelibly' with the name 'King of the English Henry III'.[399]

This desire for publicity had a spiritual purpose, but one inseparable from current politics. Henry hoped to secure the prayers of beneficiaries and admirers for success in this life as well as his passage to the next. He might also hope that everyone would wish to support someone so clearly steered by the hand of God. The question for Henry's personal rule was how far would his piety save him from danger, as Louis IX purportedly said it would. Would indeed God be willing to quell tempests on his behalf? Such questions were related to another. How far was Henry's personal piety related to a sense of duty, as a Christian king, to look after the welfare of his subjects and put right what was out of joint in the realm? That question will be returned to in later chapters.[400]

---

[398] For the sculpture of the chapter house, see Foster and Tudor-Craig, 'Sculptural decoration', and for the tiles, see Keen, 'Chapter house decorated tile pavement'.

[399] Paris, vi, 389. 'H. by the grace of God king of England' was placed on the foundation stone of Netley abbey: Colvin, *History of the King's Works*, i, 158 n. 2.

[400] See below 527–33, 566–7, 711–15.

Chapter 7

THE COURT OF HENRY III

Contemporaries who lived at the court of the Angevin kings complained bitterly of its ceaseless movement.[1] King John, the first king whose itinerary is known in detail, rarely spent more than a few days in any one place. As the historian J.E.A. Jolliffe put it, this was a 'government of roads and roadsides'.[2] Kings did not travel, as they might have done in the past, because they had eaten and drunk their way through the supplies in an area. They could perfectly well be supplied wherever they were for as long as they wished to stay. Rather it was the exigencies of controlling a vast empire stretching from Ireland to the Pyrenees that kept them constantly on the move and as much on the continent as in England itself. They fought wars now against the Welsh rulers, now against the king of France, now against rebels across their dominions. But even in times of peace John was travelling, travelling to monitor the performance of his local officials, test the loyalty of local elites, and make money both by advertising what he might sell and by punishing financially those who crossed him. The king could also hope the more he showed himself to his people, the more impressive his kingship would seem. As one of the prayers at the coronation put it, 'the glorious dignity of the royal palace' would 'dazzle the eyes of all with the great splendour of royal power'.[3] The king's lavish hospitality, the rich clothes of his courtiers and the majesty of his bejewelled and crowned person might all play a part in confirming his subjects in their obedience.

King Henry III was equally keen to impress with the magnificence of his entourage and person. Yet in one key respect his court was fundamentally different from that of his predecessors. Henry was a sedentary king. He travelled far less often and remained stationary for far longer periods than his father. Westminster, in particular, became a dominant residence in a way it had never been before. What the reign of Henry III showed was

---

[1] For itineration, see Bartlett, *England under the Norman and Angevin Kings*, 133–43; Church, 'Some aspects of the royal itinerary'; Vincent, 'Court of Henry II', 278–9, 304–9; and the work of Julie Kanter cited below under n. 7. For a study of Edward I's household, see Prestwich, *Edward I*, ch. 6. I am grateful to Hugh Thomas for allowing me to see a draft of his forthcoming book, a social and cultural history of the court of King John.

[2] Jolliffe, *Angevin Kingship*, 140.

[3] *English Coronation Records*, 32: 'dignitas gloriosa regalis palatii maximo splendore regie potestatis oculis omnium fulgeat'.

that, outside emergencies, kings did not have to travel to rule the country. The many courtiers who worked across the reigns thus had a far easier time, in terms of travel, under Henry than under John, yet they would have noticed little change in the actual structure of the court. The major offices were the same: the chancery responsible for the writing and sealing the king's charters and letters; the chamber or wardrobe responsible for receiving, storing and spending the king's money; the kitchen, pantry and buttery providing the court's food and drink; the almonry feeding the paupers; and the stables caring for the horses. The men staffing these offices, with assorted household knights, stewards and ministers, formed the core of the court, several hundred strong, many of them kitted out by the king in liveries graduated according to rank. Around this core, the court expanded and contracted like a great bellows depending on the occasion. It was at its smallest during quiet times in the summer at Windsor or Woodstock; at its fullest during the times of parliament when the great lay and ecclesiastical magnates came in to see the king.

This chapter will begin with Henry's itinerary and the homes in which he lived, the court's physical environment. It will then look at the chancery, the wardrobe, the food and drink departments, the stewards, the household knights and the place of the queen. The chapter will discuss the role of liveries, the rituals of gift-giving, and the question of access to the king and the power of his presence. The court was a highly political place, but it was also a place for pleasure. The chapter will conclude by looking at the pleasure Henry had from books, jokes, jesters and falconry.[4]

HENRY'S ITINERARY

Although less itinerant than his predecessors, Henry, travelling on horseback, still knew the roads and surrounding landscape far better than anyone today. Just occasionally, for example on the old Watling Street (now the A2) between Teynham and Ospringe in Kent, one can get a feeling for the terrain he must have known so well. One wonders whether Henry ever saw Matthew Paris's maps of Britain, in which case he would have gained some feeling for the island's overall shape.[5] He had certainly seen maps of the world for they featured on the walls of both his hall at Winchester and his chamber at Westminster. Such maps were in no way accurate geographically but would have given Henry at least some awareness of the spatial relationship between Britain, France, Spain, Germany, Italy, the

---

[4] I am not discussing here the king's council, councillors and favourites as they run through the narrative of the book. Equally I am not discussing the court *coram rege*, for which see above, 170.

[5] See Harvey, 'Matthew Paris's maps of Britain', and Connolly, *Maps of Matthew Paris*, 186–91. Connolly argues (173–82, 190–1) that one of the itineraries from London to Rome, ascribed to Matthew Paris, was prepared either for Henry III or, if a copy, for Edward I.

Mediterranean and the Holy Land.[6] It was to this wider world that Henry's thoughts in the 1250s were very much to turn.

The change in the king's itinerary during Henry's reign began at its start. That of his minority government was already totally different from King John's.[7] Between 1220 and 1226 the government spent 46 per cent of its time at Westminster or elsewhere in London. John, in years when not overseas, spent 10 per cent of his time there.[8] The controlling hand here must have been that of the justiciar, Hubert de Burgh. In a telling assessment of the centralized nature of government, he deemed it better to sit at the exchequer and fight from there the battle to rebuild royal power than to tour the country in the fashion of King John. That was partly, of course, because any attempt to revive the financial exactions associated with John's harrying visitations would have been disastrous.

During Henry's personal rule there was some shift in the pattern. Between 1234 and 1252 (omitting the years 1242–3 spent partly in France), Westminster was still dominant but it absorbed some 28 per cent of the king's time as against 46 per cent of the minority government's. This was because the traditional homes of monarchy had come more into play. After Westminster, the next most favoured residences, according to the percentage of time spent there, were Windsor with 11 per cent, Woodstock 8 per cent, Marlborough 6 per cent, Clarendon 6 per cent, Reading 4 per cent and Winchester 3 per cent, followed by Kempton and Guildford with 4 per cent combined. All these places, of course, apart from the royal abbey of Reading, founded by Henry I, were castles or palaces of the king himself. Taken together, Henry, therefore, spent 66 per cent of his time in his own homes.[9] The prominence of Clarendon is striking, and was clearly because Henry came to love it. It had featured minimally in the years down to 1231. Henry's homes were in the south. His northernmost residence was Woodstock, itself only sixty-three miles north-west of London. His westernmost residence was Clarendon, this thanks to the virtual abandonment of Corfe. John was at Corfe on fifteen occasions between 1200 and 1215, and built fine new apartments there for himself and his court.

[6] Harvey, *Medieval Maps*, 19–37.

[7] Henry's itinerary is printed in Craib, Brindle and Priestley, *Itinerary of King Henry III*. The contrast between Henry's itinerary and King John's is a major theme of the doctoral thesis of Julie Kanter (now Crockford), 'Peripatetic and sedentary kingship', from which much of the following material comes. Some of the main findings are also set out in her article 'Itineraries of John and Henry III'. For Edward I, see Prestwich, 'The royal itinerary and roads in England under Edward I'.

[8] I have calculated John's figure myself from the years 1204, 1205, 1207 and 1213, years when he was in England and where we know his itinerary for over 300 days of the year. For 1207 see also Kanter, 'Peripatetic and sedentary kingship', 167.

[9] The pattern is not much different as between 1234–41 and 1244–52, apart from a slight reshuffling of the order below Westminster. I am indebted here to BA special subject long essays by Michael Bachelor covering the first period and Andrew Steele the second.

Between 1234 and 1258, Henry went there just for a day on his western tours of 1235 and 1236. Perhaps he had unpleasant memories from the time he was quartered in the great castle as a boy. Perhaps he had heard stories of the Briouzes being starved to death there.

Apart from abandoning Corfe, Henry's most visited residences were not very different from those of his father or indeed his twelfth-century predecessors. The only new property in the mix was Kempton, Henry having obtaining the manor through an exchange with Hubert de Burgh in 1228. It seems unlikely Henry particularly wanted Kempton (he had never been there) but he came to like it, partly because it made a convenient resting place between Windsor and Westminster.[10] If, however, Henry's principal homes were also those favoured by his predecessors, the proportion of his time they absorbed was very different. As mentioned, John, when in England, spent 10 per cent of his time in London or Westminster, as against Henry's 28 per cent. The same contrast, in varying degrees, appears with the other residences. So John was 2.5 per cent of his time at Windsor, against Henry's 11 per cent, 4 per cent at Woodstock against Henry's 8 per cent, 3 per cent at Clarendon against Henry's 6 per cent. Only at Winchester did the two kings spend roughly equivalent proportions of time. Whereas Henry was 66 per cent of his time at his main homes, with John the proportion was more than reversed. This reflected another major contrast, namely that involving the length of stay in any one place. Whereas 60 per cent of Henry's time was spent in visits of a week or more, the equivalent figure for John was only 12 per cent.

Compared to his predecessors Henry, then, was very much a sedentary king. But that did not mean he simply spent all his time travelling round his homes in the south. During his personal rule there were only four years when that was the case.[11] In 1242–3 and 1253–4 he was in France. In England he was drawn from his southern round by his pilgrimages to East Anglia and Canterbury. And he was also drawn away, far less willingly, by tours of the Welsh marches, by campaigns in Wales and by expeditions to the north to deal with the affairs of Scotland. What, however, Henry rarely did was travel for the purposes of routine government. John too had been drawn north by his quarrels with the king of Scots, but he combined such descents with long visitations of the northern counties for the kind of governmental purposes we have outlined. Henry travelled straight up and down. He never saw Carlisle, despite saying he would go there. John was there on three occasions. Matthew Paris has Henry going to Dover in 1246 to secure the loyalty of the coastal area, probably because of tensions with

[10] Henry had a barge made at Kempton to cross the Thames: *CLR 1245–51*, 83. Perhaps he also went by barge up the Thames to Westminster.

[11] 1239, 1246, 1247 (with a visit to Dover), 1249 (with a visit to Canterbury and the Northampton hunting lodges).

France, but the comment is conspicuous for its uniqueness.[12] Equally rare were tours for the purposes of raising money, indeed only one falls clearly into that category: in 1235 when Henry went west to Bristol and Wells (taking in a visit to Arthur's tomb at Glastonbury) and then north to Nottingham. His purpose was to see the heads of the religious houses along the route and persuade them to contribute to his sister Isabella's dowry on her marriage to Emperor Frederick.[13] Another visit to the west in 1236 was probably to show Glastonbury and Arthur's tomb to his new queen. A final tour in 1250, reaching as far as Exeter, may likewise have been an adjunct to Henry's wish, now a crusader, to see Arthur's tomb once more. This was Henry's only visit to Exeter during his personal rule. John was there on three occasions.[14]

It is Henry's journeys which help explain the 40 per cent of his time spent in visits of less than a week and the 30 per cent of his time spent outside his principal residences (and Reading) in the south. In 1239, when he was entirely in the south, he stayed at twenty-six different places. In 1238, when he went on pilgrimage to East Anglia and twice to the Welsh marches, he stayed in fifty-five. On his journeys Henry's less-visited castles and houses came into play. On the way to Canterbury and Dover, the castle at Rochester, on the way to Woodstock, Brill (where Edward the Confessor had performed a miracle) and the houses in Oxford; on the trek further north, Northampton and Nottingham castles and the Northamptonshire and Nottinghamshire hunting lodges. Henry would also be entertained at the homes of his magnates: at Oddington, a manor of the archbishop of York, on the way from Woodstock out to the Welsh march; at Otford, a manor of the archbishop of Canterbury, on the way to Canterbury; at Wallingford, the castle of his brother, on the way to Woodstock; and now and again at Framlingham, castle of Roger Bigod, on the East Anglian pilgrimages. Henry also stayed, of course, at religious institutions great and small – on the way to and from Canterbury, at Faversham abbey and at the commandery of the hospitallers at Sutton at Hone, where the chapel, for whose roof he gave five oaks in 1234, still survives.[15] Henry visited the great

---

[12] Paris, iv, 553. See *CR 1242–7*, 424. Another purpose may have been to prevent money going out of the kingdom to the pope: *CR 1242–7*, 421–2. For Henry's descents on Winchester and Lincoln to deal with problems, see below, 483–4, 626–8. His visit to Norwich at the end of the reign is discussed in volume 2.

[13] See above, 175.

[14] During his personal rule, Henry's principal journeys outside the south were as follows: 1235, the tour mentioned above and an East Anglian pilgrimage; 1236, York; 1237, Welsh marches, York; 1238, East Anglian pilgrimage, Welsh marches (twice); 1240, Welsh marches; 1241, campaign in Wales; 1242–3, Poitou, Gascony; 1244, Newcastle; 1245, campaign in Wales; 1248, East Anglian pilgrimage; 1250, West Country; 1251, East Anglian pilgrimage, York; 1252, East Anglian pilgrimage; 1253–4, Gascony, France; 1255, Wark, Scotland; 1256, East Anglian pilgrimage, Welsh marches; 1257, campaign in Wales.

[15] *CR 1231–4*, 401. One hopes the setting of the commandery (in the care of the National Trust) was as delightful then as it is now.

abbeys of Reading and St Albans (where he had his own chamber) for their own sakes but they were also ideal resting places on the journeys to and from London. How one wishes there had been a chronicler at Reading to rival Matthew Paris.

Henry's itinerary was fitted, as far as possible, around the fixed points and places of his religious year. The chief festivals, of course, were those of the Confessor on 5 January and 13 October, which Henry always sought to spend at Westminster. On several occasions he hurried back from the north or from Wales in order to make the 13 October feast. Henry was almost equally determined to celebrate Easter at Westminster. He was there in all but four of the years between 1235 and 1258, in two of which he was abroad.[16] The pattern for Whitsun was more varied. Westminster still came out top (Henry was there in twelve of the years between 1235 and 1258), but he was at Winchester for four of the feasts and at Clarendon for one. It was at Christmas that Winchester came into its own, although that came to mean a chilly midwinter journey up to Westminster for the Confessor's feast on 5 January. Henry was at Winchester for every Christmas from 1235 to 1239 and again, apart from three unavoidable exceptions, from 1246 to 1255.[17] The gap in the early 1240s was due in part to the pall cast over Winchester by the disputed episcopal election.[18] Henry intended to spend Christmas at Winchester again in 1257 until the negotiations with France and the papacy kept him at Westminster.[19] Winchester reappeared as the favourite resort for Christmas in the last years of the reign.

As an example of a quiet Henrician year we can take 1246. Having celebrated the Christmas of 1245 at Westminster, Henry went to Merton priory before arriving back at Westminster in time for the Confessor's feast on 5 January. He remained there until the end of the month, witnessing the start of building operations on the Abbey. Then, via stops at Guildford and Windsor, Henry divided his time between Reading, Winchester and Marlborough before returning, via Reading and Windsor, to Westminster where he stayed from 17 March until 10 April, celebrating Easter there on 8 April. There followed a division of time between Windsor and Westminster and the visit to Canterbury and Dover mentioned by Matthew Paris, Henry returning to Westminster in time to celebrate Whitsun there on 27 May. In June, after a week at Windsor, Henry went with all his family to Beaulieu in Hampshire for the consecration of the abbey founded by King John. The rest of the summer (fairly typical when nothing else was on the agenda) saw

---

[16] The other two exceptions were 1235 at Reading and 1238 at Gloucester.

[17] The exceptions were when Henry was at York in 1251, in Gascony in 1253 and when just landed back from France in 1254.

[18] During the interval Henry celebrated Christmas at Westminster, save in 1242 when he was in Bordeaux and, in 1243, when, following Richard of Cornwall's marriage, he celebrated the feast at Richard's castle of Wallingford.

[19] See below, 675.

a fortnight at Clarendon, nearly three weeks at Marlborough and over three weeks at Woodstock. After that, it was home via Brill to Windsor for a stay lasting from 13 September to 4 October. And then, of course (via Kempton) up to Westminster for the 13 October feast. After staying at Westminster until the end of the month, Henry set out on another tour typical of this time of year, one taking him via Guildford and Reading (where for a week in early November) to Marlborough and Clarendon before arriving at Winchester in time for Christmas. So during the year, Henry had spent eighty-seven days at Westminster, forty-four at Windsor, thirty-nine at Clarendon, thirty-seven at Marlborough, twenty-eight at Winchester, twenty-four at Woodstock and five at Guildford. In all 72 per cent of his time. Another twenty-six days were spent at Reading. What a comfortable life.

One cardinal factor permitting Henry's easy living was, of course, the loss of the old cross-Channel empire. Unlike his predecessors since the Norman conquest, Henry had no need to spend half his time on the continent. Those predecessors had criss-crossed the channel, partly to ward off threats to their continental possessions, partly because the great castles, towns and manors of Normandy and (after 1154) of Anjou were just as much 'home' as anything in England. About Gascony, they never felt the same way, nor did Henry. Only twice during his personal rule (in 1242–3 and 1253–4) did he feel the need to spend time there. Another factor behind the ease of Henry's life, one for which he can take some credit, was the near quarter-century of peace of his personal rule. He had no need to travel England or (like John in 1210) go to Ireland to put down baronial revolt, not that Henry travelled to put down revolt even when (in 1261) he might have done so! Henry, therefore, was free to divide his time between the comforts and consolations of his palaces and palace castles in the south. In one of his moments of sharp observation Matthew Paris noted how, returning from the north in 1244, Henry decided to neglect the revolt in Wales and instead hasten to the 'accustomed delights and rest of Westminster'. 'Delight and rest'. That got very close to what Henry's itinerary was all about.[20] Of course, it was also religion. Henry's long stays at Westminster were not primarily (as they had been in the minority) because Westminster was the governmental capital. That had equally been true under John, yet he spent nowhere near the same amount of time there.[21] What tied Henry to Westminster was the Confessor.

Would Henry's rule have been more successful had he travelled the country more? There is no clear-cut answer to this question. The fine rolls show that those who wanted concessions from the king were not put off by

[20] Paris, iv, 385.
[21] There was also a contrast between Henry and his son. In the years analysed by Kanter, 'Peripatetic and sedentary kingship', 275, Edward I spent 17% of his time in London/Westminster as opposed to Henry's 28%.

having to travel or send to court to get them. In the fine rolls of 1252 more business was transacted for Lincolnshire than any other county although Henry did not go there. The fact that Henry was so often at Westminster must have helped those seeking out the court, and indeed the 1252 fine rolls suggest that proportionately more business was transacted there than anywhere else.[22] On the other hand, Henry's visit to the West Country in 1250 does seem to show the value of travelling the country both to himself and the community.[23] Displaying the benevolent face of his kingship, he made concessions to the abbot of Glastonbury, Maurice de Berkeley, 2 burgesses of Bristol and the abbot of Cerne, the latter paying 15 marks for a market charter. The king's presence was evidently welcomed by those seeking writs to pursue the common law legal actions: seven were bought by people from Dorset, seven and thirteen apiece from those from Somerset and Gloucester respectively, far more than for other counties. As with the charter for the abbot of Cerne, here Henry was making money in an acceptable way. Henry's piety was equally on display. At the abbey of Montacute his offering was a silver cup to hold the host and a precious cloth.[24] At Exeter, likewise, the monks of the cathedral received a silver cup, this one costing 20 marks. At Bristol, Henry set up an altar to the Confessor in the castle and paid the wages of a chaplain to celebrate daily for the soul of Eleanor of Brittany. Henry's piety indeed reached further west than he actually went, for he ordered measures, candles of his height, to burn both at Plympton and at St Michael's Mount in Cornwall. The trip also provided the opportunity to inspect his castles and he ordered building works at Exeter, Bristol and Gloucester.[25]

Yet one cannot be sure Henry's descent was universally popular. Doubtless he was welcomed by processions of townsmen and churchmen, but many must have worried about the consequences of his arrival. He was of course perfectly capable, when angry, of throwing back a reception in its face. When in 1258 the mayor and citizens of London came to Knightsbridge, as was customary, to greet the king on his arrival from Windsor, Henry sent a squire telling them not to enter his sight.[26] At Bristol in 1250 one burgess had to pay 50 marks to be pardoned a transgression.[27] When Henry stayed at a religious house or a baronial castle, he sometimes said thank you with a gift of game or timber. But such stays could impose heavy burdens on the hosts, notably (if Matthew Paris can be believed) in the early 1250s when Henry deliberately quartered himself in religious

---

[22] For 1252, see Kanter, 'Relationship between business'. See also Carpenter, *Struggle for Mastery*, 259, for evidence from feet of fines.

[23] For this period in the fine rolls, see *CFR 1251–2*, nos. 572–635.

[24] BL Cotton Tiberius A X, f. 169 (a brief chronicle of the house).

[25] *CLR 1245–51*, 297–301.

[26] FitzThedmar, 31.

[27] *CFR 1251–2*, no. 635.

houses in order to save money for his crusade.[28] Any benefit to the local economy was likely to be offset if the household's food and drink departments failed to pay their way and left behind a trail of debt. Accusations to that effect were common.[29] More certainly burdensome on the 1250 tour of the west were the impositions of the court, presided over by the king's marshals, with authority to try breaches of the rules on weights and measures. A surviving roll shows that in Wiltshire seven vills and eighteen individuals (including several women) were penalized. In Somerset fourteen vills suffered, in Devon four. An amercement of 7 marks was slapped on Montacute, ones of 40 marks on Exeter and Bristol. The total owed as recorded in the roll was £289.[30] Many local people must heartily have wished the king had never come.[31]

Whether, therefore, Henry would have enhanced his reputation by travelling the country more is a moot point. To have done so most effectively he would have needed to travel the country in a different way. Given the growing unpopularity of his local officials, he could have used the court *coram rege* in a systematic fashion to hear complaints of local oppression and abuse, just as the Marshalsea court heard cases about weights and measures. That was not, however, something Henry ever did.

HENRY'S HOMES

Given the sedentary nature of his court, Henry had the incentive and the opportunity, as he had also the artistic taste, to enhance its physical environment. He poured money into making his homes more beautiful, comfortable and, through their religious imagery, more meaningful. He thus created a splendid environment for the rituals at court with all their different rooms and etiquettes – the exchange of gifts, the holding of feasts, and the conduct of private audiences – through all of which he hoped to get his way. Henry was well aware of the impact a building could make. In 1247 he wanted the visiting Savoyard Gauter de Châtillon to be shown Dover castle 'so that the nobility of the castle is apparent to him and no defects are seen'.[32] At Dover it was first and foremost military might that was expected to impress. One can imagine Gauter inspecting with a practised eye the works set in train by Hubert de Burgh after the great siege of 1216–17: the three solid beaked towers, with a sally port beneath, blocking

---

[28] Unfortunately, the absence of household rolls, showing daily expenditure on food and drink, means there is no way of checking this allegation. In later years, where rolls do survive, they show Henry generally paying his way even when at a religious house.

[29] Carpenter, 'Household rolls', 29–30.

[30] TNA C 47/3/43/7; partly printed in Wild, *WA*, cix–x.

[31] For the burden of the king's presence, see Prestwich, 'The royal itinerary and roads in England under Edward I', 180.

[32] *CR 1247–51*, 8. See Liddiard, *Castles in Context*, 139–41, for another account of the castle's impact on Gauter.

the old gateway brought down during the siege, and the towering new gateway (today's Constable's tower) along the walls to the west. But Gauter could also admire the new hall and royal chamber completed in 1240, and the altars dedicated to Saints Edward, Edmund and Adrian, with appropriate imagery, which Henry had commissioned by word of mouth on a visit to the castle earlier in the year. There were also plenty of services for Gauter to attend since by 1247 five chaplains were at work in the castle.[33]

Dover castle was never a place where Henry lived for any extended period of time. When it came to his principal residences, there was, of course, a distinction between those which were and were not castles.[34] The defences of Windsor, like those at Dover, were revolutionized by the work started by Hubert de Burgh in the minority: a new gateway, two sally ports and the drum towers along the walls which still shape much of the castle's external appearance.[35] At Winchester, likewise, during Henry's personal rule, a new gatehouse was built and at least five new towers.[36] All this military architecture was very much for real. No king, after the great sieges of the civil war and the minority – Rochester, Dover and Bedford – would have wanted a castle (as Bodiam was in the next century) where the walls and towers looked elegantly martial but were militarily useless.[37] No one would have been impressed if such a castle had been built. A castle's prestige derived from the splendour of its domestic quarters certainly, but also from its military might. It was to enhance the impact of that might, with a dash of decorative bravado, and a reference perhaps to Roman buildings, that at Windsor the curtain walls were divided horizontally by strips of lighter coloured stone work. At the Tower, Henry had all the walls painted white, apparently the first king to do so.[38]

Henry's residences also had differences in function quite apart from those related to whether they were castles. Westminster stood apart as the seat of government, the home of the exchequer, the judicial bench and the most common venue for parliament. Between 1235 and 1257 thirty-nine of the

---

[33] *CLR 1245–51*, 112. For the works at Dover under Henry, see Colvin, *History of the King's Works*, ii, 633–8.

[34] For the castles, see Colvin, *History of the King's Works*, ii, 710–15 (the Tower), 735–7 (Marlborough), 858–62 (Winchester), 865–9 (Windsor), for the houses, ii, 912–16 (Clarendon), 965–6 (Kempton), 1010–15 (Woodstock) and for Westminster, i, 494–504. Colvin, *History of the King's Works*, ii, 658–9, 950–3, covers the castle and houses at Guildford separately. For them, see now Poulton, *A Medieval Royal Complex at Guildford*. For Colvin's general discussion of Henry's work on his castles and houses, see *History of the King's Works*, i, 110–30.

[35] Brindle, *Windsor Castle*, 48–57; Colvin, *History of the King's Works*, ii, 865–6.

[36] Colvin, *History of the King's Works*, ii, 859–60.

[37] For the debate about Bodiam, see Liddiard, *Castles in Context*, 7–11. For the new tower Henry built at York, see Colvin, *History of the King's Works*, ii, 116.

[38] Brindle, *Windsor Castle*, 54–5; *CLR 1226–40*, 457; *CLR 1240–5*, 14. Henry had the guttering of the newly whitened 'great tower' (presumably the present White Tower) altered so the rainwater would not trickle down the walls, but this was to avoid damage to the structure rather than the aesthetic effect.

fifty-four great councils and parliaments met there. The other residences lacked the same public purpose. In the same period three parliaments met at Winchester, three at Woodstock and two at Windsor.[39] Windsor was set apart in another way by being the most normal home of the queen and the royal children.[40] It also had a special relationship with Westminster. Again and again Henry would leave Westminster, go out for a stay at Windsor and then return to Westminster, sometimes with stops along the way at Kempton or Merton priory.[41] The tour might take in Guildford as well, and, in various combinations, the abbeys of Reading, St Albans and Waltham. Some combination of the Westminster–Windsor–Westminster pattern occurred no fewer than thirty-four times during Henry's personal rule.[42]

In terms of enhancing the appearance and comfort of his homes, Henry, as he took up the reins of power, had much to do. King John, rarely more than a few days in one place, had spent little money on his principal residences other than at Corfe. The homes Henry came to know during the minority must often have been dilapidated and depressing. He had even more to do after 1236, when he wished to provide a fitting environment for his much loved queen, this after a gap of twenty years when there had been no queen at all, not that John anyway seems to have been much concerned to provide special quarters for Isabella of Angoulême. Henry never thought, as he did with Westminster Abbey, of sweeping existing buildings away and making a completely new start. Instead, he embellished and expanded existing structures. As a result, all Henry's homes were transformed during the period of his personal rule. Old halls, chambers and chapels were remodelled, and new ones built from scratch. Around them there was an array of new kitchens, butteries, pantries, stables, almonries, sheds for firewood and cellars for storing wine. The chambers of the king and queen were wainscotted and decorated with high-quality religious and secular imagery. The floors were tiled and the windows glazed and made to open and shut. Screens kept out drafts, burning logs in capacious fireplaces provided heat and, on winter nights, shutters to the windows helped retain the warmth.[43]

[39] Maddicott, *Origins of the English Parliament*, 454–72. I am including Maddicott's possible parliaments and assuming that parliaments said to meet in London in fact met at Westminster.

[40] For Windsor and the queen, see Brindle, *Windsor Castle*, 59–60.

[41] Henry, on occasion, went out to Merton priory from Westminster and then back again. In terms of the time spent there during the personal rule, Merton does not come much below Guildford. Again, one wishes there had been a chronicler to record the visits.

[42] Carpenter and Kanter, 'King Henry III and Windsor castle', 30–1. Windsor was also a stopping point on Henry's journeys out to Reading, from where he could progress either to Woodstock or to Marlborough, Clarendon and Winchester. It was equally a stopping point on the way back to Westminster. Visits to Waltham were sometimes combined with ones to the royal manor of Havering. Havering might also be a stopping point on the journey to or from East Anglia.

[43] *CR 1256–9*, 365.

The health and comfort of the homes was helped by Henry's concern for sanitation. At Westminster he had a special conduit constructed to carry away the water with the kitchen waste since those in the halls were being overcome with the smell. At many of his homes he had new privies built, with those for his own use (doubtless with the deep drop he wanted at York in 1251) placed conveniently close to his chamber. At Westminster the privy in his wardrobe was resited as it smelt so badly. In the same or another wardrobe Henry's hair was washed and he had his bath.[44] The comfort and privacy of the king's entourage was enhanced by the separate chambers for stewards, knights, squires, bailiffs, victuallers, chaplains and friars. Some of the king's most senior ministers had their own chambers. At Westminster, John Mansel took over that of the abbot of Evesham (erstwhile keeper of the seal) until he acquired his own house at Tothill, opposite Westminster Abbey. Hubert de Burgh likewise had his own house near Westminster as did many bishops and barons.

Around the halls, chambers and chapels Henry laid out herb gardens and planted pear and cherry trees. At Woodstock, the 'pleasant and suitable herb garden' made for the queen was surrounded by a high wall 'so that no one can get in'.[45] Security was increased after the attempt on the king's life at Woodstock in 1238, and thereafter windows in the homes were often barred with iron. At Clarendon, those of the queen's new wardrobe were not only barred, but, on Henry's orders, placed so high up that someone standing in the courtyard could not see in.[46] The possibilities of relaxation were enhanced at Windsor, Clarendon, Woodstock and Guildford by their great parks. At Windsor, indeed, Henry built a new house some five miles south of the castle and around it created the nucleus of what was to become Windsor Great Park.[47] Much as he loved Westminster it must sometimes have been a relief to escape to Windsor. At Woodstock, there was already a rural retreat set beneath the palace around the spring and ponds of Everswell. This was where Henry II had conducted his amours with fair Rosamond, as Henry himself knew for he had Rosamond's chamber there repaired. At Everswell, in much more proper congress, Henry and Eleanor could be quite self-contained for around 'the cloisters by the pools' (which Henry had paved and wainscotted) they had their own chambers (which Henry had connected), as well as a kitchen and a wine cellar.

Within Henry's buildings imagery was appropriately placed. Depictions of the twelve months of the year with their emblems were placed above

---

[44] *CR 1254–6*, 326; *CLR 1251–60*, 507; *CR 1256–9*, 377–8, 380.

[45] *CLR 1245–51*, 292. It is not quite clear here whether two gardens are referred to or just one. Currently in Winchester castle there is a herb garden laid out as it might have been in Queen Eleanor's day.

[46] *CLR 1240–5*, 310.

[47] Colvin, *History of the King's Works*, ii, 1007.

the fireplace in the king's chamber at Kempton. A painting of winter appeared on the chimney breast of the queen's chamber at Westminster. 'By its sad looks and other miserable portrayals of the body' it was to be 'justly likened to winter', a striking example of the impact Henry expected from his art.[48] Religious imagery – the Virgin Mary, the Confessor and the Pilgrim, the apostles and much else besides – was ubiquitous, appearing just as much in chambers as in chapels. In 1250, after Henry had taken the cross, stories connected with the crusades also began to appear. The decoration spoke very much to Henry's regality. His coats of arms were painted on shutters and depicted in the stained-glass windows. Images of kings and queens were everywhere, at Kempton even surmounting the roof of the hall. In things great and small Henry was acutely aware of his dignity, hence the highly painted royal seats in his halls and chapels, hence the porch built at Westminster 'in keeping with so great a palace' so that he could dismount from his palfrey 'before a noble frontage'.[49]

The work on his homes Henry usually commanded during or just after a visit. One can picture him walking round with clerks, quills ready to jot down the list of things to do. Or did Henry just remember himself and give the orders verbally to the clerks of the chancery? Whichever, the resulting writs cover a vast range of work and demonstrate the energy, acuity, imagination and impatience of the king in matters great and small. In one writ, issued just after Henry had been at Clarendon in June 1251, the sheriff of Wiltshire was to carry out around twenty separate jobs ranging from having the duel between Richard and Saladin painted in the king's chamber down to making iron pegs for chains to shut the glass windows in the king's chapel.[50] Henry wanted his commissions done to the highest standards. His paintings were to be 'in the best colours' by the 'best painter'. At Winchester in 1256 we glimpse him discussing with his painter Master William (a monk of Westminster) a picture for the wardrobe at Westminster where his hair was washed. (It was to be of a king rescued from sedition by his dogs.) The superb quality of such work is best exemplified in the surviving fragments of wall painting, probably dating from the 1240s, in the chapel of Chester castle. Here there is an imposing head of a bishop with large eyes full of meaning and a moving depiction of the Visitation with Elizabeth tenderly holding the Virgin's chin.[51] Henry drove the works forward just as he did those at Westminster Abbey. The wainscotting of his new chamber at Windsor was to proceed 'day and night' so as to be ready for his arrival (this linked to precise instructions as to how

[48] *CLR 1226–40*, 444.

[49] *CR 1242–7*, 273: 'ad honestam frontem'. I am grateful to Daniel Hadas for advice on the translation here. Contrast Colvin, *History of the King's Works*, i, 504.

[50] *CLR 1245–51*, 362.

[51] *CR 1254–6*, 326. For the Chester paintings, see Cather, Park and Pender, 'Henry III's wall paintings at Chester castle', 170–89, and plates I–IV.

the wainscotting should appear). The new chapel at Windsor was to be completed as soon as possible even if it meant labouring 'in winter and in summer'. The new chamber for the knights at Westminster was to be ready by Easter, 'even if a thousand workers are needed every day'; the resited privy was to be ready for the king's arrival, even if it cost £100.[52]

The money for Henry's works, outside those at Westminster, usually came from the sheriffs with the revenues on which they could draw sometimes exactly specified.[53] In November 1255, Henry explained that he would be spending Christmas at Winchester and then celebrating the feast of the circumcision (1 January with its gift-giving ceremonies) at Guildford. Worried that the buildings at Guildford would not be ready in time, he ordered the sheriff of Sussex to provide the keepers of the works there with £100 from the issues of the judicial eyre in the county. If the money could not be given in a lump sum, it was to be sent in instalments. If the buildings were unfinished for lack of money, Henry warned, he would punish the sheriff severely. A writ, issued from Guildford on 3 January, just before Henry left for the Confessor's feast at Westminster, reveals the nature of the work being undertaken. It involved the wainscotting of the king's and queen's chapels; the making of two great windows in the king's chapel; the wainscotting of the king's new chamber and the barring of its windows; the making of a stone porch for the hall; the painting of the story of Dives and Lazarus in the king's hall opposite his seat; the making of an image with beasts in the seat itself; and the lengthening of the chamber of the king's chaplains.[54]

Little remains to show the splendour of Henry's homes. Marlborough castle is now reduced to a bare motte. At Guildford, while one can sense the pleasure of the site on its hill overlooking the park, Henry's palace buildings have quite vanished.[55] What was left of the palace at Woodstock was pulled down during the construction of Blenheim. Even the hill where it stood was flattened out during landscaping. Now only a small plinth (erected in 1961) reminds walkers through the park that this was the site of one of the premier royal palaces of medieval England. Fortunately at Windsor there survive from Henry's new chapel (almost certainly designed by the Abbey's master mason, Henry de Reyns) some spacious arcading and the three-arched entrance with its Purbeck marble columns. The two interleaving central doors have spiralling ironwork of equal harmony and complexity, the signed work of the smith Gilebertus. There are also two imposing painted heads, full faced with large staring eyes, probably the

---

[52] *CR 1237–42*, 514; *CR 1242–7*, 39, 136, 160.

[53] For overall figures for Henry's expenditure on castles and houses, see Colvin, *History of the King's Works*, i, 113, 120. Over the reign as a whole they averaged some £2,000 a year.

[54] *CLR 1251–60*, 257, 262–3.

[55] The castle's keep of course remains. For the palace and the castle, see Poulton, *A Medieval Royal Complex at Guildford*.

work of Master William, the monk of Westminster.[56] The mighty fortifications, the art and architecture of the domestic quarters, and the great park all help to explain why in the 1260s Windsor was described as 'that most beautiful castle of which there was not one more splendid within the bounds of Europe'.[57]

Just one of the great halls built by Henry survives, the spacious aisled hall, with its tall Purbeck columns supporting the arcades, being finished at Winchester in 1233. In the gable above the dais Henry had painted a wheel of fortune. The image was thus behind him but visible to everyone in the body of the hall, a warning as to what might happen to those who transgressed. As will be seen, it was a warning that Henry uttered himself to good effect during dramatic events in the hall in 1249.[58]

The one surviving royal chamber, indeed 'great chamber', built in Henry's reign is on the first floor of what is now called the Wakefield tower at the Tower of London.[59] In normal times Henry never lived at the Tower. He only went there in moments of political crisis, in 1236, in 1238 (after the Montfort marriage) and for long sojourns during the struggle to recover power in 1261. During these periods he almost certainly lived in the Wakefield tower. The chamber gives a great sense of space, grandeur and security. It is ocatagonal in plan within a round tower whose walls are 10 feet thick. Into the walls were inserted a privy chamber and a door leading to the adjoining hall. There were two windows, probably with window seats, overlooking the Thames, which then (before the construction of the Edwardian outer walls) lapped against the base of the tower. A third window lit a private chapel. On one side of the tower was a watergate, and on the other a private landing stage and a doorway leading via a spacious spiral staircase to the chamber above.[60] This was doubtless the way Henry came in. The tower had actually been built during his minority, but, after his enforced stay in 1238, Henry had the chapel painted and a wooden screen placed between it and the main body of the chamber.[61] In 1240 the walls of the chamber were to be whitewashed (perhaps over

[56] Brindle, *Windsor Castle*, 63–72, where on p. 64 there is a conjectural reconstruction of a highly decorated chamber from Henry's time based on fragments of a surviving painting found in one of the present cloister houses.

[57] Pershore, *Flores*, 481. The Pershore *Flores* were written under the eye of its abbot Eleurius, an old servant of Henry III, who knew Windsor well. The context of the comment is military. In another contemporary description Windsor is described as a palace: *Saint Richard of Chichester*, 100, 176.

[58] Colvin, *History of the King's Works*, ii, 858–60; see below, 484.

[59] For the Tower, see Curnow, 'The Wakefield tower', and Parnell, *Tower of London*, 27–32 and plate 2.

[60] The sill of the private entrance still survives pierced with weep-holes to allow the water to escape.

[61] *CLR 1226–40*, 315–16, 352, 444, 453; Colvin, *History of the King's Works*, ii, 713–14. There is currently a reproduction of the screen in the chamber.

wainscotting) and the king's arms painted on the window shutters.[62] If Henry had to go to the Tower, he could at least live in a chamber speaking to his regal state.[63]

At Clarendon, in contrast to Windsor, Winchester and the Tower, nothing of Henry's work remains above ground. Fortunately excavations have done much to reveal the charm of the palace's situation and the splendour of its Henrician decoration. When I first visited the site in the early 1980s it had become so overgrown since the excavations of the 1930s that hardly anything could be discerned of the palace's layout. Since then further excavations have taken place and the site has been cleared.[64] One can now see how the palace ran along the ridge of a hill and looked down, through terraced gardens, into the valley below. We may be sure Henry placed windows to take advantage of the view. At Nottingham he wanted the tower and chambers of the castle to have plenty of windows overlooking the river but only one window apiece overlooking the town.[65] The excavations at Clarendon revealed in the king's apartments gilded stars made of lead which were probably pinned to the ceilings and a tile depicting two knights in combat, perhaps Richard I and Saladin. Elsewhere significant portions of two pavements were discovered, both now in the British Museum. One of these had been on a first floor and had fallen through into the chamber below. It was circular in form with concentric bands of green glazed tiles alternating with bands of tiles decorated with spiralling foliage and other patterns.[66] It seems highly likely this was a pavement in the king's chapel. Fifteen letters survive from an inscription but the text is irrecoverable. The second pavement, as an evocative photograph shows, was actually found in situ.[67] This time the floor was divided into panels with different arrangements of plain and decorated tiles in each, some of the latter displaying lions, griffins and birds. Probably this was a pavement in the queen's apartments. Although there was nothing unique about either pavement, they were of the highest quality both in terms of manufacture and design, very much fit for the king and queen.[68]

Perhaps most striking of all from Clarendon is the sculptured head recovered from what were the king's apartments Looked at close up in the Salisbury museum this head of a young man apparently in the throes of death is intensely moving. The brow is furrowed, the eyes reduced to slits, the mouth slightly open revealing the teeth, the whole expression poignant, despairing. Probably it served as a stop to a moulding around a door or

---

[62] *CLR 1226–40*, 453.

[63] R.A. Brown comments that the tower has that 'duality of military strength and residential splendour characteristic of the medieval castle': Brown, 'Architectural description', 43.

[64] For Clarendon, see James and Robinson, *Clarendon Palace*.

[65] *CR 1242–7*, 68. For attitudes to landscape, see Liddiard, *Castles in Context*, 115.

[66] The tiles were made on site, excavations having revealed part of the kiln.

[67] James and Robinson, *Clarendon Palace*, plate LIV.

[68] For the tiles, see Eames, 'Tile kiln and floor tiles', 139–57 and plates.

window, with on the other side another head depicting life. While all else is lost, the Clarendon head survives to suggest the brilliantly expressive sculpture found in Henry's homes.

Virtually nothing now remains of Henry's transformative work at his most important palace of all, Westminster, but fortunately his recorded orders and the drawings made in the late eighteenth and early nineteenth centuries (some of them in fine colours) can give an impression of its magnificence and meaning.[69] The palace in Henry's time covered a substantial area.[70] It was bounded to the east by the Thames and surrounded by a crenellated wall in which there were gateways and posterns. When Henry arrived by water he disembarked at his pier in the north-east corner of the palace site. When he came by land he rode through the great gateway in its north-west corner, perhaps saluted (such was the overcrowding) by those living in tents outside. Henry did not, however, dismount at this point and walk through the outer courtyard into the great hall of William Rufus, with all its hurly burly. Rather he rode on through an inner gateway, down the length of the hall, and then dismounted by the door of the smaller hall. It was here he ordered the new porch to be built so he could descend from his palfrey (he wanted it white in 1238) 'before a noble frontage'.[71] From this point, Henry could do one of three things. He could walk up to a doorway into the south end of the great hall and look down from the dais at those below, he could walk straight on into the palace's principal chapel, that of Saint Stephen, and give thanks for his safe return, or, ignoring these two possibilities, he could turn right into the lesser hall and walk through it to the rest and relaxation of his own great chamber. From the chamber there was a doorway in its south-west corner leading to a pentice which ran, through a postern gate, across to the Abbey and its south transept doorway. From there, if Henry wished, he could go up a turret stair case, across the end of the south transept and into his own pew with its great sculpted heads of a king and queen and magical views across the Abbey. In this as in everything else Abbey and palace moved together.[72] To make the connection more delightful, between the Abbey and the palace Henry planted pear trees.

William Rufus's great hall remained far and away the largest building in the palace, however much overtopped by Henry's new Abbey. Apart from adding a chamber for his knights along its western side, Henry did little to its structure, but he oversaw important changes to its function. During his

---

[69] The drawings were made both before and after Henry's buildings were gutted by the fire of 1834. The buildings were then, of course, swept away to be replaced by the present Houses of Parliament.

[70] For the palace under Henry, see Colvin, *History of the King's Works*, i, 494–503, and Jansen, 'Henry III's palace at Westminster'.

[71] *CR 1242–7*, 273; *CR 1237–42*, 97.

[72] Wilson, 'Calling the tune?', 65–8.

reign the exchequer thus moved from the south of Saint Stephen's chapel to take up quarters in chambers adjoining the entrance to the hall, the exchequer of receipt to the left as one went in, the exchequer of audit to the right.[73] The latter's thirteenth-century doorway still survives in the hall's north-west corner. Through it Henry must have walked countless times to give rulings at the exchequer and make speeches (most notably in 1250) to the assembled sheriffs. One can also imagine him going into the exchequer of receipt to check on the cash coming in, just as, when elsewhere, he was constantly asking for information about it. The great hall was also the home of the court of common pleas and, one may suspect, when the king was in residence, of the court *coram rege*. Perhaps chancery clerks were there too, charged with making out the thousands of writs every year purchased to initiate and process the common law legal actions.

The great hall, therefore, for much of the year, was thronged with litigants, lawyers, sheriffs, knights, barons and baronial stewards, debating business, pleasure and the affairs of the kingdom. And over them all, at all times, was a reminder of the king, for at the southern end of the hall on the dais was his gilded throne. In 1245, Henry decided the two leopards on either side should be made in bronze rather than marble, on the grounds they would be 'more sumptuous' that way. At the same time he ordered the steps on which the throne was raised to be in cut stone. It was sitting on these steps that Matthew Paris had a respectful conversation with the king during a great ceremony in 1247. In 1258, Henry was doubtless enthroned here when judgement was given in the great hall against the London aldermen.[74] The whole ensemble was meant to recall Solomon's throne with its steps and golden lions. Everyone in the hall would thus be reminded of Henry's own Solomonic majesty and wisdom, or so at least he might hope. The great hall was also central to the practice of Henry's piety and hospitality. Here he fed his paupers, cramming the hall full to capacity, and here he held his magnificent feasts on the high days of the year. On the dais Henry had placed a great table made of stone – three of its Purbeck marble trestles, with their columns and capitals, have recently been found during excavations. Henry was determined to feast in proper state.[75]

Given its proximity to the great hall the chapel of Saint Stephen's was often used by Henry for meetings. It was here that Henry lost his temper with Gerard Bat, the new mayor of London, here that he begged his brother Richard of Cornwall, before assembled magnates, to accept election to the kingship of Germany, and here too that he conferred with his council before going into the great hall to see the London aldermen in

[73] The exchequer of the Jews was in an adjoining chamber.

[74] See below, 677–8.

[75] *CR 1242–7*, 293; *BA*, 422–3; 1 Kings 10:18–20; 2 Chronicles 9:7–19; Jansen, 'Henry III's palace at Westminster', 104–5; Collins, 'The king's high table'.

1258.[76] No wonder Henry gave constant attention to the chapel's decoration, with its paintings of Nebuchadnezzar, a king and a queen, the apostles, the Last Judgement and, strategically placed as one came down from the great hall, the Virgin Mary.[77]

Fortunately some drawings survive of the chamber and chapel Henry built for Queen Eleanor after their marriage in 1236. They were first-floor buildings, the chamber connecting directly with the bed end of Henry's own chamber, so he could easily slip across. Both chamber and chapel were large buildings. The former had a capacious fireplace (with the likeness of winter painted on the mantle) and double lancet windows with roundels above on the eastern side looking towards the Thames. It measured 70 x 27 feet and so was a foot wider and only 10 feet less in length than the king's own chamber. The queen's chapel, lit by single lancets, at 43 x 21 feet, was considerably larger than the private chapel of the king. These spacious quarters reflect how much Henry wished to enhance the status of his queen and provide fitting accommodation for her large entourage.

Henry's own chamber, likewise a first-floor structure, measured 80 feet 6 inches x 26 feet and was 31 feet 9 inches high.[78] The surviving drawings give an impression of its capacious length and height. The basic structure Henry had inherited from Henry II, but he added a new roof, for which timber was ordered in 1232, and, around the same time, replaced the twelfth-century windows with double lancets. Those down the walls had roundels above, the two pairs at the east end overlooking the river and lighting the king's bed had lozenges.[79] The drawings show a large fireplace and a grand doorway in the south-west corner, which would have led down to the pentice running out to the Abbey.

Henry's orders show his concern for the decoration of the chamber and give at least some idea of how it appeared in his personal rule, although there is no precise information about how the various elements were arranged. In May 1236, Henry wanted the chamber painted 'in a good green colour in the form of a curtain'. At the same time in the great gable by the doorway there was to be the motto 'he who does not give what he has will never gain what he desires', an exhortation to charity presumably visible to everyone as they left the chamber. The following year, Henry ordered a picture of lions, birds and other beasts begun 'under the great history of the chamber' to be removed and replaced by a green curtain in

---

[76] FitzThedmar, 8, 36.

[77] *CR 1231–4*, 9–10, 207; *CR 1234–7*, 239, 378; *CR 1242–7*, 279, 287; *CR 1247–51*, 311; *CR 1253–4*, 165. For Nebuchadnezzar, see below, 571.

[78] For the chamber, see Binski, *Painted Chamber*, and Wilson, 'Monument to St Edward the Confessor'.

[79] The windows evidently survived the fire which ravaged the chamber in 1263. Had they been even a decade later they (and those in the queen's chamber) would probably have been in bar rather than plate tracery.

such a way that the great history was preserved unharmed. Thereafter, between 1241 and 1243, orders were issued for the paving of the chamber, for the painting of two great lions face to face in the western gable, and for the painting of the four evangelists in fine colours, John on the east wall, Matthew on the west, Luke on the south and Mark on the north. The evangelists were to appear 'above the lions', so it sounds as though there was some kind of frieze of lions around the chamber. Then, in 1244, Henry ordered the chamber to be wainscotted, whether as a replacement for the green curtain or as an accompaniment is not clear. That the order for the great lions in the gable was issued while Henry was in Gascony shows the chamber was never far from his thoughts.[80]

Historians are agreed that Henry's bed was situated against the north-east wall of the chamber. It was well placed for both physical and spiritual comfort. To its left was the chamber's great fireplace, on whose mantle in 1259 Henry had a Tree of Jesse painted.[81] Judging from the expenditure on 'wood for the chamber' recorded in the household accounts, during winter there was always a roaring fire.[82] On the right of the bed was a doorway through to Henry's chapel, where the Montforts were married in 1238. A few months later Henry had its floor tiled and the history of Joseph painted behind his seat.[83] A small quatrefoil window in the wall behind his bed enabled Henry at any time to look through to the chapel. In May 1236, soon after his marriage, he wanted the window glazed as soon as possible, presumably to shield himself and his queen from any draft.[84]

Throughout his residences Henry paid close attention to his beds, the centrepieces of all his chambers. He certainly wanted them comfortable and tested them as carefully as anyone in a modern showroom. In 1259 he rejected a new bed sent to Windsor and ordered a replacement made of better and stronger cloth and with a better and larger mattress.[85] Henry also wanted his beds to be imposing. A 'beautiful bed' he ordered in 1249 was to be composed of a mattress, a quilt, various covers and two pillows, all made of silk and cloths of gold and scarlet.[86] The bed at Westminster was particularly magnificent. In 1239 it was provided with a cloth with an orphrey and a green double cloth; in 1243 with forty-eight ells of green linen. The following year Henry ordered the columns around the bed to be newly painted in a vivid green and starred with gold. Evidently the columns held

[80] CR 1234–7, 271, 484; CR 1237–42, 312; CR 1242–7, 19–20, 45, 169.

[81] BA, 371–2. At the same time the paintings on the walls of the chamber were renewed and cleaned.

[82] The amounts recorded each day in late October and early November 1259 were often in the region of 5s to 7s. In February and March 1266 they were sometimes between 15s and 17s.

[83] CR 1237–42, 26.

[84] CR 1234–7, 270.

[85] CR 1256–9, 365.

[86] CR 1247–51, 237. The bed was to be a gift to Gaston de Béarn.

up the curtains that Henry now ordered to be made. They were to 'befit his royal honour' and be openable and closable at his pleasure.[87] Probably the columns also supported a canopy like that borne over Henry in his coronation procession, thus adding greatly to the dignity of the ensemble. Henry's care and attention was hardly surprising. His bed at Westminster was the most important in the kingdom. Indeed, it was in a way the epicentre of the realm. With the curtains closed it was a bed for sleep and sex; with them open, to a greater degree than any bed elsewhere, it was a bed of state where the king could sit discussing the affairs of the kingdom with those to whom he had granted an audience, the frisson of the private function giving all the more intimacy and thus all the more power to the public one.

The impact of the Westminster bed was enhanced by the surrounding decoration, decoration known from water-coloured copies, made in 1819, of the paintings in the area.[88] All historians agree, on stylistic grounds, that these paintings date to after the fire that ravaged the chamber in 1263.[89] But there is equal agreement that, in terms of their subject matter, they may well have replicated the paintings commissioned by Henry before the fire. We can, therefore, get some impression of the decoration of the area during Henry's personal rule.[90]

To the left of the bed there was a large standing figure of a knight in armour, holding a spear and girt with a sword. Here Henry was continuing the Solomonic references begun with the throne in the great hall, for the knight was almost certainly paired with a knight on the other side, the two thus guarding the king's bed like the knights girt with swords guarding Solomon's bed in the Song of Songs (iii:7–10). Solomon's guardians indeed figured in paintings Henry placed around his bed in Winchester castle.[91] The Solomonic references were also there in the green colours of the bed, recalling again the Song of Songs (i:16): 'Behold, thou art fair, my beloved, yea pleasant: also our bed is green.' In the great chamber, therefore, the green of the bed matched the green of the walls, the curtain effect of the walls themselves matching what were doubtless the green curtains of the bed.

Into this Solomonic context Henry introduced the Confessor. For at the head of the bed was a magnificent painting of the Confessor's coronation with two mitred prelates placing the crown on the king's head, surrounded by a great crowd of bishops holding crosses and croziers. Above the scene, just in case anyone was unsure, an inscription proclaimed in capital letters:

---

[87] *CLR 1226–40*, 376; *CLR 1240–5*, 205; *CR 1242–7*, 169: 'curtinas . . . honestatem regiam decentes'.

[88] The copyists were Charles Stothard and Edward Crocker.

[89] The restoration of the chamber post-1263 is discussed in volume 2.

[90] For a debate about the paintings, see below, 371, n. 103.

[91] *CLR 1245–51*, 325. In the same order the new chapel in the castle was to be floored with tiles and the story of Joseph painted.

CEST LE CORONEMENT SEINT EDEWARD

The Confessorian theme continued in the large standing figures painted in the splays of the windows immediately opposite the bed. On the left was the pilgrim holding out his supplicatory hand, on the right the Confessor bestowing the ring. So Henry, lying in bed, lying, he may well have thought, in the very place the Confessor himself had lain,[92] had above his head the Confessor's coronation, the supreme moment at the start of the reign, and at his feet the numinous episode at the end which foreshadowed the Confessor's ascent to heaven. He was placing himself completely into the Confessor's caring hands.

In the splays of the other windows in the chamber Henry had painted the Virtues and the Vices, the Virtues great standing figures of queens trampling the Vices underfoot. The window just to the west of that with the Confessor and the pilgrim had 'largesse' triumphing over 'covetousness' and 'deboneretè' triumphing over 'anger'. In their post-1263 incarnations these are superb pictures, the identity of the Virtues and Vices proclaimed in large capital letters, the queens, their robes fringed with orphreys, wearing golden, floreated crowns, *deboneretè* particularly associated with Henry by bearing the royal arms of England on her shield. Here, of course, Henry invoked virtues associated with the Confessor's just and consensual rule, as he also, in the imagery of the bed, linked together (as was often done) the Confessor and Solomon.[93] The decoration of Henry's great chamber probably began sometime after 1232 when timber was being obtained for the roof.[94] It was thus conceived at the very moment when Henry's devotion to the Confessor was developing apace.[95] It fitted perfectly with the consensual politics ushered in by the fall of Peter des Roches.[96]

The Confessorian imagery moved with that in the rest of the chamber. The apostles ranged around the walls situated the Confessor in his wider biblical context, with Saint John, the Confessor's conductor to heaven, placed on the eastern wall and thus beside Henry's bed. The same biblical context was provided by the Tree of Jesse, with its portrayal of Christ's ancestors (another work of Master William), placed on the mantel of the fireplace in 1259.[97] There was also a wider context still, which introduces

---

[92] I owe this thought to Wilson, 'Monument to St Edward the Confessor', 169. More generally, see Hyams, 'What did Henry III of England think in bed'.

[93] See Binski, *Painted Chamber*, 42–3 and n. 69; Fenster and Wogan-Browne, *History of Saint Edward*, 14–16; *Lives of Edward the Confessor*, lines 890, 1373.

[94] If the roof followed that in place after 1263, then it was flat and made of wooden panels.

[95] For the scheme being conceived at this time, see Wilson, 'Monument to St Edward the Confessor', 169.

[96] See above, 160–2.

[97] *BA*, 372–3.

something else in the room during Henry's personal rule. This was a mappa mundi. It was famous and a copy (now lost) was made by Matthew Paris (something he tells us in a note written in his own hand).[98] Quite possibly the mappa mundi was the same as the magna historia already referred to.[99] The late thirteenth-century Hereford mappa mundi was thus explicitly described by its maker as a 'history' ('estorie').[100] This was not surprising because, like other world maps, it was packed with text describing the numerous places, people and beasts depicted, drawing on the bible, the classics and a rich store of fable and legend.[101] At the centre of the Hereford map (as with all mappae mundi), was Jerusalem, while above Christ is shown sitting in judgement, with the blessed and the damned on either side proceeding to their different fates. Henry's map was probably very large. The Hereford map is 4 feet 2 inches high and 4 feet 4 inches wide. The earlier Ebstorf map (dated to 1239) was some 10 feet square.[102] Perhaps Henry's mappa was placed on the right of the great chamber's main doorway where space was provided by a blocked twelfth-century window. It was thus the first thing seen on entry. The mappa placed Henry, the Confessor, the Virtues and Vices and the Apostles within the whole world of God's creation and its final end with the last judgement.[103]

---

[98] Reproduced in Connolly, *Maps of Matthew Paris*, plate 3, with discussion between 159 and 164.

[99] This is suggested in Binski, *Painted Chamber*, 44, and accepted by Connolly, *Maps of Matthew Paris*, 185, as 'likely'. Henry had another mappa mundi painted in the hall at Winchester: *CLR 1226–40*, 405.

[100] Harvey, *Hereford World Map*, 86.

[101] See the general description of such maps in Harvey, *Medieval Maps*, 19.

[102] Harvey, *Hereford World Map*, 11, 59. The Ebstorf map was destroyed by bombing in 1943 but has been reconstructed from photographs. Paris's copy of Henry's map, which he placed in his service book, was evidently small scale.

[103] While there is a considerable measure of agreement about the decoration of the great chamber at Westminster in Henry's time, there is one major area of debate. The watercolours made in 1819 show that there were a series of Old Testament scenes painted in great bands along the walls of the chamber. These depicted the wars of the Maccabees and the oppressions and downfall of tyrannical rulers. When two Irish friars saw the chamber in 1323, they described it as 'that famous chamber on whose walls all the warlike stories of the whole bible are painted with wonderful skill and explained by a complete series of texts written in French to the great admiration of the beholder and with the greatest royal magnificence' (Binski, *Painted Chamber*, 1). Paul Binski has argued that these paintings (for which there is no certain proof before 1323) were the work of Edward I in the 1290s (Binski, *Painted Chamber*, ch. 3, and his later article, 'Painted chamber at Westminster'). Christopher Wilson, on the other hand, argues that, if renewed after the fire of 1263, they were, for the most part, conceived in the mid-1230s and were the culmination of Henry III's repair and remodelling of the chamber (Wilson, 'Monument to St Edward the Confessor'). There are also other possibilities. The paintings could date to after the 1263 fire, or even have begun life when the chamber was first built by Henry II. The debate is obviously fundamental to the appearance of the chamber in Henry's time, but, in the current state of evidence and argument, I just do not think it is capable of resolution. The

Save perhaps when he was with his brother Richard at Wallingford, did Henry reflect on how his residences outshone those of his earls and barons? Several times in his personal rule he was entertained at Roger Bigod's castle at Framlingham in Suffolk. The modern photographs, taken from across the mere, make the castle seem far larger than it really is. Henry would have known how easily it had fallen to his father in 1216. He may also have considered the square towers along the curtain walls outmoded compared to the round ones he was constructing at Dover, Windsor, Winchester and the Tower. Inside the castle, there was a largish chapel but with outdated round-headed windows. The windows of the chamber looked out over the cramped courtyard instead of over the mere.[104] That view, in a reversal of proper status, was enjoyed by the hall. The contrast with his own castles may well have given Henry all the more confidence in his occasional confrontations with the earl of Norfolk.[105]

THE CHANCERY

English royal government was driven by documents.[106] It was through them that Henry bestowed patronage, dispensed justice and issued the myriad of orders on which his rule depended. At court, there was always a posse of royal messengers ready to take the king's orders to all parts of the country.[107] The office responsible for writing these documents, and

'magna historia', for example, which Henry was eager to preserve in the chamber in 1237, could have been either the Old Testament scenes, the 'mappa mundi' or something else. At first sight paintings of warlike scenes seem more likely under Edward I, very much 'mighty in war like a Maccabee' (as was said of his grandson Edward III), than under the pacific Henry III. Would, moreover, Henry III have been keen to cover the chamber with images of war and tyranny in the mid-1230s at the very time he was emerging from a disastrous civil war and accusations he had himself behaved like a tyrant? On the other hand, while there is evidence for extensive works on the paintings in the palace in the 1290s, in the king's chamber perhaps they were just repairs to existing work. The Confessor and the Maccabees have a link because, in the medieval lectionary, the book of Maccabees was the reading for October and, of course, the feast of the Confessor's translation was on 13 October. If Henry did commission the paintings in the 1230s, as his devotion to the Confessor grew apace, then the point was to contrast the Confessor's benign and peaceful rule, celebrated in the coronation scene behind the bed and the Virtues and the Vices, with the war and tyranny of the Old Testament scenes. In that sense (to add a thought of my own) there was a parallel with Matthew Paris's life of the Confessor, where images of his just and pacific rule are framed by ones illustrating the war and disorder in England before his accession and after his death (see below, 404). But these images hardly dominate the life in the way the Old Testament scenes dominated the chamber, rather to the disadvantage of the Confessor, hence the way the Irish friars did not refer to him at all.

[104] For the siege and the view over the mere, see Liddiard, *Castles in Context*, 93–5, 115.

[105] See below, 625, but not, however, in 1258. Henry never saw Bigod's castle at Chepstow, which Roger inherited from the Marshal earls.

[106] The classic work about the development of records and a record culture is Clanchy, *From Memory to Written Record*.

[107] See Hill, *King's Messengers*.

authenticating them with the great seal, was the chancery, hence Matthew Paris's description of the seal as 'the key of the kingdom'.[108] In Henry's reign the chancery was nearly always at court, travelling with him wherever he went. Henry, therefore, unlike later kings when the chancery had become fixed at Westminster, had no need to use letters authenticated by his privy seal to express his immediate will. This explains why we hear so little of the privy seal. It also explains why chancery letters are such a fruitful source for the history of the reign.

When Henry granted a charter to bestow a favour or issued an order about the decoration of a building, he was very much a self-starter. He was using the chancery to do things he wanted to do. But the chancellor or, in his absence, the keeper of the seal, was fielding all the time letters from the king's ministers, giving information and asking for decisions. In 1226 the judge William of York thus kept Ralph de Neville in close touch with the progress of the judicial eyre in the north, while adding he was now tired out and needed a holiday.[109] The chancery also had to respond to a constant flow of requests and petitions from the king's subjects. As the law book *Fleta* put it, the chancery clerks 'hear and examine the petitions and complaints of petitioners and by means of royal writs provide them with a remedy'.[110] Such petitions could be dealt with in a routine way, without consulting the king, when they involved the initiation and processing of common law legal actions. But when they raised more important issues, then they would have to go up to the king himself. The running of the chancery was thus of great moment to the king's subjects. For them, it was by far the most important element of Henry's court. Seeking its documents was the main reason why they went there. No wonder, therefore, control of the chancery became a major aim of Henry's political opponents.

By Henry's time the main documents issued by the chancery were set in form.[111] At the top of the scale, in terms of their consequence and appearance, were the charters in which Henry made permanent gifts of land and rights. Always containing a list of witnesses and often beautifully written, especially early in the reign, the great seal was attached by silken threads. Next down from charters were letters patent. These were used to announce appointments, issue proclamations and make gifts of a less than permanent nature. Without witness lists, and less finely written than charters, the great seal was usually attached not by a silken thread but by a parchment tongue. Letters close were the final type of document the

---

[108] Paris, v, 130.

[109] Meekings, *Studies in 13th-Century Justice*, ch. 5, 492–504. For the eyres, see above, 51.

[110] *Fleta*, 123. *Fleta* is a work of the late thirteenth century.

[111] For the documents issued by the chancery, see Chaplais, *English Royal Documents*. There is a great deal of information about chancery practice in Maxwell-Lyte, *Historical Notes*. In writing this section I have been helped by chapters from Adam Chambers' doctoral thesis on the Henrician chancery rolls and by a forthcoming paper by Nicholas Vincent, 'Royal diplomatic and the shape of the English state, 1066–1300'.

chancery issued. They were so named because they were folded and then tied up with a strip of parchment cut from the bottom, with just a dab of wax from a corner of the great seal being placed across the knot. They were thus closed whereas charters and letters patent were always left open with the great seal hanging beneath them. Letters close were the administrative maids of all work and were sent to the king's agents with all manner of instructions. Also in the form of letters close were the writs (in Latin 'breves'), issued in great numbers, to initiate and further legal actions according to the forms of the common law.

The production and sealing of these documents did not end the work of the chancery. It also recorded a large proportion of its output on a series of rolls, new ones being begun at the start of each regnal year, so on 28 October the day of Henry's first coronation. There were thus charter rolls, patent rolls, close rolls, liberate rolls (with letters close dealing with the expenditure of money) and fine rolls (recording offers of money to the king for concessions and letters close dealing with a range of financial business).[112]

All the charters and letters issued by the chancery ended with statements of their place and date of issue. It is thanks to the copies on the rolls, rather than the surviving originals (a tiny fraction of the whole), that this information can be used to establish both the king's itinerary and (thanks to the witness lists of charters) who was present at court. It is equally through the rolls that we can gauge the extent of the chancery's labours. In the regnal year 1250/1 the rolls recorded 3,803 separate items of business, so an average of ten a day. There were 136 entries on the charter rolls, 471 on the patent rolls, 1,247 on the close rolls, 719 on the liberate rolls and 1,230 on the fine rolls. The work was increasing. An equivalent count for the year 1232/3 has only 2,360 items of business. All of these figures, moreover, exclude the numerous standard form writs initiating the common law legal actions as they were never enrolled at all. A surviving but incomplete file of its business has 130 of such writs issued for the 1248 Berkshire eyre alone.[113]

Between 1218 and 1238 the chancery was under Ralph de Neville, first as deputy of the chancellor, Richard de Marsh, and then as chancellor himself. After Henry took the seal from Neville in 1238, the chancery was headed for the most part by a succession of royal clerks acting as keepers of the seal.[114] Neville, however, was allowed to remain as chancellor down to his death in 1244. He thus still received its substantial revenues, revenues derived from the set fees charged for issuing the charters, letters patent,

---

[112] Copies of the fine rolls, called originalia rolls, were sent to the exchequer so it knew what money to collect.

[113] Clanchy, *Berkshire Eyre*, lxvi, cxii–xiii, and nos. a1–a231. The figures cited above come from Adam Chambers. See also Clanchy, *From Memory to Written Record*, 61, 78–80, where Clanchy traces the growth in output by looking at the weight of the purchases of sealing wax. This test would not cover the great increase in the common law writs as they only received a dab from the seal.

[114] See Dibben, 'Chancellor and keeper of the seal'.

writs and letters close sought by individuals. Doubtless there was also a great deal to be made from undercover payments. With Neville's demise in 1244, Henry received the revenues himself and they were often paid directly into the wardrobe.[115] The political significance of the change is discussed in the main narrative of the book.

Just how many clerks there were working in the chancery is unknown, but there were almost certainly two divisions. On the one hand there were the clerks who wrote the writs, like those for the Berkshire eyre, initiating the common law legal procedures. Costing only 6d, these were called writs 'of course' ('de cursu'), because they were absolutely standard form. These clerks also made out the writs, costing half a mark or more, designed to speed up the judicial process in a variety of ways.[116] The work became increasingly burdensome as more and more people embraced common law litigation. Quite apart from the 'de cursu' writs for which there is no evidence, in the fine roll of 1206–7 around seventy writs were purchased, connected in some way with the common law procedures. In the roll of 1256/7 the number was 462. In that of 1271/2 it was over 1,500.[117] Almost certainly the clerks making out these writs had a fixed place in the various royal residences, at Westminster, as suggested, perhaps in the great hall.

The upper division of clerks dealt with the business very much not 'of course'. On one occasion Henry himself described them as the clerks he had retained with him 'in chief in his chancellery'.[118] They were equally described as clerks 'de precepto' or 'preceptores' after the writs they ordered.[119] These senior clerks helped the chancellor or keeper decide what documents could be issued on his own authority, and what needed to go on up to king. They also drafted the orders received from the king. There is some evidence of their presence at meetings of the king and his ministers where they drew up memoranda of the letters they needed to issue. Perhaps it was also at such formal meetings that charters were witnessed. But alongside such meetings there were probably many occasions when the king and ministers went directly to the 'de precepto' clerks with orders for letters. The varying procedures are reflected in the notes sometimes appended to letters in the chancery rolls indicating the authority for their issue, so they might be 'by the king', 'by the council' or by a named minister.

---

[115] Wild, *WA*, 45, 51, 71, 76, 78, 80, 84–5, 100, 107, 123, 130, 144.

[116] The writs thus moved cases between courts, gave specific days for hearings and commissioned judges to hear cases locally; see Moore, 'Fine rolls as evidence for the expansion of royal justice', 65–8.

[117] Carpenter, 'Between Magna Carta and the parliamentary state', 12–13. The money for purchasing these writs, as for purchasing charters, went direct to the king, but the separate charge for writing them out went to the chancery.

[118] *CR 1254–6*, 77.

[119] *Fleta*, 125.

The sealing itself was a formal occasion. If fourteenth-century practice was followed, it could not take place without the chancellor or keeper of the seal. In 1248 a note on the chancery rolls recorded John of Lexington's departure from court on a Monday 'after he had sealed', and his return on the following Thursday 'before sealing'.[120] It was, indeed, the formal act of sealing, together with actually folding the writs, that inaugurated the reign of a new keeper. So when John of Kirkby was appointed in 1272, the king gave him the seal and John 'saw writs being sealed and folded them as the custom is'.[121]

Henry's chancery officials were men of high calibre who contributed much to the intellectual level of the court. It was not their fault if they were ordered to do foolish things. Matthew Paris had high praise both for Neville and several of his successors. Silvester of Everdon, keeper of the seal from 1244 to 1246, was thus a man of good reputation and behaviour who was skilled in the ways of the chancery.[122] William of Kilkenny was modest, faithful and elegantly learned in both canon and civil law.[123] Everdon, Kilkenny and another keeper Henry of Wingham all went on to bishoprics, whereupon, unlike Neville, they gave up the seal. Paris at least believed that both Neville and Master Simon the Norman, one of his successors as keeper, tried to resist irresponsible acts of the king. In 1253, Kilkenny seems to have broadcast on his own initiative the king's confirmation of Magna Carta.[124] The senior clerks could have ideas of their own about how the chancery might be run. In 1255 one of them, Henry de Mauley, asked Henry of Bath, the senior judge of the court *coram rege*, whether it was necessary any longer to enrol writs about the repledging of land in law cases. Bath said no but was overruled and the enrolments continued. Enrolment itself was a continuous process and rarely fell into arrears.[125] Mistakes were corrected and notes made when keepers of the seal temporally left court or were replaced. Memoranda registered protests when documents were issued outside the proper procedures of the chancery.[126] Marginalia describing the content of entries facilitated searches, thereby helping the king check on orders he had issued. Knowledge that he could do so was an important weapon in controlling his officials.

Something of the camaraderie between the clerks can be sensed in the way they witnessed each other's charters and sought to help each

---

[120] Maxwell-Lyte, *Historical Notes*, 295; *CR 1247–51*, 47.

[121] *ERF*, ii, 575. For Henry folding a letter with his own hand, see *CPR 1258–66*, 416.

[122] Paris, iv, 569; and see the remarks put into the king's mouth: Paris, v, 374. For Everdon, see Summerson, 'The king's *clericulus*'.

[123] Paris, v, 130.

[124] See below, 566.

[125] This is demonstrated in Chambers, 'Aspects of chancery procedure in the chancery rolls of Henry III of England'.

[126] Chaplais, *English Royal Documents*, 56; *CPR 1258–66*, 317; *CPR 1266–72*, 66.

other to benefices, not always successfully.[127] In 1262, when the clerks were divided between those with Henry in France and those left in England, a clerk sent out from England described in a letter home how he had found his colleagues in Paris sitting at table, happy and joking. But unfortunately they had moved too slowly in trying to secure a benefice and it had gone instead to the son of the king's doctor. The writer added that he had not been able to find a carpet or tapestry fit to cover the hall of the chancellor and concluded the letter with a cheery 'Salute all our colleagues'.[128]

Not surprisingly Henry was close to the senior chancery clerks who took his orders, men such as Henry de Mauley, Adam of Chesterton, Henry of Mercinton and Adam of Aston. Henry ensured they received their annual robes, gave them gifts of game, timber and firewood (one went to Adam of Chesterton's mother), appointed them to benefices and entrusted them with work outside the chancery, notably the custody of vacant abbeys. Adam of Chesterton, in the 1260s, also became the warden of the Domus Conversorum.[129] Henry's closeness to the rolls themselves is shown in the way the fine rolls were central to the trick he played on his clerk Peter the Poitevin in the ship returning home from Gascony in 1243.[130] The episode also shows the friendly atmosphere reigning between Henry and his clerks.

THE WARDROBE[131]

The letters of the chancery allowed Henry to fire off orders to all parts of his kingdom. But the orders would have been worthless had there been no power behind the parchment. That power, or a large part of it, ultimately came from money and here the role of the wardrobe was absolutely central. Wherever Henry was he relied on the wardrobe to supply him with ready cash, cash he could spend on the court's food, drink and clothing, and on anything else he wished. There were chambers set aside for the wardrobe at all the major residences.[132] If Henry's court was magnificent, the wardrobe's cash made it so.

---

[127] For example, *CPR 1247–58*, 521; *CR 1259–61*, 218. I assume Vincent de Maulay owed his promotion to Henry de Maulay. For the clerk Adam of Chesterton passing on a benefice to him, see *CPR 1247–58*, 614, 621.

[128] *DD*, no. 370. I thank Henry Summerson for comment on this letter.

[129] For example, *CPR 1247–58*, 374, 391–2, 521, 530, 608, 621; *CR 1242–7*, 399, 493; *CR 1247–51*, 162, 246, 262, 478, 517; *CR 1251–3*, 378, 388, 404; *CR 1253–4*, 74; *CR 1254–6*, 21, 76–7, 341, 362; *CR 1256–9*, 17, 61, 177, 402, 456. I owe some of these references to Nicholas Vincent.

[130] See above, 270–1.

[131] For what follows the pioneering work in Tout, *Chapters*, i, chs. 5–6, remains essential.

[132] For Henry having its chamber at Westminster wainscotted plainly without ornamentation or picture, see *RG*, i, no. 1362.

The wardrobe's financial activities are revealed by the accounts of its keepers heard at the exchequer and enrolled on the pipe rolls.[133] They suggest that the wardrobe, in substantial periods during the personal rule, was handling between a quarter and a half of the crown's annual cash income. The average weekly expenditure between 1234 and 1256 was around £200, approaching the annual income of a middle-ranking baron.[134]

The chief official of the wardrobe was called its keeper or (in recognition of his financial role) its treasurer. There was also a deputy, called the 'controller', who kept a second roll against which the accounts of the keeper were checked. Both officials were clerks, save for during Simon de Montfort's ascendancy in 1265. Given the pivotal role of the wardrobe, the identity of its keeper was clearly a matter of great importance, and their succession too is traced in the general narrative of this book.[135] All, of course, were able men and could, a measure of Henry's trust, be employed on difficult and delicate missions outside the court. As with the chancery clerks, Henry rewarded his keepers and controllers with numerous gifts of wine, wood and game, and appointed them to benefices. They like the chancery clerks must have put pressure on him to resist papal provisions. The Poitevin Peter Chaceporc, keeper from 1241 to 1254, became archdeacon of Wells, treasurer of Lincoln and dean of both Tattenhall in Cheshire and Tottenham outside London.

There was a close relationship between the wardrobe and the chancery. Indeed, in the 1250s, William of Kilkenny moved from being controller of the wardrobe to keeper of the seal, for a while, it seems, holding the two offices in tandem. The relationship had to be close because it was through writs issued by the chancery that the wardrobe obtained much of its money. This worked in two main ways. First, a chancery writ of liberate could order the exchequer to send money to the wardrobe. Or second, a writ could command a sheriff or other official to pay revenue not to the exchequer but to the wardrobe, in which case he was promised an appropriate allowance when he came

---

[133] The accounts have now been edited for the Pipe Roll Society by Ben Wild, see Wild, *WA*, and his related articles 'A truly royal retinue', 'Secrecy, splendour and statecraft' and 'Royal finance under King Henry III'. What we lack under Henry are records of day-to-day wardrobe expenditure. These survive for two regnal years of King John: *RLJ*, 109–71; *DI*, 231–69.

[134] Wild, 'Royal finance under King Henry III', 1399. During the twelfth century the financial office with the king had been his chamber. From late in John's reign, however, in a trend completed early in Henry's minority, it comes to be called the wardrobe. In fact, the chamber had always used the wardrobe to store its money, and probably there is here no more than a chance change in nomenclature with the same officials doing the same job. Early in the minority the same money might be described in one place as paid into the chamber and in another as paid into the wardrobe, and equally officials might be described as both 'of the chamber' and 'of the wardrobe'. See Tout, *Chapters*, i, 188–91. In Henry's reign little is heard of the dedicated chamber officials. They were probably of low status and responsible for such things as lighting the fires, laying the tables and making the bed.

[135] See above, 28–9, 60, 115–16, 153, 222, and below, 672.

to the exchequer to account.[136] There was also money from loans and gifts coming into the wardrobe without any reference to the exchequer.

During the personal rule there were considerable variations in the wardrobe's sources of revenue.[137] For all but one of the accounting periods from 1234 to 1245 between 64 per cent and 77 per cent of the wardrobe's money was supplied by the exchequer.[138] Thereafter the proportion declined, the balance being made up by loans and money paid to the wardrobe direct.[139] As will be seen, objections were raised to the declining role of the exchequer and the reforms of 1258 sought to make it once again the main source of wardrobe money.[140] In terms of the total sums received by the wardrobe, they averaged some £7,750 a year between 1224 and 1226. In the 1230s they were higher, the average for the accounting periods between 1234 and 1240 varying between £9,000 and £10,500 annually. Between 1241 and 1245 the average was over £14,000, largely the result of the war of 1242–3 being funded out of the wardrobe. Between 1245 and 1252 the average was once again around £10,500.[141]

What did the wardrobe do with the money? During the personal rule the largest slice, between 40 and 50 per cent each year, went in paying for the household's food and drink.[142] Money was also spent in a great variety of other ways including alms to the poor, wages to a variety of royal servants and the purchase of cloths and jewels.[143] The officials responsible for

---

[136] The king could also, as we have seen with building works, simply order a sheriff to spend money locally, again with the promise of an allowance when he came to account. The king could, therefore, pay for anything in one of three ways: by ordering payment out of the exchequer; by ordering it out of local revenues; or by paying it out of the wardrobe.

[137] For what follows I am indebted to the analyses of the wardrobe accounts as audited by the exchequer found in Wild, *WA*, lxxi, lxxvi, lxxxxiv, xciii, cii, cxv, cxxii, cxxix.

[138] The exception was between 1238 and 1240, where only 18% came from the exchequer. This was because of revenue coming from the tax of 1237 and ecclesiastical vacancies.

[139] See below, 425, 658, 664.

[140] See below, 664–7.

[141] For the figures for each account, see Tout, *Chapters*, vi, 74–6. Wild, 'Royal finance under King Henry III', 1393, gives weekly averages. Chaceporc's death meant there were no accounts for the period from October 1252 to December 1254, so there is no detailed information about the Gascon expedition of 1253–4.

[142] Carpenter, 'Household rolls', 35.

[143] In the regnal year 1238/9 (Wild, *WA*, lxxxvi–vii, 32–8) the breakdown of expenditure, under the different cost centres, was as follows: £4,184 to the household (largely spent on food and drink); £177 on the king's daily offerings, and clothing of the poor; £429 on the expenses of the queen, Edward, the king's son, Richard de Clare and other wards in the king's care, together with the costs of the king's shoes, the purchase of eight palfreys and seven rounceys, and the acquisition and gilding of a silver arm, doubtless to hold a relic; £1,150 on gifts and liveries to knights, clerks and other envoys from diverse lands, payments to Poitevins and payments to the king's sergeants-at-arms, knights and clerks; £152 on messengers; £177 on huntsmen, falconers and dogs; £948 on a great variety of cloth both from across the sea and from England, as well as boots for the king, queen and Edward; £126 on spices for the queen and the queen of Scotland; £348 on wax for the households and chapels of the king and queen; £127 on cloths of gold and vestments; £174 on jewels.

the various types of expenditure accounted to the wardrobe for the money they received, the food and drink departments doing so probably every night.[144] Their rolls of expenditure were then presented by the keepers when they themselves came to account at the exchequer, although such accounts became less frequent as the personal rule wore on, testimony both to Henry's laxity and his confidence in his wardrobe officials. There was also a deterioration in the wardrobe's ability to pay its way. Between 1234 and 1245 it was able to do so, but at the end of Chaceporc's long accounting period between 1245 and 1252, a debt of £2,690 was owed to merchants.[145] The parliament of 1248 and the reformers in 1258 complained bitterly of the failure to pay merchants for the king's food, drink and cloth.[146]

THE HOUSEHOLD DEPARTMENTS

At the heart of the king's court was his household. Its daily costs arranged under separate departmental headings were recorded on a 'household roll'. By far the most important function of the departments was to provide the king and his entourage with their food and drink. They thus played a vital part in sustaining the morale of the court, for what was more important than good fare! Their role was equally vital in the wider political process, allowing the king to display his magnificence and demonstrate his generosity. Day by day, dining in his chamber, he could hope to influence chosen guests as they drank his fine wine and ate the succulent deer from his forests. At the great feasts, dining in his hall, he could hope to impress the wider body politic with the lavishness of his hospitality.

Unfortunately, only one complete household roll survives for Henry's reign, that for 1259/60, a highly unusual year, a large part of it spent in France. There are also fragments of rolls from 1225/6, 1262, 1266 and 1271. The rolls record the daily costs of the pantry, buttery, kitchen, saucery, scullery, hall, chamber and stables, with separate entries for the liveries of the grooms and horses. They record too the daily costs of the pantry, buttery and kitchen in feeding paupers, or 'fratres' as they are called. And there are entries for the costs of firewood burnt in the hall and chamber. When the queen was at court the rolls show the king taking over the costs of her stables, while the number of fratres fed goes up from 100 to 150. A separate entry gives the weight of wax consumed during the day.[147]

---

[144] For the nightly audit early in the reign of Edward I, see *EHD*, 584.

[145] Wild, *WA*, cvii, cxi; Wild, 'Royal finance under King Henry III', 1398–9, where the deficit for the years 1234–6 was cleared in the next account.

[146] Paris, v, 6; *DBM*, 86–7, 276–7.

[147] Wax is the one item given by weight rather than by cost. This is because the household departments were not responsible for the purchase of wax. The bill was usually paid by the exchequer.

By far the most important cost centre, sometimes responsible for around half the daily bill, was the kitchen. The master of the cooks was an important man. For a long period in the personal rule it was Master Richard of Winchester, of whom Matthew Paris wrote a dyspeptic obituary in 1255. (He had, so Paris alleged, amassed a treasure of over 5,000 marks.) Richard's job was firstly to obtain the food and to that end he sent out buyers who acquired victuals (mostly meat and fish) either by cash or credit, in the latter case giving tallies as promise for future payment.[148] Richard's other task was to oversee the cooking. Before the great Christmas feast at York in 1251, Henry gave him strict instructions about providing the necessary cooks and doing the other (unpecified) things pertaining to his office. Richard must have come up to expectations because later he received a gift of ten oaks from the king.[149] But it could be a dangerous job. Another cook, Roger by name, had his hair pulled out (hair by hair) by one of the king's half-brothers and was then strung up naked.[150]

The costs recorded on the household roll increased very greatly between the end of the minority and the first years of the personal rule.[151] Between 1224 and 1226 the daily average was around £6.50. Between 1234 and 1235 it was double that sum. When the change took place is unknown, but it must reflect the expanding size of Henry's court. Between 1236 and 1252 the average, in the various accounting periods, ranges from a low of £11.03 to a high of £15.97. In the 1250s, when Henry deliberately reduced costs so as to save for his crusade and then for the Sicilian project, they fell to £9.79 a day and then to £9.19.[152] This prompted Matthew Paris into expressing rare praise for King John. In reducing his hospitality, Henry was foolishly deviating from the path of his father, a comment which shows just how central such largesse was to the dignity and prestige of kingship.[153] Even at £9 a day the annual cost of the household at some £3,285 equalled or exceeded the total annual income of all the earls, the king's brother Richard of Cornwall only excepted. At their best sustained level of £15 a day, they were thirty times more than the 10s a day average revealed in the 1273 household roll of the earl of Oxford, a poor earl but still a very substantial magnate. At the equivalent of £5,474 a year they now roughly equalled the total annual income of Richard of Cornwall.[154]

---

[148] The costs recorded on the household roll were not the costs of purchases on the day in question but the cost of acquiring the food served on that day, either by cash or credit.

[149] *CR 1251–3*, 23; *CR 1253–4*, 210.

[150] John of Wallingford (2), 175.

[151] The total figures from the household rolls appear in the accounts of the keepers of the wardrobe heard at the exchequer.

[152] The first figure is for 1252 (although the saving may have begun earlier) and the second for 1255–6.

[153] Paris, v, 114, 199.

[154] For baronial incomes, see Maddicott, *Simon de Montfort*, 55.

These figures, moreover, understate the value of the food provided. Quite logically, they never included, since it came free, all the fare provided by the king's own properties, so the deer from his forests and the fish from his fishponds. The sheriffs too made their contribution. For the Christmas at Winchester in 1246 they had to provide 3,300 chickens, 960 partridges, 114 pheasants, 200 hares, 84 peacocks, 48 swans, 30 cranes, 320 rabbits and 56 boars with their heads whole and well boiled and pickled.[155] The accounts also omit the cost of the wine since that was largely paid for through the exchequer. Much of the supply was acquired by the keepers of the king's wine at Southampton, where wine from Gascony and elsewhere in France was unloaded.[156] Contained in tuns holding 252 gallons, it was then distributed in long carts (on one occasion five of them) between the cellars of the king's various residences. This was far from a process Henry simply delegated. In 1246 he gave orders for such a distribution by word of mouth. He also pardoned a poor man when a cask was lost through an accident to his cart.[157] Henry was concerned to see the wine merchants paid, partly at least to save himself from their complaints. In 1245 he issued urgent orders for all the debts owed 'for wine and other things' to be paid 'lest we are bothered about it on our arrival in London'.[158] As for the amounts consumed every day, five tuns (1,160 gallons) of French wine delivered into the buttery were consumed over four (non-feast) days in 1237, but there is no means of knowing whether that was the total amount.[159] The buttery served the wine but did not for the most part acquire it, hence its costs, compared to the kitchen, were usually very low. Its main expenditure was in acquiring ale, the beverage presumably drunk by the lower orders of the household and the fratres. Since ale did not keep, its acquisition was a continuous process. The one surviving buttery roll, covering a journey to Norwich near the end of the reign, shows daily purchases of 40 or 50 gallons from a wide variety of people.[160]

---

[155] *CLR 1245–51*, 93–4.

[156] Wine was also unloaded at Bristol and London, where the king's chamberlain had responsibility for acquisitions, and was sometimes bought at Boston and other fairs. Some idea of the cost is gained from the accounts of John Mansel when, early in his career, he was responsible for the king's purchases. In an eighteen-month period in the late 1230s he acquired 500 casks of Gascon and Angevin wine worth £1,130: TNA E 372/81, m. 31d. Thanks largely to money from the exchequer he paid for most of it, leaving £234 owing to various merchants. A total of 386 of the casks were taken by the bailiffs at Southampton and 114 casks by the mayor and men of Bristol. In purchases there were two different levels of price. The king was entitled by his customary right of prise to purchase at a low fixed price one tun from before the mast in each ship and one tun from behind. For everything else he was supposed to pay the full market price. In 1239 prise wine from Gascony cost 20s a tun and wine at full price 28s: *CLR 1226–40*, 397–8.

[157] *CR 1237–42*, 160; *CLR 1245–51*, 18–19; TNA E 372/81, m. 3d.

[158] *CR 1242–7*, 309.

[159] *CLR 1226–40*, 306–7.

[160] TNA E 101/684/10/1. This comes from the visit to Norwich right at the end of the reign in 1272 and is discussed in volume 2.

The daily costs on the household roll naturally varied throughout the year. While at Westminster in November 1259 they were between £14 and £20 a day; in the quiet August of 1260, when the king travelled between Windsor, Guildford and Winchester, they were often little more than £9, partly because the queen had now left court. For the great feasts the costs were much higher. The most spectacular recorded was that for the translation of the Confessor on 13 October 1260 when the cost for the day (and the bread and water of the vigil) amounted to £229, with £133 put down to the kitchen. This was the day Henry fed 5,016 paupers.

In the summer, there are frequently no entries for the hall and chamber's firewood. In the colder months, it was common for the daily cost of wood for the chamber to be around 14s, with that for the hall, if entered at all, being several times less.[161] Wood of course burns very quickly in open hearths, and vast amounts were consumed. On his way home from York in January 1252, Henry had seventy-six oak trees in the forest of Geddington cut down for his firewood and another eighteen in the forest of Silverstone. No wonder he had large sheds constructed to hold firewood and often bestowed firewood as a gift.[162]

The statement in the accounts about the stables came from the responsible office, the Marshalsea. Here too, although the number of horses is never revealed, the surviving rolls for the 1260s show a threefold increase in costs since the 1220s. Presumably the horses included the palfreys on which the king rode and the beasts of burden pulling the carts with the bag and baggage of the household. In the household ordinance of 1279 there were three long carts for the wardrobe, one long cart for the pantry, a short cart to carry flour, another to carry the mills of the saucery, a long cart and a short cart for the buttery, and one long cart and two short ones for the kitchen. In 1238 a new harness was provided for the sumpter horse of the king's chapel, including a bag for his oats.[163] Travelling much more slowly than the king and his entourage on their elegant palfreys, the baggage train of the household must have set off in good time to be ready for the court's arrival at a new destination, leaving the king free to start late or spend time hawking or visiting along the route.

THE STEWARDS OF THE HOUSEHOLD

The heads of the king's household were his stewards.[164] There were always several in office at any one time, although they were not always present

---

[161] Carpenter, 'Household rolls', 37–8.

[162] The whole subject of firewood would repay further study. One wonders why the costs were so high given Henry, as here, could use his own woods, but presumably there was the cost of cutting, carriage and storage. In the accounts 'hall' and 'chamber' are given in the singular but perhaps sometimes more than one hall and chamber were involved.

[163] *EHD*, 586; *CLR 1226–40*, 306.

[164] For the stewards in early periods, see Jolliffe, *Angevin Kingship*, ch. 10, and Church, *Household Knights of King John*, 8–11.

together. The stewards presided with the keeper of the wardrobe over the nightly audit of household expenditure. They also headed the household's military forces.[165] It was doubtless at their head that the steward Ralph fitzNicholas distinguished himself in the fighting outside Saintes in 1242. The stewards had overall responsibility for supply of the household's food and drink. Hence it was to the stewards (fitzNicholas, Paulinus Peyvre and Robert Walerand) that the chamberlain of London sent a letter asking for payment for the wine he had taken.[166] Both the high status of the stewards and their permanent presence at court is shown by their regular place in the witness lists of royal charters. Indeed, every year they nearly always attest more charters than anyone else. Their closeness to the king is reflected in the way he favoured them with the usual gifts of wood, game and wine, and also with more substantial rewards in the form of wardships and escheats. The stewards are found authorizing writs not just about the household's food and drink but a whole variety of other business. Matthew Paris describes Peyvre as one of Henry's principal councillors.[167] At court they had their own entourages. The four knights of Ralph fitzNicholas were given the same robes as the household knights of the king.[168] The stewards were adept in promoting their men. The brother of Ralph fitzNicholas became sheriff of Hampshire, the nephew of Godfrey of Crowcombe sheriff of Oxfordshire. Naturally the stewards could be very useful in helping forward business at court. It was with a sure eye that Gilbert Marshal, earl of Pembroke, early in the personal rule, granted land to both fitzNicholas and Crowcombe.[169]

The stewards were also employed outside the court. They acted as diplomats. Robert Walerand went to Rome to help forward the Sicilian enterprise.[170] They were sent on special missions. Godfrey of Crowcombe headed the posse sent in 1232 to arrest Hubert de Burgh. They held local office as sheriffs, castellans and keepers of vacant bishoprics.[171] They thus helped stiffen the sinews of royal power in the localities. They did the same through their landed estates. Thanks largely to Henry's generosity, Crowcombe acquired manors in five contiguous counties, Somerset,

---

[165] These are discussed in the next section.

[166] *RL*, ii, 95–8. In the reign of Edward I, the steward presided over the court of the household with its jurisdiction over all offences committed within a twelve-mile radius (see the discussion in Prestwich, *Edward I*, 165–8, drawing on *Fleta*, 109–13). There seems no evidence for this court under Henry III, although it may well have existed. There is evidence, as we have seen, for the court trying weights and measures offences.

[167] Paris, v, 242.

[168] *CR 1242–7*, 493; *RL*, i, 382–3.

[169] See above, 169.

[170] For his career, see Harding, 'Robert Walerand' and 432, n. 94.

[171] The extent to which they acted as sheriffs declined after 1236, however, although John fitzGeoffrey and Robert Walerand (the latter before he was steward) were sheriffs of Gloucestershire from 1238 to 1250.

Wiltshire, Gloucestershire, Oxfordshire and Warwickshire. He did all he could to improve the properties, again with Henry's help, by setting up markets and fairs, creating parks and fish ponds, and constructing a range of new buildings. Such men, a process that can be seen in detail with Philip Basset, were also busy buying up land to expand and round off the estates.[172] Paulinus Peyvre's voracious acquisition of property, and the costly buildings he erected at Toddington in Bedfordshire (a 'palace', with chapel and chambers built in stone and covered in lead, surrounded by orchards and fish ponds), earned him a not uncritical obituary from Matthew Paris.[173] When a steward had property in an area, everyone knew about it.

Until the appointment of the Savoyards, Ebulo de Montibus and Imbert Pugeys, in 1256–7, Henry's stewards were generally English.[174] John fitzGeoffrey (1237–45) and William de Cantilupe II (1239–51) were men of baronial status. Most of the others, fitzNicholas, Crowcombe, Bertram de Criel, John of Lexington, Paulinus Peyvre, Robert Walerand and John and William de Grey were from knightly backgrounds. A common route into the household, initially as a household knight, was through a connection with an established minister. Crowcombe and later Criel probably owed their starts to Hubert de Burgh, Walerand and Peyvre to William de Cantilupe II.[175] FitzNicholas, who like Crowcombe began his career in King John's reign, was a knight of the loyalist William de Ferrers, earl of Derby. Some of the stewards had family connections with the royal service. John fitzGeoffrey was the son of John's justiciar, Geoffrey fitzPeter, William de Cantilupe II the son of John's steward and Henry's guardian, William de Cantilupe I. Richard de Grey, the elder brother of John and William, had been a prominent household knight, while John of Lexington's elder brother Robert was a distinguished judge. Physically some of these men were very tough. Crowcombe's career stretched from John's reign into the 1240s, that of fitzNicholas into the 1250s. Some were men of education. Matthew Paris describe Lexington and Peyvre as impressively literate. (Both were younger sons, hence perhaps their education.)[176] He also praised Crowcombe, fitzNicholas and John de Grey.[177] It would be easy to think that Henry felt at times out of sympathy with these men of military mien. This may be to underestimate their religiosity. John of Lexington bore witness to the miracles at the tomb of Thomas, archdeacon of Northampton, and played a vital role in Henry's terrible purge of the

---

[172] See Stewart-Parker, 'The Bassets of High Wycombe'. For the example of Geoffrey de Langley, see Coss, 'Sir Geoffrey de Langley'.

[173] Carpenter, 'Career of Godfrey of Crowcombe', 47–9 (within a full study of his career); Paris, v, 242.

[174] The exception was the Norman, Amaury de St Amand. For Pugeys and Montibus, see above, 217, and below, 672.

[175] For Peyvre, see *BF*, ii, 868, 1357.

[176] Paris, iv, 294.

[177] Paris, iv, 191, 213; Paris, v, 242, 504, 523.

Lincoln Jews. The long careers of these clever, multi-talented men gave stability to Henry's court and reach to his government.

The stewards were at the head of the king's household knights, the knights 'de familia regis' as they were called.[178] These men could form the core of royal armies. They also, or at least the most senior of them, had many other functions, just like the stewards, who had often risen from their ranks. They acted as diplomats, courtiers and local officials. Simply as landholders, they upheld the king's interests in the counties, having (since John's reign) taken a special oath to report anything said against the king.[179] Nicholas de Molis, the most famous of Henry's knights, had a career stretching from John's reign into the 1260s. He was at different times sheriff of Kent, castellan of Dover, keeper of vacant bishoprics, warden of the Channel Islands, envoy to Louis IX, seneschal of Gascony and custodian of Cardigan and Carmarthen. He won a war against the king of Navarre and led a marauding expedition through the whole length of Wales. He amassed a collection of manors (several from 'the lands of the Normans'), married an heiress and founded a baronial line in the West Country. At the coronation of the queen in 1236, he and another famous 'miles strenuus', Richard Siward, carried the royal sceptres.[180]

Many knights seem to have been attached to the household simply on the basis of receiving robes from the king. Others were granted annual money fees commonly ranging from £5 to £20 a year.[181] The most senior, such as Molis, thanks to the king's generosity, built up considerable landed estates. Molis was not unusual amongst Henry's early knights in having connections with Normandy. That was equally true of Drogo de Barentin, Nicholas de Bolleville and John de Plessis. All of them quickly put down roots in England and went on to long careers in the king's service, John becoming earl of Warwick in right of his wife. Other household knights were from English families with traditions of royal service. The brothers Gilbert and Philip Basset were the sons of Alan Basset, a leading household knight of King John.[182]

---

[178] For Henry's household knights, see Walker, 'Anglo-Welsh wars', 61–99, and, down to 1234, Lightfoot, 'Household knights of King Henry III'. For those of earlier kings, see Church, *Household Knights of King John*, and J.O. Prestwich, 'Military household of the Norman kings'.

[179] For a household knight in the localities, see the case of Geoffrey of Childwick, below, 538.

[180] There is a biography of Molis [Moels] by Ethel Stokes in Cokayne, *Complete Peerage*, ix, 1–4. Molis (as it is often rendered) seems to have been Meulles near Orbec in Normandy. The family also had interests in the West Country. Molis's precise ancestry is unknown and he seems to have been self-made.

[181] See the tables of fees in Walker, 'Anglo-Welsh wars', 72–8. For the argument that the knights under John were not generally supported by fees, see Church, *Household Knights of King John*, ch. 4, and his 'Rewards of royal service'.

[182] For this branch of the Bassets, see Stewart-Parker, 'The Bassets of High Wycombe'.

At Christmas 1217 only seven knights were in receipt of Henry's robes. By the Christmas of 1220 the number had risen to twenty-five.[183] Then, in the second half of the 1220s, there was a large increase.[184] The aim was to meet continental emergencies and opportunities, and perhaps also to strengthen the regime at home. One list names eighty-five knights in receipt of fees. Another, probably related to the Gascon campaigns of 1225–6, names 123 knights summoned 'de familia regis'. Since they were expected to bring another 85 knights with them the total rises to 208. For the Christmas of 1231 (after the Welsh campaign of that year) robes were ordered for 130 knights.[185] No fewer than 201 knights received robes at the Christmas of 1236, 178 at Whitsun 1237 and 200 at the Christmas of 1237.[186]

These seem very high numbers. King John is thought to have had on call something over 100 household knights at any one time. The earliest list of Edward I's knights in receipt of robes puts their number at 101.[187] What may have happened is that the knights recruited for the French and Welsh campaigns between 1225 and 1231 were kept on the books, forming a kind of territorial army reserve. One can be fairly sure the majority were not present at court, outside perhaps Christmas and Whitsun, when they came for their robes. How far Henry maintained the high numbers in receipt of robes throughout the personal rule is unknown. (The wardrobe accounts cease to give such figures.) A cut probably took place in the early 1250s, when Matthew Paris mentions a reduction in robes as well as hospitality and almsgiving.[188] The number of knights in receipt of fees was always much smaller than those just getting robes. In the personal rule, in a typical year, between thirty and forty knights were paid by the exchequer, although we do not know (the accounts giving no details) how many more received money from the wardrobe.[189] Henry could certainly hope his household knights would strengthen his rule in the localities, and support him in military campaigns and political emergencies. Unfortunately, as John found out, the loyalty of household knights could be friable.[190] Henry himself was hardly an inspiring leader. In the great crisis of 1258 he might well have cried out, 'Where are the household knights?'

---

[183] Carpenter, *Minority*, 242, 317, 382.

[184] These figures come from the lists in TNA C 72/2, mm. 13, 15d, 20 discussed in Lightfoot, 'Household knights of King Henry III', ch. 4, and transcribed in Appendix 4, B-F. See also Critchley, 'Summonses to military service'.

[185] *CR 1231–4*, 1.

[186] Wild, 'A truly royal retinue', 139–40; Wild, *WA*, 24.

[187] Church, 'Knights of the household of King John', 157–8; Prestwich, *War, Politics and Finance*, 46.

[188] Paris, v, 114, 199.

[189] Walker, 'Anglo-Welsh wars', 80–1, and from my own inspection of the liberate rolls. The great expansion of the household forces in 1261 is discussed in volume 2.

[190] See Church, *Household Knights of King John*, ch. 5.

THE QUEEN AT COURT

The court was very far from being an exclusively male preserve. Henry throughout his reign made gifts of game and firewood to the wives of leading courtiers. We cannot be sure these women were at court, but it seems likely. At the very least Henry was asking after them. In the mid-1230s, Alice, wife of Godfrey of Crowcombe, seems a particular favourite.[191] More fundamental, of course, was the presence of the queen.[192] The chambers and chapels that Henry built and beautified for her were as much for when they were together as apart, hence the way they were connected with the apartments of the king. Eleanor's domestic establishment mirrored that of the king. She had her own wardrobe, pantry, buttery and kitchen, and her own stables. During the course of Henry's personal rule the establishment greatly expanded in size. For the twenty months after their marriage in 1236, Eleanor's wardrobe receipts totaled some £562. In the two years from 1250 the total was £3,360. While most of the money came, by Henry's order, either from the exchequer or the king's wardrobe, from the 1240s control of wardships provided more independent sources of income.[193] When Eleanor was by herself the daily costs of her household, as recorded on her two surviving household rolls (from 1252 and 1253), suggest her establishment was roughly half the size of the king's. In terms of her almsgiving, she fed 50 'fratres' every day against the 100 of her husband. When Eleanor was at court, her domestic staff kept working but now Henry took over all their costs, his own costs, as recorded on his household roll, commensurately increasing.[194] The interchange between the two courts was helped by Eleanor's close relationship with the king's ministers (notably John Mansel) and by Henry's readiness to promote Savoyards. So in the 1250s both Ebulo de Montibus and Imbert Pugeys became stewards of the royal household.

Outside the few periods where household rolls survive, we have no detailed knowledge of how often Henry and Eleanor were together. It was probably less once the children were born and Eleanor became increasingly

---

[191] *CR 1234–7*, 135, 204, 213, 218, 222, 283. Alice was the sister of Sybil Giffard for whom see above, 206. For gifts to the wives of Geoffrey de Cauz, Geoffrey de Langley, John fitzPhilip and Paulinus Peyvre, see *CR 1237–42*, 98, 113, 215; *CLR 1226–40*, 375–6.

[192] For what follows, see Howell, *Eleanor of Provence*, ch. 4 (on the queen's lifestyle) and 266–9; Carpenter, 'Household rolls', 43–5.

[193] She also gained control of a customary source of income known as 'queen's gold', a 10% levy on voluntary fines of 10 marks or more made with the king. For the changing nature of Eleanor's resources, see Howell, 'Resources of Eleanor of Provence', and Howell, *Eleanor of Provence*, 273–9.

[194] In 1260 at Saint Denis in France, Henry's costs were £13 3s without the queen on 17 January, and £22 13s on the next day with her back at court. At Arras the costs were £20 17s on 5 February with the queen, and £14 8s on the next day without her: Carpenter, 'Household rolls', 44. The only item of the queen separately totalled on the king's household roll was the cost of her stables.

based with them at Windsor.[195] A fear of miscarriage (if miscarriages are the explanation for the childless interlude between the birth of Edmund in 1245 and Katherine in 1253) may have made Eleanor less willing to travel. In 1252 between 24 June and 19 August she was with Henry at Winchester, Clarendon, Marlborough and Woodstock, but in 1253, newly pregnant, she remained at Windsor for a four-month period, during which time Henry (preoccupied with affairs at Westminster) made only two brief visits. Later, in the regnal year 1259/60, Eleanor was all but 100 days at court. She was also there throughout the periods covered by the household rolls of 1262 and (before the siege of Kenilworth) 1266.

That Eleanor spent substantial periods of time at court there seems then little doubt. Her presence naturally increased the number of women there, given those in her entourage.[196] Accounts and inventories from 1252/3 allow a glimpse of their fashionable attire: the hoods and capes lined with fur, the gowns of russet, blue and green, trimmed with borders of gold and silver and decorated with dozens of pearl buttons; the chemises, veils, wimples, slippers and boots, one pair of fine goatskin being for the queen herself. The entourage looked equally impressive when on the move, either in 'noble carriages' (as on the journey to Paris in 1259) or seated on fine palfreys with saddles ornamented with orphreys and gold studs.[197]

Eleanor's presence enhanced the court in other ways. She can be imagined there with her dwarf only 3 feet high, her jewels, her books of romances and her splendidly illuminated devotional texts, of which more later. She may have encouraged Henry to hear sermons by Franciscan friends, notably Adam Marsh, to whom she was close. Adam sometimes ended his letters to the queen by hoping God would show his favour to the king, 'your good person and your children', not that Henry always liked the sermons when he heard them.[198] The royal children made their own contribution to the atmosphere at court. By 1250, Edward was eleven, Margaret ten, Beatrice eight and Edmund five. The children were largely based at Windsor but can be found elsewhere. Together they made offerings on the feasts of the Confessor at Westminster. In 1246, in an act of dynastic continuity, they went with Henry and Eleanor to the dedication of the Cistercian abbey founded by John at Beaulieu in Hampshire. When Edward fell ill there, Eleanor insisted on staying until his recovery nearly three weeks later, this despite the rules of the order banning women from the monastic precincts. The prior and cellarer, at the next visitation of the monastery, were dismissed as a result.[199] Living alongside Edward and his siblings were a

---

[195] Eleanor can also be found apart from Henry at such places as Marlborough, Guildford and the royal manor of Havering.

[196] Howell, *Eleanor of Provence*, 105.

[197] Howell, *Eleanor of Provence*, 75–6; St Albans continuator, 438.

[198] *Letters of Adam Marsh*, 368–75, 446–7, 462–3.

[199] Winchester, 337; Howell, *Eleanor of Provence*, 101.

group of aristocratic children, several of them royal wards. In the 1250s they included Henry de Hastings, Geoffrey de Lucy and Nicholas of Seagrave.[200] The three formed a bond which held them together in the later civil war. The chambers, gardens and parks of the royal homes must often have reverberated to the sounds of children laughing, playing and fighting. One of the images in Matthew Paris's life of the Confessor shows him seated at table while an attendant separates the boys Harold and Tostig struggling on the ground beneath.[201] The Harold and Tostig fight was, of course, prophetic of their later enmity. Fortunately Edward and Edmund seem to have got on, Edmund perhaps always being somewhat in awe of his elder brother.

HENRY AT TABLE

It is a pity more is not known about the etiquettes of Henry's court, starting with those at table. In the household ordinance of 1279 a separation was made between the cooks for the king's kitchen and those of the household.[202] There seems no evidence for that under Henry, but it seems probable. There is little information about his personal likes and dislikes, though perhaps the bread baked with the special high-quality flour known as 'flos dominicus' was reserved for his table. He and the queen did agree on finding fish other than lampreys 'insipid', perhaps because lampreys had more texture than most fish.[203] As a result they were a much sought after meat substitute during Lent, although they were also favoured by Henry at other times. He was constantly ordering them to be sent from Gloucester where they were caught in the weirs on the Severn. As for wine, Henry preferred Gascon wine to that from 'elsewhere' in France and was particular over what he drank. In 1238, on his way north, a tun of wine was hurried from Northampton to Wroxton so that he could have it for his dinner on the following Sunday. In 1243 he was having special spiced wine made for him.[204] Spices in general played an important part in enlivening the food and, imported from abroad, much effort and expense went into their acquisition. In 1239 the bailiffs of Southampton were to send the king without delay four hundreds of almonds, a hundred of rice, a bale of ginger, a bale of cinnamon and 100 pounds of gingerbead, as well as four bales of dates. Also in 1239 all the raisins and dates at Winchester, as well as a cartload of figs, were to be dispatched to the king at Westminster.[205]

---

[200] Wild, *WA*, 81.

[201] *Lives of the Confessor*, 14. This is image 54 in the Cambridge University Library online version of the life, for which see above, 326, n. 305.

[202] *EHD*, 582.

[203] *CR 1234–7*, 420. There are many rather unpleasant images of lampreys online. I have not tried to eat them.

[204] *CR 1242–7*, 133–4; *CLR 1226–40*, 343.

[205] *CLR 1226–40*, 364, 367. At Winchester the fruit was in the chamber where the king's wardrobe was deposited, and the order for their despatch was sent to Roger the tailor. This

Although the overall content of the daily food is clear, there is no sign of how it was divided between the two main meals of dinner and supper.[206] We have equally no idea how often, outside the great feasts, Henry dined in the hall as opposed to his chamber, although one suspects it was not very often. If that was largely for reasons of comfort and privacy, it also had a political dimension. An invitation to dine with Henry in his chamber might be a signal mark of favour, just as its absence might be a mark of disgrace. Equally important was precisely where you sat and whether close enough to the king to partake of his own food. As bishop of Lincoln, Grosseteste's practice was to have the dish before him heaped up and frequently replenished so he could share it with those sitting to his right and left. Henry certainly gave attention to seating plans. At the Christmas feast of 1240, held in the great hall at Westminster, he placed the legate Otto (much to the disgust of Matthew Paris) centrally in the royal seat, with himself on the right and the archbishop of York on the left, and with 'the prelates and other nobles taking their place according to the order of their dignity and power, the king wishing it thus and arranging the festivities'.[207] Grosseteste's practices show other rituals of the table. Thus, before the grace, the pantler with the bread and butler with the cup came 'step by step' into his presence at the high table. Henry's own pantlers were conspicuous, indeed controversial, figures. One, in the 1250s, was the Poitevin favourite William de Sancta Ermina, who stood beside Henry at table with a towel and cut up his food. Much rewarded by the king, he was expelled from England in 1258.[208]

Matthew Paris, in describing the 1240 feast, says nothing about the queen. Did Eleanor sit separately with her ladies and lady guests, as apparently did the queens and countesses at Henry's great feast in Paris in 1254?[209] Did she, on other days, dine with Henry in his chamber or separately in her own? Did Henry sometimes dine in her chamber, as he slept sometimes in her bed? Whatever the seating arrangements, Henry wished Eleanor to be conspicuous at his feasts and not just through her clothes. It was for the Christmas in 1240 that a magnificent golden cup was made (worked on day and night to be ready in time) so that she could drink from it at the feast and 'both king and queen can be content'.[210] It was presumably for his own table

---

foreshadowed the way spices and fruit would be stored along with cloth in what came to be called the great wardrobe.

[206] For the division in Robert Grosseteste's household as bishop of Lincoln, see *Rules of Robert Grosseteste*, 404–5. At dinner the household had two dishes large and full to increase the amount left over for alms. At supper there was to be a dish of lighter nature, followed by a second course and cheese. Grosseteste's rules were designed as advice for the widowed countess of Lincoln. He urged the countess to dine whenever possible in the hall.

[207] Paris, iv, 83–4.

[208] *CR 1254–6*, 81; Paris, v, 678, 702; Ray, 'Alien courtiers of thirteenth-century England', 153–8.

[209] Paris, v, 480.

[210] *CR 1237–42*, 258.

that Henry had sent to Gloucester for the Easter celebrations of 1238 twenty silver dishes and twenty silver saucers. For Christmas at Canterbury in 1262 he had brought from Westminster two coffers with silver vessels and (presumably to decorate the high table) 'the silver knights and horses of the king'. Also prominent in feasts (especially sent for in 1255) was a great cup adorned with shields.[211]

LIVERIES AND GIFT-GIVING

Henry's alimentary largesse spoke at once to the solidarity, separation and outreach of his court: solidarity because he provided food and drink for all members of his household; separation because only a chosen few dined with him at high table or in the chamber; and outreach because Henry hoped the sight and savour of his hospitality would impress all those who came to court.[212] The same themes were present, in different ways, in another of the rituals of the court, namely the giving of robes to members of the household. Henry thus bound its members to himself and to each other. He also, in the different qualities of the robes, gave visual expression to the household's hierarchies. And he hoped to impress those coming to court with the number and finery of his men.[213]

By the time of Henry's reign, the custom by which a lord provided clothes for members of his household both at Christmas and Whitsun was long-standing.[214] On his deathbed in 1219, the old regent, William Marshal, insisted on giving his knights their Whitsun robes rather than having them sold to raise money for the poor.[215] King John himself was commended for his generosity in giving robes to his knights.[216] By the 1230s, Henry was giving robes on a large scale. Some 452 people received them at Christmas 1236, 313 at Whitsun 1237 and 419 at Christmas 1237.[217] At Christmas 1236 the beneficiaries included 201 household knights and 92 'servientes' and clerks of the king and queen. A year later, 100 'servientes' (probably meaning both servants and sergeants-at-arms) 'of the household of the king' received robes. A list naming the ninety-seven king's clerks and seventy-five 'servientes' given robes probably for a Whitsun feast between 1234 and 1236 shows the range of beneficiaries.[218] They included the

---

[211] *CLR 1226–40*, 322; *CR 1261–4*, 167; *CR 1254–6*, 434. For other silver horses, see Wild, *WA*, 119, 140, 154.

[212] For the role of symbolism and non-verbal communication in Henry's reign, see Weiler, 'Symbolism and politics'.

[213] For Giles of Rome's discussion of the purpose of liveries, see Lachaud, 'Liveries of robes', 286, 291.

[214] For much of what follows, see Lachaud, 'Liveries of robes', and Wild, 'A truly royal retinue'.

[215] Marshal, lines 18684–706.

[216] Anonymous, 105.

[217] Wild, 'A truly royal retinue', 138–40.

[218] This list is transcribed and analysed in Wild, 'A truly royal retinue', 133–8, 144–57.

keepers of the wardrobe, Walter of Kirkham and William of Haverhill, the head of court *coram rege*, William of Raleigh, the head of the chapel, Walter de Lench, Master Thomas, the king's physician, the chancellor Ralph de Neville, Thomas the clerk of the almonry, Richard the harper, William the taylor, Simon the Cook, William the scullerer, Adam the saucerer, Adam of Guildford, keeper of the king's horses, German the farrier, William buyer of oats, two guards, two trumpeters, Geoffrey 'of the tents', five huntsmen, six falconers, and six carpenters. While the queen and her ladies made women prominent at court, amongst the household officials in receipt of liveries there were just three, two washerwomen and one woman given a name, 'fair Alice'.

The hierarchy of the court was revealed in the different types of robe. Basic or 'common' robes, as they were called, consisted simply of tunics and supertunics. The high-status variety, on the other hand, included cloaks and hoods lined with expensive furs. In the 1234–6 list the robes of the king's senior clerks were made of burnet and cendal, the former a costly dark blue woollen cloth, the latter a silken cloth, perhaps used here as a lining. The majority of the 'servientes' were clad either in burrel, a coarse woollen cloth, or in cloths of blue and green, probably made into robes of two colours divided vertically. That the hierarchy of robes was well established is shown by the way an individual could be given a robe of a kind worn by one or other category of king's men: stewards, household knights, clerks, chaplains, 'valets' and 'servientes'.[219]

The acquisition of the vast amount of cloth needed to clothe the king's household was a major enterprise. Between 1241 and 1245 the wardrobe passed no less than £6,504 to Roger the Taylor, the man in charge of the business.[220] Another £736 went to his assistant William de Plessis. By the 1250s, Roger was heading a separate department, based at the Tower of London and known as the great wardrobe, where all the cloth was stored, along with other bulk purchases such as wax and spices.[221]

How far Henry made his robes distinctively royal, for example through bearing his coat of arms, is unclear. Jean de Joinville remembered that at the great court held at Saumur in 1241 there were many sergeants wearing the coat of arms of the count of Poitou, Louis IX's brother, so it is possible Henry's men were similarly attired.[222] Certainly at the York wedding of his daughter in 1251 to the king of Scots, Henry wanted Edward and his three knights to appear in robes decorated with the leopards of England.[223] Henry

---

[219] *CR 1242–7*, 145–9.

[220] *CLR 1251–60*, 25; Wild, *WA*, xcviii–ix.

[221] *CR 1251–3*, 449; *CR 1256–9*, 89. The development of the great wardrobe is traced in Tout, *Chapters*, iv, ch. 14.

[222] Joinville, cap. 94.

[223] See below, 523. However, Lachaud, 'Liveries of robes', 280–1, considers the bearing of heraldic devices to be a development of the next century.

took a close interest in the business of acquiring the cloth for the liveries. When there was conflict over the division of responsibility for purchases, Roger the Taylor was ordered 'to come straightway to speak with the king'. Later, Henry authorized personally the writ ordering Roger to account for the great wardrobe at the exchequer.[224]

Another ritual at court, speaking both to the solidarity and separation of the courtiers and connecting Henry to the wider realm, was gift-giving. Whenever Henry was received by a monastic house or entered a town, he expected to be welcomed with a gift. A steady flow of gifts also came in throughout the year, wherever Henry was. And then there were the gifts expected at Christmas and even more on 1 January. Celebrations at the start of the Roman year (1 January) were sometimes criticized by churchmen. They seemed a pagan rite contaminating the great Christian festival of 1 January, that of Christ's circumcision.[225] But New Year's gifts had long been part of the ritual at court and Henry was not going to abandon them.

One surviving inventory from 1234/5 reveals the process of gift-giving in some detail.[226] In December 1234, Henry visited the monastery of Wherwell in Hampshire and received from the abbess a chest covered with red cendal (he used it as a reliquary). In the same month he was given an ebony image of the Virgin Mary by the prioress of Amesbury, a silver gilt cup by Henry fitzNicholas, sheriff of Hampshire, two highly decorated jesses by the countess of Warenne for his hawks, and two more silver gilt cups, one worked and one plain, by the abbot of Whitby. On Christmas Day, celebrated at Westminster, no fewer than ten cups were presented by the citizens of London. And then on 1 January an array of precious cups, plates, cloths and belts, including a salt-cellar on four wheels with two candelabras, were given to the king, topped off with two goshawks and a pair of furred boots and gloves. Altogether, between November 1234 and June 1235, over 120 different gifts came in from around fifty individuals and institutions.[227] Twenty-six of the gifts were from Emperor Frederick (this was the time of his marriage to Henry's sister Isabella), but for the rest the donors were probably fairly typical of other periods of the reign, save, of course, that this was before the advent of the king's foreign relatives. They included bishops, abbots, abbesses, townsmen and magnates, together with leading ministers and their wives.[228]

---

[224] *CPR 1232–47*, 449–50; *CR 1251–3*, 449. There are, however, no signs of such an account.

[225] See Wild, 'A gift inventory', 541–3.

[226] One side of the inventory (it is on a single membrane) is published and analysed in Wild, 'A gift inventory', and the other in Vincent, 'An inventory of gifts'.

[227] Wild, 'A gift inventory', 533–4; Vincent 'An inventory of gifts', 125. Twenty-six of the gifts came from Frederick II.

[228] The king received belts from the wives of both Godfrey of Crowcombe and the king's falconer, Ralph fitzBernard.

As precious objects came in to the court, they were also going out, for Henry throughout the year was making gifts of his own. Of course, a gift from Henry could take many forms, but there was something especially resonant about one in the form of a precious object, especially when, as was most often the case, it was a ring. Worn on the finger it was a permanent reminder of Henry's benevolence, a permanent incitement to loyalty and faithful service. In that sense it was very different from a consumable gift such as wine, wood or game. On each 1 January, Henry personally distributed rings on a large scale. No fewer than 309 were given 'by hand of the king' during the New Year ceremonies of 1237 and 1238.[229] In all, between 1245 and 1252, Henry gave away 2,769 rings, 931 brooches, 814 cups, 144 belts and 65 basins, although, given the baldness of the accounts, we do not know to whom.[230] In making such gifts, Henry had no qualms about recycling what he received. The 1234/5 inventory shows that most of the gifts coming in were soon on their way out. While the incoming cups and belts could, in some periods, more or less balance those outgoing, rings, the king's most frequent gift, had to be purchased on a grand scale.[231] Between 1245 and 1252, £1,744 was spent buying them and other (unspecified) jewels.[232]

The queen herself played a major part in the cycle of gift-giving. In the year 1252/3 (where there are detailed records) she spent around £200 buying jewels and precious objects, including sixty-one rings, ninety-one brooches and thirty-three belts. Some of the brooches were decorated with pearls and saphires, the rings with rubies and emeralds. One belt, worked with shields of tiny pearls, cost over £8. The great majority of these glowing and glittering objects were given away, sixty of them on 1 January 1253.[233]

Beneath the surface pageantry, there could be tension. Religious houses could resent having to go out and welcome the king with gifts. Henry's courtiers, like the Viscount Lisle at the court of Henry VIII, must often have worried about how their gifts would be received and whether what they received in return matched their status, or hoped-for status.[234] Henry could demonstrate degrees of appreciation by his treatment of the gift. Best of all was if he kept it for himself. The prior of Durham was surely pleased when his silver basin was handed to Thomas the barber 'for the use of king', presumably for the washing of Henry's hair. If Henry did pass the gift on, the question was whether it went up or down the social scale. Again pleasing for the prior was when Henry gave another gift, a silver flagon gilded with flowers, to his sister Isabella to take with her to

<hr>

[229] Wild, *WA*, 28; Kjaer, 'Matthew Paris and the royal Christmas', 152.
[230] Wild, 'Secrecy, splendour and statecraft', 419–21.
[231] See the tables for 1245–52 in Wild, 'Secrecy, splendour and statecraft', 419–21.
[232] Wild, *WA*, 55.
[233] Howell, *Eleanor of Provence*, 69, 78–9.
[234] *C&S*, i, 547, cap. 45; *Lisle Letters*, 147–8, 150, 279.

Germany. The bishop of Carlisle was perhaps less happy when one of his goshawks was passed down at once to the household knight Emery de Sacy.[235] There was also an obvious hierarchy in what was given. The ruby ring costing all of £13 6s given by the queen to Louis IX was a world away from the rings costing 2s 6d given to cooks, bakers and doorkeepers.[236]

Henry, however, was not a manipulative king. He did not delight in tormenting his ministers and setting one against the other in the fashion of his father. At its best, the cycle of gift-giving bonded together the court, smoothed Henry's relations with bishops and barons, and played an important part in international diplomacy. Hence, in Matthew Paris's view, Henry's state was diminished when, in the early 1250s, he reduced the scale of his expenditure on gifts and liveries, as well as alms. Indeed, Paris says there were no gifts and liveries at all at the Christmas of 1251.[237] How far Henry continued such uncharacteristic parsimony is not known. If he did, it can hardly have strengthened his position before the revolution of 1258.

ACCESS AND PRESENCE

King John, at the start of his reign, is pictured in the life of Hugh, bishop of Lincoln, as being thoroughly accessible even to his lowliest subjects. 'When the beggars he met wished him prosperity, he bowed to them and thanked them most assiduously, and graciously returned the greetings of ragged crones.' Yet the life equally shows how even a bishop might be advised to approach the king not directly but through intermediaries. This was the counsel given to Hugh by William Marshal and the earl of Aumale after his quarrel with King Richard: let them approach the angry king on his behalf. In the event, Hugh disregarded the advice, entered the king's presence, seized his tunic and shook it until Richard with a smile gave him a kiss of peace. But there were not many with the status and courage to act like that.[238]

How accessible was Henry III? The layout of his palaces might make one think 'not very', or 'not very' without the kind of help spurned by Bishop Hugh. Both at Westminster and Clarendon the royal apartments were situated at the end of the complex of buildings, furthest away from the main gateway. The same was true of the new apartments in the upper ward at Windsor. At the palace castles there was the protection of the castle walls. At Woodstock, Henry could escape to Everswell, at Windsor

---

[235] Wild, 'A gift inventory', 537, 563; Vincent, 'An inventory of gifts', 137. Henry did, however, keep another of the bishop's goshawks.

[236] Carpenter, 'Meetings of kings', 22–3.

[237] Paris, v, 199. For an analysis of the wardrobe records showing a decline in the gifts of rings, brooches, cups, belts and basins, see Kjaer, 'Matthew Paris and the royal Christmas', 152–3.

[238] Adam of Eynsham, 101, 107–8, 141.

to his manor in the park.[239] In the palaces, windows were barred and gardens walled. At Rochester castle, Henry had a door made in the wall of the chapel so that 'strangers and others' could enter it without going through the middle of his chamber.[240] In the chamber, as an ultimate retreat, Henry could pull the curtains around his bed. At court, access was controlled by ushers and by the marshals of the household, distinguished by their staffs of office.[241] There were also around thirty sergeants-at-arms, six of whom (in the 1240s at least) always followed the king, clearly as a bodyguard.[242] Control of access was linked to control of order. Acts of violence were unusual. When Robert of Thwing struck a clerk of the archbishop of York in the hall at Windsor, Henry was furious and ordered his lands to be confiscated, although, characteristically, he soon remitted his 'ire and indignation'.[243]

Henry himself could use banishment from his presence both as a threat and a punishment. Get it done 'if you wish to appear before us on our next arrival in London', ran one order.[244] A succession of those in disgrace – Peter de Rivallis, Stephen of Seagrave, Betram de Criel, Richard Siward, William of Raleigh, Henry of Bath, the citizens of London – were told not to appear before the king. In 1260 even Henry's eldest son, Edward, suffered that fate. Gilbert Marshal knew he was in deep disfavour when the king's ushers barred his way into the hall at Winchester for the Christmas feast.[245] Those seeking access could some-times have to wait a long time. In 1252 the canons of St Bartholomew in London languished outside the door of the king's chamber at Westminster without ever getting in. Richard of Wich, hoping for the restoration of his temporalities as bishop of Chichester, followed the king round the country without managing to see him. On one occasion he did enter Windsor castle only to be threatened by one of the marshals for his temerity: 'How dare you come in here, when you well know you have gravely offended the king?' Richard, humble man that he was, accordingly 'waited outside in the open air with the common people', an indication perhaps that the common people were not normally allowed into the castle.[246]

In these circumstances one can well imagine why even great magnates like Gilbert Marshal felt it wise to retain leading ministers of the king.

---

[239] For the seclusion of the queen's apartments in the upper bailey at Windsor, see Brindle, *Windsor Castle*, 72.

[240] *CLR 1251–60*, 290–1.

[241] The marshals (of which two seem normally to have been in office) were drawn from the ranks of the household knights.

[242] For the wages and robes of the sergeants, see for example, *CLR 1226–40*, 449; *CR 1242–7*, 148; *CR 1251–3*, 363.

[243] *CR 1242–7*, 315.

[244] *CR 1242–7*, 274.

[245] Paris, iv, 523.

[246] *Saint Richard of Chichester*, 100, 176.

Richard of Wich himself made a friend of John Mansel, for Mansel appears as one of his executors.[247] The justiciar of Ireland, Maurice fitzGerald, on one occasion asked Mansel to speak to the king on his behalf about a whole variety of matters.[248] Throughout the chancery rolls there are concessions to individuals and institutions made at the instance of courtiers or in writs they authorize. Influence was easier to bring to bear when the king was alone and the court relatively empty. In one letter, Chancellor Neville was told it was a good moment to ask for a favour since the king was on his way to Gloucester and few magnates were with him.[249] The courtiers were also a source of news. 'Since the archbishop [of York] delights in gossip and news of the court, it would be a good idea to gratify him, and then if you want him to do your friends a favour, slip in a word about it at the end of your letter,' ran another missive to Neville.[250]

To imagine Henry as somehow shut off from his subjects behind the doors of his palaces, approachable only through intermediaries, would, however, be misleading. Indeed for Henry, the whole point was for people, or for selected people, to come in and be influenced by what they saw. Of course, when it came to access much depended on status. Unless, they were totally 'out', Henry would surely not refuse to see a bishop or a baron. Indeed, their presence at court, and within the counsels of the king, is shown by their attestation of royal charters, especially during times of parliament.[251] During parliaments Henry both addressed the assembled magnates and tried to get his way through individual meetings. In all this he was able to play a kind of ritual of the rooms, moving discussions from one place to another according to the nature of the business and the numbers of those he wished to consult. At Westminster, he is seen holding meetings in his chamber, the chapel of Saint Stephen's, the great hall and, over at the Abbey, in the infirmary chapel of Saint Katherine, the refectory and the chapter house. Long-running affairs could follow the king around the country. The dispute over the Durham election in 1226 began with Henry sitting with his council 'in the chamber beyond the exchequer at Westminster'. There were then further meetings in the chapel at Windsor, the infirmary chapel at Westminster and at Nottingham and Hereford.[252]

It is clear that 'the common people' too could get through to the king. The chancery rolls, throughout the reign, have concessions made to men of royal manors and women in distress.[253] It was thus as an act of 'benev-

[247] Saint Richard of Chichester, 68–9.

[248] CR 1242–7, 233.

[249] TNA SC 1/6/139.

[250] Meekings, Studies in 13th-Century Justice, ch. 5, 501.

[251] Thus Maddicott uses as evidence for the meeting of parliament the appearance of bishops and barons in the witness lists: Maddicott, Origins of the English Parliament, 454–72.

[252] Powicke, King Henry III, i, 267–9.

[253] For early examples, see above, 84, 101.

olence and special grace' that Henry in 1252 allowed Edith, wife of Roger fitzRoger of Drayton, to retain her inheritance, a paltry half a virgate (so perhaps twelve acres of land), despite the opinion of several people (presumably the king's judges) that she should lose it thanks to her husband's outlawry.[254] The year before, having passed through the royal manor of Clipstone, on his way north, Henry ordered 'the king's men of Clipstone' to be compensated – 'so that the king incurs no sin' – for the damage suffered through work on the manor's fishpond. It is more than likely that Edith and the men of Clipstone poured out their grievances personally to Henry, hence the very personal nature of the resulting letters with their references to the king's special grace and their concern that he commit no sin.[255] Later, in 1255, a woman from Lincoln travelled to court and flung herself tearfully at Henry's feet, complaining that her son had been murdered by the city's Jews.[256] Henry felt at ease amongst the poor. He washed their feet and fed them at court in great numbers. To them, as to the ordinary men and women whom he met, he surely spoke in English. Henry could be surprisingly relaxed about who was allowed into his presence. If Matthew Paris can be believed, the assassination attempt at Woodstock in 1238 was made by someone who earlier in the day had abused Henry to his face. When ministers wished to seize the man, Henry told them to leave him alone, as no one would believe his mad ravings.[257]

Henry's dealings with Matthew Paris show him at his most accessible and informal. When, during a great ceremony in Westminster Hall in 1247, Henry spied Matthew, he called him up and had him sit on the step beneath the throne. Paris was then asked to record the events of the day and invited to dinner.[258] One wonders whether it was Henry himself who took Paris into the great chamber so he could make his drawing of the mappa mundi. At St Albans, Paris had many friendly conversations with the king and even felt able to complain of injustices, or perceived injustices.[259] In 1257, during a week's stay, Paris was with Henry continually 'at table, in the palace and in the chamber', and took down from him a great deal of information, including the names of all of England's sainted kings. When Paris mentioned how the church was threatened with ruin, Henry made an appropriate response: 'let that not happen, especially in my time'.[260]

---

[254] *CR 1251–3*, 241. The half virgate was in Grafton just by Drayton (in Warwickshire). The distance to Woodstock, where the concession was made, is about thirty miles.

[255] *CR 1251–3*, 26. The letter with its reference to sin was actually replaced, perhaps after Henry had calmed down and taken advice, by another which just said the men should be compensated in a way that did least harm to the king.

[256] See below, 626.

[257] Paris, iv, 497.

[258] Paris, iv, 644–5.

[259] See below, 541.

[260] Paris, v, 617–18.

If, moreover, access was sometimes difficult, that made it all the more meaningful when it occurred. Those who passed through the outer halls and chapels, reached the king's chamber, were admitted by the ushers and were then invited to sit beside Henry on his bed could feel they had had achieved the ultimate in closeness to their king. His affability in such circumstances was made all the more special by the very grandeur he did so much to cultivate. Those sitting beside Henry on his bed would also have seen him at great ceremonies, crowned, enthroned and dressed in cloth of gold.[261] At the Whitsun feast in 1236 the cloth came from the emperor Frederick and was decorated with peacocks.[262] On such occasions, Henry's appearance was presumably announced by the two trumpeteers to whom he gave liveries. And perhaps too, symbolizing peace, he held a dove-topped rod like that shown on his new seal made in 1259, this in imitation of the Confessor, who appeared thus on his own seal.[263] Certainly an assortment of sceptres and rods, part of the regalia, were kept in the wardrobe.[264] In 1250, when Henry ordered a new seat to be made for himself in the middle of the table in the hall at Windsor, it was to be painted with a king, holding a sceptre, 'suitably adorned with painting in gold'.[265] Later in his reign, Henry's thrones were probably much like that depicted on the second seal, grand and high backed and decorated with arcading and colonettes, very different from the flat bench shown on the first seal made in 1218. On the 1259 seal the arms of the chair are shown flat whereas in reality they would have reached forward, supporting Henry on either side and ensuring that supplicants came before him direct and were subject to the full sight of his majesty. Henry, throughout his reign, spent money on crowns. One in 1253, bought from a foreign merchant, cost 500 marks and must have been studded with precious stones.[266] It was after all the crown which set Henry visually apart from all his subjects. How Henry hoped a formal meeting might go can be imagined from the images in Matthew Paris's life of the Confessor. Again and again the Confessor is depicted crowned and sitting on a raised throne, with those around him humbly standing or kneeling. In the only image where assembled magnates and ministers are also seated, the Confessor appears as a gigantic figure double their size, with the jewels in his crown and tunic painted.[267]

---

[261] For Matthew Paris's description of him at the ceremony of the Holy Blood in 1247, see below, 477–8.

[262] Vincent, 'An inventory of gifts', 127–8, 139.

[263] Carpenter, *Reign of Henry III*, 439–40. The 1259 seal is discussed in volume 2.

[264] Wild, *WA*, 92–3. For the regalia, see Carpenter, *Reign of Henry III*, ch. 21.

[265] *CLR 1245–51*, 296.

[266] *CLR 1251–60*, 105. The exchequer issue rolls show the bill was paid.

[267] This is no. 31 of the online images, for which see above, p. 326, n. 305.

Henricus Rex octau... [text in image]

Iste henricus .iii. mlto tempe regnauit in pace Anglia gubi
uit. eccam sci petri Westmon magnifice restaurauit. et
amator sci Edwardi special: feretrum er auro purissimo e
gemis pciosissimis gloriose fecit fabricari. pallis et cer
ipsam eccam venustauit pcipue. Alias eccas mlta ostens

1. Matthew Paris drew this picture of Henry III (described as the eighth king since the Conquest) as part of the gallery of kings at the start of his *Historia Anglorum*. It shows Henry, with his drooping left eyelid, holding Westminster Abbey. The caption celebrates his 'magnificent' rebuilding of the Abbey and the long peace of his reign.

2. Henry in his cradle as drawn by Matthew Paris. Henry was occasionally called 'Henry of Winchester' after his birthplace. His nurse from whom he probably learnt English was Helen of Winchester.

3. Henry's second coronation on Whitsunday 1220 was designed to put right the defects of the first in 1216. It was in the proper place, Westminster Abbey, and was conducted by the archbishop of Canterbury, Stephen Langton, drawn here by Matthew Paris crowning the twelve-year-old king.

4 and 5. Henry's first seal, made in 1218, marked an important stage in the assertion of royal authority. His second seal, from 1259, was needed when he abandoned the titles duke of Normandy and count of Anjou under the Treaty of Paris. Henry sought to compensate by seating himself on an elaborate throne. This only prompted the waspish question, why did he have a grander seal than before when he was duke of Normandy?

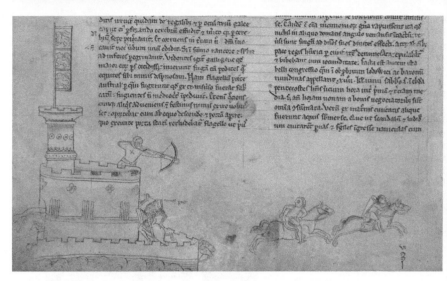

6. The victory of Henry's forces at Lincoln in 1217 was decisive in establishing him on the throne. In this dramatic drawing by Matthew Paris, the leopards of England fly over the castle, the count of Perche is killed by a thrust through his visor and defeated knights flee the town.

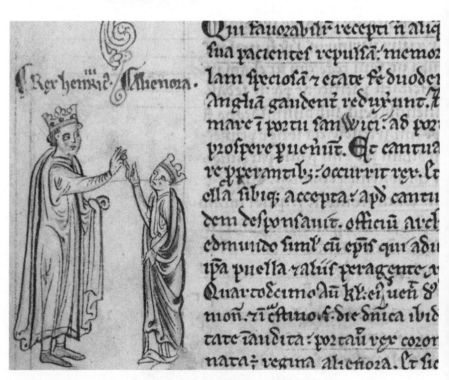

7. Henry's marriage to Eleanor of Provence in 1236. Matthew Paris captures the difference in age between the twenty-eight-year-old king and the twelve-year-old queen. Eleanor was very much Henry's to mould but she turned out to be the stronger character.

8. In 1225, Henry issued the definitive version of Magna Carta, unlike its predecessors a consensual document witnessed by the great and good of the land. Appreciating the significance, this copy made soon afterwards at Cerne abbey in Dorset gives prominence to the witness list and place and date of issue.

9 and 10. The proof for Henry of Edward the Confessor's place in heaven. On the left Edward gives his ring to a pilgrim setting off for the Holy Land. On the right, the pilgrim, now revealed as Saint John the Evangelist, ushers the Confessor into Christ's presence. The paintings, though not by Matthew Paris, are from his life of the Confessor.

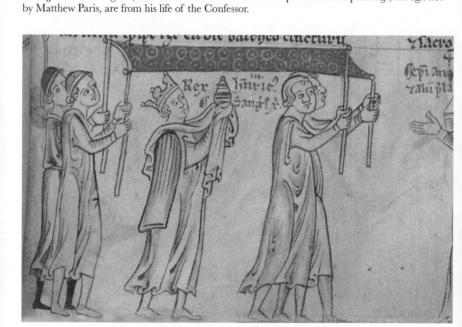

11. In 1247, Henry presented to Westminster Abbey a phial containing blood Christ had shed on the cross. Matthew Paris depicts him here on his way to the Abbey, holding the phial aloft, the solemnity of the occasion emphasised by the canopy held over his head as at a coronation.

12 and 13. Concerned with his image, the new silver penny Henry launched in 1247 had a much better designed king's head and identified Henry as 'the third' (III, to the left of the sceptre). This example was minted by Richard Bonaventure, a London moneyer and goldsmith. In his gold penny of 1257, Henry went further in demonstrating the majesty of his kingship. He is now enthroned, holding orb and sceptre. The model appropriately was a coin of Edward the Confessor.

14. The golden bulla made for Henry's second son, Edmund, as king of Sicily. On the face Edmund appears enthroned. On the reverse, shown here, he is called the son of 'the illustrious king of England' and the arms of England are displayed, a striking indication of Henry's involvement in the Sicilian project.

15. King Louis IX of France (Saint Louis) was Henry's rival, brother-in-law and ultimately friend. This early fourteenth-century statue from Mainneville in Normandy is thought to depict him. It certainly conveys the aura which surrounded his person and reputation.

16 and 17. The heads of Henry and Eleanor from above the entrance to the royal pew (now the muniment room) in Westminster Abbey. Dating from the early 1250s, with their faint smiles they breathe the spirit of 'debonereté', that calm and courteous form of conduct to which Henry aspired, not always successfully.

18. Henry conceived the chapter house of Westminster Abbey as a building where he could address the realm. Accordingly, either side of the speaking position, bands of tiles bearing the royal arms ran (and still run) right across the floor. The arms, depicted here, appear sixty-two times.

19. One striking feature of Westminster Abbey's design is the galleried triforium, with external windows, placed above the aisles and the radiating chapels. This increased the grandeur of the church and provided space for crowds at great services. The round windows were inspired by those at Amiens cathedral.

20. In his great chamber at Westminster, Henry had painted images of the Virtues and the Vices. Here, in the form of queens, 'largesse' (a virtue Henry had in over-abundance) triumphs over 'covetousness' and 'deboneretè' (with the king's arms on her shield) over anger. The paintings survive only in these watercolour copies made by Charles Stothard in 1819.

21. This cascade of fretted glass in the south transept was the vista seen on entering the Abbey. Beneath the rose window (very like that at Notre Dame in Paris) are the figures, flanked by censing angels, of the Confessor (now headless) and the pilgrim, thus letting everyone know what the Abbey was about. The high pitch and patterning of the vault is also apparent.

Some impression of how Henry liked to be addressed can be gleaned from the address clauses in letters. 'Your royal majesty', 'the serenity of your royal majesty', 'our most illustrious lord above all to be revered' was how he appeared in letters from Gascon subjects.[268] In one from Peter of Savoy he is 'your sublimitas'. In another letter the bishops of London and Worcester wished him all the success he desired 'in him through whom kings reign', and appealed to 'the goodness of your serenity and the promptitude of your benevolent conscience'.[269] In a letter from the king's 'humble and most devoted consort', he is her 'most excellent and revered lord', who is owed 'due subjection' and 'all reverence'.[270] Those coming into the king's presence were certainly expected to show subjection and reverence, especially when they were seeking pardon for offences. In 1234 at Gloucester (in a ceremony designed to conceal the king's own humiliation), Hubert de Burgh and the other rebels appeared before Henry barefoot, bare-headed, unbelted and with arms naked to the elbow.[271]

The aura of Henry's kingship gave a charge to the occasions when he physically touched his subjects, for example when distributing rings or washing the feet of paupers – the electricity of the royal touch.[272] It was a physical act, the act of homage, which inaugurated the special relationship between the king and his tenants-in-chief. Here the king clasped the hands of the kneeling tenant and received his oath of faithful service. Between 1234 and 1258 there were over 360 such ceremonies, the tenants ranging from the greatest earls down to many of knightly or less than knightly status.[273] Another physical ceremony was the kiss of peace, especially important in the conclusion to quarrels. In 1234, moved by the appearance of Hubert de Burgh and his companions, Henry 'took them in his hand and kissed them with a tender heart'.[274] The kiss was employed as a significant form of greeting on other occasions. Henry did much to defuse a tense moment in 1234 by rising to greet and kiss the archbishop of Canterbury, Edmund of Abingdon.[275] Hearing that the Franciscan master-general, John of Parma, was arriving at court, Henry rose from the table and hurried out of the palace to greet him, doing so with an embrace and

---

[268] For example, *RL*, ii, 63–4, 68, 74. For similar forms of address under Richard II, see Saul, 'Richard II and the vocabulary of kingship'. The whole subject is explored in Vincent, 'Meeting and greeting kings of England', a forthcoming paper of which he has kindly sent me a copy.

[269] They were here asking for concessions as the executors of William of York, bishop of Salisbury: TNA SC1/2/145. Their appeal did the trick: *CR 1254–6*, 272.

[270] *RL*, ii, 42–3, 210–11. Peter's letter shows him characteristically clued up about the details of his affairs.

[271] See above, 156.

[272] For Henry touching for the scrofula, see above, 296, n. 129.

[273] The figure comes from the online fine rolls via a search for 'homage'.

[274] Robert of Gloucester, ii, lines 10832–3.

[275] Lawrence, *St Edmund of Abingdon*, 240; see above, 151.

a kiss. When Henry's knights grumbled about the king humbling himself in this way, Henry explained he did so to honour Saint Francis and the holiness of John himself. Those who honoured the servants of God, he added, were not humiliating themselves, for as the Lord said, 'who receives you, receives me'. The reply was applauded and shows Henry's *deboneretè* at its best. The episode appears in the history written by the Italian Franciscan Salimbene and, since the two were close, he probably got it from John of Parma himself.[276]

As the grumbles of the knights showed, the forms of Henry's greetings could be closely watched. A refusal to stand in welcome showed the king's displeasure.[277] Advancing with a kiss, as with John of Parma, showed respect.[278] The welcome could be used to win over opponents. Attempting to gain the consent of Hugh of Northwold, bishop of Ely, to a clerical tax, Henry, in a private meeting, rose 'reverently and honorably' to greet the bishop and then sat down beside him, beginning the conversation in mellifluous tones, 'Dearest lord bishop . . .'[279] If, as is likely, the meeting took place in the king's chamber at Westminster, perhaps they sat together on the king's bed, just as Hugh had sat beside King John on his bed in Windsor castle after being admitted as abbot of Bury St Edmunds in 1215.[280] It was certainly in his chamber at Westminster that Henry, likewise in friendly fashion, began an interview with the countess of Arundel.[281] In such cases Henry might hope the chamber would work its magic, with the bishop and the countess entering at the western end of the room and then walking down its length, past the mappa mundi, the apostles and the Virtues and Vices until, coming to the bed, they saw the paintings of the coronation of the Confessor and the Confessor and the pilgrim, and realized how Henry's rule was at all times supported and elevated by the intercessions of his patron saint.

THE RELAXATIONS OF THE KING

Did Henry enjoy books, reading them, having them read, perusing their beautiful illustrations? Books (quite aside from bibles and service books) he certainly possessed. In 1237 new clasps were made for the cover of his 'great book of Romances'.[282] Later the stock of chivalric literature was

---

[276] Salimbene, 134; Coulton, *From St Francis to Dante*, 246. One can surely banish the thought that John of Parma had made the story up to flatter himself.

[277] So with Aymer de Lusignan, bishop-elect of Winchester in 1255: Paris, v, 332.

[278] Likewise, when the legate Otto arrived in 1237, Henry bowed as low as Otto's knees: Paris, iii, 396.

[279] Paris, v, 330.

[280] *Election of Abbot Hugh*, 170–1. Hugh of Northwold was abbot of Bury St Edmunds from 1215 to 1229, then becoming bishop of Ely.

[281] Paris, v, 336; see below, 553–4.

[282] *CLR 1226–40*, 288.

increased by the activities of the queen. In 1252 she bought two books of romances and had another bound.[283] After she had taken the cross with Henry in 1250, Henry obtained for her (from the Master of the Templars) 'a great book' in French about 'the deeds of Antioch', clearly a book telling the story of the siege of Antioch on the First Crusade.[284] Just how steeped Eleanor was in the chivalric world is shown by the way a poem on the life of Christ, written by her chaplain, John of Howden, managed to include a whole list of classical, biblical, Arthurian and modern heroes.[285]

Henry himself commissioned both books and poems. From 1243 he paid a pension and gave numerous gifts of wine to the poet Henry of Avranches.[286] In England, early in the reign, Avranches had written for various ecclesiastical patrons, most notably Peter des Roches, and possibly had been Henry's tutor. He had then spent time at both the papal and the imperial courts. In 1244 it was his verses, reflecting on how blessed were those who believed without seeing, that Henry had inscribed on a ring destined for the casket holding the hand of the apostle Thomas, though how Henry thought the whole poem could be put on a ring is hard to imagine.[287] Next year, Avranches was engaged on a more substantial work, writing the lives of both Edward the Confessor and Saint George, a commission Henry might have regretted had he known that George would supplant Edward as England's national saint.[288] Henry was also, of course, a patron of Matthew Paris. He commissioned Paris's life of Edward the Confessor, commanded him to write an account of a great ceremony at Westminster Abbey in 1247, and gave him much other historical information. He would have got a shock had he seen the actual text of the *Chronica Majora*, with its bitter criticisms, and doubtless it was kept safely locked away on his visits to St Albans. It is possible the abbreviated version that Paris prepared in the early 1250s, known as the *Historia Anglorum*, was conceived as something that could be presented to Henry, but, if so, the changes were not nearly extensive enough to make that possible.[289]

A few surviving books give some impression of the nature and quality of what was found at court: the Rutland psalter with a king and a queen depicted at the start of psalm 101, the book of hours belonging to Henry and Eleanor's daughter Beatrice, and the brilliantly illuminated Trinity apocalypse, just possibly owned by the queen herself. In its most famous image the central figure is a finely dressed woman striking with her sword at

---

[283] For what follows, see Howell, *Eleanor of Provence*, 83–92.

[284] *CR 1247–51*, 283; Howell, *Eleanor of Provence*, 60.

[285] Stone, 'Jean de Howden', 509–13.

[286] For Henry, see Russell, 'Master Henry of Avranches', and Henry of Avranches.

[287] *CR 1242–7*, 270; Flete, 70.

[288] *CLR 1240–5*, 293.

[289] I have reflected on Paris's revisions in my 'Chronology and truth: Matthew Paris and the *Chronica Majora*'.

a grotesque seven-headed monster.[290] Eleanor would have liked that. Henry himself enjoyed images of fabulous beasts, hence the superbly crafted and highly painted boss above the entrance to the royal pew in Westminster Abbey depicting a centaur fighting a dragon.

There is just one surviving book that was almost certainly seen by Henry and Eleanor, namely the often mentioned life of Edward the Confessor by Matthew Paris. With its dedication to Eleanor and compliments to Henry, it was clearly commissioned by Henry, probably soon after 1236 to introduce Eleanor to the Confessor's cult. The original manuscript, perhaps illuminated by Paris himself, is now lost, but there is another, judging from the style of the illuminations, dating from the 1250s. One suggestion is that it was made for Eleanor of Castile on her marriage to the king's eldest son, Edward, in 1254, but, since the text is unaltered, just as likely it was a second copy for the queen herself. Good though Paris's text is, the illustrations are the thing. They take up the top half of all sixty-four pages, sometimes being split so as to cover two connected events. Beneath them, in red ink, there is a summary of what they depict, thus making it possible to follow the story without having to plunge into the detailed text.[291] And what a story. The illuminations turn the placid reign of the Confessor into a series of gripping events. They start with the tyranny of Danish rule and the queen's escape to Normandy with her sons Alfred and Edward. There is then the combat between Cnut and Edmund Ironside followed by Alfred's return to England and his murder. (He is shown strapped to a board having his eyes pulled out.) On to the reign itself, where there are vivid portrayals of the drowning of the king of Denmark, the choking to death of Earl Godwin, the appearance of the Christ child during mass, the various miracles of healing, the giving of the ring to the pilgrim, the ring's return, the Confessor's death and (on the same page) his ascent to heaven. The story concludes with Harold's

---

[290] These books and their connections with the court are discussed in Howell, *Eleanor of Provence*, 87–91. For the Trinity Apocalypse, see McKitterick, *Trinity Apocalypse*. For a discussion of possible ownership, see Morgan, 'Illustrated apocalypses of mid thirteenth-century England', 15–16, and Short, 'Introduction', 135. In their emphasis on confession, penance and the prospect of judgement the apocalypses responded to key spiritual concerns of the period. Increasingly popular in France in the thirteenth century were *Bible Moralisées*, books with extracts from biblical texts accompanied with commentary and illustrations. John Lowden has suggested that Louis IX or his queen may have given such a Bible to Henry or Eleanor on their visit to Paris in 1254 or 1259, but there are other possibilities: Lowden, *Making of the Bibles Moralisées*, i, 185–6, 216; Morgan, 'Illustrated apocalypses of mid thirteenth-century England', 4. Grant, *Blanche of Castile*, 235–49, has a full discussion of the 'book culture' at the Capetian court.

[291] As said before, they are all available online as part of the Cambridge University Library's digital library: https://cudl.lib.cam.ac.uk/view/MS-EE-00003-00059/1. In fact, one need merely put into a search engine 'Cambridge University Library La Estoire' and it comes up. For the life, see Binski, 'Reflections on "La estoire de Seint Aedward"'; Binski, *Westminster Abbey*, ch. 2; Fenster and Wogan-Browne, *History of Saint Edward*; and Carpenter, 'King Henry III and Saint Edward the Confessor', 885–91.

victory at Stamford Bridge (made possible by the Confessor's intervention), his subsequent descent into tyranny (disregarding the advice of the
Confessor) and his death at the battle of Hastings. The final image (now
much defaced) shows the opening of the Confessor's tomb and the
discovery of his uncorrupted body. One can surely think of Henry and
Eleanor poring over the pages of this masterpiece of medieval art.

In the Paris life, when the Confessor sees in a vision the drowning of
the king of Denmark, he laughs at the good news. Henry himself certainly
had a sense of humour, and one, so it seems, of an innocent kind, more
likely to bring people together, joining in the fun, than set them apart.
There are no stories of him mocking magnates and ministers in the
fashion of his father.[292] The closest he came to that, if Roger of Wendover
can be believed, was in 1234 when he laughed at the collapse of Stephen
of Seagrave's courage confronted by the fearsome Richard Siward.[293]

Much of the humour at Henry's court depended on his fools and jesters.
Some of their names are known: Aleman, Perin Teutonicus, Hugh Eustace,
John de Blaye, Jacominus and Fortunatus de Luka, himself the brother of
Raymond de Luka, a Gascon crossbowman 'with whom the king often used
to play'.[294] These men stood high in the king's favour and had some status.
Indeed, Hugh Eustace and Fortunatus de Luka became knights.[295]

In a story relayed by Salimbene, a jester pleased the king by comparing
him to Christ, only then to explain, when Henry unfortunately asked for
more information, that just as Christ was as wise at the moment of his
conception as when thirty years old, so the king was as wise now as when
a little child. Henry, infuriated, ordered the jester to be hanged. In
response, his servants, just went through a playful form of execution and
told the jester to clear out until Henry had calmed down.[296] How far, in
reality, Henry's jesters teased and mocked we do not know. Salimbene's
story appears just after his account of John of Parma's reception, so it may
well have come from John himself. But it could just have been a story
going round the court, perhaps derived from what a jester said behind the
king's back. Henry certainly manhandled his jesters but perhaps more in
ragging, push-me, pull-me games, than because he was really angry with
them. In such cases he was quick to arrange compensation for any damage
done. Thus in 1256, Henry gave Fortunatus de Luka a new robe 'in place

---

[292] For a famous example of King John mocking his half-brother, Geoffrey, archbishop
of York, see Gervase, ii, pp. lix–lx.

[293] Wendover, iii, 271. Seagrave, seeing his manor of Alconbury in flames, had set off
with an armed band only hastily to turn tail when he realized the perpetrator was Siward!

[294] Paris, iv, 483. For 'Luca' (Laluque) in Gascony, see *RG*, i, suppl., 137.

[295] I am assuming in these cases 'istrio' means jester rather than minstrel, although of
course there may have been an overlap between the two: *CR 1247–51*, 8, 18, 56, 308; *CR
1251–3*, 286; *CR 1253–4*, 176, 194, 256; *CR 1254–6*, 176, 194, 249; *CR 1259–61*, 321; Paris, iv,
483; *CChR 1226–57*, 287. Raymond was killed during the Welsh campaign of 1245.

[296] Salimbene, 134; Coulton, *From Saint Francis to Dante*, 246–7.

of the one he lost when the king ordered him to be thrown into the bath at Bath'! Again, in the following year, Fortunatus received a new robe to replace 'a certain robe which the king lately threw into the water'.[297] Out in Gascony in 1254 a new set of robes was given to John de Blaye 'in recompense for the robes which the king tore to pieces'.[298] The kind of games leading to such actions are suggested by a scene witnessed by Matthew Paris in 1252. While exercising in the orchard at St Albans, Henry and his entourage were entertained by a chaplain, jester rather than priest, Paris thought, who bombarded them with apples and turf and squirted the juice of grapes into their faces.[299]

Not all Henry's humour was at the level of throwing jesters into baths. He was also capable of more sophisticated jokes which depended on conjuring up ideas of the absurd. When it is often hard to know whether statements in royal letters are intended as jokes, it is fortunate that an entry on the fine rolls states specifically that, in the ship coming home from Gascony in 1243, Henry was playing a joke when he had written down on the fine rolls a whole series of ridiculous debts his clerk Peter the Potevin was supposed to have incurred.[300] Probably in the same vein was the letter patent Henry issued giving his clerk William de Peretot full power to cut the long hairs of the household's clerks, with the threat, if he did not, that the king would take the scissors to his own hair.[301] Henry of Avranches seems much in tune with this type of humour in his poem calling upon a doctor to heal John Mansel's broken leg; if not the king will regard it as a hanging matter.[302] Years later, Henry's sister-in-law Queen Margaret of

---

[297] CLR 1251–60, 311; CR 1256–9, 171.

[298] CR 1253–4, 256. Henry also, by word of mouth, ordered John to be given £2 to buy a horse.

[299] Paris, v, 319–20, 329–30. The chaplain was Arnulf, archdeacon of Tours, in the service of Henry's half-brother Geoffrey de Lusignan: CPR 1247–58, 149. For Henry's gifts to one Siswsmeames, a jester of Guy de Lusignan, see CR 1251–3, 50; CLR 1251–60, 26. Henry's jester Alemanus had once been the jester of Geoffrey de Lusignan.

[300] See above, 271–2, and for the whole episode see Carpenter, 'Sense of humour of King Henry III'.

[301] CPR 1232–47, 202. See above, 168.

[302] Henry of Avranches, 137–9, 157; Liu, 'John Mansel', 33–5, where there is a translation of the poem by Lesley Boatwright. I wonder if the lengthy poem written by Michael of Cornwall in which he hurls abuse at Avranches (Henry of Avranches, 149–55), should be regarded in the same light. The charge of drunkenness (and Avranches did receive a good deal of wine from the king) is amongst the milder accusations. The poem, along with Avranches's reply (now lost), is said to have been performed (sometime between 1250 and 1254) in a kind of public contest, the audience including on one occasion the University of Cambridge, on another the abbot of Westminster and the dean of St Paul's. If Michael of Cornwall performed before the king, perhaps he diluted some of his vitriol, for example the charge that Avranches presented a robe given him by the queen to a red-haired prostitute, but equally Henry and Eleanor may well have regarded such extravagant accusations as funny. For the sometimes coarse humour at the French court, see Grant, Blanche of Castile, 159–60, 243, 249.

France seems equally in tune, when telling Henry in a letter that she was hurrying Queen Eleanor back to England lest Henry take it into his head to marry someone else![303]

Henry, therefore, seemed very capable of creating a light-hearted atmosphere at court. There was also music, not just that of the divine services echoing through the palaces but also that of Henry's minstrels, men such as John de Mez, Eustace de Reyns and Master Richard the king's harper. Master Richard was sent to 'console' Edmund, Henry's second son, during an illness in 1253. His wife was in the queen's service and received a cask of wine to celebrate the feast of her purification after the birth of a child.[304]

What of recreations outside the court? When at Westminster, Henry must often have taken his barge downriver to the Tower to inspect the animals of the royal menagerie. Here, at different times, there were the three leopards sent by Emperor Frederick, a lion, a white bear from Norway allowed to go fishing in the Thames, and, the highlight of the collection, drawn by Matthew Paris, an elephant sent by Louis IX of France.[305]

No contemporary writer refers to Henry's love of hunting and hawking, this in sharp contrast to comments made about both his father and his son Edward.[306] In fact, there is plenty of evidence that Henry loved falconry; his enthusiasm for hunting is less certain. Henry naturally maintained a hunting establishment. In the 1230s wages were being paid and robes given to six huntsmen.[307] Such men had their own packs of hounds and were hard at work every year catching deer in the royal forests, deer which were then salted and sent to the king for consumption at court.[308] When there is evidence from 1258, the two packs mentioned, each under two huntsmen, both had fifteen dogs, alongside two horses and three grooms. The first, in eighty days in the forests of Gillingham, Selwood and Melksham had caught sixty deer. The second, in the forest of Carlisle (which Henry never saw), in eighty-three days had caught eighty.[309] The number of hounds here seems a far cry from the packs, several hundred strong, found in King John's reign.[310] The annual cost of Henry's combined hunting and

---

[303] Howell, *Eleanor of Provence*, 231–2, where the date and meaning of the letter is unravelled for the first time. It is placed in context in volume 2.

[304] *CLR 1226–40*, 453; *CR 1237–42*, 83, 192; *CR 1247–51*, 459, 493; *CR 1251–3*, 330; *CR 1264–8*, 195.

[305] Borg, 'Royal menagerie', 100–1; Cassidy and Clasby, 'Matthew Paris and Henry III's elephant'; *CLR 1251–60*, 284.

[306] For John, see Anonymous, 104, 109, and for Edward, Trevet, 281–2.

[307] Wild, 'A truly royal retinue', 137–8; Wild, *WA*, 22.

[308] In 1239, for example, the huntsmen were told to catch 225 deer: *CLR 1226–40*, 362, 391, 398, 401–2, 404, 406, 431. This is a minimum figure because some orders did not specify how many deer were to be caught. Other orders were probably given by word of mouth.

[309] TNA E 101/349/30/1.

[310] See Church, 'Some aspects of the royal itinerary', 37–8.

hawking establishment was also much less than under his son. Between 1245 and 1252 it averaged just £153 a year. By the year 1280/1, Edward's costs had reached £565 and later they rose much higher.[311]

There is some evidence of Henry hunting personally. In November 1247 he ordered gaps to be made in the palisade of Clarendon park so that beasts could enter from the surrounding forest. On his next coming he would thus be able to go forth 'and take beasts in the same park'. Presumably, therefore, Henry also hunted in the great parks at Windsor, Guildford and Woodstock. Further afield, an inquiry recorded how the king and queen spent a week at Geddington in August 1255 and 'took venison [in Rockingham forest] at their pleasure'. We cannot be quite sure of this apparently delightful picture of Henry and Eleanor hunting together. It could just mean that beasts were taken by their huntsman. This presumably is the meaning when a similar inquisition spoke of game being taken by Robert Grosseteste, bishop of Lincoln. (We would certainly need to alter our ideas of the aged bishop if he hunted personally!) An earlier inquisition, however, is more specific about Henry's own involvement. It recorded how 'the lord king came twice into the forest at Rockingham and took beasts at his pleasure'. The occasions were in late November 1248 and early August 1249 when Henry was again staying at Geddington, having (if we may judge from his itinerary) made deliberate decisions to go there.[312] Yet how large a part hunting played in Henry's life remains unclear. Since he spent nearly a fortnight at Geddington during the visits of 1248 and 1249, he was hardly going out hunting on any regular basis. The order about Clarendon park stands out for its uniqueness.

A couple of times in the 1230s the king's huntsmen were told to stop their 'running' and come with all their dogs to the king, but the impression from the flow of orders on the chancery rolls is that they were chiefly employed chasing game in the royal forests around the country.[313] There is little sign of them shadowing the king's itinerary with hundreds of dogs as happened under King John.[314] There is equally no sign of Henry, unlike Edward, spending time hunting in the New Forest.[315] The occasions in 1248 and 1249 seem the only ones when he made a deliberate effort to visit Geddington. (In 1255 he and Eleanor paused there on the way north, waiting for news from Scotland.)[316]

Henry, we may suspect, neither craved the exhilaration of the chase nor the escape it afforded from daily cares. Did his neglect of hunting, if such it was, matter? After all, there is no evidence that Louis IX hunted, and there

---

[311] Oggins, *Kings and their Hawks*, 74, 83, 140–1. This is the money paid out by the wardrobe and is not the total money spent.

[312] *CR 1247–51*, 9; *CR 1231–4*, 2; *CR 1234–7*, 534.

[313] *CR 1231–4*, 2; *CR 1234–7*, 534.

[314] Church, 'Some aspects of the royal itinerary', 37–8.

[315] Kanter, 'Peripatetic and sedentary kingship', 282.

[316] During his personal rule he was there on eight occasions.

were strands of clerical opinion strongly opposed to the sport.[317] Yet Henry's attitude must have created prejudices amongst nobles who saw hunting both as a training for war and a highly important social ritual. It was as a huntsman, astride his horse, blowing his horn and with a dog running below that Simon de Montfort was depicted on his seal.[318] Henry's reputation as a rather pallid *rex pacificus* was thus confirmed. He was also unable to use inclusion in the hunt, as he might use seating at table, as a way of indicating approval and winning favour. Henry might have bonded much better with his nobles had he hunted more. That would have been even more true had he been keen on tournaments. Between 1331 and 1343 his great-grandson Edward III hosted at least thirty of them.[319]

If Henry showed limited enthusiasm for hunting with horses and hounds, his attitude was very different when it came to falconry. Here too there was prestige to be won. Indeed Henry's brother-in-law the emperor Frederick II considered 'falconry an art more noble than other forms of hunting', this because training the birds required far more knowledge and expertise than did training horses and hounds. The great book *The Art of Hunting with Birds*, written by Frederick himself, runs, in a modern translation, to over 300 pages, almost entirely based on his own observations.[320] The comparisons in costs already mentioned suggests that Henry's falconry establishment was considerably smaller than Edward's.[321] But that Henry hawked with enthusiasm there can be no doubt. In the last year of his life he gave 5 marks to John of Bicknor, 'because the king's goshawk, which is in John's keeping, took a duck in its first flight from the king's hand last season' (so probably in the autumn of 1271 when the falconry season began).[322]

Henry's chancery rolls are full of orders about the acquisition and care of birds of prey: gerfalcons, peregrine falcons, heron falcons, laner falcons, goshawks and sparrowhawks. Some of these birds could be caught from the nest in England. In 1255 the forester Hugh of Goldingham asked the king what he should do with four young falcons from nests in Handley park in Silverstone forest. (Henry's answer was that they should be sent to the keeper of his other falcons.)[323] Birds were also acquired from abroad, and especially, when it came to the gerfalcons, the largest and most prized birds of all, from Norway. In 1245 six gerfalcons, four peregrine falcons

---

[317] Le Goff, *Saint Louis*, 691–3; Buc, *L'ambiguïté du Livre*, 112–22.

[318] For the image on Simon's seal, inherited from his father, see Ambler, *Song of Simon de Montfort*, plates 10–13.

[319] Ormrod, *Edward III*, 143.

[320] Edited and translated by Casey Wood and Marjorie Fyfe with the title *The Art of Falconry*. Henry's hawking is covered comprehensively in Oggins, *Kings and their Hawks*, 73–81.

[321] Under Edward, when we have comparative figures, the falconers' costs could be double those of the huntsmen: Oggins, *Kings and their Hawks*, 83.

[322] *CLR 1260–7*, no. 1847.

[323] TNA SC 1/1/6/178; *CR 1254–6*, 82. Goldingham wrote not to the king direct but to Henry of Wingham (diplomatically called chancellor), asking him to inform the king of the question.

and two goshawks arrived at Lynn (King's Lynn) as gifts from the king of Norway. Three years later another seven gerfalcons followed. Henry, however, did not just rely on gifts. In 1252 he sent his men to Norway to buy goshawks.[324] Birds could also be acquired in England. In 1237 the sheriffs of Norfolk and Lincoln were ordered to detain all the goshawks, gerfalcons and peregrine falcons coming into their ports until the king's falconer had had his pick. Three years later the sheriffs of Lincoln, Hereford, York, Norfolk and London were to buy a total of thirty-six goshawks and thirteen gerfalcons and send them immediately to the king. No other birds were to be sold until they had been seen either by the king or by someone he sent.[325]

Some of the bought and gifted birds may have been already trained, although a degree of retraining would always have been required to suit them to their new masters. When taken from their nests or caught in the wild, the birds had to be trained from scratch, an elaborate and time-consuming process to which much of Frederick's book is devoted. In Henry's case this was the job of his falconers. In the 1230s there were a dozen or so in receipt of robes from the king.[326] Some were new men, others came from families (fitzBernard, Hauville, Erlham) long connected with the king's birds and holding office by hereditary sergeanties.[327] The main falconry establishments were at Brigstock and Geddington in Northamptonshire, although birds could also be trained elsewhere. The first part of the process was to get the birds to accept man as their natural master and a manmade habitat as their natural home. Apart from being the only source of food, this was done by spending days carrying the bird on the arm and gradually (so as to keep it calm) bringing it from darkness (with eyes stitched up and the head hooded) into light. Once 'manned', the bird had to be taught, with lures and baits, to hunt in such a way it could be retrieved by the falconer, rather than escaping into the wild. The training was especially elaborate when falcons were to attack birds, notably cranes and herons, much bigger than themselves and able to fight back.[328] Here particularly dogs entered the game, for when a falcon was still fighting with a crane or heron it had brought to earth, dogs (usually a couple) would run to its aid, the falconer accompanying them on horseback. The initial training was followed by a round of constant maintenance. The birds had to be 'mewed' each summer, that is looked after while they moulted and their new plumage grew. (Hence the name 'mews' for falconry establishments.) Outside the moulting season, the birds had to be constantly flown,

---

[324] *CR 1242–7*, 365; *CR 1247–51*, 85; *CPR 1247–58*, 157. For the count of Brittany seeking gerfalcons in Norway, see *CPR 1247–58*, 180.

[325] *CR 1234–7*, 98; *CR 1237–42*, 252; *CLR 1226–40*, 10.

[326] Wild, 'A truly royal retinue', 138, 177; Wild, *WA*, 22.

[327] The sergeanties are examined in detail in Oggins, *Kings and their Hawks*, 76–81.

[328] For Henry's gerfalcon Blakeman being trained to fly at cranes, see *RLC*, i, 470.

yet also preserved from exhaustion and accidents. Here careful feeding and checking of weight were of the essence. 'A full falcon never flies' might have been the maxim. The birds had to be kept hungry enough to want to hunt, yet not so hungry they lacked the strength to do so.

Henry, of course, never wrote a book like Frederick II's, but he certainly took a close interest in the welfare of his birds. He threatened one sheriff with severe punishment if he failed to provide money for the falconer mewing his gerfalcons. Out in Gascony, in 1242, he ordered William de Cantilupe back home to fly all his birds at opportune times. It was doubtless on Henry's instructions that, in the same year, the home government said that one of the king's goshawks was only to be flown delicately, namely once or twice a week. In Gascony again, in 1255, Henry wanted his laner and heron falcons to be taken from the mew after their moult and flown, so that they were ready on his return.[329]

In the autumn, when the falconry season began, there was a great gathering of the falconers at court. In October 1258 they included John fitz-Bernard, 'marshal of the king's hawks', another leading falconer Hugh of Erlham and eight men described as 'bearers of the king's hawks'.[330] Hawks could be flown anywhere in open countryside, but the best hawking was by rivers where cranes, herons and ducks were to be found. On occasion, therefore, Henry sought to protect and facilitate his hawking by making sure the ancient enclosures around rivers were in place and that all those with the ancient obligation to make bridges over them were ready to do so when he travelled through their parts, bridges (clearly here of a temporary nature) being essential to follow the birds as they descended with their prey.[331]

Falconry was not as social a sport as hunting with horses and hounds, but Henry often gave and received birds of prey as presents so there was some bonding there. In 1254 he was left one 'good goshawk' in the will of William de Ferrers, earl of Derby. Henry had someone skilled 'in the recognition of birds' sent to the earl's castle at Tutbury to chose the best one.[332] Let us hope the gerfalcons Henry sent to Frederick II came up to expectations.

Henry evidently had a close relationship with his favourite birds. From the early minority their names run through the chancery rolls: Blakeman, Refuse, Blanchpenny, Pilgrim, Lespaynol.[333] When he allowed his half-brother Geoffrey de Lusignan to choose one of his goshawks, 'the old hawk

---

[329] *CLR 1251–60*, 4; *CR 1237–42*, 514; *CR 1242–7*, 73; *CR 1254–6*, 267. For other orders related to mewing, see *CR 1234–7*, 415; *CR 1247–51*, 290; *CLR 1245–51*, 303, 306.

[330] TNA E 101/349/30/1.

[331] *CR 1237–42*, 244–5, 363–4. For the relationship with a chapter in Magna Carta, see Carpenter, *Magna Carta*, 205–6. Henry's reference to those obliged to make bridges 'ab antiquo et de jure' follows exactly the wording in the Charter.

[332] *CR 1253–4*, 96.

[333] Oggins, *Kings and their Hawks*, 73.

of the king' and 'the crossbow of Osmond' (presumably the name of a hawk and its bearer) were excepted. There is something deeply personal in the relationship between human and hawk. There is the wonder, as Frederick II noted, of a wild bird, normally so fearful of humans, becoming a close companion, a companion one can stroke and talk to.[334] And there is the intimacy of its weight on your arm, and the excitement of the throw from the hand (sensed in Henry's order in 1272) as the bird is launched into the air – if a goshawk, shooting off horizontally after duck or rabbit, if a gerfalcon, spiralling high into the air before stooping down at over 200 mph to crash into a crane or heron and engage in aerial combat.[335] With his birds and his falconers (much less likely than his jesters to answer back) Henry could feel totally relaxed.

CONFLICT OR COHESION

Was Henry's court characterized by conflict or cohesion, by competition or consensus? The answer is, in different degrees at different times, somewhere between the two. As will be seen, after the arrival of the king's Poitevin half-brothers in 1247, the court did become increasingly factionalized. At a lower level there must often have been competition between ministers over place and patronage. We have seen how disappointed the chancery clerks were when a benefice they were eyeing up was snaffled away by the king's surgeon. When Geoffrey de Langley became head of the royal forests he was supplanting his old patron, Robert Passelewe. When John Mansel masterminded the appointment of Philip Lovel as treasurer of the exchequer, he was keeping out the exchequer official John le Francis. The court was divided by the way ministers were retained by leading magnates. The rewards given to the king's stewards Ralph fitzNicholas and Godfrey of Crowcombe by Gilbert Marshal had probably many other parallels.[336] FitzNicholas himself was a tenant and former steward of the earl of Derby. A critique of Henry's rule drawn up in 1264 complained of the close links between magnates, English and foreign, and the king's judges, and there is a good deal of evidence to substantiate the charge.[337]

Yet there was anther side, seen in the sense of community amongst the chancery clerks. John Mansel himself may have done down John le

---

[334] *Art of Falconry*, 6.

[335] There are numerous examples on YouTube of both these forms of attack. At the East Anglia Academy of Falconry at Stonham in Suffolk, I was told that their falcons, though high in the air, can notice the slight movement of the falconer's hand getting bait out of a bag and will immediately plummet to get it.

[336] For the household knight Bartholomew Pecche and the earl of Hereford, see *CPR 1232–47*, 230.

[337] *DBM*, 272–3; Carpenter, *Reign of Henry III*, 83–4; Maddicott, *Law and Lordship*, 4–13. I will discuss this further in the first chapter of volume 2.

Francis, but he often appears as a peacemaker, striving to settle quarrels and support friends.[338] Above all, everyone at court was lucky to serve a kind and generous master who had none of his father's spikiness and aggression. Perhaps things might have been better if he had. Archbishop Edmund, expressing a common clerical critique, felt that the court was a place full of flattery and corruption.[339] In fact, John Mansel for one was quite prepared to give the king unwelcome advice, as of course were many of the great men present at court and parliament. But when Henry was flattered, as he must often have been, he lacked the intelligence and scepticism to see through it. Henry certainly had likes and dislikes. Some sons of leading ministers conspicuously failed to follow their fathers at court, or at least not until the revolution of 1258, presumably because Henry just did not want them.[340] Henry was also perfectly capable of angrily dismissing ministers for transgressions or alleged transgressions. Yet few ministers, during the personal rule, permanently forfeited the king's esteem. Godfrey of Crowcombe, Ralph fitzNicholas, Henry of Bath, John de Grey and Philip Lovel all recovered the king's favour and returned to the colours.[341] The hasty recall of Roger the almoner to court 'despite the asperity of any words we addressed to you' seems typical of the king.[342] The decorum of the court and the *debonereté* of the king made his occasional outbursts of anger all the more dramatic. But with Henry, what you saw was what you got. He was not a king to feign anger for effect. And like summer storms, the anger was soon over. Henry's court was often a happy place, too happy perhaps for his complete good.

Henry's court almost certainly outshone that of any earl or baron, even after the reduction of costs in the early 1250s. In considering its impact, its secular and religious face have to be taken together. The liveries and the gift-giving meshed with the religious services and the feeding of paupers. The halls and chambers were used for secular business yet were full of religious imagery. The chapels where the services were sung were themselves used for business, though under Henry, we may be sure, not at the same time. All these aspects of court life contributed to Henry's 'soft power'. No king put more trust in that aspect of monarchy. A central question during Henry's personal rule was how far would it get him.

---

[338] For the king describing the future chancellor Walter of Merton as Mansel's 'amicum et benevolum', see *CR 1256–9*, 150.

[339] Lawrence, *St Edmund of Abingdon*, 131.

[340] Examples are Hugh, son of Hugh Despenser; Giles, son of Richard de Argentan; Bertram, son of Bertram de Criel; and Robert, son of Ralph fitzNicholas. All were rebels in the civil war. After the revolution of 1258, Giles became steward of the royal household and Hugh justiciar.

[341] An exception is Master Simon the Norman.

[342] *CR 1242–7*, 58, and likewise p. 440 for the recall of the household knight, Peter Braunche.

Chapter 8

YEARS OF DIVISION
1243–1250

The years between Henry's return from Gascony in 1243 and his departure again for the duchy ten years later form a discrete period in his personal rule, although one separated by his decision in 1250 to take the cross. Henry could claim many positive achievements. The most visible, of course, was the rebuilding of Westminster Abbey. All those who flocked to Westminster for meetings of parliament and sessions of the bench and the exchequer witnessed the dramatic dismantling of the church of the Confessor and then, year by year, the rising up of the magnificent new structure in its place. By 1253 the main frame of the east end and transepts were in place, standing high shouldered above the surrounding buildings, proclaiming Henry's achievement, dominating the Westminster scene. At the same time work was proceeding on the jewelled and golden shrine to hold the Confessor's body. Henry also did something else to enhance the spiritual life of his people. In 1247 he gave to the Abbey a wonderful relic, none other than a portion of the blood that Christ had shed on the cross. It was more precious even than the crown of thorns King Louis had brought to Paris.

Henry had much to celebrate in his family life. Richard of Cornwall's marriage to Queen Eleanor's sister Sanchia tied him safely into the family circle, and he supported the regime with a whole series of important loans. In 1245, Eleanor gave birth to another son, Edmund, so the future of the dynasty was assured. Her Savoyard kinsmen continued to guide Henry through the mazy avenues of international politics. For a while there was also a reconciliation with Henry's brother-in-law Simon de Montfort, hence his appointment as seneschal of Gascony in 1248. If one family group was not enough, Henry, from 1247, was busy establishing another in England. These were his Poitevin half-brothers, the fruits of his mother's second marriage with Hugh de Lusignan. Henry endowed one brother with a landed inheritance and made him a fixture at court. He promoted another brother to the see of Winchester, and enriched two more with pensions and wardships. In all this Henry had shown his power and, as he hoped, secured loyal support in England, as well as a foothold in Poitou and a shield for the defence of Gascony.

Very hands on when it came to money, Henry managed in these years to keep going by cash or credit and in the early 1250s save up a considerable treasure, even though he was unable to obtain grants of taxation. In

1247 he carried through a successful recoinage. He was also successful within Britain. After a scare in 1244, he maintained good relations with the king of Scots. At York, in December 1251, in one of the happiest and grandest ceremonies of the reign, he married his daughter Margaret to the young King Alexander III. In Wales, Henry was a conqueror. He defeated the rulers of Gwynedd, secured the Four Cantrefs between the Dee and the Conwy for the crown and held them down with his castles at Deganwy and Dyserth. The treaty of Woodstock in 1247 seemed to set a seal on his achievement.

Unfortunately, this is far from the whole picture. These were years of increasing tension and division. Henry suffered a series of bruising defeats over episcopal elections and had a bishop of Winchester forced on him by the pope. The establishment of his Lusignan half-brothers proved far more disruptive than that of the Savoyards, partly because of their own behaviour, partly because they seemed to suck up far too much from a diminishing pool of royal patronage. One result was factional struggles at court which some-times pitched Henry against his queen. Another was the growing perception that England was being tyrannized by greedy and lawless foreigners. Here were some of the ingredients in the revolution of 1258. Henry also set a dangerous precedent in failing to lead the kingdom's resistance to the demands of the pope. Instead, he allowed the magnates to take the lead. In 1258 they would take the lead again, this time against Henry himself.

This was a decisive period in the development of parliament.[1] The name itself was now regularly given to assemblies bringing together the great and good of the realm. In origin the word itself, in French 'parle-ment', in Latin 'parliamentum', simply meant a 'discussion', a usage which easily expanded to describe the assembly in which the discussion took place. Up to a point the appearance of the word (for the first time in an official record in 1237) was simply a new name for an old institution, for kings since Anglo-Saxon times had convened assemblies to discuss the affairs of the realm. But it may be that the new name stuck from a feeling the assembly had changed its nature and was now playing a larger part than ever before in national life. In the 1240s parliaments both co-ordinated the kingdom's resistance to papal exactions and rejected the king's frequent demands for taxation. The great lever, the source of all parliament's power down the ages, the ability to refuse taxation, appears for the first time in real action. Henry had previously been granted taxes in 1225, 1232 and 1237. Only once after 1234 had a tax been denied him – in 1242 just before his Poitevin expedition. Between 1244 and 1252, Henry was refused taxation on four or five occasions.[2] As the reason for its refusal, parliament set out a wide-ranging critique of his rule. It also, as a condition of any tax, asked Henry to accept a programme of reform. The

---

[1] For a full discussion see Maddicott, *Origins of the English Parliament*, ch. 4.

[2] Maddicott, *Origins of the English Parliament*, 454–68.

precedents of 1225 and 1237 had made concessions as the price for any tax seem natural. But, whereas in 1225 and 1237 the concession had been Magna Carta, from the 1240s parliament was calling for far more radical reforms, ones which Henry found unacceptable as they would effectively strip him of power. This was the programme finally implemented in the revolution of 1258.

Overshadowing much of the period was the problem of Gascony. Here Henry made Simon de Montfort his lieutenant and thought for a while the duchy had been reduced to order. Instead, Montfort's abrasive policies threatened Gascony's total loss, forcing Henry ultimately to go there. He was reluctant to do so for he now had an altogether new priority. This was to go on crusade. Henry took the cross in March 1250 and became passionately committed to the cause. That commitment, as well as the conflagration in Gascony, had a major impact on domestic politics, and kept parliament to the fore. It was in parliament that Simon de Montfort answered the charges brought against him by his Gascon enemies. It was in parliament and related assemblies that Henry begged for money both for Gascony and the crusade. One result of these great debates was a confirmation of Magna Carta and the Charter of the Forest linked to the most public and publicized sentences of excommunication against contra- veners of the Charters launched in the whole of the thirteenth century.

In what follows the story of these years is told in three chapters. This one covers Henry's experiences 'at home' between 1244 and 1250, as well as his successes in Wales and Scotland. The next looks at Gascony between 1244 and 1252; and then a chapter turns to Henry's crusade and the poli- tics of the years between 1250 and 1253, politics which culminated in the confirmation of Magna Carta and the final decision to go to Gascony.

A MARRIAGE AND A BIRTH: HENRY AND HIS FAMILY, 1243–5

In early November 1243, Henry and Eleanor, with a large company, trav- elled from Westminster to Dover. There they welcomed to England the queen's mother, Beatrice of Savoy, countess of Provence, and her youngest daughter, Sanchia, who had come to marry Richard of Cornwall. From Dover the royal party moved to Canterbury where Henry arranged for thousands of candles to light up the churches. The cost was over £64 and the weight of the wax some 2,440 pounds. The entry to a cleaned and decorated London followed and this time as many candles lit up Westminster Abbey as on the feast day of the Confessor himself. The wedding itself was celebrated on 23 November. The Waverley annalist thought the subsequent feast, in the great hall, equalled that at a coronation. Matthew Paris, impressed if scandalized by the extravagance, spoke of 30,000 dishes.[3]

---

[3] Paris, iv, 261–3; Waverley, 330; *CLR 1240–5*, 211; *CR 1242–7*, 138.

Henry now reached a full and final settlement with his brother. Richard quitclaimed his right to Gascony under the grant made to him at Saintes. In return, Henry promised Richard and Sanchia and their heirs land worth £500 a year. The land was to come not from the 'ancient demesnes belonging to the crown' (an indication they were now considered inalienable) but from the first escheats that fell in. No one else was to receive escheated land until Richard had been satisfied. Until then he was to receive 1,000 marks a year, the amount to diminish as the land was assigned. Henry did not always keep his promises. This one he did. Richard had already received a significant proportion of the land when he first agreed to marry Sanchia in 1242.[4] By 1256 he had got it all. When Henry, with many mouths to feed (the more especially after the arrival of his half-brothers), formed queues of those awaiting grants of land, he always made clear that Richard topped the list. When major escheats went to others, it was with Richard's consent.[5]

Henry celebrated visually Richard's place in the family circle. A silk cloth starred with gold was to be given a border with the arms of the king, Richard and the count of Provence. When Westminster Abbey was decorated the cloth was to be hung behind the cross on the high altar.[6] The three heraldic shields to survive from the stained glass of Henry's new church likewise bear the arms of Henry, Richard and the count. Henry rewarded his brother in the years after 1243 with a series of personal gifts: wine for his cellars, game for his parks and timber for his buildings. Above all Henry supported the Cistercian house Richard founded at Hailes near Winchcombe in Gloucestershire. Indeed, Henry both gave the manor of Hailes to Richard (it was an escheat) and did not deduct its value from his 1,000 mark fee.[7]

Matthew Paris rightly commented that Henry loved his brother and wished to enrich and pacify him. In doing so, Henry showed great wisdom. The wealthiest earl in the country and the closest to the throne in blood, in the years after 1243 Richard was frequently at court and effectively Henry's chief councillor: he attested royal charters in six of the months in 1244; seven in 1245; ten in 1246; and seven again in 1247. The flow of gifts was not one way. In 1244, Richard gave his brother 'a great tapestry' and Henry ordered it to be hung behind his throne at Westminster on Christmas day. Above all, Richard now started to support the regime with his abundant money. Between 1245 and 1252 the wardrobe received

[4] See above, 251.

[5] F, 253–4 (CPR 1232–47, 437); Denholm-Young, Richard of Cornwall, 164; Stacey, Politics, Policy and Finance, 238; Ridgeway, 'Foreign favourites', 600–1. The day before the wedding, Henry gave Richard £1,000 as part of the £3,000 promised with the marriage: CLR 1240–5, 198.

[6] CR 1242–7, 153.

[7] CChR 1226–57, 280, 288, 294.

loans from him totalling nearly £7,000. Paris commented that Richard calmed many disturbances in England. Without his loyalty and support Henry's personal rule might well have ended sooner than it did.[8]

During the Christmas festivities of 1243, celebrated at Richard of Cornwall's castle of Wallingford, Henry treated Sanchia with marked consideration but she never became a particular favourite.[9] The person who really impressed Henry during her brief visit to England was his mother-in-law, Countess Beatrice. His numerous gifts included the best scarlet robe, lined with ermine, that could be found in London, this to be worn during the Christmas festivities.[10] It was thanks to Beatrice's intercession that Henry now completed the family circle by reaching a settlement with his brother-in-law Simon de Montfort.[11] He pardoned the Montforts nearly £2,000 of debt (a gigantic alleviation), and gave them once again the great castle of Kenilworth as a principal residence. Henry also did something to give Eleanor a proper marriage portion. He granted the Montforts 500 marks a year, of which 300 marks (£200) were to be entailed on their heirs. The following year, going some way to fulfilling the promise to convert this pension into land, he exchanged it for the Umfraville wardship, which meant that, until the heir came of age in 1266, Montfort would control valuable estates in the north of England.[12] This concession projected Montfort into the ranks of the richer earls. Henry also welcomed Montfort back as one of his leading councillors: a spokesman in parliament, an ambassador to Louis IX and a frequent attender at court: he attested royal charters in eight months in 1244; ten in 1245, and six in 1246. An important factor in this reconciliation was Henry's renewed affection for Eleanor. He gave her many personal gifts and often described her as his 'sister' as well as 'countess of Leicester'.[13]

Henry might also hope for much from another noble, who was in a way family since he had grown up at Henry's court. This was Richard de Clare, who came of age in 1243 and two years later was knighted by the king and invested with the earldoms of Gloucester and Hertford. He had already in 1240, by an agreement with Gilbert Marshal, taken over the lordship of Glamorgan. In 1246, Clare attested royal charters in eight months of the year; in 1247, in seven.

Most central of all to Henry's family, and, he would have thought, to the realm itself, were his queen and children. Henry was constantly offering up

---

[8] Wild, *WA*, 52, 54; Paris, *HA*, ii, 296–7; *CR 1242–7*, 279; Denholm-Young, *Richard of Cornwall*, 157.

[9] Paris, iv, 283.

[10] *CR 1242–7*, 145.

[11] Bémont, *Simon de Montfort*, 335. For what follows, see Maddicott, *Simon de Montfort*, 32–3, 35–7, 47, 52–5.

[12] *CFR 1244–5*, nos. 64, 334; *CR 1242–7*, 159, 164; *CPR 1232–47*, 419; *CChR 1226–57*, 278; Maddicott, *Simon de Montfort*, 54.

[13] For example, *CR 1242–7*, 458, 518, 521; Wilkinson, *Eleanor de Montfort*, 76–7.

alms and oblations for the health of Eleanor, Edward, Margaret and Beatrice, 'beautiful Beatrice' as he described her (when two years old) in one order.[14] His affection and concern for Eleanor were demonstrated, as so often, in work on her chapels, chambers and wardrobes, and in numerous gifts (such as the elaborate glass and silver cup fashioned in November 1244).[15] In 1244, apart from the new apartments at Windsor, work for her was going on at Havering, Ludgershall, Marlborough, Brill, Oxford (with a painting of the last supper and the crucifixion), Woodstock and Nottingham.[16] The unity between king and queen was proclaimed in a whole series of ways: in the parallel wainscoting of their chambers; in the identical silver basins and lecterns ordered for their wardrobes and chapels; in the robes of scarlet lined with minever they wore at Christmas 1243 cut from the cloth given by Thomas of Savoy; in the images of king and queen to be painted in St Stephen's chapel at Westminster; and in the stained-glass portrayals of a king and queen sitting on thrones placed in the window by the dais in the upper hall at Guildford.[17]

When Henry and Eleanor were apart, they kept in touch by letters. A couple of Eleanor's from this period survive. They were dutiful in tone. She saluted Henry as 'her most excellent lord . . . with every kind of reverential subjection'. She begged to be informed of his wishes, urged him to write frequently, and hoped he was well 'with all the affection of our heart and mind'. Eleanor, however, was clear about her own status. Just as Henry was king of England 'by the grace of God', so she was 'by the same grace, queen of England'. She began her letters by assuring Henry that their children were well, thus highlighting the central role she was playing in their welfare and upbringing.[18] Eleanor preserved the forms of subjection but, now around twenty, contemporaries believed and rightly that she wielded great influence over her husband. In 1243, beyond the dais in the new hall he was building in Dublin castle, Henry ordered a painting of 'a king and queen sitting with their baronage'. They seemed almost to be joint rulers of the realm.[19]

Above the royal family, holding it in his protective embrace, stood the Confessor. It was in 1244 that he saved Thomas of Savoy from a life-threatening illness, a miracle Henry specifically instructed Matthew Paris to record.[20] The queen continued to embrace the cult and had an image of the Virgin Mary constructed and placed on the Confessor's shrine. In September 1244, Henry arranged for Eleanor, Edward, Margaret and

[14] *CR 1242–7*, 228; *CLR 1240–5*, 150.

[15] *CR 1242–7*, 271.

[16] *CLR 1240–5*, 216, 218, 234, 252, 282.

[17] *CLR 1240–5*, 216, 218, 228, 234, 252; *CR 1242–7*, 145, 287; *CLR 1245–50*, 25.

[18] TNA SC 1/3/83; *RL*, ii, 42–3.

[19] *CR 1242–7*, 23. The order was issued from Bordeaux in April 1243, another indication of how much Henry valued Eleanor's support at that difficult time.

[20] Paris, vi, 92–4.

'beautiful Beatrice' to make offerings at the shrine when they next came to Westminster.[21] A couple of months later, Henry explained how, 'by the mercy of Jesus Christ', he reigned helped 'by the patronage of our patron and predecessor the blessed Edward'. At this time he must have been very close to the decision to rebuild Westminster Abbey.[22]

In 1244, Henry and Eleanor had still only one son, Edward, born in 1239. He had been seriously ill on more than one occasion. Child mortality rates were high. However beautiful their daughters, Henry was unceasing in offering prayers and alms 'so that God would give him a child to strengthen the kingdom'. Here, in Paris's words, he appeared as 'a most Christian of kings'.[23] A child, of course, meant a son and the Confessor having done his work in giving Edward, it was to Edmund, the second great Anglo-Saxon royal saint, that Henry turned. Once it was clear, in the summer of 1244, that Eleanor was pregnant, Henry went on pilgrimage to Bury, arranging for 1,000 candles to burn on his arrival. For Edmund's feast later in the year the number rose to 3,000. Henry also took out reinsurance at Canterbury, where 1,000 candles were placed around Becket's shrine for the queen's safe delivery.[24] And he looked for help from another quarter. Henry's archbishop of Canterbury, Edmund of Abingdon, had died in Burgundy in November 1240 on his way to Rome. By 1245, he was well on his way to canonization by the pope. So it was that, as Eleanor neared her time, Henry appealed to Edmund's sisters, nuns at Catesby in Northamptonshire, to bring to Westminster the cloak 'the blessed Edmund' had left them, evidently already a holy relic. They were rewarded with £10 for doing so. At the last, however, it was again to Bury's Saint Edmund that Henry turned. As Eleanor laboured in the pains of childbirth, Henry had his antiphon chanted for her and almost at once a servant (inevitably a Savoyard) arrived with the news that Eleanor had given birth to a son. It was 16 January 1245. All this Henry narrated in a joyful letter to the monks of Bury, adding that he had named his son Edmund, as they had requested. Henry ordered, 'no expense spared', the cloth in which Edmund was wrapped at his baptism to be made into 'the richest and noblest possible' chasuble, indeed 'far nobler and richer' than he had first envisaged. It was to be so loaded with gold and precious stones that it would burden the celebrant wearing it even more than the weight of a gospel book. Later in the year Henry had the window above his bed at Brill blocked so that a painting of St Edmund could be placed there.[25] In

[21] *CR 1242–7*, 159, 228.

[22] TNA SC 1/2/121.

[23] Paris, *HA*, ii, 499 (a later addition).

[24] Henry also arranged for Eleanor to translate a relic of St Thomas the Apostle at Westminster into its new container (made in the shape of an arm): *CR 1242–7*, 270.

[25] Howell, *Eleanor of Provence*, 44–5; *CLR 1240–5*, 244, 264, 275, 285, 306; *CR 1242–7*, 276, 288; *Cronica Buriensis*, 28–9. For the role of Edmund of Abingdon, see Creamer, 'St Edmund of Canterbury and Henry III', 130.

March 1245 he made another East Anglian pilgrimage to Bury, Walsingham and Bromholm.

HENRY'S CLASH WITH KING ALEXANDER, 1244

The death of Henry's sister Joan, wife of King Alexander of Scotland, back in 1238 had inevitably weakened the ties between the English and Scottish courts. The marriage had been childless and for his second wife Alexander looked not to England but to France, marrying in 1239 Marie, the daughter of the great French noble, Enguerrand de Coucy. None of this need have thrown Anglo-Scottish relations into crisis. Before setting off for Poitou in 1242, Henry had finally given Alexander the northern manors due under the treaty of 1237. He had also reached a preliminary agreement for the marriage of his infant daughter Margaret to Alexander's son and heir by Marie, the future Alexander III, born in 1241. According to Matthew Paris, the agreement had restored good relations between the kings.

The crisis in 1244 had its origins in a great feud amongst the nobility of Scotland, a feud Alexander failed to control.[26] One faction, headed by Patrick, earl of Dunbar, and the Comyns, accused Walter Bisset, lord of Aboyne, and his nephew John of murdering Patrick, claimant to the earldom of Athol. The nature of his demise – burnt to death in a house – made the crime seem all the more appalling. Forced into exile, the Bissets were supposed to go to the Holy Land. Instead, they went to Henry III and were soon taken into his service. John indeed became one of Henry's household knights.[27] The two were thus ideally placed to poison Henry's mind against Alexander and the nobles responsible for their downfall.

There were a whole series of charges.[28] Alexander, it was said, was harbouring Henry's enemies, including Geoffrey de Marsh. He was fortifying two castles along the Anglo-Scottish border, one at Hermitage in Liddesdale, the other at Tarset in Tynedale. At Tarset, he was hand in glove with the castle's lord, none other than the Bisset enemy Walter Comyn, earl of Menteith. Alexander, the accusations continued, was also seeking military help from his friends in France and perhaps making an alliance with Louis IX. With Earl Patrick of Dunbar as his leading councillor, he was even planning to attack the north of England.[29] Henry thought back fondly to the days of Joan. In February 1244, on the anniversary of her death, he ordered numerous paupers to be fed for the health of her soul. (The beneficiaries included 1,000 poor scholars at Oxford.)[30] The Bissets also raked up the issue of Scotland's status. They

[26] For these events, see Brown, *Wars of Scotland*, 39–42 and Oram, *Alexander II*, 158–69.
[27] *CR 1242–7*, 147.
[28] Paris, iv, 201–2, 359, 379–81; Bower, 5, 184–5; *CR 1242–7*, 221.
[29] For Patrick, see *CPR 1232–47*, 432.
[30] *CLR 1240–5*, 220; *CR 1242–7*, 164.

claimed that Alexander, the king's 'liege man', had no power without Henry's consent to disinherit a nobleman in Scotland, thus implying that Henry was still overlord of the kingdom. Henry sometimes liked to think so. Matthew Paris recorded his indignation when, at St Albans, he heard of Alexander's claim that no particle of the Scottish kingdom was held from the king of England.[31]

In 1244, faced with these conjured threats, Henry decided he must go north during the summer to check on the security of his border castles. He also tried to prevent knights, merchants, letters and arms passing between France and Scotland.[32] This was in April. In May he went further and by the 'common counsel of our kingdom' summoned his tenants-in-chief to muster in arms at Newcastle on 1 August. He also called for help from Ireland and Flanders. His aim, he explained, was to take revenge for the 'transgressions and injuries' suffered at the hands of the king of Scotland.[33]

Henry left Westminster early in June. Until his return from Scotland, he ordered twenty extra candles to burn around the shrine of the Confessor. He also had made for the Abbey a dragon banner with eyes of sapphires and a tongue 'burning like fire and in appearance continually moving'.[34] For the moment he was in martial mode. First, however, there was time for a pilgrimage to the East Anglian shrines.[35] Henry then headed westwards to join up with the road north. Eleanor went with him as far as Nottingham, where she set up her household. It was now that Henry ordered, alongside other works, a roofed passage to be made between their chambers in the castle. Earlier he had commissioned extensive work for them both at the royal manor of Geddington, where they had stayed for a few days on their way through Northamptonshire.[36] During this northern journey Henry made numerous gifts to the friars, hospitals and religious houses along the way. At Croxton, where John's entrails were buried, he provided a chasuble for the mass on his father's anniversary.[37] At York, where over a thousand of candles were to mark his entry into the cathedral, he ordered four great tapers, each weighing 100 pounds, to be placed at the four corners of the shrine of Saint William.[38]

Henry reached Newcastle on time on 1 August. There had been a good response to his summons from the earls and barons. Matthew Paris believed that the knights in the army, all well armed, numbered 1,200. Thomas of Savoy, for once showing his worth, answered Henry's call and

[31] Paris, iv, 201–2, 359.
[32] *CLR 1240–5*, 229; *CR 1242–7*, 243.
[33] *CR 1242–7*, 254–5; *CR Supp*, nos. 1–7.
[34] *CR 1242–7*, 199, 201.
[35] *CLR 1240–5*, 244.
[36] *CLR 1240–5*, 249, 252–3.
[37] *CLR 1240–5*, 250.
[38] *CLR 1240–5*, 254, 256.

came with 62 knights and over 400 horses.[39] Henry ordered a hauberk to be acquired for himself, and planned an advance to the Scottish border. The efforts made to transport siege engines suggest the first aim was take the two objectionable castles.[40]

Alexander, meanwhile, had mustered his own army for the defence of his kingdom. Matthew Paris was impressed by that too. If it numbered only 500 knights, there were vast numbers of foot-soldiers, 60,000 Paris said, with some exaggeration.[41] In the event there was no fighting. Thanks to the good offices of Richard of Cornwall and the archbishop of York, Alexander came under safe conduct to Newcastle, and an agreement was reached.[42] It was far less exigent than sometimes supposed.

In the settlement, Alexander addressed Henry as his 'liege lord'. He thus acknowledged that his duty to Henry overrode that to any other lord and obliged him to do nothing to harm Henry's interests. Alexander accordingly promised that he and his heirs would never make war on the king of England or damage him and his lands by reason of a treaty with his enemies. But, and here was the crucial point, the treaty clearly implied that Alexander's liege homage was simply for the lands he held from Henry in England, not for Scotland itself.[43] Thus, although the marriage between Alexander's son and Henry's daughter was confirmed, Henry agreed it was not to prejudice the king of Scots' freedom to contract marriages wherever he wished.[44] Such an acknowledgement would have been inconceivable had Scotland itself been subject to the king of England. Indeed, it contrasted sharply with the treaty of 1212 where King William the Lion had given to King John the right to marry his son, Alexander, 'as his liege man'.[45] There was no ambiguity over what that meant since, under the terms of the 1209 treaty of Norham, Alexander had done homage for the kingdom.

The treaty of 1244, therefore, like that of 1237, while making no explicit pronouncement on the subject, left Scotland's independence very much intact. Alexander's liege homage was just the same as that which his father had done King Richard, having recovered Scotland's independence in 1190. It was, that is, homage for lands in England.[46] In other ways, the

[39] Paris, vi, 518, with the numbers reduced at iv, 385; *CLR 1240–5*, 264. Peter of Geneva was also on the expedition: *RCWL*, i, 193.

[40] *CR 1242–7*, 216, 257–8; *CLR 1240–5*, 255.

[41] Paris, vi, 518, with the numbers reduced at iv, 380.

[42] *CPR 1232–47*, 432, 434. I am sceptical as to whether Alexander was allowed to advance with his army to within six miles of Newcastle. For this question see the comment in Bower, 5, 282 no. 34. For the settlement, see Oram, *Alexander II*, 172–4.

[43] *CChR 1226–57*, 310; *CR 1242–7*, 343.

[44] We only have the summary of a document in the Scottish treasury in 1282: *APS*, 108.

[45] *RRS*, ii, no. 505. The agreement of the 1212 treaty only survives in a later English copy. Duncan, *Scotland*, 251 n. 68, 536–7, suggests this copy was possibly drawn up and doctored on this occasion in order to help Henry press his claims. If so, it had no effect.

[46] *ASR*, 16–17.

treaty was remarkably reciprocal. Henry promised not to make war on the king of Scotland, and the undertakings of both kings were guaranteed by oaths taken by their nobles.[47] For both kings, though, the restrictions did not apply if their kingdoms needed to be defended. So there was still the possibility of a Franco-Scottish alliance after all. As for the castles, Alexander and Walter Comyn surrendered Tarset to Henry, although ultimately the Comyns got it back.[48] (What happened about Hermitage is unknown.) On the other hand, the Bissets did not recover their lands in Scotland and, based in Ireland, remained dependent on Henry's support.

Walter Bower, writing in the fifteenth century but probably using contemporary material, thought that Henry in 1244 aimed 'to reduce with all his might the whole realm of Scotland to his authority', but was then scared off by 'the bold front' of the Scots.[49] Henry, like Matthew Paris, may well have been impressed by the size of Alexander's army. He may also have remembered the disastrous results at Taillebourg only two years before when he last contemplated a battle. Yet, in truth, Henry's overlordship over Scotland was not something he felt that strongly about. It was not in the same league as the campaign of 1242 or later his crusade and the Sicilian project. Henry might stamp his feet and proclaim his rights but he was not prepared to push them in an aggressive way. This was true even in the 1250s, when the terrain was more favourable. In 1244 he mentioned from the first the possibility of a peaceful settlement and accepted one on the easiest terms once he was reassured about Alexander's intentions. He was then only too pleased to get home. The settlement brought a sensible end to the quarrel, and was welcomed by Matthew Paris, who hoped the kings would henceforth become 'indissolvable friends'.[50] The Lanercost chronicler, describing the events of 1244, called Henry a 'king of gentle heart'.[51] One major consequence of the expedition is visible to this day at York. There the castle was in a ruinous condition and Henry set in train its rebuilding, with the centrepiece a new keep, now known at Clifford's tower. In March 1245, Henry spared Master Henry de Reyns from his work at

[47] The charter issued by the Scottish nobles is found in Paris, iv, 381–3 (RRS, iii, no. 299). Henry's side of the agreement is only known from the description in 1282 of documents in the treasury at Edinburgh: 'the last confederation made between Henry king of England and Alexander king of Scots at Newcastle upon Tyne and that none of them move war against the other unless for their defence where there are not the seals of the earls of Gloucester and Hereford nor do they seem to have been appended': APS, 108. This seems to mean that Henry's agreement was sealed by other nobles but not by these two earls. Paris (iv, 383) tells us that some of the seals on Alexander's charter were appended at once, others later. Gloucester and Hereford did not come on the northern expedition as they were guarding the Welsh marches. Richard de Clare was only invested with the earldom of Gloucester in 1245 but may well have been given the title in this document.

[48] CR 1242–7, 221; CPR 1266–72, 178.

[49] Bower, 5, 184–5.

[50] Paris, iv, 385.

[51] Lanercost, 54.

Windsor and Westminster and sent him to York to make plans for the castle. The keep he designed was quatrefoil in shape, thus greatly increasing the angles of flanking fire. It was modelled on that at Étampes in France, so Master Henry was not merely an expert on the French cathedrals.[52]

WALES, 1244–7

Having reached his settlement with King Alexander at Newcastle, Henry could have headed west and visited Cumberland and Carlisle, as he had intended earlier in the year. Alternatively, he could have led his army into Wales and dealt with the rising there. Henry did neither of these things. Instead, in the words of Matthew Paris, 'having heard [of the Welsh rising] ... the king did not wish to divert there with the army he had ready. Rather, swayed by womanly counsels, he hastened to the accustomed delights and rest of Westminster.'[53] In terms of his itinerary, this was all too true. Henry left Newcastle in mid-August, reached Windsor on 6 September, and then spent over three weeks 'resting' at Westminster. Among the delights were the new curtains and painted columns ordered earlier in the year for his bed.[54] In the whole of his reign he never saw Carlisle.

The trouble in Wales had been sparked by an event at the Tower of London. Since 1241, Gruffudd, the eldest but illegitimate son of Llywelyn the Great, had been imprisoned there. During the night of 30 April–1 March 1244 he was killed in an attempt to escape. He had tied together bedsheets and lowered himself down from his tower only for the makeshift rope to break under his weight. He was, so Matthew Paris says, extremely fat, perhaps thanks to his years of comfortable captivity. When his body was found in the morning his head and neck had been stoved in between his shoulder blades. Henry ordered 500 paupers to be fed for the benefit of his soul.[55]

For Dafydd, the ruler of Gwynedd, the death of his elder brother seemed a godsend. He was no longer held in check by the threat of Gruffudd's release. True, Henry still held Owain, Gruffud's eldest son, but Owain had nothing like his father's political standing. Over the next few years Henry dithered over what to do with him. Dafydd, therefore, saw his chance. He launched a bid to recover the territory lost in 1241 and replace Henry's authority over the native rulers with his own. He was taking a great risk. Any breach of the 1241 treaty would mean Gwynedd was forfeit for ever to the English crown.[56] But Dafydd's grievances were overwhelming. By the treaty of 1241 he had surrendered in perpetuity both the castle of Deganwy, overlooking the Conwy, and the whole of Englefield,

---

[52] *CR 1242–7*, 293; Colvin, *History of the King's Works*, i, 116; ii, 889–90.
[53] Paris, iv, 385.
[54] *CR 1242–7*, 169.
[55] Paris, iv, 295–6; *CLR 1240–5*, 306.
[56] *AWR*, nos. 300–5, for the texts of 1241.

Gwynedd's easternmost cantref between the Clywd and the Dee. While Henry seems to have left Deganwy as a structure of earth and timber (it had been destroyed by Dafydd before his evacuation), at Dyserth he had built an entirely new castle. It towered above the valley of the Clwyd, and barred Dafydd's way back into Englefield. To the immediate south of Englefield, Dafydd's claims to Mold had been ignored.[57] In South Wales he was excluded from the inheritance of his wife, Isabella de Briouze, both by the king, who retained Builth, and by Humphrey de Bohun (eldest son of the earl of Hereford), who was married to one of Isabella's sisters.[58] The treaty of 1241 also stressed that the homages of the Welsh rulers belonged to the king, thus ending the hope of a Welsh principality in which homage was done to the ruler of Gwynedd.

Dafydd's situation was in one way stronger than in 1240 and 1241. Then he had received little support from the other Welsh leaders. Now, having experienced the sharp end of Henrician rule, they joined his rising. The only ones to remain on Henry's side were Gruffudd ap Madog and Gruffudd ap Gwenwynwyn, rulers respectively of northern and southern Powys. Both, however, warned Henry of the discontent amongst their men.[59] In Glamorgan, moreover, there was growing resentment at the harsh rule of Richard de Clare. In Ystrad Tywi and Ceredigion the rulers were suffering from the jurisdictional demands and territorial encroachments of the royal officials in Cardigan and Carmarthen.

Whether Dafydd formally took the homages of the other Welsh rulers is unknown, but he made an important statement of his authority. He called himself 'prince of Wales'. This was a title avoided by Llywelyn the Great, knowing it would provoke the king of England and Welsh rulers alike. Dafydd now embraced it. He thus asserted his authority over the whole of native Wales. The challenge to Henry was blatant. Dafydd also did something else. He laid his complaints before the pope. Innocent IV was remarkably sympathetic, perhaps angry at Henry's conduct over ecclesiastical elections. In a letter of 26 July 1244 he empowered the abbots of Aberconwy and Cumhyre to absolve Dafydd from his oath to observe the 1241 treaty if they found his complaints justified. Accordingly they summoned Henry to appear before them in January 1245. Innocent's letter was threatening in another way. It noted that Dafydd's parents had made him a papal ward. Was this coming close to accepting Dafydd's offer to become a vassal of the pope?[60]

Henry was naturally indignant at this papal intervention. In 1245 he persuaded Innocent to change his mind. Dafydd, the pope now said, had not

---

[57] Colvin, *History of the King's Works*, ii, 624–5, 644–5. In the crisis of 1244, Mold was returned to its lord, Roger of Mold.

[58] Paris, iv, 385.

[59] *RL*, ii, 38–9; *CACW*, 21–2.

[60] Paris, iv, 316, 323–4, 398–400; *AWR*, nos. 306–7; Dunstable, 168; Richter, 'David ap Llywelyn', 209–10.

been forced into the treaty and had never been made a ward of the pope. Indeed, he and his ancestors had been vassals of the king of England 'from time out of mind'.[61] It was one thing, however, to square the pope, another to deal with the situation on the ground. From the spring of 1244 there was war in much of Wales, with attacks on castles, ravaging of land, and slaughter of people. The justiciar of Chester, John Lestrange, declared he could not reach Dyserth without a large army as Dafydd was blocking his way. He also warned that Dafydd was about to launch an attack on Gruffudd ap Gwenwynwyn. All this was reported in June 1244 as Henry made his way to the north. His response was hardly very commanding. Earlier in the year he had at last set in train the rebuilding of the castle of Deganwy.[62] Now Henry told Lestrange that if Dyserth was attacked he would come in person or send help. For the rest he could not reply until he had met up with Simon de Montfort and other magnates.[63] Lestrange's predicament was shown in his accounts for 1244/5. He beat off several attacks on Oswestry, spent large sums munitioning the castles at Shrewsbury, Ellesmere and Dyserth, 'rescued' both Mold and Dyserth from Dafydd's sieges, and on four other occasions mustered forces to meet Dafydd's approach.[64]

Henry found all this disappointing and distasteful. He was proud of his achievements in 1241 but had no urgent wish for more. His officials were far more aggressive than he was himself. He had certainly no desire for another campaign in Wales. Matthew Paris, in describing Henry's return to Westminster, catches his mood exactly. Henry hoped that the royal officials and marcher barons on the ground, with some reinforcements, would contain the trouble. Then eventually Dafydd and his adherents would see sense and submit. Into 1245, Henry was still offering them safe conducts in the hope of negotiations. He could still call Dafydd his 'nephew' and Dafydd played along. He was, he wrote, ready to make peace and show 'all love and humility' towards 'his uncle'.[65] Henry also offered reassurance about the nature of English rule. It was never his intention to introduce new laws and customs into Wales.[66]

In these circumstances the preparations for launching an actual campaign were sluggish. Early in 1245, Henry at last announced that 'without further delay' he was planning one for the following summer. The justiciar of Ireland was to gather troops and munitions. But no date was given for any muster. In March 1245, John Lestrange complained that what once could have been done for £1,000 would now cost £10,000![67] This was

[61] *F*, 255.

[62] Colvin, *History of the King's Works*, ii, 624–5.

[63] *RL*, ii, 38–40 (*CACW*, 10, 21–2).

[64] *CLR 1245–51*, 98–9; *CheshirePR*, 75–80.

[65] *CPR 1232–47*, 428, 431, 447–9; *CR 1242–7*, 347–8; *AWR*, no. 308.

[66] *CPR 1232–47*, 430.

[67] *CR 1242–7*, 348–9; *CACW*, 22. The Bissets became much involved in raising troops and money from Ireland.

said in a letter to Henry, who was on a pilgrimage to East Anglia. The
military situation was indeed deteriorating. In February an English force
was ambushed near Margam and its leader, Herbert fitzMatthew, was
killed. Next month Dafydd took Mold. But Henry remained in no hurry.
Parliament met at Westminster on 4 June, the day of Pentecost. Only then
were the king's tenants-in-chief told of the coming campaign. But again
no date was fixed. They were just to be ready at a fortnight's notice.[68]

Henry had one special reason for delay. It was Westminster Abbey. The
great moment when work on the new church could begin was approaching
and he was determined to supervise the preparations. Quite apart from
the demolition of the old Abbey, he had to arrange the spiritually charged
and physically tricky removal of the Confessor's body to a temporary
shrine. Henry finally left Westminster on 5 July. Next day the dismantling
of the Confessor's church began.[69] The delay, in Henry's mind, had not
damaged the campaign. On the contrary, honouring the Confessor was
the best way to ensure its success. Once Henry realized he would not be
back for the Confessor's feast on 13 October, he made elaborate arrangements for its celebration in his absence. He also ordered twenty candles,
weighing four hundredweight, to burn around the shrine until his return.
An even more magnificent dragon standard was placed in the Abbey than
that ordered for the Scottish campaign the year before. It was to be wavy,
in black and yellow cendal, and larger than all the other banners at
Westminster. The dragon itself was to be red sprinkled with gold, with a
gold head and crystal and ruby eyes. All this was to completed 'as you wish
to enjoy our love and see us joyful'.[70]

Henry, with Eleanor in his company, journeyed first to Gloucester to
check on the situation in the south. There he ensured that the garrisons of
Cardigan and Carmarthen received their pay and ordered new work at
Gloucester castle, including glass windows for the chapel and chamber of
the queen.[71] Operations in Glamorgan were commanded by Richard de
Clare (knighted and invested with his earldoms at the Pentecost feast),
while those in the middle March, between Brecon and Shrewsbury, were
under the earl of Hereford.

Throughout this time, and throughout the campaign, Henry made great
efforts to raise money. He threatened Italian merchants with expulsion if
they did not make a gift of 6,000 marks, or 'at least' a loan of some proportions. He summoned Jews into his presence and threatened them with
imprisonment in Ireland if they did not pay their tallage. On security of his
gold and jewels he secured a loan of 2,000 marks from his brother Richard
of Cornwall. (This, so Matthew Paris thought, dispelled rumours that

---

[68] Paris, iv, 407–9; St Werburgh, 62; *CR 1242–7*, 357.
[69] Paris, *FH*, ii, 289; Rishanger, 429.
[70] *CR 1242–7*, 331.
[71] *CLR 1245–51*, 318; *CPR 1232–47*, 458.

Richard was lukewarm about the campaign.) Henry ordered the exchequer to send him large amounts of cash and also lists of its daily receipts. (On one occasion it was also to send a silver image of Edward the Confessor.) He commanded sheriffs to pay money from diverse sources direct into the wardrobe.[72] One delinquent sheriff was summoned to court so Henry 'with his own mouth' could pronounce judgement against him.[73] Henry's campaign certainly did not want for money.

For all the troubles elsewhere in Wales, the main threat from Dafydd was in the north. Indeed, in mid-July, Henry had to send an emergency force to raise the siege of Dyserth.[74] It was to Chester, therefore, that Henry summoned the great bulk of his tenants-in-chief. The response impressed the annalist of the local abbey of St Werburgh. He recorded Henry and Eleanor's arrival on 13 August with 'an abundant army' including the earls of Cornwall, Leicester, Winchester, Aumale and Oxford 'and almost all the nobles of the whole of England'. Later in the campaign, Henry was joined by the earl of Gloucester (having won his war in the south), the earl of Norfolk (back from the papal council at Lyon) and the justiciar of Ireland, Maurice fitzGerald. One calculation is that Henry's tenants-in-chief supplied a cavalry force roughly 660 strong made up of some 350 knights and roughly 300 sergeants. This was just as large as Edward I's force for the campaign of 1277. There were also 10,000 foot-soldiers, including the 3,000 from Ireland. On 26 August, Henry was able to declare he had 'sufficient' forces to 'oppress his enemies'.[75] The army of 1245 was the largest Henry ever mustered in Wales.[76]

The campaign had a clear strategic objective. The base was at Chester, where Eleanor established herself in the castle. The paintings in her chamber were renewed and a bridge was made to the orchard so that she and Henry could descend there 'without danger' to take exercise.[77] The army, meanwhile, advanced westwards to Deganwy, which it reached on 25 August. It remained encamped there for the next two months. The purpose was to build a great new castle. It would prevent Dafydd crossing the Conwy and advancing eastwards – no more threats to Dyserth and Mold, let alone Chester and Oswestry. The castle was also aggressive. Henry earlier in the year had spoken of the coming war as one of 'conquest'.[78] Pinioned by the castles at Deganwy and Dyserth, the three cantrefs between the Conwy and the Clywyd would now be his. He would thus have all four

[72] *CR 1242–7*, 314–15, 324, 332, 339; *CFR 1244–5*, nos. 10, 322–4. This included the money now coming in from the aid for the prospective marriage of the king's daughter Margaret to the son and heir of King Alexander II.

[73] *CR 1242–7*, 361.

[74] *CR 1242–7*, 456.

[75] *CR 1242–7*, 363.

[76] Walker, 'Anglo-Welsh wars', 507–10.

[77] *CR 1242–7*, 327–8; *CLR 1240–5*, 311.

[78] *CR 1242–7*, 348–9.

of Gwynedd's cantrefs between the Conwy and the Dee, just like his father had in 1211. The great army was needed to guard the camp from attack while the miners, masons, carpenters and labourers did their work.

Henry built his castle high up on the great rock of Deganwy from where he could gaze westwards over the Conwy estuary towards the mountains of Snowdonia and frowning cliffs of Penmaenmawr running sheer into the sea. The site had been fortified and fought since the Norman conquest. Henry's plan was to crown the two hillocks on the summit of the rock with stone keeps and then join them together with two lines of walls each with twin-towered gate houses.[79]

So for two months Henry lived surrounded by his army in a set of pavilions, one especially constructed for his chapel.[80] It was there on 13 October he had to celebrate the feast of Edward the Confessor. His absence from Westminster Abbey on this the greatest day of the year is the best testimony to his determination. And the army was sorely needed. Dafydd did not challenge Henry to any set-piece battle but his forces constantly harried the army and tried to cut off its supplies. In reply, Henry's men launched raids into Snowdonia and ravaged Anglesey, the main source of Gwynedd's corn. This last enterprise was the work of Maurice fitzGerald and his Irishmen, helped by the Bissets. The wardrobe during this time was paying out large sums for the work on Deganwy castle and for gifts and wages to knights and sergeants.[81] The danger was famine, despite all Henry's efforts to keep the army supplied.

A letter written in late September by someone at Deganwy gives a vivid description of the situation.[82] Beneath the castle 'an arm of the sea' flowed up and down, at full tide the width of a crossbow shot. Beyond it lay 'Snowden where the Welsh live'. The army was cold in its tents and had no winter clothing.[83] It was starving despite the ships coming in with victuals from Chester and Ireland. A halfpenny loaf was being sold for five pence. At one point there was just a solitary cask of wine in 'all the household of the king'. The army was also fearful, having to mount guard throughout the night against Welsh attacks. One skirmish, beginning with a struggle over a ship, full of wine, stuck in the mud at low tide, ended in disaster. English forces pursued the Welsh across the estuary and there (much to the disapproval of the letter writer) sacked the abbey of Aberconwy. On their return, loaded with plunder, they were cut off by the Welsh. The knightly leaders surrendered and initially were held captive, but then, in an act of revenge for the killing of a young Welsh noble, they were hanged, their decapitated and mutilated bodies being thrown into the estuary. Thus perished, the

[79] Colvin, *History of the King's Works*, ii, 624–6.
[80] *CLR 1240–5*, 312.
[81] Wild, *WA*, 55.
[82] Paris, iv, 481–4.
[83] Osney, 93–4.

letter continued, several household knights of Richard of Cornwall and also a Gascon crossbowman with whom Henry often liked to joke. At Deganwy itself Henry had granted him some land in return for making a wooden crossbow each year.[84] Henry must have watched this shocking disaster from his camp on the rock. He had with him two gilded helmets studded with gems.[85] There is no evidence he ever used them.

Henry finally left Deganwy on 28 October and by the end of November was back at Windsor. One view of the campaign was that he had lost many men, killed few of the Welsh and generally achieved little.[86] This was unfair. Henry left behind a castle already formidable and defensible. Over the following years he pressed on with the work, spending nearly £10,000, much the same as Edward I's expenditure on his castle at Rhuddlan. Henry had not brought Dafydd to terms, let alone expelled him from Snowdonia, but Deganwy, as Matthew Paris said, was 'a thorn in the eye of the Welsh'. A Welsh chronicler described the castle as 'the strongest in the kingdom'.[87] It obstructed advances eastwards towards England and, with Dyserth, held down the Four Cantrefs 'in obedience to royal rule'. Henry did not forget the dead. On the way home he ordered a special mass for them at Osney abbey. He also looked after the widow of his crossbowman. He had achieved his purpose. Paris has him returning home 'in all happiness and prosperity'.[88] Henry had also won the war in the south. From November 1245 he was negotiating with the rulers of Ystrad Tywi and Ceredigion. They submitted the following year without (save in one case) the need for any more military action.[89] Meanwhile, Glamorgan had been reduced to obedience by Richard de Clare, as his appearance at Deganwy showed.

While at Deganwy, Henry had ordered a special cope for presentation at the Confessor's shrine when he arrived at Westminster.[90] In the event he delayed his return until 10 December perhaps so the work of demolition of the Confessor's church could be completed. A 'joyful' Christmas followed, so Matthew Paris tells us, with many of the nobles who had borne the heat of the day in Wales. Alongside the queen, the earls of Cornwall, Gloucester, Leicester, Norfolk, Peter of Savoy and Peter of Geneva were all in attendance.[91] Perhaps it was on the following 5 January, the feast on the anniversary of the Confessor's death, that Henry laid the foundation stone of the new Abbey.

---

[84] *CChR 1226–57*, 287; *CR 1242–7*, 338, 390. The crossbowman was Raymond de Luka.

[85] *CLR 1245–51*, 30.

[86] *St Werburgh*, 64; Dunstable, 168.

[87] Colvin, *History of the King's Works*, ii, 626; *AC*, 101.

[88] Paris, iv, 486–8; *CLR 1245–51*, 8; *CR 1242–7*, 390, 489.

[89] *CPR 1232–47*, 465, 470, 474, 479.

[90] *CR 1242–7*, 344. The cope was to be partly made with orphreys found above the body of Edith, the Confessor's queen.

[91] Paris, iv, 503–4; *RCWL*, ii, 9. But see Kjaer, 'Matthew Paris and the royal Christmas', for more critical comment.

Around this time Henry received extraordinary news. Walter Marshal, earl of Pembroke, had been too ill to join the Deganwy campaign. He died on 24 November 1245. His heir was his younger brother Anselm. Just before Christmas, Anselm died as well. The five sons who had followed the great Marshal one after another – William, Richard, Gilbert, Walter and Anselm – had not produced a single legitimate child. The heirs now became the five daughters of the regent and their husbands and descendants. The division of the great inheritance between them might well have caused endless dispute. In fact, in the next couple of years, it went through comparatively smoothly, a tribute to Henry's fairness and his government's efficiency. Thus, amongst others, Roger Bigod, son of the eldest daughter, gained Chepstow, Carlow and the marshalship; Richard de Clare gained Usk and Kilkenny; and John de Munchesney gained Pembroke and Wexford.[92]

Another death soon followed, one opening up great vistas. It was the death on 25 February 1246 of Dafydd himself. He too left no children. The rump of Gwynedd west of Conwy fell into the hands of two sons of the hapless Gruffudd, Llywelyn and his elder brother Owain. The latter, on hearing of Dafydd's death, had scuttled from his semi-captivity in Shrewsbury. Surely now Henry could complete his conquest. He certainly thought about it. At his behest the friendly bishop of Bangor stated that under the 1241 treaty Dafydd had made Henry his heir if he had no children and had also agreed that all his lands would be forfeit if he broke the peace.[93] So Gwynedd was now doubly forfeit.

At this very time a great military action suggested the ease with which Henry might indeed take possession. Back in October 1245 he had placed Cardigan and Carmarthen under Nicholas de Molis, just back from his stint as seneschal of Gascony and his victory over the king of Navarre. In the summer of 1246, Molis and the knight Robert Walerand (at the start of a long career) attacked Maelgwn ap Maelgwn, the one Welsh ruler who had not submitted to Henry, and drove him from his lands in northern Ceredigion.[94] They then crossed the Dyfi and forced the ruler of Meirionydd to agree he would forfeit everything if he broke faith with the king. The campaign did not stop there. Molis marched on right through

[92] For Bigod's investiture as Marshal, see Paris, iv, 548; *CR 1242–7*, 454–5. For the Marshal descendants see Genealogical Table no. 3. The complex details of the partition are set out in *CPR 1364–7*, 263–75. Roger de Mortimer and the other descendants of the fourth sister, Eva de Briouze, argued unavailingly that the Marshalship should be partitioned: *CPR 1364–7*, 269.

[93] *LW*, 21–2.

[94] By 1242, Walerand had inherited an ancestral manor at Whaddon, south of Salisbury. He belonged to a junior branch of the family of the Domesday baron Waleran the Huntsman, whose descendants were keepers of the New Forest. Walerand had started out as a knight of Henry III's steward William de Cantilupe II. He was now in charge of the Marshal lordships in South Wales: *BF*, ii, 716, 747; *CPR 1232–47*, 370; Sanders, *English Baronies*, 96–7. For his career, see Harding, 'Robert Walerand'.

Gwynedd until he reached Deganwy, making Llywelyn, Owain and Maelgwn flee to the hills. His feat showed how the native rulers were back on Henry's side, for the army included, as well as Gruffudd ap Gwenwynwyn, Maredudd ap Rhys (of Ystrad Tywi) and Maelgwn's rival in Ceredigion, Maredudd ap Owain.[95]

Was Molis's great march then co-ordinated with Henry's own campaign in the north? No it was not. Back in April, Henry had made plans for a campaign but he soon abandoned them. During 1246 the closest he got to Wales was Woodstock![96] As early as that May he was contemplating a settlement with Llywelyn and Owain. He did not change his mind even after Molis's march.[97] The terms were demanding but the brothers were desperate for a breathing space in which to establish themselves in Gwynedd. So finally, in April 1247, they came to Woodstock and made peace.[98] The Treaty of Woodstock, like that of 1241, affirmed that the homages of all the nobles of Wales belonged to the king; so much for Dafydd's pretensions to be prince of Wales. The whole of the Four Cantrefs between the Conwy and the Dee were now surrendered in perpetuity to the king of England, not just Englefield. While, moreover, Llywelyn and Owain retained Gwynedd west of Conwy, they now held it in return for specified military service. They were to contribute 1,000 foot-soldiers and 24 well-armed knights to any campaign in Wales and the march. In addition, 500 foot-soldiers were to be forthcoming for any campaign in England, although here at the king's pay. The penalty for any breach of the treaty was forfeiture.

Henry, therefore, had gained much yet had passed up the chance of conquering Gwynedd, although he had the justification, the opportunity and the resources. Indeed, he now abandoned any idea of Gwynedd simply falling into his hands through lack of heirs. Whereas the treaty of 1241 had stated explicitly this would happen if Dafydd had no heirs by his wife (as seemed likely), in 1247 there was no equivalent provision. Gwynedd (or what was left of it) was simply to be held by Owain and Llywelyn and their heirs.[99]

Why then the passivity? It was partly because Henry had no aptitude or interest in the business of war. To have conquered Gwynedd west of Conwy, defended as it was by its great mountain ranges, would have been a major military undertaking. Henry had no wish to make it. The last thing he wanted was to spend another summer under canvas, short of

---

[95] *Cronica de Wallia*, 39–40; *Brut*, 240–1; *LW*, 14–15.

[96] For Henry's itinerary in 1246, see above, 354–5.

[97] *CPR 1232–47*, 480.

[98] *AWR*, no. 312.

[99] The jurisdictional provisions of the treaty could also have been more provocative. If a Welshman or anyone else on the side of the king wished to bring a case against Owain and Llywelyn, the parties were to come on the king's orders to a place in the march or in Wales where the case would be decided according to the laws and customs of Wales. In 1241, by contrast, cases involving Gruffudd's portion were to be heard in Henry's court, according to whatever law he decided: *AWR*, 471, cap. ii.

food and fearful of attack, while castles were built at Bangor and on Anglesey. There was, however, more to it than that. 'Blessed are the peace-makers for they shall be called the sons of God,' Christ had preached in his sermon on the mount. Henry believed that. He agreed the Treaty of Woodstock 'moved by piety'. Its aim was 'concord and perpetual peace'.

The treaty also owed something to Henry's general attitude to Wales and the Welsh. He had no desire to eliminate the native rulers. He wanted them as his loyal men, owing him homage and service. Ties of kinship were a factor here. Dafydd had been Henry's nephew. Both the rulers of Powys, Gruffudd ap Gwenwynwyn and Madog ap Gruffudd, were married to English noblewomen. Henry also understood the advice given him in 1244 by the Marshal officials in Pembroke, namely that the Welsh were best contained by men of their own tongue.[100] They accordingly urged Henry to grant to Maredudd ap Owain part of the land of Maelgwn ap Maelgwn (the latter the first object of Molis's attack) rather than try and keep it for himself. It was advice Henry followed, just as he also rehabilitated all the other rulers of the south who had rebelled against him. There was even a place for Maelgwn ap Maelgwn. After his submis-sion in November 1247, he was allowed to keep two commotes in admit-tedly what was now called 'the county of Cardigan'.[101]

Considerations of piety and prudence explain then the lenient features of the Treaty of Woodstock. For Henry, it was a great achievement. It confirmed his conquest of the Four Cantrefs, defined for the first time the service owed by the rulers of Gwynedd, repeated that all the homages of the Welsh rulers belonged to the king, and, in its moderation, held out hope of 'a perpetual peace'. There it was unsuccessful but still it was ten years before Henry had to campaign again in Wales.

THE WINCHESTER ELECTION

In the two years before his departure for Gascony in 1242, Henry had been notably successful in the field of episcopal appointments. He had promoted Boniface of Savoy to Canterbury and Peter de Aigueblanche to Hereford. The long dispute at Durham had been concluded by the election of his confessor, Nicholas of Farnham. Henry had wanted Aigueblanche to be translated to London when a vacancy occurred there in 1241, but he was soon reconciled to the election of the dean of York and head of the Basset family of High Wycombe, Fulk Basset.[102] The pattern in the years immediately after

---

[100] *RL*, i, 426–7 (*CACW*, 48).

[101] *CPR 1232–47*, 486, 488, 493.

[102] For Fulk, see Hoskins, *EEA London*, xli–li. Basset and Boniface did not take up office until 1244, the former because he could not be confirmed on account of the Canterbury vacancy, the latter because he could not be confirmed due to the papal vacancy. Fulk had succeeded his brother Gilbert after the death of both Gilbert and his infant son in 1241.

Henry's return from Gascony in 1243 was very different. He suffered a humiliating defeat in the appointment closest to his heart, that to the bishopric of Winchester, and then was equally unsuccessful in struggles over the appointments to Chichester and Coventry–Lichfield. These episodes did much to damage his reputation with the church and exacerbate the feeling that he was acting in breach of Magna Carta.[103] There is here a paradox which comes up again and again during Henry's personal rule. How was it that so Christian a king, and one bound by his coronation oath to protect the church, was prepared to act in ways so bitterly criticized by the churchmen? The paradox is easily resolvable. Henry's personal piety in no way detracted from his determination to defend the rights of the crown. He saw that as a sacred duty likewise enjoined by his coronation oath. Henry felt he had every right to influence the election of bishops so as to ensure those appointed would be of use both to himself and the realm.[104] He equally felt he had the right to take the revenues when bishoprics were vacant. That some were vacant for a long time was not because he prevented elections taking place from a desire to make money in the fashion of his predecessors. Henry could feel he was guiltless on that score. It was because he objected to those elected. Henry's conscience was also clear when it came to other complaints made by churchmen in long schedules of grievances drawn up between the 1230s and 1260s. Many of these turned on the jurisdictional conflicts between royal and ecclesiastical courts, issues over which Henry's judges and indeed his lay magnates urged him to stand firm.[105]

The Winchester dispute had a long history. On the death of Peter des Roches back in 1238, Henry had tried to persuade the Winchester monks to choose the bishop-elect of Valence. Instead they had gone for Henry's chancellor, the bishop of Chichester, Ralph de Neville. Henry's response was to sack Neville as keeper of the seal and appeal to the pope. In February 1239, Pope Gregory ordered the Winchester monks to hold a fresh election. With the death of the bishop-elect of Valence later in the year, Henry now made the bishop-elect's younger brother Boniface his candidate. He was building up his party within the convent. When the

[103] In tracing the story of the Winchester and Chichester elections I have been helped by an unpublished paper by Katherine Harvey on the subject. Her book, *Episcopal Appointments in England 1214–1344*, has passages on all the appointments mentioned in this section.

[104] For a strident statement to that effect, see below, 650.

[105] For such schedules, see *C&S*, i, 280–4, 537–48; Hoskin, 'The church and the king', 198; Creamer, 'St Edmund of Abingdon and Henry III', 137–8. For the claims of ecclesiastical institutions to the chattels of their men convicted of crimes, see below, 461. Other complaints covered writs of prohibition stopping cases proceeding in ecclesiastical courts; the claims of royal officials that they could not be excommunicated while in the king's service; and (an issue going back to the Becket dispute) the way clerks accused of crimes were not handed over at once to their bishops but were brought before the justices in eyre. For Henry's defence see Hoskin, 'The church and the king', 208–10. Part of the background is the rapid development of church courts: Hoskin, 'The church and the king', 203–4.

prior died in 1239 he replaced him with the third prior, a foreigner, Andrew the Breton, who attempted a violent purge of the king's opponents within the convent.[106] It did not work. When the election eventually took place in June 1240, three of the electoral body voted for Boniface (including the prior) and four for William of Raleigh, former head of the court *coram rege* and, since 1239, bishop of Norwich.[107]

The Winchester monks were evidently reluctant to have a foreigner and total stranger as bishop and hoped to placate the king by electing instead one of his former ministers. They had tried the same trick in 1238. It had failed then and it failed again.[108] Henry was enraged. What could Raleigh, from a minor gentry family in the West Country, give to the king and kingdom compared to the queen's uncle from one of the most famous ruling houses in Europe? The whole thing was inconceivable. When Raleigh refused to stand down, Henry accused him of being motivated by 'excessive ambition' and refused to see him.[109] Seizing on supposed irregularities in the electoral process, Henry appealed again to the pope.

Raleigh has left no explanation as to why he decided to fight it out. It seems hard to reconcile the two sides of his career, the first as a judge working closely with the king, the second as a bishop, defying the king's wishes. But of course, on a much grander and cataclysmic scale, Thomas Becket had made the same transition. Raleigh had resigned from the king's service on his election to Norwich. He proved a conscientious bishop, and both at Norwich and Winchester issued lengthy diocesan statutes full of injunctions and reforms.[110] The same passion and determination he had put into defending the laws of England against Robert Grosseteste's attempts to bend them to church law he now put into defending the justice of his election to Winchester against what he saw as the frivolous objections of the king.

The papal interregnum between the death of Gregory IX in August 1241 and the elevation of Innocent IV in June 1243 necessarily put the dispute on hold. Raleigh remained as bishop of Norwich and the Winchester revenues continued with the king. By the time of Innocent's accession, Boniface had been elected at Canterbury, but that did nothing to alter Henry's hostility to Raleigh. He urged the new pope both to confirm Boniface's election and order a new one at Winchester. On 17 September 1243, Innocent did the first but not the second. Instead, he confirmed Raleigh's election alongside that of Boniface.[111] Doubtless he

---

[106] Paris, iv, 159; *CPReg*, 200.

[107] *Reg. Innocent IV*, i, 23 (*CPReg*, 199); *RG*, i, 1206–7 (*CPR 1232–47*, 400).

[108] Paris believed that the monks had thought of electing Raleigh in 1238 but had been put off by the hostility of the king: Paris, iii, 493–5.

[109] Paris, iv, 159; *RG*, i, 1206–7 (*CPR 1232–47*, 400); *CPR 1232–47*, 410–11, 438.

[110] *C&S*, i, 403–16.

[111] *CPReg*, 199–200.

felt that the Winchester vacancy had lasted quite long enough and that Raleigh would make a good bishop.

Raleigh heard the news around 11 November 1243. He immediately resigned the see of Norwich and summoned the churchmen of the Winchester diocese to Westminster to swear obedience to him as their new bishop. At the same time he begged Henry to assent to his appointment and receive his oath of fealty. Henry now made a crucial decision. He would continue his resistance. He hated Raleigh. He thought the whole process of the papal confirmation was flawed. He considered Raleigh's assumption of episcopal authority before receiving his consent an affront to the rights and dignity of the crown.[112] He was also buoyed up by the forthcoming marriage between his brother Richard of Cornwall and Sanchia of Provence. He thus refused his assent and prepared an appeal to the pope. Here he was helped by another clever Savoyard in his service, the distinguished canonist Henry of Susa.[113] The main grounds were that the pope had been deceived. He had been led to believe that Raleigh was the king's friend, whereas in fact he was his greatest enemy.

Raleigh was in no way deterred by the king's resistance. He too raised the stakes. Declaring he dared not disobey the pope, he decided to go to Winchester and assume his episcopal duties. In a bid to stop him, Henry of Susa offered an arbitration on the merits of Henry's appeal. If it was deemed reasonable then Raleigh would abstain from entering his diocese until the pope delivered his verdict. When Raleigh heard this suggestion, the Waverley annalist says he laughed, doubtless with scorn. Next day he set off for Winchester.[114] Henry, by word of mouth, issued orders to keep him out of the city. The result was that on 24 December 1243, as Henry prepared to celebrate Christmas at Wallingford with Richard and Sanchia, Raleigh walked barefoot around the walls of Winchester and found all the gates shut and barred against him. Five days later, the day after the feast of Becket's martyrdom, Raleigh placed Winchester under an interdict and excommunicated the monks and the town officials.

Henry, through Henry of Susa, made one last effort to defuse the situation. Early in January 1244, having already secured approval from Oxford, he offered to submit the merits of the appeal to the masters teaching law at the university of Paris. If they supported the king, Raleigh was to leave the diocese; if they supported Raleigh, Henry in effect promised to accept him. Raleigh swept this away too, in the process getting in some clever and hurtful digs at the king. It was 'neither congruous to the utility of the realm nor fitting for the king's majesty' to go outside the kingdom for such an opinion, implying as it did the king distrusted his own men. What a contrast this was to the past when the princes of the world

---

[112] Raleigh was assuming spiritual authority. The temporalities remained with the king.
[113] See Powicke, *King Henry III*, i, 272.
[114] Waverley, 331.

had brought their disputes to the king's predecessors for settlement. The king's rule should be distinguished not just by arms but by laws.[115]

By the time Raleigh received the king's proposal (in early January 1244) he had already withdrawn from the diocese and taken shelter in Southwark. In February 1244 he retired to France to await the papal judgement on Henry's appeal. That came at the end of the month. Innocent IV, not surprisingly expressed astonishment at Henry's conduct, dismissed his claims and complaints, and ordered him to restore Raleigh to his castles and manors.[116]

Henry had no alternative but to back down. Had he continued to resist, as King John did over Langton, he would have been excommunicated by the pope. A horrific prospect for Henry, if not for his father. So Henry began negotiations with Raleigh over the precise terms of a settlement and was softened by his conciliatory replies. Eventually, on 21 July, Raleigh was given permission to return to England. In September 1244, during a parliament at Windsor, he was restored to his temporalities and given at least some compensation for what had been illegitimately taken away. Henry also accepted the deposition of the prior (the successor to Andrew the Breton) and the punishment of the mayor of Winchester who had kept Raleigh out of the city.[117]

Henry remained unhappy with Raleigh. He gave him no mitre and did not attend his installation at Winchester on 20 November (the day of St Edmund).[118] But Henry rarely harboured grudges for long. He celebrated the Christmas of 1246 at Winchester, his first there since 1239, and, accepting Raleigh's invitation to dinner, renewed their old friendship before all present.[119] Next year Raleigh, quite like the old days, was back at court authorizing a writ saying the king did not wish any free man to be disseized of his land without judgement.[120]

THE CHICHESTER ELECTION

When Ralph de Neville died in February 1244, Henry thought he had the ideal replacement, none other than Robert Passelewe. Passelewe's remarkable career had seen many ups and downs: a royal clerk under King John, a principal servant of Falkes de Bréauté, envoy of the 1223 dissidents at Rome and author of Falkes's tendentious complaint to the pope, he had then been unemployed until the regime of Peter des Roches brought him

[115] *CPR 1232–47*, 439–41.

[116] Paris, iv, 347–9.

[117] Paris, iv, 390–1; Waverley, 332; Dunstable, 164–5; *CPR 1232–47*, 433, 435–6; *CR 1242–7*, 227; *CFR 1243–4*, nos. 441–2.

[118] Vincent, 'Politics of church and state', 167.

[119] Paris, iv, 590.

[120] *CR 1247–51*, 100; and see 106, 146, 249.

back as acting head of the exchequer. Another period of disgrace followed until, from 1236, Passelewe began to climb his way back into the king's favour and service.[121] On Henry's return from Gascony in 1243, he established himself at court, where he authorized royal letters and appeared in the select circle of magnates and ministers attesting royal charters. In March 1244 he was appointed by the king (here making use of his rights during the vacancy) to a canonry at Chichester and the associated archdeaconry of Lewes.[122] Doubtless Henry made clear to the other canons that Passelewe would be ideal as their new bishop. They agreed easily enough. As Matthew Paris later acknowledged, they recognized that Passelewe was 'prudent and circumspect' and would ensure the favour of the king. They had seen the advantages of that in the long years of Neville's pomp and the disadvantages in recent events at Winchester. Passelewe's appointment, they hoped, would please both God and king.[123] He was certainly very capable of running a diocese in efficient fashion, all the more so as he was absolved by the king from all ties with the court, so was not expected to continue as a full-time minister. His evil conduct as a forest judge (which so appalled Grosseteste) was in the future, a point obscured by Matthew Paris's account of the election. Later the pope himself acknowledged that Passelewe was perfectly appointable as a bishop.[124]

On 19 April 1244, while at Windsor, Henry gave his consent to Passelewe's election and asked Boniface of Savoy, archbishop-elect of Canterbury, 'to do his part therein'.[125] That meant confirm the election whereupon Passelewe would swear fealty to Henry and receive the temporalities of the see. Boniface had just reached England, receiving from an overjoyed Henry wine for his cellars and a mitre, covered with jewels, costing an amazing £200.[126] Boniface, however, was under pressure and wished to show he was no mere stooge of the king. He acknowledged that he owed everything to Henry, and promised 'all the time of his life' to avoid displeasing him. But he added the rider 'as according to God we are able'. On the urgings of Grosseteste, he had already written to Henry begging him to accept William of Raleigh.[127] Now, early in June 1244, instead of simply confirming the Chichester election, he allowed Grosseteste to put Passelewe through an oral examination in theology. It was severe, one of Grosseteste's principles being that a bishop should be able 'to feed the Lord's flock in scripture's pasture with justice and judgement, knowledge

---

[121] Passelewe became sheriff of Hampshire just before Henry's departure for Poitou in 1242. He had attested royal charters that March and April.

[122] *CPR 1232–47*, 421.

[123] Paris, iv, 401–2. These were Paris's second thoughts on the matter.

[124] *CPR 1232–47*, 423; Paris, iv, 401–2; *Letters of Grosseteste*, 367–8, 372–4; *CPReg*, 215.

[125] *CPR 1232–47*, 423.

[126] *CLR 1240–5*, 212, 277.

[127] *RL*, ii, 36; *Letters of Grosseteste*, no. 86; Paris, iv, 297–8.

and doctrine'.[128] Henry heard the result of the examination on 11 June while at St Albans. Passelewe had failed. Indeed, Boniface had not only quashed the election, but had also, on the advice of the bishops, appointed instead Master Richard of Wich. Wich had been the chancellor of Archbishop Edmund and thus had some administrative experience. But he was chiefly famous as a scholar, having been a regent master in canon law at Oxford. The contrast between him and Passelewe could not have been more marked.[129]

Henry was shocked by Boniface's disloyalty. He also felt, as Matthew Paris said, that 'enormous' damage had been done to the rights of the crown for he had not been consulted at all over Wich's elevation. Paris, himself, for all his prejudice against Passelewe, thought his election had been 'indecently' quashed.[130] Boniface's very right to appoint Wich was questionable. His action was as unexpected as it was unprecedented.[131]

Henry, therefore, appealed to the pope. To no avail. At Lyon, on 5 March 1245 (the first Sunday in Lent), Pope Innocent consecrated Wich, thus once again setting at nought the king's claim to give consent to episcopal appointments. As he had done over Raleigh, Henry decided to resist. He refused to restore Wich, 'who behaves as bishop', to the temporalities of the see, and shut him out from Chichester. At one point its gates were to be guarded day and night.[132] Wich did what he could to administer the diocese and also spent time following the court, hoping in vain to gain access to the king. A shy and gentle man, when threatened by the king's marshal at Windsor he quietly left the castle and waited 'outside in the open air with the common people'. Meanwhile, according to Wich's biographer, the friar Ralph Bocking, the episcopal estates were pillaged by the king's custodians.[133]

At Lyon in March 1245, Pope Innocent had also appointed Master Roger de Wesham, dean of Lincoln, as the new bishop of Coventry and Lichfield after the election had produced two rival candidates. Once again Henry was affronted. Direct papal appointments at this time were rare. Henry would probably have accepted this one, had Innocent chosen one of his own candidates.[134] As it was, the king had once again not been consulted at all. Matthew Paris suspected that Grosseteste, present at Lyon,

---

[128] *Letters of Grosseteste*, 209.

[129] Paris, iv, 358–9, 401–2; *Saint Richard of Chichester*, 95–6, 172–3. The place 'Wich' is now Droitwich.

[130] Paris, iv, 401–2, 412–13.

[131] Harvey, *Episcopal Appointments*, 102–5. The pope confirmed Wich's appointment, drawing on his own authority (indeed the plenitude of papal power), and not because Boniface's provision had been 'rightly' done: *F*, 261.

[132] *CR 1242–7*, 306, 352.

[133] *F*, 261; Waverley, 335; *CR 1242–7*, 306, 352; *Saint Richard of Chichester*, 95–101, 172–7.

[134] Henry had in fact empowered Master Laurence de St Martin to give consent to appointments made by Pope Innocent at Lyon: *DI*, 357; Paris, iv, 412.

was behind the appointment. Wesham was just the kind of scholar-bishop he wanted, besides being a kindly and holy man. Once again Henry decided to resist. It was not until March 1246 that he restored Wesham to the temporalities of his see, 'notwithstanding his preferment by the pope being to the prejudice of the king's dignity'.[135] Four months later, on 20 July 1246, Henry at last climbed down over Wich and restored his temporalities as well. This time he gave both bishops mitres but their joint cost was a meagre 12 marks![136] Henry did make some effort to compensate Wich for the two years of revenue lost since his appointment in June 1244. But Wich on his death in 1253 still enjoined his executors to obtain the arrears or he would seek payment 'in the court of the most High'.[137]

Henry's conduct of ecclesiastical appointments blackened his reputation and, in Grosseteste's view, endangered his soul.[138] Yet some of the worst excesses were committed by Henry's agents without his consent. When Henry heard, over Christmas at Wallingford in 1243, that an armed force had seized Raleigh's goods and victuals at Winchester, he ordered them to be returned. As the writ went on to explain, the king 'does not wish there to be any cruelty'. Rather his agents were to pursue 'a middle way' so as to be 'chargeable neither with harshness nor negligence'.[139] Earlier Henry had wanted prior Andrew to treat the recalcitrant cathedral monks 'according to God and justice, no hatred or enmity entering into it'.[140] The same point applied to Henry's exploitation of the vacancies. He certainly kept a close eye on the revenues and gave some of his orders to the keepers by word of mouth. He made numerous gifts of oaks from episcopal woods. Yet over Winchester, Chichester and Coventry–Lichfield he also issued orders for the manors to be kept in a good condition. Even Matthew Paris admitted that the ruthless conduct of the keepers went beyond Henry's orders.[141]

Given the eventual outcomes, always surely likely, it could be argued that Henry was ill-advised to continue the struggles once Pope Innocent had spoken. As it was, his right both to assent to episcopal appointments and to receive an oath of fealty before bishops entered their temporalities and spiritualities was called into question by the pope. Could Raleigh himself persuade the pope to maintain the king's privileges in these areas?

---

[135] Paris, iv, 424–6, 552; *CPR 1232–47*, 476; *CR 1242–7*, 385; *CLR 1240–5*, 324. Henry also accepted the papal appointment of the bishop of Elphin in Ireland, although it was 'derogatory to the royal liberty because [it had been] made without the king's assent': *CPR 1232–47*, 460.

[136] *CLR 1245–51*, 37.

[137] *CLR 1245–51*, 150, 326; *CLR 1251–60*, 126; *CLR 1267–72*, no. 1386; *Saint Richard of Chichester*, 69, 70 n. 20.

[138] *Letters of Grosseteste*, 210; Paris, iv, 296–7.

[139] *CPR 1232–47*, 413, 438.

[140] *CR 1237–42*, 274.

[141] *CLR 1226–40*, 488; *CLR 1240–5*, 7; Paris, iv, 264; Howell, *Regalian Right*, 105, 144–6.

That was what Henry anxiously asked him to do as a condition for a final settlement.[142] For Henry, there were nonetheless compensations. He had not kept the sees vacant simply to take the revenues but the revenues had been substantial. The gross receipts from Winchester between 1238 and 1244 were nearly £23,000, not far short of the crown's ordinary annual revenue.[143] Henry was also absolutely right to show electoral bodies, bishops and popes that he would stand up for the rights of the crown. It had some effect. When the Winchester monks next had to elect someone they fell in easily enough with Henry's wishes and chose his half-brother Aymer de Lusignan.

THE ROLE OF THE QUEEN

In these fraught disputes over episcopal appointments the men involved ascribed considerable influence to Queen Eleanor. 'Urge her by letters and messengers to persuade the king to accept William of Raleigh', was Grossesteste's plea to archbishop-elect Boniface. Grosseteste also appealed to Eleanor directly. 'Like the sun rising in the world in God's heavens, so the beauty of a good wife is the adornment of her house,' he wrote, quoting the Book of Wisdom. Eleanor's 'house', Grosseteste explained, 'consists in a special sense of the church and kingdom of England'. She should produce effects like the rising sun and imitate Queen Esther, who saved her people from the death sentence pronounced by the king. What Henry does 'in response to your recommendation, you will be doing through and in him'.[144] The impact of this empowering letter on the twenty-year-old queen can be imagined. She may well have acted as enjoined. She was very close to her uncle Thomas of Savoy. It was at Thomas's 'instance' that Henry issued the letter allowing Raleigh to return to England.[145]

Eleanor was certainly involved in the Chichester embroglio. When Boniface learnt that his conduct had aroused her wrath, he sent messengers to her and then appeared in person. Eleanor's response was firm. Unless Boniface bent to the king's will, she would not remit her 'anger and indignation'. All this Eleanor narrated in a letter to Henry. If Henry had suspected she was on Boniface's side, she could not have done more to disabuse him. Yet under cover of loyalty she worked to bring the quarrel to an end. It was her intercession, so Matthew Paris believed, that finally reconciled Henry to Richard of Wich. Wich was to leave Eleanor a ring in his will.[146]

---

[142] Paris, iv, 347–51. The assent came after the election or postulation, the oath after the confirmation.

[143] Howell, *Regalian Right*, 229; see Vincent, 'Politics of church and state', 167 n. 65.

[144] *Letters of Grosseteste*, nos. 86, 103.

[145] *CPR 1232–47*, 433.

[146] *RL*, ii, 42–3; Paris, iv, 509–10; *Saint Richard of Chichester*, 68; Howell, *Eleanor of Provence*, 41–2.

THE DEMANDS OF THE POPE

Between 1244 and 1247, Henry and his kingdom were oppressed as never before by the demands of the pope. Henry was torn and tormented by how to react. His reverence for the papacy ran deep, and he could appreciate its terrible problems. Yet he also wished to protect the rights of the crown and somehow respond to the fury that papal policies provoked in England. At times Henry seemed to stand shoulder to shoulder with his subjects in equal opposition; at times he seemed to stand down and leave the rights of the kingdom to be defended by the kingdom itself, a dangerous precedent. This was a perplexing and uncomfortable passage in Henry's life.

The overarching factor in all this was the great quarrel between the pope and the emperor. On Gregory IX's death in 1241, Frederick II had hoped for a reconciliation with his successor. Henry III and Louis IX hoped for it too. Instead, as soon as he was elected in June 1243, Pope Innocent IV renewed Frederick's excommunication and broadcast his crimes throughout Catholic Europe: Frederick's capture of the cardinals back in 1241 meant he was guilty of sacrilege;[147] the way he had ignored the papal sentence of excommunication, and employed Saracens at court (even to guard his wives), tainted him with heresy; and above all he was refusing to return the duchy of Benevento and other papal states he had seized in Tuscany and Lombardy. As a result, in the summer of 1244, Pope Innocent fled from Rome to Genoa. By the end of the year he had established himself at Lyon, that great city, subject to neither the emperor nor the king of France, at the confluence of the rivers Rhone and Saone.

Not surprisingly, Innocent was determined that the English church should help in this life-and-death struggle for papal independence. Around Easter 1244 his chamber clerk Master Martin arrived in England. He was instructed to obtain the arrears of the 1,000 marks annual tribute due to the pope as England's overlord and left unpaid since Gregory IX's death. He also had powers both to gather in the arrears of the subsidy imposed by Gregory in 1240 and seek a new one worth some 10,000 marks. Equally provocative, Martin was entitled to exploit the pope's right of 'provision', his right that is to appoint to ecclesiastical positions, which meant in practice appoint largely absentee Italian clerks to cathedral prebends and the other livings otherwise in the gift of religious houses, bishops, cathedral chapters and sometimes laymen. As Innocent explained apologetically, he had no other way of providing for faithful servants working so hard for the church in this time of trial.[148]

---

[147] See above, 247.
[148] *F*, 266.

Demands like those brought by Master Martin had long been unpopular. The properties of Italians provided to English livings had been attacked in 1232. The 1240 subsidy had been criticized in detailed schedules of complaint.[149] But now, Master Martin's zeal and range of powers (they included the right to exact money from monasteries for his own support) made the protests louder than ever before. Although the burden fell chiefly on the church, the laity were equally critical. It had been the Yorkshire knight Robert of Thwing who had led the protests in 1232.[150] The complaints now drawn up by barons and knights largely overlapped with those of churchmen. A total of 60,000 marks, so they said, were being taken each year out of England by Italians, more than the annual revenue of the king, thus leaving the kingdom vulnerable to its enemies. The church was being denuded of the money it would otherwise have used to relieve poverty and provide hospitality. When the ancestors of the barons of 1244 had endowed monasteries with lands and churches, they had never expected them to be preyed upon in this way by the pope. Italians provided to English livings, the complaint continued, were either absentees or, if present, did not know the language and were useless for looking after the spiritual welfare of their flock.[151]

In the last resort the pope could have simply commanded the payment of subsidies by the English church, but he preferred to secure its consent, if not to their principle then to their methods of collection. Indeed, without an element of co-operation the taxes could hardly have been collected. To secure that co-operation Master Martin and his successors convoked a series of clerical assemblies of various compositions. At the same time the king himself summoned parliaments both to answer his own appeals for taxation and discuss the demands of the pope. As a result, papal exactions were debated in no fewer than seven parliaments between 1244 and 1247.[152]

Henry's letters in these years spoke again and again of the protests by 'the magnates of England', lay and ecclesiastical, against the 'innumerable and immoderate oppressions' of the pope. Their 'clamour', he said, was 'unprecedented'. Papal provisions in particular were 'odious' in England.[153]

---

[149] C&S, i, 287–92.

[150] Vincent, Peter des Roches, 304–6.

[151] C&S, i, 392–5; Paris, iv, 313, 371–2; CLR 1240–5, 275, 277.

[152] Maddicott, Origins of the English Parliament, 460–4. I reach seven by including the parliaments of November 1244 and February 1245. The story of papal demands and resistance to them is told in wonderful detail by Lunt, Financial Relations, 147–50, 206–25, 250–5, 541–2. Many of the primary sources for the complaints have been brought together with a preliminary commentary in C&S, i, 388–403. I have been helped by Nicholas Vincent's unpublished article, 'Henry III, Frederick II and the council of Lyon', which prints hitherto unknown material preserved in the monastic cartularies of Glastonbury and Malton (Yorkshire).

[153] CR 1242–7, 259, 355, 357, 477; Paris, iv, 535–6.

Henry was also under pressure from his own clerks, who found themselves deprived of livings by such provisions. Yet, as Henry explained to Grosseteste in a private conversation, he was determined to 'show and practice obedience, loyalty and devotion to the lord pope as our spiritual father and to the Holy Roman church as our mother . . . both in good times and bad'. Indeed, the day he did not, he wished his eyes to be plucked out and head cut off. Quite apart from the reasons he shared with all Christian princes, Henry explained, he could never forget the way Guala, as papal legate, had saved him and his throne at the start of his reign.[154] The problem was compounded by what to think about the emperor. The latter's envoy, Master Walter de Ocra, came to England in 1244 and warned of reprisals if money was sent to the pope. He also harped on his master's desire to return to the bosom of the church, so why give money if the dispute was soon to be settled? Yet Henry had also to listen to Grosseteste explaining (in a letter) how necessary it was to give help to a pope 'driven into exile, robbed of his patrimony, deprived of the means of subsistence and everywhere oppressed by persecutions and tribulations'.[155] Henry hoped profoundly that pope and emperor could be reconciled, but he recognized that could never happen while Frederick continued to occupy papal states in Italy. His proctor at the papal court, Master Laurence de St Martin, wrote an amazingly frank letter to Frederick on the subject.[156]

In this situation, Henry tried to sail a middle course. On the one hand, he made great efforts to pay the arrears of the papal tribute and by January 1245 he was more than up to date.[157] On the other hand, during his expedition to the north of England in August 1244, he addressed an astringent letter to Master Martin on the subject of provisions.[158] Martin's 'stony heart' had remained deaf to Henry's pleas. He had created 'subversion in our kingdom' and now 'our magnates' (doubtless those in Henry's army) 'complain about our patience'. Henry was beginning to see another point. The more money the church gave to the pope, the less there would be for him. He allowed Master Martin at clerical assemblies to demand the 10,000 marks required by the pope but, thinking of his own needs, refused to give him any overt support. Partly as a result Martin made no progress in securing the tax.[159] In March 1245, Henry went further and ordered a search at the ports for papal letters being brought into the country. If any were found they were to be sent to him. In May he

[154] *Letters of Robert Grosseteste*, no. 117.

[155] *Letters of Robert Grosseteste*, no. 119.

[156] Longleat House, Marquess of Bath MS. Muniments no. 10590 (Glastonbury Cartulary), fo. 4v.

[157] *CLR 1240–5*, 242, 264, 269, 285; *CR 1242–7*, 197; Lunt, *Financial Relations*, 147–8.

[158] *CR 1242–7*, 259; Powicke, *King Henry III*, i, 354.

[159] Paris, iv, 368–9; Lunt, *Financial Relations*, 207–8, although Paris's account, here cited, of the February 1245 assembly (*C&S*, i, 388–91) is untrustworthy; Dunstable, 166–8.

commissioned an inquiry into the revenues enjoyed by Italians throughout the kingdom.[160] When it came to Master Martin, however, a group of magnates took matters into their own hands. Having gathered for a tournament, they sent the baron Fulk fitzWarin (his quarrel with King John was the stuff of legend) to warn Martin to leave the country or worse would follow. Martin appealed to the king, but got nothing more than a safe conduct to Dover. He sailed on 15 July. Fulk fitzWarin, according to the story he liked to tell, only just avoided laying violent hands on him.[161]

THE COUNCIL OF LYON, 1245

By the final phase of Martin's mission in England, the whole framework of England's relations with the papacy had been transformed by Pope Innocent's decision to summon a council of the whole church to meet at Lyon towards the end of June 1245. Innocent planned to issue constitutions for the reform of the church and deal with the question of the emperor. He also wished to respond to a terrible event which had sent shock waves through Europe, namely the fall of Jerusalem in July 1244 to the Khwarazmian Turks.

In the short term Innocent's initiative took the pressure off in England. Henry was able to forbid the payment of the papal subsidy until the matter had been discussed at the Lyon council. He was reluctant, he said, to do anything contrary to the will of the pope, but knew that the demands of his magnates were congruent with his 'honour'.[162] At the council it would also be possible to raise all the ingredients of papal oppression including most obviously the issue of provisions. Early in June 1245 a parliament met in London to co-ordinate the response. It was decided to send to Lyon both magnates representing the 'baronage of all England' and knights representing 'the community'. The impression that the kingdom was going it alone without the king should not be exaggerated. The leader of the baronial delegation was Roger Bigod, earl of Norfolk. The other members – William de Cantilupe II, John fitzGeoffrey, Ralph fitzNicholas and Philip Basset – were men high in the king's service. One of the knights, Henry de Mara, was to become a prominent judge. The spokesman was the king's clerk Master William of Powicke. Bigod and the rest were also to act for the king in treating of peace between the pope and emperor.[163]

Yet the letter taken to Lyon setting out the country's grievances, although composed by a royal clerk, was still remarkable for the way it

---

[160] *CR 1242–7*, 350, 354; Paris, iv, 416–17.

[161] Paris, iv, 420–2; Paris, *HA*, ii, 503–4.

[162] *CR 1242–7*, 350, 357.

[163] Paris, iv, 418–9; *CPR 1232–47*, 453–4, 463; *DI*, 358. The role of Henry de Mara appears in what follows.

seemed to put the king on one side and give to 'the baronage of England' the duty of preserving the rights of kingdom. Henry was thus portrayed as a Catholic prince, devoting himself, without care for his body, to divine service and the service of Jesus Christ, a king, his own rights preserved, eager to do all he could to support the pope. This passive picture contrasted very much with that of 'the barons, knights and all the baronage of England'. It was they who refused to 'tolerate the [current] detestable oppressions'. It was they who 'in the king's arduous affairs bear the weight and heat of the day, and who, one with the king, are intent on the preservation of the kingdom'.[164]

Of course it suited Henry to preserve his own relations with the papacy by shielding behind his men. There were precedents for barons sending their own letters of protest to the pope. The Irish magnates had done that in 1213.[165] But it was one thing for it to happen at the behest of a strong king, as in 1213, another under a weak king on the initiative of the baronage.

Once the English delegation got to Lyon, it made another assertion of communal responsibility. During the council the pope demanded a confirmation of King John's charter making England a papal fief with the 1,000 marks a year annual tribute. John's submission had always been unpopular, and the delegation took a stand against it. In order to give their letter of protest more weight, it was issued in the name of an 'earl', a 'baron' and a 'knight' (Roger Bigod, Philip Basset and Henry de Mara), 'the agents and the envoys of the universitas of the kingdom of England'. The three declared on behalf of 'the community of all the realm' that the 'magnates and people' had never consented to John's concession. It was their 'duty to observe and uphold the rights of the realm and the crown and their liberties and laws', however much 'the exercise of authority and the honour and prerogative of power resides in the royal dignity'.[166]

The protests of the English delegation achieved something but not much. The pope promised to restrict the number of papal provisions, and seems to have reduced the subsidy he was demanding from 10,000 to 6,000 marks. But the bishops now consented to it and set their seals to John's 'detestable charter' (as Matthew Paris put it).[167] The council as a whole agreed fresh taxes to be paid by the church: a twentieth of ecclesiastical incomes for three years to support a crusade for the recovery of Jerusalem,

---

[164] C&S, i, 394; Paris, iv, 444.

[165] Richardson and Sayles, Irish Parliament, 285–7. See Simpson, 'Declaration of Arbroath', 22–3. In 1205, Philip Augustus organized letters from French barons recording his agreement to do nothing for the pope without their consent: Layettes, i, no. 762.

[166] DI, 359–60; Longleat House, Marquess of Bath MS., Muniments no. 10590 (Glastonbury Cartulary), fo. 4v: 'Dicimus etiam quod licet iurisdictionis exercitium honor et prerogat(iv)a potestatis in regia dignitate consistant, iura tamen regni, coronam ipsorumque libertates et leges iidem nobiles et populus observare et conservare tenentur' (as transcribed in Vincent, 'Henry III, Frederick II and the council of Lyon', 83).

[167] Paris, iv, 479.

and various graded payments from those non-resident in their benefices in aid of the tottering eastern empire. As for Emperor Frederick, far from any settlement, at the end of the council Pope Innocent deposed him.

THE END OF THE FIGHT

With the campaign in Wales supervening, it was not until March 1246 that a parliament considered Innocent IV's response. By this time, so it was alleged, the pope's promises over provisions had already been breached. Henry seemed at one with his subjects in indignation. He addressed 'with his own mouth' the bishops, the earls and barons, and the abbots. Each group wrote its own letter of protest, that of the earls and barons being on behalf of 'universitas' of England. Henry also sent out strict orders forbidding the payment of the 6,000-mark subsidy until the return of the delegation now sent to Rome.[168] Yet, the abbots' letter to the pope, in giving a picture of the dangerous situation in England, revealed dissatisfaction with the king: 'the people' were moved against him and would withdraw from their fidelity unless protected more effectively by royal power from papal exactions.[169]

When the new delegation returned to a parliament held at Winchester in July 1246, it came empty handed. For a moment Henry thought of continuing his resistance, but then he gave way and allowed the collection of the subsidy to go ahead. He had already issued orders for the payment of the papal tribute and for the next few years he kept it up to date.[170] He was influenced by the bishops. Grosseteste, as we have seen, wrote eloquently about the pope's needs. Richard of Cornwall too urged compliance, grateful for papal help towards meeting the costs of his recent crusade.[171] As with episcopal appointments, to have continued resistance would have risked excommunication and interdict, and Henry would never do that.

The struggle was not quite over. There remained the new taxes agreed at the council of Lyon for the crusade and the eastern empire. With Henry resisting their payment, these were considered at a parliament held in February 1247. Once again letters of protest were sent to the pope. Once again they had no effect. Innocent made his usual promises over provisions but refused to back down over taxes agreed at Lyon by the whole church.[172] That ended Henry's resistance although just how far the new taxes were collected remains unclear.[173] If the pope did not press the point, that was partly because he now had a new priority, namely to raise a subsidy, this time for the papacy itself. His agent, John Anglicus (an Englishman,

---

[168] Paris, iv, 554, 557–8.
[169] Paris, iv, 532; and 518–22, 526–36; Maddicott, *Origins of the English Parliament*, 201–2.
[170] *CLR 1245–51*, 34, 115, 142; but see Paris, iv, 479.
[171] Paris, iv, 560–1; Lunt, *Financial Relations*, 219.
[172] Paris, iv, 594–7; *F*, 266.
[173] Lunt, *Financial Relations*, 253–4.

though that hardly made it better), arrived in February 1247. This time Henry made no protest and allowed John to get to work. With the bishops reluctantly agreeing to get the consent of their clergy to a levy of 11,000 marks, the tax seems to have gone ahead. At least, some consolation, it was last sought by Innocent for direct papal purposes. The next taxes demanded of the church were to be for Henry's own crusade.[174]

At times, Matthew Paris had been impressed by the way Henry stood up to the pope. He had shown 'compassion' for his people, and acted for 'the salvation of the kingdom'. Yet Paris equally doubted the resolve of this 'waxen hearted' king.[175] There were dangers in allowing the 'universitas' of the kingdom to take the lead in protecting the rights of the realm. It is no coincidence that at this very time it was doing the same in domestic affairs where parliaments were pressing radical schemes of reform on the king. Later, five of the earls who wrote to the pope in 1246 on behalf of the kingdom were to feature on the revolutionary council set up in 1258.[176] In all this Henry's conduct was strikingly different from that of Louis IX. In France there was much the same resentment at papal taxation and papal provisions. But in protesting to the pope, Louis needed no backup from anyone else. He did so on his own authority in defence of 'the liberties and customs of the kingdom committed to him by God'.[177]

HENRY'S FINANCIAL SITUATION

Henry returned from Gascony in 1243 burdened with debts. Indeed, according to one calculation, he owed some £15,000 in loans incurred during the expedition and promises made to Gascon and other supporters. In the financial year Michaelmas 1243/4, Henry's authorized expenditure exceeded his receipts by some £3,500.[178] Some of the gap could be filled by further loans, such as those from his brother Richard of Cornwall or Sienese and Florentine merchants. In December 1243 the latter lent 2,000 marks.[179] But these only went so far. In practice the expenditure Henry authorized was often notional, with the exchequer unable to find the cash for the payments it was supposed to make. Henry recognized as much. In January 1244 one Gascon was to receive his wages from the exchequer 'if there is money to pay him'. In February others were to have just half of what they were owed.[180]

---

[174] Paris, iv, 599, 622–3; Lunt, *Financial Relations*, 220–4.

[175] Paris, iv, 509–10, 559, 594, 599.

[176] The earls of Leicester, Hereford, Norfolk, Gloucester and Aumale: Paris, iv, 533.

[177] Paris, iv, 99–112, with quotation at 112; Campbell, 'The protest of Saint Louis'; Le Goff, *Saint Louis*, 167–8, 783–4. But see Paris, iv, 590–4; Lavisse, *Histoire de France*, iii, 60–1.

[178] Stacey, *Politics, Policy and Finance*, 227, table 6.6, and see above, 224, n. 291.

[179] *CPR 1232–47*, 411.

[180] *CLR 1240–5*, 211, 217. This did not, however, stop many other writs being issued ordering the exchequer to spend money.

The situation was aggravated by fresh expenditure that Henry could not avoid. In 1244–5 he had to finance a war in Gascony against the king of Navarre, an expedition to the north of England to contain the king of Scots, and a full-scale military campaign in Wales. Faced with these pressures, Henry made efforts to retrench. In January 1244, 'in great need', he suspended work on Dublin castle and ordered all available money to be sent to England. Next year, 'burdened with expenses', he even sought to reduce the costs of Lord Edward's household.[181] But retrenchment came unnaturally to Henry, although he was better at it later. It was one thing to suspend work in Ireland, where he never went, quite another to do so in England. Henry's expenditure on the costs of his household remained high. He was also spending unprecedented amounts on his buildings. In May 1244 alone the exchequer was told to find nearly £2,000 for the new knights' chamber and other works at Westminster.[182] From 1245 there were the costs of the Abbey.[183] There was also all the money promised to Richard of Cornwall, Simon de Montfort and the queen's mother, Beatrice of Savoy. Henry's open-handed generosity to his Savoyard kin continued unabated. When he learnt that the inheritance of Peter of Geneva's wife, Maud de Lacy, was depleted by lands held in dower, he granted Peter £100 a year until the dower fell in. This pension was itself soon converted into land, partly by a grant of the royal demesne manor of Dilwyn in Herefordshire. Peter was also pardoned £450 of Maud's inherited debts to the Jews.[184]

If Henry was thus good at spending money, at least he did all he could, as during the Welsh campaign of 1245, to accumulate it. Repeating an initiative of 1240, he tried once again to build up a reserve of treasure. He demanded that the sheriffs respond to orders with speed and pay their debts 'in full'. Those who failed to do so were subject to amercement or arrest. In 1247 the exchequer was not to release those imprisoned 'without our special order since henceforth we wish to reserve that power to ourselves'.[185] This was part and parcel of the close eye Henry kept on the exchequer. He ordered decisions to be postponed until he could be present (the exchequer constantly noted matters to be discussed with him) and demanded precise information about receipts and expenditure.[186] One such letter, written by the treasurer, William of Haverhill, in the summer of 1244, while the king was on his way north, shows the detail Henry demanded and the problems that he faced.

[181] CR 1242–7, 326.

[182] CR 1242–7, 160; CLR 1240–5, 239.

[183] Colvin, History of the King's Works, i, 155–7.

[184] CPR 1232–47, 429, 450; CFR 1245–6, no. 86.

[185] CFR 1243–4, no. 1803; TNA E 368/20, m. 3.

[186] TNA E 368/15, m. 2; TNA E 368/18, mm. 1, 3–4, 6d–7; TNA E 368/19, mm. 1, 4, 6d–7d; TNA E 368/20, mm. 3, 7d–8. The orders to distrain for debts run throughout the sections of the memoranda rolls dealing with the individual county accounts.

Between 5 and 30 June, Henry was told, 5,500 marks had been received from the tallage imposed on the Jews. Of this, Richard of Cornwall had received 500 marks, a messenger of the pope's 700 marks and the king's sergeants-at-arms 400 marks. Some 2,500 marks were being carried after the king for his use while the balance was being used to help settle the debts of wardrobe and household. Having set out what more could be expected from the Jews, the treasurer added that he was taking steps to ensure the money was paid. He next explained that during the same period £1,117 had been received 'from diverse Christians'. Henry could learn from an attached schedule how £927 of it had been spent. In addition £78 had gone on making tents (presumably for the northern campaign) and £100 on the works at Westminster. All this expenditure (all of it authorized by writs of the king) left £507 owing to workers at Westminster and 700 marks to Florentine and Sienese merchants. Another £16 3s 4d was owed for feeding paupers on the feast of Peter and Paul (29 June). There were also debts of unspecified amounts owed to merchants for wine and robes and to knights (presumably for their fees). The treasurer asked Henry, 'your royal majesty', what he should do, and explained depressingly that at the moment there was only £12 4s 11d in the treasury and 'I do not believe that much money will be received into your exchequer before the feast of Michaelmas'.[187]

Faced with such problems, Henry and his advisers were fertile in schemes for increasing royal revenue and resources. By far the most lucrative was the tallage on the Jews referred to in the treasurer's letter. Imposed during the summer of 1244, the amount demanded was a colossal 60,000 marks. This sum had no precedent under Henry III (it was three times larger than the next highest tallage in 1241/2) and was presumably suggested by King John's 60,000-mark tallage of 1210. Between 1244 and 1249 nearly 40,000 marks seems to have been raised, thus making a major contribution to royal income.[188]

Alongside the tallage of the Jews, there were a whole series of other measures designed to assert the king's authority and increase his resources. In January 1244 the sheriffs were ordered to take into the king's hands all lands alienated from sergeanties without royal permission. They were also to inquire into all wardships and marriages which belonged to the king and take them too into his hands.[189] In March there was an inquiry into 'lands of the Normans' currently held by earls, barons, knights and ecclesiastics. Then in April the sheriffs were to distrain all those with land worth an annual £20 to take up a knighthood. At the same time they were to ensure that anyone using liberties belonging to the crown had either

---

[187] TNA SC 1/3/90. The letter is damaged but some of the amounts can be supplied from the corresponding orders: *CLR 1240–5*, 239, 242–3.

[188] Stacey, '1240–60: a watershed in Anglo-Jewish relations?', 136–9.

[189] *BF*, ii, 1142–3. They were also to seize all lands held by those in the power of the king of France, this prompted by a parallel measure of Louis IX; see below, 491.

sufficient warrant from the king or his predecessors or had used them before what was called 'the parliament of Runnymede'.[190] A few days later Henry commissioned detailed inquiries into offences committed in the royal forest.[191] The sheriffs were threatened with ruin if they did not carry them out. Indeed, their punishments, Henry said, would terrify everyone.

Thanks in part to the Jewish tallage, episcopal vacancies and treasure from Ireland, Henry's revenues at this time were quite buoyant. Between Michaelmas 1243 and March 1244 he was able to clear many of his Gascon debts. While there was a deficit in the financial year 1243/4 of some £3,500, in the following year it was almost reversed.[192] Unfortunately Henry had not the benefit of calculations made by modern historians. He saw only that he was often very short of money. As a result, what developed was a hand-to-mouth form of existence, with Henry ordering officials and individual debtors to pay what they owed direct to the wardrobe, rather than to the exchequer. Thus the exchequer supplied only 56 per cent of wardrobe revenue between 1245 and 1251 as opposed to 72 per cent between 1241 and 1245.[193] Not surprisingly, Henry began to think that the only real solution to his financial problems was to get a tax from parliament. His first attempt, in the aftermath of his settlement with King Alexander, was in the autumn of 1244. It was not a happy experience.

PARLIAMENT AND THE PAPER CONSTITUTION

The kind of tax Henry coveted was almost certainly similar to those granted in 1225, 1232 and 1237, namely a fractional levy on the value of everyone's movable property. That would bring in many times more than any tax levied in the form of a scutage on knights' fees. Henry, however, knew such a tax would be difficult to obtain. At the parliament of 1242 he had sought one to fund his Poitevin campaign and been rebuffed. Accordingly in 1244, as never before, Henry put his heart and soul into the business of persuasion. The accounts of the parliament give a vivid impression of him at work. In 1237, William of Raleigh had spoken for the king. Now, in 1244, Henry spoke for himself. The parliament assembled at Westminster in November. In the refectory of Westminster Abbey, 'with his own mouth', as Matthew Paris put it, Henry made the case for the tax.[194] He focused on the debts incurred by his time in Poitou and

---

[190] CR 1242–7, 239–40, 242.

[191] CPR 1232–47, 442; CFR 1243–4, no. 284; Paris, vi, 94–9; Stacey, Politics, Policy and Finance, 251.

[192] Stacey, Politics, Policy and Finance, 206–7, 226–7, 237; and see above, 224, n. 291.

[193] Wild, WA, ci, cxvi–vii.

[194] Paris, iv, 362–3, 395–6; Paris, HA, ii, 490–1; Maddicott, Origins of the English Parliament, 174, 461.

Gascony, the money he owed merchants for 'the necessaries of life', and the costs of meeting the threats from Wales and Scotland. Having heard the king, the lay and ecclesiastical magnates agreed to stand together and give a joint reply about the conditions for any grant. These were to be decided by a panel of twelve men, chosen by 'common assent' and composed of four earls, four bishops and four barons, two lay and two ecclesiastical.

The conditions put forward in 1244 built on those of 1237 but went far beyond them. In 1237 three magnates had been added to the king's council but there is no sign they acted to impede the motions of the king. They never supervised the spending of the tax conceded by the parliament as may have been envisaged. Now, in 1244, the demands had much more bite. They focused first on the two great ministers through whom much of the business of the realm had once passed. These were the justiciar and chancellor. There had been no justiciar since Stephen of Seagrave's dismissal in 1234. There had been no working chancellor since Henry had taken the great seal from Ralph de Neville in 1238. There had been no chancellor at all since Neville's death early in 1244. Now the offices were to be revived and their occupants chosen not by the king but by parliament. This was not all. These demands were linked, as will be seen, to a wider scheme of reform in which justiciar, chancellor and other elected councillors were to control much of the government of the country. Henry was to become an emasculated king. This programme was as novel as it was revolutionary. The demands of 1244 thus marked a new stage in the opposition to the rule of Henry III. In one form or another they were to be pressed on the king at parliament after parliament until finally realized in the revolution of 1258.

Henry came to the parliament of 1244 buoyed up by his success against the king of Scots. Not surprisingly, he refused absolutely to accept 'novel' demands (as Matthew Paris described them) under 'compulsion of the council'. He probably pointed out (as he certainly did later) that he and his ancestors had always been accustomed to appoint and dismiss justiciars and chancellors as they pleased. Any concession on the point would breach his coronation oath to preserve the rights of the crown.[195] It would also restrict his freedom of action. When one of the men to whom Henry entrusted the seal after 1238, Master Simon the Norman, resisted the issue of a charter that he felt contravened the rights of the crown, Henry immediately dismissed him. He could not do that with an elected chancellor.[196]

At the parliament Henry did not give up easily. Over six days he explained his case and 'humbly' promised some reforms of his own. On the last day, with the magnates departing, Henry laboured until late at night to persuade the prelates to stay on, hoping they would at least agree

---

[195] *DBM*, 252–3, 256–7.
[196] For the episode, see Powicke, *King Henry III*, ii, 780–3.

to the purely ecclesiastical tax sanctioned earlier in the year by the pope. Another meeting did indeed take place, its setting Westminster Abbey's infirmary chapel of St Katherine. The king's case was made by a delegation led by Simon de Montfort, until Henry himself could bear it no more. He burst in and, sitting down, made a passionate speech setting out the reciprocal relationship between king and realm. 'Without you I cannot live nor can you live without me. You depend on me and I on you, since if I am rich, you are rich, if I am poor, you are poor.' Quite probably this was Henry's theme throughout the parliament. He had developed a similar line of argument earlier in the year when justifying his measure over liberties. Everyone, Henry said, should wish to protect those of the crown, 'as they wish, under the wings of royal justice, to enjoy those given them by our predecessors'.[197] It was to no avail. Led by Bishop Grosseteste, the prelates stood by the answer already given by their 'peers', the earls and barons. That answer, the best Henry could obtain for all his efforts, was to consider the king's request again at a parliament due to meet in February 1245.[198]

In the interval Henry did something to appease his critics but not much. A few days after the close of the November parliament he gave his clerk Silvester of Everdon custody of the great seal. Silvester had a good reputation and was skilled, according to Matthew Paris, in the work of the chancery.[199] But it was hardly the same as appointing a proper chancellor. At least Henry's piety remained conspicuous. When he visited St Albans just before Christmas, he prayed at the high altar and offered a precious cloth and three gold necklaces at St Alban's shrine. When he heard of the death of the countess of Flanders, wife of Thomas of Savoy, he ordered her exequies to be celebrated in the choir and arranged for all the friars, hospitals, poor nuns and lepers in London to be fed for the benefit of her soul. Here he was acting, in Paris's words, as a 'rex Christianissimus'.[200]

By the time the parliament opened towards the end of February 1245 the birth of Henry and Eleanor's youngest son, Edmund, had secured the future of the dynasty. It was with all the more confidence, therefore, that Henry returned to the attack.[201] Day after day he pleaded with the assembly both personally and through intermediaries. He promised to obey Magna Carta and asked the bishops to pronounce sentences of excommunication against all those who contravened it. In the end he achieved something but not nearly as much as he wished. The parliament

[197] CR 1237–42, 242.
[198] National Library of Wales, Aberystwyth, MS Peniarth 390 (Burton formulary), fo. 40r; Paris, iv, 365–6. I am grateful to Nicholas Vincent for sending me his transcription of the account of Henry's speech in the Burton formulary. It is similar to the version given by Matthew Paris.
[199] CR 1242–7, 266; Paris, iv, 569, 587.
[200] Paris, iv, 402; CR 1242–7, 270.
[201] Paris, iv, 372–4; Maddicott, Origins of the English Parliament, 174, 461.

refused any tax on movables but conceded Henry a scutage to be levied at
the rate of £1 on each knight's fee. This was stated to be for the marriage
of Henry's eldest daughter, Margaret, now betrothed to the son of the
king of Scots, although in fact the marriage did not take place until 1251.
No conditions were demanded for the grant, but then Henry was only
getting something to which he was entitled anyway. Even the 1215 Magna
Carta had acknowledged that the king could levy an aid for the marriage
of his eldest daughter without the need for consent.

Henry had thus emerged with his authority intact. He had refused
demands incompatible with the rights of the crown. He had also avoided
those demands simply being thrust upon him. Although legally unnecessary, the consent given to the aid for his daughter's marriage was worth
having, making it easier to collect. In the event some £2,480 were paid in
between 1245 and 1247, a worthwhile sum if many times less than that
promised by a tax on movables.[202] Nonetheless, the demands of 1244
marked a watershed in Henry's rule and showed just how large the gulf
was between him and his kingdom.

The full extent of those demands is revealed in a document called by
historians 'the Paper Constitution'. The text is given by Matthew Paris in
his account of the 1244 parliament under the heading 'These things the
magnates provided with the king's consent to be henceforth inviolably
observed'.[203] In fact, Henry never consented to any such things, which is
why historians call the document 'the Paper Constitution'. Henry, however,
must have known that demands of this kind were being canvassed. They
gave him all the more reason to stand his ground.

The Paper Constitution starts with the failure to observe the liberties in
Magna Carta despite the sentence of excommunication pronounced by
Archbishop Edmund in 1237. As a remedy four councillors are to be
elected by parliament as 'conservators of liberties'.[204] These councillors,
only dismissable by parliament and with at least two of them permanently
at court, are to handle faithfully the affairs of king and kingdom, hear
everyone's complaints, and give speedy justice to anyone suffering an
injury. The councillors are also to manage the king's treasure, oversee the
expenditure of any tax conceded by parliament, and decide when parliament should be summoned. The justiciar and chancellor are likewise to be
appointed and removed by parliament. Since they are to be frequently
with the king, they can be two of the four councillors. If the seal is taken
from the chancellor it is to be immediately restored and anything sealed in

---

[202] Mitchell, *Studies in Taxation*, 243–4.

[203] Paris, iv, 366–8. For the date of the document, see Cheney, 'The "Paper Constitution"'.

[204] I have rendered as 'parliament' such terms as 'universi', 'omnes' and 'de communi
assensu'.

the interval is to be considered invalid. Writs issued 'against the king[205] and the custom of the kingdom' are likewise to be void. The constitution also extended its reach to other central government officials. Two justices of the bench, two barons of the exchequer and at least one justice of the Jews are to be chosen by parliament for 'as they handle the affairs of all, so everyone should agree in their election'. Subsequently, however, they could be chosen by the four councillors. All of these reforms were to be placed in a new charter and supported by sentences of excommunication, as well as by a general oath and a particular oath taken by the councillors.

These were revolutionary demands revealing a major escalation in the programme of opposition to the king. The aim was no longer to restrict the operations of royal government as in Magna Carta, it was to take over the running of that government altogether. Magna Carta had left the king perfectly free to appoint his own ministers and spend his money as he wished. Now his leading officials were to be appointed by parliament and were to supervise not merely the spending of any tax but also the spending of the king's treasure more generally. They were also to take over the most fundamental duty of the king, that of giving justice to his subjects.

What then was going on? What had Henry done to deserve this abasement? One suggestion is that in these years Henry had become 'dangerously isolated from the greater portion of the earls and barons'.[206] Yet Henry might think he had done much to avoid such a fate. The northern expedition of 1244 had helped bring him closer to his leading magnates as had his opposition, if under pressure, to the demands of Master Martin and the pope. In 1244, Richard of Cornwall and Simon de Montfort were leading councillors. The earls of Norfolk, Hereford and Pembroke were all found at court. The following year, Henry made Norfolk his proctor at the council of Lyon. All these men, in 1244–5, received the gifts of wood, wine or game which marked the king's favour. So did the young earls of Devon and Gloucester and the aged earl of Derby. Henry's household stewards still included the barons John fitzGeoffrey and William de Cantilupe II.[207] All four of the men Matthew Paris named as Henry's principal councillors in 1244 he praised for their skill, prudence and English birth. (They were John Mansel, Master Laurence de St Martin and the literate knights Paulinus Peyvre and John of Lexington.) By promoting them, Paris added, Henry conciliated in no little degree 'the magnates of England'.[208]

Matthew Paris's comment here leads to another point. Hostility to the queen's Savoyard relatives was one dog that did not bark at the parlia-

---

[205] It is possible that 'regem' here in Paris's transcription is a mistake for 'legem', hence the reference is to writs against the law and custom of the kingdom. If 'regem' is right, then the reference is presumably to writs in some way damaging to the rights of the king.

[206] Stacey, *Politics, Policy and Finance*, 252–3.

[207] See above, 220.

[208] Paris, iv, 294; Paris, *HA*, ii, 480–1.

ments of 1244 and 1245, despite the continuing flow of favour to them. To that extent they had been accepted into the kingdom. Indeed, Boniface of Savoy, as archbishop-elect of Canterbury, headed the episcopal contingent on the committee of twelve appointed by the 1244 parliament. If there were any objections to Peter of Savoy's influence (and he always did his sinuous best to allay them), they were defused by his absence for the whole of 1244 from England.

How then could the demand for an elected justiciar and chancellor, and quite possibly related controls as in the Paper Constitution, be put forward by men who, in varying degrees, enjoyed Henry's trust and favour? The earls on the committee in the 1244 parliament were Richard of Cornwall, Simon de Montfort, Walter Marshal and Roger Bigod. The lay barons were Richard de Montfichet, currently sheriff of Essex–Hertfordshire, and John de Balliol, who in 1248 would be appointed sheriff of Cumberland. Yet precisely because they saw him at close quarters, these men were well aware of Henry's failings. Simon de Montfort only two years before had said he needed to be set apart like Charles the Simple. They could all agree that Henry would rule in more ordered and responsible a fashion if he had by his side elected officials, which meant, of course, in considerable part, officials chosen by themselves. Given Henry's extravagance and open-handed generosity, they might well think that he would fritter away any tax unless controlled by elected councillors. The same was true of his revenues more generally.

It is, however, unlikely that the demands of 1244 originated with the great nobles enjoying entrée to Henry's court and benefiting from his favour, although they were prepared to put them forward. For the laity (we will discuss the church later) the demands rather served the groups with limited access to the court: magnates outside its circle and county knights. But how did such men make their voices heard? The question obviously leads on to another. Who attended the parliaments of Henry's personal rule?[209] Unfortunately there is no definitive answer. No lists survive of summonses, let alone of attendance. The likelihood, however, is that the form of summons followed the two-tier process outlined in the 1215 Magna Carta. There the bishops, abbots, earls and 'greater barons' were to be summoned by individual letters, with the rest of the king's tenants-in-chief being summoned 'in general' through the sheriffs. Some idea of the numbers in the first tier can be gained from parallel summonses of tenants-in-chief to perform their military service. Thus for the projected campaign of 1244 in Scotland, summonses went out to nine bishops, twenty-six abbots and priors, nine earls and seventy-two barons.[210] Quite

[209] For what follows in this and the next paragraph, see Maddicott, *Origins of the English Parliament*, 191, 198–206.

[210] *CR Supp.*, 1–3; Maddicott, 'An infinite number of nobles', 21. The ecclesiastics were expected to send their due service to the army, not come in person.

possibly a similar list was used for the individual summonses to the parliament later in the year. A good proportion of the seventy-two barons would have been men with no particular connection to the court.

The same lack of courtly connections was even more true of the lesser tenants-in-chief, a body several hundred strong, summoned generally through the sheriffs. Nearly all would have been men of knightly or less than knightly status. Even if only the more substantial turned up, that would still have meant a good number of knights being present at Henry's parliaments. Indeed, their presence is referred to both in chronicles and royal letters. These knights were not, in any formal way, representative of county communities. Only once during the personal rule were such representatives summoned to parliament, and that (in 1254) was in exceptional circumstances.[211] But the knights would have been very ready to express the discontent with Henry's rule in the shires, all the more so when faced with demands for taxation. Their influence can be seen in the appointment of knights to represent 'the community' at the council of Lyon. It can be seen too in the way Henry modified his attempt to make men take up knighthood 'after the complaints of many', complaints almost certainly voiced at the parliament of June 1245.[212] Lesser barons, knights and those below them in local society suffered, far more than the greatest nobles, from the suspension of the offices of justiciar and chancellor. They also suffered more from the weight of royal government in the shires. In 1242 there had been complaints in parliament about the amercements imposed by the justices in eyre.[213] The need to do something about the eyres was flagged up in the Paper Constitution. The Constitution said nothing about the sheriffs but when it mentioned breaches of Magna Carta the sheriffs were certainly major culprits. They stood accused of violating both the chapter on the levying of amercements and that on the holding of the county and hundred courts. The situation was aggravated by the gradual abandonment of the reforms of 1236. The number of county knights running the sheriffdoms was diminishing while the financial demands of the exchequer were on the increase.

A complaint by the knight Robert fitzNicholas from the late 1240s reveals some of the problems set by the sheriffs as well as the need for a justiciar and chancellor to sort them out. In this case the villain of the piece was the sheriff of Worcestershire. He had done nothing in response to orders from the king telling him to hold several inquiries, one into tres-

---

[211] See below, 580.

[212] Those with a knight's fee were only to be liable to take up knighthood if the fee was worth £20 a year, a distinct retreat from the order in March 1245, which said nothing about the value of the fee: *CR 1242–7*, 242, 350, 354, 356; Maddicott, *Origins of the English Parliament*, 222. For concessions to those hit by the inquiry into alienations from sergeanties, see TNA E 368/20, m. 8.

[213] Paris, iv, 186–7.

passes in Robert's park. He was forcing Robert, by seizing his chattels, to make a payment to the great local baron William de Beauchamp.[214] He was also bringing a case against Robert in the Worcester county court for having buried a body without proper supervision of the coroner, this although the body, as Robert said, was being eaten by dogs and pigs. In these travails Robert knew what to do. He wrote to the king's steward John of Lexington and asked for a series of royal letters to be sent to the sheriff, letters doubtless threatening the sheriff with punishment if he did not mend his ways. Robert was a well-connected man, the son of Lexington's colleague the steward Ralph fitzNicholas. He evidently knew that Lexington at this time was keeper of the seal and thus the right man to ask for the letters.[215] But imagine the fate of those without Robert's knowledge and connections. In all probability they would not even know who held the seal, given the way it had passed through so many hands since being taken from Neville in 1238. What made this worse was that the twenty-seven years of peace since the conclusion of the 1215–17 civil war had seen a steady increase in the scope of the king's government, as the burgeoning size of the plea rolls and pipe rolls shows. More people than ever before, as litigators and debtors, were coming within the ambit of that government. The consequence was a corresponding increase in the number of petitions coming into the centre demanding justice, favour and redress of grievances.[216] But at Henry's court there seemed no conspicuous and responsible ministers who might answer such requests and complaints.

In these circumstances the years in which Hubert de Burgh and Ralph de Neville together had run the show took on a golden glow. Hubert de Burgh was certainly out for himself, but he was also very aware of his position as 'justiciar of England, held to dispense justice to everyone', as one letter put it.[217] When the Paper Constitution said that the four elected councillors, one of whom would be the justiciar, were to hear everyone's complaints and pronounce swift justice, they defined exactly the role Hubert had aspired to play.

Neville, over his twenty years as keeper of the seal, had played a similar role. It was he who dealt with the numerous requests, like those of Robert fitzNicholas, for royal letters to sort out this problem or that. That he tried to discharge his responsibilities in an open even-handed fashion was certainly the view of Matthew Paris: a 'solitary column of truth and faith in royal affairs'.[218] Neville's career had a major impact on the demands of

---

[214] Beauchamp was also the sheriff of the county, one of the few sheriffdoms held in hereditary right. The sheriff mentioned in the letter was, therefore, his deputy.

[215] *RL*, ii, 48–9.

[216] See Moore, 'Fine rolls as evidence for the expansion of royal justice'.

[217] *RL*, i, 5.

[218] Paris, iii, 90, 206–7.

1244, just as his death earlier in the year cleared the way for the appointment of a new chancellor. Indeed, it may well be that Neville's circle contributed to the details of the Paper Constitution. The justiciar, chancellor and the other councillors were to be chosen by parliament, just as Neville claimed to have been in 1218. The seal could only be taken from the chancellor by common consent, exactly what Neville said in 1236. When the Paper Constitution went on to say that if the seal was taken from the chancellor, it was to be immediately returned, and anything sealed in the interval be regarded as void, it was surely thinking of the way the seal had been taken from Neville in 1238. When the Paper Constitution saw an elected chancellor as a barrier against writs issued 'against justice' and against the 'king and custom of the kingdom', they were most likely remembering how Neville claimed to have resisted irresponsible letters and charters that Henry had issued during the rule of Peter des Roches.[219]

The disappearance of the justiciarship and chancellorship, therefore, meant that, at the very time when, as the Paper Constitution put it, the government was dealing more and more 'with the affairs of everyone', defined and navigable channels of communication with the centre of that government were closing down. The measures of 1244 were essentially designed to open up and control a system of government which, while increasing in range, had become more enclosed and remote, and for that reason easier for those on the inside to manipulate and corrupt.

There was, therefore, a long-term background to the demands of 1244. There was also an immediate one. The initiatives of 1244 – the distraint of knighthood, the move against the usurpation of liberties and the inquiries into sergeanties, the lands of the Normans and the royal forest had created much alarm. They were followed by a flow of orders in favour of those improperly dispossessed. Henry himself, reacting to the protests, changed his mind more than once about when, where and before whom those caught by the forest inquiry should appear. Eventually, they were to come before Henry himself, half in mid-October and half at the end of the month. If the order was obeyed, then a large number of disgruntled individuals, many from the knightly class, must have come to Westminster not long before the meeting of the November parliament.[220]

The Paper Constitution had begun with a preamble about the breach of the liberties in Magna Carta despite the sentence of excommunication pronounced by Archbishop Edmund. Its four elected councillors were to be 'conservators of liberties'. All this suggests that the church too had a major influence on the demands of 1244, for its liberties were conspicuously under threat. It could also make its views felt, for the committee of twelve included the archbishop-elect of Canterbury, Boniface of Savoy, two abbots and the bishops of Lincoln, Worcester and Winchester, respectively Robert

---

[219] Carpenter, 'Chancellor Ralph de Neville', 71–6.
[220] *CFR 1243–4*, no. 284; *CR 1242–7*, 253.

Grosseteste, Walter de Cantilupe (later a staunch Montfortian) and William of Raleigh. Raleigh, only just reconciled to the king, and with his inside knowledge of the sometimes shambolic workings of Henry's government, may well have had an input into the Paper Constitution.[221]

The church felt that its liberties were grievously contravened by Henry's conduct of episcopal elections and his exploitations of vacancies, very live issues in 1244. While Magna Carta after 1215 no longer confirmed John's charter granting free elections, thus increasing Henry's leeway, the charter was well known, and anyway Henry could always be accused of breaching Magna Carta's more general guarantee of ecclesiastical liberties. The liberty of the church was also under threat in other ways. One was the challenge to the right claimed by many religious houses and some bishops to have the amercements imposed by the king's judges on their men. Equally under challenge was their right to have the chattels of their men when they were executed or outlawed. From sometime in the regnal year 1233 to 1234, the exchequer had begun to refuse such claims unless specially sanctioned by the king. In the ensuing years such sanction was made dependent on the 'express mention' of a grant of amercements and chattels in a royal charter. Since many claims were based on vague general references in charters, by 1244–5 around forty religious houses together with some bishops and cathedral chapters found their 'liberties' in this area being questioned by the exchequer. They included the monasteries of Bury St Edmunds and Ramsay, whose abbots were both on the committee of twelve.[222]

While the Paper Constitution was clearly a pragmatic solution to palpable grievances, the intellectual rationale behind the demands is less clear and may have been less than clear at the time. At least there was no need to justify the coercion of the king, for none was contemplated. The idea rather was that the Constitution should be freely conceded in return for a tax, just like Magna Carta in 1225 and 1237. When the king would have none of it, that was the end of the matter, at least for the moment. But that still begged the question of how such restrictions could be justified, especially when Henry thought they were inimical to the rights of the crown. One possible reply could lie in the duty of the baronage to defend the laws and customs of the realm, as it was currently doing faced with the demands of the pope. The Paper Constitution said its aim was to preserve the 'liberties' conceded in Magna Carta. Later parliaments justified in terms of 'custom' their right to choose the kings ministers.[223] After all, during the minority of Henry III great councils had both made such appointments (as in the case of Neville) and had also decided a variety of

---

[221] Raleigh's role was suggested by Andrew Spencer in a talk at the Leeds International Medieval Conference.

[222] *Reading Abbey Cartularies*, i, 91–2; Carpenter, *Reign of Henry III*, 85–6; TNA E 368/15, m. 3.

[223] Paris, v, 487.

other important business.[224] Of course, the king was then underage, but subsequently the Gloucester parliament of 1234 had both dismissed and appointed the king's ministers and made him reverse many of his previous acts. The parliament of 1237 had added barons to the king's council.

The solidarity of these arguments is another matter. The appeal to 'custom' was based on very recent practice. There was nothing in Magna Carta preventing the king choosing his own ministers and past kings had been entirely free to do so. At Lyon itself the English delegation acknowledged that the 'exercise of power' was the 'prerogative' of the king.[225] *Bracton* had justified the events of 1234 in terms of the baronage's duty to put reins on a lawless king, but was Henry in 1244 lawless or simply incompetent? How did one justify acting against a king of that type? One answer was being provided at this very time in Portugal, where the clerical and noble opposition appealed to Pope Innocent for the removal of King Sancho II.[226] In July 1245, during the council of Lyon, Innocent complied. He allowed Sancho to remain king but entrusted the 'care and administration' of the kingdom to his brother Alfonso. He did so not because of Sancho's tyranny but because of his 'negligence', 'idleness' and 'feebleness of heart'.[227] The English delegation at Lyon must have brought back news of Innocent's action, but there is no sign it had any impact in England.[228] Perhaps that is not surprising. However much Henry's conduct offended church and kingdom, there was not the slightest chance of the pope sanctioning his displacement. The whole problem of how to justify depriving the king of the 'care and administration' of his kingdom had to be faced again in more acute form after 1258. The Paper Constitution itself provided just one other possible answer. In its solitary (and off-hand) justification for parliamentary appointments, it declared that 'as [ministers] handle the affairs of all, so everyone shall concur in their election'. This was to be a principle developed at much more length in the great justification of Montfortian rule in *The Song of Lewes*.

Henry was able to withstand the challenge to his rule in and after 1244 partly because his financial position was less desperate than it sometimes seemed. Even without taxation he had enough money to keep going. He also in some areas trod carefully. In practice, he made little effort to challenge liberties usurped by his magnates in the field of local government. If the liberties of the church remained under challenge at the exchequer, they were not taken away, the cases over them being adjourned from one year to the next. Henry also rowed back on some of the initiatives of 1244.

[224] Carpenter, *Minority*, 407–9.

[225] See above, 447.

[226] For what follows, see Peters, *Shadow King*, ch. 4, and Ambler, *Bishops in the Political Community*, 54.

[227] Peters, *Shadow King*, 138–9.

[228] Matthew Paris makes no mention of events in Portugal.

He limited the numbers of those caught by the distraint of knighthood and stressed that no one should be dispossessed through the inquiry into the lands of the Normans.[229]

THE REBUILDING OF WESTMINSTER ABBEY

Henry, on his return to England in 1243, was spending a great deal on his court. In the year 1243/4 the costs of the daily food, drink, stables and alms giving, as recorded on the household roll, attained a daily average of nearly £16, the highest sum recorded in the whole of the reign.[230] Perhaps here Henry was hoping to compensate for his humiliating failure in Poitou and impress those gathering at Westminster for parliaments. He was also, perhaps for the same reason, paying great attention to the external show of his kingship. The new gateway at Westminster so he could descend from his palfrey 'before a noble facade'; the leopards beneath his throne made in bronze rather then marble because they would be 'more sumptuous', and the columns around his bed painted in vivid green stencilled with gold, all these, with their Solomonic references, were ordered in 1244/5.[231] In such orders so much of Henry's personality stands out. There is the attention to detail and the passion with which he drives forward his commissions, demanding, threatening, heedless of cost. It was in this period again that the new chamber at Westminster for the king's knights was to be completed by Easter 'even if it requires 1,000 workers every day'. This enthusiasm was about to be transferred to work on a much larger scale, a work very much connected with advertising the virtues of Henry's kingship to his subjects, namely the rebuilding of Westminster Abbey.

The demolition of the Confessor's church had begun in July 1245, just after Henry set off on his Welsh campaign. The decision must have been maturing throughout Henry's battering at the parliaments of November 1244 and February 1245. In response, Henry had done little of substance. His promise to keep Magna Carta was entirely verbal, without teeth and indeed without much publicity. In Henry's mind, it was the Abbey that provided the answer. It was his reply to the Paper Constitution. Parliament and the Abbey had always been closely linked. Its sessions frequently spilled over into the monks' refectory, chapter house and infirmary chapel of St Katherine. Now, with the start of the new church, Henry sought to link parliament and the Confessor together in novel fashion, something seen in a remarkable change in the times when parliament met. Before

---

[229] *CR 1242–7*, 239–40 and see above, n. 212. For concessions to those hit by the inquiry into alienations from sergeanties, see TNA E 368/20, m. 8.

[230] Carpenter, 'Household rolls', 35.

[231] *CR 1242–7*, 169, 273, 293.

1245, Henry never seems to have made its opening coincide with the main feast of the Confessor on 13 October. After 1245, he did so on five or six occasions – in 1247, 1249, 1251, 1252, 1255 and probably 1257. In 1249 and 1250 parliaments also met for the first time on the 5 January feast.[232] Clearly the idea was for the parliamentarians to fall in with Henry's wishes, inspired by the ceremony in the Abbey, the banquet afterwards and the astounding new church rising around.

THE RECOINAGE OF 1247–50

Henry may have done nothing to reform the realm in response to parliamentary demands, but in 1247 he did embark on a major enterprise for the realm's benefit. This was to give it an entirely new coinage.[233] Since Henry II's recoinage in 1179–80 the form of the silver penny had remained the same. It had the king's head and name on one side and on the other a small cross surrounded by the name and mint of the moneyer. Although John had carried out a partial recoinage in 1205, the form of the coin had not altered. Indeed, neither Richard nor John minted coins in their own names. The king on the coins was 'Henricus' all the way through from 1179 to 1247.

Between 1247 and 1250 the whole coinage of the country was replaced. The new coin boasted a new design. The cross, instead of being just in the centre, now ran its four arms to the perimeter. Hence historians speak of the 'long cross coinage' replacing 'the short cross' one. There was also another change. The identity of the king was proclaimed. The 'Henricus' thus became 'Henricus tercius' or, in later versions, 'Henricus III'.[234] The king also wore a much better designed crown and in coins later in the mintage always grasped a sceptre.[235]

The driving force behind the coinage was not Henry himself but the wealthiest noble in the kingdom, his brother, Richard of Cornwall.[236] It was Richard who suggested, financed and organized the recoinage and took the lion's share of the profits. He was not acting entirely from self-interest. The recoinage was agreed by the parliament which met at Oxford

---

[232] Maddicott, *Origins of the English Parliament*, 455–72.

[233] For secondary work on what follows, see Eaglen, *Abbey and Mint of Bury St Edmunds*, 164–94; Allen, *Mints and Money*, 189–92, 304–8, 325–6; Bolton, *Money in the Medieval Economy*, 24–7, 148–54, 176–9; Churchill and Thomas, *Brussels Hoard*; Mayhew, 'Coinage and money'; Latimer, 'Quantity of money'; Cassidy, 'Richard of Cornwall and the royal mints'. I am grateful to Richard Cassidy for a great deal of help with this section.

[234] In some of the coins from early in the mintage the 'tercius' is on the side of the cross rather than on the side with the king's head and the 'Henricus'. For copious illustrations of both short-cross and long-cross coins from the Bury St Edmunds mint, see the plates in Eaglen, *Abbey and Mint of Bury St Edmunds*.

[235] The sceptre is also found on Henry's short-cross coins.

[236] For Richard's role, see Cassidy, 'Richard of Cornwall and the royal mints'.

in April 1247.[237] There was a general acceptance that the coinage was in an 'intolerable' state, largely due to clipping. The Waverley abbey annalist asserted that, for every 3,000 old pennies, one could hardly find 20 in good condition. Indeed, it often took three bad pennies to equal the weight of two good ones. Matthew Paris added that the clipping had reduced some coins to little more than the circle around the small inner cross. For this he blamed the Jews as well as Italian and Flemish merchants. In France, Paris continued, Louis IX had ordered English coins beneath lawful weight to be seized and melted down so they did not disturb commerce.[238]

There was here a wider background. Coins were playing a far larger part in the life of the country than they had at the start of Henry's reign. From around 1209 to the 1220s between £200,000 and £300,000 worth of pennies were, at any one time, in circulation. By 1247 the amount had risen to between £460,000 and £490,000.[239] Much of this took place during 'a startling period of growth' from the mid-1230s, most of it due to the influx of silver from Flanders to pay for the export of English wool.[240] There was also, although less startling thanks to the expansion of the population, a rise in the amount of money per head. 'By the mid thirteenth century the concentrated money supply in England had probably reached the critical point that would allow coins to be used as the normal medium or agent of exchange'.[241] That use would become all the more 'normal' if the condition of the currency could be improved. This was the aim of the new design. Running the cross right to the edge of the coins would, it was hoped, make clipping more obvious and thus more difficult.

At the start of the recoinage, the exchange of old clipped coins for new ones was made compulsory. Old coins in good condition, however, could continue in circulation.[242] In practice, between 1247 and 1250, the coinage was changed completely. The great bulk of the exchange took place at the two main mints of the kingdom, those of London and Canterbury. Richard of Cornwall, clearly with a large amount of liquid wealth, made an initial loan of 10,000 marks so they could start work and have new currency ready as the old was handed in. The London and Canterbury mints began operations in November 1247 and the next month were joined by the abbot's mint at Bury St Edmunds. In the following year seventeen new mints were opened in towns around the country. At each four moneyers, four keepers of the dies, two assayers and one clerk were

---

[237] Wykes, 96–7; Maddicott, *Origins of the English Parliament*, 463–4.

[238] Waverley, 339; Paris, iv, 608–9, 632–3; Eaglen, *Abbey and Mint of Bury St Edmunds*, 163; Allen, *Mints and Money*, 372–3.

[239] Combining figures in Bolton, *Money in the Medieval Economy*, 148–9, and Allen, *Mints and Money*, 325–6.

[240] Bolton, *Money in the Medieval Economy*, 148, 151–2.

[241] Bolton, *Money in the Medieval Economy*, 27.

[242] *CR 1242–7*, 545; *CPR 1247–58*, 22; Paris, iv, 150–1; FitzThedmar, 181–2.

appointed.[243] Again Richard of Cornwall gave loans to enable work to be started. He also gave 2,000 marks so work could begin in Ireland.[244] Between November 1247 and July 1250 the English mints produced, according to one estimate, around £577,000 worth of coins, so over 138 million silver pennies. This equates to a yearly average of some fifty-eight million pennies, over four times larger than the estimated average for the years 1240 to 1247.[245] By the end of 1250 most of the new mints had closed down, leaving just those of London, Canterbury and Bury in major action. The recoinage was complete. The absence of any substantial mingling of long-cross and short-cross pennies in coin hoards shows its success.[246] The new coins had almost entirely replaced the old. This was a colossal administrative achievement.

Matthew Paris, while acknowledging the clipped state of the earlier currency, was highly critical of the recoinage. There was both the burden of travel to the mints (he does not mention the increase in their number) and the punishments inflicted on those privately exchanging just a few coins of the new money for the old. There was also the cost of the exchange itself.[247] Those handing in old coins weighing a pound did not get a pound's weight of new coins in return. They got 16d less. This was because 6d was deducted as the charge of the king and 10d as the charge of the moneyers.[248]

Paris was similarly critical of the large sums of money made by Richard of Cornwall. Under the earl's agreement with the king he was to control the mints in England, Wales and Ireland for no less than twelve years. He did indeed control them down to November 1259. For all that period he was entitled to half of the king's 6d. Between 1247 and 1259 this brought him nearly £11,000.[249] Richard also profited from the loans he had made to sustain the mints. Here, under the terms of the agreement, he could, if he wished, be repaid out of the king's half of the 6d. Indeed, between 1247 and 1250 he received all of it. An additional perk was that the money Richard gave to support the coinage (amounting eventually to over

---

[243] Allen, *Mints and Money*, 307; *De Moneta*, 100–5.

[244] *CR 1247–51*, 107–8; Cassidy, 'Richard of Cornwall and the royal mints', 141.

[245] Allen, *Mints and Money*, 306–8. The precise dates for these calculations are 1 November 1247 to 14 July 1250 and 22 February 1240 to 1 November 1247.

[246] Allen, *Mints and Money*, 447. In the Colchester hoard, deposited in the 1250s and 1270s, there are only 8 short-cross pennies in a total of 14,076. There are 9 short-cross pennies in the 52,275 pennies of the Brussels Hoard: Churchill and Thomas, *Brussels Hoard*, 15, 409.

[247] Paris, v, 18–19, 629. For measures against private exchangers, see *CR 1247–51*, 108; Paris, vi, 150–1. Paris's detail about the mint charges was incorrect.

[248] 6d as their customary payment and another 4d since the silver content of the new coins (as a test had shown) was 4d greater than the old. Once the recoinage was complete the 4d surcharge was dropped.

[249] *CPR 1232–47*, 505, 511; *CPR 1247–58*, 12–13; Cassidy, 'Richard of Cornwall and the royal mints', 141.

£20,000) was to be repaid not weight for weight but coin for coin. Any clipped coins he delivered were therefore replaced by whole ones.

There is no sign the government ever made the long-cross coinage compulsory. Yet it quickly became universal. Evidently both payers and payees preferred the new coin. That is the best testimony to the state of the currency prior to 1247 and the utility of the new coinage. How far the recoinage reduced clipping seems impossible to say. There has been no comparison between the condition of long-cross and short-cross pennies. For what it is worth, of the roughly fifty long-cross coins in my own collection, only two or three bear significant signs of clipping. Henry's pennies lasted down to Edward I's recoinage in 1279 and may well have contributed to two decades of stable prices.[250]

Henry III was a king very conscious of his name and fame. He was surely involved with the changes to his style and appearance on the new coins – the declaration that he was Henry the third, the more impressive crown and the introduction of the sceptre. Even allowing for the repayments to Richard, he seems to have made around £7,000 from his share of the charges down to 1259, enough to build a good part of his castle at Deganwy.[251] If recoinage was Richard of Cornwall's achievement, it would never have taken place without the good relations between Henry and his brother.

THE ARRIVAL OF THE LUSIGNANS

The year 1247 was a pivotal one in Henry's reign. In the previous decade he had established the Savoyard kinsmen of Queen Eleanor in England. They had largely been accepted. Now, in 1247, Henry decided to tie to the kingdom a second group of foreign relatives. These were his own half-brothers and half-sisters, the children of his mother Queen Isabella by her marriage to Hugh de Lusignan. The introduction of the Lusignans brought happiness to Henry but poisoned the politics of the court and damaged his reputation in the country. It was a major cause of the revolution of 1258.

The Lusignan party arrived in England in April 1247. It included Henry's half-sister Alice. She had come to marry John de Warenne, heir to the earldom of Surrey.[252] Since John, in his late teens, was still a minor in the king's custody, and had spent much time at court, this was a marriage Henry was very able to arrange.[253] Also in the party was the

---

[250] Bolton, *Money in the Medieval Economy*, 182. For continued clipping, see Eaglen, *Abbey and Mint of Bury St Edmunds*, 163; Allen, *Mints and Money*, 374.

[251] Cassidy, 'Richard of Cornwall and the royal mints', 141, 143; Allen, *Mints and Money*, 190–2.

[252] FitzThedmar, 12.

[253] Wild, *WA*, 47–9.

youngest of the half-brothers, Aymer. Destined for the church, he was now to stay in England and pursue his studies at Oxford University. He was later to go on to much greater things. The leader of the party, Guy de Lusignan, Henry rewarded with a pension of 300 marks a year and a promise to convert it into land from wardships or escheats. As an advance on the pension, he provided Guy with an immediate payment of £1,000.[254] At the end of the year, Henry granted a similar 300-mark pension to another half-brother, Geoffrey de Lusignan.[255] Geoffrey had not been part of the original party but had hurried to England on hearing the prizes on offer.

Pensions worth 300 marks were never sufficient to tie Guy and Geoffrey permanently to England, as Henry must have known. Early in 1248 the brothers returned home, although much more was to be seen of them in the 1250s.[256] They left behind another brother already established in the kingdom. This was William de Valence.[257]

William de Valence's stiff and formal effigy in Westminster Abbey, hands joined together in prayer (it is made of Limoges enamel covering a wooden core) gives little impression of the trouble he caused in England during the reign of Henry III. In 1247, the youngest of the brothers apart from Aymer, he was probably in his late teens and yet to be knighted. His establishment in England was made possible by an extraordinary piece of luck. In June 1247, so a couple of months after the Lusignans' arrival, Henry learnt of the death of John de Munchesney.[258] This meant that John's inheritance as one of the Marshal heirs (his mother was the youngest daughter of the old regent) would pass to his sister Joan. Her husband would thus obtain both Pembroke in Wales and Wexford in Ireland. Henry saw his chance. On 13 August 1247, at Windsor, two marriages were celebrated not one. Alice married John de Warenne, and William de Valence married Joan de Munchesney.[259]

Through Alice, Valence obtained land valued at £362 in England and Wales and £341 in Ireland, a total of £703. Henry judged this quite insufficient for his brother. After all, Peter of Savoy had gained land worth over £1,000 a year with the honour of Richmond and had then received much else besides. Henry, therefore, moved at once to increase the endowment. Valence and his heirs by Joan were promised land worth £500 a year and a pension of that size until the land was found. No land was to be given to anyone else, apart from Richard of Cornwall, until Valence was satisfied.[260]

---

[254] *CLR 1240–5*, 126; *CPR 1232–47*, 502; Wild, *WA*, 56.

[255] *CPR 1247–58*, 3.

[256] *CLR 1245–51*, 159, 166.

[257] This is Valence near Lusignan, not the Valence in the valley of the Rhône.

[258] *CFR 1246–7*, no. 356.

[259] Paris, iv, 628–9.

[260] It was understood that the land in question would be from escheats or wardships, not the royal demesne.

Another pension, this time of an annual 500 marks, was to be paid to Valence throughout his life. All this was on top of the grant of two lucrative wardships (one worth at least £140 a year) and a life grant of Hertford castle and its attendant royal manors (later valued at some £92 a year). Next year Henry granted Valence four manors from the lands of the Normans and stipulated their value was not be deducted from either of his pensions, so this was pure gain. Henry also told the exchequer to give him £200 'notwithstanding' its oath to make no payments until Gascon debts had been met. Valence's total income soon reached some £2,300 a year, making him richer than Simon de Montfort.[261]

Henry had met his half-brothers and sisters back in 1242 during his disastrous campaign in Poitou. But why did he choose this moment to bring them to England? Why bring them to England at all? The answer almost certainly lies in rumours, circulating at the February 1247 parliament, that Louis IX was preparing an invasion of Gascony. The rumours were false, yet were easily believed, given the current turmoil in the duchy. Indeed, they were believed by Matthew Paris.[262] There were also fears about the security of England itself if war broke out with France. In May, Henry revoked William the Conqueror's gift of Winchelsea and Rye to the abbey of Fécamp in Normandy, compensating the house with property elsewhere. He acted 'for the safety of the realm', recognizing that Fécamp, as he said, could scarcely fortify these two Cinque Ports effectively 'in time of war'. In this Henry had been counselled by 'the great men of the kingdom', the relevant exchange being witnessed by assorted prelates, together with the earls of Cornwall, Gloucester and Leicester and Peter of Savoy.[263] Henry also acted with counsel when it came to inviting the Lusignans. This was not one of his impulsive individual decisions. Even Matthew Paris acknowledged that the king's council desired and 'diligently procured' the Valence marriage.[264]

The aim in winning over the Lusignans was thus to provide Henry with a foothold in Poitou and support for the defence of Gascony. Of course, Lusignan power had been badly damaged by the debacle of 1242. Henry's humiliated stepfather, Hugh de Lusignan, was now preparing to leave on Louis IX's crusade. He was to die at the siege of Damietta in June 1249. His sons, however, while very ready to profit from Henry's overtures (tired of being trampled on by the French, Matthew Paris thought), still retained lands and castles in Poitou. The eldest, Hugh XI, had become count of

---

[261] *CChR 1226–57*, 329; *CPR 1247–58*, 10; *CR 1247–51*, 91; Ridgeway, 'Foreign favourites', 592, 595; Maddicott, *Simon de Montfort*, 47.

[262] Paris, iv, 594.

[263] *CChR 1226–57*, 321–2; *RCWL*, ii, 22. The arrangements either replaced or confirmed the exchange arranged in 1245: *CPR 1232–47*, 458.

[264] Paris, iv, 628.

Angoulême on Isabella's death in 1246.[265] Hugh XI himself never came to England but he too (in 1249) was given a pension worth an annual 400 marks with a promise of conversion into land.[266] In the same year Hugh's daughter Mary was married to Robert de Ferrers, heir to the earldom of Derby. This was a child marriage indeed since Robert was nine and Mary seven.[267]

The establishment of William de Valence had other advantages for Henry. He was able to place key parts of the Marshal inheritance both in Wales and Ireland in the hands of a brother. The lordship of Pembroke itself, with the great castle built by the old regent, was now in family hands. What an extraordinary turnaround since the days when Henry had been humbled by Richard Marshal. Valence, however, spent no time on his Welsh and Irish lordships. Indeed, there is no evidence he ever visited them before the revolution of 1258. Instead, Henry wanted him at court, even to the extent of sometimes forcing him to stay there. By 1249, in the ten months for which there is evidence, he was there in all but two. This set the pattern for the future. Unlike Peter of Savoy, or Guy and Geoffrey de Lusignan, Valence spent the bulk of his time at court. The grant of Hertford castle helped here since it gave Valence a base a day's ride from both Westminster and Windsor.

Aged forty in 1247, Henry was old enough to be Valence's father and shared none of his enthusiasm for tournaments. Yet the age difference is one key to the relationship. Henry felt an almost paternal love and responsibility for his younger brother. Valence's youth and innocence were part of the charm. He also gave in return. Despite moments of frustration, and occasional disobedience, he was prepared to remain at Henry's side. He wanted reward certainly, but with little experience of the world he was unlikely to tax Henry with unwelcome advice. Probably he was adept at telling Henry what he wanted to hear. He had a personality that Henry found delightfully engaging.

Henry's introduction of the Lusignans did nothing to dull his enthusiasm for the Savoyards. In 1246 he gave Peter of Savoy the house in London which was to become the palace of the Savoy. Next year, Peter brought to England two Savoyard 'girls' (as Matthew Paris described them). One married the young Richard de Burgh, lord of Connacht, the other Edmund de Lacy, heir to the earldom of Lincoln.[268] In 1248 both Thomas of Savoy and Beatrice, the queen mother, made a visit and basked again in royal favour. Henry's concern and affection for Eleanor likewise continued as strong as ever. To make quite sure Cheshire was

---

[265] Paris, iv, 628–9. For the French grip on Poitou and the Saintonge, see Chenard, *L'Administration d'Alphonse de Poitiers*, 204–17. Amongst other properties, Guy de Lusignan was lord of Cognac, Geoffrey of Jarnac and William de Valence of Montignac.

[266] *CPR 1247–58*, 35.

[267] *CR 1247–51*, 224–6; *CLR 1245–51*, 260, 279; Burton, 285.

[268] Paris, iv, 598, 628; Howell, *Eleanor of Provence*, 53; Cox, *Eagles of Savoy*, 168–9.

never separated from the crown, he made it part of her dower.[269] For the Christmas of 1247, celebrated at Winchester, he ordered identical beds with scarlet covers to be made for them both. Next year Eleanor was bought another bed of the best striped cloth 'suitable for a queen'.[270]

It was equally no part of Henry's policy to construct a foreign court from which native nobles were excluded. Rather, he hoped native nobles would be drawn into the court by marriages to his kin.[271] This was not an unreasonable aspiration. Matthew Paris described the two Savoyard 'girls' brought by Peter of Savoy as 'ignoble and unknown'. Subsequently he deleted the 'ignoble'.[272] He was right to do so. Henry was not alone in thinking that English barons were dignified rather than disparaged by marriages to high-born Savoyards. Edmund de Lacy's bride was the daughter of the marquess of Saluzzo.[273] Later another daughter of the marquess was married to the heir of the Northumberland baron William de Vescy, a marriage arranged with William's consent by the queen and Peter of Savoy.[274] Native nobles had much to gain through such marriages. Both Warin de Munchesney, with his daughter married to William de Valence, and William de Ferrers, earl of Derby, with his son married to the daughter of Hugh de Lusignan, were supported by the king in their lawsuits.[275] Both John de Warenne and Edmund de Lacy secured entry into their inheritances before coming of age. In the great crisis of 1258, Warenne stood by the king and the Lusignans, so the marriage had done its work despite Alice's death (much lamented both by Warenne and Henry) two years earlier.[276]

Henry's policy towards the Lusignans was also supported or at least accepted by the two most powerful English earls. Both Richard of Cornwall and Richard de Clare spent a good deal of time at court in 1247 and were probably amongst the councillors who supported the Valence marriage. The Lusignans were just as much Richard of Cornwall's kin as Henry's and there is no evidence they ever quarrelled, or at least not in any significant way. Doubtless that was partly thanks to Henry himself, who made clear his promises to Richard had a higher priority than those

---

[269] *CPR 1232–47*, 394, 501 (May 1247).

[270] *CR 1247–51*, 12, 86.

[271] See below, 613.

[272] Paris, iv, 628.

[273] The weddings at Woodstock in April 1247 were attended by the earls of Gloucester, Leicester and Norfolk as well as Peter of Savoy: Paris, iv, 628; *RCWL*, ii, 22 (28 April). The marquess of Saluzzo had married Beatrice of Savoy, niece of Thomas, Peter and Archbishop Boniface.

[274] *CPR 1247–58*, 237–8.

[275] Moore, 'The Thorrington dispute' and below, 537; Carpenter, *Reign of Henry III*, 32–3.

[276] Paris, v, 551. Edmund de Lacy died in 1258. Henry's numerous gifts shows Alice was a particular favourite.

to his half-brothers. Richard de Clare was only a few years older than William de Valence. They shared a love of tournaments and tried to persuade Henry to permit them.[277] In 1253 (handsomely rewarded by Henry himself), Clare agreed that his son and heir should marry another of the king's Lusignan nieces.[278]

Unfortunately, Henry's aim of creating a harmonious court composed of his foreign relatives and his native magnates proved hard to achieve. Soon deep divisions were opening up between Lusignans and Savoyards. In terms of numbers far fewer Lusignans were established in England. Eight of them received land as opposed to thirty-nine Savoyards.[279] Henry's court, however, was still transformed. Where the queen, Peter of Savoy and their followers had once shone alone, they now had to share Henry's love with William de Valence and Lusignan knights like Elyas de Rabayne and William de Sancta Ermina. Given Henry's limited political skills, tension was inevitable.

Central to that tension was conflict over patronage and here there was a wider background. Quite simply, Henry had less to give after 1247 when establishing the Lusignans than in the decade from 1236 when he was setting up the Savoyards.[280] The 'lands of the Normans' had now mostly been given away. The honour of Richmond confiscated from the duke of Brittany had gone to Peter of Savoy, and there were no equivalents to the long periods when the Clare, Lacy and Warenne earldoms were in the king's hands. And while he had fewer resources Henry had more mouths to feed. He promised pensions of 100 marks or more to twenty-eight Lusignans on top of the 40 promised to Savoyards. The pensions of the half-brothers he was committed to convert into land.[281] Meanwhile, he had to find land for Queen Eleanor, who was increasingly dissatisfied with support just from money. In 1254 he had to endow Edward with a great estate on his marriage to Eleanor of Castile. How tight the situation was is exemplified by the case of William de Valence. By 1258, despite great effort, less than half of the £500 worth of land promised back in 1247 had been found.[282] Even so Valence had done far better than anyone apart from Richard of Cornwall. Already in 1249, in one scramble for patronage, the Savoyards had come off worse. Henry's grant of Bampton in Oxfordshire to William de Valence involved depriving Imbert Pugeys of one-half of the manor and subjecting him to Valence's overlordship for the other.[283]

[277] Paris, iv, 649; Paris, v, 83.

[278] *CPR 1247–58*, 174–5; *CChR 1226–57*, 438.

[279] Ridgeway, 'King Henry III and the "aliens"', 81–2.

[280] This is a major theme of Ridgeway, 'Foreign favourites'.

[281] Ridgeway, 'King Henry III and the "aliens"', 81–2.

[282] Ridgeway, 'Foreign favourites', 595. This was partly, however, because Henry agreed that some gifts should not be deducted from the £500.

[283] *CPR 1247–58*, 35; *CChR 1226–57*, 339; Ray, 'Alien courtiers of thirteenth-century England', 138; Ridgeway, 'Foreign favourites', 600–1.

Valence's arrival threatened one other conflict, which was ominous for the future. This was with Simon de Montfort. Montfort must have worried (very rightly as it turned out) that Valence's endowment would push him down the queue for patronage. There was also a more particular difficulty, one related to Montfort's wider grievances.[284] The Montforts had never been satisfied with the £400 annual payment given to Eleanor as compensation for her dower in the Welsh and Irish lands of her first husband William Marshal. This was the sum agreed by the king and Richard Marshal in 1233 and accepted, so the Montforts said, by Eleanor only under duress. Down to 1245 the money was due from the Marshal earls, and thereafter from the numerous heirs, with the king (as he had pledged in 1233) acting as the guarantor in the case of non-payment.[285] The Montforts alleged that the £400 short-changed Eleanor by around £1,000 a year. That may have been an exaggeration, but research suggests the loss was at least £500 a year, so the grievance was real. The Montforts also maintained that William Marshal had anyway dowered Eleanor not with money but with land, and in particular with land in Pembrokeshire. At Easter 1247, at Henry's suggestion, the Montforts had begun a legal action against John de Munchesney and the other Marshal heirs for the Pembrokeshire dower. (The heirs would have to compensate John for any losses.) The case continued after Valence's succession and, of course, threatened a large part of his landed estate. In the end a day early in 1248 was given for a judgement to be pronounced in the king's presence. But no judgement was ever pronounced. Thanks to the loss of the relevant plea rolls, there is no light to be shed on the reason. The legal issue was difficult. Did the dower given by William Marshal (if such it was) override the later agreement with Richard Marshal? The politics were even more treacherous, for the numerous Marshal heirs, including some of the greatest men in the kingdom, as well as William de Valence, would be the losers if the Montforts won. It is hardly surprising Henry shied away from giving a judgement. He also tried to compensate Montfort in other ways, most strikingly by conceding him Kenilworth castle during Eleanor's lifetime. (The grant took place in January 1248 so around the time the lawsuit was due to be heard.)[286] Still, Montfort was bound to think he was

---

[284] For what follows, see Bémont, *Simon de Montfort*, 335; TNA KB 26/159, mm. 2d–3d; Maddicott, *Simon de Montfort*, 50, 52–3, 131, 133; Carpenter, *Reign of Henry III*, 35. Henry had made an attempt in 1244 to compensate the Montforts for their losses over the dower by granting them a 400-mark annual pension. But this did not continue, probably because of the grant of the 500-mark pension. Montfort fiercely and rightly rebutted any suggestion that the latter had anything to do with the dower: *CLR 1240–5*, 230–1; Maddicott, *Simon de Montfort*, 54.

[285] Whereas the Marshals had generally kept up to date with the payments, it was far more difficult to extract them from the numerous Marshal heirs, so Henry from 1246 began to pick up the tab: *CLR 1245–51*, 85, 118, 215, 226.

[286] *CPR 1247–58*, 5. For the Marshal heirs, see Genealogical Table no. 3.

suffering an injustice. Henry had encouraged him to begin the case when the chief victim was John de Munchesney and backtracked when it was William de Valence. Montfort's antipathy to Valence and his grievance over the dower both played its part in the revolution of 1258.

Quite apart from fomenting divisions at court, the events of 1247 marked a shift in Henry's relations with the country. Four marriages involving his foreign relatives took place in this year. This seemed something new and sparked in Matthew Paris a new refrain, one growing in volume over the following years. There was, he opined, indignation throughout the kingdom at the way 'the English nobility was being given away to unknown immigrants'.[287] The favours to the foreigners were certainly conspicuous. Both the Dunstable annalist and the London alderman Arnold fitzThedmar noted the arrival of the Lusignans and the wedding of William de Valence. The Burton annals commented on the young age of Robert de Ferrers and his bride. Those of Tewkesbury complained about the way abbots and priors were forced to give pensions to Aymer de Lusignan.[288] The patronage given to foreigners and their prominence at Henry's side was also obvious to the many people who came to court on business. It was equally apparent to the bishops, barons, abbots and knights who attended parliament. And it was apparent to the religious houses like St Albans though which Henry passed with his foreign relatives and their satellites at his side. A dangerous gulf was opening up between Henry and his kingdom.[289]

THE CEREMONY OF THE HOLY BLOOD, 13 OCTOBER 1247

In August 1247, as Henry, his queen and children made their way from Woodstock to Windsor for the Valence wedding, they passed through Dunstable and stayed a couple of days at the priory. The steward Paulinus Peyvre and the judge Roger of Thirkleby together settled a dispute between the prior and the burgesses of the town. Henry himself is seen in that round of gift exchange which made his journeys so pietistic and congenial, congenial both for him and, he hoped, those he met. The priory thus gave gold cups to Henry and Eleanor and gold brooches to Edward and Margaret. The cost was 22 marks 'besides other expenses'. Henry and Eleanor, for their part, gave the priory eight silk cloths and £5 to make a silver censer and a cup to hold the 'eucharist'. The censer was to purify the way as the cup 'with the body of Christ' was carried

---

[287] Paris, iv, 598, 628–9. Paris had not commented on the earlier marriages of John de Plessis and Peter and Ebulo of Geneva, in the two last cases perhaps because they involved Irish women.

[288] Dunstable, 171–7; FitzThedmar, 12; Burton, 285; Tewkesbury, 138.

[289] For a different view suggesting that Henry's foreign favourites did not arouse much opposition or interest before 1258, see Ridgeway, 'King Henry III and the "aliens"', 86.

to those lying sick in the town.[290] Henry, however, was soon planning a much bigger procession and a gift not to an individual religious house but to the kingdom itself, a gift involving not the body of Christ as created in the mass but of something, if possible, even more extraordinary.

Sometime before the end of September 1247, Henry received a gift from the patriarch of Jerusalem.[291] It was none other than a crystal cup containing a particle of the very blood Christ had shed upon the Cross. Some doubts were expressed about whether the relic was genuine. After all when Christ rose from the dead surely he resumed all the blood he had shed upon the cross. Fortunately Robert Grosseteste was at hand to lay these doubts to rest. He explained that there were two types of blood. There was that 'stored in the innermost chamber of the heart', which constituted 'the necessary blood of life'. This had indeed risen with Christ and (subject always to God's will) could not be found on earth. There was, however, also a second type of blood derived from 'nutrition', excesses of which could burst forth, for example in nose bleeds. It was this type of blood which Joseph of Arimathea had collected from Christ's body on the cross. It had passed down through his descendants until finally coming into the hands of the patriarch of Jerusalem.

The patriarch stressed he wished no reward for this momentous gift. He did, however, in his letter to Henry, expand on the terrible situation in the Holy Land, the implication being that it needed Henry's help. Here his plea elicited little immediate response. It was not until 1250 that Henry took the cross. He also did nothing to respond to the patriarch's plea for the restoration of his rights over various churches in England.[292] But Henry was overjoyed and exhilarated by the gift. The patriarch stressed that, having 'the blood of our salvation' before his eyes, Henry would have a permanent reminder of Christ's passion, a permanent sight of the blood, as the patriarch put it, poured out 'for your redemption and salvation and that of all Christians'. It was thus (as the bishop of Norwich explained in a sermon on the subject) the most sacred of all relics surviving amongst mortals. It was 'the price of the world, its effusion the salvation of human kind'.

The patriarch had said nothing specific about how Henry should treat the Holy Blood. If it was to be always before his eyes, might it not form the centrepiece of his own relic collection? But Henry was thinking along

---

[290] Dunstable, 173–4; *CLR 1245–51*, 137.

[291] For all of what follows, see Vincent, *Holy Blood*.

[292] Vincent, *Holy Blood*, 24–9, suggests that these were rights associated with the order of the Holy Sepulchre. Henry did at least place the Holy Blood in the hospital of the Holy Sepulchre in London prior to the ceremony he was planning. The text of the letter is found between 202 and 204 and it is fully discussed in ch. 3.

much bigger and more public lines. The gift of the Holy Blood honoured both him and his kingdom. It had the power to transform the spiritual life of both. As the bishop of Norwich put it, the blood had been sent 'out of the greatest reverence for the holiness of the king of England, who is known to be amongst all Christian princes, the most Christian'.[293] It had also come to England because 'as all the world knows, faith and holiness flourish there more than any other region in the wide world'.

There was a further factor behind the decisions Henry now took. He was inspired by the king of France. In 1239 Louis had acquired the crown of thorns, fragments of the Holy Cross and other relics of Christ's passion. He was now building a splendid chapel in Paris as their home. In acquiring the Holy Blood, Henry could bless England in the same way. As the bishop of Norwich again put it, 'in the possession of so great a treasure England is glorified and can rejoice no less than can France in the reception of the Holy Cross, which the king of France loves and venerates'.[294] Indeed, the blood was *more* sacred than the Holy Cross since the cross derived its sacrality from the way Christ's blood had been shed upon it.

Although no contemporary commentator made the link, there was one other aspect to Henry's eager reception of the Holy Blood. At the end of 1246, Pope Innocent had canonized Henry's erstwhile archbishop of Canterbury Edmund of Abingdon. In June 1247 he was translated to his shrine in the Cistercian abbey of Pontigny in Burgundy.[295] The canonization owed much to miracles at Pontigny and the monastery's desire for a saint, but there was also a growing cult in England, particularly at Catesby, where Edmund's sisters were custodians of his cloak, hence the way Henry himself called the cloak in aid during Eleanor's pregnancy in 1245.[296] Henry was delighted when he heard the news of the canonization.[297] Over his later differences with Edmund his conscience was probably clear.[298] Edmund had not been exiled. He had left England voluntarily and had died on his way to see the pope. That his body reposed at Pontigny, the scene of Becket's exile, was purely fortuitous. Having died soon after leaving the monastery, where he had broken his journey, he was naturally brought back there for burial. But inevitably Edmund was soon being compared to Becket as someone who had fought for the liberty of the church and been exiled in consequence. What made this worse was the

---

[293] Paris, iv, 642–3.

[294] Paris, iv, 642.

[295] The body is still at Pontigny but in an eighteenth-century shrine, grotesque or glorious according to taste.

[296] Simon Langton, however, had a hard time, so he said, getting together a delegation from Kent to testify to Edmund's miracles. Perhaps he was wondering why it was Edmund, not his brother Stephen, who was being made a saint: Lawrence, *St Edmund of Abingdon*, 19; Benoit, 'Autour des tombeaux de Saint Edme à Pontigny', 44.

[297] Paris, iv, 586.

[298] See above, 215, 476–7.

way the French royal house had taken ownership of the new saint. Both Louis IX and his mother were present at the translation. The Holy Blood allowed Henry to demonstrate that, whatever was said about his treatment of Edmund, he too was a most Christian king.[299]

The last thing Henry wished to do, therefore, was to keep the Holy Blood for himself as some private relic. Instead, in a moment of inspiration, he saw how three things could be linked together: the Holy Blood, Edward the Confessor and, yes, William de Valence. He would summon the great and good of the kingdom to Westminster Abbey on 13 October 1247, there to celebrate the feast of the Confessor's translation. On the same day he would offer the Holy Blood to the Confessor, the Abbey and the kingdom. And he would also knight William de Valence: what better way to embed him into the community of the realm. As Matthew Paris put it, 'a multiple feast was to be made serene and joyful by the presence of the magnates, prelates and others, to the honour of the king and kingdom'.

Henry prepared himself for the great ceremony by fasting the day before on bread and water and staying up in prayer during the night.[300] On 13 October itself, instead of just taking the blood across from the palace to the Abbey, he received it at St Paul's, being met there by all the clergy of London holding banners, crosses and lighted candles. Henry, dressed as a pauper, and walking on foot under a canopy borne by four men just as at his coronation, then carried the cup with the blood all the way to the Abbey, holding it above his head with both hands, and never taking his eyes from it despite the poor quality of the road.[301] At the bishop of Durham's house in the Strand he was met by the monks of Westminster and attendant bishops singing and shedding tears of emotion. As the procession neared the Abbey, the rising walls of Henry's new church came into focus. For the time being the blood must repose in what remained of the church of the Confessor, but the new Abbey would be its ultimate home.

On his arrival at Westminster, Henry carried the blood round the Abbey, round his rooms in the palace and then, 'as a gift without price enriching the whole of England', offered it to God, the Abbey 'and to his dear Edward and the holy convent who minister there to God and his saints'. Back in the palace, now dressed in cloth of gold and wearing a gold coronet, Henry sat 'gloriously' on his throne, doubtless that with

---

[299] Paris, iv, 586, 631–2, 636, 646–7; Paris, vi, 120–7; Lawrence, *St Edmund of Abingdon*, 285–6; Creamer, 'St Edmund of Canterbury and Henry III', 134–6; Grant, *Blanche of Castile*, 134–5, 221–2. The recovery of the saint for England was helped by Richard of Cornwall. After a mission to King Louis (which meant he missed the presentation of the Holy Blood) he went on a pilgrimage to Pontigny: Paris, iv, 646–7.

[300] Paris, iv, 640–5.

[301] Paris, iv, 553; *CR 1242–7*, 424; *CChR 1226–57*, 321–2.

the bronze lions in Westminster Hall, and joyfully knighted William de Valence and several other nobles. Afterwards, spying Matthew Paris, Henry told him to sit on the step beneath the throne and enjoined him to write a full account of the day lest the memory of it be lost to posterity. He also invited him and his three colleagues to the ensuing feast. Paris replied, dutifully but sincerely, that the events of the day were indeed 'truly glorious' and his account was all Henry could have wished. There was not even a hint of criticism when it came to the knighting of William de Valence.[302]

Henry, therefore, had given a relic, more precious than any other, to the realm. He must have hoped it would show its gratitude at forthcoming parliaments.

THE PARLIAMENTS OF 1248

Henry's financial needs at this time seemed as pressing as ever. He had to fund a war in Gascony and the building of Westminster Abbey on top of all the payments and pensions he had promised to the Lusignans, Savoyards, Simon de Montfort and Richard of Cornwall. He was also heavily in debt to merchants.[303] In January and February 1248 he ordered the exchequer to pay out around £680 to over thirty wine merchants. Payment of another £2,093 owed to merchants of Ypres, Douai, Spain, Gotland and Eastland for cloth, wax and fur had to be postponed until the Easter exchequer. He had to do the same with 1,675 marks worth of Gascon debts.[304]

Parliament met in London on 9 February and was well attended by bishops, earls, barons and knights.[305] There was some agreement. Henry accepted the decision of his 'magnates' that vacant churches in the gift of laymen should be exempted from the subsidy promised the church of Canterbury by the pope. (This was easier to agree since Archbishop Boniface was overseas.)[306] But when it came to the tax Henry wanted, he got nowhere.[307] The Holy Blood had not made a difference. As in 1244, Henry was faced with the demand 'from each and all' that he appoint a justiciar, chancellor and treasurer 'by the common counsel of his kingdom'. The critique of his rule focused precisely on the way he was taking food, wine and cloth from merchants without payment, to the great detriment, it was said, of the kingdom's trade. The scale of his almsgiving and his

---

[302] Note also how in the immediately preceding chapter, bar one, Matthew Paris praises Henry's 'firm faith' when asking for prayers for the recovery of Edward from illness: Paris, iv, 639.

[303] This was despite spending £3,296 in 1245–6, acquitting old debts of the wardrobe and household: Wild, *WA*, 56.

[304] *CLR 1245–51*, 161, 163, 166; *CPR 1247–58*, 7, 9–10.

[305] Maddicott, *Origins of the English Parliament*, 464–5.

[306] *CR 1247–51*, 109, and 106–7 for the parliament quashing an outlawry.

[307] Paris, v, 5–8, is the source for what follows.

lighting of candles itself seemed 'ill judged, immoderate and superfluous' when the food and wax were taken without payment.[308] The mood in the parliament cannot have been helped by the exactions of the king's judges in the localities, hearing both judicial pleas and pleas of the forest. The justices of the general eyre visited seventeen counties between 1245 and 1247.[309] The forest judges, headed by Robert Passelewe, between December 1244 and early 1248 visited twelve counties, imposing penalties worth some £10,296.[310]

The other focus of complaint was Henry's prodigal distribution of patronage to 'aliens' and the way he was marrying them off to the noble men and women of the kingdom.[311] The issue of 'the aliens' had hardly been raised in the parliaments of 1244–5. The events of 1247 had changed all that. The situation was aggravated by two measures Henry took early in 1248 showing magnates all too clearly where their money was going. In January, Henry assigned to William de Valence £3,196 worth of debts owed by the great northern baron Peter de Brus (the lord of Skelton). Peter had not incurred this burden on his own account. Rather he had inherited the debt with his wife's half of the barony of Kendal. Now he was to pay the debt off at £200 a year and was also encouraged to sell Valence land in lieu. By 1251 he had paid Valence £700. Brus considered these terms 'grievous and unjust'. The revolutionary council set up in 1258 agreed and halved the rate of payment.[312] Henry's concession to Valence was followed in February 1248 by the assignment to Thomas of Savoy and his elder brother Count Amadeus of the 700 marks owed each year by Hugh Bigod for the wardship of Baldwin de Wake.[313] Hugh Bigod was the younger brother of Roger Bigod, earl of Norfolk. In 1258 he was to become justiciar of England.

---

[308] Paris, v, 6.

[309] Crook, *Records of the General Eyre*, 105–12.

[310] Winters, 'The forest eyre 1154–1368', 181–91. The £10,296 is money owed not money paid in. Rates of repayment varied and were sometimes slow when large individual amercements were involved. In the fine rolls of 1245/6 many favoured individuals were given terms on which to pay their amercements. The sum includes the 2,000 marks owed by John de Neville for his transgressions as chief forester, although he was allowed to pay the debt off at 100 marks a year: *CFR 1245–6*, no. 223; Paris, iv, 400, 427.

[311] There were also complaints about Henry's exploitation of ecclesiastical vacancies.

[312] *CPR 1247–58*, 5, 29, 33, 41; *CPR 1258–66*, 4; TNA E 372/93 (http://aalt.law.uh.edu/AALT4/H3/E372n093/aE372n093fronts/IMG_5897.htm) and TNA E 372/95 (http://aalt.law.uh.edu/AALT4/H3/E372n095/aE372n095fronts/IMG_6199.htm). With the expulsion of William de Valence in 1258, the debt returned to the king. In 1248, Henry also assigned to Valence the debt owed by Walter de Lindsey for his half of the same barony and its rate of payment was also reduced in 1258. The debts in question were debts owed to the Jews.

[313] The assignment was to pay their annual pensions. Hugh Bigod had married Joan Wake, Baldwin's mother, who had made the initial fine for the wardship: *CFR 1241–2*, no. 105; *CPR 1247–58*, 9. Thomas and his sister, Beatrice of Savoy, were at this time in England. Peter of Savoy was at court in February and for much of the year.

Faced with these criticisms at parliament, Henry, much as in 1244, was apologetic and promised reform. The question of the tax was thus adjourned to another parliament scheduled for July. Henry almost at once set off on a pilgrimage to Bury, Walsingham and Bromholm. He also made moves to appease his critics. On the way back to Westminster for the celebration of Easter, he stayed with Roger Bigod at Framlingham and respited payment of his debts. He also made concessions to John de Burgh, including pardoning him a debt 'for the soul' of his father, Hubert. These were but two of many concessions over debts, made to lay and ecclesiastical magnates between the parliaments.[314] It was at this time that both John de Warenne and Edmund de Lacy succeeded to their inheritances despite being underage.[315]

The second parliament opened in London on 8 July and was for Henry no better than the first. It again demanded the election of a justiciar, chancellor and treasurer. When that was denied, it again refused to grant any tax. Henry now changed tack completely. He made an aggressive speech justifying his refusal to appoint officials at parliament's bidding. Matthew Paris is the only source for what was said, but *The Song of Lewes* later sets out the king's case in similar terms.[316] The magnates, Henry complained, were denying the king the right enjoyed by every head of a household to appoint whomever he wished to this or that office. (In the version in *The Song of Lewes*, it is every earl who can give castles, lands and revenues as he pleases.) Henry also set out what he saw as the proper relationship between the king and his subjects. He quoted Matthew 10:24: 'the servant is not above his lord nor the disciple above his master'. Vassals should not seek to judge 'their prince'. Rather, they should be directed by the will of their lord and master. The magnates of England should not, therefore, be subjecting the king to their 'will' and reducing him to servitude.

Henry was thus speaking far more aggressively than in 1244 when he had stressed the common interests of king and kingdom: 'if I am poor, you are poor'. Now he seemed to be setting out a very different view of the realm, one where it was more or less a private estate that the king could run as he pleased.[317] Matthew Paris blamed the new approach on Henry's advisers, and doubtless they helped him with the speech. But Henry himself was exasperated by the reiterated demand for elected officials and felt the need to rebut it. How wise his arguments were was questionable. Although the

---

[314] *CFR 1247–8*, nos. 262–3, 272, and the fine rolls generally for the concessions.

[315] Edmund de Lacy paid 1,300 marks for the concession: *CFR 1247–8*, no. 599. This makes a striking contrast to the 7,000 marks King John demanded from his father, John de Lacy, at the time of his succession, although he was not then under age: *RF*, 494–5. The concession to John de Warenne excluded the Surrey and Sussex lands given to Peter of Savoy.

[316] *Song of Lewes*, lines 485–526. *The Song of Lewes*, written after Simon de Montfort's victory in 1264, explains Henry's case only then to knock it down. Paris was actually in Norway in July 1248 so he must have received an account of the speech on his return.

[317] Maddicott, ' "1258" and "1297" ', 11–12.

context was defending the right to appoint his own officials, the statement that subjects needed to be directed by the will of their lord could have wider implications. The analogy between the king's position and the head of a household was easy to rebut. As the Paper Constitution argued, since the king's officials handled the affairs of everyone (unlike those of a magnate), everyone should concur in their choice. If, moreover, Henry was saying to his magnates 'if you don't interfere with me, I won't interfere with you', where did that leave his duty to protect everyone from oppression, baronial as well as royal?[318] Henry would have done better to have stuck to the mutual interests of himself and his subjects and the argument he was acting 'for the common utility of all the kingdom', as the prologue to the 1236 Statute of Merton put it.[319] Instead, he now gave the impression he was ruling only for himself, thus fulfilling one contemporary criterion for being a tyrant.[320]

Henry took the refusal of taxation in 1248 very much to heart. It was not until 1252 that he sought another tax from parliament.

THE AFFAIR OF THE FAIR AND THE ALTON ROBBERY CASE, 1248-9

In the autumn of 1248, Henry's desire to support Westminster Abbey exacerbated his often fraught relations with London. The episode shows both Henry's power and the way it could be limited by his magnates.[321]

In July 1245, just as he was beginning to demolish the church of the Confessor, Henry had granted the monks of Westminster the right to hold fairs for three days around both the 13 October and 5 January feasts of the 'glorious King Edward'.[322] In 1248, Henry went further and extended the duration of the fairs to sixteen days.[323] He encouraged attendance by promising that at the October fair (always the most important) he would pay at once for his own purchases. He also ordered the shops and stalls in London to be closed for the fair's duration. Perhaps there were proclamations to the same effect in other towns.[324] In all this, Henry's aim was to ensure that 'innumerable people, flocked [to Westminster] as to the most famous fairs',

---

[318] For Henry speaking of his 'special duty' to help the oppressed, see *RG*, i, no. 1206.

[319] Burton, 249. See Burt, *Edward I and the Governance of England*, 43–4.

[320] John of Salisbury, 25, 28–9, 190–3.

[321] For what follows, see FitzThedmar, 14–15; Paris, v, 28–9 (where I do not think the whole account should be transferred to the 5 January feast), 47–8; Letters, *Gazetteer*, i, 237; Rosser, *Medieval Westminster*, 96–115; Williams, *Medieval London*, 206–7; Barron, *London in the Later Middle Ages*, 40.

[322] *CChR 1226–57*, 286.

[323] No charter to this effect survives either as an original or a copy, but it is referred to in a charter of Edward I: *CChR 1257–1300*, 471. Perhaps it was discarded as being made redundant by Edward's charter.

[324] No written orders commanding attendance and closures are known, so it is hard to know how far the statements in Paris, v, 29, and FitzThedmar, 14–15, are accurate.

there to 'venerate the translation of the blessed Edward and the Holy Blood'.[325] They would also, of course, bring money to the Abbey.

None of this was popular. The bishop of Ely protested about the effect on his own fair at Ely held around 17 October. Henry was sympathetic and freed the bishop's liberties from their challenge by the exchequer.[326] But he would not budge on the fair. In October 1248 itself the Londoners attended, as Arnold fitzThedmar put it, 'not compelled and yet compelled'. Other merchants probably felt the same way. What made it worse was the stormy weather and the lack of shelter other than in tents. The merchants were cold, wet and mired in mud. Henry, moreover, was not finished with the Londoners. He assembled the mayor and citizens and asked them to grant (for an exchange) various liberties to the abbot of Westminster in Middlesex. When they refused 'without the assent of the whole commune', Henry, 'as if moved to anger', changed tack and challenged the judgement recently passed in the hustings court against a London widow Margery Viel.[327] In the end Henry was stopped by his magnates. 'Having taken counsel with the bishops and barons, in the presence of the lord king, the mayor and citizens departed quit.'[328] At least the fair itself was a success. Although the one on 5 January was abandoned under Edward I, this was in return for extending the October fair to thirty-two days. By the early fourteenth century it was making a significant contribution to the Abbey's revenues.[329]

In this episode over London, Henry was restrained by his magnates from committing what may have been an act of injustice. Yet this is far from a complete picture of his attitude to law and justice in these years. 'The king does not wish that anyone in his kingdom shall be disseised of any free tenement unjustly and without judgement,' ran one writ from 1249.[330] 'It is not the king's intention to usurp the lands of his faithful subjects by malicious methods,' ran one from 1247.[331] If Henry's interventions were often in favour of influential men, he could also act on the complaints of peasants. So he declared that it was neither 'equitable nor reasonable' for the men of Mansfield to be tallaged other than was customary. The men of Dymock in Gloucestershire were to be treated according to the 'custom of the manor and not burdened unduly'.[332]

Henry was also perfectly capable, at this time, of striking a far more inclusive note than that seen in the parliament of 1248. In a letter begging for financial aid, he declared it was natural for his faithful subjects to help

[325] Paris, v, 28–9.

[326] *CR 1247–51*, 128.

[327] FitzThedmar, 12–15.

[328] *CFR 1248–9*, no. 96; Paris, v, 47; Wild, *WA*, 54. The Londoners did, however, give the king an expensive New Year's gift.

[329] Rosser, *Medieval Westminster*, 101–6.

[330] *CR 1247–51*, 235, and 49, 100 for other examples.

[331] *CR 1247–51*, 504.

[332] *CR 1242–7*, 505; *CR 1247–51*, 141.

him protect the rights of his kingdom, breathing as they did under the wings of his protection.[333] Matthew Paris's account of the 5 January 1249 feast of the Confessor was wholly favourable. On the eve, Henry fasted on bread and water and wore woollen clothes. The next day he celebrated magnificently in the presence of a multitude of magnates (including the earls of Cornwall, Norfolk and Hereford). They had gathered, Paris believed, 'out of devotion and love of the saint, out of veneration for the holy blood of Christ and to obtain the pardon of their sins, and out of reverence for the king who had called them'.[334]

In 1249, Henry displayed his concern for law, order and justice in a dramatic fashion, indeed in the most dramatic fashion in his reign. This introduces the Alton robbery case.[335] In the thirteenth century an important road from Winchester ran north-east to Alresford and then climbed steeply to the village of Medstead, some 700 feet above sea level. From there the 'high road', as it was called, followed the ridge of the hill through thick beech woods for two or three miles before descending to Alton, whence it continued to Farnham and Guildford.[336] This passage through the woods was known as the pass of Alton. It was an obvious place for highway robbery. In 1248, Henry, when staying at Winchester, sent sergeants-at-arms to guard it. They did not do their job. That autumn, as the beech trees turned a golden brown, a group of Brabantine merchants were ambushed and plundered as they proceeded through the pass. What made this a cause célèbre was the enormous size of the haul: Henry later compensated the merchants to the tune of £132. He felt keenly the shame of the outrage within the heartland of the kingdom and close to his birthplace at Winchester. He also saw there would be damage to trade if foreign merchants were not safe in the country. Henry needed to stamp down hard.

His first move (in September 1248) was to order an inquiry 'by knights and good men' into the robbery. Headed by Henry de Mara, the knight who had represented the community at the council of Lyon, it made limited progress other than blaming unnamed outlaws. The problem was that local men were deeply implicated in the robbery and local jurors were reluctant to identify them. When the names of two ringleaders were at last disgorged they turned out to be men of gentry status from the vicinity of Alton. They were both arrested only to escape. One of them, John de Bendinges, had been a royal sergeant-at-arms in Wales in 1245 and 1246. Quite probably he was one of those appointed to guard the pass. The involvement of those in the king's service was another disturbing feature

---

[333] Paris, v, 52–3.

[334] Paris, v, 29, 47–8.

[335] For all of what follows, see Clanchy, 'Highway robbery'.

[336] This is essentially the route of the preserved steam railway the Watercress Line. The steep inclines led engine men to call the route 'over the Alps'.

of the whole affair. Indeed, a man working for one of Henry's cooks had supplied food to the outlaws in Alton wood.

With Mara having failed, Henry now looked to the justices of the general eyre who were due to hear the criminal and civil pleas for Hampshire at Winchester in January 1249. Twelve jurors from all the Hampshire hundreds, including those from Alton and the adjoining hundreds of Selborne and Odiham, were duly summoned to appear before them. Given the jurors' duty was to accuse all those guilty of crime since the last eyre, they would surely now name the Alton robbers. Then other jurors could be empanelled to judge the truth of their accusations. The eyre justices, however, although headed by the formidable Henry of Bath, encountered precisely the same difficulties as Henry de Mara.

It was at this point that Henry himself intervened and in dramatic fashion. He made a special journey from Westminster to Winchester, arriving on or shortly before 24 January. He then summoned the recalcitrant jurors to appear before him in the great hall of the castle, the hall he had built, which survives to this day. Having made a speech about the shameful nature of both the crime and the cover up, he 'suddenly and frighteningly shouted out "close the doors, close the doors immediately" '. With the jurors unable to escape, and perhaps looking up apprehensively at the wheel of fortune painted in the gable behind the dais, Henry then threatened them with imprisonment and execution if they did not tell the truth. This did the trick and the full extent of local involvement in the robbery was at last revealed.

There is only Matthew Paris's word for Henry's speech.[337] But the essence of his account is unlikely to be wrong. The roll of the justices in eyre itself reveals the punishment of corrupt jurors and also the charging of sixty-four people with offences connected with robbery, so in the end the jurors' tongues were loosened. The trial jurors, nonetheless, kept their balance and acquitted as many men as they convicted. Most of those caught and executed (perhaps thirty in all) were men of small estate, but they included one of the electors of the Selborne jury. Although the three main gentry ringleaders were eventually pardoned, including John de Bendinges, they suffered great financial losses. Most of the stolen goods, moreover, seem to have been discovered amongst Bendinges' possessions.

Matthew Paris was impressed by Henry's performance in the Alton case. Everyone, he said, greatly admired the skilful and terrifying way the king questioned the jurors. The countryside around Winchester was freed from thieves 'through the revenge of God and the measures of the king'.[338] The latter included cutting down the wood on either side of the pass. Henry also ordered his seat in the hall at Winchester to be repainted.[339]

---

[337] Paris, v, 56–60.
[338] Paris, *HA*, iii, 47; Paris, *FH*, ii, 361.
[339] *CR 1247–51*, 167; *CLR 1245–51*, 221.

THE HALF-BROTHERS: A QUARREL AND AN
EPISCOPAL ELECTION

In November 1249 even his beloved brother William de Valence felt the force of King Henry's anger. Valence had been at court for much of the year, warmed by the king's favour. That August he received from Henry a real plum, namely the wardship of the infant heir of Roger fitzJohn. This promised twenty years' control of Clavering in Essex and Warkworth castle in Northumberland. At least the annual value of the estates (put at £145) was deducted from Valence's annual fee, although the £200 he offered for the wardship was soon pardoned. The heir's mother, Ada de Balliol, so Matthew Paris heard, had offered Henry £800 for it.[340]

Trouble, however, was brewing and it was over tournaments.[341] As a young man, eager to win his knightly spurs, Valence longed to attend them. As a king, with little interest in martial exploits, concerned for the peace of the realm, and worried about Valence suffering death or injury (it was at a tournament in France that Roger fitzJohn had been killed), Henry wanted to ban them. Nonetheless, on the day of Valence's knighting and the ceremony of the Holy Blood, Henry had bowed to the prayers of the young Richard de Clare and agreed to licence tournaments, or so at least Clare thought. Clare and Valence accordingly planned to tourney against each other at Northampton, only for Henry at the last moment to change his mind. The following year, 1248, the two did better. While Henry was on his East Anglian pilgrimage, they were allowed to hold a tournament at Newbury. Valence came off worst but at least showed his mettle. He tried again in February 1249 at Northampton without permission, and gained some honour through promising to protect the participants from the king. Snow, however, caused this contest to be abandoned. The tourneyers met again the following November at Brackley, where the rebel barons had gathered in 1215. Again they lacked the king's consent, but this time they went ahead. Clare, having previously fought against Valence and other courtiers, now switched sides and gave them the victory. Paris thought this a shameful transfer from the English side to that of the aliens. But Clare's very conduct meant such divisions were not clear cut.[342]

Henry, however, was furious. He seized the lands of both Valence and Valence's brother-in-law John de Warenne and ordered everything on Valence's Irish estates to be sold. The proceeds were to go to Simon de Montfort in Gascony, perhaps a hint at the tension between the two men. One of the king's household knights, Geoffrey Gascelin, fared even worse, although Henry's actions were hardly very measured or likely to be effective.

---

[340] *CPR 1247–58*, 46–7, 124–5; Paris, v, 92; Paris, *HA*, 67; *CFR 1248–9*, no. 434; *CFR 1229–50*, no. 490.

[341] For a series of model letters about tournaments, see Carlin and Crouch, *Lost Letters*.

[342] Paris, iv, 649; Paris, v, 17–18, 54, 83; Tewkesbury, 157. For an emphasis more in line with Paris's, see Barker, *Tournament in England*, 48–50.

With dubious legality he set in train the process of Gascelin's outlawry, while at the same time seeking (with a gift of three deer) to persuade Gascelin's mother-in-law to sell off her lands so Gascelin would not inherit them![343]

As so often Henry's rage did not last for long. By Christmas both Valence and Warenne (whose wife was pregnant) were back in favour. Gascelin too made his peace.[344] Henry's confidence in his half-brothers was unshaken. When in 1250 a golden opportunity came to promote the youngest, Aymer, Henry seized it with both hands.

On arriving in England in 1247, Aymer had commenced his studies at Oxford.[345] Almost at once, an ominous foretaste of future trouble, his baker was killed, presumably in a fight. Henry took the government of the town into his hands until the mayor and citizens made their (expensive) peace. In the following years, Henry showed a continuous concern for his youngest brother. He evidently felt for him the same kind of protective affection as he did for William de Valence. Quite apart from numerous gifts of wine, deer, fish and firewood, he presented him with rich livings and pressurized religious houses to do the same. Normal rules did not apply. Some 200 marks given to Aymer from the issues of the Essex eyre were to be raised at once notwithstanding the terms Henry had previously conceded for their payment.[346] None of this made Aymer very popular, but Henry was far from finished. Only a bishopric, and a great bishopric at that, would do for his brother.

Henry's opportunity came with the death of the bishop of Winchester, William of Raleigh, in September 1250. Henry shed dry tears (according to Matthew Paris) and despatched John Mansel and Peter Chaceporc to make Aymer's case with the Winchester monks. In terms of age and experience, Aymer was completely unsuitable for such an office.[347] Henry did not see it like that. Winchester was the richest see in the country. Its diocese embraced the old heartland of the kingdom. Henry had been born in the city. The two bishops so far in his time, des Roches and Raleigh, had been at best difficult, at worst disastrous. How wonderful now to have his youngest brother there; someone he could mould and trust; someone who down the years would give loyal support to both king and kingdom.

As the election drew near, Henry installed himself at the episcopal manor of Marwell, some five miles from Winchester. He had stayed there before when trying to persuade the monks to choose the bishop-elect of

---

[343] *CFR 1249–50*, nos.51–3; *CR 1247–51*, 257, 260–1, 344–5.

[344] *CR 1247–51*, 247–9, 257, 260–1.

[345] For Aymer, see Ridgeway, 'Ecclesiastical career of Aymer de Lusignan'.

[346] *CR 1247–51*, 4, 25–6, 42, 296; Paris, v, 39, 85, 91; Tewkesbury, 138. However, when ordering the sheriff of Northamptonshire to defend and maintain Aymer in one dispute, Henry did add 'as far as [you] can with justice': *CR 1247–51*, 116.

[347] Ridgeway considers him to have been 'fairly respectably educated', though whether he had completed his university studies is not known: Ridgeway, 'Ecclesiastical career of Aymer de Lusignan', 155.

Valence back in 1238. This time he was more successful. The monks had no desire to repeat their traumatic experiences over William of Raleigh. On 4 November they chose Aymer and asked the pope to confirm their choice, a necessity given that Aymer was still underage.[348] Henry then, having come to Winchester, entered the chapter house and ascended to the seat usually taken by the prior or bishop, delivered a sermon to the assembled monks.[349] It was a curious effort, impressive in one way, inappropriate in another.

Henry took as his text a passage from psalm 85: 'justice and peace have kissed each other'. He then explained how the rigour of justice and judgement, through which the people were governed, belonged to him as king. To monks, as men of religion, belonged peace and tranquillity. Thanks to the monks agreeing to his wishes, the two had come together. Henry's words had all the more meaning when put into the context of the psalm as a whole. It begins by looking back to a time when the Lord has forgiven the Israelites their sins. Now, however, they have offended again and the psalmist has to beg once more for God's mercy and the cessation of his anger. In the final section of the psalm he looks forward to the happiness which will follow the answering of the prayer. Henry's quotation comes from this last section. He *has*, therefore, forgiven the monks, although at the same time reminded them of the consequences of his anger.

So far so impressive and appropriate. Yet Henry then set out on another tack. Just as a woman, he said, had been the first ruin of the world, so a woman had been its saviour. He was referring, of course, to Eve and the Virgin Mary. The monks at this point must have wondered what was coming next. Henry explained. The trouble at Winchester had begun when the monks refused to accept his wife's uncle, the bishop-elect of Valence as bishop. It had ended with their acceptance of the son of his mother. It is difficult to see that Eleanor of Provence would have been happy with this scenario in which she seemed to be compared to Eve. Doubtless Henry did not intend it like that, but the whole analogy seems inconsequential and ill judged. It can only have come from Henry himself, and gives a poor impression of the quality of his thought.

After being chosen by the monks, Aymer set off for Lyon, where he was confirmed by the pope although not consecrated. Because of his youth he remained bishop-elect. That did not bother Henry. He welcomed Aymer back to Winchester in July 1251 and gave, by word of mouth, the instructions for his magnificent present: a set of vestments and a chalice, staff and mitre 'suitable for so great a prelate'. The mitre alone cost £80.[350]

---

[348] Harvey, *Episcopal Appointments*, 46.

[349] Paris, v, 180–1. For a discussion of the sermon and the problem of Paris's text (the only source), see Harvey, *Episcopal Appointments*, 81–3. I think the sermon was delivered after rather than before the monks made their choice.

[350] *CR 1247–51*, 413, 472; *CLR 1251–60*, 94.

Henry in his sermon to the monks had hoped Aymer would illuminate their church with the rays of his regal birth. In fact, Aymer did win some good opinions at Winchester.[351] He did not, however, bring 'justice and peace' either to court or the kingdom. Henry may not have meant to cast aspersions on the queen but Aymer was certainly to do so.

Since his return from Gascony in 1243, Henry had chalked up considerable achievements: the birth of a second son, the triumph in Wales, the settlement with King Alexander, the building of Westminster Abbey, the gift of the Holy Blood, the transformation of the currency and, giving him so much pleasure, the establishment of his half-brothers in England. Yet he would also have been aware that there was a new edge to his relations with the church and with parliament. He had been forced to ward off radical schemes of reform designed to strip him of power, an ominous sign for the future. He had also allowed the realm to take the lead in resistance to the pope. Much of the critique of his rule seems, moreover, justified. That fatal combination of simplicity and generosity had led him to give more trust and reward to both Savoyards and Lusignans than was politic. He had failed to see how much his government needed reform both at the centre and in the localities, as the Paper Constitution clearly indicated. The period was barren of the kinds of legislative reform seen in the years between 1234 and 1237. Henry had little leisure to think of such things. By the time of his success over the Winchester election, he had something entirely new on his agenda. In March 1250, Henry took the cross and his whole heart became set on his crusade. Soon, however, that ambition became entangled with something else, namely the necessity of rescuing Gascony from the wreckage of Montfort's lieutenancy. The problems of Gascony are the subject of the next chapter.

---

[351] Ridgeway, 'Ecclesiastical career of Aymer de Lusignan', 174–6.

Chapter 9

GASCONY AND THE INTERNATIONAL CONTEXT
1243–1252

Before his departure from Gascony in the autumn of 1243, Henry III had worked hard to set the province to rights. He had toured the duchy, reconciled competing factions, maintained his rights and bolstered the defences against external attack, or at least tried to do so. But, as a would-be conqueror of Gascony had once said, it was like trying to plough the seashore.[1] For the next ten years Henry was never free from Gascon worries. They led him in 1248 to place the duchy under Simon de Montfort and, when that ended in disaster, they forced him in 1253 to go there himself, despite being now pledged to go on crusade. Henry's concentration on Gascony and commitment to the crusade reflected the more general international situation, which left him with little else to do. There was no chance of attempting to recover the lost continental empire. Indeed, the ten years between Henry's two sojourns in Gascony in 1243 and 1253 saw a significant shift in the European balance of power towards the Capetian kings of France.

Henry had always hoped to counter Capetian power through his alliance with Emperor Frederick II, yet that prospect after 1243 seemed as remote as ever. After the death of Gregory IX in 1241, Henry shared all Frederick's hopes of a reconciliation with his successor. At the great papal council held at Lyon in 1245, the English delegation worked hard to bring it about.[2] To no avail. Innocent IV's horror at Frederick's conduct, and fear that reconciliation could only mean subservience, rendered him implacable. In July 1245 he excommunicated Frederick and, going decisively beyond the anathemas of 1239, pronounced his deposition as emperor, soon broadcasting the sentences, along with lurid lists of his crimes, through Europe. This situation made Frederick all the keener on the English alliance: keen so that he could prevent Henry sending money to the pope, keen so he could prevent any acknowledgement of the successive anti-kings, Henry of Raspe and William of Holland, set up in Germany. To that end, he sent streams of letters and envoys to England.

---

[1] Vincent, 'A forgotten war', 117.
[2] Vincent, 'Henry III, Frederick II and the council of Lyon'; *CR 1242–7*, 356.

They threatened reprisals if Henry helped the pope, yet also canvassed the possibility of some settlement in which young Henry, the fruit of Frederick's marriage with Isabella, might be baptized by the pope and become ruler of Sicily.[3]

King Henry was between a rock and a hard place. He had deep respect for the papacy and feared to the depths of his being the spiritual penalties for disobedience. Yet he was desperate not to offend Frederick, a ruler of seemingly titanic power who might at any time be reconciled to the church. In these circumstances, much like Louis IX and his Savoyard uncles, though with less assurance, Henry endeavoured to steer a middle path. He tried to obstruct papal taxation of the English church (and there were no demands after 1247), but he did not absolutely prevent it.[4] He avoided contact with Raspe, Holland and the arrogant archbishop of Cologne, who crowned them. (The latter was to be depicted on his tomb depositing crowns with either hand on the heads of two little kingly figures.) He still received Frederick's envoys and, in 1247, doubtless aware of the emperor's passion for falconry, allowed one of them to choose four of his gerfalcons to take back as a present.[5] Yet Henry accepted that Frederick was beyond the pale as an acknowledged and active ally.[6] The emperor's death at the end of 1250 brought this uneasy balancing act to an end. It meant William of Holland establishing himself in Germany, while Conrad, Frederick's eldest surviving son, sought control of the kingdom of Sicily. The young Henry, under Frederick's will, was to be the ruler either of imperial Burgundy or of the kingdom of Jerusalem. Frederick's death was a watershed in European history. The Hohenstaufen attempt to wield authority in Germany, northern Italy and Sicily was at an end. For a while in the 1250s 'dazzling prospects' (in Powicke's words) opened up for both Henry and his brother Richard.[7] But it was the Capetians who ultimately profited most from the Hohenstaufen downfall.[8]

THE CAPETIAN ADVANCE AND THE SAVOYARD EMBRACE

In March 1243, out in Gascony, Henry had concluded a five-year truce with Louis IX. It was to be renewed, sometimes for periods of weeks, sometimes for years, on eleven occasions all the way down to the final

---

[3] Weiler, *Henry III of England and the Staufen Empire*, 113, 123.

[4] Lunt, *Financial Relations*, 206–25. For a full discussion, see above, 443–9. Henry's resistance was because of the intense hostility to such taxation in England, irrespective of it being used against the emperor.

[5] *CR 1247–51*, 88.

[6] For this period of Anglo-imperial relations, see Weiler, *Henry III of England and the Staufen Empire*, ch. 5.

[7] Powicke, *Henry III*, i, 187.

[8] The Capetian ascendancy is discussed in Weiler, *Henry III of England and the Staufen Empire*, 118–22.

peace of Paris in 1259.[9] The long delay before a final settlement was not surprising. Both Henry and Louis wished for peace, but on incompatible terms. Louis wanted Henry to resign his claims to the lost territories in France, whereas Henry, however vainly, still wanted to recover them. In late 1243, Louis took an important initiative. He insisted that those still with lands in Normandy and England chose their allegiance. If it was to be French, they must surrender their English lands. In January 1244, Henry replied in kind and ordered all the lands of those 'who are of the power of the king of France' to be seized.[10] Since significant cross-Channel landholders were by this time few, Louis's move was largely symbolic. His aim, quite probably, building on his victory in 1242, was to push Henry towards some final peace by making it absolutely clear he would not surrender Normandy.

Later in 1244, recovering from a dangerous illness, Louis took the cross. His prospective absence made him even keener to reach a settlement with Henry. Over the turn of the year 1245–6, on his initiative, negotiations began both to renew the truce beyond 1248, and explore the possibility of a permanent peace. According to Matthew Paris, if Henry resigned his claims to Normandy where Louis was 'confident of his right', Louis was ready to return all the other continental possessions.[11] Had this been an accurate summary of Louis's terms, Henry would have jumped at them. But it must have been wrong. There was no way Louis was going to remove his brothers Alphonse and Charles from, respectively, Poitou and Anjou. Perhaps all Louis suggested were territorial concessions of much smaller dimensions, the equivalent of those accepted in the final peace of 1259. Whatever the case, the negotiations led neither to a peace nor an extension of the truce, one further point of tension being the future of Provence, of which more later.

Louis's status as a crusader did not stop rumours of his hostile intentions. They may well explain Henry's visit to Dover in the early summer of 1246. Fears that Louis was planning to subjugate Gascony circulated at the February 1247 parliament. Later in the year Henry brought the Lusignans to England, and completed his acquisition of Winchelsea and Rye, acting 'for the safety of the realm'. Fécamp abbey, he said, would be unable to defend them 'in time of war'.[12] In the autumn, however, Henry changed tack. Aware that Louis, anxious as a crusader to depart with a clean bill of spiritual health, was offering to restore everything unjustly

---

[9] Anglo-French relations in this period are covered in detail in Amicie Pelissie du Rausas's doctoral thesis 'Les relations Franco-Anglaises sous Louis IX et Henri III 1242–1259' and I am indebted to it at many points.

[10] Paris, iv, 288; *BF*, iii, 1142–3. Since many with good title to their land found themselves dispossessed, this was one of the initiatives contributing to political tension in 1244.

[11] Paris, iv, 506; and for the documentary evidence *CPR 1232–47*, 468; *CLR 1245–51*, 13.

[12] Paris, iv, 553; *CR 1242–7*, 424; *CChR 1226–57*, 321–2.

taken, he despatched Richard of Cornwall to ask for the return of the continental possessions. Louis, at least in Matthew Paris's account, appeared sympathetic but referred the matter to his councillors and to a body of Norman bishops, who all declared that King John's forfeiture had been absolutely just.[13] It would take a complete change of circumstances in the late 1250s to finally break this impasse and bring Henry to accept Louis's terms for peace.

Louis left on his crusade in 1248 and did not return to France until 1254, after many trials and tribulations. Given that all his lands and rights were placed under papal protection as a crusader, there was no prospect of Henry acting overtly against him, although a more cynical king might have imitated Philip Augustus's treatment of King Richard in the 1190s and sought to do so. Meanwhile, one field of Capetian advance and Henrician retreat was in Flanders and Hainault, a story which also shows the extraordinary hold over Henry wielded by the Savoyards.

Although Flanders was a fief of the king of France, and Hainault of the emperor, they had long been linked to England by their cloth industries' dependence on English wool. Since 1237 the two counties had been controlled by the uncle of Henry's queen Thomas of Savoy through his marriage to countess Joan. With considerable skill, particularly during the war of 1242, he had walked a tightrope between England and France, receiving a 500-mark annual pension from Henry without ever falling out with Louis. At the end of 1244, however, Joan died and was succeeded by her sister Margaret.[14] Thomas claimed from Margaret an annual pension left him by his wife, but his control of Flanders and Hainault was at an end. Since Thomas had received his annual 500 marks from Henry as count of Flanders, logically it should now have been terminated, all the more so since Henry began to pay it, if in fits and starts, to Margaret.[15] But there was no question of Thomas being cast off and he continued to receive the 500 marks as a personal fee. At least Thomas was far from down and out. He was busy carving out a principality in northern Italy and just conceivably his power there might one day be useful.[16] Rather less justifiable was the extraordinary way Henry sided with Thomas against Margaret over the payment of the pension left by his wife. When in 1248, Thomas complained that Margaret was failing to pay it, Henry simply ordered the sheriffs, when notified by Thomas of any default, to seize Flemish men and merchandise in England until satisfaction was made. This was tantamount to handing control of the sheriffs over to Thomas and allowing him to declare war on Flanders on his own behalf. At the same time, Henry agreed that the homage Margaret owed for her annual

[13] *CLR 1245–51*, 141; Paris, iv, 645–6.
[14] For Henry's reaction to her death, see above, 454.
[15] *CLR 1245–51*, 224, 349.
[16] Cox, *Eagles of Savoy*, 155.

fee should be performed instead to Thomas 'in our name'! Even Henry felt this concession needed some justification: it was, he said, permitted by 'reason' although 'unusual in the kingdom', and not to set a precedent.[17] The 'reason' itself was not explained and the motive can only have been to give Thomas a hold over Margaret. It is difficult to think of more extraordinary concessions ever made by a king of England. They can scarcely have endeared Henry to Margaret. As fighting developed over the future succession to Flanders and Hainault between the children of her two marriages, both of doubtful legitimacy, one to Bouchard d'Avesnes and the other to Guillaume de Dampierre, Henry had to look on while Louis IX's brother Charles of Anjou obtained for a while control of much of Hainault. In the end it was left to Louis IX, on his return from crusade, to settle the quarrels in his arbitration at Péronne in 1256.[18]

Charles of Anjou made a large profit from his involvement in the Low Countries. He did even better in Provence. In his will drawn up in 1238, Raymond Berengar had left 10,000 marks apiece as 'dowry' for his daughters the queens of France and England, but the succession to Provence itself went to his youngest unmarried daughter, Beatrice. Whenever the count died, Henry and Eleanor would naturally wish to secure their 10,000 marks and challenge Beatrice's exclusive right to the succession. They were also deeply interested in who she married. Here, Eleanor's mother, Beatrice of Savoy, was a key player since Raymond had left her, as his widow, the usufruct of Provence as well as several strategic castles.[19] When Beatrice came to England towards the end of 1243 for the marriage of her daughter Sanchia (also left only money in the will), Henry was bowled over by this 'woman of impressive grace, prudent and courteous', as Matthew Paris called her. He gave her a pension of £400 a year to last for six years, a magnificent golden and jewelled eagle costing over £100 (this in reference to Savoy's eagle emblem), and agreed to loan her husband 4,000 marks on the security of five castles in Provence of Henry's choice.[20]

All this was a very substantial investment in Beatrice's goodwill, and seemed the more prudent when news arrived, before her departure, of the

[17] F, 268–9 (CPR 1232–47, 7, 9); RCWL, ii, 27; Paris, v, 2–3; Cox, Eagles of Savoy, 169–71. Henry also promised to convert Thomas's 500-mark pension into land, saving his promises to Richard of Cornwall. Thomas was in England at this time with Peter of Savoy and his sister Beatrice, the queen's mother, so he had powerful voices speaking for him.

[18] For a summary of this complex story, see Lavisse, Histoire de France, iii, pt 2, 89–91, and Le Goff, Saint Louis, 252–5. Under the settlement the countess Margaret bought out Charles's interest in Hainault. Flanders was to pass to her son Guy de Dampnierre, and Hainault to her son John d'Avesnes. Margaret herself lived until 1280 and quarrelled bitterly with Henry in the last years of his reign, as will be seen in volume 2.

[19] Layettes, i, no. 2719 (Actes des Comtes de Provence, ii, no. 292A); Howell, Eleanor of Provence, 40.

[20] Paris, iv, 261, 283–4; CPR 1247–58, 414, 416; F, 254; CLR 1241–5, 213; Howell, Eleanor of Provence, 39–40. In December 1244, 2,000 marks were set aside for Beatrice and she was sent together with her husband an 'exquisite' gift of cloth: CR 1242–7, 270, 272, 274.

count's declining health. On his demise in August 1245, Henry did everything right, as Matthew Paris acknowledged. Hiding the news at first from
Queen Eleanor so as not to upset her, he ordered 10,000 paupers to be fed
and a great service to be held in Westminster Abbey (with 150 candles).[21]
None of this helped when it came to the succession. In a remarkable coup
connived in by Beatrice, confirmed by the pope and concocted by Louis
IX, at the end of January 1246 the heiress to Provence married none other
than Charles of Anjou. Provence, therefore, was now Capetian.[22]

Henry was dismayed by this betrayal, and protested to the pope, yet at
this very time he was striking an alliance with Savoy.[23] On 16 January 1246,
by which time the rumours may well have arrived of Charles's impending
marriage, he promised Amadeus, count of Savoy (elder brother of Peter
and the rest), both £1,000 (of which £333 were paid cash down) and an
annual pension of 200 marks. In addition, Henry agreed to marry one of
the count's granddaughters to either John de Warenne or Edmund de
Lacy, heirs respectively to the earldoms of Surrey and Lincoln. In return
for all this, Amadeus was to perform homage to Henry for the castles and
towns guarding the Mont Cenis, Grand St Bernard and Petit St Bernard
passes across the Alps.[24] Henry could take possession of them to attack his
enemies whenever he wished. Amadeus, in a pact of mutual assistance,
was also to use his power to help Henry's friends and aggrieve his
enemies.[25] The Savoyards worked together to bring about this alliance.
Peter de Aigueblanche, bishop of Hereford, had urged it on Henry and his
council in the early part of 1245, and had done so again later by letter,
having gone out to Savoy. Amadeus's eventual homage (sometime in 1246)
was performed to Archbishop Boniface, standing in for the king, in the
presence of Thomas of Savoy. The count thus gained money and
prevented Henry losing faith in his family. Perhaps he also hoped, under
cover of Henry, to distance himself from any conflict over control of the
passes between the pope and Frederick II. The agreement itself stipulated
it was not to prejudice the homage he had done the emperor.

[21] Paris, iv, 284, 485; *CLR 1240–5*, 324. Here Henry expressed some anxiety as to whether
it would be possible to assemble the 10,000!

[22] Paris, iv, 505.

[23] For Henry's protest, in which he was joined by Richard of Cornwall, see *CPReg*, 327.
He challenged the will, and asked the pope to stop Charles of Anjou taking possession.
Charles and Louis were also to respect the rights of Eleanor and Sanchia.

[24] To quote Nicholas Vincent (see next note), 'the properties in question were the castle
of Avigliana and the town of Susa, guarding the southern approaches to the Mont Cenis
pass and the castle of Bard and the town of St Maurice-d'Agaune, guarding either end of
Grand-St-Bernard and the southern approaches to the Petit-St-Bernard passes'.

[25] Henry's grant is *F*, 264 (*CPR 1232–47*, 469). A copy of Amadeus's own announcement
of the treaty had been discovered by Nicholas Vincent in the Glastonbury cartulary:
Longleat House, Marquess of Bath MS., Muniments no. 10590, fo. 5. I have been helped
by Vincent's discussion of the treaty in his unpublished paper 'Henry III, Frederick II and
the council of Lyons'.

In considering the treaty, one is tempted to say that those clever Savoyards had taken a simplex Henry for a ride. The chances of him actually taking possession of his Alpine towns and castles was surely low, to put it mildly. Yet Henry might think the treaty marched well with his alliance with Thomas of Savoy. He was certainly immensely proud of Amadeus's homage and his lordship in the Alps, telling Matthew Paris all about them, and stressing they were not aimed at the emperor.[26] That the Savoyards had thrown in their lot with France over the succession to Provence made it all the more important to retain counterbalancing connections. Henry's relations with Beatrice soon recovered and before long she was quarrelling with Charles of Anjou.[27] In a world where so much seemed to be moving against Henry, how important it was, as the bishop of Hereford put it, 'that you study to acquire friends and subjects who, when opportunity offers, may be able to counter your enemies, as befits so great a prince'.[28] 'When opportunity offers', that siren call again. But ten years later Henry was to think an opportunity across the Alps very much did offer itself.[29]

There was one other Capetian advance, one particularly threatening to Gascony. Raymond VII, count of Toulouse, died in 1249, leaving as his heir his son-in-law Alphonse, count of Poitou, brother of Louis IX. Alphonse was absent on his brother's crusade, but his agents took possession both of Toulouse and the Agenais, despite Henry's claims to the latter. (It had been given to Raymond VI, count of Toulouse, in 1196 on his marriage to King Richard's sister.) So Capetian power now sat alongside the eastern frontiers of Gascony, as well as being established in the Saintonge and Poitou to the north.

THE GASCON TURMOIL, 1243–8

King Henry had left Gascony in the autumn of 1243 with no great desire to return, yet he remained very directly involved in its affairs. In February 1247, when a minister was leaving for Gascony, Henry instructed him 'by word of mouth' about the repair of the castles of Bordeaux, Bayonne and La Réole.[30] Communications could be rapid with a letter sent from La Réole able to provoke decisions at Westminster within little more than a fortnight.[31] Between 1243 and 1248, Henry had to wage two wars (against the king of Navarre and Gaston de Béarn) while ruling through no fewer

---

[26] Paris, iv, 550; Paris, *HA*, iii, 8.

[27] It was Beatrice who held the castles given to Henry in return for the loan of 4,000 marks in 1244 made to her husband: *CPR 1247–58*, 469, 540–1, 559, 584; Howell, *Eleanor of Provence*, 40, 47, 144.

[28] *DD*, no. 260.

[29] See below, 583–9.

[30] *CR 1242–7*, 503.

[31] For example, *RL*, ii, 76–81; *CR 1251–3*, 207.

than five seneschals, as one after the other found the job too much. Henry was very conscious of money (however profligate in its use), and knew all too well the large sums he devoted each year to Gascony, sums to sustain the seneschals, to repay merchants for their loans and their wine, and to meet the numerous annual fees enjoyed by members of the nobility.

Despite this cost, Henry was completely committed to Gascony's retention and good order. An immediate reason for that was the wish of Henry and Eleanor to make Gascony the centrepiece of the appanage they would one day create for their eldest son. This was why Eleanor had persuaded Henry to withdraw the promise of giving Gascony to Richard of Cornwall. Here, in the protection of Edward's interests, she received staunch support from Peter of Savoy. The heir to the throne was after all the rock on which Savoyard fortunes were founded.

Henry was also attached to Gascony in a way quite different from his predecessors. They had never thought of their continental possessions as integral to their English kingship. Henry did just that, a fundamental ideological shift. Thus, when formally granting Gascony to Edward in 1252, he laid down that 'it is not to be in anyway alienated from our crown of England but is always to be joined to it'.[32] This shift was partly the result of England now far outbalancing everything on the continent. It resulted too from the developing doctrine that certain rights and properties were inalienable from the crown. There was another difference between Henry and his predecessors. For them, Gascony was the least significant and most expendable part of a wide continental empire. For Henry, with the rest of the empire gone, it represented his sole claim to continental power. If it went, then 'never in future times', as Matthew Paris put it, would it be possible 'to cast anchor in lands across the sea'. There was far more here than some token continental presence. Paris, in explaining Henry's horror at Gascony's prospective loss, observed that the revenues from Bordeaux alone were worth 1,000 marks a year and this was probably an underestimate for in the 1260s the customs, levied chiefly on wine exports, were leased for an annual £3,000.[33] And then there were the castles and the loyal townsmen prepared to lend their money in Henry's cause.[34] Gascony was certainly a drain on Henry's English and Irish resources, but that might be reversed if the seneschals could recover the king's rights. Henry no longer had an empire stretching from Normandy to the Pyrenees, but south-west of the Gironde, between the Dordogne and the Pyrenees, he was still the major power. As he put it feelingly in his letters, the loss of

---

[32] *CChR 1226–57*, 389; *RL*, ii, 389–90 (*CPR 1247–58*, 141); Ridgeway, 'Foreign favourites', 599; Studd, 'Reconfiguring the Angevin empire', 32.

[33] Paris, v, 278; Paris, iv, 594; *CPR 1266–72*, 14; Trabut-Cussac, *L'Administration Anglaise*, 315, 321.

[34] For Henry's 'especial love' of the mayor and citizens of Bordeaux, see *CPR 1232–47*, 445.

Gascony would be 'shameful, dishonourable, ignominious', involving 'irretrievable damage to us and our heirs'.[35]

When Henry III left Gascony in September 1243 he had hoped that a mixture of fair words and firm action would check King Theobald of Navarre.[36] In fact, Theobald became all the more aggressive.[37] Starting out as count of Champagne, Theobald had gained Navarre by marriage in 1234, thus becoming ruler of the small kingdom in north-west Spain, created by the counts of Pamplona. Kings of Navarre, unlike those of Castile and Aragon, had no claims to Gascony itself, but that did not make them any less of a threat. The Pyrenees were neither a barrier nor a border. Trade and pilgrims moved constantly along the great passes through the mountains, the pilgrims on their way to and from Santiago de Compostela. Much of the area running south-west from Bayonne and the river Adour, up into the Pyrenees and down into Navarre, had its own character, as it still does today with its Basque language, distinctive architecture and pastoral farming, so that in the hills around say Ainhoa it is often impossible to know whether one is in France or Spain. There was equally no clear frontier in the thirteenth century, just a patchwork of castles, lordships and small towns and settlements which might at one time acknowledge the king of Navarre and at another the king of England, and sometimes both at the same time.

In this conducive environment, King Theobald, like his predecessors, was very much in the game of pushing his authority northwards into Gascony, into 'the lands lying beyond the passes', the 'ultrapuertos'. King Henry was naturally determined to resist these Navarrese encroachments. Already before his departure in 1243 there had been struggles over control of castles and allegiances east of Bayonne, notably at Garro and Gramont, where the formidable hill-topped castle of William Arnold controlled the passage down the river Bidouze.[38] The precise chronology of the war which broke out over these and other issues is lost, but Theobald's forces threatened Bayonne and in a wide surrounding area laid siege to castles, devastated olive groves, burnt houses, destroyed mills and killed people.[39] Henry was lucky in that his own forces were recruited and commanded by a great military expert, the household knight Nicholas de Molis, the seneschal appointed in 1243. Nicholas based himself at Bayonne (whose

---

[35] *RG*, i, no. 2455 ('verecundus, probrosus, dedecorus'); *CR 1251–3*, 240. Paris, iv, 594, described the king's attitude to Gascony's loss in similar terms: 'probrosum, ignominiosum et dampnosum'.

[36] *CR 1242–7*, 70.

[37] For much of what follows I am indebted to Vincent, 'A forgotten war', with an appendix of original documents.

[38] It seems unclear whether the castle in question was at Gramont or Old Gramont further up the Bidouze. I hope it is the former as it is the one I visited and the one described here! See Vincent, 'A forgotten war', 127 n. 94.

[39] *DD*, no. 257. The details of the devastation come from the complaints against Theobald compiled by Simon de Montfort in 1248: Vincent, 'A forgotten war', 129, 144–6.

loyalty he lauded and loans he sought to repay), and by August 1244 he was in negotiations for a settlement.[40] Ratified by Theobald in November, and by Henry in April 1245, this involved referring the disputes to the arbitration of the ubiquitous Thomas of Savoy, and agreeing a truce which was to last until September 1249.[41] Matthew Paris thought that Molis had triumphed, and he had certainly recovered the allegiance of the lord of Gramont, William Arnold, although its possession was one of Theobald's main ambitions.[42] On the other hand, Theobald retained gains he had made before and during the war, notably the castle of Mondarrin and the parishes of Iholdy and Amendaritz, and thus had advanced further into Gascony. The war had also been expensive, both in terms of damage done and the money expended: the £2,000 plus found in the records can only have been a proportion of the cost.[43]

Nicholas de Molis resigned the seneschalship in July 1245, not surprisingly for he was considerably out of pocket and had to lease his own manors to pay off some of his private debts.[44] In his place Henry appointed another household knight, the Norman William de Buelles. Buelles's boastfulness (characteristic of Normans so Matthew Paris thought) and Molis's success persuaded Henry that he could at last run Gascony more cheaply. He retained in his own hands the revenues of Bordeaux and Bayonne and only allowed Buelles what was left to do his job, making no mention of any extra help in emergencies.[45] These arrangements soon foundered in another war, this one fomented by Gaston, count of Béarn, the independent frontier lordship just to the east of the area ravaged by the war with Navarre. (Its rulers did homage not for Béarn itself but only for outlying regions.) Gaston and his mother, the countess Garsenda, had actually sided with Henry in the war of Navarre and been given £400 for their pains.[46] What Gaston had not been given was the return of Sault-de-Navailles, the town on the northern frontier of Béarn, which Henry had obtained by judgement of his court when in Gascony in 1243. Gaston's resentment over this was the principal cause of 'the war of Sault' as it was called.[47] In a period of prolonged and widespread ravage and disorder, the castle of Sault was besieged, the citizens grievously tallaged and much damage done to the men of Dax.[48] This was too much for Buelles and

---

[40] *DD*, nos. 257–8; *CPR 1232–47*, 434.

[41] Vincent, 'A forgotten war', Appendix, 140–4.

[42] Paris, iv, 396; *CPR 1232–47*, 386, 474; *CPR 1247–58*, 157; *CR 1247–51*, 357–8.

[43] Vincent, 'A forgotten war', 128–9.

[44] *CPR 1232–47*, 479.

[45] *CR 1242–7*, 329, 361; Paris, iv, 630.

[46] *CPR 1232–47*, 451.

[47] *CLR 1251–60*, 19; see *CPR 1232–47*, 382, 388, 498; Bémont, *Simon de Montfort*, 297–8; and for the dispute, see Vincent, 'A forgotten war', 126 n. 82.

[48] *CPR 1232–47*, 498; *CLR 1251–60*, 19; Bémont, *Simon de Montfort*, 301; 'Réponses de Simon de Montfort', 580.

Henry, reshuffling the pack of household knights, replaced him as sene-schal first by Drogo de Barentin and then, in February 1248, by Richard de Grey. At considerable expense, Grey reached Gascony, only then to be recalled.[49] With Gaston unsubdued, Gascony in turmoil and the truces with France and Navarre nearing their end, Henry decided to adopt an entirely new policy, one which was to have momentous consequences. He would place Gascony under Simon de Montfort.

MONTFORT IN GASCONY: TRIUMPH AND DISASTER

Montfort's appointment was made possible by the favour he enjoyed at court. Since 1244 he had been a leading and well-rewarded councillor. Eleanor too remained close to her brother.[50] The arrival of the Lusignans in 1247 had brought about a change. Montfort found himself pushed down the pecking order for patronage and stymied in his suit for lands in Pembrokeshire as Eleanor's dower. But he still appeared at court and, in January 1248, received Kenilworth castle for Eleanor's lifetime, almost certainly compensation for the failure of the lawsuit.[51] Eleanor was also pardoned the £50 a year she owed for the manor of Odiham, and given forty deer to stock the park at Hungerford.[52] Montfort stood high too in the queen's favour. In 1247 she pardoned him a debt of no less than 1,000 marks.[53]

If Montfort's relations with Henry permitted his appointment, it was encouraged by Henry's desperate need to find someone with the prestige, personality and power to win the war against Gaston de Béarn, reassert royal rights and secure Gascony as an appanage for the heir to the throne. Montfort seemed exactly to fit the bill. Queen Eleanor thought so too and begged Montfort to take the job. Indeed, it was to her, as guardian of the heir and the kingdom, that he was to be answerable if Henry died.[54] Montfort's immediate predecessors had been household knights, able men close to the king, but without any name and fame. They paled into insig-nificance before a great earl who was also married to the king's sister. Nor had anyone else in England the same stake and reputation in the south of France. Montfort had connections with Bigorre, immediately to the east

---

[49] *CR 1247–51*, 79.

[50] See above, 418.

[51] See above, 473. Montfort was at court at this time: *RCWL*, ii, 27. Henry was also making the £400 payments as compensation for Eleanor's dower in Wales and Ireland.

[52] *CR 1242–7*, 518, 521; *CR 1247–51*, 22; *CPR 1232–47*, 5; *RCWL*, ii, 27.

[53] TNA E 368/19, m. 52. The money was owed for the queen's share of Montfort's fine for the Umfraville wardship, for which see below, 575.

[54] Bémont, *Simon de Montfort*, 265, 335–6, 341; Howell, *Eleanor of Provence*, 61. Montfort also mentioned the role of the king's council. The earl of Norfolk, Peter of Savoy and the bishop of Salisbury were all at court around the time of the appointment as well as Montfort himself: *RCWL*, ii, 28–9.

of Béarn, since its ruler, the countess Petronilla, had once been married to Guy, his elder brother. Montfort also had an awesome name as the son of the Simon de Montfort who had led the Albigensian crusade and routed the heretics in Toulouse. 'He had heard evil things spoken of the race of Montfort,' remarked a citizen of Sault-de-Navailles in explaining his fear of Simon.[55] The fear was justified in another way, for Montfort was already 'a warrior, famous and experienced in warfare', as Paris put it.[56] He had distinguished himself in the fighting outside Saintes in 1242, featuring prominently in John of Garland's poem describing the engagement.[57] Perhaps Montfort had distinguished himself too on his crusade. He doubtless looked the part and talked the talk.[58] His martial mien was clearly, as Paris thought, a key reason for his appointment.

In 1248, Montfort had just taken the cross and intended to join the crusade of Louis IX. When offered the appointment, he hesitated for a moment but then entered fully into its spirit. It appealed to his love of war, his lust for power and, emulating his father, his longing for a righteous cause. Indeed, in subduing the Gascon rebels, he was, as Matthew Paris put it, 'studying in all things to take after and follow in the footsteps . . . of his magnificent father'.[59] Montfort insisted on terms that would enhance his power as well as protect him from loss, and these were embodied in a solemn charter. He was to have all the revenues of Gascony and receive help from Henry if war broke out against any of four kings – those of France, Navarre, Aragon and Castile, a good indication of the threat Gascony was deemed to be under. These were similar terms to Richard de Grey's but Montfort also got much more: Henry was to give him 2,000 marks, pay the wages of fifty knights for a year, meet the costs of work on royal castles (Montfort evidently intended a vigorous castle policy) and, above all, give him the job for a full seven years. As Montfort later explained, he was determined to finish what he started and ensure 'the people' were well secured 'in their faith', which meant that his friends could count on his support and his enemies would have no escape. Montfort saw his position as virtually regal. He was appointed 'not as a bailiff removable at the will of his lord who rendered account but as one to whom the people were in all things to be intendant as to the king himself'.[60]

Henry, having made the appointment, laboured to back it up. He sought to repay loans of over £1,300 taken from Bordeaux and elsewhere, pay the

---

[55] Bémont, *Simon de Montfort*, 298.

[56] Paris, v, 293.

[57] See above, 261.

[58] Maddicott, *Simon de Montfort*, 109.

[59] Paris, v, 104. In her new biography, Sophie Ambler suggests Montfort may have taken part in Frederick II's Italian wars in the late 1230s: *The Song of Simon de Montfort*, 66–8.

[60] Bémont, *Simon de Montfort*, 264–5, 339, 341–2. For a new account of Montfort's governorship, see Amicie Pelissie du Rausas, 'Un croisé en Gascogne.

annual fees owed to around twenty Gascon nobles (worth around £1,000 a year), and generally meet his obligations to Montfort and the knights going with him.[61] After failing in an attempt to get funds from the parliament of July 1248, Henry sold jewels, took a loan from Richard of Cornwall and made the exchequer officials swear 'on his soul' not to make any payments until the Gascon merchants were satisfied, even if he ordered them to do so: a characteristic recognition of his own fallibility (though not much different from making the Bank of England independent).[62] Henry was able to pay out directly from the wardrobe around £2,000 to the knights and sergeants-at-arms going out with Montfort. The force, which left in September, impressed Matthew Paris and had at its heart a contingent from the royal household of over fifty knights.[63]

Montfort's task was certainly difficult. He had to deal with the Gaston war; the threat from Navarre (for nothing had come from Thomas of Savoy's mediation); the factional disputes in the towns; and a divided nobility of questionable loyalty.[64] The rights he was supposed to recover were nebulous and disputed. It was easy for 'faithful service' to the king to cause offence: it had made the household knight Francis de Bren 'odious' south of Bayonne, as the king acknowledged in 1245.[65] As the citizen of La Rochelle had commented back in 1242, 'for the king of the English, even at Bordeaux and Bayonne, they do not care an egg'.[66] Now they, or at least some of them, were to be made to care very much indeed.

Having despatched Montfort with all the backing he could give, Henry waited with baited breath to see the results. He was not to be disappointed for Montfort, combining force and diplomacy, acted with remarkable despatch. First, he renewed the truce with the king of France.[67] Then, in November, at Ainhoa, in the far south of Gascony, he reached a settlement with the king of Navarre by which all disputes were referred to another process of arbitration. Around the same time, by a remarkable coup, Montfort got personal possession of Bigorre, this in return for an annual payment to the aged countess Petronella. All this left him free to stamp his authority on Gascony itself. He toured the main courts of the province, issued general edicts to secure the peace, and punished individuals who, he thought, had broken it. Two men in particular fell victim to his power, both major allies of Gaston de Béarn and much involved in the disorders. The first was Arnold William of Gramont, whose allegiance Henry and the king

---

[61] *CPR 1247–58*, 14–15; *CLR 1245–51*, 179ff; *CR 1247–51*, 45.

[62] Paris, v, 21–2; Paris, *FH*, ii, 453; *CR 1247–51*, 82, 91; *CPR 1247–58*, 23. There had been complaints at parliament at the king's failure to pay merchants and he had done something already earlier in the year to meet his debts to them: Paris, v, 5–7; *CLR 1245–51*, 163, 166.

[63] Wild, *WA*, 55; Paris, *FH*, ii, 355–6; *CR 1247–51*, 119.

[64] A particular quarrel was between the vicomte of Fronsac and Amauvin de Vayres.

[65] *CR 1242–7*, 329.

[66] 'Lettre à la Reine Blanche', 527.

[67] This was the first of a succession of short renewals until one of five years in 1250.

of Navarre had earlier disputed. When Arnold refused to answer for his breaches of the peace, Montfort simply had him arrested and imprisoned at La Réole. The second was the vicomte of Soule, who was compelled by a siege of his castle at Mauléon (in the southern dip of Gascony between Navarre and Béarn) to offer a large payment for his misdemeanours; so Henrician power, thanks to Montfort, now reached into the foothills of the Pyrenees. Montfort also taught a lesson, one designed to reverberate through Gascony, to the town of Sault-de-Navailles, Gaston's designs on which had been the main cause of the war. When the men said that, like previous sene-schals, he must come to the town and swear to uphold their customs before they would swear allegiance to him, Montfort angrily refused. Instead he summoned them to the court at St-Sever and made them swear first before taking himself just an oath to uphold the customs of Gascony in general. As he contemptuously remarked, he was not going to swear 'to every man and vill'.[68] Thus isolated and intimidated, Gaston agreed a truce, and Montfort, in January 1249, returned to England, where Henry, 'exhilarated' by his achievements, and praising his fidelity, ratified the agreement with the king of Navarre.[69] The next intelligence Henry received from Gascony was far more disturbing, although he proved its equal.

Montfort had returned to Gascony in the early summer of 1249 and on 28 June, the eve of the mayoral elections, was in Bordeaux. That night a riot broke out between the Soler and Colom factions which dominated the town.[70] Restoring order, Montfort kept the Solers in prison where their leader Rostand soon died, but released the Coloms who thus had free rein to attack their enemies. Irrespective of who was actually responsible for the riot, Montfort had good reason for acting as he did. The Coloms were major wine merchants, very ready to lend money to the king and doubtless also to Montfort. Rostand de Soler, on the other hand, so Montfort later alleged, acted as 'lord of the city'. The great tower of his house contra-vened regulations on height and dominated the skyline. (It was now demolished though Henry had allowed it.)[71] Yet by throwing in his lot with the Coloms, Montfort was overturning all previous royal policy in Gascony, which had hinged on holding a balance between the factions in the towns.[72] This would not have mattered had Montfort been able to finish off the Solers once and for all, but that he could not do. Part of the trouble was that both parties had allies amongst the factions in other major towns, so that events in Bordeaux had immediate repercussions in La Réole and Bazas. Against Bazas, Montfort now took punitive action,

[68] Bémont, *Simon de Montfort*, 297–8; 'Réponses de Simon de Montfort', 585.

[69] Paris, v, 48–9; *F*, 269–70 (*CPR 1247–58*, 36).

[70] There is a vivid description of these events in Ambler, *The Song of Simon de Montfort*, 123–5.

[71] Bémont, *Simon de Montfort*, 286, 292; *CPR 1232–47*, 473.

[72] Most recently, *CPR 1247–58*, 23.

imprisoning some citizens and forcing others to pay heavy ransoms. He also took the castle of Fronsac after a siege, accusing the vicomte of plotting to hand Gascony over to Alphonse of Poitiers.

Henry first heard news of these events from the lips of Gaillard de Solers, Rostand's son, and his followers, who had escaped to England. Susceptible and impulsive, he immediately ordered Montfort to restore their property, only then to have some of them imprisoned in the Tower (though not in the dungeons), when the Coloms and Amauvin de Vayres arrived to set the record straight.[73] At the end of November 1249, Henry addressed a remarkable letter to Montfort.[74] Its tailpiece urged on him the kind of middle way which Henry at his best often tried to follow. 'We advise you earnestly that in your actions you are neither so tepid or remiss . . . as to give others incentive to commit similar offences, nor so cruel as to inflict punishments beyond deserts, but you should follow in a straight line the path of justice as the care of a just and constant judge requires, and then you will deserve to be commended in perpetuity.'

Immediately this related to the Solers whom, Henry explained, he was sending back to Gascony for trial and who should not be judged 'by a suspect judge'. In fact, Montfort did no judging at all. He kept some of the Solers in prison and forced others to pay heavy ransoms. He felt the more able to do this because the rest of Henry's letter was a litany of thanks and praise: Montfort's 'fidelity, vigilance, strength, prudence and immense labours' had benefited 'all our posterity for ever'. He should continue his good work and bring it to a happy conclusion.[75] The gift of Gascony to Henry's son Lord Edward, made formally in September 1249, now seemed completely safe. The charter in question was witnessed by Peter of Savoy while the accompanying letter patent was deposited in his archives, a good example of his role in safeguarding Edward's interests.[76]

Montfort's success seemed even clearer towards the end of the year when who should arrive in England but Gaston de Béarn himself. He had been captured by Montfort and despatched from Gascony so that the king could deal with him in person. Gaston was a very different proposition from the Solers since he was a member of the high European nobility and indeed a cousin of the queen, his mother being the sister of Eleanor's

---

[73] CR 1247–51, 231, 241–3.

[74] CR 1247–51, 343–4.

[75] See also the reaction as described in Paris, v, 77, which refers again to him following in the footsteps of his father.

[76] CChR 1226–57, 345; RCWL, ii, 37; CPR 1247–58, 50; Ridgeway, 'English cartulary roll of Peter of Savoy', calendar, no. 32. In his letters Edward called himself simply the first-born son of King Henry, but in government records and the writings of contemporaries he was often called 'dominus Edwardus', 'Lord Edward'. As there is no definite article in Latin, there is no warrant for the usage 'the lord Edward' frequently adopted by historians. See Prestwich, Edward I, 11–12.

father. At Clarendon in December he threw himself on the king's mercy. With the queen interceding, Henry pardoned all his offences, and then ordered for him (in loving detail) a 'beautiful bed', covered with cloth of gold. In view of later events, as Montfort pointed out, this seemed a classic example of Henry's gullibility and ill judgement, which up to a point it was. On the other hand, Gaston was bound (according to Matthew Paris) by 'strict obligations', and did homage to Henry and Edward. The 'king made his enemies in Gascony his tributaries', commented the Winchester annals describing the Christmas court. Henry, moreover, combined clemency for Gaston with giving power to Montfort to keep him in check. The latter's Christmas present, besides thirty deer to stock the park at Hungerford, was a promise to support the castle-building programme with 1,000 marks, this on top of the revenues for Ireland (worth perhaps £1,000 annually) conceded for two years back in November.[77]

It seemed almost job done. When the chaplain of Alphonse of Poitiers visited Montfort and Eleanor (the first evidence she was out there with him) at La Réole in February 1250, he reported that 'he holds Gascony in good estate and all obey him and none dare undertake anything against him'.[78] Montfort had been instructed by Henry to press English claims to the Agenais, but given Alphonse was still absent on crusade there was little to be done in that direction.[79] Instead, in this calm period, both Montfort and Henry began to think (independently) that they would join the crusade themselves.

It was the calm before the storm. Early in April 1250, Henry received a frank and emotional letter from Montfort, written from Paris where he had probably gone for the renewal of the truce.[80] Protecting the poor and the rights of the king had, he said, made him unpopular with the great men of Gascony. Many knights, having failed to recover their possessions through Gaston, were now planning to ravage the land. Montfort wanted to come back to England to explain himself. There were, he knew, malicious stories reaching the king that 'the war' was all his own fault. When, however, Montfort did meet Henry at Westminster and Windsor in late May 1250, he found him completely supportive. Montfort was urged to resist the vicomte of Fronsac (evidently one of those on the pillage), and left to decide what to do with the still imprisoned vicomte of Gramont. Henry also took steps to find him £2,000, and made a significant promise over Eleanor's dower. Later, in September, he added another £1,000 for

[77] CR 1247–51, 247–9, 254; RL, ii, 57, 380; CPR 1247–58, 55–8, 60; Paris, v, 104; Bémont, Simon de Montfort, 342; Winchester, 91. Gramont (still controlled by Gaston's imprisoned ally Arnold William) was not, however, surrendered.

[78] Boutaric, Saint Louis et Alfonse de Poitiers, 73; Labarge, Simon de Montfort, 114.

[79] F, 271 (CPR 1247–58, 56).

[80] RL, ii, 52–3, 361–2; Maddicott, Simon de Montfort, 112.

the castle of Saint-André-de-Cubzac, which Montfort was building from scratch.[81]

Again Henry waited for results. Again he was in for a shock. Early in January 1251, Montfort suddenly arrived back in England 'inglorious and in haste', almost alone with his horses spent. The explosion had happened and a powerful coalition was up in arms against him, led by Gaston de Béarn.[82] Montfort begged for help to subdue the 'rebels', but Henry was concerned. He pointed to the complaints against Montfort and sent out to Gascony two former seneschals Nicholas de Molis and Drogo de Barentin to try and reach a settlement. Montfort never complained about this commission (although he complained of much else), and he probably saw it as a way of checking the rebellion and exposing the malice of his enemies. Certainly in every other way Henry remained sympathetic and supportive. He found over £2,000 to munition castles and repay debts, and then (according to Matthew Paris) sent a 'joyful' Montfort back to Gascony, 'refreshed by royal comfort' and with plenty of money to recruit mercenaries.[83]

For a while it seemed this had done the trick. In May 1251, to establish 'peace' between Montfort and his opponents, the disputes were referred to local judges chosen by Molis and Barentin. This suited Montfort, who, meanwhile, took the castle of Castillon on the Dordogne, destroyed that of Lados (whose overlordship was claimed by Gaston) and arrested his enemies around Bayonne, grievously offending the men of the town in the process.[84] In mid-December 1251 he returned to England and attended the marriage at York between Henry's daughter Margaret and King Alexander III of Scotland. Montfort asserted that the land was at peace, only for the shocking news to arrive that in fact, once again, it was at war.

Henry found himself in an appallingly difficult situation. He was still impressed by Montfort's robust defence of his conduct, and his reminder of past Gascon betrayals. But that conduct seemed to be leading to disaster. 'Fluctuating in uncertainty' (as Matthew Paris put it), he tried to

---

[81] *CR 1247–51*, 321, 357–8; *RL*, ii, 61, 382–3; *CPR 1247–58*, 67, 73; *CLR 1251–60*, 288–9; Paris, v, 128. The concession over the dower was Henry's promise to pay the £400 a year directly himself, instead (the implication was) of only doing so when the Marshal heirs defaulted. It was thus up to Henry, not the Montforts, to get the money from the heirs.

[82] The coalition included Gaillard de Solers, men from Bordeaux and La Réole, the vicomtes of Fronsac, Castillon and Bénauges, Elyas Ridel (son of the lord of Bergerac), Amaneus d'Albret and Arnold de Blanquefort. The last had been forced by Montfort to surrender his castle at Bourg and felt threatened by the new castle at Cubzak (both gave Montfort control of the mouth of the Dordogne).

[83] Bémont, *Simon de Montfort*, 268, 313. Gaston had been alienated by a further dispute over the lordship of the castle of Lados, which Montfort claimed was in the king's 'mouvance': Paris, v, 208–9; *RCWL*, ii, 42; *CPR 1247–58*, 85; *CLR 1245–51*, 326, 329, 335.

[84] For Montfort's happiness with the 'form of peace', see *Letters of Adam Marsh*, 83.

steer a middle way, although that in itself represented a major shift of course.[85] On the three previous occasions when Montfort had returned to England, Henry had sent him back with encouragement and material support. Now he offered no such endorsement. Instead, he sent out to Gascony the master of the Templars and the 'wise and circumspect clerk' Henry of Wingham (a former treasurer of Gascony). They were to report on the situation and summon all those wishing to complain about Montfort to England at Easter 1252, when Henry would do them justice. Montfort welcomed this summons since, he said, the truth would vindicate him (as Henry acknowledged it might). But he also saw the writing on the wall and offered to resign his post provided he received his expenses, thus opening up a whole new can of worms for he claimed to be substantially out of pocket.[86] When Henry baulked at paying for the castles Montfort had built or obtained, Montfort threatened to alienate them. This alarmed the queen, who busied herself with Peter of Savoy trying to broker a settlement.[87] In the end, in mid-March 1252, a complex deal was thrashed out. Montfort's revenues and expenses were to be assessed, he was to receive an immediate payment of 2,000 marks, and the king was to take responsibility for some of the castles, including those at Fronsac, Castillon, Cubzac and Bourg.[88]

After this, Henry, instead of removing Montfort, allowed him to set off for Gascony, only then (on 23 March) to despatch an urgent letter commanding his return. He had received a warning from Wingham and the master of the Templars that, if Montfort reappeared, none of the Gascons would come to England to make their complaints against him. The truce recently arranged would also be disturbed. That would be disastrous for they had found 'great disturbance' in the land. At La Réole, in particular, Gaston de Béarn and the townsmen, with support from Bazas, were laying siege to Montfort's supporters in the castle, all this provoked by Montfort's attempt to tax the town.[89]

The Gascons arrived in England in April 1252, some sailing up the Thames to London. Henry gave them private audiences – indeed Gaston alleged that some of his sufferings were so 'shameful' that his envoy (he did

---

[85] Paris, v, 276–7.

[86] Paris, v, 209–10, 290.

[87] Chapuisat, 'Pierre de Savoie', 258–9, plausibly suggests that it was the crisis in Gascony (and the threat to Edward's position) that brought Peter back to England after a long absence in March 1252.

[88] Bémont, *Simon de Montfort*, 336, 339, 342; Paris, v, 276–8; *RL*, ii, 68–9 (*CPR 1247–58*, 124); *CR 1251–3*, 186–7, 203–5; *Letters of Adam Marsh*, 129; *CLR 1251–60*, 33; Howell, *Eleanor of Provence*, 63.

[89] *CR 1251–3*, 207; *RL*, ii, 72–4, 76–81. On 22 February, Montfort was given protection as having gone on the king's service to Gascony (*CPR 1247–58*, 129), but he was in England on 7 and 19 March, so does not seem to have gone: *Letters of Adam Marsh*, 129; *RCWL*, ii, 60; but contrast Paris, v, 177, 287.

not come in person) would only reveal them to the king 'in secret'.[90] He also welcomed them publicly at court where the bishop of Bayonne and Gaillard de Solers witnessed another charter granting Edward Gascony on 28 April.[91] It was witnessed by seven bishops, eight earls (including Richard of Cornwall and Montfort), Guy de Lusignan, William de Valence, Peter of Savoy, sixteen other magnates and ministers, and nine men from Gascony. The aim was to put beyond doubt Henry's determination to hold on to the province. To that end, Gascony was not only granted to Lord Edward and his heirs, as in 1249, but was also made inseparable from the crown of England.

The formal proceedings against Montfort, beginning around 9 May 1252, took place in a great assembly of lay and ecclesiastical magnates held in the refectory of Westminster Abbey. That this large hall, adjoining the south cloister and running its whole length, was chosen for the meetings suggests the numbers of people who were present.[92] The proceedings did not amount to a formal trial, for, as Montfort contemptuously observed, the Gascons refused to engage in one, doubtless fearing the penalties for false accusations should he be acquitted. As a result, Henry was all the more exposed, for, instead of a judgement being delivered by Montfort's peers, he would have to make a decision himself, one on which the whole future of Gascony might depend.[93]

Up to this point, Henry had probably been undecided, but he now found the Gascon case terribly compelling. The complainants knew how to hit the right notes. They addressed themselves as 'faithful' men to Henry's 'serene majesty', referred to his 'compassion as a good lord' and revealed their sufferings, under a reign of arrests and seizures, down to the most personal details. So Henry learnt that the men of Bazas had been forced to do their 'naturalia' 'shamefully' in the church where they had taken refuge during Montfort's occupation.[94] Above all there were the sheer numbers and details of the complaints. Reduced to writing (thus Henry could mull them over), they came from Gaillard de Solers, the dean of St Severin Bordeaux and the towns (or factions within the towns) of Bayonne, Gosse, Dax, Sault-de-Navailles, Bazas and La Réole. Amongst the nobility, the complainants included Gaston himself and Arnold de

---

[90] Bémont, *Simon de Montfort*, 314.

[91] *CChR 1226–57*, 389; *RCWL*, ii, 63.

[92] There is a description of the refectory in Ambler, *The Song of Simon de Montfort*, 116. Only the blocked fourteenth-century windows above the cloister and the Norman wall arcade now survive. The space is partly taken up by the fives courts of Westminster school (not a game at which I was any good).

[93] As evidence for the proceedings there is a long letter written immediately afterwards by Montfort's intimate friend the friar Adam Marsh (*Letters of Adam Marsh*, 78–91) and the account by Matthew Paris: Paris, v, 287–96, although this is mixed in with material from earlier years.

[94] Bémont, *Simon de Montfort*, 284, 302, 307, 309, 311–13, 319.

Blanquefort, William de Armendarits, Amaneus d'Albret, Aquelinus de Lesparre and the vicomtes of Gramont, Castillon, Fronsac and Soule. And then there was also the presence of the archbishop of Bordeaux himself, who had turned against Montfort, having once been on his side.[95]

Faced with all this, Montfort had letters of support from Bordeaux, which was still controlled by the Colom faction. And he had himself. His defence, combining sarcasm, forensic brilliance and self-righteousness, gives a wonderful measure of the man. He was hardly guilty, he said, of Rostand de Solers's death in prison for, if Rostand was as faithful as was claimed, he must have died of grief at his son's disloyalty! He could hardly be accused of abusing his powers when he had sent Gaston back to England for the king to deal with. That made it ridiculous for the men of Dax to complain of the subsequent settlement with Gaston when it was down to the king not to him: 'from these their first words the king can see how well the men of Dax have kept their oath to tell the truth'.[96] If these were clever debating points, Montfort also rebutted the accusations point by point, showing how he had taken counsel, acted after judgement or against those who refused to accept it, and had generally harmed no one contrary to their deserts. If he was unpopular that was through striving to keep the peace, defend the poor, subdue the mighty and maintain the rights of the king. 'Why should I not act in this way? God does thus, crowning those who persevere in justice and punishing those who resort to evil,' Matthew Paris quoted him as saying.[97] Montfort believed absolutely in the righteousness of his conduct. Throughout his time in Gascony he and Eleanor were receiving counsel and consolation from Robert Grosseteste and Adam Marsh; hence Adam's long and totally supportive letter to Grosseteste about the 'trial', and his conclusion that Montfort 'grounded in the fear of the divine name and given courage by the love of God . . . places all his hope in Him who does not abandon all who hope in Him'.[98]

Montfort had begun his defence with limited support, although it included the queen's uncle Peter of Savoy, and thus probably the queen herself. But he soon won round Richard of Cornwall, the earls of Gloucester and Hereford, the king's half-brothers, the prelates and the senior members of the council. Henry, however, remained unconvinced. Indeed, he had moved decisively in the other direction. The rights and wrongs of the evidence, much of it contradictory, he must have found impossible to sort out. Only a detailed judicial inquiry or proper trial with

---

[95] The complaints, spread across archives in France and England, were first sorted and analysed in an MA dissertation by Amicie Pelissie du Rausas, 'Voices from the archives: reassembling the dossier of Gascon complaints against Simon de Montfort (1252)'. For a summary see her 'Promesses de Gascons'.

[96] Bémont, *Simon de Montfort*, 293, 342; 'Réponses de Simon de Montfort', 580.

[97] Bémont, *Simon de Montfort*, 342; Paris, v, 296.

[98] *Letters of Adam Marsh*, 56–61, 88–9, 96–9, 128–9, 324–59 (where not all the letters are datable); Maddicott, *Simon de Montfort*, 117–18.

witnesses could do that. But Henry was thoroughly alarmed by the warnings that if he persisted with Montfort he might lose Gascony altogether.[99] The Gascons also suggested a solution. Come yourself or send Edward and there will be peace.[100]

As proceedings dragged on into June, Henry wished not merely to dismiss Montfort but also to act against him. But the mood of the assembly made that impossible. Henry could not even banish Montfort from court, where he continued to attest royal charters with the other earls.[101] Powerless and frustrated, Henry's anger boiled over. Instead of sitting as an impartial judge, he now became an accuser, so that Montfort, as Marsh put it, 'suffered reproaches and vociferous abuse from the king in front of many great persons'. According to Marsh, Montfort bore this with admirable self-restraint;[102] according to Matthew Paris he was provoked into replying in kind, and the arguments between the two men covered the whole course of their relationship, and included accusations of bad faith, lies and un-Christian conduct. 'I repent of nothing so much as ever permitting you to enter England,' cried Henry. At one point, according to Marsh, Henry was forced, to much applause, to make a formal pronouncement in Montfort's favour, only then, next day, his 'wrath boiling over' to return to 'savage threats against the earl, bitter reproaches, indecent contumely'.[103]

In the end, it was left to Henry, calm but constrained, to conceive and issue (on 13 June) his own interim solution, one that Marsh stresses was very much his own, although he was clearly helped by John Mansel, who personally authorized some of the relevant writs.[104] It was not a bad solution. Henry announced he could not settle the controversies in England. So he or Edward would come out to Gascony early next year when they would give justice to everyone who wished to complain against Montfort. Meanwhile the truce was to be maintained, and prisoners in Montfort's hands were to be released on bail. In separate acts Henry made even clearer where his sympathies lay. He freed the Solers from their oath not to complain about Montfort (it was highly prejudicial to the king's dignity) and declared how unjust it was for them to be disseised without judgement. He expressed sorrow at the vicomte of Gramont's long imprisonment and ordered his release. He also sought to restore the balance in mayoral elections in Bordeaux (thus remedying Montfort's fatal partisanship). After they had done formal homage to Edward, he entertained the Gascons to a great dinner.[105]

[99] Bémont, *Simon de Montfort*, 307, 312, 317.
[100] Paris, v, 277–8.
[101] *RCWL*, ii, 63–7.
[102] For Marsh's counsel on this point, see above, 262.
[103] *Letters of Adam Marsh*, 78–9, 84–5; Paris, v, 290–1.
[104] *Letters of Adam Marsh*, 86–9; *F*, 282–3; *CPR 1247–58*, 141–2, 158–9.
[105] *RL*, ii, 87–90, 389–92; *CPR 1247–58*, 141–2, 157–9; *CR 1251–3*, 218–19, 224; Paris, v, 313–14.

As for Montfort, once the Westminster proceedings were over, Henry summoned him to Windsor, probably with the aim of negotiating his resignation. Instead, without Henry's knowledge, Montfort left for France, recruited a large body of mercenaries, and descended on Gascony where he 'gloriously triumphed', according to Matthew Paris, in a battle lasting half a day. At one point he was rescued by his knights, having been beaten from his horse. The centre of the fighting was around La Réole, where Montfort destroyed the vines of his enemies, and it was here that the master of the Temple and Nicholas de Molis caught up with him. Henry had appointed them to keep the truce, and had equipped them with letters effectively dismissing Montfort if he refused to obey it. Montfort not only refused (after all his enemies, he said, were not obeying it either) but also challenged his dismissal, against 'reason' and in breach of his charter. But his offer to go with proper compensation stood and during the autumn he agreed to resign his post in return for a payment of 7,000 marks. Since none of the schemes to assess his receipts and expenditure came to fruition, just how generous this was is hard to assess. Henry was desperate to get rid of Montfort, but he never forgot both the cost and the breach of the truce.[106]

Montfort's trial shows how Henry was very much bound by counsel and consent. He was quite unable to punish Montfort as he probably wished, not that the wish would necessarily have lasted long. It was when he pressed ahead without counsel and consent, as he did later in the 1250s, that he got into trouble. If, however, Henry was thus constrained, so was Montfort. His impulse was to act in arbitrary fashion against his enemies; probably he had done so. Yet he never sought to justify his conduct in those terms. His defence abounded with assertions that he had acted after taking counsel, and had punished people only when they refused to accept justice, or had been judicially condemned 'by right, by reason and by award of the court'.[107]

English opinion, as represented by Marsh and Paris, was completely supportive of Montfort and condemned Henry as weak, inconstant and temperamental. This was unfair. Three times between 1248 and 1251, Montfort returned to England, and each time Henry sent him back with praise, sympathy and resources.[108] It was only in the course of 1252 that Henry changed his mind. He was right to do so. Montfort was now more than halfway through his seven-year term, and yet the situation was worse than it had been at the start. Then there had been the Gaston war; now the war was general. As Sir James Ramsay remarked, Montfort 'had set

---

[106] Bémont, *Simon de Montfort*, 321–4, 340–3; Paris, v, 314–16; Maddicott, *Simon de Montfort*, 119.

[107] 'Réponses de Simon de Montfort', 576.

[108] For Marsh himself acknowledging Henry's support, see *Letters of Adam Marsh*, 337, 359.

the whole Province in flames; and no proconsul could be justified in doing that'.[109] Had Henry not acted, Gascony might have been lost.

In the summer of 1252, therefore, either Henry or Edward were pledged to go to Gascony to sort out the Montfort mess. Since Edward was only thirteen, in practice Henry had to go himself. But his heart was now set on something completely different, namely a crusade to the Holy Land.

[109] Ramsay, *Dawn of the Constitution*, 135.

Chapter 10

HENRY THE CRUSADER
1250–1253

Henry took the cross in March 1250 and hoped to fire his subjects with enthusiasm for the enterprise. He was unsuccessful. In these years Matthew Paris's critique of Henry's rule reached a crescendo. The king's financial exactions, patronage of foreigners and acts of injustice, so Paris thought, had utterly deprived him of his subjects' love.[1] The contrast here with Louis IX in France was stark. Having taken the cross, Louis, in a series of wide-ranging inquiries, sought to redress the injustices committed by himself and his officials. It was an example that Henry failed to follow. Had he embarked on a similar path of reform, he might have defused the grievances underlying the revolution of 1258.[2] This period presaged the revolution in another way, namely in the factional struggles at court. It became clear that the two groups of foreigners established there, the Lusignans and the Savoyards, did not get on. In 1252 there was open conflict between them, the king's men and the queen's men as they were called by Matthew Paris.

Henry's involvement in politics and government, as he prepared for his crusade, is very apparent. Indeed, when it comes to the letters issued by the chancery, his agency stands out in a unique way. Throughout Henry's reign, notes were sometimes appended in the chancery rolls indicating on whose authority letters were issued – 'by the king' or 'by the council' or 'by' some minister. The notes also appeared on the letters themselves, thus making them less impersonal and investing them with more authority. The frequency of the notes varied greatly. There were periods when there were few or none; periods when they were plentiful, especially during times of political crisis (as between 1232 and 1234), when they acted as cover for the chancery showing on whose authority a letter had been issued. No political crisis, however, explains the gigantic number of such notes appearing in the rolls between May 1251 and the early months of 1253 before Henry's final departure for Gascony. Sometimes their coverage is almost blanket in a way not found before or since. So, of the hundred or so letters enrolled on the liberate rolls between 22 August and 20 October 1251, all but a

---

[1] For example, Paris, v, 205, 229, 242, 370–1.
[2] To be fair Matthew Paris also thought the burdens Louis placed on the church to support his crusade were a reason for its failure.

dozen are authorized.[3] What is even more remarkable is the dominance of the king. According to one calculation, in this period he authorized on his own no fewer than 2,188 letters. After that come the stewards Robert Walerand and Ralph fitzNicholas, who authorized 175 and 122 letters respectively, and John Mansel who authorized 146. The council itself had not disappeared. It was involved in authorizing fifty-one letters, forty-one of them with the king. Still it was clearly not playing a regular part in day-to-day affairs.[4] Henry was also unrestricted by any chancellor, for the office remained vacant. When the keeper of the seal, the clerk William of Kilkenny, went out on a limb over the publication of Magna Carta in 1253, he seems briefly to have been suspended.[5]

Almost certainly the decision to append his name to so many letters was Henry's own. He thus showed how personally engaged he was in this crucial period leading up to the crusade. Henry's agency is equally apparent in his outbursts of anger and the outflow of his patronage. What was too often in shorter supply was the kind of judgement he showed in dismissing Simon de Montfort and, as will be seen, conciliating King Alexander III. Flattering favourites and clever councillors found it all too easy to appease his anger, exploit his love and divert him from any general reform of the realm.

TAKING THE CROSS

Henry had taken the cross once before at the very start of the reign, as a nine-year-old boy. He had done so, on the advice of his ministers, to gain the protection and prestige of a crusader in the life and death struggle for the throne. It had worked and Henry did not forget. Signed with the cross (he told the pope in 1253), he had been protected from the assaults of his enemies.[6] Henry was also very aware of the name and fame as a crusader achieved by his uncle Richard I. He fed paupers for the benefit of Richard's soul and sent a cloth of gold to cover his tomb at Fontevraud.[7] He knew that through crusading, he might achieve 'in heaven . . . a crown of glory that fadeth not away', as Pope Innocent III had told his father.[8] Yet, having been absolved from his crusading oath sometime in the minority, Henry made no effort to resume it. If he showed respect for the crusades by leaving his body to the Temple Church in London, he then opted for Westminster Abbey instead. In 1243, out in Bordeaux, he gave

[3] *CLR 1247–51*, 371–82.
[4] I am indebted here to the calculations of Hui Liu; see Liu, 'John Mansel', 47, 60, 225–7.
[5] See below, 566.
[6] *CR 1251–3*, 448.
[7] *CLR 1240–5*, 86; *CLR 1245–51*, 168–9.
[8] *SLI*, no. 78; cited by Lloyd, *English Society and the Crusade*, 201.

500 marks to the master of the Templars 'in aid of the Holy Land', but then agreed the money could help pay for the building of the new Temple church.[9] He did nothing to imitate the crusades of Simon de Montfort and his brother Richard of Cornwall.

The train of events leading to Henry's crusade began with the fall of Jerusalem in 1244 to the Khwarismian Turks. The disaster shook Catholic Europe to its foundations. Thousands of Christians evacuating the city had been massacred. Christ's tomb had been desecrated and the priests celebrating mass in the church of the Holy Sepulchre beheaded. These terrible details were contained in widely circulated letters from the patriarch of Jerusalem. 'The boundless filthiness and cruelty' of the Khwarismians, he declared, far surpassed that of the previous Saracen rulers of Jerusalem, who had allowed Christians the custody of the church of the Holy Sepulchre.[10] Oppressed by these events, later in the year Louis IX took the cross, having recovered from a desperate illness. In 1245, Pope Innocent made support for a general crusade a centrepiece of the council of Lyon. Yet none of this stirred Henry into action. When the bishop of Beirut came to England in 1245 to preach the crusade, he received a mitre from Henry, a chalice from Eleanor and little else.[11] In the early summer of 1247, Henry wrote to the pope asking that England be spared the crusading taxation decreed by the Lyon council.[12]

Henry's attitude was perfectly justifiable. Whatever the precedents to the contrary, there were strong views that those with heavy responsibilities at home should not crusade. Louis IX himself came under intense pressure to change his mind. At a lower level, Matthew Paris thought the abbot of Bury St Edmunds set a pernicious example to fellow monks by taking the cross. He also has Henry explaining to the bishop of Beirut how England was surrounded by enemies and should not, in the cause of the crusade, be emptied of soldiery and money.[13]

A succession of factors brought Henry to change his mind. There was no way he could forget the example of Louis's crusade because English nobles, failing an enterprise led by himself, were determined to join it. The most prominent, in the early stages, was William Longespée, Henry's erstwhile general in Gascony. He departed in July 1249 with the blessing of his mother, Ela, countess of Salisbury, 'the noble and holy abbess of Lacock'. Longespée had been at court earlier in the year, just at the time when Ela received a generous gift of firewood from the king, and doubtless he filled

[9] *RG*, i, nos. 920, 926 (*CPR 1232–47*, 370–1); Stewart, 'A lesson in patronage', 344.

[10] *Melrose*, Anderson and Anderson edition, 91–5; Broun and Harrison, *Chronicle of Melrose*, 151–2; Paris, iv, 337–44; and 300–11 for letters from Frederick II and the Master of the Hospitallers.

[11] Paris, iv, 488–9; *CR 1242–7*, 372.

[12] *F*, 266 (where misdated to 1246). For these taxes, see Lunt, *Financial Relations*, 250–5.

[13] Paris, iv, 488–9; Paris, v, 3–5, 101, 196.

the air with his crusading plans.[14] Henry was also well aware of the participation of his Poitevin kin: he gave a silver cup and a 'beautiful' bed to his father-in-law, Hugh de Lusignan, on his 'going to the Holy Land'.[15] What was equally clear to Henry was that there were funds for the crusade. Longespée was assigned over £1,000 by the pope from the crusading monies being collected in England. Richard of Cornwall was still receiving subventions from the same source, 'having magnificently fulfilled his vow'.[16] This money, received by papally authorized collectors, came from legacies left to the Holy Land and payments made for absolution from crusading vows. There was also the tax, a twentieth of ecclesiastical revenues for three years, sanctioned by the council of Lyon. While Henry had written to the pope asking England to be spared the levy, he must equally have been aware that in France it had been converted into a tax to support the crusade of King Louis.[17]

Under these pressures, Henry endeavoured to assert control over the English crusade and the money for it.[18] In the summer of 1247 he wrote to the pope asking that the English crusaders might leave a year after Louis IX and be led by his half-brother Guy de Lusignan. Henry, therefore, still avoided going himself. He was also out of touch with English sentiment. Guy (according to Paris) was 'loved' by the English since he had warned them of their danger at Saintes in 1242, but he was now under oath to sail with the king of France. In the event, quite properly, it was Longespée not Guy who led the English forces. As for Henry's request to be assigned the crusading monies, the pope was dismissive. These were already earmarked for needy crusaders.[19]

Henry's inertia was transformed into action by sensational events in the Nile Delta. In September 1249, Archbishop Boniface arrived back in England and hurried to court. He brought with him news of Louis IX's landing in Egypt and his taking of the great city of Damietta, 'glorious' achievements of a 'rex Christianissimus', as Matthew Paris put it. More detail was supplied in a series of letters, one from Louis's mother, Queen Blanche, direct to Henry himself: 'since we know that you will be overjoyed at what makes for the profit and honour of Christendom, we inform you of those things which our Lord Jesus Christ, to the exaltation of the Christian faith and of his name, has thought worthy to bring about through the king, our dearest son'.[20]

[14] *RCWL*, ii, 34; *CR 1247–51*, 138; Paris, v, 76–7.

[15] *CR 1247–51*, 49.

[16] *CPReg*, 232, 240, 242, 255.

[17] Jordan, *Louis IX and the Challenge of the Crusade*, 79–82.

[18] This theme is stressed by Stacey, 'Crusades, crusaders', 145–6.

[19] *Reg. Innocent IV*, nos. 4054, 5044 (*CPReg*, 248); Paris, iv, 218, 633.

[20] Paris, v, 81; Paris, vi, 152–69, with the queen's letter between 165 and 167; *RCWL*, ii, 37.

A less open-hearted man than Henry might have been jealous and depressed by these triumphs of his greatest enemy. Instead, he was 'exhilarated'.[21] It was almost certainly now that he decided to take the cross himself. He did so in no narrow, calculating spirit of rivalry with Louis IX. Rather, he was swept away on a tide of enthusiasm for the crusade and a desire to emulate what Louis had achieved. He would thus secure the profit and honour of Christendom, and fame and salvation for himself.

Henry's decision, and his request for an ecclesiastical tax to support the cause, was quite probably conveyed to the pope by envoys who left England early in November 1249, when Henry and Eleanor were at Canterbury for Boniface's enthronement as archbishop.[22] The pope, in his reply, pointed out that, as with the case of Louis IX, no tax could be granted until Henry formally took the cross.[23] Henry therefore decided to do so. The date he chose, the Sunday in mid-Lent, was deeply significant and a telling witness to the utter sincerity of his plans. It was indeed the same date chosen by Emperor Frederick Barbarossa (in 1188) and for the same reason. The mass for that Sunday was shot through with references to Jerusalem. 'Rejoice with Jerusalem' began the Office (giving the Sunday its name); 'Jerusalem which . . . is in bondage with her children' ran the lesson (Galations 4:22–31); 'Jerusalem is built as a city: that is a unity in itself. For thither the tribes go up, even the tribes of the Lord: to give thanks unto the name of the Lord' ran the psalm (122).[24] Henry was thinking big. He would go up to Jerusalem and deliver it from bondage. Jerusalem would indeed rejoice.

After the great mass on 6 March, Henry entered Westminster Hall and before the assembled Londoners, men and women, took the cross from the hand of Archbishop Boniface. From now on he wore a cross on his shoulder, sewn into his clothes, as visual testimony to his status.[25] Henry had already taken practical steps to clear the way for his crusade. On 5 March he set in train negotiations with France, either for a full peace or failing that for a truce of sixteen years.[26] The unprecedented length was Henry's way of emphasizing how much he wished to end all discord between himself and King Louis, his fellow crusader. The proposal was taken out to Louis's mother, Queen Blanche (acting as regent), by Richard of Cornwall, and led in the event to a truce of five years. Richard then carried the news of Henry's crusading vow on to the pope at Lyon. Pope

---

[21] This is from the chronicle of John of Wallingford, a fellow monk and helper of Matthew Paris at St Albans: John of Wallingford (2), 162.

[22] *CLR 1245–51*, 260: the bishop of Hereford and Peter Chaceporc.

[23] *F*, 272.

[24] *Sarum Missal*, 90–1.

[25] FitzThedmar, 16; Paris, v, 101–2.

[26] *F*, 272 (*CPR 1247–58*, 62).

Innocent's reaction (in a letter of 11 April) was hardly enthusiastic. With Louis already in the East and Frederick II threatening the papacy, this was not a good time for Henry to go too. Still the pope acknowledged Henry's intention of 'succouring the Holy Land magnificently and powerfully' (very much catching Henry's spirit), and conceded him a tax for the purpose, although collection was only to begin two years before the date, as yet unset, for Henry's departure.[27]

Henry was not to be put off by these papal cautions. Indeed, his mind racing ahead to the journey, he was already worrying about whether friars could accompany him on horseback, riding being contrary to the statutes of their order.[28] Queen Eleanor too entered into the crusading spirit. She had taken the cross with her husband and had every intention of going too, as her sister Queen Margaret had gone with Louis IX. In May, Eleanor secured from the Master of the Templars 'a great book' giving an account of the heroic deeds during the siege of Antioch on the First Crusade.[29] Ill perhaps or pregnant, she did not go herself, but she doubtless encouraged Henry's visit to Glastonbury later in the year. If only Henry could imbibe some of Arthur's martial prowess and repeat the great deeds at Antioch! Henry's own mind was expressed in a letter to Ireland that June. 'We bear the sign of the cross on our shoulder and propose with all our strength to avenge the injury of the Crucified, and to the exaltation of the Christian faith and our honour, powerfully and magnificently [here echoing the words of the pope] to fulfil our vow in our own person.'[30]

Events in the East soon transformed the whole nature of Henry's task. While Richard of Cornwall was sitting at the exchequer on 1 August 1250, a messenger arrived with cataclysmic news. The French army had been comprehensively defeated. Louis IX himself had been captured, indeed on the very day in April 1250, so it turned out, that Richard had dined with the pope at Lyon. Many nobles had been slain, including William Longespée. Henry immediately sent his mother a gift of deer.[31] In the next months further intelligence arrived. Louis had been released in return for a gigantic ransom and the surrender of Damietta. He had then made the heroic decision to remain in the East to rebuild the Christian position. Henry had taken the cross in the aftermath of Louis's triumph at Damietta and must have feared he would arrive in time merely to applaud the French king's achievements. Now, by contrast, he could indeed crusade 'magnificently and powerfully' himself. The kings exchanged letters. Henry expressed joy at Louis's release and his desire to join him, though

[27] *F*, 272, 274; Paris, v, 97, 159, 347.

[28] *F*, 274.

[29] *CR 1247–51*, 283; Howell, *Eleanor of Provence*, 60.

[30] *CR 1247–51*, 358.

[31] Paris, v, 147, 153–4, 159, 281–2, 347; *CR 1247–51*, 315.

adding he could do so all the more quickly if his rights in France were restored. There was no chance of that, but Louis welcomed Henry's intentions, urged him to hurry, and recalled the crusading exploits of their predecessors, without adding that King Richard's had totally eclipsed King Philip's. Helped by the death of Emperor Frederick at the end of 1250, the pope's attitude also changed. By October 1251 he was urging Henry on. 'A famous prince and special athlete of God', he should 'wield the triumphal sword to revenge the injury to Christ'. 'Beside an eternal reward, you will gain glory here, and fill all Christian people with immense joy.'[32]

Henry's enthusiasm in the summer of 1251 found visual expression. The lower chamber in his garden at Westminster, he decided, should be called 'the chamber of Antioch'. Having just made a gift to the prior of the Holy Sepulchre at Jerusalem, he ordered the history of Antioch to be painted in a chamber at the Tower of London, as he did a little later in chambers at Winchester castle and at Clarendon, where it was linked to a painting of the duel between King Richard and Saladin. That was a subject too which featured in contemporary tiles.[33] Where he walked, where he looked, Henry was constantly reminded of the crusade. At the same time, he did all he could to enhance the outward show of his kingship. In 1251 he ordered his seat in the hall at Windsor to be painted with the image of a king in golden robes holding a sceptre. At Winchester the guardians of Solomon's bed were to be painted on a tablet by Henry's bed.[34]

RELATIONS WITH SCOTLAND: THE MARRIAGE AT YORK, CHRISTMAS 1251

If Henry was to leave England on crusade, he had to be sure there would be no trouble from Wales and Scotland, dangers he had mentioned in his supposed conversation with the bishop of Beirut. He might certainly think his hold on Wales was secure. In 1252, when the justiciar of Chester, Alan la Zouche, passed through St Albans with treasure bound for the exchequer at Westminster, he boasted, as he doubtless did to the king, of how 'all Wales' lay in peace and subject to English laws. The bishop of Bangor staying at St Albans said the same thing.[35] In 1251, Henry also secured an altogether new influence in Scotland. This was through the marriage of his daughter Margaret with Alexander III, the young king of Scots.

After his settlement with King Henry in 1244, Alexander II had sought to prize the lordship of the Isle of Man and the Hebrides from the king of Norway. But Alexander died suddenly in July 1249 during an expedition

[32] Burton, 293–5; F, 282 (CPR 1247–58, 158); Lloyd, English Society and the Crusade, 212–13.
[33] CR 1247–51, 454, 464; CLR 1245–51, 358, 362; James and Robinson, Clarendon Palace, 146–7, 163.
[34] CLR 1245–51, 296, 325.
[35] Paris, v, 288.

designed to make good his claims. Henry must have been relieved. He cannot have welcomed this westward expansion of Scottish power, all the more so given his own relations with the kings of Man and Norway.[36] There was no immediate danger of Scottish ambitions being revived for Alexander's successor. His son, Alexander, by Marie de Coucy, was a boy two months short of his eighth birthday. A long minority was in prospect. Marie herself, perhaps denied a regency role like that played by Louis IX's mother, returned to France in 1251, an action that closely paralleled Isabella of Angoulême's desertion of her son Henry, although Marie at least did come over on visits.[37] Scottish politics became as factionalized as those of Henry's own minority. On the one side was the head of the government, the justiciar Alan Durward, on the other Walter Comyn, earl of Menteith and his allies. It was probably Durward who petitioned the pope for Alexander to be allowed a full coronation with crowning and anointing, this as opposed to his simple inauguration, numinous though it was, at Scone in 1249.

Might Pope Innocent agree? He had after all just canonized Queen Margaret, the wife of King Malcolm III (r.1058–93). In June 1250, amidst much ceremony, her body was translated to its shrine in Dunfermline abbey. The granddaughter of King Edmund Ironside, it was through Margaret that the Scottish line could claim descent from the Anglo-Saxon kings. In some minds there was linkage here with the campaign for a coronation. Historical writing at Dunfermline abbey thus traced the Scottish line back through Margaret to Alfred the Great and stressed how he had been anointed by the pope, a reason perhaps for the pope sanctioning the anointing of Alexander III.[38]

Henry was alarmed at these developments. If Alexander was crowned and anointed it would alter the balance of status within Britain, perhaps also the balance of power. Accordingly, he asked the pope to forbid any coronation without his, Henry's, consent, pointing out that the king of Scots was his liegeman and owed him homage. The reply, delivered in April 1251, was not entirely reassuring.[39] Pope Innocent declared that the apostolic see was little accustomed to admit such requests and would not accede to this one. He also turned down Henry's suggestion that the papally sanctioned tax on the church to support the crusade be extended to Scotland. It was unheard of that such a tax be conceded to anyone 'in the realm of another'. The only consolation was Innocent's promise not to make any concession prejudicial to royal dignity. Henry's protest suggests he was once more reviving his claim to overlordship of the Scottish kingdom, for if the king of Scots was merely his liegeman for land

[36] Brown, 'Henry the peaceable', 48.
[37] Paris, v, 265.
[38] For all this, see Taylor, 'Historical writing', 246–9.
[39] *ASR*, no. 9.

in England, there was little basis for opposing a Scottish coronation. Innocent's reply was a masterly exercise in sitting on the fence. On the one hand, he implied that Scotland was an independent state – 'the realm of another'. Yet, on the other, he seemed to acknowledge that a change in its status might prejudice Henry's royal dignity. If Innocent would not forbid a Scottish coronation, he would not facilitate one either.

Faced by Innocent's non-cooperation, the idea of a Scottish coronation lapsed. Henry himself was not without support at the Scottish court. In April 1251 he speeded the passage overseas of two envoys of the king of Scots, while at the same time ordering others returning from Rome (those sent by Durward?) to be arrested if they were found to be acting against the Scottish king and his magnates.[40] It was magnates allied to Henry who now asked that the marriage between Alexander and Henry's daughter Margaret, agreed back in 1244, could go ahead. The couple would be very much child brides since Margaret was only a year older than her prospective husband. Alan Durward presumably agreed to this move, but his opponents saw it as a means of removing him.

Henry was delighted with the proposal and agreed that the wedding should take place in York over the Christmas of 1251, even though this meant he would miss the 5 January feast of the Confessor at Westminster. In August he began to make preparations for the wedding, spiritual as well as material.[41] On a pilgrimage to St Albans he gave the monastery three silken cloths and ordered two precious necklaces to be 'firmly' fixed to the shrine 'in his memory'. This was the occasion on which he asked how many silken cloths he had given to the abbey and whether, as he had ordered, they all bore his name 'king of the English, Henry III'. The answer was thirty-one (no king had given more), and yes they did.[42] On 13 October, Henry was at Westminster for the feast of the Confessor, having ordered for the day a series of new copes (one powdered with small leopards), a stole with pearls and strips of gold, and a great hanging for the Abbey made of seven silken cloths.[43] Later in the month, Henry set off for Hailes near Winchcombe in Gloucestershire for the dedication of the Cistercian abbey, founded there with his help by Richard of Cornwall. Richard had thus fulfilled his vow made during a great storm at sea on his way back from Gascony in 1242. The ceremony on 5 November was attended by Queen Eleanor, 'nearly all the magnates of England' and thirteen bishops each celebrating mass at his own altar, Grosseteste of

---

[40] *CR 1247–51*, 430.

[41] *CLR 1245–51*, 368. The preparations are described in detail in Staniland, 'Nuptials of Alexander III'.

[42] Paris, v, 257–8; Paris, vi, 389–90, where there are slight differences between the two accounts. On this tour Henry also visited Waltham abbey.

[43] *CR 1247–51*, 493–4. Two of the copes were to be made from cloth given by Robert Passelewe.

Lincoln having the starring part at the high altar itself. The church itself had cost 10,000 marks, so Richard told Matthew Paris. If only, he lamented, all the money lavished on Wallingford castle had been as pleasing to God. Henry's gift included timber for the monk's dormitory and a magnificent cope and chasuble, the precise details of their decoration all carefully described.[44] On the day of the dedication itself, in the presence of the bishops, Richard and assembled earls, Henry promulgated a salutary reform (or so the judge Bracton thought it) designed to limit the grounds on which lawsuits could be delayed by citing the king to warrant.[45] The whole occasion enhanced the prestige of England and its royal family, a good preparation for the ceremony at York. Henry also did something else along the same lines. The day before the dedication he granted 20 marks a year for the maintenance of four candles burning continuously around the shrine of Saint Edmund at Pontigny.[46] It was not merely Scotland that had a new saint.

After a visit to Gloucester, Henry set out for the north, bestowing alms and ordering building works as he went. At Nottingham, where he made a generous gift of firewood to the Franciscans, he enhanced the castle's religious imagery, regal dignity and military might. In the chapels there were to be paintings of Saint William of York, the Confessor, Saint Katherine and the last 'dread judgement'. The king's chamber was to be wainscoted and provided with new chairs. It was also to have a new doorway with a staircase lit both by candles placed in iron holders and by windows, one with glass depicting Saint Martin giving his cloak to the beggar. In the queen's chamber there were to be glass windows while her wardrobe was to be wainscoted. And in the middle bailey, the wooden palisade was to be replaced by a crenelated wall and there was to be a new twin-towered gatehouse with a chamber and fireplace above.[47]

Henry and Eleanor, with Margaret presumably in their train, arrived in York on 22 December and made their offerings at the shrine of Saint William.[48] They were to stay in Walter de Grey's episcopal palace, while Lord Edward, on Henry's instructions, was placed in a fine house nearby. The archbishop's chamber, in which Henry slept, was fitted up with a new doorway linking it with the chamber of the queen. In both chambers there were to be screens between the doors and the royal beds, doubtless as a precaution against winter drafts. Henry also ordered a new privy chamber

---

[44] Paris, v, 262; *CR 1251–3*, 2, 11–12.

[45] *Bracton*, iv, 197 (where only nine bishops were said to be present). The ruling arose from a lawsuit between the earl of Gloucester and the abbot of Bury St Edmunds.

[46] *CChR 1226–57*, 369; Bibliothèque Nationale de France MS Latin 9887 (Pontigny cartulary), fo. 27d.

[47] *CR 1251–3*, 26; *CLR 1251–60*, 9, 11–12, 17–18; Colvin, *History of the King's Works*, ii, 759–60.

[48] For Henry's offerings of two large gold brooches, see *CR 1251–3*, 15.

with a deep drop, doubtless as a precaution against unpleasant smells.[49] As for the cathedral itself, Henry could now appreciate the new transepts that Grey was adding. (Far more must have been in place than on his last visit in 1244.) With their single lancets, Salisbury-like triforium and stunted clerestory, Henry may well have judged them very inferior to his new work at Westminster, for all the simple beauty of the north transept's five sister window. The York transepts indeed showed just how far the Abbey had transformed ecclesiastical architecture in England.

Alongside Henry and Eleanor, Margaret and Edward, the royal family was in full attendance. Guy de Lusignan, William de Valence, bishop-elect Aymer and Simon de Montfort, just back from Gascony, were all there.[50] (Henry around this time was shutting the ports to prevent William de Valence leaving the kingdom.)[51] Then there were the bishops of London, Worcester, Salisbury, Norwich and Carlisle, and the earls of Gloucester, Derby and Norfolk. On the Scottish side, Marie de Coucy arrived with a substantial contingent from France. The narrow streets of the town were packed and fights broke out between the English and the Scots, despite efforts to keep them apart.[52]

The ceremonies began on Christmas Day itself when Henry girded Alexander with the sword of knighthood, having specially ordered a 'beautiful sword' with a silver pommel, a silk scabbard and a 'beautiful belt to hang it on' for the purpose.[53] Probably at the same time Alexander did homage to Henry. According to Matthew Paris, Henry first asked that this should be homage for the kingdom, as performed, so he said, by Alexander's ancestors. When, however, Alexander objected, Henry backed down and received homage simply for the lands that Alexander held in England. Henry did not wish, Paris said, to disturb the happiness of the proceedings and create difficulties for the young king.[54] Early next morning, to avoid being swamped by the crowds, the wedding itself took place 'in the face of the church', probably outside the new north transept. For Margaret's marriage portion, Henry promised to pay 5,000 marks within the next four years.[55] At least this was a lot less than the 30,000 marks given the emperor in 1235. It was also not a promise Henry kept.

The courts were together in York for six days, dressed in festal robes ('quointises'), entertained by jesters, bonded by rounds of gift-giving, and

[49] *CR 1247–51*, 518; *CR 1251–3*, 18.

[50] *RCWL*, ii, 55–7. One presumes Richard of Cornwall was there but there seems no evidence of it.

[51] *CR 1251–3*, 5, 178, 191.

[52] The fullest account of events is found in Paris, v, 266–72. For a fine evocation of York and description of the wedding, see Howell, *Eleanor of Provence*, 77–8.

[53] *CR 1251–3*, 12; Staniland, 'Nuptials of Alexander III', 32.

[54] Paris, v, 268. Paris, however, defines the tenements held 'de regno Anglie' as including Lothian, which cannot be right.

[55] *F*, 279 (*CPR 1247–58*, 121–2). For payments: *CLR 1251–60*, 330; *CLR 1260–7*, 52; Wild, *WA*, 87, 103.

fed full by the feasts mounted by both kings and the archbishop. The latter, Paris tells us, provided 80 oxen for one course alone, and spent some 4,000 marks on gifts of gold, silk and silver.[56] Henry's own preparations had been abundant and meticulous. His known orders for 7,000 hens, 2,100 partridges, 125 swans, 115 cranes, 120 peacocks, 290 pheasants, 400 rabbits, 1,300 hares, 400 pigs, 70 boars, nearly 1,000 deer, 10,000 haddock and 68,500 loaves of bread give but a fraction of the mountains of food brought together. Equally assembled were the shoes and clothes for almsgiving to the poor.[57] Henry and Eleanor themselves were to appear in identical robes made from the best samite that could be found, edged with gold brocade. Their cloaks were to be lined with ermine and their super-tunics with minever, while the tunics themselves (no doubt for comfort) were to be in a softer variety of samite. Henry also ordered for himself three 'robes of quointises', one of them to be made from the best violet samite, with three small leopards in front and three behind. Equal atten-tion was given to Lord Edward's appearance. He was to have five sets of robes made from cloth of gold, some with sleeves and some without. At the wedding itself he was to appear with his three knights in tabards with the king's arms in cloth of gold if it could be found; if not the leopards were to be depicted in gilded skin. How all the gold must have set off Edward's flaxen hair![58]

And then there were the gifts. Henry had gold, silver and jewels costing over £500 sent to York almost certainly for distribution. Amongst much else, Alexander received a 'precious' bed (Henry soon decided to have one like it himself), silver gilt spurs and (costing £57) a gold cup, a gold chalice and six golden spoons. As for Margaret's trousseau, it included four saddles, a bed, books and vestments for her chapel, and (for distribution as alms and gifts) 10 cloths of gold, 35 brooches and 198 rings.[59]

While the courts celebrated, politics continued and the plot against Alan Durward reached its climax. He was accused of treason and ejected from the justiciarship. The other ministers too resigned their offices. A new council was formed dominated by Walter Comyn and his allies. Henry himself was in the thick of these changes. He heard the charges against Durward and added two Anglo-Scottish nobles, Robert de Ros and John de Balliol, to Alexander's council.[60]

[56] Wild, WA, 56; Paris, v, 269–70. In his Chronica Majora, Paris criticized the 'wordly vanity' of the celebrations but the account in his Historian Anglorum (perhaps designed for royal consumption) is wholly favourable. See Kjær, 'Matthew Paris and the royal Christmas', 145–7.

[57] Staniland, 'Nuptials of Alexander III', 29, 35–6, 38; CR 1247–51, 518; CLR 1251–60, 10, 14.

[58] For the hair, see Political Songs, 64, 68.

[59] CR 1251–3, 1, 11, 13–14, 17, 19; CLR 1251–3, 39–40, 55; Wild, WA, 69–70; Staniland, 'Nuptials of Alexander III', 29–31.

[60] Melrose, 569–71; Broun and Harrison, Chronicle of Melrose, 157–8; Bower, 5, 298–301.

What of Margaret herself amidst all the pageantry and politics? Leaving her home and kindly parents must have been heart-rending, and one can imagine many tears shed on parting. At least she took two of her own female attendants as well as Matilda de Cantilupe, widow of Henry's steward William de Cantilupe II.[61] Fortunately she and Alexander got on and later complained together about the treatment of their guardians. That, as will be seen, was the cause of Henry's next intervention in Scottish affairs.

Henry's conduct in 1251 deserves much praise. It laid the foundations for the harmonious relations with Alexander, which were so vital later in the reign. Whereas Alexander II had thrown in his lot with the baronial rebels in 1215, Alexander III remained staunch in his support for his father-in-law. Critical here was the way Henry withdrew his claims to overlordship over the Scottish kingdom. That made peace possible. One can well imagine a more aggressive monarch thinking this was the moment to push the claims forward. Henry also did his best to allay anxieties over his role in changing Alexander's councillors. The fact that this took place in England was, he said, to create no precedent. Later he declared he intended no prejudice to the liberties of the Scottish king and his kingdom.[62] Henry had only intervened when asked to do so by the Comyn faction. Asserting an overlordship over Scotland was low on his list of priorities. His chief concern was to safeguard the interests of his daughter. That was the primary task he gave to Ros and Balliol. He listened the more readily to the charges against Durward because of their impact on Margaret's position, the principal accusation, true or false, being that Durward was asking the pope to legitimize his wife (an illegitimate daughter of Alexander II) so that she could become the heir to the throne.[63] Henry also wanted to act as the fatherly protector and counsellor of his young son-in-law. Indeed, if we can believe a tearful conversation between them over the Christmas of 1251, described by Matthew Paris, Alexander adopted Henry 'as a father so you may supply the deficiency in my case of a father and mother'.[64] How that must have appealed to Henry, having suffered a similar deficiency himself.[65]

If, however, Henry sought no formal rights over Scotland, he was very aware of the importance of 'soft power'. The great celebrations at York were designed to impress the Scots with the power of his kingship and the strength of his dynasty; hence the display of the king's coat of arms; hence the prominence accorded to Lord Edward, on this his first appearance on the public stage. It must have been around this time that the head of the young Edward was carved inside the north door of Westminster Abbey,

---

[61] *CR 1251–3*, 19; *CPR 1247–58*, 123.

[62] *CPR 1247–58*, 122, 422; *F*, 327.

[63] Melrose, 571; Bower, 300–1.

[64] Paris, v, 271.

[65] For an analysis of Henry's approach, see Brown, 'Henry the peaceable', 52–3.

gazing out over the great church his father was creating. There was also in the celebrations at York a warning. The wealth expended on feasts and gifts might equally be used to raise armies. The Scots would do well to behave when Henry was absent on his crusade.

THE CRUSADE: FIXING THE DATE

As he returned south after the York marriage, making gifts to religious houses and ordering works on his castles and manors as he went, Henry had two major preoccupations. One was how to deal with the crisis produced in Gascony by Simon de Montfort's abrasive rule. In the summer, as we have seen, that was to lead to Montfort's 'trial' at Westminster and Henry's reluctant pledge to go to Gascony himself. The other preoccupation was how to gather support for his crusade. To that end Henry staged another great ceremony. On Sunday 14 April 1252 the Londoners and many others were convoked at Westminster. They heard sermons from bishops and friars especially chosen at Henry's request 'for their knowledge in preaching the cross'. Some of Henry's courtiers were inspired to join the enterprise, Henry rushing forward to embrace them and calling them his brothers. At the same time, the chief point of the ceremony, Henry swore that he would set out four years from the coming feast of John the Baptist, that is on 24 June 1256. Kings very rarely took personal oaths. In taking this one, according to Matthew Paris, probably a witness, Henry placed his right hand on his breast in priestly fashion, before laying it on the Gospels and kissing them in the fashion of the laity. He could not have committed his whole being as king more solemnly to the cause.[66]

Having fixed the date, Henry was able to press ahead with getting the taxation to support the expedition.[67] He was also taking steps to secure shipping, first to transport all the stores going out in advance, and then, a year later, to transport his own person.[68] Henry believed profoundly (as the pope put it) that to succeed 'human power is insufficient without divine aid, since victory in war comes not from the multitude of an army but from strength from heaven'.[69] At Henry's request, therefore, the pope ordered that in every church on every day a special prayer was to be said begging God to protect the king from evil and help him wrest the land, 'which your only son consecrated with his own blood', from the hands of the infidels. This was to follow the agonizing psalm 79: 'Oh God the heathen are come into thy inheritance: thy holy temple have they defiled and made Jerusalem an heap of stones.' During the service two bells were

[66] Paris, v, 281–2; *CR 1251–3*, 201–2, 217; *F*, 282 (*CPR 1247–58*, 158).
[67] See below, 549–54.
[68] *F*, 282 (*CPR 1247–58*, 158).
[69] *F*, 287.

to be rung at whose sound those at work or at home were to say the Lord's Prayer and other prayers as the lord inspired them. Every church once a month was to stage a procession to a neighbouring church, ending up there with the mass of the Cross, and an exhortation to the people to pray for the king, his company and the freeing of the Holy Land. Once the king had set out, everyone was exhorted to abstain from lascivious dancing and shameful games, and live more soberly with prayers, almsgiving and fasting.[70] Truly Henry wished to convert his whole kingdom into a great church praying for his success.

Henry did not neglect other spiritual aid. Apart from visits to St Albans and Waltham abbey, he went on pilgrimages to East Anglia both in 1251 and 1252.[71] And above all he pressed on with the work at Westminster Abbey. In 1251 he wanted to have 600 or 800 men labouring on the building.[72] In 1254 he announced that with 'divine aid' he intended the church to be dedicated on 13 October 1255, so, as he said, before his departure (the following year) on crusade.[73]

The response to all these efforts was limited. The English clergy and people certainly followed events in the East with deep interest. They admired intensely the exploits of their own crusaders. William Longespée became a hero celebrated in verse.[74] Yet, outside a group of dutiful courtiers, very few people joined Henry in taking the cross, either in 1250 or 1252. There was no upsurge of enthusiasm for the crusade of their king. Richard de Clare was much at court in the early 1250s, but, having witnessed the great ceremony on 6 March 1250, he left at once on a pilgrimage overseas to Santiago de Compostela and never took the cross himself.[75]

Part of the problem was Henry himself. He was not a natural crusader. As his critics pointed out, a 'petty king', he had never ridden a horse in battle, brandished a sword or wielded a spear.[76] When he took the cross in 1250, it was rumoured he did so only to squeeze money from his subjects. Henry was also at odds with those from whom he might most naturally have expected support; those, that is, like the marcher baron Roger of Mold, who had already taken the cross. The trouble was that, with their preparations made, they were eager to be off. Instead, they found themselves told by Henry and then the pope to wait several years until Henry himself was ready to go. That meant they would have to make their costly preparations all over again.[77] There was also tension over the money raised

---

[70] *F*, 286; Lloyd, *English Society and the Crusade*, 51–2.

[71] Illness in 1252 prevented Henry taking in Walsingham and Bromholm as well.

[72] *CR 1247–51*, 307, 423; *CR 1251–3*, 174; *BA*, 192–4.

[73] *RG*, i, no. 2469; *BA*, 194–5 (*CPR 1247–58*, 281, 381); *CLR 1245–51*, 329, 339, 345.

[74] Lloyd, 'Sir William Longespée'.

[75] *RCWL*, ii, 39; Tewkesbury, 140; *CPR 1247–58*, 61–2. Clare attested charters at court in five of the months in 1251 and six in 1252. The charter roll for 1249/50 is badly damaged.

[76] Paris, v, 335. For more extreme (and fanciful) criticism see Paris, iii, 619.

[77] Paris, v, 102; Paris, vi, 200–2. The pope in fact only issued the ban after the disaster to Louis.

for the crusade by papal collectors. Those already signed up feared rightly that Henry had his eyes on it. As 'the crusaders of England' they petitioned the pope to make sure he got nothing until they had received their own dues.[78] When, in 1252, the pope formally declined Henry's request for the money, he added a telling homily on the importance of general support. If he merely trusted in his own strength, the results might be disastrous. The prelates, barons, nobles and all the clergy and people of his kingdom were more useful to him 'than others'. He should treat them well, and not oppress them, so that they were ready to do his pleasure 'more in heart than in body'.[79] It had come to something when the pope had to lecture Henry in this way.

HENRY'S SPEECH TO THE SHERIFFS
AND HIS LOCAL INQUIRIES

Henry had one practical but also deeply religious way of breaking through this hostility and showing the benefits of the crusade to his subjects. Integral to the crusader's oath was the undertaking to leave home with a clean bill of spiritual health, which meant, amongst other things, putting right any wrongs one had committed. How, after all, could God look favourably on someone who left in a state of sin? Here the conduct of Henry's brother-in-law Louis IX had set a potent example, as Henry must have known. In 1247, under a chapter headed 'the pious deed of the king of France', Matthew Paris recorded how Louis, a 'rex piissimus', had sent friars throughout his realm to give redress to all those who had suffered injury at the hands of his officials. He was 'prepared to restore all things'. Paris had here grasped the key feature of Louis's 'enquêtes', namely to give 'reparation' for injuries suffered at the hands of royal officials. Indeed, their scope was wider than Paris stated, for the wrongs committed by Louis himself and his predecessors were also to be redressed.[80]

To a limited degree Henry did try, as a crusader, to put things right. He sought to free himself from debts owed to merchants for purchases of cloth, furs, wax and spices. On the day he took the cross, he tearfully begged pardon from the Londoners for all the wrongs they had suffered at

---

[78] *CPReg*, 263.

[79] Burton, 298–9. Henry also had to issue a proclamation dispelling the rumour that all those who had promised money for absolution from their vows would now have to pay additional sums: *F*, 276 (*CPR 1247–58*, 84).

[80] Paris, iv, 638–9. For Louis, his crusade and the reform of the realm, see Jordan, *Louis IX and the Challenge of the Crusade*, and Dejoux, *Les Enquêtes de Saint Louis*. The importance of reparation is a major theme of Dejoux's book. I discuss the contrast between Louis's ideas and Henry's in this area below, 713–15.

his hands.[81] The reform he promulgated at the dedication of Hailes abbey was designed to speed up the hearing of lawsuits. There was also, at this time, a remarkable increase in the number of people having recourse to the procedures of the common law. This is seen most dramatically in the purchasing of writs, usually costing between half a mark (6s 8d) and 20s, either to have a case heard locally by one of the king's judges or to transfer a case to the court *coram rege* or to the justices of the bench at Westminster. Between 1241 and 1249 an average of 174 such writs were purchased every year. In the regnal year 1249/50 the number rises to 399 and in the following year to 580. The annual average for the rest of the reign down to 1272 is 790, with a large increase in the last years more than offsetting a decline during the civil war.[82] How far this increase reflected entirely new business, how far simply a transfer of business from county courts, is impossible to say, but it certainly shows the king's justice was in demand. While there is no certain explanation for the sudden change in 1250, it probably resulted from Henry publicizing the fact that such writs were available. His motive was to raise money for the crusade (as he sought to do in other ways), but perhaps, as a crusading king, he also saw himself as giving justice to his people. That there was some co-ordinated thought behind the initiative is suggested by the way, so as to deal with the extra business, the judicial bench was now kept in session at Westminster even when general eyres were taking place in the localities. (From this period there is also a large increase in the size of the bench's plea rolls.)[83] It is, moreover, in the 1250s that the king's justices for the first time were paid regular salaries.[84]

Henry's most striking initiative in the cause of reform took place on 7 October 1250. On that day he entered the exchequer with his council and addressed the assembled sheriffs 'with his own mouth'.[85] Although he made no specific reference to his obligations as a crusader, the speech was almost certainly inspired by them. Henry's first concern was religious. The sheriffs were to maintain the liberties of 'Holy Church' and, in the spirit of so many biblical examples and injunctions, protect and give speedy justice to orphans and widows. They were also to make anyone who blasphemed the name of Jesus Christ answer on a day and at a place the king

---

[81] Paris, v, 114; *CLR 1245–51*, 284, 315–21.

[82] For all this see Moore, 'Fine rolls as evidence for the expansion of royal justice', 66–71, and Hartland and Dryburgh, 'Development of the fine rolls', 198–9; Carpenter, 'Between Magna Carta and the parliamentary state', 13. Down to 1242 the commissions to hear cases locally were to four local knights. Thereafter they were to a judge with power to co-opt others to sit with him. See Musson, 'Reappraisal of the "four knights" system'; Kanter, 'Four knights system'.

[83] Moore, 'Fine rolls as evidence for the expansion of royal justice', 60; Meekings and Crook, *King's Bench and Common Bench*, 125.

[84] Brand, *Making of the Common Law*, 146–7.

[85] Clanchy, 'Did Henry III have a policy?', 215–16.

would name. Henry's second concern was the oppressive conduct of his magnates. No peasant ('rusticus') was to be forced to pay a debt of his lord so long as the lord had the wherewithal to pay. The sheriffs were also to inquire how 'magnates' treated their men and correct their transgressions. If they were unable to do so, they were to inform the king. The third concern was with the conduct of the sheriffs themselves. They were only to let out hundreds at higher rates to those whom they were sure 'would treat the people with justice'. Finally there were a series of injunctions about preserving the rights and liberties of the crown, especially in the field of local government. No one was to have the franchise of return of writs, or hold the view of frankpledge or the sheriff's tourn, unless they had warrant either from long usage or from a charter of the king.[86]

As far as it went, this was an impressive performance. Henry showed himself informed. He knew about the ill feeling generated by the conduct of magnates. He was aware too that they were expanding their local power at his expense. And he appreciated the unpopularity of his own sheriffs who were trying to increase their revenues and very much not treating the people 'with justice'. As he wrote later (in 1253), their delinquencies necessitated their frequent removal.[87] In some ways Henry sought to follow up his speech. He tried to ensure that ecclesiastical estates

[86] The franchise of return of writs (for which see Clanchy, 'Franchise of return of writs') was usually attached to a private hundred, a hundred that is run by a lord rather than the king. (The hundred court had jurisdiction over small debts and fights and brawls not involving a breach of the king's peace.) The franchise meant any writ relevant to the hundred, so one ordering a debt to be raised, a jury to be summoned, a verdict to be enforced or a criminal to be arrested had to be handed by the sheriff over for execution to the bailiff of the lord. Both the exchequer and the law courts found the liberty extremely vexatious, with the lord's bailiff frequently doing nothing in response to the order. The view of frankpledge involved checking that peasants were in their tithing groups, the groups, ten or twelve strong, of adult males of unfree status sworn to keep the peace and ensure the good conduct of their fellows. The view took place every Michaelmas at the hundred court but might also be held at a privileged manorial court. It was highly profitable for there were many opportunities to impose amercements on the tithings. Magna Carta 1217 said the view should be held without unjust exactions. The tourn was an especially well-attended session of the hundred court. According to Magna Carta 1217, it was only to be held twice a year, at Easter and Michaelmas, the Michaelmas session being the occasion for the view of frankpledge. Another important liberty, often claimed for a private hundred or manorial court, was that of 'infangentheof', the right to have a gallows on which to hang thieves taken red-handed within the area of the hundred or manor. Alongside the private hundred and the manorial court, a third type of private court (although the distinctions between them were sometimes blurred) was that called by historians the 'honourial' court, the court held by a lord for his tenants by knight service. It had jurisdiction over disputes involving possession of the fees held by the tenants from the lord and over the services owed him. Its activities had been greatly reduced by the development of the common law legal procedures, as these easily removed cases to the court of the king, but it was still an important source of authority and money, in part from amercements imposed for non-attendance.

[87] F, 292 (CPR 1247–58, 214).

during vacancies were administered by his officials 'with justice'. Indeed, he claimed to have taken a corporal oath to that effect.[88] He sought to restrain his justiciar of Chester, Alan la Zouche, having heard 'frequent and diverse complaints' from 'the poor men' of North Wales about his rule.[89] Henry continued to be concerned for the religious health of his people. He even prohibited bakers from making bread bearing the sign of the cross, the Agnus Dei and the name of Christ, lest these holy signs and the name of the Lord be disfigured.[90]

Yet the fact remains that Henry's efforts were poor indeed when compared with those of Louis IX.[91] His apology to the Londoners degenerated into a bullying attempt to get them to confer new liberties on Westminster Abbey.[92] The reform of procedure at the dedication of Hailes abbey hardly amounted to major legislation. If Henry saw the selling of writs as a way of making his justice more available, he gained no credit from it. It went unmentioned by Matthew Paris. And was Henry's speech to the sheriffs itself anything more than window dressing? How much of it could they even remember, standing there before him, outwardly dutiful but inwardly astonished? As far as is known, they never received a text of the speech, nor was it ever proclaimed to the realm. No chronicler mentions it. The whole set of injunctions was nebulous, impossible.

To be fair, Henry was doing something on another front. Between 1246 and 1254 a series of new questions were added to those customarily put by the itinerant justices, the justices in eyre, to the local juries that came before them. Some of the questions related to the rights of the crown, but others were concerned with the way sheriffs and bailiffs had 'stifled truth and justice', for example by taking bribes and extorting money from those attending the hundred courts. A good number of officials were now accused of such offences by the juries, and many were either amerced or ordered to make fines for their transgressions. The prospect of that happening must have acted as a check on malpractice.[93] Yet these measures only went so far. Sometimes the judges simply minuted that the issues raised were to be 'discussed'. That was the case when the jurors of Larkfield hundred in Kent accused the sheriff and his bailiffs of insisting everyone

---

[88] For example, *CR 1247–51*, 313–14, 323, 326; *CFR 1250–1*, no. 82; *CR 1251–3*, 156–7. For the oath, see, *C&S*, i, 691.

[89] *CR 1247–51*, 541, 551; *CR 1251–3*, 179, 263. And see his terms of appointment: *CPR 1247–58*, 70, 151.

[90] *CR 1251–3*, 249.

[91] For comment on the failure to reform the realm, see Stacey, 'Crusades, crusaders', 146–7.

[92] See below, 542.

[93] For the above see Cam, 'Studies in the hundred rolls', 22–5; Meekings, *Wiltshire Eyre*, 27–33 (with the quotation at 32); Harding, *Shropshire Eyre*, xix–xxiv (with a positive view of the eyre's utility). I am grateful to Paul Brand and Henry Summerson for advice about procedure at the eyre.

attend coroners' inquests and amercing them 'by will' when they failed to turn up. This was an issue dealt with in the reforming legislation of 1259.[94] More generally, Henry did nothing to open up the eyres to complaints made verbally by individuals, as happened after 1258. If officials were punished, there was little emphasis on providing compensation for what had been taken, although that was a key feature of Louis's enquêtes. The eyres, at least on the criminal side, still seemed mainly a way of making money for the crown. With much else to do, they were no substitute for targeted inquiries into local abuse like those mounted by Louis.

To be fair again, Henry was at this time making some effort to mount such inquiries, and as a result discovering a far greater level of malpractice than that revealed by the eyres. In October 1249 he appointed William le Breton and William of Axmouth to inquire, through local juries, into trespasses throughout the realm. They were still at work early in 1252. Later that year the commission was renewed.[95] The returns of the inquiry survive for the hundred of Samford in Suffolk.[96] They paint an appalling picture of the abuses practised by local officials with over a hundred complaints being recorded. The chief culprit was the bailiff William Testepin, who ran the hundred under the sheriff Hamo Passelewe.[97] So money was extorted for such things as release from prison, the remission of false accusations, the return of chattels unjustly seized and the failure to provide the officials with hospitality. Passelewe himself was accused, over the six years he held office, of exacting 40s at the annual tourn where 20s had been customary, a clear breach of Magna Carta. 'And so we beg the king to show mercy to us,' concluded the jurors.[98] But no mercy was forthcoming. Henry's inquisitors were feeble indeed compared to the enquêteurs of Louis IX. William le Breton and William of Axmouth were experienced administrators but members of the regime, not outsiders like Louis's friars. It would take them ages to cover the whole country. (How far they got is unclear.)[99] There was no effort to divide the kingdom into circuits, as Louis had done. Above all, Henry's inquisitors were just that. They were to inquire only. They had power neither to punish nor to give compensation. Henry's main motive seems to have been to make money. Hamo Passelewe was pardoned his trespasses and exempted from all complaints in return for a fine of 200 marks made by

---

[94] TNA Just 1/ 361, m.44 (1255); Brand, *Kings, Barons and Justices*, 81–2. The legislation dealt with the imposition of such amercements by the justices in eyre. I have been through the surviving crown pleas of all the eyres between 1250 and 1258, for which see Crook, *Records of the General Eyre*, 115–26.

[95] *CPR 1247–58*, 51, 163.

[96] *RH*, ii, 174–8; Jacob, *Studies*, 25–6.

[97] For the Testepins, see Gallagher, *Suffolk Eyre*, no. 873.

[98] *RH*, ii, 176a.

[99] For a biography of Breton, see Meekings, *Wiltshire Eyre*, 129–30. Axmouth was a royal clerk and was killed at the battle of Lewes.

his brother, the great minister Robert Passelewe.[100] Twelve other sheriffs were forced to make fines for the pardon of their offences, but the people gained no redress.[101] In the case of Henry de Coleville, sheriff of Cambridgeshire and Huntingdonshire, Breton and Axmouth were told specifically to cease their inquiries.[102] Although most of the sheriffs were removed from office, their successors were no better. In Northamptonshire the new men became notorious for their oppressions. In Northumberland the sheriff, William Heron, actually stayed in office, going on to gain a terrible reputation as a 'hammer of the poor'. In 1253, Matthew Paris cried out against the sheriffs' oppressions. Their activities were to be a major subject of reform in 1258.[103]

If Henry did little to restrain the abuses of his own men, he did even less when it came to magnates and their officials. His speech to the sheriffs shows he knew this was an issue, as does his frequent demand that everyone should obey Magna Carta. Yet the sheriffs were entitled to wonder, if they reported back to Henry the malpractices of magnates, how much backing they would receive, especially if the offenders were his relatives or others in his favour. Indeed, the laxity and indulgence of Henry's rule was rapidly making matters worse, allowing magnates and their officials to become all the more powerful and oppressive.[104] In the 1240s and 1250s the replies of the juries to the questions posed by the king's itinerant justices revealed in county after county cases of men, in a variety of ways, being withdrawn from the jurisdiction of the sheriffs and being made subject to the jurisdiction of their lords. The culprits included the king's foreign relatives, the earls of Gloucester and Cornwall, and many other native magnates. This was part and parcel of a concerted move by magnates to compel more people to attend their courts.[105]

All this meant financial loss to the crown. Between 1256 and 1258 the sheriff of Bedfordshire and Buckinghamshire listed twenty-one vills where 'he does not dare to raise' a total of £19, 'because of the power' of the earl of Gloucester, the queen, William de Valence and the earl of Cornwall and his wife.[106] Occasionally the justices in eyre sought to do something about such encroachments but more often they just minuted that they were to be discussed with the king. If they were, no action followed, not surprisingly since the culprits were often those high in Henry's favour. The situation was

---

[100] *CFR 1250–1*, no. 1144; *CPR 1247–58*, 112. Robert's fine also covered his own activities.

[101] *CPR 1247–58*, 111–12, 128, 140; *CR 1251–3*, 28, 42, 182; *CFR 1250–1*, no. 1125; *CFR 1251–2*, nos. 90, 187, 221–5, 277, 607. Three of the sheriffs operated in Essex.

[102] *CPR 1247–58*, 125.

[103] Paris, v, 370–1, 577, 580, 663, 715. See Cassidy, 'William Heron'. The financial pressures placed on the sheriffs by the demands of the exchequer are discussed below, 659.

[104] For what follows, see Carpenter, *Reign of Henry III*, 85–8, 99–105, 327–8; Maddicott, 'Magna Carta and the local community', 54–61.

[105] *DBM*, 274–5, cap. 4. For such courts, see above, n. 86.

[106] Maddicott, 'Magna Carta and the local community', 50; Carpenter, *Reign of Henry III*, 101. In twelve of the vills the culprit was the earl of Gloucester.

aggravated by the disappearance for the most part of curial sheriffs, those close to the king with the power and resources to enforce his rights. As it was, a bailiff of Guy de Lusignan could say in 1253/4 that 'he would do no more for the sheriff than he would for [the sheriff's] daughter'.[107]

Henry was certainly capable, in these years, of acting when he thought his rights were being violated. The bishops of Worcester and Lincoln (Cantilupe and Grosseteste) were both upbraided for taking oaths from laymen and excommunicating royal officials.[108] When John de Grey married Joan, widow of Paulinus Peyvre, without permission, he was made to offer 500 marks for his pardon, although the terms of payment (thanks in part to John Mansel) were soon relaxed.[109] Henry appeared equally masterful in another episode, this one involving the marcher baron Walter of Clifford. Angered by the contents of a royal letter, Clifford had forced a royal messenger to eat it together with its seal![110] In response, Henry ordered the sheriffs to seize and sell the corn and livestock on Clifford's properties. This brought him to court, where he was convicted of showing gross contempt for the king. Rather than suffer judgement, he agreed to pay £1,000 for a pardon, although the rate of repayment was gradually reduced to £20 a year with £200 being forgiven altogether.[111] But it was one thing to react to individual acts of misconduct, quite another to carry through a more general reform of the realm. It was left to the revolutionary regime of 1258 to hear complaints against magnates and promulgate legislation restricting their ability to force men to attend their courts.[112] It was left to Edward I to launch nationwide inquiries, asking 'by what warrant' magnates held their local government liberties.[113]

[107] Carpenter, *Reign of Henry III*, 103. For the decline of the curial sheriff, see above, 223. For the powerlessness of the sheriff of Sussex faced with John de Warenne, see *SCWR*, 126–7; Spencer, *Nobility and Kingship*, 159.

[108] *CR 1247–51*, 221–2, 525, 554; *CPReg*, 265; Paris, v, 109; Tewkesbury, 139–40, 142–3, 145; Worcester, 439–40. Cantilupe was involved in a jurisdictional dispute with the sheriff of Worcestershire, William de Beauchamp.

[109] *CFR 1250–1*, no. 1213; *CFR 1251–2*, nos. 405, 571, 1312; *CFR 1252–3*, no. 5; Paris, v, 242; Dunstable, 182–3. The marriage was all the more advantageous because Joan had bought the wardship of Paulinus's lands and the marriage of his heirs: *CFR 1250–1*, no. 935. John took over Paulinus's splendid house at Toddington.

[110] Matthew Paris (v, 95) says nothing about the contents of the letter. It may have been one from the exchequer ordering the sheriff of Buckinghamshire to distrain Clifford to pay an amercement for a forest offence, see TNA E 368/23, m. 19 (http://aalt.law.uh.edu/aalt1/H3/E368n023/aE368n023fronts/IMG_4242.htm). If so, at least the messenger had only to eat the smaller exchequer seal and not the great seal!

[111] *CFR 1249–50*, nos. 327–8, 432; *CFR 1250–1*, no. 226; Carpenter, *Reign of Henry III*, 97 n. 114.

[112] The legislation dealt with forced attendance at honourial courts. For the whole issue, see Brand, *Kings, Barons, Justices*, 43–53. Lords were also forcing men to attend private hundred courts.

[113] See Sutherland, *Quo Warranto Proceedings*. Nothing came of Henry's initiatives in 1244 and 1255, for which see above, 451–2, and below, 616–17. Nor was the court *coram rege* used in any general way to hear 'quo warranto' cases.

THE HENRY OF BATH CASE, 1251

While Henry's inquisitors were at work uncovering malpractices amongst the Testepins at the bottom of the royal administration, a scandal broke out pointing to malpractice at the very top. In February 1251 the senior justice of the king's bench, Henry of Bath, was accused of corruption. In the detailed description of events offered by Matthew Paris what stands out is the king's anger and his determination to prosecute the case, despite the intercession of Bath's powerful friends. He appears very much in Alton mould. Yet in the end he calmed down and pardoned Bath in return for money. As with the inquiries going on in the localities, he drew no wider conclusions about the need to reform the realm.

Matthew Paris's picture of Henry of Bath himself is black.[114] Bath was, Paris acknowledged, a literate knight and skilled in the laws of the land, but he took bribes from both sides in cases and corruptly accumulated a large landed estate. On one judicial eyre alone he allegedly appropriated £200 worth of land. He was egged on by his greedy wife, Alina, a kinswoman of the Sandfords and the Bassets of High Wycombe.

The scandal in 1251 had its origins in a legal action won by Bath against Philip de Arcy (son of the aged baron Norman de Arcy) on the 1250 Lincolnshire eyre, a case about the wardship of Joan de Quatremars. This was an eyre over which Bath presided. That in itself was not improper. Judges often litigated in their own courts.[115] But evidently de Arcy was outraged by what happened. He came before the king and accused Bath of giving a false judgement against him. Henry was angry and refused John Mansel's offer to stand surety for the judge. Henry of Bath, Henry averred, was being accused of treason for which no clerk could stand surety. (That put Mansel in his place!) In this dangerous situation, Bath sent Alina round to her kinsfolk, and Fulk Basset, bishop of London, Philip Basset and the 'miles strenuus', Nicholas of Sandford, all rallied in his support. In the end, Henry allowed Bath to be placed in the custody of twenty-four knights, who guaranteed he would stand trial at the forthcoming parliament, that meeting in February 1251.[116] Henry, however, refused absolutely, even when approached by Richard of Cornwall, to be swayed by prayers and promises on Henry of Bath's behalf. When Bath appeared at the parliament, surrounded by his knightly friends and relations, Henry became yet more angry and accused him of disturbing the peace of the kingdom. Nicholas of Sandford, so Matthew Paris thought, had indeed threatened to take up

---

[114] See Paris, v, 213–15, 223–4, 240, 379, for his narrative of the affair. The following account combines what he says with the record evidence assembled by Meekings in Meekings and Crook, *King's Bench and Common Bench*, 95–102, with 92–5 on Bath's earlier career. Full references to what follows will be found there.

[115] Presumably, in those cases, one of their colleagues presided, although not apparently in this case as it was Bath who was accused of giving the false judgement.

[116] Maddicott, *Origins of the English Parliament*, 466.

arms on Bath's behalf. Henry now announced that all complaining against Bath should come before him to be heard. According to Paris, many did so. When one of Bath's own colleagues accused him of accepting money for the release of a prisoner, Henry stood up in a rage and promised to pardon anyone who killed the judge. He then swept out, leaving John Mansel to caution against acting on what was said in anger. The king might soon regret his words, wise advice as it turned out.

Although Paris does not mention it specifically, Henry of Bath's travails were connected with another case from the Lincolnshire eyre. Again he had proved the victor, this time against Thomas of Moulton, the son of the Lincolnshire magnate and former judge of the same name. Moulton was amerced the sum of 100 marks. He too was furious and immediately offered the king 30 marks for a writ allowing him to bring an action accusing the trial jury of a false judgement.[117] This action was eventually heard by the judge Roger of Thirkleby and the king's steward John of Lexington in June 1251, with judgement given *coram rege* in July at Woodstock. It was for Moulton and amercements of £40 and £200 were imposed respectively on the original jurors and on Henry of Bath himself. By this time, however, Henry had evidently calmed down, as Mansel predicted. In return for a fine of 2,000 marks, Bath was pardoned the king's 'indignation and rancour for all manner of trespasses'. The letter patent recording the fact was authorized by Mansel and the steward Ralph fitzNicholas.[118] This ended the de Arcy case, as far as the king was concerned, and perhaps it led to an out-of-court settlement. At any rate Henry of Bath held on to the Quatremars heiress and she married his younger son Fulk, named presumably after Fulk Basset.

While the king was appeased, Henry of Bath was still to stand trial *coram rege* against anyone wishing to complain against him. Given the loss of the plea rolls in this period we cannot know how many did so, but there is no evidence of any successful litigation. In 1256, three years after Bath had returned to office as head of the court *coram rege*, the verdict in the Moulton case was itself overturned by the king and the council. They decided that the jury of twenty-four knights, appearing before Thirkleby and Lexington, and convicting the original jury of perjury, had actually said exactly the same as the original jurors. The latter had only been convicted because the court had been deceived, whatever that meant. The letter announcing all this was authorized by Henry of Bath himself![119]

The rights and wrongs of the Bath case are impossible to unravel. Henry of Bath was not in the end convicted of any crime, yet one can well imagine he used his position to secure favourable verdicts and the imposition of

---

[117] There is a great deal about Moulton senior in Holt, *Northerners*.

[118] *CPR 1247–58*, 101; *CFR 1250–1*, no. 822. The 2,000-mark fine was payable at 200 marks a year. The £300 amercement was pardoned as part of the fine.

[119] *CPR 1247–58*, 526.

heavy penalties on his defeated opponents. Thirkleby had a reputation
for probity (unlike Bath) and had surely not misinterpreted the verdict of
the Moulton jury.[120] There had earlier been efforts to delay his hearing of
the case. He knew Matthew Paris well and may have been a source for the
latter's account of the trial. Was he indeed the judge who accused Bath of
taking bribes?

Henry comes out of the affair half-well. He pursued the matter
against powerful opposition and inflicted a heavy punishment. Here
was a warning against both judicial misconduct and attempts to bully the
king. Henry might also think Bath had no need to take bribes since he
enjoyed a salary of £100 a year, the highest of the professional judges.
Yet in the end Henry had settled the case very quickly without much
concern for its wider implications. His pardoning of Bath must have
discouraged those wishing to bring their own cases against the judge. His
overturning of the verdict in Moulton's favour looks very fishy. He even
failed in the end to make much money for the 2,000-mark fine, payable at
200 marks a year, was simply set against Bath's salary once he returned to
office. The Bath case, like the inquiries in the localities, led to no general
cleansing of the royal administration. Was there not also something
unstable and ill considered in Henry's anger, as there was also in its sudden
evaporation? The king's 'heart', as Paris put it, was easily stirred. It could
wax soft with love and hot with anger. But Henry never remained angry
for long. When he calmed down, he was easily steered by cleverer men
(like Mansel) into quieter waters. It would have been far better had Henry
combined a righteous anger with a cool, considered determination to find
the truth.[121]

Later in 1251 there was a repeat of the Bath case in miniature. This time
the object of Henry's ire was the justice of the Jews, Philip Lovel. On the
way to York for the marriage with Alexander, Henry suddenly heard accusations that Lovel was taking bribes to let Jews off the current tallage. He
indignantly dismissed him from office only to be gradually softened by the
intercession of Mansel again and King Alexander. Lovel, a clever and
circumspect man in Paris's view, was pardoned in return for a fine of 10
marks of gold, the equivalent of 100 marks of silver. (Paris was wrong in
thinking the amount was 1,000 marks.) Later, in 1252, Lovel returned as a
justice of the Jews and then became treasurer of the exchequer. The latter
appointment took place at St Albans and was stage managed, so Paris
thought, by Mansel. If Bath and Lovel had been justly accused they

---

[120] For Thirkleby's reputation and a curious last link with Henry of Bath, see St Albans
Continuator, 450–1.

[121] *CR 1256–9*, 20. Philip de Arcy went on the Gascon expediion of 1253–4. In 1256 he
received a gift of game and later, high in the king's favour, supported the royal recovery of
power in 1261. He died in 1264. Thomas of Moulton, however, joined the rebels.

should never have returned to high office. If unjustly, they should never have been sacked in the first place.[122]

In both these cases, as in others around this time, John Mansel intervened to save a fellow minister. In some ways that speaks well for the bonds holding together Henry's court. Evidently, at Mansel's level, not everyone was at each other's throat. Yet this solidarity is another reason for the absence of general reform. The king's minsters, fearful of what might be uncovered, were able to manouevre Henry away from any attempt to imitate King Louis. On his own, Henry simply lacked the single-minded drive and sense of duty to carry through a great reform of the realm in face of the vested interests of himself and his officials.[123]

DENIAL OF JUSTICE

Henry, therefore, could fairly be accused of failing to reform the realm. He was also accused of something else. Instead of acting as an impartial judge, he was denying justice to those seeking to bring legal actions against those in his favour. A critique of Henry's rule drawn up in 1264 alleged it was hard even to obtain writs to begin actions against the king's foreign relatives and well-placed native magnates. Matthew Paris stated much the same. Indeed, he believed that, 'contrary to all right and the peace of the kingdom', Henry ordered writs not to be issued damaging to the earls of Cornwall and Gloucester, Peter of Savoy and the half-brothers.[124] There is no documentary evidence to support the accusation, but that Henry was obstructive when cases were brought against those in his favour has some truth.[125] The beneficiaries included English magnates as well as the king's foreign relatives.[126] In 1251, Henry simply suspended the case in which the knight Hugh of Elmstead claimed that Warin de Munchesney had dispossessed him unjustly of the Essex manor of Thorringon, a manor Elmstead had just bought.[127] After the suspension, Elmstead gave up the case and granted the manor to Munchesney.[128] On Munchesney's death in 1255, Matthew Paris praised his zeal in protecting the liberty and peace of the kingdom, but evidently he was not above exploiting the influence gained through being the father-in-law of William de Valence.[129] A few years

---

[122] Paris, v, 261–2, 270, 320, 345; *CPR 1247–58*, 128, 149; Meekings, *Studies in 13th-Century Justice*, ch. 4, 180–1.

[123] For further reflections on the contrast between the two kings, see below, 713–15.

[124] *DBM*, 270–5; Paris, v, 594. This was in 1256.

[125] See Carpenter, *Reign of Henry III*, 30–6, 191–2; Moore, 'Thorrington dispute'.

[126] For the foreign relatives, see below, 673.

[127] For the whole story, see Moore, 'Thorrington dispute'.

[128] Since Munchesney was the overlord of Thorrington, he probably thought Elmstead had no business acquiring the manor in the first place.

[129] Paris, v, 504.

later, much to the annoyance of the judge Henry of Bracton, the king
again stopped a case going forward, this time at the instance of Richard
de Clare.[130] Such interventions, preventing cases proceeding to judgement, were specifically condemned in the critique of 1264.[131]

In the early 1250s St Albans abbey had its own difficulties getting
justice, or what it claimed to be justice, especially when up against its
tenant and neighbour, Geoffrey of Childwick.[132] (The two places are only
three miles apart.) Like his father, Childwick was a household knight and
marshal of the king. He was also married to Clarice, John Mansel's sister.
Husband and wife were equally bad, Matthew Paris thought. Puffed up by
his position, Childwick threw his weight around locally. He rode around
on a costly horse with a large retinue. He invaded the abbot's warren with
his hunting dogs, bows, arrows and nets. He maltreated a servant bringing
the abbot a gift of venison on the spurious grounds the venison had been
poached from the royal forest. As a member of the king's household,
Childwick was obliged, he said, to stamp out such malpractices. The abbot
began a legal action against Childwick for breach of the peace but was
persuaded by Mansel and the king to abandon it. The whole affair showed
'the tepidity of justice and the remissness of the king'.[133] In related litigation, according to Paris, Mansel's influence stopped the mouths of all the
pleaders at the bench, and the abbey's cellarer and legal expert, William
of Horton, had to put the abbey's case in person. The judges whispered
to Horton that there were two dominant people in the kingdom against
whom they dared not pass sentence: John Mansel himself and Richard of
Cornwall. Another claim in the critique of 1264 was that the king's judges
were in the pockets of great men, and certainly there were close connections between some judges and leading nobles.[134] Horton's conclusion was
that 'there are certain people in the land like kings against whom it is
scarcely or not at all possible to have justice'.[135]

When the victims of Henry's obstructionism had limited influence,
there might be no repercussions, at least in the short term. Hugh of
Elmstead accepted his defeat but rebelled later in the civil war. More
serious were the cases involving the great against the great, for these added
to the tensions at Henry's court. Simon de Montfort resented the way his
wife's claim, against William de Valence, for dower in Pembrokeshire had
not gone forward. Roger Bigod was involved in frustrating litigation over

---

[130] Carpenter, *Reign of Henry III*, 82–3. The case was being brought by Andrew Wake
(who was thus the loser) against the West Country baron William de Montacute.

[131] *DBM*, 272–3.

[132] For what follows, see Paris, *GA*, 315–19; Paris, v, 129–30, 233–4, translated in Vaughan,
Chronicles, 74–6, 225–6, and the full account in Meekings and Crook, *King's Bench and
Common Bench*, 104–5.

[133] Paris, v, 234.

[134] Carpenter, *Reign of Henry III*, 83–4; Maddicott, *Law and Lordship*, 4–13.

[135] Paris, *GA*, i, 340.

the Suffolk manor of Redenhall, litigation touching on the interests of the queen and Peter of Savoy. Bigod also brought an action, accusing the king's half-brother bishop-elect Aymer of depriving him of a wardship. The action was adjourned by the judges when Bigod might have expected a verdict in his favour.[136]

Henry's approach to these cases is not always clear. The arguments leading him to stop the Munchesney and Clare litigation are unknown. Quite probably he gave the matter little thought. In the Childwick case, as Matthew Paris acknowledged, he persuaded the abbot to abandon the action. He did the same in Paris's account of a more famous case involving John fitzGeoffrey in 1258. Henry often said he wanted something done so that he incurred no sin. Perhaps in these cases, given that the abbot and fitzGeoffrey gave way to his pleas, he told himself his conscience could be clear. The Montfort litigation, as we have seen, involved complex issues of law and politics, and Henry offered some compensation when it did not proceed.[137] He showed some sympathy to Bigod in the Redenhall affair and was not the direct cause of the earl's difficulties. Nonetheless, these and other cases made it easy to argue that 'justice was virtually shut out from England', as the critique of 1264 put it.[138] In the end the seeming denial of justice to John fitzGeoffrey, shielding bishop-elect Aymer, helped bring Henry's regime down.

ARBITRARY DISPOSSESSION?

If then Henry could indeed be accused of breaking Magna Carta's chapter 40 forbidding the denial of justice, was he also guilty of violating chapter 39 forbidding dispossession save by lawful process? This is certainly the impression given by Matthew Paris, who has Henry both attempting, in arbitrary fashion, to overturn established rights and justifying his ability to do so. A king who should be the mirror of justice was now spreading darkness not light.[139]

Paris's picture was closely connected to his worry about the use of the term 'non obstante' – 'notwithstanding'. His original complaint here related to the pope and certainly 'non obstante' clauses frequently appear

---

[136] Carpenter, *Reign of Henry III*, 30–2, 83, 192; Howell, *Eleanor of Provence*, 263–4; Morris, *Bigod Earls of Norfolk*, 52–3. For the case involving the wardship of Richard, son of Richard de Bere, see Carpenter, *Reign of Henry III*, 192; Morris, *Bigod Earls of Norfolk*, 52. It may have ended with Aymer buying out Bigod's rights for 100 marks. Whether Bigod was pleased when Henry agreed the money could be deducted from the payments he was supposed to be making towards his debts at the exchequer may be questioned.

[137] See above, 473–4.

[138] *DBM*, 260–1, cap. 7.

[139] Paris, v, 128, 275–6.

in the letters of Innocent IV.[140] Their use could be perfectly innocuous. So the king's clerk John le Francis was allowed to proceed to higher orders, 'notwithstanding' his defective sight and a blemish in one of his eyes. They could also be used (and this was the cause of Paris's concern) to set aside existing privileges. So the abbot and convent of Glastonbury were ordered to confer a benefice on the pope's nephew 'notwithstanding' any papally conferred indult or exemption.[141] Henry's own use of the term could be similarly innocuous, so wine might be sent to one destination 'notwithstanding' a previous order to send it to another. But Henry was also, so Paris believed, using the term in a far more sinister fashion both to manipulate the judicial process and, like the pope, to abrogate existing rights. If he could do that, privileges and property conferred by royal charters would be at his mercy. He would effectively be a tyrant.

How far all of this is true is another matter. In one example Paris gives from 1251 it may well be that the judge, Roger of Thirkleby, protested at the way he was ordered to summon a defendant, Gerard de Rodes, before the bench to answer in a lawsuit 'notwithstanding' letters of protection by which he should have been exempt. The order in question was authorized by the king and benefited Silvester of Everdon, the former keeper of the seal and now bishop of Carlisle. Paris's account ends with Thirkleby lamenting the way ecclesiastical practices were contaminating those of the king's courts. Yet, under cool examination, the episode appears in a less serious light. Rodes's exemption was overridden simply to allow the bishop a speedy settlement of the case, one for which he paid handsomely and from which Rodes himself (essentially a secondary figure in the proceedings) was no loser.[142]

In another case, this one from 1252, Matthew Paris has Henry himself making a threatening speech about the use of 'non obstante'. When the prior of the Hospitallers in England complained of an injury and showed his royal letters of protection, he was met by a high-voiced harangue. The Templars and Hospitallers, Henry cried, had become arrogant thanks to their superfluity of charters and liberties. Just as the pope quashed previous concessions by the use of 'non obstante', so Henry would recall the charters he and his predecessors had rashly granted. When the prior replied that Henry's title to rule depended on him ruling justly, Henry accused 'the English' of wishing to depose or kill him just as they had his father.[143]

---

[140] Paris, iv, 445 (note the entry over an erasure), 522; Paris, v, 127–30, 210–11, 339. For discussion of 'non obstante', see Clanchy, 'Did Henry III have a policy?', 209; Carpenter, *Reign of Henry III*, 78–9.

[141] *CPReg*, 257, 262. Numerous examples of the use of the term appear in the *Calendar of Papal Letters*.

[142] Paris, v, 210; *CR 1247–51*, 540, 566. The 'cool examination' is by Henry Summerson, see his 'The king's *clericulus*', 84–8, and also Powicke, *King Henry III*, i, 324–5. Summerson shows that Paris completely misunderstood the nature of the case. The suggestions related to Thirkleby's role are my own.

[143] Paris, v, 339.

It is impossible to know how much credence to place on this exchange.[144] In illustrating the truth of major themes – here the threat of 'non obstante' and the king's hostility to his own subjects – Paris was quite capable of placing words into Henry's mouth.[145] He gives no details of the dispute and none appear elsewhere. Indeed, around this time the prior of the Hospitallers seems in high favour.[146] Just possibly, the origins of the account lie in a muddled recollection of a dispute in 1252 between Henry and the hospital of St Thomas of Acre in London over rights of presentation during a vacancy. Here, however, after high-sounding sentiments about protecting the rights of the crown, Henry seems to have climbed down.[147]

Much more to the point is Paris's account of the long-running disputes between St Albans and Geoffrey of Childwick. Here Henry appealed to 'non obstante' in a conversation with Paris himself. In June 1249, Childwick obtained a charter from the king granting him free warren in Childwick and other lands. One of the witnesses was John Mansel. This seemed to St Albans a direct attack on its own rights, rights confirmed only the year before in a royal charter granting it free warren in all its demesne lands in England.[148] The abbot, however, made a fatal mistake. Instead of challenging Childwick's charter in a legal action, he ignored it and exercised his rights of warren as before. This gave Childwick the opportunity to bring his own action against the abbot.

At some point in the course of the litigation, perhaps on Henry's visit to St Albans, in April 1251, Paris himself, so he tells us, 'unafraid', 'reproached the king over these things'. Henry's reply was to say 'surely the pope does likewise, manifestly adding in his letters "notwithstanding any privilege or indulgence"'![149] There is at least some supporting evidence that Henry might have spoken in this way. Both in 1246 and 1249, an old theme, he secured from the pope permission to revoke alienations made contrary to his coronation oath to preserve the rights and properties of the crown. This was to be 'notwithstanding' any oath to the contrary, even if confirmed by the pope.[150] The fit with Matthew Paris's account of Henry's speeches is not exact. They made no reference to the coronation oath or papal letters. But clearly Henry was troubled by grants he had made in the past and sought help from the pope in overthrowing them. That, in his conversation with Paris, he drew parallels with the papal use of 'notwithstanding' is not impossible.

---

[144] For Clanchy's doubts, see 'Did Henry III have a policy?', 211.

[145] See Carpenter, 'Chronology and truth: Matthew Paris and the *Chronica Majora*'.

[146] *CR 1251–3*, 5, 30, 86, 108, 152, 266, 273, 281.

[147] *CR 1251–3*, 242. Henry's presentation of Roger of Missenden to the living in dispute seems to have been cancelled: *CPR 1247–58*, 135.

[148] *CChR 1226–57*, 330, 342; *RCWL*, ii, 36.

[149] Paris, v, 129–30, and 233–4 for the probable occasion.

[150] *CPReg*, 224–5, 251–2. It is not clear what oath Henry was referring to here.

Actions, however, speak louder than words and the fact is that Henry's actions never lived up to his 'non obstante' protestations. That Paris 'unafraid' felt able to raise the Childwick case shows how approachable and amenable Henry could be. He was also sensitive and sympathetic to Paris's reaction for, having blurted out the claim over 'non obstante', he then, 'speaking with more moderation, added "now, now, we will think about it"'. The results of these kingly cogitations are shown in the eventual judgement in the case. This was pronounced at Michaelmas 1251 by Henry himself but was formulated, so Paris says, by the judge William of York, now bishop of Salisbury. There was no reference at all to any claims to revoke previous charters. Indeed, there was an implication that the king might have acted unjustly. St Albans lost the case only because it had taken direct action. Even if the king granted a manor to a magnate unjustly, so the judgement ran (in Paris's account), the magnate needed to bring his case to court and make good his claim there. This judgement was cited with approval in *Bracton*.[151] St Albans did not try to revive the case again. Instead, through the good offices of Mansel, here as so often a peacemaker, it came to terms with Childwick.

Quite probably, Henry had made the grant to Childwick without realizing how it might infringe the liberties of St Albans. When, on the contrary, Henry knew he was up against established privileges, his conduct was different, as another case from this period shows. It is narrated in detail by the London alderman, Arnold fitzThedmar, and concerns Henry's second attempt (the first was back in 1248) to get the Londoners to grant liberties in Middlesex to Westminster Abbey.[152] In 1248 the Londoners had gone quit 'by the counsel of the earls and barons in the king's presence'. Now, in May 1250, Henry hoped to get his way by arranging a 'day of love' between the abbot of Westminster and the citizens. It was to no avail. The Londoners proclaimed 'with one voice' that they would not depart from their existing liberties. In an angry response (on 20 May) Henry took the government of London into his own hands and summoned the citizens to come before him at Windsor, there to face other accusations of misconduct. At Windsor, however, Henry retreated and, after some discussion between the king and his council, the Londoners recovered control of the city. Matthew Paris has both Richard of Cornwall and Simon de Montfort involved in the decision.[153] The case was postponed until the feast of the Confessor on 13 October, where it seems to have been dropped. In return the Londoners, on Henry's petition, donated some great candles to the altar of the Confessor.

This episode shows the constitutional limitations on royal power. One part of Henry doubtless wished to grant the liberties to Westminster

---

[151] *Bracton*, ii, 169.

[152] FitzThedmar, 16–17; Paris, v, 127–8; Stone, 'Book of Arnold fitzThedmar', 208–9. See above, 481–2.

[153] *CPR 1247–58*, 65; *CR 1247–51*, 285; Paris, v, 127–8.

Abbey, 'non obstante' those of London. Yet he knew it was both illegal and impractical to do so. When the Londoners refused to give way, he raked up old charges and thus sought to pressurize them by at least a quasi-judicial process. He also took the city into his own hands, something he could claim to do by established right. Yet he was still made to back down – by his council in 1250, including Earl Richard and Montfort, and by the earls and barons in 1248.[154] 'Thus the wisdom of the magnates happily recalled the king from his impetuous assault,' wrote Paris. He believed that the magnates, nonetheless, were alarmed by Henry's conduct. Would they be next if, following the example of the pope, the king tried to set aside the charters of his predecessors? But they were not next. No anxiety over 'non obstante' was expressed in the numerous schedules of complaint about Henry's rule drawn up in the period of reform and rebellion. When, in 1253, Henry granted liberties to William de Valence, he said he did not want them to harm those of the abbey of Bury St Edmunds, thus avoiding the injustice in the Childwick case.[155]

There were, during Henry's personal rule, a few occasions where he was able to get around charters he had granted. He did so, however, by securing resignations of the charters concerned rather than blatantly over-turning them. The most striking examples involved his recovery of Pevensey and then Cardigan and Carmarthen from the Marshals, this without incurring, as far as can be seen, any kind of criticism[156] More dubious was the way, in 1257, he pressurized Robert fitzNicholas into selling him the manor of Dunham so it could be given to William de Valence.[157] The one case where Henry refused directly to uphold a royal charter occurred in August 1234, right at the start of his personal rule. This was a charter granting the Leicestershire manor of Rothley to its men at an annual farm, the problem being that Henry had subsequently granted the manor to the Templars along with the burial of his body. The reason for Henry's refusal to uphold the charter, as recorded in the roll of the court *coram rege*, was 'that the charter had been made in the four-teenth year of the reign, and the king says he was then under age and deceived'.[158] Of all the extraordinary statements Henry made in his reign, this must rank near the top. That Henry had been deceived into granting the charter may be true for the terms were very favourable to the men, perhaps through the influence (doubtless at a price) of Stephen of Seagrave, whose home at Seagrave was only four miles from Rothley. But for Henry to claim that he was underage when he granted the charter was

---

[154] There may not have been much difference between the two bodies.

[155] *CR 1251–3*, 462.

[156] See above, 240–3.

[157] See below, 690.

[158] *CRR*, xv, nos. 1044, 1085. As was proper in cases turning on royal charters, Henry was here giving judgement himself.

absurd as the statement in the roll itself made clear. The charter had indeed been granted in the fourteenth year of the reign, in fact in February 1230. Henry was then twenty-three![159] How could he utter so obvious a falsehood? Was it that in some simplistic and emotional way he persuaded himself he was still underage while being controlled by the regime of Hubert de Burgh? Whatever the case, Henry certainly knew how to make himself look ridiculous.

Henry got away with revoking the charter to the men of Rothley because he was dealing with peasants, indeed the peasants of a royal manor. The court record itself, having stated that the men had returned their charter to the king, added 'and since they are rustici of the king', rather implying that unfree peasants had no right to a charter anyway.[160] Had Henry, by contrast, sought to overturn the charters granted to his magnates in so direct a fashion, he would soon have been in trouble. As it was, the occasions when charters were surrendered, as with the Marshals and Robert fitzNicholas, were few and far between. On the whole, Henry was not guilty of breaching Magna Carta chapter 39, and indeed the critique of his rule in 1264 did not accuse him of doing so. In line with the Charter, Henry constantly stressed he wished to deprive no one of possessions unjustly and without judgement.[161] When, in 1256, Richard of Cornwall advised that it would be 'most unfitting' for Henry's daughter to be married into the kingdom of Castile, where her husband might be deprived of his lands 'by the sole will and pleasure of the prince', the implication was that things were very different in England.[162] Under the terms of Magna Carta, in 1215, John was forced to make some fifty acts of restoration to men complaining of unjust dispossession.[163] Nothing like that happened after the revolution of 1258. But if Henry was innocent of breaking Magna Carta chapter 39, to be accused of breaking chapter 40 forbidding the denial of justice was bad enough.[164]

MONEY FOR THE CRUSADE AND HENRY'S GOLD TREASURE

In order to launch his crusade Henry needed money, lots of it. He was far more successful here than he was in reforming the realm or in generating crusading enthusiasm. Henry had two ways of gathering the necessary

---

[159] One wonders whether the presiding judge of the court, William of Raleigh, allowed the fourteenth year to be placed on the roll as a way of distancing himself from the king's judgement.

[160] Perhaps in not being reminded of the men's status was another way in which Henry thought he had been deceived.

[161] *CR 1247–51*, 49, 235, 341; *CR 1251–3*, 103, 484; *CR 1256–9*, 65; see *F*, 408–9.

[162] *CR 1254–6*, 389–90.

[163] Holt, *Magna Carta*, 360–1; Carpenter, *Magna Carta*, 388.

[164] Henry was not, however, guilty of openly selling justice in the fashion of his predecessors.

funds. The first was by reducing his expenditure, and this he attempted. He cut the numbers of his servants in receipt of robes and, perhaps by as much as 40 per cent, the costs of his household's daily food and drink. He also, a great sacrifice, reduced his almsgiving and the number of candles which illuminated his services. A cross to be ready for the feast of Edward the Confessor was first to cost no more than £10, then no more than £5.[165]

Yet this unaccustomed parsimony itself excited no support for the crusade. Indeed, it provoked Matthew Paris into rare praise for King John. Henry was departing from his father's standards of hospitality.[166] He was also reducing the costs of the household by extracting hospitality from religious houses.[167] In other areas, moreover, Henry seemed as extravagant as ever, especially when it came to finding patronage for his foreign relatives.[168] Paris's comment that Henry was wasting the treasure needed for his crusade on aliens seems fair enough.[169] While, moreover, Henry reduced some of his pious costs, he ordered the work on Westminster Abbey to be speeded up: money was to be got by loan or in any other way so there should be no delays. In Henry's mind, of course, completing the Abbey was a way of winning the Confessor's support for the crusade, but he was also lavishing funds on purely secular buildings. His journeys to the West Country in 1250 and to the north in 1251–2 called for extensive work on the royal castles and houses he visited along the route. As for Windsor, Henry told a sheriff to raise 400 marks for the works by any means 'as he wishes to have the king's grace and avoid his indignation'. And Henry could never resist a beautiful object. In February 1253 he spent all of 500 marks buying a new crown from an overseas merchant.[170]

Henry, however, did not just spend money. He also devoted himself to raising it. In this period, perhaps more than any other in his reign, he drove forward the financial machine. He demanded information about the exchequer's daily receipts, and (so Matthew Paris believed) ordered a scrutiny of the rolls to see how much money he had spent during his reign.[171] Through letters and through personal appearances at the exchequer, he demanded that the sheriffs collect debts more swiftly and with less regard

---

[165] *CR 1247–51*, 383, 389–90; Lachaud, 'Liveries of robes', 283; Paris, v, 114, 137, 199 (and for earlier efforts, 50); Carpenter, 'Household rolls', 35–6.

[166] Paris, v, 114.

[167] Paris, v, 199; see *C&S*, i, 471, cap. 11. The abbeys of Reading, Merton, Bury and St Albans would seem to have been the chief sufferers, although the absence of household rolls from this period means there is no precise chapter and verse.

[168] See below, 555.

[169] Paris, v, 205.

[170] *CR 1247–51*, 460, 492; *CLR 1251–60*, 105. The issue rolls for the exchequer show the order to pay the 500 marks was obeyed.

[171] *CR 1247–51*, 464; Paris, v, 215.

to liberties, those of Westminster Abbey, of course, excluded.[172] Between 1250 and 1252 he commissioned forest eyres in the northern counties under Geoffrey de Langley, extorting, Paris thought, 'infinite' sums of money. The amount owed was some £5,685, over half of it due from Yorkshire.[173] At Easter 1252 the exchequer ordered a whole group of Yorkshire men to be distrained to pay up.[174] This was the culmination of a series of forest eyres, headed first by Robert Passelewe and then by Geoffrey de Langley, since 1244 gradually covering the forest counties. The total owed the crown between 1244 and 1252 was £18,214, as against £5,558 due from all the forest eyres held previously in the reign.[175]

Henry also sought to make more money from his own manors. In 1250 and 1251 he commissioned inquiries into their annual value and the alienation of royal rights within them. Eleurius, abbot of Pershore, an able monk from Fécamp abbey in Normandy, in charge of the policy, proudly showed how the new rents imposed, at £1,028, exceeded the old by some £367.[176] In April 1252, the same month in which he fixed the date for his departure on crusade, Henry levied a tallage on his towns and manors, London's share being 1,000 marks and 20 marks of gold.[177] Henry sometimes stressed he only wanted what he could have 'with justice', but his methods could be disreputable even if he tried to hide this, perhaps even from himself. After William of Raleigh's death, he extracted £400 from the bishop's executors. This was to repay the money Henry had spent opposing Raleigh's election, money which 'men worthy to be believed' now told him could be recouped from episcopal goods, since it had been spent 'to the profit of the church'![178]

Henry's hand, in these years, fell heavily on the Jews. With the proceeds of the 60,000-mark tallage levied between 1244 and 1250 now petering out, between 1250 and 1253 he imposed four new tallages with a total value of 24,000 marks. This pressure had repercussions on Henry's Christian subjects, since the Jews, in order to pay the tallages, put more pressure on

[172] TNA E 368/24, m. 3; TNA E 368/26, m. 8; TNA E 368/27, mm. 3, 4; TNA E 368/28, m. 1d; TNA SC 1/3/89; CR 1251–3, 279–80, 424–5; Paris, v, 283. For Henry sitting personally at the exchequer and ordering the preservation of the liberties of Westminster Abbey, see TNA E 368/27, m. 4.

[173] Paris, v, 136–7, 340; Winters, 'The forest eyre 1154–1368', 197–206. The amounts assessed in the individual counties were Yorkshire, £2,507; Nottinghamshire and Derbyshire, £1,588; Cumberland, £413; Lancashire, £457; and Northumberland, £720.

[174] TNA E 368/26, mm. 17d–18. For Henry setting terms for the payment of the debts, see CFR 1250–1, nos. 135, 154, 168–71, 174–5, 212, 217, 263–80, 284, 664, 667; CFR 1251–2, nos. 96, 126, 128, 146, 150, 327.

[175] Winters, 'The Forest Eyre 1154–1368', 19–20, 25–6.

[176] CPR 1247–58, 71, 95, 99 (for the same policy in Ireland); CFR 1250–1, no. 1107; Tewkesbury, 142.

[177] CR 1251–3, 212–13; CR 1254–6, 160; Paris, v, 333–4; Mitchell, Studies in Taxation, 251.

[178] CR 1247–51, 522–3; CFR 1250–1, nos. 23, 162. For raising money with justice, see CR 1247–51, 254; CR 1251–3, 156–7; Clanchy, 'Did Henry III have a policy?', 215–16.

their Christian debtors, or handed over their debts to be collected by the king. They also sold debts of lesser men to magnates who then took control of the land on which the money was secured, a practice complained about after the revolution of 1258.[179]

Matthew Paris, with a mixture of satisfaction and sympathy, appreciated how taxation was impoverishing the Jews. He also linked it directly to the needs of the crusade.[180] It was the crusade too, as Paris likewise appreciated, which lay behind the most striking of Henry's financial policies in these years: his amassing of a gold treasure.[181] As Paris explained, since gold was the currency in the East and the specie in which soldiers were paid, Henry began to collect it.[182] In so doing he was probably following the general practice of crusaders. What was impressive was the single-minded devotion he gave to the task, one quite at odds with his usual reputation. Year after year, he accumulated gold, and refused to break into his store for other purposes. Instead of taking it with him to Gascony in 1253, he stipulated in the will he then made that, if he died, it was to be used in aid of the Holy Land.[183]

Henry had begun saving gold in 1243 when he decided to keep all the gifts and fines in gold made on his return from Gascony. Probably his aim was to devote the gold to the new feretory of Edward the Confessor. That he acquired far more than he could immediately use was why the rate of collection then declined. The revival of saving in the later 1240s reflects the way Henry was already thinking of a crusade, if at first one led by Guy de Lusignan. The rapid accumulation of gold between 1250 and 1253 was the result of Henry taking the cross himself. The gold was acquired in two ways. First, Henry, in a series of personal instructions, arranged for silver to be used to buy gold, an activity in which he both enlisted Jewish expertise (as frequent dealers in gold) and employed silver drawn from Jewish tallages.[184] More important, Henry proclaimed (as Matthew Paris noted) that he was now prepared to sell various privileges in return for gold. The most important were charters giving the right to set up markets and fairs or create free warrens (essentially private parks for hunting). Between October 1251 and May 1253 (when there are figures from the fine rolls) some 25 ecclesiastics and around 100 laymen offered gold for such concessions. During the same period 115 laymen, mostly of knightly status, offered gold for exemption from jury service and other duties. The cost of these concessions was usually either a half or 1 mark of gold, which meant (at a 10 to 1 ratio between gold and silver) they cost the equivalent

---

[179] Stacey, '1240–60: a watershed in Anglo-Jewish relations?', 136–9, 142–4; Paris, v, 114–16; *DBM*, 86–7, cap. 25; Huscroft, *Expulsion*, 91–3.

[180] Paris, v, 114–16, 136, 274.

[181] For the whole story, see Carpenter, *Reign of Henry III*, ch. 6.

[182] Paris, *HA*, iii, 99, 320; Paris, v, 274.

[183] *F*, 496.

[184] For example, *CFR 1248–9*, nos. 446–63; *CR 1247–51*, 473.

of 5 marks or 10 marks of silver. In addition towns and religious houses gave gold to confirm old liberties and secure new ones.[185]

Since there was no English gold coin in which to make these offers, they were paid either in foreign gold coins like Byzantine bezants and the Islamic money of Murcia or 'in foil', most of it probably acquired from goldsmiths and dealers, many of the latter Jews.[186] The money from the fines was received, usually cash down, into the wardrobe, bypassing the exchequer, which again shows how personal the initiative was to the king. Henry took the closest interest in the treasure's accumulation, sometimes issuing orders about it by word of mouth. In October 1252 he wanted the gold at the New Temple (where the treasure was kept) to be weighed so that he could be informed of the amount without delay.[187] When Peter Chaceporc, as keeper of the wardrobe, accounted in May 1253, the treasure had reached some 2,110 marks of gold. Probably another 729 marks of gold had been collected outside his control. The total value of the treasure, therefore, was not far short of 3,000 marks of gold, which made it worth 30,000 marks or £20,000 of silver. In modern terms it weighed a little under two-thirds of a tonne, the equal of some 56 of the 12.4 kg bars in which gold is stored in the vaults of the Bank of England. If, as seems likely, around two-thirds of this had been collected between 1250 and May 1253, Henry was then saving at the rate of 640 marks of gold, or 6,400 marks (£4,200) of silver a year. The treasure paled before the £130,000 King John had at his disposal in 1213. But still it was not far short of the 34,000 marks raised by the last tax on movables, levied in 1237. It exceeded the 25,000 marks of the tax of 1232. Its accumulation was a great achievement.

There was, however, one unfortunate consequence of Henry's attempts to save money. On a scale unseen before, the wardrobe was failing to pay merchants promptly for the court's food, drink, cloth and wax. Instead it was piling up debt. There had already been criticism on this score at the parliament of 1248 and thereafter the situation probably worsened.[188] When Peter Chaceporc, as keeper of the wardrobe, accounted in February 1252 for the period since 1245, he recognized that £2,690 was still owed to 'diverse merchants'.[189] At least, the gold treasure itself was not squeezed

---

[185] Carpenter, *Reign of Henry III*, 112–14.

[186] Carpenter, 'Gold and gold coins', 107–9. The 'oboli' of 'musc' Henry used for his offerings were coins of Murcia, the chief Almohade city on the Mediterranean coast of Spain.

[187] *CR 1251–3*, 148; TNA E 368/27, m. 3.

[188] Paris, v, 6.

[189] Wild, *WA*, cvii, cxi; Wild, 'Royal finance under Henry III', 1399. It is possible that some of the debts were paid out of the £1,190 surplus of receipts over expenditure recorded in Chaceporc's account for the period from February to October 1252: Wild, *WA*, cxix. Since this was his last account, his executors, on his death at the end of 1254, being pardoned all his debts, there is no means of knowing. See *CPR 1247–58*, p. 388; http://aalt. law.uh.edu/AALT4/H3/E372n098/bE372n098dorses/IMG_8273.htm, references I owe to Richard Cassidy.

from the realm. People were paying voluntarily for real benefits. Since the charge in gold was much the same as it would have been in silver, there was no extra cost involved other than that of acquiring the gold in the first place. The policy also brought large numbers of churchmen, magnates and knights to court, where they made the fines and paid in the money. How Henry must have hoped they would return home full of enthusiasm for his crusade, ready to support it, not just with money, but with all the prayers and processions he was planning.

THE TAXATION OF THE CHURCH

It was very different when it came to the second main way in which Henry sought to raise money for the crusade, namely by taxation of the church. The papally sanctioned tax for Louis's crusade had been very unpopular in France.[190] It was the same with the tax granted in England. As he had done with Louis, Pope Innocent gave Henry a tenth of ecclesiastical revenues for three years. This certainly was a great prize. While Henry could not know exactly what the tax would produce, he must have anticipated a yield equalling or exceeding the taxes on movables he had levied in the past.[191] Innocent had first said that collection should start two years before Henry's date of departure, but had then made it three years instead.[192] Since, in April 1252, Henry had fixed his departure for June 1256, that meant collection should start in June 1253. There was, however, a major snag. The pope had the power to command the English church to pay the tax, but was reluctant to use it. Collection would be far easier if the church freely assented to the levy. Innocent's initial concession in April 1250 had been on the understanding that it had indeed done so.[193] Henry too accepted the necessity, or at least the utility, of the church's consent. But he also, crucially, came to accept, as did the pope, that the consent given in 1250 was inadequate. Thus Henry found himself in the position of having to beg the prelates 'to freely assent to the apostolic mandate', a mandate (replacing that of 1250) which urged consent but did not enforce it.[194]

---

[190] Paris, iv, 561–2; Paris, v, 102.

[191] In the event the annual value of ecclesiastical revenues was assessed for the tax at around £102,000, so it should have yielded some £34,000: Lunt, *Financial Relations*, 260. The valuation was supposed to include both spiritual and temporal revenue (Lunt, *Valuation*, 64), although the extent to which the latter was included was limited. The story of the tax and its successors is set out by Lunt in his *Financial Relations*, 255–90, behind which lies the detailed examination in his remarkable *Valuation of Norwich*.

[192] *Reg. Innocent IV*, ii, no. 5106 (*CPReg*, 267); *CR 1251–3*, 214, 217. However, Lunt notes there was some confusion over the advance from two years to three: Lunt, *Valuation*, 60–2.

[193] *F*, 272, 274.

[194] *CR 1251–3*, 217; Paris, vi, 296–7; *C&S*, i, 450. But look at the text of *Reg. Innocent IV*, ii, no. 5106.

The trouble was that the initial assent to which Pope Innocent referred had almost certainly been given in ambiguous terms by a small number of prelates speaking merely for themselves. What was needed was consent from full and formal assemblies to the detail of the tax as well as to the principle. The detail was important because the pope had stipulated that the tax should be levied on a new valuation of ecclesiastical property, which was bound to make it more burdensome.[195] Equally important was the fullness of the assemblies, because the idea that taxation born by all the clergy should in some way receive all the clergy's consent was by now ingrained in ecclesiastical thinking.[196] The bishops could not answer just by themselves.

None of this would have mattered had the church wished to support Henry's crusade with money as well as prayers. It did not. Some of Henry's prelates readily threw themselves into the task of preaching the cross. The bishop of Chichester, Richard of Wich, died while on a preaching tour of the south and left 50 marks in his will to a kinsman (the second largest bequest), 'so that he may go [to the Holy Land] for me'.[197] Bishops from the 1240s had also been the papally appointed collectors of crusading monies. One of them, Walter de Cantilupe of Worcester, Simon de Montfort's friend, took the cross himself, though not with Henry, and tried to ensure crusaders actually went and were not pressurized, if they were fit, into redeeming their vows.[198] Here was part of the problem. As Cantilupe's concern implies, the methods used, especially by the friars, to get money from redemptions could seem scandalous.[199] The hostility to the great tax granted Henry by the pope was even more intense. However good the cause it could be contaminated by bad money. Was not the money Louis IX had extorted from the church (likewise through a papally sanctioned tax) the reason for the failure of his own crusade? At least Louis had gone to the East, but would Henry? Was not his crusade simply a way of getting money which he would then use for other purposes?[200]

The accusation was unfair, given Henry's evident sincerity, and the way the tax was to be handed over only when he actually set out, but it reflected a distrust of the king's fixity of purpose, ultimately all too justified. Henry might reply that without the tax there was no way he could crusade, but there was an answer to that. If only he would husband his own resources, his manors, escheats and wardships, instead of wasting their revenues on foreigners, he would have the resources to live in plenty,

---

[195] Lunt, *Valuation*, 64–5.

[196] See Carpenter, *Reign of Henry III*, 400–2.

[197] *Saint Richard of Chichester*, 21, 67, 134–6, 211–12; *CPR 1247–58*, 164, 168.

[198] *CPReg*, 234; Paris, v, 98–9.

[199] Paris, v, 73–4. But see how Paris later, perhaps ironically, put this in a different light: Paris, *HA*, iii, 51–2, n.3; Vaughan, *Matthew Paris*, 122.

[200] Paris, v, 170–2, 282, 327.

and indeed crusade, without burdening the church. The bishop of Lincoln, Robert Grosseteste, put this in a wider intellectual framework. Unlike many clerical thinkers, he believed kingship was God-given, part of the natural order of things. He also believed, following Aristotle, that kings needed to have abundant resources of their own. Such self-sufficiency would enable them to govern for the common good without exploiting the wealth of their subjects. A king who did not have these resources was in danger of becoming a 'clerotes', a Greek term meaning someone drawn by lot to be a ruler, and thus holding his position but by chance. Without resources, a clerotes is forced to consult just his own interests, not those of his people, and is thus driven into tyranny. Was this not Henry's situation and also Henry's fault? Should one really give money to such a man whose crusade, if it took place, might, by a just judgement of God, be doomed from the start?[201]

Henry's attempt to get ecclesiastical consent to the papal tax began in the spring of 1252, just after he had fixed the date for his departure. He summoned into his presence the bishops of the southern province, only for them to say they could do nothing in the absence of Archbishop Boniface, who was abroad. In the north, the bishops assembled their own clergy and urged them to agree to the tax, only to be told that the matter concerned the whole English church and needed general discussion.[202]

Henry would return to the charge at the parliament held in October 1252. Meanwhile he had Simon de Montfort and the Gascon crisis to deal with. There was also the weather. The summer of 1252 saw drought and heatwave, the worst in living memory. Men and animals died. Henry gave a pension to someone driven mad by 'the intemperance of the air'.[203] Famine followed. In August the king left Woodstock and set off on a pilgrimage to East Anglian shrines, doubtless to pray for his crusade and his forthcoming expedition to Gascony. On the way, with Lord Edward in his company (though not the queen who had returned to Windsor), he stayed five days at St Albans, perhaps in part to reduce costs by accepting the abbot's hospitality. Matthew Paris paints the king in fascinatingly different guises. At religion he was impressive, just as he had been on his visits in 1251. He went 'devotedly' up to the high altar to pray, and then offered a precious cloth, two necklaces, two gold rings and twelve gold coins at Alban's shrine. At government, Henry was less commanding. When news arrived of the death of his treasurer, William of Haverhill, he wished to appoint in his place the exchequer official John le Francis, for all his blemished eye. But then rumours came in (false as they turned out) of John's death and Henry chose the clerk Philip Lovel instead. All this

---

[201] For Grosseteste's thought on this matter, see Ambler, 'On kingship and tyranny', 122, and Ambler, *Bishops in the Political Community*, 54–5, 155–6.

[202] *C&S*, i, 449–50; *CR 1251–3*, 217.

[203] Paris, v, 317, 321; Tewkesbury, 147; Waverley, 344; Wykes, 103; *CR 1251–3*, 120.

(so Matthew Paris believed) was arranged by John Mansel, Philip's friend. At play and patronage, Henry's conduct was deplorable. While exercising in the orchard at St Albans, he and his court were entertained by the jolly japes of Geoffrey de Lusignan's Poitevin chaplain, who pelted them with apples and turf and squirted the juice of grapes into their faces. Yet it was on this man, jester rather than priest, that Henry, in the full glare of publicity at St Albans, bestowed one of the richest benefices of the deceased William of Haverhill.[204]

Having arrived at Bury St Edmunds on 1 September, Henry fell gravely ill and had to stay there for over a fortnight, much to the inconvenience of the monks. He recovered in time to attend the dedication of the new choir and presbytery of Ely cathedral built by Bishop Hugh of Northwold in the years after 1234. Henry, one suspects, admired this new work far more than he did Walter de Grey's transepts at York. True, the Ely work had none of Westminster Abbey's height and grandeur. It had old fashioned lancet windows and a square east end. But, against that, the extraordinary profusion of the decoration, covering every surface, was absolutely to Henry's taste. Indeed, in deciding after 1259 to put extra ribs into the vault at Westminster, and extra shafts into the columns of the main arcade, he may well have been influenced by Ely's example.[205]

After the dedication, Henry returned to the south for the Confessor's feast at Westminster on 13 October. A magnificent crown was to be ready to offer the saint on his arrival.[206] Henry also had another saint on his mind, for during his illness he had vowed to visit the shrine of Archbishop Edmund at Pontigny. In December 1252 he actually wrote to Queen Blanche, asking her for a safe conduct through France, and saying he intended to cross the Channel in the coming February.[207]

What on earth was going on? Surely Henry should have been in Gascony by then, soothing passions after the Montfortian chaos. During the summer of 1252 he had solemnly promised the Gascons that he was coming. In September he had said the army was to muster at the parliament due to be held at Westminster on 13 October. The fleet was to be ready at Portsmouth a week later. Yet when the parliament opened, Henry called off the expedition almost at once. Even before it met, there are signs he was changing his mind.[208] He had heard that Simon de Montfort was

---

[204] Paris, v, 319–20, 329–30; *CPR 1247–58*, 149. The chaplain was Arnulf, archdeacon of Tours.

[205] Paris, v, 322. For Ely's decoration, see Binski, *Becket's Crown*, 87–101.

[206] Paris, v, 304, 322; *CR 1251–3*, 156, 159.

[207] *CR 1251–3*, 433. Henry was also grateful to Edmund the Martyr and took care to send offerings for his feast day in November: *CR 1251–3*, 427.

[208] *CR 1251–3*, 240, 245, 259–60, 262; *CPR 1247–58*, 161; Paris, v, 334–5, 337–8. Paris may here have confused Henry's request to travel through France for his pilgrimage to Pontigny with a request to travel through France to Gascony.

willing to be bought out, and thought that would be enough. Gascony could look after itself.[209] Henry could turn back to his crusade.

The autumn parliament of 1252 opened on 13 October, the day of the Confessor's translation, so all present presumably attended the service in Westminster Abbey. Hundreds of craftsmen and labourers were at work on the new church, now reaching high above the palace. In this environment, how Henry must have hoped there would be a full and final consent to the crusading tenth conceded by the pope. It did not work out like that. There is only Matthew Paris's account of the debates but it rings true:[210] Henry crying out in fury when his initial demands were refused, so that all fled from his chamber; his second attempt, now calmed down by his courtiers, begging for the subsidy not as imposed by the pope but as a simple favour 'to their crusading lord'; and, when that too failed, his attempts at individual persuasion. Henry rose reverently when Bishop Northwold of Ely entered, sat him down and thanked him for his past service. This was just the kind of interview for which the chamber at Westminster had been designed, with the paintings of the coronation of the Confessor and the guardians of Solomon's bed. But if such was the venue, the bishop was unmoved and stood by the refusal of his colleagues. Henry then lost his temper again and ordered his servants to throw out 'this rustic . . . who denies me help and solace'. In this case, a reversal of the painting in the chamber, Henry's anger had triumphed over his 'debonereté'.

Both archbishops were absent from the parliament (itself cited as a reason for delay) and the opposition was led by Grosseteste. Even Henry's half-brother Aymer, bishop-elect of Winchester, joined in the resistance: 'you ought to stand by me even if all the world was against me,' Henry exclaimed, refusing to rise to greet his brother.[211] Only the bishop of Salisbury, the judge William of York, took Henry's part. The pope's concession of the tax was easily discounted. He would never have agreed had he known of Henry's oppression of the church. There were also concerns about the wider realm, burdened as it was by the exactions of sheriffs and the penalties imposed by judicial and forest eyres.

Henry made some attempt at conciliation. To the pleasure of 'many English', he removed the hated Geoffrey de Langley from the custody of the forests, but this was hardly enough.[212] He was damaged by another episode, one Matthew Paris places specifically in the Westminster chamber. When the young and deeply pious widow Isabella, countess of Arundel, complained about his appropriation of a wardship, Henry was at first

---

[209] Bémont, *Simon de Montfort*, 337–8, 341–4; *CR 1251–3*, 431–2; Maddicott, *Simon de Montfort*, 119.

[210] For what follows, see Paris, v, 324–36; Maddicott, *Origins of the English Parliament*, 468.

[211] Paris, v, 332–3.

[212] Paris, v, 340; *CPR 1247–58*, 154–5, 162.

calm and conciliatory. Why didn't she make her claim as a matter of grace and favour? But Isabella insisted on her right to the wardship and silenced Henry with a tirade about his injustices and breaches of Magna Carta. In fact Henry had been misinformed rather than mendacious, and later returned the wardship to the countess. But the episode became widely known and left a deep mark on the king, sensitive as he always was to his name and fame. Two years later, when Henry (by then in Gascony) made another concession to the countess, he stipulated in writing that she was not to repeat 'the opprobrious things' she had said 'when lately we were at Westminster'.[213]

The church's refusal of aid was not blanket. The prelates raised the possibility of conceding the tax if Henry would confirm Magna Carta, make other concessions to the church and ensure the susbsidy was spent on its stated object. But nothing was agreed. Equally, Henry made no progress when he asked for help from the laity.[214] The parliament closed with him feeling bitterly let down.

THE PROMINENCE OF FOREIGNERS

Dividing Henry from his parliaments was another issue, as Matthew Paris makes very clear: that of the place and patronage enjoyed by his foreign relatives. It was to illustrate the problem that Paris inserted into his account of the October 1252 parliament the unseemly episode in the orchard at St Albans. This is not to say that native nobles were absent from court. The earls of Norfolk and Oxford welcomed Henry at Bury St Edmunds during his East Anglian pilgrimage. Norfolk, together with the earls of Cornwall, Gloucester, Derby and Winchester, attested royal charters during the October parliament.[215] Four of the stewards of the household in 1251 were English knights: Ralph fitzNicholas, Bertram de Criel, John of Lexington and Robert Walerand.[216] Yet the king's foreign relatives were equally conspicuous and were at court for much longer periods than native nobles. During the parliament itself Peter of Savoy, William de Valence, Geoffrey de Lusignan and of course bishop-elect Aymer were all present. Their prominence at court in 1252, as against native nobles, is reflected in the following table showing the number of days in that year on which the listed individuals attested royal charters:

[213] Paris, v, 336–7; *CFR 1253–4*, no. 510. For full discussion, see Annesley, 'Isabella countess of Arundel'. The confrontation took place immediately after the parliament, but doubtless Isabella had already made her feelings felt.

[214] Paris, v, 335, implies the tax demanded from the laity was for crusade; contrast Maddicott, *Origins of the English Parliament*, 468, which states it was to be for Gascony.

[215] *RCWL*, ii, 71–3.

[216] TNA SC 1/6/163 is a letter of July 1251 addressed to all four of them as stewards.

Geoffrey de Lusignan	50 (from April)
Peter of Savoy	45 (from March)
William de Valence	40
Guy de Lusignan	16 (down to April)
The earl of Gloucester	16
The earl of Cornwall	15
The earl of Norfolk	12
The earl of Hereford	10

With the Poitevin knight Elyas de Rabayne and the Savoyards Ebulo de Montibus and Imbert Pugeys in frequent attendance, the court could take on a very alien air.

With presence went patronage. Again the king's favour was not confined to his foreign relatives. His brother, Richard of Cornwall, remained top of the queue to receive land from the king, and in this year did indeed receive some extremely valuable escheats. But next on the list were William de Valence and Geoffrey de Lusignan. The king, in October 1252, promised to provide for the latter 'before he provides for anyone else', Richard and William aside. In this year, William, Guy and John de Warenne's wife, Alice de Lusignan, the latter described as the king's 'beloved sister', all received valuable wardships. A stole ordered for bishop-elect Aymer was to cost 'at least' 100 marks. Alice, in one gift, was fitted out with silver plates and jugs, robes of scarlet and green, beds (one of gold), a palfrey, a sumpter horse and vestments for her chapel. Peter of Savoy, meanwhile, gained the marriage of the heir to the earldom of Devon for a kinswoman of the queen. The queen herself received the wardship of the Devon lands. When the chancery noted that Geoffrey de Lusignan's money fee had been paid down to Michaelmas 1252, Henry simply decided the final instalment had been a gift, which meant £100 was due to Geoffrey all over again! All told, during October 1252, the month of the crucial parliament, the king ordered around £2,000 to be paid out to his foreign relatives. Only the money assigned to Westminster Abbey had priority.[217]

There were, of course, advantages to great baronial families in connections with the king's foreign kin, as we have said.[218] Early in 1253, Richard de Clare, greatest of all the earls apart from Richard of Cornwall, agreed to marry his son and heir to a niece of the Lusignans. When the abbeys of St Albans and Reading refused to act as security for the 1,000 marks he owed as part of the contract, the king agreed to pay the sum himself.[219] There were also advantages further down the social scale. The knights of

[217] CChR 1226–57, 392; CPR 1247–48, 124–5, 148, 151, 162, 167, 469; CR 1247–51, 477; CR 1251–3, 34, 121, 171; CLR 1251–60, 53, 57, 74–80.
[218] See above, 471.
[219] CPR 1247–58, 174–5; Paris, v, 363–4; Tewkesbury, 151. The marriage was to Alice, daughter of Hugh de Lusignan, the count of La Marche.

both William de Valence and bishop-elect Aymer were largely English.[220] There was obviously much to be gained from association with such powerful men. Much, however, depended on one's situation. The attitude of a wealthy widow to a foreign match might be very different from that of an ambitious baron or knight. According to the well-informed Dunstable annalist, the marriage between John de Grey and Joan, widow of Paulinus Peyvre, was hurried through so she was not pressurized into marrying the Savoyard knight Stephen de Salines. She may well have remembered Henry's earlier treatment (however untypical) of the countess of Warwick. The way an English barony could fall into foreign hands was shown by another case from the early 1250s. Here Henry had persuaded the aged and ailing Stephen de Bayeux to marry Matilda, his eldest daughter, to Elyas de Rabayne and give her the whole of his barony, this to the disadvantage of his younger daughter Joan, who was sent off to Sixhills priory.[221] It was Stephen's elder brother and predecessor John de Bayeux who had tried to stir up Lincolnshire in support of Magna Carta's chapter on local courts.[222] Now his barony was in the hands of a Poitevin knight. Magna Carta had said that heiresses were to be married without disparagement, meaning not to be married to those beneath their social station. Matilda de Bayeux's marriage to Rabayne could seem a clear case of that happening, even if the barony was not a large one.[223] Subsequently her sister Joan suffered the same fate, for Elyas, with the king's consent, removed her from Sixhills priory and sent her overseas, where she married another Poitevin.

Matthew Paris's amazement at the way the fruits of England were being devoured by foreigners probably reflects very well the views of barons, knights, prelates and lower clergy in parliament. Paris specifically noted that one concession to Rabayne, a man 'wholly unworthy of such great honour', was made while the parliament of April 1252 was still meeting.[224] A schedule of demands drawn up by the Oxford parliament of 1258 went beyond Magna Carta and defined disparagement as marriage to men who were 'not of the nation of the kingdom of England', precisely the fate of the Bayeux girls, as of other heiresses of more consequence.[225] It was also possible to look askance at the ecclesiastical patronage of the

---

[220] Ridgeway, 'William de Valence and his *familiares*'; Ridgeway, 'The ecclesiastical career of Aymer de Lusignan', 162.

[221] For this episode, see Ridgeway, 'Dorset in the period of baronial reform', 23, and *CPR 1247–58*, 62, 65, 237; *CChR 1257–1300*, 133.

[222] See above, 185.

[223] The barony, probably worth less than £200 a year, was centred on Thoresway in Lincolnshire and also had lands in Dorset: Sanders, *English Baronies*, 88–9. The Rabayne marriage can be compared with that of John de Plessis, above, 264–6.

[224] Paris, v, 283. Paris was probably thinking here of the concessions in *CPR 1247–58*, 133–4.

[225] *DBM*, 80–1, cap. 6.

aliens. Most of that bestowed by bishop-elect Aymer went to foreign clerks in his service or the service of Henry III.[226] At Hereford, Bishop Aigueblanche packed the chapter with his relations. In 1252 his deputy in the diocese, Bernard, prior of Champagne (a kinsman of the queen), was atrociously murdered while he sang mass in the episcopal chapel.[227] In a letter to the pope at this time, and doubtless also at the various parliaments, Henry stressed his affection for his native subjects: it was 'hard', to think they would not come on his crusade 'especially when we have more faith in our own people than in aliens'.[228] His conduct hardly suggested this was the case.

The situation was further aggravated by the belief that the foreigners were behaving in an arrogant and lawless fashion. Since the king had granted Elyas de Rabayne the rights over Joan de Bayeux's marriage, arguably he was not acting illegally in marrying her to a Poitevin, but after the revolution of 1258 he was still accused of 'fraud' and deprived of Joan's half of the Bayeux barony.[229] In 1250 itself Paris devoted much space to the activities of the archbishop of Canterbury, Boniface of Savoy, 'a foreigner, illiterate ... more suited to warlike than spiritual affairs'.[230] Early in the year Boniface had begun a visitation of his province. In May he reached London only to meet resistance on the grounds that its clergy were subject to their bishop (the formidable Fulk Basset), not the archbishop of Canterbury. In response, Boniface excommunicated Fulk, the canons of St Paul's and the canons of St Batholomew's priory. At St Bartholomew's, according to Paris's dramatic account, there was a violent confrontation in the church itself with Boniface, wearing armour under his vestments, throwing punches at the aged prior and shouting 'this is how English traitors should be dealt with'. When the canons, battered and bruised, complained to the king, he refused to hear them, although they waited for a long time outside the door to his chamber.

The London chronicle of fitzThedmar speaks of a 'tumult' at St Bartholomew's, but Paris's account was grossly exaggerated.[231] He later

---

[226] Ridgeway, 'The ecclesiastical career of Aymer de Lusignan', 162.

[227] For this episode, see Barrow, *EEA Hereford*, lii–iv, lxxiv–v; Howell, *Eleanor of Provence*, 58.

[228] *CR 1251–3*, 448; Lloyd, *English Society and the Crusade*, 222.

[229] *ERF*, ii, 286 (*CFR 1257–8*, no. 926). To be fair to Elyas, Joan cannot have been entirely disinherited otherwise she could scarcely have been married to her Poitevin. Assuming she had not taken the habit at Sixhills and was simply being maintained there, Elyas was also within his rights in removing her from the priory, although it was feared that Grosseteste (as the diocesan) was going to intervene.

[230] For what follows, see Paris, v, 117–26, 205–6; Paris, vi, 188–91; Paris, *AC*, 313–14; Paris, *FH*, 366; Paris, *HA*, 78–80. For an account of the dispute, see Hoskin, *EEA London*, xlvi–viii. An additional cause of Boniface's unpopularity was the pope's concession allowing him the first fruits from churches throughout his province to help pay Canterbury's debts.

[231] FitzThedmar, 17.

excised it and acknowledged that Boniface had undertaken his visitation with good intentions if with excessive rigour. Adam Marsh, who accompanied Boniface, believed he had acted 'in a praiseworthy manner' and been the victim of scurrilous stories.[232] Fulk Basset himself complained of the excommunications but not of violence.[233] Boniface undoubtedly saw his visitation, in accordance with papal injunctions, as a way of improving the lives of his clergy and enhancing the cure of souls: hence the support he gained from conscientious churchmen like Adam Marsh.[234] It was not simply a way, as Matthew Paris thought, of extracting money in the form of 'procurations', the expenses the archbishop was entitled to exact from those he visited, although that certainly was a major cause of discontent. Henry himself was surely right to stay out of this ecclesiastical quarrel. In the event both sides appealed to the pope, who came down in Boniface's favour. Eventually, as Paris acknowledged, an acceptable compromise was reached and none of Boniface's later visitations generated so much heat and light.[235] When Boniface came to St Albans in 1253 (as a guest not a visitor), Paris was impressed by his restraint and modesty. The obituary written on Boniface's death in 1270 by Thomas Wykes praised him in similar terms: humble, modest, chaste and, though of little learning, guided by wise men.[236]

Paris then changed his mind about Boniface, rightly so. He did not, however, change his mind about the king's half-brothers.[237] The agents of the Savoyards in the localities were probably just as harsh as those of the Lusignans. Yet Peter and Boniface of Savoy were capable of a tact and diplomacy apparently foreign to the Lusignans, hence the way back in 1242 that Peter had resigned the custody of Dover castle.[238] Peter, although at odds with John de Warenne and sometimes Roger Bigod, was also better at making political allies, as the events of 1258 were to show. When Geoffrey de Lusignan arrived at St Albans in 1252 his conduct was very different from Boniface's. His marshal demanded accommodation for his master in the royal apartments and drove all the other horses out of the abbey's stables. Only three days earlier, if Paris can be believed, William de Valence had hunted without permission in the park of the bishop of Ely near Hatfield and then made free with the wine from his cellars. An uglier incident occurred at Guildford next year when Geoffrey de Lusignan, for some unknown offence, seized on one of the king's cooks,

[232] *Letters of Adam Marsh*, 146–7.

[233] Paris, v, 125–6; Hoskin, *EEA London*, no. 120.

[234] Grosseteste, however, criticized Boniface's conduct: Gieben, 'Robert Grosseteste', 371.

[235] *CPReg*, 276; Paris, *AC*, 314.

[236] Wykes, 235–6.

[237] For more discussion, see below, 673–4.

[238] See above, 251.

pulled his hair out and hanged him up naked. When Roger, the king's chief cook, protested, he got nowhere.[239]

KING'S MEN AND QUEEN'S MEN

These episodes paled into insignificance before a cause célèbre which shook the court in the autumn of 1252. It seemed to reveal the violence of the Lusignans and their friends. It also revealed the deep divisions emerging between the Lusignans and the Savoyards. Something of the battle lines had been drawn here, and the queen's position greatly strengthened, by the return to England in March 1252 of Peter of Savoy, after a long absence.[240] He was greeted by Henry at Dover but cannot have been pleased to find himself, in the witness lists of royal charters, and thus presumably in the etiquettes at court, placed beneath William de Valence and the other half-brothers, a reversal of the position back in 1249.[241] Almost at once he was in the middle of an open conflict between the king and queen, the first of which there is evidence.

In 1252, Eleanor was twenty-eight years old. She had not given birth since January 1245 and was not to do so again until November 1253. Since there is no reason to think that Henry, in his late thirties and early forties, was taking mistresses or had decided to imitate the celibacy of the Confessor, perhaps Eleanor had suffered a succession of miscarriages. It is noticeable that, whereas she went overseas with Henry in 1242 although heavily pregnant, in 1253, again pregnant, she did not do so. Henry cannot have been that anxious, given Eleanor had already produced four children including two sons. Judging from the flow of gifts and work on her apartments, his love for her was as strong as ever. At York over Christmas in 1251, for the marriage of their daughter Margaret, the two, as has been seen, slept in connected chambers and wore identical robes.

Already, however, a quarrel was brewing. On 21 December 1251, Henry presented his wardrobe clerk Artaud de Saint-Romain to the church of Flamstead in Hertfordsire. This set him on a collision course with the queen, who had already presented her clerk William of London to the living. Eleanor's right derived from the wardship, given her by the king, of the lands of Roger de Tony, which included Flamstead. Henry's argument, in all probability, was that the gift did not include the right to present to the church livings. In March 1252, while at Dover welcoming Peter of Savoy, Henry instructed Grosseteste as the diocesan bishop to induct Artaud. Ten days later, he ordered the sheriff to remove William of

---

[239] Paris, v, 343–5; Paris, vi, 406; John of Wallingford (2), 175. John of Wallingford says the cook (Roger) died from this torture, but there is some doubt about that, see *CLR 1251–60*, 367.

[240] For a detailed account of Peter's role in English affairs between 1252 and 1255, see Chapuiset, 'Pierre de Savoie', 259–64.

[241] *RCWL*, ii, 37, 60–3.

London from the church. Since William is now styled 'formerly chaplain of the queen', Henry evidently regarded him as dismissed.[242]

Eleanor, however, refused to back down. Instead, she appealed to Grosseteste, who excommunicated Artaud and placed the church of Flamstead under an interdict. Henry angrily cried out (according to Matthew Paris) against the pride of women. He could not be calmed down (according to a letter of Adam Marsh) either by Eleanor or Eleanor de Montfort, not surprisingly as the queen would not give way.[243] Henry was forced to pursue the case in both the ecclesiastical and secular courts. In the end he abandoned the struggle. William of London remained rector of Flamstead.[244]

Meanwhile a far more serious quarrel had broken out. During the autumn of 1252 Aymer, bishop-elect of Winchester, as the patron, had appointed a new prior to the hospital of Thomas Becket at Southwark. The prior took office at once, ignoring the right claimed by the archbishop of Canterbury to confirm his appointment.[245] Archbishop Boniface was abroad, so his official Eustace of Lynn took up the cudgels and excommunicated the prior. In response, Aymer sent a large force, which broke into Lambeth palace, robbed it of jewels, plate and money, and seized hold of Eustace. Although an elderly and distinguished ecclesiastic, he was put on a horse like a common criminal, without a cloak nor hold of the reins, and led to Aymer's house at Southwark. A priest, also arrested, was made to follow on foot in the mud. All this took place 'in full sight of the people'. Boniface had been humiliated in the most glaring way.

News of these events immediately reached the court at Windsor. Both the queen and Peter of Savoy leapt to the defence of their absent kinsman and demanded action against Aymer. Henry protested that the dispute was ecclesiastical.[246] But that was easily answered. Aymer's behaviour (as Boniface put it later), 'by force and arms', breached 'the peace of king and kingdom' and showed contempt 'for the reverence due the prince'.[247] Henry should have reacted. Instead, he did nothing. The result was an open breach between king and queen. On 4 November, the day after the outrage, Henry, evidently incensed by what they had said, confiscated the revenues of both Eleanor and Peter of Savoy. Both left court.[248] Henry set off for Reading and Marlborough while the queen was sent packing first to Guildford and then to Winchester.[249]

---

[242] CR 1251–3, 202, 208.

[243] Letters of Adam Marsh, 540–1.

[244] Paris, v, 298–9. Howell, Eleanor of Provence, 64–6, has a full account of the quarrel.

[245] For what follows, see Paris, v, 348–54; Paris, vi, 222–5 (Boniface's account); Hershey, Special Eyre, no. 163; Howell, Eleanor of Provence, 66–9; Ridgeway, 'Ecclesiastical career of Aymer de Lusignan', 165–6.

[246] CR 1251–3, 431.

[247] Paris, vi, 224.

[248] CR 1251–3, 273. Peter's revenues in question were those from Tickhill.

[249] Howell, Eleanor of Provence, 67.

The crisis deepened with Boniface's return to England on 18 November. He boycotted the court (where Aymer had now returned) and went to London where he excommunicated the perpetrators of the crime with great publicity.[250] Those anathamatized included men from the households of William de Valence and Geoffrey de Lusignan. On 7 December, Boniface repeated his sentence at Oxford before the assembled university. The conflict seemed to Matthew Paris one between 'king's men' and 'queen's men', Poitevins against Provençals. There was also the danger of the native earls being drawn in on one side or the other thanks, in part, to the alliances and antagonisms created by Henry's patronage. The most striking case was that of John de Warenne. He was tied to the Lusignans by his successful marriage to the much-favoured Alice. He was also hostile to Peter of Savoy thanks to the latter's custody of his lands during his minority. In Surrey and Sussex, Peter's agents in just two years had felled nearly 800 beech and oak trees, precisely the kind of conduct Magna Carta's chapter on wardships was designed to prevent. An indignant local jury reported that if this continued until Warenne came of age, 'the whole of his forest, woods and park would be almost devastated'. What made this worse was that although, on his marriage, Warenne had been allowed to succeed to his estates before coming of age, the Surrey and Sussex lands in the hands of Peter of Savoy had been excluded from the concession.[251] Hardly surprising then if Warenne supported the Lusignans in the quarrel now shaking the court. Indeed, rumour had it he was party to the violence.[252]

The affair was becoming a great public scandal and a threat to the peace of the realm. It did much to make the wider community aware of Henry's foreign favourites. It also, since general opinion saw Boniface as the injured party, spread the view that the Lusignans, in particular, were violent individuals, placed by the king above the law. Around this time the poet Michael of Cornwall described the half-brothers as 'nulla valentia sed violentia'.[253] Six years later, jurors from Brixton hundred (in which Lambeth was situated) were still able to give a detailed description of the crime committed 'by a multitude of armed Poitevins' from the households of Aymer and his brothers.[254]

Mercifully, Henry soon relented. He brought the queen back to court and before the end of November had restored her revenues and those of Peter of Savoy.[255] He also ordered the earls not to take sides in the dispute.

[250] *RCWL*, ii, 76.

[251] *CIM*, no. 16; *CPR 1247–58*, 11; *CR 1247–51*, 39. Warenne's quarrel with Savoy is illuminated in a forthcoming paper by Andrew Spencer, ' "A vineyard without a wall" '.

[252] Paris, v, 352, 359; *CR 1251–3*, 431.

[253] Russell, 'Master Henry of Avranches', 42; Henry of Avranches, 137–42. Doubtless Michael omitted this passage when the poem was performed before Aymer himself.

[254] Hershey, *Special Eyre*, no. 163.

[255] *CR 1251–3*, 283; *CPR 1258–66*, 165–6; and for what follows Howell, *Eleanor of Provence*, 68–9.

Henry turned again on Peter of Savoy, ordering him from court when he expressed his inability to settle the quarrel. But Peter was soon back and Henry and Eleanor were now working together for peace, as Matthew Paris recognized. The pair exchanged New Year's presents. The jewels Henry gave Eleanor cost £260.[256] Eleanor also gave presents to the Lusignan brothers. Boniface meanwhile had summoned a church council to meet in London on 13 January 1253. Henry, having attended the feast of the Confessor at Westminster (where a great new bell was specially rung), retired to Windsor.[257] He told the assembled prelates not to leave the capital until they had reached a settlement, nor would he return until they had done so. This worked. Aymer swore he had nothing to do with the attack, and agreed a compromise over the status of the hospital. He and Boniface exchanged a kiss of peace.[258] Boniface did not, however, recover all his property, and the affair left a lasting mark on relations between the 'regales' and 'reginales'.[259]

Whether it left a lasting mark on relations between king and queen is more doubtful. It is true that in the first half of 1253 they spent some four months apart, save for a few days in May and June. That, however, was partly because business kept Henry at Westminster, while Eleanor, now pregnant, remained at her Windsor home. Since their daughter Katherine was born on 25 November, she was presumably conceived just before Henry left Windsor on 25 February. Meanwhile Eleanor lived in some state. The daily costs of her household at Windsor were some £5 a day, over a pound more than the year before, and perhaps more than half the current costs of the household of the king.[260] That Henry had total confidence in his queen is shown by the arrangements made for the governance of the kingdom when he finally sailed to Gascony. Eleanor was a wise woman. She understood her position depended ultimately on good relations with her husband. He would never be a chivalric hero (here Eleanor looked to her son), but he had other virtues. In a poem composed for Eleanor by her chaplain, John of Howden, Henry (by then dead) appears in a list of great men. He is not credited, like the others, with any famous deed, but he is described as 'overflowing in giving like a live fountain'.[261] That was a characteristic Eleanor knew well how to exploit. She was far stronger and more intelligent than her husband.

It must have been in these years that the sculptured heads of a king and a queen were put up above the entrance to what is now the muniment

[256] John of Wallingford (1), 72; *RCWL*, ii, 79; *CLR 1251–60*, 110.

[257] *CR 1251–3*, 280.

[258] Paris, v, 359; John of Wallingford (1), 72; Tewkesbury, 151.

[259] Hershey, *Special Eyre*, no. 163.

[260] Carpenter, 'Household rolls', 35, 44–5.

[261] John of Howden, lines 4003–4. I am grateful to Alice Rio for help with the translation here.

room at Westminster Abbey, the room quite probably used by Henry and Eleanor as a chamber or a pew where they could hold meetings and view what was going on in the great church.[262] The heads are large and beautiful, with calm features and faint smiles. They exude the quality of 'debonereté', so much prized in courtly life. They are surely Henry and Eleanor as they wished to be and as they sometimes were.

MAGNA CARTA 1253 AND THE DECISION TO GO TO GASCONY

After the church council of January 1253 had reconciled Boniface and Aymer, it turned to the crusading tax. Here too progress was made with Henry encouraging the prelates to put their grievances into writing. This they had done by 6 February when Henry sent the rolls containing their complaints to the exchequer, asking for its advice. He had, he added, fixed a day at Westminster in early May to discuss the whole issue with his brother Richard and assembled magnates.[263] Meanwhile Henry sought to appease Grosseteste by addressing one of his personal grievances.[264] He also asked the pope to urge other princes to join his crusade: 'by the mercy of the crucified we are preparing for our crusade with all the strength of our mind and body'. At the end of January, Henry did something else to prove his crusading credentials. He issued legislation against the Jews.

The 'provision', in question, was 'made by the king' and was authorized by him and his council. It was thus very much Henry's personal initiative and was not agreed by 'common counsel' in parliament. Indeed, no bishops were at court when it was promulgated. The provision broke new ground in being concerned not with the financial activities of the Jews, like royal legislation in the past, but with the threat they posed to the faith. Its main aim was thus to enforce the separation between Jews and Christians. Jewish rites were to be celebrated in low voices so no Christian could hear them. Christian wet nurses and servants were not to work for Jews and vice versa. No Christian was to eat with a Jew or stay in his house. No Jew was publicly to dispute the Christian faith. All Jews were to be distinguished by wearing the tabula.[265] Timed as it was, Henry must have hoped the legislation would help win support for the tax at the forthcoming May parliament.

During the Lent of 1253 both Henry and his second son, Edmund, fell ill. Henry sent his harper, Richard, to play to Edmund and ordered twenty

---

[262] For the muniment room, see Wilson, 'Calling the tune?', 67–8.

[263] TNA E 368/27, m. 8; see Carpenter, 'Magna Carta 1253'.

[264] *CFR 1252–3*, nos. 324, 333.

[265] *CR 1251–3*, 312–13; *C&S*, i, 472–3; Stacey, '1240–1260: a watershed in Anglo-Jewish relations?', 146–7; Richardson, *English Jewry under the Angevin Kings*, 191–3; Brand, 'Jews and the law in England', 1142 ns. 1 and 3, 1143–4. The regulation on the tabula repeated a royal order of 1218. For parallels with the ecclesiastical statutes of Oxford in 1222, although Henry's provision went beyond them, see *C&S*, i, 120–1, caps. 46–7.

'measures' (a candle the height of the person to be prayed for) to be offered to Saint Edmund at Bury. He also decided on a more or less immediate pilgrimage to Saint Edmund at Pontigny. This rash and impulsive idea (as it was regarded at St Albans) was soon lost amongst the rush of other events. Henry found he would have to go to Gascony after all.[266]

In Gascony, Simon de Montfort's departure and Henry's failure to appear had created a vacuum. It was filled by Alfonso X, king of Castile. He now revived the old Castilian claim to Gascony as forming the dowry of Henry II's daughter Eleanor, when she married King Alfonso VIII. Within Gascony, Alfonso's supporters, led by Gaston de Béarn, still simmering from his treatment by Montfort, were soon in control of La Réole and St Emilion. The loyalists in Bordeaux warned Henry that unless he came soon the whole land would be lost.[267] Henry's initial reaction, in March 1253, was to hurry out fifteen or so household knights, one of whom, Drogo de Barentin, was made seneschal jointly with Peter Bonefans, a citizen of Bordeaux. This force (fitted into one ship) was hardly likely to stem the revolt.[268] Henry's own mind was still on his crusade. On 18 April, in return for Peter of Savoy swearing to come too, Henry as a king 'consecrated and anointed' promised to find him a ship for his passage, 10,000 marks on his arrival at Marseilles and twenty warhorses in the Holy Land. Meanwhile, to support Peter's 'war' and other affairs (in the Pays de Vaud), Henry promised him a further 5,500 marks, giving £1,000 borrowed from Sienese and Florentine merchants, cash down.[269] All this at a time when Henry had his own war to fight in Gascony!

The parliament opened at Westminster on 4 May and was one of the best attended in Henry's reign. Apart from the bishops, abbots, earls and barons, there was probably a large turnout of knights.[270] Peter of Savoy was there but the half-brothers (bishop-elect Aymer aside) were thankfully absent.[271] The king asked for two taxes, one to support the expedition to Gascony, the other from the church, the much-contested one for the crusade. The debates were long and acrimonious, and Henry got nothing for Gascony as such. All that was agreed was an aid for the knighting of his eldest son, Lord Edward, to which he was entitled anyway under the terms of the 1215 Magna Carta. This eventually brought in around £6,000, a useful sum, but the tenth on ecclesiastical revenues over three

---

[266] *CR 1251–3*, 330, 465; John of Wallingford (2), 177.

[267] Paris, v, 365–6, 368–70, 378–9.

[268] *CPR 1247–58*, 184, 228; *CR 1251–3*, 456; *CLR 1251–60*, 117.

[269] *F*, 288–9 (*CPR 1247–58*, 188–9); Cox, *Eagles of Savoy*, 199–202, 238–9. The arrangements for paying the rest of the money show how hard-headed Peter was and what little trust he put in mere promises.

[270] Maddicott, *Origins of the English Parliament*, 202, 468–9. For what follows, see Paris, v, 373–8; Dunstable, 186; *C&S*, i, 474–9.

[271] *RCWL*, ii, 88–9.

years was likely to bring in very much more.[272] To such a tax the prelates assembled at the parliament now at last agreed. Here at least Henry had got his way. Ultimately, as Matthew Paris said, the bishops did not wish to frustrate Henry's intention 'so pious' to go on crusade. His sincerity could hardly be doubted when, during the parliament itself, he was thinking ahead to the shipping needed for the expedition.[273]

The quid pro quo for the taxes was revealed in a great ceremony held in Westminster Hall on 13 May. There, before the king, five earls and assembled barons and knights, the archbishop of Canterbury and thirteen bishops, dressed in full pontificals and with burning candles, solemnly excommunicated all who violated Magna Carta and the Charter of the Forest. According to Matthew Paris, who was probably present, Henry refused to take a candle himself – he was not a priest he said – but he held his hand to his heart and as the candles were thrown down cried eagerly 'As God helps me, I will keep all these things faithfully, as I am a knight and as I am a crowned and anointed king.'

Lay and ecclesiastical magnates then had joined together in support of Magna Carta, 'their common inheritance'.[274] Henry had joined with them. The realm seemed at one. Yet it was more complex than that. These events highlighted the tensions between churchmen and laymen, as well as between church and state. The driving force behind the confirmation of Magna Carta in 1253 had been the church, as accounts of the parliaments of 1252–3 show. That is not surprising since the church possessed the lever of its great crusading tax. The tax granted by the laity was hardly a lever at all, since the king was entitled to it anyway. In these circumstances, the puzzle is that the church settled for so little. Of course, the Charter in its first clause gave freedom to the church. Clergy, as much as laity, could welcome its general support for just and lawful rule. But what had happened to the church's other grievances, not covered at all in the Charters, those grievances set out on the rolls handed to Henry in February, the grievances the parliament was supposed to debate? The answer is precisely nothing. The fact was there was little support for the church's demands, many related to its jurisdictional claims, amongst the laity at the parliament. Laymen, for a start, would hardly welcome being made to swear oaths so as to allow prelates to inquire into their moral failings. In resisting such demands in earlier years Henry had stressed he was acting 'on the complaints of magnates and others'.[275]

---

[272] Mitchell, *Studies in Taxation*, 257; Lunt, *Financial Relations*, 260–1, 289–90.

[273] F, 289 (*CPR 1247–58*, 191).

[274] Maddicott, *Origins of the English Parliament*, 195.

[275] *C&S*, i, 470, cap. 8, 541, cap. 9; *CR 1251–3*, 224–5; *CR 1247–51*, 554. It is possible that Henry had issued provisions in 1247 restricting the claims of ecclesiastical courts: Paris, iv, 614, but see *C&S*, i, 419 n. 3. For the lack of secular support for the church's jurisdictional claims, see Hoskin, 'The church and the king', 200–2.

Tensions were apparent in the sentence of excommunication itself. There had been sentences of excommunication before, in 1225 and 1237, but this time the bishops spelt everything out in far more detail and with far more publicity. Indeed, it was here they attempted to get beyond Magna Carta by placing within the ban royal councillors who introduced new statutes and customs to the detriment of the church.[276] After the parliament, the sentence was published in parish churches on Sundays and festival days, accompanied by the ringing of bells and the burning of candles. Grosseteste was particularly active in his diocese and had his clergy fulminate the sentence with crosses and handbells in secular courts.[277]

What none of this revealed was that the king and his secular magnates had issued their own proclamation about the excommunication, one rather different from that of the bishops. This recorded that Henry, during the pronouncement of the sentence, had saved 'with his own mouth' the ancient customs of the kingdom and the rights of the crown.[278] The proclamation also reserved to the king's court the right to correct breaches of the Charter. And it announced that king, magnates and 'the community of the people' had publicly protested before the bishops that if anything else was found in any document about the sentence, then they had never consented to it. Here Henry was standing very much with his people in resisting the pretensions of the church. He was also standing up for the rights of the crown. The episode foreshadowed events in and after 1258 when the church was left very much to pursue its own agenda of reform separate from the general reform of the realm.

The confirmation of Magna Carta in 1253 was for Henry both a warning and an opportunity. He should surely now have seized the initiative and shown how eager he was to enforce the Charter, making good on the statement that breaches were to be corrected in his court. Unfortunately, Henry's efforts were half-hearted in the extreme. It was not the king but the keeper of the seal, William of Kilkenny, who took responsibility for letters sent on 15 May to all royal officials, commanding them on pain of heavy punishment to observe the Charters in all their points lest they fell under the sentence of excommunication. Henry may well have been annoyed at this independent initiative, all the more so since the letter said nothing about protecting the rights of the crown. At any rate, the very next day Kilkenny retired from court due, it was said, to 'illness', and the seal was committed to other ministers.[279]

---

[276] F, 289; C&S, i, 477–8.
[277] C&S, i, 474–7; Paris, v, 395. Like Cheney and Powicke, I am sceptical about the authenticity of an earlier sentence of excommunication assigned to 1248: C&S, i, 418–19.
[278] F, 290; CPR 1247–58, 229; C&S, i, 478–9.
[279] For all this, see Carpenter, 'More light on Henry III's confirmation of Magna Carta in 1253'. The letter issued by Kilkenny was discovered by Felicity Hill. It was said to be 'given

It was another month before Henry did anything himself about the Charter. At last, on 23 June, the sheriffs were ordered to obey it and, on pain of punishment, make sure it was obeyed too by prelates, magnates and everyone else. Henry also reserved the rights of the crown and the liberties everyone else had enjoyed before the time of the Charter.[280] That everyone should obey the Charter was an old theme and Henry had good grounds for revisiting it now, given the malpractices of baronial officials. But a simple injunction to the sheriffs was not going to go very far in making the principle a reality. Neither in this letter nor in another issued at Portsmouth in July, while waiting for the wind to waft him across to Gascony, did Henry mention redressing breaches of the Charter in his court, let alone set up mechanisms to make that possible. Instead, at Portsmouth, Henry issued another 'provision' altogether, one which showed just how out of touch he was. It was for the keeping of the peace in his absence and mostly rehearsed familiar measures, but there was also one striking innovation. Local communities were now to make restitution from their own pockets to those who suffered robbery while passing through their districts. The assembled knights and freemen must have listened with amazement while this vague and impractical proposal was explained to them by the senior judges despatched for the purpose. In Shropshire the judge met open resistance. Matthew Paris criticized the idea as being modelled on the practice in Savoy and quite unsuitable for England. He also said, rightly, that such a major change in the law and custom of the realm should have received 'common assent'.[281] The measure, of course, came to nothing. In 1244 the Paper Constitution, in its call for the revival of the justiciarship and chancellorship, had shown his government was already out of touch and unpopular in the shires. Since then the returns to the inquiries staged between 1249 and 1252 had given hard evidence of the malpractices occurring. Both Henry's duty to give justice to his people and the obligations flowing from his assumption of the cross should have inspired measures to redress the grievances from which the realm was suffering. The extent to which they did so was very limited. Meanwhile, the introduction of his Lusignan halfbrothers was increasingly dividing Henry's court. The seeds were being sown for the revolution of 1258.

by the hand of William of Kilkenny . . . then acting in place of the chancellor'. This is a unique formula since all chancery instruments at this time were either given or witnessed by the king. Kilkenny soon returned to court and resumed the keepership of the seal.

[280] *CR 1251–3*, 482. The writ is only addressed to the sheriff of Somerset and Dorset. This was the Poitevin Elyas de Rabayne, who may well have needed such instruction (see Ridgeway, 'Dorset in the period of baronial reform', 23–4), but the letter probably went to the other sheriffs as well. There was a parallel writ to the chief justice of the forest south of Trent about observing the Forest Charter.

[281] *CR 1251–3*, 452, 492–4; *CR 1253–4*, 3; Paris, v, 368–70, 410–11; Paris, vi, 255–7. In 1254 the government said the measure had been decided by the king and his council but did not claim it had received any common assent: *CR 1253–4*, 127.

Chapter 11

THE GASCON EXPEDITION AND THE BEGINNINGS OF THE SICILIAN AFFAIR
1253–1254

After the great parliament of May 1253, Henry knew there was no escaping Gascony. His letters now spoke of 'the war and great disturbance' and the fear that Gascony, 'unless it is quickly succoured, may soon be lost forever'.[1] Diplomacy offered one ray of hope. Might the king of Castile be induced to resign his claims in return for the marriage of his sister Eleanor to Edward, Henry's son and heir. Soon after the May parliament was over, John Mansel and the bishop of Bath and Wells were commissioned to open negotiations for such a settlement but it was not until August that they departed. There could be no quick diplomatic fix. On 25 May, Henry formally told the Gascons he was coming.[2]

By this time Henry was already assembling the ships for his passage. He thought 300 would be needed.[3] But that was the easy part. What of the money and men to put in them? Here Henry took a crucial decision which shows where his priorities lay. His only treasure lay in the gold he had saved for his crusade, worth some £20,000. But this he would not break into. It was for the crusade not Gascony. The most Henry did was to place part of the treasure in pawn for a £4,000 loan from his brother, Richard of Cornwall.[4] For the rest, the expedition was funded from about £5,200 arriving from Ireland, £2,700 coming from the Jews, another £2,000 in loan from Richard and the sums donated, 'graciously' but in fact grudgingly, by various religious houses and by royal towns and manors.[5] The proceeds of the aid for the knighting of Edward were not due until after Michaelmas and would have to be sent later. If, as seems likely, Henry assembled some £15,000, or thereabouts, for the expedition, that was between £5,000 and £15,000 less than he had with him in 1230 and 1242.[6]

---

[1] *CPR 1247–58*, 229; *CR 1251–3*, 485.

[2] *F*, 290; *CPR 1247–58*, 219, 229–30; *CLR 1251–60*, 138; *CR 1251–3*, 352–3, 355; Liu, 'John Mansel', 76–7; and in general Baylen, 'John Maunsell and the Castilian treaty'.

[3] *CR 1251–3*, 355; *CLR 1251–60*, 132–3; *CPR 1247–58*, 230.

[4] Carpenter, *Reign of Henry III*, 118; *CPR 1247–58*, 236; *CLR 1251–60*, 147.

[5] *CPR 1247–58*, 204, 209, 216, 220; *CR 1251–3*, 386; *CLR 1251–60*, 145; Mitchell, *Studies in Taxation*, 255–6. Some of the Irish money had arrived the previous year.

[6] See above, 86, 255.

On the other hand, had Henry utilized the whole of his gold treasure, he would have had more money than for the earlier campaigns, a tribute to his financial management.

As for men, Henry called on his tenants-in-chief. The form of the summons does not survive but if it was like the cancelled one of August 1252, it hardly struck a compelling note.[7] On that occasion, those addressed were ordered to muster, 'on the faith in which you are held to us, understanding that it behoves you to give us help towards the preservation of our right and prevent irrecoverable damage to us and our heirs'.[8] At least Henry avoided asserting that military service was due in Gascony, a very questionable proposition. But in stressing the damage to him and his heirs and the obligation to preserve his rights, he had quite failed to portray this as a national cause, although that was precisely the way Matthew Paris was able to see it. Paris thus wrote of Gascony as the country's 'defence and barrier', and 'the last remnants of the continental lands subjected to and glorifying the noble kingdom of England'.[9] If only Henry had spoken like that.

In the event, in 1254, letters of protection were issued to over 300 individuals joining the expedition, an assortment of tenants-in-chief and household knights and officials. This was more than the 200 of 1242 and fewer than the 370 in 1230. But the number of great barons who came was small, and conspicuously less than in 1242. There were only two English earls, those of Hereford and Norfolk, the latter receiving a gift of £200 to meet his costs.[10] Henry was infuriated by the absenteeism of Richard de Clare, this despite the prospective marriage of his son into the royal family.[11] Absent too was Richard of Cornwall. This allowed him to help with the home government, but there was no real necessity for that. In 1242 a successful campaign would have made him count of Poitou. He saw little personal profit in this expedition, all the more so now that Gascony was to be not his but Lord Edward's.[12] Still, Matthew Paris was impressed by the size of the fleet which eventually sailed, thinking it consisted of three great ships and many lesser ones.[13]

Henry paid close attention to the government of England in his absence, placing the queen at the summit of his plans. Their quarrels of the year before were evidently quite forgotten. Eleanor would doubtless have liked to accompany the expedition, as she had in 1242. Then her pregnancy had not stopped her going. Now, perhaps after a series of miscarriages, it did.

---

[7] *CR 1251–3*, 240. The summons was to a group of earls, barons and household knights.

[8] *CR 1251–3*, 240.

[9] Paris, v, 278, 368.

[10] *CFR 1252–3*, no. 882.

[11] Tewkesbury, 153.

[12] See above, 417.

[13] Paris, v, 383; Tewkesbury, 153; *CPR 1247–58*, 230. For Henry's attempts to recruit over 300 sergeants-at-arms in Flanders, see *CR 1251–3*, 486.

But at least that cleared the way for her to have the 'government' of England, Wales and Ireland, with Richard of Cornwall acting as her adviser. If, moreover, Henry died, Eleanor was to be regent until Edward (who was to remain in England) came of age. To increase her material power in such circumstances she was given a much enhanced dower.[14] Henry also wrote to King Alexander asking him to let Queen Margaret come south to provide her mother with 'solace and recreation' until she gave birth, a glimpse at the closeness of the royal family.[15]

There was no time before Henry's planned departure to go on a pilgrimage to the East Anglian holy sites as he had in 1242. But he ordered Eleanor, during his absence, to celebrate the mass of the Confessor every day in his chapel at Westminster.[16] Henry also made his will, the only one known to survive. He left his soul to the Virgin Mary and all the saints, and his body to the Confessor at Westminster. He assigned 500 marks to finishing the Confessor's shrine and laid on Edward the duty of completing the Abbey itself. Queen Eleanor headed the list of executors, followed by Archbishop Boniface, Aymer, bishop-elect of Winchester, Richard of Cornwall, Peter of Savoy, John Mansel and other household officials. Half of the ten, if we include the queen, were foreigners.[17]

On 30 May, Henry assembled the Londoners in the cemetery at Westminster. He arranged for them to do homage to Edward as his heir, and bade them farewell. He then made a special trip into Kent to attend the foundation ceremony of John Mansel's Augustinian priory at Bilsington, near Canterbury, before coming back to say goodbye to the queen at Windsor. They decided she should go to Westminster so as to be close to the Confessor and the seat of government. Henry himself progressed on to Winchester, where he celebrated Whitsun with five bishops. He arrived at Portsmouth on 23 June, exactly on time to meet the fleet assembled there.[18] In the event, adverse winds meant Henry now had a long wait at considerable cost both to himself and local religious houses at which the army was parked. It was not until 6 August that he eventually set sail. Matthew Paris pictures him in tears kissing and embracing Edward many times over. The boy stood sobbing on the shore, not wanting to go until the last sail had faded from sight.[19]

---

[14] *F*, 291–2; *CPR 1247–58*, 206, 214; *CR 1251–3*, 497; Howell, *Eleanor of Provence*, 111–13. Henry was still to control membership of the home council. He allowed sheriffs to be changed (but not castellans) and reserved the right to consent to episcopal appointments. Eleanor and Richard attested royal letters jointly and used the exchequer seal. The great seal was shut up and left at home. Henry used in Gascony a specially made one for use there: *CPR 1247–58*, 200, 210; Tout, *Chapters*, i, 292–3; Chaplais, *Piers Gaveston*, 37.

[15] *CR 1251–3*, 485.

[16] *CR 1251–3*, 486.

[17] *F*, 496.

[18] FitzThedmar, 19; Liu, 'John Mansel', 194–5; TNA E 101/349/22, m. 7.

[19] Paris, v, 381, 383.

HENRY IN GASCONY

Henry landed in Gascony on 12 August 1253 and immediately opened the new seal he was to use there.[20] He was soon writing home asking both for more money and (in the same letter) for the history of Nebuchadnezzar to be painted in the best colours in St Stephen's chapel at Westminster.[21] He was surely thinking of parallels between that tyrannical king and King Alfonso. The situation was indeed alarming and Henry spent a fortnight at Bordeaux taking stock. A formidable array of townsmen and nobles were in revolt along with Gaston de Béarn. The insurrection was at its strongest not in the far south in the foothills of the Pyrenees around Béarn, but along the Dordogne and the Garonne. It thus struck at the very heart of Gascony. The key centre was the town of La Réole, where the citizens had expelled Simon de Montfort's partisans and were now absolutely solid in their rebellion. It was 'the mayor and all the jurats' of La Réole who were excommunicated in December 1253; it was likewise 'all the men of La Réole' whom Alfonso protected in the final peace.[22] Their determination was not surprising. Members of the Pins family controlling the town had been seized by Montfort and were still in his custody, despite Henry's promises to free them.[23] The clever and energetic William de Pins, prior of Le Mas d'Agenais, east of La Réole, was a leading figure in the revolt. Bitterness was increased by the Pins' long record of loyalty to the English crown, which contrasted, so they said, with Montfort's friends who had surrendered La Réole to the French back in 1224.[24] Another factor was the presence in La Réole of the Solers, who had likewise allied themselves to Alfonso. Montfort's attack on the family had begun his Gascon troubles. They had long been allies of the Pins. Indeed, Montfort had seized the latter because, so he believed, they had abetted the Solers in the disturbances in Bordeaux.[25]

What made all this worse was La Réole's strategic position. It controlled traffic up the Garonne to the Agenais and could in the right hands be a 'firm obstacle' to any advance from that quarter.[26] In the wrong hands it might be the reverse. This was all the more worrying now that the Agenais had passed to Louis IX's brother Alphonse of Poitiers. La Réole was also going to be very difficult to attack. It stood high on a cliff above the Garonne. Its castle was controlled by the citizens and worked in tandem with the church of the adjoining monastery. The latter, Henry later complained, was a kind of 'fortress', 'a tower of Babel rather than a

---

[20] CR 1253–4, 165; Paris, v, 388.
[21] CR 1253–4, 165.
[22] F, 294–5; RG, i, nos. 4281, 4283 (CPR 1247–58, 351–2).
[23] CPR 1247–58, 158–9, 319, 337, 352–3.
[24] Bémont, Simon de Montfort, 310; DD, no. 51.
[25] RL, ii, 72–4; CPR 1247–58, 158–9.
[26] DD, no. 48.

temple of God'.[27] La Réole pulled the smaller towns of the region in its wake. Alfonso had 'favourers' upriver at Lamothe-Landerron, Meilhan and Ste Bazeille.[28] Further south, a focus of the revolt was Bazas, cathedral city, regional capital and home of one of the four courts of Gascony, where the townsmen, as at La Réole, had expelled Henry's partisans.[29] The revolt in this area was supported by the greatest noble of central Gascony, Amaneus d'Albret, who was lord of Meilhan and Bazas and had major castles at Casteljaloux and Cazeneuve. Further north, between the Garonne and the Dordogne, in Entre-Deux-Mers, Bernard de Bouville, vicomte of Benauges, had joined the rebellion, as along the Dordogne had the vicomtes of Fronsac and Castillon. And then there was Gaston de Béarn himself. He had grander ambitions than simply asserting his claims to the overlordship of Sault-de-Navailles and Lados. His aim was to make himself effective master of Gascony and arbiter of its future. That emerges very clearly from his extraordinary agreement with the vicomte of Gramont in June 1253.[30] The latter was to accept whatever lord Gaston wished, whether the king of England or the king of Castile. At the moment it was the king of Castile, who, indeed, had made Gaston his seneschal of Gascony and thus its prospective ruler.[31]

What of Alfonso himself? Contemporaries, in retrospect, were quick to doubt the reality of his Gascon designs, but that was not how it looked at the time. Alfonso was a king with ambition. His father, Ferdinand III, on his deathbed in 1252, had turned to him and said, referring to his own conquests: 'If you should manage to hold it all . . . then you are as good a king as I; and if you should enlarge it, you are better than I; and if you should lose any of it, you are not as good as I.'[32] There was plenty Alfonso could do. He might conquer Muslim territories in southern Spain and North Africa. He might assert Castilian overlordship over Navarre. And he might make good ancient claims to Gascony. After all his grandfather, Alfonso VIII, had invaded and come close to conquering it in 1204–5. Alfonso himself never invaded but he gave material support to the rebels and doubtless hoped the province would fall into his hands. He turned down advances for a marriage settlement in the spring and summer of 1253, and only admitted them once it was clear Henry really was coming to Gascony with an army. Even then, Alfonso was in no hurry. He wanted to see how events panned out. At the very least he would demand a price for any agreement. He had every reason to persuade Henry of the reality of his designs.

---

[27] RG, i, nos. 4153–4 (CPR 1247–58, 339–40).
[28] RG, i, no. 4281 (CPR 1247–58, 351–2); DD, no. 264.
[29] CR 1253–4, 167, 170–1, 286; DD, no. 264.
[30] Ellis, 'Gaston de Béarn', 160–1, transcribed from De Marca, *Histoire de Béarn*, 598.
[31] For the issue of the seneschalship, see Paris, vi, 286.
[32] MacKay, *Spain in the Middle Ages*, 58–9.

Save at the beginning and end of his stay in Gascony, Henry spent little time at Bordeaux itself, a measure of the crisis confronting him. But Bordeaux was the administrative base where the wardrobe clerk John of Southwark received the customs of Bordeaux, and guarded prisoners, treasure and goods in the castle. Also based in the castle was what was coming to be called the great wardrobe, with its store of cloth under the control of the king's tailor, Roger de Ros.[33] As in 1242–3 the wardrobe was the financial centre of the expedition, and large sums of money passed through the hands of the keeper, Peter Chaceporc.[34] For Gascony generally, Henry appointed as his seneschal the former steward of the royal household John de Grey, now quite forgiven for his unlicensed marriage. When his health gave way, Henry replaced him with his elder brother Richard.[35] While the war lasted this was a military assignment, and no reference was made to the financial terms on which the office was to be held.[36]

Soon after landing, Henry tried to open negotiations with the men of La Réole and Bazas.[37] His policy was very different from Simon de Montfort's. He sought not to crush his opponents but conciliate them. When, however, his overtures were rebuffed, he saw he must act. Early in September he set up camp outside La Réole and began to lay siege to the town. He made no progress and on 13–14 September, after little more than a week, abandoned the operation. La Réole remained untaken until the end of the war almost a year later. Henry later reflected bitterly on the damage he sustained through its defiance.[38]

Elsewhere, however, Henry was making progress, for forces under the command of Roger Bigod, John de Plessis, Peter of Savoy and John de Grey were busy securing hold of towns and garrisoning their castles with household knights and sergeants-at-arms.[39] By the end of Henry's stay around twenty castles had been garrisoned in that way. Henry's forces were also engaged in ravaging the lands of his enemies. Here they were just as brutal as those of Montfort.

The first success was at St-Macaire, which Bigod and Plessis received into the king's hands at the end of August.[40] Henry, meanwhile, managed to gain possession of Gironde, the town immediately to the west of La

---

[33] Tout, *Chapters*, i, 273.

[34] See *RG*, i, nos. 2602, 3874, 3905, 3936 (*CPR 1247–58*, 314–15, 317, 320); *CR 1253–4*, 185. Because Chaceporc never accounted for this period, there is no detailed record of wardrobe receipts and expenditure to compare with that for 1242/3.

[35] *RG*, i, nos. 2063, 2107.

[36] *CPR 1247–58*, 242; *CR 1253–4*, 199–200, 317.

[37] *CR 1253–4*, 165, 286.

[38] *RG*, i, no. 4154.

[39] *CR 1253–4*, 176, 294.

[40] *CR 1253–4*, 166–8. But St-Macaire did not send a contingent to the army at La Réole (289).

Réole, commanding a bridge over the Garonne.[41] To the east of La Réole the household knight Geoffrey Gascelin held the castle at Lamothe-Landerron while Peter of Savoy and John de Grey placed a large garrison, under Philip de Arcy, in Meilhan, thus obstructing traffic bound for La Réole from the Agenais.[42] Henry had not taken La Réole but he might hope he was closing the net around it. Further south, in September, in the first major victory of the campaign, he secured Bazas. It was placed under Roger Bigod and the king's opponents were expelled.[43]

Henry now sought to build on these successes. He thanked the towns for their help at La Réole, and avowed he wished to spare them at this time of the wine-making. Nonetheless he demanded 3,740 archers be sent him for a forthcoming expedition.[44] This was to Benauges, which Henry began to besiege on 28 September. Situated in Entre-Deux-Mers, north-west of La Réole, the castle sat high on a hill and dominated the surrounding plain. It was the chief seat of the leading rebel, Bernard de Bouville. If Henry could take it, he might strike a major blow against his enemies. The task was easier than at La Réole, because the castle could be isolated and invested. But the garrison put up a staunch defence. Great mill stones (taken back to England as curiosities) were hurled down on the attackers. Henry asked for armour to protect his knees and shins to be sent to him from Bordeaux.[45] Throughout October he and his army remained camped in fields around the castle. It was to there accordingly that Henry summoned eight local bishops and the archbishop of Auch to celebrate the feast of the Confessor with him on 13 October.[46]

Benauges fell at last on 6 November, whereupon Henry garrisoned the castle and appointed a chaplain, equipped with 'simple' vestments and a little silver chalice to celebrate mass there. The triumph was only marred by Guy de Lusignan, at least according to Matthew Paris's story. Without consulting the king and his councillors, indeed, while they were at table, he allowed the women taken in the castle to join their husbands in La Réole, much to the anger of the earls and barons in the army.[47] The fall of Benauges shifted the situation immediately in Henry's favour.[48] Gaillard de Solers opened negotiations to enter the king's peace. Then, at the start of December, Amaneus d'Albret actually did so. He was made to surrender two castles (Castel Jalouz and Cazeneuve) as security for his obedience to the king 'as his liege lord'.[49]

---

[41] *CPR 1247–58*, 243, 250.

[42] *CPR 1247–58*, 242–3, 250, 254–5, 273; *CR 1251–3*, 173, 201.

[43] *CR 1253–4*, 166–7, 170–2, 179, 190; *CPR 1247–58*, 352.

[44] *CR 1253–4*, 289.

[45] Paris, v, 396; *CR 1253–4*, 174.

[46] *CR 1253–4*, 291.

[47] *CR 1253–4*, 189; Burton, 317; Paris, v, 396.

[48] For Henry's measures backing up the success, see *RG*, i, nos. 2171, 2178–9; *CR 1253–4*, 188–90, 193.

[49] *RG*, i, nos. 2188, 2210, 2411–12 (*CPR 1247–58*, 254–5).

Henry had a further accession of strength from a surprising quarter. For who should join him during the siege of Benauges but Simon de Montfort! At first sight this seems extraordinary. Henry had done all he could to get Simon out of Gascony. Why should he now want him back?[50] But the situations were very different. Montfort came not as an independent commander but as a helper of the king. On that basis his military expertise could be very useful. He was thus asked to come with as large a posse of mounted crossbowmen as could be recruited.[51]

Henry had gone to great lengths to get Montfort back. He was to be conducted to court by the earls of Norfolk and Hereford and given 200 marks for his journey. He was also promised protection from his enemies, and the right to depart at any time if he felt his stay was incompatible with his interest and his honour.[52] Early in November, once Montfort had arrived, Henry attempted a comprehensive settlement with him, one of considerable generosity. Hitherto Montfort, as Eleanor's marriage portion, had been in receipt of a 500-mark annual fee from the king, of which 200 marks were for life and 300 marks entailed on his heirs with the promise of eventual conversion into land. In fact, Montfort was not actually receiving the 500 marks because they were set against the 500 marks he owed the king each year for the wardship of the great Northumbrian barony of Umfraville. Now, however, Henry pardoned the 500-mark Umfraville payment, and thus started paying the 500-mark fee all over again. He did better than that. He increased the fee to 600 marks and made the whole of it hereditary, again with the promise of eventual conversion into land. As an absolute assurance that the money would be forthcoming, he made it the first call on the revenues of six English counties, an unprecedented concession. Their sheriffs were to take an oath to Montfort, and be appointed with his consent. They were also to hand over the money directly to him rather than first sending it to the exchequer. Apart from securing the money, the arrangement gave Montfort extensive power in the counties concerned – Warwickshire–Leicestershire (where his main bases lay), Nottinghamshire–Derbyshire, Wiltshire and Berkshire.[53] This was not all. Henry gave Kenilworth castle to Montfort and Eleanor for their joint lives (previously it had only been for Eleanor's). He promised too an additional £500 for Montfort's damages and expenses in Gascony, and took steps to pay the outstanding balance of the earlier 7,000-mark settlement (still over half of it was owed).[54]

[50] For what follows, see Maddicott, *Simon de Montfort*, 121–4.

[51] *CR 1253–4*, 291; Paris, v, 415–16.

[52] *CR 1253–4*, 168–9; *RG*, i, no. 2111 (*CPR 1247–58*, 244).

[53] Warwickshire–Leicestershire and Nottinghamshire–Derbyshire were joint sheriffdoms.

[54] *RG*, i, nos. 2153 (*CPR 1247–58*, 249–50), 2160; *CR 1253–4*, 179, 210–11; *CLR 1251–60*, 154, 167. The exchequer's issue roll for Easter 1254 (TNA E 403/10) shows a payment to Montfort of 3,000 marks towards the 7,000 marks owed.

It is easy to think that these concessions had been forced from a grudging and resentful king. Certainly Montfort had driven a hard bargain and nailed down the agreement with his usual intelligent and sceptical precision. Yet there was more to it than that. The concessions so opulent, and in the case of the sheriffs so irresponsible, stemmed from an emotional reconciliation between the two men, which Henry celebrated in his usual warm, impulsive way. Here Montfort's own attitude, in Matthew Paris's account, played a part. He had, he said, turned down an offer to become steward of France following the death of Queen Blanche. His loyalty was to King Henry and he could not serve two masters. He had also been influenced by the last advice of Robert Grosseteste.

Grosseteste had died at his manor of Buckden on 9 October 1253, with those in the surrounding area, including Fulk Basset, bishop of London, hearing the miraculous sound of bells as his spirit ascended. No less miraculous was the transition Grosseteste had made, at a late age, from the university to the diocese, from being the greatest scholar of the age to being the greatest bishop. His fiery zeal for the cure of souls and his utter certainty in his own righteousness and judgement had made him a chastizer of pope, king, nobles, monks and his own cathedral chapter. Yet, affable, cheerful and a generous host, he was a trusted friend and counsellor. He had urged Montfort, in a spirit of charity and humility, to forgive the harsh words spoken by the king in 1252 and think only of the great benefits he had received, including the marriage of Eleanor and the Umfraville custody. Montfort evidently took the advice and Matthew Paris captured exactly Henry's reaction: 'the king admiring the charity of the earl, received him with the greatest exultation'.[55] Montfort himself later admitted that the king made himself 'si bon semblant' that he thought all their quarrels were over.[56]

Henry reaped some reward from Montfort's return. He came with a substantial force and stayed at court until the end of November. He helped negotiate the settlement with Amaneus d'Albret, and then in December went on a successful mission to secure loans from the southern towns. At Bayonne, with Peter of Savoy, he made provisions about the choice of a new mayor.[57] Montfort was still contracting loans for the king in February 1254. All very different from the fire and sword of his period in charge. His return to England (by May 1254) was clearly with the king's blessing. That August he was commissioned to relay a secret message from Henry to the king of Scotland.[58] Montfort still nursed grievances over Eleanor's dower and the failure to convert his new pension into land, but he now remained part of Henry's court down to the revolution of 1258.

---

[55] Paris, v, 407–9, 415–16.

[56] Bémont, *Simon de Montfort*, 338.

[57] Paris, v, 415–16; Bémont, *Simon de Montfort*, 338; *RG*, i, nos. 2237, 2322, 2371, 2399, 3755, 3955 (*CPR 1247–58*, 264, 269, 273, 302, 321). Montfort last attests on 28 November.

[58] *RG*, i, nos. 2325, 3955 (*CPR 1247–58*, 264, 321).

There was one more consequence of Montfort's arrival, that related to Bigorre, the county along the eastern frontier of Béarn, to which Gaston himself had a claim. As part of his campaign against the latter, Montfort had got control of the county via a lease from the aged countess, Petronella. With her death he had allowed (in June 1253) her designated heir, the young Esquivat de Chabanais, to succeed to the county, although the latter owed him large sums of money and remained very much under his control. Now, in November 1253, Henry himself suddenly made a move. He decided to buy the overlordship of Bigorre for several hundred pounds from the bishop and chapter of Le-Puy-en-Velay. (They had acquired it in the eleventh century via the gift of the count.) Given that Montfort was with Henry at this time, the purchase must have been his idea. There were advantages for the king. Esquivat was secured as an ally against Gaston, and the following year did homage to Henry for the county. Henry bought from him three castles in the county of Fézensac, thus bolstering the eastern defences of Gascony. There were also advantages to Montfort, who expected to get the money owed him by Esquivat from the large sums the latter was now due to receive from the king. This added another dimension to the complex relations between the king and his brother-in-law.[59]

The securing of Bigorre was not Henry's only activity on the diplomatic front. He was also doing his best to prevent any further outside intervention. He tried to maintain good relations with Navarre and indeed asked it for military help.[60] He strove to keep Louis IX's brother Alphonse, who was ruling in Poitou, the Saintonge, the Agenais and Toulouse, out of the game, going to great lengths to ensure that a debt to him of nearly £3,000 was actually paid.[61]

With the fall of Benauges, the submission of Amaneus d'Albret and the negotiations with Gaillard de Solers, it seemed as though the Gascon revolt was collapsing. As early as October 1254, Henry was taking steps to ensure the province passed intact to Edward. With the possessions of rebels coming into his hands, he took a solemn oath not to alienate them. If he did, his gifts were to be invalid 'since we wish that all the land of Gascony . . . shall remain together in perpetuity'. The aspiration was laudable. The means of achieving it was lamentable. Henry's promise, publicly proclaimed in a letter patent, revealed all too clearly his weaknesses and indeed his own recognition of them. With its unnerving echo of the oaths taken at Burgh in 1232, there was something terribly undignified and undermining in a king acknowledging that his own acts were to be 'of no value or moment'. Henry had taken the oath 'in the hand' of Peter de Aigueblanche, the

---

[59] *RG*, i, nos. 3791, 4274, 4276, 4279 (*CPR 1247–58*, 305–6, 350–1); Bémont, *Simon de Montfort*, 370–1; Labarge, *Simon de Montfort*, 134–5; Maddicott, *Simon de Montfort*, 134–5.

[60] *CR 1253–4*, 172, 288–9; *RG*, i, no. 2136; *CPR 1247–58*, 280.

[61] *CR 1253–4*, 174, 304; *RG*, i, no. 2175 (*CPR 1247–58*, 251–2); *CPR 1247–58*, 367, 369. The money was owed for damages done by the Gascons to the men of Alphonse's territories.

Savoyard bishop of Hereford, and almost certainly it was a Savoyard idea. Behind it lay the worry of the queen, back in England with Edward, that her husband was about to cast the proceeds of the Gascon victory to the winds, or perhaps more to the point to the Lusignans.[62]

THE CASTILIAN INVASION THREAT AND THE RESPONSE IN ENGLAND

But there was no Gascon victory, or not immediately. When he submitted in early December, Amaneus d'Albret was promised help if he was attacked by either Gaston de Béarn or Alfonso of Castile. In December, Henry's own fear of a Castilian invasion reached a peak. He sent a letter home (received by Christmas) explaining his anxieties and demanding a parliament be summoned to agree on a response.[63] Henry also sent back to England to make his case to the parliament none other than Roger Bigod. Roger had taken an active part in the fighting, and been rewarded by concessions over his rights, as marshal, at the exchequer. He was also given a house for his base in Bordeaux. That Henry now gave him this important mission shows how good their relations could sometimes be.[64]

Matthew Paris considered that in all this the king's behaviour was fraudulent. He knew perfectly well that there would be no Castilian invasion and was simply using the prospect to get money from parliament. Paris's account, however, was written with the benefit of hindsight, after the threat had indeed evaporated. His idea that Bigod himself had been led astray by the king is plainly absurd.[65] The evidence that Henry and the home government believed the threat to be real is overwhelming.[66] The negotiations for a marriage settlement had run into difficulties.[67] John Mansel and the bishop of Bath and Wells must have reached Castile sometime in August. They did not return to Henry in Gascony until late January, having, as the annals of Dunstable noted, been unable to reach an agreement. They brought nothing but Alfonso's demands. These were high. Apart from the pardon and restoration of his supporters in Gascony, Henry was to convert his crusade to the Holy Land into one with Alfonso to North Africa and Morocco. Henry was also to send his son Edward or his seneschal to make war 'with great power' on the king of Navarre.[68]

---

[62] *RG*, i, no. 2599 (*CPR 1247–58*, 293). The promise was made during the siege of Benauges. The immediate occasion was the granting to Edward of all the lands falling to the king from the vicomte of Benauges, Bernard de Bouville.

[63] Paris, vi, 282; *CR 1253–4*, 107.

[64] *CR 1253–4*, 196, 304; Paris, v, 423; Paris, vi, 282–3. See Morris, *Bigod Earls of Norfolk*, 46–8, for in some ways a different emphasis. Bigod did not return to Gascony in 1254.

[65] Paris, v, 423–5, 445; Paris, vi, 284 n. 1.

[66] The reality of Henry's fears is well argued in Ellis, 'Gaston de Béarn', 179–80.

[67] Forey, 'Crusading vows', 242–3, for rumours as to Alfonso's movements.

[68] Dunstable, 188; *CPR 1247–58*, 263; Paris, vi, 284–6 (*F*, 298).

These demands must have knocked Henry sideways. They meant abandoning his cherished crusade to the Holy Land and attacking Navarre, whose help he was now seeking in Gascony, however much he still resented its encroachments during the war of the 1240s.[69] Yet, on the other side, there seemed a real danger of a Castilian invasion. Henry even had the date. It was to be in late April.[70]

Henry, therefore, appealed for help to the home government under his queen and Richard of Cornwall. He had treated them with far more courtesy than he had the governors left behind in 1242. In letters home he stressed that in matters of patronage he respected their delegated powers and would do nothing without their assent and counsel. He gave Richard a Wiltshire manor 'if he wants it' as part of Sanchia's marriage portion, and made clear he was top of the waiting list for more.[71] Eleanor's role was particularly important, for she authorized far more letters than did Richard. She would have been delighted both by the oath safeguarding Gascony for Edward and by the concession of the lucrative Vescy wardship to Peter of Savoy.[72] In his turn, Henry was delighted with Eleanor. He gave £15 a year to the messenger who brought 'the happy news of the delivery by divine grace to our beloved consort of a beautiful daughter called Katherine'.[73] Given Gascony was to be Edward's, Eleanor would have been very concerned by the threatened Castilian invasion. She and Richard now set about mobilizing help.

Their first move was to summon a parliament to meet at Westminster on 27 January 1254. Even before that they were arranging for forces to go out to Henry from Ireland.[74] When the parliament opened, Bigod had not arrived, but he was able to join proceedings later.[75] There was some scepticism about the king's appeal. It was noted that Edward had been

---

[69] The final treaty with Castile mentions castles and lands taken from the king of England by the king of Navarre; *F*, 299–300; *DD*, no. 272.

[70] Paris, vi, 283; *CR 1253–4*, 109.

[71] See *CR 1253–4*, 253.

[72] *CPR 1247–58*, 237–8, 245, 268; *RG*, i, no. 2722; *CFR 1253–4*, nos. 263–6; *CR 1256–9*, 27. William de Vescy, lord of the great Northumberland barony centred on Alnwick, had died during the expedition. Before embarking, he had agreed that Peter of Savoy could control the marriage of John de Vescy, his son and heir. The wardship gave Peter ten years' control of the barony. Peter married John to Agnes, daughter of the marquess of Saluzo, sister of the Alice whom he had already married to Edmund de Lacy. Peter agreed to pay £625 a year for the wardship but this was soon pardoned by the king.

[73] *RG*, i, no. 2350 (*CPR 1247–58*, 267).

[74] *CR 1253–4*, 14–15, 109.

[75] For the parliament and subsequent measures, see Maddicott, *Origins of the English Parliament*, 211–13, 469. The account in Paris (v, 423–5) needs to be controlled by Tewkesbury (154) and Dunstable (189), and even more by the letters showing the measures of the government and explaining the situation to Henry: *CR 1253–4*, 26, 111–12, 114–16, 119; *CPR 1247–58*, 363–4; Paris, vi, 286–7; *RL*, ii, 101–2, of which Paris, vi, 282–4, may be an earlier draft version (see Maddicott, *Origins of the English Parliament*, 211 n. 212).

summoned out to Gascony. The offers of help were, therefore, made conditional on whether the king of Castile actually did come, yet help was offered. Matthew Paris acknowledged that Richard de Clare was convinced of the danger. The earls and barons accordingly promised they would gather at Westminster on 3 May and then march to Portsmouth to embark for Gascony. (The invasion was now expected not in April but in the summer.) Richard of Cornwall pledged to go too with a contingent for which, he said, his brother would be eternally grateful. All tenants-in-chief holding land worth at least £20 a year were also ordered to muster. Several bishops, led by the archbishop of Canterbury, likewise said they would embark, while others promised financial aid.

There was, however, difficulty with the government's financial demands. The bishops said they could not consent on behalf of the lower clergy to a tax of a tenth on their incomes. The latter must give their own consent, which itself might hinge on the pope remitting part of the tax for Henry's crusade. The queen and Richard of Cornwall accordingly asked for assemblies to be convened where such assent might be forthcoming. As for the tax to be paid by the laity, since the earls, barons and other tenants-in-chief who were going in person would be exempt, it was felt that, in this case too, those who would have to pay must give their consent. The sheriffs were thus ordered to bring before the council on 26 April two knights from each county, elected in the county court, to say 'on behalf of all and everyone of the county' what tax they were prepared to give. This was to be after listening to the sheriffs explaining the king's urgent needs. The explanation cannot have been helped by the sheriffs also being told, in threatening terms, to collect all the money owed the king by Easter.[76]

Considerable constitutional significance has been attached to this summons of knights to what is elsewhere described as a parliament. It was probably the first such summons and is thus a landmark in parliamentary history. While the routine summons of tenants-in-chief to parliament had always meant knights were in attendance (for many lesser tenants-in-chief were of knightly status), they had come for themselves. Now knights were to come as representatives of their counties, a very different proposition.[77] To be sure, the circumstances were exceptional, given this was not a tax involving the bulk of the king's tenants-in-chief. Had they been involved, they would probably have answered for the realm in the traditional way. Nonetheless, the summons pointed to the future. During the period of reform and rebellion, and in the last years of the reign, knights representing the counties and burgesses the towns were to be summoned to parliament with increasing frequency.

The idea for the summons in 1254 was surely Richard of Cornwall's and shows how fertile he was in expedients and how sensitive to the national

---

[76] *CR 1253–4*, 114–5; Paris, vi, 286–7.

[77] For a full discussion, see Maddicott, *Origins of the English Parliament*, 212–18.

mood.[78] He was equally sensitive in the letters trying to rally support for the expedition. These suggested that everyone would suffer from Gascony's loss. Indeed, a Castilian invasion of England and Ireland might follow. The letters also appealed to national pride. The kingdom, amongst all worldly dominions, had been famed for the strength of its people and it would be terrible for it to fail now through the powerlessness and laziness of its men. Although the king could recruit troops abroad, he trusted far more in his own men than in aliens. In explaining the results of the parliament to Henry, Richard warned that no tax would be forthcoming unless the king caused Magna Carta to be proclaimed and observed by all the sheriffs. Thus Henry's failure to broadcast his 1253 confirmation of the Charters was to be remedied. 'Many complain that the charters are not observed by your sheriffs and other bailiffs as they ought to be,' Richard concluded.[79] Henry had been told.

While Henry awaited the results of his appeal, he stayed at Bazas. Indeed, he was there for the whole period from 19 November 1253 to 26 February 1254. He thus stamped his authority on this former rebel town and had a more central base than that provided by Bordeaux. Early in February the fears, which had prompted his appeal, seemed well justified, for Gaston de Béarn, aided by an Alfonsonist faction in the town, attempted to seize Bayonne. Fortunately, the insurgents were captured and sent to Bordeaux, where Henry, doubtless remembering Rostand de Solers's death in Montfort's custody, ordered them to be treated 'courteously' and not loaded down with irons. After this success, there were more negotiations with Gaston, La Réole and the Solers, but they led nowhere. With nothing from England since October, Henry was becoming desperately short of money. He took out loans and received 2,000 marks from Bordeaux for a charter of liberties, but he still had to pay castle garrisons from stores of wine, cloth and food. One group of sergeants-at-arms, Henry lamented, had been forced to pawn their armour, and would soon have to leave his service. In a desperate expedient to raise cash Henry told Peter Chaceporc to acquire wine at Bordeaux on credit and then sell it even at half price.[80]

Henry also had to face discontent within his army. On 8 January 1254 he dictated an angry letter to the home government about the northern baron Peter de Maulay, son of the notorious henchman of Peter des Roches. Maulay had come out late to Gascony, tried to persuade others to go home, and been rude to Henry's face. Placed in charge of the royal bodyguard of fifty knights, he had gone off without permission, leaving

---

[78] The writ as copied by Matthew Paris only has the queen as a witness (Paris, vi, 114–15), but the copy on the close rolls is 'witnessed as above', the 'above' being a writ attested by both queen and earl; *CR 1253–4*, 113–15.

[79] *CR 1253–4*, 114–16; *RL*, ii, 101–2; Paris, vi, 286–7.

[80] *CR 1253–4*, 213–5, 217, 234; *RG*, i, no. 2602 (*CPR 1247–58*, 294).

Henry alone and in great danger. In fact Henry never sent the letter and soon restored Peter to favour, but more trouble was to follow.[81] A contingent of Welsh soldiers in the army went on an unlicensed pillaging expedition and were punished by the bishop of Hereford, Peter de Aigueblanche, and the king's Lusignan half-brothers. This offended Humphrey de Bohun, earl of Hereford, who as hereditary constable claimed jurisdiction over such matters. Henry, who generally got on well with Bohun, soon apologized and granted Bohun's son, another Humphrey, 80 marks a year to sustain him in royal service.[82] The earl, however, decided to go home, and is last found at court on 9 February.

THE CASTILIAN AGREEMENT

The earls of Norfolk and Hereford, who had come with Henry, had both now departed. While Henry still had English magnates with him they were not of the first rank. The only earl in attendance was the Norman John de Plessis, earl of Warwick in right of his wife. The king's foreign relatives on the other hand had remained at Henry's side: Peter of Savoy, Bishop Aigueblanche and the king's half-brothers Geoffrey de Lusignan and William de Valence. One reason for Henry attaching himself to the Lusignans was so they could help in Gascony. At last they were showing their worth.

It was this very foreign-dominated court which now, in February 1254, took momentous decisions affecting the future of England, Gascony, the crusade and the kingdom of Sicily. John Mansel had arrived at Bazas in late January, bearing Alfonso's demanding terms. Henry took a big gulp and accepted them. In return for a renunciation of the Castilian claim to Gascony, he agreed to make good the damage done to Gaston and Alfonso's other supporters, make war on Navarre and ask the pope to change his crusade to the Holy Land into one to North Africa and Morocco. Henry also, as demanded, agreed to give his son Edward an endowment worthy of his marriage to Alfonso's sister, the marriage being the centrepiece of the treaty. The charter in Edward's favour, issued on 14 February, was witnessed by the bishop of Hereford, the earl of Warwick, Geoffrey de Lusignan, William de Valence, Peter of Savoy and not a single English magnate.[83] It gave Edward £10,000 a year made up of Gascony, the lordship of Ireland, the county of Chester, the king's conquests in North Wales, the city of Bristol and various other possessions in England.[84]

---

[81] *CR 1253–4*, 295. Peter had inherited the Fossard barony in Yorkshire, acquired by his father through marriage.

[82] Paris, v, 442–3.

[83] *F*, 296–7 (*CPR 1247–58*, 269–71).

[84] Paris, v, 488, 510. See below, 657, n. 238.

On the terms thus agreed, with much thanks and reward, Henry sent John Mansel and Bishop Aigueblanche back to Castile with full power to conclude the treaty.[85] Its most remarkable feature was the way it committed Henry to make war on two fronts, in Navarre and in Africa. But Henry could hope that Castile and Navarre would settle their differences. He might also hope that the pope would never sanction the commutation of his crusading vow into one to campaign in Africa. This was not because Henry was to go to the Holy Land. He was to do something else quite different. It was this very month, February 1254, at the very time that he was agreeing the Castilian terms, that Henry accepted a papal offer to put Edmund, his second son, on the throne of Sicily.

THE BEGINNINGS OF THE SICILIAN AFFAIR

How had this extraordinary development come about? After the death of Emperor Frederick II at the end of 1250, his son Conrad had left Germany and made himself master of the Sicilian kingdom. This was the last thing Pope Innocent IV wanted. He distrusted Conrad as the son of his bitterest enemy. He also feared his power. Conrad had been crowned king of the Romans during his father's lifetime and thus could claim authority in Germany. If he had the Sicilian kingdom as well, including as it did the southern half of Italy, the papal states in central Italy would be at his mercy. Since Sicily was a papal fief, Innocent felt able to give its kingship to whomever he liked. In November 1252 his notary, Master Albert of Parma, arrived in England empowered to offer the throne to none other than Henry III's brother, Richard of Cornwall.[86] Innocent had met Richard in 1250 and doubtless been impressed by his wisdom and his wealth. But the negotiations made little progress and at the end of January 1253, Master Albert left England empty-handed.[87] Henry, nonetheless, wrote to the pope in glowing terms about the honour conferred by the papal choice.[88] So, switching brothers, in April 1253, Innocent gave Master Albert full power to give the kingdom either to Henry himself or one of his sons. At the same time he was authorized to commute Henry's vow to crusade in the Holy Land into one for the execution of the Sicilian business.[89] There is no sign, however, that the negotiations with Henry, if they ever started, made any more progress than had those with Richard.

---

[85] *RG*, i, nos. 2349, 2351–2, 2362.

[86] For a detailed account of Albert's career in this period, see Montaubin, 'Royaume de Sicilie'.

[87] *F*, 284; Paris, v, 346–7, 361; Paris, *HA*, iii, 126–7; *CR 1251–3*, 290, 303, 449; *CLR 1251–60*, 102, 109.

[88] *CR 1251–3*, 449.

[89] *Reg. Alexandre IV*, iii, no. 3036 (89).

Matthew Paris, who saw Richard around this time, captures his objections well. They carried some weight since Richard was one of the few people in England who knew the Sicilian kingdom, having travelled through it on his way home from his crusade, meeting Frederick II on the journey.[90] There was firstly an obvious point: 'the pope is giving me what he is not strong enough to obtain. Surely Conrad lives.' Securing the kingdom would require a major military campaign with all its expenses and hazards. Richard, not anyway 'in armis strenuus', demanded the pope provide him with plentiful supplies of money, a safe conduct through France (for how else was he to get there) and various other guarantees. When these were insufficiently forthcoming, Richard remarked that it was as though the pope had said 'I offer you the moon, go up and take it'.[91] There was also another problem which prevented Henry too, for all his enthusiasm, taking up the papal offer. Still alive was not merely Conrad but also Conrad's younger half-brother, Henry, product of Frederick II's marriage to Henry and Richard's sister Isabella. He was, therefore, Henry and Richard's nephew and was indeed named after their grandfather Henry II. He was now based in Sicily where he was acting as Conrad's lieutenant. A war between uncle and nephew would be 'shameful'. Henry III would not (as the pope acknowledged) 'thirst after his own blood'.[92]

Pope Innocent, therefore, turned elsewhere and in the summer of 1253, through Master Albert, conducted negotiations with the brother of Louis IX, Charles of Anjou. Since Charles was also count of Provence, he was far better placed than either Henry or Richard to mount a campaign in Sicily. In the end, however, he too pulled out of the negotiations (although they went much further than they had with England), deciding rightly that it would be far easier to exploit opportunities opening up in Hainault than it would be to oust Conrad from Sicily.[93] This was in the late summer of 1253 and after that the Sicilian business lay fallow until December. It was then transformed by the death of Henry, son of Isabella. The great obstacle in the path of Henry III had been removed. Innocent acted at once. On 20 December 1253 he gave Master Albert full power to concede the kingdom to Edmund, Henry's second son (aged nine), if, that is, Henry was prepared to accept it.[94] Albert did not go to Gascony in person, but his envoys reached Henry in January. It did not take Henry long to decide. On 12 February, from Bazas, he sent back to Albert proctors with full

[90] I owe this point to Adrian Jobson. Henry himself would have had some idea of the geography from his mappae mundi. For a discussion, see Connolly, *Maps of Matthew Paris*, 174–5.

[91] Paris, v, 362, 457; Paris, *HA*, iii, 126–7.

[92] Paris, iv, 613; Paris, v, 347; *F*, 302.

[93] *Reg. Innocent IV*, iii, nos. 6806–19; Dunbabin, *Charles I of Anjou*, 37–8.

[94] *Reg. Alexandre IV*, iii, no. 3036 (89).

power to accept the kingdom in Edmund's name. He also appointed a team to negotiate the detailed conditions.[95] On the strength of this, on 6 March, at Vendôme in France, Albert formally entrusted Edmund with the kingdom. On 14 May, at Assissi, Innocent ratified the gift, and a few days later instructed Henry to make Edmund his golden seal as king of Sicily.

For Henry the ultimate prize seemed great. The kingdom of Sicily embraced Naples and southern Italy as well as the island of Sicily itself. Henry knew, as he told the pope, that it was 'great amongst other kingdoms'. Yes indeed, the pope rejoined, it 'abounded . . . in wealth and luxuries'.[96] Henry's establishment there would utterly transform the balance of power in Europe. Having failed to recover the Angevin empire, he would now establish his dynasty as a Mediterranean power. He could use Sicily as a base for a crusade to the Holy Land or indeed one to support Alfonso in North Africa. He would surpass the achievements even of his uncle Richard the Lionheart, who had merely meddled in Sicilian politics on his way to the Holy Land.[97] There was also for Henry the appeal of the relationship with the pope himself, who stressed that Edmund would now become their 'common son'.[98] With Henry's profound reverence for the papacy the offer of the kingdom seemed a gift from God.[99]

In conjuring up such visions, was Henry not living in a fantasy world? Was not the pope, as Matthew Paris believed, exploiting Henry's 'simplicity'? The Burton annalist put it differently: the pope and cardinals turned to Henry appreciating 'his astuteness and power'. He was, of course, being ironic.[100] After all, the difficulties of actually acquiring Sicily were the same now as when they had deterred Richard. Whatever the ebbs and flows of the situation, Conrad was still in place and a major military campaign, perhaps many campaigns, might be needed to oust him. Henry was even less than Richard 'strenuus in armis'. The contrast here with the Lionheart could not have been starker. Henry, moreover, had taken on all this when waging a war in Gascony, and when surrounded by his foreign relatives and counselled by not a single English noble. Not one was named on the team who were to negotiate the precise terms with the pope. How far Henry had consulted with his brother

[95] *RG*, i, nos.2291, 2367 (*CPR 1247–58*, 262, 269); *CR 1253–4*, 213.

[96] *CR 1251–3*, 449; *F*, 302; *Reg. Alexandre IV*, iii, no. 3036 (89–90).

[97] For sympathetic accounts of Henry's involvement in the Sicilian affair, which stress these wider international considerations and imperatives, see Lloyd, *English Society and the Crusade*, 221–32; Weiler, *Henry III of England and the Staufen Empire*, ch. 7, and Weiler, 'Henry III and the Sicilian business'.

[98] *F*, 302, 304.

[99] Burton, 324–5, for light-hearted correspondence between Henry and Innocent over who was the older.

[100] Paris, v, 457; Burton, 339.

Richard of Cornwall is unclear. This was a reckless start to a project which would depend on mobilizing the resources of the kingdom. What was going on?

To understand the Sicilian affair, one fundamental point needs appreciation: it was an enterprise of the Savoyards.[101] Peter of Savoy and the Savoyard bishop of Hereford, Peter de Aigueblanche, were at court throughout February when the crucial decisions were made. It was at this time Henry freed Peter from any payments for the Vesci wardship, a concession worth all of £625 a year.[102] The chief envoy shuttling between Henry, Master Albert and the pope was the Savoyard clerk and papal chaplain John de Ambléon.[103] The committee Henry nominated to negotiate the precise terms comprised Philip of Savoy, archbishop-elect of Lyon, Philip's brothers Peter and Thomas of Savoy, the Poitevin keeper of the wardrobe, Peter Chaceporc, and just one Englishman, John Mansel.[104] The Lusignans, though at court, were conspicuous by their absence. This was not their affair.

Amongst the Savoyards, one name stands out, that of Thomas of Savoy. It was he more than anyone else who hoped to profit from the papal offer, and had helped bring it about. In February 1254, on the English patent rolls, the orders sending John de Ambléon to the papal court and settling up the arrears of Thomas's fee sit side by side.[105] Later, in May, when the pope ratified the offer, Thomas was at the papal court acting on Henry's behalf.[106] Since leaving Flanders on his wife's death in 1244, Thomas had forged a new career for himself in northern Italy, in 1248 becoming Emperor Frederick II's vicar general in Upper Pavia. Many of the grants he received from Frederick, including the castle and town of Turin, were notional, but Thomas was determined to make them a reality. In that cause, after Frederick's death, he deftly changed sides and married a niece of Innocent IV. 'From a son of wrath, he became a son of grace,' as Matthew Paris put it.[107] Thomas's position was further enhanced by the death of his elder brother, in June 1253, which meant he became regent of Savoy, as he did also, through further deaths, of the marquisates of Saluzzo and Montferrat.[108] If the Sicilian enterprise succeeded, Thomas would surely become regent of Sicily itself. Henry had immediately conceded him, on

---

[101] This is finely brought out in Howell, *Eleanor of Provence*, 131–5, and less emphatically in Cox, *Eagles of Savoy*, 242–5. See also Chapuisat, 'Pierre de Savoie', 261–3.

[102] *RG*, i, no. 2363 (*CPR 1247–58*, 268); see *CR 1256–9*, 27; *CFR 1253–4*, no. 263, seems to have misunderstood the king's order.

[103] *CR 1253–4*, 213; *RG*, i, no. 2367 (*CPR 1247–58*, 269); *Reg. Alexandre IV*, iii, no. 3036 (89–91); *F*, 304. John was dean of Saint-André, near Chambéry.

[104] *Reg. Alexandre IV*, iii, no. 3036 (89–90).

[105] *RG*, i, nos. 2366–7 (*CPR 1247–58*, 269).

[106] *F*, 304; and see *Reg. Innocent IV*, iii, nos. 7571, 7742.

[107] Paris, v, 255–6; Cox, *Eagles of Savoy*, 184–6, 206–17.

[108] Cox, *Eagles of Savoy*, 226, 229–30; Howell, *Eleanor of Provence*, 134.

Edmund's behalf, the principality of Capua, a gift which the pope confirmed in May, at Thomas's request.[109]

How might the project succeed? From the Savoyard perspective, it did not seem so impossible. The logistical problems were alleviated by Thomas's position in northern Italy and the family's control over the Alpine passes. Of the castles and towns guarding the passes, Henry indeed was the nominal lord.[110] Some sort of settlement with France might be necessary for the transport of the army, but perhaps that might be achieved given Savoyard connections with the Capetian court. Meanwhile, if money could be got to Thomas, he could recruit forces to maintain Edmund's cause.

When it came to finance, the pope himself was prepared to help. Since, as he said, 'much money' was needed to prosecute the enterprise 'potenter et viriliter', he absolved Henry from all his pious expenses, and, more to the point, promised to pay him the equivalent of £25,000 sterling.[111] This was much less than he had promised to raise through loans for Charles of Anjou, but at least it was a start.[112] There was also a way of adding to it, if, as Henry suggested, he was conceded the proceeds of the crusading tax now being levied in England.[113] Since that promised to bring in at least £30,000, here was a sum that could indeed launch a campaign. In May 1254, Thomas of Savoy, at the papal court, asked the pope to commute Henry's crusading vow to one for the prosecution of the Sicilian affair.[114] The point of course was that this would also involve the diversion of all the crusading money.

Of course, the clever Savoyards knew this was a speculative enterprise. Henry was not clever but perhaps he realized it too. But here another factor kicked in. The pope was making no demands in return for his offer. Indeed, he was promising Henry money to come. He was equally imposing no penalties for failure. There was no talk of excommunication or interdict. Nor, although Innocent wanted help quickly, were there any deadlines. And who could say what would happen? At the top, the project might make Edmund king of Sicily, and Thomas his regent. At the bottom, it was at least a negotiating card to bargain for some lesser settlement. The Savoyards certainly looked at it in that light. Indeed, they retained a foot in both camps. In February 1254, at the very moment when Henry was accepting the papal offer, Thomas was asking the pope to give

---

[109] Innocent's confirmation is in the Archivio di Stato di Torino: Principi del Sangue diversi Mazzo, 1 no. 3; a reference I owe to Nicholas Vincent. There is also there a copy of Edmund's eventual grant dated 9 October 1254 (Mazzo 1, no. 6). Henry confirmed this grant on 12 October: *RG*, i, no. 4210 (*CPR 1247–58*, 344).

[110] See above, 494.

[111] *F*, 303.

[112] *Reg. Innocent IV*, iii, no. 6819 (280).

[113] *Reg. Alexandre IV*, iii, no. 3036 (93).

[114] *F*, 304.

Conrad more time in negotiations for a settlement.[115] After all, Thomas's niece (daughter of his elder brother Amadeus, count of Savoy) was married to Frederick's illegitimate son Manfred, who had first opposed Conrad taking over Sicily, but now supported it.[116]

In all this, however, Henry should have seen there was a clear divergence between his position and that of the Savoyards. Provided the project remained a matter of diplomacy all was well. At the very least it made Henry a bigger player on the European stage. Once, however, the project became real and Henry had to solicit help from his kingdom to raise the necessary armies, he was bound to be in trouble. The church would be appalled at the diversion of the crusade to Sicily. Parliament would be horrified at the idea of granting a tax to support such a cause. Everyone would think the whole project a madness. The Savoyards, if that happened, could just wash their hands of the English consequences. Henry could not. He would be deeply damaged. If only Henry had regarded the Sicilian project in the same calculating spirit as the Savoyards, the danger might have been averted. Yet at some point, perhaps once the papal ratification arrived, something fatal happened, for which the Savoyards themselves had not planned. Henry became obsessed with the project, in the same way he had been obsessed earlier with the crusade. As Matthew Paris wrote, 'he was so exhilarated by the shady papal promise and his heart so filled with inane joy, that proclaiming his exultation in voice, gesture and laughter, he called his son openly king of Sicily, believing that he had already subjugated of the kingdom'.[117]

In one and the same month, in February 1254, Henry had committed himself to campaigns against both Moslems in North Africa and against Christians in Sicily. He was also still talking of his crusade to the Holy Land and wanting Westminster Abbey finished in October 1255 before his departure.[118] But Sicily soon swept all other projects from Henry's mind. For three years the crusade had dominated his life. The gold treasure saved to finance it he had refused to spend in Gascony. But now he was becoming committed to Sicily despite widespread criticism of such political crusades and despite anguished appeals from the Holy Land for help.[119] In the event, Henry's enthusiasm for the crusade had turned out to be like throwing paper onto a fire. For a moment the flames burn bright and give out tremendous heat, only then to die away into ashes. It is difficult to think of King Louis, for whom the crusade was central to his life, being so diverted. To be fair to Henry, this was not the end of the story. He soon gave up the idea of having his crusading vow commuted and it

[115] *Reg. Innocent IV*, iii, no. 7758.
[116] Cox, *Eagles of Savoy*, 158–9.
[117] Paris, v, 458.
[118] *RG*, i, no. 2469; *CPR 1247–58*, 281, 381.
[119] Burton, 368–9; *F*, 308.

never was.[120] Perhaps Henry dreamt of Sicily being a base for the crusade, as indeed the pope said it might be. Perhaps, more prosaically, he did not want to offend King Alfonso. In any case, the commutation lost its point once Henry knew it would not secure the crusading tax. So Henry continued to wear his crusader's cross and his conscience was sometimes troubled over his failure. In the last years of his life, the ashes of his crusading ardour were once more fanned into life.

THE FINAL SETTLEMENT WITH CASTILE

Having agreed the Spanish terms and despatched John Mansel and Peter de Aigueblanche back to Castile, Henry must have hoped the threat of an invasion was at an end. He was soon to be disappointed. On 24 March he sent a remarkable letter to everyone in England, one so personal that he must have crafted it himself. It was the reply to the offers of help relayed in the letters of the home government after the January parliament. Henry expressed his immense joy at the promise of support, including of course the promised army. He then acknowledged that negotiations were in train for a settlement with the king of Castile, but appearances, he said, could not be trusted. Alfonso had transmitted an immense sum of money to Gascony. He was still preparing an invasion, and intended to move at Easter to Burgos, only ten days' journey away. As a result, in Gascony the king's enemies were becoming madder day by day. Henry thus still wanted an army to muster at Portsmouth three weeks after Easter ready to cross to Gascony. Those not coming in person should still provide aid. In order to encourage them to do so, Henry took the advice of the regents and asked the sheriffs publicly to proclaim Magna Carta and see it was upheld. The Charter was also (the usual royal theme) to be obeyed by everyone else. In all this Henry tried to invoke the national spirit seen in the letters of Richard of Cornwall. He hoped for help from home because the nobles of England flourished more than those of other nations in virtue and vigour. Yet Henry still viewed the whole situation in very personal terms. Help was needed 'to save our body, life and honour and to defend our land'.[121]

Again, Henry's fears were genuine although what sparked them is unclear. Perhaps he was worried that Alfonso would hear of his Sicilian plans and realize he was being double-crossed. Whatever the truth, from February through into April, Henry was evidently preparing for a continuation of the struggle and a possible invasion. In April itself he twice issued orders to muster armies. He sent out streams of writs about garrisoning castles and taking possession of new ones. With promises of money fees and other concessions he ensured that a substantial body of English magnates and knights remained with him; and he continued to recruit Gascon forces.

[120] This was first demonstrated by Forey in his 'Crusading vows'.
[121] *RG*, i, nos. 2455, 2473–4 (*CPR 1247–58*, 279–81).

In March he retained Amaneus d'Albret with twenty knights and twenty sergeant-at-arms 'for the duration of the war for defence of our land'.[122] By this time Henry had moved from Bazas to Meilhan above the Garonne where he remained from the start of March to early June. He thus put pressure on La Réole only seven miles to the east.

In the event, Henry's fears proved unjustified. Alfonso never advanced to Burgos and remained at Toledo. He realized the Gascon revolt would be difficult to reignite even if he intervened. He was prepared to settle for the status conferred by Lord Edward's marriage and the possibility, faint though it was, of Henry's help in Africa.[123] So, on 1 April 1254, Bishop Aigueblanche and John Mansel swore, on the king's behalf, to observe the terms of the treaty and received parallel oaths from Alfonso's proctors.[124] There was then an anxious wait until 22 April when Alfonso finally sealed the treaty himself and took a corporal oath to abide by it. He also issued letters to his Gascon supporters, including Gaston de Béarn and the men of La Réole, telling them to obey Henry and Edward and return what they had occupied during the war. Henry, for his part, promised to restore to Alfonso's supporters' their losses 'in castles, inheritances and things'.[125]

THE GOVERNMENT OF RICHARD OF CORNWALL

Back in England the great parliament summoned by the queen and Earl Richard to meet the Gascon crisis met at Westminster on 26 April. News cannot have arrived of Alfonso's final ratification of the treaty, but that it was likely to go through was known. Indeed, Simon de Montfort himself had now arrived back in England to say so. As a result, plans to muster an army to sail out to Gascony and succour the king were abandoned. An attempt was still made to get a tax from the lower clergy, whose proctors had been summoned to the parliament. They did indeed agree to give the king the first year of the crusading tenth but only if the pope consented, which was hardly likely.[126] If a parallel attempt was made to get a tax from the two knightly representatives elected in each county, it achieved nothing. Since the army had been abandoned, it was only logical that the tax from those not in the army should be abandoned also.[127]

---

[122] *RG*, i, no. 2411 (*CPR 1247–58*, 274.)

[123] For Henry's personal efforts to persuade Alfonso that he really was seeking a commutation of his vow to Africa, see *CR 1253–4*, 275, 316; *CR 1254–6*, 390.

[124] *F*, 297–8; *DD*, no. 270.

[125] *F*, 299–301; *DD*, nos. 271–4.

[126] *C&S*, i, 482–3. For the parliament, see Paris, v, 440; Maddicott, *Origins of the English Parliament*, 213–4, 470.

[127] For the election of the knights, see *CR 1253–4*, 42, and Maddicott, 'Earliest known knights of the shire'. For a fascinating case before the parliament about the liberties of St Albans abbey, see Paris, *GA*, i, 338–46. The queen, Earl Richard, the judges, the barons of the exchequer, the king's council and 'nearly all the bishops and magnates of the kingdom' were involved in the case and the final judgement in St Albans' favour.

Eleanor was now to join her husband. She sailed from Portsmouth on 29 May, taking with her both her sons. Edward was to marry Eleanor of Castile, and then assume the government of Gascony. Edmund, if all went well, was to become king of Sicily. With the queen were Archbishop Boniface, Walter de Cantilupe, bishop of Worcester, Richard de Clare, earl of Gloucester (now reconciled to the king), and a substantial contingent of knights and magnates. Letters of protection were issued to over 120 men, including John de Warenne and Edmund de Lacy, who went by land.[128] Eleanor also brought money, including £3,228 in silver coin and plate, and gold worth, in silver, some £10,880.[129] Henry had at last accepted that his gold treasure must be spent.

Richard of Cornwall remained behind in charge of the home government. He had not needed to fulfil his boast of coming out with 300 knights but he remained supportive of his brother. In March he loaned another 4,000 marks on security of the last part of the gold treasure.[130]

During his period as regent, Richard certainly looked after himself. He vigorously upheld the liberties of his honour of Wallingford.[131] He inspired the litigation in which the king made good his right to the valuable manor of Longborough in Gloucestershire, this at the expense of Roger de Mortimer. The manor was then assigned by the queen to Richard, and the following year he and Sanchia received it in hereditary right.[132] Richard also took an undercover payment of £100 to help St Albans abbey in a lawsuit and extracted 600 marks from London to settle a dispute over the mint.[133] But Richard's rule went beyond self-interest. His vision and wisdom had been shown in the summoning of knights to parliament, in his advice about Magna Carta and in the 'national' terms in which he tried to rally support for Gascony. He now took over the reins of government with remarkable vigour and perception, giving a striking demonstration of how different his kingship would have been from his brother's.[134]

Whereas the government under the queen had hardly moved beyond Westminster and Windsor (she was of course first pregnant and then recovering from pregnancy), Richard went on a tour to the Welsh marches, going via Oxford and coming back via Northampton. He held parliaments at Oxford and Windsor, at the former settling a dispute between Winchelsea and Yarmouth.[135] He ensured the impoverished abbey of

[128] CPR 1247–58, 374–7; Paris, v, 446–7; Tewkesbury, 154.

[129] RG, i, no. 3874 (CPR 1247–58, 314–5).

[130] CPR 1247–58, 364; CR 1253–4, 123.

[131] SCWR, 107–8.

[132] Carpenter, 'A noble in politics', 189–90. For the acquisition of the manor of Barford in Wiltshire, see CR 1253–4, 13, 24, 187.

[133] Paris, GA, i, 346. FitzThedmar, 21; CFR 1253–4, no. 944.

[134] For notice of this period, see Denholm-Young, Richard of Cornwall, 79–80.

[135] CR 1253–4, 136–7, 140–1; FitzThedmar, 21.

Selby was treated with 'justice and mercy' during a vacancy.[136] He sacked the sheriff of Yorkshire and made him give reparation for what he had unjustly taken 'from diverse people'.[137] He punished resistance to royal orders, even acting against the abbot of Westminster.[138] As far as can be seen, Richard did not follow up the king's instructions to proclaim Magna Carta but he took steps to see magnates obeyed it in their dealings with their own men, as Henry had ordered.[139] Richard also set an example by abolishing the fish weirs on his rivers in accordance with the Charter.[140]

THE END OF THE GASCON CAMPAIGN

Henry was overjoyed by the arrival of the queen and Edward. Still at Meilhan, he gave a robe to the messenger of the archbishop of Bordeaux who brought the news, and acquired cloths of gold for the pair to offer in local churches.[141] Henry received a further boost with the arrival in July of the justiciar of Ireland, John fitzGeoffrey, and £1,533 of Irish treasure. In August another £3,114 arrived from England.[142] The news of Alfonso's resignation and the terms obtained for his partisans did not end the revolt at once, but events steadily moved in that direction. In June, Henry took the homage of Esquivat de Chabanais for the county of Bigorre. He also summoned an army from the towns and advanced north to Bergerac on the Dordogne, remaining camped outside the town until mid-July. He thus asserted his rights as chief lord of the town following the death of Elyas Ridel, and sought to prevent it falling to Reginald de Pons, married to Elyas's daughter, but in the allegiance of the king of France.[143]

From Bergerac, Henry returned southwards and from 23 July until 6 August he was in camp again at Gironde just west of La Réole. He was careful to avoid provocations and issued instructions that no one, man or woman, should be disseized without his special order or without judgement of his court. But at the same time the king summoned forces from the towns to muster at La Réole on 4 and 5 August.[144] The combination of conciliation and confrontation did the trick. On 4 August itself Henry

---

[136] *CR 1253–4*, 96–7; *CFR 1253–4*, no. 945; contrast Paris, v, 467.

[137] *CR 1253–4*, 143; *CPR 1247–58*, 372.

[138] *CR 1253–4*, 49–50, 91–2, 132.

[139] *CR 1253–4*, 139.

[140] John of Wallingford (2), 131; *CR 1253–4*, 142.

[141] *CR 1253–4*, 247–8, 250, 304.

[142] *RG*, i, nos. 3869, 3905, 3936 (*CPR 1247–58*, 314, 317, 320).

[143] *CR 1253–4*, 74, 238–9, 305–6. For the affair, see Trabut-Cussac, *L'Administration Anglaise*, xxxviii–ix; Bémont's introduction to *RG*, i, suppl., cxi–xvi and nos. 4358–64, 4378, and *RG*, i, no. 3959 (which shows that Henry did not have possession in August). For the truce see BL Cotton Julius E 1 no. 227. The affair rumbled on for years and post-1259 came before the parlement of Paris.

[144] *CR 1253–4*, 260, 306.

pardoned Gaillard de Solers and his allies, restored their possessions and allowed them to live in Bordeaux. This concession included the period of their quarrel with Simon de Montfort, since that was not covered by the settlement with the king of Castile.[145] Next day, 5 August, peace was formally proclaimed. At the prayers of the king of Castile, Henry announced that he had remitted his anger against Gaston de Béarn, the vicomtes of Fronsac, Benauges and Castillon, the men of La Réole, the Ladils of Bazas, William de Pins, prior of Le Mas d'Agenais, and the men in the other towns who had supported Alfonso's cause. A little later Henry agreed to ransom the Pins still in Montfort's prison.[146] He also pardoned the leaders who had tried to rouse Bayonne in Alfonso's cause.[147] In seeing through these restorations, John Mansel played a leading part. They were followed both at Bordeaux and Bayonne by attempts to ban factional confederations.[148] At Bordeaux, in a 'dictum and arbitrium' issued in October, Henry ordered all documents about the confederations of the Coloms and Solers to be burnt, and expressed the hope that marriages would make peace between them. Although the Coloms retained control of the mayoralty, the Solers reappeared amongst the jurats who formed the town council.[149] Montfort's foolish attempt to destroy them was at an end. Henry had a further success, one helping to affirm his authority on the frontiers of Gascony. In mid-September he gave Gerard d'Armagnac an annual fee of 100 marks and received his homage for the counties of Armagnac and Fézensac, securing custody for five years of the strategic castle of Lavardens north-west of Auch.[150]

The general settlement in Gascony took time to implement and disputes continued about the restoration of property. The vicomtes of Castillon and Fronsac felt hard done by. The Alfonsonist faction in Bayonne had to appeal again for his help.[151] But on the whole the settlement worked and meant a new start in Gascony's history. William de Pins, prior of Le Mas d'Agenais, was soon involved in rebuilding the churches in La Réole and later entered the king's service and became a much employed diplomat.[152] Gaston was not formally released from Alfonso's homage until May 1255, but later in the year he gave his third daughter to Edward to be married. He did not become seneschal of Gascony, but he recovered Roquefort and the homage of Bernard de Ladils in the Bazadais.[153]

[145] *RG*, i, no. 4275; *CPR 1247–58*, 352–3.

[146] *RG*, i, nos. 4281–5; *CPR 1247–58*, 319, 337, 352–3.

[147] *RG*, i, nos. 3925, 3954 (*CPR 1247–58*, 318, 321); *CR 1253–4*, 311.

[148] *F*, 310; *RG*, i, no. 4139 (*CPR 1247–58*, 338).

[149] *RG*, i, suppl., no. 4552; *CR 1253–4*, 318–19. See the analysis of the settlement in Marsh, *English Rule in Gascony*, 147–8.

[150] *RG*, i, nos. 4065, 4299–300 (*CPR 1247–58*, 350–1, 378).

[151] *CPR 1247–58*, 453, 500, 506, 629, 639–40.

[152] *RG*, i, suppl., no. 4641; *CPR 1258–66*, 109, 124, 243, 260, 264, 266, 380.

[153] *RG*, i, suppl., no. 4610; Ellis, 'Gaston de Béarn', 207–8, 217–21, 224–8.

Edward himself, as the new ruler of Gascony, was fully involved in the settlement. He issued his own letters of pardon to the rebels and made a ceremonial entry into La Réole itself on 5 August. In October, on his way to Castile, he entered Bayonne and promulgated the ban on factions.[154] It was his marriage of course which had made all this possible. Henry had hoped it might take place in Castile on 13 October, the feast of the translation of the Confessor, but things had been left too late for that.[155] It was finally celebrated in the royal monastery of Las Huelgas in Burgos on 1 November. On the same day Alfonso knighted Edward and resigned all his claims to Gascony. Those with Edward included Richard de Clare, earl of Gloucester, John de Warenne, the future earl of Surrey, Walter de Cantilupe, bishop of Worcester, and Peter de Montfort. Peter was to die fighting against Edward and Warenne at Evesham. Walter said mass for the doomed Montfortian army before the battle.

Henry was immensely proud of his son and promised £5 a year in land to the envoy who brought the 'happy' news of his knighting.[156] Edward at fifteen had yet to reach his impressive stature, but that he was strong, vigorous and intelligent must already have been clear. Edward, in his letters, called himself 'Edward first born son and heir of lord Henry, illustrious king of England'.[157] He never received another title such as duke of Gascony or earl of Chester. There was no point. It was as the son and heir of the king that he gained his status and his power.[158]

On Edward's return from Castile in November, Henry had already left Gascony. Edward was to remain there for nearly a year, returning to England at the end of October 1255. During that time he and his agents were the immediate rulers of Gascony. Edward enjoyed all Gascony's revenues and also (by a decision of the king and council in September) 'all escheats of the land'.[159] When banning factions in Bayonne, he described himself as Henry's son and heir 'already reigning in Gascony as prince and lord'.[160] Edward's precise constitutional position, however, was never defined either in Gascony or the rest of his appanage. Henry still possessed overall authority. He had granted Gascony to Edward 'saving the allegiance to the king'. He retained the ultimate power to appoint officials and still expected oaths of loyalty (as at Bayonne) to be taken to himself as well as to Edward. His insistence that Gascony (and thus everything within it) should not be separated from the crown of England restricted Edward's powers of

[154] Trabut-Cussac, *L'Administration Anglaise*, 4–5.

[155] *CR 1253–4*, 154–5.

[156] *RG*, i, suppl., lxxvi–vii, no. 56.

[157] For example, in an original writ sewn onto the exchequer memoranda roll: TNA E 159/31, m. 13d.

[158] For a discussion of his title, see Prestwich, *Edward I*, 11–12, and for a different emphasis, see Studd, 'The Lord Edward and Henry III'.

[159] *RG*, i, no. 4099 (*CPR 1247–58*, 334).

[160] *F*, 310; Trabut-Cussac, *L'Administration Anglaise*, 8.

patronage.[161] Edward's first seneschal of Gascony, appointed by the end of October 1254, was Stephen Bauzan, a household knight of the king, who was close to the queen and had come over from France with her.[162] As Edward grew older he found his parents' control increasingly irksome.[163] The situation in Gascony itself remained fragile. In May 1255, Henry had to hurry out forces because, so he said, Edward was in great danger, partly the result of disturbances following an attempt to raise a hearth tax.[164] In July 1255, Henry averred that Bergerac was still wavering in its allegiance. It was vital not to give Gascons cause 'to depart from our faith'. In the event, Edward managed to secure Bergerac, even capturing Reginald de Pons, and proved Henry's fears about the Gascons deserting unjustified.[165]

HENRY'S ACHIEVEMENT

Matthew Paris was scornful of Henry's achievement in Gascony. He had only secured what was his already and this at a gigantic expense.[166] By contrast, the annals of Winchester praised Henry for 'subjugating' Gascony. Thomas Wykes was equally positive. Henry had taken castles 'wickedly' held against him, and solidified everything through all the province, necessarily spending large sums of money.[167] Henry's achievement was indeed great. Before his arrival there was a very real danger of Gascony slipping into the hands of Gaston de Béarn and Alfonso of Castile. Henry had prevented that disaster and laid the foundations for another 200 years of English rule. Edward's marriage had been important in removing the threat from Alfonso, but the latter would never have abdicated his claim had Henry not been already on his way to victory. Henry had won through both by military action, notably the long siege of Benauges, and by appeasement. In the end his opponents were not punished but pardoned and reintegrated into the life of the province. In this his conduct was very different from Simon de Montfort's.

Henry owed his success to support within Gascony itself. Well might he praise the citizens of Bordeaux, who 'have served us laudably and

---

[161] *RG*, i, no. 3973 (*CPR 1247–58*, 323); *F*, 301. For orders to Edward, see *RG*, i, suppl., lxxiv–ix, nos. 25, 32–4, 43–4, 57, 63, and for Ireland, no. 69 (*CPR 1247–58*, 380–1, 384, 389). For Henry asking for Edward's consent to acts of patronage, see *RG*, i, nos. 2235, 2479 (*CPR 1247–58*, 282).

[162] *CR 1253–4*, 282; *RG*, i, suppl., lxxxiii, no. 13 (*CPR 1247–58*, 379); *CLR 1245–51*, 309; *CPR 1247–58*, 376; Howell, *Eleanor of Provence*, 125.

[163] This is a major theme in Studd, 'The Lord Edward and King Henry III'.

[164] Trabut-Cussac, *L'Administration Anglaise*, 12.

[165] *CR 1254–6*, 207–8. For the affair, see Trabut-Cussac, *L'Administration Anglaise*, xxxviii–ix; Bémont's introduction to *RG*, i, suppl., cxi–cxvi, and *RG*, i, no. 3959, and *RG*, ii, nos. 4358–64, 4378. The affair rumbled on for years and post-1259 came before the parlement of Paris.

[166] Paris, v, 450–1.

[167] Winchester, 94; Wykes, 105.

faithfully, and for the defence of our land have frequently sustained great damages and expenses, exposing themselves to many dangers'.[168] In the south, Bayonne, Gascony's second city, was also the king's, if less securely, as were Dax and St Sever. The loyalist towns supplied Henry with office-holders: the aptly named Stephen le Engleys, a citizen of Bordeaux, took charge of the forest around Bordeaux and the revenues of those expelled from the city.[169] More importantly, the towns supplied Henry with troops. In September 1253, Henry asked Bordeaux to provide him with not less than 3,000 men equipped with bows and other arms.[170] The towns were also prepared to supply Henry with loans 'in his great necessity'. The debts Henry acknowledged during his time in Gascony amounted to many thousands of pounds. They ranged from £33 from the city of Dax (to help fortify the castle of Sault), £93 from St Sever, £580 from Bayonne, over £2,000 from the archbishop of Bordeaux and several thousand pounds from Bordeaux's citizens. From further afield Henry was able to borrow 2,000 marks from the merchants of Toulouse, £2,547 from those from Agen and another 2,000 marks from those of Lucca, an early tapping of their funds.[171] Henry also enjoyed the support of important nobles, who held local office and provided contingents of soldiers. Montfort's old ally Amauvin de Vayres became seneschal of southern Gascony[172]. Elias Ridel, lord of Bergerac, and his brother were paid for maintaining twenty-five knights and twenty sergeants-at-arms in the king's service.[173]

Behind all this support lay the factor which had always bound Gascony to England, the wine trade. When the citizens of Bordeaux in February 1254 secured their royal charter, it was all about ensuring that the king paid promptly for their wines while limiting his right of prise, his right, that is, to compulsorily purchase wine at low rates.[174] If the charter revealed grievances, the fact that the citizens paid 2,000 marks cash down for it, shows how vital was their English trade. Henry likewise conciliated merchants by freeing the contents of individual ships from prise alto-gether. He did the same for nobles such as Amauvin de Vayres and Elyas Ridel, thus showing the lords of Gascony were as much involved in the wine trade as were the townsmen. Viticulture was less prevalent in the south of Gascony, but since Bayonne provided the ships and the sailors for much of the trade it was equally tied into the English connection.

[168] *RG*, i, no. 2602. For other thanks, see *CR 1253–4*, 298.

[169] *CPR 1247–58*, 264–5.

[170] *CR 1253–4*, 289.

[171] These figures are based on the bonds recorded in the patent rolls, and see the summary given in Marsh, *English Rule in Gascony*, 141–3. The money was not all owed at the same time. It is difficult to give a precise figure because sometimes new bonds might embrace money in old ones.

[172] *CPR 1247–58*, 276.

[173] *RG*, i, nos. 2171, 2177–8 (*CPR 1247–58*, 251–2).

[174] *RG*, i, no. 2602.

In winning through, Henry owed a considerable debt to his foreign relatives, a debt he fulsomely acknowledged and amply repaid. Peter of Savoy was at court for ten of the eleven months between October 1253 and August 1254, and tops the list of those witnessing royal charters in the period, outside the household officials. William de Valence and Geoffrey de Lusignan were both there for eight months, and come in third and fourth in the same list. Guy de Lusignan was there for five months. The Lusignans were far more than courtiers for they led troops and lost horses in the king's service.[175] Henry wrote feelingly of William de Valence's many and great costs 'in staying in our service in Gascony', and made him again second only to Richard of Cornwall in the race for landed reward.[176] Likewise, he backdated a charter conceding £500 of land in Ireland to Geoffrey de Lusignan so that it came before the concession of the lordship to Lord Edward. Henry later made great efforts to see it was implemented despite Edward's opposition.[177]

Henry also owed much to the support of his English nobles. Both the earls of Norfolk and Hereford were active in the first phase of the campaign. Throughout its course the senior officials of the household were Robert Walerand and the brothers William and John de Grey, all from knightly families. After the two earls had gone home, Henry had with him an important group of men of baronial status who were prominent both at court and active out in the regions.[178] Henry appreciated their services (John fitzGeoffrey's were 'immense') and rewarded them with money fees and grants of markets, fairs, free warrens, deer and wine. At the end of the campaign in September 1254 it was a group of English magnates who agreed to undergo imprisonment if Henry did not pay his debts: John fitzGeoffrey, Peter de Montfort, John de Burgh, John de Warenne, Stephen Longespée and Roger of Mold.[179]

Underpinning Henry's success lay money, the expenditure of it and the promise of it. During his time in Gascony, he made around sixty grants of money fees to Gascon nobles and others further afield. The total annual cost (if the promises were fulfilled) was around £2,000. In the same period, leaving aside his obligations to Simon de Montfort, he made around thirty grants of fees to his English supporters, worth around £900

[175] CR 1253–4, 229–30; RG, i, no. 2460 (CPR 1247–58, 279). Fourth place in the witness list table was taken by John de Plessis, earl of Warwick.

[176] CR 1253–4, 214–15, 253, 303–4.

[177] CR 1253–4, RG, i, nos. 2382, 2398, 2579, 3813; RG, i, suppl., lxxviii, no. 68 (CPR 1247–58, 271, 273, 291, 308, 384).

[178] The list includes Roger of Mold, John de Burgh, Robert de St John, William de Cantilupe III, John de Courteny, John fitzGeoffrey, Philip Marmion, John de Vaux, Hamon Lestrange, William Bardolph, Stephen Longespée, John fitzAlan, Humphrey de Bohun junior, Patrick de Chaworth, Roger de Somery, Gilbert of Seagrave, Peter de Montfort, Ralph de Camoys, Robert Tregoz, William de Beauchamp and Hamo Crevequer.

[179] RG, i, no. 4302 (CPR 1247–58, 357–8).

a year. Ultimately, as in 1242–3, both the merchants who loaned money and gave goods on credit, and the nobles promised fees and wages, knew that Henry *could* pay, for he had solid and regular sources of income. Short of ready cash though he sometimes was, in Gascon terms Henry was rich. In Gascony itself he had the proceeds from the great and small customs,[180] the mint (which he reinvigorated)[181] and a series of scattered revenues from towns and surrounding bailiwicks. Forty-five sergeants-at-arms were to be paid from those of Meilhan; other payments were made from the issues of Entre-Deux-Mers, Barsac, Belin, St-Macaire and the isle of Oléron.[182] There were also, far more important, the revenues from England. Many of Henry's debts were to be paid either in England from the issues of the exchequer or in Gascony once treasure from England arrived. After the £15,000 taken with him, £8,706 were sent out in October 1253; a further £14,200 in June 1254; £1,533 from Ireland in July; and then another £3,114 in August. A total of £42,458.[183] More than anything else, this explains how Henry held on to Gascony. The sum indeed was larger than that raised by the great tax to save Gascony in 1225.

THE END OF THE SICILIAN AFFAIR?

In May 1254, Pope Innocent had confirmed the concession of the Sicilian kingdom made to Henry by Master Albert of Parma. In doing so he did not conceal the magnitude of the task. Henry needed to send Edmund to Sicily with an army absolutely as soon as possible in order to wrest the kingdom from Conrad. Yet the situation was soon to be transformed. On 24 May, Conrad died. Some of the pope's advisers, as Innocent told Henry, urged the grant to Edmund now be cancelled. He was no longer needed. The kingdom would simply fall into the pope's hands. Innocent was less sure. Manfred, Conrad's half-brother, Frederick II's illegitimate son, had a powerful position in the kingdom and might well seek to take Conrad's place. So the pope still urged Henry to send Edmund with all speed.[184]

Henry needed no convincing. Unless Edmund could make a powerful 'adventus', there was every chance that either Manfred or the pope would secure the kingdom without him. Yet Henry was well aware that he completely lacked the resources to do anything of the kind. He made this perfectly clear in an extraordinary meeting with Master Albert when the

---

[180] *CPR 1247–58*, 264–5. See above, 496.

[181] *CR 1253–4*, 167; *CPR 1247–58*, 247–8.

[182] *CR 1253–4*, 301–2.

[183] *CLR 1251–60*, 150; *RG*, i, nos. 3874, 3905, 3936 (*CPR 1247–58*, 314–15, 317, 320). In addition, Richard of Cornwall lent Henry £2,666 in March 1254 for Gascon affairs, but it is not clear whether this was received in Gascony: *CPR 1247–58*, 364.

[184] *Reg. Alexandre IV*, iii, no. 3036 (92–3); *F*, 297, 301–3.

latter arrived with the papal confirmation. As instructed by Pope Innocent, Albert urged Henry to send Edmund 'as soon as possible with a strong force to prosecute the affair vigorously and powerfully as befits so great a prince'.[185] In reply Henry was devastatingly frank. 'Viva voce', he declared he did not have the money for the enterprise and 'openly confessed his weakness and impotence'.[186] But Henry also had a solution, namely for him to be given the proceeds of the crusading tax. Having made this suggestion, Henry went on to ask Albert 'both politely and impolitely' to confirm the grant of the kingdom to Edmund. Albert, however, refused. 'Seeing the weakness and impotence of the king, which publicly he admitted, and understanding that the affair needed speed, I did not make the renewal and proceeded no further in the business.' As a result, 'the king took back the letters which he had caused before to be presented to me'. The identity of these letters is unclear. Henry certainly did not resign his claim to the kingdom at this point, but perhaps he took back letters in which he had entered into commitments in relation to the offer.

When the pope heard Master Albert's report, it must have confirmed what he already suspected. Even in May 1254, when he ratified the gift to Edmund, Innocent was beginning to doubt whether Henry would really come up with the military goods. In his letters of that month, he begged the queen and Peter of Savoy to see that Henry did indeed prosecute the project 'vigorously and powerfully'. Observing that a great deal of money was needed for the enterprise, he made Henry's readiness to save, by reducing his 'pious expenses', a test of his good faith.[187] The reason why Innocent promised Henry so much less than Charles of Anjou was probably because he realized it might just be throwing good money after bad. The same consideration explains the pope's refusal to let Henry have the crusading tax. The one thing he was not going to do was pay all the expenses himself and hand Edmund the Sicilian kingdom on a plate. The most Innocent did, when confirming the gift in May 1254, was to agree the tax should be levied for five years rather than the previous three. It was to be kept in a safe place and expended for the business of the Holy Land, as the pope decided.[188] This clearly left open the possibility that Innocent might still divert the tax to Sicily, if, that is, Henry showed himself deserving by making a real effort of his own. When Master Albert saw Henry could make no such effort, he concluded the whole enterprise was at an end.[189]

[185] *Reg. Alexandre IV*, iii, no. 3036 (92–3); *F*, 301.

[186] *Reg. Alexandre IV*, iii, no. 3036 (93). This is in a later report Albert wrote for Pope Alexander. We have no date for the meeting, but as Albert was bringing the papal confirmation of May 1254 it probably took place in Gascony during the summer. However, Montaubin, 'Royaume de Sicile', 179, thinks it might have been later.

[187] *F*, 302–3.

[188] *F*, 303.

[189] Paris, v, 458–9, asserts that Henry sent Innocent substantial sums of his own money in 1254, but there is no documentary evidence for that.

For all practical purposes, Innocent drew the same conclusions. In the ebb and flow of his struggle against Manfred in the second half of 1254, he made inroads into the Hohenstaufen camp and built up a substantial body of supporters, or seeming supporters.[190] But none of his concessions made any reference to Edmund. The pope was recruiting for himself.[191] Not surprisingly, the negotiations over the precise terms on which Edmund was to hold the kingdom, never took place or at least never reached a conclusion.[192] When Henry did at last make a move, it showed how right Innocent was. In November there arrived in Italy, to take possession of the kingdom on Edmund's behalf, the archbishop of Embrun and Bishop Aigueblanche. They were equipped not with a military force but simply with letters telling everyone to obey them. How this was to be achieved was not said, although Aigueblanche was allowed to borrow the princely sum of 300 marks.[193] It is difficult to think of anything less like the thundering 'adventus', terrifying enemies and encouraging friends, that Innocent had envisaged. In a letter to Henry on 17 November he made no reference to Edmund at all, but said that if Henry hurried he would still be able to have 'the thing' (whatever that was) and 'we will be able to assign it to you', which, of course, implied it had not been assigned already. The pope went on to warn Henry that unless he hurried he would have to concede 'the thing' to someone else.[194] The Sicilian affair looked as good as over and so much the better for that.

HENRY'S VISIT TO FONTEVRAUD, PONTIGNY AND PARIS

With the war in Gascony 'sedata', as he said in a letter of 31 August, Henry began to plan his arrival back in England. He sent orders for the purchase of jewels to offer at the feretory of the Confessor and the shrine of Thomas of Canterbury. The former were to cost £100, the latter merely to be 'fitting'.[195] At the start of October, Earl Richard had the streets of London cleaned and cleared for the king's reception.[196] He was, however, out of touch, for Henry's plans had changed. He was about to undertake the happiest and most politically consequential visit of his reign.[197]

---

[190] See Weiler, *Henry III of England and the Staufen Empire*, 149–50.

[191] See, for example, *F*, 311–12; *Reg. Innocent IV*, iii, no. 8268.

[192] This is why no record survives of the terms and why in 1255 Henry III replaced his 1254 negotiating team with a new one, without any indication it had reached a conclusion: *F*, 317–18.

[193] *RG*, i, nos. 4187, 4212–13; *CPR 1247–58*, 343–4.

[194] *F*, 312.

[195] *CR 1253–4*, 275.

[196] *CR 1253–4*, 98–9.

[197] The major narrative sources for Henry's visit to France are Burton, 327–9, and Paris, v, 475–84.

Throughout the summer of 1254, Henry had been pressing for a safe conduct so as to fulfil his long-vowed pilgrimage to Saint Edmund at Pontigny.[198] By the end of August, with Louis IX now back in France from his crusade, permission was given and Louis also suggested something else. Why not come and visit me in Paris?[199] Henry was overjoyed. As Matthew Paris observed, he longed to meet both Louis and Queen Margaret. Eleanor, of course, was invited too and felt exactly the same. This would be a meeting of sisters who were queens as well as of kings married to sisters. There was another attraction, as Matthew Paris explained. Henry wished to see France itself, its cities and churches, and the 'incomparable' royal chapel in the capital built to house the crown of thorns. Here he was 'le touriste exceptionnel'.[200] And there was one other special place Henry wished to see. On the way to Pontigny and Paris, he would be able to visit the great nunnery at Fontevraud where his grandfather and grandmother Henry II and Eleanor of Aquitaine, his uncle Richard the Lionheart and his mother, Isabella of Angoulême, lay buried.

It was, however, a long time before Henry could actually set forth. He was detained in Gascony by his debts, having taken an oath not to leave until his creditors were satisfied. The only way to escape was by borrowing more money. Between 19 September and 29 October he managed to raise £6,840 from the archbishop and citizens of Bordeaux and the citizens of Agen. Repayment was secured on specified English revenues and the gifts Henry would receive on his return to England.[201]

Henry finally left Bordeaux early in November 1254. He soon heard upsetting news from England. The workers at Westminster Abbey had deserted for lack of pay! In response, Henry sent urgent orders to put matters right and stressed he still wanted the Abbey consecrated on the feast of the Confessor's translation in 1255, although he no longer said this would be before his departure on crusade.[202] Henry issued the order about the Abbey at Cognac in the Saintonge. From there he progressed through Poitou into the Touraine and by 15 November was at Fontevraud. Were there, one wonders, aged nuns who still remembered his father's visit to the monastery in 1199 when Bishop Hugh of Lincoln had pointed to the Last Judgement scene sculpted above the doorway and warned King John not to be amongst the kings being dragged down to the fires of hell?[203] John had assured Hugh he would be with the kings on the other side going

---

[198] CR 1253–4, 244; RG, i, no. 3859 (CPR 1247–58, 312). For Henry's relations with Edmund, see above, 215, 420, 476, and Creamer, 'St Edmund of Canterbury and Henry III'.

[199] CPR 1247–58, 326.

[200] Paris, v, 475–6; Le Goff, Saint Louis, 576.

[201] RG, i, nos. 4294, 4302, 4306–7; RG, i, suppl., lxxii–iii, lxxxii, nos. 8, 17, 97 (CPR 1247–58, 353, 357–8, 378–9, 384).

[202] BA, 194 (CPR 1247–58, 381).

[203] Adam of Eynsham, 140–1. In Henry's entourage was his steward Ralph fitzNicholas, who had been a household knight under John.

up to heaven, but Henry must often have wondered where his father really was. Having entered the church, Henry prayed and offered precious cloths at the tombs of Henry II, Richard and Eleanor. Their imposing and impassive effigies radiated a power and authority so much greater than that he now possessed. John by contrast, after the loss of the continental empire, was buried not at Fontevraud, but needs must at Worcester, under a very English purbeck marble effigy. How the dynasty had fallen, how Henry had failed to restore its fortunes! Whether or not Henry had such thoughts, he was deeply moved by his visit for he decided his heart should be buried beside his ancestors. He also had his mother's body moved from the cemetery to the church and commissioned the present effigy, which covers her tomb. There Isabella appears with her hands folded quietly on her breast, some contrast to her far from quiet life.[204]

From Fontevraud, Henry journeyed 120 miles north-east to Orléans, where he arrived on 24 November. There he was met by Louis himself. The nearest Henry had come to a meeting before was at Taillebourg when he stared across the Charente at the oriflamme flying above Louis's tents. Now, seeing one another for the first time, the two kings rushed into each other's arms, kissing and embracing, and then engaged in excited and amicable conversation. After three days of celebrations, Louis offered to accompany Henry to Pontigny, only for Henry tactfully to decline, pointing to Louis's exhaustion having come back from his crusade. On the journey eastwards to Pontigny (some 115 miles from Orléans), the French nobles along the way pressed their hospitality on Henry, as Louis encouraged them to do. Henry declined much of it but stressed that, far from looking down on the French (as was suggested), it was an immense privilege and pleasure to be meeting their illustrious king. Henry wished to impress everyone with the splendour of his kingship. He did not want it dulled by seeming to be dependent on anyone else. If Matthew Paris can be believed, the French indeed admired the size of his company with its 1,000 fine horses and many more in the baggage train. Fortunately, Richard de Clare had now arrived to swell the throng. The only drawback was that by the time Henry reached Pontigny he had run out of money. He had to borrow the wax (worth 47 marks) for candles and could only promise 60 marks in the future to provide food for the monks.[205] The long low church itself was little different from when Becket and Langton, in their exiles, had worshipped there. Praying now before the shrine, Henry could thank Saint Edmund for rescuing his kingship in 1234 and curing his illness in 1252. He could show there was nothing in their later differences and reclaim the saint for England and the dynasty.

---

[204] In 1250, Henry asked the religious houses in Normandy to inscribe his mother's name in their martyrologies and celebrate masses for her, especially on her anniversary: *CPR 1247–58*, 75, 89.

[205] *RG*, i, suppl., no. 66 (*CPR 1247–58*, 384); *CLR 1251–60*, 205–6.

Henry arrived on the south-eastern outskirts of Paris on 6 December and put up at the monastery of Saint Maur-des-Fossés. Next day, the register of Eudes Rigaud, archbishop of Rouen, recorded how he had 'gone to meet the king of England coming to Paris'. Doubtless Eudes was one of a large reception party conducting the king into the city. Henry was greeted by the scholars of the university, led by the English contingent, bearing tapers, singing songs and wearing festive robes. Around them the whole city was decorated and illuminated.[206] Louis insisted that Henry should stay with him in the royal palace on the Île de la Cité. When Henry demurred, Louis laughed and said, 'I am lord and king in my kingdom and I wish to prevail!'[207]

At the palace, the kings and queens dined together in the hall and were together at night.[208] Henry was taken by Louis round the Saint Chapelle, 'the most beautiful chapel in the court of the king of France', as Matthew Paris put it. Henry prayed there, honoured the relics and made royal offerings. Henry also went on a tour round the city. He saw 'the great bridge' over the Seine, the remarkable houses three or four stories high, and (although Paris does not mention this) obviously too the cathedral of Notre-Dame. All the while people thronged the streets and hung out of windows, hoping to catch a glimpse of the English king.

Henry did not stay long at the royal palace. Louis, sensitive to his needs, asked whether he would like to move instead to the more spacious quarters offered by the Old Temple, situated on the right bank just opposite the Île de la Cité.[209] Henry accepted the invitation and could now put on his own show, helped by the timely arrival of 4,000 marks from England.[210] On the morning after his arrival at the Temple, he had the buildings filled with paupers, all of whom enjoyed an abundance of food and wine. Here Henry was displaying one of the most characteristic and distinctive features of piety, there being no sign Louis went in for these Henrician-style mass feedings.[211] At the Temple, Henry also threw an absolutely stupendous feast. It was held in the great hall where the walls were decorated with heraldic shields, one being that of Richard the

---

[206] Paris, v, 477, makes much of the flower decorations, but how would there have been flowers in December?

[207] Paris, v, 481, and see Le Goff, *Saint Louis*, 449 and n. 4. In what follows I have altered Matthew Paris's account of events in Paris in light of the evidence for Henry's whereabouts given by the attestation clauses of royal letters and in view of the statement in Burton, 329, that Henry moved to the Temple after he had stayed at the palace.

[208] Burton, 329: 'pariter pernoctantes'.

[209] Despite Matthew Paris's specific statement that Henry's residence was the Old Temple, previous commentators, including myself, have thought Henry stayed at the new quarters of the Templars to the north of the city walls. The Old Temple, as Paris stated, was beside the Place de Grève, now the Place Hôtel-de-Ville. All this has been clarified for the first time by Amicie Pelissie du Rausas in her doctoral thesis.

[210] *CPR 1247–58*, 382, 386; *CLR 1251–60*, 184–5.

[211] See Carpenter, 'Meetings of kings', 16–18.

Lionheart. An English wag said the sight of it should put the French off their food!

The feast was attended by huge numbers of people for, in honour of Henry and Eleanor, Louis had summoned all the nobles of the kingdom to Paris. This was also a gathering of the royal families. The younger sisters of the two queens, Beatrice, married to Charles of Anjou, and Sanchia, married to Richard of Cornwall, had come.[212] So had their mother, Beatrice of Savoy, countess of Provence, whom Henry had always found so wonderful. There too were the king of Navarre, Theobald of Champagne, the dukes of Burgundy and Louvain, twenty-three arch-bishops and bishops, and twenty-seven earls and eighteen countesses.[213] Against this the English contingent (for all Paris's boasting) was actually rather small. There were no bishops, and only one real earl, Richard de Clare, earl of Gloucester and Hertford, admittedly second only to Richard of Cornwall, the greatest earl in the kingdom. For the rest there was John de Plessis, earl of Warwick, an assortment of magnates and ministers, and the king's half-brothers William de Valence and Geoffrey de Lusignan.[214] All the more important for Henry to put on a magnificent show.[215]

At the feast all were seated according to rank. On the high table the king of France sat centrally with the king of England and the king of Navarre on either side. Louis had tried to get Henry to take the central place, only for Henry to decline: 'No, it is more fitting for you to be there as you are my lord and will be', a graceful reference to the homage Henry hoped one day to give for his lost possessions. We can imagine Louis and Henry sometimes talking sotto voce, head to head, sometimes joining in the joyful clamour. The feast was indeed a magnificent success, at least if Matthew Paris can be believed. Although it was a 'fish day' (so presumably Friday 11 December), the variety of the dishes, the abundance of drink, the attentiveness of the servants and the status of the guests meant there had never been such a feast, so Paris affirmed, even in the days of Asshir (founder of Tyre), Arthur and Charlemagne.

After the feast, Henry despatched gifts of silver cups, gold brooches and silken belts to the French magnates at their lodgings.[216] The gift-giving generally during the Paris visit played a vital part in bonding the courts and the kingdoms. Queen Margaret's presents included a fantastic jewel shaped like a peacock and Louis's an elephant (Henry was soon making arrangements for its journey back to England).[217] One of the belts Henry

[212] Richard remained holding the fort in England.

[213] Burton, 329; Paris, v, 480. Paris, however, only gives twelve bishops.

[214] *CPR 1247–58*, 385–6.

[215] Le Goff, *Saint Louis*, 449–50, 637–9, wrongly ascribes the feast to Louis, but there is some wonderful writing here.

[216] Back in October, Henry had ordered 300 marks worth of 'pulcra et decencia', brooches, rings and jewels, to be sent out to him in France: *CR 1253–4*, 320.

[217] Paris, v, 489; Burton, 329; *CR 1254–6*, 34.

quite probably gave at this time survives, affording an insight into both the magnificence of his presents and his state of mind.[218] The recipient was Theobald of Navarre and Champagne, who gave the belt at some stage to Fernando de la Cerda, son of Alfonso X, king of Castile.[219] When Fernando's tomb at Las Huelgas was opened in 1942, the belt was found wrapped around his body.[220] The belt is made of braid, decorated with woven heraldic shields of English earls and barons divided from one another by silver gilt bars studded with pearls. This is fine enough but the chief glory of the belt lies in the silver gilt plates attached to either end so it could be fastened around the waist, one of the plates being hinged to a folding buckle, the other being the tongue. The buckle is decorated with pearls and sapphires, and displays Theobald's arms as count of Champagne, hence the certainty he was the recipient. The plate to which it was attached has the arms of the king of England, the king of France, Richard of Cornwall and the king of Navarre, the tongue those of the king of England, the king of France and the Clare earls of Gloucester and the Ferrers earls of Derby. Since on both buckle plate and tongue the arms of the king of England have pride of place, there is no doubt Henry was the donor. He thus assured Theobald of his friendship, whatever the stipulations about an attack on Navarre in the treaty with Castile. He also celebrated through the heraldic shields both his relationship with Louis and the community he shared with his English earls and barons. Louis had brought his nobles to Paris. Henry now demonstrated he had an equal relationship with his own men. In this gift to Theobald, in a very French setting, Henry wanted to stand forth as king of England. There were no shields of his Lusignan, Provencal and Savoyard kin. The belt was conceived very much in the spirit Henry and Richard of Cornwall had evoked when rallying support for Gascony: Henry had more trust in his own men than those from other lands.[221] If only he had given that impression more often during his personal rule.

On the evening of the feast, Henry left the Old Temple (the place must have needed a great deal of clearing up) and went to the great monastery

---

[218] For a detailed description of the belt (which I follow below) as well as a discussion of its significance and date, see Wild, 'Emblems and enigmas'. For a previous discussion, see Collin, *Riddle of a 13th-Century Sword-Belt*. The precise interpretation here is my own.

[219] This was Theobald II, king of Navarre and count of Champagne, who had succeeded on the death of his father, Theobald I, in 1253.

[220] I went to Las Huelgas to see the belt only to discover it was away being conserved in Madrid! There are many images of it online.

[221] The arms of the earls on the belt have been identified as those of the earls of Devon, Surrey, Hereford, Cornwall, Gloucester and Derby (the three last also on the tongue). The earl of Derby, William de Ferrers, had died in March 1254. Perhaps his son and heir, Robert (married to Mary de Lusignan), as a ward now in the king's custody, was in the Paris party, hence the prominence of his arms on the belt. For favours to Robert and Mary, see *CR 1254–6*, 39, 104, 109–10, 259, 340.

of Saint Denis, doubtless being met by a procession of the monks. There he could admire the tombs of Capetian kings stretching back now for centuries and merging seamlessly with those of their Carolingian and Merovingian predecessors.[222] It must have been hard not to think of the broken burials of his own dynasty and the chequered fortunes they reflected. No king had been buried at Westminster since the Confessor. There Henry must make a new start.

Henry left Saint Denis next day (Saturday 12 December) and travelled, with Louis in his company, the twenty-five miles to the royal castle at Beaumont-sur-Oise. Then with private words, kisses and embraces the two kings parted. Three days later Henry was at Amiens. By 18 December he was at Boulogne waiting for a fair wind to cross the channel. In terms of his reputation in England, Henry's time in the French kingdom had been a resounding success. The Burton annalist has Henry returning home 'with immense honour'. According to Matthew Paris, after the feast, his fame was praised to the skies, thanks to the generosity of his gifts, the bounty of the day and the copiousness of his almsgiving. His stay had cost all of £1,000 and greatly reduced his treasure, but 'the honour of the king of the English and of all the English was no little exalted and much augmented'.[223] Whether Henry's conduct really had the effect Paris imagined in France is unknown, thanks to the dearth of relevant sources, but for Henry the visit could not have come at a better time. After a successful campaign, he had secured Gascony for his son. Louis, by contrast, had returned from a crusade where he had lost his chief prize (Damietta) and suffered a period of captivity. There was far more equality between the kings than at any previous time in their reigns.

By far the most important legacy of Henry's visit was the intimate relationship formed between the royal families, between Henry and Eleanor and Louis and Margaret. Without it there would have been no peace of Paris in 1259. There were many differences between Henry and Louis in terms of status, situation and character. However much recent events had evened the balance between them, Louis was still regarded by Matthew Paris as 'the king of terrestrial kings', this thanks to 'his heavenly unction, his power and the standing of his knights'.[224] Physically the kings were very different. Henry was of average height, compact of body, with a drooping eyelid. Louis was tall, willowy, angel-faced. Henry was deserted by his mother, Louis trained under his mother's care. Henry was profligate in his gift-giving. Louis never forgot his grandfather's advice to reward people according to their deserts and say 'no' just as readily as 'yes'. Henry lacked Louis's fixity of purpose, hence he ended with no crusades to his

---

[222] The actual effigies were put up in the 1260s.

[223] Paris, v, 481–2.

[224] Paris, v, 480.

credit against Louis's two.[225] For all these differences, during their many meetings, public and private in 1254, a deep joyful and enduring bond formed between the two kings.[226] They flourished in each other's company. Later, writing to Louis about a visit in 1262, Henry asked to reside near him in Paris 'so that we can more easily be delighted by your conversation and presence' ('frui vestro colloquio et aspectu'). Such words can be conventional when describing meetings, yet in this case they catch a real truth. Similar language occurs in the Burton abbey description of the 1254 visit. Having met for the first time at Orléans, Henry expresses his joy at the prospect of seeing Louis again and being 'delighted and revived by his pleasant conversation'. The remark recalled the way Saul had been revived (again the word used is *refocillo*) by listening to David's lyre.[227] These feelings were mutual. Matthew Paris has Louis quoting the Psalms to Henry –'O how sweet are your words to my throat' – and lamenting that they might never meet again. In private conversations he confided to Henry his sorrows during the crusade and how he rejoiced more in the patience God had given him than if he had conquered all the world.[228] In Henry's company he was also able to relax and enjoy himself. He laughed and joked and had no difficulty combining his own 'ascèse alimentaire' with a 'commensalité royale'.[229] We know nothing of the role of the queens but that too must have been important. Judging from her later correspondence, Margaret struck up a very personal relationship with Henry, partly founded on a mutual sense of humour.[230] In 1263 she told him how her mind had fallen into grief and sorrow at his illness and how much she rejoiced at his recovery.[231]

This unity between the courts promised political consequences. In Matthew Paris's account of their conversation, Louis observed that he, Henry and their two brothers had all married sisters. Their children would thus be like brothers and sisters.[232] The justification Louis later gave for concluding the Treaty of Paris was in similar terms: there should be peace between families so closely connected.[233] In 1254, however, there remained a great obstacle to peace. Henry was still demanding the return of

---

[225] See below, 713–15, where the contrast is further discussed.

[226] For what follows, see Carpenter, 'Meetings of kings', 24–5.

[227] 1 Samuel 16:23.

[228] Paris, v, 482; psalms 103, 119. Louis also had conversations with Henry of a more political nature. It was at the 'instance' and for 'love' of Louis, who had 'much honoured' the king and queen on their journey through France, that Henry, at Beaumont-sur-Oise on 13 December, ordered Edward to release Reginald de Pons from captivity. The letter to Edward was authorized by Thomas of Savoy (!) and the king's council: *CR 1254–6*, 284.

[229] Le Goff, *Saint Louis*, 637–9.

[230] See above, 406–7.

[231] *DD*, no. 384.

[232] Paris, v, 481–2.

[233] Joinville, cap. 678.

Normandy and the rest of the Angevin empire. Louis, during Henry's visit, gave the impression of having some sympathy with the English case. Perhaps he was just being tactful. Certainly his fair words made no difference. The fact was, as Louis said, his magnates would never allow him to return the lost territories. So, until Henry accepted that unpalatable truth there could be no peace. At the end of 1254 it was hard to see how he might be brought to do so. The Sicilian project was soon to change all that.

Henry was deeply impressed by Louis IX, yet one thing Louis was doing seems to have had limited impact on him. It was unfortunately an area where some impact would have been very salutary. On his return from crusade, Louis had redoubled his efforts to give justice to his people. In December 1254, so at the very time of Henry's visit, he promulgated a great ordinance for the reform of the realm.[234] Running to twenty-six separate chapters, it was chiefly concerned with the malpractices of the king's local officials. They were to take an oath to maintain the rights of the crown and to abstain from giving or receiving bribes, all kinds of circumstances in which they might be tempted to do so being envisaged. They were also forbidden from demanding excessive hospitality, employing too many subordinates, depriving people of property unjustly, imposing new forms of taxation and forming local attachments likely to influence their conduct. They were to stay in their areas after leaving office so people could complain against them. Further provisions were devoted to stamping out blasphemy and immoral living. Henry himself had raised some of these issues in his speech to the sheriffs in 1250. It is possible that one reform in 1257, a new oath for his councillors, owed something to Louis's ordinance. But Henry issued no ordinance to reform the conduct of his local officials. That was left to the revolution of 1258.

What finally of the impact on Henry of the churches of France? He must have looked at them with intense interest and measured against them what he was doing at Westminster. Henry had longed to see the Sainte Chapelle and it was the first thing Louis showed him. A hall church, with the whole wall space dissolved into light by its great windows filled with stained glass, it was indeed 'incomparable'. There was certainly nothing like it in England. According to one satirical poem, Henry wished to take it home in a cart.[235] But was Henry so overawed? He could think he had built his own 'incomparable' building (Matthew Paris's word again) in the chapter house at the Abbey where again windows occupied all the wall space. Indeed, the chapter house in one crucial respect excelled its French rival. Because the vault was sprung at a higher level, it meant the windows were visible in their entirety from every viewpoint, instead of having their

---

[234] Joinville, caps. 694–719. For a discussion, see Jordan, *Louis IX and the Challenge of the Crusade*, 158–71; Le Goff, *Saint Louis*, 216–20.

[235] *Political Songs*, 67.

heads obscured by the springing of the vault.[236] The Sainte Chapelle, moreover, is a small building. Henry's own chapel was Westminster Abbey itself.[237] And the Abbey, of course, housed a relic in the portion of Christ's blood every bit as precious as the crown of thorns.

Henry also saw three great churches much more directly comparable to the Abbey: the cathedrals of Notre-Dame and Amiens and the abbey of Saint Denis. At Notre-Dame he surely looked admiringly at the western towers for he probably intended something similar at the Abbey. At Amiens he could compare the great west front with his own north transept doorway at Westminster. Henry must have been impressed by Amiens's great height: 139 feet to the top of the vault as opposed to the Abbey's 104 feet. He must also have admired the lovely foliated string course running beneath the triforium and the four light clerestory windows, as against (following Reims) the two light ones at the Abbey. Amiens also has a neatness, a precision, a refinement in its architectural details very foreign to the Abbey's more free and easy style. And yet there was much at Amiens that Henry may have questioned. It had nothing like Westminster's complex arch mouldings, Purbeck marble and profusion of diaper, and, while its east end was awkwardly formed with five narrow, squashed arcades, the three at the Abbey, following Reims, were so much more stately and harmonious.

How little the visit to France impacted architecturally on Henry, and how confident he was in his own ideas, became clear when the second phase of the work at Westminster Abbey started with the building of the new choir in 1259. Such changes as the adding of extra ribs to the vault and extra shafts to columns of the main arcade owed nothing to French examples. Henry also decided against replacing the two light Reims-style windows with the four light ones he had seen at Amiens and, on a larger scale, at Saint Denis. And he equally declined to follow perhaps the most spectacular development he had seen in France. At Amiens, in its first phase, behind the triforium arches, beautiful though they were, there was just an ugly blank wall. But in the later stages, going up during Henry's visit, the wall was replaced with windows, giving the whole structure a much lighter effect. At Saint Denis, the eastern parts of the church were being remodelled in the same way, thus creating, in junction with the clerestory windows, and the stained glass, an extraordinary array of coloured light. If, as is likely, Henry, designing the Abbey, knew from Henry de Reyns about these developments, he had rejected them. Instead, he went for a galleried triforium with windows in its external wall.[238] But, having now seen Saint Denis and Amiens, might he not change his mind and remodel the triforium of the choir and nave along their lines? He did

[236] I owe this point to Christopher Wilson: Wilson, 'Chapter house', 42–6.
[237] *CR 1251–3*, 226.
[238] See above, 340–1.

not do so. The galleried triforium continued after 1259, thus giving the church so much extra space and grandeur. The only change was to replace the great octafoil external windows with three cinquefoils, thus going for an even more decorative effect.[239] At the end of 1254, Henry could return to England thinking that at Westminster he was building a church equal to anything he had seen in France.

---

[239] The external windows of the galleried triforium at Notre-Dame have three roundels, but the two in the corners are small so the effect is unlike that at Westminster.

Chapter 12

THE LAST YEARS OF THE
PERSONAL RULE
1255–1257

Henry arrived at Dover on Sunday 26 December 1254. The large reception party, headed by Richard of Cornwall, had been waiting for a long time, but welcomed him 'with joy' and abundant presents. Dunstable priory's offering, handed over by its cellarer, was a silver gilt cup worth £5.[1] Henry in his turn feasted everyone at Canterbury on 29 December, the anniversary of Becket's death. The joy at Henry's arrival, testified to in several sources, was justified. He had been absent for well over a year and had returned, if not in triumph, then at least with substantial achievements to his credit. He had won the war in Gascony and established his son Edward, now married to Eleanor of Castile, as its ruler. Henry's reception and behaviour in Paris had honoured him and his kingdom. His subjects could soon marvel at the elephant given him by Louis IX, twice drawn by Matthew Paris, for which Henry constructed a special house at the Tower of London.[2] Had Henry died in 1255 he might have been viewed as a moderately successful king. How different it was to be three years and a few months later when a great revolution brought Henry's government crashing to the ground, ending the nearly twenty-five years of his personal rule.

From Canterbury, Henry travelled to London, making a ceremonial entry into the city on 3 January. Two days later he attended the feast of the Confessor at Westminster.[3] Henry must have inspected progress on the Abbey with intense interest. He had urged on the work in his absence, but was he disappointed with the results? At any rate, no more is heard of having the church ready for consecration on 13 October 1255. Until the end of April, Henry remained largely at Westminster apart from visits to Windsor. Probably it was there he saw for the first time his new daughter Katherine, born in November 1253.[4] In April, Henry ordered a great cloth

---

[1] *CR 1254–6*, 155.
[2] *CLR 1251–60*, 197, 245. See Cassidy and Clasby, 'Matthew Paris and Henry III's elephant'.
[3] For preparations, see *CR 1254–6*, 151–2.
[4] There is a chapter on Katherine in Armstrong, 'Royal and aristocratic women at the court of Henry III', where the nature of the illness from which she suffered is fully discussed.

of gold surrounded protectively 'with a beautiful border with the shields of the arms of the king' to be made so he could offer it for her in Westminster Abbey.[5]

Henry now had two major anxieties. About one he could do nothing. He could only wait on events in Italy and the papal court to see whether the Sicilian enterprise might be revived. The other anxiety was money. He needed it to pay off the voluminous debts he had incurred in Gascony, all the more so given Edward's early difficulties there.[6] Henry would need more money, much more, if he was indeed to send an army to Sicily.

Henry faced these challenges with a court seemingly more stable than in the early 1250s, or at least there were no longer open quarrels between the Lusignans and the Savoyards. The half-brothers remained prominent and Queen Eleanor had to face them with intermittent support from Peter of Savoy, for he was now absent for long periods. Archbishop Boniface too was rarely at court. But Henry, between 1255 and 1257, remained close to his queen and very concerned for her wealth and welfare. She drew strength from the Savoyards prominent in the king's household and from her control (as she liked to think) of the entourage of her eldest son.[7]

Henry could feel supported by the two most powerful native magnates, both tied in by marriages with his foreign relatives. Henry recognized how much he depended on his brother, and the queen's brother-in-law, Richard of Cornwall. Again and again in 1255 he referred to taking his brother's advice and that of other unnamed councillors, thus indicating Richard's pre-eminent place on the council. Also present at court was the only earl who could rival Cornwall's wealth and power. This was Richard de Clare, earl of Gloucester and Hertford. Clare had annoyed Henry by failing to join the Gascon expedition back in 1253. Perhaps he was irritated by Bristol being included in Edward's endowment despite his own claims to the city.[8] But Clare had attended Edward's marriage in Burgos and then accompanied the king to Paris. The marriage of Gilbert, Richard's son and heir, to Henry's Poitevin niece Alice, daughter of Hugh de Lusignan, helped make him family, as did the way he had grown up at Henry's court. During 1255 he attested royal charters more frequently than anyone outside the household officials. Simon de Montfort himself was employed increasingly as a diplomat (with Peter of Savoy in June 1255 he renewed the truce with France) and, while rarely at court in 1255 and 1256, was a frequent presence in 1257.[9] Another accession to the council, this time from a high-status magnate family, was Walter de Cantilupe, bishop of Worcester. At odds with Henry in the early 1250s, he had joined the

[5] *CR 1254–6*, 59.
[6] See above, 595–6.
[7] For the cases of Imbert Pugeys and Ebulo de Montibus, see below, 672.
[8] Tewkesbury, 155.
[9] *CR 1254–6*, 195–6; *CPR 1247–58*, 411; *F*, 324.

Gascon expedition and played a part in the final negotiations leading to Edward's marriage. Numerous jurisdictional privileges were now heaped on his bishopric, to a large extent exempting its lands from the jurisdiction of the sheriff.[10] Also found at court in 1255 were Edmund de Lacy, heir to the earldom of Lincoln, and married to the queen's kinswoman, Agnes of Saluzzo, and John de Warenne, married to Henry's 'sister' Alice de Lusignan.[11] When Alice, always a favourite, gave birth to a son, Henry bestowed a 'good robe' on the messenger who brought the news.[12] Soon another young noble was tied into the court, or so the king could hope. This was Baldwin de Redvers, heir to the earldom of Devon, who both came of age in 1257 and (Peter of Savoy's work) married a daughter of Thomas of Savoy.

Matthew Paris appreciated the success of Henry's policies.[13] The king, he wrote, 'with ineffable cunning, having drop by drop attracted aliens to him, had successively allied himself to nearly all the nobles of England, such as the earls of Gloucester, Warenne and Lincoln and Devon'.[14] Paris then added that the earl of Cornwall was 'neutral', meaning he had done nothing to stop these associations. The consequences Paris felt were clear. With so many nobles thus entrapped by the king, the prelates, magnates and 'universitas of the kingdom' were unable to stand up for their rights, and despaired at the riches given away to foreigners. The distinction Paris makes here, if in a muddled way, is telling. It is essentially one between the court, where the native nobles had been drawn into alliances with the king's foreign relatives, and the rest of the political kingdom, well represented in parliament, which shared Paris's hostility to the foreigners and felt far more than the courtiers the pressures of royal government. The situation was sustainable so long as Henry's court held together. When it broke apart he was in deep trouble.

After Henry's return, there was no immediate sign of that happening. A degree of political calm is suggested by the paucity of notes on the chancery rolls stating on whose authority letters had been issued. The

---

[10] *CPR 1247–58*, 306; *CChR 1226–57*, 443. Henry's concession of the liberties was made for the soul of King John. 'As the bishop would not receive the liberty without making some recompense' (which was good of him), he agreed to take over the annual payment of 6 marks the king gave in alms to the nuns of Wroxall. In fact the liberate rolls show the payment (which went back to John's reign) was one of 10 marks.

[11] Edmund died in June 1258, leaving a seven-year-old son. In May 1256, Warenne was granted the third penny of the county of Surrey as his father, William de Warenne, earl of Surrey, had held it: *CR 1254–6*, 299. This would seem to mark his formal investiture with the earldom, but he still appears after that as plain John de Warenne. In March 1258 (*CPR 1247–58*, 620) he is styled John, earl of Warenne, a title often used rather than earl of Surrey. He was rarely at court after 1255, although in no way out of favour.

[12] *CR 1254–6*, 262. Here called the king's sister and countess of Warenne.

[13] Paris, v, 514–15.

[14] Paris placed the comment in 1255 but it must have been written after the Redvers marriage in 1257.

almost blanket coverage of such notes had lapsed during the course of 1253 and was not revived.[15] Henry was also working with his council. How frequently and formally it met is unknown, but it was certainly involved in a wide variety of business. Indeed, in 1257 it attempted to reform the king's finances and lay down rules for its own conduct. Some of its membership is clear: the king's foreign relatives, the bishop of Worcester, Richard of Cornwall, Richard de Clare, John fitzGeoffrey, Hugh Bigod (Roger Bigod's brother), John Mansel, the household stewards and the king's senior judges, with Henry of Bath now returning to head the court *coram rege*. Yet there was also, in Henry's relations with his council, something which foreshadowed the crash to come. For Henry remained quite able to disregard its advice and forge ahead on his own. Over the Sicilian affair he did so with cataclysmic consequences.

HENRY'S QUARREL WITH LONDON, THE PARLIAMENT OF APRIL 1255

Soon after Henry's return in 1255 he ran into a quarrel with London. It was a quarrel he won, unlike his confrontations in 1248 and 1250. In the process he upheld the rights of the crown and showed the force of his anger.

Henry had already been displeased by the size of the Londoners' welcome home present and extracted a cup worth £200 in addition to it.[16] Then on 6 January 1255 he forced the mayor and citizens to answer before him for the escape of a prisoner from Newgate. This was no ordinary prisoner. It was the wealthy clerk John of Frome, accused of murdering the proctor who was running the diocese of Hereford for Peter de Aigueblanche.[17] Since the victim was himself a Savoyard, the queen was deeply concerned with the affair. Henry himself, according to fitz-Thedmar, 'moved to anger beyond measure' at the escape, imprisoned the sheriffs in the Tower of London, and then sacked them.[18] All this became bound up with the dispute over London's tallage.

Because of the unprecedented need arising from his Gascon debts, Henry and his council had decided to tallage the king's towns and manors, and tallage them, as they said, more heavily than before. From London, 3,000 marks were demanded, a sum Matthew Paris thought was partly a punishment for the Frome escape. This raised in acute form the old dispute about London's status. Were its citizens liable to arbitrary tallages like other royal towns and like the villeins and serfs on royal demesne manors? Or did their special privileges mean they were exempt from such

[15] See above, 512–13.
[16] Paris, v, 485–6.
[17] Tewkesbury, 148.
[18] Paris, v, 486–7; Barrow, *EEA Hereford*, lii–iv and see above, 557.

impositions and could only be taxed with their consent? Faced with the king's demand, they refused the 3,000-mark tallage and offered instead 2,000 marks as a freely conceded aid. Henry, backed by Richard of Cornwall, his judges and exchequer officials, declared this claim highly prejudicial to 'the liberty which we and our predecessors have enjoyed in the city'. In his rage (as portrayed by Paris) Henry called the citizens his 'serfs', and took London's government into his hands. Under this pressure the citizens appeared before the king, the earls of Cornwall and Gloucester, the bishop of Worcester and the rest of the council at Westminster. An inspection of old rolls showed the citizens *were* liable to tallage. On the next day (9 February), they gave in and agreed to pay the 3,000 marks. The episode showed how powerful Henry could be when he moved with the support of his officials and his council.[19]

As another way of relieving his debts, Henry intended, as he said, to 'implore' his magnates to grant him 'an effective aid'.[20] To that end a parliament was summoned to meet on 18 April. Beforehand, Henry left Westminster and went on a pilgrimage to St Albans, taking with him Richard of Cornwall and William de Valence. He stayed for six days, doubtless at the monastery's cost, yet his conduct was completely fitting and Matthew Paris made no complaints. Every day and night with many candles and great devotion Henry prayed at Alban's shrine. He also offered two precious cloths and a cope of gold. No king, Paris observed, not even its founder, King Offa, had given as many cloths to the church. Indeed, he had given more than all the other kings put together.[21]

It was little help when it came to the parliament. Henry had announced (in January) that he had undertaken the war in Gascony 'for the honour and tranquillity of our kingdom of England by counsel of our magnates'.[22] That struck the right note, but Henry was also very capable of telling his subjects that they were obliged to defend *his* rights and honour out of simple fidelity to him. Perhaps that was how it came across now, for the parliament was a disaster, this despite six bishops (including Walter de Grey of York making a last appearance) and the earls of Cornwall, Gloucester, Norfolk and Winchester all being present at court.[23] Perhaps Henry did not help matters by increasing Geoffrey de Lusignan's annual fee by £100 and making him a gift of 200 marks.[24] Whatever the cause, Henry somehow managed to give the impression he was seeking to impose a tallage on the

[19] Paris, v, 486–7; *CR 1254–6*, 157–60. The whole subject of London's taxation is unravelled in Cassidy, 'The barons of London and royal taxation', with a discussion of the events of 1255 on 6–7.

[20] Piper, 'Writs of summons', 284–6 at 286; *CR 1254–6*, 154, 157–8.

[21] Paris, v, 489–90.

[22] *CR 1254–6*, 157–8.

[23] *RCWL*, ii, 95. For the parliament, see Paris, v, 493–4; Burton, 336; Winchester, 95; Dunstable, 195; Maddicott, *Origins of the English Parliament*, 470.

[24] *CLR 1251–60*, 209; *CPR 1247–58*, 407.

kingdom, as opposed to a voluntary aid. The Burton annalist even gave it a name – 'horngeld'.

In response to these provocative demands, the parliament, for its part, demanded the right to appoint and dismiss the king's justiciar, chancellor and treasurer 'according to custom and for the common utility of the kingdom'. This was a significant moment. It showed that, for all Henry's success in Gascony and the presence of English magnates at court, the revolutionary demands first seen in 1244 were still very much on the agenda. There had been no justiciar since 1234, no active chancellor since 1238. On William of Kilkenny's elevation to the bishopric of Ely, Henry at the start of 1255 had entrusted the seal to Henry of Wingham. This was a good choice and Wingham was left in place (if now answerable to the ruling council) by the revolutionaries of 1258. Under Henry he was sometimes styled in official records 'chancellor of the king', but much more often he appears simply as 'the king's clerk'.[25] However conscientious and efficient, he had no independent status. The same was true of Philip Lovel as treasurer of the exchequer. The ability of such ministers to stand up to the king would be transformed if they were appointed by parliament. The widespread dissatisfaction with Henry's government in the localities was shown later in the year when the king's judges visited Hereford.[26] The total value of the amercements imposed was 766 marks. Juries of local knights twice gave verdicts against the bishop of Hereford, Peter de Aigueblanche, once over his claims to jurisdictional liberties, once over his demands for extra services from one of his free tenants.[27] The hundred juries presented a whole series of complaints against recent sheriffs. They included holding pleas of the crown and imposing arbitrary amercements, both abuses in clear breach of Magna Carta. Although the culprits were amerced, the incumbent sheriff, the clerk John le Bretun, was not removed, and no redress was given to the victims.

At the parliament, Henry, as in the past, would make no concessions about elected ministers. But he did give some promise about keeping Magna Carta, whereupon consideration of the tax was adjourned until the Michaelmas parliament to see whether the promise was kept. Henry made some effort to follow it up. On 23 May 1255, by which time he was at Clarendon, he sent orders to his sheriffs ordering them, on pain of punishment, to have Magna Carta read in full county court. They were also to make sure it was 'inviolably' observed both by the king and everyone else. Similar orders were sent to the justices in eyre.[28] As so often,

[25] *CPR 1247–58*, 440, 521, 624 (as chancellor), 398, 407, 415, 450, 464, 473, 477, 541, 543, 563, 599, 604, 610, 616 (as clerk).

[26] For the burdens of such visitations, see below, 661.

[27] TNA JUST 1/300C, mm. 9, 10. For threats to the dean of Hereford, see *CR 1254–6*, 236.

[28] *CR 1254–6*, 194–5; TNA JUST 1/872, m.9.

however, Henry's efforts lacked real bite. It was left to the church to arrange for copies of the Charter to be made and distributed. The church also had the pope's confirmation of the 1253 sentences of excommunication published both in French and English, thus aiming at a wide audience.[29] If only Henry had taken steps to broadcast his adherence to the Charters in that way. Instead, his chief concern was defending the rights of the crown and not very effectively at that. On 22 June, while at Woodstock, Henry commissioned an inquiry by his judges into encroachments on 'the king's rights and liberties'. They were also to survey the state of the royal forests and demesne.[30] There was every reason for such an initiative, but why not, at the same time, set up judges empowered to hear complaints against violators of the Charters? Something like that was being suggested at this time by William of Horton, the St Albans abbey monk and expert in legal affairs. In his view the Charters were not being observed by the king, his judges and his bailiffs, 'because no keepers of them are appointed to hear the complaints of the community'.[31] There was, to be sure, a final clause in the 1255 articles of inquiry asking whether the sheriffs and their agents had 'aggrieved anyone by unjust extortion', but it seems to have been neglected by the judges for it prompted few answers in the surviving returns.[32] Even in recovering lost rights, the inquiry seems to have had little effect. There is no evidence much was done with the mountain of information produced, any more than much was done in response to the encroachments on royal rights revealed by the inquiries of the justices in eyre.[33] The judges in 1255 had no power to rectify let alone punish the usurpations they uncovered. Theirs was an inquiry pure and simple. Perhaps the lack of action was not surprising given that many of the encroachments were committed by leading members of the regime, including Richard de Clare, who was described in one return as acting 'in contempt of the king'.[34]

In terms of defending the rights of the crown, Henry's only follow-up to the inquiry of 1255 was an ordinance promulgated, with the consent of his council, in July the following year. This pointed out that alienations

[29] Burton, 319–22; F, 293. For the necessary link between the publication and the sentences, see Hill, 'Magna Carta, canon law and pastoral care'.

[30] CPR 1247–58, 438; Burton, 337–9. This inquiry is fully discussed in Roffe, 'The hundred rolls of 1255'.

[31] Paris, GA, i, 340.

[32] Roffe, 'The hundred rolls of 1255', 207, 210. For the surviving returns, see RH, i, 20–34; RH, ii, 38–45, 55–84; BF, ii, 1287–90. RH, ii, 68–9, has a presentation under the abuse article.

[33] See above, 530–1.

[34] RH, i, 22. For Simon de Montfort, see BF, ii, 1288. The returns, with what effect we do not know, were got out for the judges of the special eyre in 1259 to help their inquiry into liberties withdrawn from the king without warrant. The implication was that nothing had been done with them up to that point. See DBM, 162–3, cap. 9.

made by tenants-in-chief were reducing the amount of land coming into the king's hands through wardships. Henceforth, such alienations were to require the king's consent. The ordinance was not a complete innovation and its immediate effects are hard to gauge.[35] It was not much to set beside the extensive legislation that Louis IX was promulgating at this time for the reform of the realm.

HENRY'S EXPEDITION TO SCOTLAND IN THE AUTUMN OF 1255

In the summer of 1255, Henry began to face a problem which ultimately played a part in his downfall in 1258. This was the rising power of Llywelyn ap Gruffudd in Wales.[36] Under the Treaty of Woodstock in 1247, Gwynedd west of the Conwy had been shared between Llywelyn and his elder brother Owain, both doing homage to the king. Now, to the inevitable tensions between the brothers, there was added the demand of the younger brother Dafydd to have his share of the inheritance according, as he said, 'to the custom of Wales'. The king's jurisdictional rights over these quarrels had been asserted, during their regency, by the queen and Earl Richard, but their chief concern was simply to keep the peace during the king's absence. Henry on his return had appointed (in May 1255) a commission to give judgement on Owain's complaints against Llywelyn, 'according to the law and custom of those parts'.[37] But, before it could act, Owain and Dafydd had taken matters into their own hands. They launched an attack on Llywelyn, only to be defeated and captured in the battle of Bryn Derwin. Llywelyn was now sole master of Gwynedd west of Conwy. Henry's reaction, counselled by the earls of Cornwall and Gloucester and the elect of Winchester, was simply to tell the justiciar of Chester, Alan la Zouche, to protect Gruffudd of Bromfield if Llywelyn attacked him.[38] Llywelyn was encouraged to reach for more.

Henry's major preoccupation at this time was not the activity of Llywelyn in Wales, but the fate of his daughter Margaret in Scotland. His intention during the summer of 1255 had been to visit the new house he was building at Gillingham in Dorset, where glass was going into the windows of the chapel. Instead he was forced to make one of his rare journeys to the north, stopping at Woodstock on the way.[39]

---

[35] *CR 1254–6*, 429. See Bean, *Decline of English Feudalism*, 66–71; Brand, 'The fine rolls of Henry III', 50. For a case from the 1255 inquiry directly relevant to the legislation, see *RH*, ii, 43b (about the earl of Winchester). The legislation may also have been prompted by the case between the king and Robert de Ros over possession of Wark, see below, 620 and n. 48.

[36] For what follows, see Smith, *Llywelyn ap Gruffudd*, 68–73.

[37] *CPR 1247–58*, 432.

[38] *CR 1254–6*, 204.

[39] *CLR 1251–60*, 202, 220; *CPR 1247–58*, 412. For Henry's intervention, see Brown, 'Henry the peaceable', 50–1.

Back at the time of Margaret's marriage to King Alexander at York, in December 1251, Henry had helped reorder the council of the nine-year-old king. The justiciar, Alan Durward, and his allies had been removed and the government entrusted to the Comyn earls of Mentieth and Buchan and their brother-in-law the earl of Mar. At Henry's behest two Anglo-Scottish barons were also added to the council. One was Robert de Ros, grandson of William the Lion, and lord both of Wark on the Scottish border and of Sanquhar in Nithsdale. The other was John de Balliol, lord of both Barnard Castle in county Durham and, through marriage, of a large part of Galloway. Both were experienced administrators. Ros had done a long stint as chief justice of the royal forests north of Trent. Balliol since 1248 had been sheriff of Cumberland. Margaret was now especially entrusted to their care.

In 1250, Henry had gracefully withdrawn his claims to overlordship of the Scottish kingdom. His chosen role was that of Alexander's father-in-law and friend.[40] He naturally hoped that the Scottish government would help him in Gascony. He also hoped to receive the monies raised in Scotland to support the crusade.[41] But was the Scottish government friendly? There was one man who said the reverse, and, unlike that government, he had helped Henry in Gascony. Alan Durward had not taken his dismissal in 1250 lying down. In 1254 he accompanied the queen out to Gascony, leading a contingent of four knights. He went on to attend Edward's marriage at Burgos. Meanwhile, he took every opportunity to blacken the Scottish government. It can be no coincidence that in August 1254, only four days after granting Alan an annual fee of £50 a year, Henry suddenly sacked Robert de Ros and John de Balliol. At the same time, Henry commissioned Simon de Montfort to relay 'certain secrets' by word of mouth to Alexander.[42]

In fact Henry soon changed his mind and Ros and Balliol remained in office. But there was more trouble to come. It stemmed from Henry and Eleanor's growing anxiety about the welfare of their daughter Margaret. In 1255 she was fifteen. Her husband, Alexander, was a little over a year younger. The queen, as Matthew Paris put it, 'desired most ardently the safety and prosperity of her daughter, as she did those of [Alexander] whom she loved as an adoptive son'. Henry shared her feelings completely. The York wedding of the young couple had been one of the happiest events of his reign. Now, however, the queen's physician, Reginald of

---

[40] Likewise, when the queen and Earl Richard asked Alexander to convene an assembly to consider requests for help in Gascony, they did so simply 'by reason of the tie and alliance between us'. There was no mention of any feudal obligation: *CR 1253–4*, 108.

[41] *ASR*, no. 9; *F*, 303, 322; Duncan, *Scotland*, 564.

[42] *CR 1253–4*, 70, 266; *CPR 1247–58*, 321, 395, 410; *CLR 1251–60*, 208 (which suggests his closeness to Earl Richard), 219; Melrose, 575–6. Nothing seems to have come from Montfort's mission, if it ever took place, or from that found in *CR 1254–6*, 272–3.

Bath, sent by Eleanor to look after her daughter, was sending back alarming reports of Margaret's pallor and depression, and blaming her keepers for it.[43] Further intelligence doubtless came from Durward: both he and his ally David de Lindsey (ousted as chancellor in 1250) were at court in May 1255 when Henry began to contemplate an expedition to the north.[44] The finger of blame particularly pointed at Ros since he was in charge of Edinburgh castle where Margaret often lived.[45]

Initially, Henry moved slowly, probably unclear about the situation, perhaps hoping Margaret might be brought south. For most of June he was at Woodstock before travelling on to his little-visited hunting lodges in Northamptonshire. At Geddington he and Eleanor (for Eleanor of course was coming too) 'took venison in the park as they wished'.[46] Then the couple moved to Nottingham where they remained from 17 July to 2 August. It was probably there they heard news that a daring plot had met with success. John Mansel and Richard de Clare, disguising themselves as menials from the household of Robert de Ros, had gained entry into Edinburgh castle and then let in men-at-arms supplied by Patrick, earl of Dunbar. With the fortress secured, Margaret poured out her tearful story. She felt incarcerated in the castle, a sad and solitary place by the sea, without sight of green fields, and lacking healthy air. Queen Eleanor herself often worried about air quality and this must have struck a special chord. Margaret added that she could not choose her own handmaidens and was prevented from sleeping with her husband. Quite probably Ros felt he was under orders to wait until Alexander became fourteen on 4 September before letting them sleep together. Mansel and Gloucester immediately remedied this and placed the couple in the same bed.[47]

When Henry heard this news his mind was made up. He announced his 'firm intention to go to the north to see the king and queen of Scotland, whom he has not seen for a long time and whom he wishes to see with all his heart'. Margaret's younger sister Beatrice was coming too so this was to be very much a family reunion. As Henry moved north he ordered Ros to surrender Wark castle so that it could be used as a royal base. He also began a legal action challenging Ros's title to the castle, though stressing its surrender would not prejudice any defence. Indeed (pending a verdict), the castle would be returned once Henry had finished his business in the north.[48]

---

[43] Paris, *HA*, iii, 322; Paris, v, 272, 504–6. Bath died soon after this, Paris thought through poison.

[44] *CLR 1251–60*, 219; *CPR 1247–58*, 410.

[45] Paris, v, 272, 504–6; Paris, *HA*, iii, 322.

[46] *SPF*, 113. See above, 408.

[47] Paris, v, 504–6, 569; Melrose, 580–1; Broun and Harrison, *The Chronicle of Melrose*, 157–8; Dunstable, 198; Burton, 337.

[48] *CR 1254–6*, 216; *CPR 1247–58*, 423. The claim probably related to the division of the family patrimony by which Robert, a younger son, received Wark and his elder brother,

The crisis soon intensified. When the Scottish council realized what had happened – 'this treason' – they assembled an army, and threatened to besiege Edinburgh castle.[49] Henry's reaction on 10 August was to give Gloucester and Mansel power to take into the king's protection a long list of Scottish nobles who were ready to stand against the enemies of their king and queen. (The list was headed by the earl of Dunbar and included Durward and Lindsey.) Six days later, now at York, Henry summoned his tenants-in-chief 'on their faith and homage' to come to him 'day and night with all their power'. Vavasours and knights who did not hold their lands directly from the king were to come 'as they loved the king and his honour' and as they wished for thanks and favour. Henry at the same time removed John de Balliol from the custody of Carlisle castle and had his personal armour sent from the Tower of London.[50]

Henry's army brought together both foreign relatives and English magnates. Attesting royal charters during the expedition were William de Valence, Geoffrey de Lusignan, John de Plessis, earl of Warwick, Roger Bigod, earl of Norfolk (at court since July), Roger's brother Hugh Bigod, William de Fors, earl of Aumale, and John de Warenne and Edmund de Lacy.[51] Henry finally arrived at Wark on 6 September. From the castle high above the river, he could gaze across the Tweed into Scotland and worry about his daughter's fate.[52] Fortunately, Durward's party soon spirited Alexander and Margaret away from Edinburgh and brought them to Roxburgh. From there, conducted by an impressive array of magnates, they came over the border to meet Henry at Wark.[53] Alexander returned the same day, but Margaret remained with her mother and father. At some point in the next fortnight the English party itself crossed the border. They were welcomed by Alexander at Roxburgh 'with great joy', conducted in a procession to Kelso abbey, and then entertained to a banquet.[54]

Henry remained at Wark until 21 September while a new structure of government for Scotland was hammered out. Eventually, the Comyns and

---

William, inherited Helmsley. Robert was to hold Wark from William, which explains why the king ultimately brought his case against William, Robert having called him to warrant; see *Northumberland Pleas*, nos. 584, 594, 596, references I owe to Henry Summerson. In 1227, Henry had confirmed this settlement (*CChR 1226–57*, 56), but while he was under the influence of Hubert de Burgh. The arrangement meant Henry would lose the wardship of Wark during a minority.

[49] Paris, v, 506; Melrose, 581–2.

[50] *F*, 325–7 (*CPR 1247–58*, 421); *CR 1254–6*, 218–20.

[51] *RCWL*, ii, 97–8; *ASR*, 69. William de Fors was the son of the William who had caused so much trouble in the Minority. He succeeded his father in 1241 and was native born. His mother was Aveline, daughter of Richard de Montfichet of Stansted Montfichet.

[52] Today little remains of the castle other than earthworks and a few stumpy walls. It is difficult of access.

[53] *F*, 327; *CPR 1247–58*, 424, 441.

[54] Melrose, 582–3.

their allies (including Ros and Balliol) were removed from Alexander's council. In their place a new council of fifteen men was set up. It included the earl of Dunbar (who swore to the whole agreement on Alexander's behalf), as well as Alan Durward and David de Lindsey. The council was to control patronage and appointments for the next seven years until Alexander's twenty-first birthday. Durward became justiciar of Scotia and Lindsey chamberlain, which meant he received the revenues of the kingdom.[55] Queen Eleanor had, meanwhile, fallen ill and needed to stay at Wark, rather than go back with Henry to the south. It was agreed that Margaret could remain with her until her recovery. Beatrice probably stayed too. The sisters interceded together to secure a pardon on 24 September.[56]

Henry's tiptoe across the border in September 1255 was the only time he entered Scotland, a benign contrast to the destructive invasions of his son. Kelso abbey, founded by King David in 1128, was thus the only great church in Scotland that Henry ever saw. Largely built in the late twelfth century and thus by then out of date, it was nonetheless, with its towers, twin transepts and elaborate arcading, a very impressive building, fully comparable to work of the same vintage at Ely, Peterborough and Norwich. The sight of such a fine abbey must have increased Henry's respect for the Scottish kingdom, whose ruler he was doing so much to protect.[57] Henry had indeed scored a success. He had rallied his nobility behind him, rescued his daughter and son-in-law, and transformed the government of Scotland. He had done so without in any way exacerbating the situation by advancing claims to overlordship, unlike his son in the 1290s. There were certainly fears that Henry's intervention was encroaching on the kingdom's independence. The Melrose chronicle said that the agreement contained 'many things which might result in dishonour to the king and kingdom'.[58] Henry acknowledged such fears and did his best to dispel them. He stated that his involvement in the changes to the Scottish council at the time of the York marriage was in no way to prejudice the liberties of the king and kingdom. The more he was bound by paternal love to Alexander, the more he wished to preserve those liberties and rights unharmed.[59] Henry was completely sincere. Indeed, he was at this time urging the king of Castile to think in exactly the same way. Alfonso should not support the rebels in Gascony for that would be to damage the interests of his son-in-law.[60] Henry's motives were also recognized in Scotland,

---

[55] *CPR 1247–58*, 426; *ASR*, 60–9.

[56] *F*, 328 (*CPR 1247–58*, 425–6).

[57] For Kelso abbey, see Webb, *Architecture in Britain*, 53–5. Henry may also have been impressed by Roxburgh castle, but of that nothing remains apart from earthworks and a few walls.

[58] Melrose, 583;

[59] *F*, 327 (*CPR 1247–58*, 422).

[60] *CR 1254–6*, 389.

at least by the party for which he was acting. Alexander declared that his 'dearest father and lord' had come personally to the northern border 'for the honour and utility of us and our kingdom'.[61] Looking back from the 1280s, the Scottish chronicle known as the *Gesta Annalia* declared that, with 'good judgement and justice sleeping' in Scotland, King Henry had come to Wark answering the request of Alexander and his magnates 'like a faithful father'.[62] Yet it is difficult to give Henry full marks for his intervention. The administration he had set up in Scotland was highly partisan, excluding as it did some of the greatest men in the realm. Naturally it was unstable. Henry would have done better had he constructed a government of all the parties.

THE PUNISHMENT OF JOHN DE BALLIOL AND ROBERT DE ROS

Henry was determined to punish both Balliol and Ros for their transgressions, Balliol's being aggravated by 'his enormous excesses and injuries' against the peace during a jurisdictional dispute with the bishop of Durham.[63] Ros was so fearful for his safety that he secured a safe conduct to come to court.[64] When Henry got back to Westminster in October, he commenced legal actions against both men, although the loss of the rolls of the court *coram rege* between 1255 and 1258 means there are no details. Balliol got off more lightly, probably because he was less involved with Margaret, and also submitted more quickly. Eventually, during Henry's Welsh campaign of 1257, he offered £500 for the remission of the king's anger and the end of legal proceedings against him. By the following March he had paid in £366. He was then pardoned the rest of the debt as well as a 100-mark amercement.[65]

Robert de Ros was another matter.[66] He had the more direct responsibility for Margaret, and created fresh resentment by failing at once to come to court. He appeared eventually in May 1256 at Windsor and at first things went well: Wark was restored to him, saving any lawsuit of the king.[67] Then, however, disaster struck, partly again through his own actions. He refused to stand to a judgement of a court composed, he

[61] *ASR*, 60–1.

[62] Fordun, 297; Bower, 5, 314–7. For the *Gesta Annalia*, probably completed by 1285, and incorporated into the chronicles of John of Fordun and thence of Walter Bower, see Broun, 'A new look at the *Gesta Annalia*'.

[63] *CR 1254–6*, 217; Beam, *Balliol Dynasty*, 50–3, 64–5.

[64] *CPR 1247–58*, 424.

[65] *CPR 1247–58*, 575; *CFR 1256–7*, no. 894; *CFR 1257–8*, no. 374; Paris, v, 507; Beam, *Balliol Dynasty*, 67.

[66] What follows summarizes the reconstruction offered in my 'Vis et voluntas of Henry III'.

[67] *CR 1254–6*, 414; *CPR 1247–58*, 473.

alleged, of his enemies, and demanded instead trial by battle. Infuriated by this defiance, and claiming the injuries inflicted on his daughter amounted to treason, Henry now sought to hit Ros with an astronomical amercement of 100,000 marks![68] There could be no greater measure of his anger. Such a sum was totally unprecedented and was double the notorious 50,000-mark fine that King John had used to destroy Matilda de Briouze. It gave Henry the means to ruin Ros absolutely. At this point, however, the council intervened and reduced the amercement to one of a more ordinary level for a great offence, namely 1,000 marks, larger than Balliol's fine but only by some £266.

This reconstruction of events is to some extent conjectural but it gains credence from another case before the king in 1256. Here Henry imposed an amercement of £100 on the bishop of Bath and immediately ordered the exchequer to collect it. But afterwards, 'by consideration of the peers of the bishop in the king's presence', the amercement was reduced to 50 marks.[69] Much the same, it may be suggested, happened in the case of Robert de Ros. There were plenty of his peers at court in May 1256, judging from the favours given to the earls of Cornwall, Leicester, Gloucester, Norfolk and Surrey, as well as Roger de Mortimer, Hugh Bigod and Henry de Hastings.[70] Even as reduced by the council, an amercement of 1,000 marks remained a heavy burden and Ros proved unable to meet the doubtless harsh terms set for payment. This gave Henry the opportunity to seize his lands and £171 was soon raised from them.

Henry then had laid low two great Anglo-Scottish barons. In the process, in a time of financial need, he had raised £537, £366 from Balliol's fine and £171 from Ros's chattels. For one of the few times in his reign he had shown a 'vis and voluntas' worthy of his father. Indeed, Matthew Paris drew a parallel with King John's own treatment of the Northerners.[71] Yet the episode, like so many others, also shows the restraints on Henry's kingship. Left to himself, in his anger, he might have punished both men in arbitrary fashion. Instead he proceeded against them judicially. In Ros's case, he was forced by his court to slash the size of the amercement he wished to impose. He never made good his claim to Wark. Henry was also acting within the law in seizing Ros's lands, for even Magna Carta permitted distraint on land when debts were left unpaid. One thing the Charter had failed to do was stipulate that the terms set for repayment should be reasonable.

---

[68] Paris, v, 569.

[69] CFR 1255–6, no. 657. For Henry having to backtrack over getting the 50 marks paid, see CR 1254–6, 418, 443, 450.

[70] CR 1254–6, 297, 299–300, 303–4, 307, 309; CPR 1247–58, 472; CLR 1251–60, 285, 292. The charter roll for 1255/6 does not survive. It was in this month that John de Warenne seems to have been invested with the earldom of Surrey.

[71] Paris, v, 569.

Henry also remained within bounds when it came to dealing with the one nobleman who spoke up in Ros's favour. This was Roger Bigod, earl of Norfolk. The story here comes entirely from Matthew Paris but has some supporting evidence.[72] During the October parliament of 1255, when Bigod sought to intervene on Ros's behalf, Henry rounded on him in his usual high-sounding way and called him a traitor. Bigod, of course, denied the accusation and asked how Henry could hurt him if he acted justly. 'I can seize your corn, and thresh it and sell it,' Henry retorted. 'Do so,' shot back Roger, 'and I will send back your threshers without their heads'! In a way, Henry was right. He was perfectly entitled to seize corn and other chattels to secure payment of Bigod's mountainous debts. Indeed, he immediately went ahead and ordered the exchequer to do so. But it did not last for long. A month later, with the intervention of Richard de Clare, the order to the exchequer was rescinded.[73] Henry's relations with Bigod soon straightened out. In April 1256 the earl entertained Henry at Framlingham and was thanked with a present of ten oaks. In October a concession allowed him to tighten his control over Earsham hundred in Norfolk.[74]

The treatment of Ros, however, left a mark on Henry's reputation. Although Ros played little part in the later civil war, in 1258-9 he complained vociferously to the revolutionary government about what had happened.[75] He recovered full control of his lands and the king's claim to Wark was declared baseless. In pardoning the amercement, the government acknowledged it had been imposed by king and council, and so not by the arbitrary will of the king. However, it put the amount of the fine at the original 100,000 marks, thus seeking to blacken further Henry's reputation.[76] John de Balliol behaved differently. He remained in favour after his submission in 1257 and gave sterling support to Henry during the civil war.

CRUCIFIXION AND CONVERSION: HENRY AND THE JEWS IN 1255

Describing the fate of Ros and Balliol has taken the story beyond the events of 1255. There Henry was left at Wark, having just righted, as he hoped, the affairs of Scotland. He finally set off southwards on 21 September, determined to reach Westminster in time for the feast of the Confessor on 13 October. He was also determined to visit Lincoln on the

---

[72] Paris, v, 530. For the episode, see Morris, *Bigod Earls of Norfolk*, 48–51.

[73] *CR 1254–6*, 238.

[74] *CR 1254–6*, 290, 294; *CPR 1247–58*, 506.

[75] I think the Montfortian was Robert de Ros of Helmsley. Ros of Wark died in 1269.

[76] *CR 1256–9*, 460; *CChR 1257–1300*, 25; *RCWL*, ii, 127; *Northumberland Pleas*, no. 596. It is the chronicler John of Wallingford (a monk of St Albans alongside Matthew Paris) who puts the amount of the fine at 1,000 marks: John of Wallingford (1), 74.

way. What followed was one of the most terrible and tragic episodes in Henry's reign, one for which he bears a large measure of responsibility.

On 31 July 1255 a little boy named Hugh had disappeared in Lincoln. His mother, a widow named Beatrice, learnt he was last seen playing with some Jewish boys.[77] She raised the alarm and soon accused the Jews of capturing her son in order to crucify him in mocking parody of the crucifixion of Christ. There was a widespread belief that such horrors happened. The first known accusation was levelled against the Jews of Norwich in 1144, and led to the alleged victim being venerated as 'Saint William of Norwich'.[78] Thereafter, many other supposed killings followed in England and abroad.[79] What gave Beatrice's allegations the more credence was that large numbers of Jews had gathered in Lincoln, in fact for a wedding. The city authorities, however, hesitated to take action, so Beatrice, with a courage and enterprise admirable in another cause, 'set off for the king in Scotland and flinging herself at his feet, crying and lamenting, made her complaint'.[80]

According to a contemporary ballad narrating these events, Henry kept his balance. If the accusation was true, the Jews deserved to die; if it was false 'by Saint Edward', Beatrice deserved the same fate. Henry here was acting in the vein of previous monarchs across Europe, who had never endorsed belief in Jewish crucifixion stories. Henry, however, also decided that, on his return from the north, he must go to Lincoln to find out the truth. That decision had been made by 18 August.[81] There was soon much more to investigate. On 29 August little Hugh's body was discovered down a well. Beatrice had yet to return to the city, but her accusations seemed to have terrible confirmation. Hugh's injuries appeared consistent with crucifixion, and a blind woman, who wiped her eyes with fluids from the body, claimed to have recovered her sight. The dean and chapter of Lincoln carried the corpse in ululating procession with 'candles, crosses and thuribles' to the cathedral, where it was buried beside the body of the recently deceased bishop Robert Grosseteste, who was himself working miracles and being regarded as a saint.[82]

News of these extraordinary events reached Henry at Newcastle on Tyne. He immediately reaffirmed his decision to go to Lincoln, and summoned the senior judge Roger of Thirkleby to join him there.[83] Henry's concern was utterly understandable. His desire to protect and promote the faith was integral to his view of himself as 'a most Christian

---

[77] For more detail on what follows, see Carpenter, 'Crucifixion and conversion'.

[78] See Monmouth, 'William of Norwich'.

[79] Stacey, ' "Adam of Bristol" and tales of ritual crucifixion', 1.

[80] Burton, 342.

[81] *CLR 1251–60*, 237.

[82] Burton, 344.

[83] *CR 1254–6*, 221.

king'. In his speech to the sheriffs assembled at the exchequer in 1250, he had ordered them to take action against anyone 'blaspheming the name of Jesus Christ'.[84] Two years later, he had sought to prevent bakers imprinting the sign of the cross, the Agnus Dei or the name of Christ on their bread, lest, through carelessness, they were disfigured.[85] On his way to the north in 1255 he had written to the Cistercian monks, who were holding their general chapter, a deeply felt letter begging them to pray for himself, his queen and his children. Without God's help he could do nothing. With his help he hoped to rule 'to the praise of his name and the exaltation of the Catholic faith' so that 'having consummated the curriculum of this present life, we may obtain the rewards of eternal happiness'.[86]

What greater attack on Christ's name and offence to the faith could there be than the events of Lincoln. If true, he must avenge them. And there was another background, for Henry at this time was intensely concerned with all things Jewish. Already in his legislation of 1253 he had tried to protect Christians from contaminating contact with Jews. Now in 1255, having just handed the profits from the Jews to his brother Richard of Cornwall in return for a great loan, he had less material reason for protecting them, and was freer to act from purely 'religious' reasons. His personal efforts to convert Jews to Christianity were famous.[87] With the Domus Conversorum, the House for Converted Jews, he had founded back in 1232 frequently full, he was parking individual converts on religious houses throughout the country. When he got back from Gascony at the end of 1254 he found these arrangements in chaos. Taking action at once, on 20 January 1255, he begged some 140 religious houses to provide daily food or a money pension for around 160 converts.[88] The majority were single men and women but there were also some family groups, husbands and wives, and mothers and daughters. Over 70 of the 160 converts were women. Henry made clear the arrangements were temporary and he was asking a favour, yet some thirty converts were turned away. Henry sent them back with letters expressing his astonishment and dolefully reflecting how his prayers would have been even less effective had he been absent across the sea![89] The episode hardly showed Henry at his most masterful. At Lincoln he would appear in a different light.

Making little more than overnight stops on the way, Henry arrived at Lincoln on 3 October. In the city he was doubtless hit by a great wave of emotion and certainty about what had happened. And he was in a hurry.

---

[84] Clanchy, 'Did Henry III have a policy?', 215–16. For Louis IX's actions against blasphemers, see Geoffroi de Beaulieu, caps. 32–3.

[85] *CR 1251–3*, 249.

[86] *CR 1254–6*, 215–16.

[87] Stacey, 'Conversion of Jews', 263–83.

[88] *CFR 1254–5*, nos. 53, 124–5; Greatrex, 'Monastic charity for Jewish converts', 133–43; Stacey, 'Conversion of Jews', 269.

[89] *CFR 1254–5*, no. 123.

He could give just three days to the affair, if he was to be at Westminster on the thirteenth for the feast of the Confessor, just the kind of conditions which in all centuries have produced miscarriages of justice. The first step was to arrest all male Jews.[90] They were then examined and here there was a man, thanks to his combination of learning and local knowledge, supremely fitted for the task, the king's steward John of Lexington.[91] John had been pretty constantly at court since the spring.[92] He was a literate knight, a 'miles litteratus', learned in both canon and Roman law. As steward of the king's household, he was one of the judges of the court *coram rege*. He came from a distinguished family whose ancestral home at Laxton was only fifteen miles from Lincoln.[93] One brother, Robert, had been a senior royal judge, another, Stephen, was abbot of Clairvaux, while a third, Henry, was Grosseteste's successor as bishop of Lincoln. In addition, three of John's nephews were canons of the cathedral, and thus quite possibly participants in the procession bearing Hugh's body to its resting place.[94] It was John who, with a promise of his life, extracted a full confession about the crucifixion from Copin, a leading Lincoln Jew.[95]

Henry was convinced and made a decisive decision. He overruled John's promise of mercy and determined that Copin should die. Indeed, as a 'a blasphemer and murderer he deserved to die many times over'.[96] So Copin was dragged through the streets of Lincoln at the tail of a horse and then strung up on Lincoln's gallow's hill at Canwick.[97] As for the rest of the accused, they seem to have been offered a trial by an all Christian jury, something eighteen of them refused to accept, demanding a mixture of Jews as well.[98] What was to be done, however, could be left to the future. Henry was now bound for Westminster.

The rest of the tragic story is quickly told. In October the constable of Lincoln castle was ordered to despatch all the Jews 'taken for the child lately crucified' to the king at Westminster, from where they were sent to the Tower.[99] The following month (on 22 November), with Hugh's mother actively prosecuting her suit, all ninety-two were brought back to Westminster. The eighteen Jews who had refused to place themselves on a

[90] Burton, 344–5. The ballad seems to put the arrest on the day before the king's arrival: *Ballad of Hugh of Lincoln*, 51–2, stanzas 72–5.

[91] Langmuir, 'Knight's tale of young Hugh of Lincoln', 474–7.

[92] *RCWL*, ii, 96–9.

[93] For John and his family, see Crook, 'Dynastic conflict in thirteenth-century Laxton', 194–8. I follow the conventional usage in the secondary literature in speaking of John of Lexington (the old form of the place name) rather than John of Laxton.

[94] Langmuir, 'Knight's tale of young Hugh of Lincoln', 472. The evidence for these canonries is slightly later than 1255, however.

[95] *Ballad of Hugh of Lincoln*, 52–4.

[96] Paris, v, 518. The quotation is Paris's comment, not Henry's direct speech.

[97] *Ballad of Hugh of Lincoln*, 54.

[98] FitzThedmar, 23.

[99] *CR 1254–6*, 145.

jury of Christians without Jews were immediately drawn through London and hanged on a specially constructed gallows. The remaining seventy-four Jews were returned to the Tower.[100] There was now some slackening in the persecution. According to the Burton annalist, the Dominican friars intervened strenuously for the Jews, Matthew Paris ascribing the same role to the Franciscans.[101] There were no more executions. Instead, in May 1256, the remaining Jews were released after the intervention of the earl of Cornwall.[102] Richard himself had clearly a financial motive in protecting the Jews (as both Paris and the Burton annalist pointed out) but probably had never believed the accusations in the first place.[103] He had two Lincoln Jews in his employ. He also visited Lincoln during the affair but only to pray at Grosseteste's tomb.[104] Had he been with Henry on his northern journey, things might have taken a different turn. In 1256, Henry himself in letters began to speak of the Jews crucifying Hugh 'as it is said'.[105] The eventual release of the Jews shows that relations between Christians and Jews was not fixedly prejudiced. Indeed, reading between the lines of the Lincoln affair, the same point appears. Little Hugh was said to be playing with Jewish boys. The ballad has his body being disposed of by a former nurse of one of the Jews who passed for a Christian. When the Jews were arrested, their women and children were left untouched 'out of pity'.[106] Henry, according to his lights, had acted from the best of motives; yet he was the first European monarch to sanction belief in such crucifixions. His actions were a step towards the eventual expulsion of the Jews from England in 1290.

THE REVIVAL OF THE SICILIAN AFFAIR: OCTOBER, NOVEMBER 1255

Henry's last day in Lincoln was 5 October. Then, leaving the Jews imprisoned in the castle, he was off: 6 October, Sempringham; 7th, Stamford; 8th, Peterborough; 9th, Huntingdon; 10th, Royston; 11th, Hertford; and thus at Westminster in time for the feast of the Confessor on 13 October. The instructions issued earlier for the celebrations in case he did not make it give some idea of their form. Thirty-six gold coins offered for Henry, Eleanor and their children were to be fixed to the cross above the high altar; a piece of gold bullion weighing an ounce was to be offered for the king during the solemn mass of the Confessor; the two halls at Westminster (capacity over

---

[100] FitzThedmar, 23; Paris, v, 519; Burton, 346.

[101] Burton, 346–8; Paris, v, 546.

[102] Burton, 348; Paris, v, 546, 552; John of Wallingford (1), 74.

[103] Richard, however, did profit from the possessions of the executed Jews: *CR 1254–6*, 241, 285.

[104] *CR 1254–6*, 180; Burton, 344.

[105] *RL*, ii, 110; *CR 1256–9*, 236–7.

[106] *Ballad of Hugh of Lincoln*, 48 (stanzas 44, 47), 52 (stanza 74), 53 (stanza 85).

5,000) were to be filled with paupers enjoying their customary food; and all the 'processions' of the city of London, with candles and banners, together with the mayor and citizens, were to come to Westminster.[107] In the event, the great feast was attended by the bishops of Salisbury and Worcester, and the earls of Cornwall, Hereford and Norfolk.[108] Henry had hoped Edward's new wife, Eleanor of Castile, would also be present. In the event she did not arrive in time, but Henry arranged for her own celebrations at Canterbury before staging a magnificent reception for her in London and fitting out her quarters with Spanish carpets.[109]

If Henry hoped these celebrations with his successes in Scotland and Gascony would help him at the October parliament he was to be disappointed. The parliament had been summoned to reply to Henry's demand, made earlier in the year, for taxation to pay off his Gascon debts. Yet this concern was swept off the agenda by a totally new matter, one which was to dominate Henry's thinking and alienate him from his subjects as never before. This was the Sicilian affair.

When Henry returned to England at the end of 1254, the project to make Edmund king of Sicily had run into the sand. Pope Innocent himself had virtually lost interest in it. His death on 7 December 1254 and the immediate succession of Rinaldo Conti, as Alexander IV, made matters worse. Alexander's initial move was to seek a settlement with Emperor Frederick's illegitimate son Manfred, whose position had been immeasurably strengthened by a victory near Foggia on 2 December. In the ensuing negotiations, and in the concessions to Alexander's allies, absolutely no mention was made of Edmund's claims. In February 1255, Alexander referred to Manfred as 'that noble man, prince of Taranto'. Rumours reached England that a settlement had actually been reached, with Manfred paying large sums to be recognized as king of Sicily.[110] On 15 March, when Alexander at last turned down Henry's request (in dutiful compliance with the Castilian treaty) to have his crusading vow commuted to one for a campaign in Africa, the grounds were not the Sicilian project, but the desperate needs of the Holy Land, which, Henry was reminded, Christ had 'sanctified with his blood'.[111]

In the following three weeks everything changed. Henry's envoys, Peter de Aigueblanche and Robert Walerand, long hanging around the papal court, were suddenly called in. The reason was that the negotiations with Manfred had collapsed. Alexander had realized the prince aimed to master the whole of Sicily and would never make a docile servant of the papacy. So he determined to combat him. Here Henry could play a vital

---

[107] CR 1254–6, 222.
[108] All attest on 14 October: RCWL, ii, 98.
[109] CR 1254–6, 144–5; Paris, v, 509, 513–14; FitzThedmar, 22.
[110] F, 314–15; Reg. Alexandre IV, 226–30; Dunstable, 197.
[111] F, 316.

role. It was, however, a role totally different from that envisaged by Pope Innocent the year before. Innocent had genuinely thought of Henry sending an army. He had effectively thrown Henry over when he saw an army would never be forthcoming. Alexander learnt from these mistakes. What he wanted from Henry was less a military force than money. He thus explicitly withdrew Innocent's offer of £25,000 to help fund Henry's army. Instead, he demanded that Henry pay the papacy £90,300 (135,451 marks), this being the money it had allegedly spent in prosecuting the affair, topped up by 20,000 marks Henry had promised the pope as a gift. But where was Henry to get the money? Here Alexander had a solution, one explaining why he had turned to Henry in the first place. Innocent had refused to allow Henry to have the proceeds of the crusading taxation on the English church to fund his Sicilian army, not surprisingly because he suspected it would be frittered away to no purpose. The most he offered was to set the money aside until he decided what to do with it. Alexander had a better idea. He would get his hands on the money himself. It would be used to pay off the gigantic debt Henry now owed the papacy.

Of course, Alexander knew full well that if the tax was used to liquidate Henry's debt, it could not fund his Sicilian army. That would have to be done from Henry's own resources. Alexander must equally have known about the paucity of those resources and the unlikelihood of any supplement from parliament. But none of that affected Alexander's main priority which was simply to get the money. This does not mean his offer of the kingship to Edmund was totally bogus. If the papal armies won the war, funded by Henry's money, and helped by any force England might send, then Edmund might make a compliant monarch, very much under the papal thumb. At the same time, in the event of a complete victory, it would always be easy to find some breach in the agreement and dispense with Edmund altogether.

Such thinking underlay the papal bull of 9 April 1255 in which Alexander set out the terms for Edmund's kingship of Sicily. Learning from Innocent's mistakes, Henry was now given a deadline. Apart from some leeway offered through arrangements with merchants, the whole of the 135,451 marks were to be paid by Michaelmas 1256. Within the same term, the king was also to send a captain to Sicily 'with a competent force as the state of the affair requires'. However, here Alexander made his priorities absolutely clear. Henry was not to send this force, or receive possession of the kingdom, *until all the money had been paid*. The money absolutely came first. There was one other critical difference with the terms offered the year before. They had contained no sanctions. Now, unless Henry paid the money and sent the force by Michaelmas 1256, Alexander held himself free to cancel the agreement, keep all the money so far received, excommunicate the king and place the kingdom under an interdict![112] These were, of course, impossible

---

[112] Alexander's bull, an imposing document measuring 50 by 70 cms, is BL Cotton Cleopatra E i, no. 186. It is printed in *F*, 316–18.

terms, but Alexander had the measure of his man. Given all the contact between England and Rome, Henry's reputation for 'foolish simplicity' was well known. Indeed, the Franciscan master-general, John of Parma (a man close to Alexander), had probably brought back from his English visit the story of the jester who had compared Henry to Christ, this because he was as wise as a man as when a little child![113] Given also Henry's devotion to the papacy, Alexander was confident he would accept the proffered bargain. No one else would have done so.

Alexander never stated specifically that the crusading tenth (extended by Pope Innocent from three years to five) was to be used to pay off Henry's debt to the pope.[114] What was done was more underhand but equally effective. Already in April 1255, Bishop Aigueblanche was taking out loans on the king's behalf from Italian merchants. These loans were almost entirely fictitious and simply amounted to taking over papal debts. The pope then allowed the money Henry owed to be repaid from the tenth and set against the 135,451 marks debt. At the same time, Aigueblanche, masquerading as the representative of numerous English religious houses, contracted loans on their behalf so, it was said, they could prosecute their affairs at the papal court. In fact there were no such affairs and the houses were just shouldering more of the papal debts. The houses were expected to repay these loans at once but were then allowed to set against the payments the sums they owed for the crusading tax. Again the money involved was taken as reducing the king's 135,451 marks debt. Henry later estimated nearly 30,000 marks would be raised in this way, with another 41,200 marks going from the tenth direct to Sienese and other merchants. His own debt would thus be reduced by a corresponding amount.[115]

Alexander was very clear that both Henry and his councillors must sign up to his terms in person. Accordingly, he sent the bishop of Bologna to England to receive the necessary undertakings. The bishop arrived in England with Aigueblanche just in time for the October parliament.[116] Henry was overjoyed by the revival of the project. Already in June 1255 he had commissioned Thomas and Peter of Savoy to retain knights for a Sicilian army, although he gave them no money with which to do so.[117] In September, while at Wark, he gave orders for all crusaders in boroughs and villages to be formed into companies and trained how to fire cross-bows.[118] Little did they know it, but their destination was to be Sicily!

[113] Salimbene, 134; Coulton, *From Saint Francis to Dante*, 246–7; see above, 405.
[114] Alexander at this time sanctioned the commutation of Henry's vow from the Holy Land to Sicily, but the commutation never went through: *CPReg*, 314; *F*, 319–20, 322.
[115] *CR 1254–6*, 408; *CPR 1247–58*, 514–17.
[116] *CR 1254–6*, 145, is the first sign they are in England.
[117] *CPR 1247–58*, 413.
[118] *CR 1254–6*, 221.

When the parliament opened, the bishop of Bologna gave Edmund a ring in token of his coming investiture with the kingdom. Rumours circulated that Manfred was dead. Both Henry and Eleanor were elated and went around calling Edmund king. Henry, flinging himself before an altar, swore by Saint Edward that he would lead the army out to Sicily himself. He now commissioned the golden bullae with which Edmund would seal the deal and other documents as king.[119] In the event thirty-five were made, of which one survives in the British Museum. It shows a youthful Edmund sitting crowned and holding the orb and sceptre. Around him the legend runs 'EADMUNDUS : DEI : GRACIA : SICILIE : REX'. On the reverse is a shield bearing the three leopards of the king's arms within the legend 'EADMUNDUS : NATUS: REGIS : ANGLIE : ILLUSTRIS'. That behind Edmund's kingship stood the illustrious king of England was thus made very clear.[120] Looking at the bulla one senses the attraction of the project for Henry and Eleanor. Their son was to sit golden and enthroned as king of Sicily, protected by the leopards of England and by the grace of God.

Unfortunately, not many shared this vision. Aigueblanche himself had appreciated that getting general support would be not be easy. In naming the councillors who would accept and seal the agreement, he excluded English barons, including Earl Richard, and named simply the Savoyard archbishop of Canterbury, William of Kilkenny, now bishop of Ely, the abbot of Westminster and a group of courtiers.[121] But Henry, of course, needed general support for without it there would be no tax and no prospect of raising the necessary army. The parliament of October 1255 was certainly well attended with five bishops and five earls (including Simon de Montfort) all attesting royal charters during its course. Henry made great efforts to win favour with gifts of wine, game, fish and timber.[122] Yet he got nowhere. As he told the pope later, the magnates of the kingdom thought the conditions 'gravissimas' and 'durissimas', and sought to dissuade him from entering into such a dangerous bargain.[123] The impossibility of paying the money and sending an army, the dangers of losing everything and of suffering spiritual penalties were all too obvious. The opposition was led by Earl Richard himself, effectively the head of the king's council, who, of course, had turned down an earlier offer on far more advantageous terms. He now pointed out that Henry had charged ahead without the counsel and consent either of himself or the baronage,

[119] Paris, v, 515–16; Burton, 348–9.

[120] For the bullae, see Carpenter, 'Gold and gold coins', 110.

[121] The others were John Mansel, the stewards Ralph fitzNicholas (now very aged) and Bertram de Criel and the judge Roger of Thirkleby.

[122] *RCWL*, ii, 98–9; *CR 1254–6*, 148, 232–4. This parliament was the occasion for Henry's quarrel with Bigod described earlier. That cannot have helped his cause.

[123] *CR 1254–6*, 404–6.

and blamed Aigueblanche and Walerand for infatuating the king with the whole affair. The magnates as a whole argued that they had not been properly summoned to the parliament in accordance with the procedures set out in the 1215 Magna Carta, a good example of its continuing force.[124] There was even opposition from the most astute and loyal of the very councillors whom Aigueblanche had named. On 18 October, Henry had to issue an astonishing letter commanding John Mansel to seal the agreement 'as he loves our honour and wishes to avoid our perpetual indignation'.[125]

There was equally opposition in a parallel ecclesiastical assembly. This was convoked by a new figure on the Sicilian scene, the papal chaplain Master Rostand, a highly educated Gascon who was to supervise the collection of the crusading tax and explain and expand Aigueblanche's scheme for its anticipation. The assembly was naturally shocked at the conversion of money destined for the Holy Land to a war against Christians in Italy. It was appalled to find how many religious houses had been placed in debt to Italian merchants.[126] No wonder Aigueblanche was regarded with sulphurous hostility. The protests were led by the bishops of London and Worcester, Walter de Cantilupe and Fulk Basset. 'Take away my mitre, my helmet remains,' Basset allegedly replied to Henry's threats, referring to his baronial status as head of the Bassets of High Wycombe.[127] Henry's relations with the church were not helped by the conduct of his officials during the vacancy of the archbishopric of York, however much he tried to restrain them. (Walter de Grey, a last link with King John's reign, had finally died in May 1255.) There was also an incident on the way home from Scotland where Matthew Paris accused Henry, not entirely fairly, of seizing the goods of the late bishop of Durham.[128]

The opposition Henry thus faced to his Sicilian schemes was bad enough, but it was soon to get even stiffer. Far from winning the war in Italy, the pope had catastrophically lost it. In a letter to Henry on 18 September he told the sorry tale. His great ally Berthold of Hohenburg had deserted to Manfred and the papal army had disintegrated. Alexander confessed himself 'wholly impotent'. He had spent all his money and was unable to get more loans. Henry was asked to send money at once to hire knights

[124] Paris, v, 520–1.

[125] F, 331 (CPR 1247–58, 444).

[126] CPR 1247–58, 514–18. For clerical resistance to the tax, see Ambler, Bishops and the Political Community, 95–9.

[127] Paris, v, 519–27, 532; Burton, 350–60; Lunt, Financial Relations, 269.

[128] Paris, v, 501, 507–8, 516, 565; CPR 1247–58, 423, 448; CR 1254–6, 203; Howell, Regalian Right, 238. Walter de Grey was buried in the cathedral's south transept, which he had built, under a splendid canopied tomb and Purbeck marble effigy. Artefacts taken from the tomb, when it was opened in 1967–8, including an opulent episcopal ring, are on display in the Minster's Undercroft.

together with a captain to command them. He was to follow that up by despatching 'a copious and strenuous army'. So Alexander, in extremis, wanted Henry's military help after all, although still not enough to divert the crusade taxation in order to secure it.[129] The 'terrible news' of this disaster arrived while the parliament was still in session. 'Those who before had distrusted the affair on account of the difficulty of the conditions, now despaired, so much that there was scarcely anyone who remained steadfast and willing to prosecute that affair with us,' Henry confessed in a letter to the cardinals.[130]

There was one other factor which should have encouraged Henry to share his parliament's despair. This was the absence of the leading Savoyards. Thomas and Peter of Savoy had been central to the beginnings of the Sicilian affair and the advantageous terms Henry had secured in 1254. Henry had hoped to enlist them again, as has been seen. Yet the fact is that neither Thomas nor Peter were involved in the second phase of the project in anywhere like the degree they were in the first. There is no evidence of them at the papal court in 1255. Neither were they in England. Archbishop Boniface, too, during the October 1255 parliament, was away in Savoy. None of them, therefore, were party to the decision Henry now had to take. Both Thomas and Peter, having featured in Pope Innocent's version of the agreement, were explicitly dropped from the group of councillors who were to accept it under Alexander. Doubtless the brothers welcomed the revival of Edmund's cause since it made them bigger players on the Italian stage, but they would have been appalled like everyone else by the terms. If all the money went to the pope, there would be none for themselves and any force they might seek to raise. The fact was that, with the death of their kinsman Innocent IV, the brothers had lost their inside track to the papal court. Their attentions were also turning elsewhere. In February 1255 they were all together in Savoy to settle matters after the death of their father the previous year. Peter was now busy affirming his protectorate over Bern and Murat and completing his 'conquest' of the Pays de Vaud.[131] Thomas had became bogged down in northern Italy, engaged in a disastrous struggle to assert his authority over the city of Asti.[132] The Savoyards had neither the time, resources nor inclination to help Henry fight a war against Manfred. If Queen Eleanor was still enthusiastic about the project she only had Aigueblanche, of the Savoyard party, by her side. He, one may suspect, had simply been acting

[129] *F*, 328.

[130] *CR 1254–6*, 406–8.

[131] *CR 1254–6*, 195–6; *CPR 1247–58*, 411; *F*, 324. Peter was also active in advising how Edward should manage his affairs: *CR 1254–6*, 195–6, 219–20. Peter found time to go to Paris in June 1255 and arrange an extension of the truce down to October 1258. In August 1255, Henry hoped that, after helping Edward in Gascony, he would hasten to England to discuss the Sicilian business.

[132] Cox, *Eagles of Savoy*, 202–5, 227–9 and n. 71, 254–5.

under instructions. Henry had told him to seal the deal on whatever terms he could get.

After the news of the papal disaster, Henry should surely have pulled back. His refusal to do so testifies to his fatally flawed judgement, just as his ability to continue testifies to his determination and his power. It took a long time though to get his way. Henry had insisted that John Mansel seal the agreement as early as 18 October. It was not, in the event, until 6 November, just before the court left Westminster for Windsor, that the councillors named by Alexander issued their formal letter agreeing to its terms. Two days later, now at Windsor, Henry did the same. In the peaceful surroundings of the Vatican Archives' Sala di Studio, as one unfolds the gigantic text of Henry's undertaking, one experiences a sense of shock, for it is manifestly not a production of the English royal chancery. Rather the hand seems papal, the scribe one suspects being a clerk in the entourage of the bishop of Bologna. Nothing symbolizes better the way Henry was putting his seal to an agreement dictated by the pope.[133]

On 7 November, Henry thanked Aigueblanche for his labours in promoting the affair by giving him a palfrey worth £27.[134] Later, on 21 November at Windsor, Henry sealed 'all the privileges' about the kingdom and despatched them to the wardrobe for safekeeping. Here he acted on the counsel of Aigueblanche, three Lusignan brothers and a group of courtiers and judges. Richard de Clare was the only English

---

[133] The text of Henry's undertaking, now badly damaged and without a seal, is Archivio Apostolico Vaticano Instr. Misc. 80. The councillors' letter, in better condition, is AA Arm. I-XVIII no. 587. It is issued in the names of the bishops of Hereford and Ely, the abbot of Westminster, John Mansel, Ralph fitzNicholas, Bertram de Criel and Roger of Thirkleby, so the councillors named by the pope and Aigueblanche, less Archbishop Boniface, who was stated to be in Savoy. A slightly different group (the bishop of Ely being missing and the bishops of Worcester and Salisbury being included) took an oath (referred to in both undertakings) to ensure that Edmund at the age of fifteen did homage to the pope and abided by the agreement. The bishop of Worcester and probably also the bishop of Salisbury sealed AA Arm. I-XVIII no. 587 alongside the seven in whose names it was issued. This irregular procedure may reflect the irregular circumstances in which the document was produced. The document once had nine seals, of which those of the bishops of Worcester and Ely, the abbot of Westminster, Ralph fitzNicholas and Bertram de Criel survive at least in part. The councillors' letter is also in a papal-looking hand although not the same as that in the king's undertaking. The bishop of Salisbury was William of York, the former judge. Cantilupe of Worcester's participation seems more surprising. Both undertakings are cited in Lunt, *Financial Relations*, 269 n. 4. Since then they have been transcribed by Nicholas Vincent, a colossal task given their size and condition. I am grateful to him for sending me the texts. David D'Avray kindly drew up for me a twenty-eight-point guide to working in the Vatican Archives, including where to find the bar. I thank the Archive's officials for being helpful in all manner of ways, including allowing me to compare the two documents side by side. While I was working in the Archives, Pope Francis with his 'Moto Proprio *L'esperienza storica*' decided that the Archivio Segreto Vaticano (ASV) was henceforth to be called the Archivio Apostolico Vaticano (AAV).

[134] *CLR 1251–60*, 249.

magnate present.[135] Henry knew the odds, and was equally clear why he was braving them. The conditions were thought 'not merely difficult but nearly impossible', but, as he told the cardinals, 'We, however, directing our eyes to the king of heaven and ruler of the constellations, and realising that he is able to rule sea and wind, and quiet their tempests, and bring tranquillity where there is disturbance and convert darkness into light, did not wish to abandon what we had begun.'[136] On the same day as Henry sealed the privileges, he ordered a magnificent cope of samite to be offered at the altar of the Confessor 'for Edmund, son of the king, that God shall give a happy outcome to his Sicilian enterprise'. Surely with the Confessor interceding, God would find a way.[137]

In fact, Henry had signed up to the most ridiculous agreement ever made by an English monarch. Almost at once there was a fresh disaster. On 23 November 1255, Thomas of Savoy was comprehensively defeated by citizens of Asti and soon found himself a prisoner in Turin. On 1 January, at Guildford, on his way from his Winchester Christmas to the 5 January feast of the Confessor at Westminster, Henry ordered the arrest of Asti merchants in England and cried out against their fraud, sedition, machinations, conspiracy and insults. Had Thomas won his war in the north, he might have helped the Sicilian project. As it was Savoyard resources were now devoted to securing Thomas's release.[138]

PEACE WITH FRANCE AND KINGSHIP IN GERMANY

In this unpromising situation Henry placed part of his hopes in diplomacy. In the early spring of 1256 he sent pleading letters to the papal court. He now confessed there was no way he could pay the balance of the monies owed and send an army by the deadline of Michaelmas 1256. 'We do not believe that today there is any prince on earth who could raise so suddenly such an immense sum of money.' So Henry begged the pope to modify the terms. The campaign to get him to do so was now to absorb much of Henry's energy.[139]

Henry also began to think of a fundamental step to further the Sicilian project. In January 1256 he instructed John Mansel to open negotiations for a permanent peace with France.[140] Henry explained he was being urged to make peace by the king of Castile and Alfonso (whose envoys

---

[135] *F*, 332; *CR 1254–6*, 240.

[136] *CR 1254–6*, 407.

[137] *CR 1254–6*, 240.

[138] Cox, *Eagles of Savoy*, 254–5. Clever for once, to help pay Thomas's ransom, Henry granted Peter of Savoy what was clearly a bad debt, namely the 4,000 marks he was owed for the loan made to the count of Provence (secured on four Provencal castles) back in 1243: *CPR 1247–58*, 540–1; see above, 493.

[139] *CR 1254–6*, 404–8.

[140] For what follows, see *CPR 1247–58*, 457–8; *F*, 335; Paris, v, 547–8.

were in England in January 1256) certainly wanted to free Henry up for a crusade in Africa.[141] Henry, however, was being disingenuous. The real reason he was seeking peace was quite different. It was the Sicilian project.[142] Without peace with France, he would never dare to send a substantial army from the kingdom. Without peace, he could never get to Sicily in the first place. The normal route would take Henry's army to Burgundy and then south to Lyon. The army might then, exploiting Savoyard control of the passes (nominally guarded by Henry's own castles), cross the Alps into northern Italy and march south. Alternatively, the army might continue south from Lyon, take ship from Marseille, and sail on down the coast of Italy to the Sicilian kingdom. Either way, Henry needed Louis's consent, for the journey to Burgundy involved going through the heart of the French kingdom. Mansel, accordingly, was to seek both peace and a licence for the transit of troops and treasure. He got nowhere. Indeed, aware of the disasters overtaking papal armies, and sceptical anyway about the project, he hardly pressed for the licence at all. His peace feelers were roundly rejected when, labouring under a totally unrealistic brief, he demanded the return of the old continental empire. Still, the process was now under way that would lead to the peace of Paris in 1259.[143]

While Henry was beginning to contemplate a peace with France, new possibilities were opening up which, he might hope, would drive all clouds away. On 28 January 1256, a day Henry spent with his brother at Wallingford, the king of Germany, William of Holland, was killed by a fall from his horse. A week later, apprised of the news, and counselled by Earl Richard, Henry granted a pension of £200 a year to the count of Hainault, John de Avesnes, an influential figure in German affairs. This was the opening move in a project to raise as the new king of Germany none other than Richard of Cornwall himself.[144]

---

[141] Henry asked Richard of Cornwall how to respond to Alfonso's complaints and proposals (including a marriage involving Henry's daughter Beatrice). His advice, full of cautions, considerations and stratagems, is a remarkable testimony to his knowledge, shrewdness and mental ability. Henry painted in much broader and more emotional strokes. Adding nothing of his own, he simply passed on the advice to John Mansel (now in France), and told him to act as he thought best, 'as you have laboured [for the Spanish alliance] above everyone else living': *CR 1254–6*, 389–91.

[142] According to Henry, Alfonso himself accepted Sicily must come before Africa and might take six years: *CR 1254–6*, 390.

[143] Mansel and his colleague Bertram de Criel were also empowered, probably as the next best thing if the peace negotiations failed, to prolong the truce beyond the three years agreed by Simon de Montfort and Peter of Savoy in 1255: *F*, 335. Nothing came of this either.

[144] For a different view, see Hilpert, 'Richard of Cornwall's candidature', 186. For Richard's securing of the throne, see Weiler, *Henry III of England and the Staufen Empire*, 172–4. John de Avesnes, bruised by the disputes over control of Flanders and Hainault, probably saw Richard's candidature as a move against the Capetians. This was not, however, Richard's view. See below, 685.

The choice of the king of the Romans, to give the king of Germany his official title, lay with the electoral princes. Henry later rattled off their names in a conversation with Matthew Paris: the archbishops of Cologne, Mainz and Trier, the count palatine of the Rhine, the king of Bohemia and the dukes of Saxony and Brandenburg. Richard had several attractions as a candidate. Without any base in Germany, he would be no threat to the princes while, at the same time, with his fabled wealth, he would be able to pay highly for their votes. He could also foster trading relations with England.

The pope himself had the uncontested right to consent to any election. After all, whoever was chosen would hope to proceed to papal coronation as emperor of the Romans, thus inheriting wide claims to authority in Italy, especially over the north Italian towns. There seemed a good chance the pope would look favourably on Richard's candidature. In the spring of 1256, Henry felt confident enough to ask him to send a legate to Germany, evidently on Richard's behalf.[145] Papal policy was governed, as always, by one overriding ambition: to keep Sicily and the empire apart and have loyal and compliant rulers of both. Of course, Richard's candidature threatened the unification of the empire and Sicily under the same dynasty (which was why Henry was so delighted), but Alexander knew that Edmund would never be more than a puppet ruler, while Richard, as king and emperor, was likely to be far more controllable than other candidates. From Henry's point of view, Richard's kingship seemed a godsend. It would surely help forward the Sicilian project, just as a French king of the Romans would hinder it. For Richard, the German kingship was a far better bet than that of Sicily which he had contemptuously declined. Given that the Hohenstaufen candidate, in the shape of Conrad's son Conradin, was only a child, and thus out of the game, if Richard was elected he could actually take up the kingship. He would not have to fight for it. It was an orb in his grasp, not a moon unreachable in the sky. The power was limited but the status was high. And it might lead on to the imperial crown itself. On 12 June 1256 matters had gone so far that Henry despatched Richard de Clare and Robert Walerand to Germany to prosecute Richard's cause.[146]

FAMILY AFFAIRS, 1256

In February 1256, Henry went on a pilgrimage to the East Anglian holy sites, visiting Bury St Edmunds, Walsingham and Bromholm. 'Six great and beautiful brooches' were to be sent him for his offerings.[147] This was

[145] *CR 1254–6*, 408.
[146] *F*, 342; *CPR 1247–58*, 481.
[147] *CR 1254–6*, 394.

when he was entertained by Roger Bigod at Framlingham.[148] Henry was obviously praying for the success of both the Sicilian and the German projects. And he was praying too for his daughter Katherine, who was gripped by illness. Here there was success. On 27 March, at Norwich, Henry gave a robe to the messenger of the queen who brought the good news of Katherine's recovery. He also ordered, 'for Katherine lately ill', a silver image of a woman, presumably Katherine herself, to be made, probably for placing on the feretory of the Confessor at Westminster.[149] Queen Eleanor herself had not accompanied Henry on the pilgrimage, going instead to Marlborough where indeed she spent much of 1256.[150] Henry was clearly concerned for her welfare and issued a stream of orders about her drink, food (including lampreys) and general comfort.[151] In all this time Henry was pressing on with the building of Westminster Abbey. Not to have done so in his mind would have been disastrous. In February 1256, when he heard that once again his masons wished to depart for lack of pay, he ordered the exchequer to find £400 at once, giving precise instructions as to where the money might come from. All told in this year, Henry assigned nearly £4,000 to the works. He also decided to remodel the Lady chapel, begun in 1220, to bring it into line with the new structure.[152]

Henry returned to Westminster for the Easter celebrations of 1256, and the trial of Robert de Ros. A parliament at Reading followed where it was decided to release the Lincoln Jews in the Tower. Then, Henry, leaving the queen again at Marlborough, set off in July on a tour of the Welsh marches from south to north. There was some fun. At Bath (where the tour started) Henry had his jester thrown into the Roman bath, a few days later giving him a new suit of clothes in compensation. At Bristol he was entertained by watersports, although a man was drowned during their course.[153] As he went through the major towns, Henry made money by selling privileges to their men. His main aim was both to monitor the situation against the rising power of Llywelyn and install Edward in his appanage. Edward had returned to England from Gascony towards the end of 1255, and had accompanied Henry on the pilgrimage to East Anglia. He was now sixteen and perhaps already taller than his father. Henry, advised by Peter of Savoy, was keen that Edward should visit all the parts of his appanage. Given the threat from Llywelyn, it was particularly important he took command of his Welsh lordships. Accordingly on 17 July while Henry was at Bristol, Edward's main administrative base,

---

[148] *CR 1254–6*, 285, 294; *CLR 1251–60*, 273.
[149] *CR 1254–6*, 287–8.
[150] *CR 1254–6*, 265, 270, 332.
[151] *CR 1254–6*, 270, 280, 283.
[152] *CR 1254–6*, 274, 314; *CLR 1251–60*, 274, 305; Colvin, *History of the King's Works*, i, 156.
[153] *CLR 1251–60*, 311; *CPR 1247–58*, 488.

Edward himself entered Chester and then went to inspect the Four Cantrefs and the castles of Deganwy and Dyserth.[154]

The next month saw the kind of family event Henry and Eleanor found so delightful. Back in June, when the royal couple were together at Winchester, a safe conduct was given to King Alexander and Queen Margaret to come to England. Next day Henry spoke to his painter, Master William (a monk of Westminster), and laid plans for a picture in his wardrobe at Westminster, where his head was washed, a picture showing a king rescued by his dogs from sedition plotted by his men.[155] Henry, one suspects, was thinking here not of himself but of King Alexander. The government set up after Henry's visit to Scotland in 1255 was inherently unstable, excluding as it did much of the political community. When Alexander returned home in September, he took with him John Mansel, who was both to help negotiations with the 'rebels', as Henry called them, and also draw, if necessary, on military support from the northern counties if things got worse.[156] But the purpose of Alexander's visit to England was also personal. As Matthew Paris put it, Alexander and Margaret came at the invitation of Henry and Eleanor, Margaret to see her parents and Alexander to see a king 'who had adopted him with love as a son'. Indeed, Henry described Alexander as his 'son' when assigning £100 for his expenses.[157] Alexander also wished to see England itself, its castles, cities, rivers, meadows, woods and fields. When Alexander and Margaret arrived Henry 'rushed into their embraces, and engaged them in pleasant and familiar conversation'. The meeting took place at Woodstock, where Henry planned to celebrate the feast of the Assumption on 15 August. Sent from London were twenty-four cloths of gold, a great and small tapestry or carpet, the great bed given by the countess of Provence, the long chest with all the vestments and vessels of the king's chapel, two chests with silver vases and silver horses, a great cup adorned with shields, 'and the other things which the king is accustomed to have at his solemn feasts and which at present he cannot remember'.[158]

The king's efforts met with great success. The London chronicle of Arnold fitzThedmar spoke of Henry holding 'a great and most noble court' attended by nearly all his earls and barons.[159] So many people were there, Matthew Paris added, that they had to be quartered in tents, neighbouring villages and even in Oxford.[160] Those present included Richard

[154] CR 1254–6, 219–20; St Werburgh, 72–3; AC, 90–1; Studd, 'Lord Edward's lordship of Chester', 30.
[155] CPR 1247–58, 484; CR 1254–6, 326. See Ross, 'A lost painting in Henry III's palace at Westminster'.
[156] F, 347; CPR 1247–58, 525–6; CR 1254–6, 354.
[157] CLR 1251–60, 319.
[158] CR 1254–6, 434.
[159] FitzThedmar, 23.
[160] Paris, v, 573–6.

of Cornwall, all four Lusignan half-brothers, the earls of Norfolk and Hereford (the latter soon rewarded with a gift of game) and Richard de Clare, who lent some of his pavilions and did homage to Edward for his lands in Ireland.[161] The throng then made its way to London, Edward taking one route, Henry another. At St Albans, Henry, 'adoring God and the martyr devotedly according to his custom', offered four precious cloths. A joyful entry was made into a decorated London on 27 August, and next day John Mansel threw a magnificent feast at Tothill just outside Westminster Abbey, where his house was surrounded by pavilions to take the numbers involved. More than 700 dishes were needed and all were 'splendidly, abundantly and honourably fed'. No other clerk at any time could have done it, Paris added. However, he ended his account of proceedings on a sour note. Henry, he said, depleted his resources by confirming to Alexander the earldom of Huntingdon. This was unfair since (as indeed Paris acknowledged) the earldom had been held by Alexander's predecessors. For the rest, Paris's account, like that of fitz-Thedmar, was enthusiastic and admiring. Henry often seemed out of touch, but here his kingly generosity and family affections appeared at their inclusive best.[162] The following year Alexander wrote begging for news of Henry, the queen 'our dearest mother' and their children. He desired their happiness and prosperity 'with all his heart'.[163] The bonds being constructed contributed to Alexander's conduct in the later civil war.

Having said goodbye to Alexander, Henry (again leaving the queen behind) went on another pilgrimage, this time to Becket's shrine at Canterbury. He was there when the deadline set by the pope for Sicily ran out at Michaelmas 1256. Henry was back at Westminster for the feast of the Confessor on 13 October, but no parliament had been summoned. What was the point? Henry could only wait to see what was happening about Sicily and there was no use making another appeal for money meanwhile. Likewise he could only wait to see what was happening in Germany.

SUCCESS IN GERMANY, HOPE OVER SICILY, 1256–7

In respect of Germany there was soon tremendous news. On 25 November 1256, Ludwig, count palatine of the Rhine and duke of Bavaria, agreed to vote for Richard of Cornwall. In return, he was to marry a daughter of Henry III with a dowry of 12,000 marks. He also extracted a promise from

---

[161] *CLR 1251–60*, 318; *CPR 1247–58*, 492. Norfolk does not attest charters at Woodstock, but his presence may be inferred from the gift made there on 20 August: *CR 1254–6*, 349, and 352 for a gift to Hereford. Simon de Montfort seems to have been away, probably in France, but the king made major efforts around this time to settle the debts he owed him, for example *CPR 1247–58*, 493.

[162] Paris, v, 753–6.

[163] *F*, 353.

Richard not to impede the claims of his ward Frederick II's grandson Conradin, to the kingdom of Sicily. How that sat with Edmund's candidature was not explained. Still, at least Richard was perfectly free to act against Manfred, as, of course, Henry hoped he would. Next month, the archbishop of Cologne agreed to vote for Richard in return for a promise of 8,000 marks; another promise brought in the archbishop of Mainz.[164] Envoys with these pledges of support reached England in time for Henry's Christmas court. On 28 December 1256, in the chapel of St Stephen at Westminster, amidst a great storm of thunder and lightning, while others counselled caution Henry stepped forward and urged his brother to accept the offers. They came, he said, both from God and man. Richard complied. Moving many to tears, he asked to be struck down before he left the chapel if he acted other than from a desire to promote the welfare of his new kingdom.[165]

On 28 January 1257, Henry was able to announce his brother's election as king of the Romans. It had actually taken place on 13 January outside Frankfurt. Henry ordered a robe to be given to the messenger of the bishop of Cambrai who brought the news. On the following Tuesday, after dinner at his castle at Wallingford, Richard heard details which made things even better. King Ottakar of Bohemia, hitherto sitting on the fence, had given his consent to the election. Henry now declared he would accompany Richard out to Germany, evidently to attend the coronation. Although nothing came of the idea, this was just the kind of progress Henry enjoyed.[166] His appearance would also help establish Richard in Germany, and thus further the Sicilian affair.

Early in 1257, Henry received more good news, this time about Sicily. The archbishop of Messina had arrived with Pope Alexander's replies to Henry's requests. The tone of the papal letters was reproachful. Henry had done nothing to answer the appeals made for military help back in September 1255. Then the Terra di Lavoro had still been under papal control, providing entry into the rest of the kingdom. Now that too Manfred had conquered. Nonetheless, the pope wished Henry to continue with the project. Indeed, if he did not, he would bring shame to his posterity for ever and all the kings and princes in the world would realize his impotence and weakness. So the pope agreed to extend the deadline until the end of May 1257, urging Henry now to gird himself and his barons to the task. Henry was also to repair his relations with the church. But Alexander made no effort to alter the other terms despite Henry's pleas to do so. Indeed, he made quite clear the extension was to have no

[164] MGH, *Constitutiones*, nos. 379–80, 383; Denholm-Young, *Richard of Cornwall*, 88; Hilpert, 'Richard of Cornwall's candidature', 188–9; Weiler, 'Image and reality', 1114; Weiler, *Henry III and the Staufen Empire*, 173.

[165] FitzThedmar, 24–5; Paris, v, 601–3.

[166] *CR 1256–9*, 36–7, 119; Burton, 391–2; Denholm-Young, *Richard of Cornwall*, 89.

effects on the payment of the debt. For Alexander this remained the key. Given the choice between Henry's army and Henry's money, he still preferred the money. The chief reason he did not cancel the bargain, having thought it over, was that there was still money to be made.[167]

With the news coming from Rome, Henry now summoned a parliament. It was to meet in London at mid-Lent (18 March). The extension given by the pope would be worth little unless he could get a subsidy from the realm to finance a Sicilian army. Henry said the discussions at the parliament would be 'for our and your common utility and that of all the kingdom'.[168] If only the Sicilian affair could be regarded in that light.

Henry spent January and February 1257 largely at Westminster and Windsor. At the start of March he left Windsor to return to Westminster, but he did so via a pilgrimage to St Albans and Waltham abbey, being entertained by William de Valence at Hertford castle on route. There were again personal reasons for prayer. The queen was ill at Windsor as were several young nobles staying there in her household. Matthew Paris again made no complaint about Henry's visit although the king stayed for a week and brought with him Guy de Lusignan and William de Valence, as well as the Savoyards Imbert Pugeys and William de Chabanais. But then Henry's conduct once again was so completely right. His offerings included fine rings, silken cloths and a 'most noble necklace with two clasps and a cross and chain'. There was also a silver gilt cup to hold the dust found in the recently discovered original tomb of St Alban. During this visit Matthew Paris, so he tells us, was continually with the king at his table and in his chamber. Henry, 'directing amicably and diligently the pen of the writer', named for Paris the princes who had just elected Richard as king of Germany. He named too the sainted kings of England and then ran through all the English baronies he could remember, finding there were 250. Paris captures Henry dealing with business. Certain masters of the University of Oxford came before him in the chapel of Saint Oswin and made a complaint about the jurisdictional claims of the bishop of Lincoln. They were given a day for their case to be heard at the forthcoming 'great parliament'. Matthew Paris told the king 'secretly' how ruin would threaten the whole church if the University of Oxford should now suffer the same fate as the very troubled University of Paris. Henry showed suitable alarm. 'Let this not happen, especially in my time.' On a visit like this to a great monastery, Henry could display a charming combination of respectful piety, friendly accessibility and proper concern, *debonereté* at its best.[169]

---

[167] *F*, 350–1.
[168] Burton, 384.
[169] Paris, v, 617–18.

THE PARLIAMENT OF MARCH 1257

The great parliament opened at Westminster on or soon after 18 March.[170] The German part of the business went well. The archbishop of Cologne arrived, having sailed his great barge up the Thames. Richard of Cornwall gave him 500 marks and a mitre decorated with precious stones. 'He has mitred me and I will crown him,' the archbishop replied, referring to his role in the coronation.[171] Richard finally set out from London on 10 April and sailed from Yarmouth at the end of the month.[172] He was not to return to England until January 1259, by which time a revolution had taken place.

The Sicilian business was a different matter. At some point, to stir the emotions, Henry paraded before the assembly the twelve-year-old Edmund dressed in Sicilian robes.[173] The archbishop of Messina likewise took the stage. On Sunday 2 April he entered the chapter house of Westminster Abbey and urged the assembled clergy and people to support the enterprise.[174] This is the first known event in Henry's 'incomparable' chapter house. It was, of course, a house where the monks held their daily business meetings, but Henry had also designed it as a place where he could address the realm. The archbishop doubtless spoke from the king's seat, looking towards the statues of the Angel Gabriel and the Virgin Mary above the doorway, and flanked on either side by the bands of tiles running across the floor bearing the leopards of the king's arms. Unfortunately, the setting failed to work its magic. The assembled magnates refused to help and drew up a schedule of 'reasons against the king', showing just how impossible the whole enterprise was.

The indictment was comprehensive. Manfred now held the Terra di Lavoro and 'nearly all' Sicily's towns and cities. How then could England, exhausted by the king's judicial eyres and prises, and threatened by a Welsh rising and even a French invasion (with Richard of Cornwall gone), possibly fund the conquest of Sicily and find the money owed the pope? The harshness of the terms meant the king could spend 'infinite' sums of money only for the whole thing to be cancelled. And, on all of this, Henry had embarked without any kind of counsel and consent.[175] Whether Henry himself spoke to the assembly in the chapter house is unknown, although not unlikely. If so the results were the same. For his failure,

---

[170] For what follows, see Paris, v, 621–4; Burton, 386–91; Winchester, 96; Osney, 114–15; Dunstable, 199–200, 202–3; C&S, i, 524–30; Maddicott, *Origins of the English Parliament*, 471–2.

[171] Paris, v, 625–6.

[172] FitzThedmar, 26–7.

[173] Paris, v, 623. However, Maddicott, *Origins of the English Parliament*, 472, thinks Paris misdated the parade and it more likely took place at the October parliament of 1255.

[174] Burton, 386.

[175] Burton, 387–8.

Henry seems to have blamed not the message but his speaking position! He later commissioned a special lectern for the chapter house from which he could speak, one made of gilded iron work.[176]

On the same day as the speech of the archbishop of Messina, the papal envoy, Rostand, held an exclusively ecclesiastical gathering. With the payment of the tax now well under way, he published papal letters confirming its continuation from three years to five, and imposing a series of new taxes (called 'the graces'), including annates from all livings becoming vacant in the next five years.[177] In response, the bishops and clergy drew up their own schedule of objections to the Sicilian affair. It covered much the same ground as that of the magnates. England had not the wherewithal to take on such a burden, 'even if clay was turned to gold'. The church had paid for everything and seen its money 'uselessly expended and lost'.[178]

Although there was no way they could ultimately be gainsaid, the new taxes were resisted at clerical assemblies throughout 1257, much to Henry's frustration. His mood can be judged from an order the previous year when faced by the Cistercians' resistance to the original crusading tenth. The sheriffs were to do them no favours, although they were still to have 'common justice'; that the king 'wished to deny' to no one, a good example of both the latitude and limits of Henry's power.[179]

SORROW AND UNCERTAINTY

The rebuff at the parliament must have been painful enough for Henry but he soon had more personal reasons for depression. Around 3 May his daughter Katherine died, the daughter welcomed with such joy back in 1254. It had gradually become clear that Katherine suffered from more than normal childhood illnesses. She was, as Matthew Paris tells us, 'mute and incapable but very beautiful in face'. Henry and Eleanor loved her perhaps all the more. If Katherine died at Windsor, where the queen was so often based with her children, then Henry was present, having arrived there from Merton priory. Perhaps overcome with grief, he seems to have left immediately afterwards, going back to Merton. There he stayed until 14 May, when he returned to Westminster both for Katherine's burial in the Abbey and the feast of Pentecost. Henry spent £51 on alms at Katherine's funeral, enough to feed 10,000 paupers, and commissioned an

---

[176] Carpenter, 'King Henry III and the chapter house', 2.

[177] These letters were issued back in August and September 1256: *F*, 344–6; Burton, 388–9; Canterbury/Dover, 206 (which summarizes new demands). For the new exactions and resistance to them, see Lunt, *Financial Relations*, 275–8. Annates here meant the pope would have the first year's revenue from the vacant livings.

[178] Burton, 390–1.

[179] *CR 1254–6*, 418.

effigy for her tomb.[180] Whether the queen accompanied Henry to Merton and Westminster is doubtful. According to Matthew Paris, she was devastated by her daughter's death, and wasted away in bed at Windsor, seemingly beyond the help of doctors. Absence, however, did not weaken the bond between king and queen. When Henry himself fell ill towards the end of May, worry over the queen and grief over his daughter were, according to Paris, contributory factors.[181] When a decade later Henry commissioned the magnificent retable for the High Altar of Westminster Abbey, one of the miracles depicted was Christ raising the daughter of the centurion Jairus from the dead; the gesture in which he reaches down and holds her hand is an exquisite and poignant piece of painting. Included in the scene, standing over his daughter, is Jairus himself, and behind Jairus, with her arms around him, is Jairus's wife. This surely recalled how Henry and Eleanor stood grieving over Katherine. Christ would not raise Katherine from the dead but he would raise her to the life thereafter.[182]

After the rebuff at the parliament, Henry followed contradictory policies over Sicily. On 24 April, when he was at Merton priory, he sent a sharp letter to Rostand. On pain of losing all he possessed, he was to cease making payments to the Italian merchants from the crusading taxation until the king was confident the Sicilian business could proceed with success. Meanwhile the money was to be deposited at the New Temple.[183] Clearly Henry, not before time, was having second thoughts. Yet within little more than two weeks he was striking a very different note. On 9 May at Merton, Henry gave a robe to the messenger who brought the news of Richard of Cornwall's safe arrival in Germany.[184] Next day, with Richard's coronation seemingly assured (it took place on 17 May), Henry informed the pope he would soon be sending out a 'noble and strenuous' captain equipped with a great sum of money, the details the now returning archbishop of Messina could explain viva voce. In reality there was no money, but Henry had fingered a captain, none other than Henry of Castile, who had quarrelled with his brother King Alfonso, and was now being maintained in England. In the course of 1256–7 no less than £537 was assigned to his support.[185]

---

[180] *CLR 1251–60*, 373, 376, 385; Colvin, *History of the King's Works*, i, 478–9. For the tomb, see Badham and Oosterwijk, 'The tomb monument of Katherine'.

[181] Paris, v, 632, 643.

[182] For the retable, see Binski et al., *The Westminster Retable*. The link between Jairus's daughter and Katherine is my own.

[183] *CPR 1247–58*, 566; F, 356–7. The exchequer in this period was not acting on the writs of liberate ordering it to give the 1,000-mark annual pension to the pope. The order for the payment in 1255 was not implemented until the Michaelmas term of 1257: *CLR 1251–60*, 228; TNA E 403/15A.

[184] *CR 1256–9*, 52.

[185] F, 355; *CPR 1247–58*, 592. I owe the figure for Henry of Castile to Richard Cassidy.

At the end of June, with the help of Rostand himself, a co-ordinated if complex policy at last emerged.[186] The one thing absolutely clear was that Henry, by hook or by crook, wanted to continue with the project, although he saw that the terms just had to be modified. Henry thus told the pope that, since he had the Sicilian project greatly to heart, he was ready, 'according to your counsel', to make peace with France. To that end, ambassadors were being despatched who were to act with the counsel of Simon de Montfort and Peter of Savoy. The idea was that Montfort and Savoy would then go on to Rome. In a letter of excuse, Henry admitted he had not paid all the money and blamed the Welsh rising (of which more later) for the failure to despatch Henry of Castile as soon as he wished. He then suggested a whole series of ways in which the terms might be altered in order to give the project a chance of success.[187] So the penalties might be withdrawn or modified, the time limit might be extended; the payment of the debts might be suspended until the kingdom had been obtained; the money now collected from the church might be used to fund the army. Alternatively, perhaps a peace might be arranged in which Manfred resigned the kingdom on Edmund's marriage to his daughter. If none of these ways forward were acceptable, then Henry's envoys were empowered to renounce the kingdom.

Other than a further extension of the timetable on the existing terms, none of this was likely to gain much purchase, as Henry's wiser councillors must have known. It is noteworthy that neither Montfort nor Peter of Savoy actually went to Rome.[188] Why should Manfred resign the kingdom, when he was on his way to his coronation, and conceiving wider plans for Italian conquests? Why should the pope, reversing all previous policy, prefer to put the church's money into Henry's phantom army rather than into paying off the debts? Nor was the pope likely to be much impressed by the threat to resign the kingdom. It would not free Henry from his outstanding debt, let alone (as Henry absurdly hoped if the pope found another candidate) allow him to have back all he had spent! Nor was it at all likely that Henry's envoys would actually surrender the kingdom without further consultation. Had Henry been really bold, he would have stuck to his order preventing Rostand taking any more money from the kingdom. As it was, a furious Alexander told Rostand to ignore the order and threatened to proceed against king and kingdom if there was any more obstruction. Henry backed down and the money continued to flood from the country. Henry hoped vaguely for help from Richard, whom he was careful to carry with him in the French negotiations. But his brother

---

[186] For what follows, see *CR 1256–9*, 136–7; *F*, 358–61; *CPR 1247–58*, 564–8; *CLR 1251–60*, 382 (where shipping is also provided for Henry of Castile).

[187] These detailed instructions (drafted by Rostand himself) were for the benefit of envoys who might go if Montfort and Savoy could not.

[188] The chief envoys were the bishops of Bath and Wells and of Rochester: *F*, 365.

had now to spend all his money on Germany. Even if there was peace with France, Louis was unlikely to allow an army to pass through his kingdom. Indeed, Henry was soon complaining about the 'pernicious refusal' to allow anyone to go through France to Richard in Germany.[189] With a campaign in Wales looming, Henry should have cut his losses and pulled out of the project. Instead he waited for the pope's reply and, since Alexander still felt there was money to be made, the affair dragged on for another fateful year.

ARCBHISHOP BONIFACE AND RELATIONS WITH THE CHURCH, 1257

In securing the church's support for the Sicilian enterprise, or at least in securing its money, Henry must have hoped for help from Archbishop Boniface. Why else had he been appointed if not to be the loyal servant of the king? Henry was to be grievously disappointed.

Boniface had returned to England in November 1256, after an absence of over two years, much of it involved in Savoyard family affairs and the attempt to free Thomas of Savoy from his captivity in Turin. It was at Belley in Savoy that Boniface had consecrated William of Kilkenny as the new bishop of Ely.[190] Boniface's frequent absences meant he was scarcely a model archbishop, but he was absolutely ready to defend the privileges of the church against the demands of royal government. He was also, by this time, distancing himself from the Sicilian affair. He played no part in Henry's desperate attempt to modify the conditions. The bad feeling between Henry and his archbishop is shown by his total absence from court outside the parliament of March 1257. Instead of a firm supporter of his regime, Henry had an archbishop who was semi-detached as the great crisis of his reign approached.

In 1257, Boniface had come up with an offer to buy off the new papal taxes with a lump sum payment. He had made it, however, conditional on the king ceasing his oppressions and restoring the church to its ancient liberties.[191] To take matters further, Boniface summoned the bishops and clergy of the Canterbury province to a meeting in London during August. Henry was enraged for this clashed with his projected campaign against Llywelyn. He forbad the meeting and ordered the bishops, on pain of forfeiting their lands and goods, to join him in Wales.[192] Boniface was defiant and offered to prosecute the cause of the church 'in his own

[189] *CR 1256–9*, 134.
[190] Paris, v, 508, 515, 548, 564. Paris acknowledged that both Boniface and Peter of Savoy were generous in meeting Kilkenny's costs.
[191] Burton, 402.
[192] *CR 1256–9*, 142.

person if necessary, sparing no expense', provided the clergy of his province were prepared to support him.[193] The meeting went ahead, and the bishops went unpunished. They reviewed a whole series of detailed complaints against the operations of royal government. In one draft they ran to fifty separate chapters. Many turned on the extent to which churchmen were being made subject to secular justice. There were also the familiar complaints against the manipulation of ecclesiastical elections and the exploitation of vacancies.[194]

In the area of elections and vacancies, new disputes were tainting Henry's relations with the church. As he ruefully told the cardinals, the pope had taken no notice of his opposition to the election of the dean of York, Sewal de Bovill, as the new archbishop of York, and Sewal had finally been consecrated in July 1256. An argument over Ely soon followed. After William of Kilkenny's death in September 1256, the monks had gone ahead at once and elected their sub-prior, Hugh of Balsham. Henry sent Archbishop Boniface a passionate letter of protest, following up with one on similar lines to the cardinals.[195] His predecessors, he said, had conceded free elections, but saving their 'just and honest prayers' for the appointment of people valuable to king, church and kingdom. The monks of Ely had gone ahead without waiting for the king's envoys and had elected Hugh, a wastrel of servile birth, a man wholly unsuitable to the rule of a great church in a strategic area of the country. (It had once, Henry reminded the pope, been used by Danes and Saxons for attacks on the king.) If the monks had their way, it would offend the royal dignity, disinherit the king and his heirs, and make it impossible to appoint royal clerks to bishoprics 'by whose counsel and industry the arduous affairs of kingdom and church have accustomed to be wholesomely treated'. No doubt, Henry here was being egged on by his clerks, but this was an affair he took 'much to heart'. It was to no avail. The pope eventually consecrated Balsham in October 1257.[196] At least Henry was able to draw £2,500 from the revenues during the vacancy, although at the cost of yet more damage to his reputation.[197] About Ely itself he was prophetic. It was once again to be a rebel base during the coming civil war.

Meanwhile, Pope Alexander himself was becoming concerned about Henry's general treatment of the church, thanks in part to another bishop

---

[193] Burton, 403.

[194] Burton, 401–7; C&S, i, 530–48; Hoskin, 'The church and the king', 197–8.

[195] CR 1256–9, 108–9; F, 354.

[196] For the significance of the pope's intervention as a step towards the development of papal provisions, see Harvey, Episcopal Appointments, 102–3, 136 and the references given there. Boniface had earlier, as in the case of the bishop of Chichester, attempted to assert his right as primate to quash elections and appoint a new bishop (he had appointed Adam Marsh). For a full account of the Balsham affair, see Vincent, 'The thirteenth century', in Ely: Bishops and Diocese, 36–40.

[197] Howell, Regalian Right, 155, 238.

from whom Henry might have hoped for better. This was Laurence de St Martin, bishop of Rochester, whom Henry frequently employed as a diplomat. Indeed, the bishop had written home from Rome warning that Saracens might be plotting some wicked deed in England, a reference to a rumour that Manfred was planning to assassinate the king and his sons.[198] But this was not all St Martin was doing. He was also, 'on behalf of all the prelates and clergy of the kingdom of England', complaining to the pope about Henry's oppression of the church. In response, Alexander, in a pained letter, which became widely known in England, reminded Henry of the 1253 sentence against contraveners of Magna Carta and his coronation oath to protect the church. How could he pose as liberator of the Sicilian church, or get support from the church in England, when he was acting in this way? He must stop at once and restore what he had taken.[199] Alexander was responding to widespread disaffection. Together with the burdens flowing from the Sicilian affair, it would rob Henry of any support from the bishops and clergy when the crisis broke upon him in 1258.

DISASTER IN WALES, 1256 AND 1257

Back in 1255, when Llywelyn captured his brothers at the battle of Bryn Derwin and made himself sole master of Gwynedd west of Conwy, Henry had hardly reacted. Soon inaction was no longer a possibility. Llywelyn's triumphs were transforming the political shape of Wales. They distracted Henry III from the Sicilian affair, and helped bring about the revolution of 1258. Early in November 1256, Llywelyn had crossed the Conwy and taken possession of the Four Cantrefs to the east, leaving in Lord Edward's hands only the castles of Deganwy and Dyserth. He had then threatened Chester and forced Gruffudd of Bromfield, the ruler of northern Powys, to flee to the king. In South Wales, he had taken Gwerthrynion from Roger de Mortimer and given his Welsh allies Edward's lands around Builth.[200]

In striking these blows, Llywelyn had exploited discontent in the Four Cantrefs with the oppressive nature of English rule. Henry, aware of the situation, had attempted on several occasions to ensure his Welsh subjects were governed according to their own laws, but he had done nothing to reduce the 1,000-mark farm for which Alan la Zouche was expected to answer, a sum double that of his predecessor, John de Grey.[201] Money had

---

[198] *DD*, no. 288; Burton, 395.

[199] *F*, 351; Paris, v, 615–16; Paris, vi, 332. The letter was written in November 1256. Laurence de St Martin was also disaffected as a result of the king not supporting him in a jurisdictional dispute with Archbishop Boniface: Paris, v, 545, 615.

[200] St Werburgh, 72–3; *AC*, 90–1; *Brut*, 246–9; *Brut/Peniarth*, 110; Paris, v, 592–8.

[201] *CheshirePR*, 93, 97. The rent was for the county of Chester as well as the Four Cantrefs.

also been extracted from the men of the Four Cantrefs to help Henry in
Gascony.[202] Under Edward, things had probably got worse. At any rate,
his Welsh supremo, Geoffrey de Langley (already notorious as a justice of
the forest), was widely blamed for what happened. Quite possibly Edward
himself had turned a deaf ear to complaints on his visit in August 1256.
Soon afterwards, according to the Welsh chroniclers, the men of the Four
Cantrefs appealed to Llywelyn to free them from their slavery.

Llywelyn's aims were clear. He wished to recover the Four Cantrefs and
receive the homages of the other Welsh rulers. In other words he wished
to destroy the 1247 Treaty of Woodstock with its cession of the Four
Cantrefs and the homages to the king. In responding to Llywelyn's invasion, Edward got no help from his father. Henry simply sent plaintive
letters to Llwyelyn, ordering him to desist, yet also offering to do justice on
any complaints against Edward and his officials.[203] The last thing Henry
wanted at this juncture was to campaign in Wales, 'which is', as he put it
in a letter to the king of Castile, 'in the more remote parts of our
kingdom'.[204] A dignified and reproachful letter from Llywelyn, addressed
flatteringly to Richard both as king of the Romans and 'by the grace of
God emperor', showed there was no chance of him simply restoring his
ill-gotten gains. The most he would offer was either £1,000 for a seven-
year truce or, in return for a lasting peace, the surrender of the two
commotes in which the castles of Deganwy and Dyserth were actually
situated.[205] Since both proposals would have left him with the lion's
share of his conquests, emasculating Edward's Welsh lordship, they were
impossible to accept. The alternative was to hope that Edward could deal
with the situation himself and from his own resources. He was certainly,
in the spring of 1257, sending forces to Wales.[206] He was also raising
money, selling the Ferrers wardship to his mother and Peter of Savoy
for £4,000.[207]

Llywelyn, however, went from strength to strength. In January 1257, in
alliance with the rulers from South Wales (in itself an ominous sign as
Matthew Paris noted), he drove Gruffyd ap Gwenwynwyn, long loyal to
Henry, from southern Powys.[208] In Lent he took a large army south and

[202] *CPR 1247–58*, 70; *CheshirePR*, 96, 100, 103; *CFR 1253–4*, no. 8. For taxation levied
under Henry, see *CR 1254–6*, 301.

[203] *CR 1256–9*, 107–8, 112 (17 November, 10 December).

[204] *CR 1256–9*, 152.

[205] *AWR*, no. 327; *CR 1254–6*, 115; *CPR 1247–58*, 541; Paris, v, 613–14.

[206] *CPR 1247–58*, 586.

[207] *CPR 1247–58*, 554. This was the wardship of Robert de Ferrers, son and heir of
William de Ferrers, earl of Derby, who had died in 1254. Paris, v, 592–3, says Edward was
able to borrow 4,000 marks from Richard of Cornwall.

[208] There is a detailed examination of the events of 1257 in Smith, *Llywelyn ap Gruffudd*,
92–108.

ravaged the areas around Kidwelly, Gower and Swansea.[209] Worse still was to follow. In May, Edward's commander in South Wales, Stephen Bauzan, led a substantial force down the Tywi valley. The aim was to restore the Welsh ruler Rhys Fychan to the castle and lordship of Dinefwr, thus striking a blow at Maredud ap Rhys, to whom Llywelyn had given Rhys Fychan's territories. Maredudd, however, dogged the army all the way, and finally on Saturday 2 June Rhys Fychan deserted. The English attempted to retreat back to Carmarthen, but they lost their baggage train, and were then cornered and massacred. The shock to Henry was terrible. Both he and the queen knew Bauzan intimately, a favoured household knight who had passed into Edward's service and been briefly seneschal in Gascony. Henry was soon making generous concessions to Bauzan's widow.[210] But this was more than a personal disaster. The English had been humiliated. Their whole position in Wales seemed under threat. Both Richard de Clare, lord of Glamorgan, and William de Valence, lord of Pembroke, were at court in June when the news came in. The demand for action was irresistible.

On 21 June, therefore, Henry ordered a standard of red silk with gold brocade to be offered at the shrine of Saint Edward, as is 'customary when he is about to go on an expedition'.[211] Around the same time he summoned his tenants-in-chief to rendezvous at Chester on 1 August.[212] Although, therefore, the most recent disaster had been in the south, the aim was to campaign in the north. That was sensible. With Llywelyn defeated in his heartland, everything else in Wales might fall back into place. Llywelyn, however, was a jump ahead. On 13 July he inflicted a major defeat on Richard de Clare in Glamorgan, killing his men and burning one of his castles.[213] If the aim of this attack was to provoke a division of Henry's army, thus lessening the assault on Gwynedd, it worked perfectly. Clare hurried to court and on 18 July (with the king now at Woodstock) secured the command of 100 knights to protect Glamorgan and Pembroke. At the same time Humphrey de Bohun, earl of Hereford, was placed in command of forces between Clare's lands and Montgomery to the north.[214]

If Sicily and Wales were not enough on Henry's plate, at this very time there were anxieties in Scotland. There negotiations for a settlement with the Comyns had been getting nowhere.[215] On 20 July 1257, Henry appointed a high-powered delegation (including John Mansel) to meet Alexander and

[209] *AC*, 91–3; *Brut*, 248–9; Paris, v, 645–6; *CPR 1247–58*, 560.
[210] *CPR 1247–58*, 561, 570.
[211] *CR 1256–9*, 68.
[212] *CR 1256–9*, 139; Paris, vi, 373.
[213] Smith, *Llywelyn ap Gruffudd*, 45, 102; Paris, v, 642.
[214] *CR 1256–9*, 139–51; Dunstable, 203.
[215] *F*, 353.

his magnates at Stirling with a view to settling the disputes between them.[216] Meanwhile Henry and Eleanor decided to split forces. Henry would go on to Chester, while Eleanor would set out for Nottingham.[217] From there, if necessary, she was well placed to proceed further north. At Nottingham, Eleanor's apartment back in 1251 had been wainscoted, plastered, glassed and adorned with a painting of the story of Alexander. But in 1257 she found the air there unwholesome so went to stay at Tutbury castle instead. (It was in her hands through her purchase of the Ferrers wardship.) While at Tutbury she received a visit from Richard de Clare, quite probably to discuss the marriage of his daughter to Eleanor's cousin the marquis of Montferrat. Eleanor was seeking to draw Clare away from the Lusignans and into her own circle.[218]

Henry and Edward finally arrived at Chester on 5 August. A fortnight later, 'with no small army', they marched westwards into the Four Cantrefs. There was a good showing of magnates. Roger Bigod, earl of Norfolk, as marshal, organized the army.[219] The earl of Oxford mustered, as did John de Warenne, Edmund de Lacy, William de Valence, John de Balliol (who here purchased the king's grace), John fizGeoffrey, Philip Basset and John de Plessis, earl of Warwick.[220] On 26 August the army reached Deganwy, where Henry had been in 1245 while his new castle was built there. This time he had grander plans. He aimed not simply to recover the Four Cantrefs but also to conquer Anglesey. Then, if they entered his allegiance, what remained of Gwynedd west of Conwy could be shared between Dafydd and Owain.

Edward may well have been behind the strategy of the campaign. The occupation of Anglesey was a centrepiece of his campaign in 1277. This time, however, nothing like that happened. On 4 September Henry called off the invasion of Anglesey and decided to return home. As he explained to Richard de Clare in a long apologetic letter, the winter was approaching and the shipping summoned from Ireland and England had not materialized. Matthew Paris adds that there was famine in the army since the Welsh had ravaged the surrounding area.[221] Henry, however, pledged to return to Chester at Pentecost 1258 with a great array of food, shipping and troops to renew the campaign.[222] Meanwhile he hurried home to Westminster, getting there in time for the feast of the Confessor on 13 October.

The opinion of contemporary chroniclers on this Henry's last campaign in Wales was derisory. He had spent a great deal of money, achieved

[216] *F*, 362; *CPR 1247–58*, 571.
[217] *CR 1256–9*, 79–80, 85.
[218] *CLR 1251–60*, 9, 18; Dunstable, 203; Howell, *Eleanor of Provence*, 74, 142.
[219] Paris, vi, 373–4.
[220] *RCWL*, ii, 110–13.
[221] Paris, v, 649.
[222] *CR 1256–9*, 90–1.

nothing and returned without glory. The most Henry himself claimed was that he had refortified Deganwy castle. As his army retreated, Llywelyn hung about its tail and then resumed control of the Four Cantrefs.[223] Henry's Welsh ally Gruffudd of Bromfield, ruler of northern Powys, had been with Henry on the campaign and been involved in vain attempts to win over Dafydd, Llywelyn's brother.[224] Now, 'after seventeen years of unflinching loyalty to the crown', he deserted to Llywelyn.[225]

Only in South Wales was there a different picture. Here Henry thanked Richard de Clare effusively for bringing over to the king's side none other than Maredudd ap Rhys, the very man responsible for the death of Stephen Bauzan. In October he came to London, did homage to Henry and received the lands of Rhys Fychan.[226]

Henry, in his letter to Richard de Clare, insisted that the decision to abandon the campaign had been taken on the advice of his magnates and was repugnant to his wishes.[227] Matthew Paris gives a picture of Henry during the campaign 'armed elegantly', advancing with his forces, his dragon standard displayed, urging his knights to kill the Welsh.[228] The trouble, as so often, was that Henry's actions did not match his words. To abandon the campaign, on the excuse of the coming winter, *in the first week of September*, was absurd. Whatever the famine in the army, Henry could at least have remained at Chester to help Edward maintain some authority over the Four Cantrefs and prevent Gruffudd of Bromfield deserting to Llywelyn. The truth, as both Matthew Paris and the Dunstable annalist implied, was that Henry wanted to get home for the feast of Edward the Confessor.[229]

The logical deduction from Henry's plans to conquer Gwynedd in the summer of 1258 was that he had at last abandoned the Sicilian project. Yet, as events were to show, that was not the case. Henry was far more committed to the conquest of Sicily than he was to the conquest of Wales and there was no way he would abandon the first in order to pursue the second. Yet with Edward and his magnates feeling exactly the reverse, there was equally no way he could abandon Wales in favour of Sicily. So Henry was trapped. There was nothing he could do other than muddle on and hope for the best. Perhaps the Confessor would find a way.

[223] Paris, v, 651, 656–7, 664.

[224] *CPR 1247–58*, 600.

[225] Smith, *Llywelyn ap Gruffudd*, 105; St Werburgh, 74.

[226] Smith, *Llywelyn ap Gruffudd*, 99–100, 105–7; Paris, v, 646–7; *CPR 1247–58*, 577; *LW*, 161–4. These were the last charters witnessed before his death by the king's steward Ralph fitzNicholas after a career stretching back to King John's reign.

[227] *CR 1256–9*, 90–1.

[228] Paris, v, 648, 651.

[229] Paris, v, 649; Dunstable, 204.

EXPEDIENTS AND OPPRESSION IN THE LAST YEARS
OF THE PERSONAL RULE

In the last years of his personal rule, Henry was desperate for money. He had returned from Gascony burdened with debt. Soon, he needed vast sums to fund his Sicilian army. And then there was the cost of the campaign in Wales. Faced with this situation, Henry was as hands on as ever. He tried to increase his revenues, reduce his expenditure and (with the support of his council) introduce financial reform. He saved up a second gold treasure and minted his own gold coinage, the first in gold since before the Norman Conquest. He was not bankrupt. He could pay his way day to day by cash and credit. In 1258 he even had a reserve of treasure. But it was worth a few thousand pounds, not the many tens of thousands needed merely to launch a war in Sicily.

In his financial difficulties there was one source Henry was loath to tap. Many of his leading magnates owed him money, yet Henry could have been a lot more determined in making them pay up.[230] Here the experiences of John de Balliol and Robert de Ros were untypical. Of the eleven laymen chosen by the barons in 1258 to reform the realm, none had been put under real financial pressure by the crown.[231] The only occasion when Henry attempted punitive action was against the earl of Norfolk in 1255, and that was short lived as we have seen. When the exchequer, going loyally through the motions, attempted to collect the debts of such men, it was usually stopped by letters of the king, sometimes angry letters, respiting or pardoning the debts in question, or setting increasingly easy terms for their repayment. One farcical result was that while Henry, as the guarantor, was paying the Montforts £400 a year as compensation for Eleanor's dower in Wales and Ireland, he failed abjectly to recoup the money from the Marshal heirs, who included the earls of Norfolk and Gloucester, William de Valence, Humphrey de Bohun, eldest son of the earl of Hereford, and Roger de Mortimer.[232] In all this Henry was behaving very differently from his father, whose treatment of major barons

---

[230] Carpenter, *Reign of Henry III*, 75–9.

[231] The earls of Leicester, Gloucester, Norfolk and Hereford, Roger de Mortimer, John fitzGeoffrey, Hugh Bigod, Richard de Grey, William Bardolph, Peter de Montfort and Hugh Despenser.

[232] This saga runs through the memoranda rolls of the 1250s: for example, TNA E 368/31, m. 4d; E 368/32, mm. 3, 10d, 13d; E 159/30, m. 1d. For Henry's guarantee, see above, 505, n. 81. The exchequer was also trying to get the heirs to compensate Margaret, countess of Lincoln and Pembroke, for paying more than her share from her dower as the widow of Walter Marshal. It was apparently in this context that Henry for once took action against his half-brothers. In 1257 he sent Robert Walerand and Imbert Pugeys (the latter no friend of William de Valence) into the exchequer with orders that it henceforth 'exhibit full justice' to William de Valence, his other brothers and everyone else. An order to the sheriff of Hertfordshire to make Valence appear at the exchequer and reach an agreement with the countess followed: TNA E 368/ 32, m. 15d.

made the rebellion of 1215 very much 'a rebellion of the king's debtors'.[233] That was hardly the case in 1258.[234]

The picture, however, is very different if one moves beyond the great men in and around the court whose favour Henry wished to retain. Out in the shires, Henry might rather appear to be, as Matthew Paris put it, 'a vigilant and indefatigable searcher after money'.[235] Henry's financial expedients, moreover, in exacerbating his government's unpopularity, made all the more impossible the only real solution to Henry's financial problems, namely taxation conceded by parliament.

Matthew Paris put Henry's Gascon debts at over £200,000, which caught their flavour even if it was greatly exaggerated.[236] Henry had certainly acknowledged debts while in Gascony worth many thousands of pounds.[237] He was also committed to paying new pensions to his Gascon and other supporters worth around £2,000 a year. Meanwhile his overall resources had been reduced by the appanage created for Edward. Including as it did Ireland, Cheshire, Bristol, numerous English manors and a collection of wardships, Henry's annual income was potentially cut by around £7000 a year.[238]

Faced with his Gascon debts, Henry moved at once to increase his cash resources. In February 1255 he borrowed 10,000 marks (£6,666) from Earl

---

[233] Holt, *Northerners*, 34.

[234] One baron with an apparent grievance over debt was the lord of Clun and Oswestry, John fitzAlan, for whom see also below, 701, n. 7. Whereas, by a decision of Hubert de Burgh, his father had been let off payments towards the minatory 10,000 marks King John had demanded for succession to the family estates (http://aalt.law.uh.edu/AALT4/H3/E372n071/aE372n071fronts/IMG_1315.htm), from 1249 onwards John was asked to pay up. By 1258 the pipe rolls show that he had paid off £1,350. One might have thought this treatment would have made him a leading revolutionary, but in the end he supported the king during the civil war. A series of factors may have reduced the grievance. That he was liable for the debt seems to have been a decision of parliament: *CFR 1247–58*, no. 530. The rate of repayment was reduced from £200 a year to £100 (a concession made to John and his heirs probably thanks to John going with Henry to Gascony). Some later payments were respited thanks to John's service in Wales. In 1257, Henry put him in command at Montgomery: *CFR 1247–8*, no. 530; *CFR 1256–7*, no. 934; *CFR 1257–8*, no. 458 (which shows him serving in Wales at the time of the 1258 revolution); http://aalt.law.uh.edu/AALT4/H3/E372n098/aE372n098fronts/IMG_8227.htm; *CR 1256–9*, 88. John was a rich man since he had inherited through his mother the castle and honour of Arundel.

[235] Paris, v, 55, 274.

[236] Paris, v, 484.

[237] See above, 596–8.

[238] Wait, 'Household and resources of the Lord Edward', 10, 26, 30–2, 42–3, 60–2, 67–75, 160–1, shows that Henry lost annually a potential £2,000 from Ireland, £1,000 from Cheshire and the Welsh lordships, £1,400 from Bristol and the English manors and £2,500 from the Ferrers, Seagrave and Cantilupe wardships (these last conceded to Edward in 1254). The appanage also included Gascony but that entailed no loss to Henry in terms of revenue available in England. For the revenue sent to England from Ireland in the 1250s, see Lydon, 'Edward II and the revenues of Ireland', 55–6 and Lydon, 'Three exchequer documents'.

Richard, in return handing over to him the custody of the Jews. The only qualification, decided on later, doubtless after a protest from the queen, was that her own monies from the Jews should be safeguarded.[239] No less than 41 per cent of wardrobe receipts in the account from January 1255 to April 1256 came from this loan. Thus supported, Henry was able to liquidate over £6,300 of Gascon debts by payments made out of the wardrobe.[240] Orders were also given (how far obeyed is unknown) for debts to be paid by the exchequer. In April 1255 alone the total to be disbursed was over £2,700.[241]

Henry tried to retrench. In view of his 'immense and burdensome debts' he reduced his former 'sumptuous' expenditure on the wages of castle garrisons. He ordered only £10 to be spent on the repair of Oxford castle, although it needed £60, this until he had further advice from Earl Richard and others of the council.[242] Henry also kept down the costs of his household's food and drink. He had done that while saving for his crusade. He now continued in the same vein. The average daily cost of the food and drink between January 1255 and April 1256 was £9.19 a day, less even than in 1252 when it had been £9.79, and a considerable contrast to the £13.55 average between 1245 and 1252.[243] There was also in the same period, compared with the years 1245–52, a decline in the gifts of rings, brooches, cups and basins.[244]

Aside from the great loan from Richard, Henry sought other ways to increase his cash flow. Between January 1255 and April 1256 he sold jewels worth £1,206.[245] Specifically to relieve his Gascon debts, he and the council tallaged the royal demesne, as they said, more heavily than before, although trying to ensure the poor were not unfairly burdened.[246] Henry also, in a very personal initiative, came down on the sheriffs. On 9 October 1256 he entered the exchequer and 'with own mouth' laid down that henceforth they were to appear in person every Easter and Michaelmas with all the money they had collected, this on pain of heavy and escalating amercements. It was

---

[239] Wild, *WA*, cxxiv, cxxviii–xi, 81; *F*, 315; *CPR 1247–58*, 400–1; Paris, v, 488; Denholm-Young, *Richard of Cornwall*, 80, 159–60. The agreement stated the Jews were to pay Richard 8,000 marks over the next two years. The rest of the loan was secured on Henry's 'old treasure' (made up of jewels and precious objects), which Richard was allowed to pawn if not repaid.

[240] Wild, *WA*, cxxiv, cxxxi, 81.

[241] *CLR 1251–60*, 203–12; Collingwood, 'Royal finance', 57–8. There are no issue rolls in this period.

[242] *CLR 1251–60*, 271; *CR 1254–6*, 113.

[243] Carpenter, 'Household rolls', 35. The figures include other items of expenditure on the household roll.

[244] Kjaer, 'Matthew Paris and the royal Christmas', 152.

[245] Wild, *WA*, cxxviii, 80.

[246] *CR 1254–6*, 157–62; *F*, 316 (*CPR 1247–58*, 404); Mitchell, *Studies in Taxation*, 283. This was the occasion for the quarrel with London, for which see above, 614–15. The amount charged for the tallage was 8,500 marks including the 3,000 marks from London.

not perhaps a very sensible initiative, and was soon abandoned. There was no reason why the sheriffs should not send their money in through deputies.[247] Still, at least it showed Henry was monitoring the performance of the sheriffs and trying to keep them up to the mark.

The sheriffs were under pressure in another way. In 1229/30 the amount they owed the exchequer above the ancient farms of their counties had been around £750.[248] By 1242 it was £1,540, nearly all in the form of annual increments charged above the farms. By 1252 the sum had risen to £2,320. Over the next five years, while the increments in two sheriffdoms were reduced, six suffered further increases so that the total demanded in 1257 amounted to £2,500.[249] The increment from Norfolk–Suffolk (a joint sheriffdom) rose between 1252 and 1257 from 300 marks to 400 marks; that from Northamptonshire from 130 marks to 180 marks.[250]

Matthew Paris commented under 1256 on the escalating increments and how the sheriffs were becoming progressively more extortionate. He then went on to describe in detail the evil behaviour of the sheriff of Northamptonshire, the knight William de Lisle. Here Henry did act. Lisle was dismissed, imprisoned and deprived temporarily of his lands, before being saved by the intervention of John Mansel and the king and queen of Scotland. The episode might have triggered provisions dealing with the abuses of local officials along the lines of Louis IX's Ordinance of December 1254. Indeed, around this time, perhaps recalling his own conversations with the king, Matthew Paris has Henry, 'led by pious intentions', 'thirsting' to put a stop to the evils inflicted by the sheriffs.[251] But it was mere words. No measures of reform followed. In setting the terms for Lisle's successor, Henry's chief concern was the ability to raise the increment, which remained at the same high level.[252] Not surprisingly, the new sheriff, the clerk Hugh de Manneby, turned out to be just as bad as his predecessor and was finally brought to book by the revolution of 1258.[253] As the critique

[247] For the whole episode, see Carpenter, *Reign of Henry III*, ch. 7.

[248] Carpenter, *Reign of Henry III*, 172. This is the figure either from the increments demanded above the farm or from profits less any allowances given the sheriff. For the two systems of getting extra money from the sheriffs, see above, 190.

[249] Carpenter, *Reign of Henry III*, 172. Richard Cassidy, calculating the increments in a slightly different way, has sent me figures showing a comparable increase, namely £1,729 for 1242, £2,525 for 1252 and £2,777 for 1257. See his 'Bad sheriffs, custodial sheriffs', 36–8, where the success of the sheriffs in raising the revenue demanded is demonstrated.

[250] Carpenter, *Reign of Henry III*, 172.

[251] Paris, ii, 389. Paris is here revising his account of 1236 and removing what was clearly a more disobliging comment. For the date of the revision, see Vaughan, *Matthew Paris*, 121.

[252] Paris, v, 576–80; *CFR 1255–6*, no. 1117. In Lisle's case, the council, including Henry of Bath, asserted the principle (for which see *CR 1231–4*, 587–8) that no one should be deprived of possessions until convicted of a crime, although it proved hard to prize Lisle's manor of Grafton in Northamptonshire from William de Valence: *CR 1256–9*, 65, 82, 171, 174–5, 196, 293–4, 298–9.

[253] Cassidy, 'Bad sheriffs, custodial sheriffs', 38–40.

of Henry's personal rule drawn up in 1264 put it, the increments could not be raised by the sheriffs 'without oppressing those subject to them and without unlawful extortion'.[254] They inevitably meant an increase in amounts demanded from the hundreds, thus making it all the less likely they would be entrusted to bailiffs who would 'treat the people with justice', as Henry had vainly hoped in his speech to the sheriffs in 1250.[255]

The critique of 1264 also honed in on the types of people Henry had appointed as sheriff. Instead of 'prudent and knowledgeable knights of the counties' as 'of old custom', they had been 'men coming from far away and utter strangers in the counties'. In fact, in the 1240s and 1250s, a proportion of the sheriffs were still local knights, including William de Lisle. But others were indeed outsiders, clerks and professional administrators, men unconstrained by local ties and for that reason likely to be all the more ruthless in raising money both for themselves and the crown.[256] All this was very different from the way the counties had been run during the popular experiment launched in 1236. The sheriffs appointed in that year had been county knights. They had answered not for farms and increments but for all their revenues, receiving an allowance for their own support. And they had also taken an oath forbidding bribes and requiring moderation in demands for entertainment. In 1258 the reformers reintroduced the arrangements of 1236.[257]

The sheriffs were not the only unpopular local agents of the king. There were also the escheators. From 1246 to 1248, after a series of different expedients, new arrangements were devised for exploiting the escheats and wardships falling due to the king. Two chief escheators were appointed, one north of the Trent, the other south (Henry of Wingham). Under them in each county there was a sub-escheator, usually a local knight.[258] The amount of land in the escheators' hands was always limited, given the way wardships and escheats were given away by the king. But after the revolution of 1258 there were still vociferous complaints about the 'wrongs done by escheators' in breach of the chapters in Magna Carta preventing wardships being ravaged by their custodians. In the reforms proposed at the Oxford parliament in 1258, the section on the escheators came immediately after that on the sheriffs.[259]

Henry, in these last years of his personal rule, was also bearing down on the counties through the exactions of his judges. After the termination of the northern forest eyres in 1252, there had been a pause, but between

---

[254] *DBM*, 120–1, and see also 82–3, cap. 16; Carpenter, *Reign of Henry III*, 172–5. For the increments in Somerset–Dorset, see Ridgeway, 'Dorset in the period of baronial reform', 24–5.

[255] See above, 529.

[256] Carpenter, *Reign of Henry III*, 178–9.

[257] Carpenter, *Reign of Henry III*, 170–1.

[258] Waugh, 'The origins of the office of escheator', 261–5.

[259] *DBM*, 108–9, cap.18, 270–1; and see *C&S*, i, 543, cap. 24. The relevant chapters in the 1215 Magna Carta were 4, 5 and 26.

1255 and 1258 the forest justices were at work again in thirteen counties, the amercements they imposed being worth a potential £1,808 to the crown.[260] More burdensome still were the exactions of the justices of the general eyre.[261] The king's judges, or the best of them, certainly believed in their duty to uphold right and justice. They showed concern for widows and sometimes pardoned the amercements of the poor.[262] But they also saw it absolutely as their task to make money for the crown. In the 1220s the judge William of York, on eyre in Cumberland, wrote cheery letters to the chancellor, Ralph de Neville, telling him how much money was coming in every day.[263] The burden of the eyre increased during Henry's personal rule. Indeed, the judges in the 1240s devised fresh ways in which to extract money from the local communities.[264] The amercements the sheriffs were expected to collect stood at £10,153 for the eyres of 1234–6, £18,698 for the eyres of 1245–9, and £17,859 for those of 1252–8.[265] In this last period the judges were hearing pleas in twenty-five counties, Henry closely following their progress and often assigning the proceeds before they had even come in.[266] No wonder there were vociferous complaints about the burdens of the eyre, no wonder the reforming legislation of 1259 sought to limit its exactions.[267] Many of those who suffered were unfree peasants, but the juries who came before the judges, and were often amerced, included knights and substantial free tenants. Henry was alienating the people on whom his rule in the shires depended.[268]

HENRY'S SECOND GOLD TREASURE

Henry was not entirely profligate in his use of the money he was making. Indeed, in these last years of his personal rule he was trying to build up another treasure. Once again it was to be in gold. Its purpose was no longer to fund his crusade. It was to fund his Sicilian army, gold being the currency of the Sicilian kingdom.

As with his first gold treasure, this was an enterprise close to Henry's heart and under his personal control. The gold was saved by the wardrobe

---

[260] Winters, 'The forest eyre 1154–1368', 25, 206–37. For the forest eyre, see above, 51–2.

[261] Maddicott, 'Magna Carta and the local community', 47–8. For the nature of the general eyre, see above, 51, n. 169.

[262] See Turner, *The English Judiciary in the Age of Glanvill and Bracton*, ch. 6.

[263] Meekings, *Studies in 13th-Century Justice*, v, 499–500.

[264] Maddicott, 'Magna Carta and the local community', 47–8.

[265] Cassidy, 'Bad sheriffs, custodial sheriffs', 37, drawing in part on Meekings' calculations in Meekings and Crook, *Surrey Eyre*, i, 135, and Meekings, *Wiltshire Eyre*, 112. The figures are calculated from the lump sum accounted for by the sheriffs. Further money was due outside the lump sum.

[266] Crook, *Records of the General Eyre*, 120–6.

[267] Brand, *Kings, Barons and Justices*, 77–83, 87–94. For complaints about the eyre during the personal rule, Paris, iv, 186–7; Burton, 387.

[268] For the personnel of these juries, see Carpenter, *Magna Carta*, 135–7.

not the exchequer.[269] Indeed, later in the enterprise, the exchequer was not even informed about what was coming in. Driven forward by the king, the results were not unimpressive. The wardrobe accounts show that, between January 1255 and April 1256, 390 marks of gold were saved, so gold with the silver value of nearly 4,000 marks. There are no wardrobe accounts thereafter, but by August 1257 the treasure was certainly worth some 569 marks of gold, so the equivalent of 5,690 marks of silver or £3,793. It may well have been worth several thousand marks more.[270]

The treasure was accumulated partly by using silver to buy gold. Between January 1255 and April 1256, £1,055 of wardrobe cash was used in that way. Henry even swore an oath to restore whatever he took from the silver assigned for such purchases.[271] He eagerly awaited the results of his endeavours. In April 1255 he was to be sent the gold obtained from 60 marks of silver on the following Monday morning at Merton before he rose from his bed. Henry also advertised his readiness to grant privileges in return for gold. Between January 1255 and April 1256, 143 marks of gold were added to the treasure from fines and gifts. These were much the same methods as those used to accumulate the first gold treasure and were uncontroversial. But Henry also developed a striking new policy, one which did much to make him unpopular with gentry opinion in the shires.

On 13 April 1256, Henry sent out an order to the sheriffs. They were to compel all those holding by military service and with an income of £15 a year to take up knighthood. The aim may partly have been to strengthen the military might of the country prior to a Sicilian campaign. But it was also to raise money, for Henry made clear that exemptions from knighthood could be bought in return for fines of gold. The usual amount was half a mark, so the equivalent of 5 marks of silver or £3 6s 8d. There was nothing unusual in the king issuing orders to compel those qualified to take up knighthood, and his right to do so was never questioned. Two things, however, were now new. One was that the uniquely low level – an annual income of £15 – at which men became liable. In 1244 the level had been £20. The exemption could thus cost a good slice of the potential knight's annual income. The second innovation was the thoroughness with which the policy was implemented. The sheriffs had to value properties of all the potential knights in their counties and return the lists to the king. They then had to distrain those identified either to take up knighthood or make the fine for exemption. Negligence was punished. On 10 October

---

[269] See *CR 1254–6*, 416–17. See Cassidy, 'The reforming council takes control'.

[270] Carpenter, *Reign of Henry III*, 120–2.

[271] Wild, *WA*, 81; *CR 1254–6*, 178; *CR 1256–9*, 6, 26. There was one disappointment. In November 1256, Henry had finally to ratify the delivery to Richard of Cornwall of the 1,207 marks of gold from the first gold treasure, pledged against the loans Richard had made back in 1254. Henry still did not give up hope of getting it back and spoke to his brother about it, not to any effect: *CPR 1247–58*, 528; TNA E 368/32, m. 6.

1256 no fewer than twenty-two sheriffs were each amerced half a mark of gold for failing to carry out the distraint effectively.[272] The sheriffs were, in fact, damned if they did and damned if they didn't, for they were also amerced for forcing people to become knights when they had insufficient income.

The results of this policy are very apparent.[273] Between April 1256 and the end of 1257 around 415 individuals fined for respite of knighthood with another 50 fining for an inquiry into the value of their lands.[274] The silver value of the fines was around £1,640. This was a useful sum but scarcely transformative. It hardly compensated for the resulting unpopularity. Matthew Paris listed the policy as one of the oppressive measures of 1256.[275] It affected not merely those who made fines with the king but those who decided to shoulder the cost of actually assuming knighthood. Perhaps as many as a thousand men were affected in one way or the other. There were also those who escaped by bribing the sheriffs, a subject on which there was later an inquiry.[276] Here again Henry was alienating the very men he should have been doing his very best to placate.

HENRY'S FINANCIAL SITUATION AND
A SCHEME OF REFORM

What then were the results of all Henry's labours to get money? Here the calculations made by historians are subject to all kinds of qualifications and can only be very approximate, but the main outlines are clear.[277] Henry's revenue in 1255, boosted by Richard's loan, the sale of jewels and the fines and gifts in gold may well have been around £37,000.[278] Save for one exceptional year this exceeded the level in the early 1240s.[279] It helps explain how Henry was able to clear so many of his Gascon debts. The absence of any wardrobe accounts after April 1256 make calculations very approximate, but revenue in 1256 and 1257 was almost certainly lower than in 1255, perhaps by something like £6,000 a year. The fines of gold

---

[272] *CFR 1255–6*, nos. 1196–1220; Paris, v, 589.

[273] For what follows, see Carpenter, 'Between Magna Carta and the parliamentary state', 23–8, and Waugh, 'Reluctant knights and jurors', 951–2.

[274] The respite was usually to last for three years.

[275] Paris, v, 594–5.

[276] Jacob, *Studies*, 30, cap. xi.

[277] I am indebted here to the pioneering work of James Collingwood and Richard Cassidy, both of whom have laboriously added up the figures in the pipe rolls, and made complex adjustments, to arrive at some kind of estimate for annual revenue. For Collingwood's figures, see 'Royal finance', 28–9, and 67 for the additional sums from fines of gold. For Cassidy's figures and much of what follows I am indebted to his unpublished 'A golden treasure or a state of collapse?' See also his 'Adventus vicecomitum'. For wider discussion, see Barratt, 'Finance on a shoestring'.

[278] For 1255 I am indebted to Cassidy. Collingwood started his calculations in 1256.

[279] Stacey, *Politics, Policy and Finance*, 208.

cannot have compensated for the absence of any equivalent to Richard's loan and the resulting lack of revenue from the Jews. Thanks to Edward's endowment, Henry's annual income, at probably little more than £30,000, was now significantly less than in the early 1250s. Of course, Henry could hope that Edward would lift the burden of Wales and Gascony from his shoulders and Irish resources did contribute to the Welsh campaign of 1257. But Henry was still left complaining of his great needs and his lack of money.[280] He was forced to keep debtors hanging around until cash came into the exchequer, and even then often sent them home with only partial payments.[281] In July 1255 he learnt that Gascon merchants, fed up with lack of payment, would no longer sell him wine.[282] The dearth of cash in the exchequer was also reflected in the small amounts of money it was sending to the wardrobe, quite different from earlier years. Between January 1255 and April 1256 it supplied only 16 per cent of wardrobe revenue as opposed to over 50 per cent between 1245 and 1252.[283]

There were two reasons for this lack of exchequer cash. The first was that a large proportion of revenue was being disbursed, on the king's orders, by sheriffs and other officials with the result that it never reached the exchequer. In 1256, for example, some 42 per cent of the king's income was absorbed by such disbursements. This was a pattern seen from the start of the 1250s, but was very different from that between 1240 and 1245, when such expenditure accounted for around 14 per cent of revenue.[284] Major items of this expenditure in 1256 and 1257 were fees and wages, building works, purchases of cloth, wine and munitions, and, most striking of all (worth £3,425 in 1256), gifts of money to the royal family and favourites.[285]

The second reason for the exchequer's lack of cash was Henry's diversion direct into the wardrobe of money from eyres, vacant bishoprics and other debts. Sometimes it was to be sent day by day as it came in, or even day and night.[286] There was nothing new in this either, nor was there anything necessarily wrong about it. Why not secure money directly rather then wait for it to go into the exchequer and then out again to the wardrobe? Yet Henry's councillors *did* think there was something wrong, probably because the wardrobe was left living hand to mouth and scrabbling

[280] Lydon, 'Three exchequer documents', 15–18; see Barratt, 'Crisis management', 58–62.

[281] For example, *CR 1254–6*, 74; *CLR 1251–60*, 354. For Henry's inability to pay the wages of workers at Gillingham, see *CR 1254–6*, 79.

[282] *CR 1254–6*, 207–8; and see 88–9. The problem was compounded by Henry's charter to Bordeaux in 1254, which protected their wines from compulsory purchase.

[283] Wild, *WA*, cxv, cxxii, cxxix.

[284] Stacey, *Politics, Policy and Finance*, 208. For the decline in cash income, see Collingwood, 'Royal finance', 30.

[285] Collingwood, 'Royal finance', 55–6.

[286] So, for example, *CR 1254–6*, 242–3; Wild, *WA*, cxxix, 80–1. In the accounts of 1255/6 there are over twenty such payments, many of them amalgams of smaller sums.

around for money from a whole variety of sources. The result was that it too sometimes ran out of funds and could not pay its way, leaving behind a trail of debts for food, drink and cloth. Far better for the wardrobe to be financed in an orderly fashion from the exchequer. This was precisely the aim of a major reform attempted in April 1257.

The reform was promulgated by the king in the presence of Lord Edward, Guy de Lusignan, William de Valence, Peter of Savoy, John Mansel, Robert Walerand and others of the council, a rare example of the half-brothers and Peter of Savoy working constructively together.[287] Henceforth, the expenses of the king's household were to be paid for day by day. To make that possible the exchequer was to reserve for the wardrobe 20,000 marks – £13,333 – half from the first monies coming into the Easter exchequer and half from those coming in at Michaelmas. A further £1,000 was to be reserved each year for the building of Westminster Abbey. To ensure this happened, the treasurer of the exchequer, Philip Lovel, took a personal oath before the king and the councillors to make no payment on the king's orders, even if given by the king by word of mouth, until the money for the wardrobe had been accumulated. If he did do so, then he would be liable to make restoration out of his own goods!

The scheme stands with others in the reign as a withering witness to the king's sense of his own fallibility. His efforts to protect himself from himself were as unkingly as they were unrealistic. Was Lovel really going to refuse orders personally issued by the king? The actual sum to be set aside for the wardrobe would certainly have covered wardrobe expenditure in a normal year. Indeed, £10,000 would have been an adequate figure. The ban on payments until the figure was reached was sensible. But the scheme was a complete failure. For a while, in the spring and summer of 1257, orders to the exchequer to spend money were qualified by saying the cash due to the wardrobe must be raised first. The last of these was in July.[288] Thereafter payments were ordered without restriction. There had also been payments ordered without reference to the restriction from the start. The exchequer itself never sent anything like the stipulated sums to the wardrobe and the king soon resumed his old practice of drawing directly on local revenues.[289]

The only way the scheme could have worked was if all the kingdom's revenues were paid in to the exchequer. Otherwise it would never have the cash to meet the wardrobe's requirements.[290] If such a concentration of revenue was intended in 1257, it was not stipulated. That was later imposed

[287] *CR 1256–9*, 46–7.

[288] *CLR 1251–60*, 364–84.

[289] *CLR 1251–60*, 372–5 (to Montfort and the countess of Flanders), 377, 395, 405.

[290] Cash paid to the exchequer exceeded £13,000 by £1,000 or so in 1255 and 1257, but was over £1,000 short in 1256. Another problem was in deciding what was and what was not wardrobe expenditure: *CLR 1251–60*, 366–7.

in the reforms of 1258.[291] As it was, the king continued to pay debts from local revenues, thus necessarily reducing the income of the exchequer.[292] The reform would always have been difficult to work. It had limited success in 1258. But without formal restrictions on the king it had no hope. A mere oath taken by Lovel was not nearly enough. The reformers of 1258 took note.

Henry was unlucky in these years in the comparative dearth of money from episcopal vacancies. The audited totals for 1256 and 1257 averaged only £1,300 a year as against nearly £6,000 for the years 1240 to 1244, when both Canterbury and Winchester were in his hands.[293] Yet Henry also had himself to blame for his predicament. He was never very consistent about retrenchment. On the same day in May 1255 as he ordered 60 to 100 marks to be spent on a jewel for the feretory of the Confessor, he admitted he could not pay various German merchants the great sums he owed them.[294] Henry was also as lavish as ever in the distribution of patronage, especially when it came to Richard of Cornwall, the queen, his foreign relatives and Simon de Montfort.[295] While Henry avoided alienating royal demesne manors in perpetuity, he was very ready to grant them away more temporarily on favourable terms. As a result, the rents from twenty-eight manors worth £1,201 in 1241 had fallen to £755 by 1258.[296] As for wardships, the most valuable neither stayed in his hands for long nor were used to make money. In 1255 custody of the lands and heir of Warin de Munchesney was given, even before Warin was quite dead, to William de Valence, this to fulfil the promise made in Gascony to give him £500 from the first wards falling in.[297] In 1257 the plum Longespée wardship (the heiress was only two) was given at once to the queen, while the rights over Longespée's widow went to Geoffrey de Lusignan. Meanwhile, the king confirmed a concession made out in Gascony to Peter of Savoy, freeing him from the £625 a year he was due to pay for the Vescy wardship.[298] In 1258–9 the revolutionary council asserted control over wardships and laid down that they should be sold to support the king's household and pay his debts.[299]

---

[291] *DBM*, 106–7, cap. 14.

[292] *CPR 1247–58*, 552; *CLR 1251–60*, 367, 377.

[293] Collingwood, 'Royal finance', 36–7.

[294] *CR 1254–6*, 74.

[295] For Henry's treatment of the debts of his leading nobles, see Carpenter, *Reign of Henry III*, 88–93.

[296] Cassidy, 'A golden treasure or a state of collapse?', 17 and table 11.

[297] *CPR 1247–58*, 419. This was the custody of William, the son of Warin's second marriage, to whom the Munchesney inheritance passed. Valence was married to the surviving child of Warin's first marriage to Joan, the daughter of William Marshal, who thus had a share of the Marshal inheritance. The Munchesney wardship had over a year to run.

[298] *CR 1256–9*, 27.

[299] *DBM*, 103 (cap. 7), 151–3 (caps. 8, 14, 17), 220–1 (cap. 1[3]); Waugh, *Lordship of England*, 255.

Henry was also giving large sums of money to those in his favour. The issue rolls of the exchequer between Michaelmas 1256 and Easter 1258 show £1,000 given to Montfort, £766 to Guy de Lusignan, £521 to William de Valence and £420 to Geoffrey de Lusignan.[300] Much the same men also profited from local revenues. Montfort was receiving his £400 a year from the farms of the midlands counties. In March 1257 he made Henry set out in excruciating detail how 514 marks were to be paid him from the proceeds of the Yorkshire eyre.[301] Geoffrey de Lusignan had likewise fastened on the eyres and received 500 marks from their issues.[302]

Henry would doubtless have claimed that he was acting in all this with kingly generosity and strengthening key members of his regime. Peter of Savoy and the Lusignans after all had given valiant service in Gascony. A critique of his rule, drawn up in 1264, took a different view. Courtiers and aliens were enjoying so many fees from 'the assured revenues of the king' that 'the royal patrimony was almost completely exhausted'.[303]

HENRY III'S GOLD COINAGE, 1257

Henry's Welsh campaign of 1257 necessitated a great deal of expenditure by local officials, thus further diminishing their payments to the exchequer.[304] The campaign also had a major impact on Henry's gold treasure. Henry found it far harder to set aside silver to purchase gold and indeed took 2,000 marks from William of Gloucester's store without any arrangements for paying it back.[305] Worse was to follow, for Henry soon saw no alternative to breaking into the gold treasure itself.[306] His way of doing so was imaginative. If he must spend his treasure, he would do so through the medium of his own gold coins. He thus avoided the cost of changing his gold (much of it in foil) back into silver. He was also able, through the design of

---

[300] Collingwood, 'Royal finance', 75–6, drawing on TNA E 403/11; E 403/13; E 403/15A; E 403/17A.

[301] *CPR 1247–58*, 590–1. See Barratt, 'Crisis management', 60–2. In the Michaelmas term of 1257, Montfort received £600 as arrears of the £400 dower payment from 1255 and the first half of 1256, although there is some reason to think this had already been paid by the countess of Lincoln: TNA E 403/15A; *CLR 1251–60*, 285, 318; *CPR 1247–58*, 493; TNA E 159/30, m. 4d. For Henry's debts to Montfort and his efforts to pay them, see Maddicott, *Simon de Montfort*, 136–7. The statement that Montfort received £6,500 to £7,000 from Henry between October 1256 and December 1257 is incorrect since it includes £4,666 of the settlement over Gascony which had been paid up earlier. Between Easter 1254 and Easter 1258, Montfort did, however, receive £3,039 in cash from the exchequer: TNA E 403/10, 11, 13, 15A, 3114. I am grateful to Richard Cassidy for sending me a schedule of payments to Montfort from the exchequer.

[302] *CPR 1247–58*, 535; TNA E 372/102, m. 39d, a reference I owe to James Collingwood.

[303] *DBM*, 276–7.

[304] *CLR 1251–60*, 386–7.

[305] *CPR 1247–58*, 561, 570.

[306] For what follows, see Carpenter, *Reign of Henry III*, 121–8.

the coin, to impress everyone with the elevation and elegance of his king-ship. The coin was designed by William of Gloucester, doubtless in close consultation with Henry himself. It was of pure gold and weighed two silver pennies. At the usual exchange rate between gold and silver of ten to one, it was thus worth 20 silver pennies or 1s 8d. The new coins broke entirely with the design of the silver pennies. All of those since the Conquest had simply depicted the head of a king. Now, on his gold coin, Henry sat enthroned, holding orb and sceptre. The model was a coin of Edward the Confessor. Henry's gold penny thus proclaimed the dignity of his kingship and paid homage to his patron saint.

By 16 August 1257 the coin was ready and Henry at Chester ordered the sheriffs of London to proclaim that 'the gold money' of the king would run through the city and elsewhere in the kingdom, each coin being worth 20 silver pennies.[307] Ten days later 466 marks of gold in the king's new money (so 37,280 gold pennies), together with a little over 103 marks in the gold of foreign coins, were received at Chester. The king sent urgent orders for the money to be sent on to him at Deganwy and doubtless he spent much of it on the campaign.[308]

Henry had another motive for minting his treasure. He hoped that large numbers of people would change gold in leaf, plate and foreign currencies into his coin, paying of course to do so. He would thus be opening up a new source of revenue. Such hopes were soon dashed. The new coinage proved extremely unpopular. In November 1257, Henry, reacting to complaints, summoned the mayor and citizens of London to the exchequer and charged them to say whether the coinage was 'for the common benefit of his kingdom or not'. The reply was disappointing in the extreme. The coinage, Henry was told, would do great damage to his kingdom and especially to the poor whose chattels were not worth one gold coin. It had also (a point of special concern to goldsmiths) brought down the rate of exchange between gold and silver from one to ten, to one to eight or nine. Faced with this rebuff, Henry stood his ground and declared he still wished the coinage to run although no one was to be compelled to take it.[309] In the event the coinage never became common currency and minting soon ceased, which is why only six of the coins survive, making it the most valu-able British coin at auction. Henry had miscalculated. Only his own thirst for gold had created the impression a gold currency was needed. In England there was some circulation of gold coins from abroad, mostly Byzantine bezants and Islamic money of Murcia, but it was limited.[310] A large proportion of the payments made towards the gold treasure were in gold foil rather than gold coins. The situation was very different when

[307] *CR 1256–9*, 88.
[308] *CPR 1247–58*, 649–50; *CR 1256–9*, 90.
[309] FitzThedmar, 29–30.
[310] Carpenter, 'Gold and gold coins', 107–9.

Edward III minted his successful gold currency in the next century. Then great numbers of foreign gold coins were in circulation.[311]

There was little Henry could do to replace the inroads into his gold treasure. By the autumn of 1257 fines of gold from those seeking exemption from knighthood were drying up. Although old fines were still being paid, new ones between 28 October 1257 and 30 April 1258 were only worth some 13 marks of gold.[312] Equally the cash coming into the exchequer between Michaelmas 1256 and Easter 1258 was all going out again in payments, as the surviving receipt and issue rolls show.[313] So there was no chance of the exchequer building up a reserve. Henry's day-to-day situation at the time of the revolution in April 1258 was not desperate. Most of the writs commanding payments out of the exchequer were being honoured.[314] But had there been wardrobe accounts for the period after April 1256, they would probably show the king running up large debts through failing to pay for his household's food and drink. As result of such debts, so it was later alleged, English merchants were impoverished and foreign merchants refused to enter the kingdom.[315] Henry, in April 1258 still had a treasure worth 500 marks of gold, so 5,000 marks or £3,333 of silver. But this was tiny when set against the costs of the Sicilian project. Nor would it have gone far had he tried to raise military forces to resist his opponents. He was not exactly a sitting target, but he was very vulnerable.

THE COUNCILLORS' OATH OF 1257

The paucity of Henry's treasure would not have mattered had he been sailing in calm waters. He was not. The eyres and the exactions of the sheriffs had made his government unpopular in the shires. The exploitation of vacancies, the quarrels over jurisdiction and the Sicilian taxation had totally alienated churchmen. Over £30,000 probably went from the English church to the papacy and all for nothing, absolutely nothing.[316] In this situation there was just one measure of reform designed to cleanse the reputation of the regime. It was an oath taken by the king's councillors at Windsor sometime in 1257.[317]

The most striking feature of the oath was the way the council's agreement was made necessary for important acts of patronage. The councillors were

[311] Carpenter, *Reign of Henry III*, 127–8.

[312] Carpenter, *Reign of Henry III*, 124.

[313] Collingwood, 'Royal finance', 62; Cassidy, 'A golden treasure or a state of collapse?', table 7.

[314] Cassidy, 'A golden treasure or a state of collapse?', 22.

[315] Carpenter, 'Household rolls', 29–30; *DBM*, 86–7, cap. 23, 274–5, cap. 5.

[316] Lunt, *Financial Relations*, 260–1, 289–90.

[317] The oath is recorded in the annals of Burton abbey: Burton, 395–7; *DBM*, 196–7, cap. 9. For a commentary, see Powicke, *King Henry III*, i, 336–8; Maddicott, *Simon de Montfort*, 148–9, 189.

thus to refuse consent to alienations from the king's ancient demesnes.[318] They also needed to give their consent to gifts of privileges and liberties affecting the rights of the crown and anyone else. They were not to seek gifts on their own account and were not to receive them without the consent of the council should the king wish to bestow them 'by his own motion'. They would be subject to dismissal and loss of lands for a year if they themselves were convicted of taking bribes. The oath was also concerned with the administration of justice. The councillors were to ensure it was given to rich and poor alike according to the right laws and customs of the kingdom. They were to allow, in particular, petitioners to have justice against themselves, their friends and relations, not obstructing it by prayer, price, hate or favour. Alongside the councillors, the oath was to be sworn both by the senior judges and the chief officials of the exchequer, while a separate oath was to be devised by the councillors for the sheriffs. Evil officials and useless bailiffs appointed by the king were to be dismissed and better ones appointed. Clearly the councillors envisaged a reform of local government.

The oath sought to deal with much that seemed wrong with Henry's personal rule: his lavish distribution of patronage; his obstruction of the judicial process when it touched his favourites; his failure to reform local government. In all these ways the oath anticipated the reforms implemented after the 1258 revolution. It would be good to think that Henry himself was behind the oath. He had often in the past sought to place restrictions on himself. Was he now influenced by the recent Ordinance of Louis IX where the oath sworn by local officials likewise prevented them accepting gifts and bribes? Perhaps, but given Henry's track record, it must be more likely the oath was conceived by the council itself or a faction within it. According to the Burton annals, where the text is preserved, the oath coincided with the appointment to the council of Walter de Cantilupe, bishop of Worcester, and Fulk Basset, bishop of London, but that may have been as much a consequence of the oath as a cause.[319] The oath was certainly sworn by Simon de Montfort, Peter of Savoy and John Mansel. Perhaps its most likely date is June 1257, when Montfort, Richard de Clare, Bishop Cantilupe, Peter of Savoy and 'others of the council', probably including John Mansel and Hugh Bigod, were all with Henry at Windsor.[320] Significantly the Lusignans appear to have been absent. This may hint at one purpose of the oath. The restrictions on

---

[318] Whether such alienations covered leases was not clarified.

[319] They actually spent little time at court in 1257. Cantilupe had presumably been dismissed from the council following his opposition to Sicilian taxation in 1255, see above, 634, although see 636, n. 133.

[320] *DBM*, 86–7, cap. 23; *TR*, 46; *RCWL*, ii, 108; *CPR 1247–58*, 563; *CLR 1251–60*, 382. For a different view of the date see Maddicott, *Simon de Montfort*, 148. Not all the councillors necessarily took the oath at the same time. Probably it was Peter of Savoy who safeguarded the interests of the queen. The councillors were to be faithful to her and protect her rights, person and dower.

patronage were clearly open to manipulation. A dominant faction on the council might consent to rewards for themselves and refuse it to their enemies. Quite probably, Montfort, Peter of Savoy and their allies saw the restrictions as a way of doing down the Lusignans.[321]

It would be wrong, however, to view the oath simply as an instrument of faction. Just as striking as the restrictions on the king's ability to give patronage were those imposed on the councillors themselves: they were not to accept gifts and bribes and were to subject their own activities, and those of their friends and relations, to judicial redress. The stress on not taking gifts was to be found in the oath sworn by the baronial confederates at the start of the movement of reform in 1258. The following year (in February 1259), the ruling councillors issued a proclamation saying that all the wrongs done by themselves and their bailiffs should be corrected by the newly appointed justiciar. Montfort played a major part in conceiving the 1258 oath and was passionately attached to the 1259 proclamation.[322] It may well be that the councillors' oath of 1257 is the first sign of his righteous commitment to the cause of reform, a commitment in no way incompatible with the pursuit of his equally justified (in his view) material ambitions.[323] Given his close connections with the French court, Montfort was quite probably influenced here by Louis IX. (The two men had met in 1255 when Montfort was negotiating an extension of the truce.) Around this time Matthew Paris refers to Montfort, 'in the cause of justice', ordering his officials to return what they had taken 'from the people' ('a plebe') and give satisfaction for the injuries done.[324] Here he was acting very much in Louis's spirit. Perhaps the French king's example was also an argument Montfort used to get Henry to accept the oath. Montfort was often at court in the first half of 1257 so he was well placed to press the scheme on the king.[325]

If implemented, the oath would have gravely restricted Henry's ability to distribute patronage. Yet one doubts whether he really thought the council would stop him doing what he wanted, any more than he expected Philip Lovel really to prevent him spending money. The oath spoke of consent being given 'by all the council' or 'the greater and wiser part of it', but how was that to be defined? The councillors were given no specific power over Henry's seal and anyway could always be dismissed. There is

[321] For a clash between Montfort and William de Valence in 1257, see Paris, v, 634.

[322] *DBM*, 131–7; Maddicott, *Simon de Montfort*, 179–81.

[323] For an opposite view of Montfort's role, see Maddicott, *Simon de Montfort*, 148. I do not think the concession to Montfort in February 1257 (*CPR 1247–58*, 543), allowing him free disposition in his will of lands and wardships notwithstanding any laws and statutes to the contrary, is necessarily connected with the oath.

[324] Paris, *HA*, ii, 409. This is a comment, introduced over an erasure, relating to Montfort's conduct in 1238. For the date of the comment, see Vaughan, *Matthew Paris*, 121.

[325] In 1257, Montfort attested royal charters in every month between January and June and again in October and December.

no sign the oath had any effect on Henry's behaviour. The following year the council's control of the king was to be much more tightly defined.

ENGLAND OVERRUN BY FOREIGNERS

During the last phase of the personal rule those present at parliament must have been very aware of the prominence enjoyed by the king's foreign relations and their connections. The same lesson was imbibed by a larger audience thanks to the policy of distraint of knighthood. Quite apart from learning about the Sicilian affair (for they were bound to ask why on earth the king wanted gold), they also gained an insight into Henry's court, for it was to the keepers of the wardrobe that their money was paid. That the wardrobe was indeed 'in foreign hands' was obvious. The Poitevin clerk Peter Chaceporc, in office since 1241, had died at Boulogne in December 1254 on the way back to England. He made a good end and left money in a 'noble will' (as Matthew Paris put it) for the foundation of an Augustinian priory.[326] Henry, in a characteristic act of impulsive generosity, immediately forgave Chaceporc's executors all his debts, although he cannot have had the slightest idea what was owed.[327] Chaceporc was followed by another foreign clerk, Artaud de Saint-Romain, from Burgundy or Provence. On his death in the autumn of 1257, the wardrobe was entrusted to none other than Peter de Rivallis, 'an alien after an alien', as Paris put it.[328] It was to Artaud and Peter that nearly all the money from the potential knights was paid. Peter's position was bound to recall the 'Poitevin' tyranny of 1232–4, when he had ruled England with his uncle Peter des Roches. In 1258 he was dismissed by the reforming barons.

The potential knights saw more than a foreign domination of the wardrobe. The fourteen fining for respite in the first half of December 1256, for example, found a court attended by William de Valence, Guy and Geoffrey de Lusignan, and Peter of Savoy, as well as Imbert Pugeys and the king's jester, Fortunatus de Luka (he who was thrown into the bath at Bath.)[329] In April 1257, Pugeys became a steward of the royal household, where he joined another Savoyard close to the queen, appointed in the previous year, Ebulo de Montibus.[330] The chancery stayed in English hands, but the appearance of the two Savoyards amongst the stewards of the household was a new departure and increased the foreign colour of

[326] Paris, v, 483–4, 535; Tout, *Chapters*, i, 263–4.
[327] *CPR 1247–58*, 388. I owe this point to Richard Cassidy.
[328] Paris, v, 298; 655; Dunstable, 194; Tout, *Chapters*, i, 278–9.
[329] *RCWL*, ii, 102.
[330] For Ebulo, see Ray, 'A Vaudois servant of Henry III'. As Ray shows, Ebulo came from Mont-sur-Rolle, a small settlement facing south over Lake Geneva. Its castle at Mont le Grand, high above on the wooded slopes of the Jura mountains, has magnificent views over the lake.

the court, all the more so since they replaced Bertram de Criel, John of
Lexington and Ralph fitzNicholas, who all died in 1256–7. There was also
the high visibility of another alien courtier, this time a Poitevin, William
de Sancta Ermina. He stood beside Henry at table with a towel and cut
up his food.[331]

Although impossible to be sure, it seems probable that in these last years
there was also a rising chorus of complaints against the local malpractices
of the Savoyards and Lusignans. As early as 1243 a local jury complained
of the way Peter of Savoy was ravaging the woods of John de Warenne
while they were in his custody during John's minority.[332] There is no
reason to think his conduct improved thereafter. In legal proceedings after
the revolution, the peasants of Witley in Surrey complained bitterly about
how he had increased their rent.[333] Similar complaints came from the men
of the Kent and Surrey manors in the custody of Guy and Geoffrey de
Lusignan via their wardship of the lands of Geoffrey de Lucy. In Surrey
bishop-elect Aymer was accused of exacting illicit tolls (after placing a
barrier across the king's road at Esher) while a local jury described in
detail his attack 'with a multitude of armed Poitevins' on Lambeth palace
in 1252. Two prominent Kentish knights, meanwhile, complained they
could get no justice because their opponents were protected by William de
Valence.[334] Matthew Paris quoted a leading bailiff of the Lusignans,
William de Bussey, as saying 'If I do you wrong, who is there to do you
right?'[335] Not all the evil was perpetrated by officials. Indeed, it was
possible for ordinary people to experience at first hand the aloofness and
arrogance of the foreign favourites. In another case brought after the
revolution, Thomasia de Ros told how she was ejected from her property
at Hallingbury in Essex by the bailiffs of William de Valence. When
Valence came to the manor and stayed there for a day and night, she stood
outside the gate on his arrival and departure seeking redress, only to be
ignored.[336]

Of course, the numbers of those who felt the rough hand of the
Lusignans and Savoyards were few compared to those abused by English

---

[331] Paris, v, 678, 702. From 1255, William was the king's pantler: *CR 1254–6*, 81. For him
see Ray, 'Alien courtiers of thirteenth-century England', 153–8.

[332] *CIM*, no. 16.

[333] Hershey, *Special Eyre*, no. 105.

[334] These cases are reviewed in Hershey, *Special Eyre*, xxxi, lviii–lxiii, with lii–viii for an
analysis of cases in Kent and Surrey brought against other magnates and royal officials.
The knights were William de St John and Fulk Payforer, and they were obstructed by fellow
Kentish knights Roger of Leybourne (of whom much in volume 2) and Guncelin of
Badlesmere. For English knights in the service of William de Valence see Ridgeway,
'William de Valence and his *familiares*'.

[335] Paris, v, 738.

[336] TNA Just 1/1187, m. 1d; Hershey, *Special Eyre*, lx. She claimed to have been dispossessed of a messuage, a carucate of land (perhaps 120 acres), 44s of rent and a mill. She
was, therefore, a substantial freeholder.

magnates. The misdeeds of the king's foreign favourites were part of a much wider pattern in which Henry had allowed magnates to encroach on the rights of the crown and subject men to the jurisdiction of their courts.[337] Richard de Clare was doing this on a far greater scale than Peter of Savoy and the Lusignans. But an extra dimension was given to the abuse when the perpetrators were foreign. That the officials themselves were often English made no difference. William de Bussey, himself, although English, was abused as a 'Poitevin'.[338] Stories of the crimes of these men resonated far beyond the actual victims. Matthew Paris was able to give a graphic description of how Bussey had caused the death of a young man at Trumpington in Cambridgeshire through harsh imprisonment and then, as a spectacle, had hanged up his dead body.[339] There was also a perception that foreigners held far too much power as castellans of royal castles. Indeed, an account of the 1258 revolution alleged that nearly all the king's castles were 'in the hands of aliens'.[340] This was a great exaggeration but still in 1258 the Tower, Hertford, Hadleigh, Colchester, Windsor, Devizes, Gloucester and Corfe were held by foreigners.[341] Elyas de Rabayne combined his custody of Corfe with two important manors further along the Dorset coast, one near Weymouth, the other at Lyme, obtained with his marriage. A stint as sheriff of Dorset between 1251 and 1255 had further helped him dig into the area. Since bishop-elect Aymer, in 1257, had acquired Weymouth itself and the island of Portland, 'the Poitevins had established an ascendancy over the Dorset coastline', much to the displeasure of Richard de Clare, who after the revolution was to acquire Portland for himself.[342] Another demand in 1258 was that royal castles on harbours should be entrusted to men 'born of the kingdom of England', this on account of the danger if they were held 'by others'.[343] By 1258 it was easy to think that England was being laid waste by greedy and lawless foreigners.[344] Such feelings were to be a powerful force in the revolutionary years to come.

---

[337] See above, 532.

[338] TNA JUST 1/1187, m. 20, a reference brought to light by Andrew Hershey.

[339] Paris, v, 739; Carpenter, *Reign of Henry III*, 327–8; Maddicott, 'Magna Carta and the local community', 54–61.

[340] *DBM*, 90–1.

[341] The Tower of London (Imbert Pugeys); Colchester (Guy de Rochefort); Hertford (William de Valence); Hadleigh (Ebulo of Geneva); Windsor (Aymo Thurbert); Devizes (John de Plessis); Gloucester (Matthias Bezill); Corfe (Elyas de Rabayne). Both Plessis and Bezill were left in place after the revolution.

[342] Ridgeway, 'Dorset in the period of baronial reform', 23–6.

[343] *DBM*, 80–1, cap. 5. Another aspect of Lusignan unpopularity was their traffic in Jewish debts: Stacey, '1240–1260: a watershed in Anglo-Jewish relations?', 143–4.

[344] For a recent discussion, see Hennings, 'Simon de Montfort and the ambiguity of ethnicity', 144–6, 152.

Chapter 13

THE REVOLUTION OF 1258

Between the parliaments of October 1257 and April 1258, Henry spent all his time at Westminster apart from visits to Merton, Guildford and Windsor. He cancelled plans for Christmas at Winchester and a trip to Marlborough.[1] The king was anxiously awaiting the return of his envoys from both the papal court and the court of Louis IX. On both depended the future of the Sicilian enterprise. If that were not enough, Henry was also facing the prospect of war on two fronts in Britain.

Throughout the winter, under cover of a truce, preparations continued for the forthcoming campaign in Wales. On 18 March, Henry sent out orders for a general muster at Chester on 16 June. He was still thinking in terms of an invasion of Anglesey and ordered the Cinque Ports to send 200 ships, of which 100 were able to bear twenty-four horses each and the other 100 sixteen horses each.[2]

Meanwhile there was more trouble in Scotland. The regime set up on Henry's visit to Scotland in 1255 had collapsed. On the night of 18–19 October 1257 the Comyns had seized King Alexander as he lay asleep in bed at Kinross and taken control of the seal.[3] Evidently his dogs had not saved him![4] In response, Henry's first thought was of going to Scotland himself to put matters right.[5] Then, in January 1258, he told large numbers of northern magnates to be ready with all their force to rescue the king.[6] In the event, Alexander seems to have shaken himself free from Comyn control, but the situation remained uncertain. In March 1258 the Comyns entered into an alliance with Llywelyn and the other Welsh rulers. Here, for the first time, Llywelyn appears with the title Prince of Wales, an ominous indication of his ambitions.[7] In the same month Henry, accepting a diversion of forces from the Welsh campaign, ordered the northern

---

[1] *CLR 1251–60*, 407, 409.
[2] *CR 1256–9*, 294–7.
[3] Fordun, 297–8; Bower, 5, 318–21; Melrose, 589; Paris, v, 656; Brown, *Wars of Scotland*, 51–3.
[4] See above, 641.
[5] *CR 1256–9*, 168.
[6] *CR 1256–9*, 290–1.
[7] *AWR*, 499–501.

sheriffs to intervene if war broke out in Scotland.[8] Later they were to go personally to Queen Margaret and offer her help and solace.[9] Henry had not forgotten his daughter, for whom all this must have been traumatic, but his other preoccupations meant there was little he could do to influence events in Scotland.

At Christmas 1257, Henry had despatched envoys to carry on negotiations with Louis IX. The delegation was high powered and included Bishop Cantilupe of Worcester, the abbot of Westminster, Hugh Bigod, and probably Simon de Montfort, Peter of Savoy and Aymer, bishop-elect of Winchester. The hope was that they would bring back proposals for a peace treaty. On 24 January, Henry even summoned a parliament to meet a month later to consider the terms. Louis, however, postponed decisions until an assembly of his own was due to meet in early March. Henry's envoys thus returned empty handed, though leaving behind the abbot of Westminster. Henry accordingly postponed his parliament until April, by which time he might have news both from France and Rome.[10]

Henry was facing another problem potentially damaging to his international schemes. He had hoped Richard of Cornwall, as king of Germany and ultimately emperor of the Romans, would bring powerful support to the Sicilian enterprise. But during the course of 1257 it became clear that Richard had a rival, none other than King Alfonso of Castile, Edward's father-in-law. Alfonso, descended from Philip of Swabia, could claim to represent the Hohenstaufen line, and he gathered some support.[11] On 1 April 1257 the archbishop of Trier elected him to the kingship, with the consent of the duke of Saxony and the margrave of Brandenburg. The king of Bohemia, having previously voted for Richard, now switched sides. In the event Alfonso never set foot in Germany, but his candidature impeded Richard's coronation as emperor since the pope had now to choose between two rivals for the throne. The chances of Richard helping with the Sicilian project were correspondingly reduced. Henry urged the pope to expedite Richard's 'business', precisely so such help could be forthcoming.[12] He also, in a letter to Alfonso, pointed out that Richard had

---

[8] *CR 1256–9*, 300–1.

[9] *CR 1256–9*, 221. This was in May.

[10] The delegation also included Adam Marsh: *CPR 1247–58*, 609; *CLR 1251–60*, 416; Paris, v, 649–50, 659–60, 663; Paris, vi, 392; John of Wallingford (1), 77; Maddicott, *Simon de Montfort*, 140 n. 123. Paris is the only source for Montfort, Savoy and Aymer being amongst the envoys. All attest royal charters on 18 December 1257 and then not again until early February, which would fit in with the mission. Montfort and Aymer's inclusion is also suggested by *CPR 1247–58*, 610, where with the bishop of Worcester they are empowered to emend unjust exactions in the port of Dover provided the king of France did the same in his ports. Paris also includes Robert Walerand, but he attests as late as 30 December. He had been on an earlier mission, however.

[11] Philip was the brother of Emperor Henry VI and had been king of the Romans between 1198 and 1208.

[12] *CR Supp*, no. 284.

been properly elected and crowned 'with the diadem of the kingdom' in the appointed place.[13]

THE ATTACK ON THE LONDON ALDERMEN

While Henry was waiting for the return of his envoys, he launched an attack on the mayor of London, Ralph Hardel, and the twelve aldermen who governed the city.[14] The opportunity was provided by a complaint reaching the king from London's lower orders, from, as Matthew Paris put it, the 'the middle classes (mediocres), the people and the plebs'. They alleged that the mayor and his colleagues, in assessing the recent tallages on the city, had spared themselves and burdened everyone else.[15] The king was very ready to act on the complaint. He could thus right the wrongs of his poorer subjects. He could also attack the mayor and the aldermen, who had denied that the city owed tallages at all and had objected to the liberties Henry wished conferred on Westminster Abbey.

One of the accused aldermen was Arnold fitzThedmar and he left a vivid account of the quarrel, full of people and places. The dispute had begun at Windsor in January, where Henry was irritated by the mayor's objection to a sworn inquiry into the tallages. When, on Henry's return to London, the mayor and citizens came out to meet him at Knightsbridge as customary, the king sent a squire to say they were not to enter his sight. The subsequent campaign was run by John Mansel, who was there at every stage of the proceedings and masterminded the key tactic of calling in the people against the ruling elite. Thus for a week he took evidence from four men elected from each of the London wards. He then had their testimony read before the king and his councillors sitting at the exchequer. Twice also Mansel convened the people in a folkmoot at the cross of St Paul. They cried out 'Ya Ya' when asked whether Londoners could give evidence on oath, and 'Nay, nay, nay' when asked if the aldermen could defend themselves by the oath of twelve sworn men. Further meetings took place at the Guildhall, the hall of the bishop of London and the house of a canon of St Paul's, where the aldermen, realizing from 'the murmur of the people' that they had no support, saw Mansel and placed themselves in the king's mercy.

The conclusion came on 13 February when the mayor and the aldermen, on Mansel's orders, came to Westminster hall. There they were kept waiting while Henry conferred with his councillors in St Stephen's chapel.

---

[13] *CR 1256–9*, 284–5, 289–90; Paris, v, 649, 657–8. In his dealings with Alfonso, Henry relied very much on the advice of John Mansel, who of course knew Alfonso well.

[14] For what follows, see *CPR 1247–58*, 614; FitzThedmar, 30–7, 176; TNA E 159/31, m. 10; Paris, v, 663, 675; *CR 1256–9*, 299; Williams, *Medieval London*, 207–11; Cassidy, 'The barons of London and royal taxation', 7–8.

[15] For similar complaints earlier in Oxford, see *CIM*, no. 238, discussed in Hammer, 'Complaints of the lesser commune'.

Then Henry entered the hall and, sitting with his ministers 'as a tribunal', had sentence pronounced by Henry of Bath. The mayor and the aldermen were dismissed and saddled with heavy fines. Those imposed on Hardel and seven of his fellows were so burdensome they thought of selling up and leaving the city.[16] Nonetheless, Matthew Paris credited Mansel with saving them from worse punishment.

Henry had thus defeated the leading Londoners, as he had done before over the tallage of 1255. Hardel, son of the mayor of Magna Carta, was now replaced by the loyalist William fitzRichard.[17] The city was far less a base for the opposition in the first phase of the coming revolution than might have been the case. Henry had achieved his victory working closely with his leading officials. Alongside Mansel, Henry of Wingham, keeper of the seal, Philip Lovel, treasurer of the exchequer, Henry of Bath, chief justice of the court *coram rege*, and Imbert Pugeys, steward of the household and keeper of the Tower, were all involved, as were Richard de Clare and John de Plessis. The whole episode may well have given Henry a false impression of the unity of his government and the strength of his political position. Unfortunately, his support of the poor against the rich was not part of any wider programme. Nor in London did the lower orders show much gratitude. During the civil war they shouted 'Yah Yah' loudly in support of Simon de Montfort.

THE GREAT FAMINE OF 1258

On 28 March 1258, Henry III left Westminster for Merton priory for a short break. He returned between 7 and 9 April for the opening of the parliament. It was to last until early May and be the most dramatic and decisive of his reign. The tensions at the parliament were heightened by its meeting during a terrible famine.[18] The harvest of 1257 had been blighted by torrential rain. That of 1256 had also been poor. The whole weather was being adversely affected by a 'strong solar-generated global climate perturbation', caused by the abrupt easing of both the Asian monsoon and a drought in the Pacific West of the Americas.[19] Corn in 1258 was selling at 15s to 20s a quarter, some five or six times the level in 1254 and 1255.[20] Just before his account of the parliament, Matthew Paris

---

[16] The absence of wardrobe accounts for this period means we have no record of the amount.

[17] The divisions in the city were not clear cut, however, and one of Arnold fitzThedmar's pledges was the king's man John de Gisors: TNA E 159/31, m. 10.

[18] For what follows, see Paris, v, 660, 673–4, 693–4, 701–2; FitzThedmar, 37; Dunstable, 208; Osney, 118; *CR 1256–9*, 212, 225; Titow, *English Rural Society*, 97; and the discussion of the whole subject in Campbell, 'Global climates'.

[19] Campbell, 'Global climates', 117. There was also an easing of 'the North Atlantic Oscillation'. The eruption of the Samalas Volcano in Indonesia in the spring or early summer of 1257 occurred too late to affect the crisis of 1258.

[20] Bury St Edmunds, 22; Titow, *English Rural Society*, 97.

recorded that many were dying of hunger, their bodies, swollen and rotten, lying around on dunghills and in the village streets. The bitterly cold weather from February into the summer aggravated the situation and hastened the death of those living outdoors and already weakened by hunger. On 16 April, during the parliament, the king acknowledged that many paupers, dying 'miserably' of famine in fields and open places, were being left unburied because the coroners were overwhelmed and could not get round to view the bodies. The situation was especially bad in London itself, whither 'the men of the villages' (as fitzThedmar called them) flocked in search of food. As the famine worsened, thousands perished. The recently excavated graveyard of St Mary Spital, to the north-east of the city, has many of the bodies, half of them women and two-thirds under thirty-five.[21] More would have died had not corn ships arrived from Germany, although that just drew additional people into the city.

None of those attending the parliament ever went without a square meal. Indeed, they profited from the rising prices if they had corn to sell. On the other hand, they suffered if they had to buy corn (as did Dunstable priory), and rising corn prices drove up prices in general. The cost of transporting the king's wines rose from 13d to 20d a day because of the 'dearth'. Urged on by the friars in their households, concern for the poor was central to the religious life of the nobles, as it was of the king. All were engaged in a daily round of almsgiving. Now the need for it was acute. Every day, while the parliament was in session, paupers thronged around Westminster hoping for alms from the king. They thronged too around the houses of the magnates. Simon de Montfort was probably staying in the mansion of the bishop of Durham on the Strand. Peter of Savoy was at his house a little further east. Matthew Paris tells of some organized relief in London with paupers being directed to the houses of the nobles where they could receive alms.[22] The famine was not the fault of the king. Indeed, he could show himself at his most benevolent. But its appalling course heightened the feeling at the parliament that the realm was out of joint and something must be done to put it right.

THE PARLIAMENT OF APRIL 1258

Outside the great men, nothing is known about who attended the parliament of April 1258, although since taxation was an issue there was probably a very full attendance of barons and knights. There is equally no information about where exactly the parliament met although presumably it spilled over from the halls of the palace into the refectory, infirmary chapel and

[21] Campbell, 'Global climates', 110–11, citing Connell, Jones, Redfern and Walker, *Bioarchaeological Study of Medieval Burials on the Site of St Mary Spital*, 36, 38, 229, 271–2.

[22] It is a shame that Paris's account of this episode is truncated by the loss of a folio (Paris, v, 694). He appears to refer back to it at Paris, v, 702.

chapter house of the Abbey. The radiating chapels, east end and transepts of Henry's new church were now nearly complete. It is possible that Henry intended to consecrate the Abbey and translate the Confessor on 13 October 1258, for the ecclesiastical calendar in 1258 was the same as in the year of the Confessor's first translation in 1163. Between October 1257 and April 1258 the exchequer found 1,400 marks for the works.[23] In the event, the political turmoil put paid to any such ideas, but all those present at the parliament must have marvelled at the new church with its great height, flying buttresses, galleried triforium, bar-traceried lancets, rose windows and Last Judgement portal. The head of Edward gazing out over the transepts, the king's arms prominent in the stained glass and the tiled floors, showed Henry's ownership of the church. He had created it to secure in the Confessor's support for himself and his dynasty. But he was also offering the church and the Confessor to the realm as a whole. How he must have hoped the realm would now show some gratitude.

When the parliament opened there were three items on the official agenda: the campaign in Wales, the negotiations with France and the business of Sicily. The situation in Wales explained some notable absences from the parliament, including the marcher barons Humphrey de Bohun, earl of Hereford, and Roger de Mortimer. During the parliament news came in of a defeat (with loss of goods and men) suffered on 1 April by the English in William de Valence's lordship of Pembroke. Valence (according to Matthew Paris) accused both Richard de Clare (lord of nearby Glamorgan) and Simon de Montfort (although with no interests in Wales) of treacherously conniving with Llywelyn. Valence then nearly came to blows with Montfort, who rushed at him, crying out 'I am not the son of a traitor nor a traitor myself; our forbears are not alike.' The king himself separated the two but the episode revealed the tensions that would soon pull Henry's court apart. At least the decision about what to do was uncontroversial. The king's army was to muster at Chester later in the summer and meanwhile Edward was empowered to renew the truce.[24]

PEACE WITH FRANCE: THE CRUCIAL DECISION

The abbot of Westminster, Richard de Crokesley, had stayed behind in France to attend Louis IX's mid-Lent parliament. He was now back in England with Louis's terms. According to Matthew Paris (the only source), in January, Henry's envoys were still demanding the return of Normandy and the rest of the old continental empire. They were seconded by envoys from King Richard.[25] Despite Louis's sympathetic words, these demands

---

[23] *CLR 1251–60*, 396, 399, 411, 433; TNA E 403/15A; TNA E 403/3114.

[24] *AC*, 95; Paris, v, 676–7; *CR 1256–9*, 310–11; *CPR 1247–58*, 624–5.

[25] Paris, v, 649–50, 659–60, 663; John of Wallingford (1), 77; Weiler, *Henry III of England and the Staufen Empire*, 179–80. For the claim to Normandy, see also *Political Songs*, 60.

were now turned down flat. Instead, in the proposals the abbot brought back, Henry was to resign all claims to Normandy, Anjou, Touraine, Maine and Poitou. This cannot have come as a complete surprise. As early as 1228 there had been an acceptance that much of the old empire was lost.[26] But it was still a bitter thing for Henry to lose the titles duke of Normandy and count of Anjou, the first borne by his predecessors since 1066, the second since 1154. Just as bad was the forfeiture of Poitou, lost as it was on Henry's watch. No wonder he said later that through the terms of the peace 'our condition is worsened'.[27]

Louis also demanded another major concession. During the negotiations Henry had maintained that Gascony, his remaining continental possession, was an allod held in full sovereignty, not, as Louis averred, a fief held from the king of France.[28] The truth of the matter was irrecoverable, there being no record of what exactly King John had done homage for back in 1200. Louis, however, was determined to press his point and now demanded that Henry do liege homage for Bordeaux, Bayonne and the rest of Gascony. That the French kingdom stretched to the Pyrenees was no longer to be disputed. The type of homage being demanded, liege homage, was itself significant for it overrode the obligations to anyone else. It was 'against all men and women who are able to live and die'.[29] Thus the king of England should neither rebel against the king of France nor do anything to give him offence.[30] If he did, Gascony would be forfeit. There were no such obligations and no such penalty if Gascony remained an allod. And the English side should have been aware of one other consequence. As a fief held from the king of France, judicial appeals could go from Gascony to the court of the king of France in Paris. All this was underlined in Henry's title. Under the terms Louis offered, Henry could remain as 'duke of Aquitaine' although originally the style was associated with Poitou rather than Gascony.[31] Since Poitou had certainly been a French fief this reinforced the

[26] See above, 78.

[27] *CR 1256–9*, 324–5.

[28] Thus, the Canterbury/Dover annals, writing soon after the treaty, observed that it meant Henry was to hold Aquitaine (meaning here Gascony) from the king of France, 'which before he, and all his predecessors had held from no one': Canterbury/Dover, 209–20. The French view is seen in Louis VIII's concession of Bordeaux to Hugh de Lusignan in 1224. Here he reserved to himself and his heirs the 'regalia' of the city, thus implying the king already had rights over it: Martène, *Amplissima Collectio*, i, cols. 1162–4, 1184–8, references I owe to Amicie Pelissie du Rausas. The question of Gascony's status is discussed in Chaplais, 'Le traité de Paris 1259 et l'inféodation de la Gascogne allodiale'.

[29] This is how it is put in the liege homage Hugh de Lusignan owed Louis VIII in 1224, see n. 28 above. The act of homage was usually linked to an oath of fealty and in 1259 Henry performed both: *CR 1259–61*, 225; for homage and fealty, see *Bracton*, ii, 232–3. Later the king of England argued he owed homage but not fealty: Vale, *The Angevin Legacy*, 51. For the liege homage given to Henry by the kings of Scotland, see above, 423.

[30] For Edward I's later statement to this effect, see Vale, *The Angevin Legacy*, 57.

[31] Chaplais, 'Le traité de Paris 1259 et l'inféodation de la Gascogne allodiale', II, 126–7.

view that Gascony was too. The eventual treaty made clear that Henry was duke of Aquitaine as a peer of the kingdom of France.

If Henry was to make these unpalatable concessions, he would have to override the objections of his eldest son.[32] Edward's opposition is understandable. As the immediate ruler of Gascony, he would bear the brunt of its changed status. As a warrior, promising to be in a different league from his father, he might one day hope to recover the lost territories in a successful war. Back in 1254 he had been formally conceded all his father's claims to them.[33] Henry, however, was determined to go ahead. He had tried twice to recover his lost empire through war and had been resoundingly defeated on both occasions. He could hope for nothing more in that direction. He was now committed to the Sicilian enterprise and for that peace with France was essential. Under heavy pressure in 1257, Henry had contemplated abandoning the project, but in truth it still gripped his heart and probably Eleanor's also. Peace with France could also help in a very material way, this thanks to a brilliant idea of the pope. Since Henry had no resources to fund his Sicilian army, Alexander suggested that, as part of the peace treaty, Henry should ask Louis to pay the costs of hiring 1,000 knights for one year, or 500 knights for two.[34] Henry seized the suggestion. After all, he had been told by the pope's treasurer that with 1,000 knights he would be able to conquer Sicily 'in a moment'.[35] Peace with France would make the Sicilian enterprise practical in more ways than one.

Henry could also take a positive view of the liege homage due under the treaty. After all, throughout his reign he had been looking to re-enter the allegiance of the king of France. His letters to Louis described him as 'my lord, if it pleases you'. When insisting Louis take the central seat at the great banquet in Paris in December 1254, he had said 'after all, you will be my lord'.[36] Of course, Henry was hoping that Louis would be his lord for Normandy, Anjou and Poitou, not Gascony, but there might be solid advantages in Gascony's status as a fief within the framework of an overall peace. Alfonso of Castile would be deprived of Louis as an ally and Gascony itself secured from French attack.

There was another crucial factor in persuading Henry to agree to the peace. Louis was prepared to make significant concessions by ceding rights and territories adjoining the existing boundaries of Gascony. First, he offered to surrender his rights in the cities and dioceses of Limoges, Cahors and Périguex. Second, he promised an annual cash payment in place of the Agenais until the current holder, Joan, wife of Alphonse of Poitiers (Louis's brother), died. If the Agenais then escheated to the king

---

[32] Canterbury/Dover, 209–10.
[33] F, 296 (CPR 1247–58, 271).
[34] CR 1256–9, 325–6; DD, no. 229; Layettes, iii, no. 4416.
[35] DD, no. 298.
[36] DD, no. 234; Paris, v, 480.

of France, he would give it to the king of England. If not, the payment would continue.[37] Third, Louis promised the king of England the land currently held by Alphonse of Poitiers in the Saintonge south of the river Charente, if, that is, it escheated to the king of France on Alphonse's death. If it did not, Louis was either to acquire it for the king or give an exchange.

Summarized like this (and some of the detail has been omitted), it might seem as though Louis was not giving very much. This was not the view of his councillors, who urged him not to make the concessions.[38] Although the surrender of Louis's rights in the three dioceses caused endless trouble, the area, when accounts survive for the year 1306/7, still yielded £863 to the English crown.[39] As for the Saintonge and the Agenais, since Joan and Alphonse had no children after many years of marriage, there was every likelihood (if the treaty held) that the territories would pass eventually to the king of England. Thus the great city of Saintes, from which Henry had been driven so humiliatingly in 1242, would once more be in English hands. The annual payments eventually agreed for the Agenais amounted to £930 a year and made a significant contribution to Henry's resources in the 1260s.[40] In English hands from 1279, its value greatly increased and it contributed some £6,026 to the accounts in 1306/7.[41] All in all the territories brought to the crown by the treaty were worth some £7,641 in that year, amounting to nearly half of Gascony's total revenues.

All that was in the future. For the present, as Henry and his councillors pondered Louis's offers, they must have been well aware how much had to be taken on trust. Would Louis actually transfer his rights in the three dioceses? Would the Agenais be valued properly? Would it eventually be handed over with the Saintonge on the deaths of Alphonse and Joan? Would, an early test, Louis agree to find the money for the knights? Fortunately, trust there was in abundance, which introduces the final factor underpinning the whole treaty. Louis IX (in Joinville's recollection) justified his concessions on the grounds they would 'foster love between his children and mine, who are first cousins'.[42] Henry felt the same. The wonderful family party in Paris at the end of 1254 had shown how much the two kings had in common, how much they respected and loved each other. They naturally wished to live in peace. Their queens, as sisters,

---

[37] The English claimed the Agenais on the grounds that it was given by King Richard to his sister, Joan's grandmother, when she married the count of Toulouse. The treaty also set up an inquiry to see whether Quercy was held in the same way. If so, it too would pass to the king of England on Joan's death. Edward I eventually surrendered his claims in Quercy for a payment of £750 a year: *F*, 673.

[38] Joinville, cap. 678.

[39] For the accounts, see Trabut-Cussac, 'Les coutumes ou droits de douane', 135–6.

[40] *CPR 1258–66*, 174, 189.

[41] The Saintonge, finally acquired in 1286 (*F*, 672), contributed £752.

[42] Joinville, cap. 678.

shared the same feelings. Later Edward I thanked Queen Margaret 'with all his heart' for labouring for peace between Louis and Henry.[43] Without the trust between the families, in a negotiation where so much depended on trust, the peace of Paris would have been impossible.

For all his commitment to the treaty, Henry would have found it difficult to carry through against the advice of his council and parliament. Had Edward enjoyed more support he could have stopped it. But there is no sign of opposition at this stage, however much there was grumbling later. Few if any of Henry's councillors can have thought the treaty would clear the way for a campaign in Sicily. But equally they saw no point in continuing the long-lost struggle with France, even if they had claims to ancestral lands in Normandy.[44] Richard de Clare supported the treaty, although certainly in that position.[45] Equally supportive were the Lusignans. Indeed, Guy and Geoffrey were amongst the envoys taking Henry's replies out to Louis after the parliament. Their position would be easier if there was peace between the royal houses, to both of which they owed allegiance.

Two other envoys sent to Louis were Peter of Savoy and Simon de Montfort. Both had been deeply involved in the peace negotiations. Peter and his brothers must always have hoped for peace between England and France. With one niece married to Louis, another to Henry, they would no longer have to perform a balancing act between the courts. Montfort himself had a personal stake in the negotiations. In February 1257 he had secured from Henry a licence to receive his inheritance in France if Louis would give it to him.[46] Montfort's claims were wide for they included the county of Evreux in Normandy and rights in his father's conquests in the south.[47] He doubtless hoped to secure some kind of settlement alongside the more general peace. Even more, Montfort knew a peace would require his wife, as the daughter of King John, to abandon her claims to the ceded territories.[48] Just to make sure, Montfort made clear to Louis the necessity of getting such renunciations, or so Henry later alleged.[49] Montfort had thus acquired a weapon with which to force through a settlement of his material grievances. He could hold up the treaty by refusing the renunciations until Henry gave him satisfaction.

Most important of all was the attitude of Henry's brother, Richard, king of the Romans. He too would be required to make a renunciation under the terms of the treaty. Wisely Henry had kept Richard, although absent

[43] Vale, *The Angevin Legacy*, 55; and for her activity, see *DD*, no. 348.

[44] For the ancestral lands and the treaty, see Power, 'The treaty of Paris', 152–4.

[45] Canterbury/Dover, 209–10; Paris, v, 745; Power, 'The treaty of Paris', 154.

[46] *CPR 1247–58*, 542.

[47] Maddicott, *Simon de Montfort*, 141.

[48] Already in 1241, in the treaty with the Lusignans, she had been made to renounce her claims to the territories of her mother: *Cartulaire des Comtes de la Marche*, 19–21. I thank Amicie Pelissie du Rausas for bringing this document to my attention.

[49] *DBM*, 194–5, caps. 3–5.

in Germany, on board from the start. 'We wish to agree nothing without your counsel,' he wrote in June 1257.[50] Luckily Richard's attitude coincided with his brother's, if for different reasons. Wise man that he was, he too cannot have thought the peace would do much to further the Sicilian project, but it might facilitate his progress to the imperial throne and help block the candidacy of Alfonso of Castile. Indeed, alongside the peace, Richard hoped to conclude an alliance of mutual aid with Louis.[51]

Confident in his brother's acquiescence, and with support from his councillors, Henry decided to go ahead. On 8 May he sent his proctors – Peter of Savoy, Montfort, Guy and Geoffrey de Lusignan and Hugh Bigod – out to Paris with full power to swear to the proffered terms. On 28 May, fully in touch with events, King Richard gave his own proctor power to make the required renunciations.[52] Agreeing to what was to become the peace of Paris was one of the best things Henry did in his reign. Unfortunately, he wanted peace on one front only to make war on another. Fortunately, on the war front he made far less progress at the parliament.

THE SICILIAN PROVOCATION

A papal diplomat, new to the English scene, had arrived early in April 1258, just in time for the parliament, his name Master Arlot.[53] An indication of how slowly the wheels of papal diplomacy could turn, he brought the pope's reply to the various proposals for reform of the Sicilian project conceived back in June 1257. By this time the situation in Sicily had deteriorated further, with Manfred completely in the ascendant. In August 1258, brushing aside the claims of Conradin, he was crowned king. The idea, mooted in 1257, that he might marry his daughter to Edmund and give Edmund the kingdom, was clearly hopelessly out of date.

None of this made Pope Alexander any more willing to modify the terms as Henry had hoped. The king's plea that further payment of the debt should be suspended until Sicily had been conquered, with the money from the tax being used to finance Henry's army, was turned down flat. Instead, the pope demanded that all the clerical taxation should go towards paying Henry's debts, and indeed that 30,000 marks should be paid at once, an impossible demand as Henry said.[54] Meanwhile the pope had not given up on Henry's army. By March 1259, Henry was to send 2,000 knights, 500 crossbowmen and 6,000 foot-soldiers! Probably Alexander thought little would come of this. His priority was still to get Henry's cash. But it was

[50] F, 358; CPR 1247–58, 594.

[51] Layettes, iii, no. 4415.

[52] Chaplais, English Medieval Diplomatic Practice, ii, no. 289 (Layettes, v, no. 687); Layettes, iii, no. 4413.

[53] Paris, v, 673; Tewksbury, 162.

[54] CR Supp, nos. 281, 283.

worth a try. Indeed, the pope had two concrete suggestions as to how the army might be raised. The first, as mentioned, was that, under the terms of the peace treaty, Louis should pay for 500 knights for two years or 1,000 knights for one. The second was that Henry should obtain a 'common subsidy' from the realm, in other words a tax from parliament.[55]

If ever Henry should have pulled out of the whole affair it was now. He had thought of doing so the year before. Since then the business had simply gone from bad to worse. Henry should have known that the peace with France would hardly move the affair forward in any substantive way. He should have known that demanding a tax from parliament would be both dangerously provocative and utterly useless.

Instead, Henry rushed ahead and pleaded for the tax. According to the Tewkesbury annalist it was one of shocking size. The scutage agreed for the 1257 Welsh campaign had already been a cause of complaint. It had been levied despite the harvest failure, and hit the poor hard. Yet, this tax had only raised a few thousand pounds.[56] The tax demanded now (if the Tewkesbury annalist is right) was 'unprecedented, both in its weight and form'.[57] It was to be a tax levied on movables and also, as never before, on immovables, and so on the value of land. Its rate was to be that of a third, so more even than for Richard's ransom, where the rate was a quarter. Henry's taxes of 1225, 1232 and 1237 had been a fifteenth, a fortieth and a thirtieth. Henry's hope was that with some of the clerical monies the tax would raise at least £66,000.[58]

Another provocation was the behaviour of Master Arlot. The pope had agreed to postpone the penalties but only until 1 June.[59] After that an interdict, Arlot declared, was highly likely to be imposed if a tax was not forthcoming. Probably, by this stage everyone thought these were empty threats. Henry himself made no mention of the penalties in his later suggestions for the modification of the terms. Previous deadlines had passed and nothing had happened. Arlot himself had the power to extend the deadline until September and at some point he did so. Once the project was at an end, Alexander, 'with his accustomed kindness', suspended the penalties altogether.[60] But none of this made Arlot's bluster at the parliament any the less infuriating.

Equally infuriating was that, while Henry was demanding money from the parliament, he was giving it away to foreign favourites and courtiers.

---

[55] For these demands (and the replies), see *CR Supp*, nos. 280–6, and *CR 1256–9*, 325–6.

[56] Tewkesbury, 158; Paris, v, 677; Mitchell, *Studies in Taxation*, 284–7, where the proceeds of the tax seem negligible. Many tenants-in-chief, who took part in the campaign, would have levied it for themselves.

[57] Tewkesbury, 163; Maddicott, *Origins of the English Parliament*, 235 n. 5. The quotation is from Maddicott.

[58] *CR Supp*, no. 284.

[59] Dunstable, 208; Tewkesbury, 163.

[60] *F*, 366, 369, 379; *CR 1256–9*, 163.

Right at the start of the parliament who should arrive at Westminster, but Thomas of Savoy, now at last freed from his Turin prison. A week later, he was on his way back across the Channel. But he took with him the 1,000 marks which the executors of the bishop of Ely had just paid the king. It was not as though Thomas could do much to aid Henry's cause. He was a sick man, conveyed on a litter. He died in February 1259. What a dance he had led the king. Around the same time, Matthew Paris complained about 200 marks given to Henry's Poitevin pantler, William de Sancta Ermina.[61] During the parliament itself Henry was desperately trying to raise a loan from merchants of Cahors totalling some 7,500 marks. This involved sending the clerk Simon Passelewe round to the monasteries of Westminster, Waltham and St Albans, begging them to stand as sureties. Otherwise, Passelewe said, the king's chapel would be placed under an interdict.[62]

By demanding the Sicilian tax, Henry thus enraged a parliament already critical of his rule. In Matthew Paris's account it complained of his breaches of Magna Carta; his oppression of the church; his lavish patronage of foreigners; his poverty; and his inability to deal even with the Welsh. Almost certainly there were complaints too about the oppressions of the sheriffs and the burdens of the eyres. Much of this critique came from magnates and knights at the parliament unconnected with the court. But it is doubtful whether Henry had much support from his councillors either. He was very much alone.

As medicine for the kingdom's ills, the parliament propounded the same remedy as that put forward at parliament after parliament since 1244. Henry should agree to reform of the realm. If he did, then some kind of promise of taxation might be forthcoming. In the past Henry had always refused such a bargain. He knew that the envisaged reform was likely to restrict his independence, perhaps even rob him of power altogether. Not surprisingly, Henry refused again. So the parliament dragged on from 9 April through the rest of the month. In the past such stand-offs had ended in stalemate. Henry had refused reform. No tax had been granted. Everyone had gone home. Now in April 1258 it was different. Action there would be. That was partly because Henry's rule seemed to have reached a new low with the farcical state of the Sicilian affair. As the barons said in a letter to the pope, Henry had reduced the kingdom to an 'imbecilic state'.[63] Yet despite all this, there would have been no revolution

---

[61] Paris, v, 674–5, 677; *CFR 1256–7*, no. 916; *CPR 1247–58*, 622; *CLR 1251–60*, 432; *CR 1256–9*, 302. There is no documentary proof of the gift to Sancta Ermina but the money may have been paid out of the wardrobe. For a grant of land to him in March 1258, see *CR 1256–9*, 200; *CPR 1247–58*, 619. The issue rolls show he got £20 from the chattels of the hanged mayor of Winchester: TNA E 403/3114.

[62] *CPR 1247–58*, 625; Paris, v, 682–8. The cash appearing at the Easter 1258 adventus was down on that in the three previous years: Cassidy, 'Adventus vicecomitum', 616.

[63] Burton, 457.

without one further factor. This was the moment when Henry's court split apart.

THE INTOLERABLE LUSIGNANS

Henry had always hoped to create a cohesive court where the two groups of his foreign relatives mingled and intermarried with native magnates and their families. It had not been easy given the scramble for patronage and the little Henry sometimes had to offer.[64] The tensions between the Lusignans and Savoyards, between king's men and queen's men, had erupted in 1252. In more recent years there had been comparative quiet. The Lusignans, alongside Peter of Savoy, had given sterling service in Gascony in 1253–4. In 1257, Guy de Lusignan, William de Valence and Peter of Savoy joined together in trying to reform the king's finances. But the tensions remained below the surface. In 1258 they at last erupted.

There was one particular detonator. At Shere in Surrey, a village nestling below the North Downs, there was a dispute over possession of the advowson between the great curial magnate John fitzGeoffrey and the abbot of Netley. As Shere was in the diocese of Winchester, bishop-elect Aymer became involved and vigorously took the abbot's part. He decided, through his archdeacon, Peter de Sancto Mauro, to go ahead and induct the abbey's candidate as the new incumbent.[65] The date chosen was Monday 1 April. Since resistance was expected, Sancto Mauro was accompanied by a substantial band of local villagers, led by Vivian, Aymer's crossbowman. Resistance there was. In the ensuing scuffle, several of fitz-Geoffrey's men were seized and hauled off to Aymer's castle at Farnham, where one, Philip the Carpenter, died of his wounds. When the parliament opened at Westminster, fitzGeoffrey complained to the king and demanded justice. Henry, however, made a worried attempt to dampen down the whole affair. According to Matthew Paris, he 'palliated and excused the fault of the elect, and earnestly begged [fitzGeoffrey], not to create scandal and accuse him of such a grave crime, or move any complaint'. As a result, Paris continues, fitzGeoffrey took no formal action and waited 'for better times'.[66] This seems indeed to have been the case. FitzGeoffrey remained at court and even attested a royal charter on 15 April alongside Aymer himself. Aymer, meanwhile, remained in high favour and on 25 April received a present of thirty-five oaks for timber.[67]

---

[64] For the whole subject, see Ridgeway, 'Foreign favourites'.

[65] The incumbent would have been a vicar if, as seems likely, the living was now to be appropriated by the abbey. For the dispute, see Ridgeway, 'Ecclesiastical career of Aymer de Lusignan', 166–7, and Stewart, 'What happened at Shere?', and see Carpenter, *Reign of Henry III*, 192–3.

[66] Paris, v, 708–9.

[67] *CR 1256–9*, 215.

Henry had made a disastrous mistake. When fitzGeoffrey, after the revolution, began legal proceedings about the matter, the plea roll stated
bluntly that the king had 'refused to hear him and wholly denied him
justice'.[68] Henry might think otherwise. He had persuaded fitzGeoffrey not
to pursue the matter. But denial of justice was what it amounted to. Henry
had thus offended a very dangerous man. The son of King John's justiciar,
Geoffrey fitzPeter, and married to the sister of Roger and Hugh Bigod,
fitzGeoffrey was, as Matthew Paris said, 'a man of a famous family, rich
and powerful'.[69] He had been added to the king's council in 1237 at the
instance of parliament. He had then (much praised and rewarded by the
king) served as a steward of the royal household and (between 1245 and
1256) as justiciar of Ireland. Thereafter he was prominent at court and a
member of the king's council. He was also a leading councillor of Edward
and commander of his base at Bristol castle.[70] That he should be treated
in this way seemed utterly scandalous. His complaint about the affair was
the first case heard by the new justiciar (Hugh Bigod) set up by the reform
regime.[71] It featured prominently in the letters of explanation the barons
sent to the pope: 'lately to John fitzGeoffrey, a noble and powerful man
amongst us, [Aymer] has committed the most atrocious injuries, so that the
great men of the kingdom, are vehemently offended, calling to mind his
earlier deeds'.[72] That was part of it. Aymer's conduct seemed all too remi-
niscent of his armed attack on Lambeth palace in 1252.[73] It also helped
join together the grievances of the great with those of the wider realm. As
the ruling council put it after the revolution, in a letter to the pope, the
half-brothers despoiled the poor and oppressed the innocent. Their inferiors could not live under them, their equals could not live with them, and
their superiors could not rule over them. The realm (here drawing on the
famous analogy of John of Salisbury) had become like a body with its
limbs out of joint. And what was Henry doing while all this happened? 'If
anyone brought a complaint and sought judgement [against the Lusignans]',
the letter continued, with some exaggeration, 'the king turned against the
complainant in a most extraordinary manner, and he who should have
been a propitious judge . . . . became a terrible enemy.'[74]

What made all this worse was the Lusignans' prominence at court and
their absorption of Henry's limited patronage. They certainly deserved
reward for their performance in Gascony in 1253–4, but not, as it sometimes

[68] TNA Just 1/1187, m. 1.

[69] Paris, v, 708–9.

[70] Ridgeway, 'The Lord Edward and the Provisions of Oxford', 93. In 1257, fitzGeoffrey
attested royal charters in six months of the year and in January and February 1258.

[71] Hugh Bigod's plea rolls are being edited for the Selden Society by Andrew Hershey.

[72] Paris, vi, 409.

[73] For the monks of Winchester also suffering Aymer's violence, see Ridgeway,
'Ecclesiastical career of Aymer de Lusignan', 170.

[74] Burton, 458–9.

seemed, to the exclusion of everyone else. In 1257, William de Valence attested more royal charters than anyone save the household officials. Valence, Geoffrey de Lusignan, and bishop-elect Aymer were all at court during the April 1258 parliament. The month before, Geoffrey had been promised 500 marks both for his expenses in coming to England and as compensation for the lands he had never received in Ireland. During the parliament itself, another 100 marks came from the exchequer after Henry ordered it to be paid over without delay.[75]

Valence, meanwhile, likewise during the parliament, received the £100 he had lent the king to help buy Dunham manor in Nottinghamshire. This whole episode was an irritating example of what the Lusignans could get away with. Back in 1227, Henry had granted Dunham, an escheat worth all of £50 a year, to his steward Ralph fitzNicholas. On Ralph's death in 1257 he had granted it at once to William de Valence in hereditary right, alleging that Ralph's tenure had only been for life. Then things went wrong for Ralph's son, Robert fitzNicholas, was able to prove his father's tenure had been hereditary under the terms of the 1227 charter. Henry, however, was not to be deterred. He pressurized Robert into selling him the manor and, at the end of 1257, with the sale gone through, gave it back to Valence. The degree of injustice here is hard to gauge. Robert fitzNicholas rebelled in the civil war, but did not, as far as is known, seek to recover Dunham. He may have received a fair price. But the episode showed the lengths to which Henry would go to reward his brother.[76]

All this must have been hot coals to Simon de Montfort. *Nothing* at all had been done to convert *his* annual pension of £400 into land. Although Eleanor's dower payments were more or less up to date (Montfort received another £200 during the Easter term of 1258), he was still owed nearly £1,200, largely as a result of the dealings over Bigorre.[77] The dower payments themselves would have been unnecessary had Montfort been able to pursue his claim for the dower to be in land within Valence's lordship of Pembroke.[78] The tensions between the two men had erupted in May 1257, when the king intervened to prevent them coming to blows.[79]

---

[75] *CPR 1247–58*, 621–2; *CR 1256–9*, 209; *CLR 1251–60*, 432; TNA E 403/3114.

[76] *CChR 1226–57*, 54; *CPR 1247–58*, 576; *CChR 1257–1300*, 2; *CLR 1251–60*, 418–19, 432; *CFR 1257–8*, no. 210; TNA E 403/3114; Ridgeway, 'Foreign favourites', 605. It may or may not be a guarantee of the probity of the transaction that Valence's charter for Dunham (again in hereditary right) was witnessed by Edward, the earls of Hereford and Oxford, and John fitzGeoffrey: *RCWL*, ii, 116. The value of Dunham was deducted from Valence's £500 annual fee. He had now received land worth £200 a year.

[77] *CPR 1247–58*, 609; Maddicott, *Simon de Montfort*, 136.

[78] See above 473–4.

[79] Paris, v, 634; Maddicott, *Simon de Montfort*, 146. The quarrel here, perhaps over conflicting rights associated with Long Crendon in Buckinghamshire (see *CPR 1364–7*, 265), had begun with Valence's bailiffs seizing some of Montfort's property and Montfort's steward then taking it back.

Their confrontation during the parliament of 1258 was no isolated incident. Later in the proceedings, if Matthew Paris is right, Montfort complained about Valence before everyone and demanded justice. In describing the climax of the parliament, Paris brought everything back to the Lusignans. The king had prevented legal actions being brought against them and had exalted them above his native subjects.

THE BARONIAL CONFEDERATION OF 12 APRIL 1258

With the king denying justice to John fitzGeoffrey while asking for a monstrous tax to pursue his Sicilian dreams, seven magnates decided to take action. On Friday 12 April 1258 the earls of Gloucester, Norfolk and Leicester, together with Peter of Savoy, Hugh Bigod (the earl of Norfolk's brother), John fitzGeoffrey and Peter de Montfort, formed an alliance. They swore to support each other against all people, doing right and taking nothing they could not take without doing wrong, saving only the faith owed the king and the crown. Their oath was embodied in a solemn document they all sealed.[80] This was no group of young hotheads. At thirty-six, Richard de Clare was the youngest. All the rest were in their forties or fifties. Only Peter de Montfort was not from the high nobility. This was a formidable coalition.[81]

The aim of the seven was to bring down the Lusignans and force through a general reform of the realm. The alliance would protect them if the king and the Lusignans tried to strike back. Apart from Hugh Bigod and Peter de Montfort every one of the seven had clashed directly with the half-brothers. All moreover were insiders. Indeed, Roger Bigod was probably the only one not currently on the king's council.[82] For all their occasional quarrels, Bigod himself had often been on amicable terms with the king. In October 1257 he received a gift of ten 'good and great oaks' to construct his chapel at Hamstead Marshall in Berkshire.[83] The coming revolution was very much one within the court of Henry III. Nothing showed that more clearly than the presence amongst the seven of the queen's uncle Peter of Savoy.

Outside the court circle, the patronage given to the Savoyards seemed just as bad as that given to the Lusignans. Their estate officials were probably just as grasping. But within the court there were sharp distinctions. Here Peter of Savoy, an international statesman, wise and circumspect,

[80] Bémont, *Simon de Montfort*, 327–8. The document survives in an eighteenth-century drawing, of which an image is reproduced in Maddicott, *Simon de Montfort*, 153.

[81] The failure of Humphrey de Bohun, earl of Hereford, to feature was probably because he was in Wales. He later was named as one of the twelve baronial reformers, so was sympathetic to what was going on.

[82] Carpenter, *Reign of Henry III*, 94–5, 192, 195. For bishop-elect Aymer's conflicts with Roger Bigod and Richard de Clare see above, 539 and 674.

[83] *CR 1256–9*, 99–100.

seemed quite different to the hot-headed half-brothers. He had certainly offended John de Warenne, but he remained 'in' with other leading barons as his place in the confederation shows. He was close to Simon de Montfort, with whom he was acting in the negotiations with France. He and the queen had drawn Richard de Clare into their circle through arranging the marriage of his daughter to the marquis of Montferrat. The quarrel involving Peter and the queen, on one side, and Roger Bigod, on the other, over the manor of Redenhall in Norfolk was patched up at this time.[84] Behind Peter, moreover, stood Queen Eleanor.

There is no sign that personal relations between Eleanor and Henry had broken down. Earlier in 1258, Henry had been pressing ahead with her new apartments at Windsor, and busily arranging for her Lenten supplies of rice, figs, dates, pepper and gingerbread.[85] During the parliament he agreed to stand surety for the money that Richard de Clare owed the marquis of Montferrat under the marriage contract. Eleanor must also have been pleased by the money given to Thomas of Savoy. Yet Eleanor had come to hate the Lusignans. When they fled overseas later in 1258, Queen Margaret prevented them staying in France because they had 'outrageously scandalized and defamed her sister'. Later Eleanor herself complained that bishop-elect Aymer had tried many times to provoke the king against her.[86] It must have been galling to share her husband's love with the half-brothers and have to fight them for patronage.

There was also a devastating new factor influencing Eleanor's attitude.[87] One of her strengths and consolations had always been her control over Edward, now, in 1258, twenty years old. Edward's leading councillors were all close to her, most notably Peter of Savoy and John fitzGeoffrey. Indeed, she may still have 'regarded Edward's household, in some ways, as an extension of her own'.[88] Hitherto, Eleanor had been reassured by Edward's hostility to the Lusignans. In the early 1250s, Peter of Savoy had intervened to prevent Guy de Lusignan severing the isle of Oléron from Edward's Gascon appanage. Between 1254 and 1256, Edward himself had fought hard to prevent Guy and Geoffrey de Lusignan getting land in Ireland, hence the compensation Henry had to come up with. But Edward was restless. He and his entourage were gaining an evil reputation for lawless conduct.[89] He was getting tired of the staid tutelage of men much older than himself. He was irked by the restrictions placed on the way he

[84] CChR 1257–1300, 10, where Redenhall is granted to Peter of Savoy with Bigod's assent. There was soon, however, more contention: Carpenter, Reign of Henry III, 30–2, 83; Howell, Eleanor of Provence, 263–4; Morris, Bigod Earls of Norfolk, 52–3.

[85] CLR 1251–60, 422; CR 1256–9, 186; Howell, Eleanor of Provence, 150–1.

[86] Paris, v, 703; CR 1259–61, 264–5; Howell, Eleanor of Provence, 150.

[87] This was first demonstrated in Ridgeway, 'The Lord Edward and the Provisions of Oxford', a paper which opened up a completely new perspective on the crisis of 1258.

[88] Ridgeway, 'The Lord Edward and the Provisions of Oxford', 93.

[89] Paris, v, 597–8.

ran Gascony and the rest of his appanage.[90] In 1257–8 he began to recruit men of very different stamp into his entourage, men much younger than his old councillors and with none of their connections with the queen. Two in particular were close to the Lusignans, Roger of Leybourne, a knight of William de Valence, and John de Warenne, no friend anyway of Peter of Savoy.[91] To cap it all, just before the parliament of April 1258, Edward settled his quarrel in Ireland with Geoffrey de Lusignan and raised money by leasing property to William de Valence.[92] On 7 May 1258, Peter of Savoy found himself witnessing one of Edward's charters along-side Geoffrey de Lusignan. Both were described as Edward's 'uncles'.[93]

The queen was horrified by these developments.[94] She seemed to be losing her eldest son to her greatest enemies. She was prepared to support the coming revolution in the hope of putting maters right. As the Waverley annalist later put it: 'this provision [meaning the reforms of 1258] at first pleased the queen, while certain barbarous people displeasing to her were compelled to bid farewell to England'.[95]

The seven magnates bonded together on 12 April were thus determined to bring down the Lusignans. They also planned, in one way or another, to place restrictions on the king. All, save Roger Bigod, had probably taken the councillors' oath of 1257, which sought to do that in the area of patronage. Six of the seven later featured on the ruling council of fifteen formed after the revolution, and the seventh, Hugh Bigod, was placed at the head of the government as justiciar. Something of the ideology justi-fying their actions is seen in the alliance itself. It was made 'saving the faith owed to our lord the king *and to the crown*'. So loyalty to the crown might be separate from the loyalty owed to any individual monarch. There was a link here to the statement made by Roger Bigod at the council of Lyon in 1245 about the duty of the 'magnates and people' to preserve the rights, liberties and laws of the crown and kingdom.[96] That in 1258 the seven determined to do.

It seems highly likely that the driving force behind the alliance was Simon de Montfort himself.[97] Its original text was kept in his archives. He

---

[90] A theme in Studd, 'The Lord Edward and King Henry III'.

[91] See above, 561, and Andrew Spencer's forthcoming article 'A vineyard without a wall'. John's wife, the king's half-sister Alice, had died in 1256, but this did not affect his close relations with the Lusignans.

[92] Ridgeway, 'The Lord Edward and the Provisions of Oxford', 90. At some point Edward also received a loan from Aymer.

[93] *CCR 1279–88*, 180–1; Paris, v, 679; *CPR 1247–58*, 644; *CChR 1257–1300*, 13; Ridgeway, 'The Lord Edward and the Provisions of Oxford', 90 and n. 13.

[94] See Howell, *Eleanor of Provence*, 146–51, for an analysis of Eleanor's attitude.

[95] Waverley, 355.

[96] See above, 446–7.

[97] The chronicle known as the Merton *Flores* (hostile to the movement of reform) later ascribed leadership to Montfort and John fitzGeoffrey stimulated by their common hatred of William de Valence and bishop-elect Aymer: Merton, *Flores*, 252.

was close at this time to Roger Bigod and probably Richard de Clare. In Bigod's will, drawn up in 1258, both he and Clare appear as executors.[98] Montfort may well have ensured the inclusion of the most junior member of the seven, Peter de Montfort, a close ally though no relation. Simon certainly hoped the revolution would remedy his material grievances. On 5 May, only three days after Henry's submission, he extracted a promise that the reform regime would deal with his complaints over the money he was owed by the king and the lands he was to receive in place of his annual fee.[99] Yet the text of the alliance also reflected the sense of righteousness and mission which was now to characterize so much of Montfort's career. The seven swore to 'do right and take nothing that we cannot take without doing wrong'. Here was the standard they must live up to. Very similar words were soon to feature in the great oaths which underpinned the movement of reform. There was also a link to the councillors' oath of 1257. That too had been concerned with right and justice and with preventing ministers doing wrong in taking rewards.

At the parliament of April 1258 there was one conspicuous absentee, the king's brother, Richard, king of the Romans and earl of Cornwall. He was, of course, in Germany. Thomas Wykes (with connections to Richard's entourage) believed this was crucial to the course of events. The magnates, he averred, only took action because they despaired of Richard ever steering the realm once more with his wise counsel. That is surely claiming too much, but certainly had Richard been at the parliament matters might have taken another course. His absence meant Henry was all the more alone.[100]

THE WITHDRAWAL OF THE BISHOPS

The seven confederates of 12 April did not take action immediately. Between 12 and 27 April they circled round their enemies at court. In this period all but Peter de Montfort of the seven attested royal charters, sometimes alongside bishop-elect Aymer, William de Valence and Geoffrey de Lusignan.[101] Henry's other concerns went on as normal. On 15 April he sent a letter to Lesnes abbey in Essex expressing astonishment at its refusal to give sustenance and shelter to a converted Jewess and her son.[102]

It was on 28 April that Henry put his final demand for the tax. The magnates promised a reply three days later on 30 April. Meanwhile, the bishops withdrew from the parliament and went home.[103] This statement

---

[98] Morris, *Bigod Earls of Norfolk*, 218–19.

[99] *CPR 1247–58*, 627.

[100] Wykes, 118–19.

[101] *RCWL*, ii, 119–20.

[102] TNA SC 1/2/79.

[103] For a full discussion of episcopal attitudes in 1258, see Ambler, *Bishops in the Political Community*, ch. 5.

from the Tewkesbury annalist is confirmed by the witness lists of royal charters which show bishops attesting up to 19 April and not thereafter. The implication is that the tax was now to be one entirely levied on property held by the laity, and thus not requiring the assent of the church. Given the burdens the church was already bearing, probably it had been that from start. The Tewkesbury annalist also says the bishops withdrew 'lest they incur the anger of the king'. If so, they had some inkling of what was to come. They were not prepared to sanction direct action against the king, but they were not prepared to resist it either. They could not support Henry's coercion, but did not wish to impede reform of the realm. The only bishop to stand by the king in the ensuing weeks was Fulk Basset of London. There was also no chance of Archbishop Boniface appearing as a mediator and peacemaker along the lines of Archbishop Langton in 1215 and Archbishop Edmund in 1234. Boniface had clashed violently with Aymer of course. He had quarrelled too with William de Valence over possession of a wardship.[104] Like the queen and Peter of Savoy, he wanted the Lusignans marked down. His relations with Henry himself had not recovered from his refusal to cancel the London council back in August 1257. He attested not a single royal charter during the parliament, although he was staying at Lambeth palace.[105] Indeed, Boniface had been entirely absent from court since October 1257.

While, moreover, the bishops believed in the need for secular reforms, they were prepared to let the baronial leaders get on with them, in part because they were busy with their own programme for ecclesiastical reform, one they pursued (as in August 1257) at their own assemblies. They needed to go it alone because there was limited sympathy for their programme amongst the lay magnates at parliament, as the events of 1253 surrounding the confirmation of Magna Carta had shown. On 19 April 1258, Boniface summoned an ecclesiastical assembly to meet at Merton on 6 June. This went ahead although it clashed with the great parliament summoned to Oxford to begin the reform of the realm.[106]

THE REVOLUTION

Despite the withdrawal of the bishops, Henry seemed unaware of the impending crisis. There is no sign he sought to rally forces. He did not withdraw to the Tower, as in 1236 and 1238, where he would have been safe from surprise attack. On 30 April itself, the day the magnates were to give their reply to the tax, he contrived a final provocation. He promised to grant William de Valence an escheat, although (as he admitted) he did

[104] *CR 1256–9*, 276; Carpenter, *Reign of Henry III*, 192.
[105] Burton, 411–12.
[106] Burton, 411–12; *C&S*, i, 568–85.

not know its value.[107] The events of the day are described in a newsletter written soon afterwards and preserved in the annals of Tewkesbury abbey. Although one may question some of the details, the gist is perfectly believable.[108]

As the third hour of the day approached, 'there went to the court at Westminster, noble and vigorous men, earls, barons and knights, excellently protected with arms and girded with swords'. Of those taking part in the march, the account only identifies Roger Bigod but one can be sure that, of the seven confederates, Montfort, Clare, John fitzGeoffrey and Hugh Bigod were also there, shoulder to shoulder with him at the front. Peter of Savoy could well have been there too for he authorized a writ on 30 April with other unnamed members of the council.[109] The insurgents left their swords at the entrance to the royal hall but their appearance in armour was menacing enough. Where was Henry while this was happening? In his chamber perhaps, or in the chapel of Saint Stephen, where he had conferred with his councillors earlier in the year before coming down to meet the Londoners. Who came down with him now into the hall where he had so often held feasts and fed thousands of paupers? Surely at least John Mansel, Bath, Lovel and Wingham of the official establishment. Were the Lusignans there too or had they made themselves scarce? And where was the queen? She was certainly around for on this very day Henry made a concession at her instance.[110] She must have awaited the outcome anxiously, hoping it would spell the downfall of her enemies.

Although the confederates saluted him with due deference, Henry was shaken by their appearance in arms and could do no more than ask, rather pathetically, 'what is this my lords, am I, poor wretch, your prisoner?'[111] Roger Bigod gave the reply. He denied that Henry was a prisoner but demanded action against the 'intolerable' Lusignans and the reform of the realm by twenty-four men chosen by the baronage.[112] No tax was to be imposed without the consent of the twenty-four and they were to appoint someone to keep the king's seal. Henry had resisted such demands for

---

[107] *CPR 1247–58*, 625. In the event the lands were worth an annual £23, so this was a significant gift: *CChR 1257–1300*, 84. It is a testimony to the disturbance in the realm that the charter Henry promised in April 1258 was not issued until November 1267.

[108] Tewkesbury, 163–4; Carpenter, *Reign of Henry III*, 187–90. For a recent account of the revolution of 1258, see Jobson, *The First English Revolution*.

[109] *CFR 1257–8*, no. 570.

[110] *CPR 1247–58*, 626.

[111] In the Latin, there is a play on words here: 'captivus ego a vobis ne captus sum?'

[112] In the Tewkesbury account Bigod asks for the Poitevins and 'all aliens' to flee from Henry's face. It seems unlikely that he extended the proscription to all aliens since he was at this time in alliance with Peter of Savoy. Bigod also paraphrases St Luke in prophesizing glory in the heavens and peace on earth once the Poitevins and all aliens had gone: Morris, *Bigod Earls of Norfolk*, 58–9.

fourteen years. Now confronted by men in armour and fearing imprisonment, he gave way. Together with Edward, he took an oath to accept the
reforms demanded. According to Matthew Paris, the oath was sworn at
the shrine of the Confessor.[113]

The king's agreement to reform was formally announced in two letters
of 2 May. Their content, however, was very different, reflecting, it would
seem, different views as to how to proceed.[114] In one of the letters all
Henry did was to concede that by Christmas *he* would reform the state of
the kingdom by the counsel of his upstanding and faithful men. This was
to be done, moreover (surely Henry's idea), with the counsel also of a
papal legate if he came to England. (The same legate whom Henry, as will
be seen, hoped might lead an army out to Sicily.) As security for observing
the reforms, Henry subjected himself to coercion by the pope. But in
Henry's second letter, one reflecting far more the baronial view, there was
no mention of a Christmas deadline or a papal legate. Rather, twenty-four
men, twelve chosen by the barons and twelve by the king, were to meet at
Oxford in June to reform the state of the kingdom 'as they see best', with
Henry under oath to observe whatever they ordained.[115] There was here
no mention of the papal coercion either. Instead Henry was to provide
whatever security the twenty-four reformers demanded.

Henry was evidently determined to have his say in what happened
but he felt obliged to go along with the procedures in the second letter. By
2 May he had already chosen his twelve reformers. They showed his isola-
tion. To be sure, Henry hoped Richard de Clare would be one of the
number, despite him being part of the baronial confederation. On 2
May itself, Henry stood surety for the money that Clare owed for the
Montferrat marriage. But Clare ultimately refused Henry's invitation and
joined the baronial twelve instead, leaving Henry (as far as the records
go) one man short. Henry's group only had one English earl, John de
Warenne of Surrey, and only one English magnate, Fulk Basset, head of
the Bassets of High Wycombe and the only bishop on the king's twelve.
For the rest, Henry defiantly named bishop-elect Aymer, Guy de Lusignan
and William de Valence, along with King Richard's son Henry of
Almayne, John de Plessis, John Mansel, John of Darlington (the king's
confessor), the abbot of Westminster and the keeper of the seal, Henry of
Wingham.[116]

The baronial twelve on the other hand was of an altogether different
weight. To six of the original seven confederates, the earls of Leicester,
Gloucester and Norfolk, John fitzGeoffrey, Hugh Bigod and Peter de

---

[113] Paris, v, 689.

[114] *DBM*, nos. 1–2.

[115] Henry's oath is here said to have been taken on his behalf by Robert Walerand.

[116] Guy de Lusignan, unlike Geoffrey, does not attest royal charters during the
Westminster parliament but he was certainly in England.

Montfort, were added Walter de Cantilupe, bishop of Worcester, Humphrey de Bohun, earl of Hereford, the great marcher baron Roger de Mortimer and three substantial English magnates, William Bardolph, Richard de Grey and Hugh Despenser. Montfort's influence within the group would be great, for Cantilupe, Peter de Montfort, Grey and Despenser were close associates.

Peter of Savoy featured on neither list. That testified both to his break with the king and also to his desire to mend fences as soon as possible. On 2 May indeed, he was the only one of the seven confederates to witness Henry's proclamations accepting reform of the realm, doing so amongst members of Henry's twelve.[117] He wished to lay low the Lusignans, and then recover Henry's favour. Queen Eleanor's view was surely the same.

In return for Henry's acceptance of reform, the magnates made one concession recorded in the formal documents of 2 May. This was a promise over a tax. Henry thus announced that, having discussed with his magnates how to further the Sicilian business, they had replied that, if he reformed the realm, and if the pope modified the conditions so there was some hope of success, then the earls and barons would try to persuade 'the community of the realm' to grant a tax to support the Sicilian project.

The promise was so hedged around as to be virtually worthless. The barons could always decide that the pope had made insufficient modifications. But the promise had a clear purpose. It concealed Henry's coercion and gave the appearance he had voluntarily accepted reform in return for a tax, just as he had accepted Magna Carta in return for a tax in 1225. The need for any elaborate justification of the revolution was thus removed. It could go forward in the king's name and with his consent.

The truth, of course, was that Henry had been forced to accept reform. He had not done so willingly. Yet Henry had never been very grounded in reality. Perhaps he did hope something would come of the baronial promise. He had certainly not given up on the Sicilian affair. That is very clear from the reply to the pope he drew up in early May, soon after the conclusion of the Westminster parliament.[118] It was at turns soberly realistic and fancifully optimistic. Henry explained there was no way he could pay the 30,000 marks immediately demanded by Pope Alexander. Instead, he suggested, let it come from the taxation being levied on the church. Thereafter, the balance of what was owed could be raised from the issues of Sicily once it had been conquered – so that old line again.[119] As for sending an army to Sicily, the papal timetable was impossible, but surely merchants would be prepared to lend 100,000 marks on the strength of

---

[117] *DBM*, nos. 1–2.

[118] *CR Supp*, nos. 280–8; Lunt, *Financial Relations*, 281. The replies were drawn up by Rostand, John Mansel and Hugh Bigod, but obviously on Henry's instructions: *F*, 371 (*CPR 1247–58*, 629).

[119] Henry calculated he would then have paid 100,000 marks.

the remaining taxation owed by the church and the new tax to be procured by the magnates in return for reform of the realm! Then, if a legate came to England, he could organize and lead the military force raised by the money. Meanwhile, the French peace was proceeding (with its hope of the 500 or 1,000 knights) and help could be expected from the king of Germany, especially if the pope lent him support. This reply was Henry's last significant act before the shutters came down on his personal rule. It testified to his simplistic determination to pursue the Sicilian affair, a determination more than anything else responsible for bringing about his downfall.

CONCLUSION

Henry's personal rule had seen considerable achievements. On the secular side he had acquired Cheshire for the crown and wrested the Four Cantrefs from the rulers of Gwynedd. In South Wales, putting right earlier mistakes, he had recovered Cardigan and Carmarthen. In his relations with Scotland, he had ended the threat to the northern counties and established a warm relationship with his son-in-law King Alexander III. In 1253-4 he had prevented Gascony's loss after the disasters of Montfortian rule. His subsequent visit to Paris had brought honour to his kingdom. Henry's marriage to Eleanor of Provence had produced an heir, another son in reserve and two healthy daughters, one already married to the king of Scots. An achievement at least in his eyes, Henry had established two groups of foreign relatives in England, the Savoyard uncles of his wife and his own half-brothers from the house of Lusignan. Henry had transformed his homes, enhancing their comfort, their beauty and their religious and secular meaning. Continuing from the minority, he had rebuilt major castles, so that Dover, Windsor, York and the Tower were far more formidable structures than at the start of the reign. Dyserth and Deganwy, meanwhile, held down his Welsh conquests.

Within England, Henry's personal rule was a period of domestic peace. That created favourable conditions for the building of churches, the work of the friars and pastoral-minded bishops, the explosion of the money supply (boosted by Henry's recoinage of 1247) and the development of a new network of markets and fairs.[1] It provided the conditions too for the expansion of the common law, with litigants in increasing numbers bringing their cases before the king's judges both in the localities and at Westminster.[2]

In 1261, as civil war loomed, Henry wrote feelingly of his achievement. 'For the forty-five years [so from 1216], in which, by the will of God and helped by his grace, we have held the government of our kingdom . . . with our utmost desire and all our strength, we have not ceased to study and labour . . . for the peace and tranquillity of each and everyone.' The

---

[1] For markets and fairs, see Letters, *Gazetteer*. Between 1227 and 1258, Henry granted no fewer than 630 charters of 'free warren' allowing lords to set up private parks: Crook, 'The "Petition of the Barons" and charters of free warren'.

[2] Moore, 'Fine rolls as evidence for the expansion of royal justice', and above, 528.

achievement was recognized. Writing in the 1250s, Matthew Paris contrasted the 'great ruin' of England under John through war and interdict with the 'multo tempore' Henry had governed England in peace. In 1263 the Tewkesbury annalist described Henry as a 'skilful restorer of peace and quiet'.[3] Certainly, Henry's personality and policies (and sometimes lack of policies) contributed to the long peace. In the 1261 proclamation he claimed he had never taken away anyone's rights 'by force or will'. In other words, he had not contravened the key chapter in Magna Carta preventing freemen being deprived of property 'save by the lawful judgement of their peers or by the law of the land'.[4] Henry's claim was untrue during the ascendancy of Peter des Roches, but true for the most part of the subsequent years of personal rule. If, in anger, Henry often wished to act in an arbitrary fashion, again and again he allowed himself to be restrained by councillors and parliaments. There was no equivalent in 1258 to the fifty or so unjust disseisins King John was forced to reverse after Magna Carta.[5] There was equally no equivalent to the reversals of acts of injustice forced on Henry after the fall of Peter des Roches in 1234. Only one member of the ruling council set up after the revolution claimed to have lost property unjustly through an action of the king. This was Roger de Mortimer, the property being the rich manor of Lechlade in Gloucestershire. But the rights and wrongs of the matter were complex and he failed to prove his case.[6]

In other areas too Henry had obeyed the Charter. That was true, again for the most part, when it came to the reliefs of earls, barons and knights, the treatment of widows, the ban on the selling of justice and the stipulation that taxes needed the consent of the kingdom.[7] The expansion of

[3] *F*, 408–9; Carpenter, *Reign of Henry III*, 260; and Paris's comments underneath his drawings of John and Henry III in the *Historia Anglorum*'s gallery of kings: http://www.bl.uk/manuscripts/Viewer.aspx?ref=royal_ms_14_c_vii_f008v and (for Henry) above plate 1.

[4] For earls and barons being judged by their peers and being amerced in accordance with Magna Carta, see Carpenter, *Magna Carta*, 453–4.

[5] Holt, *Magna Carta*, 360–1; Carpenter, *Magna Carta*, 388–9.

[6] Carpenter, 'A noble in politics', 186–97. Mortimer's lack of progress was also due to the beneficiary being Richard of Cornwall, and it was he who was accused of committing the immediate disseisin. Acts of alleged injustice, in which Henry was directly involved, reversed after the 1258 revolution, were the rate of repayment of the debts of Peter de Brus and Walter de Lindsey, the treatment of Robert de Ros, the denial of justice to John fitzGeoffrey and (less clearly) Elyas de Rabayne's disinheritance of the Bayeux heiress: see above, 479, 557, 625.

[7] The purchase of writs, costing mostly between 6s 8d and £1, to expedite common law legal actions was not considered the selling of justice. For an assessment of how far Magna Carta was obeyed and how far breached under Henry, see Carpenter, *Magna Carta*, ch. 8. For widows, see above, 264–6. In terms of relief, between 1234 and 1258 there are around forty-five examples in the fine rolls of reliefs being charged at the £100 rate the Charter laid down for earldoms and baronies. There are also many examples of the £5 rate stipulated for a knight's fee. Many other reliefs do not indicate the size of the property in question, but the sums involved are usually small. The case of the baron John fitzAlan seems a rare breach of

common law litigation (fair and expeditious save when it touched the interests of great men) was very much in the Charter's spirit. Meanwhile, the Forest Charter had removed substantial areas of the country from the jurisdiction of forest law.[8]

The total contrast between the rule of King John and the rule of his son is shown in the offerings of money to appease the king's anger and recover his benevolence. In the fine roll of 1207/8 alone there are twelve such fines worth a potential £5,580. In the near quarter-century of Henry's personal rule there are twelve worth £2,612.[9] Henry's treatment of John de Balliol and Robert de Ros was quite exceptional. There was equally no equivalent under Henry to the fines so common under King John to recover property seized into the king's hands. There are thirteen of these in the fine roll of 1207/8 alone. The reduction in the king's ability to extract money by arbitrary means is reflected in the decline more generally in the value of fines for concessions and favours. Under John, the yearly average was around £25,500. Even leaving out the colossal total for the first regnal year (£40,700), the average was still £22,000.[10] During

the Charter although not one entirely clear cut. He had been a ward of the king and, in accordance with the Charter, was thus not charged a relief. But he nonetheless offered £1,000 for seisin of his father's lands and castles. The size of the fine seems to be explained by the way it brought him the king's corn, stock and ploughs in the lands: *CFR 1243–4*, nos. 233–7, 277. The Charter had stipulated that lands should be returned with a full complement of ploughs but said nothing about the entitlement to corn and other stock. Richard de Clare made a similar fine (of 1,200 marks) for the corn and stock in his lands: *CFR 1243–4*, no. 84. Other cases where tenants-in-chief made payments above £100 were when they were buying themselves out of a period of wardship. For fitzAlan's debts, see also above, 657, n. 234.

[8] See above, 70.

[9] I have reached the figure under Henry by putting into the fine rolls search engine (https://finerollshenry3.org.uk/content/search/search_text.html) the terms 'anger', 'rancour', 'indignation', 'grace' and 'benevolence'. (The rolls for 1244 to 1248 have been searched individually as at the moment the search facility does not work for those years.) The fines are *CFR 1235–6*, no. 152; *CFR 1237–8*, no. 59; *CFR 1238–9*, no. 13; *CFR 1242–3*, nos. 23, 24; *CFR 1250–1*, nos. 359, 822 (the Henry of Bath fine, for which see above, 535), 1,095; *CFR 1252–3*, no. 190; *CFR 1255–6*, no. 1235; *CFR 1256–7*, no. 894 (John de Balliol's fine); *CFR 1257–8*, no. 37. Under both King John and Henry III there are equivalent fines which do not mention the above terms, the most spectacular under Henry being the £1,000 fine of Walter of Clifford, for which see above, 533. In both reigns there were also fines which did not reach the fine rolls: under John the 50,000-mark fine imposed on Matilda de Briouze, under Henry the 100,000 marks imposed on Robert de Ros and reduced, I have suggested, to 1,000 marks (see above, 624). I have not included in Henry's total (as they do not mention his anger) the seventeen fines from men for having married widows without the king's permission. Their total value was only £1,535, the largest being the £500 fine of Hugh Peche for abducting Ida, widow of Stephen of Seagrave: *CFR 1246–7*, no. 424.

[10] This is an average drawn from the regnal years 1199/1200, 1200/1, 1204/5, 1205/6, 1206/7, 1207/8 and 1213/14. The totals for 1199/1200, 1204/5 and 1213/14 were calculated by Beth Hartland and Paul Dryburgh: *CFR 1224–34*, vii. I have made the other calculations myself, omitting the year 1201/2, when King John was largely overseas and the last years when England was at war. John's fine rolls between 1202 and 1204 and 1208 and 1213 are missing.

Henry's personal rule between 1234 and 1257 the average was £5,500, so four times less than under his father.[11] The contrast was partly because of Henry's respect for the letter and the spirit of Magna Carta. It was also because of his indulgent, easily appeased personality. There was a truth in the remark Roger of Wendover put into Henry's mouth: 'I prefer to be thought a king foolish and remiss than cruel and tyrannical.'[12] In that respect, Henry was the ideal king for the post-Magna Carta world.

Henry might think that during his personal rule he had done much to conciliate his leading magnates. He did not pressurize them to pay their debts. He did not challenge their liberties in the field of local government. On the contrary, he allowed them in many ways to encroach on the jurisdiction of the sheriffs and the rights of the crown.[13] This restraint was another contributor, as Henry intended, to the domestic peace. Nor during his personal rule did Henry hold his great men at arm's-length when it came to his court and council. It is true that Henry's earls spent far less time at court than did the earls of his son.[14] Given King Edward's prestige and the militaristic complexion of his court, the contrast is hardly surprising. Yet earls could be prominent under Henry: Gilbert Marshal in 1234/5, John de Lacy in 1236–7 (described by Matthew Paris as one of the king's chief councillors)[15] and, for periods in the 1240s and 1250s, Richard of Cornwall, Simon de Montfort and Richard de Clare. Indeed, over only a slightly longer period, the number of royal charters Clare attested was not much less than William de Valence. If appearing most often during military campaigns and parliaments, there were few years during the personal rule when Roger Bigod of Norfolk and Humphrey de Bohun of

---

[11] Breaking the total down, for the regnal years 1234–42 the average is £4,000; for those between 1243 and 1253, £6,500; and for 1255–7, £5,000. I have omitted the years 1242/3 and 1253/4, when Henry was overseas. The calculations between 1234 and 1242 are by Hartland and Dryburgh: *CFR 1234–42*, xii–xiii, and see their 'Development of the fine rolls', 194–5. The other calculations are by myself. Under both kings the totals in any one year can be boosted by small numbers of very large fines. Under Henry the only year when his total was over £10,000 was in 1241/2 thanks to a 10,000-mark fine by Joan, widow of Hugh Wake, for the custody of his lands: *CFR 1241–2*, no. 105. The equivalent to John's £40,700 in 1199/1200 was Henry's £7,820 in 1226/7: *CFR 1224–34*, viii, as calculated by Hartland and Dryburgh. The sum for the next regnal year was £2,768.

[12] Wendover, iii, 233.

[13] See above, 532, 617, and Carpenter, *Reign of Henry III*, 85–93, 99–102.

[14] Spencer, *Nobility and Kingship*, 45–9; Spencer, 'Dealing with inadequate kingship', 79. In what follows I am indebted to a list compiled by Andrew Spencer of the number of charters attested by the earls and foreign relatives between 1236 and 1257. See his '"A vineyard without a wall"'. The contrast can be seen in the case of John de Warenne. He came of age in 1252 and was hardly out of favour, being named as one of the king's twelve in 1258. But his attendance at court was far less frequent than under Edward, for which see Spencer, *Nobility and Kingship*, 46. His reluctance to spend time at court perhaps made Henry all the more grateful to William de Valence for sticking there from a similarly young age.

[15] Paris, iii, 412, 476.

Hereford were not found at court.[16] On Henry's council in the last years of the personal rule were the earls of Cornwall, Gloucester, Leicester, Hugh Bigod, brother of the earl of Norfolk, John fitzGeoffrey and two bishops from magnate families Walter de Cantilupe of Worcester and Fulk Basset of London. Henry was far from being remote from the upper echelons of his nobility.

In all the criticism of his personal rule levelled during the period of reform and rebellion there is but one suggestion Henry might have harboured dangerous political theories. In a speech designed to be made by a baronial envoy to the pope, the half-brothers were accused (amongst much else) of 'whispering' to the king that the prince was not subject to the laws.[17] How Henry reacted to this supposed reminder of the familiar Roman law maxim is unknown. If he was attracted by ideas about the 'plenitude' of royal power during the regime of Peter des Roches, he never appealed to them thereafter. If his speech to parliament in 1248 had threatening implications, in the event it was never more than a way of defending his right to choose his own ministers.[18] If Henry pondered how to abrogate rash concessions, and occasionally made provocative references to the papal use of 'non obstante', this was hardly a worked-out theory of absolutist kingship. Despite Matthew Paris's fears, he never in practice appealed to 'non obstante' as a way of abrogating existing rights.[19] In his denial of justice, at least as portrayed by Paris in the John fitzGeoffrey case, Henry appears not as masterful monarch, but as one wringing his hands and pleading for the complaint to be withdrawn. Henry was sincere in his confirmations of Magna Carta. His considered position was that he was subject to the law.

While Henry developed no elaborate political theory, threatening or otherwise, he could deploy solid arguments against his critics. However much parliament's demand to choose his ministers was said to be in line with custom, Henry was on strong ground when he claimed the contrary. 'The king and his ancestors by custom,' he said in 1264, have always 'appointed and removed' ministers 'at their own pleasure'. To give way on the point, he added, would violate his coronation oath to protect the rights

---

[16] Beginning in 1245, Clare attested 217 charters, Valence, starting in 1247, 249 charters. Geoffrey and Guy de Lusignan attested respectively 131 and 60 charters, and Peter of Savoy (from 1241) 200 charters. The totals for Richard of Cornwall, Simon de Montfort, Roger Bigod and Humphrey de Bohun between 1236 and 1257 were respectively 213, 176, 153 and 115.

[17] Burton, 463; Carpenter, *Reign of Henry III*, 76–9.

[18] See above, 480–1. Thus it is entirely in the context of such a defence that the speech is echoed in the Montfortian *Song of Lewes*. The Song cites the Roman law maxim 'the will of the prince has the force of law' in the same context: *Song of Lewes*, lines 485–526.

[19] See above, 539–42, and Carpenter, *Reign of Henry III*, 76–9, and for a different view, Clanchy, 'Did Henry III have a policy?' I will discuss the political ideas of the period in more detail in volume 2.

of the crown.[20] Henry could be equally effective in defending himself against the jurisdictional demands of the church.[21] In a series of clerical assemblies between 1257 and 1261 he was criticized for upsetting the proper relationship between priestly and royal power and violating the laws both of God and man, the latter notably by his breaches of Magna Carta.[22] But Henry was in no way abashed. In 1261, in detailed replies to the complaints, he took his stand on 'the customs of the kingdom', the rights of the king ('since the first foundation of the English church') and his obligation to preserve 'justice and peace', something incompatible with all the demands for clerical immunity.[23]

Henry's peace was helped by the absence of foreign war. Of course, had Henry been a king in the mould of his great-grandson, Edward III, he might have made war popular. But the financial demands needed to mount the campaigns were just as likely to generate widespread discontent as happened under both King John and Edward I. Keen though he was to recover his lost empire, Henry during his personal rule only mounted one campaign to do so, and that lasted for no more than a few months. His time in Gascony in 1253–4 was defensive, designed simply to hold onto the duchy. Within the British Isles, Henry fought just three brief campaigns, those in Wales in 1241, 1245 and 1257. He was reluctant to mount them, all really being last resorts. In 1246, Henry took the remarkable decision not to extinguish the remains of Gwynedd, although he had the right, the resources and the opportunity to do so. There was an equivalent reluctance to push claims to overlordship over Scotland. Effectively abandoned in 1237, Henry made no real effort to revive them even during the minority of Alexander III.

In all this one can see how Henry earned his reputation as a 'rex pacificus non bellicosus'.[24] There was something more here than simply a lack of martial enthusiasm and expertise. His settlements with the Welsh and the Scots showed a genuine desire for peace between rulers and peoples. He wished the truces with France to be inviolably observed 'for the peace and quiet of subjects'.[25] Of course, Henry was not a consistent peacemaker. Both in 1230 and 1242 he was passionately committed to the campaigns to recover his lost empire. In the end he wanted peace with France, so he could wage war in Sicily. Here his pacific proclivities merely ensured his lack of success. Yet Henry could claim successes on the military front both in Wales and, in 1253–4, in Gascony. His lack of aggression equally served him well.

---

[20] *DBM*, 252–3, 256–7.
[21] For what follows, see Hoskin, 'The church and the king', 205–10.
[22] See especially the preamble to the Lambeth statutes of 1261: *C&S*, i, 669–71.
[23] *C&S*, i, 687–92.
[24] Guisborough, 201.
[25] *F*, 335, and see in volume 2 the discussion of the 1267 Treaty of Montgomery.

The Gascon victory was due to diplomacy and conciliation as well as warfare. The refusal to intervene personally in Ireland was justified by the revenue it sent to England and the rewards it offered his favourites.

If Henry, then, had achievements to his credit, he had also clearly failed.[26] He had not recovered the continental empire and acknowledged his condition would be 'worsened' by the forthcoming peace with France. By 1257 his conquests in Wales were being overrun by Llywelyn and the Sicilian project was in deep trouble. Within England itself, Henry faced vehement criticisms of his rule in parliament and demands for reforms which would virtually strip him of power. He had come nowhere near achieving that utopia of the Confessor where 'there are none whom the king does not please, all are rich and all at ease'.[27] There were constant complaints that some chapters in Magna Carta were being breached, and where breached could not be enforced. A critique of Henry's rule drawn up in 1264 thus covered, in violation of the Charter, the manipulation of episcopal elections, the exploitation of ecclesiastical vacancies, the destruction of property in the king's hands during wardships, the disparagement of heirs and heiresses in marriage, and the denial of justice when litigants sought to bring cases against royal favourites.[28] Elsewhere, there were complaints about breaches of the Charter's chapters on the running of local courts and the levying of amercements. And, of course, there was the long-standing grievance over the failure to implement all the deforestations supposedly promised by the Charter of the Forest.[29] While the financial burdens Henry imposed on his kingdom nowhere near equalled those of King John, the exactions of the sheriffs and the impositions of the forest justices and the justices in eyre had created widespread discontent. On top of that, the policy of forcing all those with incomes of £15 a year to take up knighthood, or buy exemptions, had hit large sections of the gentry. The church, meanwhile, quite apart from its other grievances, had been totally alienated by the Sicilian affair and all the money extorted by the pope. While Henry was capable of ruling in concert with great councils and parliaments, he was equally capable of forging ahead without any kind of general consent. If he had some justification for doing so when making the alliance with the Lusignans in 1241–2, he had none whatsoever when it came to signing up for Sicily.

Swirling around these discontents, there was another. The feeling that Henry was handing England over to grasping and lawless foreigners was

---

[26] For a vigorous defence of Henry, see Baker, *Henry III*.

[27] See above, 324–5.

[28] *DBM*, 268–75. The relevant chapters in the 1215 Charter were 1–6 and 40. The critique was prepared for Louis IX's judgement at Amiens on the dispute between Henry and the barons.

[29] Carpenter, *Magna Carta*, 444–5, and for the whole subject, Maddicott, *Magna Carta and the Local Community*.

a major factor separating him from his people. Henry was the most English king since the Norman conquest. He lived almost entirely in England and regarded it as his homeland.[30] His adoption of the Confessor as his patron saint and the naming of his sons Edward and Edmund linked him to the Anglo-Saxon past. On occasion he celebrated the country's strengths. The nobles of England, he declared, flourished more than those of other nations in virtue and vigour. He had 'more faith' in his 'own people than in aliens'.[31] The shields on the sword belt he gave to the count of Champagne, like those in the choir of Westminster Abbey, showed him very much in the midst of his English baronage.

None of this, however, led Henry to think his patronage should be confined to native-born men. Among his great successes (in his view) were all the marriages he found for his foreign kin: on the Savoyard side, Edmund de Lacy and John de Vescy to the daughters of the marquis of Saluzzo; Baldwin de Redvers to a daughter of Thomas of Savoy; a daughter of Richard de Clare to the marquis of Montferrat, and, of course, Sanchia to Richard of Cornwall; on the Lusignan side, William de Valence to Joan de Munchesney; John de Warenne to the king's half-sister Alice; Robert de Ferrers to Mary, a niece of the king, daughter of Hugh de Lusignan; and Gilbert, Richard de Clare's son and heir, to Alice, another of Hugh's daughters.[32]

Up to a point Henry here, in his generous way, was simply trying to do his best for his foreign relations without any wider strategic purpose. But, in his mind, he also had good reasons for acting as he did. The Savoyards provided an altogether new continental profile. The Lusignans gave him a foothold in Poitou and helped with the defence of Gascony. Within the kingdom his kinsmen could play an important role as trusted councillors, lords and prelates. That trust was partly because they were family, the uncles of the queen and his own half-brothers. But this was not the whole story. Henry was perfectly capable of quarrelling with family members and excluding them from his counsels as he did with Archbishop Boniface. For Henry, it was also very personal. When he met William, the bishop-elect of Valence, Thomas and Peter of Savoy and the Lusignans, his heart, for different reasons, went out to them. They, in their turn, knew how to retain his love. The bishop-elect of Valence and Thomas and Peter of Savoy were immensely impressive men. If the personal qualities of the Lusignans are less easy to grasp, they were prepared to spend large amounts of time at court, Guy and Geoffrey on their visits to England,

[30] In his letter before sailing for Gascony in 1242, Henry asked for prayers for his safety until he returned 'home' ('ad propria'): *CR 1237–42*, 436.

[31] *CR 1251–3*, 448, and above, 557, 589.

[32] Further down the social scale Imbert Pugeys married the widow of Ralph fitzBernard, while Elyas de Rabayne married the Bayeux heiress. In Ireland, Lacy and Ridlesford heiresses went to Peter and Ebulo of Geneva. On Peter's death, his widow was married to Geoffrey de Joinville, a brother of Louis IX's biographer. There was also the marriage of the countess of Warwick to John de Plessis.

William de Valence on an almost permanent basis. Henry valued such loyalty and repaid it accordingly.

There were clearly times when Henry seemed to place more trust in his foreign relations than he did in his native nobility. In 1242, in the event of his death, it was Peter and Boniface of Savoy who were to have control of strategic castles for the benefit of the king's heirs.[33] Yet, as we have seen, Henry never aimed to construct an exclusively foreign court. Surrounding himself with foreigners so as to trample down his disloyal native subjects was not part of his vision. Henry's aim was altogether more benign and, for all his naïveté, more subtle. In remoulding the English nobility through marriages to his foreign kin, he sought to enhance its loyalty and foster peace, just as he hoped 'peace' would result from marriages between the competing factions in Bordeaux.[34] Henry was also, or so he thought, doing his nobles a favour, for surely they too would benefit from the connections with himself and such illustrious members of the European aristocracy. Many of those involved seem to have agreed. Warin de Munchesney, William de Ferrers, Richard de Clare and William de Vescy were willing participants in the unions arranged for their children.

Henry also hoped the merits of his foreign relations would appear to the wider realm. Hence he could explain how the kingdom would be more 'secure' if the bishop-elect of Valence became bishop of Durham and Boniface of Savoy archbishop of Canterbury.[35] Unfortunately many failed to share that vision. Churchmen, non-curial magnates and county knights, sections of society all present in parliament, were appalled by the way Henry was asking for their money while pouring patronage into the mouths of foreigners. *The Song of Lewes* in a powerful passage declared that the king should confine rewards to his own men. If patronage instead was given 'to those who brought nothing', the English would find themselves 'exiled by strangers'. The reputation of the aliens was further tarnished by the evil deeds of their local officials and the feeling that the king's protection placed them above the law.[36] With the ground prepared by the politics of the minority and the regime of Peter des Roches, England's sense of national identity, during Henry's personal rule, thus became shaped, sharpened and solidified by the need to stand together against the threat posed by foreigners. One of the first measures of reform after the revolution was for the king's castles to be entrusted to 'Englishmen, nearly all of them having previously been in the hands of aliens'. Foreigners, evidently, were not to be trusted. Since they were also lawless and avaricious, they were quite unworthy to marry true-born English women. Whereas Magna Carta had simply said that heiresses were not to be disparaged in marriage,

---

[33] See above, 254. They were here acting for the queen.

[34] *RG*, i, suppl., no. 4552.

[35] See above, 189, 215.

[36] *Song of Lewes*, lines 285–307; Carpenter, *Reign of Henry III*, 327–8, and above, 673.

in 1258 disparagement was defined as marriage 'to men who are not of the nation of the kingdom of England'.[37] In 1258 the Savoyards rode the revolution, but already, as the demands over castles and heiresses showed, there was hostility to foreigners in general.[38] These were feelings Simon de Montfort was later ruthlessly to exploit.

Underlying Henry's difficulties was the question of money. Throughout his personal rule he was constantly complaining of its lack. To some extent this was misleading. Henry had the resources to build Westminster Abbey, embellish his homes and give lavish rewards to his favourites. He was able to wage successful wars in Wales and (in 1253–4) in Gascony. What he lacked was anything like the wealth to recover the continental empire or place his son on the throne of Sicily. Henry's financial difficulties had a long-term cause in the decline of easy, uncontentious revenue derived from crown land, this because so much had been given away as religious and secular patronage in the twelfth century. In 1130 over £11,000 of the king's annual income came from land. It would have been worth two to three times more in thirteenth-century prices. Yet in 1230 the amount derived from land was £6,500.[39] On top of that came the restrictions inherent in the letter and spirit of Magna Carta. Henry paid a high price for the conduct of his predecessors.

These financial problems were the background to the cardinal political and constitutional development of Henry's personal rule: the sudden emergence of parliamentary power. Between 1235 and 1257, Henry convoked no fewer than fifty-four parliamentary assemblies.[40] They discussed a wide variety of business but most crucial of all was the question of taxation. Henry knew that the only way to transform his financial position was to get taxes levied on the movable property of everyone in the kingdom. But the 1215 Magna Carta had laid down that such taxes required common consent, in other words the consent of an assembly soon to be called parliament. Although the relevant chapter was left out of the Henrician versions of the Charter, it remained well known (the 1215 Charter was copied again and again) and in practice still in force. So Henry had no alternative in the 1240s and 1250s but to go again and again to parliament begging for taxation. Again and again it was denied him save on conditions he deemed unacceptable. The great lever, control of taxation, the source of parliament's power down the ages, had appeared for the first time in English history. Henry was thus caught in a vicious circle. Because he was denied taxation by parliament, he needed all the

---

[37] *DBM*, 80–1, caps. 5–6, 90–1. I will discuss the ingredients of national identity (for which see Hennings, 'Simon de Montfort and the ambiguity of ethnicity') more fully in volume 2.

[38] In this context, while probably untrue, the fact that Roger Bigod is said to demand the expulsion of all aliens is significant. See above, 696, n. 112.

[39] Barratt, 'English royal revenue', 75–7.

[40] Maddicott, *Origins of the English Parliament*, 454–72, and ch. 4 for a discussion.

more the money from the farms of the sheriffs and the amercements imposed by the judicial and forest eyres. But the resulting hostility rendered the prospects of parliamentary taxation all the more remote.

Henry might have survived all these problems had he managed to construct the happy and harmonious court he craved, one embracing both foreign relatives and native magnates. But this he lacked the political skill to do. When his court was rent asunder, with one faction uniting its grievances with those of the wider realm, his personal rule was finished. The programme of reform forced on Henry in 1258 was far more radical than Magna Carta, but then Henry's rule had set problems which the Charter, even if obeyed to the letter, simply did not deal with. The Charter had imposed virtually no controls on the king's choice of ministers, distribution of patronage and direction of policy, all areas under Henry of acute concern. Now these were to become the prerogatives of a baronial council responsible to parliament. The Charter had also been no help in key areas of local government. It said nothing about the type of person who should be sheriff and the financial terms on which he should hold office. So in ratcheting up the increments, and appointing sheriffs who were strangers in their shires, Henry was not in breach of the Charter.[41] These too were issues addressed directly by the reforms of 1258.

A remarkable invective by an unknown author in the early 1250s gives an appalling picture of the state of Henry's kingdom. Here the poor are oppressed by earls, barons, knights, rich men, corrupt judges, 'infernal sheriffs' and other 'thieves' in the service of the king. Henry's own fault is more one of omission than commission. Whereas King John is described in the invective as 'very cruel, proud, accursed and infernal', Henry appears as 'a king not even a king', 'a king only in name', who has permitted the ruin of his kingdom by failing to submit evildoers to the rigours of justice.[42] There was some truth in the picture. Henry had failed to discipline leading magnates and had allowed them to expand their local power. He had failed, in more than individual cases, to discipline his own officials. And he had failed to set in place procedures to enforce Magna Carta. He had not really laboured with 'all his desire and strength for the peace and tranquillity of each and everyone'. Above all, he had done nothing to rival the measures of his brother-in-law Louis IX. That was left to the revolutionary regime of 1258.[43] Had Henry been of different mettle and mentality, he would have introduced such reforms himself instead of waiting until they were forced

---

[41] The Henrician versions of the Charter all omitted chapter 25 of the 1215 Charter banning the imposition of increments. How much the loss was felt is shown by one fabricated copy of the 1225 Charter with the chapter put back in.

[42] Lachaud and Marguin-Hamon, 'Mouvement réformateur et mémoire de Pierre de Wakefield', 156–7, 167–77. Henry, unlike John, is not actually named, appearing just as 'the king'. The invective is also a critique of England's clergy.

[43] I will discuss in volume 2 the relationship between the reforms of 1258–9 and those of Louis IX.

upon him. He might then have conciliated his critics in parliament, secured taxation (as did Edward I) and avoided any revolution. What makes the failure all the worse is that Henry was perfectly aware of what was wrong in the realm, as his speech to the sheriffs in 1250 shows.

In terms of reform of the realm, Henry's personal rule had got off to a good start with the legislation of the years 1234 to 1237. The puzzle is why such initiatives petered out. After all, Henry seemed to view such measures for the welfare of his people as integral to his duty as king and thus as a route to personal salvation.[44] The legislation was said to be 'for the common utility of all England', 'the protection of the poor' and 'the health of our soul and the souls of our ancestors and heirs'.[45] Henry was here acting in accord with his coronation oath to maintain good laws and abolish bad. The reward, as one of the coronation prayers put it, would be that, 'after the glorious and happy days of this life', he would 'attain everlasting joy and happiness'.[46]

Unfortunately, the reforms of the years 1234 to 1237 turned out to be the fruits of the brief consensus produced by the overthrow of Peter des Roches and the arrival of Archbishop Edmund. The general agreement to the marriages of Henry and his sister was another product of this harmonious period. Although Henry had learnt his 'lesson in kingship' and never ruled again in the manner of des Roches, the idea that his salvation depended on governing for the benefit of his people and ridding the realm of ills had simply not entered the fibre of his being, however much he sometimes talked the talk. In 1267, after the civil war, Henry promulgated the Statute of Marlborough, duty bound, as he said, by 'the nature of the king's office', 'to make provision for the amelioration of his kingdom and the better administration of justice'.[47] If only he had remembered that more often during his personal rule. Matthew Paris and other contemporary writers have left many images of Henry making offerings at shrines and giving alms to the poor. There is no equivalent to Joinville's picture of Louis IX sitting under an oak tree in the woods of Vincennes and giving justice to his people.[48]

Was part of the problem the way Henry viewed the realm? He sometimes defended his right to choose his ministers on the analogy of the head of a household, who could appoint whom he liked to this or that office. But surely the responsibilities of a king extended far wider than those of the head of any private estate.[49] Henry could evoke the reciprocal relationship between his rights and those of everyone else. He could ask for prayers for

---

[44] For Louis IX's attitude here see Le Goff, *Saint Louis*, 746.

[45] Burton, 249; *CR 1231–4*, 592; F, 227. See also *RG*, i, no. 1206.

[46] *English Coronation Records*, 32–3, 258.

[47] Brand, *Kings, Barons and Justices*, 454–5; Burt, *Edward I and the Governance of England*, 45.

[48] Joinville, cap. 59.

[49] Maddicott, '"1258" and "1297"', 11–12; Burt, *Edward I and the Governance of England*, 43–4.

the health of his people as well as himself. The 'Christus Vincit', Henry heard so often, called on God's help not just for the king and queen but for 'all the princes and all the army of the English'.[50] Yet Henry far more often solicited prayers merely for himself and his family. He sometimes expected his subjects to uphold his rights and support his plans without any indication of how they might be beneficiaries. That, of course, reached a catastrophic climax in the Sicilian affair.

Edward the Confessor, in Matthew Paris's life, prays 'intently for his kingdom and his people, and that he might so reign in this life, that in the other he perish not'.[51] Why then was Henry not spurred by the Confessor's example into seeing his salvation as depending on the welfare of his people? But, while Henry certainly looked to the Confessor for success in this world and salvation in the next, the success he sought was often on his own terms not those of his patron saint. In so far as Henry was a peacemaker and an appeaser of leading nobles, he may well have been influenced by the Confessor's example. But there was also a crucial difference between the real Henry and the legendary Confessor. The Confessor, as portrayed in the lives by Ailred and Matthew Paris, was a passive king with seemingly no desire other than to rule peacefully in concert with his nobles. Henry was different. If physically lazy, he was a king with ambition. Some of the things he wished to do, like the building of the Abbey, benefited his people. Others, such as the establishment of his foreign relatives and the pursuit of the Sicilian project, did not. Henry was also very aware of the need to raise money. Here he was very far from imitating the Confessor who, according to the stories in Ailred and Paris, abolished the tax of danegeld and allowed a needy thief robbing his treasury to escape. Henry's ambitions, therefore, were incompatible with consensual rule. They also diverted his attention from any thoughts of reform. In the 1240s and 1250s he had so many other things on his agenda, all of them requiring money.

Henry's problems would have been fewer had not his ambition marched with his simplicity, his 'foolish simplicity', not his 'simplicity debonaire'.[52] Henry could act wisely. His sacking of Simon de Montfort and his own conciliatory policies helped prevent the loss of Gascony. His reluctance to press claims to the overlordship of Scotland laid the foundations for long years of Anglo-Scottish peace. His treatment of Richard of Cornwall turned him from a potential troublemaker into a pillar of the regime. But Henry could also be abysmally unwise. He found it very hard to judge the viability of projects and the real worth of men. Although he looked every inch a king, he could act in ways utterly at odds with kingship's dignity and status. The oath of Burgh in 1232 was a terrible early example, as was the trust he gave to Peter des Roches and Peter de Rivallis. The problem was aggravated by his enthu-

[50] Kanterowicz, *Laudes Regiae*, 218.
[51] Paris, *La Estoire*, lines 2534–7.
[52] See above, 166, 326.

siastic, affectionate, open-hearted personality. It was one thing, in his expansive way, to feed thousands of paupers and cover Westminster Abbey in diaper, quite another, 'overflowing in giving like a living fountain', as the poet John of Howden put it, to reward so well Hubert de Burgh, Gilbert Marshal, the Savoyards, the Lusignans and Simon de Montfort as well as many lesser favourites.[53] In Henry's chamber at Westminster the virtue of 'largesse' was pictured triumphing over the vice of 'covetousness'. But Henry never absorbed Grosseteste's teaching that it needed as well to triumph over the vice of prodigality.[54] If only Henry had imitated Louis IX's very different behaviour. As the latter's confessor Geoffroi de Beaulieu observed, Louis 'was not extravagant in giving generous gifts to the barons and knights of his kingdom'. Rather, it was because of his faith and justice that he was universally feared and respected.[55]

In driving through a reform agenda, Henry would have had limited support from his ministers. True, the councillors' oath of 1257 shows there were concerns within the regime, but they came late in the day. The activities of John Mansel and others in protecting Henry of Bath, Philip Lovel and the sheriff of Northamptonshire, William de Lisle, show how the official establishment rallied round to save its own. It had little reason to encourage Henry to embark on measures from which it might suffer. If, moreover, the activities of magnates and their officials were to be covered by any programme of reform, that would disturb the vested interests of many close to the king. Henry would have needed far more determination and imagination than he possessed to carry through any thorough reform of the realm.

There was just one moment, later in his personal rule, when Henry might have sparked into action and followed a reform agenda. As with Louis IX, this was the moment he took the cross. To a limited extent that indeed happened, hence Henry's speech to the assembled sheriffs in October 1250. But his actions were paltry compared to Louis's. This was all the less forgivable given the long tradition in England of inquiries into the running of local government, both by special commissioners and by the justices in eyre. If the main thrust of such inquiries was to defend the rights of the crown, they were also concerned with the sufferings of the people. In 1170 the inquest of sheriffs had begun by inquiring into exactions by which 'land and men have been oppressed'. In the 1240s and 1250s new questions put by the itinerant justices to local juries were likewise concerned with shrieval oppression.[56] It would not have been a huge extra step had Henry mounted

[53] For John of Howden, see above, 562.
[54] For contemporary thought about 'liberality', 'prodigality' and 'avarice', see Lachaud, *L'Éthique du Pouvoir au Moyen Âge*, 600–6.
[55] Geoffroi de Beaulieu, cap. 20.
[56] *SC*, 176; and see above, 530–1. But for the suggestion that it was 'easier' for the Capetians, with an administration less fiscally geared than that in England, to mount *enquêtes* and be concerned with the 'honesty' of local officials, see Sabapathy, *Officers and Accountability*, 121–32, especially at 122–3, 126–7. I will discuss this further in volume 2 when considering the relationship between Louis's *enquêtes* and the inquiries of 1258–60.

inquiries, like Louis's *enquêtes*, offering reparation for the abuses by himself and his officials. Part of the reason he did not goes back to the nature of his piety and to an area where there was a profound difference between the two kings. This was the concept of reparation itself.[57]

When Louis IX launched his *enquêtes*, the aim was to offer reparation for the wrongs committed by himself, his predecessors and royal officials throughout the kingdom. There were various strands of thought behind the initiative, the most immediate being the belief that a crusader, as Louis was from 1244, must not depart in a state of sin and should make reparation for anything unjustly taken. The same line of thought, when it came to departure from the world itself, led to an increasing emphasis on reparation in thirteenth-century wills. Behind all this were the new ideas about confession and penance. These gave a cutting edge to the view, going back to Saint Augustine, that, unless things wrongly obtained were returned, one remained in a state of sin. Restitution, therefore, became a central feature of penance and this for Louis IX was the key. He launched the *enquêtes* as an act of penance to save his soul. He did so, moreover, not as an individual but as a king responsible for the government of the realm and everything done in his name. Hence an absolutely key feature of the *enquêtes* was their concern for the abuses of royal officials, just as much as the wrongs committed personally by the king. Louis's sense of his responsibilities spread the benefits of reparation over all the kingdom, with commensurate benefits to the whole standing of his kingship.

The importance of reparation was stressed by English bishops. Bishop Poore's statutes for his Salisbury diocese insisted that, when it came to theft, robbery and fraud, the priests were not to enjoin penances of masses and alms 'but they should enjoin first restitution, since the sin cannot be remitted unless what has been taken is restored'.[58] Equally stressed was that the misconduct of officials might have spiritual consequences for their masters. Grosseteste thus warned the countess of Winchester to restrain the vices of her men 'because those vices will be considered your sins, and a cloud, exhaling from their foul and wanton behaviour, will dim the light of your own good works'.[59] In line with such thought, Simon de Montfort (according to Matthew Paris) ordered his ministers to return what they had taken wrongly from the people and give satisfaction for the injuries suffered. This was also a theme in his will drawn up in 1259.[60] Such ideas had some impact on Henry. In 1261 he said he was under oath to restore anything taken unjustly from vacant bishoprics. Earlier, he had compensated Richard of Wich for some, though far from all, of his losses during the dispute over

---

[57] For what follows, see Dejoux, *Les Enquêtes de Saint Louis*, ch. 8.

[58] *C&S*, i, 74 cap. 44.

[59] *Letters of Grosseteste*, 70. The invective quoted above likewise thought Henry would share the torments of his father unless he repented.

[60] Paris, *HA*, iii, 409; Maddicott, *Simon de Montfort*, 173–7.

the succession to Chichester.[61] But this seems as far as it went. Henry's inquiries in the 1250s had no restorative element.[62] He made no mention of reparation in his will drawn up in 1253, saying merely he wanted his debts paid and his servants given their due reward.[63] However much 'led by pious intentions', he lamented the malpractices of his sheriffs, but he saw no need to restore what they had taken in order to save his soul.[64] Were his confessors to blame here? Did they assure him (forgetting the injunctions of Bishop Poore) that, with all his alms and masses, with his efforts to convert the Jews, with his devotion to the Virgin and the Confessor, his conscience could be clear?[65] If so, they did him a grievous disservice.

To set in the balance against his failings, Henry had one golden weight. It was, of course, his piety. Who could be unaware of his delight in divine service, his feeding of paupers, his conversion of Jews and his distribution of silks, chalices and jewels to churches and shrines round the country? The Confessor, the Abbey and the relic of the Holy Blood had all been gifts of the king to the kingdom. Surely, Henry might hope, everyone would wish to support a king who had done so much to enhance the spiritual life of the country. The setting for much of Henry's piety was his court and the court too, Henry might hope, would impress his subjects: the great feasts and the private audiences, the liveries of the courtiers and the rounds of gift-giving, the thrones, crowns and golden robes of the king himself, and the magnificent buildings in which everything took place.

Henry, therefore, had invested heavily in 'soft power' and, in one respect, he was completely successful. His status as a most Christian king was widely recognized. Matthew Paris put into the mouth of Louis IX the remark that Henry's alms and masses would save him from all shame and dangers. Llywelyn, Paris added, had said the same thing.[66] Again and again Paris described in complimentary fashion Henry's religious rituals when he came to St Albans. The visits also showed how accessible and affable Henry could be. Paris could be complimentary too about Henry's conduct of great public events, notably the ceremony of the Holy Blood and the visit to Paris where the cost seemed worthwhile because it gave so much honour to England. Paris was equally enthusiastic about Henry's work at the Abbey, the 'magnificent' new church, the 'glorious' shrine and the 'incomparable' chapter house.[67] Henry's soft power certainly helped him when it came to

---

[61] *C&S*, i, 691; see above, 441.

[62] See above, 531–2, 617.

[63] *F*, 496.

[64] Paris, *HA*, ii, 389.

[65] See also here Church, *Henry III*, 88–9.

[66] Paris, iv, 231–2.

[67] Carpenter, 'King Henry III and the chapter house', 32 and above plate 1. For Matthew Paris in a more critical vein about public events, see above, 272 and Kjaer, 'Matthew Paris and the royal Christmas', 145–7, for his reservations about the York wedding in 1251.

escaping the consequences of Richard Marshal's death in 1234. More generally, although hard to quantify, it was surely a factor in him surviving the ups and downs of nearly twenty-five years of personal rule.

Unfortunately, Henry's subjects were perfectly capable of acknowledging his piety while criticizing other aspects of his conduct. The Osney abbey annalist having said that Henry, more than any of his predecessors, loved divine service, added dolefully that he also loved aliens more than all Englishmen and enriched them with innumerable gifts. Trevet contrasted Henry's devotion to God with his lack of wisdom in secular affairs.[68] Another chronicler, Thomas Wykes, considered that Westminster Abbey exceeded all other churches in the world yet he still reported the baronial view that Henry was 'useless and insufficient for disposing of the affairs of his kingdom'.[69] There was even the opinion that Henry's exactions tarnished the very piety for which he was famous. It was an offence to God, Matthew Paris reflected, that the silks and wax for the king's alms and candles were seized from merchants without payment. Had God not said he hated offerings derived from the spoils of robbery? In this context the expenditure on alms and candles seemed itself excessive.[70] Henry's piety did little to halt vociferous criticisms of how he treated the church. It did little to win over magnates who attended the feasts of the Confessor on 13 October and then turned down flat demands for taxation. The image of Henry sitting in majesty on his gold coin did not stop the Londoners telling him to his face it was useless. The new seal devised after the peace with France, with Henry sitting on a splendid high-backed throne, merely prompted a papal notary to ask derisorily why the seal was grander than before when Henry was duke of Normandy![71] The Confessorian imagery in the great chamber at Westminster bent neither the bishop of Ely nor the countess of Arundel to Henry's will.[72] The Solomonic references in his palaces made no one think Henry had the wisdom of Solomon. The throne up on the dais in the great hall at Westminster, made the more 'sumptuous' by its bronze lions, did not stop the barons marching in and bringing the king's personal rule to an end. Yet it would be wrong to conclude on this negative note. Without his reputation as a most Christian king, Henry would never have survived the coming period of reform, rebellion and civil war, as volume 2 of this biography will show.

[68] Osney, 253–4; Trevet, 279–80.
[69] Wykes, 118–19, 226–7.
[70] Paris, v, 6, quoting Isaiah 61:8.
[71] DD, 254.
[72] See above, 553–4.

BIBLIOGRAPHY

UNPRINTED PRIMARY SOURCES

Full references to unprinted primary sources are given in the footnotes, where BL stands for the British Library, TNA for The National Archives at Kew and WAM for Westminster Abbey Muniments.

The following are the classes of unprinted documents cited from The National Archives.

C 47 (Chancery: Miscellanea)
C 72 (Chancery: Scutage Rolls)
CP 21 (Court of Common Pleas: Essoin Rolls)
E 101 (Exchequer: King's Remembrancer, Accounts Various)
E 159 (Exchequer: King's Remembrancer, Memoranda Rolls)
E 368 (Exchequer: Lord Treasurer's Remembrancer, Memoranda Rolls)
E 372 (Exchequer: Pipe Office, Pipe Rolls)
E 403 (Exchequer of Receipt: Issue Rolls)
JUST 1 (Justices in Eyre and Assize: Plea Rolls)
KB 26 (Court of Common Pleas and King's Bench: Early Plea and Essoin Rolls)
SC 1 (Special Collections: Ancient Correspondence)
Thanks to the initiative of Robert Palmer, images of the memoranda rolls, pipe rolls, eyre rolls and rolls of the court of common pleas and court *coram rege* (King's Bench) can be found on the Anglo-American Legal Tradition website: http://aalt.law.uh.edu.

PRINTED PRIMARY SOURCES

AC Annales Cambriae, ed. J. Williams ab Ithel (Rolls Series, 20, 1860).

Actes des Comtes de Provence Recueil des Actes des Comtes de Provence appartenant à la Maison de Barcelone: Alphonse II et Raymond-Berenger V (1196–1245), ed. F. Benoit, 2 vols. (Monaco and Paris, 1925).

Adam of Eynsham, *The Life of St Hugh of Lincoln*, eds. D.L. Douie and H. Farmer, 2 vols. (London, 1962). All references are to volume 2.

Ailred, *Life of St. Edward the Confessor by St. Aelred of Rievaulx*, trans. J. Bertram (Southampton, 1997). For a new scholarly edition, see *Vita Sancti Aedwardi Regis et Confessoris*, ed. F. Marcella, Corpus Christianorum Continuatio Medievalis, Opera Omnia VII (Turnhout, 2017).

Amplissima Collectio Veterum Scriptorum et Monumentorum, Historicorum, Dogmaticorum, Moralium, Amplissima Collectio, eds. E. Martène and U. Durand, 9 vols. (Paris, 1724–33).

Anonymous, *Histoire des Ducs de Normandie et des Rois d'Angleterre*, ed. F. Michel (Paris, 1840). This volume contains the chronicle of the Anonymous of Béthune.

APS Acts of the Parliaments of Scotland. Volume I: AD MCXXIV–MCCCCXXIII, eds. T. Thomson and C.N. Innes (Edinburgh, 1814).

Art of Falconry The Art of Falconry, by Frederick II of Hohenstaufen, eds. C.A. Wood and F.M. Fyfe (Stanford, 1943), and reprinted (1969).

ASR Anglo-Scottish Relations, 1174–1328, ed. E.L.G. Stones (London, 1965).

AWR The Acts of the Welsh Rulers, 1120–1283, ed. H. Pryce with the assistance of C. Insley (Cardiff, 2005).

BA Building Accounts of King Henry III, ed. H.M. Colvin (Oxford, 1971).

Ballad of Hugh of Lincoln Sir Hugh of Lincoln, or an Examination of a Curious Tradition respecting the Jews, ed. A. Hume (London, 1849).

Barrow, *EEA Hereford English Episcopal Acta 35: Hereford, 1234–1275*, ed. J. Barrow (Oxford, 2009).

Battle *The Chronicle of Battle Abbey*, ed. E. Searle (Oxford, 1980).

BF Liber Feodorum: The Book of Fees commonly called Testa de Nevill, 3 vols., with continuous pagination (London, 1920–31).

BNB Bracton's Note Book: A Collection of Cases decided in the King's Courts during the Reign of Henry III, ed. F.W. Maitland, 3 vols. (London, 1887).

Bower Walter Bower, *Scotichronicon: Volume 5*, eds. D.E.R. Watt, S. Taylor and B. Scott (Aberdeen, 1990).

Bracton Bracton de Legibus et Consuetudinibus Angliae: Bracton on the Laws and Customs of England, ed. G.E. Woodbine, translated with revisions and notes by S.E. Thorne, 4 vols. (Cambridge, MA, 1968–77).

Brut *Brut Y Tywysogyon or The Chronicle of the Princes: Red Book of Hergest Version*, ed. T. Jones (Cardiff, 1955).

Brut/Peniarth *Brut Y Tywysogyon or The Chronicle of the Princes Peniarth MS. 20 Version*, ed. T. Jones (Cardiff, 1952). For the original Welsh text of which this is a translation, see *Brut Y Tywysogyon, Peniarth MS. 20*, ed. T. Jones (Cardiff, 1941).

Burton 'Annales de Burton, AD 1004–1263', in *Annales Monastici*, ed. H.R. Luard, 5 vols. (Rolls Series, 36, 1864–9), vol. 1.

Bury St Edmunds *The Chronicle of Bury St Edmunds, 1212–1301*, ed. A. Gransden (London, 1964).

CACW Calendar of Ancient Correspondence concerning Wales, ed. J.G. Edwards (Cardiff, 1935).

Canterbury/Dover *The Historical Works of Gervase of Canterbury: Volume 2*, ed. W. Stubbs (Rolls Series, 73, 1879–80), 106–272.

Carlin and Crouch, *Lost Letters Lost Letters of Medieval Life: English Society, 1200–1250*, eds. M. Carlin and D. Crouch (Philadelphia, PA, 2013).

Cartulaire des Comtes de la Marche Cartulaire des Comtes de la Marche, ed. G. Thomas (Angoulême, 1934).

CChR Calendar of Charter Rolls preserved in the Public Record Office, 1226–1300, 2 vols. (London, 1903–6).

CChW Calendar of Chancery Warrants preserved in the Public Record Office, 1244–1326 (London, 1927).

CCR Calendar of the Close Rolls preserved in the Public Record Office: Edward I, 1272–1307, 5 vols. (London, 1900–8).

CDI Calendar of Documents relating to Ireland, 1175–1251, ed. H.S. Sweetman (London, 1875).

CFR Calendar of the Fine Rolls of the Reign of Henry III, available both on the Henry III Fine Rolls Project's website (https://finerollshenry3.org.uk/home.html) and within the *Calendar of the Fine Rolls of the Reign of Henry III, 1216–1242*, 3 vols., ed. P. Dryburgh and B. Hartland, technical directors A. Ciula, J.M. Vieira and T. Lopez (Woodbridge, 2007–9).

Chaplais, *English Medieval Diplomatic Practice English Medieval Diplomatic Practice, Part I*, ed. P. Chaplais, 2 vols. (London, 1982).

Chaplais, *English Royal Documents English Royal Documents, King John–Henry VI, 1199–1461*, ed. P. Chaplais (Oxford, 1971).

CheshirePR Cheshire in the Pipe Rolls, 1158–1301, eds. R. Stewart-Brown and M.H. Mills (Lancashire and Cheshire Records Society, 92, 1938).

CIM Calendar of Inquisitions Miscellaneous (Chancery) preserved in the Public Record Office: Volume 1, 1216–1307 (London, 1916).

CIPM Calendar of Inquisitions Post Mortem and other analogous Documents, 1236–1307, 4 vols. (London, 1904–13). Unless stated, all references are to volume 1.

CJB A Cartulary of the Hospital of St John the Baptist, ed. H.E. Salter, 3 vols. (Oxford Historical Society, 66, 68–9, 1914–17).

Clanchy, *Berkshire Eyre The Roll and Writ File of the Berkshire Eyre of 1248*, ed. M.T. Clanchy (Selden Society, 90, 1973).

CLR Calendar of the Liberate Rolls preserved in the Public Record Office: Henry III, 1226–1272, 6 vols. (London, 1916–64).

Coggeshall *Radulphi de Coggeshall Chronicon Anglicanum*, ed. J. Stevenson (Rolls Series, 66, 1875).

CPR Calendar of Patent Rolls preserved in the Public Record Office: Henry III, 1232–1272, 4 vols. (London, 1906–13).

CPReg Calendar of Papal Registers relating to Great Britain and Ireland: Volume 1, 1198–1304, ed. W.H. Bliss (London, 1893).

CR Close Rolls of the Reign of Henry III preserved in the Public Record Office, 1227–1272, 14 vols. (London, 1902–38).

Cronica Buriensis Memorials of St Edmunds Abbey, ed. T. Arnold, 3 vols. (Rolls Series, 96, 1890–6). The *Cronica Buriensis* is found in volume 3.

Cronica de Wallia '"Cronica de Wallia" and other documents from Exeter cathedral library MS 3514', ed. T. Jones, *Bulletin of the Board of Celtic Studies*, 12 (1946–8), 27–44.

CRR Curia Regis Rolls of the Reigns of Richard I, John and Henry III preserved in the Public Record Office, 20 vols. (London, 1922–2006).

Crowland *Memoriale Fratris Walteri de Coventria*, ed. W. Stubbs, 2 vols. (Rolls Series, 58, 1872–3). All references are to volume 2.

CR Supp Close Rolls (Supplementary) of the Reign of Henry III preserved in the Public Record Office, 1244–1266, ed. A. Morton (London, 1975).

C&S Councils & Synods with other documents relating to the English Church. Volume II: 1205–1313, eds. F.M. Powicke and C.R. Cheney, 2 vols. with continuous pagination (Oxford, 1964).

DA Roll of Divers Accounts for the Early Years of the Reign of Henry III, ed. F.A. Cazel Jr (Pipe Roll Society, new series, 44, 1974).

DAI Documents on the Affairs of Ireland before the King's Council, ed. G.O. Sayles (Dublin, 1979).

DBM Documents of the Baronial Movement of Reform and Rebellion, 1258–1267, eds. R.F. Treharne and I.J. Sanders (Oxford, 1973).

DD Diplomatic Documents preserved in the Public Record Office, Volume I: 1101–1272, ed. P. Chaplais (London, 1964).

De Moneta The De Moneta of Nicholas Oresme and English Mint Documents, ed. C. Johnson (London, 1956).

John of Garland John of Garland, *De Triumphis Ecclesie*, trans. M. Hall (unpublished).

Dialogus Richard fitzNigel, Dialogus de Scaccario, The Dialogue of the Exchequer, ed. E. Amt (Oxford, 2007)

DI Documents Illustrative of English History in the Thirteenth and Fourteenth Centuries, selected from the Records of the Department of the Queen's Remembrancer of the Exchequer, ed. H. Cole (Record Commission, London, 1844).

Dunstable 'Annales Prioratus de Dunstaplia, AD 1–1297', in *Annales Monastici*, ed. H.R. Luard, 5 vols. (Rolls Series, 36, 1864–9), vol.3. There is now an English translation: *The Annals of Dunstable Priory*, trans. D. Preest, ed. H. R. Webster (Woodbridge, 2018).

Durham *Durham Annals and Documents of the Thirteenth Century*, ed. F. Barlow (Surtees Society, 155, 1940).

EHD English Historical Documents: Volume III, 1189–1327, ed. H. Rothwell (London, 1975).

Election of Abbot Hugh The Chronicle of the Election of Hugh, Abbot of Bury St Edmunds and Later Bishop of Ely, ed. R.M. Thomson (Oxford, 1974).

English Coronation Records English Coronation Records, ed. L.G. Wickham Legg (London, 1901).

ERF Excerpta Rotulis Finium in Turri Londinensi asservatis Henrico Tertio Rege, A.D. 1216–72, ed. C. Roberts, 2 vols. (Record Commission, London, 1835–6).

ERW Early Registers of Writs, eds. E. de Haas and C.D.G. Hall (Selden Society, 87, 1970).

F Foedera, Conventiones, Litterae et cujuscumque generis Acta Publica, ed. T. Rymer, new edition, vol. I, pt. i, eds. A. Clark and F. Holbrooke (Record Commission, London, 1816).

FitzThedmar Arnold fitzThedmar, *De Antiquis Legibus Liber. Cronica Maiorum et Vicecomitum Londoniarum*, ed. T. Stapleton (Camden Society, 34, 1846). A new Oxford Medieval Texts edition is forthcoming edited by I. Stone.

Fleta Fleta: Volume 2, Prologue, Book I, Book II, eds. H.G. Richardson and G.O. Sayles (Selden Society, 72, 1955).

Flete John Flete, *The History of Westminster Abbey*, ed. J. Armitage Robinson (Cambridge, 1909).

Fordun *Johannis de Fordun, Chronica Gentis Scotorum*, ed. W.F. Skene (Edinburgh, 1871).

Gallagher *Suffolk Eyre The Civil Pleas of the Suffolk Eyre of 1240*, ed. E.J. Gallagher (Suffolk Record Society, 52, 2009).

Geoffroi de Beaulieu Geoffroi de Beaulieu, *The Sanctity of Louis IX: Early Lives by Geoffrey of Beaulieu and William of Chartres*, trans. L.F. Field and eds. M.C. Gaposchkin and S.L. Field (Ithaca, NY, and London, 2015).

Gervase *The Historical Works of Gervase of Canterbury*, ed. W. Stubbs, 2 vols. (Rolls Series, 73, 1879–80). Unless stated, all references are to volume 2.

Giles, *Flowers of History Roger of Wendover's Flowers of History: Comprising the History of England from the Descent of the Saxons to A.D. 1235, formerly ascribed to Matthew Paris*, trans. J.A. Giles, 2 vols. (London, 1849).

Giles, *Matthew Paris Matthew Paris's English History from the Year 1235 to 1273*, trans. J.A. Giles, 3 vols. (London, 1852–4).

Graham, 'Letters of Cardinal Ottoboni' R. Graham, 'The letters of Cardinal Ottoboni', *English Historical Review*, 15 (1900), 87–120.

Grosseteste, *Templum Dei Grosseteste*, Robert, *Templum Dei*, eds. J. Goering and F.A.C. Mantello (Toronto, 1984).

Guala The Letters and Charters of Cardinal Guala Bicchieri, Papal Legate in England, 1216–1218, ed. N. Vincent (Canterbury and York Society, 83, 1996).

Guisborough *The Chronicle of Walter of Guisborough*, ed. H. Rothwell (Camden Society, 89, 1957).

Hailes Blount, M.N., 'A critical edition of the annals of Hailes (MS Cotton Cleopatra D iii, ff. 33–59v) with an examination of their sources' (University of Manchester, master's thesis, 1974).

Harding, *Shropshire Eyre The Roll of the Shropshire Eyre of 1256*, ed. A. Harding (Selden Society, 96, 1980).

Hennings, L., 'Simon de Montfort and the ambiguity of ethnicity in thirteenth-century politics', *Thirteenth Century England*, 16 (Woodbridge, 2017), 137–52.

Henry of Avranches *The Shorter Latin Poems of Master Henry of Avranches relating to England*, eds. J.C. Russell and J.P. Heironimus (Cambridge, MA, 1935).

Hershey, *Special Eyre The 1258–9 Special Eyre of Surrey and Kent*, ed. A.H. Hershey (Surrey Record Society, 38, 2004).

Honorii III Opera Honorii III Opera Omnia, ed. C. Horoy, *Medii Aevi Bibliotheca Patristica ab anno 1217 ad Concilii Tridentini tempora i–ii* (Paris, 1879–80).

Hoskin, *EEA London English Episcopal Acta 38: London, 1229–1280*, ed. P.M. Hoskin (Oxford, 2011).

Howden *Chronica Magistri Rogeri de Houedene*, ed. W. Stubbs, 4 vols. (Rolls Series, 51, 1868–71).

Howden, *GR Gesta Regis Henrici Secundi et Gesta Regis Ricardi Benedicti Abbatis*, ed. W. Stubbs, 2 vols. (Rolls Series, 49, 1867).

Institutes The Institutes of Justinian, ed. J. Moyles, 5th edition (Oxford, 1928).

James, *La Estoire de Seint Aedward La Estoire de Seint Aedward*, ed. M.R. James (Oxford, 1920).

James of Aragon *The Book of Deeds of James of Aragon: A Translation of the Medieval Catalan 'Llibre dels Fets'*, eds. D. Smith and H. Buffery (Aldershot, 2003).

John of Garland John of Garland, *De Triumphis Ecclesie*, trans. M. Hall (unpublished). For the original text see *Johannis de Garlandia De Triumphis Ecclesiae*, ed. T. Wright (London, 1856).

John of Howden L.W. Stone, 'Jean de Howden: poète Anglo-Normand du XIIIᵉ siècle', *Romania*, 69 (1946/7), 496–519.

John of Salisbury John of Salisbury, *Policraticus of the Frivolities of Courtiers and the Footprints of Philosophers*, ed. and trans. C.J. Nederman (Cambridge, 1990).

John of Wallingford (1) R. Vaughan, 'The chronicle of John of Wallingford', *English Historical Review*, 73 (1958), 66–77. This prints the parts of John's chronicle not copied into other published chronicles.

John of Wallingford (2) *Chronica Johannis de Oxenedes*, ed. H. Ellis (Rolls Series, 1859). In the passages cited this chronicle of St Benet Holme is copying the chronicle of John of Wallingford.

Joinville Jean de Joinville, *Vie de Saint Louis*, ed. J. Monfrin (Paris, 2010). *Joinville and Villehardouin. Chronicles of the Crusades*, ed. C. Smith (London, 2008), 141–336, has a translation into English.

Lalou, *Les Comptes sur Tablettes de Cire Les Comptes sur Tablettes de Cire de Jean Sarrazin, Chambellan de Saint Louis*, ed. E. Lalou, *Monumenta Palaeographica Medii Aevi*, Series Gallica 4 (Turnhout, 2003).

Lanercost *Chronicon de Lanercost, MCCI–MCCCXLVI. E Codice Cottoniano Nunc Primum Typis Mandatum*, ed. J. Stevenson (Maitland Club, 1839).

Layettes Layettes du Trésor des Chartes, eds. A. Teulet, H.-F. Delaborde and E. Berger, 5 vols. (Paris, 1863–1909).

Lay Subsidy Rolls Rolls of the Fifteenth of the Ninth Year of the Reign of Henry III for Cambridgeshire, Lincolnshire and Wiltshire, and Rolls of the Fortieth of the Seventeenth Year of the Reign of Henry III for Kent, eds. F.A. Cazel Jr and A.P. Cazel (Pipe Roll Society, new series, 45, 1983).

Letters, *Gazetteer Gazetteer of Markets and Fairs in England and Wales to 1516*, ed. S. Letters, 2 vols. (List and Index Society, special series, 32–3, 2003).

Letters of Adam Marsh The Letters of Adam Marsh, ed. C.H. Lawrence, 2 vols. (Oxford, 2006).

Letters of Grosseteste The Letters of Robert Grosseteste, Bishop of Lincoln, eds. F.A.C. Mantello and J. Goering (Toronto, 2010).

'Lettre à la Reine Blanche' 'Mémoire sur une lettre inédite adressée à la Reine Blanche par un habitant de La Rochelle', ed. L. Deslisle, *Bibliothèque de l'École des Chartes*, 17 (1856), 513–55.

Lisle Letters The Lisle Letters: An Abridgement, eds. M. St. Clare Byrne and B. Boland (London, 1983).

LMB Liber Memorandorum Ecclesie de Bernewelle, eds. J.W. Clark and F.W. Maitland (Cambridge, 1907).

Lunt, *Valuation The Valuation of Norwich*, ed. W.E. Lunt (Oxford, 1926).

LW Littere Wallie preserved in Liber A in the Public Record Office, ed. J.G. Edwards (Cardiff, 1940).

Margam 'Annales de Margam, AD 1066–1232', in *Annales Monastici*, ed. H.R. Luard, 5 vols. (Rolls Series, 36, 1864–9), vol. 1.

'Margam Continuation' M.L. Colker, ed., '"The Margam Chronicle" in a Dublin Manuscript', *The Haskins Society Journal*, 4 (1992), 123–48.

Marshal *History of William Marshal*, eds. A.J. Holden, S. Gregory and D. Crouch, 3 vols. (Anglo-Norman Text Society, Occasional Publications Series, 4–6, 2002–6).

Meekings *Wiltshire Eyre Crown Pleas of the Wiltshire Eyre, 1249*, ed. C.A.F. Meekings (Wiltshire Archaeological and Natural History Society Records Branch, 16, 1961).

Meekings and Crook, *Surrey Eyre The 1235 Surrey Eyre*, eds. C.A.F. Meekings and D. Crook, 2 vols. (Surrey Record Society, 31–2, 1979–83).

Melrose, Chronicle of Melrose (as translated) in *Early Sources for Scottish History AD 500–1286: Volume 2*, ed A.O. Anderson (Stamford, 1990). For a facsimile edition, see *The Chronicle of Melrose from the Cottonian Manuscript Faustina B IX in the British Museum*, eds. A.O. Anderson and M.O. Anderson (London 1936). For a detailed analysis of the stages in which the text was constructed, see D. Broun and J. Harrison, *The Chronicle of Melrose: A Stratigraphic Edition. Volume I: Introduction and Facsimile Edition* (Scottish History Society, 2007). A new edition is forthcoming edited by J. Reuben Davies.

Merton, *Flores Flores Historiarum. Volume 3*, ed. H.R. Luard (Rolls Series, 95, 1890), 239–327.

MGH, *Constitutiones Constitutiones et Acta Publica Imperatorum et Regum inde ab a MCXCVIII usque ad a MCCLXXII (1198–1272)*, ed. L. Weiland, *Monumenta Germaniae Historica*, Legum Sectio IV (Hanover, 1896).

Missale Westmonasteriensis Missale ad usum Ecclesie Westmonasteriensis, ed. J. Wickham Legg, 3 vols. (Henry Bradshaw Society, 1, 5, 12, 1891–7).

Monasticon William Dudgale, *Monasticon Anglicanum: A History of the Abbies and other Monasteries, Hospitals, Frieries, and Cathedral and Collegiate Churches, with their Dependencies, in England and Wales*, eds. J. Caley, H. Ellis and B. Bandinel, 6 vols. (London, 1817–30).

Monmouth, *William of Norwich* Thomas of Monmouth, *The Life and Passion of William of Norwich*, ed. M. Rubin (London, 2014).

MR 1231–3 Memoranda Rolls 16–17 Henry III [1231–33], ed. R.A. Brown (London, 1991).

Nangis *Chronique Latine de Guillaume de Nangis de 1113 a 1300 avec les continuations de cette Chronique de 1300 a 1368: Tome Premier*, ed. H. Géraud (Paris, 1843).

Newburgh 'The chronicle of William of Newburgh', in *Chronicles of the Reigns of Stephen, Henry II and Richard*, ed. R. Howlett, 2 vols. (Rolls Series, 82, 1884–9).

Northumberland Pleas Northumberland Pleas from the Curia Regis and Assize Rolls, 1198–1272, eds. A.H. Thompson and J.C. Hodgson (Newcastle upon Tyne Records Committee, 2, 1922).

Oram, R., *Alexander II, King of Scots, 1214–1249* (Edinburgh, 2012).

Osney 'Annales Monasterii de Oseneia, AD 1016–1347', in *Annales Monastici*, ed. H.R. Luard, 5 vols. (Rolls Series, 36, 1864–9), vol. 4.

Paris *Matthaei Parisiensis, Monachi Sancti Albani Chronica Majora*, ed. H.R. Luard, 7 vols. (Rolls Series, 57, 1872–83).

Paris, *AC Matthaei Parisiensis, Monachi Sancti Albani Abbreviatio Chronicorum Angliae*, ed. F. Madden, 3 vols. (Rolls Series, 44, 1866–9), 3, 153–348.

Paris, *FH Flores Historiarum*, ed. H.R. Luard, 3 vols. (Rolls Series, 95, 1890).

Paris, *GA Gesta Abbatum Monasterii Sancti Albani*, ed. H.T. Riley, 3 vols. (Rolls Series, 28, 1867–9).

Paris, *HA Matthaei Parisiensis, Monachi Sancti Albani Historia Anglorum*, ed. F. Madden, 3 vols. (Rolls Series, 44, 1866–9).

Paris, *La Estoire Lives of the Confessor*, ed. H.R. Luard (Rolls Series, 3, 1858). Text and translation of Matthew Paris's *La Estoire de Seint Aedward le Rei* are at 1–311 in this volume. A new translation is found in *The History of Saint Edward the King by Matthew Paris*, eds. T. Fenster and J. Wogan-Browne (Tempe, AZ, 2008). *La Estoire de Seint Aedward le Rei*, attributed to *Matthew Paris*, ed. K.Y. Wallace (London, 1983), is a scholarly edition of the French text.

Pershore, *Flores Flores Historiarum, Volume 2*, ed. H.R. Luard (Rolls Series, 95, 1890), 471–505. This is the continuation of the *Flores* composed at Pershore Abbey.

Pipe Roll 1242 The Great Roll of the Pipe for the Twenty-Sixth Year of the Reign of King Henry III, 1241–1242, ed. H.L. Cannon (New Haven, CT, 1918).

Political Songs The Political Songs of England, from the Reign of John to that of Edward II, ed. T. Wright (Camden Society, 6, 1839), with a new edition edited by P. Coss (Camden Society Classic reprints, 1996).

PR Pipe Roll. Citations to pipe rolls are to volumes published by the Pipe Roll Society. The year in the citation is that which appears on the cover of each volume.

Puylaurens *The Chronicle of William of Puylaurens: The Albigensian Crusade and its Aftermath*, eds. W.A. Sibly and M.D. Sibly (Woodbridge, 2003).

RBE Red Book of the Exchequer, ed. H. Hall, 3 vols. (Rolls Series, 99, 1896).

RCh Rotuli Chartarum in Turri Londinensi asservati, ed. T.D. Hardy (Record Commission, London, 1837).

RCWL The Royal Charter Witness Lists of Henry III, ed. M. Morris, 2 vols. (List and Index Society, 291–2, 2001).

Reading Cartulary Reading Abbey Cartularies. British Library Manuscripts: Egerton 3031, Harley 1708 and Cotton Vespasian E XXV, ed. B.R. Kemp, 2 vols. (Camden Society, 5th series, 31, 1986–7).

Reg. Alexandre IV Les Registres d'Alexandre IV. Recueil des Bulles de ce Pape Publiées ou Analysées d'après les Manuscrits Originaux du Vatican, eds. C.G.M.B. de la Roncière, J. de Loye and A. Coulon, 3 vols. (1902–59).

Reg. Gregoire IX Les Registres de Grégoire IX. Recueil des Bulles de ce Pape Publiées ou Analysées d'après les Manuscrits Originaux du Vatican, ed. L. Auvray, 4 vols. (Paris, 1896–1955).

Reg. Innocent IV Les Registres d'Innocent IV. Recueil des Bulles de ce Pape Publiées ou Analysées d'après les Manuscrits Originaux du Vatican et de la Bibliothèque Nationale, ed. E. Berger, 4 vols. (Paris, 1881–1921).

'Réponses de Simon de Montfort' 'Réponses de Simon de Montfort', in *Études Historiques sur la Ville de Bayonne, Tome Second*, eds. J. Balasque and E. Dularens (Bayonne, 1869).

RF Rotuli de Oblatis et Finibus in Turri Londoniensi asservati, Tempore Regis Johannis, ed. T.D. Hardy (Record Commission, London, 1835).

RG Rôles Gascon, eds. F. Michel and C. Bémont, 4 vols. (Paris, 1885–1906).

RH Rotuli Hundredorum. Temp. Hen. III et Edw. I, in Turr' Lond' et in Curia Receptae Scaccarij Westm., eds. W. Illingworth and J. Caley, 2 vols. (Record Commission, London, 1812–18).

RIR Receipt and Issue Rolls for the Twenty-Sixth Year of the Reign of King Henry III, 1241–2, ed. R.C. Stacey (Pipe Roll Society, new series, 49, 1992).

Rishanger *Willelmi Rishanger Chronica et Annales*, ed. H.T. Riley (Rolls Series, 28, 1865).

RL Royal and Other Historical Letters Illustrative of the Reign of Henry III, ed. W.W. Shirley, 2 vols. (Rolls Series, 27, 1862–6).

RLC Rotuli Litterarum Clausarum in Turri Londinensi asservati, 1204–27, ed. T.D. Hardy, 2 vols. (Record Commission, London, 1833–4).

RLJ Rotuli de Liberate ac de Missis et Praestitis, Regnante Johanne, ed. T.D. Hardy (Record Commission, London, 1844).

RLP Rotuli Litterarum Patentium in Turri Londinensi asservati, 1201–16, ed. T.D. Hardy (Record Commission, London, 1835).

Robert of Gloucester *Metrical Chronicle of Robert of Gloucester*, ed. W.A. Wright, 2 vols. (Rolls Series, 86, 1887).

RRS, ii *Regesta Regum Scottorum. Volume II: The Acts of William I, King of Scots, 1165–1214*, ed. G.W.S. Barrow with the collaboration of W.W. Scott (Edinburgh, 1971).

RRS, iii *Regesta Regum Scottorum, Volume III: The Acts of Alexander II, King of Scots, 1214–1249*, ed. K.J. Stringer, forthcoming.

Rules of Robert Grosseteste Walter of Henley, and Other Treatises on Estate Management and Accounting, ed. D. Oschinsky (Oxford, 1971). This volume contains the *Rules of Robert Grosseteste* between pp. 386 and 415.

Saint-Pathus Guillaume de Saint Pathus, *La Vie et les Miracles de Monseigneur Saint-Louis*, ed. M.C. Espagne (Paris, 1971).

Saint Richard of Chichester Saint Richard of Chichester: The Sources for his Life, ed. D. Jones (Sussex Record Society, 79, 1995).

Salimbene *Chronica Fr Salimbene Parmensis, Ordinis Minorum, ex Codice Bibliothecae Vaticanae nunc primum edita*, ed. A. Bertani, *Monumenta ad Provincias Parmensem et Placentinam Pertinentia* (Parma, 1858).

Sarum Missal The Sarum Missal in English, trans. A.H. Pearson (London, 1868).

SC Select Charters and Other Illustrations of English Constitutional History from the Earliest Times to the Reign of Edward I, ed. W. Stubbs, 9th edition revised by H.W.C. Davis (Oxford, 1921).

SCWR Select Cases of Procedure without Writ under Henry III, eds. H.G. Richardson and G.O. Sayles (Selden Society, 60, 141).

Selborne Charters Calendar of Charters and Documents relating to Selborne and its Priory preserved in the Muniment Room of Magdalen College, Oxford, ed. W.D. Macray (Hampshire Record Society, 4, 1891).

SLI Selected Letters of Pope Innocent III concerning England (1198–1216), eds. C.R. Cheney and W.H. Semple (London, 1953).

Song of Lewes The Song of Lewes, ed. C.L. Kingsford (Oxford, 1890).

SPF Select Pleas of the Forest, ed. G.J. Turner (Selden Society, 13, 1899).

SR Statutes of the Realm, Printed by Command of His Majesty George Third in pursuance of an address of the House of Commons of Great Britain; Volume the First (London, 1810).

St Albans Continuator *Flores Historiarum. Volume 2*, ed. H.R. Luard (Rolls Series, 95, 1890), 426–71. This is the text of the chronicle composed by Matthew Paris's successor at St Albans.

St Werburgh *Annales Cestrienses or Chronicle of the Abbey of S. Werburg Chester*, ed. R.C. Christie (Lancashire and Cheshire Record Society, 14, 1886).

Stapleton, *Magni Rotuli Magni Rotuli Scaccarii Normanniae sub Regibus Angliae*, ed. T. Stapleton, 2 vols. (Society of Antiquaries, 1840–4).

Survey of London Survey of London: Volume 13, St Margaret, Westminster, Part II, eds. M.H. Cox and P. Norman (London, 1930).

Tewkesbury 'Annales Monasterii de Theokesberia, AD 1066–1263', in *Annales Monastici*, ed. H.R. Luard, 5 vols. (Rolls Series, 36, 1864–9), vol. 1.

Thomas of Eccleston *Fratris Thomae de Eccleston Tractatus de Adventu Fratrum Minorum in Angliam*, ed. A.G. Little (Manchester, 1951).

Tours A chronicle by a canon of St Martin of Tours on *Recueil des Historiens des Gaules et de la France*, 24 vols. (Paris, 1734–1904), 18, 290–320.

TR Treaty Rolls. Volume 1: 1234–1325, ed. P. Chaplais (London, 1955).

Trevet Nicholas Trevet, *Annales Sex Regum Angliae*, ed. T. Hog (London, 1845).

Turgot Turgot of Durham, 'Life of Queen Margaret', in *Early Sources for Scottish History, A.D. 500 to 1286: Volume 2*, ed. A.O. Anderson (Stamford, 1990).

Vacarius *Liber Pauperum of Vacarius*, ed. F. du Zulueta (Selden Society, 44, 1927).

Vaughan, *Chronicles Chronicles of Matthew Paris: Monastic Life in the Thirteenth Century*, ed. and trans. R. Vaughan (Gloucester, 1984).

Walter Map Walter Map, *De Nugis Curialium: Courtiers' Trifles*, ed. M.R. James, revised C.N.L. Brooke and R.A.B. Mynors (Oxford, 1983).

Waverley, 'Annales Monasterii de Waverleia, AD 1–1291', in *Annales Monastici*, ed. H.R. Luard, 5 vols. (Rolls Series, 36, 1864–9), vol. 2.

Wendover Wendover's chronicle (his 'Flowers of History') is usually cited here from the earliest text, which is that found, with Paris's additions, in Matthew Paris's *Chronica Majora: Matthaei Parisiensis, Monachi Sancti Albani Chronica Majora*, ed. H.R. Luard, 7 vols. (Rolls Series, 57, 1872–83).

Wendover, *Flores The Flowers of History by Roger de Wendover: From the Year of Our Lord 1154, and the First Year of Henry II the Second, King of the English*, ed. H.G. Hewlett, 3 vols. (Rolls Series, 84, 1886–9).

Wendover/Paris This indicates a reference to Wendover's *Flores* and Paris's additions as found in the *Chronica Majora*. (See next but one above.)

Westminster Customary Customary of the Benedictine Monasteries of Saint Augustine, Canterbury, and Saint Peter, Westminster: Volume 2, ed. E.M. Thompson (Henry Bradshaw Society, 28, 1904).

Wild, *WA The Wardrobe Accounts of Henry III*, ed. B.L. Wild (Pipe Roll Society, new series, 68, 2012).

Williams, D.T., 'Aspects of the career of Boniface of Savoy, Archbishop of Canterbury, 1241–1270' (University of Wales, doctoral thesis, 1970).

Winchester 'Annales de Monasterii de Wintonia, AD 519–1277', in *Annales Monastici*, ed. H.R. Luard, 5 vols. (Rolls Series, 36, 1864–9), vol. 1.

Vincent, *EEA Winchester English Episcopal Acta 9: Winchester, 1205–1238*, ed. N. Vincent (Oxford, 1994).

Worcester 'Annales Prioratus de Wigornia, AD 1–1377', in *Annales Monastici*, ed. H.R. Luard, 5 vols. (Rolls Series, 36, 1864–9), vol. 4.

Worcester Cartulary The Cartulary of Worcester Cathedral Priory, ed. R.R. Darlington (Pipe Roll Society, new series, 38, 1968).

Wykes 'Chronicon vulgo dictum Chronicon Thomae Wykes, AD 1066–1289', in *Annales Monastici*, ed. H.R. Luard, 5 vols. (Rolls Series, 36, 1864–9), vol. 4.

SECONDARY SOURCES

The Oxford Dictionary of National Biography, eds. H.C.G. Matthew and B. Harrison, 60 vols. (Oxford, 2004), with the online edition at https://www.oxforddnb.com/ has biographies of all the leading actors appearing in this book.

Abulafia, D., *Frederick II: A Medieval Emperor* (London, 1988).

Adler, M., *Jews of Medieval England* (London, 1939).

Alexander, J., and Binski, P., eds., *Age of Chivalry: Art in Plantagenet England, 1200–1400* (London, 1987).

Allen, M., *Mints and Money in Medieval England* (Cambridge, 2012).

Allen, V., and Evans, R., eds., *Roadworks: Medieval Britain, Medieval Roads* (Manchester, 2016).

Ambler, S.T., *Bishops in the Political Community of England, 1213–1272* (Oxford, 2017).

Ambler, S.T., *The Song of Simon de Montfort: England's First Revolutionary and the Death of Chivalry* (London, 2019).

Ambler, S.T., 'The fine roll of 11 Henry III, 28 October 1226–27 October 1227', Henry III Fine Rolls Project, Fine of the Month for December 2007: https://finerollshenry3.org.uk/content/month/fm-12-2007.html.

Ambler, S.T., 'On kingship and tyranny: Grosseteste's memorandum and its place in the baronial reform movement', in *Thirteenth Century England*, 14 (Woodbridge, 2013), 115–28.

Andenmatten, B., Bagliani, A.P., and Pibiri, E., eds., *Pierre II de Savoie 'Le Petit Charlemagne'*, Colloque international Lausanne, 30–31 mai 1997 (Lausanne, 2000).

Annesley, S., 'Countesses in the age of Magna Carta' (King's College London, doctoral thesis, 2011)

Annesley, S., 'The impact of Magna Carta on widows: evidence from the fine rolls, 1216–1225', Henry III Fine Rolls Project, Fine of the Month for September 2007: https://finerollshenry3.org.uk/content/month/fm-11-2007.html.

Annesley, S., 'The countess and the constable: an exploration of the conflict that arose between Margaret de Burgh and Bertram de Criel', Henry III Fine Rolls Project, Fine of the Month for July 2008: https://finerollshenry3.org.uk/content/month/fm-07-2008.html.

Annesley, S., 'Isabella countess of Arundel's confrontation with King Henry III', Henry III Fine Rolls Project, Fine of the Month for August 2009: https://finerollshenry3.org.uk/content/month/fm-08-2009.html.

Armstrong, A., 'Royal and aristocratic women at the court of Henry III: an examination of the power of women and family in thirteenth-century England' (Canterbury Christ Church University, doctoral thesis, 2019).

Asaji, K., *The Angevin Empire and the Community of the Realm in England* (Kansai, 2010).

Asbridge, T.S., *The Greatest Knight: The Remarkable Life of William Marshal, the Power behind Five English Thrones* (London, 2015).

Aurell, M., *L'Empire des Plantagenêt* (editions-perrin, 2004). There is an English tranlation by David Crouch: *The Plantagenet Empire 1154–1224* (Harlow, 2007).

Bachelor, M., 'The itinerary of Henry III, 1234–1241' (King's College London, undergraduate long essay).

Badham, S., and Oosterwijk, S., 'The tomb monument of Katherine, daughter of Henry III and Eleanor of Provence (1253–7)', *The Antiquaries Journal*, 92 (2012), 169–96.

Baker, D., *With All For All: The Life of Simon de Montfort* (Stroud, 2015).

Baker, D., *Henry III: The Great King England Never Knew It Had* (Stroud, 2017).

Baldwin, J.W., 'Master Stephen Langton, future archbishop of Canterbury: the Paris schools and Magna Carta', *English Historical Review*, 123 (2008), 811–46.

Barker, J.R.V., *The Tournament in England 1100–1400* (Woodbridge, 1986).

Barlow, F., 'The king's evil', *English Historical Review*, 95 (1980), 3–27.

Barratt, N., 'The revenue of King John', *English Historical Review*, 111 (1996), 835–55.

Barratt, N., 'English royal revenue in the early thirteenth century in its wider context, 1130–1330', in *Crises, Revolutions and Self-Sustained Growth: Essays in European Fiscal History, 1130–1830*, eds. W.M. Ormrod, R. Bonney and M. Bonney (Stamford, 1999), 59–96.

Barratt, N., 'Finance on a shoestring: the exchequer in the thirteenth century', in *English Government in the Thirteenth Century*, ed. A. Jobson (Woodbridge, 2004), 71–86.

Barratt, N., 'Another fine mess: evidence for the resumption of exchequer authority in the minority of Henry III', in *The Growth of Royal Government under Henry III*, eds. D. Crook and L.J. Wilkinson (Woodbridge, 2015), 179–95.

Barratt, N., 'Crisis management: baronial reform at the exchequer', in *Baronial Reform and Revolution in England, 1258–1267*, ed. A. Jobson (Woodbridge, 2016), 56–70.

Barron, C.M., *London in the Later Middle Ages: Government and People, 1200–1500* (Oxford, 2004).

Bartlett, R.J., *England under the Norman and Angevin Kings, 1075–1225* (Oxford, 2000).

Bartlett, R.J., *Why Can the Dead Do Such Great Things? Saints and Worshippers from the Martyrs to the Reformation* (Princeton, NJ, 2013).

Barton, J.L., 'The mystery of *Bracton*', *The Journal of Legal History*, 14 (1993), 1–142.

Barthélemy, D., *La Bataille de Bouvines: Histoire et Légendes* (Paris, 2018).

Baylen, J.O., 'John Maunsell and the Castilian treaty of 1254: a study of the clerical diplomat', *Traditio*, 17 (1961), 482–91.

Bazeley, M.L., 'The extent of the English royal forest in the thirteenth century', *Transactions of the Royal Historical Society*, 4th series, iv, (1921), 140–72.

Beam, A.G., *The Balliol Dynasty, 1210–1364* (Edinburgh, 2008).

Bean, J.M.W., *The Decline of English Feudalism, 1215–1540* (Manchester, 1968).

Beauvoit, B., 'La famille de Rancon et les seigneurs de Taillebourg pendant les conflits Franco-Anglaise du XIIIᵉ siècle', *Roccafortis*, 57 (2016), 32–41.

Bémont, C., *Simon de Montfort, Comte de Leicester* (Paris, 1884).

Bémont, C., 'La campagne de Poitou, 1242–1243: Taillebourg and Saintes', *Annales du Midi*, 5 (1893), 289–314.

Benoit, J.-L., 'Autour des tombeaux de Saint Edme à Pontigny au milieu du XIIIᵉ siècle', *Bulletin de la Société des Sciences Historiques et Naturelles de l'Yonne*, 133 (2001), 33–70.

Berger, D., 'Mission to the Jews and Jewish-Christian contacts in the polemical literature of the high middle ages', *American Historical Review*, 91 (1986), 576–91.

Berger, E., *Histoire de Blanche de Castille, Reine de France* (Paris, 1895).

Binski, P., *The Painted Chamber at Westminster* (London, 1986).

Binski, P., *Westminster Abbey and the Plantagenets: Kingship and Representation of Power, 1200–1400* (New Haven, CT, and London, 1995).

Binski, P., *Becket's Crown: Art and Imagination in Gothic England, 1170–1300* (New Haven, CT, and London, 2004).

Binski, P., 'Reflections on "La estoire de Seint Aedward le rei": hagiography and kingship in thirteenth-century England', *Journal of Medieval History*, 16 (1990), 333–50.

Binski, P., 'Abbot Barking's tapestries and Matthew Paris's Life of St Edward the Confessor', *Archaeologia*, 109 (1991), 85–100.

Binski, P., 'The painted chamber at Westminster, the fall of tyrants and the English literary model of governance', *Journal of the Warburg and Courtauld Institutes*, 74 (2011), 121–54.

Binski, P., Massing, A. and Sauerberg, M.L., eds., *The Westminster Retable: History, Technique, Conservation* (Cambridge, 2009).

Bolton, J.L., *Money in the Medieval English Economy, 973–1489* (Manchester, 2012).

Borenius, T., 'The cycle of images in the castles and palaces of Henry III', *Journal of the Warburg and Courtauld Institutes*, 6 (1943), 40–50.

Borg, A.C.N., 'The royal menagerie', in *The Tower of London: Its Buildings and Institutions*, ed. J. Charlton (London, 1978), 100–3.

Boutaric, E., *Saint Louis et Alfonse de Poitiers* (Paris, 1870).

Brand, P.A., *The Making of the Common Law* (London, 1992).

Brand, P.A., *Kings, Barons and Justices: The Making and Enforcement of Legislation in Thirteenth-Century England* (Cambridge, 2003).

Brand, P.A., 'Jews and the law in England, 1275–90', *English Historical Review*, 115 (2000), 1138–58.

Brand, P.A., 'The date and authorship of *Bracton*: a response', *The Journal of Legal History*, 31 (2010), 217–45.

Brand, P.A., 'The fine rolls of Henry III as a source for the legal historian', *The Growth of Royal Government under Henry III*, eds. D. Crook and L.J. Wilkinson (Woodbridge, 2015), 44–54.

Branner, R., 'Westminster Abbey and the French court style', *Journal of the Society of Architectural Historians*, 23 (1964), 3–18.

Brindle, S., ed., *Windsor Castle: A Thousand Years of a Royal Palace* (London, 2018).

Broun, D., 'A new look at the *Gesta Annalia* attributed to John of Fordun', in *Church, Chronicle and Learning in Medieval and Early Renaissance Scotland: Essays Presented to Donald Watt on the Completion of the Publication of Bower's Scotichronicon*, ed. B.E. Crawford (Edinburgh, 1999), 9–30.

Broun, D., and Harrison, J., *The Chronicle of Melrose: A Stratigraphic Edition. Volume I: Introduction and Facsimile Edition* (Scottish History Society, 2007).

Brown, M., *The Wars of Scotland: 1214–1371* (Edinburgh, 2004).

Brown, M., 'Henry the peaceable: Henry III, Alexander III and royal lordship in the British Isles, 1249–1259', in *England and Europe in the Reign of Henry III (1216–1272)*, eds. B.K.U. Weiler and I.W. Rowlands (Aldershot, 2002), 43–66.

Brown, R.A., 'Architectural description', in *The Tower of London: Its Buildings and Institutions*, ed. J. Charlton (London, 1978), 38–54.

Browne, C., Davies, G., Michael, M.A., and Zöschg, M., eds., *English Medieval Embroidery: Opus Anglicanum*, exhibition catalogue (New Haven, CT, and London, 2016).

Buc, P., *L'Ambiguïté du Livre: Prince, Pouvoir et Peuple dans le Commentaires de la Bible au Moyen Âge* (Paris, 1994).

Burns, J.H., *The Cambridge History of Medieval Political Thought c.350–c.1450* (Cambridge, 1988).

Burt, C., *Edward I and the Governance of England, 1272–1307* (Cambridge, 2013).

Burt, C., 'Political ideas and dialogue in England in the twelfth and thirteenth centuries', *Thirteenth Century England*, 13 (Woodbridge, 2011), 1–10.

Callus, D.A., *Robert Grosseteste. Scholar and Bishop: Essays in Commemoration of the Seventh Centenary of his Death* (Oxford, 1955).

Cam, H.M., 'Studies in the hundred rolls: some aspects of thirteenth-century administration', in *Oxford Studies in Social and Legal History VI*, ed. P. Vinogradoff (Oxford, 1921), 1–198.

Campbell, B.M.S., 'Global climates, the 1257 mega-eruption of Samalas volcano, Indonesia, and the English food crisis of 1258', *Transactions of the Royal Historical Society*, 6th series, 27 (2017), 87–121.

Campbell, G.J., 'The protest of Saint Louis', *Traditio*, 15 (1959), 405–18.

Carpenter, D.A., *The Minority of Henry III* (London, 1990).

Carpenter, D.A., *The Reign of Henry III* (London, 1996).

Carpenter, D.A., *The Struggle for Mastery: Britain 1066–1284*, paperback edition (London, 2004).

Carpenter, D.A., *Magna Carta* (London, 2015).

Carpenter, D.A., 'Westminster Abbey: some characteristics of its sculpture, 1245–59', *Journal of the British Archaeological Association*, 3rd series, 35 (1972), 1–14.

Carpenter, D.A., 'Gold and gold coins in England in the mid-thirteenth century', *The Numismatic Chronicle*, 147 (1987), 106–13.

Carpenter, D.A., 'Chancellor Ralph de Neville and plans of political reform, 1215–1258', in *Thirteenth Century England*, 2 (Woodbridge, 1988), 69–80.

Carpenter, D.A., 'A noble in politics: Roger Mortimer in the period of baronial reform and rebellion, 1258–1265', in *Nobles and Nobility in Medieval Europe: Concepts, Origins, Transformations*, ed. A.J. Duggan (Woodbridge, 2000), 183–203.

Carpenter, D.A., 'The English royal chancery in the thirteenth century', in *English Government in the Thirteenth Century*, ed. A. Jobson (Woodbridge, 2004), 49–70.

Carpenter, D.A., 'The meetings of kings Henry III and Louis IX', in *Thirteenth Century England*, 10 (Woodbridge, 2005), 1–30.

Carpenter, D.A., 'The household rolls of King Henry III of England (1216–1272)', *Historical Research*, 80 (2006), 22–46.

Carpenter, D.A., 'Fines made with Henry III for the confirmation of charters, January–February 1227', Henry III Fine Rolls Project, Fine of the Month for July 2006: https://finerollshenry3.org.uk/content/month/fm-07-2006.html.

Carpenter, D.A., 'The bishop of Winchester's fine in 1227', Henry III Fine Rolls Project, Fine of the Month for August 2006: https://finerollshenry3.org.uk/content/month/fm-08-2006.html.

Carpenter, D.A., 'Dafydd ap Llywelyn's submission to King Henry III in October 1241: a new perspective', *Welsh History Review*, 23 (2007), 1–12.

Carpenter, D.A., 'King Henry III and Saint Edward the Confessor: the origins of the cult', *English Historical Review*, 122 (2007), 865–91.

Carpenter, D.A., 'The career of Godfrey of Crowcombe: household knight of King John and steward of King Henry III', in *War, Government and Aristocracy in the British Isles, c.1150–1500: Essays in Honour of Michael Prestwich*, eds. C. Given-Wilson, A.J. Kettle and L. Scales (Woodbridge, 2008), 26–54.

Carpenter, D.A., 'Hubert de Burgh, Matilda de Mowbray, and Magna Carta's protection of widows', Henry III Fine Rolls Project, Fine of the Month for March 2008: https://finerollshenry3.org.uk/content/month/fm-03-2008.html.

Carpenter, D.A., 'The peasants of Rothley in Leicestershire, the Templars and King Henry III', Henry III Fine Rolls Project, Fine of the Month for April 2009: https://finerollshenry3.org.uk/content/month/fm-04-2009.html.

Carpenter, D.A., 'King Henry III and the chapter house of Westminster Abbey', in *Westminster Abbey Chapter House: The History, Art and Architecture of 'A Chapter House beyond Compare'*, eds. W.J. Rodwell and R. Mortimer (London, 2010), 32–9.

Carpenter, D.A., 'The sense of humour of King Henry III', Henry III Fine Rolls Project, Fine of the Month for November 2011: https://finerollshenry3.org.uk/content/month/fm-11-2011.html.

Carpenter, D.A., 'Crucifixion and conversion: King Henry III and the Jews in 1255', in *Laws, Lawyers and Texts: Studies in Medieval Legal History in Honour of Paul Brand*, eds. S. Jenks, J. Rose and C. Whittick (Leiden, 2012), 129–48.

Carpenter, D.A., 'The vis et voluntas of King Henry III: the downfall and punishment of Robert de Ros', Henry III Fine Rolls Project, Fine of the Month for August 2012: https://finerollshenry3.org.uk/redist/pdf/fm-08-2012.pdf.

Carpenter, D.A., 'Chronology and truth: Matthew Paris and the *Chronica Majora*', a 'related paper' placed on the website of the Henry III Fine Rolls Project (2013): https://finerollshenry3.org.uk/redist/pdf/Chronologyandtruth3.pdf.

Carpenter, D.A., 'Magna Carta 1253: the ambitions of the church and the divisions within the realm', *Historical Research*, 86 (2013), 179–90.

Carpenter, D.A., 'More light on Henry III's confirmation of Magna Carta in 1253', *Historical Research*, 86 (2013), 191–95.

Carpenter, D.A., 'Between Magna Carta and the parliamentary state: the fine rolls of King Henry III, 1216–72', in *The Growth of Royal Government under Henry III*, eds. D. Crook and L.J. Wilkinson (Woodbridge, 2015).

Carpenter, D.A., 'The copies of Magna Carta 1216 in the Archives Nationales in Paris and the 1216 Irish Magna Carta', The Magna Carta Project, Feature of the Month for May 2015: http://magnacarta.cmp.uea.ac.uk/read/feature_of_the_month/May_2015_4.

Carpenter, D.A., and Kanter, J.E., 'King Henry III and Windsor castle', in *St George's Chapel, Windsor: History and Heritage*, eds. N. Saul and T. Tatton-Brown (Stanbridge, Wimborne Minster, 2010), 25–35.

Cassidy, R., 'Shuffling the sheriffs, 1234 and 1236', Henry III Fine Rolls Project, Fine of the Month for May 2008: https://finerollshenry3.org.uk/content/month/fm-05-2008. html.

Cassidy, R., 'Adventus vicecomitum and the financial crisis of Henry III's reign, 1250–1272', *English Historical Review*, 126 (2011), 614–27.

Cassidy, R., 'The reforming council takes control of fines of gold, 1258–59', Henry III Fine Rolls Project, Fine of the Month for October 2011: https://finerollshenry3.org.uk/content/month/fm-10-2011.html.

Cassidy, R., 'Richard of Cornwall and the royal mints and exchanges, 1247–59', *The Numismatic Chronicle*, 172 (2012), 137–56.

Cassidy, R., 'William Heron, "hammer of the poor, persecutor of the religious", sheriff of Northumberland, 1246–58', *Northern History*, 50 (2013), 9–19.

Cassidy, R., 'Bad sheriffs, custodial sheriffs, and control of the counties', in *Thirteenth Century England*, 15 (Woodbridge, 2015), 35–50.

Cassidy, R., 'The barons of London and royal taxation after Magna Carta', *The London Journal*, 42 (2017), 123–36.

Cassidy, R., 'A golden treasure or a state of collapse? Henry III's finances in the 1250s', unpublished paper.

Cassidy, R., and Clasby, M., 'Matthew Paris and Henry III's elephant', Henry III Fine Rolls Project, Fine of the Month for June 2012: https://finerollshenry3.org.uk/redist/pdf/fm-06-2012.pdf.

Cather, S., Park, D. and Pender, R., 'Henry III's wall paintings at Chester castle', in A. Thacker (ed.), *Medieval Archaeology, Art and Architecture at Chester* (British Archeological Association, Conference Transactions, 22, 2000), 170–89.

Cave, C.J.P., and Tanner, L.E., 'A thirteenth-century choir of angels in the north transept of Westminster Abbey and the adjacent figures of two kings', *Archaeologia*, 84 (1934), 63–7.

Cazel, F.A. Jr, 'The fifteenth of 1225', *Bulletin of the Institute of Historical Research*, 34 (1961), 67–80.

Cazel, F.A. Jr, 'The last years of Stephen Langton', *English Historical Review*, 79 (1964), 673–97.

Cazel, F.A. Jr, 'Religious motivation in the biography of Hubert de Burgh', in *Religious Motivation*, ed. D. Baker, *Studies in Church History*, 15 (1978), 109–20.

Chambers, A., 'Aspects of chancery procedure in the chancery rolls of Henry III of England' (King's College London, doctoral thesis), forthcoming.

Chaplais, P., *Piers Gaveston: Edward II's Adoptive Brother* (Oxford, 1994).

Chaplais, P., 'Le traité de Paris de 1259 et l'inféodation de la Gascogne allodiale', in his *Essays in Medieval Diplomacy and Administration* (London, 1981), 121–37.

Chapuisat, J-P, 'Pierre de Savoie, les affaires anglaises et la politique européenne 1252–1255' in *Pierre II de Savoie 'Le Petit Charlemagne'*, Colloque international Lausanne, 30–31 mai 1997, eds. B. Andenmatten, A.P. Bagliani, and E. Pibiri (Lausanne, 2000), 259–64.

Chenard, G., *L'Administration d'Alphonse de Poitiers (1241–1271)* (Paris, 2017).

Cheney, C.R. 'The "Paper Constitution" preserved by Matthew Paris', *English Historical Review*, 65 (1950), 213–21.

Church, S.D., *The Household Knights of King John* (Cambridge, 1999).

Church, S.D., *King John: England, Magna Carta and the Making of a Tyrant* (London, 2015).

Church, S.D., *Henry III: A Simple and God-Fearing King* (London, 2017).

Church, S.D., 'The knights of the household of King John: a question of numbers', in *Thirteenth Century England*, 4 (Woodbridge, 1992), 151–65.

Church, S.D., 'The rewards of royal service in the household of King John: a dissenting opinion', *English Historical Review*, 110 (1995), 277–302.

Church, S.D., 'The 1210 campaign in Ireland: evidence for a military revolution?', *Anglo-Norman Studies*, 20 (Woodbridge, 1998), 45–57.

Church, S.D., 'Some aspects on the royal itinerary in the twelfth century', in *Anglo-Norman Studies*, 29 (Woodbridge, 2007), 17–34.

Churchill, R., and Thomas, B., *The Brussels Hoard of 1908: The Long Cross Coinage of Henry III* (London, 2012).

Clanchy, M.T., *England and its Rulers, 1066–1272*, 2nd edition (Oxford, 1998); 3rd edition (Oxford, 2006); 4th edition (Oxford, 2014). All references are to the second edition.

Clanchy, M.T., *From Memory to Written Record: England 1066–1307*, 2nd edition (Oxford, 2009); 3rd edition (Oxford, 2012). All references are to the second edition.

Clanchy, M.T., 'The franchise of return of writs', *Transactions of the Royal Historical Society*, 5th series, 17 (1967), 59–81.

Clanchy, M.T., 'Did Henry III have a policy?', *History*, 53 (1968), 203–16.

Clanchy, M.T., 'Highway robbery and trial by battle in the Hampshire eyre of 1249', in *Medieval Legal Records edited in Memory of C.A.F. Meekings*, eds. R.F. Hunnisett and J.B. Post (London, 1978), 26–61.

Clapham, A.W., and Tanner, L.E., 'Recent discoveries in the nave of Westminster Abbey', *Archaeologia*, 83 (1933), 227–36.

Clasby, M., 'The abbot of St Albans, the royal will and Magna Carta: the amercement of the abbot of St Albans for non-attendance at the common summons of the Yorkshire forest eyre in 1212', Henry III Fine Rolls Project, Fine of the Month for September 2009: https://finerollshenry3.org.uk/content/month/fm-09-2009.html.

Clasby, M., *St Alban and his Shrine* (St Albans, 2019).

Cohen, J., *The Friars and the Jews: The Evolution of Medieval Anti-Judaism* (Ithaca, NY, 1983).

Cokayne, G.E., *The Complete Peerage of England, Scotland, Ireland, Great Britain and the United Kingdom*, eds. G.E. Cockayne, H.A. Doubleday, Lord Howard de Walden and G.H. White, 12 vols. in 13 (1910–59).

Collin, B.M., *The Riddle of a 13th-Century Sword-Belt* (East Knoyle, 1955).

Collingwood, J.A., 'Royal finance in the period of baronial reform and rebellion, 1255–1270' (University of London, doctoral thesis, 1996).

Collins, M., 'The king's high table at the palace of Westminster', *The Antiquaries Journal*, 92 (2012), 197–244.

Colvin, H.M., ed., *The History of the King's Works: The Middle Ages*, 3 vols. (London, 1963).

Connell, B., Jones, A.G., Redfern, R., and Walker, D., *A Bioarchaeological Study of Medieval Burials on the Site of St Mary Spital: Excavations at Spitalfields Market, London E1, 1991–2007* (London, 2012).

Connolly, D.K., *The Maps of Matthew Paris: Medieval Journeys through Space, Time and Liturgy* (Woodbridge, 2009).

Coss, P.R., *The Lady in Medieval England, 1000–1500* (Stroud, 1998).

Coss, P.R., *The Origins of the English Gentry* (Cambridge, 2003).

Coss, P.R., 'Sir Geoffrey de Langley and the crisis of the knightly class in thirteenth-century England', *Past & Present*, 68 (1975), 3–37.

Coulton, G.G., *From St Francis to Dante: A Translation of all that is of primary interest in the Chronicle of the Franciscan Salimbene, 1221–1288* (London, 1906).

Cox, E.L., *The Eagles of Savoy: The House of Savoy in Thirteenth-Century Europe* (Princeton, NJ, 1974).

Craib, T., Brindle, S., and Priestley, S., eds., *The Itinerary of King Henry III, 1216–1272* (English Heritage, n.d.).

Creamer, J.P., 'St Edmund of Canterbury and Henry III in the shadow of Thomas Becket', in *Thirteenth Century England*, 14 (Woodbridge, 2013), 129–40.

Critchley, J.S., 'Summonses to military service early in the reign of Henry III', *English Historical Review*, 86 (1971), 79–95.

Crook, D., *Records of the General Eyre* (London, 1982).

Crook, D., 'The struggle over the forest boundaries in Nottinghamshire, 1218–1227', *Transactions of the Thoroton Society of Nottinghamshire*, 83 (1979), 35–45.

Crook, D., 'The "Petition of the Barons" and charters of free warren, 1227–1258', in *Thirteenth Century England*, 8 (Woodbridge, 2001), 33–48.

Crook, D., 'The "lands of the Normans" in thirteenth-century Nottinghamshire: Bingham and Wheatley', *Transactions of the Thoroton Society of Nottinghamshire*, 108 (2004), 101–7.

Crook, D., 'Dynastic conflict in thirteenth-century Laxton', in *Thirteenth Century England*, 11 (Woodbridge, 2007), 193–214.

Crook, D., 'Roger of Wendover, prior of Belvoir, and the implementation of the Charter of the Forest, 1225–27', in *The Growth of Royal Government under Henry III*, eds. D. Crook and L.J. Wilkinson (Woodbridge, 2015), 166–78.

Crouch, D., *William Marshal: Court, Career and Chivalry in the Angevin Empire, 1147–1219* (London, 1990). There is a second edition, *William Marshal: Knighthood, War and Chivalry* (London, 2002), and also a third edition, *William Marshal* (London, 2016).

Crouch, D., 'The last adventure of Richard Siward', *Morgannwg*, 35 (1991), 7–30.

Crouch, D., 'Gilbert Marshal and his mortal enemies', *Historical Research*, 87 (2014), 393–403.

Curnow, P.E., 'The Wakefield tower: Tower of London', *Chateau Gaillard*, 8 (1977), 87–101.

Davies, R.R., *Conquest, Coexistence and Change: Wales 1063–1415* (Oxford, 1987).

D'Avray, D.L., *The Preaching of the Friars: Sermons Diffused from Paris before 1300* (Oxford, 1985).

D'Avray, D.L., *Dissolving Royal Marriages: A Documentary History, 860–1600* (Cambridge, 2014).

D'Avray, D.L., 'Magna Carta: its background in Stephen Langton's academic biblical exegesis and its episcopal reception', *Studii Medievali*, 3rd series, 38 (1997), 423–38.

D'Avray, D.L., 'Authentication of marital status: a thirteenth-century English royal annulment process and late medieval cases from the papal penitentiary', *English Historical Review*, 120 (2005), 987–1013.

Dejoux, M., *Les Enquêtes de Saint Louis: Gouverner et Sauvor son Âme* (Paris, 2014).

Delisle, L., 'Mémoire sur une lettre inédite adressée à la reine Blanche par un habitant de La Rochelle', *Bibliothèque de l'École des Chartes*, 17 (1856), 513–55.

De Marca, P., *Histoire de Béarn, contenant l'Origine des Rois de Navarre, des Ducs de Gascogne, Marquis de Gothie, Princes de Béarn, Comtes de Carcassonne, de Foix et de Bigorre*, 2nd edition (Pau, 1894–1912).

Denholm-Young, N., *Richard of Cornwall* (Oxford, 1947).

Denholm-Young, N., *Collected Papers of Noel Denholm-Young* (Cardiff, 1969).

Dibben, L.B., 'Chancellor and keeper of the seal under Henry III', *English Historical Review*, 27 (1912), 39–51.

Dixon-Smith, S.A., 'The image and reality of alms-giving in the great halls of Henry III', *Journal of the British Archaeological Association*, 152 (1999), 79–96.

Dixon-Smith, S.A., 'Feeding the poor to commemorate the dead: the *pro anima* almsgiving of Henry III of England, 1227–1272' (University of London, doctoral thesis, 2003).

Draper, P., 'Salisbury Cathedral: paradigm or maverick?', *British Archaeological Association Conference Transactions*, 17 (1996), 21–39.

Duby, G., *Le Dimanche de Bouvines* (Paris, 1973).

Duggan, A.J., 'The cult of St Thomas Becket in the thirteenth century', in *St Thomas Cantilupe, Bishop of Hereford: Essays in his Honour*, ed. M. Jancey (Hereford, 1982), 21–44.

Duggan, K.F., 'Communal justice in thirteenth-century England' (King's College London, doctoral thesis, 2017).

Duggan, K.F., 'The hue and cry in thirteenth-century England', in *Thirteenth Century England*, 16 (Woodbridge, 2017), 153–72.

Dunbabin, J., *Charles I of Anjou: Power, Kingship and State-Making in Thirteenth-Century Europe* (London, 1998).

Dunbabin, J., 'Robert Bacon (d.1248), theologian', *Oxford Dictionary of National Biography* (2004): https://doi.org/10/1093/ref:odnb/1007.

Duncan, A.A.M., *Scotland: The Making of the Kingdom* (Edinburgh, 1978).

Eaglen, R.J., *The Abbey and Mint of Bury St Edmunds to 1279* (London, 2006).

Eales, R.G., 'Henry III and the end of the Norman earldom of Chester', in *Thirteenth Century England*, 1 (Woodbridge, 1986), 100–13.

Eales, R.G., 'The political setting of the Becket translation of 1220', in *Martyrs and Martyrdom*, ed. D.S. Wood, *Studies in Church History*, 30 (1993), 127–39.

Eames, E.S., 'The tile kiln and floor tiles', in *Clarendon Palace: The History and Archaeology of a Medieval Palace and Hunting Lodge near Salisbury, Wiltshire*, eds. T.B. James and A.M. Robinson (Society of Antiquaries Research Report, 45, 1989).

Ehrlich, L., *Proceedings against the Crown (1216–1377)* (Oxford, 1921).

Ellis, C., *Hubert de Burgh: A Study in Constancy* (London, 1952).

Ellis, G., *Earldoms in Fee: A Study in Peerage Law and History* (London, 1963).

Ellis, J.H., 'Gaston de Béarn: a study in Anglo-Gascon relations (1229–1290)' (University of Oxford, doctoral thesis, 1952).

Engel, U., *Worcester Cathedral: An Architectural History*, 2nd edition (London, 2007).

English, B., *The Lords of Holderness, 1086–1260* (Oxford, 1979).

Evers, W.K., 'Disputes about episcopal elections in the reign of Henry III' (University of Oxford, B.Litt thesis, 1934).

Faulkner, K., 'The transformation of knighthood in early thirteenth-century England', *English Historical Review*, 111 (1996), 1–23.

Fernie, E.C., 'Edward the Confessor's Westminster Abbey', in *Edward the Confessor: The Man and the Legend*, ed. R. Mortimer (Woodbridge, 2009), 139–50.

Fletcher, C.D., *Richard II: Manhood, Youth and Politics, 1377–99* (Oxford, 2010).

Fogle, L.F., 'The *domus conversorum*: the personal interest of Henry III', *Jewish Historical Studies*, 41 (2007), 1–7.

Forey, A., 'The crusading vows of the English King Henry III', in *Military Orders and Crusades* (Aldershot, 2001), 229–47.

Foster, R., *Patterns of Thought: The Hidden Meaning of the Great Pavement of Westminster Abbey* (London, 1991).

Foster, R., and Tudor-Craig, P., 'The sculptural decoration of the Westminster chapter house portals', in *Westminster Abbey Chapter House: The History, Art and Architecture of 'A Chapter House beyond Compare'*, eds. W.J. Rodwell and R. Mortimer (London, 2010), 158–83.

Fouracre, P.J., 'Eternal light and earthly needs: practical aspects of the development of Frankish immunities', in *Property and Power in the Early Middle Ages*, eds. W. Davies and P.J. Fouracre (Cambridge, 1995), 53–81.

Frame, R., 'King Henry III and Ireland: the shaping of a peripheral lordship', in *Thirteenth Century England*, 4 (Woodbridge, 1992), 179–202.

Galbraith, V.H., *Roger of Wendover and Matthew Paris* (Glasgow, 1944).

Gaposchkin, M.C., *The Making of Saint Louis: Kingship, Sanctity and Crusade in the Later Middle Ages* (Ithaca, NY, 2008).

Gieben, S., 'Robert Grosseteste at the papal curia, Lyons, 1250: edition of the documents', *Collectanea Franciscana*, 41 (1971), 340–93.

Gillingham, J., *Richard I* (London, 1999).

Gransden, A., *Historical Writing in England, c.550–1307* (London, 1974).

Grant, L., *Blanche of Castile, Queen of France* (New Haven, CT, 2016).

Greasley, N., 'Networks and Information Gathering in the *Chronica Majora* of Matthew Paris' (University of Aberystwyth, doctoral thesis, 2017).

Greatrex, J., 'Monastic charity for Jewish converts: the requisition of corrodies by Henry III', in *Christianity and Judaism*, ed. D. Wood, *Studies in Church History*, 29 (1992), 132–43.

Green, V., *An Account of the Discovery of the Body of King John in the Cathedral Church of Worcester, July 17, 1797* (London and Worcester, 1797).

Griffiths-Jones, R., and Park, D., *The Temple Church in London: History, Art and Architecture* (Woodbridge, 2013).

Hajdu, R., 'Castles, castellans and the structure of politics in Poitou, 1152–1271', *Journal of Medieval History*, 4 (1978), 27–53.

Hammer, C.I., 'Complaints of the lesser commune, oligarchic rule and baronial reform in thirteenth-century Oxford', *Historical Research*, 85 (2012), 353–71.

Hanchett, P., 'Women in thirteenth-century Oxfordshire' (King's College London, doctoral thesis, 2007).

Harding, A., *England in the Thirteenth Century* (Cambridge, 1993).

Harding, A., 'Robert Walerand (d.1273), administrator', *Oxford Dictionary of National Biography* (2004): https://doi.org/10.1093/ref:odnb/28455.

Hartland, B., 'Administering the Irish fines, 1199–1254: the English chancery, the Dublin exchequer and the seeking of favours', in *The Growth of Royal Government under Henry III*, eds. D. Crook and L.J. Wilkinson (Woodbridge, 2015), 72–84.

Hartland, B., and Dryburgh, P., 'The development of the fine rolls', in *Thirteenth Century England*, 12 (Woodbridge, 2009), 193–205.

Harvey, K., *Episcopal Appointments in England, c.1214–1344: From Episcopal Election to Papal Provision* (London, 2014).

Harvey, K., 'The piety of King John' (King's College London, master's thesis, 2008).

Harvey, P.D.A., *Medieval Maps* (London, 1991).

Harvey, P.D.A., 'Matthew Paris's maps of Britain', in *Thirteenth Century England*, 4 (Woodbridge, 1992), 109–21.

Harvey, P.D.A., *The Hereford World Map Introduction* (London, 2010).

Hill, F.G., 'Magna Carta, canon law and pastoral care: excommunication and the church's publication of the Charter', *Historical Research*, 89 (2016), 636–50.

Hill, F.G., '*Damnatio eternae mortis* or *medicinalis non mortalis*: the ambiguities of excommunication in thirteenth-century England', in *Thirteenth Century England*, 16 (Woodbridge, 2017), 37–54.

Hill, M.C., *The King's Messengers, 1199–1377: A List of all Known Messengers, Mounted and Unmounted, who Served John, Henry III, and the First Three Edwards* (Stroud, 1994).

Hillaby, J., 'A magnate among the marchers: Hamo of Hereford, his family and clients, 1218–1253', *Jewish Historical Studies*, 31 (1990), 23–82.

Hillaby, J., 'The ritual-child-murder accusation: its dissemination and Harold of Gloucester', *Jewish Historical Studies*, 34 (1994), 69–109.

Hillaby, J., 'A *domus conversorum* in Bristol?', *Jewish Historical Studies*, 42 (2009), 1–5.

Hillaby, J., and Hillaby, C., *The Palgrave Dictionary of Medieval Anglo-Jewish History* (Basingstoke, 2013).

Hilpert, H.-E., 'Richard of Cornwall's candidature for the German throne and the Christmas 1256 parliament at Westminster', *Journal of Medieval History*, 6 (1980), 185–98.

Holt, J.C., *The Northerners: A Study in the Reign of King John* (Oxford, 1961).

Holt, J.C., *Magna Carta* (Cambridge, 1965); 2nd edition (Cambridge, 1992); 3rd edition (Cambridge, 2015). Unless stated, all references are to the second edition.

Holt, J.C., 'Magna Carta 1215–1217: the legal and social context', in his *Colonial England, 1066–1215* (London, 1997), 291–306.

Hoskin, P., 'The church and the king: canon law and kingship in England', in *The Growth of Royal Government under Henry III*, eds. D. Crook and L.J. Wilkinson (Woodbridge, 2015), 196–211.

Howell, M., *Regalian Right in Medieval England* (London, 1962).

Howell, M., *Eleanor of Provence: Queenship in Thirteenth-Century England* (Oxford, 1998).

Howell, M., 'The resources of Eleanor of Provence as queen consort', *English Historical Review*, 102 (1987), 372–93.

Howell, M., 'Royal women of England and France in the mid-thirteenth century: a gendered perspective', in *England and Europe in the Reign of Henry III (1216–1272)*, eds. B.K.U. Weiler and I.W. Rowlands (Aldershot, 2002), 163–82.

Hudson, J., *The Formation of the English Common Law: Law and Society from the Norman Conquest to Magna Carta* (London, 1996).

Huscroft, R., *Expulsion: England's Jewish Solution* (Stroud, 2006).

Hyams, P.R., 'What did Henry III of England think in bed and in French about kingship and anger?', in *Anger's Past: The Social Uses of an Emotion in the Middle Ages*, ed. B.H. Rosenwein (Ithaca, NY, and London, 1990), 92–124.

Ispir, C., 'A critical edition of the Crowland chronicle' (King's College London, doctoral thesis, 2015).

Jacob, E.F., *Studies in the Period of Baronial Reform and Rebellion, 1258–1267* (Oxford, 1925).

James, T.B., and Robinson, A.M., *Clarendon Palace: The History and Archaeology of a Medieval Palace and Hunting Lodge near Salisbury, Wiltshire* (Society of Antiquaries Research Report, 45, 1988).

Jansen, V., 'Henry III's palace at Westminster', in *Westminster: The Art, Architecture and Archaeology of the Royal Palace and Abbey, part 2*, eds. W.J. Rodwell and T. Tatton-Brown, *British Archaeological Association Conference Transactions*, 39 (2015), 89–110.

Jansen, V., 'Salisbury Cathedral and the episcopal style in the early 13th century', *British Archaeological Conference Transactions*, 17 (1996), 95–9.

Jeanroy, A., 'Un sirventès historique de 1242', in *Mélanges Léonce Couture* (Toulouse, 1902), 115–25.

Jeanroy, A., 'Un sirventès politique de 1230', in *Mélanges d'Histoire du Moyen Âge offerts à M. Ferdinand Lot par ses amis et ses élèves* (Paris, 1925), 275–83.

Jobson, A., *The First English Revolution: Simon de Montfort, Henry III and the Barons' War* (London, 2012).

Jobson, A., 'A queen in the shadows: Sanchia of Provence, Richard of Cornwall and a royal life unveiled', *Women's History Review*, forthcoming.

Jolliffe, J.E.A., *Angevin Kingship*, 2nd edition (London, 1963).

Jolliffe, J.E.A., 'The chamber and the castle treasures under King John', in *Studies in Medieval History presented to Frederick Maurice Powicke*, ed. R.W. Hunt (Oxford, 1948), 117–42.

Jones, R.R., *St Nicholas Church Grosmont Monmouthshire* (St Nicholas Church Grosmont, Parochial Church Council, 2011)

Jordan, W.C., *Louis IX and the Challenge of the Crusade: A Study in Rulership* (Princeton, NJ, 1979).

Jordan, W.C., *The French Monarchy and the Jews: From Philip Augustus to the Last Capetians* (Philadelphia, PA, 1989).

Jordan, W.C., *A Tale of Two Monasteries: Westminster and Saint Denis in the Thirteenth Century* (Princeton and Oxford, 2009).

Julian-Jones, M., 'The land of the raven and the wolf: family power and strategy in the Welsh March c.1199–1300 – The Corbets and Cantilupes' (Cardiff University, doctoral thesis, 2015).

Kanter, J.E., 'The four knights system and the evidence for it in the fine rolls', Henry III Fine Rolls Project, Fine of the Month for March 2007: https://finerollshenry3.org.uk/content/month/fm-03-2007.html.

Kanter, J.E., 'The relationship between business transacted in the fine rolls and the royal itinerary in 1252', Henry III Fine Rolls Project, Fine of the Month for March 2010: https://finerollshenry3.org.uk/content/month/fm-03-2010.html.

Kanter, J.E., 'Peripatetic and sedentary kingship: the itineraries of the thirteenth-century English kings' (King's College London, doctoral thesis, 2011).

Kanter, J.E., 'Peripatetic and sedentary kingship: the itineraries of John and Henry III', in *Thirteenth Century England*, 13 (Woodbridge, 2011), 11–26.

Kantorowicz, E.H., *Laudes Regiae: A Study in Liturgical Acclamations and Medieval Ruler Worship* (Berkeley and Los Angeles, CA, 1946).

Kay, R., 'Wendover's last annal', *English Historical Review*, 84 (1969), 779–85.

Keen, L., 'The chapter house decorated tile pavement', in *Westminster Abbey Chapter House: The History, Art and Architecture of 'A Chapter House beyond Compare'*, eds. W.J. Rodwell and R. Mortimer (London, 2010), 209–36.

Kellett, A., 'King John in Knaresborough: the first known royal Maundy', *Yorkshire Archaeological Journal*, 62 (1990), 69–90.

Kjær, L., 'Matthew Paris and the Royal Christmas: Ritualised Communication in Text and Practice', in *Thirteenth Century England*, 14 (Woodbridge, 2013), 141–54.

Knight, J.K., *The Three Castles: Grosmont, Skenfrith, White Castle*, revised edition (Cardiff, 2009).

Labarge, M.W., *Simon de Montfort* (London, 1962).

Lachaud, F., *L'Éthique du Pouvoir au Moyen Âge: L'office dans la culture politique (Angleterre, vers 1150–1330)*, (Paris, 2010).

Lachaud, F., 'Liveries of robes in England, c.1200–c.1330', *English Historical Review*, 111 (1996), 279–98.

Lachaud, F., and Marguin-Hamon, E., 'Mouvement réformateur et mémoire de Pierre de Wakefield en Angleterre au milieu de XIII siècle: L'"Invective contre le Roi Jean"', *Archives d'Histoire Doctrinal et Littéraire du Moyen Age*, 85 (2018), 149–201.

Langmuir, G.I., 'The knight's tale of young Hugh of Lincoln', *Speculum*, 47 (1972), 459–82.

Latimer, P., 'The English inflation of 1180–1220 reconsidered', *Past & Present*, 171 (2001), 3–29.

Latimer, P., 'The quantity of money in England 1180–1247: a model', *Journal of European Economic History*, 32 (2003), 637–59.

Lavisse, E., *Histoire de France depuis les Origines jusqu'à la Revolution*, 9 vols. (1902–26).

Lawrence, C.H., *St Edmund of Abingdon: A Study in Hagiography and History* (Oxford, 1960).

Lawrence, C.H., 'John of Darlington (d.1284), archbishop', *Oxford Dictionary of National Biography* (2004): https://doi.org/10.1093/ref:odnb/7159.

Le Goff, J., *La Naissance du Purgatoire* (Paris, 1981).

Le Goff, J., *Saint Louis* (Paris, 1996).

Le Pogam, P.-Y., and Vivet-Peclet, C., *Saint Louis*, exhibition catalogue (Paris, 2014).

Lethaby, W.R., *Westminster Abbey & the Kings' Craftsmen: A Study of Medieval Building* (London, 1906).

Lethaby, W.R., *Westminster Abbey Re-Examined* (London, 1925).

Letters, S., 'The Seagrave family c.1160–1295, with an edition of the calendar of the Seagrave cartulary' (University of London, doctoral thesis, 1997).

Lewis, S., *The Art of Matthew Paris in the Chronica Majora* (Berkeley and Los Angeles, CA, 1987).

Liddiard, R., *Castles in Context: Power, Symbolism and Landscape, 1066–1500* (Bollington, 2005).

Lightfoot, K.W.B., 'The household knights of King Henry III, 1216–1272' (University of Swansea, doctoral thesis, 2006).

Lipman, V.D., *The Jews of Medieval Norwich: With an Appendix of Latin Documents from the Westminster Abbey Muniment Room; and the Hebrew Poems of Meir of Norwich* (London, 1967).

Liu, H., 'John Mansel, councillor of Henry III: his life and career' (University of London, doctoral thesis, 2004).

Liu, H., 'Matthew Paris and John Mansel', in *Thirteenth Century England*, 11 (Woodbridge, 2007), 159–73.

Lloyd, J.E., *A History of Wales from the Earliest Times to the Edwardian Conquest*, 2 vols. (London, 1911).

Lloyd, S., *English Society and the Crusade, 1216–1307* (Oxford, 1988).

Lloyd, S., 'Sir William Longespée (c.1209–1250), magnate', *Oxford Dictionary of National Biography* (2004): https://doi.org/10.1093/ref:odnb/16984.

Lodge, L.A., 'Language attitudes and linguistic norms in France and England in the thirteenth-century', in *Thirteenth Century England*, 4 (Woodbridge, 1992), 73–83.

Lowden, J., *The Making of the Bibles Moralisées*, 2 vols. (University Park, 2000).

Lunt, W.E., *Financial Relations of the Papacy with England to 1327* (Cambridge, MA, 1939).

Lydon, J.F., 'Edward II and the revenues of Ireland in 1311–12', *Irish Historical Studies*, 45, (1964), 39–57.

Lydon, J.F., 'Three exchequer documents from the reign of Henry III', *Proceedings of the Royal Irish Academy: Archaeology, Culture, History, Literature*, 65 (1966–7), 1–27.

McKitterick, D., ed., *The Trinity Apocalypse* (London, 2005).

MacKay, A., *Spain in the Middle Ages: From Frontier to Empire, 1100–1500* (Basingstoke and London, 1977).

Macmillan, H., *The Blast of War 1939–1945* (London, 1967).

Maddicott, J.R., *Law and Lordship: Royal Justices as Retainers in Thirteenth- and Fourteenth-Century England*, in *Past & Present*, suppl.4 (1978).

Maddicott, J.R., *Simon de Montfort* (Cambridge, 1994).

Maddicott, J.R., *The Origins of the English Parliament, 924–1327* (Oxford, 2010).

Maddicott, J.R., 'Magna Carta and the local community, 1215–1259', *Past & Present*, 102 (1984), 25–65.

Maddicott, J.R., '"An infinite number of nobles": quality, quantity and politics in the pre-reform parliaments of Henry III', in *Thirteenth Century England*, 7 (Woodbridge, 1999), 1–16.

Maddicott, J.R., 'The earliest known knights of the shire: new light on the parliament of April 1254', *Parliamentary History*, 18 (1999), 109–30.

Maddicott, J.R., '"1258" and "1297": some comparisons and contrasts', in *Thirteenth Century England*, 9 (Woodbridge, 2003), 1–14.

Maddicott, J.R., 'The oath of Marlborough, 1209: fear, government and popular allegiance in the reign of King John', *English Historical Review*, 126 (2011), 281–318.

Maddison, J., 'The Gothic cathedral: new building in a historical context', in *A History of Ely Cathedral*, eds. P. Meadows and N. Ramsey (Woodbridge, 2003), 113–42.

Madox, T., *The History and Antiquities of the Exchequer of the Kings of England, in two periods: To wit, from the Norman Conquest, to the end of the Reign of King John; and from the end of the Reign of King John, to the end of the Reign of King Edward II*, 2nd edition, 2 vols. (London, 1769).

Maitland, F.W., *The Collected Papers of Frederic William Maitland*, ed. H.A.L. Fisher, 3 vols. (Cambridge, 1911).

Marsh, F.B., *English Rule in Gascony, 1199–1259, with Special Reference to the Towns* (Ann Arbor, MI, 1912).

Mason, E., 'The resources of the earldom of Warwick in the thirteenth-century', *Midland History*, 3 (1975), 67–76.

Maxwell-Lyte, H.C., *Historical Notes on the Use of the Great Seal of England* (London, 1926).

Mayhew, N.J., 'Coinage and money in England, 1086–c.1500', in *Medieval Money Matters*, ed. D.S. Wood (Oxford, 2004), 72–86.

Meekings, C.A.F., *Studies in 13th-Century Justice and Administration* (London, 1981).

Meekings, C.A.F., and Crook, D., *King's Bench and Common Bench in the Reign of Henry III* (Selden Society, supplementary series, 17, 2010).

Mitchell, S.K., *Studies in Taxation under John and Henry III* (New Haven, CT, 1914).

Montaubin, P., 'Royaume de Sicile, Capétiens et Plantagenets: la mission et légation d'Alberto da Parma en 1252–1255', in *Legati e Delegati Papali: Profili, Ambiti d'Azione e Tipologie di Intervento nei Secoli XII e XIII*, eds. M.P. Alberzoni and C. Zey (Milan, 2012), 159–94.

Moore, T.K., 'The Thorrington dispute: a case study of Henry III's interference with judicial process', Henry III Fine Rolls Project, Fine of the Month for July 2009: https://finerollshenry3.org.uk/content/month/fm-07-2009.html.

Moore, T.K., 'The loss of Normandy and the invention of *Terre Normannorum*, 1204', *English Historical Review*, 125 (2010), 1071–109.

Moore, T.K., 'The fine rolls as evidence for the expansion of royal justice during the reign of Henry III', in *The Growth of Royal Government under Henry III*, eds. D. Crook and L.J. Wilkinson (Woodbridge, 2015).

Morgan, N.J., 'The introduction of the Sarum calendar into the dioceses of England in the thirteenth-century', in *Thirteenth Century England*, 8 (Woodbridge, 2001), 179–206.

Morgan, N.J., 'Illustrated apocalypses of mid thirteenth-century England: historical context, patronage and readership', in *The Trinity Apocalypse*, ed. D. McKitterick (London, 2005), 3–22.

Morris, M., *The Bigod Earls of Norfolk in the Thirteenth Century* (Woodbridge, 2005).

Morris, M., *A Great and Terrible King: Edward I and the Forging of Britain* (London, 2008).

Morris, M., *King John: Treachery, Tyranny and the Road to Magna Carta* (London, 2015).

Mortimer, R., *Angevin England 1154–1258* (Oxford, 1994).

Musson, A., *Medieval Law in Context: The Growth of Legal Consciousness from Magna Carta to the Peasants' Revolt* (Manchester, 2001).

Musson, A., 'Reappraisal of the "four knights" system', in *English Government in the Thirteenth Century*, ed. A. Jobson (Woodbridge, 2004), 97–111.

Norgate, K., *The Minority of Henry III* (London, 1912).

O'Brien, B.R., *God's Peace and King's Peace: The Laws of Edward the Confessor* (Philadelphia, 1999).

Oggins, R.S., *The Kings and their Hawks: Falconry in Medieval England* (New Haven, CT, and London, 2004).

Orme, N.I., *From Childhood to Chivalry: The Education of the English Kings and Aristocracy, 1066–1530* (London, 1984).

Ormrod, W.M., *Edward III* (New Haven and London, 2013).

Orpen, G.H., *Ireland under the Normans, 1169–1333*, 4 vols. (Oxford, 1911).

Painter, S., *William Marshal: Knight-Errant, Baron, and Regent of England* (Baltimore, MD, 1933).

Painter, S., *The Scourge of the Clergy: Peter of Dreux, Duke of Brittany* (Baltimore, MD, 1937).

Painter, S., *Studies in the History of the English Feudal Barony* (Baltimore, MD, 1943).

Palmer, R.C., *The County Courts of Medieval England 1150–1350* (Princeton, NJ, 1982).

Parnell, G., *The Tower of London* (London, 1993).

Pelissie du Rausas, A., 'Voices from the archives: reassembling the dossier of Gascon complaints against Simon de Montfort (1252): A study in Anglo-Gascon history' (King's College London, master's thesis, 2013).

Pelissie du Rausas, A., 'Promesses de Gascons: les pratiques du pouvoir en Gascogne anglaise à partir du procès de Simon de Montfort, 1252', in *Aux Sources du Pouvoir: Voir, Approcher, Comprendre le Pouvoir Politique au Moyen Âge*, ed. S. Gouguenheim (Paris, 2017), 197–222.

Pelissie du Rausas, A., 'Ad partes transmarinas: The reconfiguration of Plantagenet power in Gascony, 1242–1243', in *Thirteenth Century England*, 17 (Woodbridge, forthcoming).

Pelissie du Rausas, A., 'De guerre, de trêve, de paix: Les relations franco-anglaises sous Louis IX et Henri III de la bataille de Taillebourg au traité de Paris, 1242–1259', (University of Poitiers, doctoral thesis), forthcoming.

Pelissie du Rausas, A., 'Un croisé en Gascogne. Simon VI de Montfort et la Gascogne Plantagenêt, 1248–1252', in *Simon de Montfort (†1218): Le Croisé, son Lignage et son Temps*, eds. M. Aurell, G. Lippiatt and L. Macé (Turnhout, forthcoming).

Peters, E.M., *The Shadow King: Rex Inutilis in Medieval Law and Literature, 741–1327* (New Haven, CT, and London, 1970).

Petit-Dutaillis, C., *Étude sur La Vie et le Règne de Louis VIII (1187–1226)* (Paris, 1894).

Piper, A.J., 'Writs of summons of 1246, 1247 and 1255', *Bulletin of the Institute of Historical Research*, 49 (1976), 284–6.

Piper, A.J., 'Walter of Kirkham (d.1260), administrator and bishop of Durham', *Oxford Dictionary of National Biography* (2004): https://doi.org/10.1093/ref:odnb/15668.

Pollock, F., and Maitland, F.W., *The History of English Law before the Time of Edward I*, 2nd edition, 2 vols. (Cambridge, 1968).

Poole, A.L., *From Domesday Book to Magna Carta, 1087–1216* (Oxford, 1951).

Poulton, R., ed., *A Medieval Royal Complex at Guildford: Excavations at the Castle and Palace* (Surrey Archaeological Society, 2005).

Power, D., 'The French interests of the Marshal earls of Striguil and Pembroke, 1189–1234', in *Anglo-Norman Studies XXV: Proceedings of the Battle Conference, 2002*, ed. J. Gillingham (Woodbridge, 2003), 199–216.

Power, D., 'The treaty of Paris (1259) and the aristocracy of England and Normandy', in *Thirteenth Century England*, 13 (Woodbridge, 2011), 141–58.

Powicke, F.M., *Stephen Langton* (Oxford, 1928).

Powicke, F.M., *King Henry III and the Lord Edward: The Community of the Realm in the Thirteenth Century*, 2 vols. (Oxford, 1947).

Powicke, F.M., *The Thirteenth Century, 1216–1307* (Oxford, 1953).

Powicke, F.M., *The Loss of Normandy (1189–1204): Studies in the History of the Angevin Empire*, 2nd edition (Manchester, 1961).

Prestwich, J.O., 'The military household of the Norman kings', *English Historical Review*, 96 (1981), 1–35.

Prestwich, M.C., *War, Politics and Finance under Edward I* (London, 1972).

Prestwich, M.C., *Edward I* (London, 1988).

Prestwich, M.C., *Armies and Warfare in the Middle Ages: The English Experience* (New Haven, CT, and London, 1996).

Prestwich, M.C., *Plantagenet England, 1225–1360* (Oxford, 2005).

Prestwich, M.C., 'The piety of Edward I', in *England in the Thirteenth Century*, ed. W.M. Ormrod (Stamford, 1985), 120–8.

Prestwich, M.C., 'The court of Edward II', in *The Reign of Edward II: New Perspectives*, eds. G. Dodd and A.J. Musson (Woodbridge, 2006), 61–75.

Prestwich, M.C., 'The royal itinerary and roads in England under Edward I', in *Roadworks: Medieval Britain, Medieval Roads*, eds. V. Allen and R. Evans (Manchester, 2016).

Pryce, H., 'Negotiating Anglo-Welsh relations: Llywelyn the Great and Henry III', in *England and Europe in the Reign of Henry III (1216–1272)*, eds. B.K.U. Weiler and I.W. Rowlands (Aldershot, 2002), 163–82.

Ramsay, J.H., *The Dawn of the Constitution; or the Reigns of Henry III and Edward I, A.D. 1216–1307* (Oxford, 1908).

Ramsay, J.H., *A History of the Revenues of the Kings of England 1066–1399*, 2 vols. (Oxford, 1925).

Ray, M., 'Alien courtiers of thirteenth-century England and their assimilation' (University of London, doctoral thesis, 2003).

Ray, M., 'Three alien royal stewards in thirteenth-century England: the careers and legacy of Mathias Bezill, Imbert Pugeys and Peter de Champvent', in *Thirteenth Century England*, 10 (Woodbridge, 2005), 50–70.

Ray, M., 'A Vaudois servant of Henry III, Ebal II de Mont (Ebulo de Montibus)': https://www.academia.edu/31930999/A_Vaudois_servant_of_Henry_III_Ebal_II_de_Mont_Ebulo_de_Montibus.

Ray, M., 'The lady doth protest: the marriage of John de Plessis and Margery, countess of Warwick in 1243': https://www.academia.edu/4318307/The_Lady_doth_protest_the_Marriage_of_John_de_Plessis_and_Margery_Countess_of_Warwick_1243.

Richardson, H.G., *The English Jewry under the Angevin Kings* (London, 1960).

Richardson, H.G., 'Glanvill continued', *Law Quarterly Review*, 54 (1938), 381–99.

Richardson, H.G., 'The coronation in medieval England: the evolution of the office and the oath', *Traditio*, 16 (1960), 111–202.

Richardson, H.G., 'The earliest known official use of the term "parliament"', in *The English Parliament in the Middle Ages*, eds. H.G. Richardson and G.O. Sayles (London, 1981), 747–50.

Richardson, H.G., and Sayles, G.O., *The Irish Parliament in the Middle Ages* (Philadelphia, PA, 1952).

Richter, M., 'David ap Llywelyn, the first prince of Wales', *Welsh History Review*, 5 (1971), 205–19.

Ridgeway, H.W., 'The politics of the English royal court, 1247–1265, with special reference to the role of the aliens' (University of Oxford, doctoral thesis, 1983).

Ridgeway, H.W., 'The Lord Edward and the Provisions of Oxford (1258): a study in faction', in *Thirteenth Century England*, 1 (Woodbridge, 1986), 89–99.

Ridgeway, H.W., 'King Henry III and the "aliens" 1236–1272', in *Thirteenth Century England*, 2 (Woodbridge, 1988), 81–92.

Ridgeway, H.W., 'Foreign favourites and Henry III's problems of patronage, 1247–1258', *English Historical Review*, 104 (1989), 590–610.

Ridgeway, H.W., 'William de Valence and his "familiares", 1247–72', *Historical Research*, 65 (1992), 239–57.

Ridgeway, H.W., 'The ecclesiastical career of Aymer de Lusignan, bishop elect of Winchester, 1250–1260', in *The Cloister and the World: Essays in Medieval History in Honour of Barbara Harvey*, eds. J. Blair and B.J. Golding (Oxford, 1996), 148–77.

Ridgeway, H.W., 'Henry III (1207–1272), king of England, lord of Ireland, and duke of Aquitaine, *Oxford Dictionary of National Biography* (2004): https://doi.org/10.1093/ref:odnb/12950.

Ridgeway, H.W., 'Dorset in the period of baronial reform and rebellion 1258–1267', *Historical Research*, 87 (2014), 18–42.

Ridgeway, H.W., 'An English cartulary roll of Peter of Savoy', forthcoming.

Rigold, S.E., 'The medieval hospital', in *Maison Dieu Ospringe Kent* (London, 1995), 3–14.

Roberts, M.E., 'The relic of the Holy Blood and the iconography of the thirteenth-century north transept portal of Westminster Abbey', in *England in the Thirteenth Century*, ed. W.M. Ormrod (Stamford, 1985), 129–42.

Rodwell, W.J., and Mortimer, R., eds., *Westminster Abbey Chapter House: The History, Art and Architecture of 'A Chapter House beyond Compare'* (London, 2010).

Roffe, D., 'The hundred rolls of 1255', *Historical Research*, 69 (1996), 201–10.

Ross, D.J.A., 'A lost painting in Henry III's palace at Westminster', *Journal of the Warburg and Courtauld Institutes*, 16 (1953), 160.

Rosser, G., *Medieval Westminster: 1200–1540* (Oxford, 1989).

Rubin, M., *Charity and Community in Medieval Cambridge* (Cambridge, 1987).

Rubin, M., *Corpus Christi: The Eucharist in Late Medieval Culture* (Cambridge, 1992).

Russell, J.C., 'Master Henry of Avranches as an international poet', *Speculum*, 3 (1928), 34–63.

Sabapathy, J., *Officers and Accountability in Medieval England, 1170–1300* (Oxford, 2014).

Sanders, I.J., *Feudal Military Service in England: A Study of the Constitutional and Military Powers of the Barons in Medieval England* (London, 1956).

Sanders, I.J., *English Baronies: A Study of their Origin and Descent, 1086–1327* (Oxford, 1960).

Saul, N.E., 'Richard II and the vocabulary of kingship', *English Historical Review*, 110 (1995), 854–77.

Schulman, N.M., 'Husband, father, bishop? Grosseteste in Paris', *Speculum*, 72 (1997), 330–46.

Scott, G.G., *Gleanings from Westminster Abbey* (Oxford and London, 1861).

Seabourne, G.C., 'Eleanor of Brittany and her treatment by King John and Henry III', *Nottingham Medieval Studies*, 51 (2007), 73–111.

Shacklock, A., 'Politics and devotion: Henry III and the use of native saints', in *Thirteenth Century England*, 17 (Woodbridge, forthcoming).

Short, I., 'On bilingualism in Anglo-Norman England', *Romance Philology*, 33 (1980), 467–79.

Short, I., 'Introduction', in *The Trinity Apocalypse*, ed. D. McKitterick (London, 2005), 123–38.

Simpson, G.G., 'The declaration of Arbroath revitalised', *Scottish Historical Review*, 56 (1977), 11–33.

Smalley, B., 'Robert Bacon and the early Dominican school at Oxford', *Transactions of the Royal Historical Society*, 4th series, 30 (1948), 1–19.

Smith, B., 'Irish politics, 1220–1245', in *Thirteenth Century England*, 8 (Woodbridge, 2001), 13–22.

Smith, J.B., *Llywelyn ap Gruffudd: Prince of Wales* (Cardiff, 2014).

Snellgrove, H.S., *The Lusignans in England 1247–1258* (Albuquerque, 1950).

Southern, R.W., *Robert Grosseteste: The Growth of an English Mind in Medieval Europe* (Oxford, 1986).

Spencer, A.M., *Nobility and Kingship in Medieval England: The Earls of Edward I, 1272–1307* (Cambridge, 2014).

Spencer, A.M., 'Dealing with inadequate kingship: uncertain responses from Magna Carta to deposition, 1199–1327', *Thirteenth Century England*, 16 (Woodbridge, 2017), 71–87.

Spencer, A.M., '"A vineyard without a wall": the Savoyards, John de Warenne and the failure of Henry III's kingship', in *Thirteenth Century England*, 17 (Woodbridge, forthcoming).

Spurgeon, C.J., 'Hubert's Folly: the abortive castle of the Kerry campaign, 1228', in *The Medieval Castle in Ireland and Wales: Essays in Honour of Jeremy Knight*, ed. J.R. Kenyon and C. O'Conor (Dublin, 2003).

Stacey, R.C., *Politics, Policy and Finance under Henry III, 1216–1245* (Oxford, 1987).

Stacey, R.C., '1240–60: a watershed in Anglo-Jewish relations?', *Historical Research*, 61 (1988), 135–50.

Stacey, R.C., 'Crusades, crusaders, and the baronial gravamina of 1263–1264', in *Thirteenth Century England*, 3 (Woodbridge, 1991), 137–50.

Stacey, R.C., 'The conversion of Jews to Christianity in thirteenth-century England', *Speculum*, 67 (1992), 263–83.

Stacey, R.C., 'Peter Chaceporc (d.1254), administrator', *Oxford Dictionary of National Biography* (2004): https://doi.org/10.1093/ref:odnb/5009.

Stacey, R.C., '"Adam of Bristol" and tales of ritual crucifixion in medieval England', in *Thirteenth Century England*, 11 (Woodbridge, 2007), 1–15.

Staniland, K., 'The nuptials of Alexander III of Scotland and Margaret Plantagenet', *Nottingham Medieval Studies*, 30 (1986), 20–45.

Stanley, A.P., 'On an examination of the tombs of Richard II and Henry III in Westminster Abbey', *Archaeologia*, 45 (1880), 309–27.

Steel, A., 'The itinerary of Henry III, 1244–1252' (King's College London, undergraduate long essay).

Stevenson, W.B., 'England and Normandy, 1204–1259' (University of Leeds, doctoral thesis, 1976).

Stewart, S.M., 'What happened at Shere?', *Southern History*, 22 (2000), 1–20.

Stewart, Z., 'A lesson in patronage: King Henry III, the knights templar, and a royal mausoleum at the Temple Church in London', *Speculum*, 94 (2019), 334–84.

Stewart-Brown, R., 'The end of the Norman earldom of Chester', *English Historical Review*, 35 (1920), 26–54.

Stewart-Parker, 'The Bassets of High Wycombe: politics, lordship, locality and culture in the thirteenth century' (King's College London, doctoral thesis, 2015).

Stokes, E., 'Moels', in Cokayne, *Complete Peerage*, ix, 1–4.

Stone, I., 'The book of Arnold fitz Thedmar' (King's College London, doctoral thesis, 2016).

Strayer, J.R., *The Administration of Normandy under Saint Louis* (Cambridge, MA, 1932).

Strickland, M., 'William Longespée, third earl of Salisbury', *Oxford Dictionary of National Biography* (2004): https://doi.org/10.1093/ref:odnb/16983.

Studd, J.R., 'The Lord Edward and King Henry III', *Bulletin of the Institute of Historical Research*, 50 (1977), 4–19.

Studd, J.R., 'The Lord Edward's lordship of Chester, 1254–72', *Transactions of the Historic Society of Lancashire and Cheshire*, 128 (1979), 1–25.

Studd, J.R., 'Reconfiguring the Angevin empire, 1224–1259', in *England and Europe in the Reign of Henry III (1216–1272)*, eds. B.K.U. Weiler and I.W. Rowlands (Aldershot, 2002), 31–42.

Summerson, H.R.T., 'The structure of law enforcement in thirteenth-century England', *American Journal of Legal Studies*, 23 (1979), 313–27.

Summerson, H.R.T., 'The king's *clericus*: the life and career of Silvester de Everdon, bishop of Carlisle, 1247–1254', *Northern History*, 28 (1992), 70–91.

Sutherland, D.W., *Quo Warranto Proceedings in the Reign of Edward I, 1278–1294* (Oxford, 1963).

Tatton-Brown, T., and Crook, J., *Salisbury Cathedral: The Making of a Medieval Masterpiece* (London, 2009).

Taylor, A., *The Shape of the State in Medieval Scotland 1124–1290* (Oxford, 2016).

Taylor, A., 'Historical writing in twelfth- and thirteenth-century Scotland: the Dunfermline compilation', *Historical Research*, 83 (2010), 228–52.

Thomas, H.M., *The English and the Normans: Ethnic Hostility, Assimilation and Identity 1066–c.1220* (Oxford, 2003).

Thomas, H.M., *A Social and Cultural History of the Court of King John of England, 1199–1216*, forthcoming.

Thurston, H., *Maundy Thursday* (London, 1936).

Titow, J.Z., *English Rural Society, 1200–1350* (London, 1969).

Tout, T.F., *Chapters in the Administrative History of Mediaeval England: The Wardrobe, the Chamber and the Small Seals*, 6 vols. (Manchester, 1920–33).

Trabut-Cussac, J.-P., *L'administration anglaise en Gascogne sous Henry III et Édouard I de 1254 à 1307* (Geneva, 1972).

Trabut-Cussac, J.-P., 'Les coutumes ou droits de douanes perçus à Bordeaux sur les vins et les marchandises par l'administration anglaise de 1252 à 1307', *Annales du Midi*, 62 (1950), 135–50.

Turner, R.V., *The King and his Courts: The Roll of John and Henry III in the Administration of Justice, 1199–1240* (Ithaca, New York, 1968).

Turner, R.V., *The English Judiciary in the Age of Glanvill and Bracton, c.1176–1239* (Cambridge, 1985).

Turner, R.V., *Men Raised from the Dust: Administrative Service and Upward Mobility in Angevin England* (Philadelphia, PA, 1988).

Turner, R.V., *King John* (London and New York, 1994).

Tyerman, C., *England and the Crusades, 1095–1588* (Chicago, IL, and London, 1988).

Vale, M., *The Angevin Legacy and the Hundred Years War* (Oxford, 1990).

Vale, M., *The Princely Court: Medieval Courts and Culture in North-West Europe, 1270–1380* (Oxford, 2001).

Valente, C., *The Theory and Practice of Revolt in Medieval England* (Farnham, 2003).

Van Cleve, T.C., *The Emperor Frederick II of Hohenstaufen, Immutator Mundi* (Oxford, 1972).

Vasselot de Regne, C., 'Le "Parentat" Lusignan (Xe–XIVe siècles), structures, parenté vécue, solidarités et pouvoir d'un lignage arborescent', 2 vols. (University of Nantes, doctoral thesis, 2018).

Vaughan, R., *Matthew Paris* (Oxford, 1958).

Vincent, N., *Peter des Roches: An Alien in English Politics, 1205–1238* (Cambridge, 1996).

Vincent, N., *The Holy Blood: King Henry III and the Westminster Blood Relic* (Cambridge, 2001).

Vincent, N., *A Brief History of Britain 1066–1485* (London, 2011).

Vincent, N., 'Jews, Poitevins and the bishop of Winchester', in *Christianity and Judaism*, ed. D.S. Wood, *Studies in Church History*, 29 (1992), 119–32.

Vincent, N., 'Simon de Montfort's first quarrel with King Henry III', in *Thirteenth Century England*, 4 (Woodbridge, 1992), 167–77.

Vincent, N., 'Isabella of Angoulême: John's Jezebel', in *King John: New Interpretations*, ed. S.D. Church (Woodbridge, 1999), 165–219.

Vincent, N., 'The pilgrimages of the Angevin kings of England, 1154–1272', in *Pilgrimage: The English Experience from Becket to Bunyan*, eds. C. Morris and P. Roberts (Cambridge, 2002), 12–45.

Vincent, N., 'The politics of church and state as reflected in the Winchester pipe rolls, 1208–1280', in *The Winchester Pipe Rolls and Medieval English Society*, ed. R.H. Britnell (Woodbridge, 2003), 157–82.

Vincent, N., 'King Henry III and the Blessed Virgin Mary', in *The Church and Mary*, ed. R.N. Swanson, *Studies in Church History*, 39 (2006), 126–46.

Vincent, N., 'A forgotten war: England and Navarre, 1243–4', in *Thirteenth Century England*, 11 (Woodbridge, 2007), 109–46.

Vincent, N., 'The court of Henry II', in *Henry II: New Interpretations*, eds. C. Harper-Bill and N. Vincent (Woodbridge, 2007), 278–334.

Vincent, N., 'Stephen Langton, archbishop of Canterbury', in *Étienne Langton, Prédicateur, Bibliste, Théologien*, eds. L.-J. Bataillon, N. Bériou, G. Dahan and R. Quinto (Turnhout, 2010), 51–123.

Vincent, N., 'The thirteenth century', in *Ely: Bishops and Diocese, 1109–2009*, ed. P. Meadows (Woodbridge, 2010), 26–69.

Vincent, N., 'An inventory of gifts to King Henry III, 1234–5', in *The Growth of Royal Government under Henry III*, eds. D. Crook and L.J. Wilkinson (Woodbridge, 2015), 121–48.

Vincent, N., 'Meeting and greeting kings of England', forthcoming.

Vincent, N., 'Royal diplomatic and the shape of the English state, 1066–1300', forthcoming.

Vincent, N., 'Henry III, Frederick II and the council of Lyons', unpublished paper.

Von Wurstemberger, L., *Peter der Zweite, Graf von Savoyen, Markgraf in Italien: Sein Haus und seine Lande; ein Charakterbild des Dreizehnten Jahrhunderts*, 4 vols. (Bern, 1856–8).

Wait, H.A., 'The household and resources of the Lord Edward, 1239–72' (University of Oxford, doctoral thesis, 1988).

Walker, R.F., 'The Anglo-Welsh wars, 1217–67' (University of Oxford, doctoral thesis, 1954).

Walker, R.F., 'Hubert de Burgh and Wales, 1218–1232', *English Historical Review*, 87 (1972), 465–94.

Walker, R.F., 'The supporters of Richard Marshal, earl of Pembroke, in the rebellion of 1233–1234', *Welsh History Review*, 17 (1994), 41–65.

Warren, W.L., *King John* (London, 1961).

Warren, W.L., *Henry II* (London, 1973).

Watkins, C.S., *History and the Supernatural in Medieval England* (Cambridge, 2007).

Watt, J.A., 'The English episcopate, the state and the Jews: the evidence of the thirteenth-century conciliar decrees', in *Thirteenth Century England*, 2 (Woodbridge, 1988), 137–47.

Waugh, S.L., *The Lordship of England: Royal Wardships and Marriages in English Society and Politics, 1217–1327* (Princeton, NJ, 1988).

Waugh, S.L., 'Reluctant knights and jurors: respites, exemptions and public obligations in the reign of Henry III', *Speculum*, 58 (1983), 937–86.

Waugh, S.L., 'The origins and early development of the articles of the escheator', *Thirteenth Century England*, 5 (Woodbridge, 1995), 89–114.

Waugh, S.L., 'The origins of the office of escheator', in *The Growth of Royal Government under Henry III*, eds. D. Crook and L.J. Wilkinson (Woodbridge, 2015), 227–65.

Webb, D.M., *Pilgrimage in Medieval England* (London, 2000).

Webb, G., *Architecture in Britain: The Middle Ages* (Harmondsworth, 1956).

Webster, P., *King John and Religion* (Woodbridge, 2015).

Weiler, B., *Henry III of England and the Staufen Empire, 1216–1272* (Woodbridge, 2006).

Weiler, B., *Kingship, Rebellion and Political Culture: England and Germany, c.1215–c.1250* (London, 2007).

Weiler, B., 'Image and reality in Richard of Cornwall's German career', *English Historical Review*, 113 (1998), 1111–42.

Weiler, B., 'Henry III and the Sicilian business: a reinterpretation', *Historical Research*, 74 (2001), 127–50.

Weiler, B., 'Symbolism and politics in the reign of Henry III', in *Thirteenth Century England*, 9 (Woodbridge, 2003), 15–42.

Weiler, B., 'Matthew Paris on the writing of history', *Journal of Medieval History*, 35 (2009), 254–78.

Weiler, B., 'History, prophecy and the apocalypse in the chronicles of Matthew Paris', *English Historical Review*, 133 (2018), 253–83.

Whitwell, R.J., 'The revenue and expenditure of England under Henry III', *English Historical Review*, 18 (1903), 710–11.

Wild, B.L., 'A gift inventory from the reign of Henry III', *English Historical Review*, 125 (2010), 529–59.

Wild, B.L., 'Secrecy, splendour and statecraft: the jewel accounts of King Henry III of England, 1216–72', *Historical Research*, 83 (2010), 409–31.

Wild, B.L., 'A captive king: Henry III between the battles of Lewes and Evesham, 1264–5', in *Thirteenth Century England*, 13 (Woodbridge, 2011), 41–56.

Wild, B.L., 'A truly royal retinue: using wardrobe rolls to determine the size and composition of the household of Henry III of England', *The Court Historian*, 16 (2011), 127–57.

Wild, B.L., 'Emblems and enigmas: revisiting the "sword" belt of Fernando de la Cerda', *Journal of Medieval History*, 37 (2011), 378–96.

Wild, B.L., 'The empress's new clothes: a *rotulus pannorum* of Isabella, sister of King Henry III, bride of Emperor Frederick II', in *Medieval Clothing and Textiles VII*, eds. G. Owen-Crocker and R. Netherton (Woodbridge, 2011), 1–31.

Wild, B.L., 'Royal finance under King Henry III, 1216–72: the wardrobe evidence', *Economic History Review*, 65 (2012), 1380–1402.

Wilkinson, L.J., *Eleanor de Montfort: A Rebel Countess in Medieval England* (London, 2012).

Wilkinson, L.J., 'The imperial marriage of Isabella of England, Henry III's sister', in *The Rituals and Rhetoric of Queenship: Medieval to Early Modern*, eds. L. Oakley-Brown and L.J. Wilkinson (Dublin, 2009), 20–36.

Williams, G.A., *Medieval London: From Commune to Capital* (London, 1963).

Williams, G.A., 'The succession to Gwynedd, 1238–1247', *Bulletin of the Board of Celtic Studies*, 20 (1964), 393–413.

Williamson, D.M., 'Some aspects of the legation of cardinal Otto in England, 1237–41', *English Historical Review*, 64 (1949), 145–74.

Wilson, C., 'Calling the tune? The involvement of King Henry III in the design of the abbey church at Westminster', *Journal of the British Archaeological Association*, 161 (2008), 59–93.

Wilson, C., 'The chapter house at Westminster Abbey: harbinger of a new dispensation in English architecture?', in *Westminster Abbey Chapter House: The History, Art and Architecture of 'A Chapter House beyond Compare'*, eds. W.J. Rodwell and R. Mortimer (London, 2010), 40–65.

Wilson, C., 'A monument to St Edward the Confessor: Henry III's great chamber at Westminster and its paintings', in *Westminster: The Art, Architecture and Archaeology of the Royal Palace and Abbey, part 2*, eds. W.J. Rodwell and T. Tatton-Brown, *British Archaeological Association Conference Transactions*, 39 (2015), 40–65.

Winters, J.F., 'The forest eyre, 1154–1368' (University of London, doctoral thesis, 1999).

Young, C.R., *The Royal Forests of Medieval England* (Philadelphia, PA, 1979).

INDEX

Printed and bound by CPI Group (UK) Ltd, Croydon, CR0 4YY

27/11/2024

14600225-0001